Microelectronic Circuit Design

Electronics and VLSI Circuits

Senior Consulting Editor
Stephen W. Director, University of Michigan, Ann Arbor

Consulting Editor
Richard C. Jaeger, Auburn University

Microelectronic Circuit Design

Richard C. Jaeger
Auburn University

WCB
McGraw-Hill

Boston, Massachusetts   Burr Ridge, Illinois   Dubuque, Iowa
Madison, Wisconsin   New York, New York   San Francisco, California   St. Louis, Missouri

WCB/McGraw-Hill

A Division of The McGraw-Hill Companies

MICROELECTRONIC CIRCUIT DESIGN

Copyright © 1997 by The McGraw-Hill Companies, Inc. All rights reserved. Printed in the United States of America. Except as permitted under the United States Copyright Act of 1976, no part of this publication may be reproduced or distributed in any form or by any means, or stored in a data base or retrieval system, without the prior written permission of the Publisher.

This book is printed on acid-free paper.

6 7 8 9 DOW DOW 9 0 3 2

ISBN 0-07-032482-4

This book was set in Times Roman by Publication Services.
The editor was Lynn B. Cox; the editing supervisor was Eva Marie Strock;
the interior designer was Mel Haber;
the cover designer was Francis Owens;
the production supervisor was Natalie Durbin.
R. R. Donnelley & Sons, Wilard, was the printer and binder.

Library of Congress Cataloging-in-Publication Data

Jaeger, Richard C.
    Microelectronic circuit design / Richard C. Jaeger.
        p.   cm. — (McGraw-Hill series in electrical and computer engineering)
  Includes bibliographical references and index.
  ISBN 0-07-032482-4
    1. Integrated circuits—Design and construction.
  2. Semiconductors—Design and construction.   3. Electronic circuit design.   I. Title. II. Series.
  TK7874.J333   1996
  621.3815—dc20   96-26208
                                          CIP

INTERNATIONAL EDITION
Copyright 1997. Exclusive rights by The McGraw-Hill Companies, Inc. for manufacture and export. This book cannot be re-exported from the country to which it is consigned by McGraw-Hill. The International Edition is not available in North America.

When ordering this title, use ISBN 0-07-114386-6

http://www.mhhe.com

To Joan, my loving wife and partner

Contents

Preface

The overall objective of this book is to develop a comprehensive understanding of the basic techniques of modern electronic circuit design—analog and digital, discrete and integrated. Even though most readers may not ultimately be engaged in the design of integrated circuits (ICs) themselves, a thorough understanding of the internal circuit structure is prerequisite to avoiding many of the pitfalls that prevent effective and reliable application of integrated circuits.

Digital electronics has evolved into an important area of circuit design, but it is included almost as an afterthought in most introductory electronics texts. This book presents a much more balanced coverage of analog and digital circuits. I have integrated my extensive industrial background in precision analog and digital design with my many years of classroom experience. A broad spectrum of topics is included, and material can easily be selected to satisfy either a two-semester or three-quarter sequence in electronics.

OVERVIEW

The book is divided into three parts. Part I, **Solid-State Devices and Circuits,** introduces electronics and solid-state devices. Chapter 1 is an historical overview of electronics, a subject that unfortunately has been eliminated from many recent textbooks. I feel that it is important to instill in readers a perspective of just how far electronics has advanced in a relatively short period and to provide a view of the true economic impact of electronics. I also believe strongly that readers should have a basic understanding of the origin of electrons and holes in solid-state materials. Chapter 2 treats solid-state electronics thoroughly enough to provide a basic understanding of the mechanisms that control electron and hole concentrations and of how one manipulates the doping concentrations to produce a *pn* junction or bipolar transistor. Hence, the material here is more extensive than that in many current textbooks.

Chapters 3 to 5 emphasize the economically important devices: the diode, MOSFET, and BJT. In my view, moving from the diode to the MOSFET is a smoother and less confusing transition than attempting to work with the less intuitive internal behavior of the bipolar device. The MOSFET is presented with a derivation of the linear region i-v characteristic; although enough discussion is provided so that readers will understand the basic fundamentals of device operation, the major focus is on device behavior from the terminals. A similar approach is used to develop the transport (simplified Gummel-Poon) model for the BJT.

Part II, **Digital Circuit Design,** emphasizes digital circuits before analog circuits, to point out the relative importance of digital circuit design in modern electronics. Placement of this discussion first also helps students outside of electrical engineering, particularly computer engineering or computer science majors, who may take only the first course in a sequence of electronics courses. Also, in classroom testing, I have found that dealing with digital circuit concepts first is less confusing for students, and design can be emphasized.

The material in Part II deals primarily with the internal design of logic gates and storage elements. Chapter 6 introduces the subject of logic gates and reviews boolean algebra. Chapters 7 and 8 comprehensively discuss NMOS and CMOS logic design. Chapter 9 covers memory cells and peripheral circuits in depth. Chapter 10, Bipolar Logic Circuits, includes detailed discussion of emitter-coupled logic and transistor-transistor logic. However, the material on bipolar logic has been reduced in deference to the importance of MOS technology. In addition, little discussion is given to design at the logic block level, a topic fully covered in digital system design courses.

Parts I and II deal only with the large-signal characteristics of the transistors. This constraint lets readers become comfortable with device behavior and i-v characteristics before they have to grasp the concept of splitting circuits into different pieces (and possibly different topologies) to perform dc and ac small-signal analyses. (The concept of a small signal is not formally introduced until Chapter 13.)

Although the treatment of digital circuits here is more extensive than in most textbooks, Part III, **Analog Circuit Design,** represents more than 50 percent of the book. Chapter 11 begins the traditional discussion; Chapter 12 thoroughly covers the operational amplifier and its many limitations. Knowledge of this basic material can be used to realize more complex circuits; it is used in subsequent chapters with MOSFETs and BJTs.

Design concepts and device and circuit comparisons are emphasized wherever possible. Significantly stronger emphasis is given to MOS analog circuits than in many textbooks. The treatment of bipolar and FET analog circuits is merged from Chapter 14 onward, permitting continual comparison of design options and reasons for choosing one device over another in a particular circuit. The hybrid-pi model and pi-models for the BJT and FET are used throughout.

Chapters 13 to 17 discuss in depth single-stage and multistage amplifier design using transistors. Chapter 16 discusses techniques important in IC design, explores the classic 741 operational amplifier, and details A/D and D/A converters.

Chapter 18 takes the classic two-port approach in presenting feedback. However, a section that stresses the errors which can occur when the approach is incorrectly applied is also included. Feedback amplifier stability and oscillators are discussed, as is the method of determining loop gain using successive voltage and current injection.

DESIGN

Part II launches directly into the issues associated with the design of NMOS and CMOS logic gates. The effects of device and passive element tolerances are discussed throughout the book. In today's world, low-power, low-voltage design—often supplied from batteries—is playing an increasingly important role. Low-voltage design issues are discussed throughout this book, and the text includes many problems in this important area. The use of the computer, including MATLAB, spreadsheets, and standard high-level languages, to explore design options is a thread running throughout the text.

Methods for making design estimates and decisions are stressed throughout the analog sections. Expressions for amplifier behavior are simplified beyond

the standard hybrid-pi model expressions whenever appropriate. For example, the expression for the voltage gain of an amplifier is simply written in most textbooks as $|A_V| = g_m R_L$, which tends to hide the power supply voltage as the fundamental design variable. Rewriting this expression in approximate form as $g_m R_L \approx 10 V_{CC}$ for the BJT and $g_m R_L \approx V_{DD}$ for the FET emphasizes the dependence of amplifier design on the choice of power supply voltage and provides a simple first-order design estimate for the voltage gain of the common-emitter and common-source amplifiers. Similar results are developed for the differential- and common-mode behavior of differential amplifiers and simple operational amplifiers. These approximation techniques and methods for performance estimation are included as often as possible.

Worst-case and Monte Carlo analysis techniques are introduced in Part I. Design using standard components and tolerance assignment is discussed in examples and included in many problems, particularly in the analog portion of the book. Comparisons and design trade-offs between the properties of BJTs and FETs are included throughout Part III.

PROBLEMS AND INSTRUCTOR SUPPORT

Specific design, computer, and SPICE problems are included at the end of each chapter and indicated by the icons 🔆, 💻, and 💾, respectively. The problems are keyed to the topics in the text and also graded into three levels of difficulty, with the more difficult or time-consuming problems indicated by * and **. Problem numbers in blue indicate that the answer is available in the back of the book. The accompanying *Instructor's Manual* has solutions to all the problems. In addition, copies of the original versions of all graphs and figures are available as PowerPoint files and can be retrieved from the World Wide Web.

COMPUTER USAGE AND SPICE

The computer is used as a tool throughout the book. I firmly believe that using a computer involves more than just using the SPICE circuit analysis program. In today's computing environment, it is often appropriate to use the computer to explore a complex design space rather than to try to reduce a complicated set of equations to some manageable analytic form. Examples of this process of setting up equations for iterative evaluation by computer through the use of spreadsheets, MATLAB, and/or standard high-level language programs are illustrated in many places in the book. MATLAB is also used for Nyquist and Bode plot generation and is useful for Monte Carlo analysis.

Results from SPICE simulation are included as appropriate in the book, and numerous SPICE problems appear. A PSPICE Simulation Data section is included with most chapters. These sections give the statement listings used to generate the simulation results presented in the figures in that chapter. Appendix B contains SPICE model parameters for various solid-state devices. However, I do not consider SPICE "embedded" in the text, and I omitted a detailed SPICE appendix because details of the SPICE language can be found in many supplementary textbooks.

CHAPTER SUMMARY

Part I, Solid-State Electronics and Devices.

Chapter 1 is a historical perspective of the field of electronics, beginning with vacuum tubes and advancing to very-large-scale integration (VLSI) and its impact on the global economy. The chapter also classifies electronic signals and reviews important tools from network analysis.

Chapter 2 discusses semiconductor materials, including covalent-bond and energy-band models. It also discusses intrinsic-carrier density; electron and hole populations; *n*- and *p*-type material; impurity doping; and mobility, resistivity, and carrier transport by both drift and diffusion.

Chapter 3 introduces the structure and *i-v* characteristics of solid-state diodes and discusses Schottky diodes, variable-capacitance diodes, photodiodes, solar cells, and LEDs. The concept of modeling and the use of different levels of modeling to achieve various approximations to reality are covered, and the concepts of bias, operating point, and the load line are all introduced. Iterative mathematical solutions are used to find the operating point, including spreadsheets and MATLAB. Diode applications include rectifiers, clipping and clamping circuits, and dc-to-dc converters. The dynamic switching characteristics of diodes are also presented.

Chapter 4 presents MOS and junction field-effect transistors (JFETs), starting with a qualitative description of the MOS capacitor. I believe that the concept of a voltage-controlled resistor is easier to grasp than the more complex operation of the BJT. Models are developed for the FET *i-v* characteristics, and a complete discussion of the regions of operation of the device is presented. Body effect is actively covered, as are biasing, load-line analysis, and several applications of FETs.

Chapter 5 covers the bipolar junction transistor (BJT) and presents an heuristic development of the transport (simplified Gummel-Poon) model of the BJT based on superposition. The various regions of operations are discussed in detail. Common-emitter and common-base current gains are defined, and base transit-time, diffusion capacitance, and cutoff frequency are all discussed.

Part II, Digital Circuit Design.

Chapter 6 is a compact introduction to digital electronics. Terminology discussed includes V_{OH}, V_{OL}, V_{IH}, V_{IL}, noise margin, rise and fall time, propagation delay, fan out, fan in, and power-delay product. A short review of boolean algebra is followed by a discussion of simple diode AND and OR gates. This brief chapter has been designed to stand alone, so it can be easily followed by either the discussion of MOS logic design in Chapters 7 and 8 or by the bipolar logic material in Chapter 10.

Chapter 7 follows the historical evolution of MOS logic gates, focusing on the design of NMOS saturated-load, linear-load, and depletion-mode-load circuit families. The impact of body effect on MOS logic circuit design is discussed in detail. The concept of reference inverter scaling is used to effect the design of other inverters, NAND gates, NOR gates, and complex logic functions throughout Chapters 7 and 8. Capacitance in MOS circuits is discussed, and analyses of the propagation delay and power-delay product of NMOS logic are presented.

CMOS is today's most important VLSI technology, and *Chapter 8* is an in-depth look at the design of CMOS logic gates, including inverters, NAND gates, NOR gates, and complex logic gates. In this case, the designs are based on the simple scaling of the delay of a reference inverter. Noise margin and latchup are discussed, and the power-delay products of various MOS logic families are compared.

Chapter 9 ventures into the design of memory and more advanced logic circuits, including the six-, three-, and one-transistor memory cells. Basic sense-amplifier circuits are introduced, as are the peripheral address and decoding circuits needed in memory designs. Cascade buffer design, dynamic logic circuits, ROMs, and PLAs are several of the advanced techniques covered.

Chapter 10 discusses modern bipolar logic circuits, including emitter-coupled logic (ECL) and transistor-transistor logic (TTL). The use of the differential pair as a current switch and the large-signal properties of the emitter follower are introduced. Operation of the BJT as a saturated switch is also covered, followed by discussion of low voltage and standard TTL.

Part III, Analog Circuit Design. *Chapter 11* provides a brief introduction to analog electronics. The concepts of voltage gain, current gain, and power gain are developed. Much care has been taken throughout the book to ensure consistency in the use of the notation that defines these quantities as well as in the use of dc, ac, and total signal notation. Two-port theory and Bode plots are reviewed, and amplifiers are classified by frequency response. MATLAB is introduced as a tool for producing Bode plots.

Chapter 12 is a comprehensive introduction to the design of circuits involving operational amplifiers. Classic ideal op-amp circuits are presented, and then the effects of using real amplifiers in single-stage and multistage designs are discussed in detail. Design, including the effects of device and component tolerances, is explored, and tolerance assignment is discussed and included in an array of problems. Design of the frequency response of op-amp circuits is also explored, and macromodeling of operational amplifiers is included. The chapter ends with a discussion of continuous-time filters and switched-capacitor circuits.

Chapter 13 starts with the general discussion of linear amplification using the BJT and FET as C-E and C-S amplifiers. Biasing for linear operation and the concepts of small-signal modeling are introduced, and small-signal models of the diode, BJT, and FET are all developed. The limits for small-signal operations are carefully defined. Appropriate points for signal injections and extraction are identified, and the use of coupling and bypass capacitors and inductors to separate the ac and dc designs is explored. The important 10 to 20 V_{CC} and 1 to 2 V_{DD} design estimates for the voltage gain of amplifiers are introduced, and the role of transistor amplification factor in bounding circuit performance is covered.

Chapter 14 begins with an in-depth comparison of the characteristics of single-transistor amplifiers, including small-signal amplitude limitations. Amplifiers are classified as inverting amplifiers (C-E, C-S), non-inverting amplifiers (C-B, C-G), and followers (C-C, C-D). The treatment of MOS and bipolar devices is merged from Chapter 14 on, and design tradeoffs between the use of BJTs and FETs in amplifier circuits is an important thread woven throughout Part III.

Chapter 15 explores the design of multistage amplifiers, including ac- and dc-coupled circuits. An evolutionary approach to multistage op-amp design is used.

MOS and bipolar differential amplifiers are first introduced. Subsequent addition of a second gain stage and then an output stage convert the differential amplifiers into simple op amps. Class-A, -B, and -AB operations are defined. Electronic current sources are designed and used for biasing basic operational amplifiers. Darlington, cascode, and cascade C-E circuits are presented. Discussions of important FET-BJT design tradeoffs are included wherever appropriate.

Chapter 16 focuses on techniques of particular importance in integrated circuit design. A variety of current mirror circuits are introduced and applied in bias circuits and as active loads in operational amplifiers. Numerous circuits and analog design techniques are explored through the detailed analysis of the classic 741 operational amplifier. A detailed discussion of the characteristics and circuit implementations of D/A and A/D converters completes this chapter.

Chapter 17 presents the frequency response of analog circuits. The behavior of each of the three categories of single-stage amplifiers (C-E/C-S, C-B/C-G, and C-C/C-D) is discussed in detail, and BJT behavior is contrasted with that of the FET. The frequency response of the transistor is discussed, and high-frequency, small-signal models are developed for both the BJT and FET. The short-circuit and open-circuit time-constant techniques are used to obtain estimates of the lower- and upper-cutoff frequencies of complex multistage amplifiers. Miller multiplication, cascode amplifier frequency response, and tuned amplifiers are all covered. Basic single-pole op-amp compensation is discussed, and the unity-gain-bandwidth product is related to amplifier slew rate.

Chapter 18 discusses feedback amplifier design, using the classic two-port approach to account for the loading of the amplifier and feedback network on each other. Loop-gain calculations are also discussed, including a unique section on the use of the successive voltage and current injection technique for determining loop gain. This method does not require that the feedback loop be broken and is a useful technique in the laboratory and for SPICE simulation of high-gain feedback amplifiers. Another unique section discusses errors that must be avoided when applying the two-port analysis methods to the shunt-series and series-series feedback topologies.

Stability is covered as well, and Nyquist diagrams and Bode plots (with MATLAB) are used to explore the phase and gain margin of amplifiers. Relationships between the Nyquist and Bode techniques are explicitly discussed. The Barkhausen criteria for oscillation are introduced, and oscillator circuits, including *RC*, *LC*, and crystal implementations, are presented. The discussion of amplitude stabilization in oscillators includes techniques for calculating the amplitude of the oscillation.

The five *appendixes* introduce integrated circuit fabrication (Appendix A), summarize the device models and sample SPICE parameters (Appendix B), present tables of standard component values (Appendix C), show data sheets for representative solid-state devices and operational amplifiers (Appendix D), and lists fundamental material constants (Appendix E).

CHAPTER FLEXIBILITY

The chapters are designed to be used in various sequences, and as noted earlier, there is more than enough material for a two-semester or three-quarter sequence in electronics. One can obviously proceed directly through the book. Alternatively, Chapter 5, on BJTs, can be used immediately after Chapter 3, on diodes (that is, a 1-2-3-5-4 chapter sequence). Presently, the order actually used at Auburn University is 1-2-3-4-6-7-8-9-5-10 and 11 to 18.

The chapters were also written so Part II can be skipped and Part III can be used directly after completion of the coverage of solid-state devices in Part I. If so desired, many quantitative details in Chapter 2 can be skipped.

ACKNOWLEDGMENTS

I want to thank the many people who had an impact on the material and its preparation for this book. First, I wish to thank my wife and companion, Joan C. Jaeger, who not only put up with the seemingly endless preparation of this text but who actually produced 90 percent of the original versions of the figures using Mac-Draw software. The students and faculty at Auburn University helped immensely in polishing the manuscript and managed to survive the many manuscript revisions. J. D. Irwin, head of electrical engineering at Auburn, has always been extremely supportive of faculty efforts to develop improved texts.

I wish to thank all the following reviewers for their many positive suggestions that were incorporated into the text: Frank S. Barnes, University of Colorado at Boulder; Alok K. Berry, George Mason University; Roy H. Cornely, New Jersey Institute of Technology; Artice M. Davis, San Jose State University; Mahmoud El Nokali, University of Pittsburgh; David R. Hertling, Georgia Institute of Technology; Lazaro M. Hong, University of Arizona; James Kaiser, Duke University; Robert J. Kennerknecht, the California Polytechnic State University; W. Marshall Leach, Jr., Georgia Institute of Technology; Frank J. Lofy, University of Wisconsin at Platteville; Rao Mulpuri, George Mason University; Farid N. Najm, University of Illinois at Urbana-Champaign; Donald L. Parker, Texas A&M University; Jaime Ramirez-Angulo, New Mexico State University; Sedki M. Riad, Virginia Polytechnic Institute and State University; Andrew Rys, Kansas State University; Gregory J. Sonek, University of California at Irvine; Darrell L. Vines, Texas Tech University; William L. Wilson, Jr., Rice University; William Zarnstorff, University of Wisconsin at Madison. Dr. B. M. Wilamowski of the University of Wyoming reviewed the next-to-last version of the manuscript in its entirety and provided many helpful suggestions.

I want to thank the faculty at the University of Florida, who gave me my formal training in electronics, and, more specifically, Professor A. J. Brodersen, who guided me through my graduate program. I also wish to thank Dr. T. J. Harrison for originally hiring me into the IBM Corporation. My ten years at IBM were instrumental in expanding my knowledge of precision analog circuit design and in developing my experience with VLSI design and some of the best IC technology in the world. During this time, Dr. G. A. Hellwarth greatly influenced my view of analog design.

Developmental editor Richard E. Mickey provided important suggestions and changes that helped polish the final version of the manuscript. I also want to thank McGraw-Hill Electrical Engineering Editors Anne Brown and Lynn B. Cox and Electrical Engineering Series Editor S. W. Director at the University of Michigan for their continuing support and encouragement during this lengthy project.

Richard C. Jaeger
Auburn University, 1997

CHAPTER 1

Introduction to Electronics

More than 100 years have now passed since the first radio transmissions by Marconi, which were followed after only a few years by the invention of the first electronic amplifying device, the triode vacuum tube. In this period of time, electronics—loosely defined as the design and application of electron devices—has had such a significant impact on our lives that we often overlook just how pervasive electronics has really become. One measure of the degree of this impact can be found in the gross domestic product (GDP) of the world. In 1992, the world GDP was approximately US $10 trillion, and of this total, fully 10 percent, or $1 trillion, was directly traceable to electronics. See Table 1.1 [1].

We commonly encounter electronics in the form of telephones, radios, televisions, and audio equipment, but electronics can be found in even seemingly mundane appliances such as vacuum cleaners and blenders. Wherever one looks in industry, electronics will be found. The corporate world obviously depends heavily on data processing systems to manage their operations. In fact, it is hard to see how the computer industry could have evolved without the use of its own products. In addition, the design process depends ever more heavily on computer-aided-design (CAD) systems, and manufacturing relies on electronic systems for process control—be it in petroleum refining, automobile tire production, food processing, power generation, and so on.

Table 1.1

The Worldwide Electronics Market ($1013 billion) in 1992 [1]

Category	Share (%)
Data processing hardware	23
Data processing software and services	18
Professional electronics	10
Telecommunications	9
Consumer electronics	9
Active components	9
Passive components	7
Computer integrated manufacturing	5
Instrumentation	5
Office electronics	3
Medical electronics	2

1.1 HISTORY OF ELECTRONICS: FROM VACUUM TUBES TO ULTRA-LARGE-SCALE INTEGRATION

Because most of us have grown up with electronic products all around us, we often lose perspective of how far the industry has come in a relatively short time. At the beginning of the twentieth century, there were no commercial electron devices, and transistors were not even invented until the late 1940s! Explosive growth was triggered first by the commercial availability of the bipolar transistor in the late 1950s, and then the realization of the integrated circuit (IC) in 1961. Since that time, signal processing using electron devices and electronic technology has become a pervasive force in our lives.

Table 1.2 lists a number of important milestones in the evolution of the field of electronics. The Age of Electronics begins in the early 1900s with the invention of the first electronic two-terminal devices, called **diodes.** The **vacuum diode,** or diode **vacuum tube,** was invented by Fleming in 1904; in 1906 Pickard created a diode by forming a point

Table 1.2	
Milestones in Electronics	
Year	**Event**
1884	American Institute of Electrical Engineers (AIEE) formed
1895	Marconi makes first radio transmissions
1904	Fleming invents diode vacuum tube—Age of Electronics begins
1906	Pickard creates solid-state point-contact diode (silicon)
1906	Deforest invents triode vacuum tube (audion)
1910–1911	"Reliable" tubes fabricated
1912	Institute of Radio Engineers (IRE) founded
1907–1927	First radio circuits developed from diodes and triodes
1920	Armstrong invents super heterodyne receiver
1925	TV demonstrated
1925	Lilienfeld files patent application on the field-effect device
1927–1936	Multigrid tubes developed
1933	Armstrong invents FM modulation
1935	Heil receives British patent on a field-effect device
1940	Radar developed during World War II—TV in limited use
1947	Bardeen, Brattain, and Shockley at Bell Laboratories invent bipolar transistors
1950	First demonstration of color TV
1952	Shockley describes the unipolar field-effect transistor
1952	Commercial production of silicon bipolar transistors begins at Texas Instruments
1956	Bardeen, Brattain, and Shockley receive Nobel Prize for invention of bipolar transistors
1958	Integrated circuit developed simultaneously by Kilby at Texas Instruments and Noyce and Moore at Fairchild Semiconductor
1961	First commercial digital IC available from Fairchild Semiconductor
1963	AIEE and IRE merge to become the Institute of Electrical and Electronic Engineers (IEEE): *Your* Professional Society!
1967	First semiconductor RAM (64 bits) discussed at the IEEE International Solid-State Circuits Conference (ISSCC)
1968	First commercial IC operational amplifier—the μA-709—introduced by Fairchild Semiconductor
1970	One-transistor dynamic memory cell invented by Dennard at IBM
1971	4004 microprocessor introduced by Intel
1972	First 8-bit microprocessor—the 8008—introduced by Intel
1974	First commercial 1-kilobit memory chip developed
1974	8080 microprocessor introduced
1978	First 16-bit microprocessor developed
1984	Megabit memory chip introduced
1995	Experimental gigabit memory chip presented at the IEEE ISSCC

contact to a silicon crystal. (Our study of electron devices begins with the introduction of the solid-state diode in Chapter 3.)

The invention of the three-element vacuum tube known as the **triode** was an extremely important milestone. The addition of a third element to a diode enabled electronic amplification to take place with good isolation between the input and output ports of the device. Fabrication of tubes that could be used reliably in circuits followed this invention by a few years and enabled rapid circuit innovation. Amplifiers and oscillators were developed that significantly improved radio transmission and reception. Armstrong invented the super heterodyne receiver in 1920 and FM modulation in 1933. Electronics developed rapidly during World War II, with great advances in the field of radio communications and the development of radar. Although first demonstrated in 1930, television did not begin to come into widespread use until the 1950s.

An important event in electronics occurred in 1947, when John Bardeen, Walter Brattain, and William Shockley at the Bell Telephone Laboratories invented the **bipolar transistor.**[1] Although field-effect devices had actually been conceived by Lilienfeld in 1925, Heil in 1935, and Shockley in 1952 [2], the technology to produce such devices on a commercial basis did not yet exist. Bipolar devices, however, were rapidly commercialized.

Then in 1958, the nearly simultaneous invention of the **integrated circuit (IC)** by Kilby at Texas Instruments and Noyce and Moore at Fairchild Semiconductor produced a new technology that would profoundly change our lives. The miniaturization achievable through IC technology made available complex electronic functions with high performance at low cost. The attendant characteristics of high reliability, low power, and small physical size and weight were additional important advantages.

Most of us have had some experience with personal computers, and nowhere is the impact of the integrated circuit more evident than in the area of digital electronics. For example, 64-megabit (Mb) dynamic memory chips, similar to those in Fig. 1.1(c), contain more than 66 million transistors. Creating this much memory using individual vacuum tubes [depicted in Fig. 1.1(a)] or even discrete transistors [shown in Fig. 1.1(b)] would be an almost inconceivable feat.

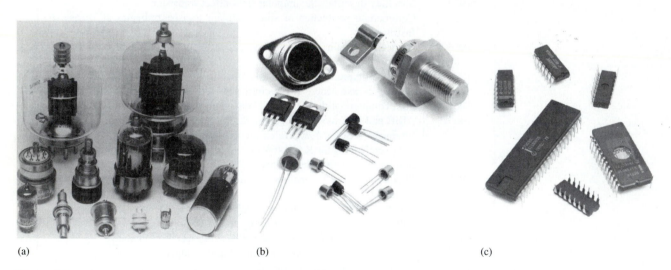

(a)   (b)   (c)

Figure 1.1 Comparison of (a) vacuum tubes, (b) individual transistors, and (c) high-density integrated circuits. [(a) Mark J. Wilson, American Radio Relay League, *The ARRL Handbook*, 1992.]

Levels of Integration

The dramatic progress of integrated circuit miniaturization is shown graphically in Figs. 1.2 to 1.4. The complexities of memory chips and microprocessors have grown exponentially with time. In the three decades since 1965, memory density has grown by a factor of more than 10 million from the 64-bit chip to the 1-gigabit (Gb) memory chip, as indicated in Fig. 1.2. Similarly, the number of transistors on a microprocessor chip has increased by a factor of more than 5000 since 1970, as shown in Fig. 1.3.

---

[1] The term **transistor** is said to have originated as a contraction of "transfer resistor," based on the voltage-controlled resistance of the characteristics (MOS) transistor.

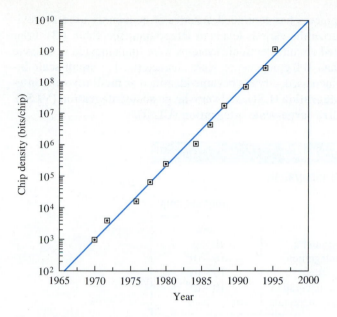

Figure 1.2 Memory chip density as a function of time. Each data point represents the first time a given chip size was presented at the IEEE International Solid-State Circuits Conference (ISSCC).

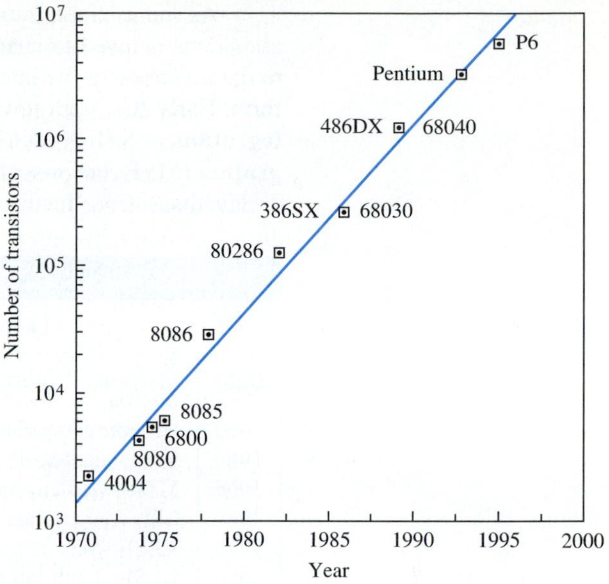

Figure 1.3 Microprocessor complexity versus time.

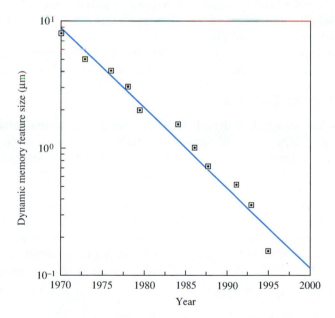

Figure 1.4 Feature size in dynamic memory chips versus time. (*Courtesy ISSCC*)

Since the commercial introduction of the integrated circuit, these increases in density have been achieved through a continued reduction in the minimum line width, or **minimum feature size,** that can be defined on the surface of the integrated circuit (see Fig. 1.4). Today, most corporate semiconductor laboratories around the world are actively working on deep submicron processes with feature sizes ranging from 0.1 to 0.2 μm—less than one one-hundredth the diameter of a human hair.

As the miniaturization process has continued, a series of commonly used abbreviations has evolved to characterize the various levels of integration (see Table 1.3). Prior to the invention of the integrated circuit, electronic systems were implemented in discrete form. Early ICs, with fewer than 100 components, were characterized as **small-scale integration,** or **SSI.** As density increased, circuits became identified as **medium-scale integration (MSI), large-scale integration (LSI),** and **very-large-scale integration (VLSI).** Today, discussions focus on **ultra-large-scale integration (ULSI).**

Table 1.3
Levels of Integration

Date	Historical Reference	Components/chip
1950	Discrete components	1–2
1960	SSI—Small-scale integration	$<10^2$
1966	MSI—Medium-scale integration	10^2–10^3
1969	LSI—Large-scale integration	10^3–10^4
1975	VLSI—Very-large-scale integration	10^4–10^9
1990	ULSI—Ultra-large-scale integration	$>10^9$

1.2 CLASSIFICATION OF ELECTRONIC SIGNALS

The signals that electronic devices are designed to process can be classified into two broad categories: analog and digital. **Analog signals** can take on a continuous range of values, and thus represent continuously varying quantities: purely **digital signals** can appear at only one of several discrete levels. Examples of these types of signals are described in more detail in the next two subsections, along with the concepts of digital-to-analog and analog-to-digital conversion, which make possible the interface between the two systems.

Digital Signals

When we speak of digital electronics, we are most often referring to electronic processing of **binary digital signals,** or signals that can take on only one of two discrete amplitude levels, as illustrated in Fig. 1.5. The status of binary systems can be represented by two symbols: a logical 1 is usually assigned to represent one level, and a logical 0 is assigned to the second level.[2] The two logic states generally correspond to two separate voltages—V_H and V_L—representing the high and low amplitude levels, and a number of voltage ranges are in common use. Although $V_H = 5$ V and $V_L = 0$ V have represented the primary standard for many years, these are now giving way to lower voltage levels because of power consumption and semiconductor device limitations. Systems employing $V_H = 3.3, 2.5,$ and 1.5 V, with $V_L = 0$ V, are now rapidly appearing in electronic systems.

Figure 1.5 A time-varying binary digital signal.

[2] This assignment facilitates the use of boolean algebra, reviewed in Chapter 6.

However, the binary voltage levels can also be negative or even bipolar. One high-performance logic family called ECL uses $V_H = -0.8$ V and $V_L = -2.0$ V, and the standard RS-422 and RS-232 communication links between a small computer and its peripherals use $V_H = +12$ V and $V_L = -12$ V. Also, the time-varying binary signal in Fig. 1.5 could equally well represent the amplitude of a current or that of an optical signal being transmitted down a fiber in an optical digital communication system.

Part II of this text discusses the design of a number of families of digital circuits using various semiconductor technologies. These include CMOS,[3] NMOS, and PMOS logic, which use field-effect transistors, and the TTL and ECL families, which are based on bipolar transistors.

Analog Signals

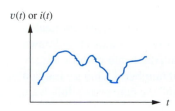

$v(t)$ or $i(t)$

Figure 1.6 An analog signal.

In contrast to discrete digital signals, the physical world is really analog in nature. Our senses of vision, hearing, smell, taste, and touch are all analog processes. Analog signals directly represent variables such as temperature, humidity, pressure, light intensity, or sound—all of which may take on any value, typically within some finite range. The time-varying voltage or current plotted in Fig. 1.6 could be the electrical representation of temperature, flow rate, or pressure versus time, or the continuous audio output from a microphone. Some analog transducers produce output *voltages* in the range of 0 to 5 or 0 to 10 V, whereas others are designed to produce an output *current* that ranges between 4 mA and 20 mA. At the other extreme, signals brought in by a radio antenna can be as small as a fraction of a microvolt.

To process the information contained in these analog signals, electronic circuits are used to selectively modify the amplitude, phase, and frequency content of the signals. In addition, significant increases in the voltage, current, and power level of the signal are usually needed. All these modifications to the signal characteristics are achieved using various forms of amplifiers, and Part III of this text discusses the analysis and design of a wide range of amplifiers using bipolar and field-effect transistors and operational amplifiers.

Bridging the Analog and Digital Domains

For analog and digital systems to be able to operate together, we must be able to convert signals from analog to digital form and vice versa. The electronic circuits that perform these translations are called digital-to-analog (D/A) and analog-to-digital (A/D) converters.

Digital-to-Analog Conversion

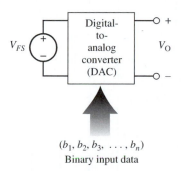

Figure 1.7 Block diagram representation for a D/A converter.

The **digital-to-analog converter,** often referred to as a **D/A converter** or **DAC,** provides an interface between the digital signals of computer systems and the continuous signals of the analog world. The D/A converter takes digital information, most often in binary form, as input and generates an output voltage or current that may be used for electronic control or analog information display. In the DAC in Fig. 1.7, an *n*-bit binary input word ($b_1, b_2, \ldots, b_n$) is treated as a binary fraction and multiplied by a full-scale reference voltage V_{FS} to set the output of the D/A converter. The behavior of the DAC can be expressed mathematically as

$$V_O = (b_1 2^{-1} + b_2 2^{-2} + \cdots + b_n 2^{-n})V_{FS} \qquad \text{for } b_i \in \{1, 0\} \qquad (1.1)$$

Examples of typical values of the full-scale voltage V_{FS} are 2.5 V, 5 V, 5.12 V, 10 V, and 10.24 V. The smallest voltage change that can occur at the output takes place

---

[3] For now, let us accept these initials as proper names without further definition. The details of each of these circuits are developed in Part II.

when the **least significant bit** b_n, or **LSB,** in the digital word changes from a 0 to a 1. This minimum voltage change is also referred to as the **resolution of the converter** and is given by

$$V_{\text{LSB}} = 2^{-n}V_{FS} \qquad (1.2)$$

At the other extreme, b_1 is referred to as the **most significant bit,** or **MSB,** and has a weight of one-half V_{FS}.

> **EXERCISE:** A 10-bit D/A converter has $V_{\text{REF}} = 5.12$ V. What is the output voltage for a binary input code of (1100010001)? What is V_{LSB} ? What is the size of the MSB?
>
> **ANSWERS:** 3.925 V; 5 mV; 2.56 V

Analog-to-Digital Conversion

The **analog-to-digital converter** (**A/D converter** or **ADC**) is used to transform analog information in electrical form into digital data. The ADC in Fig. 1.8 takes an unknown continuous analog input signal, usually a voltage v_X, and converts it into an n-bit binary number that can be easily manipulated by a computer. The n-bit number is a binary fraction representing the ratio between the unknown input voltage v_X and the converter's full-scale voltage V_{FS}.

For example, the input-output relationship for an ideal three-bit A/D converter is shown in Fig. 1.9(a). As the input increases from zero to full scale, the output digital code

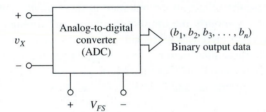

Figure 1.8 Block diagram representation for an A/D converter.

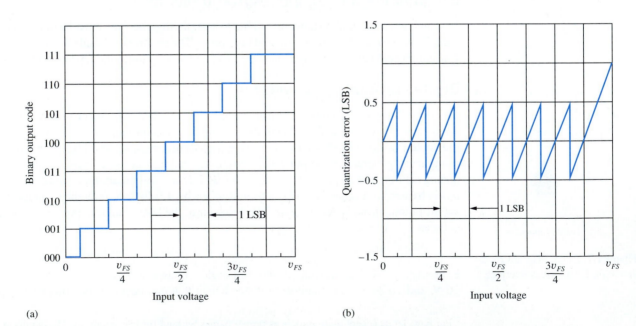

Figure 1.9 (a) Input-output relationship and (b) quantization error for 3-bit ADC.

word stair-steps from 000 to 111. The output code is constant for an input voltage range equal to 1 LSB of the ADC. Thus, as the input voltage increases, the output code first underestimates and then overestimates the input voltage. This error, called **quantization error,** is plotted against input voltage in Fig. 1.9(b).

For a given output code, we know only that the value of the input voltage lies somewhere within a 1-LSB quantization interval. For example, if the output code of the 3-bit ADC is 100, corresponding to a voltage $V_{FS}/2$, then the input voltage can be anywhere between $\frac{7}{16}V_{FS}$ and $\frac{9}{16}V_{FS}$, a range of $V_{FS}/8$ V or 1 LSB. From a mathematical point of view, the ADC circuitry in Fig. 1.8 picks the values of the bits in the binary word to minimize the magnitude of the quantization error V_ε between the unknown input voltage v_X and the nearest quantized voltage level:

$$V_\varepsilon = \left| v_X - (b_1 2^{-1} + b_2 2^{-2} + \cdots + b_n 2^{-n})V_{FS} \right| \qquad (1.3)$$

A more thorough description of the characteristics and behavior of D/A and A/D converters, as well as a discussion of the basic circuit techniques that are used to implement the converters, are in Chapter 16.

> **EXERCISE:** An 8-bit A/D converter has $V_{REF} = 5$ V. What is the digital output code word for an input of 1.2 V? What is the voltage range corresponding to 1 LSB of the converter?
>
> **ANSWERS:** 00111101; 19.5 mV

1.3 NOTATIONAL CONVENTIONS

In many circuits we will be dealing with both dc and time-varying values of voltages and currents. The following standard notation will be used to keep track of the various components of an electrical signal. Total quantities will be represented by lowercase letters with capital subscripts, such as v_T and i_T in Eq. (1.4). The dc components are represented by capital letters with capital subscripts as, for example, V_{DC} and I_{DC} in Eq. (1.4); changes or variations from the dc value are represented by v_{ac} and i_{ac}.

$$v_T = V_{DC} + v_{ac}$$
$$i_T = I_{DC} + i_{ac} \qquad (1.4)$$

As examples, the total base-emitter voltage v_{BE} of a transistor is written as

$$v_{BE} = V_{BE} + v_{be} \qquad (1.5)$$

or the total drain current i_D of a field-effect transistor is written as

$$i_D = I_D + i_d \qquad (1.6)$$

Unless otherwise indicated, the equations describing a given network will be written assuming a consistent set of units: volts, amperes, and ohms. For example, the equation $5 \text{ V} = (10,000\ \Omega)I_1 + 0.6 \text{ V}$ will be written as $5 = 10,000 I_1 + 0.6$.

> **EXERCISE:** Suppose the voltage at a circuit node is described by
>
> $$v_A = (5 \sin 2000\pi t + 4 + 3 \cos 1000\pi t) \text{ V}$$
>
> What are the expressions for V_A and v_a?
>
> **ANSWERS:** $V_A = 4$ V; $v_a = (5 \sin 2000\pi t + 3 \cos 1000\pi t)$ V

Resistance and Conductance Representations

In the circuits throughout this text, resistors will be indicated symbolically as R_x or r_x, and the values will be expressed in Ω, $k\Omega$, $M\Omega$, and so on. During analysis, however, it may be more convenient to work in terms of conductance, and the following convention will be followed:

$$G_x = \frac{1}{R_x} \qquad \text{and} \qquad g_\pi = \frac{1}{r_\pi} \tag{1.7}$$

For example, conductance G_x always represents the reciprocal of the value of R_x, and g_π represents the reciprocal of r_π. The values next to a resistor symbol will always be expressed in terms of resistance (Ω, $k\Omega$, $M\Omega$).

Dependent Sources

In electronics, **dependent** (or **controlled**) **sources** are used extensively. The four common types of dependent sources are summarized in Fig. 1.10, in which the standard diamond shape is used for controlled sources. The **voltage-controlled current source (VCCS),** **current-controlled current source (CCCS),** and **voltage-controlled voltage source (VCVS)** are used routinely in this text to model transistors and amplifiers or to simplify more complex circuits. Only the **current-controlled voltage source (CCVS)** sees limited use.

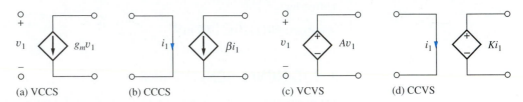

(a) VCCS　　　(b) CCCS　　　(c) VCVS　　　(d) CCVS

Figure 1.10 Controlled sources. (a) Voltage-controlled current source (VCCS). (b) Current-controlled current source (CCCS). (c) Voltage-controlled voltage source (VCVS). (d) Current-controlled voltage source (CCVS).

1.4 IMPORTANT CONCEPTS FROM CIRCUIT THEORY

Analysis and design of electronic circuits make continuous use of a number of important techniques from basic network theory. Circuits are most often analyzed using a combination of **Kirchhoff's voltage law,** abbreviated **KVL,** and **Kirchhoff's current law,** abbreviated **KCL.** Occasionally, the solution relies on systematic application of **nodal** or **mesh analysis. Thévenin** and **Norton circuit transformations** are often used to help simplify circuits, and the notions of voltage and current division also represent basic tools of analysis. Models of active devices invariably involve dependent sources, as mentioned in the last section, and we need to be familiar with dependent sources in all forms. Amplifier analysis also uses two-port network theory. A detailed review of two-port networks is deferred until the introductory discussion of amplifiers in Chapter 11. If the reader feels uncomfortable with any of the concepts just mentioned, this is a good time for review. To help, examples of these important circuit techniques are given in the next several sections.

Voltage and Current Division

Voltage and current division are routinely used to simplify circuits. **Voltage division** is demonstrated by the circuit in Fig. 1.11 in which the voltages v_1 and v_2 can be expressed as

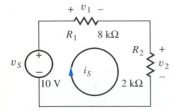

Figure 1.11 A resistive voltage divider.

$$v_1 = i_S R_1 \qquad \text{and} \qquad v_2 = i_S R_2 \tag{1.8}$$

Applying KVL to the single loop,

$$v_S = v_1 + v_2 = i_S(R_1 + R_2) \qquad \text{and} \qquad i_S = \frac{v_S}{R_1 + R_2} \tag{1.9}$$

Combining Eqs. (1.8) and (1.9) yields the basic voltage division formula:

$$v_1 = v_S \frac{R_1}{R_1 + R_2} \qquad \text{and} \qquad v_2 = v_S \frac{R_2}{R_1 + R_2} \tag{1.10}$$

For the resistor values in Fig. 1.11,

$$v_1 = 10 \text{ V} \frac{8 \text{ k}\Omega}{8 \text{ k}\Omega + 2 \text{ k}\Omega} = 8.00 \text{ V} \qquad \text{and} \qquad v_2 = 10 \text{ V} \frac{2 \text{ k}\Omega}{8 \text{ k}\Omega + 2 \text{ k}\Omega} = 2.00 \text{ V}$$
$$\tag{1.11}$$

Note that the relationship in Eq. (1.10) can be applied only when the current through the two resistor branches is the same. Also, note that the formula is correct if the resistances are replaced by complex impedances and the voltages are represented as **phasors.**

$$\mathbf{V}_1 = \mathbf{V}_S \frac{Z_1}{Z_1 + Z_2} \qquad \text{and} \qquad \mathbf{V}_2 = \mathbf{V}_S \frac{Z_2}{Z_1 + Z_2} \tag{1.12}$$

Current division is also very useful. Let us find the currents i_1 and i_2 in the circuit in Fig. 1.12. Using KCL at the single node,

$$i_S = i_1 + i_2 \qquad \text{where } i_1 = \frac{v_S}{R_1} \text{ and } i_2 = \frac{v_S}{R_2} \tag{1.13}$$

and solving for v_s yields

$$v_S = i_S \frac{1}{\dfrac{1}{R_1} + \dfrac{1}{R_2}} = i_S \frac{R_1 R_2}{R_1 + R_2} = i_S(R_1 \parallel R_2) \tag{1.14}$$

in which the notation $R_1 \parallel R_2$ represents the parallel combination of resistors R_1 and R_2. Combining Eqs. (1.13) and (1.14) yields the current division formulas:

$$i_1 = i_S \frac{R_2}{R_1 + R_2} \qquad \text{and} \qquad i_2 = i_S \frac{R_1}{R_1 + R_2} \tag{1.15}$$

For the values in Fig. 1.12,

$$i_1 = 5 \text{ mA} \frac{3 \text{ k}\Omega}{2 \text{ k}\Omega + 3 \text{ k}\Omega} = 3.00 \text{ mA} \qquad i_2 = 5 \text{ mA} \frac{2 \text{ k}\Omega}{2 \text{ k}\Omega + 3 \text{ k}\Omega} = 2.00 \text{ mA}$$
$$\tag{1.16}$$

In this case, note that the same voltage must appear across both resistors in order for the current division expressions to be valid.

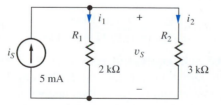

Figure 1.12 Current division in a simple network.

Thévenin and Norton Circuit Representations

Let us now review the method for finding **Thévenin** and **Norton equivalent circuits,** including a dependent source; the circuit in Fig. 1.13 serves as our illustration. Because the

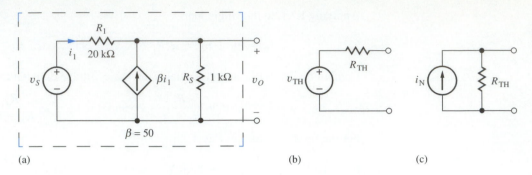

Figure 1.13 (a) Two-terminal circuit and its (b) Thévenin and (c) Norton equivalents.

linear network in the dashed box has only two terminals, it can be represented by either the Thévenin or Norton equivalent circuits in Figs. 1.13(b) or 1.13(c).

Let us find the Thévenin circuit first. Voltage source v_{TH} is the open-circuit voltage at the output terminals, and R_{TH} represents the equivalent resistance present at the output terminals with all independent sources set to zero. The open-circuit output voltage can be found by applying KCL at the output node:

$$\beta i_1 = \frac{v_O - v_S}{R_1} + \frac{v_O}{R_S} \tag{1.17}$$

which can be rewritten as

$$\beta i_1 = G_1(v_O - v_S) + G_S v_O \tag{1.18}$$

by applying the notational convention from Sec. 1.3. Current i_1 is given by

$$i_1 = G_1(v_S - v_O) \tag{1.19}$$

Substituting Eq. (1.19) into Eq. (1.18) and combining terms yields

$$G_1(\beta + 1)v_S = [G_1(\beta + 1) + G_S]v_O \tag{1.20}$$

The Thévenin equivalent output voltage is then found to be

$$v_O = \frac{G_1(\beta + 1)}{[G_1(\beta + 1) + G_S]} v_S \tag{1.21}$$

Multiplying numerator and denominator by $(R_1 R_S)$ yields

$$v_O = \frac{(\beta + 1)R_S}{[(\beta + 1)R_S + R_1]} v_S \tag{1.22}$$

For the values in this problem,

$$v_O = \frac{(50 + 1)\, 1\ k\Omega}{[(50 + 1)\, 1\ k\Omega + 20\ k\Omega]} v_S = 0.718 v_S \tag{1.23}$$

To find the **Thévenin equivalent resistance** R_{TH}, the independent sources in the network are first set to zero. Remember, however, that any dependent sources must remain active. A test voltage or current source is then applied to the network terminals and the corresponding current or voltage calculated. In Fig. 1.14, v_S is set to zero, voltage source v_X is applied to the network, and the current i_X must be determined so that

$$R_{TH} = \frac{v_X}{i_X} \tag{1.24}$$

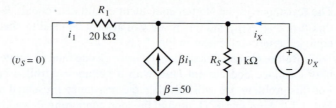

Figure 1.14 A test source v_X is applied to the network to find R_{TH}.

can be calculated. Applying KCL,

$$i_X = -i_1 - \beta i_1 + G_S v_X \qquad \text{in which } i_1 = -G_1 v_X \qquad (1.25)$$

Combining and simplifying these two expressions yields

$$i_X = [(\beta + 1)G_1 + G_S] v_X \qquad (1.26)$$

and

$$R_{TH} = \frac{v_X}{i_X} = \frac{1}{(\beta + 1)G_1 + G_S} \qquad (1.27)$$

The denominator of Eq. (1.27) represents the sum of two conductances, which corresponds to the parallel combination of two resistances. Therefore, Eq. (1.27) can be rewritten as

$$R_{TH} = \frac{1}{(\beta + 1)G_1 + G_S} = \frac{R_S \dfrac{R_1}{(\beta + 1)}}{R_S + \dfrac{R_1}{(\beta + 1)}} = R_S \left\| \frac{R_1}{(\beta + 1)} \right. \qquad (1.28)$$

For the values in this example,

$$R_{TH} = R_S \left\| \frac{R_1}{(\beta + 1)} \right. = 1 \text{ k}\Omega \left\| \frac{20 \text{ k}\Omega}{(50 + 1)} \right. = 1 \text{ k}\Omega \left\| 392 \text{ }\Omega \right. = 282 \text{ }\Omega \qquad (1.29)$$

The Norton equivalent circuit is found by determining the current coming out of the network when a short circuit is applied to the terminals. For the circuit in Fig. 1.15, the output current will be

$$i_N = i_1 + \beta i_1 \qquad \text{and} \qquad i_1 = G_1 v_S \qquad (1.30)$$

The short circuit across the output forces the current through R_S to be 0.

Combining the two expressions in Eq. (1.30) yields

$$i_N = (\beta + 1)G_1 v_S = \frac{(\beta + 1)}{R_1} v_S \qquad (1.31)$$

or

$$i_N = \frac{(50 + 1)}{20 \text{ k}\Omega} v_S = \frac{v_S}{392 \text{ }\Omega} = (2.55 \text{ mS}) v_S \qquad (1.32)$$

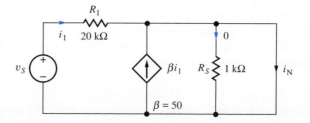

Figure 1.15 Circuit for determining short-circuit output current.

The resistance in the Norton equivalent circuit also equals R_{TH} found in Eq. (1.29). Note that $v_{\text{TH}} = i_N R_{\text{TH}}$, and this result can always be used to check the calculations. The two equivalent circuits appear in Fig. 1.16.

Before closing this section, let us work one final example combining the use of Kirchhoff's voltage and current laws with a voltage-controlled current source in the circuit. For this problem, we will calculate the resistance presented to source v_S in the circuit of Fig. 1.17. Applying KVL around the loop containing v_S yields

$$v_S = i_S R_1 + i_2 R_2 = i_S R_1 + (i_S + g_m v_1) R_2 \tag{1.33}$$

However, the voltage v_1 is related to the current i_S by

$$v_1 = i_S R_1 \tag{1.34}$$

Combining Eqs. (1.33) and (1.34) gives

$$v_S = i_S (R_1 + R_2 + g_m R_1 R_2) \tag{1.35}$$

and

$$R = \frac{v_S}{i_S} = R_1 + R_2 (1 + g_m R_1) \tag{1.36}$$

For the values in this particular circuit, we find

$$R = 3000\ \Omega + 2000\ \Omega\ [1 + (0.1\ \text{S})(3000\ \Omega)] = 605\ \text{k}\Omega \tag{1.37}$$

Note that this value is much larger than that of either of the individual resistors in the circuit.

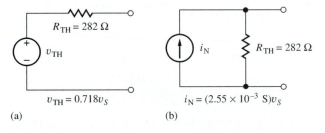

(a)   (b)

Figure 1.16 Completed (a) Thévenin and (b) Norton equivalent circuits for the two-terminal network in Fig. 1.13(a).

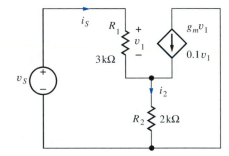

Figure 1.17 Circuit containing a voltage-controlled current source.

1.5 FREQUENCY SPECTRUM OF ELECTRONIC SIGNALS

Fourier analysis and the **Fourier series** represent extremely powerful tools in electrical engineering. Results from Fourier theory show that very complex signals are actually composed of a continuum of sinusoidal components, each having a distinct amplitude, frequency, and phase. The **frequency spectrum** of a signal presents the amplitude and phase of the components of the signal versus frequency.

Nonrepetitive signals have continuous spectra with signals that may occupy a broad range of frequencies. For example, the amplitude spectrum of a television signal measured during a small-time interval is depicted in Fig. 1.18. The TV video signal is designed to occupy the frequency range from 0 to 4.5 MHz.[4] Other types of signals occupy different regions of the frequency spectrum. Table 1.4 identifies the frequency ranges associated with various categories of common signals.

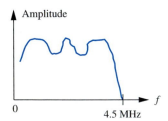

Figure 1.18 Spectrum of a TV signal.

---

[4] This signal is combined with a much higher carrier frequency prior to transmission.

T a b l e 1.4	
Frequencies Associated with Common Signals	
Category	**Frequency Range**
Audible sounds	20 Hz – 20 kHz
Baseband video (TV) signal	0 – 4.5 MHz
AM radio broadcasting	540 – 1600 kHz
High-frequency radio communications	1.6 – 54 MHz
VHF television (Channels 2–6)	54 – 88 MHz
FM radio broadcasting	88 – 108 MHz
VHF radio communication	108 – 174 MHz
VHF television (Channels 7–13)	174 – 216 MHz
UHF television (Channels 14–69)	470 – 806 MHz
Cellular telephones	824 – 892 MHz
Satellite television	3.7 – 4.2 GHz

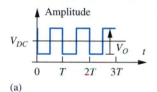

(a)

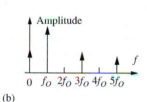

(b)

Figure 1.19 A periodic signal (a) and its amplitude spectrum (b).

In contrast to the continuous spectrum in Fig. 1.18, Fourier series analysis shows that *any periodic* signal, such as the square wave of Fig. 1.19, contains spectral components only at discrete frequencies[5] that are related directly to the period of the signal. For example, the square wave of Fig. 1.19 having an amplitude V_O and period T can be represented by the Fourier series

$$v(t) = V_{DC} + \frac{2\,V_O}{\pi}(\sin \omega_o t + \tfrac{1}{3} \sin 3\omega_o t + \tfrac{1}{5} \sin 5\omega_o t + \cdots) \qquad (1.38)$$

in which $\omega_o = 2\pi/T$ (rad/s) is the **fundamental radian frequency** of the square wave. We refer to $f_o = 1/T$ (Hz) as the **fundamental frequency** of the signal, and the frequency components at $2f_o, 3f_o, 4f_o, \ldots$ are called the second, third, fourth, and so on **harmonic frequencies.**

1.6 AMPLIFIERS

The characteristics of analog signals are most often manipulated using linear amplifiers that affect the amplitude and/or phase of the signal without changing its frequency. Although a complex signal may have many individual components, as just described in Sec. 1.5, linearity permits us to use the **superposition principle** to treat each component individually.

For example, suppose the amplifier with voltage gain A in Fig. 1.20 is fed a sinusoidal input signal component v_S with amplitude V_S, frequency ω_S, and phase ϕ:

$$v_s = V_s \sin(\omega_s t + \phi) \qquad (1.39)$$

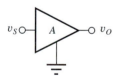

Figure 1.20 Electronic symbol for an amplifier with voltage gain A.

Then, if the amplifier is linear, the output corresponding to this signal component will also be a sinusoidal signal at the same frequency but with a different amplitude and phase:

$$v_o = V_o \sin(\omega_s t + \phi + \theta) \qquad (1.40)$$

Using phasor notation, the input and output signals would be represented as

$$\mathbf{V_s} = V_s \underline{/\phi} \qquad \text{and} \qquad \mathbf{V_o} = V_o \angle (\phi + \theta) \qquad (1.41)$$

---

[5] There are an infinite number of components, however.

The **voltage gain** of the amplifier is defined in terms of these phasors:

$$A = \frac{\mathbf{V_o}}{\mathbf{V_s}} = \frac{V_o \angle (\phi + \theta)}{V_s \angle \phi} = \frac{V_o}{V_s} \angle \theta \tag{1.42}$$

This amplifier has a voltage gain with magnitude equal to V_o/V_s and a phase shift of θ. In general, the magnitude and phase will be a function of frequency. Note that amplifiers also often provide current gain and power gain as well as voltage gain, but these concepts will not be explored further until Chapter 11.

At this point, a note regarding the phase angle is needed. In Eqs. (1.39) and (1.40), ωt, ϕ, and θ must have the same units. With ωt normally expressed in radians, ϕ should also be in radians. However, in electrical engineering texts, ϕ is often expressed in degrees. We must be aware of this mixed system of units and remember to convert degrees to radians before making any numeric calculations.

> **EXERCISE:** The input and output voltages of an amplifier are expressed as
>
> $$v_s = 0.001 \ \sin(2000\pi t) \text{ V} \quad \text{and} \quad v_o = -5\cos(2000\pi t + 25°) \text{ V}$$
>
> in which v_s and v_o are specified in volts when t is seconds. What are $\mathbf{V_S}$, $\mathbf{V_O}$, and the voltage gain of the amplifier?
>
> **ANSWERS:** $0.001 \angle 0°$; $5 \angle -65°$; $5000 \angle -65°$

Amplifiers in a Familiar Electronic System

The block diagram of an FM radio receiver in Fig. 1.21 is an example of an electronic system that uses a number of amplifiers. The signal from the antenna can be very small, often in the microvolt range. The signal's amplitude and power level are increased sequentially by three groups of amplifiers: the radio frequency (RF), intermediate frequency (IF), and audio amplifiers. At the output, the amplifier driving the loudspeaker could be delivering a 100-W audio signal to the speaker, whereas the power originally available from the antenna may only amount to picowatts.

The local oscillator, which tunes the radio receiver to select the desired station, represents another special class of amplifiers; these are investigated at the end of Chapter 18. The mixer circuit actually changes the frequency of the incoming signal and is thus a nonlinear circuit. However, its design draws heavily on linear amplifier circuit concepts. Finally, the FM detector may be formed from either a linear or nonlinear circuit. Chapters 11 to 18 provide in-depth exploration of the design techniques used in linear amplifiers and oscillators and the foundation needed to understand more complex circuits such as mixers, modulators, and detectors.

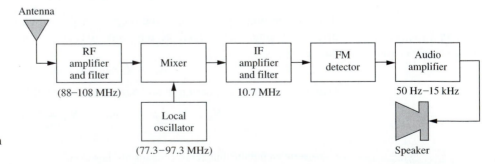

Figure 1.21 Block diagram for an FM radio receiver.

Amplifier Frequency Response

In addition to modifying the voltage, current, and/or power level of a given signal, amplifiers are often designed to selectively process signals of different frequency ranges. Amplifiers are classified into a number of categories based on their frequency response; five possible categories are shown in Fig. 1.22. The **low-pass amplifier,** Fig. 1.22(a), passes all signals below some upper cutoff frequency f_H, whereas the **high-pass amplifier,** Fig. 1.22(b), amplifies all signals above the lower cutoff frequency f_L. The **band-pass amplifier** passes all signals between the two cutoff frequencies f_L and f_H, as in Fig. 1.22(c). The **band-reject amplifier** in Fig. 1.22(d) rejects all signals having frequencies lying between f_L and f_H. Finally, the **all-pass amplifier** in Fig. 1.22(e) amplifies signals at any frequency. The all-pass amplifier is actually used to tailor the phase of the signal rather than its amplitude. Circuits that are designed to amplify specific ranges of signal frequencies are usually referred to as **filters.**

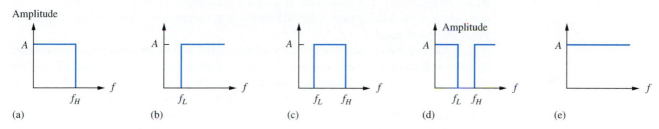

Figure 1.22 Ideal amplifier frequency responses: (a) Low-pass, (b) high-pass, (c) band-pass, (d) band-reject, and (e) all-pass characteristics.

EXERCISE: (a) The band-pass amplifier in Fig. 1.22(c) has $f_L = 1.5$ kHz, $f_H = 2.5$ kHz, and $A = 10$. If the input voltage is given by

$$v_s = [0.5 \sin(2000\pi t) + \sin(4000\pi t) + 1.5 \sin(6000\pi t)]\text{V}$$

what is the output voltage of the amplifier?
(b) Suppose the same input signal is applied to the low-pass amplifier in Fig. 1.22(a), which has $A = 6$ and $f_H = 1.5$ kHz. What is the output voltage?

ANSWERS: $10.0 \sin 4000\pi t$ V; $3.00 \sin 2000\pi t$ V

1.7 NUMERIC PRECISION

Many numeric calculations will be performed throughout this book. Keep in mind that the circuits being designed can all be built in discrete form in the laboratory or can be implemented in integrated circuit form. In designing circuits, we will be dealing with components that have tolerances ranging from less than ± 1 percent to greater than ± 50 percent, and calculating results to a precision of more than three significant digits represents a meaningless exercise except in very limited circumstances. Thus, the results in this text are consistently represented with three significant digits: 2.03 mA, 5.72 V, 0.0436 μA, and so on. For example, see the answers in Eqs. (1.16), (1.23), (1.29), and (1.37), and so on.

SUMMARY

The age of electronics began in the early 1900s with Pickard's creation of the crystal diode detector, Fleming's invention of the diode vacuum tube, and then Deforest's development of the triode vacuum tube. Since that time, the electronics industry has grown to account for as much as 10 percent of the world gross domestic product. The real catalysts for this explosive growth occurred following World War II. The first was the invention of the bipolar transistor by Bardeen, Brattain, and Shockley in 1947; the second was the simultaneous invention of the integrated circuit by Kilby and by Noyce and Moore in 1958. Integrated circuits quickly became a commercial reality, and the complexity, whether measured in memory density (bits/chip), microprocessor transistor count, or minimum feature size, has changed exponentially since the mid-1960s. We are now in an era of ultra-large-scale integration (ULSI), having already put lower levels of integration—SSI, MSI, LSI, and VLSI—behind us.

Electronic circuit design deals with two major categories of signals. Analog electrical signals may take on any value within some finite range of voltage or current. Digital signals, however, can take on only a finite set of discrete levels. The most common digital signals are binary signals, which are represented by two discrete levels. Bridging these two worlds are the digital-to-analog and analog-to-digital conversion circuits (DAC and ADC, respectively). The DAC converts digital information into an analog voltage or current, whereas the ADC creates a digital number at its output that is proportional to an analog input voltage or current.

Fourier demonstrated that complex signals can be represented as a linear combination of sinusoidal signals. Analog signal processing is applied to these signals using linear amplifiers; these modify the amplitude and phase of analog signals. Linear amplifiers do not alter the frequency content of the signal, other than changing the relative amplitudes and phases of the frequency components. Amplifiers are often classified by their frequency response into low-pass, high-pass, band-pass, band-reject, and all-pass categories. Electronic circuits that are designed to amplify specific ranges of signal frequencies are usually referred to as filters.

Key Terms

All-pass amplifier
Analog signal
Analog-to-digital converter
  (A/D converter or ADC)
Band-pass amplifier
Band-reject amplifier
Binary digital signal
Bipolar transistor
Current-controlled current source
  (CCCS)
Current-controlled voltage source
  (CCVS)
Current division
Dependent (or controlled) source
Digital signal
Digital-to-analog converter
  (D/A converter or DAC)
Diode
Filters
Fourier analysis
Fourier series

Frequency spectrum
Fundamental frequency
Fundamental radian frequency
Harmonic frequency
High-pass amplifier
Integrated circuit (IC)
Kirchhoff's current law (KCL)
Kirchhoff's voltage law (KVL)
Large-scale integration (LSI)
Least significant bit (LSB)
Low-pass amplifier
Medium-scale integration (MSI)
Mesh analysis
Minimum feature size
Most significant bit (MSB)
Nodal analysis
Norton circuit transformation
Norton equivalent circuit
Phasor
Quantization error
Resolution of the converter

Small-scale integration (SSI)
Superposition principle
Thévenin circuit
  transformation
Thévenin equivalent circuit
Thévenin equivalent
  resistance
Transistor
Triode
Ultra-large-scale integration
  (ULSI)
Vacuum diode
Vacuum tube
Very-large-scale integration
  (VLSI)
Voltage-controlled current
  source (VCCS)
Voltage-controlled voltage
  source (VCVS)
Voltage division
Voltage gain

References

1. B. Courtois, "CAD and testing of ICs and systems: Where are we going?", *Journal of Microelectronic Systems Integration,* vol. 2, no. 3, pp. 139–200, 1994.
2. J. T. Wallmark, "The field-effect transistor—an old device with new promise," *IEEE Spectrum,* March 1964.

Additional Reading

Commemorative Supplement to the Digest of Technical Papers, 1993 IEEE International Solid-State Circuits Conference Digest, vol. 36, February 1993.

Digest of Technical Papers of the IEEE Custom Integrated International Circuits Conference, April–May of each year.

Digest of Technical Papers of the IEEE International Electronic Devices Meeting, December of each year.

Digest of Technical Papers of the IEEE International Solid-State Circuits Conference, February of each year.

Digest of Technical Papers of the IEEE International Symposia on VLSI Technology and Circuits, June of each year.

Electronics, Special Commemorative Issue, Apr. 17, 1980.

Garratt, G. R. M. *The Early History of Radio from Faraday to Marconi.* Institution of Electrical Engineers (IEE), London, United Kingdom: 1994.

"200 Years of Progress," *Electronic Design,* vol. 24, no. 4, Feb. 16, 1976.

Problems

1.1 History of Electronics: From Vacuum Tubes to Ultra-Large-Scale Integration

1.1. Make a list of 24 items in your environment that contain electronics. A PC and its peripherals are considered one item. (Do not confuse electromechanical timers, common in clothes dryers or the switch in a simple thermostat, with electronic circuits.)

1.2. The straight line in Fig. 1.2 is described by $B = 45.8 \times 10^{0.239(Y-1965)}$. If a straight-line projection is made using this equation, what will be the number of memory bits/chip in the year 2020?

1.3. (a) How many years does it take for memory chip density to increase by a factor of 2, based on the equation in Prob. 1.2? (b) By a factor of 10?

1.4. The straight line in Fig. 1.3 is described by $N = 1300 \times 10^{0.15(Y-1970)}$. Based on a straight-line projection of this figure, what will be the number of transistors in a microprocessor in the year 2020?

1.5. (a) How many years does it take for microprocessor circuit density to increase by a factor of 2, based on the equation in Prob. 1.4? (b) By a factor of 10?

1.6. If you make a straight-line projection from Fig. 1.4, what will be the minimum feature size in integrated circuits in the year 2020? The curve can be described by $F = 8.9 \times 10^{-0.063(Y-1970)}\mu$m. Do you think this is possible? Why or why not?

1.7. The filament of a small vacuum tube uses a power of approximately 1.5 W. Suppose that 75 million of these tubes are used to build the equivalent of a 64-Mb memory. How much power is required for this memory? If this power is supplied from a 220-V ac source, what is the current required by this memory?

1.2 Classification of Electronic Signals

1.8. Classify each of the following as an analog or digital quantity: (a) status of a light switch, (b) status of a thermostat, (c) water pressure, (d) gas tank level, (e) bank overdraft status, (f) light bulb intensity, (g) stereo volume, (h) full or empty cup, (i) room temperature, (j) TV channel selection, and (k) tire pressure.

1.9. A 12-bit D/A converter has a reference voltage of 10.00 V. What is the voltage corresponding to the LSB? To the MSB? What is the output voltage if the binary input code is equal to (100100100100)?

1.10. A 10-bit D/A converter has a reference voltage of 2.5 V. What is the voltage corresponding to the LSB? What is the output voltage if the binary input code is equal to (0101100101)?

1.11. An 8-bit A/D converter has $V_{FS} = 5$ V. What is the value of the voltage corresponding to the LSB? If the input voltage is 2.77 V, what is the binary output code of the converter?

1.12. A 15-bit A/D converter has $V_{FS} = 10$ V. What is the value of the LSB? If the input voltage is 6.83 V, what is the binary output code of the converter?

1.3 Notational Conventions

1.13. If $i_B = 0.002(1 + \cos 1000t)$ A, what are I_B and i_b?

1.14. If $V_{CE} = 5$ V and $v_{ce} = (2 \cos 5000t)$ V, write the expression for v_{CE}.

1.15. If $V_{DS} = 5$ V and $v_{ds} = (2 \sin 2500t + 4 \sin 1000t)$ V, write the expression for v_{DS}.

1.4 Important Concepts from Circuit Theory

1.16. Use voltage and current division to find V_1, V_2, I_2, and I_3 in the circuit in Fig. P1.16 if $V = 10$ V, $R_1 = 4.7$ kΩ, $R_2 = 2.2$ kΩ, and $R_3 = 18$ kΩ.

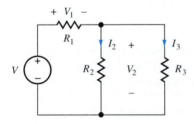

Figure P1.16

1.17. Use voltage and current division to find V_1, V_2, I_2, and I_3 in the circuit in Fig. P1.16 if $V = 18$ V, $R_1 = 39$ kΩ, $R_2 = 43$ kΩ, and $R_3 = 11$ kΩ.

1.18. Use current and voltage division to find I_1, I_2, and V_3 in the circuit in Fig. P1.18 if $I = 5$ mA, $R_1 = 4.7$ kΩ, $R_2 = 2.2$ kΩ, and $R_3 = 3.6$ kΩ.

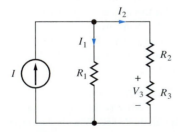

Figure P1.18

1.19. Use current and voltage division to find I_1, I_2, and V_3 in the circuit in Fig. P1.18 if $I = 250$ μA, $R_1 = 100$ kΩ, $R_2 = 68$ kΩ, and $R_3 = 82$ kΩ.

1.20. Find the Thévenin equivalent representation of the circuit in Fig. P1.20 if $g_m = 0.002$ S and $R_1 = 100$ kΩ.

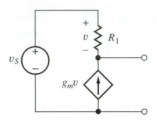

Figure P1.20

1.21. Find the Norton equivalent representation of the circuit in Fig. P1.20 if $g_m = 0.025$ S and $R_1 = 40$ kΩ.

1.22. Find the Thévenin equivalent representation of the circuit in Fig. P1.22 if $\beta = 150$, $R_1 = 100$ kΩ, and $R_2 = 39$ kΩ.

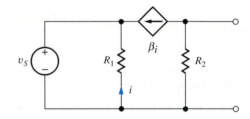

Figure P1.22

1.23. Find the Norton equivalent representation of the circuit in Fig. P1.22 if $\beta = 80$, $R_1 = 75$ kΩ, and $R_2 = 56$ kΩ.

1.24. What is the resistance presented to source v_S by the circuit in Fig. P1.22 if $\beta = 150$, $R_1 = 100$ kΩ, and $R_2 = 39$ kΩ.

1.25. Find the Thévenin equivalent representation of the circuit in Fig. P1.25 if $g_m = 0.002$ S, $R_1 = 100$ kΩ, and $R_2 = 1$ MΩ.

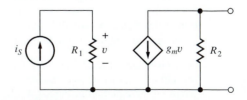

Figure P1.25

1.5 Frequency Spectrum of Electronic Signals

1.26. A signal voltage is expressed as $v(t) = (5 \sin 1000\pi t + 3 \cos 2000\pi t)$ V. Draw a graph of the amplitude spectrum for $v(t)$ similar to the one in Fig. 1.19(b).

*1.27. Voltage $v_1 = 2 \sin 20000\pi t$ is multiplied by voltage $v_2 = 2 \sin 2000\pi t$. Draw a graph of the amplitude spectrum for $v = v_1 \times v_2$ similar to the one in Fig. 1.19(b). (Note that multiplication is a nonlinear mathematical operation. In electronics it is often called *mixing* because it produces a signal that contains output frequencies that are not in the input signal but depend directly on the input frequencies.)

1.6 Amplifiers

1.28. The input and output voltages of an amplifier are expressed as $v_s = 10^{-5} \sin(2 \times 10^7 \pi t)$V and $v_o = 2 \sin(2 \times 10^7 \pi t + 36°)$ V. What are the magnitude and phase of the voltage gain of the amplifier?

*1.29. The input and output voltages of an amplifier are expressed as

$$v_s = [10^{-3} \sin(3000\pi t) + 2 \times 10^{-3} \sin(5000\pi t)] \text{ V}$$

and

$$v_o = [10^{-1} \sin(3000\pi t - 12°) + 10^{-2} \sin(5000\pi t - 45°)] \text{ V}$$

(a) What are the magnitude and phase of the voltage gain of the amplifier at a frequency of 2500 Hz? (b) At 1500 Hz?

Amplifier Frequency Response

1.30. An amplifier has a voltage gain of 5 for frequencies below 5000 Hz, and zero gain for frequencies above 5000 Hz. Classify this amplifier.

1.31. An amplifier has a voltage gain of 0 for frequencies below 1000 Hz, and zero gain for frequencies above 5000 Hz. In between these two frequencies the amplifier has a gain of 10. Classify this amplifier.

1.32. An amplifier has a voltage gain of 32 for frequencies above 10 kHz, and zero gain for frequencies below 10 kHz. Classify this amplifier.

1.33. The amplifier in Prob. 1.30 has an input signal given by $v_S(t) = (5 \sin 2000\pi t + 3 \cos 8000\pi t + 2 \cos 15000\pi t)$ V. Write an expression for the output voltage of the amplifier.

1.34. The amplifier in Prob. 1.31 has an input signal given by $v_S(t) = (0.5 \sin 2500\pi t + 0.75 \cos 8000\pi t + 0.6 \cos 12000\pi t)$ V. Write an expression for the output voltage of the amplifier.

1.35. The amplifier in Prob. 1.32 has an input signal given by $v_S(t) = (0.5 \sin 2500\pi t + 0.75 \cos 8000\pi t + 0.8 \cos 12000\pi t)$ V. Write an expression for the output voltage of the amplifier.

 1.36. An amplifier has an input signal that can be represented as

$$v(t) = \tfrac{4}{\pi}(\sin \omega_o t + \tfrac{1}{3} \sin 3\omega_o t + \tfrac{1}{5} \sin 5\omega_o t) \text{ V}$$

where $f_o = 1000$ Hz

(a) Use MATLAB to plot the signal for $0 \le t \le 5$ ms. (b) The signal $v(t)$ is amplified by an amplifier that provides a voltage gain of 5 at all frequencies. Plot the output voltage for this amplifier for $0 \le t \le 5$ ms. (c) A second amplifier has a voltage gain of 5 for frequencies below 2000 Hz but zero gain for frequencies above 2000 Hz. Plot the output voltage for this amplifier for $0 \le t \le 5$ ms. (d) A third amplifier has a gain of 5 at 1000 Hz, a gain of 3 at 3000 Hz, and a gain of 1 at 5000 Hz. Plot the output voltage for this amplifier for $0 \le t \le 5$ ms.

1.7 Numeric Precision

1.37. (a) Express the following numbers to 3 significant digits of precision: 3.2947, 0.995171, -6.1551. (b) To 4 significant digits. (c) Check these answers using your calculator.

1.38. (a) What is the voltage developed by a current of 1.763 mA in a resistor of 20.70 kΩ? Express the answer with 3 significant digits. (b) Express the answer with 2 significant digits. (c) Repeat for $I = 102.1$ μA and $R = 97.80$ kΩ.

Solid-State Electronics

The evolution of solid-state materials and the subsequent development of the technology for integrated circuit fabrication have revolutionized electronics. Using silicon as well as other crystalline semiconductor materials, we can now fabricate integrated circuits (ICs) that have hundreds of millions of electronic components on a single 2 cm $\times$ 2 cm die. Most of us have some familiarity with the very high-speed microprocessor and memory components that form the building blocks for personal computers and workstations. As this edition is being written, technology for the 1-gigabit (Gb) memory chip is being developed in a number of research laboratories around the world. The memory array alone on this chip will contain more than 10^9 transistors and 10^9 capacitors—more than 2 billion electronic components on a single die!

Our ability to build such phenomenal electronic system components is based on a detailed understanding of solid-state physics as well as on development of fabrication processes necessary to turn the theory into a manufacturable reality. Integrated circuit manufacturing is an excellent example of a process requiring a broad understanding of many disciplines. IC fabrication requires knowledge of physics, chemistry, electrical engineering, mechanical engineering, materials engineering, and metallurgy, to mention just a few disciplines. The breadth of understanding required is a challenge, but it makes the field of solid-state electronics an extremely exciting and vibrant area of specialization.

The material in this chapter provides the background necessary for understanding the behavior of the solid-state devices presented in subsequent chapters. We begin our study of solid-state electronics by exploring the characteristics of crystalline materials, with an emphasis on silicon, the most commercially important semiconductor. We look at electrical conductivity and resistivity and discuss the mechanisms of electronic conduction. The technique of impurity doping is discussed, along with its use in controlling conductivity and resistivity type.

2.1 SOLID-STATE ELECTRONIC MATERIALS

Electronic materials generally can be divided into three categories: **insulators, conductors,** and **semiconductors.** The primary parameter used to distinguish among these materials is the **resistivity** ρ, with units of $\Omega \cdot$ cm. As indicated in Table 2.1, insulators have resistivities greater than 10^5 $\Omega \cdot$ cm, whereas conductors have resistivities below 10^{-3} $\Omega \cdot$ cm. For example, diamond, one of the highest quality insulators, has a very large resistivity, 10^{16} $\Omega \cdot$ cm. On the other hand, pure copper, a good conductor, has a resistivity of only 3×10^{-6} $\Omega \cdot$ cm. Semiconductors occupy the full range of resistivities between the insulator and conductor boundaries; moreover, the resistivity can be controlled by adding various impurity atoms to the semiconductor crystal.

Elemental semiconductors are formed from a single type of atom (column IV of the periodic table of elements; see Table 2.2), whereas **compound semiconductors** can be formed from combinations of elements from columns III and V or columns II and VI. These later materials are often referred to as III–V (3–5) or II–VI (2–6) compound semiconductors. Table 2.3 presents some of the most useful possibilities. There are also ternary materials such as mercury cadmium telluride, gallium aluminum arsenide, gallium indium arsenide, and gallium indium phosphide.

Historically, germanium was one of the first semiconductors to be used. However, it was rapidly supplanted by silicon, which today is the most important semiconductor material. Silicon has a wider bandgap energy,[1] allowing it to be used in higher-temperature applications than germanium, and oxidation forms a stable insulating oxide on silicon,

Table 2.1	
Electrical Classification of Solid Materials	
Materials	**Resistivity ($\Omega \cdot$ cm)**
Insulators	$10^5 < \rho$
Semiconductors	$10^{-3} < \rho < 10^5$
Conductors	$\rho < 10^{-3}$

---

[1] The meaning of bandgap energy is discussed in detail in Secs. 2.3 and 2.8.

Table 2.2

Portion of the Periodic Table, Including the Most Important Semiconductor Elements (shaded)

IIIA	IVA	VA	VIA
5 10.811 **B** Boron	6 12.01115 **C** Carbon	7 14.0067 **N** Nitrogen	8 15.9994 **O** Oxygen
13 26.9815 **Al** Aluminum	14 28.086 **Si** Silicon	15 30.9738 **P** Phosphorus	16 32.064 **S** Sulfur

IIB

	IIIA	IVA	VA	VIA
30 65.37 **Zn** Zinc	31 69.72 **Ga** Gallium	32 72.59 **Ge** Germanium	33 74.922 **As** Arsenic	34 78.96 **Se** Selenium
48 112.40 **Cd** Cadmium	49 114.82 **In** Indium	50 118.69 **Sn** Tin	51 121.75 **Sb** Antimony	52 127.60 **Te** Tellurium
80 200.59 **Hg** Mercury	81 204.37 **Ti** Thallium	82 207.19 **Pb** Lead	83 208.980 **Bi** Bismuth	84 (210) **Po** Polonium

Table 2.3

Semiconductor Materials

Semiconductor	Bandgap Energy E_G (eV)
Carbon (diamond)	5.47
Silicon	1.12
Germanium	0.66
Tin	0.082
Gallium arsenide	1.42
Indium phosphide	1.35
Boron nitride	7.50
Silicon carbide	3.00
Cadmium selenide	1.70

giving silicon significant processing advantages over germanium during fabrication of ICs. In addition to silicon, gallium arsenide and indium phosphide are commonly encountered today, although germanium is still used in some limited applications. The compound semiconductor materials gallium arsenide (GaAs) and indium phosphide (InP) are the most important material for optoelectronic applications, including light-emitting diodes (LEDs), lasers, and photo detectors.

Many research laboratories are now exploring the formation of diamond, boron nitride, silicon carbide, and silicon germanium materials. Diamond and boron nitride are excellent insulators at room temperature, but they, as well as silicon carbide, can be used as semiconductors at much higher temperatures (600°C). Adding a small percentage (<10 percent) of germanium to silicon has been shown recently to offer improved device performance in a process compatible with normal silicon processing.

EXERCISE: What are the chemical symbols for antimony, arsenic, aluminum, boron, gallium, germanium, indium, phosphorus, and silicon?

ANSWERS: Sb, As, Al, B, Ga, Ge, In, P, Si

2.2 DRIFT CURRENTS IN SEMICONDUCTORS

Electrical resistivity ρ and its reciprocal, **conductivity** σ, characterize current flow in a material when an electric field is applied. Charged particles move or *drift* in response to the electric field, and the resulting current is called *drift current*. The **drift current density** j is defined as

$$j = Q\mathbf{v} \qquad (C/cm^3)(cm/s) = A/cm^2 \qquad (2.1)$$

where Q = charge density
        $\mathbf{v}$ = velocity of charge in electric field

In order to find the charge density, we explore the structure of silicon using both the covalent bond model and (later) the energy band model for semiconductors. We relate the velocity of the charge carriers to the applied electric field in Sec. 2.4.

2.3 COVALENT BOND MODEL

Atoms can bond together in **amorphous, polycrystalline,** or **single-crystal** forms. Amorphous materials have a totally disordered structure, whereas polycrystalline material consists of a large number of small crystallites. Most of the highly useful properties of semiconductors, however, occur in high-purity, single-crystal material. Silicon—column IV in the periodic table—has four **electrons** in the outer shell. Single-crystal material is formed by the covalent bonding of each silicon atom with its four nearest neighbors in a highly regular three-dimensional array of atoms, as shown in Fig. 2.1. Much of the behavior we discuss can be visualized using the simplified two-dimensional **covalent bond model** of Fig. 2.2.

At temperatures approaching absolute zero, all the electrons reside in the covalent bonds shared between the atoms in the array, with no electrons free for conduction. The outer shells of the silicon atoms are full, and the material behaves as an insulator. As the temperature increases, thermal energy is added to the crystal and some bonds break, freeing a small number of electrons for conduction, as in Fig. 2.3. The density of these free electrons is equal to the **intrinsic carrier density n_i** (cm^{-3}), which is determined by material properties and temperature:

$$n_i^2 = BT^3 \exp\left(-\frac{E_G}{kT}\right) \qquad \text{cm}^{-6} \tag{2.2}$$

where E_G = semiconductor bandgap energy in eV (electron volts)
        k = Boltzmann's constant, 8.62×10^{-5} eV/K
        T = absolute temperature, K
        B = material-dependent parameter, 1.08×10^{31} K$^{-3} \cdot$ cm^{-6} for Si

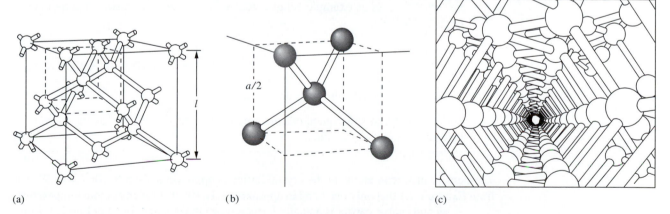

(a)   (b)   (c)

Figure 2.1 Silicon crystal lattice structure. (a) Diamond lattice unit cell. The cube side length l = 0.543 nm. (b) Enlarged top corner of the diamond lattice, showing the four nearest neighbors bonding within the structure. (c) View along a crystallographic axis. [(a) and (b) adapted from *Electrons and Holes in Semiconductors* by William Shockley, © 1950 by Litton Educational Publishing. (c) adapted from *The Architecture of Molecules* by Linus Pauling and Roger Hayward, copyright © 1964 by W. H. Freeman and Company, used with permission; and *Semiconductor Devices: Physics and Technology* by S. M. Sze, copyright © 1985 by Bell Telephone Laboratories, by permission of John Wiley & Sons, Inc.]

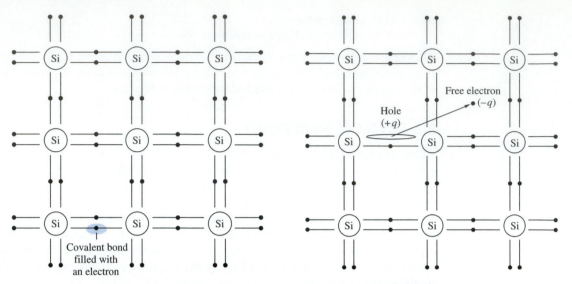

Figure 2.2 Two-dimensional silicon lattice with shared covalent bonds. At temperatures approaching 0 K, all bonds are filled, and the outer shells of the silicon atoms are completely full.

Figure 2.3 An electron–hole pair is generated whenever a covalent bond is broken.

Bandgap energy E_G is the minimum energy needed to break a covalent bond in the semiconductor crystal, thus freeing electrons for conduction. Table 2.3 lists values of the bandgap energy for various semiconductors.

The *density of conduction (or free) electrons* is represented by the symbol n (electrons/cm^3), and for **intrinsic material** $n = n_i$. The term *intrinsic* refers to the generic properties of pure material. Although n_i is an intrinsic property of each semiconductor, it is extremely temperature-dependent for all materials. Figure 2.4 has examples of the strong variation of intrinsic carrier density with temperature for germanium, silicon, and gallium arsenide.

EXAMPLE 2.1: As an example, let us calculate the value of n_i in silicon at room temperature (300 K):

$$n_i^2 = 1.08 \times 10^{31} (\text{K}^{-3} \cdot \text{cm}^{-6})(300 \text{ K})^3 \exp\left(\frac{-1.12}{(8.62 \times 10^{-5} \text{ eV/K})(300 \text{ K})}\right)$$

$$n_i^2 = 4.52 \times 10^{19}/\text{cm}^6 \qquad \text{or} \qquad n_i = 6.73 \times 10^9/\text{cm}^3$$

For simplicity, in subsequent calculations we use $n_i = 10^{10}/\text{cm}^3$ as the room temperature value of n_i for silicon.   ◆

The density of silicon atoms in the crystal lattice is approximately $5 \times 10^{22}/\text{cm}^3$. We see from Example 2.1 that only one bond in approximately 10^{13} is broken at room temperature.

A second charge carrier is actually formed when the covalent bond in Fig. 2.3 is broken. As an electron, which has charge $-q$ equal to -1.602×10^{-19} C, moves away from the covalent bond, it leaves behind a **vacancy** in the bond structure in the vicinity of its parent silicon atom. The vacancy is left with an effective charge of $+q$. An electron from an adjacent bond can fill this vacancy, creating a new vacancy in another position. This process allows the vacancy to move through the crystal. The moving vacancy behaves just

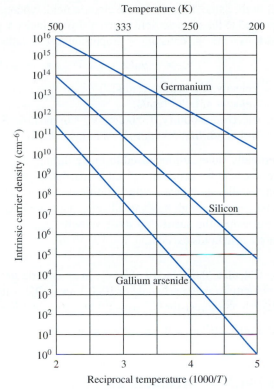

Temperature (K)

Figure 2.4 Intrinsic carrier density versus temperature from Eq. (2.2), using $B = 1.08 \times 10^{31} \text{ K}^{-3} \cdot \text{cm}^{-6}$ for Ge, $B = 2.31 \times 10^{30}$ $\text{K}^{-3} \cdot \text{cm}^{-6}$ for Si, and $B = 1.27 \times 10^{29} \text{ K}^{-3} \cdot \text{cm}^{-6}$ for GaAs.

as a particle with charge $+q$ and is called a **hole. Hole density** is represented by the symbol p (holes/cm^3).

As described above, two charged particles are created for each bond that is broken: one electron and one hole. For intrinsic silicon,

$$n = n_i = p \tag{2.3}$$

and the product of the electron and hole concentrations is

$$pn = n_i^2 \tag{2.4}$$

The **pn product** is given by Eq. (2.4) whenever a semiconductor is in **thermal equilibrium.** (This very important result is used later.) In thermal equilibrium, material properties are dependent only on the temperature T, with no other form of stimulus applied. Equation (2.4) does not apply to semiconductors operating in the presence of an external stimulus such as an applied voltage or current or an optical excitation.

> **EXERCISE:** Calculate the intrinsic carrier density in silicon at 50 K and 325 K. On the average, what is the length of one side of the cube of silicon that is needed to find one electron and one hole at $T = 50$ K?
>
> **ANSWERS:** 4.34×10^{-39}/cm^3; 4.01×10^{10}/cm^3; 6.13×10^{10} m

2.4 MOBILITY

As discussed earlier, charged particles move in response to an applied electric field. This movement is termed drift, and the resulting current flow is known as drift current. Positive charges drift in the same direction as the electric field, whereas negative charges drift in a direction opposed to the electric field. Carrier drift velocity $\mathbf{v}$ (cm/s) is proportional to the electric field $\mathbf{E}$ (V/cm); the constant of proportionality is called the **mobility** μ:

$$\mathbf{v}_n = -\mu_n \mathbf{E} \qquad \text{and} \qquad \mathbf{v}_p = \mu_p \mathbf{E} \qquad (2.5)$$

where $\mathbf{v}_n$ = velocity of electrons (cm/s)
  $\mathbf{v}_p$ = velocity of holes (cm/s)
  μ_n = **electron mobility,** 1350 cm^2/V · s in intrinsic Si
  μ_p = **hole mobility,** 500 cm^2/V · s in intrinsic Si

Conceptually, holes are localized to move through the covalent bond structure, but electrons are free to move about the crystal. Thus, one might expect hole mobility to be less than electron mobility, as appears in the definitions in Eq. (2.5). Note that the relationship in Eq. (2.5) breaks down at high fields in all semiconductors because the velocity of carriers reaches a limit called the **saturated drift velocity $\mathbf{v}_{\text{sat}}$.** In silicon, v_{sat} is approximately 10^7 cm/s for electric fields exceeding 3×10^4 V/cm.

> **EXERCISE:** Calculate the velocity of a hole in an electric field of 10 V/cm. What is the electron velocity in an electric field of 1000 V/cm? The voltage across a resistor is 1 V, and the length of the resistor is 2 μm. What is the electric field in the resistor?
>
> **ANSWERS:** 5.00×10^3 cm/s; 1.35×10^6 cm/s; 5.00×10^3 V/cm.

2.5 RESISTIVITY OF INTRINSIC SILICON

We are now in a position to calculate the electron and hole drift current densities j_n^{drift} and j_p^{drift}. For simplicity, we assume a one-dimensional current and avoid the vector notation of Eq. (2.1):

$$j_n^{\text{drift}} = Q_n v_n = (-qn)(-\mu_n E) = qn\mu_n E \qquad \text{A/cm}^2$$
$$j_p^{\text{drift}} = Q_p v_p = (+qp)(+\mu_p E) = qp\mu_p E \qquad \text{A/cm}^2 \qquad (2.6)$$

in which $Q_n = (-qn)$ and $Q_p = (+qp)$ represent the charge densities (C/cm^3) of electrons and holes, respectively. The total drift current density is then given by

$$j_T^{\text{drift}} = j_n + j_p = q(n\mu_n + p\mu_p)E = \sigma E \qquad (2.7)$$

This equation defines σ, the **electrical conductivity:**

$$\sigma = q(n\mu_n + p\mu_p) \qquad (\Omega \cdot \text{cm})^{-1} \qquad (2.8)$$

For intrinsic silicon, the charge density of electrons is given by $Q_n = -qn_i$, whereas the charge density for holes is $Q_p = +qn_i$. The values of the mobilities in intrinsic silicon were given in Eq. (2.5), and

$$\sigma = (1.60 \times 10^{-19})[(10^{10})(1350) + (10^{10})(500)] \qquad (C)(\text{cm}^{-3})(\text{cm}^2/\text{V} \cdot \text{s})$$
$$= 2.96 \times 10^{-6} \ (\Omega \cdot \text{cm})^{-1}$$

The resistivity ρ is equal to the reciprocal of the conductivity, so for intrinsic silicon

$$\rho = \frac{1}{\sigma} = 3.38 \times 10^5 \ \Omega \cdot \text{cm} \qquad (2.9)$$

From Table 2.1, we see that intrinsic silicon can be characterized as an insulator, albeit near the low end of the insulator resistivity range.

EXERCISE: Calculate the resistivity of intrinsic silicon at 50 K if the electron mobility is 6500 cm^2/V · s and the hole mobility is 2000 cm^2/V · s.

ANSWER: 1.69×10^{53} Ω · cm

2.6 IMPURITIES IN SEMICONDUCTORS

The real advantages of semiconductors emerge when **impurities** are added to the material in minute but well-controlled amounts. This process is called **impurity doping,** or just **doping,** and the material that results is termed a **doped semiconductor.** Impurity doping allows us to change the resistivity over a very wide range and to determine whether the electron or hole population controls the resistivity of the material. The following discussion focuses on silicon, although the concepts of impurity doping apply equally well to other materials. The impurities that we use with silicon most often are from columns III and V of the periodic table.

Donor Impurities in Silicon

Donor impurities in silicon are from column V, having five valence electrons in the outer shell. The most commonly used elements are phosphorus, arsenic, and antimony. When a donor atom replaces a silicon atom in the crystal lattice, as shown in Fig. 2.5, four of the five outer shell electrons fill the covalent bond structure; it then takes very little thermal energy to free the extra electron for conduction. At room temperature, essentially every donor atom contributes (donates) an electron for conduction. Each donor atom that becomes ionized by giving up an electron will have a net charge of $+q$ and represents an immobile fixed charge in the crystal lattice.

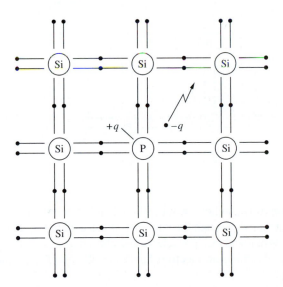

Figure 2.5 An extra electron is available from a phosphorus donor atom.

Acceptor Impurities in Silicon

Acceptor impurities in silicon are from column III and have one less electron than silicon in the outer shell. The primary acceptor impurity is boron, which is shown in place of a silicon atom in the lattice in Fig. 2.6(a). Because boron has only three electrons in its outer shell, a vacancy exists in the bond structure. It is easy for a nearby electron to move into this

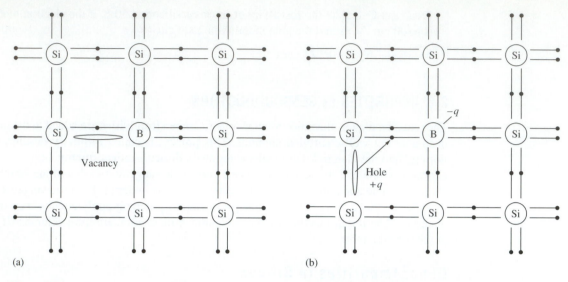

(a)

Figure 2.6 (a) Covalent bond vacancy from boron acceptor atom.

Figure 2.6 (b) Hole created after the boron atom accepts an electron.

(b)

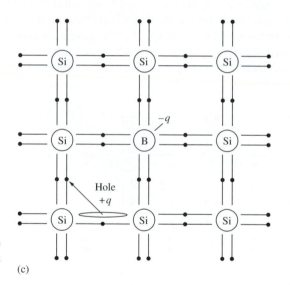

Figure 2.6 (c) Mobile hole moving through the silicon lattice.

(c)

vacancy, creating another vacancy in the bond structure. This mobile vacancy represents a hole that can move through the lattice, as illustrated in Fig. 2.6(b) and (c), and the hole may simply be visualized as a particle with a charge of $+q$. Each impurity atom that becomes ionized by accepting an electron has a net charge of $-q$, immobile in the lattice, as in Fig. 2.6(b).

2.7 ELECTRON AND HOLE CONCENTRATIONS IN DOPED SEMICONDUCTORS

We now discover how to calculate the **electron** and **hole concentrations** in a semiconductor containing donor and acceptor impurities. In doped material, the electron and hole concentrations are no longer equal. If $n > p$, the material is called **n-type,** and if $p >$

n, the material is referred to as **p-type.** The carrier with the larger population is called the **majority carrier,** and the carrier with the smaller population is termed the **minority carrier.**

To make detailed calculations of electron and hole densities, we need to keep track of the donor and acceptor impurity concentrations:

$$N_D = \textbf{donor impurity concentration} \qquad \text{atoms/cm}^3$$

$$N_A = \textbf{acceptor impurity concentration} \qquad \text{atoms/cm}^3$$

Two additional pieces of information are needed. First, the semiconductor material must remain charge neutral, which requires that the sum of the total positive charge and negative charge be zero. Ionized donors and holes represent positive charge, whereas ionized acceptors and electrons carry negative charge. Thus **charge neutrality** requires

$$q(N_D + p - N_A - n) = 0 \qquad (2.10)$$

Second, the product of the electron and hole concentrations in intrinsic material was given in Eq. (2.4) as $pn = n_i^2$. It can be shown theoretically that $pn = n_i^2$ even for doped semiconductors in thermal equilibrium, and Eq. (2.4) is valid for a very wide range of doping concentrations.

n-Type Material ($N_D > N_A$)

Solving Eq. (2.4) for p and substituting into Eq. (2.10) yields a quadratic equation for n:

$$n^2 - (N_D - N_A)n - n_i^2 = 0$$

Now solving for n,

$$n = \frac{(N_D - N_A) \pm \sqrt{(N_D - N_A)^2 + 4n_i^2}}{2} \qquad \text{and} \qquad p = \frac{n_i^2}{n} \qquad (2.11)$$

In practical situations $(N_D - N_A) \gg 2n_i$, and n is given approximately by $n \approx (N_D - N_A)$. The formulas in Eq. (2.11) should be used for $N_D > N_A$ (see Prob. 2.17).

p-Type Material ($N_A > N_D$)

For the case of $N_A > N_D$, we substitute for n in Eq. (2.10) and use the quadratic formula to solve for p:

$$p = \frac{(N_A - N_D) \pm \sqrt{(N_A - N_D)^2 + 4n_i^2}}{2} \qquad \text{and} \qquad n = \frac{n_i^2}{p} \qquad (2.12)$$

Again, the usual case is $(N_A - N_D) \gg 2n_i$, and p is given approximately by $p \approx (N_A - N_D)$. Equation (2.12) should be used for $N_A > N_D$.

Because of practical process-control limitations, impurity densities that can be introduced into the silicon lattice range from approximately 10^{14} to 10^{21} atoms/cm^3. Thus, N_A and N_D normally will be much greater than the intrinsic carrier concentration in silicon at room temperature. From the approximate expressions above, we see that the majority carrier density is set directly by the net impurity concentration: $p \approx (N_A - N_D)$ for $N_A > N_D$ or $n \approx (N_D - N_A)$ for $N_D > N_A$.

Thus, in both *n*- and *p*-type semiconductors, the majority carrier concentrations are established "at the factory" by the values of N_A and N_D and therefore are independent of temperature. In contrast, the minority carrier concentrations, although small, are proportional to n_i^2 and highly temperature-dependent.

> **EXERCISE:** Silicon is doped with an antimony concentration of 2×10^{16}/cm^3. Is antimony a donor or acceptor impurity? Find the electron and hole concentrations at 300 K. Is this material *n*- or *p*-type?

ANSWERS: Donor; $2 \times 10^{16}/\text{cm}^3$; $5 \times 10^3/\text{cm}^3$; n-type

EXERCISE: Silicon is doped with a phosphorus concentration of $1 \times 10^{17}/\text{cm}^3$. Find the electron and hole concentrations at $T = 50$ K if $n_i = 4.34 \times 10^{-34}/\text{cm}^2$.

ANSWERS: $1 \times 10^{17}/\text{cm}^3$; ≈ 0

2.8 ENERGY BAND MODEL

This section discusses the **energy band model** for a semiconductor, which provides a useful alternative view of the electron–hole creation process and the control of carrier concentrations by impurities. Quantum mechanics predicts that the highly regular crystalline structure of a semiconductor produces periodic quantized ranges of allowed and disallowed energy states for the electrons surrounding the atoms in the crystal. Figure 2.7 is a conceptual picture of this band structure in the semiconductor, in which the regions labeled **conduction band** and **valence band** represent allowed energy states for electrons. Energy E_V corresponds to the top edge of the valence band and represents the highest permissible energy for a valence electron. Energy E_C corresponds to the bottom edge of the conduction band and represents the lowest available energy level in the conduction band. Although these bands are shown as continuums in Fig. 2.7, they actually consist of a very large number of closely spaced, discrete energy levels.

Electrons are not permitted to assume values of energy lying between E_C and E_V. The difference between E_C and E_V is called the *bandgap energy E_G*:

$$E_G = E_C - E_V \tag{2.13}$$

Table 2.3 gives examples of the bandgap energy for a number of semiconductors.

Electron–Hole Pair Generation in an Intrinsic Semiconductor

In silicon at very low temperatures (≈ 0 K), the valence band states are completely filled with electrons, and the conduction band states are completely empty, as shown in Fig. 2.8. The semiconductor in this situation does not conduct current when an electric

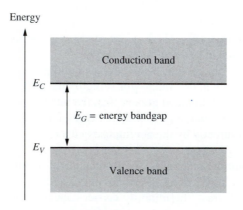

Figure 2.7 Energy band model for a semiconductor with bandgap E_G.

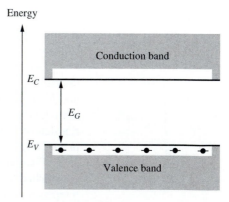

Figure 2.8 Semiconductor at 0 K with filled valence band and empty conduction band. This figure corresponds to the bond model in Figure 2.2.

field is applied. There are no free electrons in the conduction band, and no holes exist in the completely filled valence band to support current flow. The band model of Fig. 2.8 corresponds directly to the completely filled bond model of Fig. 2.2.

As temperature rises above 0 K, thermal energy is added to the crystal. A few electrons gain the energy required to surmount the energy bandgap and jump from the valence band into the conduction band, as shown in Fig. 2.9. Each electron that jumps the bandgap creates an electron–hole pair. This **electron–hole pair generation** situation corresponds directly to that presented in Fig. 2.3.

Energy Band Model for a Doped Semiconductor

Figures 2.10 to 2.12 present the band model for **extrinsic material** containing donor and/or acceptor atoms. In Fig. 2.10, a concentration N_D of donor atoms has been added to the semiconductor. The donor atoms introduce new localized energy levels within the bandgap at a **donor energy level E_D** near the conduction band edge. The value of $(E_C - E_D)$ for phosphorus is approximately 0.045 eV, so it takes very little thermal energy to promote the extra electrons from the donor sites into the conduction band. The density of conduction-band states is so high that the probability of finding an electron in a donor state is practically zero, except for heavily doped material (large N_D) or at very low temperature. Thus at room temperature, essentially all the available donor electrons are free for conduction. Figure 2.10 corresponds to the bond model of Fig. 2.5.

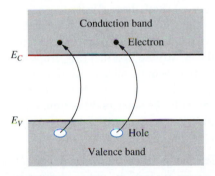

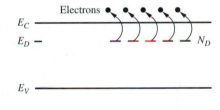

Figure 2.9 Creation of electron–hole pair by thermal excitation across the energy bandgap. This figure corresponds to the bond model of Figure 2.3.

Figure 2.10 Donor level with activation energy $(E_C - E_D)$. This figure corresponds to the bond model of Figure 2.5.

In Fig. 2.11, a concentration N_A of acceptor atoms has been added to the semiconductor. The acceptor atoms introduce energy levels within the bandgap at the **acceptor energy level E_A** near the valence band edge. The value of $(E_A - E_V)$ for boron is approximately 0.044 eV, and it takes very little thermal energy to promote electrons from the valence band into the acceptor energy levels. At room temperature, essentially all the available acceptor sites are filled, and each promoted electron creates a hole that is free for conduction. Figure 2.11 corresponds to the bond model of Fig. 2.6(b).

Compensated Semiconductors

The situation for a **compensated semiconductor,** one containing both acceptor and donor impurities, is depicted in Fig. 2.12 for the case in which there are more donor atoms than acceptor atoms. Electrons seek the lowest energy states available, and they fall from donor

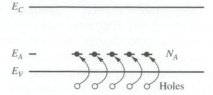

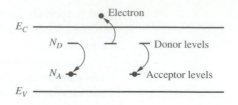

Figure 2.11 Acceptor level with activation energy $(E_A - E_V)$. This figure corresponds to the bond model of Figure 2.6(b).

Figure 2.12 Compensated semiconductor containing both donor and acceptor atoms with $N_D > N_A$.

sites, filling all the available acceptor sites. The remaining free electron population is given by $n = (N_D - N_A)$.

2.9   MOBILITY AND RESISTIVITY IN DOPED SEMICONDUCTORS

The introduction of impurities into a semiconductor such as silicon actually degrades the mobility of the carriers in the material. Impurity atoms have slightly different sizes than the silicon atoms that they replace and hence disrupt the periodicity of the lattice. In addition, the impurity atoms are ionized and represent regions of localized charge that were not present in the original crystal. Both these effects cause the electrons and holes to scatter as they move through the semiconductor and reduce the mobility of the carriers in the crystal.

Figure 2.13 shows the dependence of mobility on the *total* impurity doping density $N = (N_A + N_D)$ in silicon. We see that mobility drops rapidly as the doping level in the crystal increases. Mobility in heavily doped material can be more than an order of magnitude less than that in lightly doped material. On the other hand, doping vastly increases the density of majority carriers in the semiconductor material and thus has a dramatic effect on resistivity that overcomes the influence of decreased mobility.

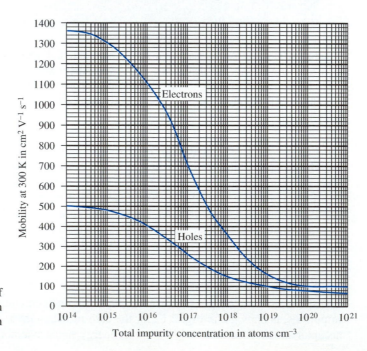

Figure 2.13 Dependence of electron and hole mobility on total impurity concentration in silicon at 300 K.

EXERCISE: What are the electron and hole mobilities in a silicon sample with an acceptor impurity density of 10^{16}/cm^3?

ANSWERS: 1110 cm^2/V · s; 400 cm^2/V · s

EXERCISE: What are the electron and hole mobilities in a silicon sample with an acceptor impurity density of 4×10^{16}/cm^3 and a donor impurity density of 6×10^{16}/cm^3?

ANSWERS: 710 cm^2/V · s, 260 cm^2/V · s.

EXAMPLE 2.2: Let us calculate the resistivity of silicon doped with a donor density $N_D = 2 \times 10^{15}$/cm^3 ($N_A = 0$). Note that this represents replacement of less than 10^{-5}% of the atoms in the silicon crystal.

SOLUTION: In this case, $N_D > N_A$ and much much greater than n_i, so

$$n = N_D = 2 \times 10^{15} \text{ electrons/cm}^3$$

$$p = \frac{n_i^2}{n} = 10^{20}/2 \times 10^{15} = 5 \times 10^4 \text{ holes/cm}^3$$

Because $n > p$, the silicon is n-type material. From Fig. 2.13, the electron and hole mobilities for an impurity concentration of 2×10^{15}/cm^3 are

$$\mu_n = 1260 \text{ cm}^2/\text{V} \cdot \text{s} \qquad \mu_p = 460 \text{ cm}^2/\text{V} \cdot \text{s}$$

The conductivity and resistivity are now found to be

$$\sigma = 1.6 \times 10^{-19}[(1260)(2 \times 10^{15}) + (460)(5 \times 10^4)] = 0.403 \ (\Omega \cdot \text{cm})^{-1}$$

and $\rho = 2.48 \ \Omega \cdot \text{cm}$ ◆

Comparing these results to those for intrinsic silicon, we note that the introduction of a minute fraction of impurities into the silicon lattice has changed the resistivity by 5 orders of magnitude, changing the material from an insulator to a midrange semiconductor.

Impurity doping also determines whether the material is n- or p-type, and simplified expressions can be used to calculate the conductivity of most extrinsic material. Note that $\mu_n n \gg \mu_p p$ in the expression for σ in Example 2.2. For doping levels normally encountered, this inequality will be true for n-type material, and $\mu_p p \gg \mu_n n$ will be valid for p-type material. The majority carrier concentration controls the conductivity of the material so that

$$\sigma \approx q\mu_n n \approx q\mu_n(N_D - N_A) \qquad \text{for } n\text{-type material}$$
$$\sigma \approx q\mu_p p \approx q\mu_p(N_A - N_D) \qquad \text{for } p\text{-type material}$$

(2.14)

EXAMPLE 2.3: An n-type silicon wafer has a resistivity of 0.054 $\Omega \cdot$ cm. It is known that the silicon contains only donor impurities. What is the donor concentration N_D?

SOLUTION: For this problem, an iterative trial-and-error solution is necessary. Because the resistivity is low, it should be safe to assume that

$$\sigma = q\mu_n n = q\mu_n N_D \qquad \text{and} \qquad \mu_n N_D = \frac{\sigma}{q}$$

We know that μ_n is a function of the doping concentration N_D, but the functional dependence is available only in graphical form. This is an example of a type of problem often encountered in engineering. The solution requires an iterative trial-and-error approach involving both mathematical and graphical evaluations. To solve the problem, we need to establish a logical progression of steps in which the choice of one parameter allows us to evaluate other parameters that lead to the solution. One method for this problem is:

1. Choose a value of N_D.
2. Find μ_n from the mobility graph.
3. Calculate $\mu_n N_D$.
4. If $\mu_n N_D$ is not correct, go back to step 1.

Obviously, we hope we can make educated choices that will lead to convergence of the process after a few trials. For this problem,

$$\frac{\sigma}{q} = (0.054 \times 1.6 \times 10^{-19})^{-1} = 1.2 \times 10^{20} \ (V \cdot s \cdot cm)^{-1}$$

Trial	N_D (cm^{-3})	μ_n (cm^2/V $\cdot$ s)	$\mu_n N_D$ (V $\cdot$ s $\cdot$ cm)$^{-1}$
1	1×10^{16}	1100	1.1×10^{19}
2	1×10^{18}	350	3.5×10^{20}
3	1×10^{17}	710	7.1×10^{19}
4	5×10^{17}	440	2.2×10^{20}
5	4×10^{17}	470	1.9×10^{20}
6	2×10^{17}	580	1.2×10^{20}

After six iterations, we find $N_D = 2 \times 10^{17}$ donor atoms/cm^3. ◆

EXERCISE: Silicon is doped with a phosphorus concentration of 2×10^{16}/cm^3. What are N_A and N_D? What are the electron and hole mobilities? What are the mobilities if boron in a concentration of 3×10^{16}/cm^3 is added to the silicon?

ANSWERS: $N_A = 0$/cm^3; $N_D = 2 \times 10^{16}$/cm^3; $\mu_n = 1030$ cm^2/V $\cdot$ s, $\mu_p = 370$ cm^2/V $\cdot$ s; $\mu_n = 870$ cm^2/V $\cdot$ s; $\mu_p = 310$ cm^2/V $\cdot$ s.

EXERCISE: Silicon is doped with a boron concentration of 4×10^{18}/cm^3. Is boron a donor or acceptor impurity? Find the electron and hole concentrations at 300 K. Is this material n-type or p-type? Find the electron and hole mobilities. Is this material n- or p-type?

ANSWERS: Acceptor; $n = 25$/cm^3, $p = 4 \times 10^{18}$/cm^3; p-type; $\mu_n = 220$ cm^2/V $\cdot$ s and $\mu_p = 110$ cm^2/V $\cdot$ s.

EXERCISE: Silicon is doped with an indium concentration of 7×10^{19}/cm^3. Is indium a donor or acceptor impurity? Find the electron and hole concentrations, the electron and hole mobilities, and the resistivity of this silicon material at 300 K. Is this material *n*- or *p*-type?

ANSWERS: Acceptor; $n = 1.4/\text{cm}^3$, $p = 7 \times 10^{19}/\text{cm}^3$; $\mu_n = 100 \text{ cm}^2/\text{V} \cdot \text{s}$ and $\mu_p = 70 \text{ cm}^2/\text{V} \cdot \text{s}$; $\rho = 0.00127 \ \Omega \cdot \text{cm}$; *p*-type.

2.10 DIFFUSION CURRENTS

As described above, the electron and hole populations in a semiconductor are controlled by the impurity doping concentrations N_A and N_D. Up to this point we have tacitly assumed that the doping is uniform in the semiconductor, but this need not be the case. Changes in doping are encountered often in semiconductors, and there will be gradients in the electron and hole concentrations. Gradients in these free carrier densities give rise to a second current flow mechanism, called **diffusion.** The free carriers tend to move (diffuse) from regions of high concentration to regions of low concentration in much the same way as a puff of smoke in one corner of a room rapidly spreads throughout the entire room.

A simple one-dimensional gradient in the electron or hole density is shown in Fig. 2.14. The gradient in this figure is positive in the $+x$ direction, but the carriers diffuse in the $-x$ direction, from high to low concentration. Thus the diffusion current densities are proportional to the negative of the carrier gradient:

$$j_p^{\text{diff}} = (+q)D_p\left(-\frac{\partial p}{\partial x}\right) = -qD_p\frac{\partial p}{\partial x}$$

$$j_n^{\text{diff}} = (-q)D_n\left(-\frac{\partial n}{\partial x}\right) = +qD_n\frac{\partial n}{\partial x}$$

$$\text{A/cm}^2 \qquad (2.15)$$

The proportionality constants D_p and D_n are the **hole** and **electron diffusivities,** with units (cm^2/s). Diffusivity and mobility are related by **Einstein's relationship:**

$$\frac{D_n}{\mu_n} = \frac{kT}{q} = \frac{D_p}{\mu_p} \qquad (2.16)$$

The quantity $(kT/q = V_T)$ is called the **thermal voltage V_T**, and its value is approximately 0.025 V at room temperature. We encounter the parameter V_T in several different contexts throughout this book.

EXERCISE: Calculate the value of the thermal voltage V_T for $T = 50$ K, 325 K.

ANSWERS: 4.3 mV; 28 mV

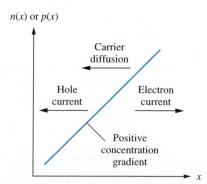

Figure 2.14 Carrier diffusion in the presence of a concentration gradient.

> **EXERCISE:** An electron gradient of $+10^{16}/(\text{cm}^3 \cdot \mu\text{m})$ exists in a semiconductor. What is the diffusion current density at room temperature if the electron diffusivity $= 20 \text{ cm}^2/\text{s}$?
>
> **ANSWER:** $+320 \text{ A/cm}^2$

2.11 TOTAL CURRENT

Generally, currents in a semiconductor have both drift and diffusion components. The total electron and hole current densities j_n^T and j_p^T can be found by adding the corresponding drift and diffusion components from Eqs. (2.6) and (2.15):

$$j_n^T = q\mu_n nE + qD_n \frac{\partial n}{\partial x}$$

$$j_p^T = q\mu_p pE - qD_p \frac{\partial p}{\partial x} \tag{2.17}$$

Using Einstein's relationship from Eq. (2.16), Eq. (2.17) can be rewritten as

$$j_n^T = q\mu_n n \left(E + V_T \frac{1}{n} \frac{\partial n}{\partial x} \right)$$

$$j_p^T = q\mu_p p \left(E - V_T \frac{1}{p} \frac{\partial p}{\partial x} \right) \tag{2.18}$$

Equation (2.17) or (2.18) combined with Gauss' law

$$\nabla \cdot (\varepsilon E) = Q \tag{2.19}$$

where ε = permittivity (F/cm)
E = electric field (V/cm)
Q = charge density (C/cm^3)

gives us a powerful mathematics approach for analyzing the behavior of semiconductors and forms the basis for many of the results presented in later chapters.

SUMMARY

Materials are found in three primary forms: amorphous, polycrystalline, and crystalline. An amorphous material is totally disordered or random material that shows no short-range order. In polycrystalline material, large numbers of small crystallites can be identified. A crystalline material exhibits a highly regular bonding structure among the atoms over the entire macroscopic crystal.

Electronic materials can be separated into three classifications based on their electrical resistivity. Insulators have resistivities above $10^5 \ \Omega \cdot \text{cm}$, whereas conductors have resistivities below $10^{-3} \ \Omega \cdot \text{cm}$. Between these two extremes lie semiconductor materials. Today's most important semiconductor is silicon (Si), which is used for fabrication of very-large-scale-integrated (VLSI) circuits. Two compound semiconductor materials, gallium arsenide (GaAs) and indium phosphide (InP), are the most important materials for optoelectronic applications including light-emitting diodes (LEDs), lasers, and photo detectors.

The highly useful properties of semiconductors arise from the periodic nature of crystalline material, and two conceptual models for these semiconductors were introduced: the covalent bond model and the energy band model. At very low temperatures approaching 0 K, all the covalent bonds in a semiconductor crystal will be intact and the material will actually be an insulator. As temperature is raised, the added thermal energy causes a small number of covalent bonds to break. The amount of energy required to break a covalent bond is equal to the bandgap energy E_G. When a covalent bond is broken, two charge carriers are produced: an electron, with charge $-q$, which is free to move about the conduction band; and a hole, with charge $+q$, which is free to move through the valence band. Pure material is referred to as intrinsic material, and the electron density n and hole density p in an intrinsic material are both equal to the intrinsic carrier density n_i, which is approximately equal to 10^{10} carriers/cm^3 in silicon at room temperature. In a material in thermal equilibrium, the product of the electron and hole concentrations is a constant: $pn = n_i^2$.

The hole and electron concentrations can be significantly altered by replacing small numbers of atoms in the original crystal with impurity atoms. Silicon, a column IV element, has four electrons in its outer shell and forms covalent bonds with its four nearest neighbors in the crystal. In contrast, the impurity elements (from columns III and V of the periodic table) have either three or five electrons in their outer shells. Column V elements such as phosphorus, arsenic, and antimony, with an extra electron in the outer shell, act as donors and add electrons directly to the conduction band. A column III element such as boron has only three outer shell electrons and creates a free hole in the valence band. The donor and acceptor impurity densities are usually represented by N_D and N_A, respectively.

If n exceeds p, the semiconductor is referred to as n-type material, and electrons are the majority carriers and holes are the minority carriers. If p exceeds n, the semiconductor is referred to as p-type material, and holes become the majority carriers and electrons, the minority carriers.

Electron and hole currents each have two components: a drift current and a diffusion current. Drift current is the result of carrier motion caused by an applied electric field; diffusion currents arise from gradients in the electron or hole concentrations. Drift currents are proportional to the electron and hole mobilities (μ_n and μ_p, respectively), and the magnitudes of the diffusion currents are proportional to the electron and hole diffusivities (D_n and D_p, respectively). Diffusivity and mobility are related by the Einstein relationship: $D/\mu = kT/q$. The expression kT/q has units of voltage and is often referred to as the thermal voltage V_T. Doping the semiconductor disrupts the periodicity of the crystal lattice, and the mobility—and hence diffusivity—both decrease monotonically as the impurity doping concentration is increased.

The ability to add impurities to change the conductivity type and to control hole and electron concentrations is at the heart of our ability to fabricate high-performance, solid-state devices and high-density integrated circuits. In the next several chapters we see how this capability is used to form diodes, field-effect transistors (FETs), and bipolar junction transistors (BJTs).

Key Terms

Acceptor energy level	Compensated semiconductor	Diffusion current density
Acceptor impurities	Compound semiconductor	Donor energy level
Acceptor impurity concentration	Conduction band	Donor impurities
Amorphous material	Conductivity	Donor impurity concentration
Bandgap energy	Conductor	Doped semiconductor
Charge neutrality	Covalent bond model	Doping

Drift current density
Einstein's relationship
Electrical conductivity
Electron
Electron concentration
Electron diffusivity
Electron–hole pair generation
Electron mobility
Elemental semiconductor
Energy band model
Extrinsic material
Hole

Hole concentration
Hole density
Hole diffusivity
Hole mobility
Impurities
Impurity doping
Insulator
Intrinsic carrier density
Intrinsic material
Majority carrier
Minority carrier
Mobility

n-type material
p-type material
pn product
Polycrystalline material
Resistivity
Saturated drift velocity
Semiconductor
Single-crystal material
Thermal equilibrium
Thermal voltage
Vacancy
Valence band

Additional Reading

Jaeger, R. C. *Introduction to Microelectronic Fabrication.* Addison-Wesley, Reading, MA: 1988.

Pierret, R. F. *Semiconductor Fundamentals.* Addison-Wesley, Reading, MA: 1983.

Sze, S. M. *Physics of Semiconductor Devices.* Wiley, New York: 1981.

Yang, E. S. *Microelectronic Devices.* McGraw-Hill, New York: 1988.

Important Equations

$$n_1^2 = BT^3 \exp\left(-\frac{E_G}{kT}\right) \quad \text{cm}^{-6} \tag{2.2}$$

where E_G = semiconductor bandgap energy in eV (electron volts)

k = Boltzmann's constant, 8.62×10^{-5} eV/K

T = absolute temperature, K

B = material-dependent parameter, $1.08 \times 10^{31}/\text{K}^{-3} \cdot \text{cm}^{-6}$ for Si

$$\sigma = q(n\mu_n + p\mu_p) \quad (\Omega \cdot \text{cm})^{-1} \tag{2.8}$$

Doped Semiconductors

$$q(N_D + p - N_A - n) = 0 \tag{2.10}$$

_n_-Type Material ($N_D > N_A$)

$$n = \frac{(N_D - N_A) \pm \sqrt{(N_D - N_A)^2 + 4n_i^2}}{2} \quad \text{and} \quad p = \frac{n_i^2}{n} \tag{2.11}$$

_p_-Type Material ($N_A > N_D$)

$$p = \frac{(N_A - N_D) \pm \sqrt{(N_A - N_D)^2 + 4n_i^2}}{2} \quad \text{and} \quad n = \frac{n_i^2}{p} \tag{2.12}$$

Currents

$$j_n^{\text{drift}} = Q_n v_n = (-qn)(-\mu_n E) = qn\mu_n E \quad \text{A/cm}^2$$

$$j_p^{\text{drift}} = Q_p v_p = (+qp)(+\mu_p E) = qp\mu_p E \quad \text{A/cm}^2 \tag{2.6}$$

$$j_p^{\text{diff}} = (+q)D_p\left(-\frac{\partial p}{\partial x}\right) = -qD_p\frac{\partial p}{\partial x}$$

$$\quad \text{A/cm}^2 \tag{2.15}$$

$$j_n^{\text{diff}} = (-q)D_n\left(-\frac{\partial n}{\partial x}\right) = +qD_n\frac{\partial n}{\partial x}$$

$$j_n^T = q\mu_n nE + qD_n \frac{\partial n}{\partial x}$$

$$j_p^T = q\mu_p pE - qD_p \frac{\partial p}{\partial x}$$

(2.17)

Problems

2.1 Solid-State Electronic Materials

2.1. Pure aluminum has a resistivity of 2.6 $\mu\Omega \cdot$ cm. Based on its resistivity, should aluminum be classified as an insulator, semiconductor, or conductor?

2.2 Drift Currents in Semiconductors

2.2. Use Eq. (2.2) to calculate the actual temperature that corresponds to the value $n_i = 10^{10}/\text{cm}^3$ in silicon.

2.3. The maximum drift velocity of electrons in silicon is 10^7 cm/s. If the silicon has a charge density of 0.5 C/cm^3, what is the maximum current density in the material?

2.4. A current density of -1000 A/cm^2 exists in a semiconductor having a charge density of 0.02 C/cm^3. What are the carrier velocities?

2.3 Covalent Bond Model

2.5. Calculate the intrinsic carrier densities in silicon and germanium at (a) 100 K, (b) 300 K, and (c) 500 K. Use the bandgap information from Table 2.3, and assume that $B = 2.31 \times 10^{30}/(\text{K}^3 \cdot \text{cm}^6)$ for germanium.

2.6. (a) At what temperature will $n_i = 10^{15}/\text{cm}^3$ in silicon? (b) Repeat the calculation for $n_i = 10^{18}/\text{cm}^3$.

2.4 Mobility

2.7. Electrons and holes are moving in a uniform, one-dimensional electric field $E = +3000$ V/cm. The electrons and holes have mobilities of 710 and 260 cm^2/V $\cdot$ s, respectively. What are the electron and hole velocities? If $n = 10^{17}/\text{cm}^3$ and $p = 10^3/\text{cm}^3$, what are the electron and hole current densities?

2.5 Resistivity of Intrinsic Silicon

2.8. At what temperature will intrinsic silicon become a conductor based on the definitions in Table 2.1? Assume that $\mu_n = 100$ cm^2/V $\cdot$ s and $\mu_p = 50$ cm^2/V $\cdot$ s.

2.9. At what temperature will intrinsic silicon become an insulator, based on the definitions in Table 2.1?

Assume that $\mu_n = 2000$ cm^2/V $\cdot$ s and $\mu_p = 750$ cm^2/V $\cdot$ s.

2.6 Impurities in Semiconductors

2.10. Draw a two-dimensional conceptual picture [similar to Fig. 2.6(a)] of the silicon lattice containing one donor atom and one acceptor atom in adjacent lattice positions. Are there any free electrons or holes?

*2.11. GaAs is composed of equal numbers of atoms of gallium and arsenic in a lattice similar to that of silicon. (a) Suppose a silicon atom replaces a gallium atom in the lattice. Do you expect the silicon atom to behave as a donor or acceptor impurity? Why? (b) Suppose a silicon atom replaces an arsenic atom in the lattice. Do you expect the silicon atom to behave as a donor or acceptor impurity? Why?

2.12. A current density of 10,000 A/cm^2 exists in a 0.01-$\Omega \cdot$ cm n-type silicon sample. What is the electric field needed to support this drift current density?

2.13. The maximum drift velocity of carriers in silicon is approximately 10^7 cm/s. What is the maximum drift current density that can be supported in an n-type silicon with a doping of $10^{16}/\text{cm}^3$?

2.7 Electron and Hole Concentrations in Doped Semiconductors

2.14. Suppose a semiconductor has $N_A = 10^{15}/\text{cm}^3$, $N_D = 10^{14}/\text{cm}^3$, and $n_i = 5 \times 10^{13}/\text{cm}^3$. What are the electron and hole concentrations?

2.15. Suppose a semiconductor has $N_D = 10^{16}/\text{cm}^3$, $N_A = 4 \times 10^{16}/\text{cm}^3$, and $n_i = 10^{11}/\text{cm}^3$. What are the electron and hole concentrations?

2.16. Suppose a semiconductor has $N_A = 10^{17}/\text{cm}^3$, $N_D = 2 \times 10^{17}/\text{cm}^3$, and $n_i = 10^{17}/\text{cm}^3$. What are the electron and hole concentrations?

2.17. Equations (2.11) and (2.12) are actually valid for any combination of N_A and N_D. Try to calculate the hole and electron concentrations in silicon with your calculator using Eq. (2.11) for the case of

$N_A = 2.5 \times 10^{18}/cm^3$ and $N_D = 0$. Did you get the correct result? If not, why not?

2.8 Energy Band Model

2.18. Draw a figure similar to Fig. 2.11 for the case $N_A > N_D$ in which there are two acceptor atoms for each donor atom.

*2.19. Electron–hole pairs can be created by means other than the thermal activation process as described in Figs. 2.3 and 2.8. For example, energy may be added to electrons through optical means by shining light on the sample. If enough optical energy is absorbed, electrons can jump the energy bandgap, creating electron–hole pairs. What is the maximum wavelength of light that we should expect silicon to be able to absorb? (*Hint:* Remember from physics that energy E is related to wavelength λ by $E = hc/\lambda$ in which Planck's constant $h = 6.626 \times 10^{-34}$ J · s and the velocity of light $c = 3 \times 10^{10}$ cm/s.)

2.9 Mobility and Resistivity in Doped Semiconductors

2.20. Silicon is doped with a donor concentration of $5 \times 10^{16}/cm^3$. Find the electron and hole concentrations, the electron and hole mobilities, and the resistivity of this silicon material at 300 K. Is this material n- or p-type?

2.21. Silicon is doped with an acceptor concentration of $10^{18}/cm^3$. Find the electron and hole concentrations, the electron and hole mobilities, and the resistivity of this silicon material at 300 K. Is this material n- or p-type?

2.22. Silicon is doped with an indium concentration of $7 \times 10^{19}/cm^3$. Is indium a donor or acceptor impurity? Find the electron and hole concentrations, the electron and hole mobilities, and the resistivity of this silicon material at 300 K. Is this material n- or p-type?

2.23. A silicon wafer is uniformly doped with 4.5×10^{16} phosphorus atoms/cm³ and 5.5×10^{16} boron atoms/cm³. Find the electron and hole concentrations, the electron and hole mobilities, and the resistivity of this silicon material at 300 K. Is this material n- or p-type?

2.24. Repeat Example 2.3 for p-type silicon. Assume that the silicon contains only acceptor impurities. What is the acceptor concentration N_A?

*2.25. A p-type silicon wafer has a resistivity of 0.75 $\Omega \cdot$ cm. It is known that silicon contains only acceptor impurities. What is the acceptor concentration N_A?

2.26. A silicon sample is doped with 5.0×10^{19} donor atoms/cm³ and 5.0×10^{19} acceptor atoms/cm³. (a) What is its resistivity? (b) Is this an insulator, conductor, or semiconductor? (c) Is this intrinsic material? Explain your answers.

*2.27. n-type silicon wafers with a resistivity of 2.0 $\Omega \cdot$ cm are needed for integrated circuit fabrication. What donor concentration N_D is required in the wafers? Assume $N_A = 0$.

2.28. (a) What is the minimum donor doping required to convert silicon into a conductor based on the definitions in Table 2.1? (b) What is the minimum acceptor doping required to convert silicon into a conductor?

*2.29. It is conceptually possible to produce extrinsic silicon with a higher resistivity than that of intrinsic silicon. How would this occur?

*2.30. Measurements of a silicon wafer indicate that it is p-type with a resistivity of 1 $\Omega \cdot$ cm. It is also known that it contains only boron impurities. (a) What additional acceptor concentration must be added to the sample to change its resistivity to 0.25 $\Omega \cdot$ cm? (b) What concentration of donors would have to be added to the original sample to change the resistivity to 0.25 $\Omega \cdot$ cm? Would the resulting material be classified as n- or p-type silicon?

*2.31. A silicon wafer has a doping concentration of 1×10^{16} phosphorus atoms/cm³. (a) Determine the conductivity of the wafer. (b) What concentration of boron atoms must be added to the wafer to make the conductivity equal to 5.0 $(\Omega \cdot$ cm$)^{-1}$?

*2.32. A silicon wafer has a background concentration of 1×10^{16} boron atoms/cm³. (a) Determine the conductivity of the wafer. (b) What concentration of phosphorus atoms must be added to the wafer to make the conductivity equal to 5.5 $(\Omega \cdot$ cm$)^{-1}$?

2.10 Diffusion Currents

2.33. Calculate the value of the thermal voltage V_T for $T = 77$ K, 150 K, and 300 K.

2.34. The electron concentration in a region of silicon is shown in Fig. P2.34. If the electron mobility is 350 cm²/V · s and the base width $W_B = 1$ μm, determine the electron diffusion current density. Assume room temperature.

2.35. Suppose the hole concentration in silicon sample is described mathematically by

$$p(x) = 10^4 + 10^{18} \exp\left(-\frac{x}{L_p}\right) \text{ holes/cm}^3, \quad x \geq 0$$

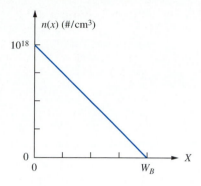

Figure P2.34

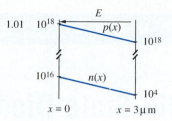

Figure P2.37

in which L_p is known as the diffusion length for holes and is equal to 2.0 μm. Find the diffusion current density for holes as a function of distance for $x \geq 0$ if $D_p = 15$ cm^2/s. What is the diffusion current at $x = 0$ if the cross-sectional area is 10 μm^2?

2.11 Total Current

*2.36. A 5-μm-long block of p-type silicon has an acceptor doping profile given by $N_A(x) = 10^{14} + 10^{18} \exp(-10^4 x)$, where x is measured in cm. Use Eq. (2.18) to demonstrate that the material must have a nonzero internal electric field E. What is the value of E at $x = 0$ and $x = 5$ μm? (*Hint:* In thermal equilibrium, the total electron and total hole currents must each be zero.)

2.37. Figure P2.37 gives the electron and hole concentrations in a 3-μm-wide region of silicon. In addition, there is a constant electric field of 25 V/cm present in the sample. What is the total current density at $x = 0$? What are the individual drift and diffusion components of the hole and electron current densities at $x = 1.5$ μm? Assume that the electron and hole mobilities are 350 and 150 cm^2/V · s, respectively.

Miscellaneous

*2.38. Single crystal silicon consists of three-dimensional arrays of the basic unit cell in Fig. 2.1(a). (a) How many atoms are in each unit cell? (b) What is volume of the unit cell in cm^3? (c) Show that the atomic density of silicon is 5×10^{22} atoms/cm^3. (d) The density of silicon is 2.33 g/cm^3. What is the mass of one unit cell? (e) Based on your calculations here, what is the mass of a proton? Assume that protons and neutrons have the same mass and that electrons are much much lighter. Is your answer reasonable? Explain.

Solid-State Diodes and Diode Circuits

The first electronic circuit element that we explore is the solid-state *pn* junction diode, which is formed by fabricating adjoining regions of *p*-type and *n*-type semiconductor material. Another type of diode, called the Schottky barrier diode, is formed by a non-ohmic contact between a metal such as aluminum, palladium, or platinum and an *n*-type or *p*-type semiconductor. Both types of solid-state diodes are discussed in this chapter. The vacuum diode, which was used before the advent of semiconductor diodes, still finds application in very high voltage situations.

The *pn* junction diode is a nonlinear element, and for many of us, this will be our first encounter with a nonlinear device. The diode is a two-terminal circuit element similar to a resistor, but its *i-v* characteristic, the relationship between the current through the element and the voltage across the element, is not a straight line. This nonlinear behavior allows electronic circuits to be designed to provide many useful operations, including rectification, mixing (a form of multiplication), and wave shaping. Diodes can also be used to perform elementary logic operations such as the AND and OR functions.

The chapter begins with a basic discussion of the structure and behavior of the *pn* junction diode and its terminal characteristics. Next is an introduction to the concept of modeling, and several different models for the diode are introduced and used to analyze the behavior of diode circuits. We begin to develop the intuition needed to make choices between models of various complexities in order to simplify electronic circuit analysis and design. Diode circuits are then explored, including the detailed application of the diode in rectifier and wave-shaping circuits. The characteristics of Zener diodes, photo diodes, solar cells, and light-emitting diodes are also discussed.

3.1 THE *pn* JUNCTION DIODE

The ***pn* junction diode** is formed by fabrication of a *p*-type semiconductor region in intimate contact with an *n*-type semiconductor region, as illustrated in Fig. 3.1. The diode is constructed using the impurity doping process studied in Chapter 2.

An actual diode can be formed by starting with an *n*-type wafer with doping N_D and selectively converting a portion of the wafer to *p*-type by adding acceptor impurities with $N_A > N_D$. The point at which the material changes from *p*-type to *n*-type is called the metallurgical junction. The *p*-type region is also referred to as the **anode** of the diode, and the *n*-type region is called the **cathode** of the diode.

Figure 3.2 gives the circuit symbol for the diode, with the left-hand end corresponding to the *p*-type region of the diode and the right-hand side corresponding to the *n*-type region. We will see shortly that the "arrow" points in the direction of positive current in the diode.

Photograph of an assortment of diodes.

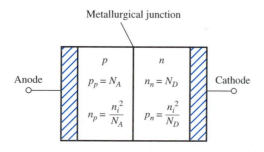

Figure 3.1 Basic *pn* junction diode.

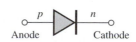

Figure 3.2 Diode circuit symbol.

pn Junction Electrostatics

Consider a *pn* junction diode similar to Fig. 3.1 having $N_A = 10^{17}/\text{cm}^3$ on the *p*-type side and $N_D = 10^{16}/\text{cm}^3$ on the *n*-type side. The hole and electron concentrations on the two sides of the junction will be:

$$p\text{-type side:} \quad p_p = 10^{17} \text{ holes/cm}^3 \qquad n_p = 10^3 \text{ electrons/cm}^3$$

$$n\text{-type side:} \quad p_n = 10^4 \text{ holes/cm}^3 \qquad n_n = 10^{16} \text{ electrons/cm}^3 \tag{3.1}$$

As shown in Fig. 3.3(a), a very large concentration of holes exists on the *p*-type side of the metallurgical junction, whereas a much smaller hole concentration exists on the *n*-type side. Likewise, there is a very large concentration of electrons on the *n*-type side of the junction and a very low concentration on the *p*-type side.

From our knowledge of diffusion from Chapter 2, we know that mobile holes will diffuse from the region of high concentration on the *p*-type side toward the region of low concentration on the *n*-type side and that mobile electrons will diffuse from the *n*-type side to the *p*-type side, as in Figs. 3.3(b) and (c). If the diffusion processes were to continue unabated, there would eventually be a uniform concentration of holes and electrons throughout the entire semiconductor region, and the *pn* junction would cease to exist. Note that the two

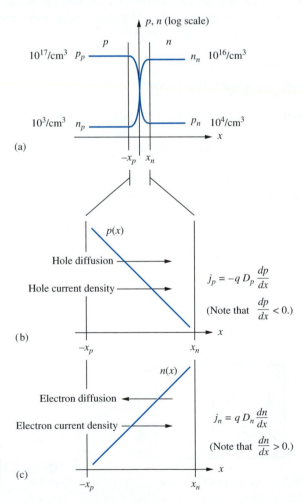

Figure 3.3 (a) Carrier concentrations; (b), (c) diffusion currents in the space charge region.

diffusion current densities are both directed in the positive x direction, but this is inconsistent with zero current in the open-circuited terminals of the diode.

A second, competing process must be established to balance the diffusion current. The competing mechanism is a drift current, as discussed in Chapter 2, and its origin can be understood by focusing on the region in the vicinity of the **metallurgical junction** shown in Fig. 3.4. As mobile holes move out of the *p*-type material, they leave behind immobile negatively charged acceptor atoms. Correspondingly, mobile electrons leave behind immobile ionized donor atoms with a localized positive charge. A **space charge region (SCR),** depleted of mobile carriers, develops in the region immediately around the metallurgical junction. This region is also often called the **depletion region,** or **depletion layer.**

From electromagnetics, we know that a region of space charge ρ_c (C/cm^3) will be accompanied by an electric field E measured in V/cm through Gauss' law,

$$\nabla \cdot E = \frac{\rho_c}{\varepsilon_s} \tag{3.2}$$

written assuming a constant semiconductor permittivity ε_s (F/cm). In one dimension, Eq. (3.2) can be rearranged to give

$$E(x) = \frac{1}{\varepsilon_s} \int \rho(x)\,dx \tag{3.3}$$

Figure 3.5 illustrates the space charge and electric field in the diode for the case of uniform (constant) doping on both sides of the junction. As illustrated in Fig. 3.5(a), the value of the space charge density on the *p*-type side will be $-qN_A$ and will extend from the metallurgical junction at $x = 0$ to $-x_p$, whereas that on the *n*-type side will be $+qN_D$

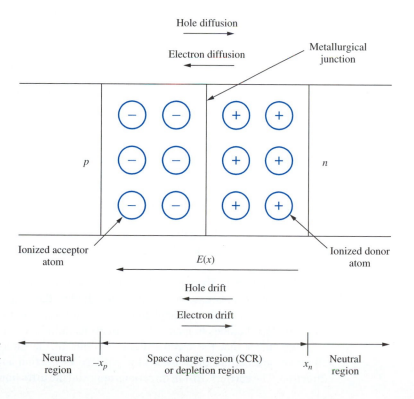

Figure 3.4 Space charge region formation near the metallurgical junction.

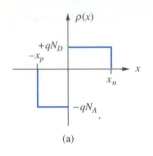

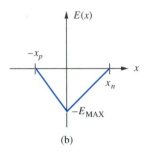

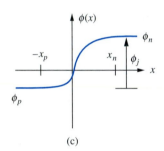

Figure 3.5 (a) Charge density (C/cm^3), (b) electric field (V/cm), and (c) electrostatic potential (V) in the space charge region of a *pn* junction.

and will extend from 0 to $+x_n$. The overall diode must be charge neutral, so

$$qN_A x_p = qN_D x_n \tag{3.4}$$

The electric field is proportional to the first integral of the space charge density and will be zero in the (charge) neutral regions outside of the depletion region. Using this zero-field boundary condition yields the triangular electric field distribution in Fig. 3.5(b).

Figure 3.5(c) represents the integral of the electric field and shows that a **built-in potential** (or voltage), or **junction potential** ϕ_j, exists across the *pn* junction space charge region according to:

$$\phi_j = -\int E(x)\,dx \qquad V \tag{3.5}$$

ϕ_j represents the difference in the internal chemical potentials between the *n* and *p* sides of the diode, and it can be shown [1] to be given by

$$\phi_j = V_T \ln\left(\frac{N_A N_D}{n_i^2}\right) \tag{3.6}$$

where the **thermal voltage** $V_T = kT/q$ was originally defined in Chapter 2.

Equations (3.3) to (3.5) can be used to determine the total width of the depletion region w_{do} in terms of the built-in potential:

$$w_{do} = (x_n + x_p) = \sqrt{\frac{2\varepsilon_s}{q}\left(\frac{1}{N_A} + \frac{1}{N_D}\right)\phi_j} \qquad m \tag{3.7}$$

From Eq. (3.7), we see that the doping on the more lightly doped side of the junction will be the most important in determining the **depletion-layer width.**

EXAMPLE 3.1: As an example of the magnitudes involved, let us calculate the built-in potential and depletion region width for a silicon diode with $N_A = 10^{17}/cm^3$ on the *p*-type side and $N_D = 10^{16}/cm^3$ on the *n*-type side using Eqs. (3.6) and (3.7).

$$\phi_j = V_T \ln\left(\frac{N_A N_D}{n_i^2}\right) = (0.025\ V)\ln\left(\frac{(10^{17}/cm^3)(10^{16}/cm^3)}{(10^{20}/cm^6)}\right) = 0.748\ V$$

For silicon, $\varepsilon_s = 11.7\varepsilon_o$, where $\varepsilon_o = 8.85 \times 10^{-14}$ F/cm represents the permittivity of free space.

$$w_{do} = \sqrt{\frac{2\varepsilon_s}{q}\left(\frac{1}{N_A} + \frac{1}{N_D}\right)\phi_j}$$

$$w_{do} = \sqrt{\frac{2 \cdot 11.7 \cdot \left(8.85 \times 10^{-14}\ \frac{F}{cm}\right)}{1.60 \times 10^{-19}\ C}\left(\frac{1}{10^{17}/cm^3} + \frac{1}{10^{16}/cm^3}\right)0.748\ V}$$

$$= 0.326\ \mu m$$

◆

The numbers in Example 3.1 are fairly typical of a *pn* junction diode. For the normal doping levels encountered in solid-state diodes, the built-in potential ranges between 0.5 V and 1.0 V, and the total depletion-layer width w_{do} can range from a fraction of 1 μm in heavily doped diodes to many tens of microns in lightly doped diodes.

Remember that the electric field *E* points in the direction that a positive carrier will move, so electrons drift toward the positive *x* direction and holes drift in the negative *x* direction. The carriers drift in directions opposite the diffusion of the same carrier species.

Because the terminal currents must be zero, a dynamic equilibrium is established in the junction region. Hole diffusion is precisely balanced by hole drift, and electron diffusion is exactly balanced by electron drift. This balance is stated mathematically in Eq. (3.8), in which the total hole and electron current densities must each be identically zero:

$$j_n^T = qn\mu_n E + qD_n \frac{\partial n}{\partial x} = 0$$

$$\text{A/cm}^2 \tag{3.8}$$

$$j_p^T = qp\mu_p E - qD_p \frac{\partial p}{\partial x} = 0$$

The difference in potential in Fig. 3.5(c) represents a barrier to both hole and electron flow across the junction. When a voltage is applied to the diode, the potential barrier is modified, and the delicate balances in Eq. (3.8) are disturbed, resulting in a current in the diode terminals.

EXAMPLE 3.2: Find x_n, x_p, and E_{MAX} for the diode in Example 3.1.

SOLUTION: Using Eq. (3.4), we can write

$$w_{do} = x_n + x_p = x_n\left(1 + \frac{N_D}{N_A}\right) \qquad \text{and} \qquad w_{do} = x_n + x_p = x_p\left(1 + \frac{N_A}{N_D}\right)$$

and solving for x_n and x_p gives

$$x_n = \frac{w_{do}}{\left(1 + \dfrac{N_D}{N_A}\right)} = \frac{0.326\ \mu\text{m}}{\left(1 + \dfrac{10^{16}}{10^{17}}\right)} = 0.296\ \mu\text{m}$$

and

$$x_p = \frac{w_{do}}{\left(1 + \dfrac{N_A}{N_D}\right)} = \frac{0.326\ \mu\text{m}}{\left(1 + \dfrac{10^{17}}{10^{16}}\right)} = 0.0296\ \mu\text{m}$$

From Eq. (3.3) and Fig. 3.5(b) and (c),

$$\phi_j = \tfrac{1}{2}E_{MAX}w_{do} \qquad \text{and} \qquad E_{MAX} = \frac{2\phi_j}{w_{do}} = \frac{2(0.748\ \text{V})}{0.327\ \mu\text{m}} = 45.7\ \text{kV/cm}$$

◆

EXERCISE: Using Eq. (3.3) and Fig. 3.5(a) and (b), show that the maximum field is given by

$$E_{MAX} = \frac{qN_A x_p}{\varepsilon_s} = \frac{qN_D x_n}{\varepsilon_s}$$

Use this formula to find E_{MAX}.

ANSWER: 45.9 kV/cm

3.2 THE *i-v* CHARACTERISTICS OF THE DIODE

A voltage is applied to the diode in Fig. 3.6. The voltage v_D represents the voltage applied to the diode terminals; i_D is the current through the diode. The neutral regions of the diode represent a low resistance to current, and essentially all the external applied voltage is dropped across the space charge region.

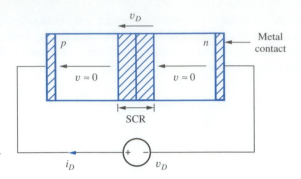

Figure 3.6 Diode with external applied voltage v_D.

The applied voltage disturbs the balance between the drift and diffusion currents at the junction specified in Eq. (3.8). A positive applied voltage reduces the potential barrier for electrons and holes, as in Fig. 3.7, and current easily crosses the junction. A negative voltage increases the potential barrier, and although the balance in Eq.(3.8) is disturbed, the increased barrier results in a very small current.

The most important details of the diode i-v characteristic appear in Fig. 3.8. The diode characteristic is definitely not linear. For voltages less than zero, the diode is essentially nonconducting, with $i_D \approx 0$. As the voltage increases above zero, the current remains nearly zero until the voltage v_D exceeds approximately 0.5 to 0.7 V. At this point, the diode current increases rapidly, and the voltage across the diode becomes almost independent of current. The voltage required to bring the diode into significant conduction is often called either the **turn-on** or **cut-in voltage** of the diode.

Figure 3.9 is an enlargement of the region around the origin in Fig. 3.8. We see that the i-v characteristic passes through the origin; the current is zero when the voltage is zero.

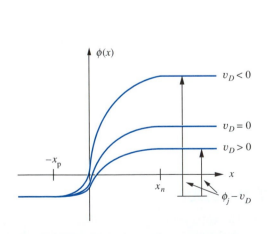

Figure 3.7 Electrostatic junction potential for different applied voltages.

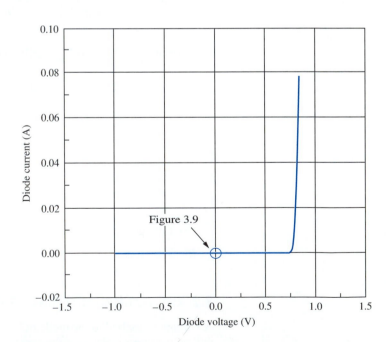

Figure 3.8 Graph of the i-v characteristics of a pn junction diode.

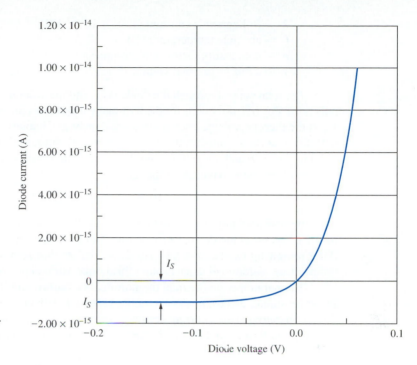

Figure 3.9 Diode behavior near the origin with $I_S = 10^{-15}$ A and $n = 1$.

For negative voltages the current is not actually zero but reaches a limiting value labeled as $-I_S$ for voltages less than -0.1 V. I_S is called the **reverse saturation current,** or just **saturation current,** of the diode.

3.3 THE DIODE EQUATION: A MATHEMATICAL MODEL FOR THE DIODE

A voltage is applied to the diode in Fig. 3.10; in the figure the diode is represented by its circuit symbol from Fig. 3.2. Although we will not attempt to do so here, Eq. (3.8) can be solved for the hole and electron concentrations and the terminal current in the diode as a function of the voltage v_D across the diode. The resulting **diode equation,** given in Eq. (3.9), provides a **mathematical model** for the i-v characteristics of the diode:

$$i_D = I_S \left[\exp\left(\frac{qv_D}{nkT}\right) - 1 \right] = I_S \left[\exp\left(\frac{v_D}{nV_T}\right) - 1 \right] \qquad (3.9)$$

where I_S = reverse saturation current of diode (A)

v_D = voltage applied to diode (V)

q = electronic charge (1.60×10^{-19} C)

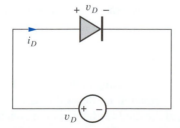

Figure 3.10 Diode with applied voltage v_D.

k = Boltzmann's constant (1.38×10^{-23} J/K)

T = absolute temperature (K)

n = nonideality factor (dimensionless)

$V_T = kT/q$ = thermal voltage (V)

The total current through the diode is i_D, and the voltage drop across the diode terminals is v_D. Positive directions for the terminal voltage and current are indicated in Fig. 3.10. V_T is the thermal voltage encountered previously in Chapter 2 and will be assumed equal to 0.025 V at room temperature. I_S is the (reverse) saturation current of the diode encountered in Fig. 3.9, and n is a dimensionless parameter discussed in more detail shortly. The saturation current is typically in the range

$$10^{-18} \text{ A} \le I_S \le 10^{-9} \text{ A} \tag{3.10}$$

From device physics, it can be shown that the diode saturation current is proportional to n_i^2, where n_i is the density of electrons and holes in intrinsic semiconductor material. After reviewing Eq. (2.2) in Chapter 2, we realize that I_S will be strongly dependent on temperature. Additional discussion of this temperature dependence is in Sec. 3.5.

The parameter n is termed the **nonideality factor,** and it is unity for an ideal diode. For most silicon diodes, n is in the range 1.0 to 1.1, although it approaches a value of 2 in diodes operating at high current densities. From this point on, we assume that $n = 1$ unless otherwise indicated, and the diode equation will be written as

$$i_D = I_S \left[\exp\left(\frac{v_D}{V_T}\right) - 1 \right] \tag{3.11}$$

The mathematical model in Eq. (3.11) provides a highly accurate prediction of the *i-v* characteristics of the *pn* junction diode. The model is useful for understanding the detailed behavior of diodes. It also provides a basis for understanding the *i-v* characteristics of the bipolar transistor in Chapter 5.

> **EXERCISE:** A diode has a reverse saturation current of 40 fA. Calculate i_D for diode voltages of 0.55 and 0.7 V. What is the diode voltage if $i_D = 6$ mA?
>
> **ANSWERS:** 143 μA; 57.9 mA; 0.643 V

3.4 DIODE CHARACTERISTICS UNDER REVERSE, ZERO, AND FORWARD BIAS

When a dc voltage is applied to an electronic device, we say that we are providing a dc bias voltage or simply a bias to the device. Bias controls the operating region of the device. For a diode, there are two regions of operation, **reverse bias** and **forward bias,** corresponding to $v_D < 0$ V and $v_D > 0$ V, respectively. The **zero bias** condition, with $v_D = 0$ V, represents the boundary between the forward and reverse bias regions. When the diode is operating with reverse bias, we consider the diode "off" or nonconducting because the current is very small. For forward bias, the diode is usually in a highly conducting state and is considered "on."

Reverse Bias

For $v_D < 0$, the diode is said to be operating under reverse bias. Only a very small reverse leakage current, approximately equal to I_S, flows through the diode. This current is small enough that we usually think of the diode as being in the nonconducting or off state when it is reverse-biased. For example, suppose that a dc voltage $V = -4V_T = -0.1$ V is applied to the diode terminals so that $v_D = -0.1 V$. Substituting this value into Eq. (3.11) gives

$$i_D = I_S \left[\exp\left(\frac{v_D}{V_T}\right) - 1 \right] = I_S[\overset{\text{negligible}}{\exp(-4)} - 1] \approx -I_S \tag{3.12}$$

because $\exp(-4) = 0.018$. For a reverse bias greater than $4V_T$—that is, $v_D \leq -4V_T = -0.1$ V—the exponential term $\exp(v_D/V_T)$ is much less than 1, and the diode current will be approximately equal to $-I_S$, a very small current. The current I_S was identified in Fig. 3.9.

> **EXERCISE:** A diode has a reverse saturation current of 5 fA. Calculate i_D for diode voltages of -0.04 V and -2 V (see Sec. 3.6).
>
> **ANSWERS:** -3.99 fA; -5 fA

The situation depicted in Fig. 3.9 and Eq. (3.12) actually represents an idealized picture of the diode. In a real diode, the reverse leakage current is several orders of magnitude larger than I_S due to the generation of electron–hole pairs within the depletion region. In addition, i_D does not saturate but increases gradually with reverse bias as the width of the depletion layer increases with reverse bias.

Zero Bias

Although it may seem to be a trivial result, it is important to remember that the i-v characteristic of the diode passes through the origin. For zero bias with $v_D = 0$, we find $i_D = 0$. As for a resistor, there must be a voltage across the diode terminals in order for a nonzero current to exist.

Forward Bias

For the case $v_D > 0$, the diode is said to be operating under **forward bias**, and a large current can be present in the diode. Suppose that a voltage $v_D \geq +4V_T = +0.1$ V is applied to the diode terminals. The exponential term $\exp(v_D/V_T)$ is now much greater than 1, and Eq. (3.9) reduces to

$$i_D = I_S \left[\exp\left(\frac{v_D}{V_T}\right) \overset{\text{negligible}}{- 1} \right] \approx I_S \exp\left(\frac{v_D}{V_T}\right) \tag{3.13}$$

The diode current grows exponentially with applied voltage for a forward bias greater than approximately $4V_T$.

The diode i-v characteristic for forward voltages is redrawn in semilogarithmic form in Fig. 3.11. The straight line behavior predicted by Eq. (3.13) for voltages $v_D \geq 4V_T$ is apparent. A slight curvature can be observed near the origin, where the -1 term in Eq. (3.13) is no longer negligible. The slope of the graph in the exponential region is very important. Only a 60-mV increase in the forward voltage is required to increase the diode current by a factor of 10. This is the reason for the almost vertical increase in current noted in Fig. 3.8 for voltages above the turn-on voltage.

EXAMPLE 3.3: Use Eq. (3.13) to accurately calculate the voltage change required to increase the diode current by a factor of 10.

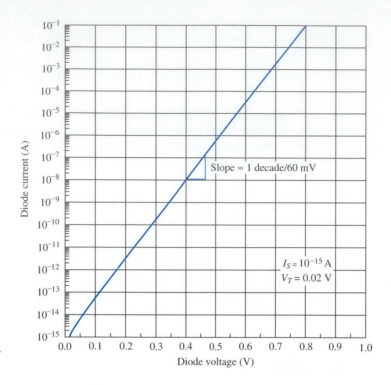

Figure 3.11 Diode *i-v* characteristic on semilog scale.

SOLUTION: Let

$$i_{D1} = I_S \exp\left(\frac{v_{D1}}{V_T}\right) \qquad \text{and} \qquad i_{D2} = I_S \exp\left(\frac{v_{D2}}{V_T}\right)$$

Taking the ratio of the two currents and setting it equal to 10 yields

$$\frac{i_{D2}}{i_{D1}} = \exp\left(\frac{v_{D2} - v_{D1}}{V_T}\right) = \exp\left(\frac{\Delta v_D}{V_T}\right) = 10$$

and

$$\Delta v_D = V_T \ln 10 = 2.3 V_T$$

$\Delta v_D = 2.3 V_T = 57.5$ mV (≈ 60 mV) at room temperature.   ◆

Sixty mV/decade is a figure we should remember because it often plays an important role in our thinking about both diode and bipolar junction transistor circuit design.

Figure 3.12 compares the characteristics of three diodes with different values of saturation current. The saturation current of diode A is 10 times larger than that of diode B, and the saturation current of diode B is 10 times that of diode C. The spacing between each pair of curves is approximately 60 mV. If the saturation current of the diode is reduced by a factor of 10, then the diode voltage must increase by approximately 60 mV to reach the same operating current level. Figure 3.12 also shows the relatively low sensitivity of the forward diode voltage to changes in the parameter I_S. For a fixed diode current, a change of two orders of magnitude in I_S results in a diode voltage change of only 120 mV.

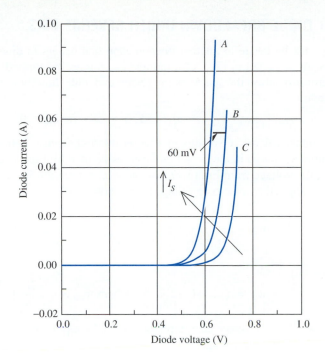

Figure 3.12 Diode characteristics for three different reverse saturation currents (a) 10^{-12} A, (b) 10^{-13} A, and (c) 10^{-14} A.

3.5 DIODE TEMPERATURE COEFFICIENT

Another important number to keep in mind is the temperature coefficient associated with the diode voltage v_D. Solving Eq. (3.11) for the diode voltage under forward bias

$$v_D = V_T \ln\left(\frac{i_D}{I_S} + 1\right) = \frac{kT}{q} \ln\left(\frac{i_D}{I_S} + 1\right) \cong \frac{kT}{q} \ln\left(\frac{i_D}{I_S}\right) \quad \text{V} \quad (3.14)$$

and taking the derivative with respect to temperature yields

$$\frac{dv_D}{dT} = \frac{k}{q} \ln\left(\frac{i_D}{I_S}\right) - \frac{kT}{q} \frac{1}{I_S} \frac{dI_S}{dT} = \frac{v_D}{T} - V_T \frac{1}{I_S} \frac{dI_S}{dT} = \frac{v_D - V_{GO} - 3V_T}{T} \quad \text{V/k} \quad (3.15)$$

where it is assumed that $i_D \gg I_S$ and $I_S \propto n_i^2$. In the numerator of Eq. (3.15), v_D represents the diode voltage, V_{GO} is the voltage corresponding to the silicon bandgap energy at 0 K, $(V_{GO} = E_G/q)$, and V_T is the thermal potential. The last two terms result from the temperature dependence of n_i^2 as defined by Eq. (2.2). Evaluating the terms in Eq. (3.15) for a silicon diode with $v_D = 0.65$ V, $E_G = 1.12$ eV, and $V_T = 0.025$ V yields

$$\frac{dv_D}{dT} = \frac{(0.65 - 1.12 - 0.075) \text{ V}}{300 \text{ K}} = -1.82 \text{ mV/K} \quad (3.16)$$

The forward voltage of the diode exhibits a negative temperature coefficient of approximately -1.8 mV/°C at room temperature.

EXERCISES:
1. Verify Eq. (3.15) using the expression for n_i^2 from Eq. (2.2).
2. A silicon diode is operating at $T = 300$ K, with $i_D = 1$ mA, and $v_D = 0.680$ V. Use the result from Eq. (3.16) to estimate the diode voltage at 275 K and at 350 K.

ANSWERS: 0.726 V; 0.589 V

3.6 DIODE BREAKDOWN UNDER REVERSE BIAS

We must be aware of another phenomenon that occurs in diodes operated under reverse bias. As depicted in Fig. 3.13, the reverse voltage v_R applied across the diode terminals is dropped across the space charge region and adds directly to the built-in potential of the junction:

$$v_j = \phi_j + v_R \qquad \text{for } v_R > 0 \tag{3.17}$$

The increased voltage results in a larger internal electric field that must be supported by additional charge in the depletion layer, as defined by Eqs. (3.2) to (3.5). Using Eq. (3.7) with the voltage from Eq. (3.17), the general expression for the depletion-layer width w_d for an applied reverse-bias voltage v_R becomes

$$w_d = (x_n + x_p) = \sqrt{\frac{2\varepsilon_s}{q}\left(\frac{1}{N_A} + \frac{1}{N_D}\right)(\phi_j + v_R)}$$

or   (3.18)

$$w_d = w_{do}\sqrt{1 + \frac{v_R}{\phi_j}} \qquad \text{where } w_{do} = \sqrt{\frac{2\varepsilon_s}{q}\left(\frac{1}{N_A} + \frac{1}{N_D}\right)\phi_j}$$

The width of the space charge region increases approximately in proportion to the square root of the applied voltage.

> **EXERCISE:** The diode in Example 3.1 had a zero-bias depletion-layer width of 0.326 μm and a built-in voltage of 0.748 V. What will be the depletion-layer width for a 10-V reverse bias? What is the new value of E_{MAX}?
>
> **ANSWERS:** 1.24 μm; 174 kV/cm

As the reverse voltage increases, the electric field within the device grows, and the diode eventually enters the **breakdown region.** The onset of the breakdown process is fairly abrupt, and the current increases rapidly for any further increase in the applied voltage, as shown in the *i-v* characteristic of Fig. 3.14.

The magnitude of the voltage at which breakdown occurs is called the **breakdown voltage V_Z** of the diode and is typically in the range

$$2 \text{ V} \le V_Z \le 2000 \text{ V} \tag{3.19}$$

The value of V_Z is determined primarily by the doping level on the more lightly doped side of the *pn* junction, but the heavier the doping, the smaller the breakdown voltage of the diode.

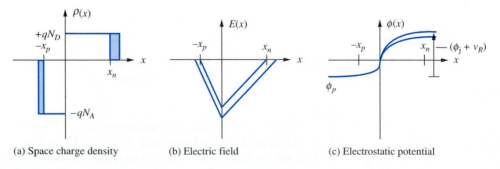

(a) Space charge density   (b) Electric field   (c) Electrostatic potential

Figure 3.13 The *pn* junction diode under reverse bias.

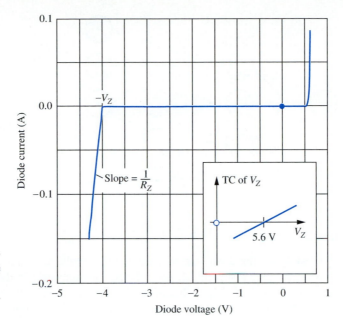

Figure 3.14 *i-v* characteristic of a diode including the reverse-breakdown region. The inset shows the temperature coefficient (TC) of V_Z.

Two separate breakdown mechanisms have been identified: *avalanche breakdown* and *Zener breakdown*. These are discussed in the following two sections.

Avalanche Breakdown

Silicon diodes with breakdown voltages greater than approximately 5.6 V enter breakdown through a mechanism called **avalanche breakdown.** As the width of the depletion layer increases under reverse bias, the electric field increases, as indicated in Fig. 3.13. Free carriers in the depletion region are accelerated by this electric field, and as the carriers move through the depletion region, they collide with the fixed atoms. At some point, the electric field and the width of the space charge region become large enough that some carriers gain energy sufficient to break covalent bonds upon impact, thereby creating electron–hole pairs. The new carriers created can also accelerate and create additional electron–hole pairs through this **impact-ionization process,** as illustrated in Fig. 3.15 on page 60.

Zener Breakdown

True **Zener breakdown** occurs only in heavily doped diodes. The high doping results in a very narrow depletion-region width, and application of a reverse bias causes carriers to tunnel directly between the conduction and valence bands, again resulting in a rapidly increasing reverse current in the diode.

Breakdown Voltage Temperature Coefficient

We can differentiate between the two types of breakdown because the breakdown voltages associated with the two mechanisms exhibit opposite temperature coefficients (TC). In avalanche breakdown, V_Z increases with temperature; in Zener breakdown, V_Z decreases with temperature. For silicon diodes, a zero temperature coefficient is achieved at approximately 5.6 V. The avalanche breakdown mechanism dominates in diodes that exhibit breakdown voltages of more than 5.6 V, whereas diodes with breakdown voltages below 5.6 V enter breakdown via the Zener mechanism.

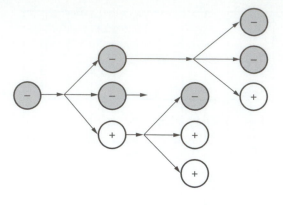

Figure 3.15 The avalanche breakdown process. (Note that the positive and negative charge carriers will actually be moving in opposite directions in the electric field in the depletion region.)

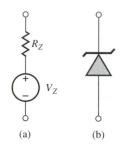

Figure 3.16 (a) Model for reverse-breakdown region of diode. (b) Zener diode symbol.

Diode Model for the Breakdown Region

In breakdown, the diode can be modeled by a voltage source of value V_Z in series with resistor R_Z, which sets the slope of the i-v characteristic in the breakdown region, as indicated in Fig. 3.16. The value of R_Z is normally small ($R_Z \leq 100\ \Omega$), and the reverse current flowing in the diode must be limited by the external circuit or the diode will be destroyed.

From the i-v characteristic in Fig. 3.14 and the model in Fig. 3.16, we see that the voltage across the diode is almost constant, independent of current, in the reverse-breakdown region. Some diodes are actually designed to be operated in **reverse breakdown.** These diodes are called **Zener diodes** and have the special circuit symbol given in Fig. 3.16(b).

3.7 *pn* JUNCTION CAPACITANCE

Forward- and reverse-biased diodes also have a capacitance associated with the *pn* junction. This capacitance is important under dynamic signal conditions because it prevents the voltage across the diode from changing instantaneously.

Reverse Bias

Under reverse bias, w_d increases beyond its zero-bias value, as expressed by Eq. (3.18), and hence the amount of charge in the depletion region also increases. Because the charge in the diode is changing with voltage, a capacitance results. Using Eqs. (3.4) and (3.7), the total space charge on the *n*-side of the diode is given by

$$Q_n = qN_D x_n A = q\left(\frac{N_A N_D}{N_A + N_D}\right) w_d A \qquad \text{C} \qquad (3.20)$$

where A is the cross-sectional area of the diode and w_d is described by Eq. (3.18). The capacitance of the reverse-biased *pn* junction is given by

$$C_j = \frac{dQ_n}{dv_R} = \frac{C_{jo}}{\sqrt{1 + \dfrac{v_R}{\phi_j}}} \qquad \text{where } C_{jo} = \frac{\varepsilon_s A}{w_{do}} \qquad \text{F} \qquad (3.21)$$

in which C_{jo} represents the **zero-bias junction capacitance** of the diode. The capacitance decreases as the reverse bias increases, exhibiting an inverse square root relationship.

Equation (3.21) shows that the capacitance of the diode changes with applied voltage. This voltage-controlled capacitance can be very useful in certain electronic circuits. Diodes

Figure 3.17 Circuit symbol for the variable capacitance diode (varactor).

can be designed with impurity profiles (called *hyper-abrupt profiles*) specifically optimized for operation as voltage-controlled capacitors. As for the case of Zener diodes, a special symbol exists for the variable capacitance diode, as shown in Fig. 3.17. Remember that this diode is to be operated under reverse bias.

Forward Bias

When the diode is operating under forward bias, additional charge is stored in the neutral regions near the edges of the space charge region. The amount of charge Q_D stored in the diode is proportional to the diode current:

$$Q_D = i_D \tau_T \quad \text{C} \tag{3.22}$$

The proportionality constant τ_T is called the diode **transit time** and ranges from 10^{-15} s to more than 10^{-6} s (1 fs to 1 μs) depending on the size and type of diode. Because we know that i_D is dependent on the diode voltage through the diode equation, there is an additional capacitance, the **diffusion capacitance C_D,** associated with the forward region of operation:

$$C_D = \frac{dQ_D}{dv_D} = \frac{(i_D + I_S)\tau_T}{V_T} \approx \frac{i_D \tau_T}{V_T} \quad \text{F} \tag{3.23}$$

in which V_T is the thermal voltage. The diffusion capacitance is also proportional to current and can become quite large at high currents.

> **EXERCISE:** A diode has a transit time of 10 ns. What is the diffusion capacitance of the diode for currents of 10 μA, 0.8 mA, and 50 mA at room temperature?
>
> **ANSWERS:** 4 pF; 320 pF; 20 nF

3.8 SCHOTTKY BARRIER DIODE

In the **Schottky barrier diode,** one of the semiconductor regions of the *pn* junction diode is replaced by a non-ohmic rectifying metal contact, as indicated in Fig. 3.18. It is easiest to form a Schottky contact to *n*-type silicon, and for this case the metal region becomes the diode anode. An *n*+ region is added to ensure that the cathode contact is ohmic. The symbol for the Schottky diode appears in Fig. 3.18(b).

The Schottky diode turns on at a much lower voltage than its *pn*-junction counterpart, as indicated in Fig. 3.19. It also has significantly reduced internal charge storage under forward bias. We encounter an important use of the Schottky diode in bipolar logic circuits in Chapter 10.

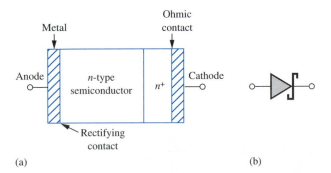

Figure 3.18 (a) Schottky barrier diode structure. (b) Schottky diode symbol.

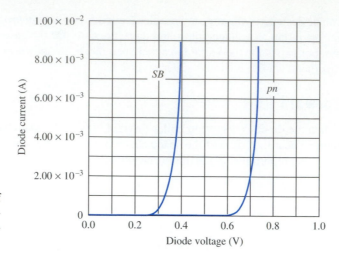

Figure 3.19 Comparison of *pn* junction (*pn*) and Schottky diode (*SB*) *i-v* characteristics.

3.9 DIODE CIRCUIT ANALYSIS

We now begin our analysis of circuits containing diodes and introduce simplified circuit models for the diode. Figure 3.20 presents a series circuit containing a voltage source, resistor, and diode. Note that V and R may represent the Thévenin equivalent of a more complicated two-terminal network. Also note the notational change in Fig. 3.20. In the circuits that we analyze in the next few sections, the applied voltage and resulting diode voltage and current will all be dc quantities. (Recall that the dc components of the total quantities i_D and v_D are indicated by I_D and V_D, respectively.)

One common objective of diode circuit analysis is to find the **quiescent operating point,** or **Q-point,** for the diode. The Q-point consists of the dc current and voltage (I_D, V_D) that define the point of operation on the diode's *i-v* characteristic. We start the analysis by writing the loop equation for the circuit of Fig. 3.20:

$$V = I_D R + V_D \tag{3.24}$$

Equation (3.24) represents a constraint placed on the diode operating point by the circuit elements. The diode *i-v* characteristic in Fig. 3.8 represents the allowed values of I_D and V_D as determined by the solid-state diode itself. Simultaneous solution of these two sets of constraints defines the Q-point.

We explore several methods for determining the solution to Eq. (3.24), including graphical analysis and the use of models of varying complexity for the diode. These techniques will include:

- Graphical analysis using the load-line technique
- Analysis with the mathematical model for the diode
- Simplified analysis with an ideal diode model
- Simplified analysis using the constant voltage drop model

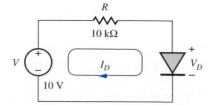

Figure 3.20 Diode circuit containing a voltage source and resistor.

Load-Line Analysis

In some cases, the *i-v* characteristic of the solid-state device may be available only in graphical form, as in Fig. 3.21. We must then use a graphical approach (**load-line analysis**) to find the simultaneous solution of Eq. (3.24) with the graphical characteristic. Equation (3.24) defines the *load line* for the diode. The Q-point can be found by plotting the graph of the load line on the *i-v* characteristic for the diode. The intersection of the two curves represents the quiescent operating point, or Q-point, for the diode.

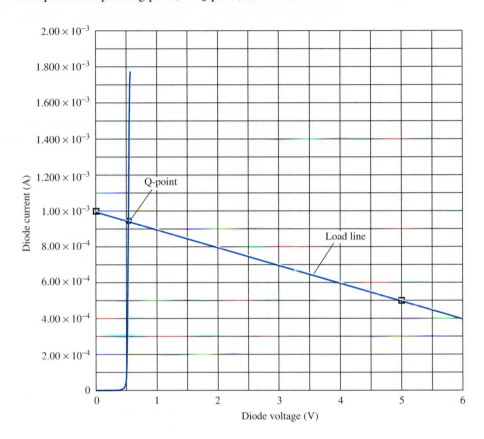

Figure 3.21 Diode *i-v* characteristic and load line.

EXAMPLE 3.4: Use load-line analysis to find the Q-point for the series diode circuit in Fig. 3.20 using the *i-v* characteristic in Fig. 3.21.

SOLUTION: Using the values from Fig. 3.20, Eq. (3.24) can be rewritten as

$$10 = I_D 10^4 + V_D \qquad (3.25)$$

Two points are needed to define the line. The simplest choices are:

$$I_D = (10 \text{ V}/10^4 \text{ }\Omega) = 1 \text{ mA} \qquad \text{for } V_D = 0$$

and

$$V_D = 10 \text{ V} \qquad \text{for } I_D = 0$$

Unfortunately, the second point is not on the diode characteristic as presented in Fig. 3.21, but we are free to choose any point that satisfies Eq. (3.25). Let's pick $V_D = 5$ V:

$$I_D = (10 - 5) \text{ V}/10^4 \text{ }\Omega = 0.5 \text{ mA} \qquad \text{for } V_D = 5$$

These points and the resulting load line are plotted in Fig. 3.21. The Q-point is given by the intersection of the load line and the diode characteristic:

$$Q\text{-point} = 0.95 \text{ mA}, 0.6 \text{ V}$$

◆

Note that the values from the example are not exactly on the load line because they do not precisely satisfy the load-line equation. This is often a problem with graphical analysis. Using $V_D = 0.6$ V in Eq. (3.25) yields an improved estimate for the Q-point: (0.94 mA, 0.6 V).

Analysis Using the Mathematical Model for the Diode

We can use our **mathematical model** for the diode to approach the solution of Eq. (3.25) more directly. The particular diode characteristic in Fig. 3.21 is represented quite accurately by diode Eq. (3.11), with $I_S = 10^{-13}$ A, $n = 1$, and $V_T = 0.025$ V:

$$I_D = 10^{-13} \left[\exp\left(\frac{V_D}{V_T}\right) - 1 \right] = 10^{-13}[\exp(40V_D) - 1] \tag{3.26}$$

Eliminating I_D by substituting Eq. (3.26) into Eq. (3.25) yields

$$10 = 10^4 \cdot 10^{-13}[\exp(40V_D) - 1] + V_D \tag{3.27}$$

An alternate equation can be obtained by eliminating the voltage V_D using Eq. (3.14) instead of Eq. (3.11):

$$10 = 10^4 I_D + 0.025 \ln\left[1 + \frac{I_D}{I_S}\right] \tag{3.28}$$

The expressions in Eqs. (3.27) and (3.28), called *transcendental equations,* do not have closed-form analytical solutions, so we settle for a numerical answer to the problem.

One approach to finding a numerical solution to Eq. (3.27) or (3.28) is through simple trial and error. We can guess a value of V_D and see if it satisfies Eq. (3.27). Based on the result, a new guess can be formulated and Eq. (3.27) evaluated again. The human brain is quite good at finding a sequence of values that will converge to the desired solution.

On the other hand, it is often preferable to use a computer to find the solution to Eq. (3.27), particularly if we need to find the answer to several different problems or parameter sets. The computer, however, requires a much more well-defined iteration strategy than brute force trial and error.

One possible numerical iteration strategy uses Newton's method for finding the zeros of an equation. Equation (3.27) can be rewritten as

$$f = 10 - 10^4 \cdot 10^{-13}[\exp(40V_D) - 1] - V_D \tag{3.29}$$

where we desire to find the value of V_D for which $f = 0$. Newton's method provides a numerical iteration strategy.

An initial guess V_D^0 is chosen for the value of V_D, and the value of f corresponding to V_D^0 is calculated. Unless we are extremely lucky, the value of f will not be zero. Referring to Fig. 3.22, the slope f' of the function f at $V_D = V_D^0$ is used to estimate an improved value V_D^1 that will force f closer to zero. It is desired that $f(V_D^1) = 0$, and

$$f'(V_D^0) = \frac{f(V_D^0) - 0}{V_D^0 - V_D^1} \quad \text{or} \quad V_D^1 = V_D^0 - \frac{f(V_D^0)}{f'(V_D^0)} \tag{3.30}$$

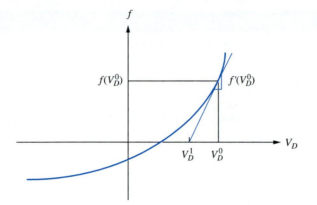

Figure 3.22 Newton update for finding a zero of the function f.

The iterative numerical procedure becomes:

1. Make an initial guess V_D^0.

2. Evaluate f and f' for this value of V_D.

3. Calculate a new guess for V_D using Eq. (3.30).

4. Repeat steps 2 and 3 until convergence is obtained.

This numerical iteration process can be done manually with a calculator or be easily implemented using a spreadsheet. Spreadsheets are quite useful in circuit design for finding solutions to iterative problems as well as for exploring the design space associated with many circuit design problems. As an example of the use of a spreadsheet, let us implement the preceding numeric iteration method. The function f, its derivative f', the iterative update for V_D, and the current I_D are all given by

$$f = 10 - 10^{-9}[\exp(40V_D) - 1] - V_D$$
$$f' = -4 \times 10^{-8} \exp(40V_D) - 1 \tag{3.31}$$
$$V_D^{i+1} = V_D^i - \frac{f(V_D^i)}{f'(V_D^i)} \qquad \text{and} \qquad I_D = 10^{-13}[\exp(40V_D) - 1]$$

Table 3.1 gives the results of spreadsheet calculations. The initial guess of $V_D = 0.8$ V is shown in **bold** type in row 0. In any given row, f, f', and I_D are calculated from their respective expressions in Eq. (3.31) using the value of V_D in the same row. Except for the initial guess in row 0, the value of V_D in any row is calculated from V_D, f, and f' in the previous row. Once the formulas are entered into one row of the spreadsheet, the row may simply be copied into the cells in as many rows as desired, and the iteration process proceeds automatically. For the particular case in Table 3.1, the diode voltage and current calculations converge to within four significant digits in 13 iterations. For these diode problems, it is best to choose an initial value of V_D that is larger than the expected solution. (See Prob. 3.37.)

Note that one can achieve answers to an almost arbitrary precision using the numerical approach. However, in most real circuit situations, we will not have an accurate value for the saturation current of the diode, and there will be significant tolerances associated with the sources and passive components in the circuit. For example, the saturation current specification for a given diode type may vary by factors ranging from 10:1 to as much as 100:1. In addition, resistors commonly have ± 5 percent to ± 10 percent tolerances, and we do not know the exact operating temperature of the diode (remember the -1.8 mV/K

Table 3.1

Diode Iteration Problem Using a Spreadsheet

Iteration #	V_D	f	f'	I_D
0	**0.8000**	-7.895×10^4	-3.159×10^6	7.896×10^0
1	0.7750	-2.904×10^4	-1.162×10^6	2.905×10^0
2	0.7500	-1.068×10^4	-4.276×10^5	1.069×10^0
3	0.7250	-3.927×10^3	-1.575×10^5	3.936×10^{-1}
4	0.7001	-1.442×10^3	-5.806×10^4	1.452×10^{-1}
5	0.6753	-5.281×10^2	-2.150×10^4	5.374×10^{-2}
6	0.6507	-1.918×10^2	-8.048×10^3	2.012×10^{-2}
7	0.6269	-6.817×10^1	-3.103×10^3	7.754×10^{-3}
8	0.6049	-2.281×10^1	-1.289×10^3	3.220×10^{-3}
9	0.5872	-6.455×10^0	-6.357×10^2	1.587×10^{-3}
10	0.5770	-1.148×10^0	-4.238×10^2	1.057×10^{-3}
11	0.5743	-5.989×10^{-2}	-3.804×10^2	9.486×10^{-4}
12	0.5742	-1.876×10^{-4}	-3.780×10^2	9.426×10^{-4}
13	0.5742	-1.858×10^{-9}	-3.780×10^2	9.426×10^{-4}
		$10 - 10^{-9}$ $[\exp(40V_D) - 1]$ $- V_D$	-4×10^{-8} $\exp(40V_D) - 1$	10^{-13} $[\exp(40V_D) - 1]$

temperature coefficient) or the precise value of the parameter *n*. Hence, it does not make sense to try to obtain answers with a precision of more than two or three significant digits.

An alternative to the use of a spreadsheet is to write a simple program using a high-level language. The solution to Eqs. (3.28) and (3.29) also can be found using the "solver" routines in many calculators, which use iteration procedures even more sophisticated than that just described. MATLAB also provides the function fzero, which will calculate the zeros of a function as outlined in Example 3.5.

EXAMPLE 3.5: Use MATLAB to find the solution to Eq. (3.29).

SOLUTION: First, create an M-file for the function 'diode':

```
function xd = diode(vd)
xd = 10-(10^(9))*(exp(40*vd)-1)-vd;
```

Then find the solution near 1 V:

```
fzero('diode',1)
```

ANSWER: 0.5742 V

The Ideal Diode Model

Graphical load-line analysis provides insight into the operation of the diode circuit of Fig. 3.20, and the mathematical model can be used to provide more accurate solutions to the load-line problem. The next method discussed provides simplified solutions to the diode circuit of Fig. 3.20 by introducing simplified diode circuit models of varying complexity.

The diode, as described by its i-v characteristic in Fig. 3.8 or by Eq. (3.11), is obviously a nonlinear device. However, most, if not all, of the circuit analysis that we have learned thus far assumed that the circuits were composed of linear elements. To use this wealth of analysis techniques, we will use **piecewise linear** approximations to the diode characteristic.

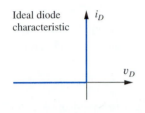

Ideal diode characteristic

The **ideal diode model** is the simplest model for the diode. The i-v characteristic for the **ideal diode** in Fig. 3.23 consists of two straight-line segments. If the diode is conducting a forward or positive current (forward-biased), then the voltage across the diode is zero. If the diode is reverse-biased, with $v_D < 0$, then the current through the diode is zero. These conditions can be stated mathematically as

$$v_D = 0 \text{ for } i_D > 0 \qquad \text{and} \qquad i_D = 0 \text{ for } v_D \le 0 \qquad (3.32)$$

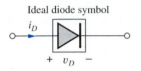

Ideal diode symbol

The special symbol in Fig. 3.23 is used to represent the ideal diode in circuit diagrams.

We can now think of the diode as having two states. The diode is either conducting in the *on* state, or nonconducting and *off*. For circuit analysis, we use the models in Fig. 3.24 for the two states. If the diode is on, then it is modeled by a "short" circuit, a wire. For the off state, the diode is modeled by an "open" circuit, no connection.

Figure 3.23 Ideal diode i-v characteristics and circuit symbol.

Let us now analyze the circuit of Fig. 3.20 assuming that the diode can be modeled by the ideal diode of Fig. 3.24. The diode has two possible states, and our analysis of diode circuits proceeds as follows:

1. Select a model for the diode.
2. Make an (educated) guess concerning the region of operation of the diode based on the circuit configuration.
3. Analyze the circuit using the diode model appropriate for the assumption in step 2.
4. Check the results to see if they are consistent with the assumptions.

For this analysis, we select the ideal diode model. The diode in the original circuit is replaced by the ideal diode, as in Fig. 3.25(b). Next we must guess the state of the diode. Because the voltage source appears to be trying to force a positive current through the diode, our first guess will be to assume that the diode is on. The ideal diode of Fig. 3.25(b) is replaced by its piecewise linear model for the on region in Fig. 3.26, and the diode current is given by

$$I_D = \frac{(10 - 0)\ \text{V}}{10\ \text{k}\Omega} = 1.00\ \text{mA}$$

 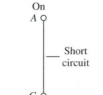

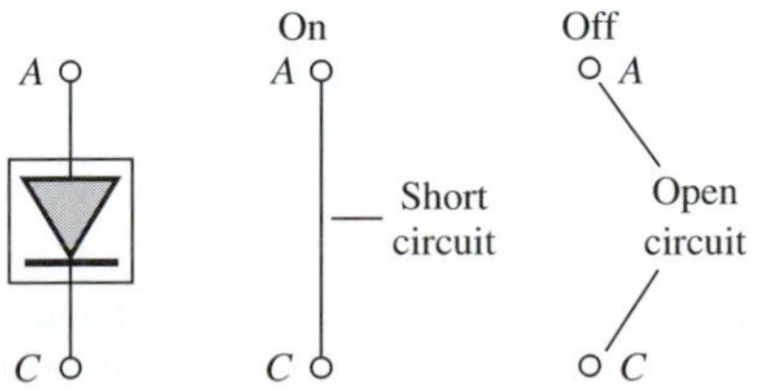

Figure 3.24 Circuit models for on and off states of the ideal diode.

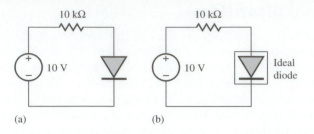

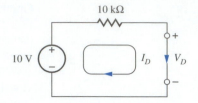

Figure 3.25 (a) Original diode circuit. (b) Circuit modeled by an ideal diode.

Figure 3.26 Ideal diode replaced with its model for the on state.

The current $I_D \geq 0$, which is consistent with the assumption that the diode is on. The Q-point is therefore equal to (1 mA, 0 V). Based on the ideal diode model, we find that the diode is forward-biased and operating with a current of 1 mA.

A Reverse-Biased Diode Circuit

A second circuit example in which the diode terminals have been reversed appears in Fig. 3.27; the ideal diode model is again used to model the diode [Fig. 3.27(b)]. The voltage source now appears to be trying to force a current backward through the diode. Because the diode cannot conduct in this direction, we assume the diode is off. The ideal diode of Fig. 3.27(b) is replaced by the open circuit model for the off region, as in Fig. 3.28. Writing the loop equation for this case,

$$-10 - V_D + 10^4 I_D = 0$$

Because $I_D = 0$ and $V_D = -10$ V, the calculated diode voltage is negative, which is consistent with the starting assumption that the diode is off. The Q-point is $(0, -10$ V). The analysis shows that the diode in the circuit of Fig. 3.27 is indeed reverse-biased.

Although these two problems may seem rather simple, the complexity of diode circuit analysis increases rapidly as the number of diodes increases. If the circuit has N diodes, then the number of possible states is 2^N. A circuit with 10 diodes has 1024 different possible circuits that could be analyzed! Only through practice can we develop the intuition needed to avoid analysis of many incorrect cases. We analyze more complex circuits shortly, but first let's look at a slightly better piecewise linear model for the diode.

Constant Voltage Drop Model

We know from our earlier discussion that there is a small, nearly constant voltage across the forward-biased diode. The ideal diode model ignores the presence of this voltage. However,

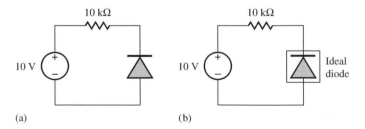

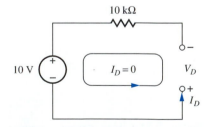

Figure 3.27 (a) Circuit with reverse-biased diode. (b) Circuit modeled by ideal diode.

Figure 3.28 Ideal diode replaced with its model for the off region.

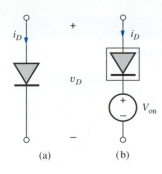

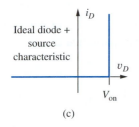

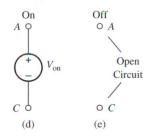

Figure 3.29 Constant voltage drop model for diode. (a) Actual diode. (b) Ideal diode plus voltage source V_{on}. (c) Composite i-v characteristic. (d) CVD model for the on state. (e) Model for the off state.

the piecewise linear model for the diode can be improved by adding a constant voltage V_{on} in series with the ideal diode, as shown in Fig. 3.29(b). This is the **constant voltage drop (CVD) model.** V_{on} offsets the i-v characteristic of the ideal diode, as indicated in Fig. 3.29(c). The piecewise linear models for the two states become a voltage source V_{on} for the on state and an open circuit for the off state. We now have

$$v_D = V_{\text{on}} \text{ for } i_D > 0 \qquad \text{and} \qquad i_D = 0 \text{ for } v_D \leq V_{\text{on}} \qquad (3.33)$$

We may consider the ideal diode model to be the special case of the constant voltage drop model for which $V_{\text{on}} = 0$. From the i-v characteristics presented in Fig. 3.7, we see that a reasonable choice for V_{on} is 0.6 to 0.7 V. We use a voltage of 0.6 V as the turn-on voltage for our diode circuit analysis.

Let us analyze the diode circuit from Fig. 3.20 using the CVD model for the diode. The diode in Fig. 3.30(a) is replaced by its CVD model in Fig. 3.30(b). The 10-V source once again appears to be forward biasing the diode, so assume that the diode is on, resulting in the simplified circuit in Fig. 3.30(c). The diode current is given by

$$I_D = \frac{(10 - V_{\text{on}}) \text{ V}}{10 \text{ k}\Omega} = \frac{(10 - 0.6) \text{ V}}{10 \text{ k}\Omega} = 0.940 \text{ mA} \qquad (3.34)$$

which is slightly smaller than that predicted by the ideal diode model.

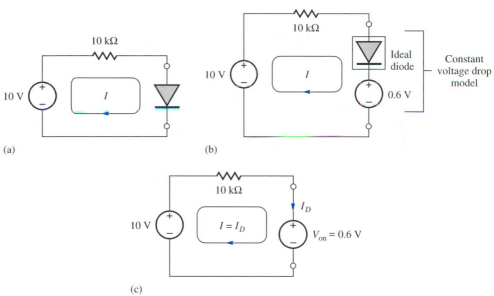

Figure 3.30 Diode circuit analysis using constant voltage drop model. (a) Original diode circuit. (b) Circuit with diode replaced by the constant voltage drop model. (c) Circuit with ideal diode replaced by the piecewise linear model.

Model Comparison and Discussion

We have analyzed the circuit of Fig. 3.20 using four different approaches; the various results appear in Table 3.2. All four sets of predicted voltages and currents are quite similar. Even the simple ideal diode model overestimates the current by less than 10 percent compared to the mathematical model. We see that the current is quite insensitive to the

Table 3.2		
Comparison of Diode Circuit Analysis Results		
Analysis Technique	**Diode Current**	**Diode Voltage**
Load-line analysis	0.94 mA	0.6 V
Mathematical model	0.942 mA	0.547 V
Ideal diode model	1.00 mA	0 V
Constant voltage drop model	0.940 mA	0.600 V

actual choice of diode voltage. This is a result of the exponential dependence of the diode current on voltage as well as the large source voltage (10 V) in this particular circuit.

Rewriting Eq. (3.34),

$$I_D = \frac{10 - V_{on}}{10 \text{ k}\Omega} = \frac{10 \text{ V}}{10 \text{ k}\Omega}\left(1 - \frac{V_{on}}{10}\right) = (1.00 \text{ mA})\left(1 - \frac{V_{on}}{10}\right) \qquad (3.35)$$

we see that the value of I_D is approximately 1 mA for $V_{on} \ll 10$ V. Variations in V_{on} have only a small effect on the result. However, the situation would be significantly different if the source voltage were only 1 V for example (see Prob. 3.41).

3.10 MULTIPLE DIODE CIRCUITS

The load-line technique is only applicable to single diode circuits, and the mathematical model, or numerical iteration technique, becomes much more complex for circuits with more than one nonlinear element. In fact, the SPICE electronic circuit simulation program referred to throughout this book is designed to provide numerical solutions to just such complex problems. In this section we discuss the use of the simplified diode models for hand analysis of more complicated diode circuits.

Example of a Circuit Containing Two Diodes

Consider the circuit containing two diodes in Fig. 3.31, which is redrawn in Fig. 3.32. For simplicity, the positive and negative voltage sources have been replaced with +15 V written at node C and −10 V at node F. We often use this "shorthand" representation to help avoid clutter in circuit diagrams as they become more complex. Such representations should always be interpreted to mean that a voltage source with the given value is connected between the node and the reference terminal for the circuit.

Following the four steps in the previous section, the ideal diode model has been chosen for the analysis, and, in Fig. 3.32(b), the circuit is redrawn using this model. With two diodes, there will be four potential piecewise linear models for the circuit corresponding to

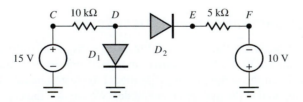

Figure 3.31 Circuit containing two diodes.

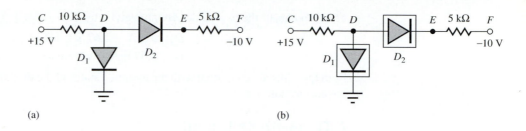

Figure 3.32 (a) Simplified representation of the circuit from Fig. 3.31. (b) Diodes replaced by the ideal diodes.

(a)   (b)

T a b l e 3.3	
Possible Diode States for Circuit in Fig. 3.32(b)	
D_1	D_2
Off	Off
Off	On
On	On
On	Off

the four diode states in Table 3.3. We must try to use some intuition to make a choice of states. It appears that the $+15$ V source will try to force a current in the positive direction through both diodes D_1 and D_2; the -10 V source will also try to force a current through D_2 in the positive direction. A reasonable initial choice for this circuit, therefore, is to assume that both diodes are on, and the circuit is redrawn in Fig. 3.33 using the piecewise linear models for the ideal diode in the on state.

The currents in the circuit can now be found using a combination of Ohm's law and Kirchhoff's current law. Because the voltage at node D is zero due to the short circuit in diode D_1, the currents I_1 and I_{D2} can be written directly using Ohm's law:

$$I_1 = \frac{(15 - 0)\text{ V}}{10\text{ k}\Omega} = 1.50\text{ mA} \qquad \text{and} \qquad I_{D2} = \frac{0 - (-10)\text{ V}}{5\text{ k}\Omega} = 2.00\text{ mA} \quad (3.36)$$

At node D, $I_1 = I_{D1} + I_{D2}$, so $I_{D1} = 1.50 - 2.00 = -0.50$ mA. The result, $I_{D2} > 0$, is consistent with D_2 being on, but $I_{D1} < 0$ is not allowed by the diode. Our assumed state must be incorrect, so we must change our assumptions and try again.

A Second Iteration

Because the current in D_2 was correct and that in D_1 was incorrect, an appropriate second guess would be D_1 off and D_2 on. Note, however, that there is no guarantee that this will in fact be correct.

Analysis of the new circuit in Fig. 3.34 proceeds as follows. Because I_{D1} is now assumed to be zero, $I_{D2} = I_1$ and a single-loop equation can be written for I_1:

$$15 - 10{,}000\,I_1 - 5000\,I_{D2} - (-10) = 0$$
$$25 = 10{,}000\,I_1 + 5000\,I_1 \qquad \text{because } I_{D2} = I_1 \qquad (3.37)$$
$$I_1 = \frac{25\text{ V}}{15{,}000\ \Omega} = 1.67\text{ mA}$$

The voltage across diode D_1 is given by

$$V_{D1} = 15 - 10{,}000\,I_1 = 15 - 16.7 = -1.67\text{ V} \qquad (3.38)$$

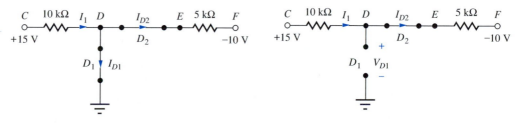

Figure 3.33 Circuit with both diodes assumed to be on.

Figure 3.34 Circuit with D_1 off and D_2 on.

The Q-points of the two diodes are now given by

$$D_1: (0 \text{ mA}, -1.67 \text{ V}): \text{ off } ✔$$
$$D_2: (1.67 \text{ mA}, 0 \text{ V}): \text{ on } ✔$$

Both Q-points are consistent with the assumed states of the diodes, so we have finally found the correct solution.

A Three-Diode Circuit

Figure 3.35 is a second example of a circuit with several diodes. We will use the CVD model for improved accuracy. With three diodes, there are eight possibilities. For this circuit, it appears that the +10-V supply will tend to forward-bias D_1 and D_2, and the −10-V supply will tend to forward-bias D_2 and D_3. The −20-V supply will also try to forward-bias D_1, so our initial circuit model will assume that all three diodes are on, as in Fig. 3.36. Here we skipped the step of physically drawing the circuit with the ideal diode symbols but instead incorporated the piecewise linear models directly into the figure.

Working from right to left, we see that the voltages at nodes C, B, and A are given by

$$V_C = -0.6 \text{ V} \qquad V_B = -0.6 + 0.6 = 0 \text{ V} \qquad V_A = 0 - 0.6 = -0.6 \text{ V}$$

With the node voltages specified, it is easy to find the current through each resistor:

$$I_1 = \frac{10 - 0}{10} \frac{\text{V}}{\text{k}\Omega} = 1 \text{ mA} \qquad I_2 = \frac{-0.6 - (-20)}{10} \frac{\text{V}}{\text{k}\Omega} = 1.94 \text{ mA}$$
$$I_3 = \frac{-0.6 - (-10)}{10} \frac{\text{V}}{\text{k}\Omega} = 0.94 \text{ mA}$$

$$(3.39)$$

Using Kirchhoff's current law, we also have

$$I_2 = I_{D1} \qquad I_1 = I_{D1} + I_{D2} \qquad I_3 = I_{D2} + I_{D3} \qquad (3.40)$$

Combining Eqs. (3.39) and (3.40) yields the three diode currents:

$$I_{D1} = 1.94 \text{ mA} > 0 ✔ \qquad I_{D2} = -0.94 \text{ mA} < 0 ✗ \qquad I_{D3} = 1.86 \text{ mA} > 0 ✔$$

$$(3.41)$$

I_{D1} and I_{D3} are consistent with the original assumptions, but I_{D2} represents a contradiction.

For our second attempt, let us assume D_1 and D_3 are on and D_2 is off, as in Fig. 3.37. We now have

$$+10 - 10,000 I_1 - 0.6 - 10,000 I_2 + 20 = 0 \qquad \text{with } I_1 = I_{D1} = I_2 \quad (3.42)$$

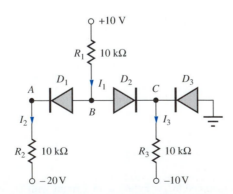

Figure 3.35 Example of a circuit containing three diodes.

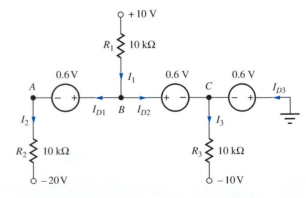

Figure 3.36 Circuit model for circuit of Fig. 3.35 with all diodes on.

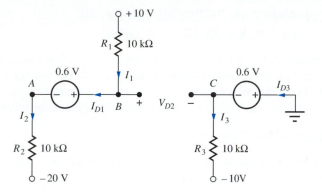

Figure 3.37 Circuit with diodes D_1 and D_3 on and D_2 off.

which yields

$$I_{D1} = \frac{29.4}{20} \frac{V}{k\Omega} = 1.47 \text{ mA} > 0 \; \checkmark$$

Also

$$I_{D3} = I_3 = \frac{-0.6 - (-10)}{10} \frac{V}{k\Omega} = 0.940 \text{ mA} > 0 \; \checkmark$$

The voltage across diode D_2 is given by

$$V_{D2} = 10 - 10{,}000 \, I_1 - (-0.6) = 10 - 14.7 + 0.6 = -4.10 \text{ V} < 0 \; \checkmark$$

I_{D1}, I_{D3}, and V_{D2} are now all consistent with the circuit assumptions, so the Q-points for the circuit are

$$D_1: (1.47 \text{ mA}, 0.6 \text{ V}) \qquad D_2: (0 \text{ mA}, -4.10 \text{ V}) \qquad D_3: (0.940 \text{ mA}, 0.6 \text{ V})$$

$$(3.43)$$

The Q-point values that would have obtained using the ideal diode model are (see Prob. 3.48):

$$D_1: (1.50 \text{ mA}, 0 \text{ V}) \qquad D_2: (0 \text{ mA}, -5.00 \text{ V}) \qquad D_3: (1.00 \text{ mA}, 0 \text{ V}) \quad (3.44)$$

The values of I_{D1} and I_{D3} differ by less than 6 percent. However, the reverse-bias voltage on D_2 differs by 20 percent. This shows the difference that the choice of models can make. The results from the circuit using the CVD model should be a more accurate estimate of how the circuit will actually perform than would result from the ideal diode case. Remember, however, that these calculations are both just approximations based on our models for the actual behavior of the real diode circuit.

> **EXERCISE:** Find the Q-points for the three diodes in Fig. 3.35 if R_1 is changed to 2.5 kΩ.
>
> **ANSWERS:** (2.14 mA, 0.6 V); (1.14 mA, 0.6 V); (0 mA, -1.37 V)

> **EXERCISE:** Use SPICE to calculate the Q-points of the diodes in Fig. 3.35. Use $I_S = 1$ fA.
>
> **ANSWERS:** (1.47 mA, 0.665 V); (0 mA, -4.01 V); (0.935 mA, 0.653 V)

3.11 ANALYSIS OF DIODES OPERATING IN THE BREAKDOWN REGION

Figure 3.38 is a single-loop circuit containing a 20-V source supplying current to a Zener diode with a reverse breakdown voltage of 5 V. The voltage source has a polarity that will tend to reverse-bias the diode. Because the source voltage exceeds the Zener voltage rating of the diode, $V_Z = 5$ V, we should expect the diode to be operating in its breakdown region.

Load-Line Analysis

The i-v characteristic for this Zener diode is given in Fig. 3.39, and a correct load-line analysis will find the Q-point for the diode, independent of the region of operation. The normal polarities for I_D and V_D are indicated in Fig. 3.38. The loop equation is

$$-20 = V_D + 5000\, I_D \tag{3.45}$$

In order to draw the load line, we choose two points on the graph:

$$V_D = 0,\ I_D = -4\ \text{mA} \qquad \text{and} \qquad V_D = -5\ \text{V},\ I_D = -3\ \text{mA}$$

In this case the load line intersects the diode characteristic at a Q-point in the breakdown region: $(-2.9\ \text{mA}, -5.2\ \text{V})$.

Analysis with the Piecewise Linear Model

The assumption of reverse breakdown requires that the diode current I_D be less than zero or that the Zener current I_Z equal $-I_D > 0$. We will analyze the circuit with the piecewise linear model and test this condition to see if it is consistent with the reverse-breakdown assumption.

In Fig. 3.40, the Zener diode has been replaced with its piecewise linear model from Fig. 3.16 in Sec. 3.6, with $V_Z = 5$ V and $R_Z = 100\ \Omega$. Writing the loop equation this time

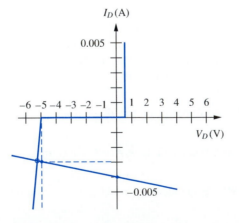

Figure 3.38 Circuit containing a Zener diode with $V_Z = 5$ V and $R_Z = 100\ \Omega$.

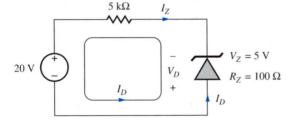

Figure 3.39 Load line for Zener diode.

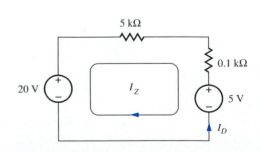

Figure 3.40 Circuit with piece-wise linear model for Zener diode.

in terms of I_Z:

$$20 - 5100\,I_Z - 5 = 0 \qquad \text{or} \qquad I_Z = \frac{(20 - 5)\,\text{V}}{5100\,\Omega} = 2.94\,\text{mA} \qquad (3.46)$$

Because I_Z is greater than zero ($I_D < 0$), the solution is consistent with our assumption of Zener breakdown operation.

It is worth noting that each diode has three possible states if the breakdown region is included, further increasing analysis complexity.

Voltage Regulation

A useful application of the Zener diode is as a **voltage regulator,** as shown in the circuit of Fig. 3.41. The function of the Zener diode is to maintain a constant voltage across load resistor R_L. As long as the diode is operating in reverse breakdown, a voltage approximately equal to V_Z will appear across R_L. To ensure that the diode is operating in the Zener breakdown region, we must have $I_Z > 0$.

The circuit of Fig. 3.41 has been redrawn in Fig. 3.42 with the model for the Zener diode, with $R_Z = 0$. Using nodal analysis, the Zener current is expressed by

$$I_Z = I_S - I_L \qquad (3.47)$$

The currents I_S and I_L are equal to

$$I_S = \frac{V_S - V_Z}{R} = \frac{(20 - 5)\,\text{V}}{5\,\text{k}\Omega} = 3\,\text{mA} \qquad \text{and} \qquad I_L = \frac{V_Z}{R_L} = \frac{5\,\text{V}}{5\,\text{k}\Omega} = 1\,\text{mA}$$

$$(3.48)$$

resulting in a Zener current $I_Z = 2\,\text{mA}$ ($I_Z > 0$, which is again consistent with our assumptions). If the calculated value of I_Z is less than zero, then the Zener diode no longer controls the voltage across R_L, and the voltage regulator is said to have "dropped out of regulation."

For proper regulation to take place, the Zener current must be positive, which places a lower bound on the value of R_L:

$$I_Z = I_S - I_L = \frac{V_S - V_Z}{R} - \frac{V_Z}{R_L} = \frac{V_S}{R} - V_Z\left(\frac{1}{R} + \frac{1}{R_L}\right) > 0 \qquad (3.49)$$

Solving for R_L yields a lower bound on the value of load resistance for which the Zener diode will continue to act as a voltage regulator.

$$R_L > \frac{R}{\left(\dfrac{V_S}{V_Z} - 1\right)} = R_{\text{MIN}} \qquad (3.50)$$

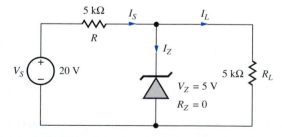

Figure 3.41 Zener diode voltage regulator circuit.

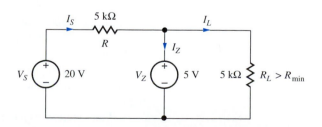

Figure 3.42 Circuit with the model for the Zener diode.

> **EXERCISE:** What is the value of R_{MIN} for the Zener voltage regulator circuit in Figs. 3.41 and 3.42? What is the output voltage for $R_L = 1 \text{ k}\Omega$? For $R_L = 2 \text{ k}\Omega$?
>
> **ANSWERS:** 1.67 kΩ; 3.33 V; 5.00 V

Analysis Including Zener Resistance

The voltage regulator circuit in Fig. 3.41 has been redrawn in Fig. 3.43 and includes a nonzero Zener resistance R_Z. The output voltage is now a function of the current I_Z through the Zener diode. For small values of R_Z, however, the change in output voltage will be small.

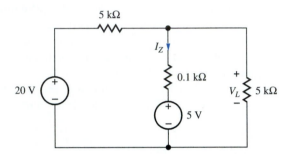

Figure 3.43 Zener diode regulator circuit, including Zener resistance.

EXAMPLE 3.6: Find the output voltage for the Zener diode regulator in Figs. 3.41 to 3.43 if $R_Z = 100 \ \Omega$ and $V_Z = 5$ V.

SOLUTION: A single nodal equation can be written for V_L:

$$\frac{V_L - 20 \text{ V}}{5000 \ \Omega} + \frac{V_L - 5 \text{ V}}{100 \ \Omega} + \frac{V_L}{5000 \ \Omega} = 0$$

Multiplying the equation by 5000 Ω and collecting terms yields

$$52 V_L = 270 \text{ V} \qquad \text{and} \qquad V_L = 5.19 \text{ V}$$

The Zener diode current is equal to

$$I_Z = \frac{V_L - 5 \text{ V}}{100 \ \Omega} = \frac{5.19 \text{ V} - 5 \text{ V}}{100 \ \Omega} = 1.90 \text{ mA} \qquad > 0 \ ✔$$

$I_Z > 0$ confirms operation in reverse breakdown. We see that the output voltage of the regulator is slightly higher than for the case with $R_Z = 0$, and the Zener diode current is reduced slightly. ◆

3.12 HALF-WAVE RECTIFIER CIRCUITS

Rectifier circuits are an important application of diodes. The basic rectifier circuit converts an ac voltage to a pulsating dc voltage. A filter is added to eliminate the ac components of the waveform and produce a nearly constant dc voltage output. Rectifier circuits are commonly used to convert the 120-V ac, 60-Hz power line source to the dc voltages needed to run electronic devices such as personal computers, stereo systems, radio receivers, and the like.

This section explores half-wave rectifier circuits with capacitor filters that form the basis for many dc power supplies. Up to this point, we have looked at only steady-state dc circuits in which the diode remained in one of its three possible states (on, off, or

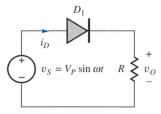

Figure 3.44 Half-wave rectifier circuit.

reverse breakdown). Now, however, the diode state will be changing with time, and a given piecewise linear model for the circuit will be valid for only a certain time interval.

A single diode is used to form the **half-wave rectifier circuit** in Fig. 3.44. A sinusoidal voltage source $v_S = V_P \sin \omega t$ is connected to the series combination of diode D_1 and load resistor R.

During the first half of the cycle, for which $v_S > 0$, the source forces a current through diode D_1 in the forward direction, and D_1 will be on. During the second half of the cycle, $v_S < 0$. Because a negative current cannot exist in the diode (unless it is in breakdown), it turns off. These two states are modeled in Fig. 3.45 using the ideal diode model.

When the diode is on, voltage source v_S is connected directly to the output and $v_O = v_S$. When the diode is off, the current in the resistor is zero, and the output voltage is zero. In this circuit, the diode is conducting 50 percent of the time and is off 50 percent of the time. The output voltage waveform is shown in Fig. 3.46(b), and the current is called pulsating direct current.

In some cases, the forward voltage drop across the diode can be important. Figure 3.47 shows the circuit model for the on state using the CVD model. For this case, the output

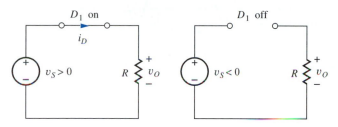

Figure 3.45 Ideal diode models for the two half-wave rectifier states.

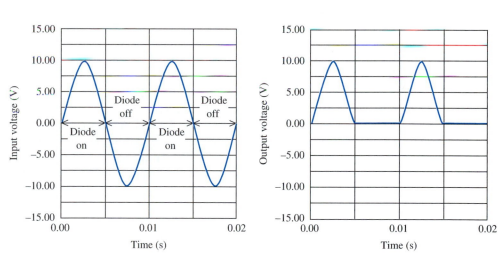

Figure 3.46 Sinusoidal input voltage v_S and pulsating dc output voltage v_O for the half-wave rectifier circuit.

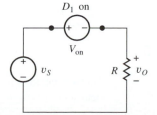

Figure 3.47 CVD model for rectifier on state.

voltage is one diode-drop smaller than the input voltage during the conduction interval:

$$v_O = (V_P \sin \omega t) - V_{\text{on}} \tag{3.51}$$

The output voltage remains zero during the off-state interval. The input and output waveforms for the half-wave rectifier, including the effect of V_{on}, are shown in Fig. 3.48 for $V_P = 10$ V and $V_{\text{on}} = 0.7$ V.

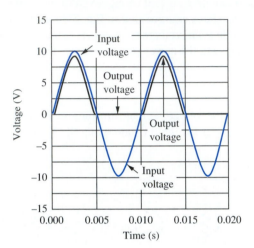

Figure 3.48 Half-wave rectifier output voltage with $V_P = 10$ V and $V_{\text{on}} = 0.7$ V.

In many applications, a transformer is used to convert from the 120-V ac, 60-Hz voltage available from the power line to the desired ac voltage level, as in Fig. 3.49. The transformer can step the voltage up or down depending on the application; it also enhances safety by providing isolation from the power line. From circuit theory we know that the output of an ideal transformer can be represented by an ideal voltage source, and we use this knowledge to simplify the representation of subsequent rectifier circuit diagrams.

The unfiltered output of the half-wave rectifier in Fig. 3.46 is not suitable for operation of most electronic circuits because constant power supply voltages are required to establish proper bias for the electronic devices. A **filter capacitor** (or more complex circuit) can be added to filter the output of the circuit in Figs. 3.44 or 3.49 in order to remove the time-varying components from the waveform.

To understand operation of the rectifier filter, we first consider the operation of the **peak-detector** circuit in Fig. 3.50. This circuit is similar to that in Fig. 3.49 except that the resistor is replaced with a capacitor C that is initially discharged [$v_O(0) = 0$].

Models for the circuit with the diode in the on and off states are in Fig. 3.51. The input and output voltage waveforms associated with this circuit are in Fig. 3.52. As the

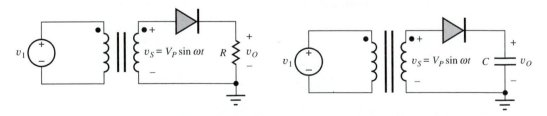

Figure 3.49 Transformer-driven half-wave rectifier.

Figure 3.50 Rectifier with capacitor load (peak detector).

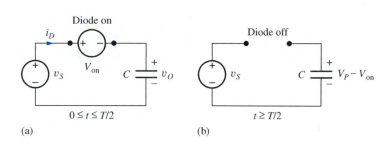

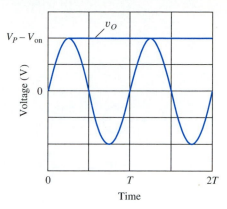

Figure 3.51 Peak-detector circuit models (constant voltage drop model). (a) The diode is on for $0 \le t \le T/2$. (b) The diode is off for $t > T/2$.

Figure 3.52 Input and output waveforms for the peak-detector circuit.

input voltage starts to rise, the diode turns on and connects the capacitor to the source. The capacitor voltage equals the input voltage minus the voltage drop across the diode.

At the peak of the input voltage waveform, the current through the diode tries to reverse direction because $i_D = C[d(v_s - V_{on})/dt] < 0$, the diode cuts off, and the capacitor is disconnected from the rest of the circuit. There is no circuit path to discharge the capacitor, so the voltage on the capacitor remains constant. Because the amplitude of the input voltage source v_S can never exceed V_P, the capacitor remains disconnected from v_S for $t > T/2$. Thus, the capacitor in the circuit in Fig. 3.50 charges up to a voltage one diode-drop below the peak of the input waveform and then remains constant, thereby producing a dc output voltage

$$V_{dc} = V_P - V_{on} \qquad (3.52)$$

Half-Wave Rectifier with *RC* Load

To make use of this output voltage, a load must be connected to the circuit as represented by the resistor R in Fig. 3.53. Now there is a path available to discharge the capacitor during the time the diode is not conducting. Models for the conducting and nonconducting time intervals are shown in Fig. 3.54; the waveforms for the circuit are shown in Fig. 3.55. The capacitor is again assumed to be initially discharged. During the first quarter cycle, the diode conducts, and the capacitor is rapidly charged toward the peak value of the input voltage source. The diode cuts off at the peak of v_S, and the capacitor voltage then discharges exponentially through the resistor R, as governed by the circuit in Fig. 3.54(b). The discharge continues until the input voltage exceeds the output voltage v_O, which occurs near the peak of the next cycle. The process is then repeated once every cycle.

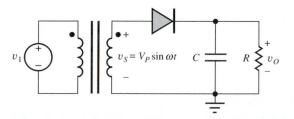

Figure 3.53 Half-wave rectifier circuit with filter capacitor.

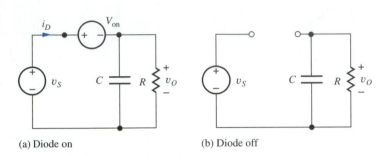

(a) Diode on   (b) Diode off

Figure 3.54 Half-wave rectifier circuit models.

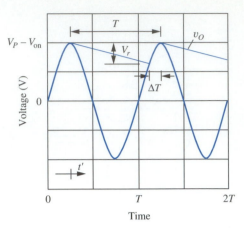

Figure 3.55 Input and output voltage waveforms for the half-wave rectifier circuit.

Ripple Voltage and Conduction Interval

The output voltage is no longer constant as in the ideal peak-detector circuit but has a **ripple voltage V_r.** In addition, the diode only conducts for a short time ΔT during each cycle. This time ΔT is called the **conduction interval,** and its angular equivalent is the **conduction angle θ_c.** The variables ΔT and V_r are important values related to dc power supply design, and we will now develop expressions for these parameters.

During the discharge period, the voltage across the capacitor is described by

$$v_o(t') = (V_P - V_{on}) \exp\left(-\frac{t'}{RC}\right) \qquad \text{for } t' = \left(t - \frac{T}{4}\right) \geq 0 \qquad (3.53)$$

in which the t' time axis is referenced to $t = T/4$. The ripple voltage V_r is given by

$$V_r = (V_P - V_{on}) - (V_P - V_{on}) \exp\left(-\frac{T - \Delta T}{RC}\right)$$

or $\hspace{11cm}$ (3.54)

$$V_r = (V_P - V_{on})\left[1 - \exp\left(-\frac{T - \Delta T}{RC}\right)\right]$$

A small value of V_r is desired in most power supply designs; a small value requires RC to be much greater than $T - \Delta T$. Using $\exp(-x) \approx 1 - x$ for small x results in an approximate expression for the ripple voltage:

$$V_r \approx (V_P - V_{on})\left[1 - \left(1 - \frac{T - \Delta T}{RC}\right)\right] = (V_P - V_{on})\frac{T}{RC}\left(1 - \frac{\Delta T}{T}\right) \qquad (3.55)$$

A small ripple voltage also requires $\Delta T \ll T$, and the final simplified expression for the ripple voltage becomes

$$V_r \approx (V_P - V_{on})\frac{T}{RC} = \frac{(V_P - V_{on})}{R}\frac{T}{C} \qquad (3.56)$$

The approximation of the exponential used in Eqs. (3.54) and (3.55) is equivalent to assuming that the capacitor is being discharged by a constant current so that the discharge waveform is a straight line. As indicated in Eq. (3.56), the ripple voltage V_R can be considered to be determined by an equivalent dc current equal to

$$I_{dc} = \frac{V_P - V_{\text{on}}}{R} \tag{3.57}$$

discharging the capacitor C for a time period T (that is, $\Delta V = (I_{dc}/C)\,T$).

An approximate expression can also be obtained for the conduction interval ΔT. At $t' = T - \Delta T$,

$$(V_P - V_{\text{on}}) \exp\left(-\frac{T - \Delta T}{RC}\right) = V_P \cos\omega(T - \Delta T) - V_{\text{on}} \tag{3.58}$$

Expanding the cosine term, recognizing that $\cos\omega T = 1$ and $\sin\omega T = 0$, and assuming that $\Delta T \ll T$ yields

$$(V_P - V_{\text{on}})\left(1 - \frac{T}{RC}\right) = V_P \cos\omega\,\Delta T - V_{\text{on}} \tag{3.59}$$

For small $\omega\,\Delta T$, Eq. (3.59) can be reduced to

$$(V_P - V_{\text{on}})\left(1 - \frac{T}{RC}\right) = V_P\left(1 - \frac{(\omega\,\Delta T)^2}{2}\right) - V_{\text{on}} \tag{3.60}$$

which can be solved for ΔT and simplified using Eq. (3.56):

$$\Delta T \approx \frac{1}{\omega}\sqrt{\frac{2T}{RC}\frac{(V_P - V_{\text{on}})}{V_P}} = \frac{1}{\omega}\sqrt{\frac{2V_r}{V_P}} \tag{3.61}$$

The conduction angle θ_c is given by

$$\theta_c = \omega\,\Delta T = \sqrt{\frac{2V_r}{V_P}} \tag{3.62}$$

Example 3.7: Find the value of the dc output voltage, ripple voltage, conduction interval, and conduction angle for a half-wave rectifier that is being supplied from a transformer with a secondary voltage of 12.6 V_{rms} (60 Hz) with $R = 15\ \Omega$ and $C = 25{,}000\ \mu\text{F}$. Assume the diode on voltage $V_{\text{on}} = 1$ V.

Solution: The ideal dc output voltage in the absence of ripple is given by Eq. (3.52):

$$V_{dc} = V_P - V_{\text{on}} = (12.6\sqrt{2} - 1)\ \text{V} = 16.8\ \text{V}$$

The ripple voltage is calculated using Eq. (3.56) with the discharge interval $T = \frac{1}{60}$ s:

$$V_r \approx \frac{(V_p - V_{\text{on}})}{R}\frac{T}{C} = \frac{16.8\ \text{V}}{15\ \Omega}\frac{\frac{1}{60}\ \text{s}}{2.5 \times 10^{-2}\ \text{F}} = 0.747\ \text{V}$$

Note that this ripple voltage represents 4.4 percent of the dc output voltage. The conduction angle is calculated using Eq. (3.62)

$$\theta_c = \omega\,\Delta T = \sqrt{\frac{2V_r}{V_P}} = \sqrt{\frac{2 \cdot 0.75}{17.8}} = 0.290\ \text{rad or } 16.6°$$

and the conduction interval is

$$\Delta T = \frac{\theta_c}{\omega} = \frac{\theta_c}{2\pi f} = \frac{0.29}{120\pi} = 0.769 \text{ mS}$$

out of a total period $T = 16.7$ mS. We see that the condition $\Delta T \ll T$ is satisfied. ◆

Example 3.7 illustrates a simple dc power supply design. The nominal dc current delivered by the supply is

$$I_{dc} = \frac{V_P - V_{on}}{R} = \frac{16.8 \text{ V}}{15 \ \Omega} = 1.12 \text{ A}$$

Maintaining a low ripple percentage in a relatively high current supply requires a significant filter capacitance C. In this case, $C = 0.025$ F. An 11-A supply would require a capacitance of one-quarter of a farad!

Diode Current

In rectifier circuits, a nonzero current is present in the diode for only a very small fraction of the period T, yet an almost constant dc current is flowing out of the filter capacitor to the load. The total charge lost from the capacitor during each cycle must be replenished by the current through the diode during the short conduction interval ΔT, which leads to high peak diode currents. Figure 3.56 shows the results of SPICE simulation[1] of the diode current. The repetitive current pulse can be modeled approximately by a triangle of height I_P and width ΔT, as in Fig. 3.57.

Equating the charge supplied through the diode during the conduction interval to the charge lost from the filter capacitor during the complete period yields

$$Q = I_P \frac{\Delta T}{2} = I_{dc}T \qquad \text{or} \qquad I_P = I_{dc} \frac{2T}{\Delta T} \qquad (3.63)$$

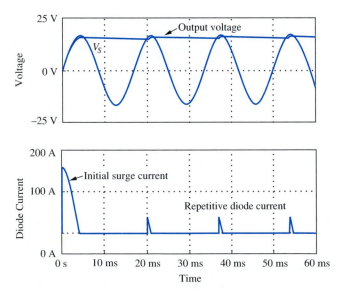

Figure 3.56 SPICE simulation of the half-wave rectifier circuit.

---

[1] The SPICE simulation data precede the problems at the end of each chapter.

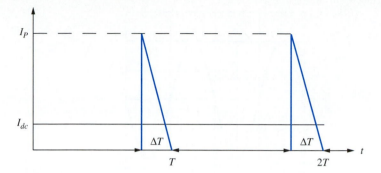

Figure 3.57 Triangular approximation to diode current pulse.

For the example above, the peak diode current would be

$$I_P = 1.12\frac{2 \cdot 16.7}{0.769} = 48.6 \text{ A} \qquad (3.64)$$

which agrees well with the simulation results in Fig. 3.56. The diode must be built to handle these high peak currents, which occur over and over. This high peak current is also the reason for the relatively large choice of V_{on} used in the example. (See Prob. 3.56.)

> **EXERCISE:** (a) What is the forward voltage of a diode operating at a current of 48.6 A at 300 K if $I_S = 10^{-15}$ A? (b) At 50 C?
>
> **ANSWERS:** 0.961 V; 1.01 V

Surge Current

When the power supply is first turned on, there can be an even larger current through the diode, as is visible in Fig. 3.56. During the first quarter cycle, the current flowing through the diode is given approximately by

$$i_d(t) = i_c(t) \approx C\left[\frac{d}{dt}V_P \sin \omega t\right] = \omega C V_P \cos \omega t \qquad (3.65)$$

The peak value of this initial **surge current** occurs at $t = 0^+$ and is given by

$$I_{SC} = \omega C V_P = 2\pi(60 \text{ Hz})(0.025 \text{ F})(17.8 \text{ V}) = 168 \text{ A} \qquad (3.66)$$

Using the numbers from Example 3.7 yields an initial surge current of almost 170 A! This value, again, agrees well with the simulation results in Fig. 3.56. If the input signal v_S does not happen to be crossing through zero when the power supply is turned on, the situation can be even worse, and rectifier diodes selected for power supply applications must be capable of withstanding very large surge currents as well as the large repetitive current pulses required each cycle.

Peak-Inverse-Voltage (PIV) Rating

We must also be concerned about the breakdown voltage rating of the diodes used in rectifier circuits. This is called the **peak-inverse-voltage (PIV)** rating of the rectifier diode. The worst-case situation for the half-wave rectifier is depicted in Fig. 3.58, in which it is assumed that the ripple voltage V_r is very small. When the diode is off, as in Fig. 3.54(b), the reverse bias across the diode is equal to $V_{dc} - v_S$. The worst case occurs when v_S reaches its negative peak of $-V_P$. The diode must therefore be able to withstand a reverse bias of

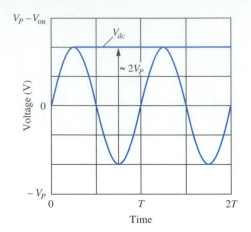

Figure 3.58 Peak reverse voltage across the diode in a half-wave rectifier.

at least

$$\text{PIV} \geq V_{dc} - v_S^{\min} = V_P - V_{\text{on}} - (-V_P) = 2V_P - V_{\text{on}} \approx 2\,V_P \qquad (3.67)$$

From Eq. (3.67), we see that diodes used in the half-wave rectifier circuit must have a PIV rating equal to twice the peak voltage supplied by the source v_S. The PIV value corresponds to the minimum value of Zener breakdown voltage for the rectifier diode. A safety margin of at least 25 to 50 percent is usually specified for the diode PIV rating in power supply designs.

Diode Power Dissipation

In high-current power supply applications, the power dissipation in the rectifier diodes can become significant. The average power dissipation in the diode is defined by

$$P_D = \frac{1}{T} \int_0^T v_D(t) i_D(t)\, dt \qquad (3.68)$$

This expression can be simplified by assuming that the voltage across the diode is approximately constant at $v_D(t) = V_{\text{on}}$ and by using the triangular approximation to the diode current $i_D(t)$ shown in Fig. 3.57. Eq. (3.68) becomes

$$P_D = \frac{1}{T} \int_0^T V_{\text{on}} i_D(t)\, dt = \frac{V_{\text{on}}}{T} \int_{T-\Delta T}^T i_D(t)\, dt = V_{\text{on}} \frac{I_P}{2} \frac{\Delta T}{T} \qquad (3.69)$$

which, using Eq. (3.63), can be reduced to

$$P_D = V_{\text{on}} I_{dc} \qquad (3.70)$$

The power dissipation is equivalent to the constant dc output current multiplied by the on-voltage of the diode. For the half-wave rectifier example, $P_D = (1\text{ V})(1.1\text{ A}) = 1.1$ W. This rectifier diode would probably need a heat sink to maintain its temperature at a reasonable level.

Another source of power dissipation is caused by resistive loss within the diode. Diodes have a small internal series resistance R_S, and the average power dissipation in this resistance can be calculated using

$$P_D = \frac{1}{T} \int_0^T i_D^2(t) R_S\, dt \qquad (3.71)$$

Evaluation of this integral (left for Prob. 3.58) for the triangular current wave form in Fig. 3.57 yields

$$P_D = \tfrac{1}{3}I_P^2 R_S \frac{\Delta T}{T} = \frac{4}{3}\frac{T}{\Delta T}I_{dc}^2 R_S \tag{3.72}$$

Using the number from the rectifier example with $R_S = 0.20\ \Omega$ yields $P_D = 7.3$ W! This is significantly greater than the component of power dissipation caused by the diode on-voltage calculated using Eq. (3.70). The component of power dissipation described by Eq. (3.72) can be significantly reduced by minimizing the peak current I_P through the use of the minimum required size of filter capacitor or by using the full-wave rectifier circuits, which are discussed in Sec. 3.13.

Half-Wave Rectifier with Negative Output Voltage

The circuit of Fig. 3.53 can also be used to produce a negative output voltage if the top rather than the bottom of the capacitor is grounded, as depicted in Fig. 3.59(a). However, we usually draw the circuit as in Fig. 3.59(b). These two circuits are equivalent. In the circuit in Fig. 3.59(b), the diode conducts on the negative half cycle of the transformer voltage v_S, and the dc output voltage is $V_{dc} = -(V_P - V_{on})$.

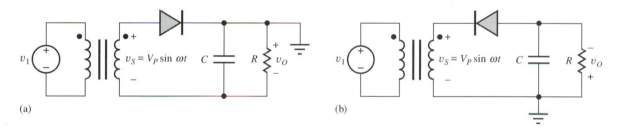

(a)   (b)

Figure 3.59 Half-wave rectifier circuits that develop negative output voltages.

3.13 FULL-WAVE RECTIFIER CIRCUITS

Full-wave rectifier circuits cut the capacitor discharge time in half and offer the advantage of requiring only one-half the filter capacitance to achieve a given ripple voltage. The full-wave rectifier circuit in Fig. 3.60 uses a **center-tapped transformer** to generate two voltages that have equal amplitudes and are 180 degrees out of phase. With the voltage v_S applied to the anode of D_1, and $-v_S$ applied to the anode of D_2, the two diodes form a pair of half-wave rectifiers operating on alternate half cycles of the input waveform. Proper phasing is indicated by the dots on the two halves of the transformer.

Figure 3.60 Full-wave rectifier circuit using two diodes and a center-tapped transformer.

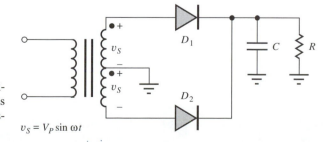

For $v_S > 0$, D_1 will be functioning as a half-wave rectifier, and D_2 will be off, as indicated in Fig. 3.61. The current exits the upper terminal of the transformer, goes through diode D_1, through the RC load, and returns back into the center tap of the transformer.

For $v_S < 0$, D_1 will be off, and D_2 will be functioning as a half-wave rectifier as indicated in Fig. 3.62. During this portion of the cycle, the current path leaves the bottom terminal of the transformer, goes through D_2, down through the RC load, and again returns into the transformer center tap. The current direction in the load is the same during both halves of the cycle; one-half of the transformer is utilized during each half cycle.

The load, consisting of the filter capacitor C and load resistor R, now receives two current pulses per cycle, and the capacitor discharge time is reduced to less than $T/2$, as indicated in the graph in Fig. 3.63. An analysis similar to that for the half-wave rectifier yields the same formulas for dc output voltage, ripple voltage, and ΔT, except that the discharge interval is $T/2$ rather than T. For a given capacitor value, the ripple voltage is one-half as large, and the conduction interval and peak current are reduced. The peak-inverse-voltage waveform for each diode is similar to the one shown in Fig. 3.58 for the half-wave rectifier, with the result that the PIV rating of each diode is the same as in the half-wave rectifier. These results are summarized in Eqs. (3.73) to (3.77) for $v_S = V_P \sin \omega t$:

$$V_{dc} = V_P - V_{\text{on}} \tag{3.73}$$

$$V_r = \frac{(V_P - V_{\text{on}})}{R} \frac{T}{2C} \tag{3.74}$$

$$\Delta T = \frac{1}{\omega} \sqrt{\frac{T}{RC} \frac{(V_P - V_{\text{on}})}{V_P}} = \frac{1}{\omega} \sqrt{\frac{2V_r}{V_P}} \tag{3.75}$$

$$\theta_c = \omega \, \Delta T = \sqrt{\frac{2V_r}{V_P}} \qquad I_P = I_{DC} \frac{T}{\Delta T} \tag{3.76}$$

$$\text{PIV} = 2 \, V_P \tag{3.77}$$

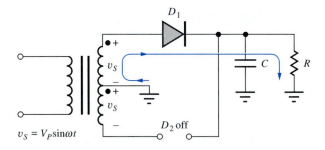

Figure 3.61 Equivalent circuit for $v_S > 0$.

$v_S = V_P \sin \omega t$

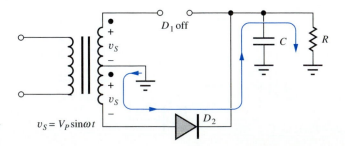

Figure 3.62 Equivalent circuit for $v_S < 0$.

$v_S = V_P \sin \omega t$

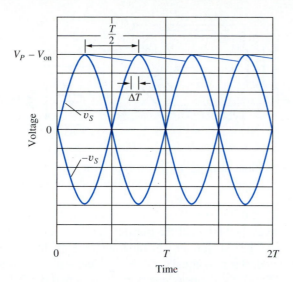

Figure 3.63 Voltage waveforms for the full-wave rectifier.

Full-Wave Rectifier with Negative Output Voltage

By reversing the polarity of the diodes, as in Fig. 3.64, a full-wave rectifier circuit with a negative output voltage is realized. Other aspects of the circuit remain the same as the previous full-wave rectifiers.

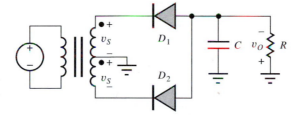

Figure 3.64 Full-wave rectifier with negative output voltage.

3.14 FULL-WAVE BRIDGE RECTIFICATION

The requirement for a center-tapped transformer in the full-wave rectifier can be eliminated through the use of two additional diodes in the **full-wave bridge rectifier circuit** configuration shown in Fig. 3.65. For $v_S > 0$, D_2 and D_4 will be on and D_1 and D_3 will be off, as indicated in Fig. 3.66. Current exits the top of the transformer, goes through D_2 into the RC load, and returns to the transformer through D_4. The full transformer voltage, now minus two diode voltage drops, appears across the load capacitor yielding a dc output voltage

$$V_{dc} = V_P - 2 V_{\text{on}} \tag{3.78}$$

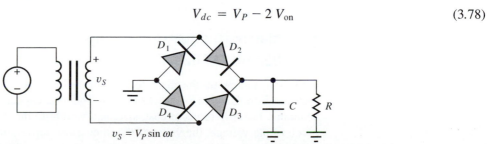

Figure 3.65 Full-wave bridge rectifier circuit.

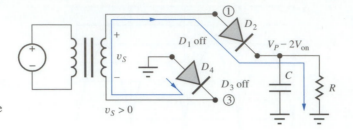

Figure 3.66 Full-wave bridge rectifier circuit for $v_S > 0$.

The peak voltage at node 1, which represents the maximum reverse voltage appearing across D_1, is equal to $(V_P - V_{on})$. Similarly, the peak reverse voltage across diode D_4 is $(V_P - 2V_{on}) - (-V_{on}) = (V_P - V_{on})$.

For $v_S < 0$, D_1 and D_3 will be on and D_2 and D_4 will be off, as depicted in Fig. 3.67. Current leaves the bottom of the transformer, goes through D_3 into the RC load, and back through D_1 to the transformer. The full transformer voltage is again being utilized. The peak voltage at node 3 is now equal to $(V_P - V_{on})$ and is the maximum reverse voltage appearing across D_4. Similarly, the peak reverse voltage across diode D_2 is $(V_P - 2V_{on}) - (-V_{on}) = (V_P - V_{on})$.

From the analysis of the two half cycles, we see that each diode must have a PIV rating given by

$$\text{PIV} = V_P - V_{on} \approx V_P \tag{3.79}$$

As with the previous rectifier circuits, a negative output voltage can be generated by reversing the direction of the diodes, as in the circuit in Fig. 3.68.

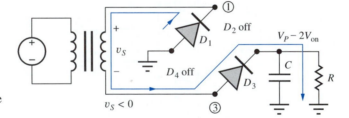

Figure 3.67 Full-wave bridge rectifier circuit for $v_S < 0$.

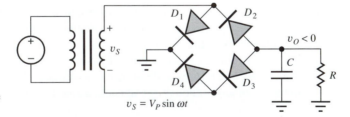

Figure 3.68 Full-wave bridge rectifier circuit with $v_O < 0$.

3.15 RECTIFIER COMPARISON AND DESIGN TRADEOFFS

Table 3.4 summarizes the characteristics of the half-wave, full-wave, and full-wave bridge rectifiers introduced in Secs. 3.12 to 3.14. The filter capacitor often represents a significant economic factor in terms of cost, size, and weight in the design of rectifier circuits. For a given ripple voltage, the value of the filter capacitor required in the full-wave rectifier is one-half that for the half-wave rectifier.

		Table 3.4	
		Comparison of Rectifiers with Capacitive Filters	
Rectifier Parameter	**Half-Wave Rectifier**	**Full-Wave Rectifier**	**Full-Wave Bridge Rectifier**
Filter capacitor	$C = \dfrac{V_P - V_{on}}{V_r}\dfrac{T}{R}$	$C = \dfrac{V_P - V_{on}}{V_r}\dfrac{T}{2R}$	$C = \dfrac{V_P - 2V_{on}}{V_r}\dfrac{T}{2R}$
PIV rating	$2V_P$	$2V_P$	V_P
Peak diode current (constant V_r)	Highest I_P	Reduced $\dfrac{I_P}{2}$	Reduced $\dfrac{I_P}{2}$
Comments	Least complexity	Smaller capacitor Requires center-tapped transformer Two diodes	Smaller capacitor Four diodes

The reduction in peak current in the full-wave rectifier can significantly reduce heat dissipation in the diodes. The addition of the second diode and the use of a center-tapped transformer represent additional expenses that offset some of the advantage. However, the benefits of full-wave rectification usually outweigh the minor increase in circuit complexity.

The bridge rectifier eliminates the need for the center-tapped transformer and the PIV rating of the diodes is reduced, which can be particularly important in high-voltage circuits. The cost of the extra diodes is usually negligible, particularly since four-diode bridge rectifiers can be purchased in single-component form.

3.16 dc-to-dc CONVERTERS

Multiple power supply voltages are required in most electronic systems. One method of generating these voltages is to use several half-wave or full-wave rectifier circuits. However, the output voltage of these circuits is determined by the transformer voltage, and hence multiple transformer outputs are required. In addition, the rectifier circuits most often operate at 60 Hz, and the transformers have a significant size and weight.

A more flexible method is to use high-efficiency **dc-to-dc converters** that can operate at much higher frequencies, thereby reducing the size and weight of the inductances in the circuit. The dc-to-dc converter uses a dc input voltage and provides an electronically controlled output voltage with a continuously variable range. This section describes two examples of dc-to-dc converters: the **boost converter,** which provides an output voltage that is greater than the input voltage, and the **buck converter,** whose output voltage is less than its input voltage.

The Boost Converter

The circuit for the basic boost converter is in Fig. 3.69(a). At the heart of the converter are the inductor L and switch S, which is periodically turned on and off, as indicated in Fig. 3.69(b). The switch is closed during the time interval T_{on} and open during the time interval T_{off}. Switching is periodic with period $T = T_{on} + T_{off}$. Diode D also operates as a switch and is off when S is on and vice versa. A dc input voltage is supplied by source V_S, and R and C represent the load resistance and filter capacitor, respectively.

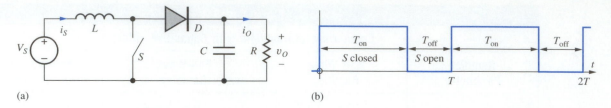

(a)   (b)

Figure 3.69 (a) dc-to-dc boost converter. (b) Periodic switch timing: Switch S is closed during T_{on} and open during T_{off}.

In the following analyses, we assume that the circuit has been operating for a long time and that any start-up transients have died out. The circuit will then be operating in the periodic steady state.

Switch S Closed

During the time interval T_{on}, switch S is closed, and the output voltage, which we will find to be greater than zero, reverse-biases diode D, resulting in the equivalent circuit in Fig. 3.70(a). For simplicity, the ideal model is used for the diode. The dc input voltage V_S now appears directly across the inductor, and the inductor current at the end of the T_{on} interval is

$$i_L(T_{on}) = i_L(0^+) + \int_0^{T_{on}} \frac{V_S}{L}\,dt = i_L(0^+) + \frac{V_S}{L}t\Big|_0^{T_{on}} = i_L(0^+) + \frac{V_S}{L}T_{on} \quad (3.80)$$

During time interval $(0, T_{on})$, the inductor current increases at a constant rate, as depicted in Fig. 3.71. Because the current in the inductor cannot change instantaneously, $i_L(0^+)$ is equal to the current just before the switch changes state.

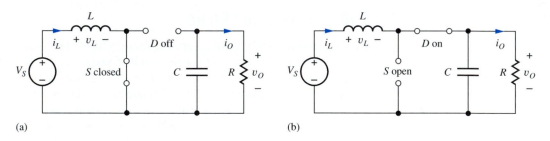

(a)   (b)

Figure 3.70 (a) Model valid during T_{on} when switch S is closed. (b) Model for T_{off} interval when switch S is open.

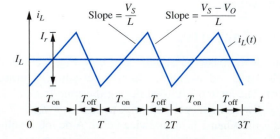

Figure 3.71 Periodic inductor current waveform: $i_L = I_L + i_r(t)$.

Switch S Open

When the switch opens, the diode turns on, providing a path for the inductor current through the diode to load resistor R and filter capacitor C, as depicted in Fig. 3.70(b). To simplify the analysis, we assume that the ripple voltage at the output is small enough for the output voltage to be approximated by a dc voltage, $v_O \approx V_O$. Using this assumption, the voltage across the inductor is again constant and equal to $V_S - V_O$. The inductor current at the end of the T_{off} time interval ($t = T_{\text{on}} + T_{\text{off}} = T$) is

$$i_L(T) = i_L(T_{\text{on}}) + \int_{T_{\text{on}}}^{T_{\text{on}}+T_{\text{off}}} \frac{V_S - V_O}{L}\, dt = i_L(T_{\text{on}}) + \frac{V_S - V_O}{L} t \Big|_{T_{\text{on}}}^{T_{\text{on}}+T_{\text{off}}} \tag{3.81}$$

$$i_L(T) = i_L(0^+) + \frac{V_S}{L} T_{\text{on}} + \frac{V_S - V_O}{L} T_{\text{off}} \tag{3.82}$$

For V_O exceeding V_S, the inductor current decreases with time during the T_{off} interval—again, as shown in Fig. 3.71. Also, because the circuit is operating periodically with period T, the inductor current at the times $t = 0^+$ and $t = T$ must be identical. Thus,

$$i_L(T) = i_L(0^+) \qquad \text{and} \qquad \frac{V_S}{L} T_{\text{on}} = \frac{V_O - V_S}{L} T_{\text{off}} \tag{3.83}$$

Rearranging this equation yields the basic relationship between the input and output voltage for the boost converter:

$$V_S(T_{\text{on}} + T_{\text{off}}) = V_O T_{\text{off}} \qquad \text{or} \qquad V_O = V_S \frac{T}{T_{\text{off}}} = \frac{V_S}{1 - \dfrac{T_{\text{on}}}{T}} = \frac{V_S}{1 - \delta} \tag{3.84}$$

in which $\delta = T_{\text{on}}/T$ is termed the **duty cycle** of the switching waveform. The output voltage can be changed by varying the duty cycle of the switch. Because $0 \le \delta \le 1$, the output voltage $V_O \ge V_S$; the converter "boosts" the output voltage above the input voltage.

Inductor Design

It is surprising to note that the expression for the output voltage in Eq. (3.84) is independent of L. An additional design parameter is needed in order to choose the value of inductor L. This parameter is the **ripple current** in the inductor. Because the voltage across the inductor is constant during both the T_{on} and T_{off} time intervals, the inductor current is a sawtooth waveform, as depicted in Fig. 3.71 [see Eqs. (3.80) and (3.81)]. The magnitude of the ripple current I_r is given by either

$$I_r = \frac{V_S}{L} T_{\text{on}} \qquad \text{or} \qquad I_r = \frac{V_O - V_S}{L} T_{\text{off}} \tag{3.85}$$

which must be equal. Rearranging Eq. (3.85) yields an expression for the value of the inductor:

$$L = \frac{V_S}{I_r} T_{\text{on}} = \frac{V_S T}{I_r} \left(\frac{T_{\text{on}}}{T}\right) = \frac{V_S}{I_r f} \delta \tag{3.86}$$

in which $f = 1/T$ is the switching frequency. From Eq. (3.86), we see that the higher the choice of operating frequency, the smaller the required value of inductance. dc-to-dc converters can be operated at frequencies well above 60 Hz in order to reduce the size of L, and f is normally chosen to be above the range of human hearing. Frequencies of 25 to 100 kHz are common.

dc Input Current

In the boost circuit, the average inductor current I_L is larger than the dc load current. For the ideal converter, there is no loss mechanism within the circuit. Therefore, the power delivered to the input of the converter must equal the power delivered to load resistor R:

$$V_S I_S = V_O I_O \quad \text{or} \quad I_S = I_O \frac{V_O}{V_S} = I_O \frac{T}{T_{\text{off}}} = \frac{I_O}{1 - \delta} \tag{3.87}$$

From this equation we see that the dc current in the inductor is greater than the dc load current by the same factor as the increase in output voltage. Note that the inductor must be properly designed to operate with this potentially large value of average current.

Ripple Voltage and Filter Capacitance

In the boost converter, filter capacitor C is designed to control the ripple voltage V_r in a manner similar to that of the half-wave rectifier in Fig. 3.55 and Eq. (3.56). During time interval T_{on}, diode D is off, as in Fig. 3.70(a), and the capacitor must supply the total load current. If the ripple voltage is designed to be small, the discharge current is approximately constant and given by $I_O \approx V_O/R$. Based on this approximation, the ripple voltage can be expressed as

$$V_r \approx \frac{I_O}{C} T_{\text{on}} = \frac{V_O T_{\text{on}}}{RC} = \frac{V_O T}{RC} \left(\frac{T_{\text{on}}}{T} \right) = \frac{V_O T}{RC} \delta \tag{3.88}$$

Table 3.5 summarizes the design relationships for the dc-to-dc boost converter.

T a b l e 3.5		
Boost Converter Design		
Output voltage	$V_O = V_S \dfrac{T}{T_{\text{off}}} = \dfrac{V_S}{1 - \dfrac{T_{\text{on}}}{T}} = \dfrac{V_S}{1 - \delta}$	
Source current	$I_S = I_O \left(\dfrac{T}{T_{\text{off}}} \right) = \dfrac{I_O}{1 - \dfrac{T_{\text{on}}}{T}} = \dfrac{I_O}{1 - \delta}$	
Inductor	$L = \dfrac{V_S}{I_r} T_{\text{on}} = \dfrac{V_S T}{I_r} \left(\dfrac{T_{\text{on}}}{T} \right) = \dfrac{V_S}{I_r f} \delta$	
Filter capacitor	$C = \dfrac{V_O T}{V_r R} \left(\dfrac{T_{\text{on}}}{T} \right) = \dfrac{V_O T}{V_r R} \delta$	

EXERCISE: What is the duty cycle of the switching waveform in Fig. 3.69(b)?

ANSWER: $\frac{2}{3}$ or 66.7%

EXERCISE: What are T, T_{on}, T_{off}, R, L, C, and I_L for a boost converter with the following specifications: $V_S = 5$ V, $V_O = 20$ V, $I_O = 1$ A, $I_r = 0.1$ A, $V_r = 0.25$ V, and $f = 50$ kHz? What are the values of v_L during the T_{on} and T_{off} time intervals?

ANSWERS: 20 μs; 15 μs; 5 μs; 20 Ω; 0.75 mH; 60 μF; 4 A; +5 V; −15 V

The Buck Converter

The buck converter in Fig. 3.72 is designed to produce an output voltage that is smaller than the input voltage. Operation of the buck converter in Fig. 3.72 is similar to that of the boost converter, and switch S operates periodically with the same timing as in Fig. 3.69(a).

Switch S Closed

During the time interval T_{on}, switch S is closed, and the positive input voltage reverse-biases diode D, resulting in the equivalent circuit in Fig. 3.72(b). We again assume that the ripple voltage at the output is small enough that the output voltage can be approximated by a constant voltage, $v_O \approx V_O$. Using this assumption, the voltage across the inductor is equal to $V_S - V_O$, and the inductor current at the end of the first T_{on} interval will be

$$i_L(T_{on}) = i_L(0^+) + \int_0^{T_{on}} \frac{V_S - V_O}{L} \, dt = i_L(0^+) + \frac{V_S - V_O}{L} T_{on} \qquad (3.89)$$

Because the current in the inductor cannot change instantaneously, $i_L(0^+)$ is equal to the current just before the switch changes state.

Switch S Open

When the switch opens, the diode turns on, providing a continuous path for the inductor current from ground through the diode to load resistor R and filter capacitor C, as depicted in Fig. 3.72(c). The voltage across the inductor is now equal to $-V_O$. The inductor current at the end of the T_{off} time interval is

$$i_L(T) = i_L(T_{on}) + \int_{T_{on}}^{T_{on}+T_{off}} \frac{-V_O}{L} \, dt = i_L(0^+) + \frac{V_S - V_O}{L} T_{on} - \frac{V_O}{L} T_{off} \quad (3.90)$$

However, the circuit is again operating periodically with period T. Therefore, the inductor current at the times $t = 0^+$ and $t = T$ must be identical. Thus,

$$i_L(T) = i_L(0^+) \qquad \text{and} \qquad \frac{V_O - V_S}{L} T_{on} = \frac{V_O}{L} T_{off} \qquad (3.91)$$

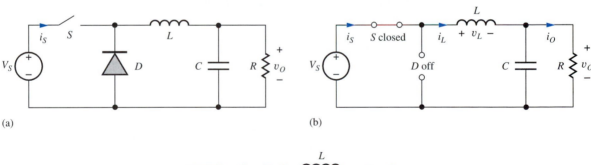

(a)

(b)

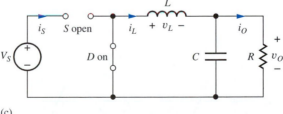

(c)

Figure 3.72 (a) dc-to-dc buck converter. (b) Model valid during T_{on} when switch S is closed. (c) Model for T_{off} interval when switch S is open.

Rearranging this equation yields the basic relationship between the input and output voltage for the boost converter:

$$V_O = V_S \frac{T_{on}}{T} = V_S \delta \tag{3.92}$$

where δ is the switch duty cycle. Because $T_{on} \leq T$, the output voltage $V_O \leq V_S$. In this converter, the inductor voltage "bucks" the input voltage, and the converter output voltage is less than the input voltage. The output voltage of the buck converter is directly proportional to the duty cycle δ.

Inductor Design

The relationship between the input and output voltages expressed by Eq. 3.84 is, again, independent of L, and the design of the inductor value is determined by the ripple current specification.

The inductor current waveform for the buck converter is very similar to that of the boost converter, as drawn in Fig. 3.73. The magnitude of the ripple current I_r is given by

$$I_r = \frac{V_S - V_O}{L} T_{on} = \frac{V_O}{L} T_{off} \tag{3.93}$$

Rearranging Eq. (3.93) yields an expression for the value of the inductor:

$$L = \frac{V_O}{I_r} T_{off} = \frac{V_O T}{I_r} \left(\frac{T_{off}}{T} \right) = \frac{V_O T}{I_r} \left(1 - \frac{T_{on}}{T} \right) = \frac{V_O}{I_r f}(1 - \delta) \tag{3.94}$$

In the buck converter, the dc current I_L is equal to the dc load current I_O. The current that must be supplied from the source V_S is given by

$$V_S I_S = V_O I_O \quad \text{or} \quad I_S = I_O \frac{V_O}{V_S} = I_O \frac{T_{on}}{T} = I_O \delta \tag{3.95}$$

From this equation, we see that the dc input current to the converter is less than the load current.

Ripple Voltage and Filter Capacitance

In the buck converter, only the ripple current must be absorbed by filter capacitor C. The positive change in voltage across the capacitor, which must also equal the negative voltage change, is equal to the ripple voltage V_r:

$$V_r = \frac{1}{C} \int_{T_{on}/2}^{T_{on}+(T_{off}/2)} i_r \, dt = \frac{\Delta Q}{C} \quad \text{where } \Delta Q = \frac{1}{2} \left(\frac{I_r}{2} \right) \left(\frac{T_{on} + T_{off}}{2} \right) = \frac{I_r T}{8} \tag{3.96}$$

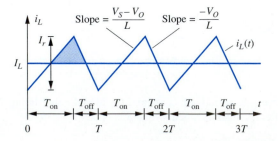

Figure 3.73 Inductor current waveform: $i_L = I_L + i_r(t)$.

The integral of the capacitor current represents the total change in charge ΔQ on the filter capacitor and corresponds to the area of the shaded triangular region in Fig. 3.73. Expressions for the value of the capacitor can be found using Eqs. (3.94) and (3.96):

$$C = \frac{I_r T}{8 V_r} = \frac{V_O}{V_r} \frac{T^2}{8L}(1 - \delta) \tag{3.97}$$

Table 3.6 summarizes the relationships needed for design of the buck converter.

T a b l e 3.6	
Buck Converter Design	
Output voltage	$V_O = V_S \dfrac{T_{\text{on}}}{T} = V_S \delta$
Source current	$I_S = I_O \dfrac{T_{\text{on}}}{T} = I_O \delta$
Inductor	$L = \dfrac{V_O T}{I_r}\left(\dfrac{T_{\text{off}}}{T}\right) = \dfrac{V_O}{I_r f}(1 - \delta)$
Filter capacitor	$C = \dfrac{I_r T}{8 V_r} = \dfrac{V_O}{V_r}\dfrac{T^2}{8L}(1 - \delta)$

EXERCISE: What are T, T_{on}, T_{off}, R, L, C, and I_S for a buck converter with the following specifications: $V_S = 10$ V, $V_O = 5$ V, $I_O = 1$ A, $I_r = 0.1$ A, $V_r = 0.25$ V, and $f = 40$ kHz?

ANSWERS: 25 μs; 12.5 μs; 12.5 μs; 5 Ω; 0.625 mH; 1.25 μF; 0.50 A

3.17 WAVE-SHAPING CIRCUITS

This section explores several additional circuit applications that use the nonlinear characteristics of the diode. These include the **clamping** or **dc-restoring circuit,** the **clipping** or **limiter circuit,** and a circuit for generating **piecewise linear transfer functions.** For simplicity in the following analyses, we use the ideal diode model.

The Clamping or dc-Restoring Circuit

Examples of the clamping or dc-restoring circuit are shown in Fig. 3.74, and an example of the waveforms for these two circuits is in Fig. 3.75 for a triangular input signal. Consider first the waveforms for the circuit in Fig. 3.74(a). The time-varying signal v_S is coupled through capacitor C to the output. As the input signal v_S starts to rise, the diode turns on and maintains the output at 0 V (for an ideal diode), and the capacitor charges up to $v_C = V_P$ during the first quarter cycle of the input waveform. As v_S begins to fall, the output follows the input, now offset by the fixed voltage V_P. There is no discharge path, and the voltage on the capacitor remains constant. After the first quarter cycle, the shape of the output waveform is exactly the same as the input signal, but the dc level has been shifted by V_P.

For the circuit in Fig. 3.74(b), the initial transient lasts for three-quarters of a cycle. When the input signal first goes positive, the diode is reverse-biased, and v_O follows v_S.

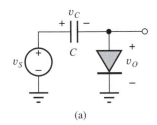

(a)

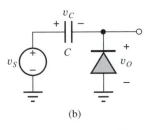

(b)

Figure 3.74 Diode clamping circuits.

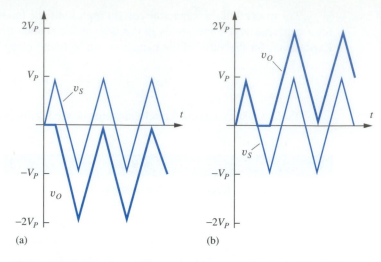

(a)   (b)

Figure 3.75   Waveforms for the two clamping circuits in Fig. 3.74.

However, as v_S swings negative, the diode turns on and again "clamps" the voltage to zero, and the capacitor charges to $v_C = -V_P$.

Once the initial transient lasting less than one cycle is over in these two circuits, the output waveform is then an undistorted replica of the input waveform. Both waveforms have been *clamped* to 0 V. The waveform for circuit (a) is shifted to be a fully negative signal and that of circuit (b) is a totally positive signal. These waveforms are said to have had their dc levels *restored* by the clamping circuit. Figure 3.76 presents two additional circuits in which the clamping level is shifted away from zero by the source V_C.

Electronic signals often lose their dc levels during signal transmission or storage. For example, dc levels are lost during radio transmission, and a TV broadcast signal must have its dc level restored in the TV receiver. It is also impossible to send dc signals through the recording and playback heads for cassette tape recorders or compact disk players. dc restoration may be required if these devices are used to store digital data.

Clipping or Limiting Circuits

Clipping circuits are designed to change the shape or distort the input waveform. Figures 3.77 and 3.78 show two examples of clipping circuits. Note that the clipping circuits have a dc path between the input and output, whereas the clamping circuits used capacitive

Figure 3.76 Circuits with clamping levels offset from zero.

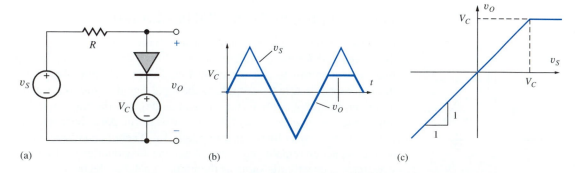

(a)   (b)   (c)

Figure 3.77 An example of a positive clipping circuit. (a) Circuit with clipping voltage V_C. (b) Voltage waveforms for a triangular input signal. (c) Voltage transfer characteristic (VTC) for the circuit in (a).

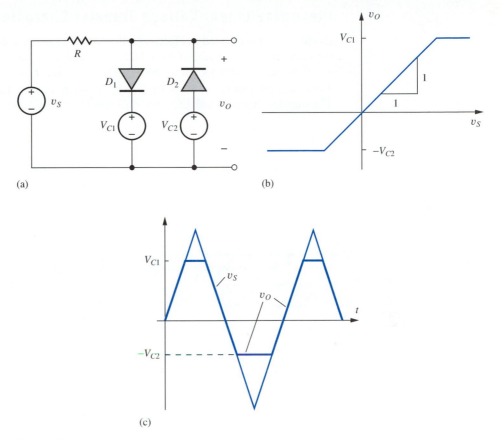

Figure 3.78 (a) Clipping circuit with positive and negative clipping levels. (b) Voltage transfer characteristic (VTC). (c) Output voltage waveform with positive and negative clipping levels.

coupling between the input and output. In the circuit in Fig. 3.77, the output follows the input until v_S exceeds the clipping voltage V_C, as depicted in the graph in part (b). The diode then turns on, and the output becomes fixed or *limited* by the voltage V_C. For the negative excursion of the input signal, the diode is off, and the output voltage equals the input voltage. The output waveform is similar to the input signal, except that the circuit has *clipped* the top off the signal.

The graph in Fig. 3.77(c) is called the **voltage transfer characteristic (VTC)** for this clipping circuit. For voltages less than V_C, the slope of the transfer characteristic is unity, indicating that $v_O = v_S$. The slope of the transfer function is called the **gain G** of the circuit defined by

$$G = \frac{dv_O}{dv_S} \tag{3.98}$$

For the circuit in Fig. 3.77, $G = 1$ for $v_S \leq V_C$, and $G = 0$ for $v_S > V_C$.

Dual Clipping Levels

Diode D_2 and source V_{C2} have been added to the circuit in Fig. 3.78 in order to set a second clipping level in the negative direction. In this circuit, the output has both the top and bottom clipped off the input waveform. The gain of this circuit is unity for $V_{C2} \leq v_S \leq V_{C1}$ and is zero for v_S outside this region.

Piecewise Linear Voltage Transfer Characteristics

Diodes can also be used to electronically switch resistors in and out of circuits to control the gain in various regions of the VTC. One example is shown in Fig. 3.79. For $v_S < 0$, D_1 is off, D_2 is on, and the slope of the transfer function is $G = 0.25$. For $0 \leq v_S \leq 2$ V, both diodes are off, and $G = 1$. For $v_S > 2$ V, D_1 is on, and the gain of the circuit is $G = 0.5$. The transfer function with the three different slopes is shown in Fig. 3.79(b).

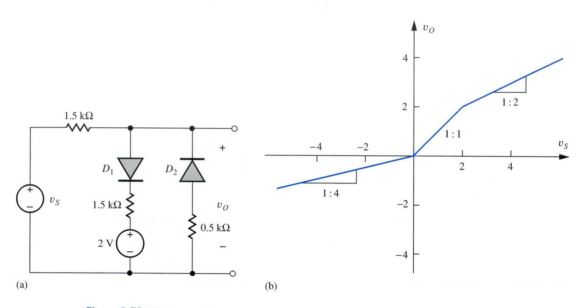

(a)   (b)

Figure 3.79 Diodes used to generate a piecewise linear voltage transfer function.

3.18 DYNAMIC SWITCHING BEHAVIOR OF THE DIODE

Up to this point, we have tacitly assumed that diodes can turn on and off instantaneously. However, an unusual phenomenon characterizes the dynamic switching behavior of the *pn* junction diode. SPICE simulation is used to illustrate the switching of the diode in the circuit in Fig. 3.80, in which diode D_1 is being driven from voltage source v_1 through resistor R_1.

The source is zero for $t < 0$. At $t = 0$, the source voltage rapidly switches to $+1.5$ V, forcing a current into the diode to turn it on. The voltage remains constant until $t = 7.5$ ns. At this point the source switches to -1.5 V in order to turn the diode back off.

The simulation results are presented in Fig. 3.81. Following the voltage source change at $t = 0+$, the current increases rapidly. The internal capacitance of the diode prevents the diode voltage from changing instantaneously. The current actually overshoots its final value

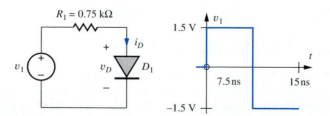

Figure 3.80 Circuit used to explore diode-switching behavior.

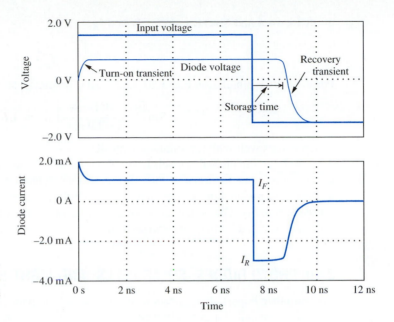

Figure 3.81 SPICE simulation results for the diode circuit in Fig. 3.80. (The diode transit time is equal to 5 ns.)

and then decreases as the diode turns on and the diode voltage increases to approximately 0.7 V. At any given time, the current flowing into the diode is given by

$$i_D(t) = \frac{v_1(t) - v_D(t)}{0.75 \text{ k}\Omega} \tag{3.99}$$

The initial peak of the current value occurs when v_1 reaches 1.5 V and v_D is still nearly zero:

$$i_{D\text{MAX}} = \frac{1.5 \text{ V}}{0.75 \text{ k}\Omega} = 2.0 \text{ mA} \tag{3.100}$$

After the diode voltage reaches its final value with $V_{\text{on}} \approx 0.7$ V, the current stabilizes at a forward current I_F of

$$I_F = \frac{1.5 - 0.7}{0.75 \text{ k}\Omega} = 1.1 \text{ mA} \tag{3.101}$$

At $t = 7.5$ ns, the input source rapidly changes polarity to -1.5 V. The diode current also rapidly reverses direction and is much greater than the reverse saturation current of the diode. The diode does not turn off immediately. In fact, the diode actually remains forward-biased by the charge stored in the diode, with $v_D = V_{\text{on}}$, even though the current has changed direction! The reverse current I_R is equal to

$$I_R = \frac{-1.5 - 0.7}{0.75 \text{ k}\Omega} = -2.9 \text{ mA} \tag{3.102}$$

The current remains at -2.9 mA for a period of time called the diode **storage time** τ_S, during which the internal charge stored in the diode is removed. Once the stored charge has been removed, the voltage across the diode begins to drop and charges toward the final value of -1.5 V. The current in the diode drops rapidly to zero as the diode voltage begins to fall.

The turn-on time and recovery time are determined primarily by the charging and discharging of the nonlinear depletion-layer capacitance C_j through the resistance R_S. The storage time is determined by the diode transit time defined in Eq. (3.22) and by the values of the forward and reverse currents I_F and I_R:

$$\tau_S = \tau_T \ln\left[1 - \frac{I_F}{I_R}\right] \tag{3.103}$$

For the SPICE simulation Fig. 3.80, Eq. (3.103) predicts a storage time of

$$\tau_S = 5\ln\left[1 - \frac{1.1\text{ mA}}{-2.9\text{ mA}}\right]\text{ ns} = 1.6\text{ ns} \tag{3.104}$$

which agrees well with the simulation results.

Always remember that solid-state devices do not turn off instantaneously. The unusual storage time behavior of the diode is an excellent example of the switching delays that occur in *pn* junction devices in which carrier flow is dominated by the minority-carrier diffusion process. This behavior is not present in field-effect transistors, in which current flow is dominated by majority-carrier drift.

3.19 PHOTO DIODES, SOLAR CELLS, AND LIGHT-EMITTING DIODES

Several other important applications of diodes include photo detectors in communication systems, solar cells for generating electric power, and light-emitting diodes (LEDs). These applications all rely on the solid-state diode's ability to interact with optical photons.

Photo Diodes and Photo Detectors

If the depletion region of a *pn* junction diode is illuminated with light of sufficiently high frequency, the photons can provide enough energy to cause electrons to jump the semiconductor bandgap, creating electron–hole pairs. For photon absorption to occur, the incident photons must have an energy E_p that exceeds the bandgap of the semiconductor:

$$E_p = h\nu = \frac{hc}{\lambda} \geq E_G \tag{3.105}$$

where h = Planck's constant (6.626×10^{-34} J · s)
  ν = frequency of optical illumination
  λ = wavelength of optical illumination
  c = velocity of light (3×10^8 m/s)

The *i-v* characteristic of a diode with and without illumination is shown in Fig. 3.82. The original diode characteristic is shifted vertically downward by the photon-generated current. Photon absorption creates an additional current crossing the *pn* junction that can be modeled by a current source i_{PH} in parallel with the *pn* junction diode, as shown in Fig. 3.83.

Based on this model, we see that the incident optical signal can be converted to an electrical signal voltage using the simple **photo-detector circuit** in Fig. 3.84. The diode is reverse-biased to enhance the width and electric field in the depletion region. The photon-generated current i_{PH} will flow through resistor R and produce an output voltage given by

$$v_O = i_{PH}R \tag{3.106}$$

In optical fiber communication systems, the amplitude of the incident light is modulated by rapidly changing digital data, and i_{PH} is a time-varying signal. The time-varying signal voltage at v_O is fed to additional electronic circuits to demodulate the signal and recover the original data that were transmitted down the optical fiber.

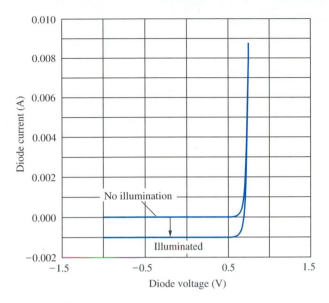

Figure 3.83 Model for optically illuminated diode. i_{PH} represents the current generated by absorption of photons in the vicinity of the *pn* junction.

Figure 3.82 Diode *i-v* characteristic with and without optical illumination.

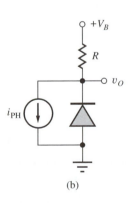

Figure 3.84 Basic photo-detector circuit (a) and model (b).

Power Generation from Solar Cells

In **solar cell** applications, the optical illumination is constant, and a dc current I_{PH} is generated. The goal is to extract power from the cell, and the *i-v* characteristics of solar cells are usually plotted in terms of the cell current I_C and cell voltage V_C, as defined in Fig. 3.85.

The *i-v* characteristic of the *pn* junction used for solar cell applications is plotted in terms of these terminal variables in Fig. 3.86. Also indicated on the graph are the short-circuit current I_{SC}, the open-circuit voltage V_{OC}, and the maximum power point P_{max}. I_{SC} represents the maximum current available from the cell, and V_{OC} is the voltage across the open-circuited cell when all the photo current is flowing into the internal *pn* junction. For the solar cell to supply power to an external circuit, the product $I_C \times V_C$ must be positive, corresponding to the first quadrant of the characteristic. An attempt is made to operate the cell near the point of maximum output power P_{max}.

Light-Emitting Diodes (LEDs)

Light-emitting diodes, or **LEDs,** rely on the annihilation of electrons and holes through recombination rather than on the generation of carriers, as in the case of the photo diode. When a hole and electron recombine, an energy equal to the bandgap of the semiconductor can be released in the form of a photon. This recombination process is present in the forward-biased *pn* junction diode. Silicon is an **indirect-gap semiconductor,** and the recombination process actually involves the interaction of photons and lattice vibrations called phonons. Hence, the optical emission process in silicon is not nearly as efficient as that in **direct-gap semiconductors** such as the III-V compound semiconductor GaAs or the ternary materials such as $GaIn_{1-x}As_x$ and $GaIn_{1-x}P_x$. LEDs in these compound semiconductor materials provide visible illumination, and the color of the output can be controlled by varying the material composition by varying the fraction x of arsenic or phosphorus in the material.

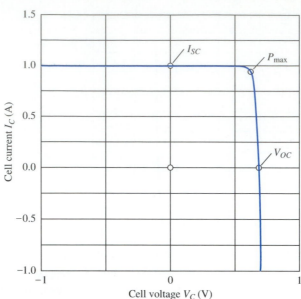

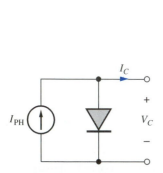

Figure 3.85 *pn* Diode under steady-state illumination as a solar cell.

Figure 3.86 Terminal characteristics for a *pn* junction solar cell.

SUMMARY

This chapter investigated the behavior of the solid-state diode. A *pn* junction diode is formed when *p*-type and *n*-type semiconductor regions are formed in intimate contact with each other. In the *pn* diode, large concentration gradients exist in the vicinity of the metallurgical junction, giving rise to large electron and hole diffusion currents. Under zero bias, no current can exist at the diode terminals, and a space charge region forms in the vicinity of the *pn* junction. The region of space charge results in a built-in potential and internal electric field, and the internal electric field produces electron and hole drift currents that exactly cancel the corresponding components of diffusion current.

When a voltage is applied to the diode, the balance in the junction region is disturbed, and the diode conducts a current. The resulting *i-v* characteristics of the diode are accurately modeled by the diode equation:

$$i_D = i_S \left[\exp\left(\frac{v_D}{nV_T} \right) - 1 \right]$$

where I_S = reverse saturation current of diode
        n = nonideality factor (typically 1)
        V_T = thermal voltage (0.025 V at room temperature)

Under reverse bias, the diode current equals $-I_S$, a very small current. For forward bias, however, large currents are possible, and the diode represents an almost constant voltage drop of 0.6 to 0.7 V. At room temperature, an order of magnitude change in diode current requires a change of less than 60 mV in the diode voltage. At room temperature, the silicon diode voltage exhibits a temperature coefficient of approximately -1.8 mV/°C.

One must also be aware of the reverse-breakdown phenomenon that is not included in the diode equation. If too large a reverse voltage is applied to the diode, the internal electric field becomes so large that the diode enters the breakdown region, either through Zener breakdown or avalanche breakdown. In the breakdown region, the diode again represents an almost fixed voltage drop, and the current must be limited by the external circuit or the diode can easily be destroyed. Diodes called Zener diodes are designed to operate in breakdown and can be used in simple voltage regulator circuits.

As the voltage across the diode changes, the charge stored in the vicinity of the space charge region of the diode changes, and a complete diode model must include a capacitance. Under reverse bias, the capacitance varies inversely with the square root of the applied voltage. Under forward bias, the capacitance is proportional to the operating current and the diode transit time. The capacitances prevent the diode from turning on and off instantaneously and cause a storage time delay during turn-off.

Direct use of the nonlinear diode equation in circuit calculations usually requires iterative numeric techniques. Several methods for simplifying the analysis of diode circuits were discussed, including the graphical load-line method and use of the ideal diode and constant voltage drop models.

Important applications of diodes include half-wave, full-wave, and full-wave bridge rectifier circuits used to convert from ac to dc voltages in power supplies. Simple power supply circuits use capacitive filters, and the design of the filter capacitor determines power supply ripple voltage and diode conduction angle. Diodes used as rectifiers in power supplies must be able to withstand large peak repetitive currents as well as surge currents when the power supplies are first turned on. The reverse-breakdown voltage of rectifier diodes is referred to as the peak-inverse-voltage, or PIV, rating of the diode.

dc-to-dc converters provide a flexible means of producing the multiple supply voltages required in many electronic systems. High efficiency dc-to-dc converters use an inductor and a periodically operated switch to generate a dc output voltage that is larger than the input voltage in the case of the boost converter, or an output that is smaller than the input in the case of a buck converter.

Diodes are also useful in building circuits that provide clipping, clamping, and generation of piecewise linear voltage transfer characteristics. Finally, the ability of the *pn* junction device to generate and detect light was discussed, and the basic characteristics of photo diodes, solar cells, and light-emitting diodes were presented.

Key Terms

Anode	Depletion region	Metallurgical junction
Avalanche breakdown	Diffusion capacitance	Nonideality factor
Boost converter	Diode equation	Peak detector
Breakdown region	Direct-gap semiconductor	Peak inverse voltage (PIV)
Breakdown voltage	Duty cycle	Photo-detector circuit
Buck converter	Filter capacitor	Piecewise linear model
Built-in potential (or voltage)	Forward bias	Piecewise linear transfer function
Cathode	Full-wave bridge rectifier circuit	*pn* junction diode
Center-tapped transformer	Full-wave rectifier circuit	Q-point
Clamping circuit	Gain	Quiescent operating point
Clipping circuit	Half-wave rectifier circuit	Rectifier circuits
Conduction angle	Ideal diode	Reverse bias
Conduction interval	Ideal diode model	Reverse breakdown
Conduction time	Impact-ionization process	Reverse saturation current
Constant voltage drop (CVD) model	Indirect-gap semiconductor	Ripple current
Cut-in voltage	Junction potential	Ripple voltage
dc-to-dc converter	Light-emitting diode (LED)	Saturation current
dc-restoring circuit	Limiter circuit	Schottky barrier diode
Depletion layer	Load-line analysis	Solar cell
Depletion-layer width	Mathematical model	Space charge region (SCR)

Storage time	Turn-on voltage	Zener breakdown
Surge current	Voltage regulator	Zener diode
Thermal voltage	Voltage transfer characteristic	Zero bias
Transit time	(VTC)	Zero-bias junction capacitance

Reference

1. G. W. Neudeck, *The PN Junction Diode,* Addison-Wesley, Reading, MA: 1983.

Additional Reading

PSPICE, MicroSim Corporation, Laguna Hills, CA.

Quarles, T., A. R. Newton, D. O. Pederson, and A. Sangiovanni-Vincentelli, *SPICE3 Version 3f3 User's Manual.* UC Berkeley: May 1993.

Sedra, A. S., and K. C. Smith. *Microelectronic Circuits.* 3d ed. HRW, Philadelphia: 1991.

PSPICE Simulation Data

*Figure 3.55 Half-Wave Rectifier Current (See Fig. 3.53)

```
VS 1 0 DC 0 AC 0 SIN(0 16.8 60)
D1 1 2 D1
R 2 0 15
C 2 0 25000U
.MODEL D1 D IS=1E-10 RS=0
*Tighten tolerances to get proper current pulse representations
.OPTIONS ABSTOL=1E-12 RELTOL=1E-6 VNTOL=1E-6
.TRAN 1US 60MS
.PROBE V(1) V(2) I(VS)
.END
```

*Figure 3.81 Diode-Switching Delay (See Fig. 3.80)

```
V1 1 0 PWL(0 0 0.01N 1.5 7.5N 1.5 7.52N -1.5 15N -1.5)
R1 1 2 0.75K
D1 2 0 DIODE
.TRAN .01NS 15NS
.MODEL DIODE D TT=5NS IS=1E-15 CJO=0.5PF
.PROBE V(1) V(2) I(V1)
.OPTIONS RELTOL=1E-6
.OP
.END
```

Problems

3.1 The *pn* Junction Diode

3.1. A diode is doped with $N_A = 10^{18}$/cm^3 on the *p*-type side and $N_D = 10^{15}$/cm^3 on the *n*-type side. (a) What are the values of p_p, p_n, n_p, and n_n? (b) What are the depletion-region width w_{do} and built-in voltage?

3.2. A diode is doped with $N_A = 10^{19}$/cm^3 on the *p*-type side and $N_D = 10^{18}$/cm^3 on the *n*-type side. (a) What is the depletion-layer width w_{do}? (b) What are the values of x_p and x_n? (c) What is the value of the built-in potential of the junction? (d) What is the value of E_{MAX}? Use Eq. (3.3) and Fig. 3.5.

3.3. Repeat Prob. 3.2 for a diode with $N_A = 10^{15}/\text{cm}^3$ on the p-type side and $N_D = 10^{19}/\text{cm}^3$ on the n-type side.

3.4. Repeat Prob. 3.2 for a diode with $N_A = 10^{18}/\text{cm}^3$ on the p-type side and $N_D = 10^{18}/\text{cm}^3$ on the n-type side.

3.5. A diode has $w_{do} = 1\ \mu\text{m}$ and $\phi_j = 0.6$ V. (a) What reverse bias is required to double the depletion-layer width? (b) What is the depletion-region width if a reverse bias of 5 V is applied to the diode?

3.6. Suppose a drift current density of 1000 A/cm^2 exists in the neutral region on the n-type side of a diode that has a resistivity of 0.5 $\Omega \cdot$ cm. What is the electric field needed to support this drift current density?

3.7. The maximum velocity of carriers in silicon is approximately 10^6 cm/s. What is the maximum drift current density that can be supported in a region of n-type silicon with a doping of $10^{15}/\text{cm}^3$?

3.8. Suppose that $N_A(x) = N_o \exp(-x/L)$ in a region of silicon extending from $x = 0$ to $x = 15\ \mu\text{m}$, where N_o is a constant. Assume that $p(x) = N_A(x)$. Assuming that j_p must be zero in thermal equilibrium, show that a built-in electric field must exist and find its value for $L = 1\ \mu\text{m}$ and $N_o = 10^{18}/\text{cm}^3$.

3.9. What carrier gradient is needed to generate a diffusion current density of $j_n = 1000$ A/cm^2 if $\mu_n = 500$ cm^2/V $\cdot$ s?

3.10. Use a spreadsheet to iteratively find the solution to Eq. 3.28 for $I_S = 10^{-13}$ A.

3.11. (a) Use MATLAB to find the solution to Eq. 3.28 for $I_S = 10^{-13}$ A. (b) Repeat for $I_S = 10^{-15}$ A.

3.2–3.4 The i-v Characteristics of the Diode; The Diode Equation: A Mathematical Model for the Diode; and Diode Characteristics Under Reverse, Zero, and Forward Bias

3.12. To what temperature does $V_T = 0.025$ V actually correspond?

3.13. (a) Plot a graph of the diode equation similar to Fig. 3.8 for a diode with $I_S = 10^{-12}$ A and $n = 1$. (b) Repeat for $n = 2$. (c) Repeat (a) for $I_S = 10^{-14}$ A.

*3.14. What are the values of I_S and n for the diode in the graph in Fig. P3.14? Assume $V_T = 0.025$ V.

3.15. A diode has $I_S = 10^{-17}$ A and $n = 1$. (a) What is the diode voltage if the diode current is 100 μA?

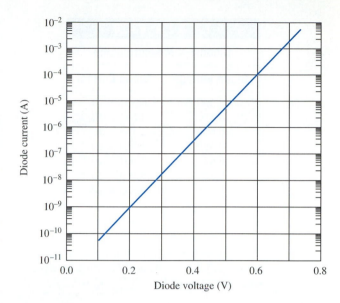

Figure P3.14

(b) What is the diode voltage if the diode current is 10 μA? (c) What is the diode current for $v_D = 0$ V? (d) What is the diode current for $v_D = -0.06$ V? (e) What is the diode current for $v_D = -4$ V?

3.16. A diode has $I_S = 10^{-17}$ A and $n = 1$. (a) What is the diode current if the diode voltage is 0.675 V? (b) What will be the diode voltage if the current increases by a factor of 3?

3.17. A diode has $I_S = 10^{-10}$ A and $n = 2$. (a) What is the diode voltage if the diode current is 50 A? (b) What is the diode voltage if the diode current is 100 A?

3.18. A diode is operating with $i_D = 250\ \mu$A and $v_D = 0.75$ V. (a) What is I_S if $n = 1$? (b) What is the diode current for $v_D = -3$ V?

3.19. The saturation current for diodes with the same part number may vary widely. Suppose it is known that 10^{-14} A $\le I_S \le 10^{-12}$ A. What is the range of forward voltages that may be exhibited by the diode if it is biased with $i_D = 1$ mA?

3.20. The i-v characteristic for a diode has been measured under carefully controlled temperature conditions ($T = 307$ K), and the data are in Table P3.20. Use a spreadsheet or write a computer program to find (by trial and error) the values of I_S and n that provide the best fit of the diode equation to the measurements in the least-squares sense. [That is, find the values of I_S and n that minimize the function $M = \sum_{m=1}^{n}(i_D^m - I_{Dm})^2$, where i_D is the

T a b l e P3.20

Diode _i-v_ Measurements

Diode Voltage	Diode Current
0.500	6.591×10^{-7}
0.550	3.647×10^{-6}
0.600	2.158×10^{-5}
0.650	1.780×10^{-4}
0.675	3.601×10^{-4}
0.700	8.963×10^{-4}
0.725	2.335×10^{-3}
0.750	6.035×10^{-3}
0.775	1.316×10^{-2}

diode equation from Eq. (3.1) and I_{Dm} are the measured data.] For your values of I_S and n, what is the minimum value of $M = \sum_{m=1}^{n}(i_D^m - I_{Dm})^2$?

3.5 Diode Temperature Coefficient

3.21. A diode with $I_S = 2.5 \times 10^{-16}$ A at 30°C is biased at a current of 1 mA. (a) What is the diode voltage? (b) If the diode voltage temperature coefficient is −1.8 mV/K, what will be the diode voltage at 50°C?

3.22. A diode has $I_S = 10^{-15}$ A and $n = 1$. (a) What is the diode voltage if the diode current is 100 μA at $T = 25$°C? (b) What is the diode voltage at $T = 50$°C? (c) At 0°C? Assume the diode voltage temperature coefficient is −2 mV/K.

*3.23. The temperature dependence of I_S is described approximately by

$$I_S = CT^3 \exp\left(-\frac{E_G}{kT}\right)$$

What is the diode voltage temperature coefficient based on this expression and Eq. (3.15) if $E_G = 1.21$ eV, $V_D = 0.7$ V, and $T = 300$ K?

3.24. The saturation current of a silicon diode is described by the expression in Prob. 3.23. (a) What temperature change will cause I_S to double? (b) To increase by 10 times? (c) To decrease by 100 times?

3.6 Diode Breakdown under Reverse Bias

*3.25. A diode has $w_{do} = 1$ μm and $\phi_j = 0.6$ V. If the diode breaks down when the internal electric field reaches 300 kV/cm, what is the breakdown voltage of the diode?

*3.26. Silicon breaks down when the internal electric field exceeds 300 kV/cm. At what reverse bias do you expect the diode of Prob. 3.1 to break down?

3.27. What are the breakdown voltage V_Z and Zener resistance R_Z of the diode depicted in Fig. P3.27?

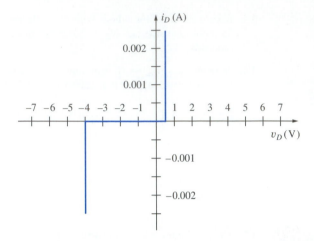

Figure P3.27

**3.28. A diode is fabricated with $N_A \gg N_D$. What value of doping is required on the lightly doped side to achieve a reverse-breakdown voltage of 1000 V if the semiconductor material breaks down at a field of 300 kV/cm?

3.7 _pn_ Junction Capacitance

3.29. What is the zero-bias junction capacitance/cm² for a diode with $N_A = 10^{15}$/cm³ on the _p_-type side and $N_D = 10^{20}$/cm³ on the _n_-type side? What is the diode capacitance with a 5-V reverse bias if the diode area is 0.01 cm²?

3.30. A diode is operating at a current of 100 μA. (a) What is the diffusion capacitance if the diode transit time is 100 ps? (b) How much charge is stored in the diode? (c) Repeat for $i_D = 25$ mA.

3.31. A _pn_ junction diode has a cross-sectional area of 10^4 μm². The _p_-type side has a doping concentration of 10^{19}/cm³ and the _n_-type side has a doping concentration of 10^{16}/cm³. What is the zero-bias capacitance of the diode? What is the capacitance at a reverse bias of 2 V?

3.32. A variable capacitance diode with $C_{jo} = 20$ pF and $\phi_j = 0.75$ V is used to tune a resonant LC circuit as shown in Fig. P3.32. The impedance of the RFC (radio frequency choke) can be considered infinite. What are the resonant frequencies $\left(f_o = \frac{1}{2\pi\sqrt{LC}}\right)$ for $V_{dc} = 1$ V and $V_{dc} = 10$ V?

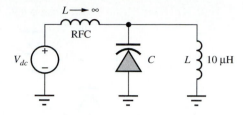

Figure P3.32

3.8 Schottky Barrier Diode

3.33. Suppose a Schottky barrier diode can be modeled by the diode equation in Eq. (3.11) with $I_S = 10^{-7}$ A. (a) What is the diode voltage at a current of 50 A? (b) What would be the voltage of a *pn* junction diode with $I_S = 10^{-14}$ A?

3.9 Diode Circuit Analysis
Load-Line Analysis

3.34. Plot the load line and find the Q-point for the diode circuit in Fig. P3.34 if $V = 5$ V and $R = 10$ kΩ. Use the *i-v* characteristic in Fig. P3.27.

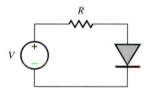

Figure P3.34

 3.35. Simulate the circuit in Prob. 3.34 with SPICE and compare the results to those in Prob. 3.34. Use $I_S = 10^{-15}$ A.

3.36. Use the *i-v* characteristic in Fig. P3.27. (a) Plot the load line and find the Q-point for the diode circuit in Fig. P3.34 if $V = 6$ V and $R = 4$ kΩ. (b) For $V = -6$ V and $R = 3$ kΩ. (c) For $V = -3$ V and $R = 3$ kΩ. (d) For $V = 12$ V and $R = 8$ kΩ. (e) For $V = -25$ V and $R = 10$ kΩ.

Iterative Analysis and the Mathematical Model

3.37. Repeat the iterative procedure used in the spreadsheet in Table 3.1 for initial guesses of 0.7 V, 0.5 V, and 0.2 V. How many iterations are required for each case? Did any problem arise? If so, what is the source of the problem?

3.38. (a) Use direct trial and error to find the solution to the diode circuit in Fig. 3.20 using Eq. (3.27). (b) Repeat using Eq. (3.28).

 3.39. Use a spreadsheet or write a program in a high-level language to numerically find the Q-point for the circuit in Fig. 3.20 using Eq. (3.28) instead of (3.27).

 3.40. Use MATLAB to numerically find the Q-point for the circuit in Fig. 3.20 using Eq. (3.28) instead of (3.27).

Ideal Diode and Constant Voltage Drop Models

*3.41. Find the Q-point for the circuit in Fig. 3.20 using the same four methods as in Sec. 3.9 if the voltage source is 1 V. Compare the answers in a manner similar to Table 3.2.

3.42. Find the Q-point for the diode in Fig. P3.42 using (a) the ideal diode model and (b) the constant voltage drop model with $V_{on} = 0.6$ V. (c) Discuss the results. Which answer do you feel is most correct?

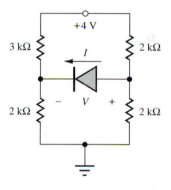

Figure P3.42

 3.43. Simulate the circuit of Fig. P3.42 and find the diode Q-point. Compare the results to those in Prob. 3.42.

3.44. (a) Find I and V in the four circuits in Fig. P3.44 using the ideal diode model. (b) Repeat using the constant voltage drop model with $V_{on} = 0.7$ V.

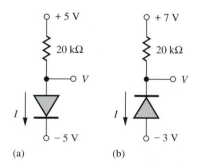

Figure P3.44

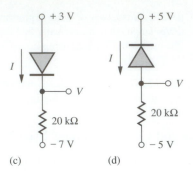

(c)   (d)

Figure P3.44 *(continued)*

3.10 Multiple Diode Circuits

3.45. Find the Q-points for the diodes in the four circuits in Fig. P3.45 using (a) the ideal diode model and (b) the constant voltage drop model with $V_{on} = 0.75$ V.

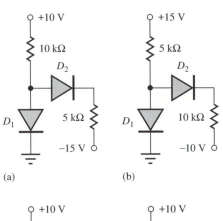

(a)   (b)

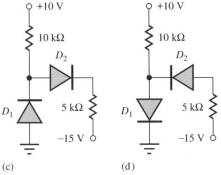

(c)   (d)

Figure P3.45

3.46. Find the Q-point for the diodes in the two circuits in Fig. P3.46 using (a) the ideal diode model and (b) the constant voltage drop model with $V_{on} = 0.6$ V.

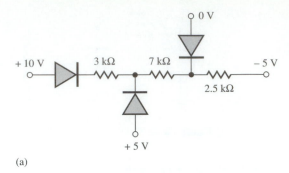

(a)

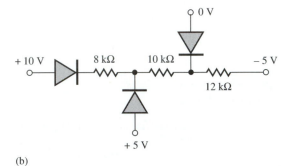

(b)

Figure P3.46

3.47. Simulate the diode circuits in Fig. P3.46 and compare your results to those in Prob. 3.46.

3.48. Verify that the values presented in Eq. (3.44) are correct.

3.49. Simulate the circuit in Fig. 3.35 and compare the results with Eq. (3.43).

3.11 Analysis of Diodes Operating in the Breakdown Region

3.50. Find the Q-point for the Zener diode in Fig. P3.50.

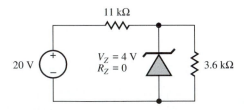

Figure P3.50

3.51. Draw the load line for the circuit in Fig. P3.50 on the characteristics in Fig. P3.27 and find the Q-point.

3.52. What is maximum load current I_L that can be drawn from the Zener regulator in Fig. P3.52 if it is to maintain a regulated output? What is the minimum value of R_L that can be used and still have a regulated output voltage?

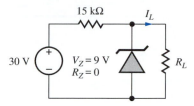

Figure P3.52

3.53. What is power dissipation in the Zener diode in Fig. P3.52 for $R_L = \infty$?

3.54. What is power dissipation in the Zener diode in Fig. P3.54 for (a) $R_L = 75\ \Omega$? (b) $R_L = \infty$?

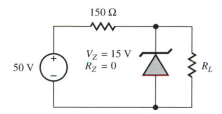

Figure P3.54

3.12 Half-Wave Rectifier Circuits

 *3.55. (a) Use a spreadsheet or MATLAB or write a computer program to find the numeric solution to the conduction angle equation (Eq. 3.58) for a 60 Hz half-wave rectifier circuit that uses a filter capacitance of 100,000 μF. The circuit is designed to provide 5 V at 5 A. {That is, solve $[(V_P - V_{on})\exp(-t/RC) = V_P\cos\omega t - V_{on}]$. Be careful! There are an infinite number of solutions to this equation. Be sure your algorithm finds the desired answer to the problem.} Assume $V_{on} = 1$ V. (b) Compare to calculations using Eq. (3.62).

3.56. A power diode has a reverse saturation current of 10^{-9} A and $n = 2$. What is the forward voltage drop at the peak current of 48.6 A that was calculated in the example in Sec. 3.12?

3.57. What is the actual average value (the dc value) of the rectifier output voltage for the waveform in Fig. P3.57 if V_r is 5 percent of $V_P - V_{on} = 15$ V?

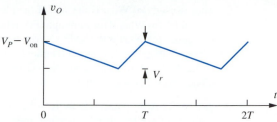

Figure P3.57

*3.58. Show that evaluation of Eq. (3.71) will yield the result in Eq. (3.72).

3.59. Draw the voltage waveforms, similar to those in Fig. 3.55, for the negative output rectifier in Fig. 3.59(b).

3.60. The half-wave rectifier in Fig. P3.60 is operating at a frequency of 60 Hz, and the RMS value of the transformer output voltage is 6.3 V. (a) What is the value of the dc output voltage V_O if the diode voltage drop is 1 V? (b) What is the minimum value of C required to maintain the ripple voltage to less than 0.25 V if $R = 0.5\ \Omega$? (c) What is the PIV rating of the diode in this circuit? (d) What is the surge current when power is first applied? (e) What is the amplitude of the repetitive current in the diode?

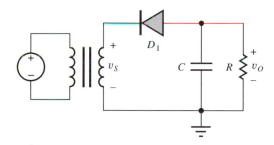

Figure P3.60

 3.61. Simulate the behavior of the half-wave rectifier in Fig. P3.60 for $V_S = 10\sin 120\pi t$, $R = 0.25\ \Omega$ and $C = 0.5$ F. (Use IS $= 10^{-10}$ A, RS $= 0$, and RELTOL $= 10^{-6}$.) Compare the simulated values of dc output voltage, ripple voltage, and peak diode current to hand calculations.

3.62. Repeat Prob. 3.60 for a frequency of 400 Hz.

3.63. Repeat Prob. 3.60 for a frequency of 100 kHz.

 3.64. A 2000-V, 1-A, dc power supply is to be designed with a ripple voltage ≤ 1 percent. Assume that a half-wave rectifier circuit (60 Hz) with a capacitor filter is used. (a) What is the size of the filter capacitor C? (b) What is the minimum PIV rating for the diode? (c) What is the RMS value of the transformer voltage needed for the rectifier? (d) What is the peak value of the repetitive current in the diode? (e) What is the surge current at $t = 0^+$?

3.65. A 5-V, 25-A dc power supply is to be designed with a ripple of less than 2.5 percent. Assume that a half-wave rectifier circuit (60 Hz) with a capacitor filter is used. (a) What is the size of the filter capacitor C? (b) What is the PIV rating for the diode? (c) What is the RMS value of the transformer voltage needed for the rectifier? (d) What is the value of the peak repetitive diode current in the diode? (e) What is the surge current at $t = 0^+$?

*3.66. A half-wave rectifier circuit (60 Hz) with capacitor filter is used to provide the input voltage to an IC voltage regulator, as shown in Fig. P3.66. The voltage regulator circuit will eliminate the ripple and provide a constant 12-V output voltage as long as the input voltage does not at any time drop below 14 V and the load resistance is at least 10 Ω. The transformer provides an output voltage of 12.6 V_{rms}, and $V_{on} = 0.8$ V for the diode. To minimize power dissipation in the voltage regulator, the rectifier circuit should be designed for the maximum permissible ripple voltage. What is the minimum value for the filter capacitor C? Assume that $I_S = I_L$.

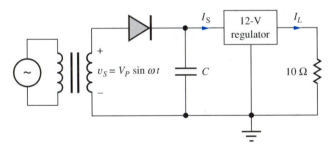

Figure P3.66

*3.67. Draw the voltage waveforms at nodes v_O and v_1 for the "voltage-doubler" circuit in Fig. P3.67 for the first two cycles of the input sine wave. What is the steady-state output voltage if $V_P = 17$ V?

3.68. Simulate the voltage-doubler rectifier circuit in Fig. P3.67 for $C = 500$ μF and $v_S = 1500 \sin 2\pi(60)t$ with a load resistance of $R_L = 3000$ Ω added between v_O and ground. Calculate the ripple voltage and compare to the simulation.

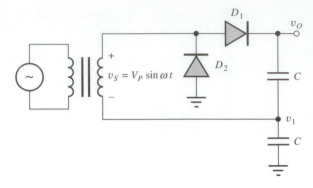

Figure P3.67

3.13 Full-Wave Rectifier Circuits

3.69. The full-wave rectifier in Fig. P3.69 is operating at a frequency of 60 Hz, and the RMS value of the transformer output voltage is 6.3 V. (a) What is the value of the dc output voltage if the diode voltage drop is 1 V? (b) What is the minimum value of C required to maintain the ripple voltage to less than 0.25 V if $R = 0.5$ Ω? (c) What is the PIV rating of the diode in this circuit? (d) What is the surge current when power is first applied? (e) What is the amplitude of the repetitive current in the diode?

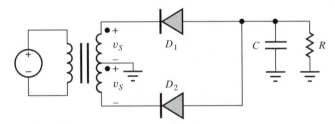

Figure P3.69

3.70. Simulate the behavior of the full-wave rectifier in Fig. P3.69 for $R = 3$ Ω and $C = 22,000$ μF. Assume that the RMS value of v_S is 10.0 V and the frequency is 400 Hz. (Use IS $= 10^{-10}$ A, RS $= 0$, and RELTOL $= 10^{-6}$.) Compare the simulated values of dc output voltage, ripple voltage, and peak diode current to hand calculations.

3.71. Repeat Prob. 3.64 for a full-wave rectifier circuit.

*3.72. The full-wave rectifier circuit in Fig. P3.72(a) was designed to have a maximum ripple of approximately 1 V, but it is not operating properly. The measured waveforms at the three nodes in the circuit are shown in Fig. P3.72(b). What is wrong with the circuit?

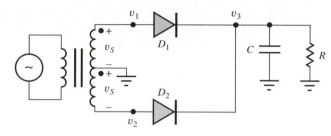

Figure P3.72(a)

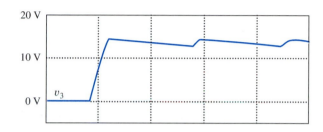

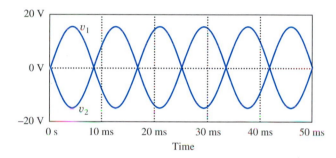

Figure P3.72(b) Waveforms for the circuit in Fig. P3.72(a).

3.14 Full-Wave Bridge Rectification

3.73. Repeat Prob. 3.64 for a full-wave bridge rectifier circuit.

*3.74. What are the dc output voltages V_1 and V_2 for the rectifier circuit in Fig. P3.74 if $v_S = 50 \sin 377t$ and $C = 10{,}000\ \mu F$?

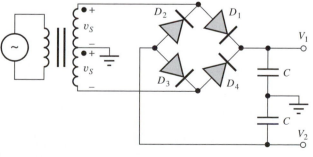

Figure P3.74

3.75. Simulate the rectifier circuit in Fig. P3.74 for $C = 100$ mF and $v_S = 35 \sin 2\pi(60)t$ with a 500-Ω load connected between each output and ground.

3.76. Repeat Prob. 3.69 if the full-wave bridge circuit in Fig. 3.68 is used instead of the rectifier in Fig. P3.69.

3.16 dc-to-dc Converters
Boost Converters

3.77. Design a boost converter operating at a frequency of 45 kHz to generate $+15$ V from a $+5$-V supply. The converter will have an output current of 0.5 A and a ripple voltage of less than 0.1 V. Assume that the ripple current is 10 percent of the dc inductor current.

3.78. Draw a graph of the waveform for the current in the switch in Fig. 3.69 for the converter in the boost converter exercise (page 92). (b) Repeat for the current in diode D.

*3.79. (a) Derive an expression, similar to Eq. 3.84, for the output voltage of a boost converter using the CVD model for the diode. (b) What are the output voltage, ripple voltage, and ripple current of a boost converter operating with $V_S = 5$ V, $V_{on} = 0.75$ V, $R = 20\ \Omega$, $L = 0.75$ mH, $C = 60\ \mu F$, $f = 50$ kHz, and $\delta = \frac{3}{4}$? Compare your answer to the boost converter exercise in the text.

**3.80. The ideal boost converter has no loss (that is, its efficiency is 100 percent). (a) Derive an expression for the efficiency η of the boost converter, including the CVD model for the diode if $\eta = 100\% \cdot P_O/P_S = 100\% \cdot V_O I_O/V_S I_S$. (b) What is the efficiency of the boost converter in the exercise on page 92 if the diode voltage is 0.75 V? (c) Derive an expression for the efficiency η of the boost converter including both the on-voltage of the diode and a fixed voltage drop across the on switch.

Buck Converters

3.81. (a) Draw a graph of the waveform for the current in the source V_S in Fig. 3.72(a) for the converter in the buck converter exercise (page 95). (b) Repeat for the current in diode D.

3.82. Draw a graph, similar to Fig. 3.71, showing the waveforms of both the inductor current and output voltage for the buck converter in Fig. 3.72(a). Use the values from the buck converter exercise (page 95).

3.83. Design a buck converter operating at a frequency of 30 kHz to generate $+15$ V from a $+50$-V supply. The converter will have an output current of 0.5 A and a ripple voltage of less than 0.1 V. Assume that the ripple current is 10 percent of the dc inductor current.

3.84. Design a buck converter operating at a frequency of 50 kHz to generate +15 V from a +170-V supply. The converter will have an output current of 2.5 A and a ripple voltage of less than 0.5 V. Assume that the ripple current is 15 percent of the dc inductor current.

*3.85. (a) Derive an expression, similar to Eq. 3.92, for the output voltage of a buck converter using the CVD model for the diode. (b) What are the output voltage, ripple voltage, and ripple current of a buck converter operating with $V_S = 10$ V, $V_{on} = 0.75$ V, $R = 5\ \Omega$, $L = 1.25$ mH, $C = 1.25\ \mu$F, $f = 40$ kHz, and $\delta = \frac{1}{2}$? Compare your answer to the buck converter exercise (page 95).

**3.86. The ideal buck converter has no loss (that is, its efficiency is 100 percent). (a) Derive an expression for the efficiency η of the buck converter, including the CVD model for the diode if $\eta = 100\% \cdot P_O/P_S = 100\% \cdot V_O I_O/V_S I_S$. (b) What is the efficiency of the buck converter in the exercise on page 95 if the on-voltage of the diode is 0.75 V? (c) Derive an expression for the efficiency η of the boost converter, including both the on-voltage of the diode and a fixed voltage drop across the on switch.

3.17 Wave-Shaping Circuits

3.87. The circuit inside the box in Fig. P3.87 contains only resistors and diodes. The terminal V_O is connected to some point in the circuit inside the box. (a) Is the largest possible value of V_O most nearly 0 V, −6 V, +6 V, or +15 V? Why? (b) Is the smallest possible value of V_O most nearly 0 V, −9 V, +6 V, or +15 V? Why?

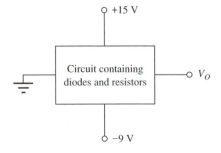

Figure P3.87

3.88. Draw waveforms for v_O for the two circuits in the Fig. P3.88. The diodes are ideal. Use the general input provided for Probs. 3.88 to 3.96.

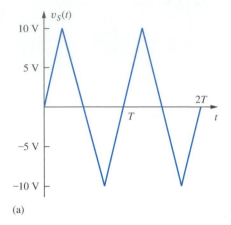

(a)

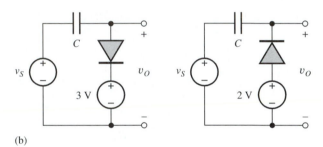

(b)

Figure P3.88 Input waveform for Probs. 3.88 to 3.96. For simulation, use $T = 0.001$ S.

3.89. Draw the waveform for v_O for the circuit in Fig. P3.89. The diode has an on-voltage of 0.7 V and $R_Z = 0$.

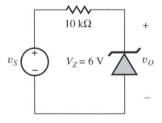

Figure P3.89

3.90. Draw the waveform for v_O for the circuit in Fig. P3.90. The diodes have an on-voltage of 0.7 V and $R_Z = 0$.

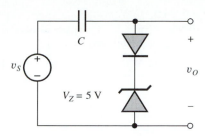

Figure P3.90

3.91. Draw the waveform for v_O for the circuit in Fig. P3.91. The diodes have an on-voltage of 0.7 V and $R_Z = 0$.

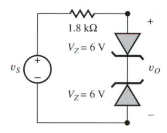

Figure P3.91

3.92. (a) Draw the waveform for v_O for the circuit in Fig. P3.92. The diodes are ideal. (b) Repeat using the CVD model with $V_{on} = 0.7$ V.

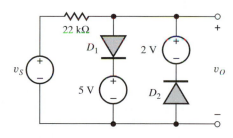

Figure P3.92

 3.93. Simulate the behavior of the circuit in Fig. P3.92 using the input voltage waveform in Fig. P3.88.

3.94. Draw the waveform for v_O for the circuit in Fig. P3.94. The diodes are ideal.

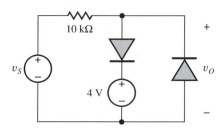

Figure P3.94

3.95. Draw the waveform for v_O for the circuit in Fig. P3.94 if the diodes have $V_{on} = 0.7$ V.

3.96. (a) Draw the waveform for v_O for the circuit in Fig. P3.96. The diodes are ideal. (b) Repeat using the CVD model with $V_{on} = 0.7$ V.

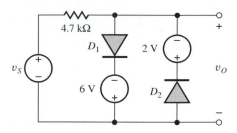

Figure P3.96

 3.97. Use SPICE to generate the voltage transfer characteristic for the circuit in Fig. P3.96.

3.98. Draw the voltage transfer characteristic for the circuit in Fig. P3.98. The diodes are ideal.

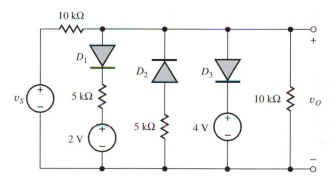

Figure P3.98

 3.99. Use SPICE to generate the voltage transfer characteristic for the circuit in Fig. P3.98.

 3.100. Simulate the behavior of the two circuits in Fig. P3.88 using a sine wave input voltage with an amplitude of 10 V and a frequency of 1000 Hz. Use $C = 100\ \mu$F.

3.101. Draw the voltage transfer characteristic for the circuit in Fig. P3.101 (page 114). The diodes are ideal.

 3.102. Use SPICE to generate the voltage transfer characteristic for the circuit in Fig. P3.101. Compare to the results of Prob. 3.101.

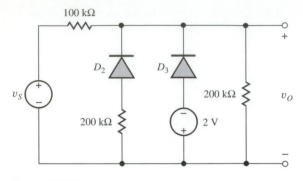

Figure P3.101

3.18 Dynamic Switching Behavior of the Diode

*3.103. (a) Calculate the current at $t = 0+$ in the circuit in Fig. P3.103. (b) Calculate I_F, I_R, and the storage time expected when the diode is switched off if $\tau_T = 7$ ns.

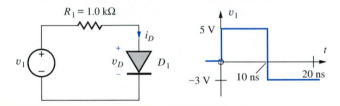

Figure P3.103

3.104. (a) Simulate the switching behavior of the circuit in Fig. P3.103. (b) Compare the simulation results to the hand calculations in Prob. 3.103.

**3.105. The simulation results presented in Fig. 3.76 were performed with the diode transit time $\tau_T = 5$ ns. (a) Repeat the simulation of the diode circuit in Fig. P3.105(a) with the diode transit time changed to $\tau_T = 50$ ns. Does the storage time that you observe change in proportion to the value of τ_T in your simulation? Discuss. (b) Repeat the simulation with the input voltage changed to the one

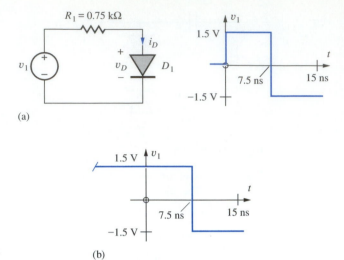

(a)

(b)

Figure P3.105

in Fig. P3.105(b), in which it is assumed that v_1 has been at 1.5 V for a long time, and compare the results to those obtained in (a). What is the reason for the difference between the results in (a) and (b)?

3.19 Photo Diodes, Solar Cells, and LEDs

*3.106. The output of a diode used as a solar cell is given by

$$I_C = 1 - 10^{-15}[\exp(40V_C) - 1] \text{ amperes}$$

What operating point corresponds to P_{max}? What is P_{max}? What are the values of I_{SC} and V_{OC}?

**3.107. The bandgaps of silicon and gallium arsenide are 1.12 eV and 1.42 eV, respectively. What are the wavelengths of light that you would expect to be emitted from these devices based on direct recombination of holes and electrons? To what "colors" of light do these wavelengths correspond?

Field-Effect Transistors

Chapter 4 explores the characteristics of **field-effect transistors (FETs).** The **metal-oxide-semiconductor field-effect transistor (MOSFET)** is without doubt the most commercially successful solid-state device. It is the primary component in high-density VLSI chips, including microprocessors and memories. A second type of FET, the **junction field-effect transistor (JFET),** is based on a *pn* junction structure.

P-**channel MOS (PMOS) transistors** were the first MOS devices to be successfully fabricated in large-scale integrated circuits (LSI). The first microprocessor chips used PMOS technology. Greater performance was later obtained with the commercial introduction of *n*-**channel MOS (NMOS)** technology in both enhancement-mode and depletion-mode devices.

This chapter discusses the qualitative and quantitative *i-v* behavior of MOSFETs and JFETs and investigates the differences between the various types of transistors. Techniques for biasing the transistors in various regions of operation are also presented.

4.1 CHARACTERISTICS OF THE MOS CAPACITOR

At the heart of the MOSFET is the **MOS capacitor** structure depicted in Fig. 4.1. The top electrode of the MOS capacitor is formed of a metal, typically aluminum or heavily doped polysilicon (polycrystalline silicon). We refer to this electrode as the **gate (*G*)** for reasons that will become apparent shortly. A thin insulating layer, typically silicon dioxide, isolates the metal gate from the substrate or body—the semiconductor region that acts as the second electrode of the capacitor. Silicon dioxide is a stable, high-quality electrical insulator readily formed by thermal oxidation of the silicon substrate. The ability to form this high-quality insulator is one of the basic reasons that silicon is the dominant semiconductor material today. The semiconductor region may be *n*-type or *p*-type, as in Fig. 4.1.

The qualitative behavior of the MOS capacitor is the basis for operation of the MOSFET. The semiconductor forming the bottom electrode of the capacitor has a substantial resistivity and a limited supply of holes and electrons. Because the semiconductor therefore can be depleted of carriers, as discussed in Chapter 2, the capacitance of this structure is a nonlinear function of voltage v_G. Figure 4.2 shows the conditions in the region of the substrate immediately below the gate electrode for three different bias voltages.

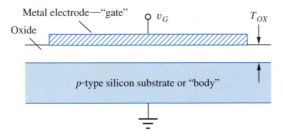

Figure 4.1 MOS capacitor structure on *p*-type silicon.

Accumulation Region

The situation for a large negative bias on the gate with respect to the substrate is depicted in Fig. 4.2(a). The large negative charge on the metal plate is balanced by holes attracted to the silicon-silicon dioxide interface directly below the gate. For the bias condition shown, the hole density at the surface exceeds that which is present in the original *p*-type substrate, and the surface is said to be operating in the **accumulation region** or just in **accumulation.**

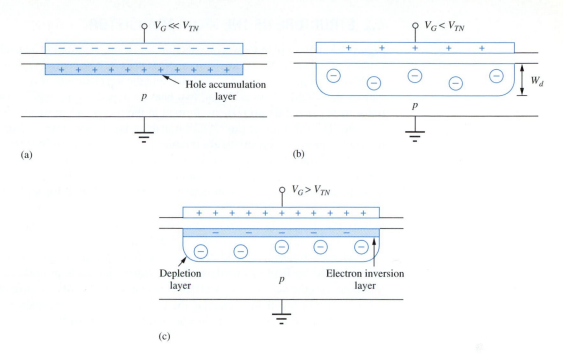

Figure 4.2 MOS capacitor operating in (a) accumulation, (b) depletion, (c) inversion.

This accumulation layer is extremely shallow, existing primarily as a charge sheet directly below the gate.

Depletion Region

Now consider the situation as the gate voltage is slowly increased. First, holes are repelled from the surface. Eventually, the hole density near the surface is reduced below the majority-carrier level set by the substrate doping level, as depicted in Fig. 4.2(b). This condition is called **depletion** and the region, the **depletion region.** The region beneath the metal electrode is depleted of free carriers in much the same way as the depletion region that exists near the metallurgical junction of the *pn* junction diode. In Fig. 4.2(b), positive charge on the gate electrode is balanced by the negative charge of the ionized acceptor atoms in the depletion layer. The depletion-region width w_d can range from a fraction of a micron to many tens of microns depending on the applied voltage and substrate doping levels.

Inversion Region

As the voltage on the top electrode increases further, electrons are attracted to the surface. At some voltage level, the electron density at the surface will exceed the hole density. At this voltage, the surface has inverted polarity from the *p*-type of the original substrate to an *n*-type **inversion layer,** or **inversion region,** directly underneath the top plate. This inversion region is an extremely shallow layer, existing primarily as a charge sheet directly below the gate. The high density of electrons in the inversion layer is supplied by the electron–hole generation process within the depletion layer.

The positive charge on the gate is balanced by the combination of negative charge in the inversion layer plus negative ionic acceptor charge in the depletion layer. The voltage at which the surface inversion layer forms plays an extremely important role in field-effect transistors and is called the **threshold voltage V_{TN}.**

4.2 STRUCTURE OF THE NMOS TRANSISTOR

Figure 4.3 shows a plan view, cross section, and circuit symbol of an **n-channel MOSFET,** usually called an **NMOS transistor,** or **NMOSFET.** The central region of the MOSFET is the MOS capacitor discussed in Sec. 4.1, and the top electrode of the capacitor is called the gate of the MOSFET. In addition, two heavily doped n-type regions (n^+ regions), called the **source (S)** and **drain (D),** are formed in the p-type substrate aligned with the edge of the gate. The substrate of the NMOS transistor is a fourth device terminal and is referred to synonymously as the **substrate terminal,** or the **body terminal (B).**

The terminal voltages and currents for the NMOS device are also defined in Fig. 4.3(b). The drain current i_D, source current i_S, gate current i_G, and body current i_B are all defined, with the positive direction of current indicated for an NMOS transistor. The important terminal voltages are the gate-source voltage $v_{GS} = v_G - v_S$, the drain-source voltage $v_{DS} = v_D - v_S$, and the source-bulk voltage $v_{SB} = v_S - v_B$. These voltages are all ≥ 0 during normal operation of the NMOSFET.

Note that the source and drain regions form pn junctions with the substrate. These two junctions are kept reverse-biased at all times in order to provide isolation between the junctions and the substrate as well as between adjacent MOS transistors. Thus, the bulk voltage must be less than or equal to the voltages applied to the source and drain terminals to ensure that these pn junctions are properly reverse-biased.

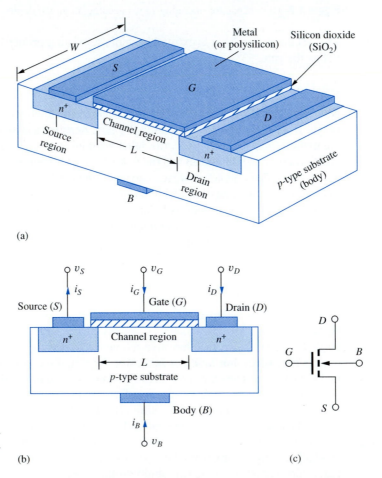

(a)

(b)

(c)

Figure 4.3 (a) NMOS transistor structure; (b) cross section; and (c) circuit symbol.

The semiconductor region between the source and drain regions directly below the gate is called the **channel region** of the FET. Two dimensions of critical import are defined in Fig. 4.3. *L* represents the channel length which is measured in the direction of current in the channel. *W* is the channel width, which is measured perpendicular to the direction of current. We will later find that the values chosen for *W* and *L* are an important aspect of digital and analog IC design.

4.3 QUALITATIVE *i-v* BEHAVIOR OF THE NMOS TRANSISTOR

Before attempting to derive an expression for the current-voltage characteristic of the NMOS transistor, let us try to develop a qualitative understanding of what we might expect by referring to Fig. 4.4. In the figure, the source, drain, and body of the NMOSFET are all grounded.

For a dc gate-source voltage, $v_{GS} = V_{GS}$, well below the threshold voltage V_{TN}, as in Fig 4.4(a), back-to-back *pn* junctions exist between the source and drain, and only a small leakage current can flow between these two terminals. For V_{GS} near but still below threshold, a depletion region forms beneath the gate and merges with the depletion regions of the source and drain, as indicated in Fig. 4.4(b). The depletion region is devoid of free carriers, so a current still cannot appear between the source and drain. Finally, however, when the gate-channel voltage exceeds the threshold voltage V_{TN}, as in Fig. 4.4(c), electrons flow in from the source and drain to form an inversion layer that connects the n^+ source region to the n^+ drain. A resistive connection exists between the source and drain terminals. If a positive voltage were now applied between these terminals, electrons in the channel would drift in the electric field, creating a current in the terminals.

The current in the NMOS transistor always enters the drain terminal, travels down the channel, and exits the source terminal. The gate terminal is insulated from the channel; thus, there is no dc gate current, and $i_G = 0$. The drain-bulk and source-bulk (and induced channel-to-bulk) *pn* junctions must be reverse-biased at all times to ensure that only a small reverse-bias leakage current exists in these diodes. This current is usually negligible with respect to the channel current i_{DS} and is neglected. Thus we assume that $i_B = 0$.

In the device in Fig. 4.4, a channel must be induced by the applied gate voltage for conduction to occur. The gate voltage "enhances" the conductivity of the channel; this type of MOSFET is named an **enhancement-mode device.** Later we identify an additional type of MOSFET called a **depletion-mode device.**

4.4 LINEAR REGION CHARACTERISTICS OF THE NMOS TRANSISTOR

In this section, we develop an expression for the current in the terminals of the NMOS device in terms of the applied voltages. It was argued earlier that both i_G and i_B are zero. Therefore, the current entering the drain must be equal to the current leaving the source and

$$i_S = i_D = i_{DS} \tag{4.1}$$

An expression for the drain-source current i_{DS} can be developed by considering the flow of charge in the channel in Fig. 4.5. The electron charge per unit length (a line charge) at any point in the channel is given by

$$Q' = -WC_{ox}''(v_{ox} - V_{TN}) \qquad \text{C/cm for } v_{ox} \geq V_{TN} \tag{4.2}$$

where $C_{ox}'' = \varepsilon_{ox}/T_{ox}$, oxide capacitance per unit area (F/cm^2)
   ε_{ox} = oxide permittivity (F/cm)[1]
   T_{ox} = oxide thickness (cm)

The voltage v_{ox} represents the voltage across the oxide and will be a function of position in the channel

$$v_{ox} = v_{GS} - v(x) \tag{4.3}$$

where $v(x)$ = voltage at any point x in the channel referred to the source

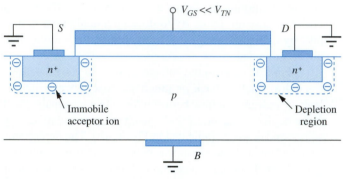

(a)

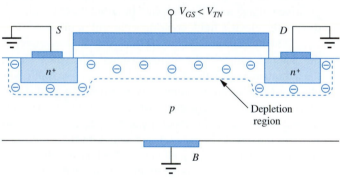

(b)

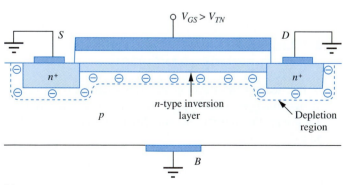

(c)

Figure 4.4 (a) $V_{GS} \ll V_{TN}$.
(b) $V_{GS} < V_{TN}$.
(c) $V_{GS} > V_{TN}$.

---

[1] For silicon dioxide, $\varepsilon_{ox} = 3.9\,\varepsilon_o$, where $\varepsilon_o = 8.854 \times 10^{-14}$ F/cm.

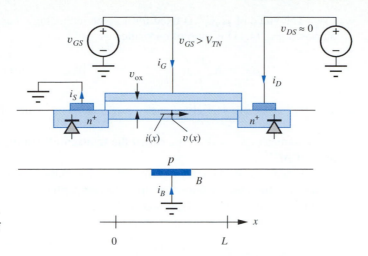

Figure 4.5 Model for determining i-v characteristics of the NMOS transistor.

Note that v_{ox} must exceed V_{TN} for an inversion layer to exist, so Q' will be zero until $v_{ox} > V_{TN}$. At the source end of the channel, $v_{ox} = v_{GS}$, and it decreases to $v_{ox} = v_{GS} - v_{DS}$ at the drain end of the channel.

The electron drift current at any point in the channel is given by the product of the charge per unit length times the velocity v_x:

$$i(x) = Q'(x)\, v_x(x) \tag{4.4}$$

The charge Q' is represented by Eq. (4.2), and the velocity v_x of electrons in the channel is determined by the electron mobility and the transverse electric field in the channel:

$$i(x) = Q' v_x = [-WC''_{ox}(v_{ox} - V_{TN})][-\mu_n E_x] \tag{4.5}$$

The transverse electric field is equal to the negative of the spatial derivative of the voltage in the channel

$$E_x = -\frac{dv(x)}{dx} \tag{4.6}$$

Combining Eqs. (4.3) to (4.6) yields an expression for the current at any point in the channel.

$$i(x) = -\mu_n C''_{ox} W(v_{GS} - v(x) - V_{TN}) \frac{dv(x)}{dx} \tag{4.7}$$

or

$$i(x)\, dx = -\mu_n C''_{ox} W(v_{GS} - v(x) - V_{TN})\, dv(x) \tag{4.8}$$

We know the voltages applied to the device terminals are $v(0) = 0$ and $v(L) = v_{DS}$, and we can integrate Eq. (4.8) between 0 and L:

$$\int_0^L i(x)\, dx = -\int_0^{v_{DS}} \mu_n C''_{ox} W(v_{GS} - v(x) - V_{TN})\, dv(x) \tag{4.9}$$

Because there is no mechanism to lose current as it goes down the channel, the current must be equal to the same value i_{DS} at every point x in the channel, $i(x) = -i_{DS}$, and Eq. (4.9) finally yields

$$i_{DS} L = \mu_n C''_{ox} W \left(v_{GS} - V_{TN} - \frac{v_{DS}}{2}\right) v_{DS} \tag{4.10}$$

or

$$i_{DS} = \mu_n C''_{ox} \frac{W}{L} \left(v_{GS} - V_{TN} - \frac{v_{DS}}{2}\right) v_{DS} \tag{4.11}$$

The value of $\mu_n C''_{\text{ox}}$ is fixed for a given technology. For circuit analysis and design purposes, Eq. (4.11) is most often written as

$$i_{DS} = K'_n \frac{W}{L}\left(v_{GS} - V_{TN} - \frac{v_{DS}}{2}\right)v_{DS} \qquad \text{where } K'_n = \mu_n C''_{\text{ox}}$$

(4.12)

or as $\qquad\qquad i_{DS} = K_n\left(v_{GS} - V_{TN} - \frac{v_{DS}}{2}\right)v_{DS} \qquad \text{where } K_n = K'_n \frac{W}{L}$

The parameters K_n and K'_n are called the **transconductance parameters** and both have units of A/V^2.

Equations (4.11) and (4.12) represent the classic expressions for the drain-source current for the NMOS transistor in its **linear region** of operation, in which a resistive channel directly connects the source and drain. This resistive connection will last as long as the voltage across the oxide exceeds the threshold voltage at every point in the channel:

$$v_{GS} - v(x) \geq V_{TN} \qquad \text{for } 0 \leq x \leq L \tag{4.13}$$

The voltage in the channel is maximum at the drain end where $v(L) = v_{DS}$. Thus, Eqs. (4.11) and (4.12) are valid as long as

$$v_{GS} - V_{TN} \geq v_{DS} \tag{4.14}$$

Recapitulating for the linear region:

$$i_{DS} = K'_n \frac{W}{L}\left(v_{GS} - V_{TN} - \frac{v_{DS}}{2}\right)v_{DS}$$

(4.15)

for $\qquad\qquad v_{GS} - V_{TN} \geq v_{DS} \geq 0 \qquad \text{and} \qquad K'_n = \mu_n C''_{\text{ox}}$

Additional insight can be gained by regrouping the terms in Eq. (4.11):

$$i_{DS} = \left[WC''_{\text{ox}}\left(v_{GS} - V_{TN} - \frac{v_{DS}}{2}\right)\right]\left[\mu_n \frac{v_{DS}}{L}\right] \tag{4.16}$$

For small drain-source voltages, the first term represents the average charge per unit length in the channel because the average channel voltage $v(x) = v_{DS}/2$. The second term represents the drift velocity in the channel, where the average electric field is equal to the voltage v_{DS} across the channel divided by the channel length L.

It should be mentioned that the linear region is sometimes called the **triode region** because of its similarity to the behavior of the electronic vacuum triodes that historically preceded it.

> **Exercise:** Calculate the drain current in an NMOS transistor for $V_{GS} = 0$ V, 1 V, 2 V, and 3 V, with $V_{DS} = 0.1$ V if $W = 10$ μm, $L = 1$ μm, $V_{TN} = 1.5$ V, and $K'_n = 25$ μA/V^2.
>
> **Answers:** 0; 0; 11.3 μA; 36.3 μA

Interpretation of the Linear Region *i-v* Characteristic

The *i-v* characteristics in the linear region generated from Eq. (4.15) are drawn in Fig. 4.6 for the case of $V_{TN} = 1$ V and $K_n = 250$ μA/V^2. The curves in Fig. 4.6 represent a portion of the **output characteristics** for the NMOS device. The output characteristics for a three-terminal device represent a graph of the current through the output port of the device, in this case the drain current, as a function of the voltage across the output port, in this case the

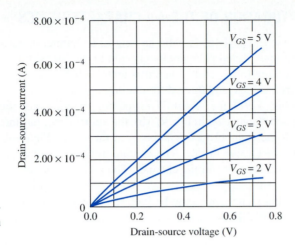

Figure 4.6 NMOS i-v characteristics in the linear region ($V_{SB} = 0$).

drain-source voltage. A family of curves is generated, with each curve corresponding to a different value of the gate-source voltage, the input-port voltage. The output characteristics will be slightly different for each value of source-bulk voltage.

The characteristics in Fig. 4.6 appear to be a family of nearly straight lines, hence the name linear region (of operation). However, some curvature can be noted in the characteristics, particularly for $V_{GS} = 2$ V.

Let us explore the linear region behavior in more detail using Eq. (4.15). For small drain-source voltages such that $v_{DS} \ll v_{GS} - V_{TN}$, Eq. (4.15) can be reduced to

$$i_{DS} \approx \mu_n C''_{\text{ox}} \frac{W}{L} (v_{GS} - V_{TN}) v_{DS} \tag{4.17}$$

in which the current i_{DS} through the MOSFET is now directly proportional to the voltage v_{DS} across the MOSFET. The FET behaves much like a resistor connected between the drain and source terminals, but the resistor value is controlled by the gate-source voltage. It has been said that this voltage-controlled resistance behavior originally gave rise to the name transistor, a contraction of "transfer-resistor."

The resistance of the FET in the linear region near the origin, called the **on-resistance** R_{on}, is defined in Eq. (4.18) and can be found using Eq. (4.15):

$$R_{\text{on}} = \left[\frac{\partial i_{DS}}{\partial v_{DS}} \bigg|_{v_{DS} \to 0} \right]_{\text{Q-point}}^{-1} = \frac{1}{K'_n \dfrac{W}{L} (V_{GS} - V_{TN})} \tag{4.18}$$

Note that R_{on} is also equal to the ratio v_{DS}/i_{DS} from Eq. (4.17).

Near the origin, the i-v curves are indeed straight lines. However, curvature develops as the assumption $v_{DS} \ll v_{GS} - V_{TN}$ starts to be violated. For the lowest curve in Fig. 4.6, $V_{GS} - V_{TN} = 2 - 1 = 1$ V, and we should expect linear behavior only for values of v_{DS} below 0.1 to 0.2 V. On the other hand, the curve for $V_{GS} = 5$ V exhibits quasi-linear behavior throughout most of the range of Fig. 4.6.

EXERCISE: Calculate the on-resistance of an NMOS transistor for $V_{GS} = 2$ V and 5 V if $V_{TN} = 1$ V and $K_n = 250\ \mu\text{A/V}^2$.

ANSWERS: 4 kΩ; 1 kΩ

4.5 SATURATION OF THE *i-v* CHARACTERISTICS

As discussed, Eq. (4.15) is valid as long as a channel directly connects the source to the drain. An unexpected phenomenon occurs in the MOSFET as the drain voltage increases above the limit in Eq. (4.15), and this unusual behavior is depicted in Fig. 4.7 for a fixed gate-source voltage and three different drain-source voltages.

In Fig. 4.7(a), the MOSFET is operating in the linear region with $v_{DS} < v_{GS} - V_{TN}$, as discussed previously. In Fig. 4.7(b), the value of v_{DS} has increased to $v_{DS} = v_{GS} - V_{TN}$, for which the channel just disappears at the drain. Figure 4.7(c) shows the channel for an even larger value of v_{DS}. The channel region has disappeared, or *pinched off,* before reaching the drain end of the channel. The resistive channel region is no longer in contact with the drain.

At first glance, one may be inclined to expect that the current should become zero in the MOSFET. However, this is not the case. As depicted in Fig. 4.8, the voltage at the

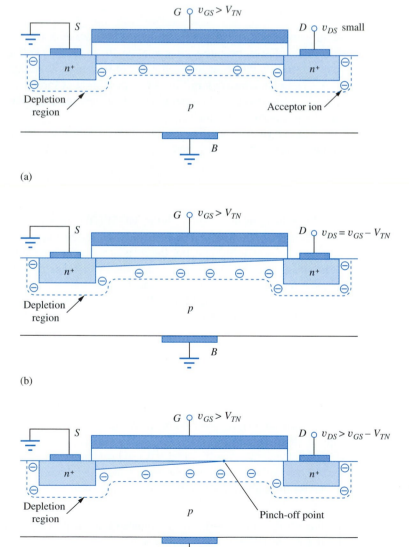

(a)

(b)

Figure 4.7 (a) MOSFET in the linear region. (b) MOSFET with channel just pinched off at the drain. (c) Channel pinch-off for $v_{DS} > v_{GS} - V_{TN}$.

(c)

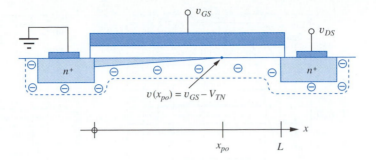

Figure 4.8 Inversion layer in the saturation region, also known as the pinch-off region.

pinch-off point in the channel is always equal to

$$v_{GS} - v(x_{po}) = V_{TN} \qquad \text{or} \qquad v(x_{po}) = v_{GS} - V_{TN} \qquad (4.19)$$

There is still a voltage equal to $v_{GS} - V_{TN}$ across the inverted portion of the channel, and electrons will be drifting down the channel from left to right. When the electrons reach the pinch-off point, they are injected into the depleted region between the end of the channel and the drain, and the electric field in the depletion region then sweeps the electrons on to the drain. Once the channel has reached pinch-off, the voltage drop across the inverted channel region is constant. Hence, the drain current becomes constant, and the MOSFET enters the **saturation region** of operation. This region is also often referred to as the **pinch-off region.**

Evaluating Eq. (4.15) with $v_{DS} = v_{GS} - V_{TN}$ yields the NMOS current in the saturation region of operation:

$$i_{DS} = \frac{K_n'}{2} \frac{W}{L} (v_{GS} - V_{TN})^2 \qquad \text{for } v_{DS} \geq (v_{GS} - V_{TN}) \geq 0 \qquad (4.20)$$

This is the classic square-law expression for the drain-source current in the saturated *n*-channel MOSFET. The current depends on the square of $v_{GS} - V_{TN}$ but is independent of the drain-source voltage.

The value of v_{DS} for which the transistor saturates is given the special name v_{DSAT}, defined by

$$v_{DSAT} = v_{GS} - V_{TN} \qquad (4.21)$$

V_{DSAT} is referred to as the **saturation voltage,** or **pinch-off voltage.**

Equation (4.20) can be interpreted in a manner similar to that of Eq. (4.16):

$$i_{DS} = \left[W C_{ox}'' \frac{(v_{GS} - V_{TN})}{2} \right] \left[\mu_n \frac{(v_{GS} - V_{TN})}{L} \right] \qquad (4.22)$$

The inverted channel region has a voltage of $v_{GS} - V_{TN}$ across it, as depicted in Fig. 4.8. Thus, the first term represents the magnitude of the average charge in the inversion layer, and the second term is the magnitude of the velocity of electrons in an electric field equal to $(v_{GS} - V_{TN})/L$.

An example of the complete output characteristics for an NMOS transistor with $V_{TN} = 1$ V and $K_n = 25 \, \mu\text{A/V}^2$ appears in Fig. 4.9, in which the locus of pinch-off points is determined by $v_{DS} = v_{DSAT}$. To the left of the pinch-off locus, the transistor is operating in the linear region, and it is operating in the saturation region for operating points to the right of the locus. For $v_{GS} \leq V_{TN} = 1$ V, the transistor is cut off and the drain current is zero. As the gate voltage is increased in the saturation region, the curves spread out due to the square-law nature of Eq. (4.20).

Figure 4.10 gives an individual output characteristic for $V_{GS} = 3$ V, showing the behavior of the individual linear and saturation region equations. The linear region

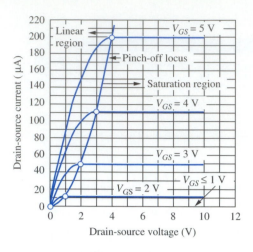

Figure 4.9 Output characteristics for an NMOS transistor with $V_{TN} = 1$ V and $K_n = 25 \times 10^{-6}$ A/V^2.

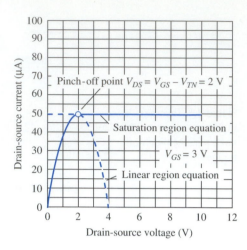

Figure 4.10 Output characteristic showing intersection of the linear region and saturation region equations at the pinch-off point.

expression in Eq. (4.15) is represented by the parabola in Fig. 4.10. Note that it does not represent a valid model for the i-v behavior for $V_{DS} > V_{GS} - V_{TN} = 2$ V for this particular device.

> **EXERCISE:** Calculate the drain current for an NMOS transistor operating with $V_{GS} = 5$ V and $V_{DS} = 10$ V if $V_{TN} = 1$ V and $K_n = 1$ mA/V^2.
>
> **ANSWER:** 8.00 mA

4.6 CHANNEL-LENGTH MODULATION

The output characteristics of the device in Fig. 4.9 indicate that the drain current is constant once the device enters the saturation region of operation. However, this is not quite true. Rather, the i-v curves have a small positive slope, as indicated in Fig. 4.11. The drain current increases slightly as the drain-source voltage increases. The increase in drain current visible in Fig. 4.11 is the result of a phenomenon called **channel-length modulation,** which can be understood from Fig. 4.12, in which the saturated channel region of the

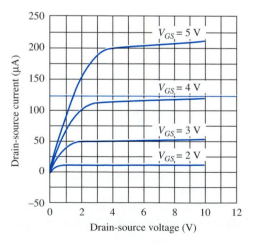

Figure 4.11 Output characteristics including the effects of channel-length modulation.

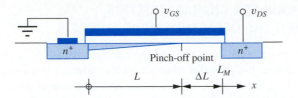

Figure 4.12 Channel-length modulation.

NMOS transistor is depicted for the case of $v_{DS} > v_{DSAT}$. The channel pinches off before it makes contact with the drain. Thus, the actual length of the resistive channel is given by $L = L_M - \Delta L$. As v_{DS} increases above v_{DSAT}, the length of the depleted channel region ΔL also increases, and the actual value of L decreases. Therefore, the value of L in the denominator of Eq. (4.20) actually has a slight dependence on v_{DS}, and the drain current increases as v_{DS} increases. The expression in Eq. (4.20) can be heuristically modified to include this drain-voltage dependence as

$$i_{DS} = \frac{K'_n}{2}\frac{W}{L}(v_{GS} - V_{TN})^2(1 + \lambda v_{DS}) \tag{4.23}$$

in which λ is called the **channel-length modulation parameter.** The value of λ is dependent on the channel length, and typical values are

$$0.001 \text{ V}^{-1} \leq \lambda \leq 0.1 \text{ V}^{-1} \tag{4.24}$$

In Fig. 4.11, λ is approximately 0.01, which yields a 10 percent increase in current for a voltage change of 10 V.

> **EXERCISE:** Calculate the drain current for an NMOS transistor operating with $V_{GS} = 5$ V and $V_{DS} = 10$ V if $V_{TN} = 1$ V, $K_n = 1$ mA/V^2, and $\lambda = 0.02$.
>
> **ANSWER:** 9.60 mA

NMOS Transistor Mathematical Model Summary

Equations (4.25) through (4.28) represent the complete model for the i-v behavior of the NMOS transistor. For all regions,

$$K_n = \mu_n C''_{\text{ox}}\frac{W}{L} \qquad i_G = 0 \qquad i_B = 0 \tag{4.25}$$

Cutoff region :
$$i_{DS} = 0 \qquad \text{for } v_{GS} \leq V_{TN} \tag{4.26}$$

Linear region :

$$i_{DS} = K_n\left(v_{GS} - V_{TN} - \frac{v_{DS}}{2}\right)v_{DS} \qquad \text{for } v_{GS} - V_{TN} \geq v_{DS} \geq 0 \tag{4.27}$$

Saturation region :

$$i_{DS} = \frac{K_n}{2}(v_{GS} - V_{TN})^2(1 + \lambda v_{DS}) \qquad \text{for } v_{DS} \geq (v_{GS} - V_{TN}) \geq 0 \tag{4.28}$$

> **EXERCISE:** What is the region of operation and drain current of an NMOS transistor having $V_{TN} = 1$ V, $K_n = 1$ mA/V^2, and $\lambda = 0.02$ for (a) $V_{GS} = 0$ V, $V_{DS} = 1$ V; (b) $V_{GS} = 2$ V, $V_{DS} = 0.5$ V; (c) $V_{GS} = 2$ V, $V_{DS} = 2$ V?
>
> **ANSWER:** cutoff, 0 A; linear, 375 μA; saturation, 520 μA

4.7 TRANSFER CHARACTERISTICS AND THE DEPLETION-MODE MOSFET

The *i-v* characteristics of the transistor are also commonly presented in another graphical format called the **transfer characteristic,** which plots drain current versus gate-source voltage for a fixed drain-source voltage. An example of this form of characteristic is given in Fig. 4.13 for two saturated NMOS transistors. Up to now, we have been assuming that the threshold voltage of the NMOS transistor is positive, as in the right-hand curve in Fig. 4.13. This curve corresponds to an enhancement-mode device with $V_{TN} = +2$ V.

However, it is also possible to fabricate NMOS transistors with values of $V_{TN} \leq 0$. These transistors are called depletion-mode devices and the transfer characteristic for such a device with $V_{TN} = -2$ V is depicted in the left-hand curve in the figure. Note that a nonzero drain current exists in this depletion-mode MOSFET for $v_{GS} = 0$, and a negative value of v_{GS} is required to turn the device off.

The cross section of the structure of a depletion-mode NMOSFET is shown in Fig. 4.14. A process called *ion-implantation* is used to form a built-in *n*-type channel in the device so that the source and drain are connected through the resistive channel region. A negative voltage must be applied to the gate in order to deplete the *n*-type channel region and quench the current path between the source and drain (hence the name depletion-mode device).

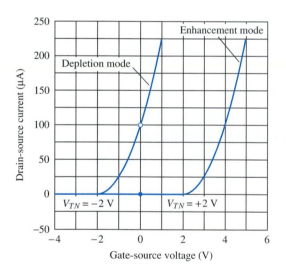

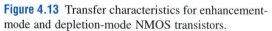

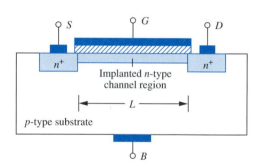

Figure 4.13 Transfer characteristics for enhancement-mode and depletion-mode NMOS transistors.

Figure 4.14 Cross section of a depletion-mode NMOS transistor.

4.8 BODY EFFECT OR SUBSTRATE SENSITIVITY

Thus far, it has been assumed that the source-bulk voltage v_{SB} is zero. With $v_{SB} = 0$, the MOSFET behaves as if it were a three-terminal device. We will find many circuits, however, in which the bulk and source of the MOSFET must be connected to different voltages so that $v_{SB} \neq 0$. A non zero value of v_{SB} affects the *i-v* characteristics of the MOSFET by changing the value of the threshold voltage. This effect is called **substrate sensitivity,** or

body effect, and can be modeled by

$$V_{TN} = V_{TO} + \gamma\left(\sqrt{v_{SB} + 2\phi_F} - \sqrt{2\phi_F}\right) \tag{4.29}$$

where V_{TO} = zero-substrate-bias value for V_{TN} (V)
γ = **body-effect parameter** ($\sqrt{V}$)
$2\phi_F$ = **surface potential parameter** (V)

For typical NMOS transistors,

$$-5\text{ V} \le V_{TO} \le +5\text{ V}$$

$$0 \le \gamma \le 3\sqrt{V}$$

$$0.3\text{ V} \le 2\phi_F \le 1\text{ V}$$

We will use $2\phi_F = 0.6$ V throughout the rest of this text, and Eq. (4.29) will be represented as:

$$V_{TN} = V_{TO} + \gamma\left(\sqrt{v_{SB} + 0.6} - \sqrt{0.6}\right) \tag{4.30}$$

Figure 4.15 plots an example of the threshold-voltage variation with source-bulk voltage for an NMOS transistor, with $V_{TO} = 1$ V and $\gamma = 0.75\sqrt{V}$. We see that $V_{TN} = V_{TO}$ for $v_{SB} = 0$, and the value of V_{TN} more than doubles for $v_{SB} = 5$ V. In a later chapter, we will see that this behavior has a profound effect on the design of MOS logic circuits.

> **EXERCISE:** Calculate the threshold voltage for the MOSFET of Fig. 4.15 for source-bulk voltages of 0 V, 1.5 V, and 3 V.
>
> **ANSWER:** 1.00 V; 1.51 V; 1.84 V

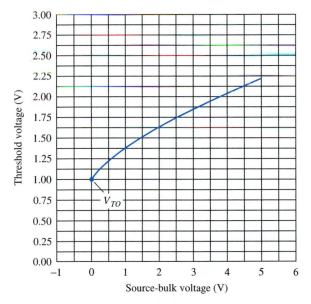

Figure 4.15 Threshold variation with source-bulk voltage for an NMOS transistor, with $V_{TO} = 1$ V, $2\phi_F = 0.6$ V and $\gamma = 0.75\sqrt{V}$.

4.9 PMOS TRANSISTORS

MOS transistors with *p*-type channels (PMOS transistors) can also easily be fabricated. In fact, the first commercial MOS transistors and integrated circuits used PMOS devices because it was easier to control the fabrication process of the PMOS technology. The PMOS device is fabricated by forming *p*-type source and drain regions in an *n*-type substrate, as depicted in the device cross section in Fig. 4.16. The qualitative behavior of the transistor is essentially the same as that of NMOS devices except that the normal voltage and current polarities are reversed. The normal directions of current in the **PMOS transistor** are indicated in Fig. 4.16. A negative voltage on the gate relative to the source ($v_{GS} < 0$ or $v_{SG} > 0$) is required to attract holes and create a *p*-type inversion layer in the channel region. In order to initiate conduction in the enhancement-mode PMOS transistor, the gate-source voltage must be more negative than the threshold voltage of the *p*-channel device, denoted by V_{TP}. To keep the source-substrate and drain-substrate junctions reverse-biased, v_{SB} and v_{DB} must also be less than zero. This requirement is satisfied by $v_{SD} \geq 0$ ($v_{DS} \leq 0$).

An example of the output characteristic for an enhancement-mode PMOS transistor is given in Fig. 4.17. For $v_{GS} \geq V_{TP} = -1$ V ($v_{SG} \leq -V_{TP} = +1$ V), the transistor is off. For more positive values of v_{SG}, the drain current increases in magnitude.

PMOS Transistor Mathematical Model Summary

The mathematical model for the PMOS transistor is summarized below in Eqs. (4.31) through (4.35). For all regions,

$$K_p = \mu_p C''_{ox} \frac{W}{L} \qquad i_G = 0 \text{ and } i_B = 0 \tag{4.31}$$

Cutoff region : $i_{SD} = 0 \qquad$ for $v_{SG} \leq -V_{TP}$ ($v_{GS} \geq V_{TP}$)   (4.32)

Linear region :

$$i_{SD} = K_p \left(v_{SG} + V_{TP} - \frac{v_{SD}}{2} \right) v_{SD} \qquad \text{for } v_{SG} + V_{TP} \geq v_{SD} \geq 0 \tag{4.33}$$

Saturation region :

$$i_{SD} = \frac{K_p}{2} (v_{SG} + V_{TP})^2 (1 + \lambda v_{SD}) \qquad \text{for } v_{SD} \geq (v_{SG} + V_{TP}) \geq 0 \tag{4.34}$$

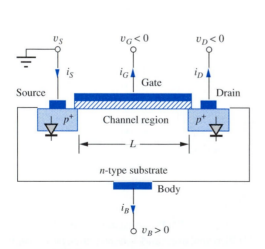

Figure 4.16 Cross section of an enhancement-mode PMOS transistor.

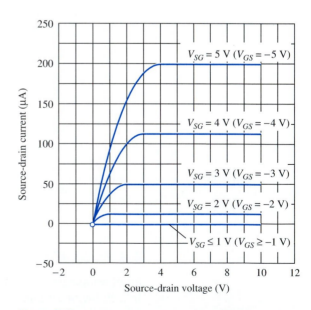

Figure 4.17 Output characteristics for a PMOS transistor with $V_{TP} = -1$ V.

Threshold voltage :

$$V_{TP} = V_{TO} - \gamma\left(\sqrt{v_{BS} + 2\phi_F} - \sqrt{2\phi_F}\right) \tag{4.35}$$

For the enhancement-mode PMOS transistor, $V_{TP} < 0$. Depletion-mode PMOS devices can also be fabricated; $V_{TP} \geq 0$ for these devices.

The drain-current expressions for the PMOS transistor are similar to those for the NMOS transistor except that the drain-current direction is reversed and the values of v_{SG}, v_{SD}, and v_{BS} are now positive. Two signs must be changed in the expressions, however. The parameter γ is normally specified as a positive value for both n- and p-channel devices, and a positive bulk-source potential will cause the PMOS threshold voltage to become more negative. The sign on the threshold voltage must also be changed.

An important parametric difference appears in the expressions for K_p and K_n. In the PMOS device, the charge carriers in the channel are holes, and so current is proportional to hole mobility μ_p. Hole mobility is typically only 40 percent of the electron mobility, so for a given set of voltage conditions, the PMOS device will conduct only 40 percent of the current of the NMOS device!

4.10 MOSFET CIRCUIT SYMBOLS AND MODEL SUMMARY

The circuit symbols for four different types of MOSFETs are given in Fig 4.18: (a) NMOS enhancement-mode, (d) PMOS enhancement-mode, (b) NMOS depletion-mode, and (e) PMOS depletion-mode transistors. The four terminals of the MOSFET are identified as source (S), drain (D), gate (G), and bulk (B). The arrow on the **bulk terminal** indicates the polarity of the bulk-drain, bulk-source, and bulk-channel diodes; the arrow points inward for an NMOS device and outward for the PMOS transistor. Enhancement-mode devices are indicated by the dashed line in the channel region, whereas depletion-mode devices have a solid line, indicating the existence of the built-in channel. The gap between the gate and channel represents the insulating oxide region.

In many circuit applications, the MOSFET substrate terminal is connected to its source. The shorthand notation in Fig. 4.18(c) and (f) is often used to represent these three-terminal MOSFETs. The arrow identifies the source terminal and points in the direction of normal positive current.

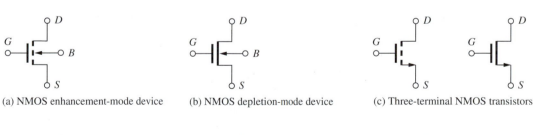

(a) NMOS enhancement-mode device   (b) NMOS depletion-mode device   (c) Three-terminal NMOS transistors

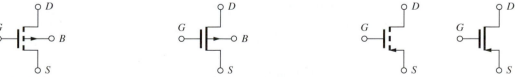

(d) PMOS enhancement-mode device   (e) PMOS depletion-mode device   (f) Three-terminal PMOS transistors

Figure 4.18 IEEE Standard MOS transistor circuit symbols.

The symmetry of MOS devices should be noted in the cross sections of Figs. 4.3 and 4.16. The terminal that is acting as the source is actually determined by the applied potentials. Current can traverse the channel in either direction, depending on the applied voltage. For NMOS transistors, the $n+$ region that is at the highest voltage will be the drain, and the one at the lowest voltage will be the source. For the PMOS transistor, the $p+$ region at the lowest voltage will be the drain, and the one at the highest voltage will be the source. In later chapters, we shall see that this symmetry is highly useful in certain applications, particularly dynamic random-access memory (DRAM) circuits.

Mathematical Model Summary

A summary of the mathematical models for both the NMOS and PMOS transistors is given below. The terminal voltages and currents are defined in Fig. 4.19.

NMOS Transistor Model Summary

For all regions,

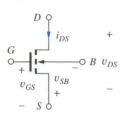

(a) NMOS transistor

$$K_n = K'_n \frac{W}{L} = \mu_n C''_{ox} \frac{W}{L} \qquad i_G = 0 \text{ and } i_B = 0 \tag{4.36}$$

Cutoff region :
$$i_{DS} = 0 \qquad \text{for } v_{GS} \leq V_{TN} \tag{4.37}$$

Linear region :

$$i_{DS} = K_n \left(v_{GS} - V_{TN} - \frac{v_{DS}}{2} \right) v_{DS} \qquad \text{for } v_{GS} - V_{TN} \geq v_{DS} \geq 0 \tag{4.38}$$

Saturation region :

$$i_{DS} = \frac{K_n}{2} (v_{GS} - V_{TN})^2 (1 + \lambda v_{DS}) \qquad \text{for } v_{DS} \geq (v_{GS} - V_{TN}) \geq 0 \tag{4.39}$$

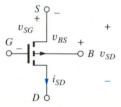

(b) PMOS transistor

Figure 4.19 (a) NMOS and (b) PMOS transistor circuit symbols.

Threshold voltage :

$$V_{TN} = V_{TO} + \gamma \left(\sqrt{v_{SB} + 2\phi_F} - \sqrt{2\phi_F} \right) \tag{4.40}$$

PMOS Transistor Model Summary

For all regions,

$$K_p = K'_p \frac{W}{L} = \mu_p C''_{ox} \frac{W}{L} \qquad i_G = 0 \text{ and } i_B = 0 \tag{4.41}$$

Cutoff region :
$$i_{SD} = 0 \qquad \text{for } v_{SG} \leq -V_{TP} \tag{4.42}$$

Linear region :

$$i_{SD} = K_p \left(v_{SG} + V_{TP} - \frac{v_{SD}}{2} \right) v_{SD} \qquad \text{for } v_{SG} + V_{TP} \geq v_{SD} \geq 0 \tag{4.43}$$

Saturation region :

$$i_{SD} = \frac{K_p}{2} (v_{SG} + V_{TP})^2 (1 + \lambda v_{SD}) \qquad \text{for } v_{SD} \geq (v_{SG} + V_{TP}) \geq 0 \tag{4.44}$$

Threshold voltage :

$$V_{TP} = V_{TO} - \gamma \left(\sqrt{v_{BS} + 2\phi_F} - \sqrt{2\phi_F} \right) \tag{4.45}$$

Table 4.1 summarizes the threshold-voltage values for the four types of NMOS and PMOS transistors.

T a b l e 4.1		
Categories of MOS Transistors		
	NMOS Device	**PMOS Device**
Enhancement-mode	$V_{TN} > 0$	$V_{TP} < 0$
Depletion-mode	$V_{TN} \leq 0$	$V_{TP} \geq 0$

4.11 BIASING THE MOSFET

We have found that the MOSFET has three primary regions of operation: cutoff, linear, and saturation. For circuit applications, we want to establish a well-defined **quiescent operating point, or Q-point,** for the MOSFET in a particular region of operation. The Q-point for the MOSFET is represented by the dc values (I_{DS}, V_{DS}) that locate the operating point on the MOSFET output characteristics. For binary logic circuits, the Q-point is usually set to be in either the cutoff or the linear regions. For analog circuits, the Q-point is most often located in the saturation region, the region in which relatively high voltage gain can be achieved.

For hand analysis and design of Q-points, channel-length modulation is usually ignored by assuming $\lambda = 0$. A review of Fig. 4.11 indicates that including λ changes the drain current by 5 to 10 percent. Generally, we do not know the values of transistor parameters to this accuracy, and the tolerances on the bias elements are typically 5 to 10 percent as well. Thus, neglecting λ will not significantly affect the validity of our analysis. On the other hand, we will later see that λ plays an extremely important role in limiting the gain of analog amplifier circuits, and the effect of λ must often be included in the analysis of these circuits.

We now look at basic circuits for biasing the MOSFET. A simple circuit including an NMOS transistor is shown in Fig. 4.20, in which a dc voltage source V_{GG} is used to establish a fixed gate-source bias for the MOSFET, and source V_{DD} supplies drain current to the NMOS transistor through resistor R_L.

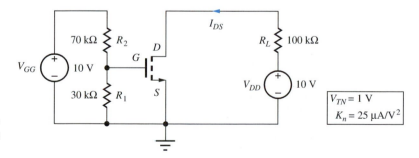

Figure 4.20 Constant gate-voltage bias using a voltage divider.

EXAMPLE 4.1: We can find the Q-point using the mathematical model for the NMOS transistor. To simplify the analysis, we replace the gate-bias network consisting of

V_{GG}, R_1, and R_2 with its Thévenin equivalent circuit in Fig. 4.21, in which

$$V_{EQ} = \frac{R_1}{R_1 + R_2} V_{GG} \quad \text{and} \quad R_{EQ} = \frac{R_1 R_2}{R_1 + R_2} \qquad (4.46)$$

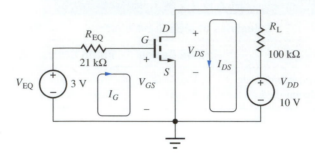

Figure 4.21 Simplified MOS-FET bias circuit.

We can determine the Q-point by applying Kirchhoff's voltage law (KVL) to the loops containing V_{GS} and V_{DS}:

$$V_{EQ} = I_G R_{EQ} + V_{GS}$$
$$V_{DD} = I_{DS} R_L + V_{DS} \qquad (4.47)$$

We know for the MOSFET, however, that $I_G = 0$ so that $V_{GS} = V_{EQ} = 3$ V.

To find I_{DS}, we must assume a region of operation, determine the Q-point, and then see if the resulting Q-point is consistent with the assumed region of operation. Let us assume that the MOSFET is saturated. This choice simplifies the mathematics because I_{DS} is independent of V_{DS}. Then,

$$I_{DS} = \frac{K_n}{2}(V_{GS} - V_{TN})^2 = \frac{25 \times 10^{-6}}{2} \frac{\mu A}{V^2}(3-1)^2\ V^2 = 50\ \mu A$$

and

$$V_{DS} = 10\ V - (50 \times 10^{-6}\ A)(10^5\ \Omega) = 5\ V$$
$$V_{GS} - V_{TN} = 2\ V$$

We see that V_{DS} exceeds $V_{GS} - V_{TN}$ so that the transistor is indeed saturated. Thus, the Q-point is (50 μA, 5 V), with $V_{GS} = 3$ V. ◆

EXERCISE: Find the Q-point for the circuit in Fig. 4.21 if R_L is changed to 50 kΩ.

ANSWER: (50.0 μA, 7.50 V)

EXERCISE: Find the Q-point for the circuit in Fig. 4.21 if $R_1 = 27$ kΩ, $R_2 = 75$ kΩ, and $R_L = 100$ kΩ.

ANSWER: (33.9 μA, 6.61 V)

EXAMPLE 4.2: The Q-point for the MOSFET circuit in Fig. 4.20 can also be found graphically with a load-line method very similar to the one used for analysis of diode circuits. The second expression in Eq. (4.47) represents the load line for this MOSFET circuit:

$$V_{DD} = I_{DS}R_L + V_{DS}$$

or
$$10 = 10^5 I_{DS} + V_{DS} \qquad (4.48)$$

As for the diode circuits in Chapter 3, the load-line is constructed by finding two points on the line: For $V_{DS} = 0$, $I_{DS} = 100\ \mu A$, and for $I_{DS} = 0$, $V_{DS} = 10$ V. The resulting line is drawn on the output characteristics of the MOSFET in Fig. 4.22.

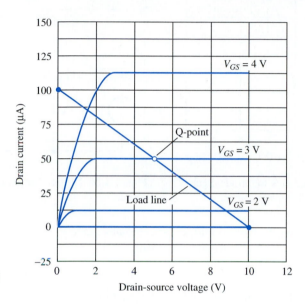

Figure 4.22 Load line for the circuit in Figs. 4.20 and 4.21.

The family of NMOS curves intersects the load line at many different points (actually infinitely many). The gate-source voltage is the parameter that determines which of the intersection points is the actual Q-point. In this circuit, we already found $V_{GS} = 3$ V; the Q-point is indicated by the circle in the Fig. 4.22. Reading the values from the graph yields $V_{DS} = 5$ V and $I_{DS} = 50\ \mu A$. This is the same Q-point that we found using our mathematical model for the MOSFET. We see from the graph that the Q-point is in the saturation region of the transistor's output characteristics. ◆

EXERCISE: Draw the new load line and find the Q-point if R_L is changed to 66.7 kΩ.

ANSWER: (50.0 μA, 6.67 V)

EXAMPLE 4.3: One important application of the MOSFET (as well as other electronic devices) is as an electronic current source. The *i-v* characteristic of an ideal current source is shown in Fig. 4.23, in which the ideal source provides a constant output current regardless of the polarity of the voltage across the source.

The output characteristics of an NMOS transistor with a fixed gate-source bias $V_{GS} = 3$ V is also given in Fig. 4.23. If the value of V_{DD} is chosen to be larger than the value needed to pinch off the MOSFET [in this case, $V_{DD} \geq (V_{GS} - V_{TN}) = 3 - 1 = 2$ V], then the output current will be constant at 50 μA. For $V_{DD} \geq 2$ V, the MOSFET represents an **electronic current source** with a 50-μA output current.

Figure 4.24 shows the NMOS transistor from Fig. 4.23 biased with a 3-V dc source. This simple two-terminal MOSFET circuit will behave as an electronic

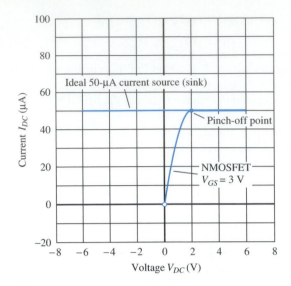

Figure 4.23 Output characteristics for an ideal current source and the MOSFET current source.

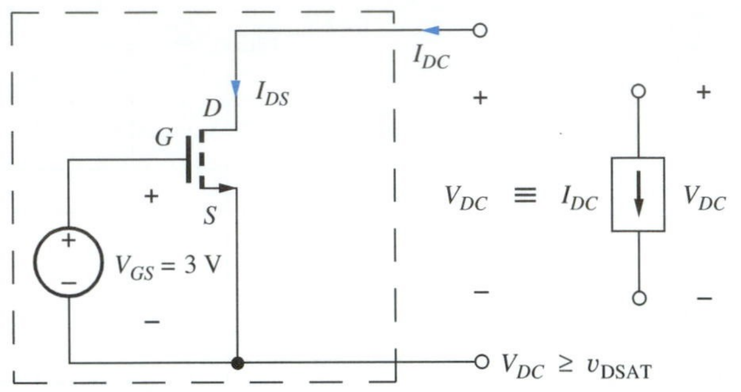

Figure 4.24 NMOS transistor as an electronic current source.

current source as long as the external voltage V_{DC} exceeds 2 V. This MOSFET circuit behaves as a current source with

$$I_{DC} = I_{DS} = 50\ \mu\text{A}$$

but over a more limited range of terminal voltage. Here, the current enters the source, and it is often referred to as a **current sink**. The fixed gate-source bias voltage in Fig. 4.24 can be derived from a larger voltage source V_{GG} using a resistive voltage divider similar to that in Fig. 4.20. ◆

EXERCISE: A current source with $I_{DC} = 25\ \mu\text{A}$ is needed, and an NMOS transistor is available with $K_n = 25\ \mu\text{A/V}^2$ and $V_{TN} = 1$ V. What is the required value of V_{GS}? What is the minimum value of V_{DS} needed for current source behavior?

ANSWERS: 2.41 V; 1.41 V

EXAMPLE 4.4: The circuit in Fig. 4.20 provides a fixed gate-source bias voltage to the transistor. Theoretically, this works fine. However, in practice the values of V_{TN} and K_n for the MOSFET will not be accurately known. In addition, we must be concerned about resistor- and power-supply tolerances as well as component value drift with time and temperature in an actual circuit.

The four-resistor bias circuit in Fig. 4.25(a) will stabilize the MOSFET Q-point in the face of many types of circuit parameter variations. A single voltage source V_{DD} is now used to supply both the gate-bias voltage and the drain current. In the equivalent circuit in Fig. 4.25(b), the voltage source has been split into two equal-valued sources, and we recognize that the gate-bias voltage is determined by V_{EQ} and R_{EQ}, exactly as in Figs. 4.20 and 4.21. A Thévenin transformation is applied to this circuit, resulting in the equivalent circuit given in Fig. 4.26. This is the final circuit to be analyzed.

Note that this circuit uses the three-terminal representation for the MOSFET, in which it is assumed that the bulk terminal is tied to the source. If the bulk termi-

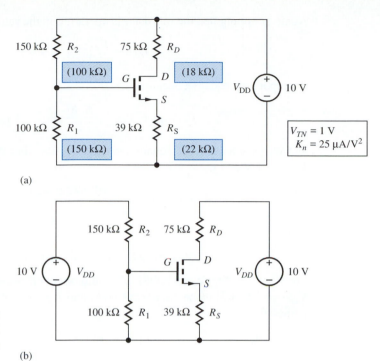

(a)

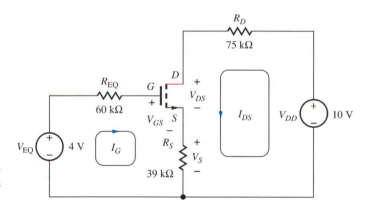

(b)

Figure 4.25 (a) Four-resistor bias network for a MOSFET. (b) Equivalent circuit with replicated sources.

Figure 4.26 Equivalent circuit for the four-resistor bias network.

nal were grounded, the analysis would become more complex because the threshold voltage would then be a function of the voltage developed at the source terminal of the device. This case will be investigated in more detail in Example 4.8.

To determine the Q-point for the circuit in Fig. 4.26, we write the following two loop equations:

$$V_{EQ} = I_G R_{EQ} + V_{GS} + (I_G + I_{DS})R_S \tag{4.49}$$

$$V_{DD} = I_{DS}R_D + V_{DS} + (I_G + I_{DS})R_S \tag{4.50}$$

Because we know that $I_G = 0$, these equations reduce to

$$V_{EQ} = V_{GS} + I_{DS}R_S \tag{4.51}$$

$$V_{DD} = I_{DS}(R_D + R_S) + V_{DS} \tag{4.52}$$

Again assuming that the transistor is operating in the saturation region with

$$I_{DS} = \frac{K_n}{2}(V_{GS} - V_{TN})^2 \tag{4.53}$$

the input loop equation becomes

$$V_{EQ} = V_{GS} + \frac{K_n R_s}{2}(V_{GS} - V_{TN})^2 \tag{4.54}$$

and we have a quadratic equation to solve for V_{GS}. For the values in Fig. 4.25 with $V_{TN} = 1$ V and $K_n = 25$ μA/V^2,

$$4 = V_{GS} + \frac{(25 \times 10^{-6})(3.9 \times 10^4)}{2}(V_{GS} - 1)^2 \tag{4.55}$$

and

$$V_{GS}^2 + 0.05V_{GS} - 7.21 = 0 \qquad \text{for which} \qquad V_{GS} = \pm 2.66 \text{ V} \tag{4.56}$$

For $V_{GS} = -2.66$ V, the MOSFET would be cut off because $v_{GS} < V_{TN}$. Therefore, $V_{GS} = +2.66$ V is the answer we seek, and $I_{DS} = 34.4$ μA using Eq. (4.53). V_{DS} is then found to be

$$10 = (34.4 \text{ μA})(75 \text{ kΩ} + 39 \text{ kΩ}) + V_{DS} \qquad \text{or} \qquad V_{DS} = 6.08 \text{ V}$$

We have

$$V_{DS} = 6.08 \text{ V}, V_{GS} - V_{TN} = 1.66 \text{ V} \qquad V_{DS} \geq (V_{GS} - V_{TN}) \; ✔$$

The saturation region assumption is consistent with the resulting Q-point: (34.4 μA, 6.08 V) with $V_{GS} = 2.66$ V. ◆

EXERCISE: Find the Q-point in the circuit in Fig. 4.26 if R_S is changed to 62 kΩ.

ANSWER: (25.2 μA, 6.55 V)

EXAMPLE 4.5: Let us redesign the four-resistor bias network in the previous example to increase the current while keeping V_{DS} approximately the same; the desired Q-point will be (100 μA, 6 V). By rearranging Eq. (4.52), we can see that the sum of R_D and R_S in the bias network of Fig. 4.26 is determined by the Q-point values:

$$R_D + R_S = \frac{V_{DD} - V_{DS}}{I_{DS}} = \frac{10 \text{ V} - 6 \text{ V}}{100 \text{ μA}} = 40 \text{ kΩ} \tag{4.57}$$

Equation (4.51) can be used to find the required value of R_S

$$R_S = \frac{V_{EQ} - V_{GS}}{I_{DS}} = \frac{V_S}{I_{DS}} \tag{4.58}$$

but we must first find the value of V_{GS}.

The gate-source voltage needed to establish $I_{DS} = 100$ μA can be found by rearranging the expression for the MOSFET drain current, Eq. (4.53):

$$V_{GS} = V_{TN} + \sqrt{\frac{2I_{DS}}{K_n}} = 1 \text{ V} + \sqrt{\frac{2(100 \text{ μA})}{25 \frac{\text{μA}}{\text{V}^2}}} = 3.83 \text{ V} \tag{4.59}$$

Substituting this value in Eq. (4.58) yields

$$R_S = \frac{4\text{ V} - 3.83\text{ V}}{100\ \mu\text{A}} = \frac{0.17\text{ V}}{100\ \mu\text{A}} = 1.7\text{ k}\Omega \qquad (4.60)$$

Although this represents a reasonable value of resistance, the voltage developed at the source of the MOSFET—only 0.17 V—is quite small and is highly sensitive to changes in V_{TN} or K_n. If we pick a larger value of V_{EQ}, and hence a larger value of V_S, the circuit design will be far less dependent on the device parameters. (See Probs. 4.43 and 4.44.)

To solve this problem, we can increase V_{EQ} from 4 to 6 V, which will also increase V_S by 2 V. The new value of R_S is

$$R_S = \frac{6\text{ V} - 3.83\text{ V}}{100\ \mu\text{A}} = \frac{2.17\text{ V}}{100\ \mu\text{A}} = 21.7\text{ k}\Omega \qquad (4.61)$$

From Appendix C, the nearest standard 5 percent resistor value is $R_S = 22$ kΩ and from Eq. (4.57), $R_D = 18$ kΩ, which happens to be a standard resistor value. The values of R_1 and R_2 must be modified to set V_{EQ} to 6 V. If we simply interchange the values of R_1 and R_2 in Fig. 4.25, we will have $V_{EQ} = 6$ V, with R_{EQ} remaining 60 kΩ. Our final design values, $R_1 = 150$ kΩ, $R_2 = 100$ kΩ, $R_S = 22$ kΩ, and $R_D = 18$ kΩ, are indicated by the shaded numbers in parentheses in Fig. 4.25(a). ◆

EXERCISE: Find the actual Q-point in the circuit in Fig. 4.25(a) for $R_1 = 150$ kΩ, $R_2 = 100$ kΩ, $R_S = 22$ kΩ, and $R_L = 18$ kΩ.

ANSWER: (99.1 μA, 6.04 V)

EXAMPLE 4.6: One possible bias circuit for a depletion-mode MOSFET device appears in Fig. 4.27. Because the depletion-mode transistor conducts with $V_{GS} = 0$, a separate gate-bias voltage is not required. This is an advantage offered by the depletion-mode device. Let us find the value of R_S required to achieve $I_{DS} = 100\ \mu$A. In this case, we must determine the value of V_{GS} needed to establish the design value of I_{DS}.

Assuming saturation region operation,

$$V_{GS} = V_{TN} + \sqrt{\frac{2I_{DS}}{K_n}} = -3\text{ V} + \sqrt{\frac{2\,(100\ \mu\text{A})}{200\ \dfrac{\mu\text{A}}{\text{V}^2}}} = -2\text{ V} \qquad (4.62)$$

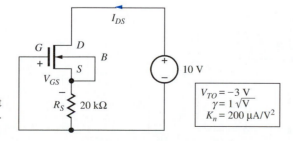

Figure 4.27 A bias circuit using an NMOS depletion-mode device.

Because we know that the gate current is zero, the input-loop equation yields

$$V_{GS} = -I_{DS}R_S \quad \text{or} \quad R_S = -\frac{V_{GS}}{I_{DS}} = -\frac{-2 \text{ V}}{100 \text{ μA}} = 20 \text{ kΩ} \quad (4.63)$$

The assumption of saturation region operation should be checked. The drain-source voltage is $V_{DS} = V_{DD} - V_S = 10 \text{ V} - 2 \text{ V} = 8 \text{ V}$, whereas $V_{GS} - V_{TN} = -2 \text{ V} - (-3 \text{ V}) = +1 \text{ V}$. Because $V_{DS} > (V_{GS} - V_{TN})$, our assumption was correct, and $R_S = 20 \text{ kΩ}$ will set the final Q-point to $(100 \text{ μA}, 8 \text{ V})$ with $V_{GS} = -2 \text{ V}$. ◆

EXERCISE: What is the Q-point in Fig. 4.27 if $V_{DD} = 15 \text{ V}$?

EXERCISE: Find the Q-point in the circuit in Fig. 4.27 if R_S is changed to 10 kΩ.

ANSWERS: $(100 \text{ μA}, 13 \text{ V})$; $(170 \text{ μA}, 8.30 \text{ V})$

EXAMPLE 4.7: The NMOS transistor in Fig. 4.27 was connected as a three-terminal device. We now determine how the Q-point is altered when the substrate is connected as shown in Fig. 4.28. In this case, the source-bulk voltage $V_{SB} = -V_{GS}$, and we must solve the following set of three equations:

$$I_{DS} = \frac{K_n}{2}(V_{GS} - V_{TN})^2$$

$$V_{GS} = -I_{DS}R_S = -V_{SB} \quad (4.64)$$

$$V_{TN} = V_{TO} + \gamma\left(\sqrt{V_{SB} + 2\phi_F} - \sqrt{2\phi_F}\right)$$

Using the values in Fig. 4.28, these expressions become

$$V_{GS} = -(2 \times 10^4)I_{DS}$$

$$V_{SB} = +(2 \times 10^4)I_{DS}$$

$$V_{TN} = -3 + 1\left(\sqrt{V_{SB} + 0.6} - \sqrt{0.6}\right) \quad (4.65)$$

$$I_{DS} = 10^{-4}(V_{GS} - V_{TN})^2$$

Although it may be possible to solve these equations analytically, it will be more expedient to find the Q-point by iteration using the computer with a spreadsheet or MATLAB, or with a calculator. The expressions in (4.65) have been arranged in a

Figure 4.28 Bias circuit in which body effect must be considered.

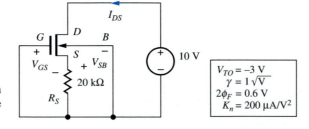

logical order for an iterative solution:

1. Estimate the value of I_{DS}.

2. Calculate the values of V_{GS} and V_{SB}.

3. Calculate the resulting value of V_{TN}.

4. Calculate I'_{DS} using the results of step 2 and step 3, and compare to the original estimate for I_{DS}.

5. If the calculated $I'_{DS} \neq$ estimated I_{DS}, then go back to step 1.

In this case, no specific method for choosing the improved estimate for I_{DS} is provided (although the problem could be structured to use Newton's method), but it is easy to converge to the solution after a few trials, using the power of the computer to do the calculations.

Table 4.2 shows the results of using a spreadsheet to iteratively find the solution to Eqs. (4.65) by trial and error. The first iteration sequence used by the author is shown; it converges to a drain current of 73.8 μA. Note in the second row that $I'_{DS} = 0$ because $V_{GS} < V_{TN}$. Care must be exercised to be sure that the spreadsheet equations are properly formulated to account for all regions of operation.

Table 4.2
Depletion-Mode Circuit Iteration

I_{DS}	V_{GS}	V_{TN}	$I_{DS'}$
1.00×10^{-4}	-2.000	-2.162	2.63×10^{-6}
2.00×10^{-4}	-4.000	-1.630	0.00
9.00×10^{-5}	-1.800	-2.225	1.81×10^{-5}
8.00×10^{-5}	-1.600	-2.291	4.78×10^{-5}
7.00×10^{-5}	-1.400	-2.360	9.22×10^{-5}
7.50×10^{-5}	-1.500	-2.325	6.81×10^{-5}
7.25×10^{-5}	-1.450	-2.343	7.97×10^{-5}
7.10×10^{-5}	-1.420	-2.353	8.71×10^{-5}
7.20×10^{-5}	-1.440	-2.346	8.21×10^{-5}
7.30×10^{-5}	-1.460	-2.339	7.73×10^{-5}
7.40×10^{-5}	-1.480	-2.332	7.27×10^{-5}
7.35×10^{-5}	-1.470	-2.336	7.50×10^{-5}
7.38×10^{-5}	-1.475	-2.334	7.38×10^{-5}

Now that the analysis is complete, we see that the presence of body effect in the circuit has caused the threshold voltage to increase from -3 V to -2.33 V and the drain current to decrease by approximately 26 percent. ◆

EXERCISE: Find the new drain current in the circuit in Fig. 4.28 if $\gamma = 0.75 \sqrt{V}$.

ANSWER: 79.2 μA.

EXAMPLE 4.8: The increase in threshold voltage of the MOSFET in Fig. 4.28 due to body effect has caused the current to be smaller than the original design value in Example 4.6. Let us choose a new design value for R_S that will set the drain-source current back to the original value of 100 μA.

The value of V_{GS} required to set $I_{DS} = 100 \ \mu A$ is

$$V_{GS} = V_{TN} + \sqrt{\frac{2I_{DS}}{K_n}} = V_{TN} + \sqrt{\frac{2(100 \ \mu A)}{200 \ \frac{\mu A}{V^2}}} = V_{TN} + 1 \ V \qquad (4.66)$$

but for this circuit,

$$V_{SB} = I_{DS}R_S = -V_{GS} \qquad \text{and} \qquad V_{SB} = -V_{TN} - 1 \ V \qquad (4.67)$$

The threshold voltage is also related to V_{SB} through Eq. (4.29)

$$V_{TN} = V_{TO} + \gamma \left(\sqrt{v_{SB} + 2\phi_F} - \sqrt{2\phi_F} \right) \qquad (4.68)$$

Combining Eqs. (4.67) and (4.68) yields an expression for the source-bulk voltage:

$$-V_{SB} - 1 \ V = -3 + (1 \ \sqrt{V}) \left(\sqrt{V_{SB} + 0.6 \ V} - \sqrt{0.6 \ V} \right) \qquad (4.69)$$

By moving all the constants to the left-hand side of the equation and then squaring both sides, we obtain a quadratic equation for V_{SB}:

$$(2.78 - V_{SB})^2 = \left(\sqrt{V_{SB} + 0.6 \ V} \right)^2$$

$$V_{SB}^2 - 6.56V_{SB} + 7.13 = 0 \qquad (4.70)$$

The roots are $V_{SB} = 1.38 \ V$ or $5.18 \ V$. The larger value would cut off the device because $V_{GS} = -V_{SB}$, so V_{SB} must equal $1.38 \ V$. The new value of R_S can now be found based on Eq. (4.67):

$$R_S = \frac{V_{SB}}{I_{DS}} = \frac{1.38 \ V}{100 \ \mu A} = 13.8 \ k\Omega \qquad (4.71)$$

From Appendix C, the nearest standard 5 percent resistor value is $13 \ k\Omega$. Thus, the value of R_S must be reduced from $20 \ k\Omega$ to $13 \ k\Omega$ to compensate for the influence of the MOS body effect.

We have tacitly assumed that the MOSFET is saturated by our choice of model equations. Let us make a final check of the operating region: $V_{DS} = V_D - V_S = 10 \ V - 1.38 \ V = 8.72 \ V$ and $V_{GS} - V_{TN} = -1.38 \ V - (-3 \ V) = +1.62 \ V$. Thus $V_{DS} > V_{GS} - V_{TN}$ is satisfied, and our assumption was correct. ◆

EXERCISE: What is the actual drain current in the circuit in Fig. 4.28 for $R_S = 13 \ k\Omega$?

ANSWER: $104 \ \mu A$

EXAMPLE 4.9: Another important application for transistors is to provide electronic voltage sources. An example using an n-channel depletion-mode MOSFET is in Fig. 4.29. In this circuit, the goal is for the MOSFET to supply a constant output voltage even though the load current i_L may change, which requires a low Thévenin equivalent resistance in the source. We first find the output voltage v_L, and then calculate the output resistance for the circuit in Fig. 4.29.

The circuit of Fig. 4.29 has been simplified to that in Fig. 4.30 using a Thévenin transformation of the gate-bias network. Applying KVL to the input loop and remembering that $i_G = 0$ yields:

$$5 = 73,000i_G + v_{GS} + v_L \qquad \text{or} \qquad v_L = 5 - v_{GS} \qquad (4.72)$$

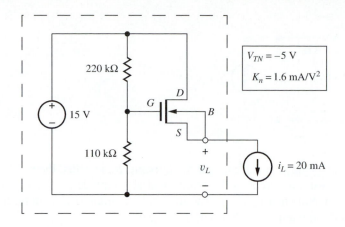

Figure 4.29 An electronic voltage source using a depletion-mode MOSFET.

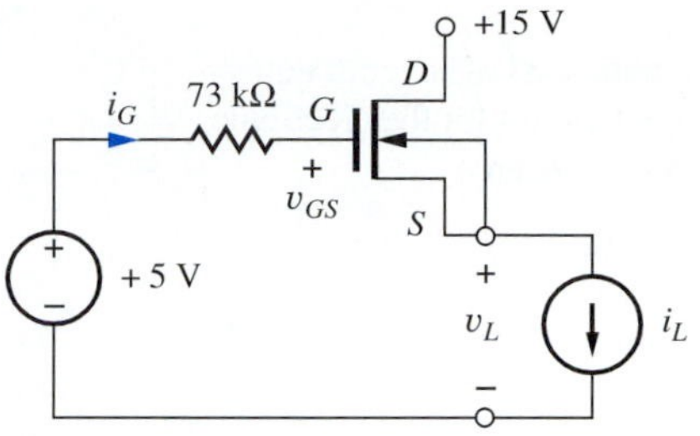

Figure 4.30 Circuit of Fig. 4.29 simplified using a Thévenin transformation.

(Because the load current and voltage may be changing with time, the circuit variables have been written in terms of total quantities.) In this circuit, i_{DS} is forced to be equal to 20 mA by the current source i_L. Assuming saturation region operation and solving Eq. (4.39) for V_{GS} (with $\lambda = 0$) gives

$$V_{GS} = V_{TN} + \sqrt{\frac{2I_{DS}}{K_n}} \qquad (4.73)$$

Evaluating Eq. (4.73) yields

$$V_{GS} = -5 + \sqrt{\frac{2(2.0 \times 10^{-2})}{1.6 \times 10^{-3}}} = 0 \text{ V}$$

and

$$v_L = 5 \text{ V}$$

Before we are done, we need to check the operating region assumption. For this circuit, $V_{GS} - V_{TN} = +5$ V and $V_{DS} = 15 - 5 = 10$ V. Because $V_{DS} > V_{GS} - V_{TN}$, the operating region assumption was correct. Thus, for a load current of 20 mA, this circuit produces an output voltage of 5 V.

Now let us investigate the behavior of the circuit for small changes in i_L. The output resistance of this circuit can be defined as

$$R_o = \left.\frac{\partial v_L}{\partial i_L}\right|_{Q-\text{point}} \qquad (4.74)$$

Using Eqs. (4.72) and (4.73) the expression for the output voltage can be written

$$v_L = 5 - v_{GS} = 5 - V_{TN} - \sqrt{\frac{2i_{DS}}{K_n}} \qquad (4.75)$$

and taking the derivative of this expression (with $i_L = i_{DS}$) as defined in Eq. (4.74):

$$R_o = \frac{1}{2}\left.\sqrt{\frac{2}{K_n i_{DS}}}\right|_{Q-\text{point}} = \frac{1}{2}\frac{(V_{GS} - V_{TN})}{I_{DS}} = \frac{1}{2}\frac{5 \text{ V}}{0.02 \text{ A}} = 125 \ \Omega \qquad (4.76)$$

The output resistance of this circuit is a relatively low value of 125 Ω.

An equivalent circuit representation for our electronic voltage source is given in Fig. 4.31. The value of R_o calculated using Eqs. (4.76) and (4.77) is valid only

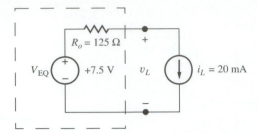

Figure 4.31 Thévenin equivalent circuit for the electronic voltage source.

for small changes in current near the Q-point. R_o is called the **small-signal output resistance** of this circuit. We explore small-signal modeling of circuits in great detail in Part III. Note that $V_{EQ} = 7.5$ V, not 5.0 V, in order to account for the voltage drop across R_o so that $v_L = 5$ V when $i_L = 20$ mA. ◆

EXERCISE: Use the model of Fig. 4.31 to find the output voltage v_L if i_L increases to 22 mA.

ANSWER: 4.75 V

EXERCISE: What value of K_n would be required to achieve $R_o = 10 \ \Omega$ in the circuit in Fig. 4.29?

ANSWER: 250 mA/V^2

EXAMPLE 4.10: An example of another type of bias circuit is given in Fig. 4.32, in which a PMOS transistor is biased using two resistors and a voltage source. Writing loop equations for the values of V_{SD} and V_{SG} yields

$$V_{SD} = 12 \text{ V} - (100 \text{ k}\Omega)I_{SD} \tag{4.77}$$

$$V_{SG} = V_{SD} - (1 \text{ M}\Omega)I_G \tag{4.78}$$

Because $I_G = 0$, $V_{SD} = V_{SG}$. Once again assuming saturation and using Eq. (4.44) with $\lambda = 0$, the first expression above yields

$$V_{SG} = 12 \text{ V} - (100 \text{ k}\Omega)\frac{100 \ \mu A}{2V^2}(V_{SG} - 2 \text{ V})^2$$

and $\qquad V_{SG} = 3.32 \text{ V}, 0.58 \text{ V}$

Because $-V_{TP} = 2$ V, $V_{SG} = 0.58$ V is not sufficient to turn on the PMOS transistor, so the answer must be $V_{SG} = 3.32$ V, which gives

$$I_{SD} = 87.1 \ \mu A \qquad \text{and} \qquad V_{SD} = 3.29 \text{ V}$$

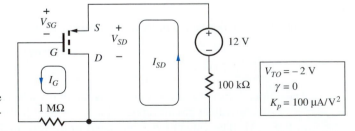

Figure 4.32 Another possible bias circuit for a MOS transistor.

We see that $V_{SD} = V_{SG}$ within round-off error. Also, $V_{SG} + V_{TP} = 1.29$ V and $V_{SD} > V_{SG} + V_{TP}$, so the assumption of saturation operation is correct. The final Q-point is (87.1 μA, 3.29 V).

It is worth remembering that an enhancement-mode device that is operating with $V_{GS} = V_{DS}$ (or $V_{SG} = V_{SD}$) will always be in saturation. It is easiest to see this by considering an NMOS device. For saturation, it is required that

$$V_{DS} \geq V_{GS} - V_{TN}$$

If $V_{GS} = V_{DS}$, this condition becomes

$$V_{DS} \geq V_{DS} - V_{TN}$$

which is always true if V_{TN} is a positive number, and $V_{TN} > 0$ corresponds to an NMOS enhancement-mode device. A similar argument holds true for enhancement-mode PMOS devices operating with $V_{SD} = V_{SG}$. ◆

EXERCISE: Find the Q-point of the PMOS transistor in Fig. 4.32 if $V_{TP} = -1$ V and $K_p = 500$ μA/V^2.

ANSWER: (103 μA, 1.76 V)

EXAMPLE 4.11: In all the previous circuit examples, we found that the transistors were operating in the saturation region. The circuit in Fig. 4.33 is an example of circuit analysis involving the linear region of the device.

We want to determine the Q-point for the PMOSFET in Fig. 4.33. In this circuit we immediately see that $V_{SG} = 4$ V. Writing the output-loop equation in terms of I_{SD} gives

$$4 - V_{SD} = 1600\, I_{SD} \tag{4.79}$$

Let us first assume that the transistor is operating in the saturation region as we have done in the past examples. Therefore, the MOSFET current is given by

$$I_{SD} = \frac{250\ \mu A}{2\ V^2}[4\ V + (-1\ V)]^2 = 1.13\ mA \tag{4.80}$$

and $V_{SD} = 2.19$ V. However, $V_{SG} + V_{TP} = 4 + (-1) = 3$ V. Because $V_{SG} + V_{TP} > V_{SD}$ (3 V > 2.19 V), the assumption of saturation region operation is incorrect, and we must try again.

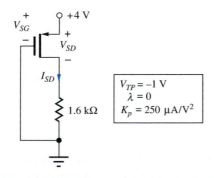

Figure 4.33 A linear region bias problem.

Substituting the linear region expression in Eq. (4.79) yields:

$$4 - V_{SD} = 1600 \, K_p \left(V_{SG} + V_{TP} - \frac{V_{SD}}{2} \right) V_{SD} \tag{4.81}$$

or

$$4 - V_{SD} = (1600)\left(\frac{250 \,\mu\text{A}}{\text{V}^2}\right)\left[4 + (-1) - \frac{V_{SD}}{2} \right] V_{SD}$$

and after rearranging

$$V_{SD}^2 - 11 V_{SD} + 20 = 0 \tag{4.82}$$

Finding the roots of the quadratic equation yields two possibilities:

$$V_{SD} = \cancel{8.7\,\text{V}}, 2.3 \text{ V}$$

The first voltage, 8.7, exceeds the magnitude of the power supply voltage and is not a possible result. So $V_{SD} = 2.3$ V and

$$I_{SD} = 250 \, \frac{\mu\text{A}}{\text{V}^2} \left[4 \text{ V} + (-1 \text{ V}) - \frac{2.3 \text{ V}}{2} \right] (2.3 \text{ V}) = 1.06 \text{ mA}$$

Using this value of current to double check our answer:

$$V_{SD} = 4 - 1600 \, I_{DS} = 2.3 \text{ V}$$

and checking the region of operation:

$$V_{SG} + V_{TP} = 4 \text{ V} + (-1 \text{ V}) = 3 \text{ V} \qquad \text{and} \qquad V_{SG} + V_{TP} > V_{SD}$$

Thus, the PMOS transistor in Fig. 4.33 is operating in the linear region at the Q-point (1.06 mA, 2.3 V).

The past eleven examples of bias circuits represent but a few of the many possible ways to bias a MOS transistor. Nevertheless, the techniques demonstrated are those we will need to analyze most of the circuits we will encounter. ◆

4.12 CAPACITANCES IN MOS TRANSISTORS

All electronic devices have internal capacitances that limit the high-frequency performance of the device. In logic applications, these capacitances limit the switching speed of the circuits, and in amplifiers, the capacitances limit the frequency at which useful amplification can be obtained.

NMOS Transistor Capacitances in the Linear Region

Figure 4.34 shows the various capacitances associated with the MOS field-effect transistor operating in the linear region, in which a channel connects source and drain. A simple model for these capacitances was presented by Meyer [1]. In the Meyer model, the total gate-channel capacitance C_{GC} is given by the product of the **gate-channel capacitance per unit area C_{ox}''** (F/cm^2 or F/m^2) and the area of the gate:

$$C_{GC} = C_{ox}'' WL \tag{4.83}$$

In the linear region, C_{GC} is partitioned into two equal parts. The gate-source capacitance C_{GS} and the gate-drain capacitance C_{GD} each consist of one-half of the gate-channel ca-

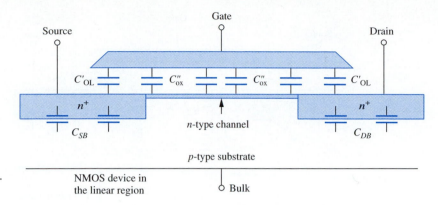

Figure 4.34 NMOS capacitances in the linear region.

pacitance plus the overlap capacitances between the gate-source or gate-drain diffusions:

$$C_{GS} = C'_{OL}W + \frac{C''_{ox}(WL)}{2} \quad \text{and} \quad C_{GD} = C'_{OL}W + \frac{C''_{ox}(WL)}{2} \quad (4.84)$$

The **overlap capacitance C'_{OL}** is normally specified as an oxide capacitance per unit width (for example, F/cm or F/m). The nonlinear capacitances of the reverse-biased pn junctions, indicated by the source-bulk and drain-bulk capacitances C_{SB} and C_{DB}, respectively, are shown between the source and drain diffusions and the substrate of the MOSFET. C_{SB} and C_{DB} will be present regardless of the region of operation.

Capacitances in the Saturation Region

In the saturation region of operation, depicted in Fig. 4.35, the portion of the channel beyond the pinch-off point disappears. The Meyer model for the values of C_{GS} and C_{GD} becomes:

$$C_{GS} = C'_{OL}W + \tfrac{2}{3}C''_{ox}(WL) \quad \text{and} \quad C_{GD} = C'_{OL}W \quad (4.85)$$

C_{GS} now contains two-thirds of C_{GC}, but C_{GC} no longer contributes to C_{GD}.

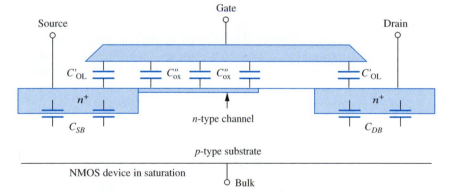

Figure 4.35 NMOS capacitances in the saturation region.

Capacitances in Cutoff

In the cutoff region of operation, the conducting channel region is gone. The values of C_{GS} and C_{GD} now contain only the overlap capacitances:

$$C_{GS} = C'_{OL}W \quad \text{and} \quad C_{GD} = C'_{OL}W \quad (4.86)$$

A small capacitance C_{GB} now appears between the gate and bulk terminal, as indicated in Fig. 4.36.

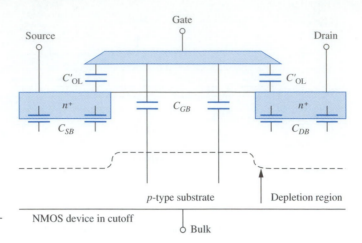

Figure 4.36 NMOS capacitances in the cutoff region.

It should be clear from Eqs. (4.82) to (4.85) that MOSFET capacitances depend on the region of operation of the transistor and are nonlinear functions of the voltages applied to the terminals of the device. In subsequent chapters we analyze the impacts of these capacitances on the behavior of digital and analog circuits. Complete models for these nonlinear capacitances are included in circuit simulation programs such as SPICE, and circuit simulation is an excellent tool for exploring the detailed effects of these capacitances.

4.13 THE JUNCTION FIELD-EFFECT TRANSISTOR (JFET)

Another type of field-effect transistor can be formed without the need for an insulating oxide by using *pn* junctions, as illustrated in Fig. 4.37. This device, the **junction field-effect transistor,** or **JFET,** consists of a *n*-type block of semiconductor material and two *pn* junctions that form the gate.

In the **n-channel JFET,** current again enters the channel region at the drain and exits from the source. The resistance of the channel region is controlled by changing the physical width of the channel through modulation of the depletion layers that surround the *pn* junctions between the gate and the channel. In its linear region, the JFET can be thought of simply as a voltage-controlled resistor with its channel resistance determined by

$$R_{\text{CH}} = \frac{\rho}{t}\frac{L}{W} \tag{4.87}$$

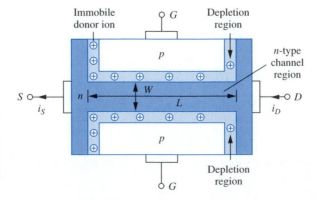

Figure 4.37 Basic *n*-channel JFET structure and important dimensions. (Note that for clarity the depletion layer in the *p*-type material is not indicated in the figure.)

where ρ = resistivity of channel region
$\quad\quad\quad L$ = channel length
$\quad\quad\quad W$ = width of channel between pn junction depletion regions
$\quad\quad\quad t$ = depth of channel into page

When a voltage is applied between the drain and source, the channel resistance determines the current through Ohm's law.

With no bias applied, as in Fig. 4.37, a resistive channel region exists connecting the drain and source. Application of a reverse bias to the gate-channel diodes will cause the depletion layers to widen, reducing the channel width and decreasing the current. Thus, the JFET is inherently a depletion-mode device—a voltage must be applied to the gate to turn the device off.

The JFET with Bias Applied

Figure 4.38(a) shows a JFET with 0 V on the drain and source and with the gate voltage $v_{GS} = 0$. The channel width is W. During normal operation, a reverse bias must be maintained across the pn junctions in order to provide isolation between the gate and channel. This reverse bias requires $v_{GS} \leq 0$ V.

In Fig. 4.38(b), v_{GS} has decreased to a negative value, and the depletion layers have increased in width, increasing the resistance of the channel region. The width of the channel has now decreased, with $W' < W$. Because the gate-source junction is reverse-biased, the

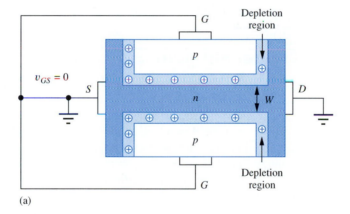

(a)

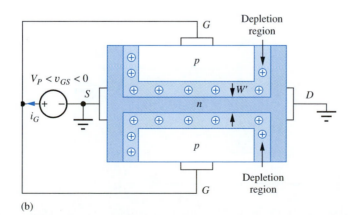

Figure 4.38 (a) JFET with zero gate-source bias. (b) JFET with negative gate-source voltage that is less negative than the pinch-off voltage V_P. Note $W' < W$.

(b)

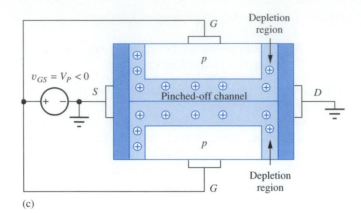

Figure 4.38 *(continued)*
(c) JFET at pinch-off with $v_{GS} = V_P$.

(c)

gate current will equal the reverse saturation current of the *pn* junction, normally a very small value, and it will be assumed that $i_G \approx 0$.

For more negative values of v_{GS}, the channel width continues to decrease, increasing the resistance of the channel region. Finally, the condition in Fig. 4.38(c) is reached for $v_{GS} = V_P$, the pinch-off voltage. V_P is the (negative) value of gate-source voltage for which the conducting channel region completely disappears. The channel becomes pinched-off when the depletion regions from the two *pn* junctions merge at the center of the channel. At this point, the resistance of the channel region has become infinitely large. Further increases in v_{GS} do not substantially affect the internal appearance of the device in Fig. 4.38(c). However, v_{GS} must not exceed the Zener breakdown voltage of the gate-channel junction.

JFET Channel with Drain-Source Bias

Figure 4.39(a) to (c) shows conditions in the JFET for increasing values of drain-source voltage v_{DS} and a fixed value of v_{GS}. For a small value of v_{DS}, as in Fig. 4.39(a), the resistive channel connects the source and drain; the JFET is operating in its linear region and the drain current will be dependent on the drain-source voltage v_{DS}. Assuming $i_G \approx 0$, the current entering the drain must exit from the source, as in the MOSFET. Note, however, that the reverse bias across the gate-channel junction is larger at the drain end of the channel than at the source end, and so the depletion layer is wider at the drain end of the device than at the source end.

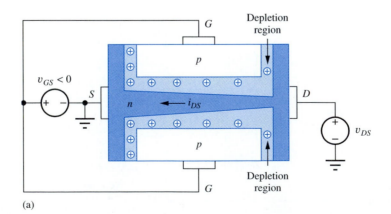

Figure 4.39 (a) JFET with small drain source.

(a)

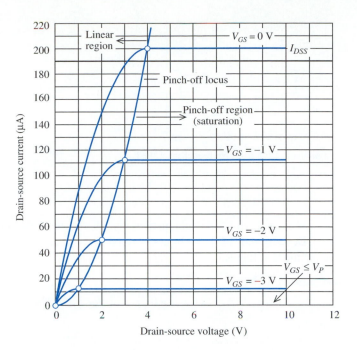

Figure 4.41 Output characteristics for a JFET with $I_{DSS} = 200$ μA and $V_P = -4$ V.

The *p*-Channel JFET

A **p-channel** version of the JFET can be fabricated by reversing the polarities of the *n*- and *p*-type regions in Fig. 4.37, as depicted in Fig. 4.42. As for the PMOSFET, the direction of current in the channel is opposite to that of the *n*-channel device, and the polarities of the operating bias voltages are reversed.

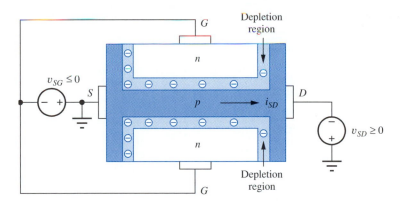

Figure 4.42 *p*-channel JFET with bias voltages.

Circuit Symbols and JFET Model Summary

The circuit symbols and terminal voltages and currents for *n*-channel and *p*-channel JFETs are presented in Fig. 4.43. The arrow identifies the polarity of the gate-channel diode. The JFET structures in Figs. 4.37 and 4.42 are inherently symmetric, as were those of the MOSFET, and the source and drain are actually determined by the voltages in the circuit in which the JFET is used. However, the arrow that indicates the gate-channel junction is often offset to indicate the preferred source terminal of the device.

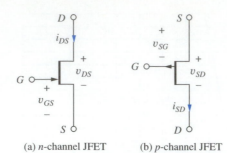

Figure 4.43 (a) *n*-channel and (b) *p*-channel JFET circuit symbols.

(a) *n*-channel JFET   (b) *p*-channel JFET

A summary of the mathematical models for the *n*-channel and *p*-channel JFETs follows. Because the JFET is a three-terminal device, the pinch-off voltage is independent of the terminal voltages.

n-Channel JFET

$$i_G \approx 0 \qquad \text{for } v_{GS} \leq 0 \ (V_P < 0) \tag{4.95}$$

Cutoff region:

$$i_{DS} = 0 \qquad \text{for } v_{GS} \leq V_P \tag{4.96}$$

Linear region:

$$i_{DS} = \frac{2I_{DSS}}{V_P^2}\left(v_{GS} - V_P - \frac{v_{DS}}{2}\right)v_{DS} \qquad \text{for } v_{GS} - V_P \geq v_{DS} \geq 0 \tag{4.97}$$

Saturation region:

$$i_{DS} = I_{DSS}\left(1 - \frac{v_{GS}}{V_P}\right)^2 (1 + \lambda v_{DS}) \qquad \text{for } v_{DS} \geq v_{GS} - V_P \geq 0 \tag{4.98}$$

p-Channel JFET

$$i_G \approx 0 \qquad \text{for } v_{SG} \leq 0 \ (V_P > 0) \tag{4.99}$$

Cutoff region:

$$i_{SD} = 0 \qquad \text{for } v_{SG} \leq -V_P \tag{4.100}$$

Linear region:

$$i_{SD} = \frac{2I_{DSS}}{V_P^2}\left(v_{SG} + V_P - \frac{v_{SD}}{2}\right)v_{SD} \qquad \text{for } v_{SG} + V_P \geq v_{SD} \geq 0 \tag{4.101}$$

Saturation region:

$$i_{SD} = I_{DSS}\left(1 + \frac{v_{SG}}{V_P}\right)^2 (1 + \lambda v_{SD}) \qquad \text{for } v_{SD} \geq v_{SG} + V_P \geq 0 \tag{4.102}$$

Overall, JFETs behave in a manner very similar to that of depletion-mode MOSFETs, and the JFET is biased in the same way as a depletion-mode MOSFET. In addition, most circuit designs must ensure that the gate-channel diode remains reverse-biased. This is not a concern for the MOSFET. In certain circumstances, however, forward bias of the JFET diode can actually be used to advantage. For instance, we know that the diode can be forward-biased by up to 0.4 to 0.5 V without significant conduction. In other applications, the gate diode can be used as a built-in diode clamp, and in some oscillator circuits, forward conduction of the gate diode is used to help stabilize the amplitude of the oscillation. This effect is explored in more detail during the discussion of oscillator circuits in Chapter 18.

The gate-source and gate-drain capacitances of the JFET are determined by the depletion-layer capacitances of the reverse-biased *pn* junctions forming the gate of the transistor and will exhibit a bias dependence similar to that described by Eq. (3.21) in Chapter 3.

SUMMARY

Chapter 4 discussed the structures and *i-v* characteristics of two types of field-effect transistors (FETs): the metal-oxide-semiconductor FET, or MOSFET, and the junction FET, or JFET. At the heart of the MOSFET is the MOS capacitor, formed by a metallic gate electrode insulated from the semiconductor by an insulating oxide layer. The potential on the gate controls the carrier concentration in the semiconductor region directly beneath the gate; three regions of operation of the MOS capacitor were identified: accumulation, depletion, and inversion. A MOSFET is formed when two *pn* junctions are added to the semiconductor region of the MOS capacitor. The junctions act as the source and drain terminals of the MOS transistor and provide a ready supply of carriers for the channel region of the MOSFET. The source and drain junctions must be kept reverse-biased at all times in order to isolate the channel from the substrate.

MOS transistors can be fabricated with either *n*-type or *p*-type channel regions and are referred to as NMOS or PMOS transistors, respectively. In addition, MOSFETs can be fabricated as either enhancement-mode or depletion-mode devices. For an enhancement-mode device, a gate-source voltage exceeding the threshold voltage must be applied to the transistor to establish a conducting channel between source and drain. In the depletion-mode device, in contrast, a channel is built into the device during its fabrication, and a voltage must be applied to the transistor's gate to quench conduction.

The JFET uses *pn* junctions to control the resistance of the conducting channel region. The gate-source voltage modulates the width of the depletion layers surrounding the gate-channel junctions and thereby changes the width of the channel region. A JFET can be fabricated with either *n*- or *p*-type channel regions, but because of its structure, the JFET is inherently a depletion-mode device.

Although structurally different, the *i-v* characteristics of MOSFETs and JFETs are very similar, and each type of FET has three regions of operation. In cutoff, a channel does not exist, and the terminal currents are zero. In the linear region of operation, the drain current in the FET depends on both the gate-source and drain-source voltages of the transistor. For small values of drain-source voltage, the transistor exhibits an almost linear relationship between its drain current and drain-source voltage. In the linear region, the FET can be used as a voltage-controlled resistor, in which the on-resistance of the transistor is controlled by the gate-source voltage of the transistor. Because of this behavior, the name *transistor* was developed as a contraction of "transfer resistor."

For values of drain-source voltage exceeding the saturation or pinch-off voltage, the drain current of the FET becomes almost independent of the drain-source voltage; that is, it "saturates." In this saturation or pinch-off region, the drain-source current exhibits a square-law dependence on the voltage applied between the gate and source terminals. Variations in drain-source voltage do cause small changes in drain current in saturation due to channel-length modulation.

Mathematical models for the *i-v* characteristics of both MOSFETs and JFETs were presented. The MOSFET is actually a four-terminal device and has a threshold voltage that depends on the source-bulk voltage of the transistor. Key parameters for the MOSFET include the transconductance parameters K_n or K_p, the zero-bias threshold voltage V_{TO}, body effect parameter γ, and channel-length modulation parameter λ as well as the width W and length L of the channel. The JFET was modeled as a three-terminal device with constant pinch-off voltage. Key parameters for the JFET include saturation current I_{DSS}, pinch-off voltage V_P, and channel-length modulation parameter λ.

Both the MOSFET and JFET are symmetrical devices. The source and drain terminals of the device are actually determined by the voltages applied to the terminals. For a given geometry and set of voltages, the n-channel transistor will conduct two to three times the current of the p-channel device because of the difference between the electron and hole mobilities in the channel.

A variety of examples of bias circuits were presented, and the mathematical model was used to find the quiescent operating point, or Q-point, for various types of MOSFETs. The Q-point represents the dc values of drain current and drain-source voltage: (I_D, V_{DS}). The i-v characteristics are often displayed graphically in the form of either the output characteristics, which plot i_{DS} versus v_{DS}, or the transfer characteristics, which graph i_{DS} versus v_{GS}. Examples of finding the Q-point using graphical load-line and iterative numerical analyses were discussed. The examples included application of the field-effect transistor as both electronic current and voltage sources.

The gate-source, gate-drain, drain-bulk, source-bulk, and gate-bulk capacitances of MOS transistors were discussed, and the Meyer model for the gate-source and gate-bulk capacitances was introduced. All the capacitances are nonlinear functions of the terminal voltages of the transistor. The capacitances of the JFET are determined by the capacitance of the reverse-biased gate-channel junctions and also exhibit a nonlinear dependence on the terminal voltages of the transistor.

Key Terms

Accumulation region
Body effect
Body-effect parameter γ
Body terminal (B)
Bulk terminal (B)
C_{GS}, C_{GD}, C_{GB}, C_{DB}, C_{SB}, C''_{ox}, C'_{OL}
Capacitance per unit width
Channel capacitance C_{GC}
Channel length L
Channel-length modulation
Channel-length modulation parameter λ
Channel region
Channel width W
Current sink
Depletion-mode device
Depletion region
Drain (D)
Electronic current source
Enhancement-mode device

Field-effect transistor (FET)
Gate (G)
Gate-channel capacitance
Inversion layer
Inversion region
Junction field-effect transistor (JFET)
Linear region
Metal-oxide-semiconductor field-effect transistor (MOSFET)
MOS capacitor
n-channel JFET
n-channel MOS (NMOS)
n-channel MOSFET
n-channel transistor
NMOSFET
NMOS transistor
On-resistance (R_{on})
Output characteristics
Overlap capacitance
Oxide thickness

p-channel JFET
p-channel MOS (PMOS)
Pinch-off region
Pinch-off point
Pinch-off voltage
PMOS transistor
Quiescent operating point
Q-point
Saturation region
Saturation voltage
Small-signal output resistance
Source (S)
Substrate sensitivity
Substrate terminal
Surface potential parameter $z\phi_F$
Threshold voltage
Transconductance parameter
Transfer characteristic
Triode region

Reference

Meyer, J. E. "MOS models and circuit simulations," *RCA Review,* vol. 32, pp. 42–63, March 1971.

Problems

Use the parameters in Table P4.1 as needed in the following problems.

T a b l e P4.1		
MOS Transistor Parameters		
	NMOS Device	**PMOS Device**
V_{TO}	+0.75 V	−0.75 V
γ	0.75 $\sqrt{\text{V}}$	0.5 $\sqrt{\text{V}}$
$2\phi_F$	0.6 V	0.6 V
K'	25 μA/V^2	10 μA/V^2

$\varepsilon_{ox} = 3.9\varepsilon_o$ and $\varepsilon_s = 11.7\varepsilon_o$ where $\varepsilon_o = 8.854 \times 10^{-14}$ F/cm

4.1–4.3 Characteristics of the MOS Capacitor and Transistor

4.1. Calculate K_n' for an NMOS transistor with $\mu_n = 500$ cm^2/V · s for an oxide thickness of (a) 50 nm, (b) 20 nm, (c) 10 nm.

4.2. Equation 4.2 indicates that the charge per unit length in the channel of a saturated transistor decreases as one proceeds from source to drain. However, it was argued that the current entering the drain terminal is equal to the current exiting from the source terminal. How can a constant current exist everywhere in the channel between the drain and source terminals if the first statement is indeed true?

4.4 Linear Region Characteristics of the NMOS Transistor

4.3. Identify the source, drain, gate, and bulk terminals, and find the current I in the transistors in Fig. P4.3. Assume $V_{TN} = 0.75$ V.

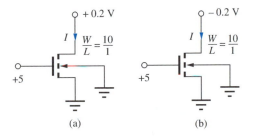

(a)   (b)

Figure P4.3

4.4. (a) What is the drain current in the transistor in Fig. P4.3(a) if the drain voltage is changed to 0.5 V? Assume $V_{TN} = 0.75$ V. (b) If the gate volt-age is changed to 3 V and the drain voltage remains at 0.2 V?

On-Resistance

4.5. What is the on-resistance of an NMOS transistor with $W/L = 100/1$ if $V_{GS} = 5$ V and $V_{TN} = 0.75$ V?

 4.6. (a) What is the W/L ratio required for an NMOS transistor to have an on-resistance of 1 kΩ when $V_{GS} = 5$ V and $V_{SB} = 0$? Assume $V_{TN} = 0.75$ V. (b) Repeat for a PMOS transistor with $V_{GS} = -5$ V and $V_{SB} = 0$. Assume $V_{TP} = -0.75$ V.

4.7. (a) Calculate the on-resistance for an NMOS transistor having $W/L = 100/1$ and operating with $V_{GS} = 5$ V and $V_{TN} = 0.75$ V. (b) Repeat for a similar PMOS transistor with $V_{GS} = -5$ V and $V_{TP} = -0.75$ V. (c) What W/L ratio is required for the PMOS transistor to have the same R_{on} as the NMOS transistor in (a)?

 4.8. The switch in a dc-to-dc boost converter (see Sec. 3.16) can easily be implemented with the NMOS transistor M_S in Fig. P4.8. Suppose that M_S must conduct a current $I_{DS} = 4$ A with $V_{DS} \leq 0.1$ V when it is on. What is the maximum on-resistance of M_S? If $V_G = 5$ V is used to turn on M_S and $V_{TN} = 2$ V, what is the minimum value of K_n required to achieve the necessary on-resistance?

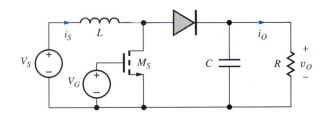

Figure P4.8

 **4.9. Simulate the boost converter (see Sec 3.16) in Fig. P4.8 with $V_S = 5$ V, $T_{on} = 15$ μS, $T_{off} = 5$ μS, $R = 20$ Ω, $C = 50$ μF, and $L = 0.75$ mH for $0 \leq t \leq 5$ mS. Assume M_S has $V_{TN} = 2$ V, $K_n = 15$ A/V^2, and V_G switches between 0 V and 5 V with 1 ns rise and fall times. Graph v_O, i_O, i_S, and the diode current as a function of time.

 4.10. The switch in a dc-to-dc buck converter (see Sec. 3.16) can easily be implemented with the PMOS transistor M_S in Fig. P4.10. Suppose M_S must conduct a current $I_{SD} = 0.5$ A with $V_{SD} \leq 0.1$ V when it is on. What is the maximum on-resistance of M_S?

If $V_G = 0$ V is used to turn on M_S with $V_S = 10$ V and $V_{TP} = -2$ V, what is the minimum value of K_p required to achieve the required on-resistance?

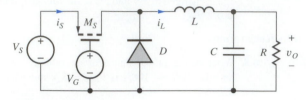

Figure P4.10

⌷S ****4.11.** Simulate the buck converter in Fig. P4.10 with $V_S = 10$ V, $T_{on} = 12.5$ μS, $T_{off} = 12.5$ μS, $R = 5$ Ω, $C = 2$ μF, and $L = 0.625$ mH for $0 \le t \le 5$ mS. Assume M_S has $V_{TP} = -2$ V, $K_p = 15$ A/V², and V_G switches between 10 V and 0 V with 1 ns rise and fall times. Graph v_O, i_L, i_S, and the diode current as a function of time.

4.5 Saturation of the *i-v* Characteristics

*4.12. The output characteristics for an NMOS transistor are given in Fig. P4.12. What are the values of K_n and V_{TN} for this transistor? Is this an enhancement-mode or depletion-mode transistor? What is W/L for this device?

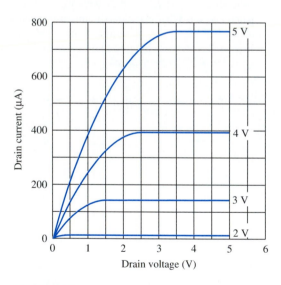

Figure P4.12

▯ 4.13. Add the $V_{GS} = 3.5$ V and $V_{GS} = 4.5$ V curves to the *i-v* characteristic of Fig. P4.12. What are the values of i_{DSAT} and v_{DSAT} for these new curves?

Regions of Operation

4.14. Find the region of operation and drain current in an NMOS transistor with $W/L = 10/1$ for $V_{TN} =$

0.75 V and (a) $V_{GS} = 2$ V and $V_{DS} = 0.2$ V, (b) $V_{GS} = 2$ V and $V_{DS} = 2.5$ V, (c) $V_{GS} = 0$ V and $V_{DS} = 4$ V.

4.15. Identify the region of operation of an NMOS transistor with $K_n = 250$ μA/V² and $V_{TN} = 1$ V for (a) $V_{GS} = 5$ V and $V_{DS} = 6$ V, (b) $V_{GS} = 0$ V and $V_{DS} = 6$ V, (c) $V_{GS} = 2$ V and $V_{DS} = 2$ V, (d) $V_{GS} = 1.5$ V and $V_{DS} = 0.5$ V, (e) $V_{GS} = 2$ V and $V_{DS} = -0.5$ V, (f) $V_{GS} = 3$ V and $V_{DS} = -6$ V.

4.16. Identify the source, drain, gate, and bulk terminals for the transistor in the circuit in Fig. P4.16. Assume $V_{DD} > 0$.

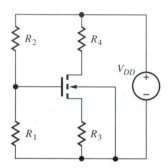

Figure P4.16

4.17. Identify the source, drain, gate, and bulk terminals for each transistor in the circuits in Fig. P4.17. Assume $V_{DD} > 0$.

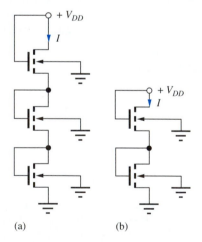

(a)   (b)

Figure P4.17

4.6 Channel-Length Modulation

4.18. (a) Calculate the drain current in an NMOS transistor if $K_n = 250$ μA/V², $V_{TN} = 1$ V, $\lambda = 0.025$ V⁻¹, $V_{GS} = 5$ V, and $V_{DS} = 6$ V. (b) Repeat assuming $\lambda = 0$.

4.19. (a) Calculate the drain current in an NMOS transistor if $K_n = 500\ \mu A/V^2$, $V_{TN} = 1.5$ V, $\lambda = 0.02\ V^{-1}$, $V_{GS} = 4$ V, and $V_{DS} = 5$ V. (b) Repeat assuming $\lambda = 0$.

4.20. (a) Find the drain current for the transistor in Fig. P4.20 if $\lambda = 0$. (b) Repeat if $\lambda = 0.025\ V^{-1}$.

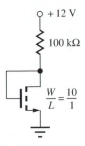

Figure P4.20

4.21. (a) Find the current I in Fig. P4.21 if $V_{DD} = 10$ V and $\lambda = 0$. (b) Repeat for $\lambda = 0.02\ V^{-1}$. Both transistors have $W/L = 10/1$.

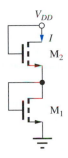

Figure P4.21

4.7 Transfer Characteristics and the Depletion-Mode MOSFET

4.22. An NMOS depletion-mode transistor is operating with $V_{DS} = V_{GS} > 0$. What is the region of operation for this device?

4.23. (a) Calculate the drain current in an NMOS transistor if $K_n = 250\ \mu A/V^2$, $V_{TN} = -2$ V, $\lambda = 0$, $V_{GS} = 5$ V, and $V_{DS} = 6$ V. (b) Repeat assuming $\lambda = 0.025\ V^{-1}$.

4.24. (a) Calculate the drain current in an NMOS transistor if $K_n = 200\ \mu A/V^2$, $V_{TN} = -3$ V, $\lambda = 0$, $V_{GS} = 0$ V, and $V_{DS} = 6$ V. (b) Repeat assuming $\lambda = 0.025\ V^{-1}$.

4.25. Find the current in the transistors in Fig. P4.25 if $V_{TN} = -2$ V.

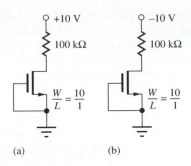

(a)   (b)

Figure P4.25

4.8 Body Effect or Substrate Sensitivity

4.26. Repeat Prob. 4.14 for $V_{SB} = 1.5$ V with the values from Table P4.1

4.27. (a) An NMOS transistor with $W/L = 5/1$ has $V_{TO} = 1$ V, $2\phi_F = 0.6$ V, and $\gamma = 0.7\ \sqrt{V}$. The transistor is operating with $V_{SB} = 3$ V, $V_{GS} = 2.5$ V, and $V_{DS} = 5$ V. What is the drain current in the transistor? (b) Repeat for $V_{DS} = 0.5$ V

4.28. An NMOS transistor with $W/L = 13.8/1$ has $V_{TO} = 1.5$ V, $2\phi_F = 0.75$ V, and $\gamma = 0.5\ \sqrt{V}$. The transistor is operating with $V_{SB} = 5$ V, $V_{GS} = 2$ V, and $V_{DS} = 5$ V. What is the drain current in the transistor?

4.29. A depletion-mode NMOS transistor has $V_{TO} = -1.5$ V, $2\phi_F = 0.75$ V, and $\gamma = 1.5\ \sqrt{V}$. What source-bulk voltage is required to change this transistor into an enhancement-mode device with a threshold voltage of $+0.75$ V?

*4.30. The measured body-effect characteristic for an NMOS transistor is given in Table P4.2. What are the best values of V_{TO}, γ, and $2\phi_F$ (in the least-squares sense; see Prob. 3.20) for this transistor?

T a b l e P4.2			
V_{SB} (V)	V_{TN} (V)	V_{SB} (V)	V_{TN} (V)
0	0.710	3.0	1.604
0.5	0.912	3.5	1.724
1.0	1.092	4.0	1.822
1.5	1.232	4.5	1.904
2.0	1.377	5.0	2.005
2.5	1.506		

4.9 PMOS Transistors

4.31. Calculate K_p' for a PMOS transistor with $\mu_p = 200\ cm^2/V \cdot s$ for an oxide thickness of (a) 50 nm, (b) 20 nm, (c) 10 nm.

*4.32. The output characteristics for a PMOS transistor are given in Fig. P4.32. What are the values of K_p and V_{TP} for this transistor? Is this an enhancement-mode or depletion-mode transistor? What is the value of W/L for this device?

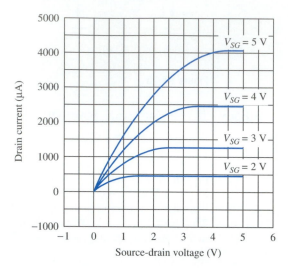

Figure P4.32

4.33. Find the region of operation and drain current in a PMOS transistor with $W/L = 10/1$ for $V_{BS} = 0$ V and (a) $V_{SG} = 1.1$ V and $V_{SD} = 0.2$ V, (b) $V_{SG} = 1.3$ V and $V_{SD} = 0.2$ V. (c) Repeat (a) and (b) for $V_{BS} = 1$ V.

4.34. Identify the source, drain, gate, and bulk terminals for the transistors in the two circuits in Fig. P4.34.

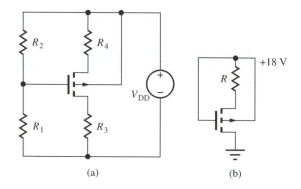

Figure P4.34

4.35. (a) What is the on-resistance and voltage V_O for the parallel combination of the NMOS ($W/L = 10/1$) and PMOS ($W/L = 25/1$) transistors in

Fig. P4.35 for $V_{in} = 0$ V? (b) For $V_{in} = 5$ V? This circuit is called a transmission gate.

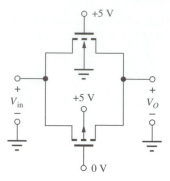

Figure P4.35

4.36. The PMOS transistor in Fig. P4.34(b) is conducting current. Is $V_{TP} > 0$ or < 0 for this transistor? Based on this value of V_{TP}, what type of transistor is in the circuit? Is the proper symbol used in this circuit for this transistor? If not, what should it be?

4.11 Biasing the MOSFET

4.37. An NMOS transistor is operating with $V_{SB} = 4$ V, $V_{GS} = 1.5$ V, and $V_{DS} = 4$ V. What are the region of operation and drain current in this device if $W/L = 20/1$?

4.38. Draw the load line for the circuit in Fig. P4.38 on the output characteristics in Fig. P4.12 and locate the Q-point. Assume $V_{DD} = +4$ V. What is the operating region of the transistor?

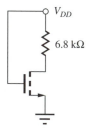

Figure P4.38

Load-Line Analysis

4.39. Draw the load line for the circuit in Fig. P4.39 on the output characteristics in Fig. P4.32 and locate the Q-point. What is the operating region of the transistor?

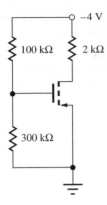

Figure P4.39

4.40. Draw the load line for the circuit in Fig. P4.40 on the output characteristics in Fig. P4.12 and locate the Q-point. Assume $V_{DD} = +6$ V. What is the operating region of the transistor?

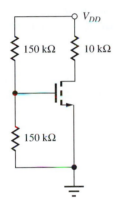

Figure P4.40

4.41. Find the Q-point for the transistors in the circuits in Fig. P4.41 if $V_{DD} = +12$ V.

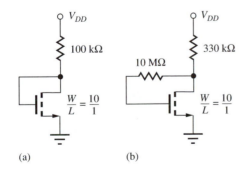

(a)   (b)

Figure P4.41

4.42. What is the minimum value of the supply voltage required to ensure saturation of the transistor in the circuit in (a) Fig. 4.27? (b) Fig. 4.28?

*4.43. Suppose the design of Example 4.5 were implemented with $V_{EQ} = 4$ V, $R_S = 1.7$ kΩ, and $R_D = 38.3$ kΩ. (a) What would be the Q-point if $K_n = 35$ µA/V^2? (b) If $K_n = 25$ µA/V^2 but $V_{TN} = 0.75$ V?

4.44. (a) Simulate the circuit in Example 4.4 and compare the results to the calculations. (b) Repeat for the circuit design in Example 4.5.

4.45. (a) Design a four-resistor bias network for an NMOS transistor to give a Q-point of (50 µA, 4 V) with $V_{DD} = 12$ V and $R_{EQ} \approx 250$ kΩ. Use the parameters from Table P4.1. (b) Repeat for a PMOS transistor.

4.46. (a) Design a four-resistor bias network for a PMOS transistor to give a Q-point of (1 mA, 5 V) with $V_{DD} = -15$ V and $R_{EQ} \geq 100$ kΩ. Use the parameters from Table P4.1. with $W/L = 20/1$. (b) Repeat for an NMOS transistor with $V_{DD} = +15$ V.

4.47. Design a bias network for a depletion-mode NMOS transistor to give a Q-point of (250 µA, 5 V) with $V_{DD} = 15$ V if $V_{TN} = -5$ V and $K_n = 1$ mA/V^2.

*4.48. Design a bias network for a depletion-mode NMOS transistor to give a Q-point of (2 mA, 5 V) with $V_{DD} = 15$ V if $V_{TN} = -2$ V and $K_n = 250$ µA/V^2. (You may wish to consider the four-resistor bias network).

Body Effect

4.49. Find the solution to Eqs. (4.65) using MATLAB. (b) Repeat for $\gamma = 0.75 \sqrt{V}$.

4.50. Find the solution to Eqs. (4.65) using a spreadsheet if $\gamma = 0.75 \sqrt{V}$. (b) Repeat for $\gamma = 1.25 \sqrt{V}$.

4.51. (a) Find the Q-point for the transistor in Fig. P4.51 if $V_{DD} = 12$ V, $R = 100$ kΩ, $W/L = 10/1$, and $\gamma = 0$. (b) Repeat for $\gamma = 1 \sqrt{V}$.

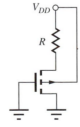

Figure P4.51

4.52. Find the Q-point for the transistor in Fig. P4.52 for $R_1 = 100$ kΩ, $R_2 = 220$ kΩ, $R_3 = 24$ kΩ, $R_4 = 12$ kΩ, and $V_{DD} = 12$ V. Assume that $V_{TO} = 1$ V, $\gamma = 0$, and $W/L = 5/1$.

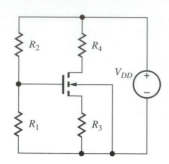

Figure P4.52

*4.53. (a) Repeat Prob. 4.52 with $\gamma = 0.75\sqrt{V}$. (b) Repeat Prob. 4.52 with $R_4 = 48$ kΩ.

4.54. (a) Use SPICE to simulate the circuit in Prob. 4.52 and compare the results to hand calculations. (b) Repeat for Prob. 4.53(a). (c) Repeat for Prob. 4.53(b).

4.55. (a) Find the Q-point for the transistor in Fig. P4.55(a) if $V_{DD} = -15$ V, $R = 75$ kΩ, and $W/L = 1/1$. (b) Find the Q-point for the transistor in Fig. P4.55(b) if $R = 75$ kΩ and $W/L = 1/1$.

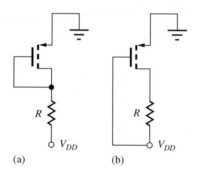

(a)   (b)

Figure P4.55

4.56. (a) Find the current I in Fig. P4.56 if $V_{DD} = 5$ V assuming that $\gamma = 0$, $V_{TO} = 1$ V, and the transis-

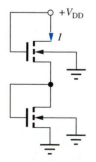

Figure P4.56

tors both have $W/L = 10/1$. (b) Repeat for $V_{DD} = 10$ V. *(c) Repeat (a) with $\gamma = 0.5\sqrt{V}$.

*4.57. (a) Find the current I and voltage V_O in Fig. P4.57 if $W/L = 20/1$ for both transistors and $V_{DD} = 10$ V. (b) What is the current if $W/L = 80/1$?

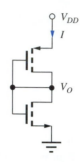

Figure P4.57

4.58. (a) Simulate the circuits in Fig. P4.55 with $V_{DD} = -15$ V and compare the Q-point results to hand calculations. (b) Repeat for Fig. P4.56 with $V_{DD} = 10$ V. (c) Repeat for Fig. P4.57 with $V_{DD} = 10$ V.

**4.59. (a) Find the current I in Fig. P4.59 assuming that $\gamma = 0$ and $W/L = 20/1$ for each transistor. (b) Repeat (a) for $W/L = 50/1$. **(c) Repeat (a) with $\gamma = 0.5\sqrt{V}$.

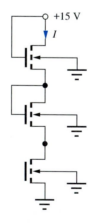

Figure P4.59

**4.60. (a) Simulate the circuit in Fig. P4.59 using SPICE, and compare the results to those in Prob. 4.59(a). (b) Repeat for Prob. 4.59(b). **(c) Repeat for Prob. 4.59(c).

**4.61. (a) Find the current I in Fig. P4.61 assuming that $\gamma = 0$ and $W/L = 40/1$ for each transistor. (b) Repeat (a) for $W/L = 75/1$ **(c) Repeat (a) with $\gamma = 0.5\sqrt{V}$.

+15 V

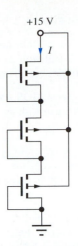

Figure P4.61

*4.62. (a) Simulate the circuit in Prob. 4.61(a) and compare the results to those in Prob. 4.61(a). (b) Repeat for Prob. 4.61(b). (c) Repeat for Prob. 4.61(c).

4.63. (a) Find the Q-point for the transistor in Fig. P4.63 if $R = 50$ kΩ. Assume that $\gamma = 0$ and $W/L = 20/1$. (b) What is the permissible range of values for R if the transistor is to remain in saturation?

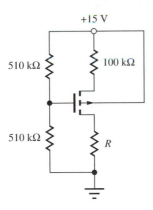

Figure P4.63

*4.64. (a) Find the Q-point for the transistor in Fig. P4.63 if $R = 50$ kΩ. Assume that $\gamma = 0.5\sqrt{V}$ and $W/L = 20/1$. (b) What is the permissible range of values for R if the transistor is to remain in saturation?

 4.65. Simulate the circuit of Prob. 4.64(a) and find the Q-point with $R = 100$ kΩ.

*4.66. The depletion-mode MOSFET in Fig. P4.66 is to be used as a current source. The transistor has $W/L = 25/1$, $V_{TO} = -5$ V, and $\gamma = 0.5\sqrt{V}$. What value

of R is required to set the current to 100 μA? What is the minimum value for V?

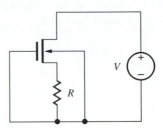

Figure P4.66

 4.67. The drain current in the circuit in Fig. 4.20 was found to be 50 μA. The gate-bias circuit in the example could have been designed with many different choices for resistors R_1 and R_2. Some possibilities for (R_1, R_2) are (3 kΩ, 7 kΩ), (12 kΩ, 28 kΩ), (300 kΩ, 700 kΩ) and (1.2 MΩ, 2.8 MΩ). Which of these choices would be the best and why?

4.68. Find the Q-point for the transistor in Fig. P4.68 if $R = 20$ kΩ, $V_{TO} = 1$ V, and $W/L = 1/1$.

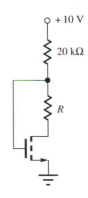

Figure P4.68

4.69. Find the Q-point for the transistor in Fig. P4.68 if $R = 10$ kΩ, $V_{TO} = 1$ V, and $W/L = 1/1$.

4.70. Find the Q-point for the transistor in Fig. P4.70 if $V_{TO} = +4$ V, $\gamma = 0$, and $W/L = 10/1$.

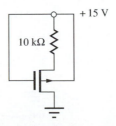

Figure P4.70

4.71. Find the Q-point for the transistor in Fig. P4.70 if $V_{TO} = +4$ V, $\gamma = 0.25 \sqrt{V}$, and $W/L = 10/1$.

4.72. Find the Q-point for the transistor in Fig. P4.72 if $V_{TO} = -1$ V and $W/L = 10/1$.

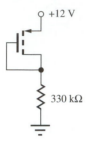

Figure P4.72

4.73. What value of W/L is required to set $V_{DS} = 0.50$ V in the circuit in Fig. P4.73 if $V = 5$ V and $R = 100$ kΩ?

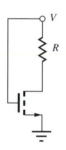

Figure P4.73

4.74. What value of W/L is required to set $V_{DS} = 0.25$ V in the circuit in Fig. P4.73 if $V = 3.3$ V and $R = 150$ kΩ?

4.75. What is the Q-point for each transistor in Fig. P4.75?

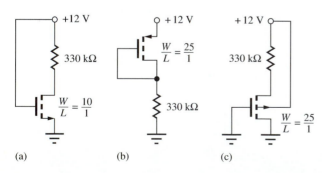

(a)   (b)   (c)

Figure P4.75

4.12 Capacitances in MOS Transistors

4.76. Calculate C''_{ox} and C_{GC} for a MOS transistor with $W = 20$ μm and $L = 2$ μm with an oxide thickness of (a) 50 nm, (b) 20 nm, (c) 10 nm.

4.77. Calculate C''_{ox} and C_{GC} for a MOS transistor with $W = 5$ μm and $L = 0.5$ μm with an oxide thickness of 20 nm.

4.78. In a certain MOSFET, the value of C'_{OL} can be calculated using an effective overlap distance of 1 μm. What is the value of C'_{OL} for an oxide thickness of 20 nm?

4.79. What are the values of C_{GS} and C_{GD} for a transistor with $C''_{ox} = 1.4 \times 10^{-3}$ F/m^2 and $C'_{OL} = 4 \times 10^{-9}$ F/m if $W = 10$ μm and $L = 1$ μm operating in (a) the linear region, (b) the saturation region, (c) cutoff?

4.80. A large-power MOSFET has an effective gate area of 25×10^6 μm^2. What is the value of C_{GC} if T_{ox} is 100 nm?

4.13 The Junction Field-Effect Transistor (JFET)

4.81. The JFET in Fig. P4.81 has $I_{DSS} = 500$ μA and $V_P = -3$ V. Find the Q-point for the JFET for (a) $R = 0$ and $V = 5$ V, (b) $R = 0$ and $V = 0.25$ V, (c) $R = 8.2$ kΩ and $V = 5$.

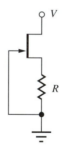

Figure P4.81

4.82. Find the Q-point for the JFET in Fig. P4.82 if $I_{DSS} = 5$ mA and $V_P = -5$ V.

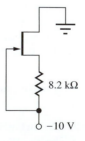

Figure P4.82

4.83. Find the on-resistance of the JFET in Fig. P4.83 if $I_{DSS} = 1$ mA and $V_P = -5$ V. Repeat for $I_{DSS} = 100$ μA and $V_P = -2$ V.

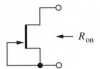

Figure P4.83

4.84. The JFET in Fig. P4.84 has $I_{DSS} = 1$ mA and $V_P = -4$ V. Find I_{DS}, I_G, and V_S for the JFET if (a) $I = 0.5$ mA and (b) $I = 2$ mA.

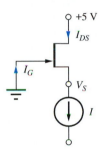

Figure P4.84

*4.85. The JFETs in Fig. P4.85 have $I_{DSS1} = 200$ μA, $V_{P1} = -2$ V, $I_{DSS2} = 500$ μA, and $V_{P2} = -4$ V. (a) Find the Q-point for the two JFETs if $V = 9$ V. (b) What minimum value of V will ensure that both J1 and J2 are in pinch-off?

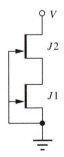

Figure P4.85

*4.86. The JFETs in Fig. P4.86 have $I_{DSS} = 200$ μA and $V_P = +2$ V. (a) Find the Q-point for the two JFETs if $R = 10$ kΩ and $V = 15$ V. (b) What minimum value of V will ensure that both J1 and J2 are in pinch-off if $R = 10$ kΩ?

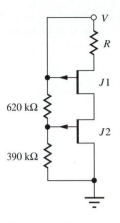

Figure P4.86

4.87. (a) The JFET in Fig. P4.87(a) has $I_{DSS} = 250$ μA and $V_P = -2$ V. Find the Q-point for the JFET. (b) The JFET in Fig. P4.87(b) has $I_{DSS} = 250$ μA and $V_P = +2$ V. Find the Q-point for the JFET.

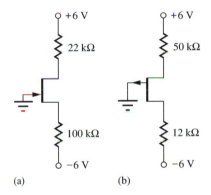

Figure P4.87

4.88. Simulate the circuit in Prob. 4.87(a) and compare the results to hand calculations. (b) Repeat for Prob. 4.87(b).

4.89. The JFET in Fig. P4.89 has $I_{DSS} = 250$ μA and $V_P = -2$ V. Find the Q-point for the JFET for (a) $R = 100$ kΩ and (b) $R = 10$ kΩ.

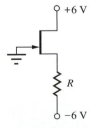

Figure P4.89

4.90. The JFET in Fig. P4.90 has $I_{DSS} = 500$ μA and $V_P = +3$ V. Find the Q-point for the JFET for (a) $R = 0$ Ω, (b) $R = 10$ kΩ, (c) $R = 100$ kΩ.

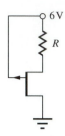

6 V

R

Figure P4.90

 4.91. Simulate the circuit in Prob. 4.85(a) and compare the results to hand calculations.

 4.92. Simulate the circuit in Prob. 4.86(a) and compare the results to hand calculations.

 4.93. Use SPICE to plot the i-v characteristic for the circuit in Fig. P4.85 for $0 \leq V \leq 15$ V if the JFETs have $I_{DSS1} = 200$ μA, $V_{P1} = -2$ V, $I_{DSS2} = 500$ μA, and $V_{P2} = -4$V.

Bipolar Junction Transistors

Following its invention and demonstration in the late 1940s by Bardeen, Brattain, and Shockley at Bell Laboratories, the **bipolar junction transistor,** or **BJT,** became the first commercially successful three-terminal solid-state device. Its commercial success was based on its structure. In the structure of the BJT, the active base region of the transistor is below the surface of the semiconductor material, making it much less dependent on surface properties and cleanliness. Thus, it was initially easier to manufacture BJTs than MOS transistors. Commercial bipolar transistors were available in the late 1950s. The first integrated circuits, resistor-transistor logic gates, and operational amplifiers consisting of a few transistors and resistors appeared in the early 1960s.

The bipolar transistor is composed of a sandwich of three doped semiconductor regions and comes in two forms: the *npn* transistor and the *pnp* transistor. Performance of the bipolar transistor is dominated by *minority-carrier* transport via diffusion and drift in the central region of the transistor. Because carrier mobility and diffusivity are higher for electrons than holes, the *npn* transistor is an inherently higher-performance device than the *pnp* transistor. In Part III of this book, we will learn that the bipolar transistor typically offers a much higher voltage gain capability than the FET. On the other hand, the BJT input resistance is much lower, and a dc-bias current must be supplied to the control electrode.

Our study of the BJT begins with a discussion of the *npn* transistor, followed by a discussion of the *pnp* device. The **transport model,** a simplified version of the Gummel-Poon model, is developed and used as our mathematical model for the behavior of the BJT. Four regions of operation of the BJT are defined and simplified models developed for each region. Examples of circuits that can be used to bias the bipolar transistor are presented. The chapter closes with a discussion of the worst-case and Monte Carlo analyses of the effects of tolerances on electronic circuits.

5.1 PHYSICAL STRUCTURE OF THE BIPOLAR TRANSISTOR

The bipolar transistor structure consists of three alternating layers of *n*- and *p*-type semiconductor material. These layers are referred to as the **emitter (E), base (B),** and **collector (C)** of the transistor. Either an ***npn*** or a ***pnp* transistor** can be fabricated. The behavior of the device can be seen from the simplified cross section of the *npn* transistor in Fig. 5.1(a). During normal operation, a majority of the current enters the collector terminal, crosses the base region, and exits from the emitter terminal. A small current also enters the base terminal, crosses the base-emitter junction of the transistor, and exits the emitter.

The most important part of the bipolar transistor is the active base region between the dotted lines directly beneath the heavily doped ($n+$) emitter. Carrier transport in this region dominates the *i-v* characteristics of the BJT. Figure 5.1(b) illustrates the rather complex physical structure actually used to realize an *npn* transistor in integrated circuit form. Most of the structure in Fig. 5.1(b) is required to fabricate the external contacts to the collector, base, and emitter regions and to isolate one bipolar transistor from another. In the sections that follow, a mathematical model is developed for the *i-v* characteristics of *npn* and *pnp* transistors.

5.2 THE TRANSPORT MODEL FOR THE *npn* TRANSISTOR

Figure 5.2 is a conceptual model for the active region of the *npn* bipolar junction transistor structure. At first glance, the BJT appears to simply be two *pn* junctions connected back to back. However, the central region (the base) is very thin (0.1 to 100 μm), and the close

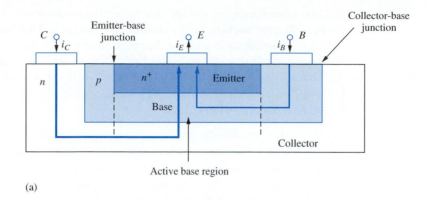

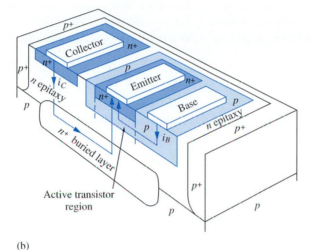

Figure 5.1 (a) Simplified cross section of an *npn* transistor with currents that occur during "normal" operation. (b) Cross section of an integrated *npn* bipolar junction transistor.

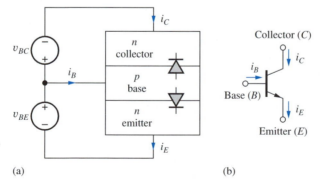

Figure 5.2 (a) Idealized *npn* transistor structure for a general-bias condition. (b) Circuit symbol for the *npn* transistor.

proximity of the two junctions leads to coupling between the two diodes. This coupling is the essence of the bipolar device. The lower *n*-type region (the emitter) injects electrons into the *p*-type base region of the device. In a modern silicon transistor, almost all these injected electrons travel across the narrow base region and are removed (or collected) by the upper *n*-type region (the collector).

The base-emitter voltage v_{BE} and the base-collector voltage v_{BC} applied to the two *pn* junctions in Fig. 5.2 determine the currents in the bipolar transistor and are defined as positive when they forward-bias their respective *pn* junctions. The three terminal currents are the **collector current i_C**, the **emitter current i_E**, and the **base current i_B**. The arrows indicate the directions of positive current in most *npn* circuit applications. The circuit symbol for the *npn* transistor appears in Fig. 5.2(b), in which the arrow identifies the emitter terminal and indicates that current normally exits the emitter of the *npn* transistor.

Forward Characteristics

Equations that describe the static *i-v* characteristics of the device can be constructed using a superposition of currents within the transistor structure.[1] In Fig. 5.3, an arbitrary voltage v_{BE} is applied to the base-emitter junction, and the voltage applied to the base-collector junction is set to zero. The base-emitter voltage establishes emitter current i_E, which equals the total current crossing the base-emitter junction. This current is composed of two components. The largest portion, the **forward-transport current i_F**, enters the collector, travels completely across the very narrow base region, and exits the emitter terminal. The collector current i_C is equal to i_F, which has the form of an ideal diode current

$$i_C = i_F = I_S\left[\exp\left(\frac{v_{BE}}{V_T}\right) - 1\right] \tag{5.1}$$

The parameter I_S is the **transistor saturation current**—that is, the saturation current of the bipolar transistor. I_S is proportional to the cross-sectional area of the active base region of the transistor, and can have a wide range of values:

$$10^{-18}\ \text{A} \le I_S \le 10^{-9}\ \text{A}$$

In Eq. (5.1), V_T should be recognized as the thermal voltage introduced in Chapter 2 and given by $V_T = kT/q = 0.025$ V at room temperature.

In addition to i_F, a second, much smaller component of current crosses the base-emitter junction. This current forms the base current i_B of the transistor, and it is directly proportional to i_F:

$$i_B = \frac{i_F}{\beta_F} = \frac{I_S}{\beta_F}\left[\exp\left(\frac{v_{BE}}{V_T}\right) - 1\right] \tag{5.2}$$

[1] The differential equations that describe the internal physics of the BJT are linear second-order differential equations. These equations are linear in terms of the hole and electron concentrations; the currents are directly related to these carrier concentrations. Thus, superposition can be used with respect to the currents flowing in the device.

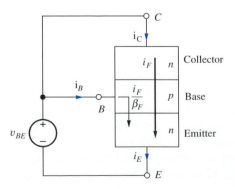

Figure 5.3 *npn* transistor with v_{BE} applied and $v_{BC} = 0$.

The parameter β_F is called the **forward** (or **normal**[2]) **common-emitter current gain.** Its value typically falls in the range

$$20 \le \beta_F \le 500$$

The emitter current i_E can be calculated by treating the transistor as a super node for which

$$i_C + i_B = i_E \tag{5.3}$$

Adding Eqs. (5.1) and (5.2) together yields

$$i_E = \left(I_S + \frac{I_S}{\beta_F}\right)\left[\exp\left(\frac{v_{BE}}{V_T}\right) - 1\right] \tag{5.4}$$

which can be rewritten as

$$i_E = I_S\left(\frac{\beta_F + 1}{\beta_F}\right)\left[\exp\left(\frac{v_{BE}}{V_T}\right) - 1\right] = \frac{I_S}{\alpha_F}\left[\exp\left(\frac{v_{BE}}{V_T}\right) - 1\right] \tag{5.5}$$

The parameter α_F is called the **forward** (or **normal**[3]) **common-base current gain,** and its value typically falls in the range

$$0.95 \le \alpha_F < 1.0$$

The parameters α_F and β_F are related by

$$\alpha_F = \frac{\beta_F}{\beta_F + 1} \qquad \text{or} \qquad \beta_F = \frac{\alpha_F}{1 - \alpha_F} \tag{5.6}$$

Equations (5.1), (5.2), and (5.5) express the fundamental physics-based characteristics of the bipolar transistor. The three terminal currents are all exponentially dependent on the base-emitter voltage of the transistor. This is a much stronger nonlinear dependence than the square-law behavior of the FET.

For the bias conditions in Fig. 5.3, the transistor is actually operating in a region of high current gain, called the forward-active region[4] of operation, which is discussed more fully in Sec. 5.9. Two extremely useful auxiliary relationships are valid in the forward-active region. The first can be found from the ratio of the collector and base current in Eqs. (5.1) and (5.2):

$$\frac{i_C}{i_B} = \beta_F \qquad \text{or} \qquad i_C = \beta_F i_B \qquad \text{and} \qquad i_E = (\beta_F + 1)i_B \tag{5.7}$$

using Eq. (5.3). The second relationship is found from the ratio of the collector and emitter current in Eqs. (5.1) and (5.5):

$$\frac{i_C}{i_E} = \alpha_F \qquad \text{or} \qquad i_C = \alpha_F i_E \tag{5.8}$$

Equation (5.7) expresses an important and useful property of the bipolar transistor: The transistor "amplifies"(magnifies) its base current by the factor β_F . Because the current gain $\beta_F \gg 1$, injection of a small current into the base of the transistor produces a much

---

[2] β_N is sometimes used to represent the normal common-emitter current gain.
[3] α_N is sometimes used to represent the normal common-base current gain.
[4] Four regions of operation are fully defined in Sec. 5.4.

larger current in both the collector and the emitter terminals. Equation (5.8) indicates that the collector and emitter currents are almost identical, because $\alpha_F \approx 1$.

Reverse Characteristics

Now consider the transistor in Fig. 5.4, in which a general voltage v_{BC} is applied to the base-collector junction, and the base-emitter junction is zero-biased. The base-collector voltage establishes the collector current i_C, now crossing the base-collector junction. The largest portion of the collector current, the reverse-transport current i_R, enters the emitter, travels completely across the narrow base region, and exits the collector terminal. Current i_R has a form identical to i_F:

$$i_R = I_S\left[\exp\left(\frac{v_{BC}}{V_T}\right) - 1\right] \qquad \text{and} \qquad i_E = -i_R \tag{5.9}$$

except the controlling voltage is now v_{BC}.

In this case, a fraction of the current i_R must also be supplied as base current through the base terminal:

$$i_B = \frac{i_R}{\beta_R} = \frac{I_S}{\beta_R}\left[\exp\left(\frac{v_{BC}}{V_T}\right) - 1\right] \tag{5.10}$$

Parameter $\boldsymbol{\beta_R}$ is called the **reverse (or inverse[5]) common-emitter current gain.**

In Chapter 4, we discovered that the FET was an inherently symmetric device. For the bipolar transistor, Eqs. (5.1) and (5.9) show the symmetry that is inherent in the current that traverses the base region of the bipolar transistor. However, the impurity doping levels of the emitter and collector regions of the BJT structure are quite asymmetric, and this fact causes the base currents in the forward and reverse modes to be significantly different. For typical BJTs, β_R is in the range

$$0 < \beta_R \leq 20 \qquad \text{whereas} \quad 20 \leq \beta_F \leq 500$$

The collector current in Fig. 5.4 can be found by combining the base and emitter currents, as was done to obtain Eq. (5.5):

$$i_C = -I_S\left(1 + \frac{1}{\beta_R}\right)\left[\exp\left(\frac{v_{BC}}{V_T}\right) - 1\right] = -\frac{I_S}{\alpha_R}\left[\exp\left(\frac{v_{BC}}{V_T}\right) - 1\right] \tag{5.11}$$

in which the parameter $\boldsymbol{\alpha_R}$ is called the **reverse (or inverse[6]) common-base current gain:**

$$\alpha_R = \frac{\beta_R}{\beta_R + 1} \qquad \text{or} \qquad \beta_R = \frac{\alpha_R}{1 - \alpha_R} \tag{5.12}$$

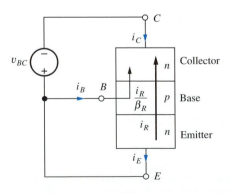

Figure 5.4 Transistor with v_{BC} applied and $v_{BE} = 0$.

---

[5] β_I is sometimes used to represent the inverse common-emitter current gain.
[6] α_I is sometimes used to represent the inverse common-base current gain.

Typical values of α_R fall in the range

$$0 < \alpha_R \leq 0.95$$

Values of the common-base current gain α and the common-emitter current gain β are compared in Table 5.1. Because α_F is typically greater than 0.95, β_F can be quite large. Values ranging from 20 to 500 are quite common for β_F, although it is possible to fabricate special-purpose transistors[7] with β_F as high as 5000. In contrast, α_R is typically less than 0.5, which results in values of β_R of less than 1.

T a b l e 5.1 Common-Emitter and Common-Base Current Gain Comparison	
α_F **or** α_R	$\beta_F = \dfrac{\alpha_F}{1 - \alpha_F}$ **or** $\beta_R = \dfrac{\alpha_R}{1 - \alpha_R}$
0.1	0.11
0.5	1
0.9	9
0.95	19
0.99	99
0.998	499

EXERCISE: What values of β correspond to $\alpha = 0.970, 0.993, 0.250$?

ANSWERS: 32.3; 142; 0.333

EXERCISE: What values of α correspond to $\beta = 40, 200, 3$?

ANSWERS: 0.976; 0.995; 0.750

The Full-Transport Model Equations for Arbitrary Bias Conditions

Combining the expressions for the two collector, emitter, and base currents from Eqs. (5.1) and (5.11), (5.4) and (5.9), and (5.2) and (5.10) yields expressions for the total collector, emitter, and base currents for the *npn* transistor that are valid for the completely general-bias voltage situation in Fig. 5.2:

$$i_C = I_S \left[\exp\left(\frac{v_{BE}}{V_T}\right) - \exp\left(\frac{v_{BC}}{V_T}\right) \right] - \frac{I_S}{\beta_R} \left[\exp\left(\frac{v_{BC}}{V_T}\right) - 1 \right]$$

$$i_E = I_S \left[\exp\left(\frac{v_{BE}}{V_T}\right) - \exp\left(\frac{v_{BC}}{V_T}\right) \right] + \frac{I_S}{\beta_F} \left[\exp\left(\frac{v_{BE}}{V_T}\right) - 1 \right] \qquad (5.13)$$

$$i_B = \frac{I_S}{\beta_F} \left[\exp\left(\frac{v_{BE}}{V_T}\right) - 1 \right] + \frac{I_S}{\beta_R} \left[\left(\frac{v_{BC}}{V_T}\right) - 1 \right]$$

---

[7] These devices are often called "super-beta" transistors.

From this equation set, we see that three parameters are required to characterize an individual BJT: I_S, β_F, and β_R. (Remember that temperature is also an important parameter because $V_T = kT/q$.)

The first term in both the emitter and collector current expressions in Eqs. (5.13) is

$$i_T = I_S \left[\exp\left(\frac{v_{BE}}{V_T}\right) - \exp\left(\frac{v_{BC}}{V_T}\right) \right] \tag{5.14}$$

which represents the current being transported completely across the base region of the transistor. Equation (5.14) demonstrates the symmetry that exists between the base-emitter and base-collector voltages in establishing the dominant current in the bipolar transistor.

Equations (5.13) actually represent a simplified version of the more complex **Gummel-Poon model** [1, 2] and form the heart of the BJT model used in the SPICE simulation program. The full Gummel-Poon model accurately describes the characteristics of BJTs over a wide range of operating conditions, and it has largely supplanted its predecessor, the **Ebers-Moll model** [3] (see Prob. 5.76).

EXAMPLE 5.1: As an example of circuit analysis using the transport model equations, we use the model to find the terminal voltages and currents in the circuit in Fig. 5.5, in which an *npn* transistor is biased by two dc voltage sources. First, let us determine the boundary conditions that this particular circuit places on the transport equations. In this circuit the base-emitter and base-collector voltages are

$$V_{BE} = V_{BB} = 0.75 \text{ V}$$

$$V_{BC} = V_{BB} - V_{CC} = 0.75 \text{ V} - 5.00 \text{ V} = -4.25 \text{ V}$$ ◆

Substituting these voltage into Eqs. (5.13) yields

$$i_C = 10^{-16} \text{ A}\left[\exp\left(\frac{0.75 \text{ V}}{0.025 \text{ V}}\right) - \exp\left(\frac{-4.75 \text{ V}}{0.025 \text{ V}}\right)^{0}\right] - \frac{10^{-16}}{1} \text{ A}\left[\exp\left(\frac{-4.75 \text{ V}}{0.025 \text{ V}}\right)^{0} - 1\right]$$

$$i_E = 10^{-16} \text{ A}\left[\exp\left(\frac{0.75 \text{ V}}{0.025 \text{ V}}\right) - \exp\left(\frac{-4.75 \text{ V}}{0.025 \text{ V}}\right)^{0}\right] + \frac{10^{-16}}{50} \text{ A}\left[\exp\left(\frac{0.75 \text{ V}}{0.025 \text{ V}}\right) - 1\right]$$

$$i_B = \frac{10^{-16}}{50} \text{ A}\left[\exp\left(\frac{0.75 \text{ V}}{0.025 \text{ V}}\right) - 1\right] + \frac{10^{-16}}{1} \text{ A}\left[\exp\left(\frac{-4.75 \text{ V}}{0.025 \text{ V}}\right)^{0} - 1\right]$$

and evaluating these expressions gives

$$I_C = 1.07 \text{ mA} \qquad I_E = 1.09 \text{ mA} \qquad I_B = 21.4 \text{ }\mu\text{A}$$

Note that the collector-base junction in Fig. 5.5 is reverse-biased, so the terms containing V_{BC} become negligibly small.

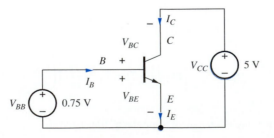

Figure 5.5 *npn* transistor circuit example: $I_S = 10^{-16}$ A, $\beta_F = 50$, $\beta_R = 1$.

In this example, the transistor is again biased in the forward-active region of operation for which

$$\beta_F = \frac{I_C}{I_B} = \frac{1.07 \text{ mA}}{0.0214 \text{ mA}} = 50 \quad \text{and} \quad \alpha_F = \frac{I_C}{I_E} = \frac{1.07 \text{ mA}}{1.09 \text{ mA}} = 0.982$$

In Sec. 5.8 to 5.12 we completely define four different regions of operation of the transistor and find simplified models for each region. First, however, let us develop the transport model for the *pnp* transistor in a manner similar to that for the *npn* transistor.

> **EXERCISE:** Repeat the example problem for $I_S = 10^{-15}$A, $\beta_F = 100$, $\beta_R = 0.50$, $V_{BE} = 0.70$ V, and $V_{CC} = 10$ V.
>
> **ANSWERS:** $I_C = 1.45$ mA, $I_E = 1.46$ mA, and $I_B = 14.5$ μA

5.3 THE *pnp* TRANSISTOR

The *pnp* transistor is fabricated by reversing the layers of the transistor, as diagrammed in Fig. 5.6 on p. 176. The transistor has been drawn with the emitter at the top of the diagram, as it appears in most circuit diagrams throughout this book. The arrows again indicate the normal directions of positive current in the *pnp* transistor in most circuit applications. The voltages applied to the two pn junctions are the emitter-base voltage v_{EB} and the collector-base voltage v_{CB}. These voltages are again positive when they forward-bias their respective pn junctions. Collector current i_C and base current i_B exit the transistor terminals, and the emitter current i_E enters the device. The circuit symbol for the *pnp* transistor appears in Fig. 5.6(b). The arrow identifies the emitter of the *pnp* transistor and points in the direction of normal positive-emitter current.

Equations that describe the static *i-v* characteristics of the *pnp* transistor can be constructed using superposition of currents within the structure just as for the *npn* transistor. In Fig. 5.7 on p. 176, voltage v_{EB} is applied to the emitter-base junction, and the collector-base voltage is set to zero. The emitter-base voltage establishes forward-transport current i_F that traverses the narrow base region and base current i_B that crosses the emitter-base junction of the transistor:

$$i_C = i_F = I_S \left[\exp\left(\frac{v_{EB}}{V_T}\right) - 1 \right]$$

$$i_B = \frac{i_F}{\beta_F} = \frac{I_S}{\beta_F} \left[\exp\left(\frac{v_{EB}}{V_T}\right) - 1 \right] \tag{5.15}$$

and
$$i_E = i_C + i_B = I_S \left(1 + \frac{1}{\beta_F}\right)\left[\exp\left(\frac{v_{EB}}{V_T}\right) - 1 \right]$$

In Fig. 5.8 on p. 176, a voltage v_{CB} is applied to the collector-base junction, and the emitter-base junction is zero-biased. The collector-base voltage establishes the reverse-transport current i_R and base current i_B:

$$-i_E = i_R = I_S \left[\exp\left(\frac{v_{CB}}{V_T}\right) - 1 \right]$$

$$i_B = \frac{i_R}{\beta_R} = \frac{I_S}{\beta_R} \left[\exp\left(\frac{v_{BC}}{V_T}\right) - 1 \right] \tag{5.16}$$

$$i_C = -I_S \left(1 + \frac{1}{\beta_R}\right)\left[\exp\left(\frac{v_{BC}}{V_T}\right) - 1 \right]$$

where the collector current is given by $i_C = i_E - i_B$.

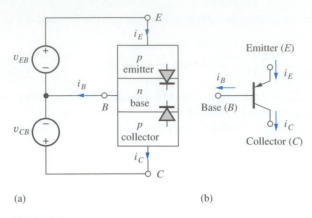

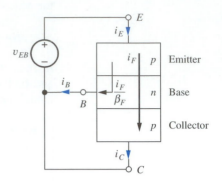

(a) (b)

Figure 5.6 (a) Idealized *pnp* transistor structure for a general-bias condition. (b) Circuit symbol for the *pnp* transistor.

Figure 5.7 *pnp* transistor with v_{EB} applied and $v_{CB} = 0$.

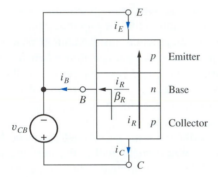

Figure 5.8 *pnp* transistor with v_{CB} applied and $v_{EB} = 0$.

For the general-bias voltage situation in Fig. 5.6, Eqs. (5.15) and (5.16) are combined to give the total collector, emitter, and base currents of the *pnp* transistor:

$$i_C = I_S \left[\exp\left(\frac{v_{EB}}{V_T}\right) - \exp\left(\frac{v_{CB}}{V_T}\right) \right] - \frac{I_S}{\beta_R} \left[\exp\left(\frac{v_{CB}}{V_T}\right) - 1 \right]$$

$$i_E = I_S \left[\exp\left(\frac{v_{EB}}{V_T}\right) - \exp\left(\frac{v_{CB}}{V_T}\right) \right] + \frac{I_S}{\beta_F} \left[\exp\left(\frac{v_{EB}}{V_T}\right) - 1 \right] \qquad (5.17)$$

$$i_B = \frac{I_S}{\beta_F} \left[\exp\left(\frac{v_{EB}}{V_T}\right) - 1 \right] + \frac{I_S}{\beta_R} \left[\exp\left(\frac{v_{CB}}{V_T}\right) - 1 \right]$$

These equations represent the simplified Gummel-Poon or transport model equations for the *pnp* transistor and can be used to relate the terminal voltages and currents of the *pnp* transistor for any general-bias condition. Note that these equations are identical to those for the *npn* transistor except that V_{EB} and V_{CB} replace V_{BE} and V_{BC}, respectively, and are a result of our careful choice for the direction of positive currents in Figs. 5.2 and 5.6.

EXERCISE: Find I_C, I_E, and I_B for a *pnp* transistor if $I_S = 10^{-16}$ A, $\beta_F = 75$, $\beta_R = 0.40$, $V_{EB} = 0.75$ V, and $V_{CB} = +0.70$ V.

ANSWERS: $I_C = 0.563$ mA; $I_E = 0.938$ mA; $I_B = 0.376$ mA

5.4 EQUIVALENT CIRCUIT REPRESENTATIONS FOR THE TRANSPORT MODELS

For circuit simulation, as well as hand analysis purposes, the transport model equations for the *npn* and *pnp* transistors can be represented by the equivalent circuits shown in Fig. 5.9(a) and (b), respectively. In the *npn* model in Fig. 5.9(a), the total transport current i_T traversing the base is determined by I_S, v_{BE}, and v_{BC}, and is modeled by the current source i_T:

$$i_T = i_F - i_R = I_S \left[\exp\left(\frac{v_{BE}}{V_T}\right) - \exp\left(\frac{v_{BC}}{V_T}\right) \right] \tag{5.18}$$

The diode currents correspond directly to the two possible components of the base current:

$$i_B = \frac{I_S}{\beta_F} \left[\exp\left(\frac{v_{BE}}{V_T}\right) - 1 \right] + \frac{I_S}{\beta_R} \left[\exp\left(\frac{v_{BC}}{V_T}\right) - 1 \right] \tag{5.19}$$

Directly analogous arguments hold for the circuit elements in the *pnp* circuit model of Fig. 5.9(b).

> **EXERCISE:** Find i_T if $I_S = 10^{-15}$ A, $V_{BE} = 0.75$ V, and $V_{BC} = -2.0$ V.
>
> **ANSWER:** 10.7 mA

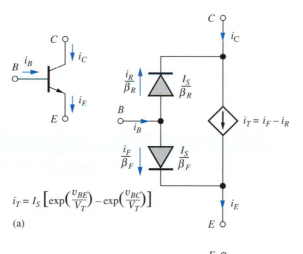

$$i_T = I_S \left[\exp\left(\frac{v_{BE}}{V_T}\right) - \exp\left(\frac{v_{BC}}{V_T}\right) \right]$$

(a)

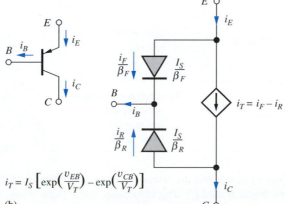

$$i_T = I_S \left[\exp\left(\frac{v_{EB}}{V_T}\right) - \exp\left(\frac{v_{CB}}{V_T}\right) \right]$$

(b)

Figure 5.9 (a) Transport model equivalent circuit for the *npn* transistor. (b) Transport model equivalent circuit for the *pnp* transistor.

5.5 THE OPERATING REGIONS OF THE BIPOLAR TRANSISTOR

In the bipolar transistor, each *pn* junction may independently be forward-biased or reverse-biased, so there are four possible regions of operation, as defined in Table 5.2. The operating point establishes the region of operation of the transistor and can be defined by any two of the four terminal voltages or currents.

When both junctions are reverse-biased, the transistor is essentially nonconducting or *cut off* (**cutoff region**) and can be considered an open switch. If both junctions are forward-biased, the transistor is operating in the **saturation region**[8] and appears as a closed switch. Cutoff and saturation (shaded in Table 5.2) are most often used to represent the two states in binary logic circuits implemented with BJTs. For example, switching between these two operating regions occurs in the transistor-transistor logic circuits that we shall study in Chapter 10 on bipolar logic circuits.

In the **forward-active region** (also called the **normal-active region**), in which the base-emitter junction is forward-biased and the base-collector junction is reverse-biased, the BJT can provide high current, voltage, and power gains. The forward-active region is most often used to achieve high-quality amplification. In addition, in the fastest form of bipolar logic, called emitter-coupled logic, the transistors switch between the cutoff and the forward-active regions.

In the **reverse-active region** (or **inverse-active region**), the base-emitter junction is reverse-biased and the base-collector junction is forward-biased. In this region, the transistor exhibits low common-emitter current gain, and the reverse-active region is not often used. However, we will see an important application of the reverse-active region in transistor-transistor logic circuits in Chapter 10. Reverse operation of the transistor has also found use in analog-switching applications.

The transport model equations describe the behavior of the bipolar transistor for any combination of terminal voltages and currents. However, the complete sets of equations

Table 5.2

Regions of Operation of the Bipolar Transistor

Base-Emitter Junction	Base-Collector Junction	
	Forward Bias	**Reverse Bias**
Forward Bias	**Saturation region** (closed switch)	**Forward-active region** (Normal-active region) (good amplifier)
Reverse Bias	**Reverse-active region** (Inverse-active region) (poor amplifier)	**Cutoff region** (open switch)

[8] It is important to note that the saturation region of the bipolar transistor does *not* correspond to the saturation region of the FET. This unfortunate use of terms is historical in nature and something we just have to accept.

in (5.13) and (5.17) are quite imposing. In subsequent sections, bias conditions specific to each of the four regions of operation will be used to obtain simplified sets of relationships that are valid for the individual regions.

> **EXERCISE:** What is the region of operation of (a) an *npn* transistor with $V_{BE} = 0.75$ V and $V_{BC} = -0.70$ V? (b) A *pnp* transistor with $V_{CB} = 0.70$ V and $V_{EB} = 0.75$ V?
>
> **ANSWERS:** Forward-active region; saturation region

5.6 THE *i-v* CHARACTERISTICS OF THE BIPOLAR TRANSISTOR

Two complementary views of the *i-v* behavior of the BJT are represented by the device's **output** and **transfer characteristics.** (Remember that similar characteristics were presented for the FETs in Chapter 4.) The output characteristics represent the relationship between the collector current and collector-emitter or collector-base voltage of the transistor, whereas the transfer characteristic relates the collector current to the base-emitter voltage. A knowledge of both *i-v* characteristics is basic to understanding the overall behavior of the bipolar transistor.

Output Characteristics

Circuits for measuring or simulating the **common-emitter output characteristics** are shown in Fig. 5.10. In these circuits, the base of the transistor is driven by a constant current source, and the output characteristics represent a graph of i_C vs. v_{CE} for the *npn* transistor (or i_C vs. v_{EC} for the *pnp*) with base current i_B as a parameter.

First, consider the *npn* transistor operating with $v_{CE} \geq 0$, represented by the first quadrant of the graph in Fig. 5.11. For $i_B = 0$, the transistor is nonconducting or cut off. As i_B increases above 0, i_C also increases. For $v_{CE} \geq v_{BE}$, the *npn* transistor is in the forward-active region, and collector current is independent of v_{CE} and equal to $\beta_F i_B$. Remember, it was demonstrated earlier that $i_C \approx \beta_F i_B$ in the forward-active region. For $v_{CE} \leq v_{BE}$, the transistor enters the saturation region of operation in which the total voltage between the collector and emitter terminals of the transistor is small.

In the third quadrant for $v_{CE} \leq 0$, the roles of the collector and emitter reverse. For $v_{BE} \leq v_{CE} \leq 0$, the transistor remains in saturation. For $v_{CE} \leq v_{BE}$, the transistor enters the reverse-active region, in which the *i-v* characteristics again become independent of v_{CE}, and now $i_C \approx -(\beta_R + 1)i_B$. The reverse-active region curves have been plotted for a relatively large value of reverse common-emitter current gain, $\beta_R = 5$, to enhance their visibility. As noted earlier, the reverse-current gain β_R is often less than 1.

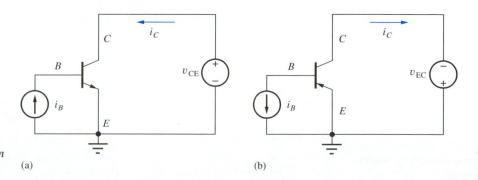

Figure 5.10 Circuits for determining common-emitter output characteristics: (a) *npn* transistor, (b) *pnp* transistor.

(a)   (b)

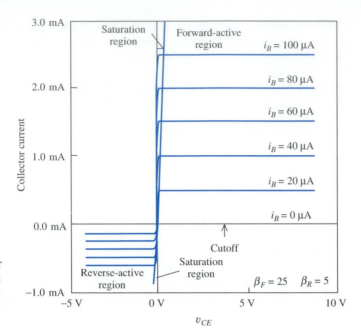

Figure 5.11 Common-emitter output characteristics for the bipolar transistor (i_C vs. v_{CE} for the *npn* transistor or i_C vs. v_{EC} for the *pnp* transistor).

Using the polarities defined in Fig. 5.10(b) for the *pnp* transistor, the output characteristics will appear exactly the same as in Fig. 5.11, except that the horizontal axis will be the voltage v_{EC} rather than v_{CE}. Remember that $i_B > 0$ and $i_C > 0$ correspond to currents exiting the base and collector terminals of the *pnp* transistor.

Circuits for measuring or simulating the **common-base output characteristics** of the *npn* and *pnp* transistors are shown in Fig. 5.12. In these circuits, the emitter of the transistor is driven by a constant current source, and the output characteristics plot i_C vs. v_{CB} for the *npn* (or i_C vs. v_{BC} for the *pnp*), with the emitter-current i_E as a parameter. For $v_{CB} \geq 0$ V in Fig. 5.13, the transistor operates in the forward-active region with i_C independent of v_{CB}, and we saw earlier that $i_C \approx i_E$. For v_{CB} less than zero, the base-collector diode of the transistor becomes forward-biased, and the collector current grows exponentially (in the negative direction) as the base-collector diode begins to conduct.

Using the polarities defined in Fig. 5.12(b) for the *pnp* transistor, the output characteristics appear exactly the same as in Fig. 5.13, except that the horizontal axis is the voltage v_{BC} rather than v_{CB}. Again, remember that $i_B > 0$ and $i_C > 0$ correspond to currents exiting the emitter and collector terminals of the *pnp* transistor.

Transfer Characteristics

The **common-emitter transfer characteristic** of the BJT defines the relationship between the collector current and the base-emitter voltage of the transistor. An example of the trans-

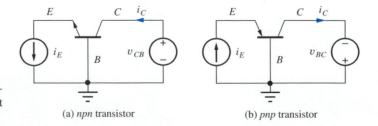

Figure 5.12 Circuits to determine common-base output characteristics.

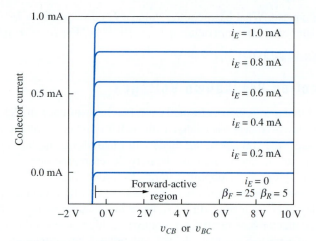

Figure 5.13 Common-base output characteristics for the bipolar transistor (i_C vs. v_{CB} for the *npn* transistor or i_C vs. v_{BC} for the *pnp* transistor).

fer characteristic for an *npn* transistor is shown in graphical form in Fig. 5.14, with both linear and semilog scales for the particular case of $v_{BC} = 0$. The transfer characteristic is virtually identical to that of a *pn* junction diode. This behavior can also be expressed mathematically by setting $v_{BC} = 0$ in the collector-current expression in Eq. (5.13):

$$i_C = I_S \left[\exp\left(\frac{v_{BE}}{V_T}\right) - 1 \right] \tag{5.20}$$

Because of the exponential relationship in Eq. (5.20), the semilog plot exhibits the same slope as that for a *pn* junction diode. Only a 60-mV change in v_{BE} is required to change the collector current by a factor of 10, and for a fixed collector current, the base-emitter voltage of the silicon BJT will exhibit a -1.8-mV/°C temperature coefficient, just as for the silicon diode (see Sec. 3.5).

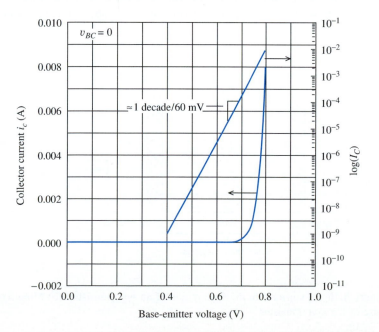

Figure 5.14 BJT transfer characteristic in the forward-active region.

> **EXERCISE:** What base-emitter voltage I_S corresponds to $I_C = 100 \ \mu A$ in an *npn* transistor at room temperature if $I_S = 10^{-16}$ A? For $I_C = 1$ mA?
>
> **ANSWERS:** 0.691 V; 0.748 V

Junction Breakdown Voltages

The bipolar transistor is formed from two back-to-back diodes, each of which has a Zener breakdown voltage associated with it. If the reverse voltage across either *pn* junction is too large, the corresponding diode will break down. In the transistor structure in Fig. 5.1, the emitter region is the most heavily doped region and the collector is the most lightly doped region. These doping differences lead to a relatively low breakdown voltage for the base-emitter diode, typically in the range of 5 to 10 V. On the other hand, the collector-base diode can be designed to break down at much larger voltages. Transistors can be fabricated with collector-base breakdown voltages as high as several hundred volts.

Transistors must be selected with breakdown voltages commensurate with the reverse voltages that will be encountered in the circuit. In the forward-active region, for example, the collector-base junction is operated under reverse bias and must not break down. In the cutoff region, both junctions are reverse-biased, and the relatively low breakdown voltage of the emitter-base junction must not be exceeded.

5.7 MINORITY-CARRIER TRANSPORT IN THE BASE REGION

Current in the BJT is predominantly determined by the transport of *minority carriers* across the base region. In the *npn* transistor in Fig. 5.15, transport current i_T results from the diffusion of minority carriers—electrons in the *npn* transistor or holes in the *pnp*—across the base. Base current i_B is composed of hole injection back into the emitter and collector, as well as a small additional current I_{REC} needed to replenish holes lost to recombination with electrons in the base. These three components of base current are shown in Fig. 5.15(a).

An expression for the transport current i_T can be developed using our knowledge of carrier diffusion and the values of base-emitter and base-collector voltages. It can be shown from device physics (beyond the scope of this text) that the voltages applied to the

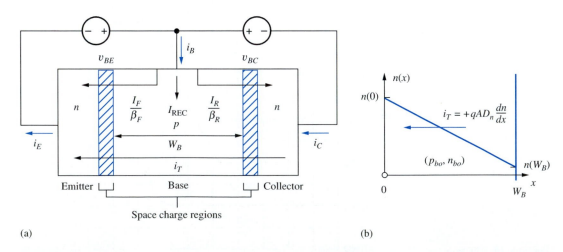

(a)   (b)

Figure 5.15 (a) Currents in the base region of an *npn* transistor. (b) Minority-carrier concentration in the base of the *npn* transistor.

base-emitter and base-collector junctions define the minority-carrier concentrations at the two ends of the base region through the following relationships:

$$n(0) = n_{bo} \exp\left(\frac{v_{BE}}{V_T}\right) \quad \text{and} \quad n(W_B) = n_{bo} \exp\left(\frac{v_{BC}}{V_T}\right) \tag{5.21}$$

in which n_{bo} is the **equilibrium electron density** in the p-type base region.

The two junction voltages establish a minority-carrier concentration gradient across the base region, as illustrated in Fig. 5.15(b). For a narrow base, the minority-carrier density decreases linearly across the base, and the diffusion current in the base can be calculated using Eq. (2.15):

$$i_T = qAD_n\frac{dn}{dx} = -qAD_n\frac{n_{bo}}{W_B}\left[\exp\left(\frac{v_{BE}}{V_T}\right) - \exp\left(\frac{v_{BC}}{V_T}\right)\right] \tag{5.22}$$

where A = cross-sectional area of base region
W_B = **base width**

Because the carrier gradient is negative, current i_T is directed in the negative x direction, exiting the emitter terminal.

Comparing Eqs. (5.22) and (5.19) yields a value for the bipolar transistor saturation current I_S:

$$I_S = qAD_n\frac{n_{bo}}{W_B} = \frac{qAD_nn_i^2}{N_{AB}W_B} \tag{5.23}$$

where N_{AB} = doping concentration in base of transistor
n_i = intrinsic-carrier concentration ($10^{10}/\text{cm}^3$)
n_{bo} = n_i^2/N_{AB} using Eq. (2.12)

Remembering from Chapter 2 that mobility μ, and hence diffusivity $D = (kT/q)\mu$ (cm^2/s), is larger for electrons than holes ($\mu_n > \mu_p$), we see from Eq. (5.22) that the *npn* transistor will conduct a higher current than the *pnp* transistor for a given set of applied voltages.

> **Exercise:** (a) What is the value of D_n at room temperature if $\mu_n = 500$ $\text{cm}^2/\text{V} \cdot \text{s}$? (b) What is I_S for a transistor with $A = 50$ μm^2, $W = 1\,\mu\text{m}$, $D_n = 12.5$ cm/s and $N_{AB} = 10^{18}/\text{cm}^3$?
>
> **Answers:** 12.5 cm/s; 10^{-18} A

Base Transit Time

To turn on the bipolar transistor, minority-carrier charge must be introduced into the base to establish the carrier gradient in Fig. 5.15(b). The **forward transit time** τ_F represents the time constant associated with storing the required charge Q in the base region and is defined by

$$\tau_F = \frac{Q}{I_T} \tag{5.24}$$

Figure 5.16 depicts the situation in the neutral base region of an *npn* transistor operating in the forward-active region with $v_{BE} > 0$ and $v_{BC} = 0$. The area under the triangle represents the excess minority charge Q that must be stored in the base to support the diffusion current. For the dimensions in Fig. 5.16,

$$Q = qA[n(0) - n_{bo}]\frac{W_B}{2}$$

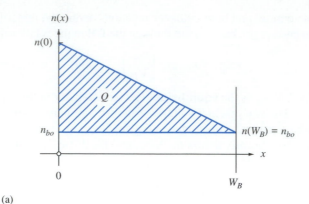

(a)

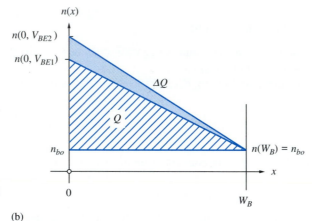

Figure 5.16 (a) Excess minority charge Q stored in the bipolar base region. (b) Stored charge Q changes as v_{BE} changes.

(b)

and using Eq. (5.21)

$$Q = qAn_{bo}\left[\exp\left(\frac{v_{BE}}{V_T}\right) - 1\right]\frac{W_B}{2} \tag{5.25}$$

For the conditions in Fig. 5.16(a),

$$i_T = \frac{qAD_n}{W_B}n_{bo}\left[\exp\left(\frac{v_{BE}}{V_T}\right) - 1\right] \tag{5.26}$$

Substituting Eqs. (5.25) and (5.26) into Eq. (5.24), the forward transit time is found to be

$$\tau_F = \frac{W_B^2}{2D_n} = \frac{W_B^2}{2V_T\mu_n} \tag{5.27}$$

The base transit time in Eq.(5.27) places an upper limit on the useful operating frequency f of the transistor,

$$f \le \frac{1}{2\pi\tau_F} \tag{5.28}$$

From Eq. (5.27), we see that the transit time is inversely proportional to the minority-carrier mobility in the base, and the difference between electron and hole mobility leads to an inherent speed advantage for the *npn* transistor. Thus, an *npn* transistor may be expected to be 2 to 2.5 times as fast as a *pnp* transistor for a given geometry and doping. Equation (5.27) also indicates the importance of shrinking the base width W_B of the transistor as much as possible. Early transistors had base widths of 10 μm or more, whereas the base width of transistors in research laboratories today is 0.025 μm (25 nm) or less.

EXAMPLE 5.2: Find the saturation current and base transit time for an *npn* transistor with a 100 μm × 100 μm emitter region, a base doping of $10^{17}/\text{cm}^3$, and a base width of 1 μm. Assume $\mu_n = 500 \text{ cm}^2/\text{V} \cdot \text{s}$.

SOLUTION: Using Eq. (5.23) for I_S,

$$I_S = \frac{qAD_n n_i^2}{N_{AB}W_B} = \frac{(1.6 \times 10^{-19} \text{ C})(10^{-2} \text{ cm})^2 \left(0.025 \text{ V} \times 500 \frac{\text{cm}^2}{\text{V} \cdot \text{s}}\right)\left(\frac{10^{20}}{\text{cm}^6}\right)}{\left(\frac{10^{17}}{\text{cm}^3}\right)(10^{-4} \text{ cm})}$$

$$= 2 \times 10^{-15} \text{ A}$$

in which $D_n = (kT/q)\mu_n$ has been used. Using Eq.(5.27),

$$\tau_F = \frac{\left(10^{-4} \text{ cm}\right)^2}{2\,(0.025 \text{ V})\,500\dfrac{\text{cm}^2}{\text{V} \cdot \text{s}}} = 4 \times 10^{-10} \text{ s}$$

which limits the use of this particular transistor to frequencies below 400 MHz. ◆

Diffusion Capacitance

For the base-emitter voltage and hence the collector current in the BJT to change, the charge stored in the base region also must change, as illustrated in Fig. 5.16(b). This change in charge with v_{BE} can be modeled by a capacitance C_D, called the **diffusion capacitance,** placed in parallel with the forward-biased base-emitter diode as defined by

$$C_D = \left.\frac{dQ}{dv_{BE}}\right|_{Q-\text{point}} = \frac{1}{V_T}\frac{qAn_{bo}W_B}{2}\exp\left(\frac{V_{BE}}{V_T}\right) \tag{5.29}$$

This equation can be rewritten as

$$C_D = \frac{1}{V_T}\left[\frac{qAD_n n_{bo}}{W_B}\exp\left(\frac{V_{BE}}{V_T}\right)\right]\left(\frac{W_B^2}{2D_n}\right) \cong \frac{I_T}{V_T}\tau_F \tag{5.30}$$

Because the transport current actually represents the collector current in the forward-active region, the expression for the diffusion capacitance is normally written as

$$C_D = \frac{I_C}{V_T}\tau_F \tag{5.31}$$

From Eq. (5.31), we see that the diffusion capacitance C_D is directly proportional to current and inversely proportional to temperature T. For example, a BJT operating at a current of 1 mA with $\tau_F = 4 \times 10^{-10}$ s has a diffusion capacitance of

$$C_D = \frac{I_C}{V_T}\tau_F = \frac{10^{-3} \text{ A}}{0.025 \text{ V}}\left(4 \times 10^{-10} \text{ s}\right) = 16 \times 10^{-12} \text{ F} = 16 \text{ pF}$$

This is a substantial capacitance, but it can be even larger if the transistor is operating at significantly higher currents.

5.8 SIMPLIFIED MODEL FOR THE CUTOFF REGION

Four regions of operation for the BJT were identified in Table 5.2. The easiest region to understand is the cutoff region, in which both junctions are reverse-biased. For an *npn* transistor, the cutoff region requires $v_{BE} \le 0$ and $v_{BC} \le 0$. Let us further assume that

$$v_{BE} < -\frac{4kT}{q} \qquad \text{and} \qquad v_{BC} < -4\frac{kT}{q} \qquad \text{where} \quad -4\frac{kT}{q} = -0.1\text{V}$$

These two conditions allow us to neglect the exponential terms in Eqs. (5.13), yielding the following simplified equations for the *npn* terminal currents in cutoff:

$$i_C = I_S\left[\exp\!\left(\frac{v_{BE}}{V_T}\right)^{\!0} - \exp\!\left(\frac{v_{BC}}{V_T}\right)^{\!0}\right] - \frac{I_S}{\beta_R}\left[\exp\!\left(\frac{v_{BC}}{V_T}\right)^{\!0} - 1\right]$$

$$i_E = I_S\left[\exp\!\left(\frac{v_{BE}}{V_T}\right)^{\!0} - \exp\!\left(\frac{v_{BC}}{V_T}\right)^{\!0}\right] + \frac{I_S}{\beta_F}\left[\exp\!\left(\frac{v_{BE}}{V_T}\right)^{\!0} - 1\right] \qquad (5.32)$$

$$i_B = \frac{I_S}{\beta_F}\left[\exp\!\left(\frac{v_{BE}}{V_T}\right)^{\!0} - 1\right] + \frac{I_S}{\beta_R}\left[\exp\!\left(\frac{v_{BC}}{V_T}\right)^{\!0} - 1\right]$$

or

$$i_C = +\frac{I_S}{\beta_R} \qquad i_E = -\frac{I_S}{\beta_F} \qquad i_B = -\frac{I_S}{\beta_F} - \frac{I_S}{\beta_R}$$

In cutoff, the three terminal currents—i_C, i_E, and i_B—are all constant and typically smaller than the saturation current I_S of the transistor. The simplified model for this situation is shown in Fig. 5.17(b). In cutoff, only very small leakage currents appear in the three transistor terminals. In most cases, these currents are negligibly small and can be assumed to be zero.

We usually think of the transistor operating in the cutoff region as being "off" with essentially zero terminal currents, as indicated by the three-terminal open-circuit model in Fig. 5.17(c). The cutoff region represents an open switch and is often used as one of the two states required for binary logic circuits.

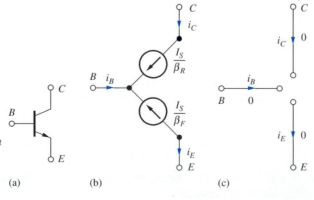

Figure 5.17 Modeling the *npn* transistor in cutoff: (a) *npn* transistor, (b) constant leakage current model, (c) open-circuit model.

(a)   (b)   (c)

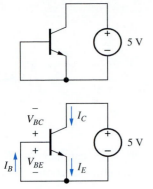

Figure 5.18 *npn* transistor bias in the cutoff region. (For calculations, use $I_S = 10^{-16}$A, $\alpha_F = 0.95$, $\alpha_R = 0.25$.)

EXAMPLE 5.3: Figure 5.18 is an example of a circuit in which the transistor is biased in the cutoff region. In this circuit, the voltages $V_{BE} = 0$ and $V_{BC} = -5$ V are consistent with the definition of the cutoff region. Thus, we expect the currents to be negligibly small. If we use the open-circuit model in Fig. 5.17(c), the currents I_C, I_E, and I_B are all predicted to be zero.

If a more exact indication of the currents in the circuit is required, we can fall back on the transport model equations. For the circuit in Fig. 5.18, the base-emitter voltage is exactly zero, and $V_{BC} \ll 0$. Therefore, Eqs. (5.13) reduce to

$$I_C = I_S\left(1 + \frac{1}{\beta_R}\right) = \frac{I_S}{\alpha_R} = \frac{10^{-16}\text{ A}}{0.25} = 4 \times 10^{-16}\text{ A}$$

$$I_E = I_S = 10^{-16}\text{ A}$$

$$I_B = -\frac{I_S}{\beta_R} = -\frac{10^{-16}\text{ A}}{\frac{1}{3}} = -3 \times 10^{-16}\text{ A}$$

The calculated currents in the terminals are very small but nonzero. Note, in particular, that the base current is not zero and that small currents exit both the emitter and base terminals of the transistor. As a check on our results, we see that Kirchhoff's current law is satisfied for the transistor treated as a supernode: $i_C + i_B = i_E$. Here again we see an example of the use of different levels of modeling to achieve different degrees of precision in the answer [$(I_C, I_E, I_B) = (0, 0, 0)$ or $(4 \times 10^{-16}$ A, 10^{-16} A, -3×10^{-16} A)]. ◆

5.9 MODEL SIMPLIFICATIONS FOR THE FORWARD-ACTIVE REGION

Probably the most important region of operation of the BJT is the forward-active region, in which the emitter-base junction is forward-biased and the collector-base junction is reverse-biased. In this region, the transistor can exhibit high voltage and current gains and is useful for analog amplification. From Table 5.2, we see that the forward-active region of an *npn* transistor corresponds to $v_{BE} \geq 0$ and $v_{BC} \leq 0$. In most cases, the forward-active region will have

$$v_{BE} > 4\frac{kT}{q} = 0.1\text{ V} \qquad \text{and} \qquad v_{BC} < -4\frac{kT}{q} = -0.1\text{ V}$$

and we can make the following simplifications to Eqs. (5.13):

$$i_C = I_S\left[\exp\left(\frac{v_{BE}}{V_T}\right) - \exp\left(\frac{v_{BC}}{V_T}\right)^{0}\right] - \frac{I_S}{\beta_R}\left[\exp\left(\frac{v_{BC}}{V_T}\right)^{0} - 1\right]$$

$$i_E = I_S\left[\exp\left(\frac{v_{BE}}{V_T}\right) - \exp\left(\frac{v_{BC}}{V_T}\right)^{0}\right] + \frac{I_S}{\beta_F}\left[\exp\left(\frac{v_{BE}}{V_T}\right) - 1\right] \qquad (5.33)$$

$$i_B = \frac{I_S}{\beta_F}\left[\exp\left(\frac{v_{BE}}{V_T}\right) - 1\right] + \frac{I_S}{\beta_R}\left[\exp\left(\frac{v_{BC}}{V_T}\right)^{0} - 1\right]$$

These simplifications yield:

$$i_C = I_S \exp\left(\frac{v_{BE}}{V_T}\right) + \frac{I_S}{\beta_R}$$

$$i_E = \frac{I_S}{\alpha_F} \exp\left(\frac{v_{BE}}{V_T}\right) - \frac{I_S}{\beta_F} \qquad (5.34)$$

$$i_B = \frac{I_S}{\beta_F} \exp\left(\frac{v_{BE}}{V_T}\right) - \frac{I_S}{\beta_F} - \frac{I_S}{\beta_R}$$

The exponential term in each of these expressions is usually huge compared to the other terms. By neglecting the small terms, we find the most useful simplifications of the BJT model for the forward-active region:

$$i_C = I_S \exp\left(\frac{v_{BE}}{V_T}\right)$$

$$i_E = \frac{I_S}{\alpha_F} \exp\left(\frac{v_{BE}}{V_T}\right) \qquad (5.35)$$

$$i_B = \frac{I_S}{\beta_F} \exp\left(\frac{v_{BE}}{V_T}\right)$$

In these equations, the fundamental, exponential relationship between all the terminal currents and the base-emitter voltage v_{BE} is once again clear. In the forward-active region, the terminal currents all have the form of diode currents in which the controlling voltage is the base-emitter junction potential. It is also important to note that the currents are all independent of the base-collector voltage v_{BC}. The collector current i_C can be modeled as a voltage-controlled current source that is controlled by the base-emitter voltage and independent of the collector voltage.

By taking ratios of the terminal currents in Eq. (5.35), the two auxiliary relationships for the forward-active region are found:

$$i_C = \alpha_F i_E \qquad \text{and} \qquad i_C = \beta_F i_B \qquad (5.36)$$

Observing that $i_E = i_C + i_B$ and using Eq. (5.36) yields a third important result:

$$i_E = (\beta_F + 1)i_B \qquad (5.37)$$

The results from Eqs.(5.36) and (5.37) are placed in a circuit context in Fig. 5.19. In the circuit in Fig. 5.19(a), the emitter current is forced by the current source to be $I_E = 100\ \mu\text{A}$. This current will forward-bias the emitter-base junction so that $V_{BE} > 0$. Also, $V_{BC} = -5$ V, so the bias conditions satisfy the definition of the forward-active re-

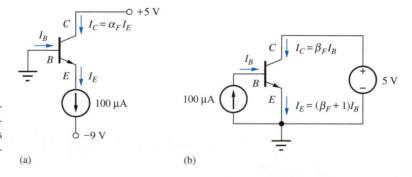

Figure 5.19 Two *npn* transistors operating in the forward-active region ($\alpha_F = 0.95$ is assumed for the example calculations).

(a)   (b)

gion. The base and collector currents can be found using Eqs. (5.36) and (5.37) with $I_E = 100 \ \mu A$:

$$I_C = \alpha_F I_E = 0.95 \cdot 100 \ \mu A = 95 \ \mu A$$

Solving for β_F gives

$$\beta_F = \frac{\alpha_F}{1 - \alpha_F} = \frac{0.95}{1 - .95} = 19 \qquad \beta_F + 1 = 20$$

and

$$I_B = \frac{I_E}{\beta_F + 1} = \frac{100 \ \mu A}{20} = 5 \ \mu A$$

We see that most of the current being forced out of the emitter by the current source comes directly through the transistor from the collector. This is the common-base mode in which $i_C = \alpha_F i_E$ with $\alpha_F \approx 1$.

In the circuit in Fig. 5.19(b), base current I_B is now forced to equal the 100-μA current source. This current enters the base and exits the emitter, forward-biasing the base-emitter junction. We expect that $V_{BE} \approx 0.7$ V, and $V_{BC} = V_{BE} - 5 = -4.3$ V. Thus, the bias conditions again satisfy the definition of the forward-active region, and the collector and emitter currents can be found using Eqs. (5.36) and (5.37) with $I_B = 100 \ \mu A$:

$$I_C = \beta_F I_B = 19 \cdot 100 \ \mu A = 1.90 \ mA$$
$$I_E = (\beta_F + 1) I_B = 20 \cdot 100 \ \mu A = 2.00 \ mA$$

A large amplification of the current takes place when the current is injected into the base terminal in Fig. 5.19(b) in contrast to when it is injected into the emitter terminal in Fig. 5.19(a). This is the common-emitter mode, in which $i_C = \beta_F i_B$ and $i_E = (\beta_F + 1) i_B$. Large amplification occurs because $\beta_F \gg 1$.

As illustrated in the preceding simple examples, Eqs. (5.36) and (5.37) can often be used to greatly simplify the analysis of circuits operating in the forward-active region. However, remember this caveat well: **The results in Eqs. (5.36) and (5.37) are valid *only* for the forward-active region of operation!**

Based on Eq. (5.36), the BJT is often considered a current-controlled device. However, from Eqs. (5.35), we see that the fundamental physics-based behavior of the BJT in the forward-active region is that of a (nonlinear) voltage-controlled current source. The base current should be considered as an unwanted defect current that must be supplied to the base in order for the transistor to operate. In an ideal BJT, β_F would be infinite, the base current would be zero, and the collector and emitter currents would be identical, just as for the FET. (Unfortunately, it is impossible to fabricate such a BJT.)

Equations (5.35) lead to the simplified circuit model for the forward-active region shown in Fig. 5.20. The current in the base-emitter diode is amplified by the common-emitter current gain β_F and appears in the collector terminal. However, remember that the base and collector currents are exponentially related to the base-emitter voltage. Because the base-emitter diode is forward-biased in the forward-active region, the transistor model of Fig. 5.20 can be further simplified to that of Fig. 5.21, in which the diode is replaced by its constant voltage drop (CVD) model, in this case $V_{BE} = 0.7$ V. The dc base and emitter voltages differ by the 0.7-V diode voltage drop in the forward-active region.

Frequency Dependence of the Common-Emitter Current Gain

The forward-biased diffusion and reverse-biased *pn* junction capacitances of the bipolar transistor cause the current gain of the transistor to be frequency-dependent. An example

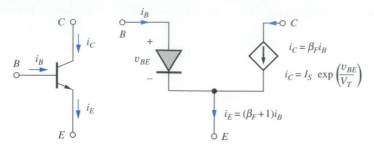

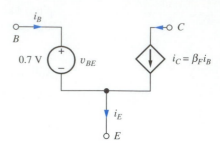

Figure 5.20 Simplified model for the *npn* transistor for the forward-active region.

Figure 5.21 Further simplification of the *npn* model for the forward-active region.

of this dependence is given in Fig. 5.22. At low frequencies, the current gain has a constant value β_F, but as frequency increases, the current gain begins to decrease. The **unity-gain frequency** f_T is defined to be the frequency at which the magnitude of the current gain is equal to 1. The behavior in the graph is described mathematically by

$$\beta(f) = \frac{\beta_F}{\sqrt{1 + \left(\dfrac{\beta_F f}{f_T}\right)^2}} = \frac{\beta_F}{\sqrt{1 + \left(\dfrac{f}{f_\beta}\right)^2}} \tag{5.38}$$

where $f_\beta = f_T/\beta_F$ is the **β-cutoff frequency.** For the transistor in Fig. 5.22, $\beta_F = 125$ and $f_T = 300$ MHz.

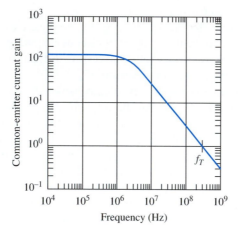

Figure 5.22 Magnitude of the common-emitter current gain β vs. frequency.

EXERCISE: What is the β-cutoff frequency for the transistor in Fig. 5.22?

ANSWER: 2.4 MHz

Transconductance

An important transistor parameter called the **transconductance** relates changes in i_C to changes in v_{BE} and is defined by

$$g_m = \left.\frac{di_C}{dv_{BE}}\right|_{Q-\text{point}} \tag{5.39}$$

For Q-points in the forward-active region, Eq. (5.39) can be evaluated using the collector-current expression from Eq. (5.35):

$$g_m = \frac{d}{dv_{BE}}\left\{ I_S \exp\left(\frac{v_{BE}}{V_T}\right)\right\}\Bigg|_{Q-point} = \frac{1}{V_T} I_S \exp\left(\frac{V_{BE}}{V_T}\right) = \frac{I_C}{V_T} \tag{5.40}$$

Equation (5.40) represents the fundamental relationship for the transconductance of the bipolar transistor, in which we find g_m is directly proportional to collector current. This is an important result that is used many times in bipolar circuit design. It is worth noting that the expression for the diffusion capacitance defined in Eq. (5.31) can be rewritten as

$$C_D = g_m \tau_F \tag{5.41}$$

EXERCISE: What is the value of the BJT transconductance g_m at $I_C = 100$ μA and $I_C = 1$ mA?

ANSWERS: 4 mS; 40 mS

EXAMPLE 5.4:   Suppose we want to find the Q-point for the transistor in the circuit in Fig. 5.23. In this circuit, the base-collector junction is reverse-biased by the +9-V source ($V_{BC} = -9$ V). The combination of the resistor and the −9-V source will forward-bias the base-emitter junction. Thus, the transistor appears to be biased in the forward-active region. As a result of this estimate, the simplified model for the forward-active region has been substituted into the circuit in Fig. 5.23(b).

The currents can now be found by using KVL around the base-emitter loop:

$$V_{BE} + 8200I_E - V_{EE} = 0$$

and using $V_{BE} = 0.7$ V,

$$0.7 + 8200I_E - 9 = 0 \quad \text{or} \quad I_E = \frac{8.3 \text{ V}}{8200 \text{ }\Omega} = 1.01 \text{ mA}$$

At the emitter node, $I_E = (\beta_F + 1)I_B$, so

$$I_B = \frac{1.01 \text{ mA}}{50 + 1} = 19.8 \text{ μA} \quad \text{and} \quad I_C = \beta_F I_B = 0.990 \text{ mA}$$

Because all the currents are positive, the assumption of forward-active region operation was correct. The collector-emitter voltage is equal to

$$V_{CE} = V_{CC} - (-V_{BE}) = 9 + 0.7 = 9.7 \text{ V}$$

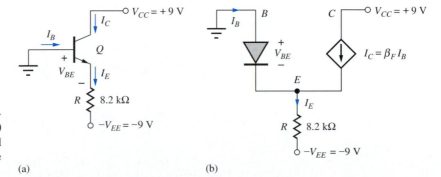

Figure 5.23 (a) *npn* Transistor circuit (assume $\beta_F = 50$ and $\beta_R = 1$). (b) Simplified model for the forward-active region.

(a)   (b)

Figure 5.24 displays the results of simulation of the collector current of the transistor in Fig. 5.23 versus the supply voltage V_{CC}. For $V_{CC} > 0$, the collector-base junction will be reverse-biased, and the transistor will be in the forward-active region. In this region, the circuit behaves essentially as a 1-mA ideal current source in which the output current is independent of V_{CC}. Note that the circuit actually behaves as a current source for V_{CC} down to approximately -0.5 V. By the definitions in Table 5.2, the transistor enters saturation for $V_{CC} < 0$, but the transistor does not actually enter heavy saturation until the base-collector junction begins to conduct for $V_{BC} \geq +0.5$ V. ◆

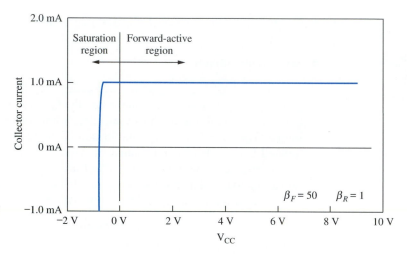

Figure 5.24 Simulation of output characteristics of circuit of Fig. 5.23(a).

EXERCISE: Find the three terminal currents in the transistor in Fig. 5.23 if the resistor value is changed to 5.6 kΩ.

ANSWER: 1.48 mA, 29.1 μA, 1.45 mA.

5.10 SIMPLIFIED MODEL FOR THE REVERSE-ACTIVE REGION

In the reverse-active region, also called the inverse-active region, the roles of the emitter and collector terminals are reversed. The base-collector diode is forward-biased and the base-emitter junction is reverse-biased. Equations (5.42) indicate the simplifications for these bias conditions.

$$i_C = I_S \left[\exp\left(\frac{v_{BE}}{V_T}\right)^{0} - \exp\left(\frac{v_{BC}}{V_T}\right) \right] - \frac{I_S}{\beta_R} \left[\exp\left(\frac{v_{BC}}{V_T}\right) - 1 \right]$$

$$i_E = I_S \left[\exp\left(\frac{v_{BE}}{V_T}\right)^{0} - \exp\left(\frac{v_{BC}}{V_T}\right) \right] + \frac{I_S}{\beta_F} \left[\exp\left(\frac{v_{BE}}{V_T}\right)^{0} - 1 \right] \qquad (5.42)$$

$$i_B = \frac{I_S}{\beta_F} \left[\exp\left(\frac{v_{BE}}{V_T}\right)^{0} - 1 \right] + \frac{I_S}{\beta_R} \left[\exp\left(\frac{v_{BC}}{V_T}\right) - 1 \right]$$

Using these simplifications and neglecting the -1 terms relative to the exponential terms yields the simplified equations for the reverse-active region:

$$i_C = -\frac{I_S}{\alpha_R} \exp\left(\frac{v_{BC}}{V_T}\right)$$

$$i_E = -I_S \exp\left(\frac{v_{BC}}{V_T}\right) \tag{5.43}$$

$$i_B = \frac{I_S}{\beta_R} \exp\left(\frac{v_{BC}}{V_T}\right)$$

Ratios of these equations yield $i_E = -\beta_R i_B$ and $i_E = \alpha_R i_C$.

Equations (5.43) lead to the simplified circuit model for the reverse-active region shown in Fig. 5.25. The base current in the base-collector diode is amplified by the reverse common-emitter current gain β_R and enters the emitter terminal.

In the reverse-active region, the base-collector diode is now forward-biased, and the transistor model of Fig. 5.25 can be further simplified to that of Fig. 5.26, in which the diode is replaced by its CVD model with a voltage of 0.7 V. The base and collector voltages differ only by one 0.7-V diode drop in the reverse-active region.

The collector and emitter terminals of the *npn* transistor in Fig. 5.23 have been interchanged in the circuit in Fig. 5.27 (the transistor may have been plugged into the circuit backward by accident). The transistor is now operating in the reverse-active region with $v_{BC} = 0.7$ V and $v_{BE} = -9$ V and is replaced with its simplified model in Fig. 5.27(b). The current $(-I_C)$ is now equal to

$$(-I_C) = \frac{-0.7\,\text{V} - (-9\,\text{V})}{8200\,\Omega} = 1.01\,\text{mA}$$

The current through the 8.2-kΩ resistor is unchanged compared to that in Fig. 5.23. However, significant differences exist in the currents in the base terminal and the +9-V source. At the collector node, $(-I_C) = (\beta_R + 1)I_B$, and at the emitter, $(-I_E) = \beta_R I_B$. Thus,

$$I_B = \frac{1.01\,\text{mA}}{2} = 0.505\,\text{mA} \qquad \text{and} \qquad -I_E = (1)I_B = 0.505\,\text{mA}$$

These currents are very different from those found for Fig. 5.23. Note that the calculated current directions are all consistent with the assumption of reverse-active region operation.

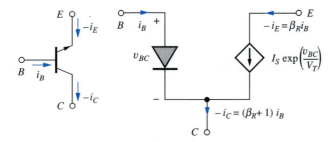

Figure 5.25 Simplified *npn* circuit model for the reverse-active region.

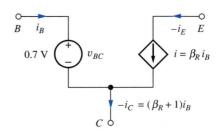

Figure 5.26 Simplified *npn* model for the reverse-active region.

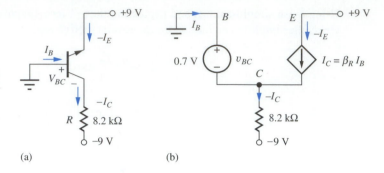

Figure 5.27 (a) Circuit of Fig. 5.23 with *npn* transistor orientation reversed. (b) Circuit simplification using the model for the reverse-active region. (Analysis of the circuit uses $\beta_F = 50$ and $\beta_R = 1$.)

(a)   (b)

EXERCISE: Find the three terminal currents in the transistor in Fig. 5.27 if the resistor value is changed to $5.6\,\text{k}\Omega$.

ANSWER: 1.48 mA, 0.741 mA, 0.741 mA

5.11 MODELING OPERATION IN THE SATURATION REGION

The fourth and final region of operation is called the saturation region. In this region, both junctions are forward-biased, and the transistor typically operates with a small voltage between collector and emitter terminals. In the saturation region, the dc value of v_{CE} is called the saturation voltage of the transistor: v_{CESAT} for the *npn* transistor or v_{ECSAT} for the *pnp* transistor.

In order to determine v_{CESAT}, we assume that both junctions are forward-biased so that i_C and i_B from Eqs. (5.13) can be approximated as

$$i_C = I_S \exp\left(\frac{v_{BE}}{V_T}\right) - \frac{I_S}{\alpha_R} \exp\left(\frac{v_{BC}}{V_T}\right)$$

$$i_B = \frac{I_S}{\beta_F} \exp\left(\frac{v_{BE}}{V_T}\right) + \frac{I_S}{\beta_R} \exp\left(\frac{v_{BC}}{V_T}\right)$$

(5.44)

Simultaneous solution of these equations using $\beta_R = \alpha_R/(1 - \alpha_R)$ yields expressions for the base-emitter and base-collector voltages:

$$v_{BE} = V_T \ln \frac{i_B + (1 - \alpha_R)i_C}{I_S\left[\dfrac{1}{\beta_F} + (1 - \alpha_R)\right]}$$

(5.45)

$$v_{BC} = V_T \ln \frac{i_B - \dfrac{i_C}{\beta_F}}{I_S\left[\dfrac{1}{\alpha_R}\right]\left[\dfrac{1}{\beta_F} + (1 - \alpha_R)\right]}$$

By applying KVL to the transistor in Fig. 5.28, we find that the collector-emitter voltage of the transistor is $v_{CE} = v_{BE} - v_{BC}$, and substituting the results from Eqs.(5.45) into this equation yields an expression for the saturation voltage of the *npn* transistor:

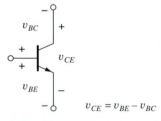

Figure 5.28 Relationship between the terminal voltages of the transistor.

$$v_{\text{CESAT}} = V_T \ln\left[\left(\frac{1}{\alpha_R}\right)\frac{1 + \dfrac{i_C}{(\beta_R + 1)i_B}}{1 - \dfrac{i_C}{\beta_F i_B}}\right] \quad \text{for } i_B > \frac{i_C}{\beta_F}$$

(5.46)

This equation is important and highly useful in the design of saturated digital switching circuits. For a given value of collector current, Eq. (5.46) can be used to determine the base current required to achieve a desired value of v_{CESAT}.

Note that Eq. (5.46) is valid only for $i_B > i_C/\beta_F$. This is an auxiliary condition that can be used to define saturation region operation. The ratio i_C/β_F represents the base current needed to maintain transistor operation in the forward-active region. If the base current exceeds the value needed for forward-active region operation, the transistor will enter saturation. The actual value of i_C/i_B is often called the **forced beta** $\boldsymbol{\beta_{FOR}}$ of the transistor, where $\beta_{FOR} \leq \beta_F$.

EXAMPLE 5.5: Calculate the saturation voltage for an *npn* transistor with $I_C = 1$ mA, $I_B = 0.1$ mA, $\beta_F = 50$, and $\beta_R = 1$.

SOLUTION: Because $I_C/I_B = 10 < \beta_F$, the transistor will indeed be saturated, so Eq.(5.45) can safely be used. Using $\alpha_R = \beta_R/(\beta_R+1) = 0.5$ and $I_C/I_B = 10$ yields

$$V_{CESAT} = V_T \ln \left[\left(\frac{1}{\alpha_R} \right) \frac{1 + \dfrac{I_C}{(\beta_R + 1)I_B}}{1 - \dfrac{I_C}{\beta_F I_B}} \right] = (0.025 \text{ V}) \ln \left[\left(\frac{1}{0.5} \right) \frac{1 + \dfrac{1 \text{ mA}}{2(0.1 \text{ mA})}}{1 - \dfrac{1 \text{ mA}}{50(0.1 \text{ mA})}} \right]$$

$$= 0.068 \text{ V}$$

◆

We see that the value of V_{CE} in Example 5.5 is indeed quite small. However, it is nonzero even for $i_C = 0$ (see Prob. 5.34)! It is impossible to force the forward voltages across both *pn* junctions to be exactly equal. This is an important difference between the BJT and the MOSFET. In the linear region of the MOSFET, the voltage between drain and source becomes zero when the drain current is zero.

Figure 5.29 shows the simplified model for the transistor in saturation in which the two diodes are assumed to be forward-biased and replaced by their respective on-voltages. The forward voltages of both diodes are normally higher in saturation than in the forward-active region, as indicated in the figure by $V_{BESAT} = 0.75$ V and $V_{BCSAT} = 0.7$ V. In this case, V_{CESAT} is 50 mV. In saturation, the terminal currents are determined by the external circuit elements; no simplifying relationships exist between i_C, i_B and i_E other than $i_C + i_B = i_E$.

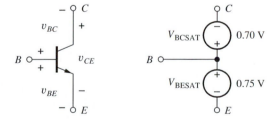

Figure 5.29 Simplified model for the *npn* transistor in saturation.

EXERCISE: Use Eqs. (5.45) to find V_{BESAT} and V_{BCSAT} for the transistor in Example 5.5 if $I_S = 10^{-15}$ A.

ANSWERS: 0.694 V, 0.627 V

5.12 THE EARLY EFFECT AND EARLY VOLTAGE

In the transistor output characteristics in Figs. 5.11 and 5.13, the current saturated at a constant value in the forward-active region. However, in a real transistor, there is actually a positive slope to the characteristics, as shown in Fig. 5.30. The collector current is not entirely independent of v_{CE}.

It has been observed experimentally that when the output characteristic curves are extrapolated back to the point of zero collector current, the curves all intersect at a common point, $v_{CE} = -V_A$. This phenomenon is called the **Early effect** [4], and the voltage V_A is called the **Early voltage** after James Early from Bell Laboratories, who first identified the source of the behavior. A relatively small value of Early voltage (14 V) has been used in Fig. 5.30 to exaggerate the characteristics. Values for the Early voltage more typically fall in the range

$$25 \text{ V} \leq V_A \leq 150 \text{ V}$$

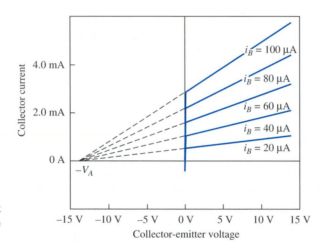

Figure 5.30 Transistor output characteristics identifying the Early voltage V_A.

Modeling the Early Effect

The dependence of the collector current on collector-emitter voltage is easily included in the simplified mathematical model for the forward-active region of the BJT by modifying Eqs. (5.35) as follows:

$$i_C = I_S \left[\exp\left(\frac{v_{BE}}{V_T}\right) \right] \left[1 + \frac{v_{CE}}{V_A} \right]$$

$$\beta_F = \beta_{FO} \left[1 + \frac{v_{CE}}{V_A} \right] \tag{5.47}$$

$$i_B = \frac{I_S}{\beta_{FO}} \left[\exp\left(\frac{v_{BE}}{V_T}\right) \right]$$

β_{FO} represents the value of β_F extrapolated to $V_{CE} = 0$. In these expressions, the collector current and current gain now have the same dependence on v_{CE}, but the base current remains independent of v_{CE}. This is consistent with Fig. 5.30, in which the separation of the constant-base-current curves in the forward-active region increases as v_{CE} increases, indicating that the current gain β_F is increasing with v_{CE}.

EXERCISE: A transistor has $I_S = 10^{-15}$ A, $\beta_{FO} = 75$, and $V_A = 50$ V and is operating with $V_{BE} = 0.7$ V and $V_{CE} = 10$ V. What are I_B, β_F, and I_C? What would be β_F and I_C if $V_A = \infty$?

ANSWERS: 19.3 μA, 90, 1.74 mA; 75, 1.45 mA

Origin of the Early Effect

Modulation of the base width W_B of the transistor by the collector-base voltage is the cause of the Early effect. As the reverse bias across the collector-base junction increases, the width of the collector-base depletion layer increases, and the width W_B of the base decreases. This mechanism, termed **base-width modulation,** is depicted in Fig. 5.31, in which the collector-base space charge region width is shown for two different values of collector-base voltage corresponding to base widths of W_B and W_B'. Equation (5.22) demonstrated that collector current is inversely proportional to the base width W_B, so a decrease in W_B results in an increase in the transport current i_T. This decrease in W_B as V_{CB} increases is the cause of the Early effect.

The Early effect reduces the output resistance of the bipolar transistor and places an important limit on the amplification factor of the BJT. These limitations are discussed in detail in Part III, Chapter 13.

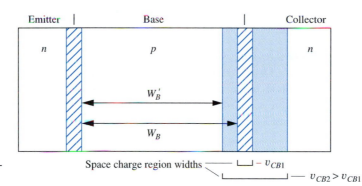

Figure 5.31 Base-width modulation, or Early effect.

5.13 BIASING THE BJT

The goal of biasing is to establish a known quiescent operating point, or Q-point. In the bipolar transistor, the Q-point is represented by the dc values of the collector current and collector-emitter voltage (I_C, V_{CE}) for the *npn* transistor, or emitter-collector voltage (I_C, V_{EC}) for the *pnp*. The Q-point establishes the initial operating region of the transistor. From Eqs. (5.40) and (5.41), we know that I_C controls the values of the diffusion capacitance and transconductance. In later chapters, we will find that the Q-point also controls the values of the input and output resistances of the transistor.

In the last several sections, we presented simplified models for the four operating regions of the BJT. In general, we will not explicitly insert the simplified circuit models for the transistor into the circuit but instead will use the mathematical relationships that were derived for the specific operating region of interest. For example, in the forward-active region, the results $V_{BE} = 0.7$ V and $I_C = \beta_F I_B$ will be utilized to directly simplify the circuit analysis.

In the dc biasing examples that follow, the Early voltage is assumed to be infinite. In general, including the Early voltage in bias circuit calculations substantially increases

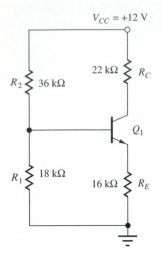

Figure 5.32 The four-resistor bias network. (Assume $\beta_F = 75$ for analysis.)

the complexity of the analysis but typically changes the results by less than 15 percent. In most cases, the tolerances on the values of resistors and independent sources will be 5 to 10 percent, and the transistor current-gain β_F may vary by a factor of 4:1 to 10:1. For example, the current gain of a transistor may be specified to be a minimum of 50 with a typical value of 100 but no upper bound specified (see Appendix D). These tolerances will swamp out any error due to neglect of the Early voltage. Thus, basic hand design will be done ignoring the Early effect, and if more precision is needed, the calculations can be refined through SPICE analysis.

EXAMPLE 5.6: One of the best circuits for stabilizing the Q-point of a transistor is the four-resistor bias network in Fig. 5.32. R_1 and R_2 form a resistive voltage divider across the power supplies (12 V and 0 V) and attempt to establish a fixed voltage at the base of transistor Q_1. R_E and R_C are used to define the emitter current and collector-emitter voltage of the transistor.

Our goal is to find the Q-point of the transistor: (I_C, V_{CE}). The first steps in analysis of the circuit in Fig. 5.32 are to split the power supply into two equal voltages, as in Fig. 5.33(a), and then to simplify the circuit by replacing the base-bias network by its Thévenin equivalent circuit, as shown in Fig. 5.33(b). V_{EQ} and R_{EQ} are given by

$$V_{EQ} = V_{CC}\frac{R_1}{R_1 + R_2} \qquad R_{EQ} = \frac{R_1 R_2}{R_1 + R_2} \qquad (5.48)$$

For the values in Fig. 5.33, $V_{EQ} = 4$ V and $R_{EQ} = 12\,k\Omega$.

Detailed analysis begins by assuming a region of operation in order to simplify the BJT model equations. Because the most common region of operation for this bias circuit is the forward-active region, we will assume it to be the region of operation. Using Kirchhoff's voltage law around loop 1:

$$V_{EQ} = R_{EQ}I_B + V_{BE} + R_E I_E \qquad (5.49)$$

or
$$4 = 12{,}000I_B + V_{BE} + 16{,}000I_E \qquad (5.50)$$

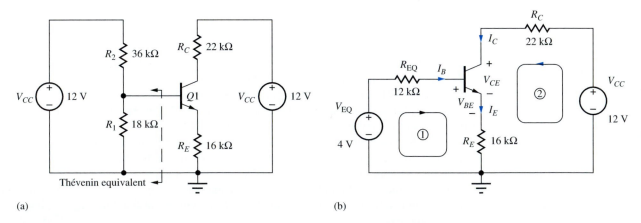

Figure 5.33 (a) Four-resistor bias circuit with replicated sources. (b) Thévenin simplification of the four-resistor bias network. (Assume $\beta_F = 75$.)

Because we are assuming forward-active region operation in which $V_{BE} = 0.7$ V and $I_E = (\beta_F + 1)I_B$, Eq. (5.50) becomes

$$4 = 12{,}000I_B + 0.7 + 16{,}000(\beta_F + 1)I_B \tag{5.51}$$

Using $\beta_F = 75$ and solving for I_B yields

$$I_B = \frac{4\text{ V} - 0.7\text{ V}}{1.23 \times 10^6\ \Omega} = 2.68\ \mu\text{A} \qquad I_C = \beta_F I_B = 201\ \mu\text{A}$$

$$I_E = (\beta_F + 1)I_B = 204\ \mu\text{A}$$

To find V_{CE}, loop 2 is used:

$$V_{CE} = V_{CC} - R_C I_C - R_E I_E = V_{CC} - \left(R_C + \frac{R_E}{\alpha_F}\right)I_C \tag{5.52}$$

because $I_E = I_C/\alpha_F$. For the values in the circuit,

$$V_{CE} = 12 - 38{,}200I_C = 12\text{ V} - 7.68\text{ V} = 4.32\text{ V} \tag{5.53}$$

All the calculated currents are greater than zero, and using the result in Eq. (5.53), $V_{BC} = V_{BE} - V_{CE} = 0.7 - 4.32 = -3.62$ V. Thus, the base-collector junction is reverse-biased, and the assumption of forward-active region operation was correct. The Q-point resulting from our analysis is $(205\ \mu\text{A},\ 4.17\text{ V})$.

Before leaving this bias example, let us draw the load line for the circuit and locate the Q-point on the output characteristics. The load-line equation for this circuit already appeared as Eq. (5.52):

$$V_{CE} = V_{CC} - \left(R_C + \frac{R_E}{\alpha_F}\right)I_C = 12 - 38{,}200I_C \tag{5.54}$$

Two points are needed to plot the load line. Choosing $I_C = 0$ yields $V_{CE} = 12$ V, and picking $V_{CE} = 0$ yields $I_C = 314\ \mu\text{A}$. The resulting load line is plotted on the transistor common-emitter output characteristics in Fig. 5.34. The base current was already found to be 2.7 μA, and the intersection of the $I_B = 2.7$-μA

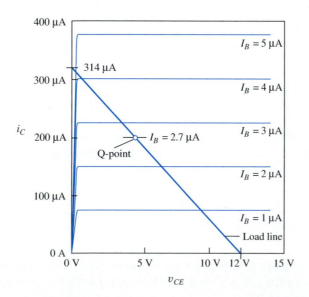

Figure 5.34 Load line for the four-resistor bias circuit.

characteristic with the load line defines the Q-point. In this case we must estimate the location of the $I_B = 2.7$-μA curve.   ◆

> **EXERCISE:** Find the Q-point for the circuit in Fig. 5.34 if $R_1 = 180$ kΩ and $R_2 = 360$ kΩ.
>
> **ANSWERS:** $(185\ \mu\text{A}, 4.93\ \text{V})$

Design Objectives for the Four-Resistor Bias Network

Now that we have analyzed a circuit involving the four-resistor bias network, let us explore the design objectives of this bias technique by solving for the emitter current from Eq. (5.49):

$$I_E = \frac{V_{\text{EQ}} - V_{BE} - R_{\text{EQ}}I_B}{R_E} \approx \frac{V_{\text{EQ}} - V_{BE}}{R_E} \qquad \text{for } R_{\text{EQ}}I_B \ll (V_{\text{EQ}} - V_{BE}) \quad (5.55)$$

The value of the Thévenin equivalent resistance R_{EQ} is normally designed to be small enough to neglect the voltage drop caused by the base current flowing through R_{EQ}. Under these conditions, I_E is set by the combination of V_{EQ}, V_{BE}, and R_E. In addition, V_{EQ} is normally designed to be large enough that small variations in the assumed value of V_{BE} will not materially affect the value of I_E.

In the original bias circuit reproduced in Fig. 5.35, the assumption that the voltage drop $I_B R_{\text{EQ}} \ll (V_{\text{EQ}} - V_{BE})$ is equivalent to assuming $I_B \ll I_2$ so that $I_1 \approx I_2$. For this case, the base current of Q_1 does not disturb the voltage divider action of R_1 and R_2. Using the approximate expression in Eq. (5.55) estimates the emitter current in the circuit in Fig. 5.33 to be

$$I_E = \frac{4\ \text{V} - 0.7\ \text{V}}{16{,}000\ \Omega} = 206\ \mu\text{A}$$

which is essentially the same as the result that was calculated using the more exact expression. This is the result that should be achieved with a proper bias network design. If the Q-point is independent of I_B, it will also be independent of current gain β (a poorly controlled transistor parameter). The emitter current will then be approximately the same for a transistor with a current gain of 50 or 500.

Generally, a very large number of possible combinations of R_1 and R_2 will yield the desired value of V_{EQ}. An additional constraint is needed to finalize the design choice. An obvious choice is to limit the power used in the base-voltage-divider network by choosing $I_2 \leq I_C/5$. This choice ensures that the power dissipated in bias resistors R_1 and R_2 is less than 17 percent of the total quiescent power consumed by the circuit and will at the same time ensure that $I_2 \gg I_B$ for $\beta \geq 50$.

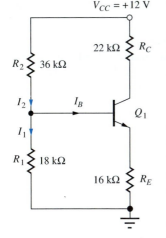

Figure 5.35 Currents in the base-bias network.

> **EXERCISE:** Find the Q-point for the circuit in Fig. 5.32 if β_F is 500.
>
> **ANSWERS:** $(212\ \mu\text{A}, 3.94\ \text{V})$

EXAMPLE 5.7: Suppose the circuit of Fig. 5.35 is to be redesigned to give a Q-point of $(750\ \mu\text{A}, 5\ \text{V})$ using a 15-V supply with a transistor having a minimum current gain of 100.

We assume that the voltage drop in R_{EQ} can be neglected. To find V_{EQ}, we must know the voltage across the emitter resistor R_E. It is common to divide the remaining power supply voltage $V_{CC} - V_{CE} = 10$ V equally between R_E and R_C. Thus, $V_E = 5$ V and $V_{EQ} = V_E + V_{BE} = 5.7$ V (neglecting $I_B R_{EQ}$). A relationship between R_1 and R_2 can be found using the formula for V_{EQ}:

$$\frac{R_1}{R_1 + R_2} = \frac{V_{EQ}}{V_{CC}} = \frac{5.7}{15} \tag{5.56}$$

Because the transistor has a minimum current gain of 100, $I_B \leq 7.5$ μA, and a choice of $I_2 \geq 75$ μA is reasonable. Let us choose $I_2 = 100$ μA. Because $I_2 \gg I_B$, $I_1 \approx I_2$ so that

$$V_{CC} = I_2 R_2 + I_1 R_1 \approx I_2(R_1 + R_2)$$

or
$$R_1 + R_2 = \frac{V_{CC}}{I_2} = \frac{15 \text{ V}}{100 \text{ μA}} = 150 \text{ k}\Omega$$

Using Eq. (5.56) yields $R_1 = 57$ kΩ and $R_2 = 93$ kΩ. Finally, the values of R_C and R_E are given by

$$R_C = \frac{5 \text{ V}}{I_C} = \frac{5 \text{ V}}{750 \text{ μA}} = 6.67 \text{ k}\Omega \quad \text{and} \quad R_E = \frac{5 \text{ V}}{I_E} = \frac{5 \text{ V}}{758 \text{ μA}} = 6.60 \text{ k}\Omega$$

These values will yield a Q-point very close to the design goals.

However, if we were going to build this circuit in the laboratory, we must use standard values for the resistors. Referring to the table of resistor values in Appendix C, we find that the closest available values are $R_1 = 56$ kΩ, $R_2 = 91$ kΩ, $R_E = 6.8$ kΩ, and $R_C = 6.8$ kΩ. The final design using these values is in Fig. 5.36, for which SPICE predicts the Q-point to be (735 μA, 4.96 V), with $V_{BE} = 0.65$ V. ◆

EXAMPLE 5.8: Let us explore the impact of changing the collector resistor in the circuit of Fig. 5.32 from 22 kΩ to 56 kΩ, as shown in Fig. 5.37.

The analysis starts by again assuming that the transistor is in the forward-active region. Loop 1 in Fig. 5.37 is identical to that in Fig. 5.33, so that I_B is determined by Eq. (5.51) with $\beta_F = 75$:

$$I_B = \frac{4 \text{ V} - 0.7 \text{ V}}{1.23 \times 10^6 \text{ }\Omega} = 2.68 \text{ μA} \qquad I_C = \beta_F I_B = 201 \text{ μA}$$

$$I_E = (\beta_F + 1)I_B = 204 \text{ μA}$$

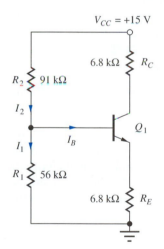

$V_{CC} = +15$ V

Figure 5.36 Final bias circuit design for a Q-point of (750 μA, 5 V).

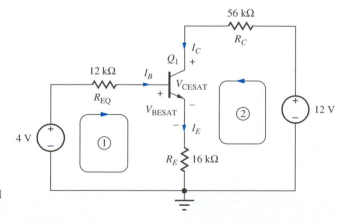

Figure 5.37 Bias circuit with collector resistor R_C increased to 56 kΩ ($\beta_F = 75$).

Using loop 2 to determine an expression for V_{CE} as in Eq. (5.52) yields:

$$V_{CE} = V_{CC} - \left(R_C + \frac{R_E}{\alpha_F}\right)I_C = 12 - 72{,}200I_C = -2.51 \text{ V}$$

The calculated value of V_{CE} is negative, which violates the assumption of forward-active region operation. (In addition, it is physically impossible for V_{CE} to become negative in this circuit.) Therefore, we must choose a new region of operation and reanalyze the circuit.

Because V_{CE} was negative, our second analysis attempt will assume that Q_1 is saturated (V_{CE} as small as possible). Writing the equations for loops 1 and 2:

$$4 = 12{,}000I_B + V_{BESAT} + 16{,}000I_E \qquad\qquad (5.57)$$
$$12 = 56{,}000I_C + V_{CESAT} + 16{,}000I_E$$

Using $V_{BESAT} = 0.75$ V, $V_{CESAT} = 0.05$ V, and $I_E = I_B + I_C$ results in

$$3.25 = 28{,}000I_B + 16{,}000I_C$$
$$11.95 = 16{,}000I_B + 72{,}000I_C$$

Solving these simultaneous equations gives

$$I_C = 160 \ \mu\text{A} \qquad I_B = 24 \ \mu\text{A} \qquad \text{and yields} \qquad I_E = 184 \ \mu\text{A}$$

The three terminal currents are all positive, and $I_C/I_B < \beta_F$ (that is, $\beta_{FOR} < \beta_F$). Therefore, saturation region operation is correct. The values of V_{BESAT} and V_{CESAT} can be calculated using Eqs. (5.57) as a check on the hand analysis and are found to be close to the assumed values: $V_{BESAT} = 0.77$ V and $V_{CESAT} = 0.096$ V.

Using SPICE analysis to check our hand calculations yields

$$I_C = 160 \ \mu\text{A} \qquad I_B = 28 \ \mu\text{A} \qquad I_E = 188 \ \mu\text{A}$$

The slight discrepancies are caused by round-off and the differences in V_{BESAT} and V_{CESAT} between our hand analysis and SPICE. ◆

EXAMPLE 5.9: Resistors consume large areas in integrated circuits, and the use of resistors is therefore avoided as much as possible in IC design. Various versions of the circuit in Fig. 5.38, called a **current mirror,** have evolved to become the primary class of bias circuits in ICs. The current mirror depends on the ability to fabricate transistors with virtually identical *i-v* characteristics in an integrated circuit. In the analysis that follows, Q_1 and Q_2 will be assumed to be **matched transistors,** which means that their respective values for parameters I_S, β_F, β_R, V_A, and so on are identical.

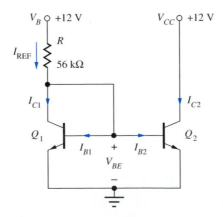

Figure 5.38 The basic current mirror circuit.

The transistors in this circuit operate in the forward-active region and have the same value of base-emitter voltage V_{BE}. Thus, the collector currents should be nearly the same. Analysis of circuit behavior begins by writing an expression for the current I_{REF} developed in resistor R using KCL at the collector node of Q_1:

$$I_{REF} = \frac{V_B - V_{BE}}{R} \qquad \text{and} \qquad I_{REF} = I_{C1} + I_{B1} + I_{B2} \tag{5.58}$$

Because the two transistors are matched and have the same V_{BE}, $I_{B1} = I_{B2}$ and $I_{C1} = I_{C2}$ [see Eqs. (5.35)]. Using $I_C = \beta_F I_B$ yields

$$I_{REF} = (\beta_F + 2)I_{B2} \qquad \text{and} \qquad I_{C2} = \beta_F I_{B2} = \beta_F \frac{I_{REF}}{\beta_F + 2} = \frac{I_{REF}}{1 + \dfrac{2}{\beta_F}} \tag{5.59}$$

For $\beta_F \gg 2$, Eq. (5.59) reduces to

$$I_{C2} \approx I_{REF} \qquad \text{where } I_{REF} = \frac{V_B - V_{BE}}{R} \tag{5.60}$$

For a current gain of 100, the collector current I_{C2} should match the reference current I_{REF} within 2 percent. Hence, the collector current of Q_2 mirrors the collector current of Q_1. For the values in Fig. 5.38 with $V_{BE} = 0.7$ V, $I_{C2} \approx I_{REF} = 202$ μA.

However, SPICE simulation with $\beta_F = 100$ and $V_A = 60$ V gives $I_{C1} = 198$ μA and $I_{C2} = 236$ μA, indicating that something has been overlooked in the analysis! When tight matching is required, we must improve our transistor model in order to better predict the behavior of the circuit. The two transistors in Fig. 5.38 operate with very different values of collector-emitter voltage, and we need to include the Early effect using Eqs. (5.47), as reproduced below. This is one example of a case in which the Early effect and Early voltage should not be neglected.

$$I_C = I_S \left[\exp\left(\frac{V_{BE}}{V_T}\right) \right]\left[1 + \frac{V_{CE}}{V_A} \right]$$

$$\beta_F = \beta_{FO}\left[1 + \frac{V_{CE}}{V_A} \right] \tag{5.61}$$

$$I_B = \frac{I_S}{\beta_{FO}}\left[\exp\left(\frac{V_{BE}}{V_T}\right) \right]$$

With these equations, the current I_{REF} can be expressed as

$$I_{REF} = I_S\left[\exp\left(\frac{V_{BE}}{V_T}\right) \right]\left[1 + \frac{V_{BE}}{V_A} \right] + 2\frac{I_S}{\beta_{FO}}\left[\exp\left(\frac{V_{BE}}{V_T}\right) \right]$$

or

$$I_S\left[\exp\left(\frac{V_{BE}}{V_T}\right) \right] = \frac{I_{REF}}{1 + \dfrac{V_{BE}}{V_A} + \dfrac{2}{\beta_{FO}}} \tag{5.62}$$

and the output current I_{C2} is then

$$I_{C2} = I_S\left[\exp\left(\frac{V_{BE}}{V_T}\right) \right]\left[1 + \frac{V_{CE2}}{V_A} \right] = I_{REF}\frac{1 + \dfrac{V_{CE2}}{V_A}}{1 + \dfrac{V_{BE}}{V_A} + \dfrac{2}{\beta_{FO}}} \tag{5.63}$$

For $\beta_F = 100$, $V_{BE} = 0.7$ V, and $V_A = 60$ V,

$$I_{C2} = I_{REF}\frac{1 + \dfrac{12\text{ V}}{60\text{ V}}}{1 + \dfrac{0.7\text{ V}}{60\text{ V}} + \dfrac{2}{100}} = I_{REF}\frac{1 + 0.2}{1 + 0.012 + 0.02} = 1.16 I_{REF} \qquad (5.64)$$

In Eq. (5.64), the output current and the reference current differ by 16 percent, due primarily to the finite Early voltage of the transistor. The current-gain error term is only a small contributor to the total mismatch between I_{REF} and I_{C2}. The Early effect accounts for the difference between the prediction of Eq. (5.59) and the SPICE results.

One reason for using this example is to demonstrate that the choice of model can have a significant impact on the results of analysis. The results of circuit analysis are only as good as the models chosen. The model used to develop Eq. (5.59) with $V_A = \infty$ and the model in SPICE containing a finite value of V_A represent different levels of modeling of the BJT. With experience, a circuit designer will develop insight that helps in the choice of the appropriate level of model. One attempts to use the simplest model that gives satisfactory results but must be ready to use a more complex model to check the results.

Simulation with the more general SPICE models is a useful tool for checking understanding and hand analysis of electronic circuits. Likewise, hand calculations should be used to check SPICE. Always be sure you understand any differences between hand analysis and circuit simulation results. Our own lack of understanding of detailed circuit behavior is the usual source of any major discrepancies between hand calculations and SPICE results. ◆

EXAMPLE 5.10: The simple two-resistor bias circuit in Fig. 5.39 can be used to bias either *npn* or, as in this case, *pnp* transistors. To find the Q-point, an equation is written involving V_{EB}, I_B, and I_C:

$$9 = V_{EB} + 18{,}000 I_B + 1000(I_C + I_B) \qquad (5.65)$$

To simplify the analysis, we select a region of operation. Picking the forward-active region and assuming that the transistor is characterized by $\beta_F = 50$ and $V_{EB} = 0.7$ V,

$$9 = 0.7 + 18{,}000 I_B + 1000(51)I_B \qquad (5.66)$$

and

$$I_B = \frac{9\text{ V} - 0.7\text{ V}}{69{,}000\ \Omega} = 120\ \mu\text{A} \qquad I_C = 50 I_B = 6.01\text{ mA} \qquad (5.67)$$

The emitter-collector voltage is given by

$$V_{EC} = 9 - 1000(I_C + I_B) = 2.88\text{ V} \qquad \text{and} \qquad V_{BC} = 2.18\text{ V} \qquad (5.68)$$

Because I_B, I_C, and V_{BC} are all greater than zero, the assumption of forward-active region operation is valid, and the Q-point is (6.01 mA, 2.88 V). ◆

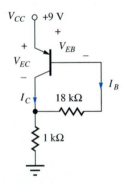

Figure 5.39 Two-resistor bias circuit with a *pnp* transistor.

The bias circuit examples that have been presented in this section have only scratched the surface of the possible techniques that can be used to bias *npn* and *pnp* transistors. However, the analysis techniques have illustrated the basic approaches that need to be followed in order to determine the Q-point of any bias circuit.

5.14 TOLERANCES IN BIAS CIRCUITS

When a circuit is actually built in discrete form in the laboratory or fabricated as an integrated circuit, the components and device parameters all have tolerances associated with their values. Discrete resistors can easily be purchased with 10 percent, 5 percent, or 1 percent tolerances, whereas typical resistors in ICs can exhibit even wider variations (± 30 percent). Power supply voltage tolerances are often 5 to 10 percent.

For a given bipolar transistor type, parameters such as current gain may cover a range of 5:1 to 10:1, or may be specified with only a nominal value and lower bound. The BJT (or diode) saturation current may vary by a factor varying from 10:1 to 100:1, and the Early voltage may vary by ± 20 percent. In FET circuits, the values of threshold voltage and the transconductance parameter can vary widely, and in op-amp circuits all the op-amp parameters (for example, open-loop gain, input resistance, output resistance, input bias current, unity gain frequency, and the like) typically exhibit wide specification ranges.

In addition to this initial value uncertainty, the values of the circuit components and parameters change as temperature changes and the circuit ages. It is important to understand the effect of these variations on our circuits and be able to design circuits that will continue to operate correctly in the face of these element variations. Worst-case analysis and Monte Carlo analysis are two approaches that can be used to quantify the effects of tolerances on circuit performance.

Worst-Case Analysis

Worst-case analysis has often been used to ensure that a design will function under an expected set of component variations. In Q-point analysis, for example, the values of components are simultaneously pushed to their various extremes in order to determine the worst possible range of Q-point values. Unfortunately, a design based on worst-case analysis is usually an unnecessary overdesign and economically undesirable. But it is important to understand the technique and its limitations.

We will use the four-resistor bias network as an example of worst-case analysis. We assume that the various parameter values can be represented by

$$P_{\text{NOM}}(1 - \varepsilon) \le P \le P_{\text{NOM}}(1 + \varepsilon) \tag{5.69}$$

in which P_{NOM} is the nominal value of the parameter such as a resistor value or independent source value, and ε is the fractional tolerance on the component. For example, a resistor R with nominal value of 10 kΩ and a 5 percent tolerance could have a value anywhere in the following range:

$$10,000 \ \Omega(1 - 0.05) \le R \le 10,000 \ \Omega(1 + 0.05)$$

or
$$9500 \ \Omega \le R \le 10,500 \ \Omega$$

The circuit in Fig. 5.40 is the simplified version of the four-resistor bias circuit in Figs. 5.32 and 5.33. Let us assume that the 12-V power supply has a 5 percent tolerance and the resistors have 10 percent tolerances. Also, assume that the transistor current gain has a nominal value of 75 with a 50 percent tolerance.

Let us first find the worst-case values (largest and smallest) of collector current based on our previous analysis results. Assuming that the voltage drop in R_{EQ} can be neglected and β_F is large, I_C is given by

$$I_C \approx I_E = \frac{V_{\text{EQ}} - V_{BE}}{R_E} \tag{5.70}$$

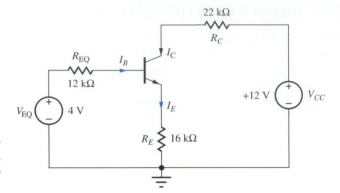

Figure 5.40 Simplified four-resistor bias circuit of Fig. 5.33(b) assuming nominal element values.

To make I_C as large as possible, V_{EQ} should be at its maximum extreme and R_E should be a minimum value. To make I_C as small as possible, V_{EQ} should be at its minimum extreme and R_E should be a maximum value. The variations in V_{BE} will be assumed to be negligible but could also be included if desired.

The extremes of R_E are $0.9 \times 16 \text{ k}\Omega = 14.4 \text{ k}\Omega$, and $1.1 \times 16 \text{ k}\Omega = 17.6 \text{ k}\Omega$. The extreme values of V_{EQ} are somewhat more complicated:

$$V_{EQ} = V_{CC}\frac{R_1}{R_1 + R_2} = \frac{V_{CC}}{1 + \dfrac{R_2}{R_1}} \tag{5.71}$$

To make V_{EQ} as large as possible, the numerator of Eq. (5.71) should be large and the denominator small. Therefore, V_{CC} and R_1 must be as large as possible and R_2 as small as possible. Conversely, to make V_{EQ} as small as possible, V_{CC} and R_1 must be small and R_2 must be large. Using this approach, the maximum and minimum values of V_{EQ} are

$$V_{EQ}^{MAX} = \frac{12 \text{ V}(1.05)}{1 + \dfrac{36 \text{ k}\Omega(0.9)}{18 \text{ k}\Omega(1.1)}} = 4.78 \text{ V}$$

and

$$V_{EQ}^{MIN} = \frac{12 \text{ V}(.95)}{1 + \dfrac{36 \text{ k}\Omega(1.1)}{18 \text{ k}\Omega(0.9)}} = 3.31 \text{ V}$$

Substituting these values in Eq. (5.70) gives the following extremes for I_C:

$$I_C^{MAX} = \frac{4.78 \text{ V} - 0.7 \text{ V}}{14,400 \text{ }\Omega} = 283 \text{ }\mu\text{A}$$

and

$$I_C^{MIN} = \frac{3.31 \text{ V} - 0.7 \text{ V}}{17,600 \text{ }\Omega} = 148 \text{ }\mu\text{A}$$

The worst-case values of I_C differ by a factor of almost 2:1! The maximum I_C is 38 percent greater than the nominal value of 210 μA, and the minimum value is 37 percent below the nominal value.

The worst-case range of V_{CE} will be calculated in a similar manner, but we must be careful to watch for possible cancellation of variables:

$$V_{CE} = V_{CC} - I_C R_C - I_E R_E \approx V_{CC} - I_C R_C - \frac{V_{EQ} - V_{BE}}{R_E}R_E \tag{5.72}$$

$$V_{CE} \approx V_{CC} - I_C R_C - V_{EQ} + V_{BE}$$

The maximum value of V_{CE} in Eq. (5.72) occurs for minimum I_C. Using (5.72), the extremes of V_{CE} are

$$V_{CE}^{MAX} \approx 12 \text{ V}(1.05) - (148 \text{ }\mu\text{A})(22 \text{ k}\Omega \times 0.9) - 3.31 \text{ V} + 0.7 \text{ V} = 7.06 \text{ V}$$

$$V_{CE}^{MIN} \approx 12 \text{ V}(0.95) - (283 \text{ }\mu\text{A})(22 \text{ k}\Omega \times 1.1) - 4.78 \text{ V} + 0.7 \text{ V} = 0.471 \text{ V} \quad \text{Saturated!}$$

The transistor remains in the forward-active region for the upper extreme, but the transistor saturates (weakly) at the lower extreme. Because the forward-active region assumption is violated in the latter case, the calculated values of V_{CE} and I_C would not actually be correct for this case. However, the apparent failure of the bias circuit to maintain the transistor in the desired region of operation is evident.

In a real circuit, the parameters will have some statistical distribution, and it is unlikely that the various components will all reach their extremes at the same time. Thus, the worst-case analysis technique will overestimate (often badly) the extremes of circuit behavior. A better approach is to attack the problem statistically using the method of Monte Carlo Analysis.

Monte Carlo Analysis

Monte Carlo analysis uses randomly selected versions of a given circuit to predict its behavior from a statistical basis. For Monte Carlo analysis, values for each parameter in the circuit are selected at random from the possible distributions of parameters, and the circuit is then analyzed using the randomly selected element values. Many random parameter sets are generated, and the statistical behavior of the circuit is built up from analysis of the many test cases.

In this section, the parameters are assumed to be uniformly distributed between the extremes. In other words, the probability that any given value of the parameter will occur is the same. In fact, when the parameter tolerance expression in Eq.(5.69) was first encountered, you probably visualized it in terms of a uniform distribution.

In mathematical terms, the probability density function $p(r)$ for a uniformly distributed resistor r is represented graphically in Fig. 5.41. The probability that a resistor value lies between r and $(r + dr)$ is equal to $p(r)\,dr$. The total probability P must equal unity, so

$$P = \int_{-\infty}^{+\infty} p(r)\,dr = 1 \tag{5.73}$$

Using this equation with the uniform probability density of Fig. 5.41 yields $p(r) = 1/(2\varepsilon R_{\text{NOM}})$ as indicated in the figure.

Monte Carlo analysis can easily be implemented with a spreadsheet, MATLAB, or a simple computer program using the **uniform random number generators,** or just **random number generators,** that are built into the software. These random number generators

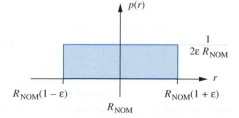

Figure 5.41 Probability density function for a uniformly distributed resistor.

produce a sequence of pseudo-random numbers that are uniformly distributed between 0 and 1 with a mean of 0.5, as in Fig. 5.42.

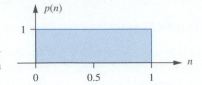

Figure 5.42 Probability density function for a uniform random number generator.

For example, the Excel spreadsheet contains the function called RAND() (used with a null argument), and MATLAB uses rand.[9] Both functions generate random numbers with the distribution in Fig. 5.42. Other software products contain random number generators with similar names. To use RAND() to generate the distribution in Fig. 5.41, the mean must be centered on R_{NOM} and the width of the distribution set to $(2\varepsilon) \times R_{NOM}$:

$$R = R_{NOM}(1 + 2\varepsilon(\text{RAND}() - 0.5)) \tag{5.74}$$

To perform a Monte Carlo analysis of the circuit in Fig. 5.40, random values are assigned to V_{CC}, R_1, R_2, R_C, R_E, and β_F and then used to determine I_C and V_{CE}. Using the tolerances from the worst-case analysis, the power supply, resistors, and current gain are represented as

$$
\begin{aligned}
&1. \quad V_{CC} = 12(1 + 0.1(\text{RAND}() - 0.5)) \\
&2. \quad R_1 = 18{,}000(1 + 0.2(\text{RAND}() - 0.5)) \\
&3. \quad R_2 = 36{,}000(1 + 0.2(\text{RAND}() - 0.5)) \\
&4. \quad R_E = 16{,}000(1 + 0.2(\text{RAND}() - 0.5)) \\
&5. \quad R_C = 22{,}000(1 + 0.2(\text{RAND}() - 0.5)) \\
&6. \quad \beta_F = 75(1 + (\text{RAND}() - 0.5))
\end{aligned}
\tag{5.75}
$$

Note that each variable must invoke a separate call of the function RAND() so that the random values will be independent of each other.

In the spreadsheet results presented in Fig. 5.43, the random elements in Eqs. (5.75) are used to evaluate the equations that characterize the bias circuit:

$$
\begin{aligned}
&7. \quad V_{EQ} = V_{CC}\frac{R_1}{R_1 + R_2} \\
&8. \quad R_{EQ} = \frac{R_1 R_2}{R_1 + R_2} \\
&9. \quad I_B = \frac{V_{EQ} - V_{BE}}{R_{EQ} + (\beta_F + 1)R_E} \\
&10. \quad I_C = \beta_F I_B \\
&11. \quad I_E = \frac{I_C}{\alpha_F} \\
&12. \quad V_{CE} = V_{CC} - I_C R_C - I_E R_E
\end{aligned}
\tag{5.76}
$$

Because the computer is doing the work, the complete expressions rather than the approximate relations for the various calculations are used in Eqs. (5.76).[10] Once Eqs. (5.75) and

---

[9] In MATLAB, rand generates a single random number, rand(n) is an $n \times n$ matrix of random numbers and rand(n,m) is an $n \times m$ matrix of random numbers.

[10] Note that V_{BE} could also be treated as a random variable.

Monte Carlo Spreadsheet

Case #	VCC (1)	R1 (2)	R2 (3)	RE (4)	RC (5)	βF (6)	VEQ (7)	REQ (8)	IB (9)	IC (10)	VCE (12)
1	12.277	16827	38577	15780	23257	67.46	3.729	11716	2.87E-06	1.93E-04	4.687
2	12.202	18188	32588	15304	23586	46.60	4.371	11673	5.09E-06	2.37E-04	2.891
3	11.526	16648	35643	14627	20682	110.73	3.669	11348	1.87E-06	2.07E-04	4.206
4	11.658	17354	33589	14639	22243	44.24	3.971	11442	5.00E-06	2.21E-04	3.420
5	11.932	19035	32886	16295	20863	62.34	4.374	12056	3.61E-06	2.25E-04	3.500
6	11.857	18706	32615	15563	21064	60.63	4.322	11888	3.83E-06	2.32E-04	3.286
7	11.669	18984	39463	17566	21034	42.86	3.790	12818	4.07E-06	1.75E-04	4.859
8	12.222	19291	37736	15285	22938	63.76	4.135	12765	3.53E-06	2.25E-04	3.577
9	11.601	17589	34032	17334	23098	103.07	3.953	11596	1.85E-06	1.90E-04	3.873
10	11.533	17514	33895	17333	19869	71.28	3.929	11547	2.63E-06	1.88E-04	4.505
11	11.436	19333	34160	15107	22593	68.20	4.133	12346	3.34E-06	2.28E-04	2.797
12	11.962	18810	33999	15545	22035	53.69	4.261	12110	4.25E-06	2.28E-04	3.330
13	11.801	19610	37917	14559	21544	109.65	4.023	12925	2.11E-06	2.31E-04	3.426
14	12.401	17947	34286	15952	21086	107.84	4.261	11780	2.09E-06	2.26E-04	4.002
15	11.894	16209	35321	17321	23940	45.00	3.741	11111	3.89E-06	1.75E-04	4.607
16	12.329	16209	37873	16662	23658	112.01	3.695	11351	1.63E-06	1.83E-04	4.923
17	11.685	19070	35267	15966	21864	64.85	4.101	12377	3.29E-06	2.13E-04	3.559
18	11.456	18096	37476	15529	20141	91.14	3.730	12203	2.17E-06	1.98E-04	4.370
19	12.527	18752	38261	15186	21556	69.26	4.120	12584	3.26E-06	2.26E-04	4.180
20	12.489	17705	36467	17325	20587	83.95	4.082	11919	2.35E-06	1.97E-04	4.979
21	11.436	18773	34697	16949	21848	65.26	4.015	12182	3.01E-06	1.96E-04	3.768
22	11.549	16830	38578	16736	19942	109.22	3.508	11718	1.57E-06	1.71E-04	5.247
23	11.733	16959	39116	15944	21413	62.82	3.548	11830	2.86E-06	1.80E-04	4.965
24	11.738	18486	35520	17526	20455	70.65	4.018	12158	2.70E-06	1.90E-04	4.457
25	11.679	18908	38236	15160	21191	103.12	3.864	12652	2.05E-06	2.12E-04	3.958
Mean	11.848	18014	35102	15973	21863	67.30	4.024	11885	3.44E-06	2.09E-04	3.880
Std. Dev.	0.296	958	2596	1108	1309	23.14	0.264	520	1.14E-06	2.18E-05	0.657

(X) = Equation number in text

Figure 5.43 Example of a Monte Carlo analysis using a spreadsheet.

(5.76) have been entered into one row of the spreadsheet, the row may be copied into as many additional rows as the number of statistical cases that are desired. The analysis is automatically repeated for the random selections to build up the statistical distributions, with each row representing one analysis of the circuit. At the end of the columns, the mean and standard deviation can be calculated using built-in spreadsheet functions, and the overall spreadsheet data can be used to build histograms for the circuit performance.

An example of a portion of the spreadsheet output for 25 cases of the circuit in Fig. 5.40 is shown in Fig. 5.43, whereas the full results of the analysis of 500 cases of the four-resistor bias circuit are given in the histograms for I_C and V_{CE} in Fig. 5.44. The mean values for I_C and V_{CE} are 207 μA and 4.06 V, respectively, which are close to the values originally estimated from the nominal circuit elements. The standard deviations are 19.6 μA and 0.64 V, respectively. The worst-case calculations from the previous section are indicated by the bold arrows in the figures. It can be seen that the worst-case values of V_{CE} lie well beyond the edges of the statistical distribution, and that saturation does

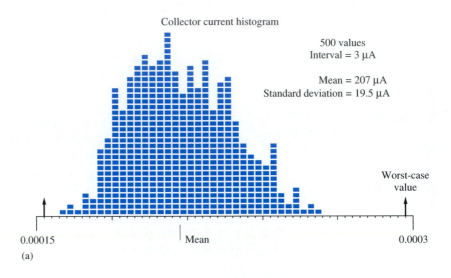

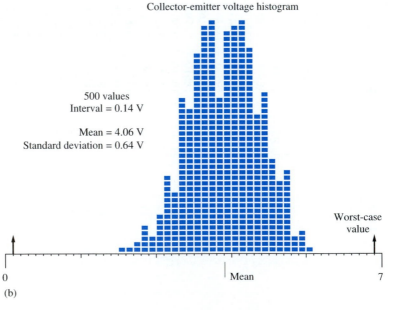

Figure 5.44 (a) Collector-current histogram. (b) Collector-emitter voltage histogram.

not actually occur for the worst statistical case evaluated. If the Q-point distribution results in the histograms in Fig. 5.44 were not sufficient to meet the design criteria, the parameter tolerances could be changed and the Monte Carlo simulation redone.

Some implementations of the SPICE circuit analysis program—PSPICE, for example—actually contain a Monte Carlo option in which a full circuit simulation is automatically performed for any number of randomly selected test cases. These programs are a powerful tool for performing much more complex statistical analysis than is possible by hand. Using these programs, statistical estimates of delay, frequency response, and so on of circuits with large numbers of transistors can be performed.

SUMMARY

The bipolar junction transistor (BJT) was invented in the late 1940s at the Bell Telephone Laboratories by Bardeen, Brattain, and Shockley and became the first commercially successful three-terminal solid-state device. The basic physical structure of the BJT consists of a three-layer sandwich of alternating p-type and n-type semiconductor materials and can be fabricated in either npn or pnp form. The emitter of the transistor injects carriers into the base. These carriers traverse the base region and are collected by the collector.

A mathematical model called the transport model (a simplified Gummel-Poon model) characterizes the i-v characteristics of the bipolar transistor for general terminal-voltage and current conditions. The transport model requires three unique parameters to characterize a particular BJT: the saturation current I_S and the forward and reverse common-emitter current gains β_F and β_R. β_F is a relatively large number, ranging from 20 to 500, and characterizes the significant current amplification capability of the BJT. Practical fabrication problems cause the bipolar transistor structure to be inherently asymmetric, and the value of β_R is much smaller than β_F, typically between 0 and 2.

Four regions of operation—cutoff, forward-active, reverse-active, and saturation—were identified for the BJT based on the bias voltages applied to the base-emitter and base-collector junctions. The transport model can be simplified for each individual region of operation. Cutoff and saturation are most often used in binary digital-switching circuits, whereas the transistor can provide high voltage and current gain for amplification of analog signals in the forward-active region. The reverse-active region finds limited use in some analog- and digital-switching applications.

The i-v characteristics of the bipolar transistor are often presented graphically in the form of the output characteristics, i_C vs. v_{CE} or v_{CB}, and the transfer characteristics, i_C vs. v_{BE} or v_{EB}. In the forward-active region, the collector current increases slightly as the collector-emitter voltage increases. The origin of this effect is base-width modulation, known as the Early effect, and it can be included in the model for the forward-active region through addition of the parameter called the Early voltage V_A. The transconductance g_m of the bipolar transistor relates differential changes in collector current and base-emitter voltage and was shown to be directly proportional to the dc collector current I_C.

The collector current of the bipolar transistor is determined by minority carrier diffusion across the base of the transistor, and expressions were developed that relate the saturation current and base transit time of the transistor to physical device parameters. The base width plays a crucial role in determining the base transit time and the high-frequency operating limits of the transistor.

Minority-carrier charge is stored in the base of the transistor during its operation, and changes in this stored charge with applied voltage result in diffusion capacitances being associated with forward-biased junctions. The value of the diffusion capacitance is proportional to the collector current I_C. The capacitances of the bipolar transistor cause the current gain to be frequency-dependent. At the beta cutoff frequency f_β, the current gain has fallen to 71 percent of its low frequency value, whereas the value of the current gain is only 1 at the unity-gain frequency f_T.

A number of biasing circuits were analyzed to determine the Q-point of the transistor, including the four-resistor circuit that provides highly stable control of the operating point. Design of the four-resistor network was investigated in detail, and an example of load-line analysis of the four-resistor bias network was also presented. The current-mirror circuit, which is extremely important for biasing integrated circuits, relies on the use of closely matched transistors for proper operation.

Techniques for analyzing the influence of element tolerances on circuit performance include the worst-case analysis and statistical Monte Carlo analysis methods. In worst-case analysis, element values are simultaneously pushed to their extremes, and the resulting predictions of circuit behavior are often overly pessimistic. The Monte Carlo method analyzes a large number of randomly selected versions of a circuit to build up a realistic estimate of the statistical distribution of circuit performance. Random number generators in high-level computer languages, spreadsheets, or MATLAB can be used to randomly select element values for use in the Monte Carlo analysis. Some circuit analysis packages such as PSPICE provide a Monte Carlo analysis option as part of the program.

Key Terms

Base
Base current
Base width
Base-width modulation
β-cutoff frequency
Bipolar junction transistor (BJT)
Collector
Collector current
Common-base output characteristic
Common-emitter output characteristic
Common-emitter transfer characteristic
Current mirror
Cutoff region
Diffusion capacitance
Early effect
Early voltage
Ebers-Moll model
Emitter

Emitter current
Equilibrium electron density
Forced beta
Forward-active region
Forward common-emitter current gain
Forward common-base current gain
Forward transit time
Forward transport current
Gummel-Poon model
Inverse-active region
Inverse common-emitter current gain
Inverse common-base current gain
Matched transistors
Monte Carlo analysis
Normal-active region
Normal common-emitter current gain
Normal common-base current gain

npn transistor
Output characteristic
Quiescent operating point
Q-point
pnp transistor
Random number generator
Reverse-active region
Reverse common-base current gain
Reverse common-emitter current gain
Saturation region
Transconductance
Transfer characteristic
Transistor saturation current
Transport model
Uniform random number generator
Unity-gain frequency
Worst-case analysis

References

1. H. K. Gummel and H. C. Poon, "A compact bipolar transistor model," *ISSCC Digest of Technical Papers,* pp. 78, 79, 146, February 1970.
2. H. K. Gummel, "A charge control relation for bipolar transistors," *Bell System Technical Journal,* January 1970.
3. J. J. Ebers and J. L. Moll, "Large signal behavior of junction transistors," *Proc. IRE.,* pp. 1761–1772, December 1954.
4. J. M. Early, "Effects of space-charge layer widening in junction transistors," *Proc. IRE.,* pp. 1401–1406, November 1952.

PSPICE Simulation Data

Figure 5.10 *npn* common-emitter output characteristics

```
*
IB 0 1 DC 0
VCE 2 0 DC 0
Q1 2 1 0 0 BJT
.DC VCE -4 9 .025 IB 0 100U 20U
.MODEL BJT NPN IS=1E-15 BF=25 BR=5
.PROBE V(1) I(VCE)
.END
```

Figure 5.12 *npn* common-base output characteristics

```
*
IE 1 0 DC 0
VCB 2 0 DC 0
Q1 2 0 1 0 BJT
.DC VCB -0.85 9 .025 IE 0 1M .2M
.MODEL BJT NPN IS=1E-15 BF=25 BR=5
.PROBE V(1) I(VCB)
.END
```

Figure 5.24 *npn* current source

```
VCC 1 0 DC 5
VEE 3 0 DC -9
RE 2 3 8.2K
Q1 1 0 2 0 NPNBJT
.OP
.DC VCC -.8 9 .025
.MODEL NPNBJT NPN IS=1E-15 BF=50 BR=1 VA=100
.PROBE V(2) I(VCC)
.END
```

Figure 5.30 *npn* early voltage (See Fig. 5.10)

```
IB 0 1 DC .001
VCE 2 0 DC 5
Q1 2 1 0 0 NBJT
.DC VCE 0 14 .025 IB 0 100U 20U
.MODEL NBJT NPN IS=1E-15 BF=25 BR=5 VA=14
.PROBE V(1) I(VCE)
.END
```

Problems

If not otherwise specified, use $I_S = 10^{-15}$ A, $V_A = 50$ V, $\beta_F = 100$, $\beta_R = 1$, and $V_{BE} = 0.70$ V.

5.1 Physical Structure of the Bipolar Transistor

5.1. Figure P5.1 is a cross section of an *npn* bipolar transistor similar to that in Fig. 5.1. Indicate the letter (*A* to *G*) that identifies the base contact, collector contact, emitter contact, *n*-type emitter region, *n*-type collector region, and the active or intrinsic transistor region.

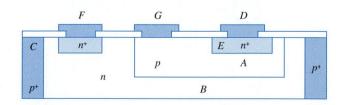

Figure P5.1

5.2 The Transport Model for the *npn* Transistor

5.2. (a) Label the collector, base, and emitter terminals of the transistor in the circuit in Fig. P5.2. (b) Label the base-emitter and base-collector voltages, V_{BE} and V_{BC}, respectively. (c) If $V = 0.630\,\text{V}$, $I_C = 275\,\mu\text{A}$, and $I_B = 5\,\mu\text{A}$, find the values of I_S, β_F, and β_R for the transistor if $\alpha_R = 0.5$.

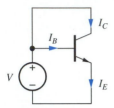

Figure P5.2

5.3. Fill in the missing entries in Table P5.3.

α	β
	0.200
0.400	
0.750	
	10.0
0.980	
	200
	1000
0.9998	

Table P5.3

5.4. (a) Find the current I in Fig. P5.4(a). (Use the parameters specified at the beginning of the problem set.)

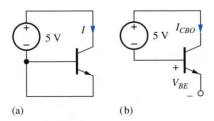

(a)   (b)

Figure P5.4

(b) Find the current I_{CBO} and the voltage V_{BE} in Fig. P5.4(b).

5.5. For the transistor in Fig. P5.5, $I_S = 2 \times 10^{-15}$ A, $\beta_F = 100$, and $\beta_R = 0.25$. (a) Label the collector, base, and emitter terminals of the transistor. (b) What is the transistor type? (c) Label the base-emitter and base-collector voltages, V_{BE} and V_{BC}, respectively, and label the normal directions for I_E, I_C, and I_B. (d) What is the relationship between V_{BE} and V_{BC}? (e) Write the simplified form of the transport model equations that apply to this particular circuit configuration. Write an expression for I_E/I_B. Write an expression for I_E/I_C. (f) Find the values of I_E, I_C, I_B, V_{BC}, and V_{BE}.

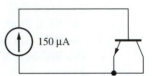

Figure P5.5

5.6. The *npn* transistor is connected in a "diode" configuration in Fig. P5.6(a). Use the transport model equations to show that the *i-v* characteristics of this connection are similar to those of a diode as defined by Eq. (3.11). What is the reverse saturation current of this "diode" if $I_S = 2 \times 10^{-15}$ A, $\beta_F = 100$, and $\beta_R = 0.25$?

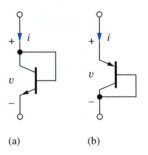

(a)   (b)

Figure P5.6

5.7. Calculate i_T for an *npn* transistor with $I_S = 10^{-16}$ A for (a) $V_{BE} = 0.75$ V and $V_{BC} = -3$ V and (b) $V_{BC} = 0.75$ V and $V_{BE} = -3$ V.

5.3 The *pnp* Transistor

5.8. Figure P5.8 is a cross section of a *pnp* bipolar transistor similar to the *npn* transistor in Fig. 5.1. Indicate the letter (A to G) that represents the base contact, collector contact, emitter contact, *p*-type emitter region, *p*-type collector region, and the active or intrinsic transistor region.

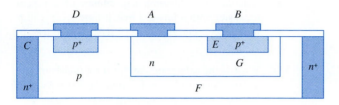

Figure P5.8

5.9. For the transistor in Fig. P5.9, $I_S = 10^{-15}$ A, $\alpha_F = 0.985$, and $\alpha_R = 0.25$. (a) What type of transistor is in this circuit? (b) Label the collector, base, and emitter terminals of the transistor. (c) Label the emitter-base and collector-base voltages, and label the normal direction for I_E, I_C, and I_B. (d) Write the simplified form of the transport model equations that apply to this particular circuit configuration. Write an expression for I_E/I_C. Write an expression for I_E/I_B. (e) Find the values of I_E, I_C, I_B, β_F, β_R, V_{EB}, and V_{CB}.

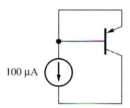

100 μA

Figure P5.9

5.10. Repeat Prob. 5.6 for the "diode-connected" *pnp* transistor in Fig. P5.6(b).

5.11. For the transistor in Fig. P5.11, $I_S = 2 \times 10^{-15}$ A, $\beta_F = 75$, and $\beta_R = 2$. (a) Label the collector, base, and emitter terminals of the transistor. (b) What is the transistor type? (c) Label the emitter-base and collector-base voltages, and label the normal direction for I_E, I_C, and I_B. (d) Write the simplified form of the transport model equations that apply to this particular circuit configuration. Write an expression for I_E/I_B. Write an expression

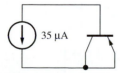

35 μA

Figure P5.11

for I_E/I_C. (e) Find the values of I_E, I_C, I_B, V_{CB}, and V_{EB}.

5.5 The Operating Regions of the Bipolar Transistor

5.12. Indicate the region of operation in the following table for an *npn* transistor biased with the indicated voltages.

Base-Emitter Voltage	Base-Collector Voltage	
	0.7 V	−5.0 V
−5.0 V		
0.7 V		

5.13. Indicate the region of operation in the following table for a *pnp* transistor biased with the indicated voltages.

Emitter-Base Voltage	Collector-Base Voltage	
	0.7 V	−0.65 V
0.7 V		
−0.65 V		

5.6 The *i-v* Characteristics of the Bipolar Transistor

*5.14. The common-emitter output characteristics for an *npn* transistor are given in Fig. P5.14. What are the values of β_F at (a) $I_C = 5$ mA and $V_{CE} = 5$ V? (b) $I_C = 7$ mA and $V_{CE} = 7.5$ V? (c) $I_C = 10$ mA and $V_{CE} = 14$ V?

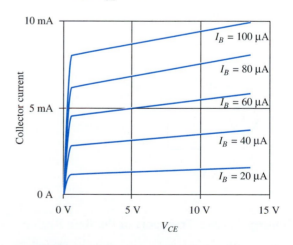

Figure P5.14

Breakdown Voltages

5.15. In the circuits in Fig. P5.15, the Zener breakdown voltages of the collector-base and emitter-base junctions of the *npn* transistors are 85 V and 6.3 V, respectively. What is the current in the resistor in each circuit? (*Hint:* The equivalent circuits for the transport model equations may help in visualizing the circuit.)

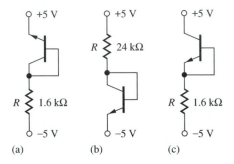

Figure P5.15

5.16. An *npn* transistor is biased as indicated in Fig. 5.10(a). What is the largest value of V_{CE} that can be applied without junction breakdown if the breakdown voltages of the collector-base and emitter-base junctions of the *npn* transistors are 60 V and 5 V, respectively?

5.17. (a) For the circuit in Fig. P5.17, what is the maximum value of I according to the transport model equations if $I_S = 1 \times 10^{-15}$ A, $\beta_F = 50$, and $\beta_R = 0.5$? (b) Suppose that $I = 1$ mA. What happens to the transistor? (*Hint:* The equivalent circuits for the transport model equations may help in visualizing the circuit.)

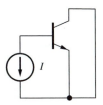

Figure P5.17

5.7 Minority Carrier Transport in the Base Region

5.18. (a) What is the forward transit time τ_F for an *npn* transistor with a base width $W_B = 2$ μm and a base

doping of 10^{18}/cm³? (b) Repeat the calculation for a *pnp* transistor.

5.19. Calculate the diffusion capacitance of a bipolar transistor with a forward transit time $\tau_F = 150$ ps for collector currents of (a) 2 μA, (b) 200 μA, (c) 20 mA.

5.20. What is the saturation current for a transistor with a base doping of 5×10^{18}/cm³, a base width of 0.5 μm, and a cross-sectional area of 25 μm²?

5.21. An *npn* transistor is needed that will operate at a frequency of at least 2 GHz. What base width is required for the transistor if the base doping is 5×10^{18}/cm³?

5.8 Simplified Model for the Cutoff Region

5.22. What are the three terminal currents I_E, I_B, and I_C in the transistor in Fig. P5.22 if $I_S = 1 \times 10^{-15}$ A, $\beta_F = 75$, and $\beta_R = 2$?

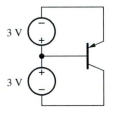

Figure P5.22

***5.23.** An *npn* transistor with $I_S = 1 \times 10^{-16}$ A, $\alpha_F = 0.95$ and $\alpha_R = 0.5$ is operating with $V_{BE} = 0.3$ V and $V_{BC} = -5$ V. This transistor is not truly operating in the region defined to be cutoff, but we still say the transistor is off. Why? Use the transport model equations to justify your answer. In what region is the transistor actually operating according to our definitions?

5.9 Model Simplifications for the Forward-Active Region

5.24. What are the values of β_F and I_S for the transistor in Fig. P5.24?

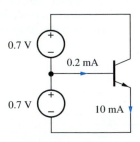

Figure P5.24

5.25. What are the values of β_F and I_S for the transistor in Fig. P5.25?

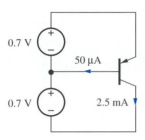

Figure P5.25

5.26. What are the emitter, base, and collector currents in the circuit in Fig. 5.23 if $V_{EE} = 3.3\,\text{V}$, $R = 47\,\text{k}\Omega$, and $\beta_F = 90$?

**5.27. A transistor has $f_T = 500$ MHz and $\beta_F = 80$. (a) What is the β-cutoff frequency f_β of this transistor? (b) Use Eq. (5.38) to find an expression for the frequency dependence of α_F—that is $\alpha_F(f)$. [*Hint:* Write an expression for $\beta(s)$.] What is the α-cutoff frequency for this transistor?

*5.28. (a) Start with the transport model equations for the *pnp* transistor, Eqs. (5.17), and construct the simplified version of the *pnp* equations that apply to the forward-active region [similar to Eqs. (5.35)]. (b) Draw the simplified model for the *pnp* transistor similar to the *npn* version in Fig. 5.21.

5.10 Simplified Model for the Reverse-Active Region

5.29. What are the values of β_R and I_S for the transistor in Fig. P5.29?

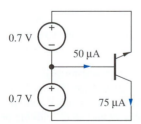

Figure P5.29

5.30. What are the values of β_R and I_S for the transistor in Fig. P5.30?

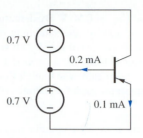

Figure P5.30

5.31. Find the emitter, base, and collector currents in the circuit in Fig. 5.27 if the negative power supply is $-3.3\,\text{V}$, $R = 47\,\text{k}\Omega$, and $\beta_R = 0.75$.

5.11 Modeling Operation in the Saturation Region

5.32. What is the saturation voltage of an *npn* transistor operating with $I_C = 1$ mA and $I_B = 1$ mA if $\beta_F = 50$ and $\beta_R = 1$? What is the forced β of this transistor? What is the value of V_{BE} if $I_S = 10^{-15}$ A?

5.33. Derive an expression for the saturation voltage V_{ECSAT} of the *pnp* transistor in a manner similar to that used to derive Eq. (5.46).

5.34. (a) What is the collector-emitter voltage for the transistor in Fig. P5.34(a) if $I_S = 2 \times 10^{-15}$ A, $\alpha_F = 0.99$, and $\alpha_R = 0.5$? (b) What is the emitter-collector voltage for the transistor in Fig. P5.34(b) for the same transistor parameters?

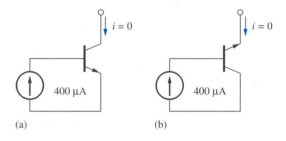

(a)   (b)

Figure P5.34

5.35. (a) What base current is required to achieve a saturation voltage of $V_{CESAT} = 0.1$V in an *npn* power transistor that is operating with a collector current of 20 A if $\beta_F = 15$ and $\beta_R = 0.9$? What is the forced β of this transistor? (b) Repeat for $V_{CESAT} = 0.04$ V.

**5.36. An *npn* transistor with $I_S = 1 \times 10^{-16}$ A, $\alpha_F = 0.975$, and $\alpha_R = 0.5$ is operating with $V_{BE} =$

0.70 V and $V_{BC} = 0.50$ V. By definition, this transistor is operating in the saturation region. However, in the discussion of Fig. 5.24 it was noted that this transistor actually behaves as if it is still in the forward-active region even though $V_{BC} > 0$. Why? Use the transport model equations to justify your answer.

5.37. The current I in both circuits in Fig. P5.37 is 250 μA. Find the value of V_{BE} for both circuits if $I_S = 1 \times 10^{-16}$ A, $\beta_F = 50$, and $\beta_R = 0.5$.

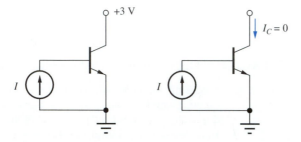

Figure P5.37

5.12 The Early Effect and Early Voltage

5.38. An *npn* transistor with $I_S = 10^{-16}$ A, $\beta_F = 100$, and $V_A = 65$ V is biased in the forward-active region with $V_{BE} = 0.72$ V and $V_{CE} = 10$ V. (a) What is the collector current I_C? (b) What would be the collector current I_C if $V_A = \infty$? (c) What is the ratio of the two answers in parts (a) and (b)?

5.39. An *npn* transistor is operating in the forward-active region with a base current of 3 μA. It is found that $I_C = 240$ μA for $V_{CE} = 5$ V and $I_C = 265$ μA for $V_{CE} = 10$ V. What are the values of β_{FO} and V_A for this transistor?

5.40. The common-emitter output characteristics for an *npn* transistor are given in Fig. P5.14. What are the values of β_{FO} and V_A for this transistor?

5.41. (a) Recalculate the currents in the transistor in Fig. 5.19 if $I_S = 5 \times 10^{-15}$ A, $\beta_{FO} = 19$, and $V_A = 50$ V. What is V_{BE}? (b) What was V_{BE} for $V_A = \infty$?

5.42. Recalculate the currents in the transistor in Fig. 5.23 if $\beta_{FO} = 50$ and $V_A = 50$ V.

5.13 Biasing the BJT

Four-Resistor Biasing

5.43. (a) Find the Q-point for the circuit in Fig. P5.43(a). Assume that $\beta_F = 50$ and $V_{BE} = 0.7$ V. (b) Repeat the calculation if all the resistor values are

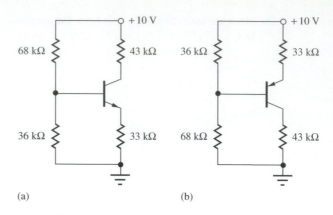

(a)   (b)

Figure P5.43

decreased by a factor of 5. (c) Repeat (a) for Fig. P5.43(b). (d) Repeat (b) for Fig. P5.43(b).

5.44. (a) Find the Q-point for the circuit in Fig. P5.43(a) if the 33-kΩ resistor is replaced with a 22-kΩ resistor. Assume that $\beta_F = 75$. (b) Repeat (a) for the circuit in Fig. P5.43(b).

5.45. (a) Simulate the circuits in Fig. P5.43 and compare the SPICE results to your hand calculations of the Q-point. Use $I_S = 1 \times 10^{-16}$ A, $\beta_F = 50$, $\beta_R = 0.25$, and $V_A = \infty$. (b) Repeat for $V_A = 60$ V. (c) Repeat (a) for the circuit in Fig. 5.43(b). (d) Repeat (b) for the circuit in Fig. 5.43(b).

5.46. Find the Q-point in the circuit in Fig. 5.32 if $R_1 = 6.2$ kΩ, $R_2 = 12$ kΩ, $R_C = 5.1$ kΩ, $R_E = 7.5$ kΩ, $\beta_F = 100$, and the positive power supply voltage is 10 V.

5.47. Find the Q-point in the circuit in Fig. 5.32 if $R_1 = 120$ kΩ, $R_2 = 240$ kΩ, $R_E = 100$ kΩ, $R_C = 150$ kΩ, $\beta_F = 100$, and the positive power supply voltage is 15 V.

5.48. (a) Design a four-resistor bias network for an *npn* transistor to give $I_C = 10$ μA and $V_{CE} = 6$ V if $V_{CC} = 18$ V and $\beta_F = 75$. (b) Replace your exact values with the nearest values from the resistor table in Appendix C and find the resulting Q-point.

5.49. (a) Design a four-resistor bias network for an *npn* transistor to give $I_C = 1$ mA, $V_{CE} = 5$ V, and $V_E = 2$ V if $V_{CC} = 12$ V and $\beta_F = 100$. (b) Replace your exact values with the nearest values from the resistor table in Appendix C and find the resulting Q-point.

5.50. (a) Design a four-resistor bias network for a *pnp* transistor to give $I_C = 13$ mA and $V_{EC} = 5$ V if $V_{CC} = -15$ V and $\beta_F = 50$. (b) Replace your exact values with the nearest values from the resistor table in Appendix C and find the resulting Q-point.

 5.51. (a) Design a four-resistor bias network for a *pnp* transistor to give $I_C = 85$ μA, $V_{EC} = 2$ V, and $V_E = 1$ V if $V_{CC} = 5$ V and $\beta_F = 60$. (b) Replace your exact values with the nearest values from the resistor table in Appendix C and find the resulting Q-point.

Current Mirrors

5.52. Find I in the circuit in Fig. P5.52 if (a) $\beta_{FO} = 20$ and $V_A = \infty$. (b) If $\beta_{FO} = 20$ and $V_A = 35$ V.

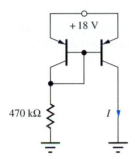

Figure P5.52

5.53. (a) Find I in the circuit in Fig. P5.53. Assume $\beta_{FO} = \infty$, $V_A = \infty$, and $V_{BE} = 0.65$ V. (b) Repeat if $\beta_{FO} = 50$.

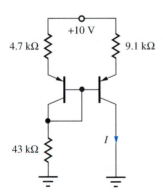

Figure P5.53

*5.54. Find I_1 and I_2 in the circuit in Fig. P5.54 for (a) $\beta_{FO} = 50$ and $V_A = \infty$ and (b) $\beta_{FO} = 50$ and $V_A = 50$ V.

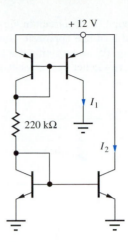

Figure P5.54

 5.55. Simulate the current-mirror circuit in Fig. P5.52 and compare the SPICE results to hand calculations. Use $I_S = 1 \times 10^{-16}$ A, $\beta_{FO} = 50$, $\beta_R = 0.25$, and $V_A = 60$ V.

 5.56. Simulate the current-mirror circuit in Fig. P5.53 and compare the SPICE results to hand calculations. Use $I_S = 1 \times 10^{-16}$ A, $\beta_{FO} = 50$, $\beta_R = 0.25$, and $V_A = 60$ V.

 5.57. Simulate the current-mirror circuit in Fig. P5.54 and compare the SPICE results to hand calculations. Use $I_S = 1 \times 10^{-16}$ A, $\beta_{FO} = 50$, $\beta_R = 0.25$, and $V_A = 60$ V.

Load Line Analysis

*5.58. Find the Q-point for the circuit in Fig. P5.58 using the graphical load-line approach. Use the characteristics in Fig. P5.14.

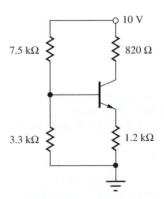

Figure P5.58

*5.59. Find the Q-point for the circuit in Fig. P5.59 using the graphical load-line approach. Use the characteristics in Fig. P5.14, assuming that the graph is a plot of i_C vs. v_{EC} rather than i_C vs. v_{CE}.

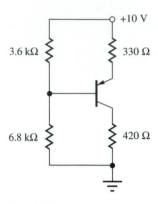

+10 V

3.6 kΩ   330 Ω

6.8 kΩ   420 Ω

Figure P5.59

Two-Resistor Biasing

5.60. Find the Q-point for the circuit in Fig. P5.60 for (a) $\beta_F = 30$, (b) $\beta_F = 100$, (c) $\beta_F = 250$, (d) $\beta_F = \infty$.

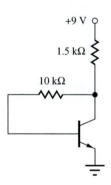

+9 V

1.5 kΩ

10 kΩ

Figure P5.60

*5.61. Write the load-line expression for the circuit in Fig. P5.60. Draw the load line on the characteristics in Fig. P5.14. Find the Q-point by drawing a curve that plots I_B vs. V_{CE}.

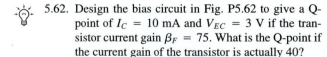

5.62. Design the bias circuit in Fig. P5.62 to give a Q-point of $I_C = 10$ mA and $V_{EC} = 3$ V if the transistor current gain $\beta_F = 75$. What is the Q-point if the current gain of the transistor is actually 40?

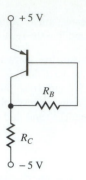

+5 V

R_B

R_C

−5 V

Figure P5.62

 5.63. Design the bias circuit in Fig. P5.63 to give a Q-point of $I_C = 10$ μA and $V_{CE} = 0.90$ V if the transistor current gain is $\beta_F = 60$ and $V_{BE} = 0.65$ V. What is the Q-point if the current gain of the transistor is actually 125?

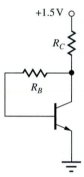

+1.5 V

R_C

R_B

Figure P5.63

*5.64. Find the Q-point for the circuit in Fig. P5.64 if the Zener diode has $V_Z = 5$ V and $R_C = 500$ Ω. Use $\beta_F = 100$.

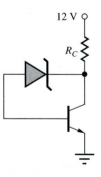

12 V

R_C

Figure P5.64

5.14 Tolerances in Bias Circuits

5.65. Find the worst-case values of the collector current and collector-emitter voltage for the circuit in Fig. 5.36 if the resistor and power supply tolerances are 5 percent.

*5.66. Perform a Monte Carlo analysis of the circuit in Fig. 5.36 assuming that the resistor and power supply tolerances are 5 percent.

*5.67. (a) Perform a worst-case analysis of the circuit in Fig. 5.39 assuming the resistor tolerances are 5 percent and $\beta_F = 100 \pm 50$ percent. (b) Perform a 100-case Monte Carlo analysis of the same circuit and compare the results to part (a).

*5.68. Repeat the Monte Carlo analysis of the circuit in Fig. 5.35 for resistor tolerances of 5 percent.

**5.69. The collector current of the circuit described by the histograms in Fig. 5.44 must be 210 μA ± 40 μA. (a) What percentage of the circuits will have to be discarded or rebuilt because they do not meet this specification? (b) Approximately what percentage of the circuits fail to meet a specification of $V_{CE} = 4.0$ V ± 20 percent?

**5.70. Choose the resistor tolerances in the circuit in Fig. 5.33 so that 99 percent of the circuits will meet the specification $I_C = 210$ μA ± 5 percent. Demonstrate your success using Monte Carlo analysis. Assume that the resistors all have the same tolerance. Do not change the tolerance on β and V_{CC}.

*5.71. Perform a worst-case analysis of the circuit in Fig. 5.39 assuming $\beta_F = 100 \pm 50$ percent, the resistors have a 20 percent tolerance, and V_{CC} has a 5 percent tolerance.

**5.72. (a) Perform a Monte Carlo analysis of the circuit in Fig. 5.39 assuming $\beta_{FO} = 100 \pm 50$ percent, $V_A = 75$ V ± 33 percent, the resistors have a 20 percent tolerance, and V_{CC} has a 5 percent tolerance. (b) Compare the results to the worst-case analysis in Prob. 5.71.

Bias Circuit Applications

5.73. The Zener diode in Fig. P5.73 has $V_Z = 7$ V and $R_Z = 100$ Ω. What is the output voltage if $I_L = 20$ mA? Use $I_S = 1 \times 10^{-16}$ A, $\beta_F = 50$, and $\beta_R = 0.5$ to find a precise answer.

*5.74. Create a model for the Zener diode and simulate the circuit in Prob. 5.73. Compare the SPICE results to your hand calculations. Use $I_S = 1 \times 10^{-16}$ A, $\beta_F = 50$, and $\beta_R = 0.5$.

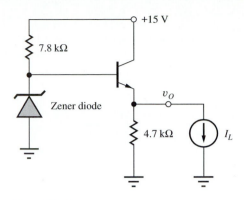

Figure P5.73

**5.75. The circuit in Fig. P5.75 has $V_{EQ} = 7$ V and $R_{EQ} = 100$ Ω. What is the output resistance R_O of this circuit for $i_L = 20$ mA if R_O is defined as $R_O = -dv_O/di_L$? Assume $\beta_F = 50$.

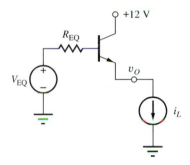

Figure P5.75

Additional Problem

*5.76 Show that the expressions for the emitter and collector currents in Eqs. (5.13) can be transformed to the equations below. These equations are known as the *Ebers-Moll model* for the BJT.

$$i_C = \alpha_F I_{ES}\left[\exp\left(\frac{v_{BE}}{V_T}\right) - 1\right] - I_{CS}\left[\exp\left(\frac{v_{BC}}{V_T}\right) - 1\right]$$

$$i_E = I_{ES}\left[\exp\left(\frac{v_{BE}}{V_T}\right) - 1\right] - \alpha_R I_{CS}\left[\exp\left(\frac{v_{BC}}{V_T}\right) - 1\right]$$

where $I_{ES} = I_S/\alpha_F$
$\quad\quad\quad I_{CS} = I_S/\alpha_R$

[*Hint:* Add and subtract 1 from the first terms in both equations in Eqs. (5.13).]

PART II

Digital Circuit Design

CHAPTER 6

Introduction to Digital Electronics

Digital electronics has had a profound effect on our lives through the pervasive application of microprocessors and microcontrollers in consumer and industrial products. The microprocessor chip forms the heart of personal computers and workstations, and digital technology is the basis of modern telecommunications. Microcontrollers are found in everything from CD players to refrigerators to washing machines to vacuum cleaners, and in today's luxury automobiles often more than 50 microprocessors work together to control the vehicle. In fact, approximately 20 percent of the total cost of such an automobile comes from electronics.

The bulk of these applications are now dominated by **complementary MOS,** or **CMOS, technology,** whereas bipolar logic circuits have historically been used in mainframe and supercomputer systems. The rapid advance of digital electronics, described in Chapter 1, was facilitated by circuit designers who developed robust bipolar unit-logic families such as **transistor-transistor logic (TTL)** and **emitter-coupled logic (ECL)** that could be easily interconnected to form highly reliable digital systems. High-density integrated circuits were later developed using first PMOS (1970), then NMOS (1975), and later CMOS (1985) technologies.

This chapter explores the requirements and general characteristics of digital logic gates. Subsequent chapters investigate the detailed implementation of logic gates in both MOS and bipolar technologies. The initial discussion in this chapter focuses on the characteristics of the inverter. Important logic levels associated with binary logic are defined, and the concepts of the voltage transfer characteristic and noise margin are introduced. Later, the temporal behavior and time delays of the gates are addressed. A review of boolean algebra, used for representation and analysis of complex logic functions, is included, and simple AND gates, OR gates, and NAND gates are implemented using diode logic and bipolar transistors.

6.1 IDEAL LOGIC GATES

In the discussions in this book, we limit consideration to binary logic, which requires only two discrete states for operation. In addition, the positive logic convention will be used throughout: The higher voltage level will correspond to a logic 1, and the lower voltage level will correspond to a logic 0.

The logic symbol and **voltage transfer characteristic (VTC)** for an ideal binary inverter are given in Fig. 6.1. The positive and negative power supplies, shown explicitly as V_+ and V_-, respectively, are not included in most logic diagrams. For input voltages v_I below the **reference voltage V_{REF},** the output v_o will be in the **high logic level at the gate output V_{OH}.** As the input voltage increases and exceeds V_{ref}, the output voltage changes abruptly to the **low logic level at the gate output V_{OL}.** The output voltages corresponding to V_{OH} and V_{OL} generally fall between the supply voltages V_- and V_+ but may not be equal to either voltage. For an input equal to V_+ or V_-, the output does not necessarily reach either V_- or V_+. The actual levels depend on the individual logic family. The reference voltage V_{REF} is determined by the internal circuitry of the gate.

In most digital designs, the power supply voltage is predetermined either by technology constraints or system power-level criteria. For example, $V_+ = 5.0$ V (with $V_- = 0$) has been the standard power supply for logic for many years. However, because of the power-dissipation, heat-removal, and breakdown-voltage limitations of advanced technology, a new power supply voltage equal to 3.3 V is gaining widespread use. In addition, many low power systems must be designed to operate from battery voltages as low as 1.0 to 1.5 V, and future logic systems will operate from supply voltages of only 1.8 to 2.5 V.

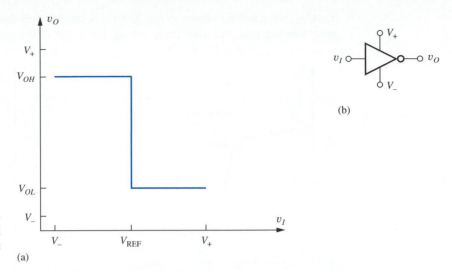

(a)

(b)

Figure 6.1 (a) Voltage transfer characteristic for an ideal inverter. (b) Inverter logic symbol.

6.2 LOGIC LEVEL DEFINITIONS AND NOISE MARGINS

Conceptually, a simple inverter circuit consists of a load resistor and a switch controlled by the input voltage v_I, as indicated in Fig. 6.2(b). When closed, the switch forces v_O to V_{OL}, and when open, the resistor sets the output to V_{OH}. In Fig. 6.2(b), $V_{OL} = 0$ V and $V_{OH} = V_+$.

The voltage-controlled switch can be realized by either the MOS transistor in Fig. 6.2(c) or the bipolar transistor in Fig. 6.2(d). Transistors M_S and Q_S switch between two states: nonconducting or off and conducting or on. Load resistor R sets the output voltage to $V_{OH} = V_+$ when switching transistor M_S or Q_S is off. If the input voltage exceeds the threshold voltage of M_S or the turn-on voltage of the base-emitter junction of Q_S, the transistors conduct a current that causes the output voltage to drop to V_{OL}. When transistors are used as switches, as in Figs. 6.2(c) and (d), $V_{OL} \neq 0$ V. Detailed discussion of the design of these circuits is deferred until Chapters 7 and 10.

In the inverter circuit, the transition between V_{OH} and V_{OL} does not occur in the abrupt manner indicated in Fig. 6.1 but is more gradual, as indicated by the more realistic

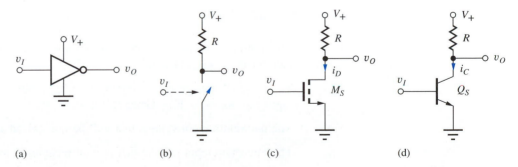

(a)   (b)   (c)   (d)

Figure 6.2 (a) Inverter operating with power supplies of 0 V and V_+. (b) Simple inverter circuit comprising a load resistor and switch. (c) Inverter with NMOS transistor switch. (d) Inverter with BJT switch.

transfer characteristic shown in Fig. 6.3(a). A single, well-defined value of V_{ref} does not exist. Instead, two additional input voltage levels are important.

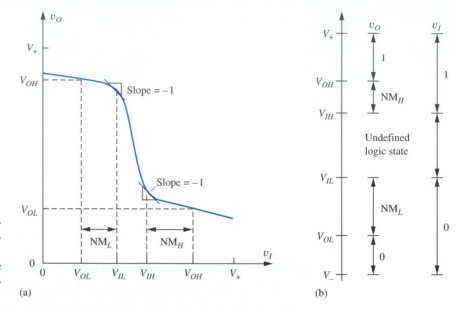

Figure 6.3 (a) Voltage transfer characteristic for the inverters in Fig. 6.2 with $V_- = 0$. (b) Voltage levels and logic state relationships for positive logic.

When the input v_I is below the **input low logic level** V_{IL}, the output is defined to be in the high output or 1 state. As the input voltage increases, the output voltage v_o falls until it reaches the low output or 0 state as v_I exceeds the voltage of the **input high logic level** V_{IH}. The input voltages V_{IL} and V_{IH} are defined by the points at which the slope of the voltage transfer characteristic equals -1. Voltages below V_{IL} are reliably recognized as logic 0s at the input of a logic gate, and voltages above V_{IH} are recognized reliably as logic 1s at the input. Voltages corresponding to the region between V_{IL} and V_{IH} do not represent valid logic input levels and generate logically indeterminate output voltages. The transition region of high negative slope between these two points[1] represents an undefined logic state. An alternate representation of the voltages and voltage ranges in Fig. 6.3(a) appears in Fig. 6.3(b), along with quantities that represent the voltage noise margins. The various terms are defined more fully below.

Logic Voltage Levels

V_{OL} The nominal voltage corresponding to a low logic state at the output of a logic gate for $v_I = V_{OH}$. Generally, $V_- \leq V_{OL}$.

V_{OH} The nominal voltage corresponding to a high logic state at the output of a logic gate for $v_I = V_{OL}$. Generally, $V_{OH} \leq V_+$.

V_{IL} The maximum input voltage that will be recognized as a low input logic level.

V_{IH} The minimum input voltage that will be recognized as a high input logic level.

---

[1] This region corresponds to a region of relatively high voltage gain. See Probs. 6.6 and 6.7.

Noise Margins

NM$_L$ The noise margin associated with a low input level is defined by

$$NM_L = V_{IL} - V_{OL} \tag{6.1}$$

NM$_H$ The noise margin associated with a high input level is defined by

$$NM_H = V_{OH} - V_{IH} \tag{6.2}$$

The **noise margin in the high state NM$_H$** and **noise margin in the low state NM$_L$** represent "safety margins" that prevent the gate from producing erroneous logic decisions in the presence of noise sources. The noise margins are needed to absorb voltage differences that may arise between the outputs and inputs of various logic gates due to a variety of sources. These may be extraneous signals coupled into the gates or simply parameter variations between gates in a logic family.

Figure 6.4 shows several interconnected inverters and tries to show why noise margin is important. The signal and power interconnections on a printed circuit board or integrated circuit, which we most often draw as zero resistance wires (or short circuits), really consist of distributed *RLC* networks. In Fig. 6.4 the output of the first inverter, v_{O1}, and the input of the second inverter, v_{I2}, are not necessarily equal. As logic signals propagate from one logic gate to the next, their characteristics become degraded by the resistance, inductance, and capacitance of the interconnections, *R*, *L*, and *C*. Rapidly switching signals may induce transient voltages and currents directly onto nearby signal nodes and lines through capacitive and inductive coupling indicated by C_c and *M*. In an RF environment, the interconnections may even act as small antennae that can couple additional extraneous signals into the logic circuitry.

Similar problems occur in the power distribution network. Both direct current and transient currents during gate switching generate voltage drops across the various components (R_p, L_p, C_p) of the power distribution network.

The noise margins also help absorb parameter variations that occur between individual logic gates. During manufacture, there will be unavoidable variations in device and circuit parameters, and variations will occur in the power supply voltages and operating temperature during application of the logic circuits. Normally, the logic manufacturer specifies worst-case values for V_{IL}, V_{OL}, V_{IH}, and V_{OH}. In our analysis, however, we will generally restrict ourselves to finding nominal values of V_{IL}, V_{OL}, V_{IH}, and V_{OH}.

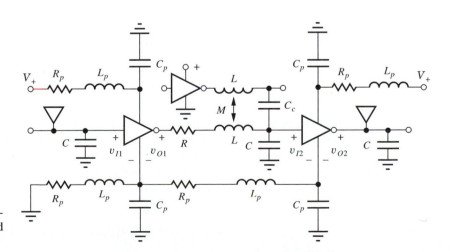

Figure 6.4 Inverters embedded in a signal and power and distribution network.

For subsequent discussions of MOS logic, V_- will usually be taken to be 0 V, and V_+ will be either 3.3 V or 5 V. These voltages are also commonly used in bipolar logic. However, other values are possible. For example, emitter-coupled logic, discussed in Chap. 10 on bipolar logic design, has historically used $V_+ = 0$ V and $V_- = -5.2$ V or -4.5 V, and new low-power ECL gates have been developed to operate with a total supply voltage span of only 2 V.

> **EXERCISE:** A certain TTL gate has the following values for its logic levels: $V_{OH} = 3.6$ V, $V_{OL} = 0.4$ V, $V_{IH} = 2.0$ V, $V_{IL} = 0.8$ V. What are the noise margins for this TTL gate?
>
> **ANSWERS:** $NM_H = 1.6$ V, $NM_L = 0.4$ V

Logic Gate Design Goals

As we explore the design of logic gates, we should keep in mind a number of goals.

1. From Fig. 6.1, we see that the ideal logic gate is a highly nonlinear device that attempts to quantize the input signal into two discrete output levels. In the actual gate in Figs. 6.2 and 6.3, we should strive to minimize the width of the undefined input voltage range, and the noise margins should generally be as large as possible.

2. Logic gates should be unidirectional in nature. The input should control the output to produce a well-defined logic function. Voltage changes at the output of a gate should not affect the input side of the circuit.

3. The logic levels must be regenerated as the signal passes through the gate. In other words, the voltage levels at the output of one gate must be compatible with the input voltage levels of the same or similar logic gates.

4. The output of one gate should also be capable of driving the inputs of more than one gate. The number of inputs that can be driven by the output of a logic gate is called the **fan-out** capability of that gate. The term **fan in** refers to the number of input signals that may be applied to the input of a gate.

5. In most design situations, the logic gate should consume as little power (and area in an IC design) as needed to meet the speed requirements of the design.

6.3 DYNAMIC RESPONSE OF LOGIC GATES

Figure 6.5 shows idealized time domain waveforms for an inverter. The input and output signals are switching between the two static logic levels V_{OL} and V_{OH}. Because of capacitances in the circuits, the waveforms exhibit nonzero rise and fall times, and propagation delays occur between the switching times of the input and output waveforms.

Rise Time and Fall Times

The **rise time** t_r for a given signal is defined as the time required for the signal to make the transition from the **"10%" point** to the **"90%" point** on the waveform, as indicated in Fig. 6.5. The **fall time** t_f is defined as the time required for the signal to make the transition between the 90% point and the 10% point on the waveform. The voltages corresponding to the 10% and 90% points are defined in terms of V_{OL} and V_{OH}:

$$V_{10\%} = V_{OL} + 0.1\,\Delta V$$
$$V_{90\%} = V_{OL} + 0.9\,\Delta V = V_{OH} - 0.1\,\Delta V$$

(6.3)

where $\Delta V = V_{OH} - V_{OL}$

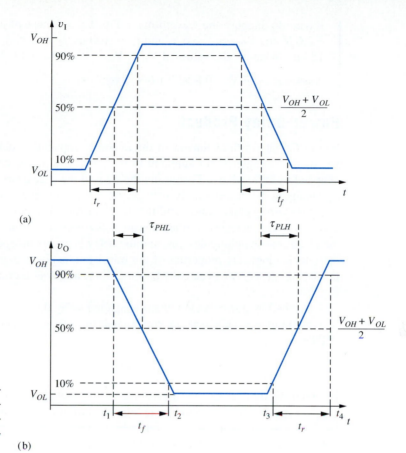

Figure 6.5 Switching waveforms for an *idealized* inverter: (a) input voltage signal, (b) output voltage waveform.

Rise and fall times usually have unequal values; the characteristic shapes of the input and output waveforms also differ.

Propagation Delay

Propagation delay is measured as the difference in time between the input and output signals reaching the **"50%" points** in their respective transitions. The 50% point is the voltage level corresponding to one-half the total transition between V_{OH} and V_{OL}:

$$V_{50\%} = \frac{V_{OH} + V_{OL}}{2} \tag{6.4}$$

The **propagation delay** on the **high-to-low output transition** is τ_{PHL} and that of the **low-to-high transition** is τ_{PLH}. In the general case, these two delays will not be equal, and the **average propagation delay** τ_P is defined by

$$\tau_P = \frac{\tau_{PLH} + \tau_{PHL}}{2} \tag{6.5}$$

Average propagation delay is one figure of merit that is commonly used to compare the performance of different logic families. In Chapters 7, 8, and 10 we explore the propagation delays for various MOS and bipolar logic circuits.

EXERCISE: Suppose the waveforms in Fig. 6.5 are those of an ECL gate with $V_{OL} = -2.6$ V and $V_{OH} = -0.6$ V, and $t_1 = 100$ ns, $t_2 = 105$ ns, $t_3 = 150$ ns, and $t_4 = 153$ ns. What are the values of $V_{10\%}$, $V_{90\%}$, $V_{50\%}$, t_r, and t_f?

ANSWERS: -2.4 V; -0.8 V; -1.6 V; 3 ns; 5 ns

Power-Delay Product

Figure 6.6 shows the behavior of the average propagation delay of a general logic gate versus the average power supplied to the gate. The power consumed by a gate can be changed by increasing or decreasing the sizes of the transistors and resistors in the gate or by changing the power supply voltage. At low power levels, gate delay is dominated by intergate wiring capacitance, and the delay decreases as power increases. As device size and power are increased further, circuit delay becomes limited by the inherent speed of the electronic switching devices, and the delay becomes independent of power. In bipolar logic technology, the properties of the transistors begin to degrade at even higher power levels, and the delay can actually become worse as power increases further, as indicated in Fig. 6.6.

In the low power region, the propagation delay decreases in direct proportion to the increase in power. This behavior corresponds to a region of constant **power-delay product (PDP),**

$$PDP = P\tau_P \tag{6.6}$$

in which P is the average power dissipated by the logic gate. The PDP represents the energy (Joules) required to perform a basic logic operation and is another figure of merit widely used to compare logic families. Early logic families had power-delay products of 10 to 100 pJ (1 pJ $= 10^{-12}$ J), whereas many of today's IC logic families now have PDPs in the 10 to 100 fJ range (1 fJ $= 10^{-15}$ J).

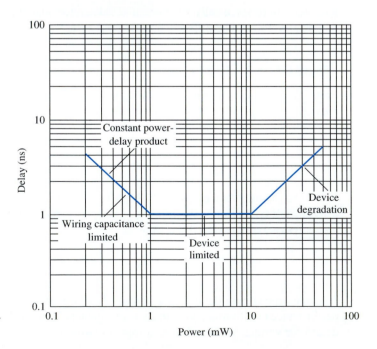

Figure 6.6 Logic gate delay versus power dissipation.

EXERCISE: (a) What is the power-delay product at low power for the logic gate characterized by Fig. 6.6? (b) What is the PDP at $P = 3$ mW? (c) At 20 mW?

ANSWER: 1 pJ; 3 pJ; 40 pJ

6.4 REVIEW OF BOOLEAN ALGEBRA

In 1849, G. Boole [1] presented a powerful mathematical formulation for dealing with logical thought and reasoning, and the formal algebra we use today to manipulate binary logic expressions is known as **boolean algebra.** Tables 6.1 to 6.6 and the following discussion summarize boolean algebra.

Table 6.1 lists the basic logic operations that we need. The logic function at the gate output is represented by variable Z and is a function of logical input variables A and B: $Z = f(A, B)$. To perform general logic operations, a logic family must provide logical inversion (NOT) plus at least one other function of two input variables, such as the OR or AND functions. We will find in Chapter 7 that NMOS logic can easily be used to implement **NOR gates** as well as **NAND gates,** and in Chapter 10 we will see that the basic TTL gate provides a NAND function whereas OR/NOR logic is provided by the basic ECL gate. Note in Table 6.1 that the NOT function is equivalent to the output of either a single input NOR gate or NAND gate.

Truth tables and logic symbols for the five functions in Table 6.1 appear in Tables 6.2 to 6.6 and Figs. 6.7 to 6.9. The truth table presents the output Z for all possible combinations of the input variables A and B. The inverter, $Z = \overline{A}$, has a single input, and the output represents the logical inversion or complement of the input variable, as indicated by the overbar (Table 6.2; Fig. 6.7).

Table 6.1

Basic Boolean Operations

Operation	Boolean Representation
NOT	$Z = \overline{A}$
OR	$Z = A + B$
AND	$Z = A \cdot B = AB$
NOR	$Z = \overline{A + B}$
NAND	$Z = \overline{A \cdot B} = \overline{AB}$

Table 6.2

NOT (Inverter) Truth Table

A	$Z = \overline{A}$
0	1
1	0

$A \rightarrow\!\!\!\triangleright\!\!\circ\ Z = \overline{A}$

Figure 6.7 Inverter symbol.

Tables 6.3 and 6.4 are the truth tables for a two-input **OR gate** and a two-input **AND gate,** respectively, and the corresponding logic symbols appear in Fig. 6.8. The OR

Table 6.3

OR Gate Truth Table

A	B	$Z = A + B$
0	0	0
0	1	1
1	0	1
1	1	1

Table 6.4

AND Gate Truth Table

A	B	$Z = AB$
0	0	0
0	1	0
1	0	0
1	1	1

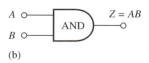

A ○——
B ○—— OR $\rangle$—○ $Z = A + B$
(a)

A ○——
B ○—— AND $\rangle$—○ $Z = AB$
(b)

Figure 6.8 (a) OR gate symbol. (b) AND gate symbol.

operation is indicated by the $+$ symbol; its output Z is a 1 when either one or both of the input variables A or B is a 1. The output is a 0 only if both inputs are 0. The AND operation is indicated by the $\cdot$ symbol, as in $A \cdot B$, or in a more compact form as simply AB, and the output Z is a 1 only if both the input variables A and B are in the 1 state. If either input is 0, then the output is 0. We shall use AB to represent A AND B throughout the rest of this text.

Tables 6.5 and 6.6 are the truth tables for the two-input **NOR gate** and the two-input **NAND gate,** respectively, and the logic symbols appear in Fig. 6.9. These functions represent the complements of the OR and AND operations—that is, the OR or AND operations followed by logical inversion. The NOR operation is represented as $Z = \overline{A + B}$, and its output Z is a 1 only if both inputs are 0. For the NAND operation, $Z = \overline{AB}$, output Z is a 1 except when both the input variables A or B are in the 1 state.

(a)

(b)

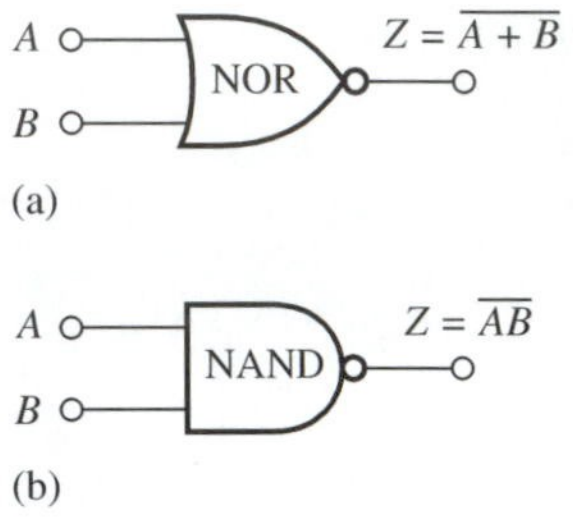

Figure 6.9 (a) NOR gate symbol. (b) NAND gate symbol.

Table 6.5

NOR Gate Truth Table

A	B	$Z = \overline{A + B}$
0	0	1
0	1	0
1	0	0
1	1	0

Table 6.6

NAND Gate Truth Table

A	B	$Z = \overline{AB}$
0	0	1
0	1	1
1	0	1
1	1	0

In Chapters 7 and 8, we will find that a major advantage of MOS logic is its capability to readily form more complex logic functions, particularly logic expressions represented in a complemented **sum-of-products** form:

$$Z = \overline{AB + CD + E} \quad \text{or} \quad Z = \overline{ABC + DE} \quad (6.7)$$

The boolean identities that are shown in Table 6.7 can be very useful in finding simplified logic expressions, such as those expressions in Eq. (6.7). This table includes the identity operations as well as the basic commutative, associative, and distributive laws of boolean algebra.

Table 6.7

Useful Boolean Identities

$A + 0 = A$	$A \cdot 1 = A$	Identity operation
$A + B = B + A$	$AB = BA$	Commutative law
$A + (B + C) = (A + B) + C$	$A(BC) = (AB)C$	Associative law
$A + BC = (A + B)(A + C)$	$A(B + C) = AB + AC$	Distributive law
$A + \overline{A} = 1$	$A \cdot \overline{A} = 0$	
$A + A = A$	$A \cdot A = A$	
$A + 1 = 1$	$A \cdot 0 = 0$	
$\overline{A + B} = \overline{A}\,\overline{B}$	$\overline{AB} = \overline{A} + \overline{B}$	

EXAMPLE 6.1: Use the relations in Table 6.7 to simplify the expression

$$Z = A\overline{B}C + ABC + \overline{A}BC$$

SOLUTION:

$$Z = A\overline{B}C + ABC + \overline{A}BC$$

$$Z = A\overline{B}C + ABC + ABC + \overline{A}BC \quad \text{using } ABC = ABC + ABC$$

$$Z = A(\overline{B} + B)C + (\overline{A} + A)BC \quad \text{using distributive law}$$

$$Z = A(1)C + (1)BC \quad \text{using } (\overline{B} + B) = (B + \overline{B}) = 1$$

$$Z = AC + BC \quad \text{since } A(1)C = AC(1) = AC$$

$$Z = (A + B)C \quad \text{using distributive law}$$

◆

6.5 DIODE LOGIC

Diode logic is one of the simplest circuit techniques that can be used to implement the AND and OR functions. Although of somewhat limited utility, diode logic provides a simple introduction to logic circuit implementation and can be used in circuit design to logically combine several input signals.

Diode OR Gate

Figure 6.10 is the circuit diagram of a simple diode **OR gate** along with circuit voltages for the case $A = 1 = 5$ V and $B = 0 = 0$ V. In Fig. 6.10(b), diode D_1 is conducting, diode D_2 is reverse-biased, and the output voltage is one diode voltage drop below the 5 V input at A. Using the constant-voltage-drop model from Chapter 3 with $V_{on} = 0.6$ V, $v_0 = 5$ V $- 0.6$ V $= 4.4$ V and $Z = 1$. Although the output voltage is not equal to the full 5-V input level, 4.4 V is usually sufficiently large to be interpreted as a logical 1. If at least one of the inputs in the circuit in Fig. 6.10 is at $+5$ V, then the output of this gate will be at 4.4 V. If both inputs are at 0 V, then D_1 and D_2 will both be nonconducting and $v_0 = 0$. Thus, the diode circuit in Fig. 6.10 is a basic form of OR logic.

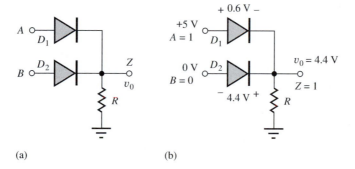

Figure 6.10 (a) Diode OR gate. (b) OR gate with $A = 1$ and $B = 0$.

Diode AND Gate

By reversing the diodes and power supply, as in Fig. 6.11, the circuit becomes an **AND gate.** In Fig. 6.11(b), we again look at the circuit for the case $A = 1 = 5$ V and $B = 0 = 0$ V. Diode D_1 is now reverse-biased, diode D_2 is conducting, and the output voltage is one

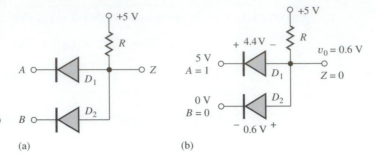

Figure 6.11 (a) Diode AND gate. (b) AND gate with $A = 1$, $B = 0$, and $Z = 0$.

diode voltage drop above ground potential:

$$v_O = (0 + 0.6) \text{ V} = 0.6 \text{ V} \qquad \text{and} \qquad Z = 0$$

Although the output voltage is not equal to 0 V, the 0.6-V level is sufficiently low to be interpreted as a logical 0. If either one or both of the inputs is at 0 V, then the output of the gate is 0.6 V. Only if both inputs are at +5 V will the output also be at +5 V, corresponding to $Z = 1$. Thus, the circuit in Fig. 6.11 functions as a basic AND gate.

Although the diode OR gate and AND gates provide simple implementations of their respective logic function, they both suffer from the same problem. The gates do not satisfy design goal 3 discussed in Sec. 6.2 because the logic levels are not regenerated at the output of the gate. When several similar gates are connected in series, the output level is degraded one diode drop by each gate in the chain. If too many diode logic gates are cascaded, then the output voltage no longer represents the proper binary state. However, there are often cases where the circuit designer would like to form the AND or OR combination of several logical variables in a simple control circuit, and diode logic will suffice.

A Diode-Transistor Logic (DTL) Gate

The level-restoration problem can be solved by adding a diode and transistor to form the **diode-transistor logic (DTL)** gate shown schematically in Fig. 6.12. We will analyze bipolar logic gates in detail in Chapter 10; here is a brief overview of the operation of this gate.

The situation in Fig. 6.13(a) corresponds to the case in which both inputs are in the logical 1 state, $V_{OH} = V_+ = 3.3$ V. In this particular circuit, diodes D_1 and D_2 are both off, and node 1 is at 1.3 V:

$$V_1 = V_{D3} + V_{BE} = 0.6 \text{ V} + 0.7 \text{ V} = 1.3 \text{ V}$$

The current I through resistor R_B and diode D_3 becomes the base current I_B of transistor Q_1. The value of I_B is designed to cause Q_1 to saturate so that $v_O = V_{\text{CESAT}}$ (for example, 0.05 to 0.1 V).

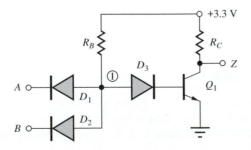

Figure 6.12 A two-input diode-transistor logic (DTL) NAND gate.

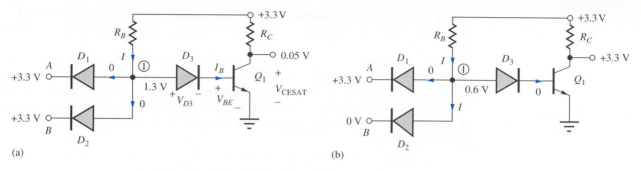

Figure 6.13 A diode-transistor NAND gate: (a) both inputs high, (b) one input low.

In Fig. 6.13(b), input B is now at 0 V, corresponding to a logical 0. Diode D_2 is conducting, holding node 1 at 0.6 V. Now diode D_3 and transistor Q_1 must both be off, because the voltage at node 1 is now less than the two diode voltage drops required to turn on both D_3 and Q_1. The base current of Q_1 is now zero; it will be off with $I_C = 0$, and the output voltage will be at +3.3 V, corresponding to a logical 1. A similar situation holds for the circuit if both inputs are low. The truth table for this gate is identical to Table 6.6. The DTL circuit represents a two-input NAND gate with $Z = \overline{AB}$.

SUMMARY

Binary logic circuits use two voltage levels to represent the boolean logic variables 1 and 0. In the positive logic convention used throughout this book, the more positive voltage represents a 1 and the more negative level represents a 0. The output of an ideal logic gate would take on only two possible voltage levels: V_{OH}, corresponding to the 1 state, and V_{OL}, corresponding to the 0 state. The output of the ideal gate would abruptly change state as the input crossed through a fixed reference voltage V_{REF}. Logic gates implemented with electronic circuits can only approximate this ideal behavior. The transition between states as the input voltage changes is much more gradual, and a precise reference voltage is not defined. V_{IL} and V_{IH} are defined by the input voltages at which the slope of the voltage transfer characteristic is equal to -1, and these voltages define the boundaries of the transition region between the logical 1 and 0 levels.

Noise margins are very important in logic gates and represent a measure of the gate's ability to reject extraneous signals. The high state and low state noise margins are defined by $NM_H = V_{OH} - V_{IH}$ and $NM_L = V_{IL} - V_{OL}$, respectively. The unwanted signals can be voltages or currents coupled into the circuit from adjacent logic gates, from the power distribution network, or by electromagnetic radiation. The noise margins must absorb manufacturing process tolerance variations and power supply voltage variations.

Keep in mind a number of logic gate design goals. The logic gate should quantize the input signal into two discrete output levels and minimize the width of the undefined input voltage range. Logic levels must be regenerated as the signal passes through the gate, and the noise margins generally should be as large as possible. The gate should be unidirectional in nature and have a significant fan-out and/or fan-in capability. Finally, a logic gate should consume as little power and area as needed to meet the speed requirements of the design.

In the time domain, the transition between logic states cannot occur instantaneously. Capacitances exist in any real circuit and slow down the state transitions, thereby degrading the logic signals. Rise time t_r and fall time t_f characterize the time required for a given signal to change between the 0 and 1 or 1 and 0 states, respectively, and the average propagation delay τ_P characterizes the time required for the output of a given gate to respond to changes in its input signals. The propagation delays on the high-to-low (τ_{PHL}) and low-to-high (τ_{PLH}) transitions are typically not equal, and τ_P is equal to the average of these two values.

The power-delay product PDP, expressed in pJ or fJ, is an important figure of merit for comparing logic families. At low power levels the power-delay product is a constant, and the propagation delay of a given logic family decreases as power is increased. At intermediate power levels, the propagation delay becomes independent of power level, and at high power levels, the propagation delay of bipolar logic families actually degrades as power is increased.

Boolean algebra, developed by G. Boole in the mid-1800s, is a powerful mathematical tool for manipulating binary logic expressions. Basic logic gates provide some combination of the NOT, AND, OR, NAND, or NOR logic functions. A complete logic family must provide at least the NOT function and either the AND or OR functions. Simple AND and OR gates can be constructed using diodes, but a transistor must be added to achieve the inversion operation. The combination of a diode AND gate and a bipolar transistor forms a DTL NAND gate.

Key Terms

AND gate
Average propagation delay
 (τ_p)
Boolean algebra
Complementary MOS (CMOS)
 technology
Diode logic
Diode-transistor logic (DTL)
Emitter-coupled logic (ECL)
Fall time t_f
Fan in
Fan out
High logic level at the gate input
 (V_{IH})

High logic level at the gate output
 (V_{OH})
Low logic level at the gate input
 (V_{IL})
Low logic level at the gate output
 (V_{OL})
NAND gate
Noise margin in high state (NM_H)
Noise margin in low state (NM_L)
NOR gate
OR gate
Power-delay product (PDP)
Propagation delay—high-to-low
 transition (τ_{PHL})

Propagation delay—low-to-
 high transition (τ_{PLH})
Reference voltage (V_{ref})
Rise time t_r
Sum-of-products representation
Transistor-transistor logic (TTL)
Truth table
Voltage transfer characteristic
 (VTC)
10% point
50% point
90% point

Reference

G. Boole, *An Investigation of the Laws of Thought, on Which Are Founded the Mathematical Theories of Logic and Probability,* 1849. Reprinted by Dover Publications, Inc., New York: 1954.

Additional Reading

Nelson, V. P., et al. *Analysis and Design of Logic Circuits.* Prentice-Hall, Englewood Cliffs, N.J.: 1994.

Problems

General Introduction

6.1. Integrated circuit chips packaged in plastic can typically dissipate only 1 W per chip. Suppose we have an IC design that must fit on one chip and requires 100,000 logic gates. (a) What is the average power that can be dissipated by each logic gate on the chip? (b) If a supply voltage of 5 V is used, how much current can be used by each gate?

6.2. A high-performance microprocessor design requires 10 million logic gates and is placed in a package that can dissipate 40 W. (a) What is the average power that can be dissipated by each logic gate on the chip? (b) If a supply voltage of 3.3 V is used, how much current can be used by each gate? (c) What is the total current required by the IC chip?

6.1–6.2 Gates, Logic Level Definitions, and Noise Margins

6.3. (a) The ideal inverter in Fig. 6.2(b) has $R = 100\text{ k}\Omega$ and $V_+ = 5$ V. What are V_{OH} and V_{OL}? What is the power dissipation of the gate for $v_O = V_{OH}$ and $v_O = V_{OL}$? (b) Repeat for $V_+ = 3.3$ V.

6.4. Plot a graph of the voltage transfer characteristic for an ideal inverter with $V_+ = 3.3$ V, $V_- = 0$ V, and $V_{REF} = 1.1$ V. Assume $V_{OH} = V_+$ and $V_{OL} = V_-$.

6.5. (a) Plot a graph of the overall voltage transfer function for two cascaded ideal inverters if each individual inverter has a voltage transfer characteristic as defined in Prob. 6.4. (b) What is the overall logic expression $Z = f(A)$ for the two cascaded inverters?

6.6. Plot a graph of the voltage gain A_v of the ideal inverter in Fig. 6.1 as a function of input voltage v_I. $(A_v = dv_O/dv_I)$

6.7. The voltage transfer characteristic for an inverter is given in Fig. P6.7. What are V_{OH}, V_{OL}, V_{IH}, V_{IL}, and the voltage gain A_v of the inverter in the transition region? $(A_v = dv_O/dv_I)$

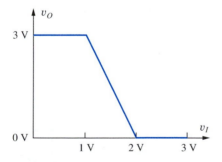

Figure P6.7

6.8. Plot a graph of the overall voltage transfer characteristic for two cascaded inverters if each individual inverter has the voltage transfer function defined in Fig. P6.7.

6.9. Suppose $V_{OH} = 5$ V, $V_{OL} = 0$ V, and $V_{REF} = 2.0$ V for the ideal logic gate in Fig. 6.1. What are the values of V_{IH}, V_{IL}, NM_H, and NM_L?

6.10. Suppose $V_{OH} = 3.3$ V and $V_{OL} = 0$ V for the ideal logic gate in Fig. 6.1. Considering noise margins, what would be the best choice of V_{REF}, and why did you make this choice?

6.11. The static voltage transfer characteristic for a practical CMOS inverter is given in Fig. P6.11. What are the values of V_{OH}, V_{OL}, V_{IH}, V_{IL}, NM_H, and NM_L?

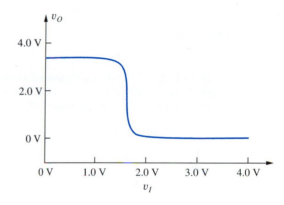

Figure P6.11

6.12. The graph in Fig. P6.12 gives the results of a SPICE simulation of an inverter. What are V_{OH} and V_{OL} for this gate?

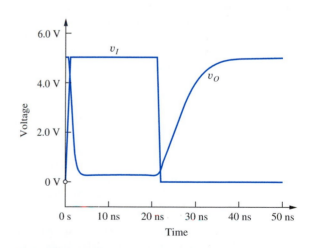

Figure P6.12

6.13. The graph in Fig. P6.13 on p. 240 gives the results of a SPICE simulation of an inverter. What are V_{OH} and V_{OL} for this gate?

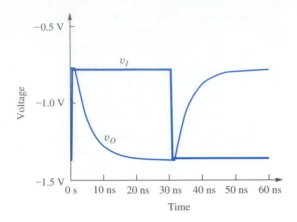

Figure P6.13

6.14. An ECL gate exhibits the following characteristics: $V_{OH} = -0.8$ V, $V_{OL} = -2.0$ V, and $NM_H = NM_L = 0.5$ V. What are the values of V_{IH} and V_{IL}?

6.3 Dynamic Response of Logic Gates

6.15. A logic family has a power-delay product of 100 fJ. If a logic gate consumes a power of 100 μW, estimate the propagation delay of the logic gate.

6.16. Integrated circuit chips packaged in plastic can typically dissipate only 1 W per chip. Suppose we have an IC design that must fit on one chip and requires 250,000 logic gates. (a) What is the average power that can be dissipated by each logic gate on the chip? (b) If a supply voltage of 5 V is used, how much current can be used by each gate? (c) If the average gate delay for these circuits must be 2 ns, what is the power-delay product required for the circuits in this design?

6.17. A high-performance microprocessor design requires 8 million logic gates and is placed in a package that can dissipate 40 W. (a) What is the average power that can be dissipated by each logic gate on the chip? (b) If a supply voltage of 3.3 V is used, how much current can be used by each gate? (c) If the average gate delay for these circuits must be 1 ns, what is the power-delay product required for the circuits in this design?

6.18. Plot the power-delay product versus power for the logic gate with the power-delay characteristic depicted in Fig. 6.6.

*6.19. (a) Derive an expression for the rise time of the circuit in Fig. P6.19(a) in terms of the circuit time constant. Assume that $v(t)$ is a 1-V step function, changing state at $t = 0$. (b) Derive a similar ex-

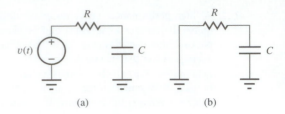

Figure P6.19

pression for the fall time of the capacitor voltage in Fig. P6.19(b) if the capacitor has an initial voltage of 1 V at $t = 0$.

6.20. The graph in Fig. P6.12 gives the results of a SPICE simulation of an inverter. (a) What are V_{OH} and V_{OL} for this gate? (b) What are the rise and fall times for v_I and v_O? (c) What are the values of τ_{PHL} and τ_{PLH}? (d) What is the average propagation delay for this gate?

6.21. The graph in Fig. P6.13 gives the results of a SPICE simulation of an inverter. (a) What are V_{OH} and V_{OL} for this gate? (b) What are the rise and fall times for v_I and v_O? (c) What are the values of τ_{PHL} and τ_{PLH}? (d) What is the average propagation delay for this gate?

6.4 Review of Boolean Algebra

6.22. Use the results in Table 6.2 to prove that $(A + B)(A + C) = A + BC$.

6.23. Use the results in Table 6.2 to simplify the logic expression $Z = AB\overline{C} + ABC + \overline{A}BC$.

6.24. Make a truth table for the expression in Prob. 6.23.

6.25. Use the results in Table 6.2 to simplify the logic expression $Z = \overline{A}\,\overline{B}C + ABC + \overline{A}BC + A\overline{B}C$.

6.26. Make a truth table for the expression in Prob. 6.25.

6.27. Make a truth table and write an expression for the logic function in Fig. P6.27.

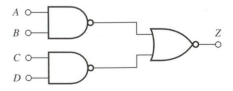

Figure P6.27

6.28. Make a truth table and write an expression for the logic function in Fig. P6.28.

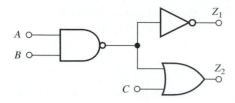

Figure P6.28

6.29. (a) What is the fan out of the NAND gate in Fig. P6.28? (b) Of each NAND gate in Fig. P6.27?

6.5 Diode Logic

6.30. What logic functions Z are provided by the two circuits in Fig. P6.30?

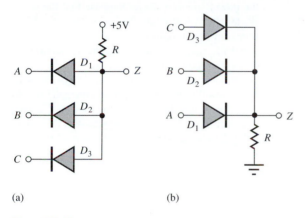

(a)   (b)

Figure P6.30

6.31. What logic functions Z are provided by the two circuits in Fig. P6.31? Assume the input voltage levels are $1 = 0$ V and $0 = -2$ V.

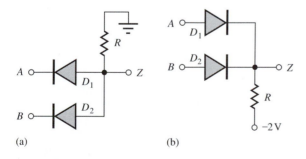

(a)   (b)

Figure P6.31

6.32. (a) The DTL gate in Fig. 6.13(a) has $R_C = 3$ kΩ, $R_B = 10$ kΩ, and $V_{CESAT} = 0.05$ V. What are the

values of the base current I_B and collector current I_C? Is this transistor saturated if $\beta_F = 20$? (b) What is the value of I in Fig. 6.13(b)? (c) What is the power dissipation in the circuit in Fig. 6.13(a)? (d) In Fig. 6.13(b)?

6.33. The DTL gate in Fig. 6.13(a) has $R_C = 3$ kΩ and $R_B = 30$ kΩ. What is the minimum value of β_F for which the transistor is saturated?

6.34. Add a diode to the circuit in Fig. 6.12 to form a three-input DTL NAND gate.

6.35. Two stages of diode logic precede the ideal inverter in Fig. P6.35. What is the expression for the logic output variable $Z = f(A, B, C)$?

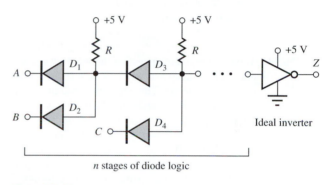

Figure P6.35

*6.36. The ideal inverter in Fig. P6.35 has a reference voltage of 2.5 V. What is the maximum number of diode logic circuits that may be cascaded ahead of the inverter without producing logic errors if the forward voltage of the diode is 0.75 V?

*6.37. Four stages of diode logic circuits are cascaded ahead of the ideal inverter in Fig. P6.35. If the forward voltage of the diodes is 0.70 V, what must be the minimum reference voltage of the inverter if it is to yield valid logic signals at its output?

General Problems

6.38. A high-speed microprocessor must drive a 64-bit data bus in which each line has a capacitive load C of 40 pF, and the logic swing is 5 V. The bus drivers must discharge the load capacitance from 5 V to 0 V in 1 ns, as depicted in Fig. P6.38 on p. 242. Draw the waveform for the current in the output of the bus driver as a function of time for the indicated waveform. What is the peak current in the microprocessor chip if all 64 drivers are switching simultaneously?

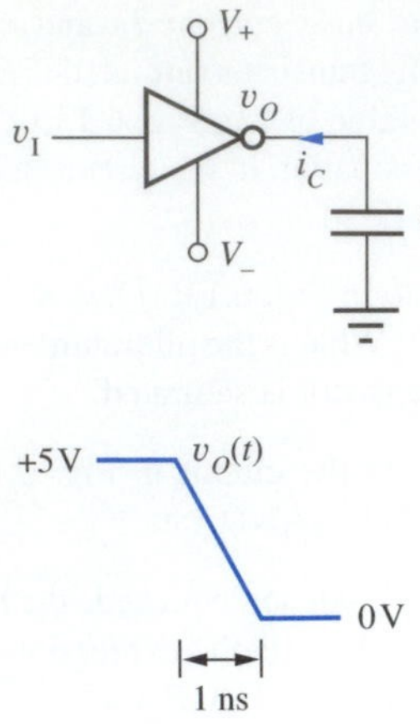

Figure P6.38 Bus driver and switching waveform.

*6.39. A particular interconnection between two logic gates in an IC chip runs one-half the distance across a 7.5-mm-wide die. The interconnection line is insulated from the substrate by silicon dioxide. If the line is 1.5 μm wide and the oxide ($\varepsilon_{ox} = 3.9\varepsilon_o$ and $\varepsilon_o = 8.85 \times 10^{-14}$ F/cm) beneath the line is 1 μm thick, what is the total capacitance of this line assuming that the capacitance is three times that predicted by the parallel plate capacitance formula? Assume that the silicon beneath the oxide represents a conducting ground plane.

**6.40. Ideal constant-electric-field scaling of a MOS technology reduces all the dimensions and voltages by the same factor α. Assume that the circuit delay ΔT can be estimated from

$$\Delta T = C\frac{\Delta V}{I}$$

in which the capacitance C is proportional to the total gate capacitance of the MOS transistor, $C = C''_{ox} WL$, ΔV is the logic swing, and I is the MOSFET drain current in saturation. Show that constant-field scaling results in a reduction in delay by a factor of α and a reduction in power by a factor of α^2 so that the PDP is reduced by a factor of α^3. Show that the power density actually remains constant under constant-field scaling.

**6.41 For many years, MOS devices were scaled to smaller and smaller dimensions without changing the power supply voltage. Suppose that the width W, length L, and oxide thickness T_{OX} of a MOS transistor are all reduced by a factor of 2. Assume that V_{TN}, v_{GS}, and v_{DS} remain the same. (a) Calculate the ratio of the drain current of the scaled device to that of the original device. (b) By what factor has the power dissipation changed? (c) By what factor has the value of the total gate capacitance changed? (d) By what factor has the circuit delay ΔT changed? (Use the delay formula in Prob. 6.40.)

C H A P T E R 7

MOS Logic Design

Chapter 7 explores the characteristics and design of basic logic gates in MOS technology. Although we focus our study on the static design of NMOS logic gates, which are circuits that use only n-channel MOS devices, the concepts and techniques discussed are also applicable to PMOS logic design, in which the logic gates are implemented using only p-channel devices. The discussion begins by investigating the design of the MOS inverter in order to gain an understanding of its voltage transfer characteristic and noise margins. Inverters with four different load configurations are considered: the resistor load, saturated load, linear load, and depletion-mode load circuits. NOR, NAND, and more complex logic gates are shown to be easily designed as simple extensions of the reference inverter designs. Later, the rise time, fall time, and propagation delays of the gates are analyzed.

The drain current of the MOS device depends on its gate-source voltage v_{GS}, drain-source voltage v_{DS}, and source-bulk voltage v_{SB}, and on the device parameters, which include the transconductance parameter K_n', threshold voltage V_{TN}, and width-to-length or **W/L ratio.** The power supply voltage constrains the range of v_{GS} and v_{DS}, and the technology sets the values of K_n' and V_{TN}. Thus, the circuit designer's job is to choose the circuit topology and the W/L ratios of the MOS transistors to achieve the desired logic function.

In most logic design situations, the power supply voltage is predetermined by either technology reliability constraints or system-level criteria. For example, as mentioned in Chapter 6, $V_{DD}{}^{1} = 5.0$ V has been the standard power supply for logic for many years. However, a new 3.3-V power supply level is now gaining widespread use as well. In addition, many low-power and portable systems must operate from battery voltages as low as 1.0 to 1.5 V.

7.1 DESIGN OF THE MOS INVERTER WITH RESISTIVE LOAD

Complex digital systems can consist of millions of logic gates, and it is helpful to remember that each individual logic gate is generally interconnected in a larger network. The output of one logic gate drives the input of another logic gate, as shown schematically by the four inverters in Fig. 7.1. Thus, a gate has $v_O = V_{OH}$ when an input voltage $v_I = V_{OL}$ is applied to its input, and vice versa. For MOS design, we first need to find V_{OH} and then apply it as an input to the gate in order to determine V_{OL}.

The basic inverter circuit shown in Fig. 7.2 consists of an NMOS switching device M_S designed to force v_O to V_{OL} and a **resistor load** element to "pull" the output up toward

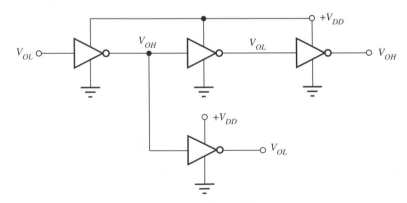

Figure 7.1 A network of inverters.

$^{1}V_{DD}$ and V_{SS} have traditionally been used to denote the positive and negative power supply voltages in MOS circuits.

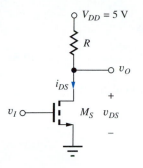

Figure 7.2 NMOS inverter with resistive load.

the power supply V_{DD}. The NMOS transistor is designed to switch between the linear region for $v_I = V_{OH}$ and the cutoff (nonconducting) state for $v_I = V_{OL}$. The circuit designer must choose the values of the load resistor R and the W/L ratio of **switching transistor M_S** so the inverter meets a set of design specifications. In this case, these two design variables permit us to choose the V_{OL} level and set the total power dissipation of the logic gate.

Let us explore the inverter operation by considering the requirements for the design of such a logic gate. Writing the equation for the output voltage, we find

$$v_O = v_{DS} = V_{DD} - i_{DS}R \tag{7.1}$$

When the input voltage is at a low state, $v_I = V_{OL}$, M_S should be cut off, with $i_{DS} = 0$, so that

$$v_O = V_{DD} = V_{OH} \tag{7.2}$$

Thus, in this particular logic circuit, the value of V_{OH} is set by the power supply voltage $V_{DD} = 5$ V.

To ensure that transistor M_S is cut off when the input is equal to V_{OL}, as in Fig. 7.3(a), the gate-source voltage of M_S ($v_{GS} = V_{OL}$) must be less than its threshold voltage V_{TN}. For $V_{TN} = 1$ V, a normal design point would be for V_{OL} to be in the range of 25 to 50 percent of V_{TN} or 0.25 to 0.50 V to ensure adequate noise margins. Let us assume a design value of $V_{OL} = 0.25$ V.

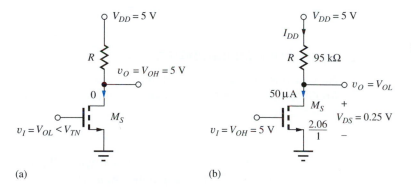

Figure 7.3 Inverters in the (a) $v_I = V_{OL}$ (0) and (b) $v_I = V_{OH}$ (1) logic states.

(a)   (b)

Design of the *W/L* Ratio of *M_S*

The value of W/L required to set $V_{OL} = 0.25$ V can be calculated if we know the parameters of the MOS device. For now, the values $V_{TN} = 1$ V and $K'_n = 25 \times 10^{-6}$ A/V^2 will be used. In addition, we need to know a value for the desired operating current of the inverter. The current is determined by the permissible power dissipation of the NMOS gate when $v_O = V_{OL}$. Using $P = 0.25$ mW (see Probs. 7.1 and 7.2[2]), the current in the gate can be found from $P = V_{DD} \times I_{DD}$. For our circuit,

$$0.25 \times 10^{-3} = 5 \times I_{DD} \qquad \text{or} \qquad I_{DD} = 50 \ \mu\text{A} = i_{DS}$$

Now we can determine the value for the W/L ratio of the NMOS switching device from the MOS drain current expression using the circuit conditions in Fig. 7.3(b). In this case, the input is set equal to $V_{OH} = 5$ V, and the output of the inverter should then be at V_{OL}. The expression for the drain current in the linear region of the device is used because $v_{GS} - V_{TN} = 5$ V $- 1$ V $= 4$ V, and $v_{DS} = V_{OL} = 0.25$ V, yielding $v_{DS} < v_{GS} - V_{TN}$.

---

[2] It would be worth exploring these problems before continuing.

$$i_{DS} = K_n'\left(\frac{W}{L}\right)_S (v_{GS} - V_{TN} - 0.5 v_{DS}) v_{DS}$$

or
(7.3)

$$5 \times 10^{-5} \text{ A} = \left(25 \times 10^{-6} \frac{\text{A}}{\text{V}^2}\right)\left(\frac{W}{L}\right)_S (5 \text{ V} - 1 \text{ V} - 0.125 \text{ V})(0.25 \text{ V})$$

Solving Eq. (7.3) for $(W/L)_S$ gives $(W/L)_S = 2.06/1$.

Load Resistor Design

The value of the load resistor R is chosen to limit the current when $v_O = V_{OL}$ and is found from

$$R = \frac{V_{DD} - V_{OL}}{i_{DS}} = \frac{(5 - 0.25) \text{ V}}{5 \times 10^{-5} \text{ A}} = 95 \text{ k}\Omega \tag{7.4}$$

These design values are shown in the circuit in Fig. 7.3(b).

> **EXERCISE:** Redesign the logic gate in Fig. 7.3 to operate at a power of 0.5 mW while maintaining $V_{OL} = 0.25$ V.
>
> **ANSWER:** $(W/L)_S = 4.12/1$, $R = 47.5 \text{ k}\Omega$

Load-Line Visualization

An important way to visualize the operation of the inverter is to draw the load line on the MOS transistor output characteristics as in Fig. 7.4. Equation (7.1), repeated here, represents the equation for the load line:

$$v_{DS} = V_{DD} - i_{DS}R$$

When the transistor is cut off, $i_{DS} = 0$ and $v_{DS} = V_{DD} = 5$ V, and when the transistor is on, the MOSFET is operating in the linear region, with $v_{GS} = V_{OH} = 5$ V and $v_{DS} = v_O = V_{OL} = 0.25$ V. The MOSFET switches between the two operating points on the load line, as indicated by the circles in Fig. 7.4. At the right-hand end of the load line,

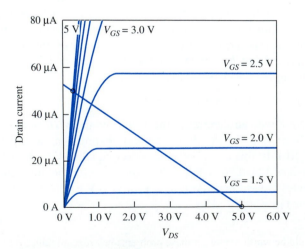

Figure 7.4 MOSFET output characteristics and load line.

the MOSFET is cut off. At the Q-point near the left end of the load line, the MOSFET represents a relatively low resistance, and the current is determined primarily by the load resistance. (Note how the Q-point is nearly independent of v_{GS}.)

On-Resistance of the Switching Device

When the logic gate output is in the low state, the output voltage can also be calculated from a resistive voltage divider formed by the load resistor R and the **on-resistance** R_{on} of the MOSFET, as in Fig. 7.5.

$$V_{OL} = V_{DD} \frac{R_{on}}{R_{on} + R} = V_{DD} \frac{1}{1 + \dfrac{R}{R_{on}}} \tag{7.5}$$

where

$$R_{on} = \frac{v_{DS}}{i_D} = \frac{1}{K'_n \dfrac{W}{L}\left(v_{GS} - V_{TN} - \dfrac{v_{DS}}{2}\right)} \tag{7.6}$$

R_{on} must be much smaller than R in order for V_{OL} to be small. It is important to recognize that R_{on} represents a nonlinear resistor because the value of R_{on} is dependent on v_{DS}, the voltage across the resistor terminals. All the NMOS gates that we study in this chapter demonstrate **"ratioed" logic**—that is, designs in which the on-resistance of the switching transistor must be much smaller than that of the load transistor in order to achieve a small value of V_{OL} ($R_{on} \ll R$).

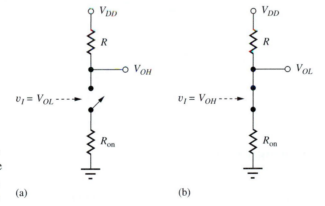

Figure 7.5 Simplified representation of an inverter: (a) the off or nonconducting state, (b) the on or conducting state.

(a)   (b)

EXAMPLE 7.1: What is the on-resistance for the NMOSFET in Fig. 7.3 when the output is at V_{OL}?

SOLUTION: R_{on} can be found using Eq. (7.6).

$$R_{on} = \frac{1}{\left(25 \times 10^{-6} \dfrac{A}{V^2}\right)\left(\dfrac{2.06}{1}\right)\left(5 - 1 - \dfrac{0.25}{2}\right) V} = 5.0 \text{ k}\Omega$$

We can check this value by using it to calculate V_{OL}:

$$V_{OL} = V_{DD}\frac{R_{on}}{R_{on} + R} = 5\text{ V}\frac{5\text{ k}\Omega}{5\text{ k}\Omega + 95\text{ k}\Omega} = 0.25\text{ V}$$

$R_{on} = 5\text{ k}\Omega$ does indeed give the correct value of V_{OL}. Note that $R_{on} \ll R$.

◆

Noise Margin Analysis

Figure 7.6 is a SPICE simulation of the voltage transfer function for the completed inverter design. Now we are in a position to find the values of V_{IL} and V_{IH} that correspond to the points at which the slope of the voltage transfer characteristic for the inverter is equal to -1, as defined in Sec. 6.2. Our analysis begins with the expression for the load line, repeated here from Eq. (7.1):

$$v_O = V_{DD} - i_{DS}R \tag{7.7}$$

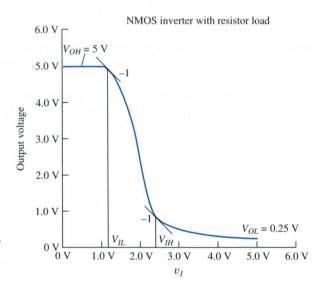

Figure 7.6 Simulated voltage transfer characteristic of an NMOS logic gate with resistive load.

Calculation of V_{IL}

Referring back to Fig. 7.2 with $v_I = V_{IL}$, v_{GS} ($= v_I$) is small and v_{DS} ($= v_O$) is large, so we expect the MOSFET to be operating in saturation, with drain current given by

$$i_{DS} = (K_n/2)(V_{GS} - V_{TN})^2 \qquad \text{where } K_n = K_n'(W/L) \text{ and } v_{GS} = v_I$$

Substituting this expression for i_{DS} in load-line Eq. (7.7),

$$v_O = V_{DD} - \frac{K_n}{2}(v_I - V_{TN})^2 R \tag{7.8}$$

and taking the derivative of v_O with respect to v_I results in

$$\frac{dv_O}{dv_I} = -K_n(v_I - V_{TN})R \tag{7.9}$$

Setting this derivative equal to -1 for $v_I = V_{IL}$ yields

$$V_{IL} = V_{TN} + \frac{1}{K_n R} \qquad \text{with } v_O = V_{DD} - \frac{1}{2K_n R} \qquad (7.10)$$

For the inverter design in Fig. 7.3(b),

$$V_{TN} = 1 \text{ V} \qquad K'_n \frac{W}{L} = 25 \times 10^{-6} \frac{2.06}{1} \frac{\text{A}}{\text{V}^2} = \frac{51.5 \ \mu\text{A}}{\text{V}^2} \qquad R = 95 \text{ k}\Omega$$

and

$$V_{IL} = 1 \text{ V} + \frac{1}{\left(51.5 \ \dfrac{\mu\text{A}}{\text{V}^2}\right)95 \text{ k}\Omega} = 1.20 \text{ V}$$

$$(7.11)$$

$$v_O = 5 \text{ V} - \frac{1}{2\left(51.5 \ \dfrac{\mu\text{A}}{\text{V}^2}\right)95 \text{ k}\Omega} = 4.90 \text{ V}$$

These values agree well with the simulation results in Fig. 7.6.

We should check our assumption of saturation region operation to see if it is consistent with the results in Eq. (7.10): $v_{DS} = 4.90$ and $v_{GS} - V_{TN} = 1.2 - 1.0 = 0.2$. Because $v_{DS} > (v_{GS} - V_{TN})$, our assumption was correct.

Calculation of V_{IH}

For $v_I = V_{IH}$, v_{GS} is large and v_{DS} is small, so we now expect the MOSFET to be operating in the linear region with drain current given by $i_{DS} = K_n[v_{GS} - V_{TN} - (v_{DS}/2)]v_{DS}$. Substituting this expression for i_{DS} into Eq. (7.7) and realizing that $v_O = v_{DS}$ yields

$$v_O = V_{DD} - K_n R\left(v_I - V_{TN} - \frac{v_O}{2}\right)v_O$$

or

$$(7.12)$$

$$\frac{v_O^2}{2} - v_O\left[v_I - V_{TN} + \frac{1}{K_n R}\right] + \frac{V_{DD}}{K_n R} = 0$$

Solving for v_O and then setting $dv_O/dv_I = -1$ for $v_I = V_{IH}$ yields

$$V_{IH} = V_{TN} - \frac{1}{K_n R} + 1.63\sqrt{\frac{V_{DD}}{K_n R}} \qquad \text{for } v_O = \sqrt{\frac{2V_{DD}}{3K_n R}} \qquad (7.13)$$

For the inverter in Fig. 7.3(b), these expressions yield $V_{IH} = 2.44$ V, with $v_O = 0.83$ V, which also agree well with the simulation results in Fig. 7.6.

| **EXERCISE:** Verify the calculated values of V_{IH} and v_O.

As mentioned earlier, V_{IL}, V_{OL}, V_{IH}, and V_{OH}, as specified by a manufacturer, actually represent guaranteed specifications for a given logic family and take into account the full range of variations in technology parameters, temperature, power supply, loading conditions, and so on. We have only computed V_{IL}, V_{OL}, V_{IH}, and V_{OH} under nominal conditions at room temperature, but these values will give the nominal value of the noise margins in our circuit:

$$NM_L = V_{IL} - V_{OL} = 1.20 \text{ V} - 0.25 \text{ V} = 0.95 \text{ V}$$

$$NM_H = V_{OH} - V_{IH} = 5.00 \text{ V} - 2.44 \text{ V} = 2.56 \text{ V}$$

Thus, this inverter can tolerate noise and process variations equivalent to 0.95 V in the low input state and more than 2.5 V in the high state. It is common for the values of the two noise margins to be substantially different, as illustrated here.

Load Resistor Problems

The NMOS inverter with resistive load has been used to introduce the concepts associated with static logic gate design. Although a simple discrete component logic gate could be built using this circuit, IC realizations do not use resistive loads because the resistor would take up far too much area.

To explore the load resistor problem further, consider the rectangular block of semiconductor material in Fig. 7.7 with a resistance given by

$$R = \frac{\rho L}{tW} \qquad (7.14)$$

where ρ = resistivity
      L, W, t = length, width, thickness of resistor, respectively

In an integrated circuit, a resistor might typically be fabricated with a thickness of 1 μm in a silicon region with a resistivity of 0.001 $\Omega \cdot$ cm. For these parameters, the 95-kΩ load resistor in the previous section would require the ratio of L/W to be

$$\frac{L}{W} = \frac{Rt}{\rho} = \frac{(9.5 \times 10^4 \ \Omega)(1 \times 10^{-4} \text{ cm})}{0.001 \ \Omega \cdot \text{cm}} = \frac{9500}{1}$$

If the resistor width W were made a minimum line width of 1 μm, which we will call the **minimum feature size F,** then the length L would be 9500 μm, and the area would be 9500 μm^2.

For the switching device M_S, W/L was found to be 2.06/1. If the device channel length is made equal to the minimum feature size of 1 μm, then the gate area of the NMOS device is only 2.06 μm^2. Thus, the load resistor would consume more than 4000 times the area of the switching transistor M_S. This is simply not an acceptable utilization of area in IC design. The solution to this problem is to replace the load resistor with a transistor.

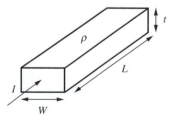

Figure 7.7 Geometry for a simple rectangular resistor.

Transistor Alternatives to the Load Resistor

The two-terminal resistor is replaced with a three-terminal MOSFET, and four possibilities are shown in Fig. 7.8. One possibility is to connect the gate to the source, as in Fig. 7.8(a). However, for this case $v_{GS} = 0$, and MOSFET M_L will be nonconducting, assuming it is an enhancement-mode device with $V_{TN} > 0$. A similar problem exists if the gate is grounded,

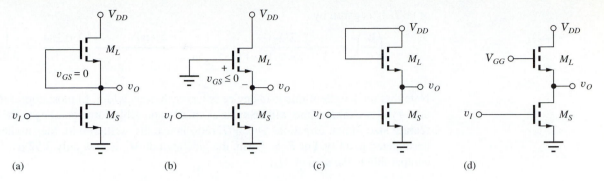

(a) (b) (c) (d)

Figure 7.8 NMOS inverter load device options: (a) NMOS inverter with gate of the load device connected to its source, (b) NMOS inverter with gate of the load device grounded, (c) saturated load inverter, (d) linear load inverter.

as in Fig. 7.8(b). Here again, the connection forces $v_{GS} \leq 0$, and the load device is turned off. Neither of these two connections work because an enhancement-mode load device can never conduct current under these conditions.

A workable choice is to connect the gate to the drain, as in Fig. 7.8(c). Here $v_{DS} = v_{GS}$, and the load device will operate in the saturation region because $v_{GS} - V_{TN} = v_{DS} - V_{TN} \leq v_{DS}$ for $V_{TN} \geq 0$. Because the connection forces the load transistor to always operate in the saturation region, we refer to this inverter as the **saturated load inverter.** Another solution, called the **linear load inverter,** is shown in Fig. 7.8(d). A final alternative is to modify the technology so that enhancement-mode and depletion-mode transistors can be simultaneously fabricated. The next several sections explore these various alternatives to the use of a resistor as the load element in the inverter.

7.2 STATIC DESIGN OF THE NMOS SATURATED LOAD INVERTER

For the design of the saturated load inverter, we use the same circuit conditions that were used for the case of the resistive load. To limit the logic gate current and power to the desired level, we choose the W/L ratio of M_L. Because M_L is forced to operate in saturation by the circuit connection, its drain current is given by

$$i_{DS} = \frac{K_n'}{2} \left(\frac{W}{L} \right)_L (v_{GS} - V_{TN})^2 \tag{7.15}$$

For the circuit conditions given in Fig. 7.9, the load device M_L has $v_{GS} = 4.75$ V for $V_{OL} = 0.25$ V. Using the 50-μA operating current calculated earlier, we find that the value

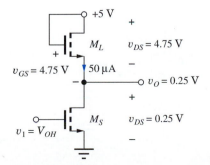

Figure 7.9 Voltages needed for determining the sizes of M_S and M_L.

of $(W/L)_L$ is given by

$$\left(\frac{W}{L}\right)_L = \frac{2i_{DS}}{K'_n(v_{GS} - V_{TN})^2} = \frac{2 \cdot 50\ \mu A}{25\ \dfrac{\mu A}{V^2}(4.75 - 1)^2\ V^2} = \frac{0.284}{1} = \frac{1}{3.52}$$

Note that the length of this load device is larger than its width. In most digital IC designs, one of the two dimensions will be made as small as possible corresponding to the minimum feature size in one direction. The W/L ratio is usually written with the smallest number normalized to unity. For $F = 1\ \mu m$, the gate area of M_L is now only 3.52 μm^2, which is comparable to the area of M_S.

Reevaluation of V_{OH} and $(W/L)_S$

Unfortunately, the use of the saturated load device has a detrimental effect on other characteristics of the logic gate. The value of V_{OH} will no longer be equal to V_{DD}. It is often helpful to our understanding of the behavior of MOS logic circuits to imagine a capacitive load attached to the logic gate, as in Fig. 7.10. Consider the logic gate with $v_I = V_{OL}$ so that M_S is turned off. When M_S turns off, load device M_L charges capacitor C until the current through M_L becomes zero, which occurs when $v_{GS} = V_{TN}$:

$$v_{GS} = V_{DD} - V_{OH} = V_{TN} \qquad \text{or} \qquad V_{OH} = V_{DD} - V_{TN} \tag{7.16}$$

Thus, for the NMOS inverter using a saturated load, the output voltage reaches a maximum value equal to one threshold voltage drop below the power supply voltage V_{DD}. For our example, the high logic level has been reduced to $V_{OH} = 5 - 1 = 4$ V.

Remember that V_{OH} is the voltage that drives switching transistor M_S in the inverter to force the output to the low level. Because V_{OH} is reduced in the saturated load circuit compared to the inverter of Fig. 7.3, the value of $(W/L)_S$ must be increased in order to compensate for the reduced value of V_{OH}:

$$i_{DS} = K'_n\left(\frac{W}{L}\right)_S (v_{GS} - V_{TN} - 0.5v_{DS})v_{DS} = K'_n\left(\frac{W}{L}\right)_S (V_{OH} - V_{TN} - 0.5v_{DS})v_{DS} \tag{7.17}$$

and

$$50\ \mu A = \frac{25\ \mu A}{V^2}\left(\frac{W}{L}\right)_S [4 - 1 - 0.5(0.25)]\ V\ (0.25\ V)$$

$$\left(\frac{W}{L}\right)_S = \frac{2.78}{1}$$

The reduction of V_{OH} from 5 to 4 V requires a 35 percent increase in the size of M_S in order to maintain the low output voltage level at 0.25 V.

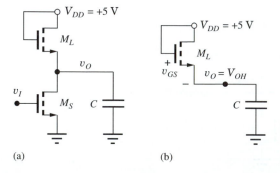

Figure 7.10 (a) Inverter with load capacitance. (b) High output level is reached when $v_I = V_{OL}$ and M_S is off.

(a)   (b)

Exercise: (a) What value of $(W/L)_S$ is required to achieve $V_{OL} = 0.15$ V in Fig. 7.9? Assume that $i_{DS} = 50 \, \mu\text{A}$. What is the value of $(W/L)_L$ required to set $i_{DS} = 50 \, \mu\text{A}$? (b) For $V_{OL} = 0.10$?

Answers: 4.56/1, 1/3.70; 6.78/1, 1/3.80

Body Effect in the Saturated Load Device

Up to this point, the dependence of the threshold voltage of the MOSFET on its source-bulk voltage has been neglected. Unfortunately, body effect in the MOS load device also has a significant effect on the design of NMOS logic gates using saturated load devices.

Figure 7.11 shows a cross section of two MOSFETs that form a saturated load inverter when they are fabricated using IC technology. The substrate is common to both NMOS transistors; thus, the substrate voltage must be the same for both M_S and M_L in the inverter. The most common voltage applied to the substrate terminal in NMOS logic is 0 V (although negative voltages -5 V and -8 V have been used in the past). For $V_B = 0$ V, v_{SB} for the switching device M_S is always zero, but v_{SB} for the load device M_L changes as v_O changes. In fact, $v_{SB} = v_O$, as indicated in Fig. 7.12.

As the output voltage increases toward V_{OH}, the value of v_{SB} becomes larger. Hence, the threshold voltage increases as determined by the body-effect relation represented by Eq. (4.29) in Chapter 4:

$$V_{TN} = V_{TO} + \gamma(\sqrt{v_{SB} + 2\phi_F} - \sqrt{2\phi_F}) \tag{7.18}$$

where V_{TO} = zero-bias value of V_{TN} (V)

γ = body-effect parameter ($\sqrt{\text{V}}$)

$2\phi_F$ = surface potential parameter (V)

The body effect causes a further reduction in V_{OH}. When v_O reaches V_{OH}, the following relationship must be true because $v_{SB} = V_{OH}$:

$$V_{OH} = V_{DD} - V_{TNL}$$
$$V_{OH} = V_{DD} - [V_{TO} + \gamma(\sqrt{V_{OH} + 2\phi_F} - \sqrt{2\phi_F})] \tag{7.19}$$

Now we must distinguish between the threshold voltage of the load device and that of the switching transistor. V_{TNL} and V_{TNS} are used to represent the values of threshold voltage for the load and switching devices, respectively. For the rest of the discussion in this chapter, we use the set of NMOS device parameters given in Table 7.1 (p. 254).

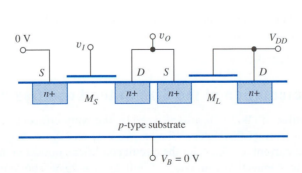

Figure 7.11 Cross section of two integrated MOSFETs forming an inverter.

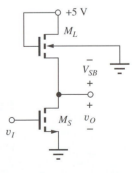

Figure 7.12 Source-bulk voltage for the load device.

Table 7.1

NMOS Enhancement-Mode Device Paramenters

V_{TO}	1 V
γ	$0.5 \sqrt{V}$
$2\phi_F$	0.6 V
K_n'	25 $\mu A/V^2$

Using Eq. (7.19) with the parameters from Table 7.1 and $V_{DD} = 5$ V, we can solve for V_{OH}, which yields the following quadratic equation:

$$(V_{OH} - 4 - 0.5\sqrt{0.6})^2 = 0.25(V_{OH} + 0.6)$$

or

$$V_{OH}^2 - 9.03V_{OH} + 19.1 = 0 \qquad (7.20)$$

and

$$V_{OH} = 3.39 \text{ V}, \ 5.64 \text{ V}$$

In this circuit, the steady-state value of V_{OH} cannot exceed the power supply voltage V_{DD} (actually it cannot exceed $V_{DD} - V_{TNL}$), so the answer must be $V_{OH} = 3.39$ V. We can check our result for V_{OH} by computing the threshold voltage of the load device using Eq. (7.18):

$$V_{TNL} = 1 \text{ V} + 0.5 \ \sqrt{V}\left(\sqrt{(3.39 + 0.6) \text{ V}} - \sqrt{0.6 \text{ V}}\right) = 1.61 \text{ V}$$

and

$$V_{OH} = V_{DD} - V_{TNL} = 5 - 1.61 = 3.39 \text{ V} \ \checkmark$$

which checks with the calculation in Eq. (7.20).

Because of the body effect, the value of V_{OH} in the inverter is even smaller than the value used in Eq. (7.17) to calculate $(W/L)_S$ of the switching device. To compensate for the further reduction in V_{OH}, $(W/L)_S$ must again be increased. Using $V_{OH} = 3.39$ V in Eq. (7.17) yields the new value of $(W/L)_S = 3.53/1$.

> **EXERCISE:** Verify that the value $(W/L)_S = 3.53/1$ is in fact correct.

> **EXERCISE:** Find V_{OH} for the inverter in Fig. 7.12 if $V_{TO} = 0.75$ V. Assume the other parameters remain constant.
>
> **ANSWER:** 3.60 V

Recalculation of the Size of the Load Device

The value of $(W/L)_L$ is also affected by the body effect. To complete the gate design, we need to correct this value. When $v_I = V_{OH}$ and $v_O = V_{OL}$, M_L must be conducting the design current of 50 μA for the circuit conditions indicated in Fig. 7.13. M_L remains saturated by connection with $v_{GS} = 5 - 0.25 = 4.75$ V. The source-bulk voltage v_{SB} of M_L is now 0.25 V, and the threshold voltage of the load device is found to be

$$V_{TNL} = 1 \text{ V} + 0.5 \ \sqrt{V}\left(\sqrt{(0.25 + 0.6) \text{ V}} - \sqrt{0.6 \text{ V}}\right) = 1.07 \text{ V} \qquad (7.21)$$

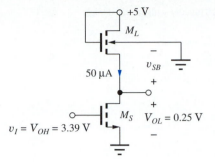

Figure 7.13 Bias conditions used to determine $(W/L)_L$.

$(W/L)_L$ can now be calculated using

$$i_{DS} = \frac{K_n'}{2}\left(\frac{W}{L}\right)_L (v_{GSL} - V_{TNL})^2$$

$$50\ \mu A = \frac{25\frac{\mu A}{V^2}}{2}\left(\frac{W}{L}\right)_L (4.75 - 1.07)^2\ V^2 \qquad (7.22)$$

$$\left(\frac{W}{L}\right)_L = \frac{1}{3.39}$$

The increased threshold voltage of the load device allows the area of the load device to actually be reduced slightly. The completed inverter design is compared to the circuit in Fig. 7.14 that was designed ignoring the body effect. The logic levels of the final design in Fig. 7.14(b) are $V_{OL} = 0.25$ V and $V_{OH} = 3.4$ V.

Figure 7.15 shows the results of SPICE simulation of the voltage transfer function for the final design in Fig. 7.14(b). For low values of input voltage, the output is constant at 3.4 V. As the input voltage increases, the slope of the transfer function abruptly changes at the point at which the switching transistor begins to conduct, as the input voltage exceeds the threshold voltage of M_S. As the input voltage continues to increase, the output voltage decreases rapidly and ultimately reaches the design value of 0.25 V for an input of 3.4 V.

V_{IH} and V_{IL}

We now calculate the values of the V_{IH} and V_{IL} for the inverter with a saturated load device. Remember that V_{IH} and V_{IL} are defined by the points in the transfer function at which the

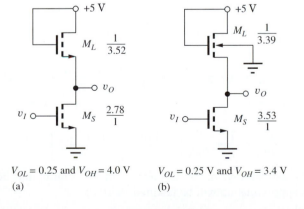

Figure 7.14 Inverter designs with saturated load devices: (a) no body effect, (b) body effect included.

(a) $V_{OL} = 0.25$ and $V_{OH} = 4.0$ V

(b) $V_{OL} = 0.25$ V and $V_{OH} = 3.4$ V

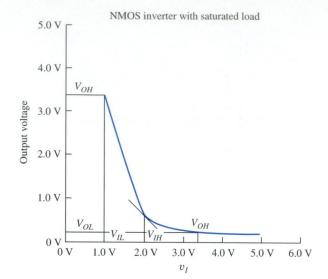

Figure 7.15 SPICE simulation of the voltage transfer function for the NMOS inverter with saturated load.

slope is equal to -1. In Fig. 7.15, the slope of the transfer function abruptly changes as M_S begins to conduct at the point where $v_I = V_{TNS}$. This point defines V_{IL}:

$$V_{IL} = V_{TNS} = 1 \text{ V} \qquad \text{for } V_{OH} = V_{DD} - V_{TNL} = 3.4 \text{ V}$$

Next let us find V_{IH}. To find a relationship between v_I and v_O, we observe that the drain currents in the switching and load devices must be equal. At $v_I = V_{IH}$, the input is at a relatively high voltage and the output is at a relatively low voltage. Thus, we can guess that M_S will be in the linear region, and we already know that the circuit connection forces M_L to operate in the saturation region. Equating drain currents in the switching and load transistors:

$$i_{DSS} = i_{DSL}$$

$$K_S\left(v_I - V_{TNS} - \frac{v_O}{2}\right)v_O = \frac{K_L}{2}(V_{DD} - v_O - V_{TNL})^2 \qquad (7.23)$$

$$K_S = K'_n\left(\frac{W}{L}\right)_S \qquad \text{and} \qquad K_L = K'_n\left(\frac{W}{L}\right)_L$$

The point of interest is $dv_O/dv_I = -1$, but solving for v_O can be quite tedious. Because the derivatives are smooth, continuous, and nonzero, we assume that $dv_O/dv_I = (dv_I/dv_O)^{-1}$, and solve for v_I in terms of v_O:

$$v_I = V_{TNS} + \frac{v_O}{2} + \frac{K_L}{2K_s}\frac{1}{v_O}(V_{DD} - v_O - V_{TNL})^2$$

$$v_I = V_{TNS} + \frac{v_O}{2} + \frac{K_L}{2K_S}\left[\frac{(V_{DD} - V_{TNL})^2}{v_O} - 2(V_{DD} - V_{TNL}) + v_O\right]$$

and

$$\frac{dv_I}{dv_O} \approx \frac{1}{2} + \frac{K_L}{2K_S}\left[-\frac{(V_{DD} - V_{TNL})^2}{v_O^2} + 1\right] \qquad (7.24)$$

In this last expression, the dependence of V_{TNL} on v_O has been neglected for simplicity. (This approximation will be justified shortly.)

Setting the derivative equal to -1 at $v_I = V_{IH}$ yields

$$-1 = \frac{1}{2} + \frac{K_L}{2K_S}\left[-\frac{(V_{DD} - V_{TNL})^2}{v_O^2} + 1\right]$$

and solving for v_O yields:

$$v_O = \frac{V_{DD} - V_{TNL}}{\sqrt{1 + 3\dfrac{K_S}{K_L}}} = \frac{V_{DD} - V_{TNL}}{\sqrt{1 + 3\dfrac{K_n'(W/L)_S}{K_n'(W/L)_L}}} = \frac{V_{DD} - V_{TNL}}{\sqrt{1 + 3\dfrac{(W/L)_S}{(W/L)_L}}} \qquad (7.25)$$

$$V_{IH} = V_{TNS} + \frac{v_O}{2} + \frac{(W/L)_L}{2(W/L)_S}\frac{1}{v_O}(V_{DD} - v_O - V_{TNL})^2$$

For the inverter design of Fig. 7.14(b) with $V_{TNL} = 1$ V, we find

$$v_O = \frac{V_{DD} - V_{TNL}}{\sqrt{1 + 3\dfrac{(W/L)_S}{(W/L)_L}}} = \frac{(5 - 1)\text{ V}}{\sqrt{1 + 3(3.53)(3.39)}} = 0.66 \text{ V}$$

$$V_{IH} = 1 + \frac{0.66 \text{ V}}{2} + \frac{1}{2(3.53)(3.39)}\frac{1}{0.66 \text{ V}}(5 - 0.66 - 1)^2 \text{ V}^2 = 1.97 \text{ V}$$

With these values, we can check our assumption of the operating region of M_S:

$$V_{GS} - V_{TNS} = 1.97 - 1 = 0.97 \text{ V} \qquad \text{and} \qquad V_{DS} = 0.66 \text{ V}$$

Because $V_{DS} < V_{GS} - V_{TN}$, the linear region assumption was correct.

In Fig. 7.15, we can see that the calculated values of V_{IH} and V_{IL} agree well with SPICE simulation results. Thus, the approximation of neglecting the voltage dependence of the threshold voltage of the load device does not introduce significant error.

However, if we want, we can use an iterative procedure to improve on the preceding estimates. The calculated value of V_{OL} can be used to determine a better estimate for V_{TNL}, and this new value of V_{TNL} can then be used to improve the estimate of V_{IH}. For $v_O = 0.66$ V,

$$V_{TNL} = 1 \text{ V} + 0.5 \sqrt{\text{V}}\left(\sqrt{(0.66 + 0.6)\text{ V}} - \sqrt{0.6 \text{ V}}\right) = 1.17 \text{ V}$$

and the new values of v_O and V_{IH} from Eq. (7.25) are equal to

$$v_O = 0.63 \text{ V} \qquad \text{and} \qquad V_{IH} = 1.99 \text{ V}$$

This process can be continued, but it has already converged, as indicated in Table 7.2. (Note that this procedure is another example of an algorithm that is very easy to implement using MATLAB or a spreadsheet.)

T a b l e 7.2

Iterative Update of V_{OL} and V_{IH}

Iteration No.	V_O	V_{TNL}	V_O'	V_{IH}
0	$\cdots$	1.00 V	0.66 V	1.97 V
1	0.66 V	1.17 V	0.63 V	1.99 V
2	0.63 V	1.17 V	0.63 V	1.99 V

7.3 NMOS INVERTER WITH A LINEAR LOAD DEVICE

Figure 7.8(d) provides a second workable choice for the load transistor M_L. In this case, the gate of the load transistor is connected to a separate voltage V_{GG}. V_{GG} is normally chosen to be at least one threshold voltage greater than the supply voltage V_{DD}:

$$V_{GG} \geq V_{DD} + V_{TNL}$$

For this value of V_{GG}, the output voltage in the high output state V_{OH} is equal to V_{DD}.

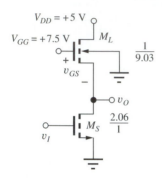

$V_{DD} = +5$ V

$V_{GG} = +7.5$ V

M_L $\dfrac{1}{9.03}$

v_{GS}

v_O

M_S $\dfrac{2.06}{1}$

v_I

Figure 7.16 Linear load inverter design.

The region of operation of M_L in Fig. 7.16 can be found by comparing $V_{GS} - V_{TNL}$ to V_{DS}. For the load device with its output at v_O and $V_{GG} \geq V_{DD} + V_{TNL}$:

$$
\begin{aligned}
v_{GS} - V_{TNL} &= V_{GG} - v_O - V_{TNL} \\
&\geq V_{DD} + V_{TNL} - v_O - V_{TNL} \qquad (7.26) \\
&\geq V_{DD} - v_O
\end{aligned}
$$

So $v_{GS} - V_{TNL} \geq V_{DD} - v_O$, but $v_{DS} = V_{DD} - v_O$, which demonstrates that the load device always operates in the linear region.

The W/L ratios for M_S and M_L can be calculated using methods similar to those in the previous sections; the results are shown in Fig. 7.16. Because V_{OH} is now equal to $V_{DD} = 5$ V, M_S is again 2.06/1. However, for $v_O = V_{OL}$, v_{GS} of M_L is large, and $(W/L)_L$ must be reduced to (1/9.03) in order to limit the current to the desired level. (Verification of these values is left for Prob. 7.20.)

Introduction of the additional power supply voltage V_{GG} overcomes the reduced output voltage problem associated with the saturated load device. However, the cost of the additional power supply level as well as the increased wiring congestion introduced by distribution of the extra supply voltage to every logic gate cause this form of load topology to be used rarely.

7.4 NMOS INVERTER WITH A DEPLETION-MODE LOAD

The saturated load and linear load circuits were developed for use in integrated circuits because all the devices had the same threshold voltages in early NMOS and PMOS technologies. However, once ion-implantation technology was perfected, it became possible to selectively adjust the threshold of the load transistors to alter their characteristics to become those of NMOS depletion-mode devices with $V_{TN} < 0$, and the use of a circuit similar to Fig. 7.8(a) became feasible.

The circuit topology for the NMOS inverter with a **depletion-mode load device** is shown in Fig. 7.17. Because the threshold voltage of the NMOS depletion-mode device is negative, a channel exists even for $v_{GS} = 0$, and the load device conducts current until its drain-source voltage becomes zero. When the switching device M_S is off ($v_I = V_{OL}$), the output voltage rises to its final value of $V_{OH} = V_{DD}$.

For $v_I = V_{OH}$, the output is low at $v_O = V_{OL}$. In this state, current is limited by the depletion-mode load device, and it is normally designed to operate in the saturation region, requiring:

$$v_{DS} \geq v_{GS} - V_{TNL} = 0 - V_{TNL} \qquad \text{or} \qquad v_{DS} \geq -V_{TNL}$$

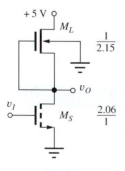

$+5$ V

M_L $\dfrac{1}{2.15}$

v_O

v_I

M_S $\dfrac{2.06}{1}$

Figure 7.17 NMOS inverter with depletion-mode load.

Calculation of $(W/L)_L$

As an example of inverter design, if we assume $V_{DD} = 5$ V, $V_{OL} = 0.25$ V, and $V_{TNL} = -3$ V, then the operating voltage for the load device with $v_O = V_{OL}$ is $V_{DS} = 4.75$ V, which is greater than $-V_{TNL} = 3$ V, and the MOSFET operates in the saturation region. The drain current of the depletion-mode load device operating in the saturation region with $V_{GS} = 0$ is given by

$$i_{DSL} = \frac{K_n'}{2}\left(\frac{W}{L}\right)_L (v_{GSL} - V_{TNL})^2 = \frac{K_n'}{2}\left(\frac{W}{L}\right)_L (V_{TNL})^2 \qquad (7.27)$$

Just as for the case of the saturated load inverter, body effect must be taken into account in the depletion-mode MOSFET, and we must calculate V_{TNL} before $(W/L)_L$ can be properly determined. For depletion-mode devices, we use the parameters in Table 7.3, and

$$V_{TNL} = -3\text{ V} + 0.5\ \sqrt{\text{V}}\left(\sqrt{(0.25 + 0.6)\text{ V}} - \sqrt{0.6\text{ V}}\right) = -2.93\text{ V}$$

Using the design current of 50 μA with $K_n' = 25\ \mu\text{A/V}^2$ and the depletion-mode threshold voltage of -2.93 V, we find

$$(W/L)_L = 0.466/1 = 1/2.15$$

Table 7.3	
Characteristics for NMOS Depletion-Mode Devices	
V_{TO}	-3 V
γ	$0.5\ \sqrt{\text{V}}$
$2\phi_F$	0.6 V
K_n'	$25\ \mu\text{A/V}^2$

Calculation of $(W/L)_S$

When $v_I = V_{OH} = V_{DD}$, the switching device once again has the full supply voltage applied to its gate, and its W/L ratio will be identical to the design of the NMOS logic gate with resistor load: $(W/L)_S = 2.06/1$. The completed depletion-mode load inverter design appears in Fig. 7.17, and the logic levels of the final design are $V_{OL} = 0.25$ V and $V_{OH} = 5.0$ V.

Figure 7.18 shows the results of SPICE simulation of the voltage transfer function for the final inverter design with the depletion-mode load. For low values of input

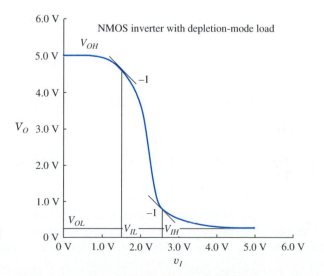

Figure 7.18 SPICE simulation results for the voltage transfer function of the NMOS depletion-load inverter of Fig. 7.17.

voltage, the output is 5 V. As the input voltage increases, the slope of the transfer function gradually changes as the switching transistor begins to conduct for an input voltage exceeding the threshold voltage. As the input voltage continues to increase, the output voltage decreases rapidly and ultimately reaches the design value of 0.25 V for an input of 5.0 V.

V_{IL} for the Inverter with Depletion-Mode Load

We are now in a position to calculate the values of V_{IH} and V_{IL} for the inverter with a depletion-mode load. Again remember that we are interested in the points in the transfer function at which the slope is equal to -1.

We first find V_{IL}. For v_I near V_{IL}, v_{DS} of M_S will be large and that of M_L will be small, so we assume that the switching device is saturated and the load device is in its linear region. Equating drain currents,

$$i_{DSS} = i_{DSL}$$

$$\frac{K_S}{2}(v_I - V_{TNS})^2 = K_L\left(0 - V_{TNL} - \frac{V_{DD} - v_O}{2}\right)(V_{DD} - v_O) \tag{7.28}$$

To simplify the algebra, let us define the ratio $K_R = K_S/K_L$, which represents the relative current drive capability of the switching and load devices in the inverter. Solving for v_O and taking the derivative yields Eq. (7.29), in which we have again assumed that $dV_{TNL}/dv_I \approx 0$.

$$v_O = V_{DD} + V_{TNL} + \sqrt{V_{TNL}^2 - K_R(v_I - V_{TNS})^2}$$

$$\frac{dv_O}{dv_I} \approx \frac{-K_R(v_I - V_{TNS})}{\sqrt{V_{TNL}^2 - K_R(v_I - V_{TNS})^2}} \tag{7.29}$$

Setting the derivative equal to -1 at $v_I = V_{IL}$ yields

$$V_{IL} = V_{TNS} - \frac{V_{TNL}}{\sqrt{K_R^2 + K_R}} \tag{7.30}$$

Because we expect v_O to approach 5 V, we should improve our estimate of V_{TNL}:

$$V_{TNL} = -3 \text{ V} + 0.5 \sqrt{\text{V}}\left(\sqrt{(5.0 + 0.6) \text{ V}} - \sqrt{0.6 \text{ V}}\right) = -2.20 \text{ V}$$

Using this value of threshold voltage, we find that the values of v_O and V_{IL} are 4.78 V and 1.46 V, respectively, which agree well with the simulation results in Fig. 7.18.

> **EXERCISE:** What is the value of K_R for the inverter in Fig. 7.17?
>
> **ANSWER:** 4.43
>
> **EXERCISE:** Verify the calculations $V_{IL} = 1.46$ V and $v_O = 4.78$ V for the inverter in Fig. 7.17.

As always, the preceding analysis was based on assumptions concerning the operating regions of the load and switching devices, and these assumptions should be checked! The values of v_{DS} for M_S and M_L are 4.78 V and 0.22 V, respectively, which can be used to confirm our operating region assumptions:

$$M_S: v_{GS} - V_{TNS} = 1.46 - 1 = 0.46 \text{ V}$$

$$\text{and} \quad v_{DS} = 4.78 \text{ V} \rightarrow \text{saturation region } \checkmark$$

$$M_L: v_{GS} - V_{TNL} = 0 - (-2.20) = 2.20 \text{ V}$$

$$\text{and} \quad v_{DS} = 0.22 \text{ V} \rightarrow \text{linear region } \checkmark$$

Iterative Update of V_{IL} and v_O

We can see from Fig. 7.18 that the calculated values of v_O and V_{IL} are quite close to the SPICE simulation results. Nevertheless, let us try to improve our answers using an iterative numerical update procedure. By examining Eqs. (7.29) and (7.30), we see that one possible iterative sequence is:

1. Choose a starting value for V_{TNL}.
2. Calculate the corresponding value of V_{IL} using Eq. (7.30).
3. Use the values V_{TNL} and V_{IL} to calculate a new estimate of v_O using Eq. (7.29).
4. Use v_O to calculate an updated value for V_{TNL}.
5. Repeat steps 2 and 3 until the convergence is achieved.

Starting with $V_{TNL} = -2.20$ V, we obtain the results in Table 7.4. The update process converges in three iterations. As was evident from the simulation results, our initial calculation was very close to the actual answer in Table 7.4.

Table 7.4			
Iterative Update of V_{IL} and v_O			
Iteration No.	V_{TNL}	V_{IL}	v_O
1	−2.20 V	1.45 V	4.79 V
2	−2.23 V	1.50 V	4.74 V
3	−2.23 V	1.50 V	4.74 V

V_{IH} for the Depletion-Mode Load Inverter

To find V_{IH}, the drain currents of the switching and load devices are again required to be equal. For $v_I = V_{IH}$, the input will be at a relatively large voltage and the output will be at a relatively small voltage. Thus, we again assume that M_S will be in the linear region and expect that M_L will operate in the saturation region because it should have a large value of v_{DS}.

$$i_{DSS} = i_{DSL}$$

$$K_S \left(v_I - V_{TNS} - \frac{v_O}{2} \right) v_O = \frac{K_L}{2} (V_{TNL})^2 \tag{7.31}$$

We are again interested in the point at which $dv_I/dv_O = -1$. Solving for v_I in terms of v_O yields:

$$v_I = V_{TNS} + \frac{v_O}{2} + \frac{K_L}{2K_S} \frac{V_{TNL}^2}{v_O} \tag{7.32}$$

$$\frac{dv_I}{dv_O} \approx \frac{1}{2} - \frac{1}{2K_R} \frac{V_{TNL}^2}{v_O^2} \qquad \text{where } K_R = \frac{K_S}{K_L} \tag{7.33}$$

In this last expression, we have once again neglected the variation of V_{TNL} with v_O. Setting the derivative equal to -1 at $v_I = V_{IH}$ yields

$$v_O = -\frac{V_{TNL}}{\sqrt{3K_R}}$$

$$\tag{7.34}$$

$$V_{IH} = V_{TNS} + 2v_O = V_{TNS} - \frac{2V_{TNL}}{\sqrt{3K_R}}$$

We also know that V_{TNL} is a function of v_O:

$$V_{TNL} = V_{TO} + \gamma \left[\sqrt{v_O + 2\phi_F} - \sqrt{2\phi_F} \right] \tag{7.35}$$

V_{IH} can be found by a simple iterative process:

1. Choose an initial value of V_{TNL}.
2. Calculate the corresponding values of v_O and V_{IH} from Eq. (7.34).
3. Use the new value of v_O and Eq. (7.35) to improve the estimate of V_{TNL}.
4. Repeat steps 2 and 3 until the process converges.

Starting with $V_{TNL} = -3$ V, we obtain the results in Table 7.5, which also agree very well with those observed in the simulation results in Fig. 7.18.

T a b l e 7.5

Iterative Update of v_O and V_{IH}

Iteration No.	v_O	V_{TNL}	v_O'	V_{IH}
1	$\cdots$	-3.00 V	0.82 V	2.64 V
2	0.82 V	-2.79 V	0.77 V	2.53 V
3	0.77 V	-2.80 V	0.77 V	2.53 V

Once again, the operating region assumptions should be checked. The values of v_{DS} for M_S and M_L are 0.77 V and 4.23 V, respectively, which can be used to confirm our choice of operating regions:

$$M_S: v_{GS} - V_{TNS} = 2.53 - 1 = 1.53 \text{ V}$$

$$\text{and} \qquad v_{DS} = 0.77 \text{ V} \rightarrow \text{linear region} ✔$$

$$M_L: v_{GS} - V_{TNL} = 0 - (-2.80) = 2.80 \text{ V}$$

$$\text{and} \qquad v_{DS} = 4.23 \text{ V} \rightarrow \text{saturation region} ✔$$

Noise Margins

The inverter with the depletion-mode load device is the most important form of NMOS logic, so we will explore the noise margins for this circuit in more detail. Using the result in Eq. (7.34) and remembering that this gate is designed with $V_{OH} = V_{DD}$, we express the high-state noise margin by

$$\text{NM}_H = V_{OH} - V_{IH} = V_{DD} - V_{TNS} + \frac{2V_{TNL}}{\sqrt{3K_R}} \tag{7.36}$$

In applying Eq. (7.36), we must remember that V_{TNL} must be evaluated for the value of v_O that corresponds to an input of $v_I = V_{IH}$!

To find the noise margin in the low-output state, expressions for both V_{OL} and V_{IL} are needed. V_{IL} was found previously in Eq. (7.30), and V_{OL} can be determined from Eq. (7.31) by realizing that $v_O = V_{OL}$ when $v_I = V_{DD}$:

$$K_S\left(V_{DD} - V_{TNS} - \frac{V_{OL}}{2}\right)V_{OL} = \frac{K_L}{2}(V_{TNL})^2 \tag{7.37}$$

and

$$V_{OL} = V_{DD} - V_{TNS} - \sqrt{(V_{DD} - V_{TNS})^2 - \frac{V_{TNL}^2}{K_R}} \tag{7.38}$$

Remember here that V_{TNL} must be evaluated for $v_O = V_{OL}$! Using this result with Eq. (7.30) yields NM_L:

$$\text{NM}_L = V_{IL} - V_{OL}$$

$$= 2V_{TNS} - V_{DD} - \frac{V_{TNLH}}{\sqrt{K_R^2 + K_R}} + \sqrt{(V_{DD} - V_{TNS})^2 - \frac{V_{TNLL}^2}{K_R}} \tag{7.39}$$

The additional subscripts on V_{TNL} remind us that two different values of V_{TNL} are involved in this expression: one for V_{OL} and one for V_{OH}! For the inverter design of Fig. 7.17, $K_R = 2.06 \times 2.15 = 4.43$, and we find:

$$\text{NM}_H = 5\text{ V} - 1\text{ V} + \frac{2(-2.93\text{ V})}{\sqrt{3(4.43)}} = 2.39\text{ V}$$

$$\text{NM}_L = 2(1\text{ V}) - 5\text{ V} - \frac{-2.20\text{ V}}{\sqrt{4.43^2 + 4.43}} + \sqrt{(5\text{ V} - 1\text{ V})^2 - \frac{(-2.93\text{ V})^2}{4.43}}$$

$$= 1.20\text{ V}$$

Figure 7.19 (p. 264) depicts the results of calculations of V_{OL}, NM_H, and NM_L versus the parameter K_R for the inverter with a depletion-mode load. As K_R increases, V_{OL} monotonically decreases and NM_H increases. NM_L increases rapidly, peaks, and then becomes only weakly dependent on K_R for $K_R > 2$. The values in the graphs agree well with the hand calculations for our inverter design with $K_R = 4.43$.

NMOS Inverter Summary and Comparison

Figure 7.20 and Table 7.6 summarize the four NMOS inverter designs discussed in Secs. 7.1 to 7.4. The gate with the resistive load takes up too much area to be implemented in IC form. The saturated load configuration is the simplest circuit, using only NMOS transistors. However, it has a disadvantage in that the high logic state no longer reaches the power

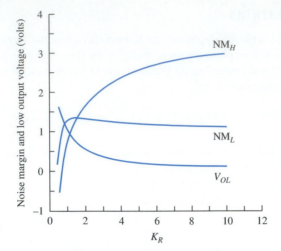

Figure 7.19 V_{OL} and noise margin versus $K_R = K_S/K_L$ for the NMOS inverter with a depletion-mode load device.

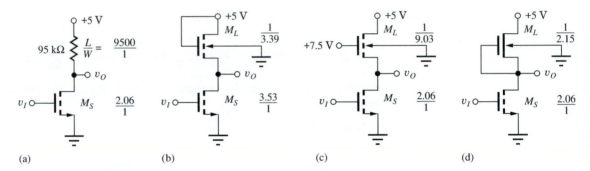

Figure 7.20 Comparison of various NMOS inverter designs: (a) Inverter with resistor load, (b) saturated load inverter, (c) linear load inverter, (d) inverter with depletion-mode load.

	Table 7.6			
	Inverter Characteristics			
	Inverter with Resistor Load	**Saturated Load Inverter**	**Linear Load Inverter**	**Inverter with Depletion-Mode Load**
V_{OH}	5.0 V	3.4 V	5.0 V	5.0 V
V_{OL}	0.25 V	0.25 V	0.25 V	0.25 V
Relative area (μm^2)	9500	6.92	9.36	4.21

supply. Also, in Sec. 7.11, the speed of the saturated load gate will be demonstrated to be poorer than that of other circuit implementations. The linear load circuit solves the logic level and speed problems but requires an additional costly power supply voltage that causes wiring congestion problems in IC designs.

Following successful development of the ion-implantation process and invention of depletion-mode load technology, NMOS circuits with depletion-mode load devices quickly became the circuit of choice. The additional process complexity was used to produce a simple inverter topology that gives $V_{OH} = V_{DD}$ with the smallest overall transistor sizes. The depletion-mode load tends to act as a current source during most of the output transition, and it will be found that depletion-mode logic is also the fastest of the four inverter configurations. We will refer to the gate designs of Fig. 7.20 as our **reference inverter designs** and use these circuits as the basis for more complex designs in subsequent sections.

Because of its many advantages, depletion-mode NMOS logic was the dominant technology for many years in the design of microprocessors. However, the large static power dissipation inherent in NMOS logic eventually limited further increases in IC chip density, and a rapid shift took place to the more complex CMOS technology, which is discussed in detail in the next chapter.

7.5 NMOS LOGIC GATES

A complete logic family must provide not only the logical inversion function but also the ability to form some combination of at least two input variables such as the AND or OR function. In NMOS logic, an additional transistor can be added to the simple inverter to form either a NOR or a NAND logic gate. The NOR gate represents the combination of an OR operation followed by inversion, and the NAND function represents the AND operation followed by inversion.

In the following discussion, remember that we use the positive logic convention to relate voltage levels to logic variables: a high logic level corresponds to a logical 1 and a low logic level corresponds to a logical 0:

$$V_{OH} = 1 \quad \text{and} \quad V_{OL} = 0$$

NOR Gates

In Fig. 7.21, the switching transistor M_S of the inverter has been replaced with two devices, M_A and M_B, to form a two-input **NOR gate.** If either, or both, of the inputs A and B is in the high logic state, a current path will exist through at least one of the two switching devices, and the output will be in the low logic state. Only if inputs A and B are both in the low state will the output of the gate be in the high logic state. The truth table for this gate, Table 7.7, corresponds to that of the NOR function $Y = \overline{A + B}$.

We will pick the size of the devices in our logic gates based on the reference inverter design defined at the end of Sec. 7.4 [Fig. 7.20(d)]. The size of the various transistors must be chosen to ensure that the gate meets the desired logic level and power specifications under the worst-case set of logic inputs.

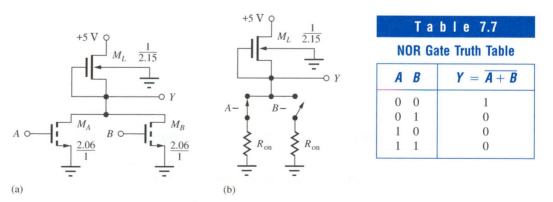

Table 7.7		
NOR Gate Truth Table		
A	**B**	**Y = $\overline{A + B}$**
0	0	1
0	1	0
1	0	0
1	1	0

(a)   (b)

Figure 7.21 (a) Two-input NMOS NOR gate: $Y = \overline{A + B}$. (b) Simplified model with switching transistor A on.

Consider the simplified schematic for the two-input NOR gate in Fig. 7.21(b). The worst-case condition for the output low state occurs when either M_A or M_B is conducting alone, so the on-resistance R_{on} of each individual transistor must be chosen to give the desired low output level. Thus, $(W/L)_A$ and $(W/L)_B$ should each be equal to the size of M_S in the reference inverter (2.06/1). If M_A and M_B both happen to be conducting ($A = 1$ and $B = 1$), then the combined on-resistance will be equivalent to $R_{on}/2$, and the actual output voltage will be somewhat lower than the original design value of $V_{OL} = 0.25$ V.

When either M_A or M_B is conducting alone, the current is limited by the load device, and the voltages are exactly the same as in the reference inverter.[3] Thus, the W/L ratio of the load device is the same as in the reference inverter (1/2.15). The completed NOR gate design is given in Fig. 7.21(a).

EXERCISE: Draw the schematic of a three-input NOR gate. What are the W/L ratios for the transistors based on Fig. 7.21?

ANSWER: 1/2.15, 2.06/1, 2.06/1, 2.06/1

NAND Gates

In Fig. 7.22(a), a second NMOS transistor has been added in series with the original switching device of the basic inverter to form a two-input **NAND gate.** Now, if inputs A and B are *both* in a high logic state, a current path exists through the series combination of the two switching devices, and the output is in a low logic state. If either input A or input B is in the low state, then the conducting path is broken and the output of the gate is in the high state. The truth table for this gate, Table 7.8, corresponds to that of the NAND function $Y = \overline{AB}$.

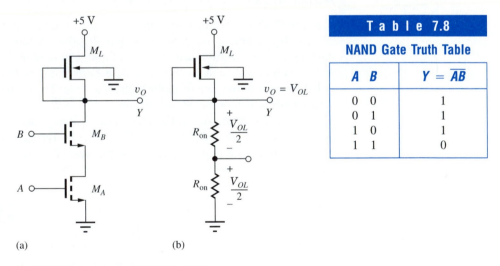

T a b l e 7.8		
NAND Gate Truth Table		
A	**B**	**Y = $\overline{AB}$**
0	0	1
0	1	1
1	0	1
1	1	0

(a) (b)

Figure 7.22 Two-input NMOS NAND gate: $Y = \overline{AB}$.

Selecting the Sizes of the Switching Transistors

The sizes of the devices in the NAND logic gate are again chosen based on the reference inverter design from Fig. 7.20(d). The W/L ratios of the various transistors must be selected

---

[3] Actually, the worst-case situation for current in the load device occurs when M_A and M_B are both on because the voltage is slightly higher across the load device, and its value of V_{SB} is smaller. However, this effect is small enough to be neglected. See Prob. 7.26.

to ensure that the gate still meets the desired logic level and power specifications under the worst-case set of logic inputs. Consider the simplified schematic for the two-input NAND gate in Fig. 7.22(b). The output low state occurs when both M_A and M_B are conducting. The combined on-resistance will now be equivalent to $2 R_{on}$, where R_{on} is the on-resistance of each individual transistor conducting alone. In order to achieve the desired low level, $(W/L)_A$ and $(W/L)_B$ must both be approximately twice as large as the W/L ratio of M_S in the reference inverter because the on-resistance of each device in the linear region is inversely proportional to the W/L ratio of the transistor:

$$R_{on} = \frac{v_{DS}}{i_{DS}} = \frac{1}{K_n' \dfrac{W}{L}\left(v_{GS} - V_{TN} - \dfrac{v_{DS}}{2}\right)} \tag{7.40}$$

A second way to approach the choice of device sizes is to look at the voltage across the two switching devices when v_O is in the low state. For our design, $V_{OL} = 0.25$ V. If we assume that one-half of this voltage is dropped across each of the switching transistors and that $(v_{GS} - V_{TN}) \gg v_{DS}/2$, then it can be seen from

$$i_{DS} = K_n'\left(\frac{W}{L}\right)_S (v_{GS} - V_{TN} - 0.5v_{DS})v_{DS} \approx K_n'\left(\frac{W}{L}\right)_S (v_{GS} - V_{TN})v_{DS} \tag{7.41}$$

that the W/L of the transistors must be approximately doubled in order to keep the current at the same value. Figure 7.23(a) shows the NAND gate design based on these arguments.

Two approximations have crept into this analysis. First, the source-bulk voltages of the two transistors are not equal, and therefore the values of the threshold voltages are slightly different for M_A and M_B. Second, $V_{GSA} \neq V_{GSB}$. From Fig. 7.23(a), $V_{GSA} = 5$ V, but $V_{GSB} = 4.875$ V. The results of taking these two effects into account are shown in Fig. 7.23(b). (Verification of these W/L values is left for Prob. 7.27.) The corrected device sizes have changed by only a small amount. The values in Fig. 7.23(a) represent an adequate level of design for most purposes.

Choosing the Size of the Load Device

When both M_A and M_B are conducting, the current is limited by the load device, but the voltages applied to the load device are exactly the same as those in the reference inverter design. Thus, the W/L ratio of the load device is the same as in the reference inverter.

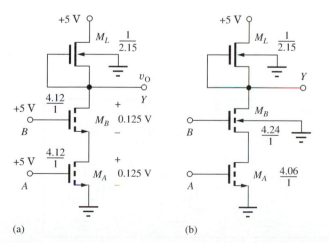

Figure 7.23 NMOS NAND gate: $Y = \overline{AB}$: (a) approximate design, (b) corrected design.

The completed NAND gate design, based on the simplified device sizing, is given in Fig. 7.23(a).

> **EXERCISE:** Draw the schematic of a three-input NAND gate. What are the W/L ratios for the transistors based on Fig. 7.20?
>
> **ANSWER:** 1/2.15, 6.18/1, 6.18/1, 6.18/1

7.6 COMPLEX NMOS LOGIC

A major advantage of MOS logic over various forms of bipolar logic comes through the ability to directly combine NAND and NOR gates into more complex configurations. Three examples of **complex logic gate** design are discussed in this section.

EXAMPLE 7.2: Consider the circuit in Fig. 7.24. The output Y will be in a low state whenever a conducting path is developed through the switching transistor network. For this circuit, the output voltage will be low if any one of the following paths is conducting: A or BC (B and C) or BD (B and D). The output Y is represented logically as

$$\overline{Y} = A + BC + BD \qquad \text{or} \qquad Y = \overline{A + BC + BD} \qquad \text{or} \qquad Y = \overline{A + B(C + D)}$$

which directly implements a complemented **sum-of-products logic function.**

Device sizing will again be based on the worst-case logic state situations. Referring to the reference inverter design, device M_A must have $W/L = 2.06/1$ because it must be able to maintain the output at 0.25 V when it is the only device that is conducting. In the other two paths, M_B will appear in series with either M_C or M_D. Thus, in the worst case, there will be two devices in series in this path, and the simplest choice will be $M_B = M_C = M_D = 4.12/1$. The load device size remains unchanged.

◆

EXAMPLE 7.3: In the second example in Fig. 7.25, there are two possible conducting paths through the switching transistor network: AB (A and B) or CDB (C and D and B). The output will be low if either path is conducting, resulting in

$$\overline{Y} = AB + CDB \qquad \text{or} \qquad Y = \overline{AB + CDB} \qquad \text{or} \qquad Y = \overline{(A + CD)B}$$

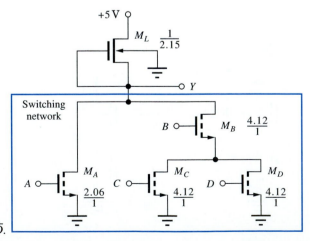

Figure 7.24 Complex NMOS logic gate: $Y = \overline{A + BC + BD}$.

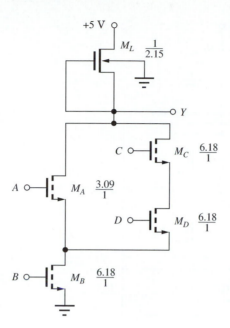

Figure 7.25 NMOS implementation of $Y = \overline{AB + CDB}$ or $Y = \overline{(A + CD)B}$.

Transistor sizing can be done in two ways. In the first method, we find the worst-case path in terms of transistor count. For this example, path CDB has three transistors. By making each transistor three times the size of the reference switching transistor, the CDB path will have an on-resistance equivalent to that of M_S in the reference inverter. Thus, each of the three transistors should have $W/L = 6.18/1$.

The second path contains transistors M_A and M_B. In this path, we want the sum of the on-resistances of the devices to be equal to the on-resistance of M_S in the reference inverter:

$$\frac{R_{\text{on}}}{\left(\dfrac{W}{L}\right)_A} + \frac{R_{\text{on}}}{\left(\dfrac{W}{L}\right)_B} = \frac{R_{\text{on}}}{\left(\dfrac{W}{L}\right)_S} \tag{7.42}$$

In Eq. (7.42), R_{on} represents the on-resistance of a transistor with $W/L = 1/1$. Because $(W/L)_B$ has already been chosen,

$$\frac{R_{\text{on}}}{\left(\dfrac{W}{L}\right)_A} + \frac{R_{\text{on}}}{6.18} = \frac{R_{\text{on}}}{2.06}$$

Solving for $(W/L)_A$ yields a value of 3.09/1. Because the operating current of the gate is to be the same as the reference inverter, the geometry of the load device remains unchanged. The completed design values appear in Fig. 7.25.

A slightly different approach is used to determine the transistor sizes for the same logic gate in Fig. 7.26 (p. 270). The switching circuit can be partitioned into two sub-networks connected in series: transistor B in series with the parallel combination of A and CD. We make the equivalent on-resistance of these two subnetworks equal. Because the two subnetworks are in series, $(W/L)_B = 2(2.06/1) = 4.12/1$. Next, the on-resistance of each path through the $(A + CD)$ network should also be equivalent to that of a 4.12/1 device. Thus $(W/L)_A = 4.12/1$ and $(W/L)_C = (W/L)_D = 8.24/1$. These results appear in Fig. 7.26.

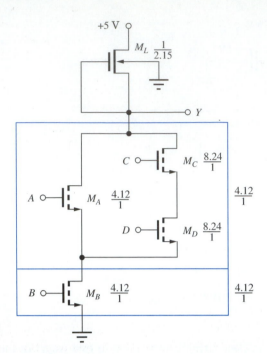

Figure 7.26 An alternate transistor sizing for the logic gate in Fig. 7.25.

Selecting Between the Two Designs

If the unity dimension corresponds to the minimum feature size F, then the total gate area of the switching transistors for the design in Fig. 7.26 is 24.7 F^2. The previous implementation of Fig. 7.25 had a total gate area of 21.6 F^2. With this yardstick, the second design requires 14 percent more area than the first. Minimum area utilization is often a key consideration in IC design, and the device sizes in Fig. 7.25 would be preferred over those in Fig. 7.26.

EXAMPLE 7.4: A final example is given Fig. 7.27. In this circuit, a fifth transistor has been added to the switching network of Fig. 7.25, and now there are *four* possible

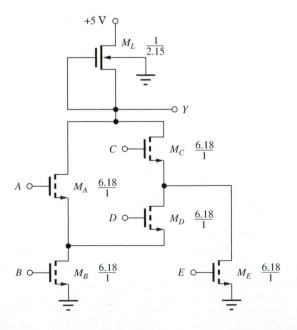

Figure 7.27 NMOS implementation of $Y = \overline{AB + CDB + CE + ADE}$.

conducting paths through the switching transistor network: AB or CDB or CE or ADE. The output will be low when any one of these paths is conducting, resulting in

$$\overline{Y} = AB + CDB + CE + ADE \qquad \text{or} \qquad Y = \overline{AB + CDB + CE + ADE}$$

This network cannot be broken into series and parallel branches, and transistor sizing will follow the worst-case path approach. Path CDB has three transistors in series, so each W/L will be set to three times that of the switching transistor in the reference inverter, or 6.18/1. Path ADE also has three transistors in series, and, because D has $(W/L) = 6.18/1$, the W/L ratios of A and E can also be 6.18/1. The remaining paths, AB and CE, need to be checked. Each has two transistors with $W/L = 6.18/1$ in series for an equivalent $W/L = 3.09/1$. Because the W/L of 3.09/1 is greater than 2.06/1, the low output state will be maintained at $V_{OL} < 0.25$ V when paths AB or CE are conducting.

Note that the current is directed through transistor D in one direction when path CDB is conducting, but in the opposite direction when path ADE is active! From the device cross section in Fig. 7.11, we see that the MOS transistor is a symmetrical device. The only way to actually tell the drain terminal from the source terminal is from the values of the applied potentials. For the NMOS transistor, the drain terminal will be the terminal at the higher voltage, and the source terminal will be the terminal at the lower potential. This bidirectional nature of the MOS transistor is a key to the design of high-density dynamic random access memories (DRAMs), which are discussed in Chapter 9. ◆

7.7 POWER DISSIPATION

In this section we consider the two primary contributions to power dissipation in NMOS inverters. The first is the steady-state power dissipation that occurs when the logic gate output is stable in either the high or low states. The second is power that is dissipated in order to charge and discharge the total equivalent load capacitance during dynamic switching of the logic gate.

Static Power Dissipation

The overall **static power dissipation** of a logic gate is the average of the power dissipations of the gate when its output is in the low state and the high state. The power supplied to the logic gate is expressed as $P = V_{DD}i_{DD}$, where i_{DD} is the current provided by the source V_{DD}. In the circuits considered so far, i_{DD} is equal to the current through the load device, and the total power supplied by source V_{DD} is dissipated in the load and switching transistors. The average power dissipation depends on the fraction of time that the output spends in the two logic states. If we assume that the average logic gate spends one-half of the time in each of the two output states (a 50 percent duty cycle), then the average power dissipation is given by

$$P_{\text{av}} = \frac{V_{DD}I_{DDH} + V_{DD}I_{DDL}}{2} \tag{7.43}$$

where I_{DDH} = current in gate for $v_O = V_{OH}$
$\qquad I_{DDL}$ = current for $v_O = V_{OL}$

For the NMOS logic gates considered in this chapter, the current in the gate becomes zero when the v_O reaches V_{OH}. Thus, $I_{DDH} = 0$, and the average power dissipation becomes equal to one-half the power dissipation when the output is low, given by

$$P_{av} = \frac{V_{DD}I_{DDL}}{2} \tag{7.44}$$

If some other duty factor is deemed more appropriate (for example, 33 percent), it simply changes the factor of 2 in the denominator of Eq. (7.44).

> **EXERCISE:** What is the average power dissipation of the gates in Fig. 7.20?
>
> **ANSWER:** 0.125 mW

Dynamic Power Dissipation

A second, very important source of power dissipation is **dynamic power dissipation,** which occurs during the process of charging and discharging the load capacitance of a logic gate. Consider the simple circuit in Fig. 7.28(a), in which a capacitor is being charged toward the positive voltage V_{DD} through a nonlinear resistor (such as a MOS load device).

Let us assume the capacitor is initially discharged; at $t = 0$ the switch closes, and the capacitor then charges toward its final value. We also assume that the nonlinear element continues to deliver current until the voltage across it reaches zero (for example, a depletion-mode load). The total energy E_D delivered by the source is given by

$$E_D = \int_0^{\infty} P(t)\,dt \tag{7.45}$$

The power $P(t) = V_{DD}i(t)$, and because V_{DD} is a constant,

$$E_D = \int_0^{\infty} V_{DD}i(t)\,dt = V_{DD}\int_0^{\infty} i(t)\,dt \tag{7.46}$$

The current supplied by source V_{DD} is also equal to the current in capacitor C, and so

$$E_D = V_{DD}\int_0^{\infty} C\frac{dv_C}{dt}\,dt = CV_{DD}\int_{V_C(0)}^{V_C(\infty)} dv_C \tag{7.47}$$

Integrating from $t = 0$ to $t = \infty$, with $V_C(0) = 0$ and $V_C(\infty) = V_{DD}$ results in

$$E_D = CV_{DD}^2 \tag{7.48}$$

We know that the energy E_S stored in capacitor C is given by

$$E_S = \frac{CV_{DD}^2}{2} \tag{7.49}$$

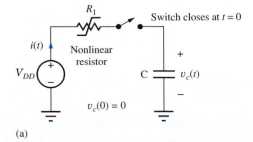
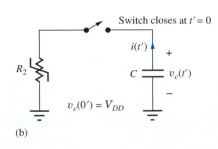

Figure 7.28 Simple circuit model for dynamic power calculation: (a) charging C, (b) discharging C.

(a)

(b)

and thus the energy E_L lost in the resistive element must be

$$E_L = E_D - E_S = \frac{CV_{DD}^2}{2} \tag{7.50}$$

Now consider the circuit in Fig. 7.28(b), in which the capacitor is initially charged to V_{DD}. At $t' = 0$, the switch closes and the capacitor discharges toward zero through another nonlinear resistor (such as an enhancement-mode MOS transistor). Again, we wait until the capacitor reaches its final value, $V_C = 0$. The energy E_S that was stored on the capacitor has now been completely dissipated in the resistor. The total energy E_{TD} dissipated in the process of first charging and then discharging the capacitor is equal to

$$E_{TD} = \frac{CV_{DD}^2}{2} + \frac{CV_{DD}^2}{2} = CV_{DD}^2 \tag{7.51}$$

Thus, every time a logic gate goes through a complete switching cycle, the transistors within the gate dissipate an energy equal to E_{TD}. Logic gates normally switch states at some relatively high frequency f (switching events/second), and the dynamic power P_D dissipated by the logic gate is then

$$P_D = CV_{DD}^2 f \tag{7.52}$$

In effect, an average current equal to $(CV_{DD}f)$ is supplied from the source V_{DD}.

> **EXERCISE:** What is the dynamic power dissipated by alternately charging and discharging a 1-pF capacitor between 5 V and 0 V at a frequency of 10 MHz?
>
> **ANSWER:** 0.25 mW

Note that the power dissipation in this exercise is the same as the static power dissipation that we allocated to the $v_O = V_{OL}$ state in our original NMOS logic gate design. In high-speed logic systems, the dynamic component of power can become dominant—we see in the next chapter that this is in fact the primary source of power dissipation in CMOS logic gates!

Power Scaling in MOS Logic Gates

During logic design in complex systems, gates with various power dissipations are often needed to provide different levels of drive capability and to drive different values of load capacitance at different speeds. For example, consider the saturated load inverter in Fig. 7.29(a). The static power dissipation is determined when $v_O = V_{OL}$. M_S is operating in the

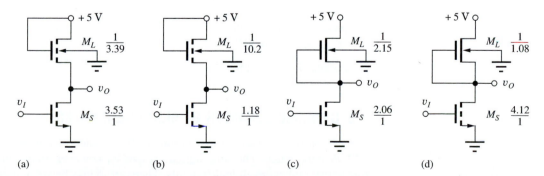

Figure 7.29 Inverter power scaling. The NMOS inverter of (b) operates at one-third the power of circuit (a), and the NMOS inverter of (d) operates at twice the power of circuit (c).

linear region, M_L is saturated, and the drain currents of the two transistors are given by

$$i_{DSL} = \frac{K_n'}{2}\left(\frac{W}{L}\right)_L (v_{GSL} - V_{TNL})^2$$

$$i_{DSS} = K_n'\left(\frac{W}{L}\right)_S \left(v_{GSS} - V_{TNS} - \frac{v_{DSS}}{2}\right)v_{DSS}$$

(7.53)

in which the W/L ratios have been chosen so that $i_{DSS} = i_{DSL}$ for $v_O = V_{OL}$. In Fig. 7.29(a), the inverter was designed to achieve $V_{OL} = 0.25$ V for $V_{OH} = 3.4$ V, with $i_{DS} = 50$ μA. The drain currents are given by

$$i_{DL} = \frac{K_n'}{2}\left(\frac{W}{L}\right)_L (4.75 - 1.07)^2 \text{ A}$$

$$i_{DS} = K_n'\left(\frac{W}{L}\right)_S \left(3.4 - 1 - \frac{0.25}{2}\right)0.25 \text{ A}$$

(7.54)

Both drain currents are directly proportional to their respective W/L ratios. If we double the W/L ratio of the load device *and* the switching device, then the drain currents both double, with no change in operating voltage levels.

Or, if we reduce the W/L ratios of both the load device and the switching device by a factor of 3, then the drain currents are both reduced by a factor of 3, with no change in operating voltage levels. Thus, if the W/L ratios of M_L and M_S are changed by the same factor, the power level of the gate can easily be scaled up and down without affecting the values of V_{OH} and V_{OL}. With this technique, the inverter in Fig. 7.29(b) has been designed to operate at one-third the power of the inverter of Fig. 7.29(a) by reducing the value of W/L of each device by a factor of 3. This **power scaling** is a property of ratioed logic circuits. The power level can be scaled up or down without disturbing the voltage levels of the design.

Similar arguments can be used to scale the power levels of any of the NMOS gate configurations that we have studied, and the depletion-mode load inverter in Fig. 7.29(d) has been designed to operate at twice the power of the inverter of that of Fig. 7.29(c) by increasing the value of W/L of each device by a factor of 2. As we will see shortly, this same technique can also be used to scale the dynamic response time of the inverter to compensate for various capacitive load conditions.

EXERCISE: What are the new W/L ratios for the transistors in the gate in Fig. 7.29(a) for a power of 0.1 mW?

ANSWER: 1/8.48 and 1.41/1

EXERCISE: What are the new W/L ratios for the transistors in the gate in Fig. 7.29(c) for a power of 10 mW?

ANSWER: 18.6/1 and 82.4/1

7.8 DYNAMIC BEHAVIOR OF MOS LOGIC GATES

Thus far in this chapter the discussion has been concerned only with the static design of NMOS logic gates. The time domain response, however, plays an extremely important role in the application of logic circuits. There are delays between input changes and output transitions in logic circuits because every node is shunted by capacitance to ground and is not able to change voltage instantaneously. This section reviews the sources of capacitance in the MOS circuit and then explores the dynamic or time-varying behavior of logic gates. Calculations of rise time t_r, fall time t_f, and the average propagation delay τ_p (all defined in Sec. 6.3) are presented, and expressions are then developed for estimating the response time of various inverter configurations.

Capacitances in Logic Circuits

Figure 7.30(a) shows two NMOS inverters including the various capacitances associated with each transistor. Each device has capacitances between its gate-source, gate-drain, source-bulk, and drain-bulk terminals. Some of the capacitances do not appear in the schematic because they are shorted out by the various circuit connections (for example, C_{SB1}, C_{GD2}, C_{SB3}, C_{GD4}). In addition to the **MOS device capacitances,** the figure includes a wiring capacitance C_W, representing the capacitance of the electrical interconnection between the two logic gates. For simplicity in analyzing the delay times in logic circuits, the capacitances on a given node will be lumped together into a fixed effective nodal capacitance C, as indicated in Fig. 7.30(b), and our hand analysis will cast the behavior of circuits in terms of this effective capacitance C. The MOS device capacitances are non-linear functions of the various node voltages; they are highly dependent on circuit layout in an integrated circuit. We will not attempt to find a precise expression for C in terms of all the capacitances in Fig. 7.30(a), but we assume that we have an estimate for the value of C. Simulation tools exist that will extract values of C from a given IC layout, and more accurate predictions of time-domain behavior can be obtained using SPICE circuit simulations.

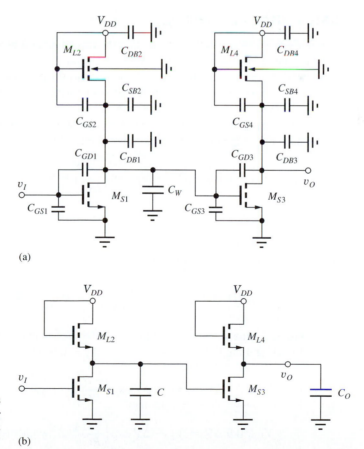

Figure 7.30 (a) Capacitances associated with an inverter pair. (b) Lumped-load capacitance model for inverters.

7.9 DYNAMIC RESPONSE OF THE NMOS INVERTER WITH A RESISTIVE LOAD

Figure 7.31 shows the circuit from our earlier discussion of the inverter with a resistive load. For hand analysis, the logic input signal is represented by an ideal step function, and we now calculate the rise time, fall time, and delay times for this inverter.

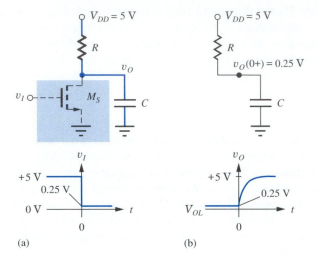

Figure 7.31 Model for rise time in resistively loaded inverter.

(a)   (b)

Calculation of t_r and τ_{PLH}

For analysis of the rise time, assume that the input and output voltages have reached their steady-state levels for $t < 0$: $v_I = V_{OH} = 5$ V and $v_O = V_{OL} = 0.25$ V. At $t = 0$, the input drops from $v_I = 5$ V to $v_I = 0.25$ V. Because the gate-source voltage of the switching transistor drops below V_{TNS}, the MOS transistor abruptly stops conducting. The output then charges from $v_O = V_{OL} = 0.25$ V to $v_O = V_{OH} = V_{DD} = 5$ V. In this case, the waveform is that of the simple RC network formed by the load resistor R and the load capacitor C. Using our knowledge of single-time constant circuits:

$$v_O(t) = V_F - (V_F - V_I)\exp\left(\frac{-t}{RC}\right) = 5.0 - 4.75\exp\left(\frac{-t}{RC}\right) \text{ V} \qquad (7.55)$$

where $V_I = 0.25$ V, initial value of capacitor voltage
$V_F = 5.0$ V, final value of capacitor voltage

This expression may be rewritten in a more convenient form for our purposes as

$$v_O(t) = V_F - \Delta V \exp\left(\frac{-t}{RC}\right) \qquad \text{and} \qquad \Delta V = V_F - V_I \qquad (7.56)$$

The rise time is determined by the difference between the time t_1 when $v_O(t_1) = V_I + 0.1\,\Delta V$ and the time t_2 when $v_O(t_2) = V_I + 0.9\,\Delta V$. Using Eq. (7.56),

$$V_I + 0.1\,\Delta V = V_F - \Delta V \exp\left(\frac{-t_1}{RC}\right) \qquad \text{yields } t_1 = -RC\ln 0.9 \qquad (7.57)$$

$$V_I + 0.9\,\Delta V = V_F - \Delta V \exp\left(\frac{-t_2}{RC}\right) \qquad \text{yields } t_2 = -RC\ln 0.1 \qquad (7.58)$$

and

$$t_r = t_2 - t_1 = RC \ln 9 = 2.2RC \tag{7.59}$$

The delay time τ_{PLH} is determined by $v_O(\tau_{PLH}) = V_1 + 0.5\,\Delta V$, which yields

$$\tau_{PLH} = -RC \ln 0.5 = 0.69RC \tag{7.60}$$

Note that this expression applies only to the simple RC network.

> **EXERCISE:** Find the t_r and τ_{PLH} for the resistively loaded inverter with $C = 0.1$ pF and $R = 95$ kΩ.
>
> **ANSWERS:** 21 ns, 6.6 ns

Calculation of τ_{PHL} and t_f

Now consider the other switching situation, with $v_I = V_{OL} = 0.25$ V and $v_O = V_{OH} = 5$ V, as displayed in Fig. 7.32. At $t = 0$, the input abruptly changes from $v_I = 0.25$ V to $v_I = 5$ V. At $t = 0^+$, M_S has $v_{GS} = 5$ V and $v_{DS} = 5$ V, so it conducts heavily and discharges the capacitance until the value of v_O reaches V_{OL}.

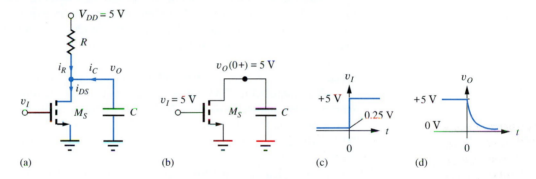

(a)   (b)   (c)   (d)

Figure 7.32 Simplified circuit for determining t_f and τ_{PHL}.

Figure 7.33 shows the currents i_R and i_{DS} in the load resistor and switching transistor as a function of v_O during the transition between V_{OH} and V_{OL}. The current available to

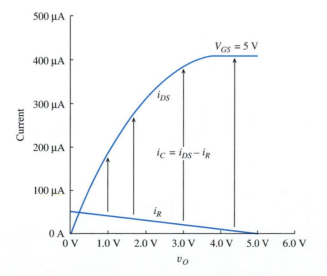

Figure 7.33 Drain current and resistor current versus v_O.

discharge the capacitor C is the difference in these two currents:

$$i_C = i_{DS} - i_R$$

Because the load element is a linear resistor, the current in the resistor increases linearly as v_O goes from V_{OH} to V_{OL}. However, when M_S first turns on, a large drain current occurs, rapidly discharging the load capacitance C. V_{OL} is reached when the current through the capacitor becomes zero and $i_R = i_D$. Note that the drain current is much greater than the current in the resistor for most of the period of time corresponding to τ_{PHL}. This leads to values of τ_{PHL} and t_f that are much shorter than τ_{PLH} and t_r associated with the rising output waveform. This is characteristic of NMOS (or PMOS) logic circuits. Another way to visualize this difference is to remember that the on-resistance of the MOS transistor must be much smaller than R in order to force V_{OL} to be a low value. Thus, the apparent "time constant" for the falling waveform will be much smaller than that of the rising waveform.

Calculation of t_f and τ_{PHL} is more complicated here than for the case of the resistor charging the capacitive load because the NMOS transistor changes regions of operation during the output voltage transition. Thus, the differential equation that models the V_{OH} to V_{OL} transition changes at the point at which the transistor changes operating regions.

First, let us simplify our model for the circuit. From Fig. 7.33, we can see that $i_{DS} \gg i_R$ except for v_O very near V_{OL}. Therefore, the current through the resistor will be neglected so that we can assume that all the drain current of the NMOS transistor is available to discharge the load capacitance, as in Fig. 7.32(b). The input signal v_I is assumed to be a step function changing to $v_I = 5$ V at $t = 0$. At $t = 0$, the output voltage V_C on the capacitor is $V_{OH} = V_{DD} = 5$ V, and the gate voltage is forced to $V_G = 5$ V.

The graph in Fig. 7.34 shows the important instants in time that need to be considered. At time t_1 the output has dropped by 10% of the logic swing ΔV, and time t_4 is the time at which the output has dropped by 90% of ΔV. Thus, $t_f = t_4 - t_1$. At t_3, the output is at the 50% point, given by $V_{50\%} = (V_{OH} + V_{OL})/2$, so $\tau_{PHL} = t_3$. Time t_2 is also very important. At this point $v_O = V_{DD} - V_{TNS}$, and this is the time at which the transistor changes from saturation region operation to linear region operation. Thus, the differential equation that models the circuit behavior changes at this point.

Calculation of τ_{PHL}

Let us first focus on calculation of τ_{PHL} and then calculate t_f. At $t = 0^+$, the NMOS transistor in Fig. 7.32(b) is operating in the saturation region, and the capacitor current is

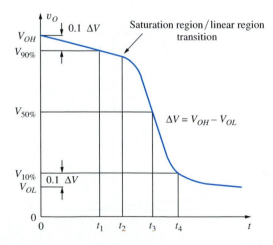

Figure 7.34 Times needed for calculation of τ_{PHL} and t_f for the inverter with resistor load. Fall time $t_f = t_4 - t_1$; propagation delay $\tau_{PHL} = t_3$.

described by

$$\frac{K_S}{2}(v_{GS} - V_{TNS})^2 = -C\frac{dv_C}{dt} \qquad \text{with } v_C(0^+) = V_{OH} \qquad (7.61)$$

in which $v_{GS} = 5$ V and $V_{TNS} = 1$ V are both constant. Thus, the drain current is constant, and the capacitor discharges at a constant rate until the MOSFET enters the linear region of operation at time t_2, when $v_C = v_{GS} - V_{TNS} = 5 - 1 = 4$ V. The MOSFET enters the linear region after the capacitor voltage drops by one threshold voltage. For these values, the time t_2 required for the transistor to reach the linear region is

$$t_2 = \frac{2CV_{TNS}}{K_S(V_{DD} - V_{TNS})^2} = 2R_{ons}C\frac{V_{TNS}}{(V_{DD} - V_{TNS})} \qquad (7.62)$$

for

$$R_{ons} = \frac{1}{K_S(V_{DD} - V_{TNS})}$$

which represents the equivalent on-resistance of the NMOS switching transistor, with $v_{GS} = V_{DD}$ and $v_{DS} = 0$. For the specific values just mentioned, we find that

$$t_2 = \frac{R_{ons}C}{2} = \frac{C}{8K_S} \qquad (7.63)$$

Once the transistor enters the linear region, the equation characterizing the discharge changes to

$$K_S\left(v_{GS} - V_{TNS} - \frac{v_C}{2}\right)v_C = -C\frac{dv_C}{dt} \qquad (7.64)$$

because the $v_{DS} = v_C$ for the MOSFET. Rearranging this equation with $v_{GS} = V_{DD}$ and integrating yields

$$\int_{V_2}^{V_3} \frac{dv_C}{(2(V_{DD} - V_{TNS}) - v_C)v_C} = \int_{t_2}^{t_3} \frac{K_S}{2C}\,dt \qquad (7.65)$$

in which the limits of integration are defined by

$$V_2 = v_C(t_2) = V_{DD} - V_{TNS} \qquad \text{and} \qquad V_3 = v_C(t_3) = 0.5(V_{DD} + V_{OL})$$

The solution to this equation may be found using:

$$\int \frac{dx}{(a-x)x} = \frac{1}{a}\int\left[\frac{1}{a-x} + \frac{1}{x}\right]dx = \frac{1}{a}\ln\left(\frac{x-a}{x}\right) \qquad (7.66)$$

Using Eq. (7.66), $t_3 - t_2$ can be found to be

$$t_3 - t_2 = \frac{C}{K_S(V_{DD} - V_{TNS})}\ln\left\{\left(\frac{V_2}{V_3}\right)\left[\frac{V_3 - 2(V_{DD} - V_{TNS})}{V_2 - 2(V_{DD} - V_{TNS})}\right]\right\} \qquad (7.67)$$

$$t_3 - t_2 = \frac{C}{K_S(V_{DD} - V_{TNS})}\ln\left[4\left(\frac{V_{DD} - V_{TNS}}{V_{DD} + V_{OL}}\right) - 1\right]$$

$$= R_{ons}C\ln\left[4\left(\frac{V_{DD} - V_{TNS}}{V_{DD} + V_{OL}}\right) - 1\right] \qquad (7.68)$$

The propagation time τ_{PHL} is just equal to t_3 and is given by

$$\tau_{PHL} = t_3 = (t_3 - t_2) + t_2 = R_{\text{ons}}C\left\{\ln\left[4\left(\frac{V_{DD} - V_{TNS}}{V_{DD} + V_{OL}}\right) - 1\right] + \frac{1}{2}\right\} \quad (7.69)$$

Using $V_{TNS} = 1$ V, $V_{DD} = 5$ V, and $V_{OL} = 0.25$ V, we find

$$\tau_{PHL} = 1.2R_{\text{ons}}C = \frac{1.2C}{K_S(V_{DD} - V_{TNS})} = \frac{0.30C}{K_S} \quad (7.70)$$

This is an extremely useful equation. Not only does it describe the behavior of the NMOS circuit, but we will also see later that Eqs. (7.69) and (7.70) characterize the delay behavior of CMOS logic gates, which form today's most important logic family.

Calculation of t_f

Fall time t_f can be written as:

$$t_f = t_4 - t_1 = (t_4 - t_2) - (t_2 - t_1)$$

During the time interval $t_1 - t_2$, the MOSFET is saturated, and the current discharging the capacitor is constant. Therefore, using

$$\Delta t = C\frac{\Delta V}{I}$$

$$t_2 - t_1 = C\frac{(V_{DD} - 0.1\,\Delta V) - (V_{DD} - V_{TNS})}{\frac{K_s}{2}(V_{DD} - V_{TNS})^2} \quad (7.71)$$

$$t_2 - t_1 = 2R_{\text{ons}}C\frac{V_{TNS} - 0.1\Delta V}{V_{DD} - V_{TNS}}$$

During the interval t_2 to t_4, the MOSFET is operating in the linear region, and the circuit is described by Eq. (7.65):

$$\int_{V_2}^{V_4} \frac{dv_C}{(2(V_{DD} - V_{TNS}) - v_C)v_C} = \int_{t_2}^{t_4} \frac{K_S}{2C}\,dt \quad (7.72)$$

in which the limits of integration are now defined by

$$V_2 = v_C(t_2) = V_{DD} - V_{TNS} \quad \text{and} \quad V_4 = v_C(t_3) = V_{DD} - 0.9\,\Delta V$$

Using the results from (7.66) and (7.67),

$$t_4 - t_2 = R_{\text{ons}}C\ln\left[2\left(\frac{V_{DD} - V_{TNS}}{V_{DD} - 0.9\,\Delta V}\right) - 1\right]$$

and our estimate for the fall time is given by:

$$t_f = t_4 - t_1 = R_{\text{ons}}C\left\{\ln\left[2\left(\frac{V_{DD} - V_{TNS}}{V_{DD} - 0.9\,\Delta V}\right) - 1\right] + 2\frac{V_{TNS} - 0.1\,\Delta V}{V_{DD} - V_{TNS}}\right\} \quad (7.73)$$

EXAMPLE 7.5: Find the t_f and τ_{PHL} for the resistively loaded inverter with $C = 0.1$ pF and $R = 95$ kΩ.

SOLUTION: We remember that $V_{OH} = 5$ V, $V_{OL} = 0.25$ V, $V_{DD} = 5$ V, and $K_S = (2.06)(25 \times 10^{-6}$ A/V^2) for this inverter design. First, calculate the value of R_{ons}:

$$R_{\text{ons}} = \frac{1}{K_S(V_{DD} - V_{TNS})} = \frac{1}{(2.06)\left(25\ \frac{\mu A}{V^2}\right)(5 - 1)\ V} = 4.85\ k\Omega$$

Substituting these values into Eqs. (7.70) and (7.73):

$$\tau_{PHL} = 1.2 R_{\text{ons}} C = 1.2(4.85 \times 10^3\ \Omega)(1 \times 10^{-13}\ F) = 0.58\ \text{ns}$$

$$t_f = (4.85\ k\Omega)(0.1\ pF)\left\{ \ln\left[2\left(\frac{4\ V}{5\ V - 4.275\ V}\right) - 1\right]\right.$$

$$\left. + 2\left(\frac{1\ V - 0.4275\ V}{5\ V - 1\ V}\right)\right\} = 1.3\ \text{ns}$$

◆

Remember from an earlier exercise that $\tau_{PLH} = 6.6$ ns and $t_r = 21$ ns for this gate. We see that τ_{PLH} is approximately 11 times τ_{PHL} and that t_r is more than 10 times t_f!

7.10 NMOS INVERTER WITH A SATURATED LOAD

The mathematical complexity of the analysis increases for inverters that use transistors as load elements. For hand calculations, we obtain useful analytical results by neglecting the body effect. If more accurate estimates are needed, they can be obtained using circuit simulation with SPICE.

As mentioned earlier, static NMOS logic gates are "ratioed" designs, in which the current drive capability of the switching transistor must be much greater than that of the load transistor in order to achieve a small value of V_{OL}. Thus, we are always able to assume that the drain current of the switching transistor is much greater than that of the load device ($i_{DS} \gg i_{DL}$) during the high-to-low switching transient, except for v_O very near V_{OL}. Therefore, we can assume that all the drain current of the switching transistor is available to discharge the load capacitance, as in Fig. 7.32. For analysis of the saturated load inverter, the input signal v_I is assumed to be a step function changing at $t = 0$, reaching a value equal to $(V_{DD} - V_{TN}) = 4$ V. At $t = 0^+$, the voltage v_C on the capacitor is equal to $V_{OH} = (V_{DD} - V_{TN}) = 4$ V, and v_I forces $v_{GS}(0^+) = V_{DD} - V_{TN} = 4$ V.

Calculation of τ_{PHL}

The graph in Fig. 7.35 (p. 282) shows the important instants in time for this inverter. Time t_1 represents the time at which the output has dropped by 0.1 ΔV, and time t_4 is the time at which the output has dropped by 0.9 ΔV. Thus, $t_f = t_4 - t_1$. At t_3, $v_O = (V_{OH} + V_{OL})/2$, so $\tau_{PHL} = t_3$. The time t_2 is also very important. At time t_2, $v_O = V_{DD} - V_{TNL} - V_{TNS}$, and the transistor changes from saturation region operation to linear region operation.

Let us again focus first on calculating τ_{PHL} and then calculate t_f. At $t = 0^+$, the NMOS switching transistor is operating in the saturation region, and the capacitor current is

$$\frac{K_S}{2}(v_{GS} - V_{TNS})^2 = -C\frac{dv_C}{dt}$$

$$\frac{K_S}{2}(V_{DD} - V_{TNL} - V_{TNS})^2 = -C\frac{dv_C}{dt} \qquad (7.74)$$

in which $v_{GS} = V_{DD} - V_{TNL} = 4$ V and $V_{TNS} = 1$ V are both constant. Thus, the drain current is constant, and the capacitor discharges at a uniform rate until the MOSFET enters

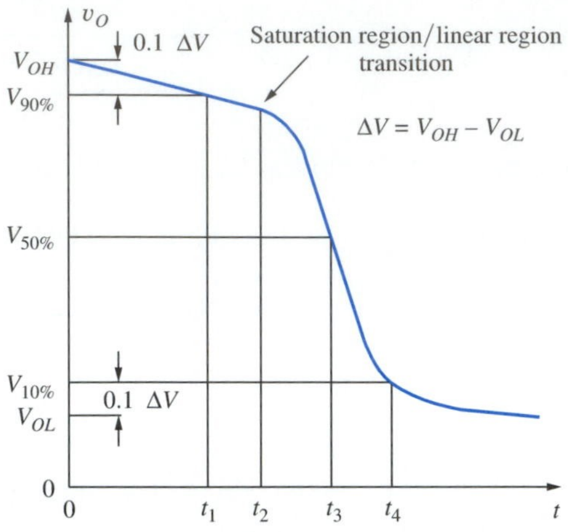

Figure 7.35 The high-to-low transition for the inverter with saturated load and the times needed for calculation of τ_{PHL} and t_f. This figure is the same as Fig. 7.34, but the values associated with the various voltage levels are different.

the linear region of operation at time t_2, when $v_C = v_{GS} - V_{TNS} - V_{TNL} = 3$ V. The MOSFET enters the linear region after the capacitor voltage drops by one threshold voltage V_{TNS}.

For these values, the time required for the transistor to reach the linear region is

$$t_2 = \frac{2CV_{TNS}}{K_S(V_{DD} - V_{TNL} - V_{TNS})^2} = 2R_{\text{ons}}C\frac{V_{TNS}}{(V_{DD} - V_{TNL} - V_{TNS})} \tag{7.75}$$

for

$$R_{\text{ons}} = \frac{1}{K_S(V_{DD} - V_{TNL} - V_{TNS})}$$

which is the equivalent on-resistance of the NMOS switching transistor with $V_{GS} = V_{DD} - V_{TNL}$ and $V_{DS} = 0$. For the specific values mentioned above, we find that

$$t_2 = 2R_{\text{ons}}C\frac{1\text{ V}}{(5-1-1)\text{ V}} = \frac{2R_{\text{ons}}C}{3} \qquad R_{\text{ons}} = \frac{1}{3K_S} \qquad t_2 = \frac{2C}{9K_S} \tag{7.76}$$

Once the transistor enters the linear region, the equation characterizing the discharge changes to

$$K_S\left(v_{GS} - V_{TNS} - \frac{v_C}{2}\right)v_C = -C\frac{dv_C}{dt} \tag{7.77}$$

because the $v_{DS} = v_C$ for the MOSFET. Rearranging this equation with $v_{GS} = V_{DD} - V_{TNL}$ and integrating yields

$$\int_{V_2}^{V_3} \frac{dv_C}{(2(V_{DD} - V_{TNL} - V_{TNS}) - v_C)v_C} = \int_{t_2}^{t_3} \frac{K_S}{2C}\,dt \tag{7.78}$$

in which the limits of integration are defined by

$$V_2 = v_C(t_2) = V_{DD} - V_{TNL} - V_{TNS}$$

and

$$V_3 = v_C(t_3) = (V_{DD} - V_{TNL} + V_{OL})/2$$

This is the same equation as in Eq. (7.65) except that $(V_{DD} - V_{TNS})$ has been replaced with $(V_{DD} - V_{TNL} - V_{TNS})$. Using the results from Eqs. (7.66) and (7.67) yields:

$$t_3 - t_2 = \frac{C}{K_S(V_{DD} - V_{TNL} - V_{TNS})}\ln\left[4\left(\frac{V_{DD} - V_{TNL} - V_{TNS}}{V_{DD} - V_{TNL} + V_{OL}}\right) - 1\right]$$

$$= R_{\text{ons}}C\ln\left[4\left(\frac{V_{DD} - V_{TNL} - V_{TNS}}{V_{DD} - V_{TNL} - V_{OL}}\right) - 1\right] \tag{7.79}$$

The propagation time τ_{PHL} is just equal to t_3 and is given by

$$\tau_{PHL} = t_3 = (t_3 - t_2) + t_2 = R_{\text{ons}}C\left[\ln\left(4\frac{V_{DD} - V_{TNL} - V_{TNS}}{V_{DD} - V_{TNL} + V_{OL}} - 1\right) + \frac{2}{3}\right] \tag{7.80}$$

Using $V_{TNS} = V_{TNL} = 1$ V, $V_{DD} = 5$ V, and $V_{OL} = 0.25$ V we find

$$\tau_{PHL} = 1.27 R_{\text{ons}}C = \frac{1.27C}{K_S(V_{DD} - V_{TNL} - V_{TNS})} = \frac{0.42C}{K_S} \tag{7.81}$$

Fall Time Calculation

The fall time is calculated from

$$t_f = t_4 - t_1 = (t_4 - t_2) - (t_2 - t_1)$$

During the time interval $t_2 - t_1$, the MOSFET is saturated, and the current discharging the capacitor is constant. Therefore,

$$t_2 - t_1 = C\frac{(V_{DD} - V_{TNL} - 0.1\,\Delta V) - (V_{DD} - V_{TNL} - V_{TNS})}{\frac{K_S}{2}(V_{DD} - V_{TNL} - V_{TNS})^2} \tag{7.82}$$

$$t_2 - t_1 = 2R_{\text{ons}}C\frac{V_{TNS} - 0.1\,\Delta V}{V_{DD} - V_{TNL} - V_{TNS}}$$

During the interval $t_4 - t_2$, the MOSFET is operating in the linear region, and the circuit is again described by Eq. (7.65):

$$\int_{V_2}^{V_4}\frac{dv_C}{(2(V_{DD} - V_{TNL} - V_{TNS}) - v_C)v_C} = \int_{t_2}^{t_4}\frac{K_S}{2C}\,dt \tag{7.83}$$

in which the limits of integration are now given by

$$V_2 = v_c(t_2) = V_{DD} - V_{TNL} - V_{TNS}$$

and

$$V_4 = v_c(t_4) = V_{DD} - V_{TNL} - 0.9\,\Delta V$$

Using the results from (7.67),

$$t_4 - t_2 = R_{\text{ons}}C\ln\left[\frac{V_{DD} - V_{TNL} - V_{TNS} + 0.9\,\Delta V}{V_{DD} - V_{TNL} - 0.9\,\Delta V}\right]$$

and our estimate for the fall time is given by:

$$t_f = t_4 - t_1$$

$$= R_{\text{ons}}C\left\{\ln\left[\frac{V_{DD} - V_{TNL} - V_{TNS} + 0.9\,\Delta V}{V_{DD} - V_{TNL} - 0.9\,\Delta V}\right] + 2\frac{V_{TNS} - 0.1\,\Delta V}{V_{DD} - V_{TNL} - V_{TNS}}\right\} \tag{7.84}$$

Calculation of τ_{PLH}

Figure 7.36 shows the inverter with a saturated load. At $t = 0$, the input signal turns off M_S. The load device always operates in saturation, and the source current charges the capacitor from an initial value of V_{OL} to the final value of $V_{DD} - V_{TNL}$. The voltage at the output of the gate is governed by the following differential equation:

$$C\frac{dv_O}{dt} = i_{DSL}$$

$$C\frac{dv_O}{dt} = \frac{K_L}{2}(V_{DD} - v_O - V_{TNL})^2 \tag{7.85}$$

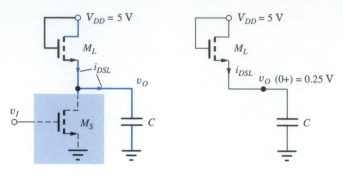

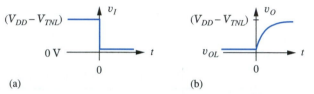

Figure 7.36 Low-to-high switching transient for an inverter with a saturated load device.

(a)

(b)

To find a solution to this equation, we neglect the body effect in the load device and assume that the threshold voltage is constant. Letting $z = (V_{DD} - V_{TNL} - v_O)$, Eq. (7.85) can be rewritten as

$$\frac{dz}{z^2} = -\frac{K_L}{2C} dt$$

which has the solution

$$\frac{K_L}{2C} t = \frac{1}{V_{DD} - V_{TNL} - v_O} + \alpha$$

Using $v_O = V_{OL}$ at $t = 0$ allows us to determine the constant α and yields the solution we want:

$$v_O(t) = V_{DD} - V_{TNL} - \cfrac{1}{\cfrac{1}{V_{DD} - V_{TNL} - V_{OL}} + \cfrac{K_L}{2C} t} \tag{7.86}$$

Equation (7.86) can be used to find values for τ_{PLH} and rise time based on the times in Fig. 7.37. For τ_{PLH}, we require that Eq. (7.86) satisfy

$$v_O(\tau_{PLH}) = \frac{V_{OH} + V_{OL}}{2} = \frac{V_{DD} - V_{TNL} + V_{OL}}{2}$$

or

$$\frac{V_{DD} - V_{TNL} + V_{OL}}{2} = V_{DD} - V_{TNL} - \cfrac{1}{\cfrac{1}{V_{DD} - V_{TNL} - V_{OL}} + \cfrac{K_L}{2C} \tau_{PLH}}$$

Solving for τ_{PLH} yields

$$\tau_{PLH} = \frac{2C}{K_L} \frac{1}{(V_{DD} - V_{TNL} - V_{OL})} = 2R_{onL}C \tag{7.87}$$

where $R_{onL} = \cfrac{1}{K_L(V_{DD} - V_{TNL} - V_{OL})}$ is the on-resistance of the load transistor with $v_{GS} = V_{DD} - V_{OL}$.

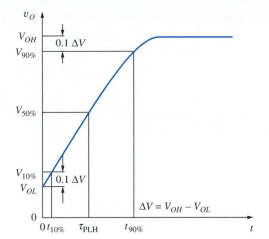

Figure 7.37 Low-to-high switching transient for an inverter with a saturated load device.

Rise Time Calculation

To find the rise time t_r, we need to calculate the time required for the output to reach the 10% and 90% points on the transition:

$$V_{10\%} = V_{OL} + 0.1\,\Delta V = V_{OL} + 0.1(V_{OH} - V_{OL}) = 0.9V_{OL} + 0.1V_{OH}$$

$$V_{10\%} = 0.9V_{OL} + 0.1(V_{DD} - V_{TNL})$$

$$V_{90\%} = V_{OH} - 0.1\,\Delta V = V_{OH} - 0.1(V_{OH} - V_{OL}) = 0.9V_{OH} + 0.1V_{OL}$$

$$V_{90\%} = 0.9(V_{DD} - V_{TNL}) + 0.1V_{OL}$$

Using Eq. (7.86) to find $t_{10\%}$,

$$\frac{V_{DD} - V_{TNL} + 9V_{OL}}{10} = V_{DD} - V_{TNL} - \cfrac{1}{\cfrac{1}{V_{DD} - V_{TNL} - V_{OL}} + \cfrac{K_L}{2C}t_{10\%}}$$

$$t_{10\%} = \frac{2C}{9K_L}\frac{1}{(V_{DD} - V_{TNL} - V_{OL})}$$

and for $t_{90\%}$

$$\frac{9(V_{DD} - V_{TNL}) + V_{OL}}{10} = V_{DD} - V_{TNL} - \cfrac{1}{\cfrac{1}{V_{DD} - V_{TNL} - V_{OL}} + \cfrac{K_L}{2C}t_{90\%}}$$

$$t_{90\%} = \frac{18C}{K_L}\frac{1}{(V_{DD} - V_{TNL} - V_{OL})} \tag{7.88}$$

$$t_r = t_{90\%} - t_{10\%} = \frac{160C}{9K_L}\frac{1}{(V_{DD} - V_{TNL} - V_{OL})} = \frac{160}{9}R_{\text{on}L}C$$

EXAMPLE 7.6: Find τ_{PLH}, τ_{PHL}, t_r, and t_f for the inverter with a saturated load from Fig. 7.14(a) with a load capacitance $C = 0.1$ pF.

SOLUTION: For the saturated load inverter without body effect, $V_{DD} = 5$ V, $V_{OL} = 0.25$ V, $V_{TN} = 1$ V for both transistors, $K_S = 2.78$ (25 μA/V^2), and $K_L = $ (25 μA/V^2)/3.52.

Substituting these values into Eqs. (7.81), (7.84), (7.87), and (7.88):

$$\tau_{PHL} = \frac{1.27(0.1 \text{ pF})}{(2.78)\left(25 \, \dfrac{\mu A}{V^2}\right)(5-2) \text{ V}} = 0.61 \text{ ns}$$

$$t_f = \frac{0.1 \text{ pF}}{(2.36)\left(25\dfrac{\mu A}{V^2}\right)(5-2) \text{ V}} \left\{ \ln\left[\frac{5-1-1+0.9(3.75) \, \dfrac{V}{V}}{5-1-0.9(3.75) \, \dfrac{V}{V}}\right] + 2\frac{5-0.1(3.75) \, \dfrac{V}{V}}{5-2}\right\}$$

$$= 1.2 \text{ ns}$$

$$\tau_{PLH} = \frac{2(0.1 \text{ pF})}{\dfrac{25}{3.52} \dfrac{\mu A}{V^2}} \frac{1}{(5-1-0.25) \text{ V}} = 7.5 \text{ ns}$$

$$t_r = \frac{160(0.1 \text{ pF})}{9\left(\dfrac{25}{3.52} \dfrac{\mu A}{V^2}\right)} \frac{1}{(5-1-0.25) \text{ V}} = 67 \text{ ns}$$

◆

As expected, we see that τ_{PLH} is an order of magnitude greater than t_{PHL} and also that the rise time is much longer than the fall time. These results are consistent with our assumption that we can neglect the load device current with respect to the switching device current during the high-to-low transition. The rise time is much greater than τ_{PLH} because the pull-up transient takes a long time to approach final value as the saturated load device approaches cutoff.

7.11 NMOS INVERTER WITH THE DEPLETION-MODE LOAD

Figure 7.38 shows the inverter with a depletion-mode load. At $t = 0$, the input signal turns off M_S. The current from the source of the load device charges the capacitor from an

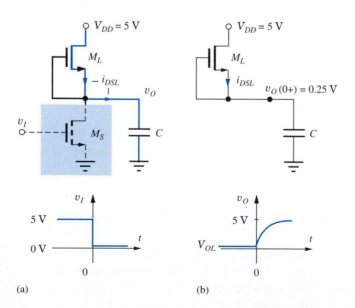

Figure 7.38 Low-to-high switching transient for an inverter with a depletion-mode load device.

initial value of V_{OL} to the final value of $V_{DD} = 5$ V. Figure 7.39 shows important times for the low-to-high switching transition for the depletion-mode load case. The times t_1 and t_4 correspond to the 10% and 90% points on the positive transition and determine the rise time. Time t_3 is the 50% point, and $\tau_{PLH} = t_3$, assuming that the input signal is a step function. Time t_2 is the point at which the depletion-mode device comes out of saturation when its drain-source voltage reaches $V_{DS} = -V_{TNL}$ because $V_{GS} = 0$. In this figure, $t_2 < t_3$, but it is possible for $t_3 > t_2$ for some values of V_{TNL}.

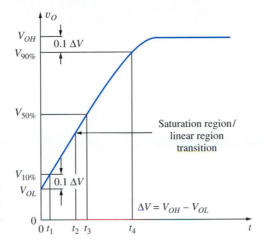

Figure 7.39 Important times in the low-to-high switching transient of an inverter with a depletion-mode load device.

Calculation of τ_{PLH}

We begin calculating τ_{PLH} by writing the propagation delay $\tau_{PLH} = t_3$ as

$$\tau_{PLH} = t_2 + (t_3 - t_2) \tag{7.89}$$

because t_2 is the time at which the load device changes regions of operation. The depletion-mode load device operates in saturation for $0 \le t \le t_2$, and is in the linear region for $t > t_2$. The depletion-mode load starts in saturation, and, because $v_{GS} = 0$,

$$i_{DSL} = \frac{K_L}{2}(V_{TNL})^2 \tag{7.90}$$

as long as

$$v_{DS} > v_{GS} - V_{TNL} \quad \text{or} \quad v_{DS} > -V_{TNL} \text{ because } v_{GS} = 0$$

Because $v_{DS} = V_{DD} - v_O$, we find that the load device will be in saturation for

$$v_O < V_{DD} + V_{TNL}$$

(Remember that $V_{TNL} < 0$ for the depletion-mode device.) Time t_2 is the time required for the transistor to reach the edge of saturation:

$$t_2 = \frac{C}{i_D}[v(t_2) - v(0)] \quad \text{or} \quad t_2 = \frac{2C}{K_L(V_{TNL})^2}[V_{DD} + V_{TNL} - V_{OL}] \tag{7.91}$$

During the time interval $t_2 - t_3$, the load device is operating in the linear region, with $v_{GS} = 0$ and $v_{DS} = V_{DD} - v_C$:

$$i_{DSL} = K_L\left(0 - V_{TNL} - \frac{V_{DD} - v_C}{2}\right)(V_{DD} - v_C)$$

Once again, $i_D = C\dfrac{dv_C}{dt}$, and we have

$$\int_{V_2}^{V_3} \frac{dv_C}{(-2V_{TNL} - (V_{DD} - v_C))(V_{DD} - v_C)} = \int_{t_2}^{t_3} \frac{K_L}{2C}\, dt \qquad (7.92)$$

in which $V_2 = V_{DD} + V_{TNL}$ and $V_3 = (V_{DD} + V_{OL})/2$. Using the result in Eq. (7.67),

$$t_3 - t_2 = \frac{C}{K_L(-V_{TNL})}\ln\left[\left(\frac{V_{DD} - V_3 + 2V_{TNL}}{V_{DD} - V_2 + 2V_{TNL}}\right)\left(\frac{V_{DD} - V_2}{V_{DD} - V_3}\right)\right] \qquad (7.93)$$

$$t_3 - t_2 = \frac{C}{K_L(-V_{TNL})}\ln\left[4\left(\frac{-V_{TNL}}{V_{DD} - V_{OL}}\right) - 1\right]$$

$$= R_{\text{on}L}C\ln\left[4\left(\frac{-V_{TNL}}{V_{DD} - V_{OL}}\right) - 1\right] \qquad (7.94)$$

where the on-resistance of the depletion-mode device is given by

$$R_{\text{on}L} = \frac{1}{K_L(-V_{TNL})}$$

and

$$\tau_{PLH} = (t_3 - t_2) + t_2 = R_{\text{on}L}C\left\{\ln\left[4\left(\frac{-V_{TNL}}{V_{DD} - V_{OL}}\right) - 1\right] + 2\frac{V_{DD} + V_{TNL} - V_{OL}}{(-V_{TNL})}\right\} \qquad (7.95)$$

Rise Time Calculation

The rise time is written as

$$t_r = t_4 - t_1 = (t_4 - t_2) - (t_2 - t_1)$$

because the transistor is in saturation during the time between t_1 and t_2, and it is in the linear region from t_2 to t_4. If we define $V_2 = V_C(t_2)$, then $V_2 = V_{DD} + V_{TNL}$. At t_4, the output voltage is at the 90% point and

$$V_{90\%} = V_{DD} - 0.1\,\Delta V$$

Once again using Eq. (7.67) and more algebra,

$$t_4 - t_2 = \frac{C}{K_L(-V_{TNL})}\ln\left[\left(-\frac{2V_{TNL}}{0.1\,\Delta V}\right) - 1\right]$$

$$t_4 - t_2 = R_{\text{on}L}C\ln\left[\left(-\frac{20V_{TNL}}{\Delta V}\right) - 1\right]$$

and

$$t_2 - t_1 = \frac{2C}{K_L(V_{TNL})^2}[V_{DD} + V_{TNL} - (V_{OL} + 0.1\,\Delta V)]$$

$$t_r = R_{\text{on}L}C\left\{\ln\left[\left(-\frac{20V_{TNL}}{\Delta V}\right) - 1\right] + 2\frac{V_{DD} + V_{TNL} - V_{OL} - 0.1\,\Delta V}{(-V_{TNL})}\right\} \qquad (7.96)$$

Fall Time and τ_{PHL} Calculations

Because $V_{OH} = V_{DD}$ for the depletion-mode load inverter, the conditions during the high-to-low switching transient are essentially identical to those for the inverter with a resistor load. Hence the fall time and propagation delay time on the negative transition are equivalent to those given by Eqs. (7.69) and (7.73):

$$\tau_{PHL} = R_{\text{ons}}C\left[\ln\left(4\frac{V_{DD} - V_{TNS}}{V_{DD} + V_{OL}} - 1\right) + \frac{1}{2}\right] \tag{7.97}$$

$$t_f = R_{\text{ons}}C\left\{\ln\left[2\left(\frac{V_{DD} - V_{TNS}}{V_{DD} - 0.9\,\Delta V}\right) - 1\right] + 2\frac{V_{TNS} - 0.1\,\Delta V}{V_{DD} - V_{TNS}}\right\} \tag{7.98}$$

$$R_{\text{ons}} = \frac{1}{K_S(V_{DD} - V_{TNS})}$$

EXAMPLE 7.7: Find τ_{PLH}, τ_{PHL}, t_r, and t_f for the inverter with a depletion-mode load with the design from Fig. 7.20(d) for a load capacitance of 0.1 pF.

SOLUTION: For the depletion-mode load without body effect, $V_{DD} = 5$ V, $V_{OL} = 0.25$ V, $V_{TNS} = 1$ V, $V_{TNL} = -3$ V, $K_S = 2.06$ (25 μA/V^2), and $K_L = $ (25 μA/V^2)/2.15.

Substituting these values into Eqs. (7.95) to (7.98):

$$\tau_{PLH} = \frac{0.1\ \text{pF}}{\dfrac{25}{2.15}\dfrac{\mu\text{A}}{\text{V}^2}(3\ \text{V})}\left\{\ln\left[4\left(\frac{3}{5 - 0.25}\frac{\text{V}}{\text{V}}\right) - 1\right] + 2\left(\frac{5 - 3 - 0.25}{3}\frac{\text{V}}{\text{V}}\right)\right\}$$

$$= 4.6\ \text{ns}$$

$$t_r = \frac{0.1\ \text{pF}}{\dfrac{25}{2.15}\dfrac{\mu\text{A}}{\text{V}^2}(3\ \text{V})}\left\{\ln\left[\left(-\frac{20(-3)\ \text{V}}{(4.75)\ \text{V}}\right) - 1\right]\right.$$

$$\left. + 2\frac{(5 - 3 - 0.25 - 0.475)\ \text{V}}{3\ \text{V}}\right\} = 9.6\ \text{ns}$$

$$\tau_{PHL} = \frac{0.1\ \text{pF}}{(2.15)\left(25\dfrac{\mu\text{A}}{\text{V}^2}\right)(5 - 1)\ \text{V}}\left[\ln\left(4\frac{(5 - 1)\ \text{V}}{(5 + 0.25)\ \text{V}} - 1\right) + \frac{1}{2}\right] = 0.57\ \text{ns}$$

$$t_f = \frac{0.1\ \text{pF}}{(2.15)\left(25\dfrac{\mu\text{A}}{\text{V}^2}\right)(5 - 1)\ \text{V}}\left\{\ln\left[2\left(\frac{(5 - 1)\ \text{V}}{(5 - 0.9(4.75))\ \text{V}}\right) - 1\right]\right.$$

$$\left. + 2\frac{(1 - 0.1(4.75))\ \text{V}}{(5 - 1)\ \text{V}}\right\} = 1.19\ \text{ns}$$

◆

7.12 A FINAL COMPARISON OF LOAD DEVICES

Figure 7.40 is a comparison of the i-v characteristics of the various load devices that we have studied, with and without the influence of body effect on the transistor characteristics.

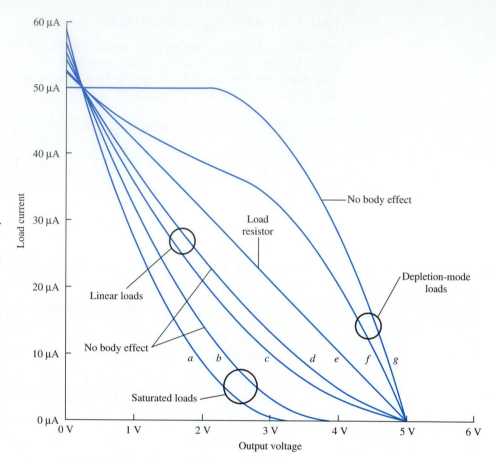

Figure 7.40 A comparison of NMOS load device characteristics with current normalized to 50 μA for $v_o = V_{OL} = 0.25$ V: (*a*) saturated load device including body effect, (*b*) saturated load device with no body effect, (*c*) linear load device including body effect, (*d*) linear load device with no body effect, (*e*) 95-kΩ resistor load, (*f*) depletion-mode load device including body effect, (*g*) depletion-mode load device without body effect.

The device sizes have been chosen so that the output current in each load is 50 μA when v_O is at the output low level of 0.25 V. As a reference for comparison, curve (e) is the straight line corresponding to the constant 95-kΩ load resistor.

For all the MOS load device cases, body effect degrades the performance of the load device. Both saturated load characteristics, (*a* and *b* in Fig. 7.40) deliver substantially less current than the resistor throughout the full output voltage transition. Thus, we expect gates with saturated loads to have the poorest values of t_{PLH}. We also can observe that the load current of the saturated load devices goes to zero before the output reaches 5 V. The linear loads *c* and *d* are an improvement over the saturated load devices but still provide less current than the resistive load. The depletion-mode load devices *f* and *g* provide the largest current throughout the transition, and thus they should exhibit the smallest value of t_{PLH}. The ideal depletion-mode load *g* functions as a current source for $v_O < 2.1$ V. Note however that body effect substantially degrades the current source characteristics of the depletion-mode device.

In our hand calculations, we neglected body effect. Based on the curves in Fig. 7.40, we can expect that the equations that were derived for t_f and τ_{PHL} may show substantial disagreement with actual measurements. This figure reinforces the need for circuit simulation if detailed analysis of digital logic circuits is required.

The following section is a summary of the delay equations derived for the various inverters in Secs. 7.10 to 7.12; Figs. 7.41 and 7.42 give the results of circuit simulation of the response of the three types of inverters, including body-effect.

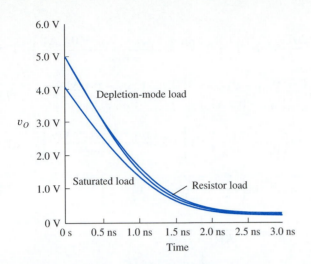

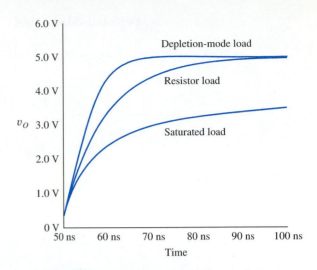

Figure 7.41 SPICE simulation results for fall time and τ_{PHL} for the inverters with resistor load, saturated load, and depletion-mode load for a load capacitance $C = 0.1$ pF.

Figure 7.42 SPICE simulation results for rise time and τ_{PLH} for the inverters with resistor load, saturated load, and depletion-mode load for a load capacitance $C = 0.1$ pF.

Summary of Dynamic Responses of NMOS Inverters

Resistor Load

$$t_r = 2.2RC \tag{7.59}$$

$$t_f = R_{\text{ons}}C\left\{\ln\left[2\left(\frac{V_{DD} - V_{TNS}}{V_{DD} - 0.9\,\Delta V}\right) - 1\right] + 2\frac{V_{TNS} - 0.1\,\Delta V}{V_{DD} - V_{TNS}}\right\} \tag{7.73}$$

$$\tau_{PLH} = 0.69RC \tag{7.60}$$

$$\tau_{PHL} = R_{\text{ons}}C\left[\ln\left(4\frac{V_{DD} - V_{TNS}}{V_{DD} + V_{OL}} - 1\right) + \frac{1}{2}\right] \tag{7.69}$$

$$R_{\text{ons}} = \frac{1}{K_S(V_{DD} - V_{TNS})}$$

Saturated Load

$$t_r = \frac{160}{9}R_{\text{onL}}C \tag{7.88}$$

$$t_f = R_{\text{ons}}C\left\{\ln\left[\frac{V_{DD} - V_{TNL} - V_{TNS} + 0.9\,\Delta V}{V_{DD} - V_{TNL} - 0.9\,\Delta V}\right] + 2\frac{V_{TNS} - 0.1\,\Delta V}{V_{DD} - V_{TNL} - V_{TNS}}\right\} \tag{7.84}$$

$$\tau_{PLH} = 2R_{\text{onL}}C \tag{7.87}$$

$$\tau_{PHL} = R_{\text{ons}}C\left[\ln\left(4\frac{V_{DD} - V_{TNL} - V_{TNS}}{V_{DD} - V_{TNL} + V_{OL}} - 1\right) + \frac{2}{3}\right] \tag{7.80}$$

$$R_{\text{onL}} = \frac{1}{K_L(V_{DD} - V_{TNL} - V_{OL})}$$

$$R_{\text{ons}} = \frac{1}{K_S(V_{DD} - V_{TNL} - V_{TNS})}$$

Depletion-Mode Load

$$t_r = R_{\text{on}L}C\left\{\ln\left[\left(-\frac{20V_{TNL}}{\Delta V}\right)-1\right]+2\frac{V_{DD}+V_{TNL}-V_{OL}-0.1\,\Delta V}{-V_{TNL}}\right\} \tag{7.96}$$

$$t_f = R_{\text{ons}}C\left\{\ln\left[2\left(\frac{V_{DD}-V_{TNS}}{V_{DD}-0.9\,\Delta V}\right)-1\right]+2\frac{V_{TNS}-0.1\,\Delta V}{V_{DD}-V_{TNS}}\right\} \tag{7.98}$$

$$\tau_{PLH} = R_{\text{on}L}C\left\{\ln\left[4\left(\frac{-V_{TNL}}{V_{DD}-V_{OL}}\right)-1\right]+2\frac{V_{DD}+V_{TNL}-V_{OL}}{-V_{TNL}}\right\} \tag{7.95}$$

$$\tau_{PHL} = R_{\text{ons}}C\left[\ln\left(4\frac{V_{DD}-V_{TNS}}{V_{DD}+V_{OL}}-1\right)+\frac{1}{2}\right] \tag{7.97}$$

$$R_{\text{on}L} = \frac{1}{K_L(-V_{TNL})}$$

$$R_{\text{ons}} = \frac{1}{K_S(V_{DD}-V_{TNS})}$$

It can be seen in Fig. 7.41 that the fall times and propagation delay times of the various inverter configurations are all similar, because the current in the switching transistor is the primary factor determining the characteristics of these waveforms. Much greater differences appear in the waveforms in Fig. 7.42 because of the large differences in the currents supplied by the load devices.

Tables 7.9 and 7.10 contain values of inverter delay based on the delay equations and the SPICE simulation results. The results of our hand calculations are surprisingly good. The biggest discrepancy appears in the rise time estimate for the depletion-mode load device, but this should not be a surprise after seeing the results in Fig. 7.40. We see that the depletion-mode load provides the best propagation delay and that the saturated load is similar to a gate with a resistor load, except for the long rise time.

Table 7.9
Analytical Inverter Delay Estimates

	τ_{PHL}	τ_{PLH}	τ_P	t_f	t_r
Resistor load	0.6 ns	6.6 ns	3.7 ns	1.3 ns	21.0 ns
Saturated load	0.6 ns	7.5 ns	4.1 ns	1.2 ns	67.0 ns
Depletion-mode load	0.6 ns	4.6 ns	2.6 ns	1.2 ns	9.6 ns

Table 7.10
SPICE Simulation of Inverter Delays Including Body Effect

	τ_{PHL}	τ_{PLH}	τ_P	t_f	t_r
Resistor load	0.8 ns	6.6 ns	3.7 ns	1.3 ns	21 ns
Saturated load	0.4 ns	6.5 ns	3.5 ns	1.1 ns	65 ns
Depletion-mode load	0.7 ns	5.5 ns	3.1 ns	1.5 ns	13 ns

SUMMARY

Chapter 7 presented a basis for MOS logic gate design, focusing on NMOS technology. Inverter design was introduced by considering the static behavior of an NMOS inverter with resistor load. However, the resistor is not feasible for use as a load element in ICs because it consumes too much area. In ICs, the resistor load in the logic gate is replaced with a second MOS transistor, and three possibilities were investigated in detail: the saturated load device, the linear load device, and the depletion-mode load device. The geometry of the load device, $(W/L)_L$, is designed to limit the current and power dissipation of the logic gate to the desired level, whereas the geometry of the switching device, $(W/L)_S$, is chosen to provide the desired value of V_{OL}. Transistors are usually designed with either W or L set equal to the minimum feature size achievable in a given technology.

The saturated load device is the most economical configuration because it does not require any modification to the basic MOS fabrication process. However, saturated load circuits offer the poorest performance in terms of propagation delay. The linear load configuration offers improved performance but requires an additional power supply voltage, which is both expensive and causes substantial wiring congestion in ICs. Depletion-mode load circuits require additional processing in order to create MOSFETs with a second value of threshold voltage. However, substantial performance improvement can be obtained, and NMOS depletion-mode load technology was the workhorse of the microprocessor industry for many years.

Multi-input NOR and NAND gates can both easily be implemented in MOS logic. The NOR gate is formed by placing additional transistors in parallel with the switching transistor of the basic inverter, whereas the NAND gate is formed by several switching devices connected in series. A major advantage of MOS logic is its ability to implement complex sum-of-product logic equations in a single logic gate, which includes both parallel and series connections of the switching transistors. A single load device is required for each logic gate, and one switching transistor is required for each logic input variable. Once the reference inverter for a logic family is designed, NAND, NOR, and complex gates can all be designed by applying simple scaling rules to the geometry of the reference inverter.

The influence of the MOSFET body effect cannot be avoided in integrated circuits, and it plays an important role in the design of NMOS (or PMOS) logic gates. Body effect reduces the value of V_{OH} in saturated load logic and generally degrades the current delivery capability of all the load device configurations, thereby increasing the delay of all the logic gates. The MOS body effect has a minor influence on the design of the W/L ratios of the switching transistors in complex logic gates.

Equations were developed for the rise time, fall time, and propagation delays of the various types of NMOS logic gates, and it was shown that all the time delays of MOS logic circuits are directly proportional to the total equivalent capacitance connected to the output node of the gate. The total effective capacitance is a complicated function of operating point and is due to the capacitance of the interconnections between gates as well as the capacitances of the MOS devices, which include the gate-source (C_{GS}), gate-drain (C_{GD}), drain-bulk (C_{DB}), and source-bulk (C_{SB}) capacitances.

Power dissipation of a logic gate has a static component and a dynamic component. Dynamic power dissipation is proportional to the switching frequency of the logic gate, the total capacitance, and the square of the logic voltage swing. At low switching frequencies, static power dissipation is most important, but at high switching rates the dynamic component becomes dominant. For a given load capacitance, the power and speed of a logic gate may be changed by proportionately scaling the geometry of the load and switching transistors. For example, doubling the W/L ratios of all devices doubles the power of the gate without changing the static voltage levels of the design. This behavior is characteristic of "ratioed" MOS logic.

Key Terms

Complex logic gates
Depletion-mode load inverter
Dynamic power dissipation
Linear load inverter
Load transistor
Minimum feature size (F)
MOS device capacitances

NAND gate
NOR gate
On-resistance
Power scaling
Ratioed logic
Reference inverter design
Resistor load inverter

Saturated load inverter
Sum-of-products logic function
Static power dissipation
Switching transistor
W/L ratio

PSPICE Simulation Data

*Figure 7.4 NMOS OUTPUT CHARACTERISTICS

```
VIN 1 0 DC 2
VDS 3 0 DC 5
VSEN 3 2 DC 0
M1 2 1 0 0 MOS1 L=1U W=2.06U
.DC VDS 0 6 .1 VIN 1 5 .5
.MODEL MOS 1 NMOS KP=2.5E-5 VTO=1
.PROBE V(1) V(2) I(VSEN)
.END
```

*Figure 7.6 NMOS INVERTER WITH RESISTOR LOAD

```
VIN 1 0 DC 0
VDD 3 0 DC 5
M1 2 1 0 0 MOS1 L=1U W=2.06U
R 3 2 95K
.DC VIN 0 5 .05
.MODEL MOS1 NMOS KP=2.5E-5 VTO=1 GAMMA=.5
.PROBE V(1) V(2)
.END
```

*Figures 7.15 and 7.18 SATURATED AND DEPLETION MODE INVERTERS

```
VIN 1 0 DC 2
VDD 3 0 DC 5
*Gate with saturated load
M1 2 1 0 0 MOS1 L=1U W=3.53U
M2 3 3 2 0 MOS1 L=3.39U W=1U
*Gate with depletion-mode load
M3 4 1 0 0 MOS1 W=2.06U L=1U
M4 3 4 4 0 MOSD W=1U L=2.15U
.DC VIN 0 5 .01
.MODEL MOS1 NMOS KP=2.5E-5 VTO=1 GAMMA=.5
.MODEL MOSD NMOS KP=2.5E-5 VTO=-3 GAMMA=.5
.PROBE V(1) V(2) V(4)
.END
```

*Figure 7.40 NMOS LOAD CHARACTERISTICS

VDC 1 0 DC 5
VO 9 0 DC 0
*Resistor Load
R 1 2 95K
VR 2 9 DC 0
*Saturated Loads
M1 1 1 3 3 MOS1 L=3.53U W=1U
V1 3 9 DC 0
M2 1 1 4 0 MOS1 L=3.39U W=1U
V2 4 9 DC 0
*Depletion-Mode Loads
M3 1 5 5 5 MOSD L=2.25U W=1U
V3 5 9 DC 0
M4 1 6 6 0 MOSD L=2.15U W=1U
V4 6 9 DC 0
*Linear Loads
VGG 10 0 DC 7.5
M5 1 10 7 7 MOS1 L=9.20U W=1U
V5 7 9 DC 0
M6 1 10 8 0 MOS1 L=9.04U W=1U
V6 8 9 DC 0
*Sweep Vo
.DC VO 0 5 .01
.MODEL MOS1 NMOS KP=2.5E-5 VTO=1 GAMMA=.5
.MODEL MOSD NMOS KP=2.5E-5 VTO=-3 GAMMA=.5
.PROBE I(V1) I(V2) I(V3) I(V4) I(V5) I(V6) I(VR)
.END

*Figures 7.41 and 7.42 NMOS INVERTER DELAY CHARACTERISTICS

VDD 3 0 DC 5
VIN5 1 0 PULSE (0 5 0 0.01NS 0.01NS 50NS)
VIN4 5 0 PULSE (0 4 0 0.01NS 0.01NS 50NS)
* Resistive load inverter
M0 6 1 0 0 MOS1 L=1U W=2.06U
R1 3 6 95K
CR 6 0 0.1P
* Saturated load inverter
M1 2 5 0 0 MOS1 L=1U W=3.53U
M2 3 3 2 0 MOS1 L=3.39U W=1U
CS 2 0 0.1P
* Depletion mode load inverter
M3 4 1 0 0 MOS1 W=2.06U L=1U
M4 3 4 4 0 MOSD W=1U L=2.15U
CD 4 0 0.1P
.MODEL MOS1 NMOS KP=2.5E-5 VTO=1 GAMMA=.5
.MODEL MOSD NMOS KP=2.5E-5 VTO=-3 GAMMA=.5
.TRAN 1NS 120NS
.PROBE V(1) V(2) V(4) V(6)
.END

Problems

Use $K'_n = 25\ \mu\text{A/V}^2$, $K'_p = 10\ \mu\text{A/V}^2$, $V_{TN} = 1$ V, and $V_{TP} = -1$ V unless otherwise indicated.

7.1 Design of MOS Inverters with Resistive Loads

7.1. Integrated circuit chips packaged in plastic DIPs (dual-in-line packages) can typically dissipate 1 W per chip. Suppose that we have an IC design that must fit on one chip and requires 100,000 logic gates. Assume that one-half the logic gates on the chip are conducting current at any given time. (a) What is the average power that can be dissipated by each logic gate on the chip? (b) If a supply voltage of 5 V is used, how much current can be used by each gate?

7.2. A high-performance microprocessor design requires 5 million logic gates and will be placed in a package that can dissipate 20 W. (a) What is the average power that can be dissipated by each logic gate on the chip? (b) If a supply voltage of 3.3 V is used, how much current can be used by each gate? Assume that two-thirds of the logic gates on the chip are in the conducting state at any given time.

7.3. Calculate the value of K'_n and K'_p for NMOS and PMOS transistors with a gate oxide thickness of 20 nm. Assume that $\mu_n = 500\ \text{cm}^2/\text{V}\cdot\text{s}$, $\mu_p = 200\ \text{cm}^2/\text{V}\cdot\text{s}$, and the permittivity of the gate oxide is $3.9\varepsilon_O$ ($\varepsilon_O = 8.854 \times 10^{-14}$ F/cm).

7.4. Find V_{OH}, V_{OL}, and the power dissipation (for $v_O = V_{OL}$) for the logic inverter with resistor load in Fig. P7.4.

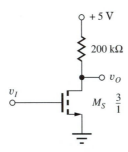

7.5. What are the noise margins for the circuit in Fig. P7.4 ?

 7.6. The resistive load inverter in Fig. 7.2 is to be redesigned for $V_{OL} = 0.5$ V. (a) What are the new values of R and $(W/L)_S$ assuming that the power

dissipation remains the same? (b) What are the values of NM_L and NM_H?

 7.7. (a) Redesign the resistive load inverter of Fig. 7.2 for operation at a power level of 0.25 mW with $V_{DD} = 3.3$ V. Assume $V_{TO} = 0.7$ V. Keep the other design parameters the same. What is the new size of M_S and the value of R? (b) What are the values for NM_H and NM_L?

 7.8. Design an inverter with a resistive load for $V_{DD} = 3.3$ and $V_{OL} = 0.2$ V. Assume $I_D = 33\ \mu\text{A}$, $K'_n = 60\ \mu\text{A/V}^2$, and $V_{TN} = 0.75$ V.

7.2. Static Design of the NMOS Saturated Load Inverter

7.9. (a) Calculate the on-resistance of an NMOS transistor with $W/L = 10/1$ for $V_{GS} = 5$ V, $V_{SB} = 0$, $V_{TO} = 1$ V, and $V_{DS} = 0$ V. (b) Calculate the on-resistance of a PMOS transistor with $W/L = 10/1$ for $V_{SG} = 5$ V, $V_{SB} = 0$, $V_{TO} = -1$ V, and $V_{SD} = 0$ V. (c) What do we mean when we say that a transistor is "on" even though I_D and $V_{DS} = 0$? (d) What must be the W/L ratios of the NMOS and PMOS transistors if they are to have the same on-resistance as parts (a) and (b) with $|V_{GS}| = 3.0$ V?

7.10. Find V_{OH} for an NMOS logic gate with a saturated load if $V_{TO} = 0.75$ V, $\gamma = 0.75\ \sqrt{V}$, $2\phi_F = 0.7$ V, and $V_{DD} = 5$ V.

7.11. Find V_{OH} for an NMOS logic gate with a saturated load if $V_{TO} = 0.5$ V, $\gamma = 0.85\ \sqrt{V}$, $2\phi_F = 0.6$ V, and $V_{DD} = 3$ V.

7.12. Find V_{OH}, V_{OL}, and the power dissipation (for $v_O = V_{OL}$) for the logic inverter with the saturated load in Fig. P7.12. Assume $\gamma = 0$.

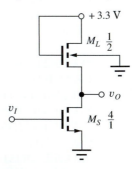

*7.13. What are the noise margins for the circuit in Fig. P7.12?

*7.14. (a) Redesign the saturated load inverter of Fig. 7.14(b) for operation at a power level of 0.25 mW with $V_{DD} = 3.3$ V. Assume $V_{TO} = 0.7$ V. Keep the other design parameters the same. What are the new sizes of M_L and M_S? (b) What are the new values for NM_H and NM_L?

7.15. Redesign the NMOS logic gate with saturated load of Fig. 7.14(b) to give $V_{OL} = 0.5$ V and $P = 0.5$ mW for $v_O = V_{OL}$.

7.16. (a) Design a saturated load inverter similar to that of Fig. 7.14(a) with $V_{DD} = 3.3$ V and $V_{OL} = 0.2$ V. Assume $I_D = 33$ μA. (b) Recalculate the values of W/L including body effect, as in Fig. 7.14(b).

7.17. The logic input of the saturated load inverter of Fig. 7.14(a) is connected to +5 V. What is v_O for this input voltage?

*7.18. The logic input of the saturated load inverter of Fig. 7.14(b) is connected to +5 V. What is v_O for this input voltage? (This problem will probably require an iterative solution.)

7.19. The saturated load inverter of Fig. 7.20(b) was designed using $K'_n = 25$ μA/V^2, but due to process variations during fabrication, the value actually turned out to be $K'_n = 18$ μA/V^2. What will be the new values of V_{OH}, V_{OL}, and the power dissipation in the gate for this new value of K'_n?

7.3 NMOS Inverter with a Linear Load Device

7.20. Calculate the W/L ratio for the linear load device using the circuit and device parameters that apply to Sec. 7.3, and show that the values presented in Fig. 7.16 are correct.

7.21. What is the minimum value of V_{GG} required for linear region operation of M_L in Fig. 7.20(c) if $V_{TO} = 1$ V, $\gamma = 0.5 \sqrt{V}$, and $2\phi_F = 0.6$ V.

7.22. Find V_{OH}, V_{OL}, and the power dissipation (for $v_O = V_{OL}$) for the linear load inverter in Fig. P7.22.

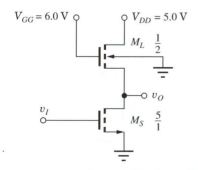

Figure P7.22

7.4 NMOS Inverter with a Depletion-Mode Load

7.23. We know that body effect deteriorates the behavior of NMOS logic gates with depletion-mode loads. Assume that the depletion-mode load device has $V_{TO} = -3$ V and is operating in an inverter circuit with $V_{DD} = 5$ V. What is the largest value of the body-effect parameter γ that still will allow $V_{OH} = V_{DD}$?

7.24. The depletion-load inverter of Fig. 7.20(d) was designed using $K'_n = 25$ μA/V^2, but due to process variations during fabrication, the value actually turned out to be $K'_n = 40$ μA/V^2. What will be the new values of V_{OH}, V_{OL}, and the power dissipation in the gate for this new value of K'_n?

7.25. (a) Redesign the inverter with depletion-mode load of Fig. 7.20(d) for operation with $V_{DD} = 3.3$ V. Assume $V_{TO} = 0.7$ V for the switching transistor and $V_{TO} = -3$ V for the depletion-mode load. Design for $V_{OL} = 0.25$ V and $P = 0.25$ mW. (b) What are the new values for NM_H and NM_L?

7.5 NMOS Logic Gates

7.26. (a) What is the value of V_{OL} in the two-input NOR gate in Fig. 7.21(a) when both $A = 1$ and $B = 1$? (b) What is the current in the gate for this input condition?

7.27. Calculate the W/L ratios of the switching devices in the NAND gate in Fig. 7.23(b) and verify that they are correct.

**7.28. The two-input NAND gate in Fig. 7.23 was designed with equal values of R_{on} (approximately equal voltage drops) in the two series-connected switching transistors, but an infinite number of other choices are possible. Show that the equal R_{on} design requires the minimum total gate area for the switching transistors.

7.29. Draw the schematic for a four-input NOR gate with a saturated load device. What are the W/L ratios of all the transistors, based on the reference inverter in Fig. 7.20?

7.30. Draw the schematic for a four-input NAND gate with a depletion-mode load device. What are the W/L ratios of all the transistors, based on the reference inverter in Fig. 7.20?

7.6 Complex NMOS Logic

*7.31. A new logic gate design is presented in Fig. P7.31. Find V_{OH} and V_{OL} for this design. (*Hint:* For V_{OL}, note that the drain currents of M_S and M_L must be equal, one device will be operating in the linear

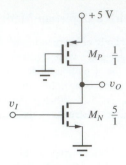

Figure P7.31

region, and one will be operating in the saturation region.)

**7.32. (a) What is the truth table for the logic function Y for the gate in Fig. P7.32? (b) Write an expression for the logical output of this gate. (c) What are the sizes of the transistors M_S and M_P in order for $V_{OL} \le$ 0.25 V? (d) Qualitatively describe how the sizes of M_S and M_P will change if body effect is included in the models for the transistors. (e) What is name for this logic function?

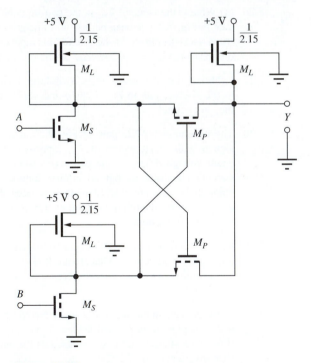

Figure P7.32

7.33. (a) What is the logic function that is implemented by the gate in Fig. P7.33? (b) What are the W/L ratios for the transistors, based on the reference inverter design of Fig. 7.20(d)?

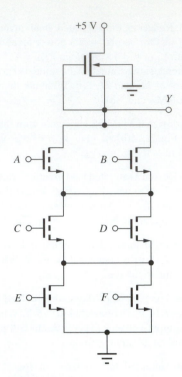

Figure P7.33

7.34. (a) What is the logic function that is implemented by the gate in Fig. P7.34? (b) What are the W/L ratios for the transistors, based on the reference inverter design of Fig. 7.20(d)?

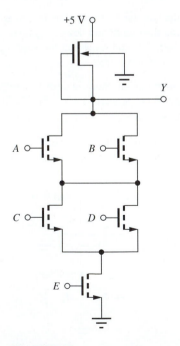

Figure P7.34

7.35. (a) What is the logic function that is implemented by the gate in Fig. P7.35? (b) What are the W/L ratios for the transistors if the gate is to dissipate three times as much power as the reference inverter design of Fig. 7.20(d)?

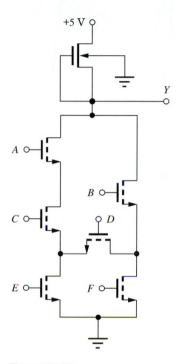

Figure P7.35

7.36. Design a depletion-load gate that implements the logic function $Y = \overline{A[B + C(D + E)]}$, based on the reference inverter design of Fig. 7.20(d).

7.37. Design a depletion-load gate that implements the logic function $Y = \overline{A(BC + DE)}$ and consumes one-half the power of the reference inverter design of Fig. 7.20(d).

7.38. Design a saturated-load gate that implements the logic function $Y = \overline{A(BC + DE)}$, based on the reference inverter design of Fig. 7.20(b).

7.39. Design a saturated-load gate that implements the logic function $Y = \overline{A(B + CD) + E}$, based on the reference inverter design of Fig. 7.20(b).

7.40. What is the logic function for the gate in Fig. P7.40? What are the W/L ratios of the transistors that form the gate if the gate is to consume twice as much power as the reference inverter in Fig. 7.20(d)?

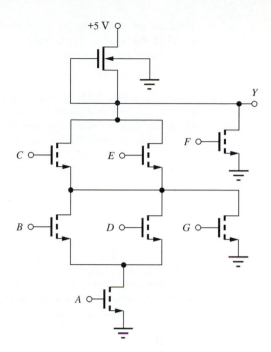

Figure P7.40

7.41. (a) Design a depletion-load gate that implements the logic function $Y + \overline{A(B + CD) + E}$, based on the reference inverter design of Fig. 7.20(d). (b) Redesign the W/L ratios of this gate to account for body effect and differences in values of V_{DS} for the various transistors.

7.42. Recalculate the W/L ratios of the transistors in the gate in Fig. 7.24 to account for the body effect and differences in the V_{DS} of the various transistors.

*7.43. Recalculate the W/L ratios of the transistors in the gate in Fig. 7.25 to account for the body effect and differences in the V_{DS} of the various transistors.

*7.44. Recalculate the W/L ratios of the transistors in the gate in Fig. 7.26 to account for the body effect and differences in the V_{DS} of the various transistors.

*7.45. Recalculate the W/L ratios of the transistors in the gate in Fig. 7.27 to account for the body effect and differences in the V_{DS} of the various transistors.

7.7 Power Dissipation

7.46. Scale the sizes of the resistors and transistors in the four inverters in Fig. 7.20 to change the power dissipation level to 1 mW.

7.47. What are the W/L ratios of the transistors in the gate in Fig. P7.40 if the gate is to consume four times as much power as the reference inverter in Fig. 7.20(d)?

7.48. What are the W/L ratios for the transistors in Fig. P7.33 if the gate is to dissipate one-quarter as much power as the reference inverter design of Fig. 7.20(d)?

*7.49. For many years, MOS devices were scaled to smaller and smaller dimensions without changing the power supply voltage. Suppose that the width W, length L, and oxide thickness t_{ox} are all reduced by a factor of 2. Assume that V_{TN}, v_{GS}, and v_{DS} remain the same. Calculate the ratio of the drain current of the scaled device to that of the original device. How has the power dissipation changed?

7.50. A high-speed NMOS microprocessor has a 64-bit address bus and performs a memory access every 50 ns. Assume that all address bits change during every memory access, and that each bus line represents a load of 10 pF. (a) How much power is being dissipated by the circuits that are driving these signals if the power supply is 5 V? (b) 3.3 V?

7.8 Dynamic Behavior of MOS Logic Gates

**7.51. The capacitive load on a logic gate becomes dominated by the channel capacitance as the transistors are made wider and wider. Assume that W is very large and show that τ_{PHL} and τ_{PLH} become independent of W and are both proportional to (L^2/μ), where L is the channel length. This result shows the importance of achieving as small a channel length as possible.

7.52. A logic family has a power-delay product of 100 fJ. If a logic gate consumes a power of 100 μW, what is the expected propagation delay of the logic gate?

7.53. The graph in Fig. P7.53 gives the results of a SPICE simulation of an inverter. (a) What are the rise and fall times for v_I and v_O? (b) What are the values of τ_{PHL} and τ_{PLH}? (c) What is the average propagation delay for this gate?

7.54. One method to estimate the average propagation delay of an inverter is to construct a long ring of inverters, as shown in the Fig. P7.54. This circuit is called a *ring oscillator*, and the output of any inverter in the chain will be similar to a square wave. (a) Suppose that the chain contains 301 inverters and the average propagation delay of an inverter is 100 ps. What will be the period of the square wave generated by the oscillator? (b) Why should the number of inverters be odd? What could happen if an even number of inverters were used in the ring oscillator?

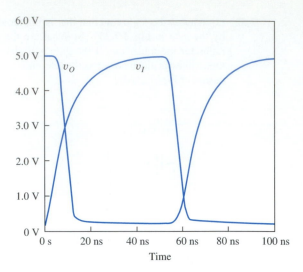

Figure P7.53

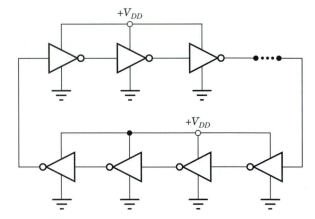

Figure P7.54 Ring oscillator formed from a chain of an *odd* number of inverters.

7.9–7.11 Dynamic Response of NMOS Inverters

Resistor Load

7.55. What are the rise time, fall time, and average propagation delay of the NMOS gate in Fig. 7.3(b) if a load capacitance $C = 0.5$ pF is attached to the output of the gate?

7.56. What are the rise time, fall time, and average propagation delay of the NMOS gate in Fig. 7.3(b) if a load capacitance $C = 0.5$ pF is attached to the output of the gate and V_{DD} is reduced to 3.3 V?

Saturated Load

*7.57. What are the rise and fall times and average propagation delays of the NMOS gate in Fig. P7.57 if $C = 0.5$ pF and $V_{DD} = 5$ V?

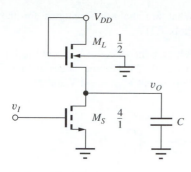

Figure P7.57

7.58. What are the rise and fall times and average propagation delays of the NMOS gate in Fig. P7.57 if $C = 0.3$ pF and $V_{DD} = 3.3$ V?

7.59. Use SPICE to determine the characteristics of the NMOS inverter with a saturated load device for the design given in Fig. 7.20(b). (a) Simulate the voltage transfer function. (b) Determine t_r, t_f, τ_{PHL}, and τ_{PLH} for this inverter with a square wave input and $C = 0.25$ pF. Compare your results to the formulas developed in the text.

7.60. Use SPICE to simulate the behavior of a chain of five saturated load inverters from Fig. 7.20(b). The input to the first inverter should be a square wave with 0.1-ns rise and fall times and a period of 100 ns. (a) Calculate t_r, t_f, τ_{PHL}, and τ_{PLH} using the input and output waveforms from the first inverter in the chain, and compare your results to the formulas developed in the text. What value of C [Fig. 7.30(b)] did you use? (b) Determine t_r, t_f, τ_{PHL}, and τ_{PLH} from the waveforms at the input and output of the fourth inverter in the chain, and compare your results to the formulas developed in the text. What value of C [Fig. 7.30(b)] did you use? (c) Discuss the differences between the results in (a) and (b).

Linear Load

7.61. Use SPICE to determine the characteristics of the NMOS inverter with a linear load device for the design given in Fig. 7.20. (a) Simulate the voltage transfer function. (b) Determine t_r, t_f, τ_{PHL}, and τ_{PLH} for this inverter with a square wave input and $C = 0.15$ pF. Compare your results to the formulas developed in the text.

7.62. Use SPICE to simulate the behavior of a chain of five linear load inverters from Fig. 7.20. The input to the first inverter should be a square wave with 0.1-ns rise and fall times and a period of 100 n. (a) Calculate t_r, t_f, τ_{PHL}, and τ_{PLH} using the input and output waveforms from the first inverter in the chain and compare your results to the formulas de-

veloped in the text. What value of C [Fig 7.30(b)] did you use? (b) Determine t_r, t_f, τ_{PHL}, and τ_{PLH} from the waveforms at the input and output of the fourth inverter in the chain, and compare your results to the formulas developed in the text. What value of C [Fig 7.30(b)] did you use? (c) Discuss the differences between the results in (a) and (b).

Depletion-Mode Load

7.63. What are the sizes of the transistors in the NMOS depletion-mode load inverter if it must drive a 1-pF capacitance with an average propagation delay of 3 nS? Assume $V_{DD} = 3.0$ V and $V_{OL} = 0.25$ V. What are the rise and fall times for the inverter? Use $V_{TNL} = -3$ V ($\gamma = 0$).

7.64. Use SPICE to determine the characteristics of the NMOS inverter with a depletion-mode load device for the design given in Fig. 7.20(d). (a) Simulate the voltage transfer function. (b) Determine t_r, t_f, τ_{PHL}, and τ_{PLH} for this inverter with a square wave input and $C = 0.2$ pF. Compare your results to the formulas developed in the text.

7.65. Use SPICE to simulate the behavior of a chain of five depletion-mode load inverters from Fig. 7.20(d). The input to the first inverter should be a square wave with 0.1-ns rise and fall times and a period of 100 ns. (a) Calculate t_r, t_f, τ_{PHL}, and τ_{PLH} using the input and output waveforms from the first inverter in the chain, and compare your results to the formulas developed in the text. What value of C [Fig 7.30(b)] did you use? (b) Determine t_r, t_f, τ_{PHL}, and τ_{PLH} from the waveforms at the input and output of the fourth inverter in the chain, and compare your results to the formulas developed in the text. (c) Discuss the differences between the results in (a) and (b).

7.66. Use SPICE to determine the characteristics of the two-input NMOS NAND gate with a depletion-mode load device for the design given in Fig. 7.23(b). (a) Simulate the voltage transfer function by varying the voltage at input A with the voltage at input B fixed at 5 V. (b) Repeat the simulation in (a), but now vary the voltage at input B with the voltage at input A fixed at 5 V. Plot the results from (a) and (b) and note any differences. (c) Determine t_r, t_f, τ_{PHL}, and τ_{PLH} for this inverter with a square wave input at input A with the voltage at input B fixed at 5 V. (d) Determine t_r, t_f, τ_{PHL}, and τ_{PLH} for this inverter with a square wave input at input B with the voltage at input A fixed at 5 V. (e) Compare the results from (c) and (d). (f) Determine t_r, t_f, τ_{PHL}, and τ_{PLH} for this inverter with a single square wave input applied to both inputs A and B. Compare the results to those in (c) and (d).

7.12 A Final Comparison of Load Devices

7.67. Currents in the various load devices are shown in Fig. 7.40. The resistor load has a value of 95 kΩ. The W/L ratios of the devices were chosen to set the current in each load device to 50 μA when $v_O = V_{OL} = 0.25$ V. Calculate the values of the W/L ratios of the load devices that were used in the figure for: (a) saturated load device including body effect, (b) saturated load device with no body effect, (c) linear load device including body effect, (d) linear load device with no body effect, (e) depletion-mode load device including body effect, (f) depletion-mode load with no body effect.

PMOS Problems

7.68. Design four PMOS logic gates similar to the ones in Fig. 7.20. Do not do a complete mathematical redesign, but design the PMOS circuits by scaling the W/L ratios in Fig. 7.20, assuming that $K'_p = 10 \ \mu$A/V^2.

*7.69. What are the values of V_{OL} and V_{OH} for the inverter in Fig. P7.69?

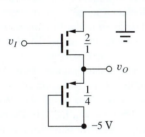

Figure P7.69

7.70. Calculate the noise margins for the circuit in Fig. P7.69.

7.71. Design the transistors in the inverter of Fig. P7.71 so that $V_{OH} = -0.33$ V and the power dissipation = 0.1 mW. Use the values in Table 7.1 on page 254, except $V_{TO} = -0.7$ V and $K'_p = 10 \ \mu$A/V^2.

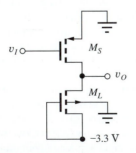

Figure P7.71

*7.72. What are the noise margins for the circuit in Prob. 7.71?

7.73. What are the values of V_{OH} and V_{OL} for the inverter of Fig. P7.73? Use the values in Table 7.1 on page 254, except $V_{TO} = -1$ V and $K'_p = 10 \ \mu$A/V^2.

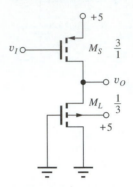

Figure P7.73

7.74. What is the logic function Y for the gate in Fig. P7.74?

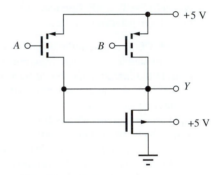

Figure P7.74

7.75. What is the logic function Y for the gate in Fig. P7.75?

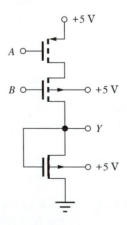

Figure P7.75

7.76. Simulate the voltage transfer characteristic for the PMOS gate in Fig. P7.69, and compare the results to those of Prob. 7.69.

7.77. Simulate the voltage transfer characteristic for the PMOS gate in Fig. P7.71, and compare the results to those of Prob. 7.71.

7.78. Simulate the voltage transfer characteristic for the PMOS gate in Fig. P7.73, and compare the results to those of Prob. 7.73.

7.79. Simulate the delay of the PMOS gate in Fig. P7.69 with a load capacitance of 1 pF, and determine the rise time, fall time, and average propagation delay.

7.80. Simulate the delay of the PMOS gate in Fig. P7.73 with a load capacitance of 1 pF, and determine the rise time, fall time, and average propagation delay.

Complementary MOS (CMOS) Logic Design

For many years, **complementary MOS (CMOS)** technology was available only in unit-logic form, with several gates packaged together in a single dual in-line package (DIP), but it was not widely used in complex integrated circuits. CMOS requires that both NMOS and PMOS transistors be built into the same substrate, and the increased complexity and cost this represents were the primary reasons why CMOS technology was little used. As time passed, however, the size of transistors in ICs continued to decrease, so an ever-larger number of gates could be placed on a given size IC chip. By the early 1980s, the total power consumption of NMOS ICs was becoming prohibitive. The problem was so severe that it was hampering progress in increasing the density of ICs. To solve the static power dissipation problem, the microprocessor industry at this point rapidly moved to CMOS technology. Today, CMOS is the industrywide standard technology.

This chapter investigates the design of CMOS logic circuits, starting with characterization of the CMOS inverter, and follows with a discussion of the design of NOR, NAND, and complex gates based on a CMOS reference inverter. CMOS gate design is demonstrated to be determined primarily by logic delay considerations. CMOS noise margins and power-delay product are discussed, and the transmission gate is also introduced.

The physical structure of CMOS technology is presented, and parasitic bipolar transistors are shown to exist within the integrated CMOS structure. If these bipolar devices become active, a potentially destructive phenomenon called latchup can occur.

8.1 CMOS INVERTER TECHNOLOGY

As noted, CMOS requires a fabrication technology that can produce both NMOS and PMOS transistors together on one IC substrate. The basic IC structure used to accomplish this task is shown in Fig. 8.1. In this cross section, NMOS transistors are shown fabricated in a normal manner in a p-type silicon substrate. A lightly doped n-type region, called the n-well, is formed in the p-type substrate, and PMOS transistors are then fabricated in the n-well region, which becomes the body of the PMOS device. Note that a large-area diode exists between the n-well and p-type substrate. This pn diode must always be kept reverse-biased by the proper connection of V_{DD} and V_{SS} (for example, 5 V and 0 V).

The connections between the transistors needed to form a CMOS inverter are shown in Fig. 8.1 and correspond to the circuit schematic for the CMOS inverter in Fig. 8.2. The inverter circuit consists of one NMOS and one PMOS transistor. The NMOS transistor functions in a manner identical to that of the switching device in the NMOS gates that we have studied previously. However, the PMOS load device is also switched on and off under control of the logic input signal v_I.

The CMOS logic gate can be conceptually modeled by the circuit in Fig. 8.2(b), in which the position of the two switches is controlled by the input voltage v_I. The circuit is designed so there will never be a conducting path between the positive and negative power supplies under steady-state conditions. When the NMOS transistor is on, the PMOS transistor is off; if the PMOS transistor is on, the NMOS device is off.

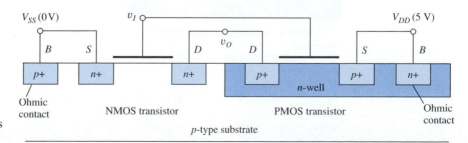

Figure 8.1 n-well CMOS structure for forming both NMOS and PMOS transistors in a single silicon substrate.

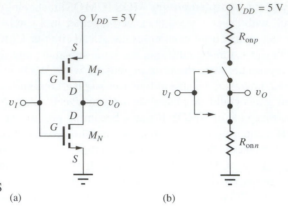

Figure 8.2 (a) A CMOS inverter uses one NMOS and one PMOS transistor. (b) Simplified model for the CMOS logic gate.

In the CMOS inverter of Fig. 8.2, the source of the PMOS transistor is connected to V_{DD}, the source of the NMOS transistor is connected to V_{SS} (0 V in this case), and the drain terminals of the two MOSFETs are connected together to form the output node. Also, the substrates of both the NMOS and PMOS transistors are connected to their respective sources, and so body effect is eliminated in both devices.

Before we explore the design of the CMOS inverter, we need parameters for the CMOS devices, as given in Table 8.1. The NMOS parameters are the same as those given in Chapter 7. In CMOS technology, the transistors are normally designed to have equal and opposite threshold voltages: $V_{TON} = +1$ V and $V_{TOP} = -1$ V. Remember that $K'_n = \mu_n C''_{ox}$ and $K'_p = \mu_p C''_{ox}$ and that hole mobility in the channel of the PMOSFET is approximately 40 percent of the electron mobility in the NMOSFET channel. The values in Table 8.1 reflect this difference because the value of K' for the NMOS device is shown as 2.5 times that for the PMOS transistor. Processing differences are also reflected in the different values for γ and $2\phi_F$ in the two types of transistors.

Remember that the threshold voltage of the NMOS transistor is denoted by V_{TN} and that of the PMOS transistor by V_{TP}:

$$V_{TN} = V_{TON} + \gamma_N(\sqrt{V_{SBN} + 2\phi_{FN}} - \sqrt{2\phi_{FN}})$$

and

$$V_{TP} = V_{TOP} - \gamma_P(\sqrt{V_{BSP} + 2\phi_{FP}} - \sqrt{2\phi_{FP}}) \tag{8.1}$$

For $v_{SBN} = 0$, $V_{TN} = V_{TON}$, and for $v_{BSP} = 0$, $V_{TP} = V_{TOP}$.

EXERCISES: (a) What are the values of K_p and K_n for transistors with $W/L = 20/1$? (b) An NMOS transistor has $V_{SB} = 3.3$ V. What is the value of V_{TN}? (c) A PMOS transistor has $V_{BS} = 3.3$ V. What is the value of V_{TP}?

ANSWERS: 200 μA/V², 500 μA/V²; 1.60 V; −1.87 V

T a b l e 8.1		
CMOS Transistor Parameters		
	NMOS Device	**PMOS Device**
V_{TO}	1 V	−1 V
γ	0.50 $\sqrt{V}$	0.75 $\sqrt{V}$
$2\phi_F$	0.60 V	0.70 V
K'	25 μA/V²	10 μA/V²

8.2 STATIC CHARACTERISTICS OF THE CMOS INVERTER

We now explore the static behavior of CMOS logic gates. Consider the CMOS inverter with an input $v_I = +5$ V (1 state), as shown in Fig. 8.3(a). For this input condition, $v_{GS} = +5$ V for the NMOS transistor, and $v_{SG} = 0$ V for the PMOS transistor. For the NMOS device, $v_{GS} > V_{TN}$ (1 V), so a channel exists in the NMOS transistor, but the PMOS transistor is off because $v_{SG} = 0$ V for the PMOS device. Thus, the load capacitor C is eventually fully discharged through the NMOS transistor, and v_O reaches 0 V. Because the PMOS transistor is off, a dc current path does not exist through M_N and M_P!

If v_I is now set to 0 V (0 state), as in Fig. 8.3(b), v_{GS} becomes 0 V for the NMOS transistor, and it is cut off. For the PMOS transistor, $v_{SG} = 5$ V, which exceeds its threshold voltage; a channel exists in the PMOS transistor; and the load capacitor C charges to a value equal to the positive power supply voltage V_{DD} (5 V). Once a steady-state condition is reached, the currents in M_N and M_P must both be zero because the NMOS transistor is off.

Several important characteristics of the CMOS inverter are evident. The values of V_{OH} and V_{OL} are equal to the positive and negative power supply voltages, and the logic swing ΔV is equal to the full power supply span. For the circuit in Fig. 8.3, $V_{OH} = 5$ V, $V_{OL} = 0$ V, and the logic swing $\Delta V = 5$ V. Of even greater importance is the observation that the static power dissipation is zero, because $I_D = 0$ in both logic states!

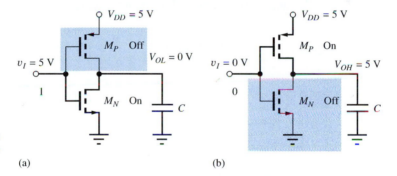

Figure 8.3 CMOS inverters in the two possible binary states.

(a)   (b)

CMOS Voltage Transfer Characteristics

Figure 8.4 shows the result of simulation of the voltage transfer characteristic (VTC) of the **symmetrical CMOS inverter,** designed with $K_P = K_N$. The VTC can be divided into five different regions, as shown in the figure and summarized in Table 8.2. For an input voltage less than $V_{TN} = 1$ V in region 1, the NMOS transistor is off, and the output is maintained at $V_{OH} = 5$ V by the PMOS device.

Similarly, for an input voltage greater than $(V_{DD} - |V_{TP}|)$ (4 V) in region 5, the PMOS device is off, and the output is maintained at $V_{OL} = 0$ V by the NMOS transistor. In region 2, the NMOS transistor is saturated, and the PMOS transistor is in the linear region. In region 3, both transistors are saturated. The boundary between regions 2 and 3 is defined by the boundary between the saturation and linear regions of operation for the PMOS transistor. Saturation of the PMOS device requires:

$$v_{SD} \geq v_{SG} + V_{TP}$$
$$(5 - v_O) \geq (5 - v_I) - 1 \tag{8.2}$$
$$v_O \leq v_I + 1$$

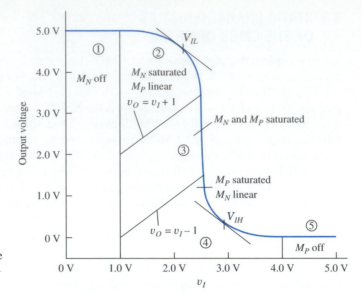

Figure 8.4 CMOS voltage transfer characteristic may be broken down into the five regions outlined in Table 8.2.

	Table 8.2			
	Regions of Operation of Transistors in a Symmetrical CMOS Inverter			
Region	**Input Voltage v_I**	**Output Voltage v_O**	**NMOS Transistor**	**PMOS Transistor**
1	$v_I \leq V_{TN}$	$V_{OH} = V_{DD}$	Cutoff	Linear
2	$V_{TN} < v_I \leq v_O + V_{TP}$	High	Saturation	Linear
3	$v_I \approx V_{DD}/2$	$V_{DD}/2$	Saturation	Saturation
4	$v_O + V_{TN} < v_I \leq (V_{DD} - |V_{TP}|)$	Low	Linear	Saturation
5	$v_I \geq (V_{DD} - |V_{TP}|)$	$V_{OL} = 0$	Linear	Cutoff

In a similar manner, the boundary between regions 3 and 4 is defined by saturation of the NMOS device:

$$v_{DS} \geq v_{GS} - V_{TN}$$
$$v_O \geq v_I - 1 \tag{8.3}$$

In region 4, the voltages place the NMOS transistor in the linear region, and the PMOS transistor remains saturated. Finally, for the input voltage near $V_{DD}/2$ (region 3), both transistors are operating in the saturation region.

> **EXERCISE:** Suppose $v_I = 2$ V for the CMOS inverter in Fig. 8.3. (a) What is the range of values of v_O for which M_N is saturated and M_P is in the linear region? (b) For which values are both transistors saturated? (c) For which values is M_P saturated and M_N in the linear region?
>
> **ANSWERS:** (3 V $\leq v_O \leq$ 5 V); (1 V $\leq v_O \leq$ 3 V); (0 V $\leq v_O \leq$ 1 V)
>
> **EXERCISE:** The $(W/L)_N$ of M_N in Fig. 8.3 is 10/1. What is the value of $(W/L)_P$ required to form a symmetrical inverter?
>
> **ANSWER:** 25/1

Figure 8.5 shows the results of simulation of the voltage transfer characteristics for a CMOS inverter with a symmetrical design ($K_P = K_N$) for several values of V_{DD}. Note that the output voltage levels V_{OH} and V_{OL} are always determined by the two power supplies. As the input voltage rises from 0 to V_{DD}, the output remains constant for $v_I < V_{TN}$ and $v_I > (V_{DD} - |V_{TP}|)$. For this symmetrical design case, the transition between V_{OH} and V_{OL} is centered at $v_I = V_{DD}/2$. The straight line on the graph represents $v_O = v_I$, which occurs for $v_I = V_{DD}/2$ for the symmetrical inverter.

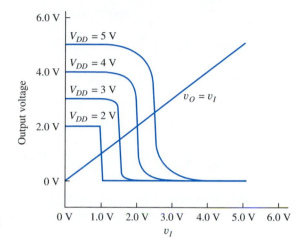

Figure 8.5 Voltage transfer characteristics for a symmetrical CMOS inverter ($K_R = 1$) with $V_{DD} = 5$ V, 4 V, 3 V, and 2 V.

If $K_p \neq K_n$, then the transition shifts away from $V_{DD}/2$. To simplify notation, a parameter K_R is defined: $K_R = K_n/K_p$. K_R represents the relative current drive capability of the NMOS and PMOS devices in the inverter. Voltage transfer characteristics for inverters with $K_R = 5$, 1, and 0.2 are shown in Fig. 8.6. For $K_R > 1$, the NMOS current drive capability exceeds that of the PMOS transistor, so the transition region shifts to $v_I < V_{DD}/2$. Conversely, for $K_R < 1$, PMOS current drive capability is greater than that of the NMOS device, and the transition region occurs for $v_I > V_{DD}/2$.

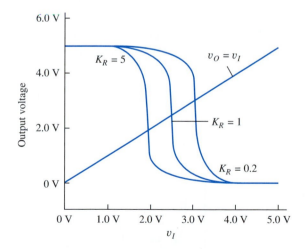

Figure 8.6 CMOS voltage transfer characteristics for $K_R = 5$, 1, and 0.2 for $V_{DD} = 5$ V.

EXERCISES: Equate the expressions for the drain currents of M_N and M_P to show that $v_O = v_I$ occurs for a voltage equal to $V_{DD}/2$ in a symmetrical inverter. What voltage corresponds to $v_O = v_I$ in an inverter with $K_R = 10$ and $V_{DD} = 4$ V?

ANSWER: 1.48 V

Noise Margins for the CMOS Inverter

Because of the importance of the CMOS logic family, we explore the noise margins of the inverter in some detail. V_{IL} and V_{IH} are identified graphically in Figs. 8.4 and 8.7 as the points at which the voltage transfer characteristic has a slope of -1. First, we will find V_{IH}.

For v_I near V_{IH}, the v_{DS} of M_P will be large and that of M_N will be small. Therefore, we assume that the PMOS device is saturated and the NMOS device is in its linear region. The two drain currents must be equal, so:

$$i_{DSN} = i_{SDP}$$

$$K_n\left(v_I - V_{TN} - \frac{v_O}{2}\right)(v_O) = \frac{K_p}{2}(V_{DD} - v_I + V_{TP})^2 \tag{8.4}$$

For M_N, $v_{GS} = v_I$ and $v_{GS} = v_O$. For M_P, $v_{SG} = V_{DD} - v_I$ and $v_{SD} = V_{DD} - v_O$. Now

$$K_R(2v_I - 2V_{TN} - v_O)(v_O) = (V_{DD} - v_I + V_{TP})^2 \tag{8.5}$$

in which $K_R = K_n/K_p$. Solving for v_O yields

$$v_O = v_I - V_{TN} \pm \sqrt{(v_I - V_{TN})^2 - \frac{(V_{DD} - v_I + V_{TP})^2}{K_R}} \tag{8.6}$$

Taking the derivative with respect to v_I and setting it equal to -1 at $v_I = V_{IH}$ is quite involved (and is most easily done with a symbolic algebra package[1] on the computer), but eventually yields the following result:

$$V_{IH} = \frac{2K_R(V_{DD} - V_{TN} + V_{TP})}{(K_R - 1)\sqrt{1 + 3K_R}} - \frac{(V_{DD} - K_R V_{TN} + V_{TP})}{K_R - 1} \tag{8.7}$$

The high-level noise margin is then equal to

$$NM_H = V_{OH} - V_{IH} = V_{DD} - V_{IH} \tag{8.8}$$

For the special case of $K_R = 1$,

$$V_{IH} = \frac{5V_{DD} + 3V_{TN} + 5V_{TP}}{8} \quad \text{and} \quad NM_H = \frac{3V_{DD} - 3V_{TN} - 5V_{TP}}{8} \tag{8.9}$$

V_{IL} can be found in a similar manner using $i_{DSN} = i_{SDP}$. For v_I near V_{IL}, the v_{DS} of M_P will be small and that of M_N will be large, so we assume that the NMOS device is

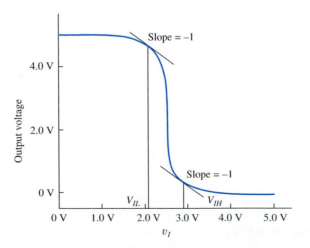

Figure 8.7 CMOS voltage transfer characteristic, with V_{IL} and V_{IH} indicated.

---

[1] For example, Mathematica, MAPLE, Macsyma, and so on.

saturated and the PMOS device is in its linear region. Equating drain currents:

$$K_P\left(V_{DD} - v_I + V_{TP} - \frac{V_{DD} - v_O}{2}\right)(V_{DD} - v_O) = \frac{K_n}{2}(v_I - V_{TN})^2$$

(8.10)

or

$$(V_{DD} - 2v_I + 2V_{TP} - v_O)(V_{DD} - v_O) = K_R(v_I - V_{TN})^2$$

Again, we solve for v_O, take the derivative with respect to v_I, and set the result equal to -1 at $v_I = V_{IL}$. This process yields:

$$V_{IL} = \frac{2\sqrt{K_R}(V_{DD} - V_{TN} + V_{TP})}{(K_R - 1)\sqrt{K_R + 3}} - \frac{(V_{DD} - K_R V_{TN} + V_{TP})}{K_R - 1}$$

(8.11)

and

$$NM_L = V_{IL} - V_{OL} = V_{IL} - 0 = V_{IL}$$

(8.12)

For the special case of $K_R = 1$,

$$V_{IL} = \frac{3V_{DD} + 5V_{TN} + 3V_{TP}}{8} \qquad \text{and} \qquad NM_L = V_{IL}$$

(8.13)

Figure 8.8 is a graph of the CMOS noise margins versus K_R from Eqs. (8.8) and (8.11) for the particular case $V_{DD} = 5$ V, $V_{TN} = 1$ V, and $V_{TP} = -1$ V. For a symmetrical inverter design ($K_R = 1$), the noise margins are both equal to approximately 2.1 V, almost equal to $V_{DD}/2$!

EXERCISE: What is the value of K_R for a CMOS inverter in which $(W/L)_P = (W/L)_N$? Calculate the noise margins for this value of K_R and $V_{DD} = 5$ V.

ANSWERS: 2.5; $NM_L = 1.70$ V, $NM_H = 2.57$ V

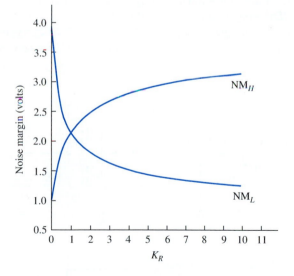

Figure 8.8 Noise margins versus K_R for the CMOS inverter with $V_{DD} = 5$ V and $V_{TN} = -V_{TP} = 1$ V.

8.3 DYNAMIC BEHAVIOR OF THE CMOS INVERTER

Static power dissipation and the values of V_{OH} and V_{OL} do not really represent design parameters in CMOS circuits. Instead, the choice of sizes of the NMOS and PMOS transistors is dictated by the dynamic behavior of the logic gate—namely, by the desired average

propagation delay τ_p. We can get an estimate of the propagation delay in the CMOS inverter by studying the circuit in Fig. 8.9, in which the inverter is driven by an ideal step function. For $t < 0$, the NMOS transistor is off and the PMOS transistor is on, forcing the output into the high state with $v_O = V_{OH} = V_{DD}$. At $t = 0$, the input abruptly changes from 0 V to 5 V, and for $t = 0^+$, the NMOS transistor is on ($v_{GS} = +5$ V) and the PMOS transistor is off ($v_{SG} = 0$ V). Thus, the circuit simplifies to that in Fig. 8.9(b). The capacitor voltage is equal to V_{DD} at $t = 0^+$, and the capacitor voltage begins to fall as C is discharged through the NMOS transistor. The NMOS device starts conduction in the saturation region with $v_{DS} = v_{GS} = V_{DD}$, and enters the linear region of operation when $v_{DS} = (v_{GS} - V_{TN}) = (V_{DD} - V_{TN})$. The NMOS device continues to discharge C until its v_{DS} becomes zero. Therefore, $V_{OL} = 0$ V.

A significant amount of effort can be saved by realizing that the set of operating conditions in Fig. 8.9 is exactly the same as was used to determine τ_{PHL} for the NMOS inverter with either a resistive or depletion-mode load. Using Eq. (7.69),

$$\tau_{PHL} = R_{onn}C\left\{\ln\left[4\left(\frac{V_{DD} - V_{TN}}{V_{DD} + V_{OL}}\right) - 1\right] + \frac{1}{2}\right\} \qquad \text{where } R_{onn} = \frac{1}{K_n(V_{DD} - V_{TN})}$$

$$(8.14)$$

For the CMOS inverter with $V_{DD} = 5$ V, $V_{TN} = 1$ V, and $V_{OL} = 0$, τ_{PHL} becomes

$$\tau_{PHL} = 1.29R_{onn}C = \frac{0.322C}{K_n} \qquad (8.15)$$

Now consider the inverter driven by a step function that switches from $+5$ V to 0 V at $t = 0$, as in Fig. 8.10. For $t < 0$, the PMOS transistor is off and the NMOS transistor is on, forcing the output into the low state with $v_O = V_{OL} = 0$. At $t = 0$, the input abruptly changes from 5 V to 0 V. For $t = 0^+$, the PMOS transistor will be on ($v_{SG} = 5$ V) and the NMOS transistor will be off ($v_{GS} = 0$ V). Thus, the circuit simplifies to that in Fig. 8.10(b). The voltage on the capacitor at $t = 0^+$ is equal to zero, and it begins to rise toward V_{DD} as charge is supplied through the PMOS transistor. The PMOS device begins conduction in the saturation region and subsequently enters the linear region of operation.

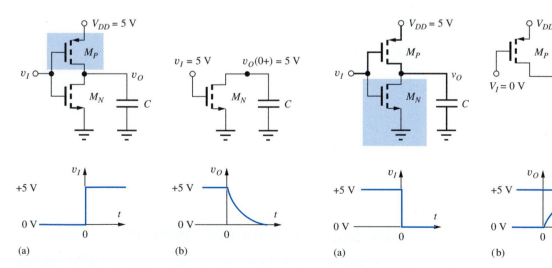

(a)   (b)   (a)   (b)

Figure 8.9 High-to-low output transition in a CMOS inverter.

Figure 8.10 Low-to-high output transition in a CMOS inverter.

This device continues to conduct until v_{DS} becomes zero, when $v_O = V_{OH} = V_{DD}$. The same set of equations that was used to arrive at Eqs. (8.14) and (8.15) apply to this circuit, and for the CMOS inverter with $V_{DD} = 5$ V, and $V_{TP} = -1$ V, τ_{PLH} becomes

$$\tau_{PLH} = 1.29 R_{onp} C \qquad \text{for } R_{onp} = \frac{1}{K_p(V_{DD} + V_{TP})} \qquad (8.16)$$

$$\tau_{PLH} = \frac{0.322C}{K_p} \qquad (8.17)$$

The only difference between Eqs. (8.15) and (8.17) is the value of R_{onn} and R_{onp}. From Table 8.1, we expect K_n' to be approximately 2.5 times the value of K_p'. In CMOS, a "symmetrical" inverter with $\tau_{PLH} = \tau_{PHL}$ can be designed if we set $(W/L)_P = (K_n'/K_p')(W/L)_N = 2.5(W/L)_N$ in order to compensate for the difference in mobilities. Because of the layout design rules in many MOS technologies, it is often convenient to design the smallest transistor with $(W/L) = (2/1)$. We use the symmetrical inverter design in Fig. 8.11, which has $(W/L)_N = (2/1)$ and $(W/L)_P = (5/1)$ as our **CMOS reference inverter** in the subsequent design of more complex CMOS logic gates.

Because we have designed this gate to have $\tau_{PLH} = \tau_{PHL}$, the average propagation delay is given by

$$\tau_p = \frac{\tau_{PHL} + \tau_{PLH}}{2} = \tau_{PHL} = \frac{0.322C}{K_n} \qquad (8.18)$$

EXERCISE: Calculate the propagation delay of the reference inverter in Fig. 8.11 for $C = 1$ pF.

ANSWER: 6.4 ns

In a CMOS inverter, the **rise** and **fall times** are approximately twice the corresponding propagation delay times, and we use

$$t_f = 2\tau_{PHL} \qquad \text{and} \qquad t_r = 2\tau_{PLH} \qquad (8.19)$$

Based on the results of the preceding exercise for the 1-pF load capacitance, the expected rise and fall times are 12.8 ns.

To increase or decrease the speed of the CMOS inverter, the sizes of the transistors are changed. The inverter in Fig. 8.12(a) has a delay of 1 ns because the W/L ratios of both transistors are 6.4 times larger than those in the reference inverter design in Fig. 8.11. The

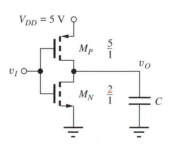

Figure 8.11 Symmetrical reference inverter design.

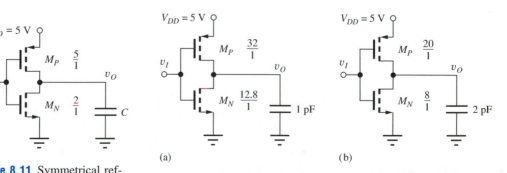

(a)   (b)

Figure 8.12 Scaled inverters: (a) $\tau_p = 1$ ns, (b) $\tau_p = 3.2$ ns.

inverter in Fig. 8.12(b) has a delay of 3.2 ns because its transistors are four times larger than those in the reference inverter, but it is driving twice as much capacitance:

$$\tau_p = (6.4 \times 2/4) \text{ ns}$$

EXERCISE: An inverter must drive a 5-pF load capacitance with $\tau_p = 1$ ns. Scale the reference inverter to achieve this delay.

ANSWER: $(W/L)_P = 160/1$ and $(W/L)_N = 64/1$

8.4 STATIC AND DYNAMIC POWER DISSIPATION IN CMOS

CMOS logic is often considered to have zero static power dissipation. When the CMOS inverter is resting in either logic state, no direct current path exists between the two power supplies (V_{DD} and ground). However, in very low power applications or in IC designs with extremely large numbers of gates, static power dissipation can be important. The actual static power dissipation is nonzero due to the leakage currents associated with the reverse-biased drain-to-substrate junctions of the NMOS and PMOS transistors as well as with the large area of reverse-biased n-well (or p-well) regions. The leakage current of these pn junctions flows between the supplies and contributes directly to static power dissipation. Except for battery-powered applications, however, power dissipation resulting from leakage is usually not a serious concern.

There are two components of dynamic power dissipation in CMOS logic gates. As the gate charges and discharges load capacitance C at a frequency f, the power dissipation is equal to that given by Eq. (7.52) in Chapter 7:

$$P_D = CV_{DD}^2 f \tag{8.20}$$

Power P_D is usually the largest component of power dissipation in CMOS gates operating at high frequency.

A second mechanism for power dissipation also occurs during switching of the CMOS logic gate and can be explored by referring to Fig. 8.13, which shows the current through a symmetrical CMOS inverter (with $C = 0$) as a function of the input voltage v_I. The current is zero for $v_I < V_{TN}$ and $v_I > (V_{DD} - |V_{TP}|)$ because either the NMOS or

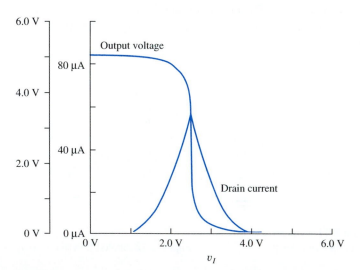

Figure 8.13 Supply current versus input voltage for a symmetrical CMOS inverter.

PMOS transistor is off for these conditions. For an input voltage exceeding V_{TN}, a current path exists through both the NMOS and PMOS devices, and the current reaches a peak for $v_I = v_O = V_{DD}/2$. As v_I increases further, the current decreases back to zero. In the time domain, a pulse of current occurs between the power supplies as the output switches state, as shown in Fig. 8.14. In very high speed CMOS circuits, this second component of dynamic power dissipation can approach 20 to 30 percent of that given by Eq. (8.20).

In the technical literature, this current pulse between supplies is often referred to as a "short circuit current." This reference is a misnomer, however, because the current is limited by the device characteristics and a short circuit does not actually exist between the power supplies.

EXERCISE: Calculate the value of the maximum current similar to that in Fig. 8.13 for the inverter design in Fig. 8.11.

ANSWER: 56.3 μA

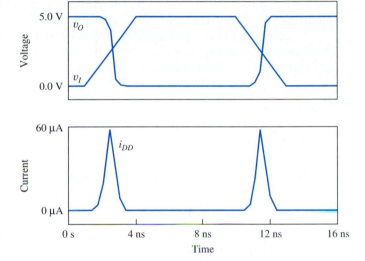

Figure 8.14 SPICE simulation of the transient current pulses between the power supplies during switching of a CMOS inverter.

8.5 CMOS NOR AND NAND GATES

The next several sections explore the design of CMOS gates, including the NOR gate, the NAND gate, and complex CMOS gates. The structure of a general static CMOS logic gate is given in Fig. 8.15 and consists of an NMOS transistor-switching network and a

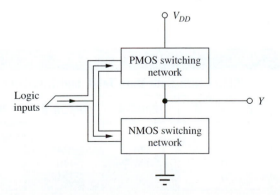

Figure 8.15 Basic CMOS logic gate structure.

PMOS transistor-switching network. For each logic input variable in a CMOS gate, there is one transistor in the NMOS network *and* one transistor in the PMOS network. Thus, a CMOS logic gate has two transistors for every input variable. When a conducting path exists through the NMOS network, a path must not exist through the PMOS network and vice versa. In other words, the conducting paths must represent logical complements of each other.

CMOS NOR Gate

The realization of a two-input CMOS **NOR gate** is shown in Fig. 8.16. For the NOR gate, the output should be low when either input A or input B is high. Thus the NMOS portion of the gate is identical to that of the NMOS NOR gate. However, in the CMOS gate, we must ensure that a static current path does not exist through the logic gate, and this requires the use of two PMOS transistors in series in the PMOS transistor network.

The complementary nature of the conducting paths can be seen in Table 8.3. A conducting path exists through the NMOS network for $A = 1$ or $B = 1$ as indicated by the blue entries in the table. However, a path exists through the PMOS network only when both $A = 0$ and $B = 0$ (no conducting path through the NMOS network).

In general, a parallel path in the NMOS network corresponds to a series path in the PMOS network, and a series path in the NMOS network corresponds to a parallel path in the PMOS network. (Bridging paths correspond to bridging paths in both networks.) We will study a rigorous method for implementing these two networks shortly.

Transistor Sizing

We can determine the sizes of the transistors in the two-input NOR gate by using our knowledge of NMOS gate design. In the CMOS case, we try to maintain the delay times equal to the reference inverter design under the worst-case input conditions. For the NMOS network with $AB = 10$ or 01, transistor A or transistor B must individually be capable of discharg-

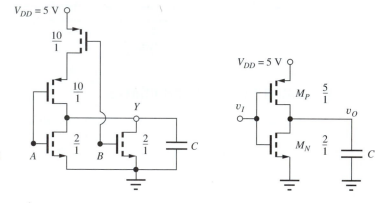

Figure 8.16 Two-input CMOS NOR gate and reference inverter.

	Table 8.3					
CMOS NOR Gate Truth Table and Transistor States						
A *B*	$Y = \overline{A + B}$	**NMOS-*A***	**NMOS-*B***	**PMOS-*A***	**PMOS-*B***
---	---	---	---	---	---
0 0	1	Off	Off	On	On
0 1	0	Off	On	On	Off
1 0	0	On	Off	Off	On
1 1	0	On	On	Off	Off

ing the load capacitance C, so each must be the same size as the NMOS device of the reference inverter. The PMOS network conducts only when $AB = 00$ and there are two PMOS transistors in series. To maintain the same **on-resistance** as the reference inverter, each PMOS device must be twice as large: $(W/L)_P = 2(5/1) = 10/1$. The resulting W/L ratios are indicated in Fig. 8.16.

Body Effect

In the preceding design, we ignored the influence of body effect. In the series-connected PMOS network, the source of the interior PMOS transistor cannot be connected to its substrate. During switching, its threshold voltage changes as its source-to-bulk voltage changes. However, once the steady-state condition is reached, with $v_O = V_{OH}$ for example, all the PMOS source and drain nodes will be at a voltage equal to V_{DD}. Thus, the total on-resistance of the PMOS transistors is not affected by the body effect once the final logic level is reached. During the transient response, however, the threshold voltage changes as a function of time and $|V_{TP}| > |V_{TOP}|$, which slows down the rise time of the gate slightly. An investigation of this effect is left for Probs. 8.26 to 8.29.

Three-Input NOR Gate

Figure 8.17 is the schematic for a three-input version of the NOR gate, and Table 8.4 is the truth table. As in the case of the NMOS gate, the output is low when NMOS transistor A or transistor B or transistor C is conducting. The only time that a conducting path exists through the PMOS network is for $A = B = C = 0$. The NMOS transistors must each individually be able to discharge the load capacitance in the desired time, so the W/L ratios are each 2/1 based on our reference inverter design. The PMOS network now has three devices in series, so each must be three times as large as the reference inverter device $(W/L = 15/1)$.

It is possible to find the PMOS network directly from the truth table. From Table 8.3 for the two-input NOR gate, we see that $Y = \overline{AB}$ and, using the identities in Table 6.7, the expression for $\overline{Y} = A + B$. For the three-input NOR gate described by Table 8.4, $Y = \overline{A}\,\overline{B}\,\overline{C}$ and $\overline{Y} = A+B+C$. The PMOS network directly implements the logic function $Y = \overline{A}\,\overline{B}\,\overline{C}$, written in terms of the complements of the input variables, and the NMOS network implements the logic function $\overline{Y} = A + B + C$, written in terms of the uncomplemented input variables. In effect, the PMOS transistors directly complement the input variables for us! The two functions $\overline{Y}$ and Y for the NMOS and PMOS networks need to be written in minimum form in order to have the minimum number of transistors in the two networks.

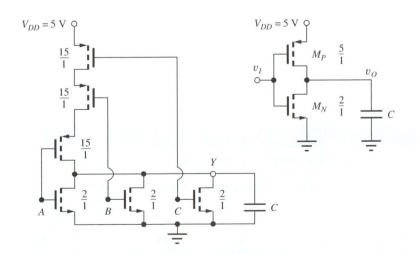

A B C	$Y = \overline{A} + \overline{B} + \overline{C}$
0 0 0	1
0 0 1	0
0 1 0	0
0 1 1	0
1 0 0	0
1 0 1	0
1 1 0	0
1 1 1	0

Table 8.4 Three-Input NOR Gate Truth Table

Figure 8.17 Three-input CMOS NOR gate and reference inverter.

The complementing effect of the PMOS devices has led to a shorthand representation for CMOS logic gates that is used in many VLSI design texts. This notation is shown by the right-hand symbol in each transistor pair in Fig. 8.18. The NMOS and PMOS transistor symbols differ only by the circle at the input of the PMOS gate. This circle identifies the PMOS transistor and indicates the logical inversion operation that is occurring to the input variable. In this book, however, we will continue to use the standard symbol.

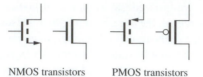

Figure 8.18 Shorthand notation for NMOS and PMOS transistors.

NMOS transistors   PMOS transistors

CMOS NAND Gates

The structure and truth table for a two-input static CMOS **NAND gate** are given in Fig. 8.19 and Table 8.5, respectively. From the truth table for the NAND gate, we see that $Y = \overline{AB}$, and the output should be low only when both input A and input B are high. Thus, the NMOS switching network is identical to that of the NMOS NAND gate with transistors A and B in series.

Expanding the equation for Y in terms of complemented variables, we have $Y = \overline{A} + \overline{B}$. If either input A or input B is low, the output must be pulled high through a PMOS transistor, resulting in two transistors in parallel in the PMOS switching network. Once again, there is one transistor in the NMOS network and one transistor in the PMOS network for each logic input variable.

Transistor Sizing

We determine the sizes of the transistors in the two-input NAND gate by again using our knowledge of NMOS design. There are two transistors in series in the NMOS network, so each should be twice as large as in the reference inverter or 4/1. In the PMOS network,

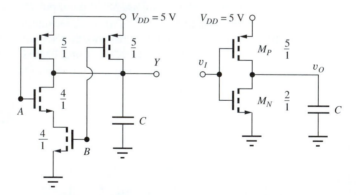

Figure 8.19 Two-input CMOS NAND gate and reference inverter.

T a b l e 8.5						
CMOS NAND Gate Truth Table and Transistor States						
A	B	$Y = \overline{AB}$	NMOS-A	NMOS-B	PMOS-A	PMOS-B
0	0	1	Off	Off	On	On
0	1	1	Off	On	On	Off
1	0	1	On	Off	Off	On
1	1	0	On	On	Off	Off

each transistor must individually be capable of discharging the load capacitance C, so each must be the same size as the PMOS device in the reference inverter. These W/L ratios are indicated in Fig. 8.19.

The Multi-Input NAND Gate

As another example, the circuit for a five-input NAND gate is given in Fig. 8.20. The NMOS network consists of a series stack of five transistors with one MOS device for each input variable. The PMOS network consists of a group of PMOS devices in parallel, also with one transistor for each input. To maintain the speed on the high-to-low transition in the five-input gate, the NMOS transistors must each be five times larger than that of the reference inverter, whereas the PMOS transistors are each identical to that of the reference inverter.

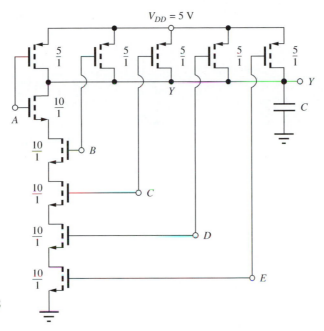

Figure 8.20 Five-input CMOS NAND gate: $Y = \overline{ABCDE}$.

8.6 COMPLEX GATES IN CMOS

Just as with NMOS design, the real power of CMOS is not realized if the designer uses only NANDs, NORs, and inverters. The ability to implement **complex logic gates** directly in CMOS is a significant advantage for CMOS design, just as it is in NMOS. This section investigates complex gate design by exploring two examples.

EXAMPLE 8.1: For our first example here, we shall implement the logic function $Y = \overline{A + BC + BD}$ or $\overline{Y} = A + BC + BD$, which is identical to that implemented by the NMOS gate in Fig. 7.24, Chapter 7. The NMOS network in Fig. 8.21(a) for $\overline{Y}$ is exactly the same as that of the NMOS gate.

We take a graphical approach to find the PMOS network. In this case, we have been given the NMOS network and will construct the corresponding PMOS network from the graph of the NMOS, which is shown in Fig. 8.21(b). Each node in the NMOS network corresponds to a node in the graph, including node 0 for ground and node 2 for the output. Each NMOS transistor is represented by an arc connecting the source and drain nodes of the transistors and is labeled with the logical input variable.

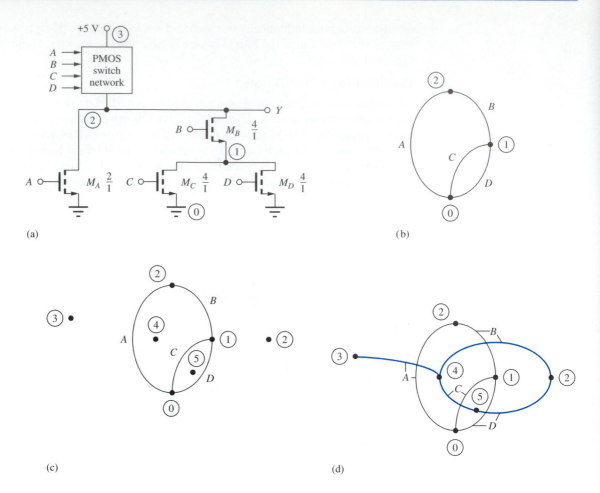

Figure 8.21 Steps in constructing graphs for NMOS and PMOS networks. (a) NMOS network. (b) NMOS graph. (c) NMOS graph with new nodes added. (d) Graph with PMOS arcs added.

The PMOS network is constructed by first placing a new node inside of every enclosed path [nodes 4 and 5 in Fig. 8.21(c)]. In addition, two exterior nodes are needed: one representing the output and one representing V_{DD} [nodes 2 and 3 in Fig. 8.21(c)]. An arc, ultimately corresponding to a PMOS transistor, is then added to the graph for each arc in the NMOS graph. The new arcs cut through the NMOS arcs and connect the pairs of nodes that are separated by the NMOS arcs. A given PMOS arc has the same logic label as the NMOS arc that is intersected. This construction results in a minimum PMOS logic network, which has only one PMOS transistor per logic input. The completed graph is given in Fig. 8.21(d), and the corresponding PMOS network is shown in Fig. 8.22. A transistor is added to the PMOS switching network corresponding to each arc in the PMOS graph.

To complete the design of this CMOS gate, we must choose the W/L ratios of the transistors. In the NMOS switching network, the worst-case path contains two transistors in series, and transistors B, C, and D should each be twice as large as those of the reference inverter. Transistor A should be the same size as the NMOS transistor in the reference inverter because it must be able to discharge the load capacitance by itself. In the PMOS switching network, the worst-case path has three transistors in series, and PMOS transistors A, C, and D should be three times as large as the PMOS device in the reference inverter. The size of transistor B is determined using

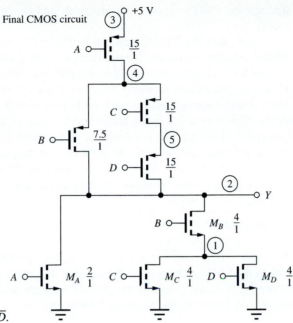

Figure 8.22 CMOS implementation of $Y = \overline{A + BC + BD}$.

the on-resistance method from Sec. 7.6, in which R_{on} represents the on-resistance of a reference transistor with $W/L = 1/1$:

$$\frac{R_{on}}{\left(\dfrac{15}{1}\right)} + \frac{R_{on}}{\left(\dfrac{W}{L}\right)_B} = \frac{R_{on}}{\left(\dfrac{5}{1}\right)} \qquad \text{or} \qquad \left(\frac{W}{L}\right)_B = \frac{7.5}{1}$$

Figure 8.23 gives a second implementation of the same logic network; here nodes 2 and 3 in the PMOS graph have been interchanged. The conducting paths

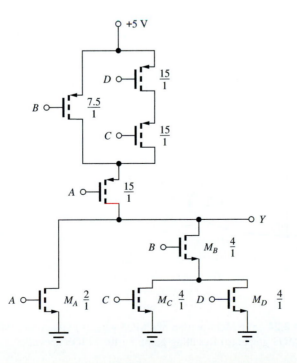

Figure 8.23 Circuit equivalent to gate in Fig. 8.22.

through the PMOS network are identical, and hence the logic function is also the same.

Note that the PMOS network in Fig. 8.22 could also be obtained from the NMOS network by successive application of the series/parallel transformation rule. The NMOS network consists of two parallel branches: transistor A and transistors B, C, and D. The PMOS network, therefore, has two branches in series, one with transistor A and a second representing the branch with B, C, and D. The second branch in the NMOS network is the series combination of transistor B and a third branch consisting of the parallel combination of C and D. In the PMOS network, this corresponds to transistor B being in parallel with the series combination of transistors C and D. This process can be used to create the PMOS network from the NMOS network or vice versa. However, it can run into trouble when bridging branches are present, as in Example 8.2. ◆

EXAMPLE 8.2: As a second example of complex gate design, let us design the CMOS version of the gate in Fig. 7.27, Chapter 7, which is the NMOS implementation of $Y = \overline{AB + CE + ADE + CDB}$. Once again, the NMOS switching network topology in the CMOS gate will be the same as that of the NMOS logic implementation. Figure 8.24 is the graph of the NMOS network and the corresponding graph for the PMOS network; the resulting CMOS gate design is given in Fig. 8.25. In this

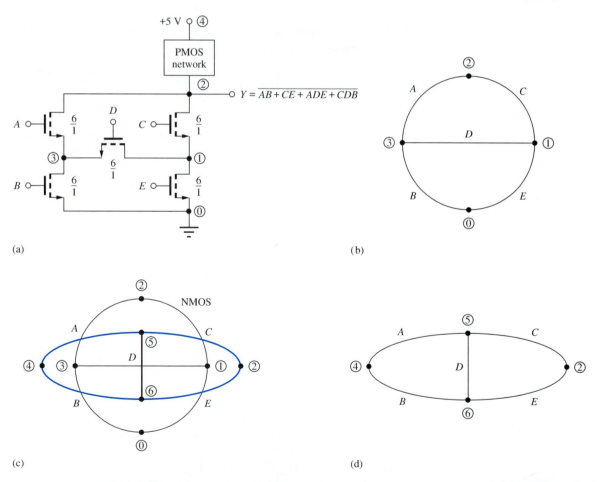

Figure 8.24 (a) NMOS portion of CMOS gate. (b) Graph for NMOS network. (c) Construction of the PMOS graph. (d) Resulting graph for the PMOS network.

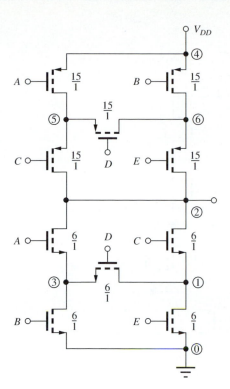

Figure 8.25 CMOS implementation of $Y = \overline{AB + CE + ADE + CDB}$.

unusual case, the NMOS and PMOS network topologies are identical. Transistor D is a bridging transistor in both networks. The worst-case path in each network contains three devices in series, and all the transistors in the CMOS gate are three times the size of the corresponding transistors in the reference inverter. ◆

8.7 MINIMUM SIZE GATE DESIGN AND PERFORMANCE

Because there is one NMOS and one PMOS transistor for each logic input variable in static CMOS, there is an area penalty in CMOS logic with respect to NMOS logic that requires only a single-load device regardless of the number of input variables. In addition, series paths in the PMOS or NMOS switching networks require large devices in order to maintain logic delay. However, in most logic designs, only the critical logic delay paths need to be scaled to maintain maximum performance. If gate delay is not the primary concern, then considerable area savings can be achieved if all transistors are made of minimum geometry. For example, the gate of Fig. 8.22 is shown implemented with minimum size transistors in Fig. 8.26 (p. 324). Here, area is being traded directly for increased logic delay. The total gate area for Fig. 8.26 is $16F^2$, where F is the minimum feature size, whereas that of Fig. 8.22 is $66.5F^2$, an area four times larger.

Let us estimate the worst-case propagation delay of this minimum size logic gate relative to our reference inverter design. In the NMOS switching network, the worst-case path contains two transistors in series, with $W/L = 2/1$, which is equivalent to the R_{on} of a 1/1 device as compared to the reference inverter, in which $W/L = 2/1$. Thus, the high-to-low propagation delay for this gate is twice that of the reference inverter τ_{PHLI}: $\tau_{PHL} = 2\tau_{PHLI}$. The worst-case path in the PMOS switching network contains three minimum geometry transistors in series, yielding an effective W/L ratio of 2/3, versus 5/1 for the reference inverter. Thus the low-to-high propagation delay is related to that of the reference inverter

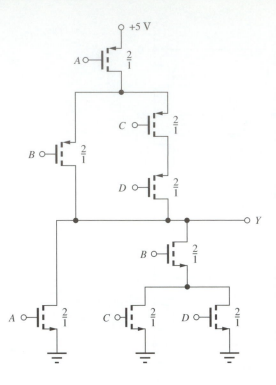

Figure 8.26 Minimum size implementation of a complex CMOS gate.

τ_{PLHI} by:

$$\tau_{PLH} = \frac{\left(\frac{5}{1}\right)}{\left(\frac{2}{3}\right)}\tau_{PLHI} = 7.5\tau_{PLHI}$$

The average propagation delay of the minimum size logic gate is

$$\tau_p = \frac{(\tau_{PLH} + \tau_{PHL})}{2} = \frac{(2\tau_{PLHI} + 7.5\tau_{PLHI})}{2} = \frac{9.5\tau_{PLHI}}{2} = 4.75\tau_{PLHI}$$

remembering that the original inverter was a symmetrical design with

$$\tau_{PHL} = \tau_{PLH}$$

Thus, the propagation delay of the minimum size gate will be 4.75 times slower than the reference inverter design when driving the same load capacitance.

8.8 POWER-DELAY PRODUCT

The **power-delay product (PDP),** defined in Sec. 6.3, is an important figure of merit for comparing various logic technologies:

$$\text{PDP} = P_{\text{av}}\tau_P \tag{8.21}$$

For CMOS, the power consumed when charging and discharging the load capacitance C is usually the dominant source of power dissipation. For this case, $P_{\text{av}} = CV_{DD}^2 f$. The switching frequency $f = (1/T)$ can be related to the rise time t_r, fall time t_f, and the propagation delay τ_P of the CMOS waveform by referring to Fig. 8.27, in which we see that the period T must satisfy

$$T \geq t_r + t_a + t_f + t_b \tag{8.22}$$

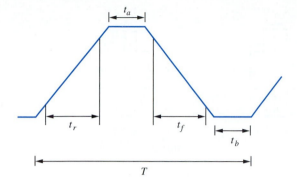

Figure 8.27 CMOS switching waveform at high frequency.

For the highest possible switching frequency, the times t_a and t_b approach 0, and the rise and fall times account for approximately 80 percent of the total transition time. Assuming a symmetrical inverter design with equal rise and fall times and using Eqs. (8.18) and (8.19) permits Eq. (8.22) to be approximated by

$$T \geq \frac{2t_r}{0.8} = \frac{2(2\tau_P)}{0.8} = 5\tau_P \tag{8.23}$$

A lower bound on the power-delay product for CMOS is then given by

$$\text{PDP} \geq \frac{CV_{DD}^2}{5\tau_P}\tau_P = \frac{CV_{DD}^2}{5} \tag{8.24}$$

The importance of using lower power supply voltages is obvious in Eq. (8.21), from which it is clear that the PDP is reduced in proportion to the square of any reduction in power supply. Moving from a power supply voltage of 5 V to one of 3.3 V reduces the power-delay product by a factor of 2.5. The importance of reducing the capacitance is also clear in Eq. (8.24). The lower the effective load capacitance, the smaller the power-delay product.

> **EXERCISE:** (a) What is the power-delay product for the symmetrical reference inverter in Fig. 8.11 operating from $V_{DD} = 5$ V and driving an average load capacitance of 100 fF? (b) Repeat for a 3.3 V supply.
>
> **ANSWERS:** 0.5 pJ; 180 fJ

8.9 THE CMOS TRANSMISSION GATE

The **CMOS transmission gate** in Fig. 8.28 is a circuit useful in both analog and digital design. The circuit consists of NMOS and PMOS transistors, with source and drain terminals connected in parallel and gate terminals driven by opposite phase logic signals indicated by A and $\overline{A}$. The transmission gate is used so often that it is given the special circuit symbol shown in Fig. 8.28(c). For $A = 0$, both transistors will be off, and the transmission gate represents an open circuit.

When the transmission gate is in the conducting state ($A = 1$), the input and output terminals are connected together through the parallel combination of the on-resistances of the two transistors, and the transmission gate represents a *bidirectional* resistive connection between the input and output terminals. The individual on-resistances $R_{\text{on}p}$ and $R_{\text{on}n}$, as well as the equivalent on-resistance R_{EQ}, all vary as a function of the input voltage v_I, as

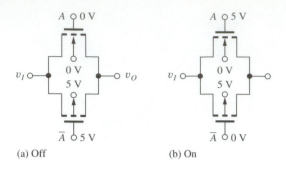

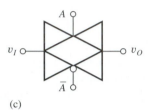

Figure 8.28 CMOS transmission gate in (b) on state and (a) off state. (c) Special circuit symbol for the transmission gate.

shown in Fig. 8.29. The value of R_{EQ} is equal to the parallel combination of R_{onp} and R_{onn}:

$$R_{EQ} = \frac{R_{onp} R_{onn}}{R_{onp} + R_{onn}} \tag{8.25}$$

In Fig. 8.29, the PMOS transistor is cut off ($R_{onp} = \infty$) for $v_I \leq 1.36$ V, and the NMOS transistor is cut off for $v_I \geq 3.64$ V. For the parameters used in Fig. 8.29, the equivalent on-resistance is always less than 20 kΩ, but it can be made smaller by increasing the W/L ratios of the n- and p-channel transistors.

> **EXERCISE:** What W/L ratios are required in the transmission gate in Fig. 8.29 to ensure that $R_{EQ} \leq 1$ kΩ if the W/L ratios of both transistors are the same?
>
> **ANSWER:** $W/L = 20/1$

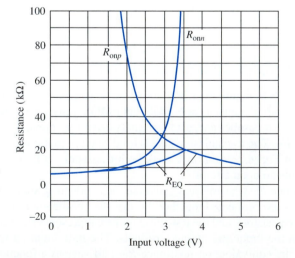

Figure 8.29 On-resistance of a transmission gate, including body effect ($V_{TON} = 0.75$ V, $V_{TOP} = -0.75$ V, $\gamma = 0.5$ V$^{0.5}$, $2\phi_F = 0.6$ V, $K_p = 20\ \mu\text{A/V}^2$, $K_n = 50\ \mu\text{A/V}^2$).

8.10 CMOS LATCHUP

The CMOS structure contains **parasitic bipolar transistors** that have the potential to destroy the CMOS circuitry. These bipolar devices are not normally active, but it is important to realize that they do exist and to understand the potential problem referred to as **latchup**. In the cross section of the CMOS structure in Fig. 8.30, a *pnp* transistor is formed by the source region of the PMOS transistor, the *n*-well, and the *p*-type substrate, and an *npn* transistor is formed by the source region of the NMOS transistor, the *p*-type substrate, and the *n*-well. The physical structure connects the *npn* and *pnp* transistors together in the equivalent circuit shown in Fig. 8.31(a). R_n and R_p model the series resistances existing between the external power supply connections and the internal base terminals of the bipolar transistors.

If the currents in R_n and R_p in the circuit model in Fig. 8.31 are zero, then the base-emitter voltages of both bipolar transistors are zero and both devices are off, and the total supply voltage $(V_{DD} - V_{SS})$ appears across the reverse-biased well-to-substrate junction that forms the collector-base junction of the two parasitic bipolar transistors. However, if a current should develop in the base of either the *npn* or the *pnp* transistor, latchup can be triggered and high currents can destroy the structure. In the latchup state, the current is limited only by the external circuit components.

The problem can be more fully understood by referring to Fig. 8.31(b), in which R_n and R_p have been neglected for the moment. Suppose a base current i_{BN} begins to flow in the base of the *npn* transistor. This base current is amplified by the *npn* current gain β_N and must be supplied from the base of the *pnp* transistor. The *pnp* base current is then amplified further by the current gain β_P of the *pnp* transistor, yielding a collector current

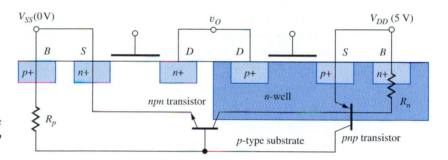

Figure 8.30 CMOS structure with parasitic *npn* and *pnp* transistors identified.

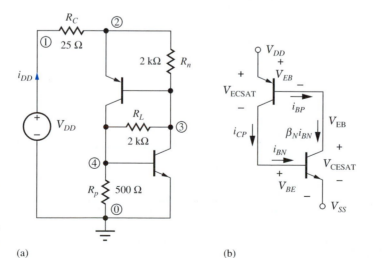

Figure 8.31 (a) Circuit including shunting resistors R_n and R_p for SPICE simulation. See text for description of R_L. (b) Regenerative structure formed by parasitic *npn* and *pnp* transistors.

(a)   (b)

equal to

$$i_{CP} = \beta_P i_{BP} = \beta_P(\beta_N i_{BN}) \tag{8.26}$$

However, the *pnp* collector current i_{CP} is also equal to the *npn* base current i_{BN}. If the product of the two current gains $\beta_P\beta_N$ exceeds unity, then all the currents will grow without bound. This situation is called *latchup*. Once the circuit has entered the latchup state, both transistors saturate, and the voltage across the structure collapses to one diode drop plus one saturation voltage:

$$V = V_{EB} + V_{\text{CESAT}} = V_{BE} + V_{\text{ECSAT}} \tag{8.27}$$

The shunting resistors R_n and R_p shown in Figs. 8.30 and 8.31(b) actually play an important role in determining the latchup conditions in a real CMOS structure. As mentioned before, latchup would not occur in an ideal structure for which $R_n = 0 = R_p$—modern CMOS technology uses special substrates and processing to minimize the values of these two resistors.

The results of SPICE simulation of the behavior of the circuit in Fig. 8.31(a) for representative circuit elements are presented in Fig. 8.32. Resistor R_L is added to the circuit to provide a leakage path across the collector-base junctions to initiate the latchup phenomenon in the simulation. Prior to latchup in Fig. 8.32, all currents are very small, and the voltage $V(2)$ at node 2 is directly proportional to the input voltage V_{DD}. At the point that latchup is triggered, the voltage across the CMOS structure collapses to approximately 0.8 V, and the current increases abruptly to $(V_{DD} - 0.8)/R_C$. The current level is limited only by the external circuit component values. Large currents and power dissipation can rapidly destroy most CMOS structures.

Under normal operating conditions, latchup does not occur. However, if a fault or transient occurs that causes one of the source or drain diffusions to momentarily exceed the power supply voltage levels, then latchup can be triggered. Ionizing radiation or intense optical illumination are two other possible sources of latchup initiation.

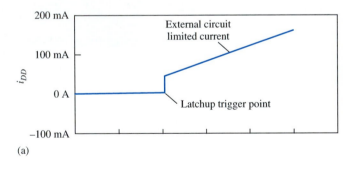

(a)

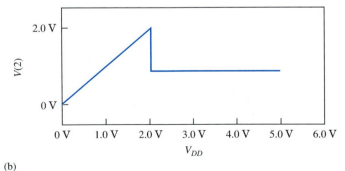

(b)

Figure 8.32 SPICE simulation of latchup in the circuit of Fig. 8.31(a): (a) current from V_{DD}, (b) voltage at node 2.

Note that this section actually introduced another form of modeling. Figure 8.30 is a cross section of a complex three-dimensional distributed structure, whereas Figs. 8.31(a) and 8.31(b) are attempts to represent or model this complex structure using a simplified network of discrete transistors and resistors. Note too that Fig. 8.31 is only a crude model of the real situation, so significant deviations between model predictions and actual measurements should not be surprising. It is easy to forget that circuit schematics generally represent only idealized models for the behavior of highly complex circuits.

SUMMARY

In this chapter, we discussed the design of CMOS logic circuits. The shape of the voltage transfer characteristic (VTC) of the CMOS inverter is almost independent of power supply voltage, and the noise margins of a symmetrical inverter can approach one-half the power supply voltage. The design of the W/L ratios of the transistors in a CMOS gate is determined primarily by the desired propagation delay τ_P, which is related directly to the device parameters K_n' and V_{TN} and the total load capacitance C.

In CMOS logic, each gate contains both an NMOS and a PMOS switching network, and every logical input is connected to at least one NMOS and one PMOS transistor. NAND gates, NOR gates, and complex CMOS logic gates can all be designed using the reference inverter concept, similar to that introduced in Chapter 7. As for NMOS circuitry, complex CMOS gates can directly implement boolean logic equations expressed in a sum-of-products form. In contrast to NMOS logic, which has highly asymmetric rise and fall times, symmetrical inverters in which t_f and t_r are equal can be designed in CMOS.

Body effect has a smaller influence on CMOS design than on NMOS design because the source-bulk voltages of all the transistors in a CMOS gate become zero in the steady state. However, the source-bulk voltages are nonzero during switching transients, and the body effect degrades the rise and fall times and propagation delays of CMOS logic.

Except for very low power applications, CMOS power dissipation is determined by the energy required to charge and discharge the effective load capacitance at the desired switching frequency. A simple expression for the power-delay product of CMOS was developed. For a given capacitive load, the power and delay of the CMOS gate may be scaled up or down by simply modifying the W/L ratios of the NMOS and PMOS transistors.

During switching of the CMOS logic gate, a pulse of current occurs between the positive and negative power supplies. This current causes an additional component of power dissipation in the CMOS gate that can be as much as 20 to 30 percent of the dissipation resulting from charging and discharging the load capacitance. For low-power applications, particularly where battery life is important, leakage current from the reverse-biased wells and drain-substrate junctions can become an important source of power dissipation. The leakage current actually places a lower bound on the power required to operate a CMOS circuit.

An important potential failure mechanism in CMOS is the phenomenon called latchup, which is caused by the existence of parasitic *npn* and *pnp* bipolar transistors in the CMOS structure. A lumped circuit model for latchup was developed and used to simulate the latchup behavior of a CMOS inverter. Special substrates and IC processing are used to minimize the possibility of latchup in modern CMOS technologies.

Finally, a new bidirectional circuit element, the CMOS transmission gate, was introduced. The transmission gate uses a parallel connection of an NMOS and a PMOS transistor. When the transmission gate is on, it provides a low-resistance connection between its input and output terminals over the entire input voltage range.

Key Terms

CMOS transmission gate
CMOS reference inverter
Complementary MOS (CMOS)
Complex logic gate
Fall time

Latchup
NAND gate
NOR gate
On-resistance
Parasitic bipolar transistors

Power-delay product
Propagation delay
Rise time
Symmetrical CMOS inverter

PSPICE Simulation Data *Figures 8.4, 8.7, 8.13 CMOS INVERTER CURRENT

```
VIN 1 0 DC 0
VDD 3 0 DC 5
M1 2 1 0 0 MOSN
M2 2 1 3 3 MOSP
.DC VIN 0 5 .05
.MODEL MOSN NMOS KP=2.5E-5 VTO=1
.MODEL MOSP PMOS KP=1.0E-5 VTO=-1
.PROBE V(1) V(2) I(VDD)
.END
```

*Figure 8.5 CMOS INVERTER TRANSFER CHARACTERISTICS

```
VIN 1 0 DC 0
VDD 3 0 DC 5
M1 2 1 0 0 MOSN W=2U L=1U
M2 2 1 3 3 MOSP W=5U L=1U
.DC VIN 0 5 .05 VDD 5 1 1
.MODEL MOSN NMOS KP=2.5E-5 VTO=1 LAMBDA=.05
.MODEL MOSP PMOS KP=1.0E-5 VTO=-1 LAMBDA=.05
.PROBE V(1) V(2) I(VDD)
.END
```

*Figure 8.6 CMOS INVERTER VTC VS KR

```
VIN 1 0 DC 0
VDD 3 0 DC 5
M1 2 1 0 0 MOSN
M2 2 1 3 3 MOSP
M3 4 1 0 0 MOSN W=5U L=1U
M4 4 1 3 3 MOSP
M5 5 1 0 0 MOSN
M6 5 1 3 3 MOSP W=5U L=1U
.DC VIN 0 5 .01
.MODEL MOSN NMOS KP=2.5E-5 VTO=1 LAMBDA=.05
.MODEL MOSP PMOS KP=2.5E-5 VTO=-1 LAMBDA=.05
.PROBE V(1) V(2) V(3) V(4) V(5) I(VDD)
.END
```

*Figure 8.14 CMOS INVERTER CURRENT

```
VIN 1 0 PULSE(0 5 1NS 3NS 3NS 6NS)
```

```
VDD 3 0 DC 5
M1 2 1 0 0 MOSN W=2U L=1U
M2 2 1 3 3 MOSP W=5U L=1U
.MODEL MOSN NMOS KP=2.5E-5 VTO=1 LAMBDA=.05
.MODEL MOSP PMOS KP=1.0E-5 VTO=-1 LAMBDA=.05
.OPTIONS ABSTOL=1E-12 RELTOL=1E-6 VNTOL=1E-6
.TRAN 0.0025NS 16NS
.PROBE V(1) V(2) I(VDD)
.END
```

*Figure 8.32 CMOS LATCHUP

```
VCC 1 0
R1 1 2 25
RL 3 4 2000
RN 2 3 2000
RP 4 0 500
Q1 3 4 0 NBJT
Q2 4 3 2 PBJT
.DC VCC 0 4 .01
.MODEL NBJT NPN BF=25 BR=.25 IS=1E-15
.MODEL PBJT PNP BF=60 BR=.25 IS=1E-15
.PROBE I(VCC) V(1) V(2) V(3) V(4)
.END
```

Problems

Use $K'_n = 25\,\mu\text{A/V}^2$, $K'_p = 10\,\mu\text{A/V}^2$, $V_{TN} = 1$ V, and $V_{TP} = -1$ V unless otherwise indicated. *For simulation purposes, use the values in Appendix B.*

8.1 CMOS Inverter Technology

8.1. Calculate the values of K'_n and K'_p for NMOS and PMOS transistors with a gate oxide thickness of 160 Å. Assume that $\mu_n = 500$ cm^2/V · s, $\mu_p = 200$ cm^2/V · s, and the relative permittivity of the gate oxide is 3.9. ($\varepsilon_0 = 8.854 \times 10^{-14}$ F/cm)

8.2. Draw a cross section similar to that in Fig. 8.1 for a CMOS process that uses a *p*-well instead of an *n*-well. Show the connections for a CMOS inverter, and draw an annotated version of the corresponding circuit schematic. (*Hint:* Start with an *n*-type substrate and interchange all the *n*- and *p*-type regions.)

*8.3. (a) The *n*-well in a CMOS process covers an area of 1 cm × 0.5 cm, and the junction saturation current density is 500 pA/cm^2. What is the total leakage current of the reverse-biased well? (b) Suppose the drain and source regions of the NMOS and PMOS transistors are 4 μm × 10 μm,

and the saturation current density of the junctions is 100 pA/cm^2. If the chip has 5 million inverters, what is the total leakage current due to the reverse-biased junctions when $v_O = 5$ V? Assume $V_{DD} = 5$ V and $V_{SS} = 0$ V. (c) When $v_O = 0$ V?

*8.4. A particular interconnection between two logic gates in an IC chip runs one-half the distance across a 5-mm-wide die. If the line is 2 μm wide and the oxide ($\varepsilon_r = 3.9$, $\varepsilon_0 = 8.854 \times 10^{-14}$ F/cm) beneath the line is 1 μm thick, what is the total capacitance of this line, assuming that the capacitance is three times that predicted by the parallel plate capacitance formula. Assume that the silicon beneath the oxide represents a conducting ground plane.

8.2 Static Characteristics of the CMOS Inverter

8.5. (a) Calculate the voltage at which $v_O = v_I$ for a CMOS inverter with $K_n = K_p$. (*Hint:* Always remember that $i_{DSN} = i_{DSP}$.) Use $V_{DD} = 5$ V, $V_{TN} = 1$ V, $V_{TP} = -1$ V. (b) Repeat the calculation in (a) for a CMOS inverter with $K_n = 2.5K_p$.

8.6. (a) The CMOS inverter in Fig. P8.6 with $(W/L)_N = 20/1$ and $(W/L)_P = 50/1$ is operating with $V_{DD} = 0$ V and $-V_{SS} = -5.2$ V. What are V_{OL} and V_{OH}? (b) If $(W/L)_N = 10/1$ and $(W/L)_P = 10/1$?

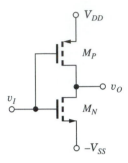

Figure P8.6

 8.7. Simulate the VTC for a CMOS inverter with $K_n = 2.5K_p$. Find the input voltage for which $v_O = v_I$ and compare to the value calculated by hand.

8.8. The CMOS gate in Fig. P8.8 is called pseudo-NMOS. Find V_{OH} and V_{OL} for this gate.

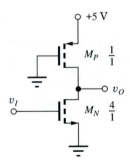

Figure P8.8

**8.9. A CMOS inverter is to be designed to drive a single TTL inverter (which will be studied in a later chapter). When $v_O = V_{OL}$, the CMOS inverter must sink a current of 1.5 mA and maintain $V_{OL} = 0.6$ V. When $v_O = V_{OH}$, the CMOS inverter must source a current of 60 μA and maintain $V_{OH} = 2.4$ V. What are the minimum W/L ratios of the NMOS and PMOS transistors required to meet these specifications? Assume $V_{DD} = 5$ V.

8.10. The outputs of two CMOS inverters are accidentally tied together, as shown in Fig. P8.10. What is the output voltage at the common node if the NMOS and PMOS transistors have W/L ratios of 20/1 and

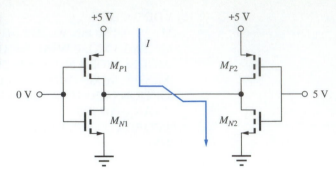

Figure P8.10

40/1, respectively? What is the current in the circuit?

8.11. What are the noise margins of a minimum size CMOS inverter in which both W/L ratios are 2/1 and $V_{DD} = 5$ V and $V_{TN} = -V_{TP} = 1$ V?

8.12. What are the noise margins for a symmetrical CMOS inverter operating with $V_{DD} = 3.3$ V and $V_{TN} = -V_{TP} = 0.75$ V?

8.13. What are the noise margins for a CMOS inverter having $(W/L)_N = (W/L)_P$ operating with $V_{DD} = 3.3$ V and $V_{TN} = -V_{TP} = 0.75$ V?

8.3 Dynamic Behavior of the CMOS Inverter

8.14. What are the rise time, fall time, and propagation delay for a minimum size CMOS inverter in which both W/L ratios are 2/1? Assume a load capacitance of 0.5 pF and $V_{DD} = 3.3$ V.

8.15. What are the sizes of the transistors in the CMOS inverter if it must drive a 1-pF capacitance with an average propagation delay of 3 ns? Design the inverter for equal rise and fall times. Use $V_{DD} = 5$ V, $V_{TN} = 1$ V, $V_{TP} = -1$ V.

8.16. Design a symmetrical CMOS reference inverter to provide a delay of 1 ns when driving a 10-pF load. (a) Assume $V_{DD} = 5$ V. (b) Assume $V_{DD} = 3.3$ V and $V_{TN} = -V_{TP} = 0.70$ V.

*8.17. Use SPICE to determine the characteristics of the CMOS inverter for the design given in Fig. 8.11 if $C = 100$ fF. (a) Simulate the voltage transfer function. (b) Determine t_r, t_f, τ_{PHL}, and τ_{PLH} for this inverter with a square wave input. What must be the total effective load capacitance C based on the propagation delay formula developed in the text?

**8.18. Use SPICE to simulate the behavior of a chain of five CMOS inverters similar to those in Fig. 8.12(b). The input to the first inverter should be a square wave with 0.1-ns rise and fall times and a period of 100 ns. (a) Calculate t_r, t_f, τ_{PHL}, and τ_{PLH} using the input and output waveforms from the first inverter in the chain and compare your results to the formulas developed in the text. (b) Determine t_r, t_f, τ_{PHL}, and τ_{PLH} from the waveforms at the input and output of the fourth inverter in the chain, and compare your results to the formulas developed in the text. (c) Discuss the differences between the results in (a) and (b).

8.4 Static and Dynamic Power Dissipation in CMOS

8.19. A certain packaged IC chip can dissipate 2 W. Suppose we have a CMOS IC design that must fit on one chip and requires 1 million logic gates. What is the average power that can be dissipated by each logic gate on the chip? If the average gate must switch at 5 MHz, what is the maximum capacitive load on a gate for $V_{DD} = 5$ V? For $V_{DD} = 3.3$ V?

8.20. A high-performance CMOS microprocessor design requires 5 million logic gates and will be placed in a package that can dissipate 20 W. (a) What is the average power that can be dissipated by each logic gate on the chip? (b) If a supply voltage of 3.3 V is used, what is the average current that must be supplied to the chip?

8.21. A high-speed CMOS microprocessor has a 64-bit address bus and performs a memory access every 10 ns. Assume that all address bits change during every memory access and that each bus line represents a load of 25 pF. (a) How much power is being dissipated by the circuits that are driving these signals if the power supply is 5 V? (b) Repeat for 3.3 V.

*8.22. (a) A CMOS inverter has $(W/L)_N = 20/1$, $(W/L)_P = 20/1$, and $V_{DD} = 5$ V. What is the peak current in the logic gate and at what input voltage does it occur? (b) Repeat for $V_{DD} = 3.3$ V.

*__8.23.__ (a) A CMOS inverter has $(W/L)_N = 2/1$, $(W/L)_P = 5/1$, and $V_{DD} = 3.3$ V. Assume $V_{TN} = -V_{TP} = 0.7$ V. What is the peak current in the logic gate and at what input voltage does it occur? (b) Repeat for $V_{DD} = 2.0$ V.

8.5 CMOS NOR and NAND Gates

8.24. (a) Draw the circuit schematic for a four-input NOR gate. What are the W/L ratios of the transistors based on the reference inverter design in Fig. 8.17? (b) What should be the W/L ratios if the NOR gate must drive twice the load capacitance with the same delay as the reference inverter?

8.25. (a) Draw the circuit schematic for a four-input NAND gate. What are the W/L ratios of the transistors based on the reference inverter design in Fig. 8.19? (b) What should be the W/L ratios if the NOR gate must drive three times the load capacitance with the same delay as the reference inverter?

**8.26. Use SPICE to determine the characteristics of the two-input CMOS NOR gate given in Fig. 8.16 with a load capacitance of 1 pF. Assume that $\gamma = 0$ for all transistors. (a) Simulate the voltage transfer function by varying the voltage at input A with the voltage at input B fixed at 5 V. (b) Repeat the simulation in (a) but now vary the voltage at input B with the voltage at input A fixed at 5 V. Plot the results from (a) and (b) and note any differences. (c) Determine t_r, t_f, τ_{PHL}, and τ_{PLH} for this inverter with a square wave input at input A with the voltage at input B fixed at 5 V. (d) Determine t_r, t_f, τ_{PHL}, and τ_{PLH} for this inverter with a square wave input at input B with the voltage at input A fixed at 5 V. (e) Compare the results from (c) and (d). (f) Determine t_r, t_f, τ_{PHL}, and τ_{PLH} for this inverter with a single square wave input applied to both inputs A and B. Compare the results to those in (c) and (d).

**8.27. Repeat (a) and (b), Prob. 8.26, using the nonzero values for the parameter γ from the device parameter tables.

**8.28. Use SPICE to determine the characteristics of the two-input CMOS NAND gate given in Fig. 8.19 with a load capacitance of 1 pF. Assume that $\gamma = 0$ for all transistors. (a) Simulate the voltage transfer function by varying the voltage at input A with the voltage at input B fixed at 5 V. (b) Repeat the simulation in (a) but now vary the voltage at input B with the voltage at input A fixed at 5 V. Plot the results from (a) and (b) and note any differences. (c) Determine t_r, t_f, τ_{PHL}, and τ_{PLH} for this inverter with a square wave input at input A with the voltage at input B fixed at 5 V. (d) Determine t_r, t_f, τ_{PHL}, and τ_{PLH} for this inverter with a square wave input at input B with the voltage at input A fixed at 5 V. (e) Compare the results from (c) and (d). (f) Determine t_r, t_f, τ_{PHL}, and τ_{PLH} for this inverter with a single square wave input applied to both inputs A and B. Compare the results to those in (c) and (d).

**8.29. Repeat (a) and (b), Prob. 8.28, using the nonzero values for the parameter γ from the device parameter tables.

8.6 Complex Gates in CMOS

8.30. What are the worst case rise and fall times and average propagation delays of the CMOS gate in Fig. 8.23 for a load capacitance of 1.25 pF?

**8.31. (a) How many transistors are needed to implement the CMOS gate in Fig. 8.26 using depletion-mode NMOS? (b) Compare the total gate area of the CMOS and NMOS designs if they are both designed for a 10-ns average propagation delay for a load capacitance of 1 pF.

8.32. (a) What is the logic function implemented by the gate in Fig. P8.32? (b) Design the PMOS transistor network. Select the device sizes for both the NMOS and PMOS transistors to give a delay similar to that of the CMOS reference inverter.

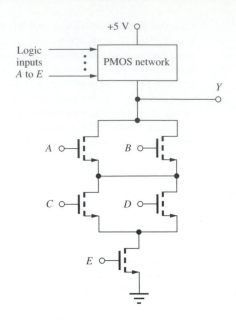

Figure P8.33

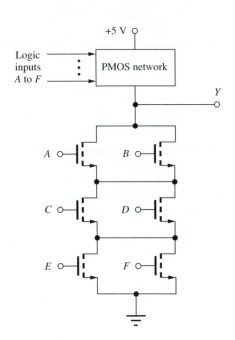

Figure P8.32

8.33. (a) What is the logic function implemented by the gate in Fig. P8.33? (b) Design the PMOS transistor network. Select the device sizes for both the NMOS and PMOS transistors to give a delay of approximately one-third the delay of the CMOS reference inverter.

8.34. (a) What is the logic function implemented by the gate in Fig. P8.34? (b) Design the PMOS transistor network. Select the device sizes for both the NMOS and PMOS transistors to give a delay of approximately one-half the delay of the CMOS reference inverter.

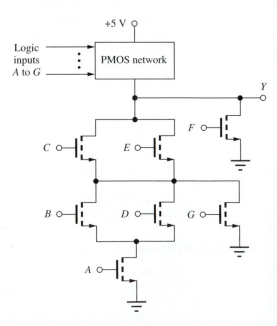

Figure P8.34

8.35. (a) What is the logic function implemented by the gate in Fig. P8.35? (b) Design the NMOS transistor network. Select the device sizes for both the NMOS and PMOS transistors to give a delay similar to that of the CMOS reference inverter.

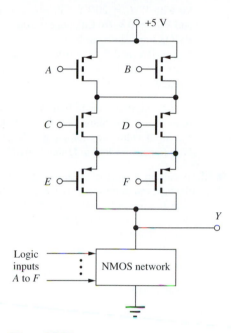

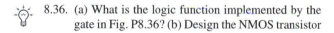

Figure P8.35

8.36. (a) What is the logic function implemented by the gate in Fig. P8.36? (b) Design the NMOS transistor

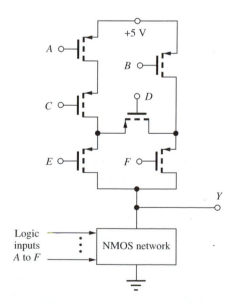

Figure P8.36

network. Select the device sizes for both the NMOS and PMOS transistors to give a delay of approximately one-third the delay of the CMOS reference inverter.

8.37. Design a CMOS logic gate that implements the logic function $Y = \overline{ABC + DE}$, based on the CMOS reference inverter. Select the transistor sizes to give the same delay as that of the reference inverter if the load capacitance is the same as that of the reference inverter.

8.38. Design a CMOS logic gate that implements the logic function $Y = \overline{A(B + C(D + E))}$, based on the CMOS reference inverter. Select the transistor sizes to give the same delay as that of the reference inverter if the load capacitance is the same as that of the reference inverter.

8.39. Design a CMOS logic gate that implements the logic function $Y = \overline{A(BC + DE)}$ and is twice as fast as the CMOS reference inverter when loaded by a capacitance of $2C$.

8.40. Design a CMOS logic gate that implements the logic function $Y = \overline{A(B + CD) + E}$ and has the same logic delay as the CMOS reference inverter when driving a capacitance of $4C$.

8.7 Minimum Size Gate Design and Performance

8.41. The three-input NOR gate in Fig. 8.17 is implemented with transistors all having $W/L = 2/1$. What is the propagation delay for this gate for a load capacitance $C = 400$ fF? Assume $V_{DD} = 5$ V. What would be the delay of the reference inverter for $C = 400$ fF?

8.42. The five-input NAND gate in Fig. 8.20 is implemented with transistors all having $W/L = 2/1$. What is the propagation delay for this gate for a load capacitance $C = 180$ fF? Assume $V_{DD} = 5$ V. What would be the delay of the reference inverter for $C = 180$ fF?

8.43. What are the worst-case values of τ_{PHL} and τ_{PLH} for the gate in Fig. 8.25 when it is implemented using only 2/1 transistors and drives a load capacitance of 1 pF? Assume $V_{DD} = 5$ V.

8.44. What is the worst-case value of τ_{PHL} for the gate in Fig. P8.32 when it is implemented using only 2/1 transistors and drives a load capacitance of 1 pF? Assume $V_{DD} = 5$ V.

8.45. (a) Use a transient simulation in SPICE to find the average propagation delay of a cascade connection of 10 minimum size inverters ($W/L = 2/1$) in series. Assume each has a capacitive load C of 200 fF and $V_{DD} = 5$ V. (b) Repeat for a cascade of 9 symmetrical reference inverters with the same design as in Fig. 8.11, and compare the average propagation delays.

8.8 Power-Delay Product

8.46. Plot the power-delay characteristic for the CMOS inverter family based on an inverter design in which $(W/L)_N = (W/L)_P$. Assume the load capacitance $C = 0.2$ pF. Use $V_{DD} = 5$ V and vary the power by changing the W/L ratios.

**8.47. Ideal constant-electric-field scaling of a MOS technology reduces all the dimensions and voltages by the same factor α. Assume that the capacitor C in Eq. (8.24) is proportional to the total gate capacitance of the MOS transistor: $C = C''_{ox} W L$, and show that constant-field scaling results in a reduction of the PDP by a factor of α^3.

**8.48. For many years, MOS technology was scaled by reducing all the dimensions by the same factor α, but keeping the voltages constant. Assume that the capacitor C in Eq. (8.24) is proportional to the total gate capacitance of the MOS transistor: $C = C''_{ox} W L$, and show that this geometry scaling results in a reduction of the PDP by a factor of α.

**8.49. Use SPICE to simulate the behavior of a chain of five CMOS inverters with the same design as in Fig. 8.11 with $C = 0.25$ pF. The input to the first inverter should be a square wave with 0.1-ns rise and fall times and a period of 30 ns. (a) Calculate t_r, t_f, τ_{PHL}, and τ_{PLH} using the input and output waveforms from the first inverter in the chain, and compare your results to the formulas developed in the text. (b) Determine t_r, t_f, τ_{PHL}, and τ_{PLH} from the waveforms at the input and output of the fourth inverter in the chain, and compare your results to the formulas developed in the text. (c) Discuss the differences between the results in (a) and (b).

**8.50. Use SPICE to simulate the behavior of a chain of five CMOS inverters with the same design as in Fig. 8.11 with $C = 1$ pF. The input to the first inverter should be a square wave with 0.1-ns rise and fall times and a period of 40 ns. (a) Determine t_r, t_f, τ_{PHL}, and τ_{PLH} from the waveforms at the input and output of the fourth inverter in the chain, and compare your results to the formulas developed in the text. (b) Repeat the simulation for

$(W/L)_P = (W/L)_N = 2/1$, and compare the results to those obtained in (a).

8.9 The CMOS Transmission Gate

8.51. (a) Calculate the on-resistance of an NMOS transistor with $W/L = 20/1$ for $V_{GS} = 5$ V, $V_{SB} = 0$ V, and $V_{DS} = 0$ V. (b) Calculate the on-resistance of a PMOS transistor with $W/L = 20/1$ for $V_{SG} = 5$ V, $V_{SB} = 0$ V, and $V_{SD} = 0$ V. (c) What do we mean when we say that a transistor is "on" even though I_{DS} and $V_{DS} = 0$?

8.52. A transmission gate is built with transistors that have $K_p = K_n$. Show that R_{EQ} is independent of the input voltage v_I for input voltages for which both transistors are on. Ignore body effect.

*8.53. A certain analog multiplexer application requires the equivalent on-resistance R_{EQ} of a transmission gate to always be less than 250 Ω. What are the minimum values of W/L for the NMOS and PMOS transistors if $V_{TON} = 0.75$ V, $V_{TOP} = -0.75$ V, $\gamma = 0.5\sqrt{V}$, $2\phi_F = 0.6$ V, $K'_p = 10\mu A/V^2$, and $K'_n = 25\ \mu A/V^2$?

8.10 CMOS Latchup

8.54. Simulate CMOS latchup using the circuit in Fig. 8.31(a) and plot graphs of the voltages at nodes 2, 3, and 4 as well as the current supplied by V_{DD}. Discuss the behavior of the voltages and identify important voltage levels, current levels, and slopes on the graphs.

Additional Problems

8.55. (a) Verify Eq. 8.9. (b) Verify Eq. (8.13).

**8.56. (a) Calculate the sensitivity $S_{K_n}^{\tau_p} = (K_n/\tau_p)(d\tau_p/dK_n)$ of the propagation delay τ_p in Eq. (8.18) to changes in K_n. If the IC processing causes K_n to be 25 percent below its nominal value, what will be the percentage change in τ_p? (b) Calculate the sensitivity $S_{V_{TN}}^{\tau_p} = (V_{TN}/\tau_p)(d\tau_p/dV_{TN})$ of the propagation delay τ_p in Eq. (8.18) to changes in V_{TN}. If the IC processing causes V_{TN} to change from a nominal value of 0.75 V to 0.85 V, what will be the percentage change in τ_p?

8.57 Calculate logic delay versus input signal rise time for a minimum size inverter with a load capacitance of 1 pF for $0.1\ ns \le t_r \le 5$ ns.

C H A P T E R   9

MOS Memory and Advanced Logic Circuits

337

Thus far, our study of logic circuits has concentrated on understanding the design of basic inverters and combinational logic circuits. In addition to logic, however, digital systems generally require data storage capability in the form of high-speed registers, high-density **random-access memory (RAM),** and **read-only memory (ROM).** Many alternative logic circuit techniques exist in addition to those already discussed, and this chapter uses memory subcircuits as a vehicle to introduce several advanced logic circuit design concepts.

In digital systems, the term RAM is used to refer to memory with both read and write capability. This is the type of memory used when information needs to be changed with great frequency. The information in any given storage location in RAM can be directly read or altered just as quickly as the information at any other location.

In the mid-1960s, the first random-access memory chip using MOS technology was discussed at the International Solid-State Circuits Conference (ISSCC) [1], and in 1974, the first commercial 1024-bit (1-Kb) memory was introduced [2]. As this book was being written, an experimental 1-gigabit (Gb) chip was described at the ISSCC, and the technology for future 1-Gb memories has been discussed at several recent International Electron Devices Meetings (IEDM). Thus, within just 30 years from the introduction of the first commercial RAM chips, we have a chip with more than 1 million times the storage capacity of the original RAMs.

Early memory designs were **static RAM,** or **SRAM,** circuits in which the information remains stored in memory as long as the power supply voltage is maintained. The SRAM cell requires the equivalent of six transistors per memory bit and features nondestructive readout of its stored information.

In 1970, an elegant circuit called the **dynamic RAM,** or **DRAM,** circuit, which requires only one transistor per bit was invented [3]. In a DRAM, information is temporarily stored as a charge on a capacitor, and the data must be periodically refreshed in order to prevent information loss. The process of reading the data out of most DRAMs destroys the information, and the data must be put back into memory as part of the read operation.

For many years, high-density memory has served as the IC industry's vehicle for driving technology to ever smaller dimensions. The 1-Gb chip just mentioned is a DRAM design that contains more than 1 billion MOSFETs and 1 billion capacitors in the memory array as well as a tremendous number of transistors in the peripheral circuits. Thus, future 1-Gb DRAMs will contain in excess of 2 billion electronic components on a single integrated circuit die!

Because the SRAM cell takes up considerably more area that the DRAM cell, an SRAM memory chip typically has only one-fourth the number of bits as a DRAM memory of the same technology generation. For example, using the same IC technology, it would be possible to fabricate a 64-Mb DRAM and a 16-Mb SRAM. The majority of RAM chips with densities below 4 Mb have provided a single output bit, but because the capacity of recent memory chips has become so large, the external interface to many memory chips is now designed to be four, eight, or more bits wide.

Read-only memories or ROMs, also sometimes called **read-only storage,** or **ROS,** represent another important class of memory. In these memories, data is permanently stored within the physical structure of the array. However, ROM technology can also be used to perform logic using the programmable logic array, or PLA, structure.

Basic combinational logic circuits were introduced in previous chapters. In this chapter, several alternative techniques are explored, including pass-transistor logic and dynamic logic circuitry, and special techniques for driving large capacitive loads are described. Digital systems also require high-speed storage in the form of individual flip-flops and registers, and this chapter introduces the basic circuits used to realize RS and D flip-flops.

9.1 RANDOM-ACCESS MEMORY (RAM)

Random-access memory (RAM) provides the high-speed temporary storage used in digital computers, and most digital systems seem to have an insatiable demand for it. Today's high-function word processing and desktop publishing software often require many megabytes of RAM for operation, and the operating systems require several more megabytes. Thus, it is common even for a personal computer to have 10 to 20 megabytes (MB) (1 byte = 8 bits) or more of RAM. In contrast, high-end computer mainframes may contain gigabytes of RAM.

It is mind-boggling to realize that a single 1-Gb memory chip contains 128 MB of storage—the equivalent of many hard disks—and that the chips contain more than 2 billion electronic components that must all be working! Only the very regular repetitive structure of the memory array permits the design and realization of such complex IC chips. This section explores the basic structure of an IC memory; subsequent sections look at individual memory cells and subcircuits in more detail.

A 256-Mb Memory Chip

Figure 9.1(a) is a microphotograph of a 256-Mb memory chip [4] and its block structure. Internally, the 256-Mb array is divided into eight 32-Mb subarrays. To select a group of bits within the large array, the memory address is decoded by **column** and **row address decoders.** In Fig. 9.1, the column decoders occupy the center of the die and separate it into upper and lower halves. Row decoders and **wordline drivers** bisect each 32-Mb subarray. Each 32-Mb subarray is further subdivided into 16 2-Mb sections, each of which contains 16 blocks of 128 kilobits (Kb). Thus, the 128-Kb array represents the basic building block of this 256-Mb memory.

Figure 9.2 (p. 341) is a block diagram of a basic memory array that could correspond to one of the 128-Kb (2^{17}-bit) subarrays in Fig. 9.1. The array contains 2^{M+N} storage locations, and the address is split into M bits of row address plus N bits of column address. Each $(M + N)$-bit address corresponds to a single storage location or memory cell within the array. For the 128-Kb memory segment in Fig. 9.1, $M = 10$ and $N = 7$. When a given bit is addressed, information can be written into the storage cell or the contents of the cell may be read out. Each 128-Kb array has a set of **sense amplifiers** to read and write the information of the selected memory cells.

When a row is selected, the contents of a 128-bit-wide word (2^7) are actually accessed in parallel. These horizontal rows are normally referred to as **wordlines (WL).** The lines running in the vertical direction contain the cell data and are called **bitlines (BL).** One or two bitlines may run through each cell, and bitlines can be shared between adjacent cells. The 7-bit column address is used to select the individual bit or group of bits that is actually transferred to the output during a **read operation,** or modified during a **write operation.**

In addition to the storage array, memory chips require several other types of peripheral circuits. Address decoder circuits are obviously required to select the desired row and column. In addition, the wordlines present heavy capacitive loads to the address decoders, and special wordline driver circuits are needed to drive these lines. Also, during a read operation the signal coming from the cell can be quite small, and sense amplifiers are required to detect the state of the memory cell and restore the signal to a full logic level for use in

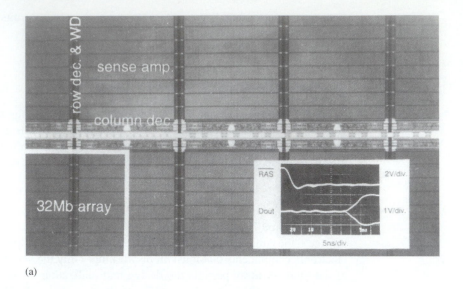

(a)

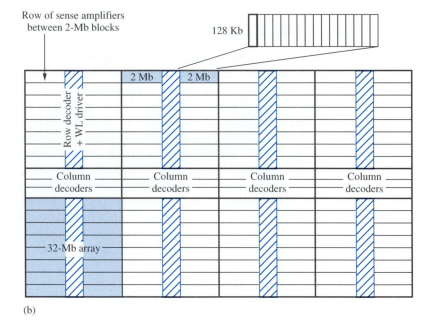

(b)

Figure 9.1 256-Mb RAM chip: (a) RAM micrograph and measured output waveforms, (b) functional identification of areas of the chip. (Micrograph from Mikio Asakura et al., *1994 ISSCC Digest of Technical Papers,* February 1994, vol. 37, © 1994 IEEE.)

the external interface. The next several sections explore the individual circuits used to implement static and dynamic memory cells as well as sense amplifier and address decoder circuits. Both static and dynamic decoder circuits are discussed.

EXERCISE: (a) How many 128-Kb segments form the 256-Mb memory? (b) A 1-Gb memory made by doubling the dimensions of the main arrays in Fig. 9.1 (32 Mb → 128 Mb, 2 Mb → 8 Mb, 128 Kb → 512 Kb). How many 512 Kb segments are required in the 1-Gb memory?

ANSWERS: 2048; 2048

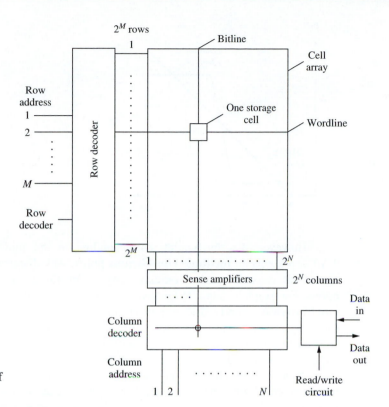

Figure 9.2 Block diagram of a basic memory array.

9.2 STATIC MEMORY CELLS

The basic electronic storage element consists of two inverters in series, with the output of the second inverter connected back to the input of the first, as shown in Fig. 9.3. If the input of the first inverter is a 0, as in Fig. 9.3(a), then its output will be a 1 and the output of the second inverter will be a 0. In Fig. 9.3(b), an alternate representation of the circuit in Fig. 9.3(a), the input of the first inverter is a 1, its output is a 0, and the output of the second inverter is a 1. For both cases, the output of the second inverter may be connected back to the input of the first inverter to form a logically stable configuration. These circuits have two stable states and are termed **bistable circuits.** The pair of **cross-coupled inverters** is also often called a **latch.**

The behavior of the circuit can be understood more completely by looking at the voltage transfer characteristic (VTC) in Fig. 9.4 for two cascaded inverters. A line with unity slope has been drawn on the figure, indicating three possible operating points with $v_O = v_I$. The points with $v_O = V_{OL}$ and $v_O = V_{OH}$ are the two stable Q-points noted above and represent the two data states of the binary latch.

Figure 9.3 Two inverters forming a static storage element or latch.

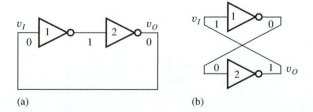

(a)   (b)

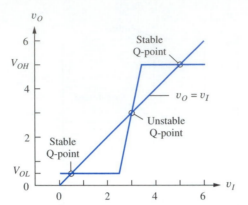

Figure 9.4 VTC for two inverters in series, indicating the three possible operating points for a latch with $v_O = v_I$.

However, the third point, corresponding to the midpoint of the VTC ($v_O \approx$ 3 V), represents an **unstable equilibrium point.** Any disturbance to the voltages in the circuit will cause the latch to quickly make a transition to one of its two stable operating points. For example, suppose the inverter is operating with $v_I = v_O = 3$ V, and then the input increases slightly. The output will immediately move toward V_{OH} due to the positive feedback or regenerative nature of the circuit. A small negative change from the 3-V equilibrium point would drive the output immediately to V_{OL}. Using nonlinear analysis techniques beyond the scope of this text, it can actually be shown that any imbalance in the voltages between the two output nodes of the latch will be reinforced; the node at the higher potential will become a logic 1, and the node at the lower potential will become a logic 0.

The two stable points in the VTC are obviously useful for storing binary data. However, in Sec. 9.4 we will see that the latch can be forced to operate at the unstable equilibrium point and find that this third point is highly useful in designing sense amplifiers.

Memory Cell Isolation and Access—The 6-T Cell

The cross-coupled inverter pair is the basic storage element needed in Fig. 9.2 to build a static memory. In Fig. 9.5, two additional transistors are added to the latch to isolate it from other memory cells and to provide a path for information to be written to and read from the memory cell. In NMOS or CMOS technology, each inverter requires two transistors, so the memory circuit in Fig. 9.5 is usually referred to as the **six-transistor (6-T) SRAM cell.** Note that the 6-T cell provides both true and complemented data outputs, D and $\overline{D}$.

Figure 9.6 presents NMOS and CMOS realizations of the static memory cell. For the NMOS cells in Figs. 9.6(a) and (b), one inverter will be on in the conducting state and one

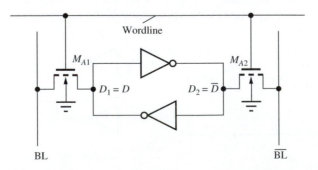

Figure 9.5 Basic memory cell formed from the two-inverter latch and two access transistors M_{A1} and M_{A2}.

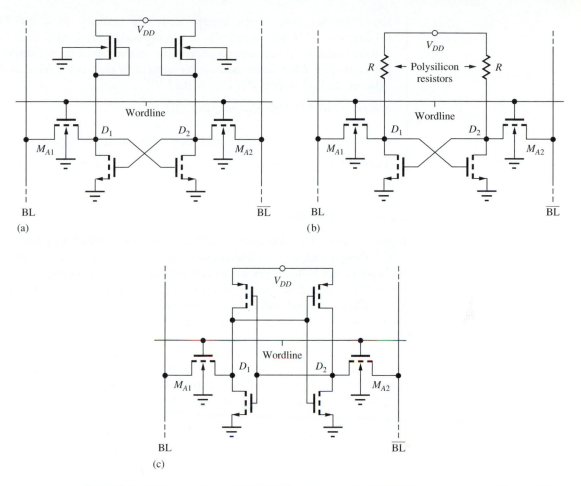

Figure 9.6 (a) Six-transistor (6-T) NMOS memory cell. (b) NMOS memory cell with polysilicon load resistors. (c) Six-transistor CMOS memory cell.

inverter will be off. For high-density memories, the load elements in the NMOS cell must limit the current to a very low level. The load devices normally supply a small current designed only to exceed the leakage currents of the cell. Recent static cell designs have actually replaced the NMOS load devices in Fig. 9.6(a) with undoped polysilicon resistors having very high resistances ($\approx$ TΩ), as shown in Fig. 9.6(b).

Figure 9.6(c) is a 6-T CMOS cell implementation. The advantage of CMOS inverters is that only very small leakage currents exist in the cell because a static current path does not exist through either inverter. Because of higher mobility and lower on-resistance for a given W/L ratio, the access devices M_{A1} and M_{A2} are shown as NMOS transistors in all the circuits in Fig. 9.6. However, PMOS transistors can successfully be used in some designs.

The 6-T cell presents an interesting set of conflicting design requirements. During the read operation, the state of the memory cell must be determined through the access transistors without upsetting the data in the cell. However, during a write operation, the data in the cell must be forced to the desired state using the same access devices. The design of these cells is explored in more detail in the next two subsections. In the following discussion, a 0 in the memory cell will correspond to a low level (0 V) on the left-hand data storage node (D_1) and a high level (V_{DD}) on the right-hand data node (D_2); a 1 in the memory cell will correspond to a high level (V_{DD}) at D_1 and a low level (0 V) at D_2.

EXERCISES: (a) How many storage cells are actually in a 256-Mb memory? (b) Suppose a 256-Mb memory is to use the resistively loaded cells in Fig. 9.6(b), and the total static power consumption of the memory must be $\leq$ 50 mW with a 3.3-V power supply. What is the permissible current in each cell? What is the minimum value of the load resistor R if $V_{OL} = 0.25$ V?

ANSWERS: 268,435,456; 56.4 pA; 48.8 GΩ

EXERCISE: Draw a PMOS version of the storage cell in Fig. 9.6(b).

ANSWER: Simply reverse the direction of the source and substrate arrows in all the devices and change V_{DD} to $-V_{SS}$.

Read Operation

Figure 9.7 is a 6-T CMOS memory cell in the 0 state, in which V_{DD} has been chosen to be 3 V. Although a number of different strategies can be used to read the state of the cell, we will assume that both bitlines are initially precharged to approximately one-half V_{DD} by the sense amplifier circuitry, while M_{A1} and M_{A2} are turned off by holding the wordline WL at 0 V. The exact precharge level is determined by the sense amplifiers and is discussed in the next section. Precharge levels equal to V_{DD}, $\frac{1}{2}V_{DD}$, and $\frac{2}{3}V_{DD}$ have all been proposed for memory design.

Once the bitline voltages have been precharged to the desired level, cell data can be accessed through transistors M_{A1} and M_{A2} by raising the wordline voltage to a high logic level (3 V). The conditions immediately following initiation of such a read operation are shown in Fig. 9.8, in which the substrate terminals of the access transistors have been omitted for clarity.[1] M_{P1} and M_{N2} are off. M_{A1} will be operating in the linear region (for typical values of V_{TN}) because $V_{GS} = 3$ V and $V_{DS} = 1.5$ V, and the current i_1 enters the cell from the bitline into the cell. M_{A2} is saturated because both V_{GS} and V_{DS} are equal to 1.5 V, and the current i_2 exits the cell into $\overline{\text{BL}}$.

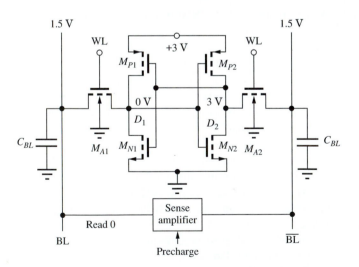

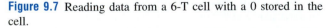

Figure 9.7 Reading data from a 6-T cell with a 0 stored in the cell.

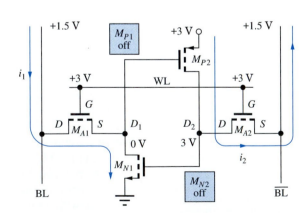

Figure 9.8 Conditions immediately following activation of the wordline.

[1] Note that the capacitances at nodes D_1 and D_2 prevent the voltages at these nodes from changing at $t = 0^+$.

As current increases through M_{A1} and M_{A2}, the voltage on data node D_1 tends to rise, and the voltage at D_2 tends to fall. For the data stored in the cell not to be disturbed, a conservative design ensures that the voltage at D_1 remains below the threshold voltage of M_{N2}, and that the voltage at D_2 remains high enough ($> 3 - |V_{-TP}|$) to maintain M_{P1} off. Currents i_1 and i_2 in the two bitlines cause the sense amplifier to rapidly assume the same state as the data stored in the cell, and the BL and $\overline{\text{BL}}$ voltages become 0 V and 3 V, respectively.

The voltages in the circuit after the sense amplifier reaches steady-state are shown in Fig. 9.9. The bitline voltages match the original cell voltages, and the bistable latch in the storage cell has restored the cell voltages to the original full logic levels. In the final steady-state condition, both M_{A1} and M_{A2} will be on in the linear region but not conducting current because $V_{DS} = 0$.

It is important to note that in Fig. 9.8 the source terminal of M_{A1} is connected to the cell, whereas the source of M_{A2} is connected to the bitline. This is an example of the bidirectional nature of the FET. Remember that the source and drain of the FET are always determined by the relative polarities of the voltages in the circuit.

Rather than try to analyze the details of this complex circuit by hand, we present in Fig. 9.10 the waveforms resulting from a SPICE simulation of the circuit in Figs. 9.7 to 9.9. The simulation assumes a total capacitance on each bitline of 500 fF, and the W/L ratios of all transistors in the memory cell are 1/1. In Fig. 9.10, the bitlines

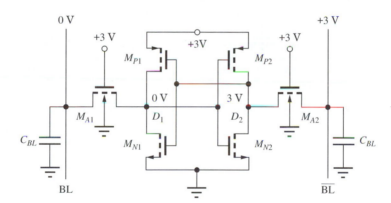

Figure 9.9 Final state after the sense amplifier has reached steady-state.

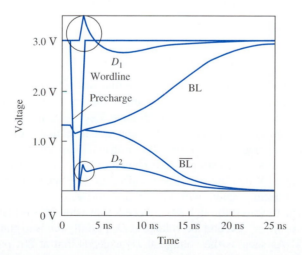

Figure 9.10 SPICE memory cell waveforms during a read operation.

can be observed to be precharged to slightly less than one-half V_{DD}, approximately 1.3 V. At $t = 1$ ns, the precharge signal is turned off, and at $t = 2$ ns the wordline begins its transition from 0 V to 3 V. As the two access transistors turn on, BL and $\overline{\text{BL}}$ begin to diverge as the sense amplifier responds and reinforces the data stored in the cell. As the bitlines increase further, the cell voltages at D_1 and D_2 return to the full 3 V and 0 V levels. The state of the memory cell is disturbed but not destroyed during the read operation. Thus the 6-T cell provides data storage with nondestructive readout.

Note that the time delay from the midpoint of the wordline transition to the point when the bitlines reach full logic levels is approximately 20 ns. Also, the two rapid positive transients at D_1 and D_2 (in the circles) result from direct coupling of the rapid transition of the wordline signal through the MOSFET gate capacitances to the internal nodes of the latch. This capacitive coupling of the wordline signal causes the initial transients both to be in the same direction.

Reading a 1 stored in the memory cell in Fig. 9.11 simply reverses the conditions in Figs. 9.7 to 9.10. The two cell currents i_1 and i_2 reverse directions, and the sense amplifier flips to the opposite state. Note that the source and drain terminals and direction of current in the two access transistors have all reversed.

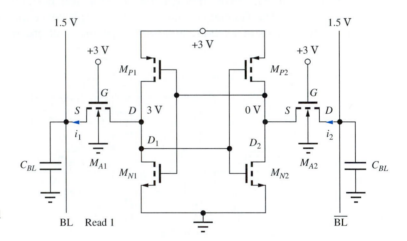

Figure 9.11 Reading data from 6-T cell with a 1 stored in the cell.

EXERCISE: Calculate $i_1(0+)$ and $i_2(0+)$ in Fig. 9.8 if all devices have $W/L = 2/1$. Assume $K'_n = 25$ μA/V^2, $V_{TO} = 0.7$ V, $\gamma = 0.5$ $\sqrt{\text{V}}$, and $2\phi_F = 0.6$ V.

ANSWERS: 116 μA, 5.29 μA

Writing Data into the 6-T Cell

For a write operation, the bitlines are initialized with the data that is to be written into the cell. In Fig. 9.12, a zero is being written into a cell that already contains a zero. It can be seen that the access transistors both have $V_{DS} = 0$. The currents i_1 and i_2 are zero, and virtually nothing happens, except for the transients that occur due to internode coupling of the wordline signal through the MOS transistor capacitances (see Prob. 9.7).

The more interesting case is shown in Fig. 9.13, in which the state of the cell must be changed. When the wordline is raised to 3 V, access transistor M_{A1} conducts current in the saturation region, with $V_{GS} = 3$ V and $V_{DS} = 3$ V, and the voltage at D_1 tends to discharge toward 0 through M_{A1}. Access transistor M_{A2} is also in saturation, with $V_{GS} = 3$ V and $V_{DS} = 3$ V, and the voltage at D_2 initially tends to charge toward a voltage of $(3 - V_{TN})$ V. As soon as the voltage at D_2 exceeds that at D_1, positive feedback takes over,

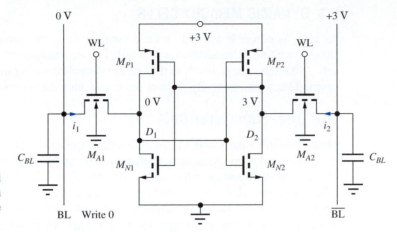

Figure 9.12 A memory cell set up for a write 0 operation with a 0 already stored in the cell.

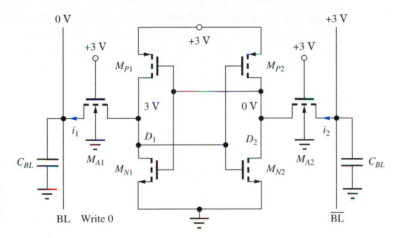

Figure 9.13 A memory cell set up for a write 0 operation with a 1 previously stored in the cell.

and the cell rapidly completes the transition to the new desired state, with $D_1 = 0$ V and $D_2 = 3$ V.

Figure 9.14 shows waveforms from a SPICE simulation of this write operation. As the wordline transition begins at $t = 0.5$ ns, the fixed levels on the bitlines are transferred to nodes D_1 and D_2 through the two access transistors. Minimum area transistors are normally used throughout the memory cell array, and the capacitances on the memory cell nodes are quite small. This small nodal capacitance is the reason why the voltages at D_1 and D_2 reach the desired state in approximately 10 ns in this simulation.

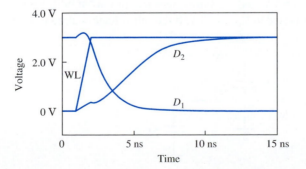

Figure 9.14 SPICE bitline and data node waveforms as a 0 is written into the 6-T cell.

9.3 DYNAMIC MEMORY CELLS

As long as power is applied to static memory cells, the information stored in the cells should be retained. In addition, static cells feature nondestructive readout of data from the cell. Although voltage levels in the cell are disturbed during the read operation, the cross-coupled latch automatically restores the levels once the access transistors are turned off.

The One-Transistor Cell

Much smaller memory cells can be built if the requirement for static data storage is relaxed. In 1970, the elegant dynamic random-access memory (DRAM) cell, which requires only one transistor and one capacitor, was invented by Robert H. Dennard [3] at the IBM Thomas J. Watson Research Center. At that time, Dennard was probably one of the few people who really believed that the **one-transistor (1-T) cell** could really be made to work. Today, it is the storage cell used in all high-density DRAMs. We explore the operation of the cell in this section.

In the 1-T cell in Fig. 9.15, data is stored as the presence or absence of charge on **cell capacitor** C_C. Because leakage currents exist in the drain-bulk and source-bulk junctions of the transistor and in the transistor channel, the information stored on C_C is eventually corrupted. To prevent this loss of information, the state of the cell is periodically read and then written back into the cell to reestablish the desired cell voltages. This operation is referred to as the **refresh operation.** Each storage cell in a DRAM must typically be refreshed every 2 to 10 ms.

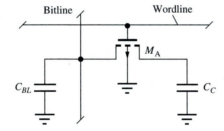

Figure 9.15 One-transistor (1-T) storage cell in which binary data is represented by the presence or absence of charge on C_C.

Data Storage in the 1-T Cell

In the analysis that follows, a 0 will be represented by 0 V on capacitor C_C, and a 1 will be represented by a high level on C_C. These data are written into the 1-T cell by placing the desired voltage level on the single bitline and turning on access transistor M_A.

Storing a 0

Consider first the situation for storing a 0 in the cell, as in Fig. 9.16. In this case, the bitline is held at 0 V, and the bitline terminal of the MOSFET acts as the source of the FET. The gate is raised to $V_{DD} = 3$ V. If the cell voltage is already zero, then the drain-source voltage

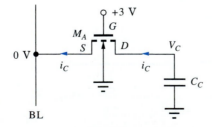

Figure 9.16 Writing a 0 into the 1-T cell.

of the MOSFET is zero, and the current is zero. If the cell contains a 1 with $V_C > 0$, then the MOSFET completely discharges C_C, also yielding $V_C = 0$.

> **EXERCISE:** (a) What is the cell current i_C in Fig. 9.16 just after access transistor M_A is turned on if $V_C = 1.9$ V, $K_n = 50$ μA/V^2, and $V_{TO} = 0.7$ V? (b) Estimate the fall time of the voltage on the capacitor using Eqs. (8.14) and (8.19), with $C_C = 50$ fF.
>
> **ANSWERS:** 128 μA; 1.13 ns

Storing a 1

Now consider the case of writing a 1 into the 1-T cell in Fig. 9.17. The bitline is first set to V_{DD} (3 V), and the wordline is then raised to V_{DD}. The bitline terminal of M_A acts as its drain, and the cell capacitance terminal acts as the FET source. Because $V_{DS} = V_{GS}$, and M_A is an enhancement mode device, M_A will operate in the saturation region. If a full 1 level already exists in the cell, then the current is zero in M_A. However, if V_C is less than a full 1 level, current through M_A will charge up the capacitor to a potential one threshold voltage below the gate voltage.

We see from this analysis that the voltage levels corresponding to 0 and 1 in the 1-T cell are 0 V and $V_G - V_{TN}$. The threshold voltage must be evaluated for a source-bulk voltage equal to V_C:

$$V_C = V_G - V_{TN} = V_G - [V_{TO} + \gamma(\sqrt{V_C + 2\phi_F} - \sqrt{2\phi_F})] \tag{9.1}$$

Equation (9.1) is identical to Eq. (7.19) used to determine V_{OH} for the saturated load NMOS logic circuit.

Note once again the important use of the bidirectional characteristics of the MOSFET. Charge must be able to flow in both directions through the transistor in order to write the desired data into the cell. To read the data, current must also be able to change directions.

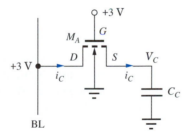

Figure 9.17 Conditions for writing a 1 into the 1-T cell.

> **EXERCISE:** Find the cell voltage V_C if $V_{DD} = 3$ V, $V_{TO} = 0.7$ V, $\gamma = 0.5 \sqrt{V}$, and $2\phi_F = 0.6$ V. What is V_C if $\gamma = 0$?
>
> **ANSWERS:** 1.89 V; 2.3 V

> **EXERCISE:** If a cell is in a 1 state, how many electrons are stored on the cell capacitor if $C_C = 25$ fF?
>
> **ANSWER:** 2.95×10^5 electrons

The results in the preceding exercises are typical of the situation for the 1 level in the cell. A significant part of the power supply voltage is lost because of the threshold voltage of the MOSFET, and the body effect has an important role in further reducing the cell voltage for the 1 state. If there were no body effect in the first exercise, then V_C would increase to 2.3 V.

Reading Data from the 1-T Cell

To read the information from the 1-T cell, the bitline is first precharged (**bitline precharge**) to a known voltage, typically V_{DD} or one-half V_{DD}. The access transistor is then turned on, and the cell capacitance is connected to the bitline through M_A. A phenomenon called **charge sharing** occurs. The total charge, originally stored separately on the **bitline capacitance** C_{BL} and cell capacitance C_C, is shared between the two capacitors following the switch closure, and the voltage on the bitline changes slightly. The magnitude and sign of the change are related to the stored information.

Detailed behavior of data readout can be understood using the circuit model in Fig. 9.18. Before access transistor M_A is turned on, the switch is open, and the total initial charge Q_I on the two capacitors is

$$Q_I = C_{BL}V_{BL} + C_CV_C \tag{9.2}$$

After access transistor M_A is activated, corresponding to closing the switch, current through the on-resistance of M_A equalizes the voltage on the two capacitors. The final value of the stored charge Q_F is given by

$$Q_F = (C_{BL} + C_C)V_F \tag{9.3}$$

Because no mechanism for charge loss exists, Q_F must equal Q_I. Equating Eqs. (9.2) and (9.3) and solving for V_F yields

$$V_F = \frac{C_{BL}V_{BL} + C_CV_C}{C_{BL} + C_C} \tag{9.4}$$

The signal to be detected is the change in the voltage on the bitline from its initial precharged value:

$$\Delta V = V_F - V_{BL} = \frac{C_C}{C_{BL} + C_C}(V_C - V_{BL}) = \frac{(V_C - V_{BL})}{\dfrac{C_{BL}}{C_C} + 1} \tag{9.5}$$

Equation (9.5) can be used to guide our selection of the precharge voltage. If V_{BL} is set midway between the 1 and 0 levels, then ΔV will be positive if a 1 is stored in the cell and negative if a 0 is stored. Study of Eq. (9.5) also shows that the signal voltage ΔV can be quite small. If there are 128 rows in our memory array, then there will be 128 access transistors connected to the bitline, and the ratio of bitline capacitance to cell capacitance can be quite large.

If we assume that $C_{BL} \gg C_C$, Eq. (9.4) shows that the final voltage on the bitline and cell is

$$V_F = \frac{C_{BL}V_{BL} + C_CV_C}{C_{BL} + C_C} \approx V_{BL} \tag{9.6}$$

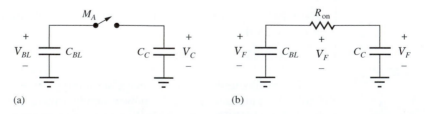

(a)   (b)

Figure 9.18 Model for charge sharing between the 1-T storage cell capacitance and the bitline capacitance: (a) circuit model before activation of access transistor, (b) circuit following closure of access switch.

Thus, the content of the cell is destroyed during the process of reading the data from the cell—the 1-T cell is a cell with destructive readout. To restore the original contents following a read operation, the data must be written back into the cell.

Except for the case of an ideal switch, charge transfer cannot occur instantaneously. If the on-resistance were constant, the voltages and currents in the circuit in Fig. 9.18 would change exponentially with a time constant τ determined by R_{on} and the series combination of C_{BL} and C_C:

$$\tau = R_{on}\frac{C_C C_{BL}}{C_C + C_{BL}} \approx R_{on}C_C \qquad \text{for } C_{BL} \gg C_C \qquad (9.7)$$

EXERCISE: (a) Find the change in bitline voltage for a memory array in which $C_{BL} = 49\ C_C$ if the bitline is precharged midway between the voltages corresponding to a 1 and a 0. Assume that 0 V corresponds to a 0 and 1.9 V corresponds to a 1. (b) What is τ if $R_{on} = 5\ k\Omega$ and $C_C = 25\ fF$?

ANSWERS: $+19.0\ \text{mV}, -19.0\ \text{mV}; 0.125\ \text{ns}$

The preceding exercise reinforces the fact that the voltage change that must be detected by the sense amplifier for a 1-T cell is quite small. Designing a sense amplifier to rapidly detect this small change is one of the major challenges of DRAM design. Also, note that the **charge transfer** occurs rapidly.

The Three-Transistor Cell

The 1-T cell is the dominant memory cell in modern ICs. However, the cell used in the first commercial 1024-bit dynamic memory [7] was actually a version of the **three-transistor (3-T) cell** shown conceptually in Fig. 9.19. Binary information is stored on cell capacitor C_C in a manner identical to the way it is stored in a 1-T cell. However, two transistors are added to provide nondestructive readout of the information. If a high voltage level is stored on C_C, then buffer transistor M_B will be in the conducting state; if a low voltage level is stored on C_C, M_B will be off. When the read line is activated, the current through read access transistor M_R will depend on the voltage stored on C_C. M_B provides a relatively large output current, and the sense amplifiers have more drive than they do in the 1-T cell. In addition, reading the data does not disturb the level stored on C_C. Like the 1-T cell, however, data must be periodically refreshed because leakage currents in write access transistor M_W will eventually corrupt the cell data. Note that if a high level is stored on C_C, $\overline{BL}$ will tend to be forced to a low level. This data inversion must be recognized but is easily taken care of in the peripheral circuits of the memory.

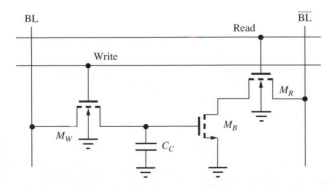

Figure 9.19 Three-transistor (3-T) dynamic memory cell.

The actual IC implementation of the 3-T memory array combines the read and write lines into a single wordline and uses a complex multilevel wordline signal that will not be described here. The interested reader can find more detail in references [2] and [11].

> **EXERCISE:** Suppose M_W and M_B in Fig. 9.19 are 2/1 devices, and M_R is an 8/1 device. (a) If the voltage stored on C_C is 1.9 V, and the voltages on the read line and $\overline{\text{BL}}$ are 3 V, what are the regions of operation of M_B and M_R? Use $K'_n = 25\ \mu\text{A/V}^2$ with $V_{TO} = 0.7$ V, $\gamma = 0.5\ \sqrt{\text{V}}$, and $2\phi_F = 0.6$ V. (b) What are the drain currents of M_B and M_R? (c) What is the drain-source voltage of M_B?
>
> **ANSWERS:** Both saturated; 36.0 μA; 1.38 V

The Four-Transistor Dynamic Memory Cell

We saw earlier that the 6-T static cell provides a large signal current to drive the sense amplifiers. This is one reason why static memory designs generally provide shorter access times than dynamic memories. The **four-transistor (4-T) cell** in Fig. 9.20 is a compromise between the 6-T and 1-T cells. The load devices of the 6-T cell are eliminated, and the information is stored on the capacitances at the interior nodes. The cross-coupled transistors provide high current for sensing, as well as both true and complemented outputs. If BL, $\overline{\text{BL}}$, and the wordline are all forced high, the two access transistors temporarily act as load devices for the 4-T cell, and the cell levels are automatically refreshed.

The conditions for writing information into the 4-T cell using a 3-V power supply are shown in Fig. 9.21. Following wordline activation, node D charges up to $3 - V_{TN} = 1.9$ V through access transistor M_{A1}, and node $\overline{D}$ discharges to 0 V through M_{A2} and M_{N2}. The regenerative nature of the two cross-coupled transistors enhances the speed of the write operation.

Figure 9.22 shows conditions during a read operation, in which the bitline capacitances have been precharged to 1.5 V. The voltages stored in the cell initially force M_{N1}

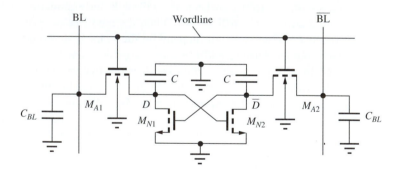

Figure 9.20 Four-transistor (4-T) dynamic memory cell.

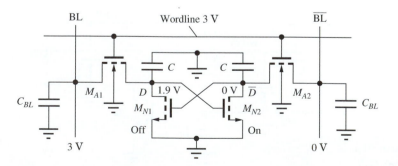

Figure 9.21 Writing data into the 4-T memory cell.

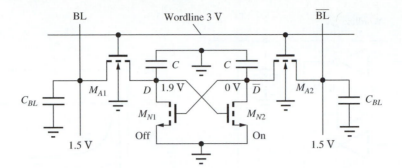

Figure 9.22 Reading data from the 4-T cell.

to be off and M_{N2} on. When the wordline is raised to 3 V, charge sharing occurs on BL, and the D node drops to approximately 1.5 V. However, the voltage on $\overline{\text{BL}}$ rapidly divides between M_{A2} and M_{N2}. In a conservative design, the W/L ratios of M_{N2} and M_{A2} keep the voltage at $\overline{D}$ from exceeding the threshold voltage of M_{N1} to ensure that M_{N1} remains off. As the sense amplifier responds and drives the bitlines to 0 and 3 V, the 1 level within the cell is also restored to its original value through the access transistors. When the wordline drops, the cross-coupled transistors fully discharge the 0 node to 0 V.

> **EXERCISE:** What is the drain current of M_{A2} in Fig. 9.22 just after the wordline is raised to 3 V if all the devices have $W/L = 2/1$? Use $K'_n = 50\ \mu\text{A/V}^2$, $V_{TO} = 0.7$ V, $\gamma = 0.5\ \sqrt{V}$, and $2\phi_F = 0.6$ V.
>
> **ANSWER:** 233 μA

9.4 SENSE AMPLIFIERS

The sense amplifiers for the cells discussed in the previous sections must detect the small currents that run through the access transistors of the cell or the small voltage difference that arises from charge sharing and rapidly amplify the signal up to full on-chip logic levels. One sense amplifier is associated with each bitline or bitline pair. The regenerative properties of the latch circuit are used to achieve high-speed sensing.

A Sense Amplifier for the 6-T Cell

A basic sense amplifier that can be used with the 6-T cell consists of a two-inverter latch plus an additional **precharge transistor,** as shown in Fig. 9.23. Transistor M_{PC} is used to force the latch to operate at the unstable equilibrium point with equal voltages at BL and $\overline{\text{BL}}$. When the precharge device is on, it operates in the linear region and represents a low-resistance connection between the two bitlines. As long as transistor M_{PC} is on, the two nodes of the sense amplifier are forced to remain at equal voltages.

Figure 9.24 shows waveforms from a SPICE simulation of the precharge operation. The voltages on BL and $\overline{\text{BL}}$ begin at 0 V and 3 V. These levels are arbitrary, but they result from a preceding read or write operation. At $t = 1$ ns, the precharge signal turns on, forcing the two bitlines toward the same potential. The time required for the latch to reach the $v_O = v_I$ state in the simulation, approximately 30 ns, is limited by the W/L ratio of the precharge device, the capacitance of the bitlines, and the current drive capability of the inverters in the latch. In the simulation in Fig. 9.24, the precharge transistor is a 50/1 device, $C_{BL} = 500$ fF, and all devices in the sense amplifier have $W/L = 50/1$. One problem with

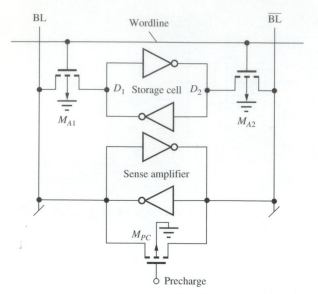

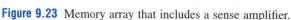

Figure 9.23 Memory array that includes a sense amplifier.

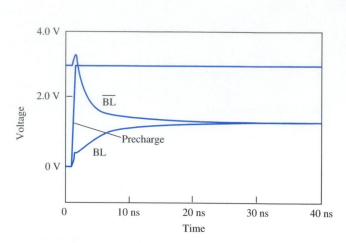

Figure 9.24 Results of SPICE simulation of the bitline voltage waveforms during the precharge operation.

this simple sense amplifier is its relatively slow precharge of the bitlines. Precharge must remain active until the bitline voltages are equal, or sensing errors may occur.

Once equilibrium is reached, the precharge transistor can be turned off, and the precharge level will be maintained temporarily on the bitline capacitances. The wordline can then be activated to read the cell, as demonstrated previously in Fig. 9.10.

A Sense Amplifier for the 1-T Cell

The two-inverter latch that was used with the 6-T static memory cell in Fig. 9.23 can also be used as the sense amplifier for the 1-T cell. The 1-T cell and a latch with precharge transistor M_{PC} are shown attached to the bitline in Fig. 9.25, and the waveforms associated with the sensing operation are shown in Fig. 9.26. Because the cross-coupled latch is highly sensitive, it remains connected across two bitlines in order to balance the capacitive load on the two nodes of the latch and to share the sense amplifier between two columns of cells.

In the circuit in Fig. 9.25, the 1-T cell is shown connected to BL. In most designs, a dummy cell with its own access transistor and storage capacitor would be connected to $\overline{BL}$ to try to balance the switching transients on the two sides of the latch as well as to improve the response time of the sense amplifier. Use of the dummy cell is discussed in more detail in the section on clocked sense amplifiers.

During the **precharge phase** of the circuit, as shown by the waveforms in Fig. 9.26, the bitlines are forced to a level determined by the relative W/L ratios of the NMOS and PMOS transistors in the sense amplifier. Following turnoff of the precharge transistor, the data in the storage cells is accessed by raising the wordline, enabling charge sharing between cell capacitance C_C and bitline capacitance C_{BL}. In the simulation, the sense amplifier amplifies the small difference and generates almost the full 3-V logic levels on the two bitlines in approximately 25 ns.

A closer inspection of the bitline waveform indicates that the desired charge sharing is actually not occurring in this circuit. The voltage on the storage node does not drop instantaneously because of the large on-resistance of the access transistor. Let us explore

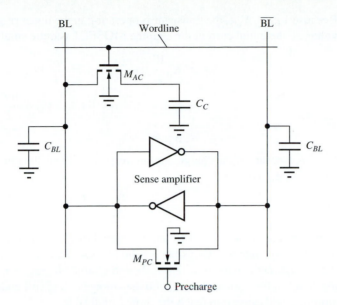

Figure 9.25 Simple sense amplifier for the 1-T cell.

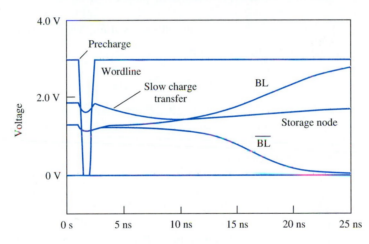

Figure 9.26 Single-ended sensing of the 1-T cell.

this problem further by looking at the voltages applied to the access transistor immediately following activation of the wordline, as in Fig. 9.27.

For M_{AC}:

$$V_{TN} = 0.70 + 0.5\left(\sqrt{1.3 + 0.6} - \sqrt{0.6}\right) = 1.0 \text{ V}$$

$$V_{GS} = 3 - 1.3 = 1.7 \text{ V}$$

and

$$V_{DS} = 1.9 - 1.3 = 0.6 \text{ V}$$

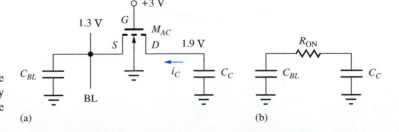

Figure 9.27 Voltages on the access transistor immediately following activation of the wordline.

Because $V_{GS} > V_{DS}$, the transistor is operating in the linear region as desired, but for these voltages, the initial current through the MOSFET is quite small. Assuming $W/L = 1/1$,

$$i_{DS} = K_n' \frac{W}{L} \left(v_{GS} - V_{TN} - \frac{v_{DS}}{2} \right) v_{DS}$$

$$= (25 \times 10^{-6}) \left(\frac{1}{1} \right) \left(1.7 - 1.0 - \frac{0.6}{2} \right) 0.6$$

$$= 6\,\mu A$$

A measure of the charge-sharing response time is the initial discharge rate of the cell capacitance, given by

$$\frac{\Delta v}{\Delta t} = \frac{i_{DS}}{C_C} \tag{9.8}$$

In the simulation, $C_C = 25$ fF and the initial discharge rate is 0.24 V/nS. This relatively low discharge rate is responsible for the incomplete charge transfer and shallow slope on the storage node waveform. Even though charge sharing is not complete in this circuit, the small initial current drawn from the storage cell is still enough to unbalance the sense amplifier and cause it to reach the proper final state.

> **EXERCISE:** What are the initial values of R_{on} and $\tau = R_{on}C_C$ in the circuit in Fig. 9.27?
>
> **ANSWERS:** 100 kΩ, 2.5 ns

The Boosted Wordline Circuit

In high-speed memory circuits, every fraction of a nanosecond is precious, and some DRAM designs use a separate voltage level for the wordline. The additional level raises the voltage corresponding to a 1 level in the 1-T cell and substantially increases i_{DS} during cell access. The waveforms for the circuit of Fig. 9.25 are repeated in Fig. 9.28 for the case in which the wordline is driven to +5 V instead of +3 V (referred to as a **boosted wordline**). In this case the cell voltage becomes 3.7 V and the initial current from the cell is increased to 90 μA, 15 times larger (see Prob. 9.13)! A much more rapid charge transfer is evident in the storage node waveform in Fig. 9.28, where the sense amplifier has developed a 1.5-V difference between the two bitlines approximately 10 ns after the wordline is raised. In the original case in Fig. 9.26, approximately 15 ns were required to reach the same bitline differential.

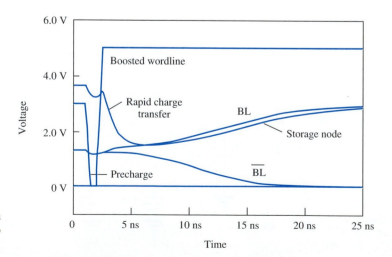

Figure 9.28 1-T sensing with wordline voltage boosted to 5 V.

Clocked CMOS Sense Amplifiers

In the sense amplifiers in Figs. 9.23 and 9.25, there is considerable current between the two power supplies during the precharge phase. In addition, a relatively long time is required for precharge. Because a large number of sense amplifiers will be active simultaneously—128 in the 256-Mb memory chip example—minimizing power dissipation in the individual sense amplifier is an important design consideration. By introducing a more sophisticated clocking scheme, sense amplifier power dissipation can be reduced.

Clocked sense amplifiers were originally introduced in NMOS technology to reduce power dissipation in saturated load and depletion-mode load sense circuits. The same techniques are also routinely used in CMOS sense amplifiers; an example of such a circuit is shown in Fig. 9.29. For sensing 1-T cells, a dummy cell is used that has one-half the capacitance of the 1-T cell. In Fig. 9.29, the bottom plate of all the capacitors has been connected to V_{DD} instead of to 0 V. This change represents another design alternative but does not alter the basic theory of operation.

During precharge, V_{PC} is held at 0 V, and the bitlines are precharged to V_{DD} through the two PMOS transistors. After the precharge signal is removed, the access transistor of the addressed cell is activated, and the corresponding bitline drops slightly. The magnitude of the change depends on the data stored in the cell. A relatively large change occurs if cell voltage is 0, and a small change occurs if the cell voltage is $V_{DD} - V_{TN}$.

A dummy cell is required in this circuit to ensure that a voltage difference of the proper polarity will always develop between the two bitlines following cell access. Dummy cell capacitance is designed to be one-half the capacitance of the data storage cell, and cell voltage is always preset to 0 V by V_{PC}. During charge sharing, the selected dummy cell causes the corresponding bitline to drop by an amount equal to one-half the voltage drop that occurs when a 0 is stored in the 1-T cell. Thus, a positive voltage difference exists between BL and $\overline{\text{BL}}$ if a 1 is stored in the 1-T cell, and a negative difference exists if a 0 is stored in the cell.

Following charge sharing, the lower part of the CMOS latch is activated by turning on M_{NL}, and the small difference between the two bitline voltages is amplified by the full cross-coupled CMOS latch. Simulated waveforms for the clocked CMOS sense amplifier

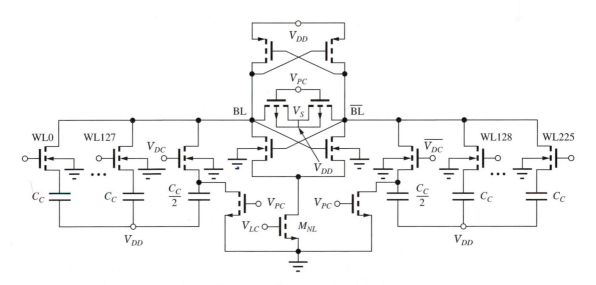

Figure 9.29 Clocked CMOS sense amplifier showing an array of 1-T memory cells and a dummy cell on each side of the sense amplifier. The right-hand dummy cell ($C_C/2$) is used with cells 0 to 127 and the left-hand dummy cell is used with cells 128 to 255.

are shown in Fig. 9.30. For clarity, the three clock signals, precharge V_{PC}, wordline WL, and latch clock V_{LC} have each been staggered by 1 ns in the simulation. Note that both BL and $\overline{BL}$ are driven above 3 V by the coupling of the clock signal to the bitlines, but the voltage difference is maintained and the latch responds properly.

No static current paths exist through the latch during the precharge period, and hence only transient switching currents exist in the sense amplifier. Although there are many variants and refinements to the circuit in Fig. 9.29, the basic circuit ideas presented here form the heart of the sense amplifiers in most dynamic RAMs.

To achieve high-speed precharge and sensing with minimum size transistors, the bit-line capacitance C_{BL} in either static or dynamic RAMs must be kept as small as possible. This requirement restricts the number of cells that can be connected to each bitline. Many clever techniques have been developed to segment the bitlines in order to reduce the size of C_{BL}, and the interested reader is referred to the references. In particular, information can be found in the annual digests of the IEEE International Solid-State Circuits Conference [5], the Custom Integrated Circuits Conference (CICC) [6], and the Symposium on VLSI Circuits [7], as well as in the yearly Special Issues of the *IEEE Journal of Solid State Circuits* [8]. New information on memory-cell technology is discussed yearly at the IEEE International Electron Devices Meeting [9], the Symposium on VLSI Technology [7], and in the *IEEE Transactions on Electron Devices*[10].

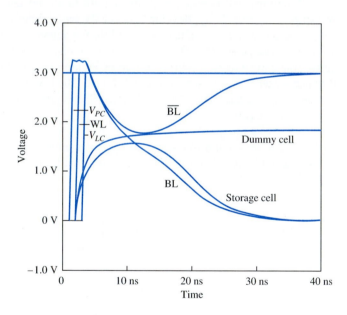

Figure 9.30 Simulated behavior of the clocked CMOS sense amplifier.

9.5 ADDRESS DECODERS

Two additional major blocks in design of a memory are the *row address* and *column address decoders* shown in the block diagram in Fig. 9.2. The row address circuits decode the row address information to determine the single wordline that is to be activated. The decoded column address information is then used to select a bit or group of bits from the selected word. This section first explores NOR and NAND row address decoders and then discusses the use of an NMOS pass-transistor tree decoder for selecting the desired data from the wide internal memory word. Dynamic logic techniques for implementing these decoders are also introduced.

NOR Decoder

Figure 9.31 is the schematic for a 3-bit **NOR decoder.** The circuit must fully decode all possible combinations of the input variables and is equivalent to at least eight (2^3) 3-input NOR gates (2^N N-input gates in the general case.) In the circuit in Fig. 9.31, true and complemented address information is fed through an array of NMOS transistors. Each row of the decoder contains three FETs, with each gate connected to one of the desired address bits or its complement and the three drains connected in parallel to the output line being enabled. At the end of each row is a depletion-mode load device to pull the row output high, which occurs only if all the inputs to that row are low.

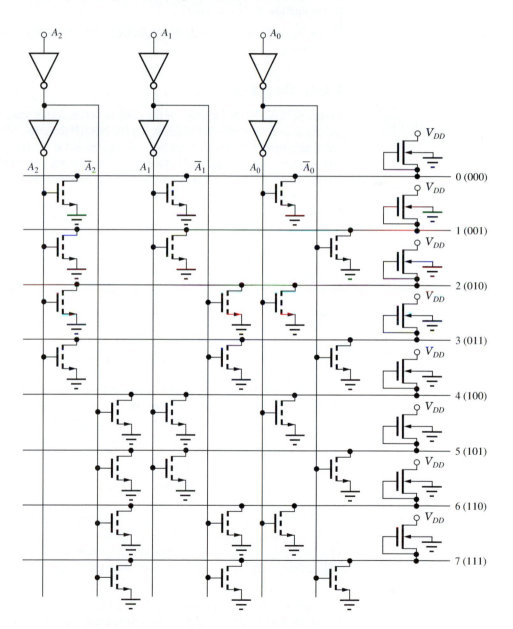

Figure 9.31 NMOS static NOR address decoder.

Only one output line will be high for any given combination of input variables; the rest will be low. Each row corresponds to one possible address combination:

$$\text{Row } 0 = \overline{A_2 + A_1 + A_0}$$

$$\text{Row } 1 = \overline{A_2 + A_1 + \overline{A_0}}$$

$$\vdots$$

$$\text{Row } 7 = \overline{\overline{A_2} + \overline{A_1} + \overline{A_0}}$$

EXERCISE: What are the sizes of the transistors for the NOR decoder in Fig. 9.31 based on the reference inverter in Fig. 7.20(d)? What is the static power dissipation of this decoder?

ANSWERS: Depletion-mode load devices: 1/2.15; NMOS switching devices: 2.06/1; 1.75 mW

NAND Decoder

Figure 9.32 is a NAND version of the same decoder. Again, true and complemented address information is fed through the array. For the **NAND decoder,** all outputs are high except for the single row in which all three transistor gates are at a 1 level. Because additional driver circuits are normally required between the decoder and the highly capacitive wordline, the logical inversion that is needed to actually drive wordlines in a memory array is easily accommodated. In Fig. 9.32, the rows correspond to

$$\text{Row } 0 = \overline{\overline{A_2}\,\overline{A_1}\,\overline{A_0}}$$

$$\text{Row } 1 = \overline{\overline{A_2}\,\overline{A_1}\,A_0}$$

$$\vdots$$

$$\text{Row } 7 = \overline{A_2 A_1 A_0}$$

As for standard NOR and NAND gates, the stacked series structure of the NAND gate tends to be slower than the corresponding parallel NOR structure, particularly if minimum-size devices are used throughout the decoder.

The NMOS static decoder circuits in Figs. 9.31 and 9.32 cause power consumption problems in high-density memories. In the memory array, 1 wordline will be high for a given address, and $2^N - 1$ will be low. For static NMOS circuits, $2^N - 1$ of the individual NOR gates in the NOR decoder dissipate power simultaneously. A similar problem occurs if NMOS inverters are used at the output of the NAND decoder.

Standard CMOS circuits offer low power dissipation but cause layout and area problems when there are a large number of inputs because each input must be connected to both an NMOS and a PMOS transistor, which doubles the number of devices in the array. A full CMOS decoder can be more efficiently implemented as a combination of an NMOS NOR array and a PMOS NAND array. However, because memories are generally used in clocked systems, they can use dynamic decoders, which consume low power and require only a few PMOS transistors. We introduce these next.

EXERCISE: What are the sizes of the load devices in the NAND decoder in Fig. 9.32 if the *W/L* ratios of the switching devices are all 2/1? Base your design on the reference inverter in Fig. 7.20(d).

ANSWER: 1/6.64

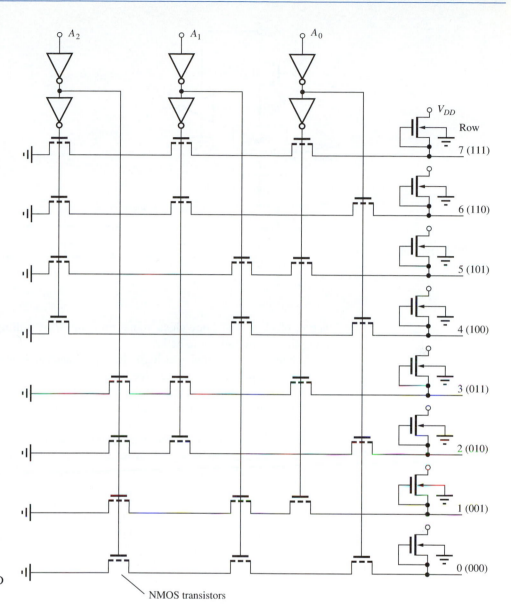

Figure 9.32 NMOS NAND decoder circuit.

Dynamic Domino CMOS Logic

Two-phase and **four-phase dynamic logic circuits** were first developed as a means of reducing power in PMOS and NMOS logic. **Dynamic logic** uses separate precharge and **evaluation phases** governed by a system clock signal to eliminate the dc current path that exists in single-channel static logic gates. However, the logical outputs are valid only during a portion of the evaluation phase of the clock. In addition, static power represents only one component of power dissipation in high-speed systems, and the power required to drive the clock signals that must connect to every dynamic logic gate can be significant.

The circuit in Fig. 9.33 represents a general dynamic logic gate in a circuit family called **domino CMOS.** Operation of the domino CMOS circuit begins with the clock signal in the low state. M_{NC} is off, which disables the current path to ground through the logic

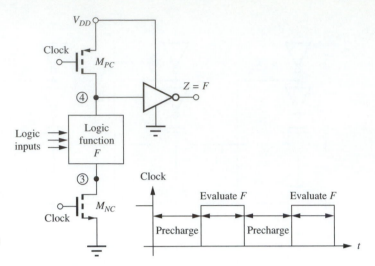

Figure 9.33 Dynamic domino CMOS logic.

function block F. The same clock signal turns on M_{PC}, pulling node 4 high to V_{DD} and forcing the inverter output to be low.

When the clock signal goes high, the capacitance at node 4 is selectively discharged. If a conducting path exists through the logic network F (that is, if $F = 1$), then node 4 is discharged to zero, and the output of the inverter rises to a 1 level. If $F = 0$, no discharge path exists, the voltage at node 4 remains high, and the output of the inverter remains at a 0.

Simulated waveforms for the single-input domino CMOS gate in Fig. 9.34 are shown in Fig. 9.35 for the case of $A = 1$. After the clock goes high, the output rises following the logic delay to discharge the capacitances at nodes 3 and 4 plus the delay through the inverter. The output drops back to zero following the clock signal's return to zero.

The inputs to a given domino CMOS gate, generated by other domino gates, make only low-to-high transitions following the clock transition, and the functional evaluation during the positive clock phase ripples through the gates like a series of dominos falling over—hence the name domino logic. Figure 9.36 shows the ripple-through effect for the

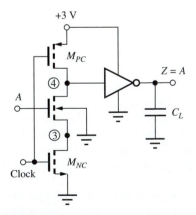

Figure 9.34 Domino CMOS gate with a single input.

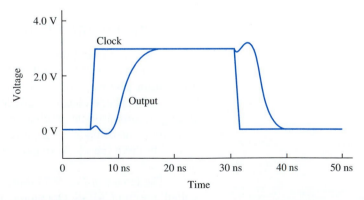

Figure 9.35 Waveforms for the clocked domino circuit.

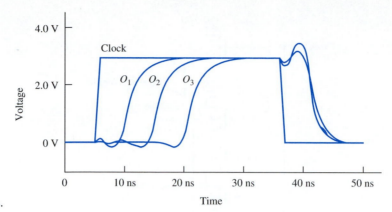

Figure 9.36 Outputs of three cascaded domino CMOS gates.

case of three domino gates in series. Output O_1 follows the rising edge of the clock and drives the input of O_2, and output O_3 responds to the change in O_2. Note that the outputs are all reset to zero at the same time, following the falling edge of the clock.

External inputs that are not from other domino gates should remain stable during the evaluation phase of the clock. As with most CMOS circuits, power dissipation is set by the dynamic power consumed in charging and discharging the capacitances at the various nodes. A major advantage of the domino CMOS circuit is the requirement for only two PMOS transistors per logic stage, no matter how complex the function F.

The observant reader has probably noticed that domino CMOS gates do not form a complete logic family because only true output functions are available. However, this does not represent a problem in system designs in which a register transfer structure exists, as in Fig. 9.37. In this logic structure, data are stored in a static register (1), which can be designed to produce both true and complemented data values at its outputs. Domino CMOS performs the combinational logic functions on the positive phase of the clock signal, and the results of the logic operations are clocked into register (2) on the falling edge of the clock signal. (Another option appears in Prob. 9.36.)

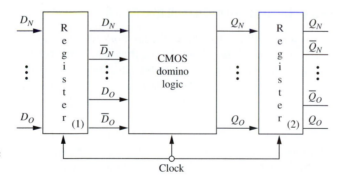

Figure 9.37 Section of logic in a complex digital system.

> **EXERCISE:** (a) Draw the circuit schematic for a domino CMOS gate for $Z = AB + C$.
> (b) What power is required in a domino CMOS clock driver circuit that drives a 50-pF load at 10 MHz if $V_{DD} = 5$ V?
>
> **ANSWER:** 6.25 mW

Decoders in Domino CMOS Logic

Figure 9.38 is the schematic for one row of a domino CMOS NAND decoder for a 3-bit address. In this circuit, a discharge path exists through the function block only for address $A_0 A_1 A_2 = 111$, and only the single-addressed wordline makes a low-to-high transition

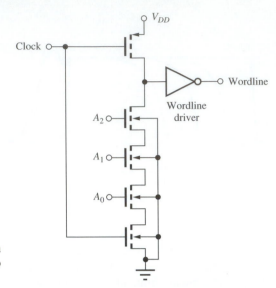

Figure 9.38 One row of an NAND decoder in domino CMOS logic.

at the output of the inverter. This structure ensures that the voltage changes on only one of the high-capacitance wordlines during a given row access. The output inverter can be designed to drive the high-capacitance load rapidly. Design techniques for these inverters are discussed in Sec. 9.9.

Figure 9.39 is the circuit schematic for a full 3-bit address decoder using the NAND decoder array of Fig. 9.32; here the load devices in Fig. 9.32 have been replaced with clocked PMOS transistors, and an NMOS clock transistor has been added to the beginning of each row. A CMOS inverter is connected to each output line to complete the domino CMOS implementation.

Pass-Transistor Column Decoder

The column address decoder of the memory in Fig. 9.2 must choose a group of data bits—usually 1, 4, or 8 bits—from the much wider word that has been selected by the row address decoder. One form of a one-bit selection circuit using NMOS **pass-transistor logic** is shown in Fig. 9.40 (p. 366). For a large number of data bits, the pass-transistor circuit technique requires far fewer transistors than would the more direct approach using standard NOR and NAND gates.

In the pass-transistor implementation, true and complement address information is fed through a transistor array, with one level of the array corresponding to each address bit. Although all transistors with a logic 1 on their respective gates will be on, the tree structure ensures that only a single path is completed through the array for each combination of inputs. In Fig. 9.40, an address of 101 is provided to the array, and the transistors indicated in blue type all have a logic 1 on their respective gates, creating a conducting channel region in each. In this case, a completed conducting path connects input column 5 to the data output.

Examples of the conducting paths through a three-level pass-transistor array for input data of 0 and 1 are shown in Fig. 9.41 (p. 366) for the case of $V_{DD} = 3$ V. For a 0 input equal to 0 V, the output node capacitor C is discharged to zero through the series combination of the three pass transistors. However, for a 1 input voltage of 3 V, the output of the first pass transistor is one threshold voltage below the gate voltage of 3 V. Using the NMOS parameters

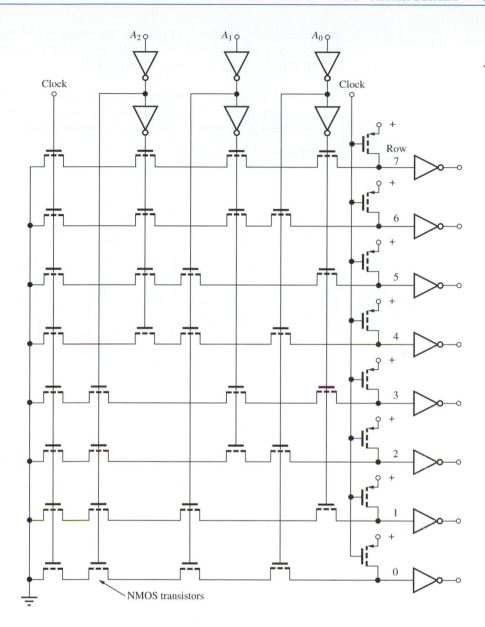

Figure 9.39 Complete 3-bit domino CMOS NAND address decoder.

from earlier in the chapter, we find that the output voltage is

$$V_O = V_G - V_{TN} = 3 - 1.1 = 1.9 \text{ V}$$

The other node voltages can reach this same potential, so the output capacitance will charge to $V_G - V_{TN} = 1.9$ V, regardless of the number of levels in the array. The data buffer at the output must be designed to have a switching threshold below 1.9 V in order to properly restore the logic level at the output.

Full logic levels can also be achieved in pass-transistor logic for both 1 and 0 inputs by replacing each NMOS transistor with a CMOS transmission gate. However, this significantly increases the area and complexity of the design with little actual benefit because the data buffer can easily be designed to compensate for the loss in signal level through the NMOS (or PMOS) pass-transistor array. In addition to doubling the number of transistors in the array, the full CMOS version requires distribution of both true and complement address information to each transmission gate. However, design techniques to simplify the layout of CMOS transmission gate arrays do exist [12].

> **EXERCISE:** What are the voltage levels at the nodes in Fig. 9.41(a) and 9.41(b) if the gate voltages are 5 V instead of 3 V? Assume $V_{TO} = 0.70$ V, $\gamma = 0.5 \sqrt{\text{V}}$, and $2\phi_F = 0.6$ V. What is the largest γ for which the output of the pass-transistor is 3 V?
>
> **ANSWERS:** 0 V, 3 V; $1.16 \sqrt{\text{V}}$

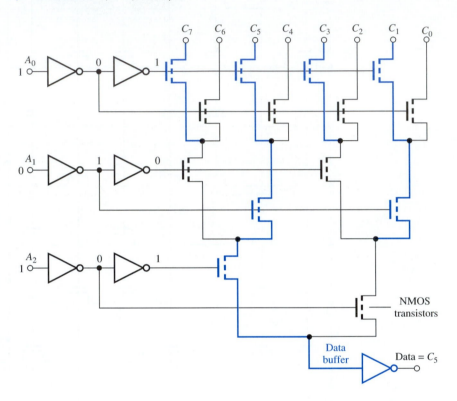

Figure 9.40 3-bit column data selector using pass-transistor logic.

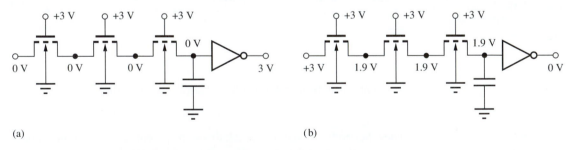

(a)   (b)

Figure 9.41 Data transmission through the pass-transistor decoder: (a) 0 input data, (b) 1 input data.

9.6 READ-ONLY MEMORY (ROM)

Read-only memory (ROM) is another form of memory often required in digital systems, and many common applications exist. Many microprocessors use microcoded instruction sets that reside in ROM, and a portion of the operating system for personal computers usually resides in ROM. The fixed programs for microcontrollers, often called *firmware,* are also usually stored in ROM, and cartridges for home video games are simply ROMs that contain the firmware programs that define the characteristics of the particular game. Plug-in modules for hand-held scientific calculators are another application of read-only memory.

Most ROMs are organized as an array of 2^N words, where each word contains the number of bits required by the intended application. Common values are 4, 8, 12, 16, 18, 24, 32, 48, 64, and so on. Figure 9.42 shows the structure of a static NMOS ROM using depletion-mode load devices. This particular ROM contains four 4-bit words. Each column corresponds to one bit of the stored word, and an individual word W_i is selected when the corresponding wordline is raised to a 1 state by an address decoder similar to that in RAM. For example, this ROM could be driven by the NOR decoder circuit in Fig. 9.31.

An NMOS transistor can be placed at the intersection of each row and column within the array. In this ROM, the gate of the transistor is tied to the wordline and the drain is connected to the output data line. If connections to an NMOS transistor exist at a given array site, then the corresponding output data line is pulled low when the word is selected. If no FET exists, then the data line is maintained at a high level by the load device. Thus, the presence of an FET corresponds to a 0 stored in the array and the absence of an FET corresponds to a 1 stored in ROM. The particular data pattern stored in the array is often referred to as the **array personalization.** Table 9.1 contains the contents of the ROM array in Fig. 9.42.

Information can be personalized in the ROM array in many ways; we mention three possibilities here. Suppose an FET is fabricated at every possible site within the array. One method of storing the desired data is to eliminate the contact between the drain and data

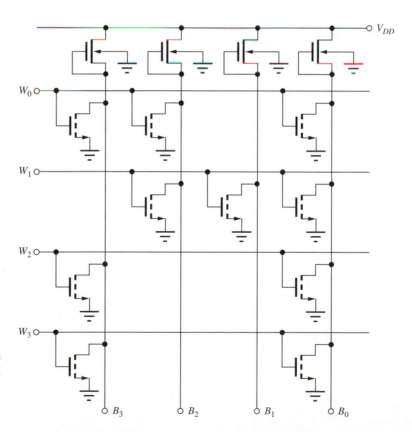

Figure 9.42 Basic structure of an NMOS static ROM with four 4-bit words: $W_0 = 0010$; $W_1 = 1000$; $W_2 = 0110$; $W_3 = 0110$.

line wherever a 1 bit is to be stored. This design yields a high capacitance on the wordline because a gate is connected to the wordline at every possible site, but a low capacitance exists on the output line because only selected drain diffusions are connected to the output lines. A second technique is to use ion implantation to alter the MOSFET threshold voltage of the FETs wherever a 1 is to be stored. If the threshold is raised high enough, then the MOSFET cannot be turned on, and therefore cannot pull the corresponding data line low. A third method is to personalize the array by eliminating gate contacts instead of drain contacts.

Standard NMOS ROM circuits exhibit substantial static power dissipation. To eliminate this power dissipation, ROMs can be designed using dynamic circuitry such as domino CMOS, as demonstrated by the ROM in Fig. 9.43, which contains six 8-bit words. When the clock signal is low, the capacitance on the output data lines is precharged high. As the clock is raised to a high level, the PMOS transistors turn off, and the data bits of the addressed word are selectively discharged to zero if a transistor connection exists at a given

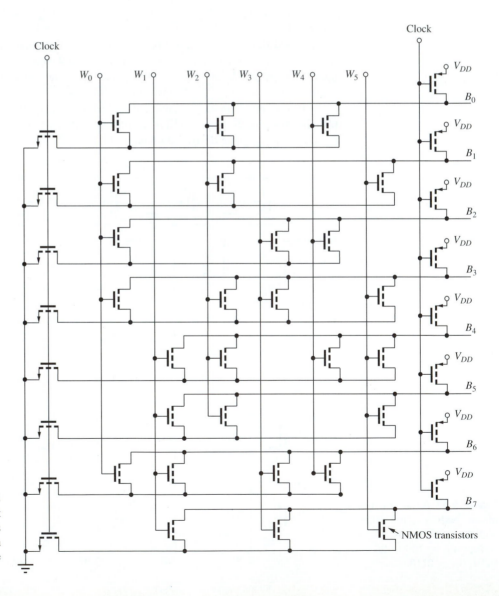

Figure 9.43 Domino CMOS ROM containing six 8-bit words. The array contains NMOS transistors in which substrate connections have been eliminated for clarity.

Table 9.2	
Contents of ROM in Fig. 9.43	
Word	**Data**
0	10110000
1	00001111
2	11000100
3	00110011
4	10101010
5	01000101

intersection point in the array. A full domino implementation will add an inverter to each output bitline. Table 9.2 lists the contents of the ROM personalization in Fig. 9.43.

The ROMs in Figs. 9.42 and 9.43 use the NOR gate structure and are often called NOR arrays. It is also possible to use a NAND array structure, as shown in Fig. 9.44. In the NAND array, all the wordlines except the desired word are raised high. Thus all the MOSFETs in the array are turned on except for the unselected row. If a MOSFET exists at a given cross-point in the unselected row, then the conducting path is broken, and the data for that column will be a 1. If the MOSFET has been replaced by a connection (possibly resistive)—by making the MOSFET a depletion-mode device for example—then the corresponding data bit will be pulled low. Note that the NAND ROM array could be driven directly by the NAND decoder in Fig. 9.32.

EXERCISE: Draw the schematic of an additional row in the ROM in Fig. 9.43 with contents of 11001101. What are the contents of the ROM in Fig. 9.44?

ANSWERS: NMOS transistors connected to B_5, B_4, and B_1 (0010, 0100, 1011, 0100).

The ROMs mentioned above are all personalized at the mask level (see Appendix A), which must be done during IC design and subsequent fabrication. If a design error occurs, the IC must be redesigned and the complete fabrication process repeated. To solve this problem, **programmable read-only memories (PROMs),** which can be programmed once from the external terminals, have been developed. **Erasable programmable read-only memories (EPROMs)** are another type of ROM. These can be erased using intense ultraviolet light and reprogrammed many times. **Electrically erasable read-only memories (EEROMs)** can be both erased and reprogrammed from the external terminals. High-density **flash memories,** which allow selective electrical erasure and reprogramming of large blocks of cells, have recently been developed.

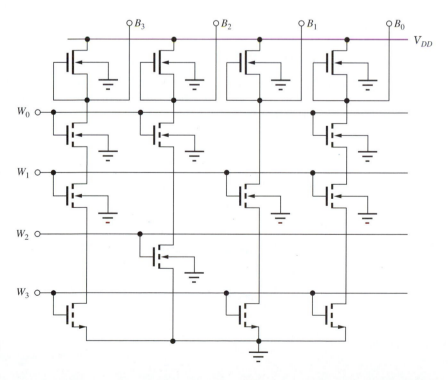

Figure 9.44 ROM based on a NAND array.

9.7 THE PROGRAMMABLE LOGIC ARRAY (PLA)

Read-only memory arrays can be used to perform logic using a structure called the **programmable logic array (PLA).** In its most straightforward form, two ROMs, an **AND array,** and an **OR array** are used to produce sum-of-products logic functions, as shown in Fig. 9.45. True and complemented versions of the input data are fed through the AND array, which is used to form the desired product terms. These product terms are then used as inputs to an OR array to produce the final sum-of-products functions.

A domino CMOS implementation of a PLA appears in Fig. 9.46, in which four product terms are generated:

$$P_0 = A$$

$$P_1 = \overline{A}B$$

$$P_2 = A\overline{B}$$

$$P_3 = \overline{B}$$

The final outputs of the PLA in Fig. 9.46 are:

$$O_0 = A\overline{B} + \overline{A}B = A \oplus B$$

$$O_1 = \overline{A}B + \overline{B}$$

$$O_2 = A + \overline{B}$$

Although this simple PLA has an equal number of inputs and outputs, this need not necessarily be the case. A PLA can be designed for whatever number of product and sum terms are needed for a particular application. Domino CMOS generates true AND and OR functions and represents a natural circuit technology for direct implementation of the PLA shown in Fig. 9.46. However, other forms exist, such as a NOR-NOR implementation, which can be used in NMOS depletion-mode load technology, for example. More powerful PLA logic blocks can be built by including storage elements such as flip-flops within the array structure.

Two-Bit Partitioning

The effective logic power of the PLA can also be increased by using more complex functions of the basic input variables as the inputs to the AND array. The **two-bit partitioning** network in Fig. 9.47 forms all possible combinations of the two input variables. These logic

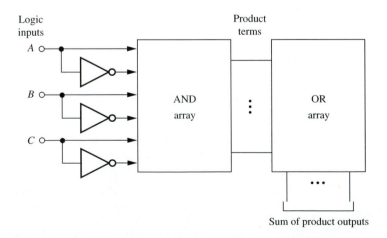

Figure 9.45 Programmable logic array.

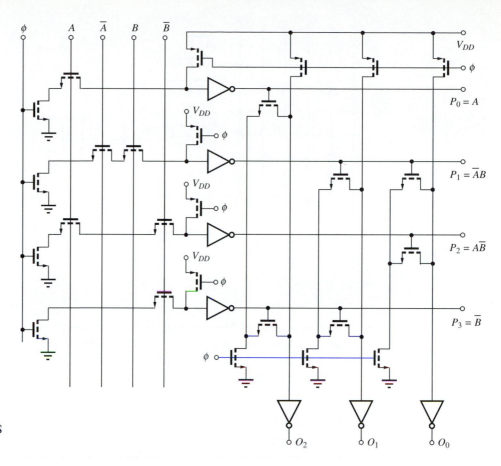

Figure 9.46 Domino CMOS programmable logic array.

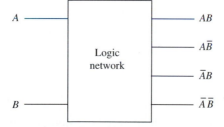

Figure 9.47 Two-bit partitioning network.

combinations replace the true and complemented logic inputs in the array of Fig. 9.45. N-bit partitioning could also be used (3-bit, 4-bit, and so on), but the logic network needed to generate the 2^N input combinations becomes more complex, and most of the benefit is derived from partitioning at the two-bit level.

Cutting and Folding

Actual utilization of the array sites in a PLA may be fairly low, as in the example in Fig. 9.46 (43 percent), and several strategies have been developed to compress PLA arrays and increase their effective density. An example of **cutting and folding** the OR array of a PLA is shown in Figs. 9.48 and 9.49. An X at a cross-point in the array indicates the presence of a transistor. The appearance of an X indicates that the given input term will appear in the sum term at the output.

To reduce the area of the array, the rows are reordered to identify disjoint columns that can be shared. In the case of the particular PLA personalization in Fig. 9.48, the columns

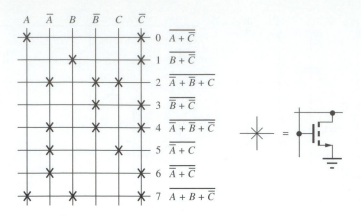

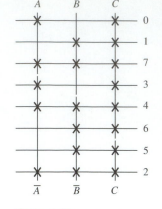

Figure 9.48 OR array of a simple PLA (40% array utilization).

Figure 9.49 PLA of Figure 9.48 following compression by cutting and folding operations.

containing the variable pairs A and $\overline{A}$, B and $\overline{B}$, and C and $\overline{C}$ can all be shared. In Fig. 9.49, the array has been compressed by reordering the input rows so each column can be shared by two input variables. Inputs to the array now come from both the top and bottom, and each goes through only a portion of the array. In the original array in Fig. 9.48, 19 of the 48 possible transistor sites are occupied, for a 40 percent array utilization. In Fig. 9.49, 79 percent (19 of 24) of the possible transistor sites are utilized, and the overall array area has been cut in half!

The operations needed to optimize the layout of large PLAs are complex but easily done using computer algorithms. Highly sophisticated programs have been developed that can go directly from a sum-of-products input description to the IC layout of a highly efficient, compressed PLA implementation of the logic. As with ROMs, programming of the standard PLA is done during fabrication, but **field programmable logic arrays (FPLAs)** are also available.

9.8 FLIP-FLOPS

Temporary storage in the form of high-speed registers is another requirement in most digital systems. The external data interface to these registers may be in either parallel or serial form and includes various **flip-flops (FFs)** and shift registers. There are many different types of flip-flops and shift registers, and this section presents several examples of circuits that can be used in static parallel registers. However, an exhaustive discussion of the various possibilities is not attempted.

RS Flip-Flop

The **RS (reset-set) flip-flop (RS-FF)** can be formed in a straightforward manner by using either two NOR gates or two NAND gates to replace the inverters in the simple latch. The desired state is stored by setting ($Q = 1$) or resetting ($Q = 0$) the flip-flop with the RS control inputs.

Figure 9.50 is the circuit for an RS-FF constructed using two-input NOR gates and corresponding to the truth table in Table 9.3. If the R and S inputs are low, they are both inactive, and the previously stored state of the flip-flop is maintained. However, if S is high

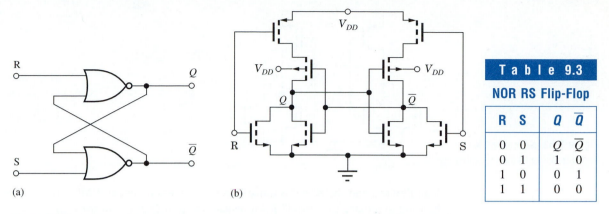

Table 9.3

NOR RS Flip-Flop

R	S	Q	$\overline{Q}$
0	0	Q	$\overline{Q}$
0	1	1	0
1	0	0	1
1	1	0	0

Figure 9.50 (a) RS flip-flop using NOR gates. (b) RS flip-flop using two CMOS NOR gates.

and R is low, output $\overline{Q}$ is forced low, and Q then becomes high, setting the latch. If R is high and S is low, node Q is low, and $\overline{Q}$ is then forced high, resetting the latch. Finally, if both R and S are high, both output nodes are forced low, and the final state is determined by the input that is maintained high for the longest period of time. The RS = 11 state is usually avoided in logic design.

The RS-FF can also be implemented using two-input NAND gates, as shown in Fig. 9.51 and Table 9.4. In this case, the latch maintains its state as long as both the $\overline{R}$ and $\overline{S}$ inputs are high, thus maintaining a conducting channel in both NMOS transistors. If the $\overline{R}$ input is set to 0 and $\overline{S}$ is a 1, then the $\overline{Q}$ output becomes a 1, causing the Q output to be reset to 0. If $\overline{R}$ returns to a 1, the reset condition is maintained within the latch. If the $\overline{S}$ input becomes a 0 and $\overline{R}$ remains a 1, the Q output is set to a 1 and the $\overline{Q}$ output becomes 0. If $\overline{S}$ returns to a 1, the latch remains "set." In the NAND implementation, both outputs are forced to 1 when $\overline{R}$ and $\overline{S}$ are both 0.

The flip-flops in Figs. 9.50 and 9.51 utilize full CMOS implementations of the NOR and NAND gates. If static power dissipation can be tolerated when the R and S inputs are both active, then the simplified implementation of Fig. 9.52 can be used. This is essentially the two-inverter latch used in the static memory circuits, with R and S transistors added to force either the Q or $\overline{Q}$ output low. If both R and S are 1, both outputs will be 0, and both

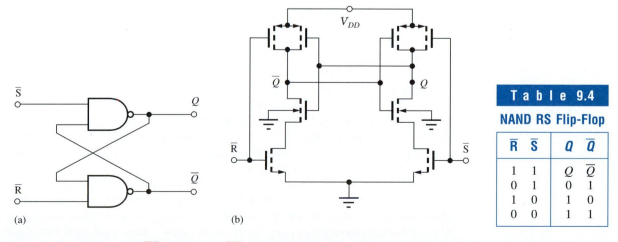

Table 9.4

NAND RS Flip-Flop

$\overline{R}$	$\overline{S}$	Q	$\overline{Q}$
1	1	Q	$\overline{Q}$
0	1	0	1
1	0	1	0
0	0	1	1

Figure 9.51 (a) A NAND $\overline{RS}$ flip-flop. (b) $\overline{RS}$ flip-flop implemented with two NAND gates.

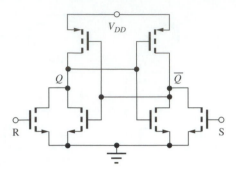

Figure 9.52 Simplified RS flip-flop using two NOR gates.

load devices and the R and S transistors will conduct current. PMOS transistors can also be used to replace the NMOS RS transistors to pull Q or $\overline{Q}$ toward V_{DD}.

The D-Latch

Another form of storage element is the **D latch,** shown in Fig. 9.53. When the clock input $C = 1$, transmission gate 1 is on and transmission gate 2 is off. The state of the D input is stored on the capacitance at the input of the first inverter and transferred through the inverter pair to the $\overline{Q}$ and Q outputs. The Q output follows the D input as long as $C = 1$. When the clock changes state to $C = 0$, the D input is disabled, and the state of the inverter pair is latched through transmission gate 2. The state at Q and $\overline{Q}$ remains constant as long as $C = 0$.

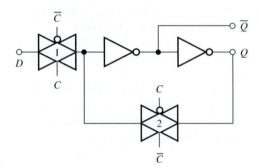

Figure 9.53 D latch.

A Master-Slave D Flip-Flop

The **master-slave D flip-flop (D-FF)** in Fig. 9.54 is a storage element in which the data is stable during both phases of the clock. Master-slave D-FFs can be directly cascaded to form a shift register. This D-FF is formed by a cascade connection of two D-type latches operating on opposite phases of the clock.

When the clock $C = 1$, transmission gates 1 and 4 are closed and 2 and 3 are open, resulting in the simplified circuit in Fig. 9.54(b). The D input is connected to the input of the first inverter pair, and the D input data appears at the output of the second inverter. The second pair of inverters is connected as a latch, holding the information previously placed on the input to the second inverter pair.

When the clock changes states and $C = 0$, as depicted in Fig. 9.54(c), transmission gate 1 disables the D input, and transmission gate 2 latches the information that was on the D input just before the clock state change. During the clock transition, data from the D input is maintained temporarily on the nodal capacitances associated with the first two inverters. Transmission gate 3 propagates the stored data onto the $\overline{Q}$ and Q outputs. Q is now equal to the data originally on the D input when C was equal to 1.

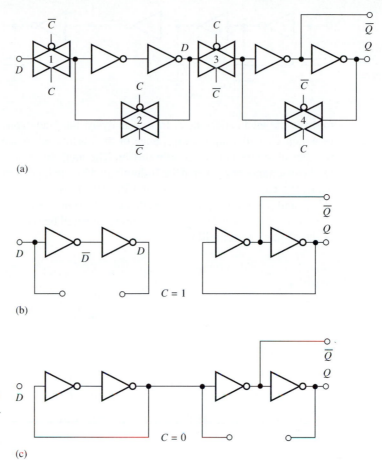

Figure 9.54 Master-slave D flip-flop. (a) Complete master-slave D flip-flop. (b) D flip-flop with $C = 1$. (c) D flip-flop with $C = 0$.

Note that the data at the output of the master-slave flip-flop is constant during both phases of the clock, except for the time required for the latches to change state. A path should never exist completely from the D input to the Q or $\overline{Q}$ outputs.

9.9 CASCADE BUFFERS

In today's high-density ICs, the input capacitance of a logic gate may be in the range of only 10 to 100 fF, and the propagation delay of a CMOS gate driving such a small load capacitance can be well below 1 ns. However, there are many cases in which a much higher load capacitance is encountered. For example, the wordlines in RAMs and ROMs represent a relatively large capacitance; long interconnection lines and internal data buses in microprocessors also represent significant load capacitances. In addition, the circuits that must drive off-chip data buses may have to drive capacitances as large as 10 to 50 pF, a capacitance 1000 times larger than the internal load capacitance. We know that the propagation delay of a CMOS gate is proportional to its load capacitance, so if a minimum size inverter is used to drive such a large capacitance, then the delay will be extremely long. If the inverter is scaled up in size to reduce its own delay, then its input capacitance increases, slowing down the propagation delay of the previous stage.

It has been shown [13, 14] that a minimum overall delay can be achieved by using an optimized cascade of several inverter stages, as depicted in Fig. 9.55. The W/L ratios of the transistors are increased by the **taper factor** β in each successive inverter stage in order

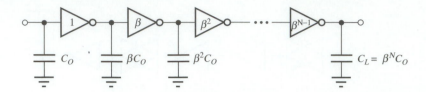

Figure 9.55 Cascade buffer for driving large capacitive loads.

to drive the load capacitance. In this analysis, the load capacitance is then $C_L = \beta^N C_o$, in which C_o is the input capacitance of the normal reference inverter stage and N is the number of stages in the **cascade buffer.** The analysis is simplified by assuming that the total capacitance at a given node is dominated by the input capacitance of the next inverter. Thus, the capacitive load on the first inverter is βC_o, the load on the second inverter is $\beta^2 C_o$, and so on. If the propagation delay of the unit size inverter driving a load capacitance of C_o is τ_o, then the delay of each inverter stage will be $\beta \tau_o$, and the total propagation delay of the N-stage buffer will be

$$\tau_B = N\beta\tau_o \tag{9.9}$$

in which

$$\beta^N = \frac{C_L}{C_O} \tag{9.10}$$

Solving Eq. (9.10) for β yields

$$\beta = \left(\frac{C_L}{C_O}\right)^{1/N} \tag{9.11}$$

and substituting this result into Eq. (9.9) yields an expression for the total propagation delay of the buffer:

$$\tau_B = N\left(\frac{C_L}{C_O}\right)^{1/N}\tau_o \tag{9.12}$$

In Eq. (9.12), N increases as additional stages are added to the buffer, but the value of the capacitance ratio term decreases with increasing N. The opposite behavior of these two factors leads to the existence of an optimum value of N for a given capacitance ratio.

Optimum Number of Stages

The number of stages that minimizes the overall buffer delay can be found by differentiating Eq. (9.12) with respect to N and setting the derivative equal to zero. The optimization can be simplified by taking logarithms of both sides of Eq. (9.12) before taking the derivative:

$$\ln \tau_B = \ln N + \frac{1}{N}\ln\left(\frac{C_L}{C_o}\right) + \ln \tau_o \tag{9.13}$$

Taking the derivative with respect to N yields:

$$\frac{d\ln\tau_B}{dN} = \frac{1}{N} - \frac{1}{N^2}\ln\left(\frac{C_L}{C_o}\right) \tag{9.14}$$

and setting Eq. (9.14) equal to zero gives the optimum value of N:

$$N_{opt} = \ln\left(\frac{C_L}{C_o}\right) \tag{9.15}$$

Substituting Eq. (9.15) into (9.11) yields the optimum value of the taper factor β_{opt} and the optimum buffer delay τ_{Bopt}:

$$\beta_{opt} = \left(\frac{C_L}{C_o}\right)^{[1/\ln(C_L/C_o)]} = \varepsilon \quad \text{and} \quad \tau_{Bopt} = \ln\left(\frac{C_L}{C_o}\right)\varepsilon\tau_o \qquad (9.16)$$

The optimum value of the taper factor is equal to the natural base $\varepsilon \approx 2.72$.

EXAMPLE 9.1: Design a cascade buffer to drive a load capacitance of 50 pF if $C_o = 50$ fF.

SOLUTION: The optimum value of N is $N_{opt} = \ln C_L/C_o = \ln(1000) = 6.91$, and the optimum delay is $\tau_{Bopt} = 6.91 \times (2.72) \times t_o = 18.8\, t_o$. N must be an integer, but either $N = 6$ or $N = 7$ can be used because the delay minimum is quite broad, as illustrated by the following numeric results. Using these two values of N yields:

$N = 6$: $\qquad\qquad\qquad\qquad \tau_B = 6(1000^{1/6})\tau_o = 19.0\tau_o$

$N = 7$: $\qquad\qquad\qquad\qquad \tau_B = 7(1000^{1/7})\tau_o = 18.8\tau_o$

Little is lost by using the smaller value of N. The choice between $N = 6$ and $N = 7$ will probably be made based on buffer area (see Prob. 50). Choosing $N = 6$ gives the buffer design in Fig. 9.56. ◆

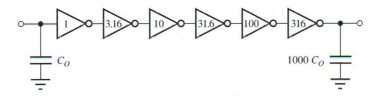

Figure 9.56 Optimum buffer design.

The buffer optimization just discussed is based on a set of very simple assumptions for the change in nodal capacitance with buffer size. Many refinements to this analysis have been published in the literature, and these more complex analyses indicate that the optimum tapering factor lies between 3 and 4. The results in Eqs. (9.15) and (9.16) should be used as an initial guide, with the final design determined using circuit simulation based on a given set of device and technology parameters.

| **EXERCISE:** Prove that $z^{1/\ln z} = \varepsilon$.

SUMMARY

Chapter 9 presented an introduction to MOS memory circuits including both random-access memory (RAM) and read-only memory (ROM), sometimes called read-only storage (ROS). Static RAMs (SRAMs) maintain the integrity of the data as long as power is applied to the circuit, whereas dynamic RAM (DRAM) circuits store the information temporarily as the charge on a capacitor. A six-transistor cell is usually used in SRAMs, whereas the one-transistor cell is now used in all high-density DRAMs. However, dynamic memories can also be based on three- and four-transistor dynamic memory cells. The internal organization of IC memories was also explored, and examples of the major building blocks of a memory chip, including row and column address decoders, sense amplifiers, wordline drivers, and output buffers were presented.

A number of new logic circuit techniques were introduced in this chapter. Static NAND and NOR array structures for use in address decoder circuits were presented, and the concept of dynamic logic was introduced. Dynamic logic circuits, such as domino CMOS, can be used effectively to reduce power consumption in many applications; a domino CMOS decoder was presented. Pass-transistor logic was introduced as one method for simplifying the design of the column decoding circuitry in a RAM.

The structure of ROM is very similar to that of RAM, but the data is embedded in the physical design of the circuitry. ROMs can be used to perform logic using the programmable logic array, or PLA. Two-bit partitioning, as well as cutting and folding operations, can be used to compress the size of PLA implementations.

Bistable storage elements based on the cross-coupled inverter pair were introduced, including the RS flip-flop, the dynamic D flip-flop, and the master-slave D flip-flop. Flip-flops use the two stable equilibrium points of a cross-coupled pair of inverters, often called a latch. The bistable latch also forms the heart of many sense amplifier circuits. The unstable equilibrium point of the latch plays a key role in the design of high-speed sensing circuits. Both static and clocked dynamic sense amplifiers can be used in memory designs.

High capacitance loads are often encountered in logic design, and cascade buffers are used to minimize the propagation delay associated with driving these large capacitance values. Cascade buffers are widely used in wordline drivers, and for on-chip and off-chip bus drivers.

Key Terms

AND array
Array personalization
Bistable circuit
Bitline
Bitline precharge
Bitline capacitance
Boosted wordline
Cascade buffer
Cell capacitance
Charge sharing
Charge transfer
Clocked sense amplifier
Clock phase
Column address decoder
Cross-coupled inverter
Cutting and folding
Domino CMOS
Dynamic logic
Dynamic random-access memory (DRAM)
D latch

Electrically erasable read-only memory (EEROM)
Erasable programmable read-only memory (EPROM)
Evaluation phase
Field programmable logic array (FPLA)
Flash memory
Flip-flop (FF)
Four-transistor (4-T) cell
Latch
Master-slave D flip-flop (D-FF)
NAND decoder
NOR decoder
One-transistor (1-T) cell
OR array
Pass-transistor logic
Precharge phase
Precharge transistor
Programmable logic array (PLA)
Programmable read-only memory (PROM)

Random-access memory (RAM)
Read-only memory (ROM)
Read-only storage (ROS)
Read operation
Refresh operation
Row address decoder
RS flip-flop (RS-FF)
Sense amplifier
Six-transistor (6-T) SRAM cell
Static random-access memory (SRAM)
Taper factor
Three-transistor (3-T) cell
Two-bit partitioning
Unstable equilibrium point
Wordline driver
Wordline capacitance
Write operation

References

1. J. Wood and R. G. Wood, "The use of insulated-gate field-effect transistors in digital storage systems," *ISSCC Digest of Technical Papers,* pp. 82–83, February 1965.

2. W. M. Regitz and J. A. Karp, "A three transistor-cell, 1024-bit, 500 ns MOS RAM," *ISSCC Digest of Technical Papers,* pp. 36–39, February 1970.

3. Robert H. Dennard; patent 3,387,286 assigned to the IBM Corporation.
4. Mikio Asakura et al., "A 34 ns 256 Mb DRAM with boosted sense-ground scheme," *ISSCC Digest of Technical Papers,* pp. 140–141, 324, February 1994.
5. *Digest of Technical Papers of the IEEE International Solid-State Circuits Conference* (ISSCC), February of each year.
6. *Digest of the IEEE Custom Integrated Circuits Conference,* April of each year.
7. *Digests of the Symposium on VLSI Circuits and the Symposium on VLSI Technology,* May/June of each year.
8. *IEEE Journal of Solid-State Circuits,* monthly.
9. *Digest of the IEEE International Electron Devices Meeting* (IEDM), December of each year.
10. *IEEE Transactions on Electron Devices,* monthly.
11. J. A. Karp, W. M. Regitz, and S. Chou, "A 4096-bit dynamic MOS RAM," *ISSCC Digest of Technical Papers,* pp. 10–11, February 1972.
12. Carver Mead and Lynn Conway, *Introduction to VLSI Systems,* Addison-Wesley, Reading, MA: 1980.
13. H. C. Lin and L. W. Linholm, "An optimized output stage for MOS integrated circuits," *IEEE JSSC,* vol. SC–10, pp. 106–109, April 1975.
14. R. C. Jaeger, "Comments on 'An optimized output stage for MOS integrated circuits,'" *IEEE JSSC,* vol. SC–10, pp. 185–186, June 1975.

PSPICE Simulation Data *All simulations use the following NMOS and PMOS Transistor Models

```
.MODEL MOSN NMOS KP=2.5E-5 VTO=.70 GAMMA=0.5
+ LAMBDA=.05 TOX=20N
+ CGSO=4E-9 CGDO=4E-9 CJ=2.0E-4 CJSW=5.0E-10
.MODEL MOSP PMOS KP=1.0E-5 VTO=-.70 GAMMA=0.75
+ LAMBDA=.05 TOX=20N
+ CGSO=4E-9 CGDO=4E-9 CJ=2.0E-4 CJSW=5.0E-10
```

*Figure 9.10 CMOS SRAM.
```
VPC 7 0 DC 3 PULSE(3 0 1NS .5NS .5NS 100NS)
VWL 6 0 DC 0 PULSE(0 3 2NS .5NS .5NS 100NS)
VDD 3 0 DC 3
CBL1 4 0 500FF
CBL2 5 0 500FF
*Storage Cell
MCN1 2 1 0 0 MOSN W=1U L=1U AS=1P AD=1P
MCP1 2 1 3 3 MOSP W=1U L=1U AS=1P AD=1P
MCN2 1 2 0 0 MOSN W=1U L=1U AS=1P AD=1P
MCP2 1 2 3 3 MOSP W=1U L=1U AS=1P AD=1P
MA1 4 6 2 0 MOSN W=1U L=1U AS=1P AD=1P
MA2 5 6 1 0 MOSN W=1U L=1U AS=1P AD=1P
*
*Sense Amplifier
MSN1 4 5 0 0 MOSN W=10U L=1U AS=10P AD=10P
MSP1 4 5 3 3 MOSP W=10U L=1U AS=10P AD=10P
MSN2 5 4 0 0 MOSN W=10U L=1U AS=10P AD=10P
MSP2 5 4 3 3 MOSP W=10U L=1U AS=10P AD=10P
MRS 5 7 4 0 MOSN W=10U L=1U AS=10P AD=10P
*
.OP
```

```
.TRAN 0.01NS 100NS
.NODESET V(1)=3 V(2)=0
*** ADD MODELS HERE ***
.PROBE V(1) V(2) V(3) V(4) V(5) V(6) V(7)
.END
```

*Figure 9.14 Writing the CMOS SRAM.

```
VWL 6 0 DC 0 PULSE(0 3 1NS 1NS 1NS 100NS)
VDD 3 0 DC 3
VBL1 4 0 DC 0
VBL2 5 0 DC 3
CBL1 4 0 500FF
CBL2 5 0 500FF
*Storage Cell
MCN1 2 1 0 0 MOSN W=1U L=1U AS=4P AD=4P
MCP1 2 1 3 3 MOSP W=1U L=1U AS=4P AD=4P
MCN2 1 2 0 0 MOSN W=1U L=1U AS=4P AD=4P
MCP2 1 2 3 3 MOSP W=1U L=1U AS=4P AD=4P
MA1 4 6 2 0 MOSN W=1U L=1U AS=4P AD=4P
MA2 5 6 1 0 MOSN W=1U L=1U AS=4P AD=4P
*
.OP
.TRAN 0.01NS 20NS
.NODESET V(1)=0 V(2)=3
*** ADD MODELS HERE ***
.PROBE V(1) V(2) V(3) V(4) V(5) V(6)
.END
```

*Figure 9.24 Sense amplifier precharge.

```
VPC 7 0 DC 3 PULSE(0 3 1NS 0.5NS 0.5NS 100NS)
VWL 6 0 DC 0
VDD 3 0 DC 3
CBL1 4 0 500FF
CBL2 5 0 500FF
*Storage Cell
MCN1 2 1 0 0 MOSN W=1U L=1U AS=2P AD=2P
MCP1 2 1 3 3 MOSP W=1U L=1U AS=2P AD=2P
MCN2 1 2 0 0 MOSN W=1U L=1U AS=2P AD=2P
MCP2 1 2 3 3 MOSP W=1U L=1U AS=2P AD=2P
MA1 4 6 2 0 MOSN W=1U L=1U AS=2P AD=2P
MA2 5 6 1 0 MOSN W=1U L=1U AS=2P AD=2P
*
*Sense Amplifier
MSN1 4 5 0 0 MOSN W=50U L=1U AS=100P AD=100P
MSP1 4 5 3 3 MOSP W=50U L=1U AS=100P AD=100P
MSN2 5 4 0 0 MOSN W=50U L=1U AS=100P AD=100P
MSP2 5 4 3 3 MOSP W=50U L=1U AS=100P AD=100P
MRS 5 7 4 0 MOSN W=50U L=1U AS=100P AD=100P
*
.OP
.TRAN 0.01NS 100NS
.NODESET V(1)=3 V(2)=0 V(5)=3 V(4)=0
```

```
*** ADD MODELS HERE ***
.PROBE V(1) V(2) V(3) V(4) V(5) V(6) V(7)
.END
```

*Figure 9.26 DRAM sense amplifier.
```
VPC 2 0 DC 3 PULSE(3 0 1NS .5NS .5NS 100NS)
VWL 6 0 DC 0 PULSE(0 3 2NS .5NS .5NS 100NS)
VDD 3 0 DC 3
CBL1 5 0 500FF
CBL2 4 0 500FF
*Storage Cell
MA1 5 6 1 0 MOSN W=1U L=1U AS=1P AD=1P
CC 1 0 50FF
MPS 3 2 1 0 MOSN W=1U L=1U AS=1P AD=1P
*Sense Amplifier
MSN1 4 5 0 0 MOSN W=10U L=1U AS=10P AD=10P
MSP1 4 5 3 3 MOSP W=10U L=1U AS=10P AD=10P
MSN2 5 4 0 0 MOSN W=10U L=1U AS=10P AD=10P
MSP2 5 4 3 3 MOSP W=10U L=1U AS=10P AD=10P
MPC 5 2 4 0 MOSN W=10U L=1U AS=10P AD=10P
*
.OP
.TRAN 0.01NS 100NS
*** ADD MODELS HERE ***
.PROBE V(1) V(2) V(3) V(4) V(5) V(6)
.END
```

*Figure 9.28 Boosted DRAM sense amplifier.
```
VPC 2 0 DC 3 PULSE(3 0 1NS .5NS .5NS 100NS)
VWL 6 0 DC 0 PULSE(0 5 2NS .5NS .5NS 100NS)
VDD 3 0 DC 3
CBL1 5 0 500FF
CBL2 4 0 500FF
*Storage Cell
MA1 5 6 1 0 MOSN W=1U L=1U AS=1P AD=1P
CC 1 0 50FF
MPS 7 7 1 0 MOSN W=1U L=1U AS=1P AD=1P
VPS 7 0 DC 5 PULSE(5 0 1NS .5NS .5NS 100NS)
*Sense Amplifier
MSN1 4 5 0 0 MOSN W=10U L=1U AS=10P AD=10P
MSP1 4 5 3 3 MOSP W=10U L=1U AS=10P AD=10P
MSN2 5 4 0 0 MOSN W=10U L=1U AS=10P AD=10P
MSP2 5 4 3 3 MOSP W=10U L=1U AS=10P AD=10P
MPC 5 2 4 0 MOSN W=10U L=1U AS=10P AD=10P
*
.OP
.TRAN 0.01NS 100NS
*** ADD MODELS HERE ***
.PROBE V(1) V(2) V(3) V(4) V(5) V(6)
.END
```

*Figure 9.30 Clocked CMOS sense amplifier.
VPC 2 0 DC 0 PULSE(0 3 1NS .5NS .5NS 100NS)
VWL 6 0 DC 0 PULSE(0 3 2NS .5NS .5NS 100NS)
VLC 9 0 DC 0 PULSE(0 3 3NS .5NS .5NS 100NS)
VDD 3 0 DC 3
CBL1 5 0 500FF
CBL2 4 0 500FF
*Storage Cell
MA1 5 6 1 0 MOSN W=1U L=1U AS=1P AD=1P
CC 1 0 50FF
*Dummy Cell
MA2 4 6 7 0 MOSN W=1U L=1U AS=1P AD=1P
CD 7 0 25FF
*Sense Amplifier
MPC1 5 2 3 3 MOSP W=10U L=1U AS=10P AD=10P
MPC2 4 2 3 3 MOSP W=10U L=1U AS=10P AD=10P
MP1 5 4 3 3 MOSP W=10U L=1U AS=10P AD=10P
MP2 4 5 3 3 MOSP W=10U L=1U AS=10P AD=10P
MS1 5 4 8 0 MOSN W=10U L=1U AS=10P AD=10P
MS2 4 5 8 0 MOSN W=10U L=1U AS=10P AD=10P
ML 8 9 0 0 MOSN W=10U L=1U AS=10P AD=10P
*
.OP
.TRAN 0.01NS 100NS
*** ADD MODELS HERE ***
.PROBE V(1) V(2) V(3) V(4) V(5) V(6) V(7) V(8) V(9)
.END

*Figure 9.35 Domino CMOS gate.
*
VDD 5 0 DC 3
VC 1 0 DC 0 PULSE(0 3 5NS .5NS .5NS 25NS)
VIN 2 0 DC 3
MN1 3 1 0 0 MOSN W=5U L=1U AS=5P AD=5P
MN2 4 2 3 0 MOSN W=5U L=1U AS=5P AD=5P
MN3 6 4 0 0 MOSN W=5U L=1U AS=5P AD=5P
MP1 4 1 5 5 MOSP W=5U L=1U AS=5P AD=5P
MP2 6 4 5 5 MOSP W=5U L=1U AS=5P AD=5P
CL 6 0 100FF
*
.OP
.TRAN 0.01NS 100NS
*** ADD MODELS HERE ***
.PROBE V(1) V(2) V(3) V(4) V(5) V(6)
.END

*Figure 9.36 Three cascaded domino CMOS gates.
*
VC 1 0 DC 0 PULSE(0 3 5NS 1NS 1NS 30NS)
VIN 2 0 DC 3
XI1 1 2 3 GATE

```
XI2 1 3 4 GATE
XI3 1 4 5 GATE
CL 5 0 100FF
.SUBCKT GATE 1 2 6
VDD 5 0 DC 3
MN1 3 1 0 0 MOSN W=5U L=1U AS=5P AD=5P
MN2 4 2 3 0 MOSN W=5U L=1U AS=5P AD=5P
MN3 6 4 0 0 MOSN W=5U L=1U AS=5P AD=5P
MP1 4 1 5 5 MOSP W=5U L=1U AS=5P AD=5P
MP2 6 4 5 5 MOSP W=5U L=1U AS=5P AD=5P
.ENDS
*
.OP
.TRAN 0.01NS 100NS
*** ADD MODELS HERE ***
.PROBE V(1) V(2) V(3) V(4) V(5)
.END
```

Problems

Unless otherwise specified, use $V_{TON} = 0.7$ V, $V_{TOP} = -0.7$ V, $\gamma = 0.5\sqrt{V}$, $2\phi_F = 0.6$ V.

9.1 Random-Access Memory (RAM)

9.1. How many bits are actually in a 256-Mb memory chip? In a 1-Gb chip?

9.2. How many 128-Kb blocks must be replicated to form the 256-Mb memory in Fig. 9.1?

9.3. A 256-Mb static CMOS memory chip uses the standard 6-T CMOS cell. How much leakage is permitted per memory cell if the total standby current of the memory is to be less than 1 mA?

9.2 Static Memory Cells

9.4. Find the voltages corresponding to D and $\overline{D}$ in an NMOS memory cell with resistor loads if $R = 10^{10}\ \Omega$, $V_{DD} = 3$ V, and $W/L = 2/1$. Use $V_{TO} = 0.75$ V, $\gamma = 0.5\sqrt{V}$, and $2\phi_F = 0.6$ V.

 *9.5. Simulate the response time of the 6-T cell in Fig. 9.6(c) from an initial condition of $D_1 = 1.55$ V and $D_2 = 1.45$ V with the access transistors off. How long does it take for the cell voltages to reach 90 percent of their final values? Use $V_{DD} = 3$ V and a symmetrical cell design, with W/L of the NMOS transistors $= 2/1$. Use the SPICE models from Appendix B.

*9.6. Assume that the two bitlines are fixed at 1.5 V in the circuit in Figs. 9.7 and 9.8 and that a steady-state condition has been reached, with the wordline voltage equal to 3 V. Assume that the inverter transistors all have $W/L = 1/1$, $V_{TN} = 0.7$ V, $V_{TP} = -0.7$ V, and $\gamma = 0$. What is the largest value of W/L for M_{A1} and M_{A2} (use the same value) that will ensure that the voltage at $D_1 \leq 0.7$ V and the voltage at $D_2 \geq 2.3$ V?

9.7. Simulate and plot a graph of the transients that occur when writing a 0 into a cell containing a 0, as in Fig. 9.12. Discuss the results.

9.3 Dynamic Memory Cells

9.8 The 1-T cell in Fig. P9.8 uses a bitline voltage of 5 V and a wordline voltage of 5 V. (a) What are the cell voltages stored on C_C for a 1 and 0 if $V_{TO} = 1$ V, $\gamma = 0.5\sqrt{V}$, and $2\phi_F = 0.6$ V? (b) What would be the minimum wordline voltage needed in order for the cell voltage to reach 5 V for a 1?

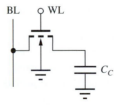

Figure P9.8

9.9. Substrate leakage currents usually tend to destroy only one of the two possible states in the 1-T cell.

For the circuit in Fig. P9.8, which level is the most sensitive to leakage currents and why?

*9.10. The gate-source and drain-source capacitances of the MOSFET in Fig. P9.8 are each 100 fF, and $C_C = 75$ fF. The bitline and wordline have been stable at 3 V for a long time. The wordline signal is shown in Fig. P9.10. What is the voltage stored on C_C before the wordline drops? Estimate the drop in voltage on the C_C due to coupling of the wordline signal through the gate-source capacitance. Use $V_{TO} = 0.80$ V, $\gamma = 0.5 \sqrt{\text{V}}$, and $2\phi_F = 0.6$ V.

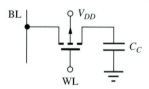

Figure P9.10

9.11. A 1-T cell has $C_C = 60$ fF and $C_{BL} = 7.5$ pF. (a) If the bitlines are precharged to 2.5 V and the cell voltage is 0 V, what is the change in bitline voltage ΔV following cell access? (b) What is the final voltage in the cell?

9.12. A 1-T cell memory can be fabricated using PMOS transistors in the array shown in Fig. P9.12. (a) What are the voltages stored on the capacitor corresponding to logic 0 and 1 levels for a technology using $V_{DD} = 5$ V? (b) Repeat for $V_{DD} = 3$ V.

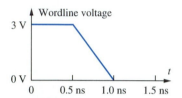

Figure P9.12

9.13. (a) Calculate the cell voltage for the boosted wordline version of the 1-T cell in Fig. 9.25 and show that the value in the text is correct. (b) Verify that the value of the current entering the sense amplifier node from the 1-T cell immediately following activation of the wordline is 90 μA, as stated in the text.

9.14. The bottom electrode of the storage capacitor in the 1-T cell is often connected to a voltage V_{PP} rather than ground, as shown in Fig. P9.14. Suppose that $V_{PP} = 5$ V. (a) What are the voltages stored in the cell at node V_C for $0 = 0$ V on the bitline and $1 = 3$ V on the bitline? Assume the wordline can

be driven to 3 V. (b) Which level will deteriorate due to leakage in this cell?

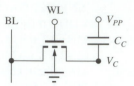

Figure P9.14

*9.15. The 1-T cell in Fig. P9.15 uses bitline and wordline voltages of 0 V and 5 V. (a) What are the cell voltages stored on C_C for a 1 and 0 if $V_{TO} = -0.80$ V, $\gamma = 0.65$ V$^{0.5}$, and $2\phi_F = 0.6$ V? (b) What would be the minimum wordline voltage needed for the stored cell voltage to reach 0 V for a 0 state?

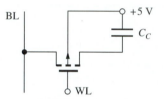

Figure P9.15

*9.16. In the discussion of the 1-T cell in the text, an improvement factor of 15 was stated for current drive from the boosted wordline cell compared to the normal cell. How much of this factor of 15 is attributable to the increased V_{DS} across the access transistor, and what portion is attributable to the increased gate voltage?

9.17. Simulate the refresh operation of the 4-T dynamic cell in Fig. P9.17. For initial conditions, assume that node D has decreased to 1 V and node $\overline{D}$ is at 0 V. Use $BL = 3$ V, $\overline{BL} = 3$ V, $W/L = 2/1$ for all transistors, and the bitline capacitance is 500 fF.

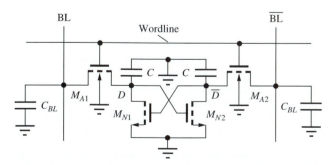

Figure P9.17

9.18. (a) Repeat the exercise related to Fig. 9.19 if all devices have $W/L = 2/1$. (Be careful—M_B may no longer be in saturation.) (b) What is the minimum value of γ for which M_B remains in saturation?

9.19. Calculate the steady state output current from the 3-T cell in Fig. 9.19 if a 1 is stored in the cell and the power supply voltage is 5 V instead of 3 V. Assume $V_{TO} = 1$ V, $\gamma = 0.65$ $V^{0.5}$, $2\phi_F = 0.6$ V, and all W/L ratios $= 2/1$.

9.20. Simulate the read access operation of the 4-T cell in Fig. P9.20 and discuss the waveforms that you obtain. What is the access time of the cell from the time the wordline is activated until the data is valid at the output of the sense amplifier? Use $W/L = 2/1$ for all devices and assume $C_{BL} = 1$ pF, with $V_{DD} = 3$ V.

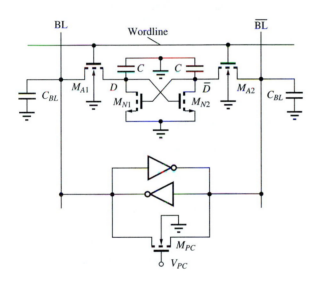

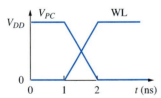

Figure P9.20

9.4 Sense Amplifiers

9.21. A simple CMOS sense amplifier is shown in Fig. P9.21. Suppose $V_{DD} = 5$ V and the W/L ratios of all the NMOS and PMOS transistors are 5/1 and 10/1, respectively. What is the total current through the sense amplifier when the precharge transistor is on? How much power will be consumed by 1024 of these sense amplifiers operating simultaneously?

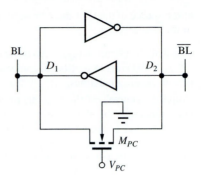

Figure P9.21

9.22. A transient drop can be observed in the waveforms for the two bitlines in Fig. 9.26 due to capacitive coupling of the precharge signal through the gate capacitance of the precharge device. Calculate the expected voltage change ΔV on the bitlines due to this coupling and compare to the simulation results in the figure. The BL capacitances are each 500 fF. See Appendix B for transistor models.

9.23. The two bitlines in Fig. 9.30 are driven above V_{DD} by capacitive coupling of the precharge signal through the gate capacitance of the precharge devices. (a) Calculate the expected voltage change ΔV on the bitlines due to this coupling and compare to the simulation results in the figure. (b) What is the largest possible value of ΔV? See PSPICE listings at chapter end for transistor models.

9.24. Figure P9.24 shows the basic form of a charge-transfer sense amplifier that can be used for amplifying the output of a 1-T cell. Assume that the switch closes at $t = 0$, that the capacitor C_C is initially discharged, and that C_L is initially charged to +3 V. Also assume that charge sharing between C_C and C_{BL} occurs instantaneously. Find the total change in the output voltage Δv_O that occurs once the circuit returns to steady-state conditions following the switch closure. Assume $C_C = 50$ fF, $C_{BL} = 1$ pF, $C_L = 100$ fF, and $W/L = 50/1$. (*Hint:* The MOSFET will restore the BL potential to the original value, and the total charge that flows out

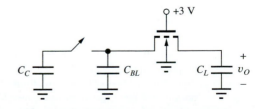

Figure P9.24 Charge transfer sense amplifier.

of the source of the FET must be supplied from the drain.)

9.25. Simulate the circuit in Fig. P9.24 using a MOSFET ($W/L = 4/1$) for the switch and compare the results to your hand calculations.

**9.26. Convince yourself of the statement that any voltage imbalance in the cross-coupled latch will be reinforced by simulating the CMOS latch of Fig. P9.26 using the following initial conditions: (a) $D_1 = 1.45$ V and $D_2 = 1.55$ V, (b) $D_1 = 1$ V and $D_2 = 1.25$ V, (c) $D_1 = 2.75$ V and $D_2 = 2.70$ V. Assume all W/L ratios are 2/1 and $V_{DD} = 5$ V, and use bitline capacitances of 1 pF.

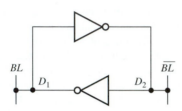

Figure P9.26

*9.27. The W/L ratios of the NMOS and PMOS transistors are 2/1 and 4/1, respectively, in the CMOS inverters in Fig. P9.27. The bitline capacitances are 400 fF, W/L of M_{PC} is 10/1, and $V_{DD} = 3$ V. (a) Simulate the switching behavior of the symmetrical latch in Fig. P9.27 and explain the behavior of the voltages at nodes D_1 and D_2. (b) Now suppose that a design error occurred and the W/L ratio of M_{N2} is 2.2/1 instead of 2/1. Simulate the latch again and explain any changes in the behavior of the voltages at nodes D_1 and D_2.

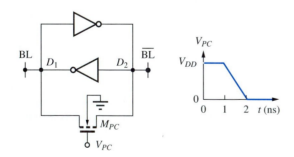

Figure P9.27

*9.28. Simulate the response of the NMOS clocked sense amplifier in Fig. P9.28 if $V_{DD} = 3$ V. What are the final voltage values on the two bitlines? How long does it take the sense amplifier to develop a difference of 1.5 V between the two bitlines? Assume that all clock signals have amplitudes equal to V_{DD}

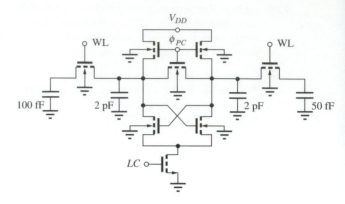

Figure P9.28

and rise or fall times of 1 ns. Assume that the three signals are delayed successively by 0.5 ns in a manner similar to Fig. 9.30.

*9.29. Repeat Prob. 9.28 for $V_{DD} = 5$ V.

9.30. Simulate the transfer function of two cascaded CMOS inverters with all 2/1 devices and find the three equilibrium points. Use $V_{DD} = 3$ V.

9.5 Address Decoders

9.31. (a) How many transistors are required to implement a full 10-bit NOR address decoder similar to that of Fig. 9.31? (b) How many transistors are required to implement a full 10-bit NAND address decoder similar to that of Fig. 9.32?

9.32. Calculate the number of transistors required to implement a 7-bit column decoder using (a) NMOS pass-transistor logic and (b) standard NOR logic.

9.33. Draw the schematic of a 3-bit OR address decoder using domino CMOS.

9.34. What are the voltages at the nodes in the pass-transistor networks in Fig. P9.34? For NMOS transistors, use $V_{TO} = 0.75$ V, $\gamma = 0.55 \sqrt{V}$, and $2\phi_F = 0.6$ V. For PMOS transistors, $V_{TO} = -0.75$ V.

*9.35. (a) Suppose that inputs A_0, A_1, and A_2 are all 0 in the domino CMOS gate in Fig. P9.35, and the clock has just changed to the evaluate phase. If A_0 now changes to a 1, what happens to the voltage at node B if $C_1 = 2C_2$? (*Hint:* Remember the charge-sharing phenomena.) (b) Now A_1 changes to a 1—what happens to the voltage at node B if $C_3 = C_2$? (c) If the output inverter is a symmetrical design, what is the minimum ratio of C_1/C_2 (assume $C_3 = C_2$) for which the gate maintains a valid output? Assume $V_{DD} = 5$ V.

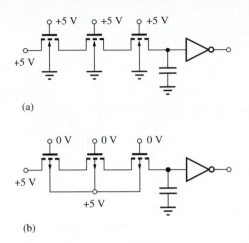

(a)

(b)

Figure P9.34

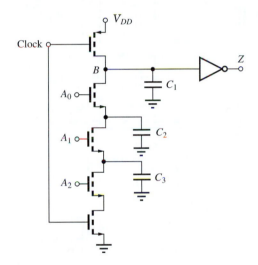

Figure P9.35

 9.36. Draw the mirror image of the gate in Fig. P9.35 by replacing NMOS transistors with PMOS transistors and vice versa. Assume the logic inputs remain the same and write an expression for the logic function Z.

9.6 Read-Only Memory (ROM)

9.37. What are the six output data words for the ROM in Fig. P9.37 on p. 388?

 9.38. Identify and simulate the worst-case delay path in the ROM in Fig. P9.37 on page 388.

9.39. What are the contents of the ROM in Fig. P9.39? (All FETs are NMOS.)

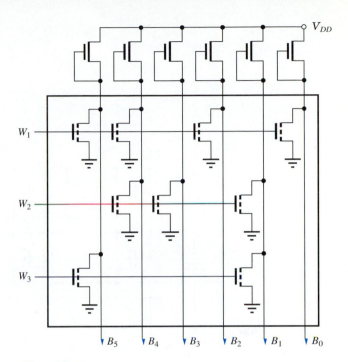

Figure P9.39

9.40. What are the contents of the ROM in Fig. P9.40? (All FETs are NMOS.)

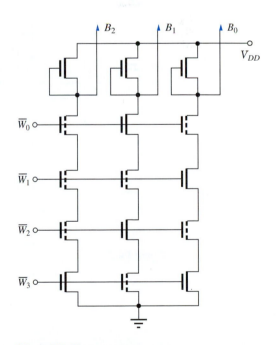

Figure P9.40

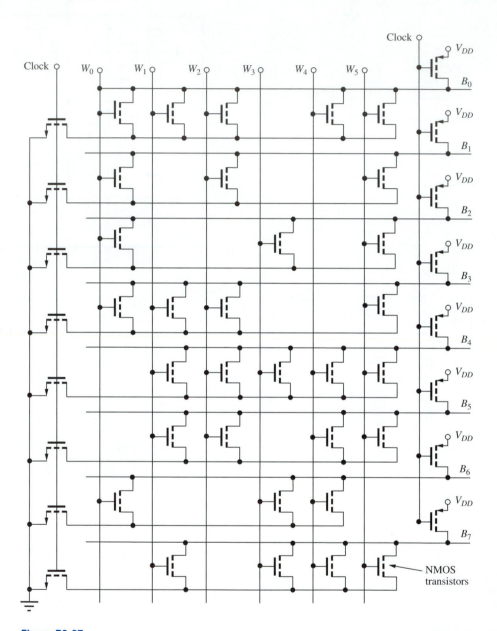

Figure P9.37

9.7 The Programmable Logic Array (PLA)

9.41. (a) What are the logic expressions for the 3 PLA outputs in Fig. P9.41 on p. 390? (b) Minimize the expressions.

9.42. A NOR array is shown in Fig. P9.42. What are the eight output terms?

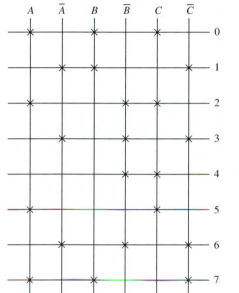

Figure P9.42

9.43. (a) What is the array utilization factor in Fig. P9.42? (b) Compress the array in Fig. P9.42 using cutting and folding operations.

9.44. Identify and simulate the worst-case delay path in the PLA in Fig. P9.41 on page 390.

9.8 Flip-Flops

9.45. What is the logic function of inputs 1 and 2 in the flip-flop in Fig. P9.45?

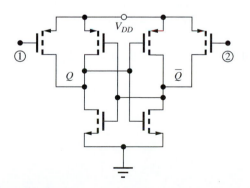

Figure P9.45

9.46. What is the minimum size of the transistors connected to the R and S inputs in Fig. P9.46 that will ensure that the latch can be forced to the desired state? Do not be concerned with speed of the latch.

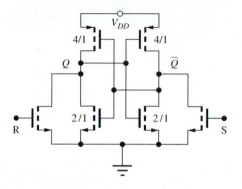

Figure P9.46

9.47. Simulate the propagation delay through the D latch to Q and $\overline{Q}$ in Fig. 9.53. Assume that D is stable and the clock signal is a square wave. Assume the transistors all have $W/L = 2/1$ and use $V_{DD} = 5$ V.

9.48. Simulate the master-slave D-flip-flop with the slowly rising clock ($T = 20$ μs) in Fig. P9.48. Assume all $W/L = 2/1$. What happens to data on the D input?

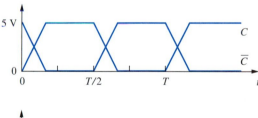

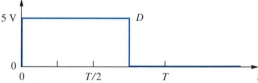

Figure P9.48

9.9 Cascade Buffers

9.49. Design an optimized cascade buffer to drive a load capacitance of 4000 C_o. (a) What is the optimum number of stages? (b) What are the relative sizes of each inverter in the chain (see Fig. 9.56)? (c) What is the delay of the buffer in terms of τ_o?

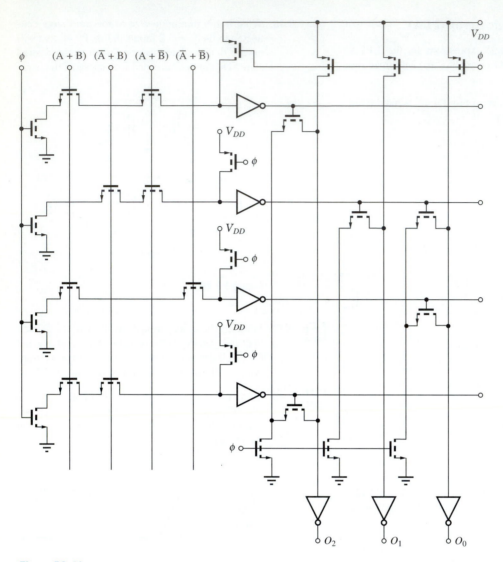

Figure P9.41

**9.50. Assume that the area of each inverter in the cascade buffer is proportional to the taper factor β and that the unit size inverter has an area A_o. Write an expression for the total area of an N-stage cascade buffer. In the example in Fig. 9.56, buffers with $N = 6$ and $N = 7$ have approximately the same delay. Compare the areas of these two buffer designs using your formula.

CHAPTER 10

Bipolar Logic Circuits

Chapter 10 explores details of the two bipolar circuit families that have been used extensively in logic circuit design since the mid-1960s. **Emitter-coupled logic (ECL)** historically has been the fastest form of logic available. The circuit uses bipolar transistors operating in a differential circuit that is often called a current switch. For binary logic operation, two states are needed, and in ECL, the transistors operate in the forward-active region with either a relatively large collector current or a very small collector current, actually near cutoff. The transistors avoid saturation and an attendant delay time that substantially slows down BJT switching speed.

Transistor-transistor logic (TTL or **T^{2}L)** was the dominant logic family for systems designed through the mid-1980s, when it began being replaced by CMOS. TTL was the family that established 5 V as the standard power supply level. The main transistors in TTL switch between the **forward-active**—but essentially nonconducting—and **saturation regions** of operation. In the TTL circuit, we find one of the few actual applications for the **reverse-active region** of operation of the BJT. Because various transistors in the TTL circuit enter saturation, TTL delays tend to be poorer than those that can be achieved with ECL. However, an improved circuit, Schottky-clamped TTL, is substantially faster than standard TTL or can achieve delays similar to standard TTL at much less power dissipation.

10.1 THE CURRENT SWITCH (EMITTER-COUPLED PAIR)

We begin our study of bipolar logic circuits with emitter-coupled logic, or ECL. At the heart of an ECL gate is the **current switch circuit** in Fig. 10.1, consisting of two identical transistors, Q_1 and Q_2; two matched-load resistors, R_C; and current source I_{EE}. This circuit is also known as an **emitter-coupled pair.** The input logic signal v_I is applied to the base of Q_1 and is compared to the **reference voltage** V_{REF}, which is connected to the base of transistor Q_2. If v_I is greater than V_{REF} by a few hundred millivolts, then the current from source I_{EE} is supplied through the emitter of Q_1. If v_I is less than V_{REF} by a few hundred millivolts, then the current from source I_{EE} is supplied by the emitter of Q_2. The input voltage v_I "switches" the current from source I_{EE} back and forth between Q_1 and Q_2. This behavior is conceptually illustrated in Fig. 10.2, in which transistors Q_1 and Q_2 have been replaced by a single-pole, double-throw switch whose position is controlled by the input v_I.

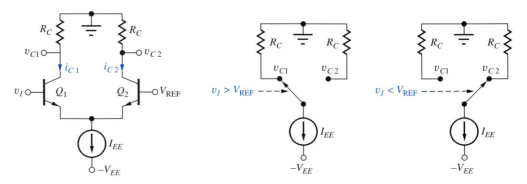

Figure 10.1 Current switch circuit used in an ECL gate.

Figure 10.2 Conceptual representation of the current switch.

Mathematical Model for Static Behavior of the Current Switch

The behavior of the current switch can be understood in more detail using the transport model for the forward-active region from Chapter 5, in which the collector currents in the two transistors are represented by

$$i_{C1} = I_S \exp\left(\frac{v_{BE1}}{V_T}\right) \qquad \text{and} \qquad i_{C2} = I_S \exp\left(\frac{v_{BE2}}{V_T}\right) \tag{10.1}$$

It is assumed in Eq. (10.1) that $v_{BE} > 4V_T$. If the transistors are identical, so that the saturation currents are the same, then the ratio of these two collector currents can be written as

$$\frac{i_{C2}}{i_{C1}} = \frac{I_S \exp\left(\dfrac{v_{BE2}}{V_T}\right)}{I_S \exp\left(\dfrac{v_{BE1}}{V_T}\right)} = \frac{\exp\left(\dfrac{v_{BE2}}{V_T}\right)}{\exp\left(\dfrac{v_{BE1}}{V_T}\right)} = \exp\left(\frac{v_{BE2} - v_{BE1}}{V_T}\right) = \exp\left(-\frac{\Delta v_{BE}}{V_T}\right) \tag{10.2}$$

Now, suppose that v_{BE2} exceeds v_{BE1} by 300 mV: $\Delta v_{BE} = (v_{BE1} - v_{BE2}) = -0.3$ V. For $V_T = 0.025$ V, we find that i_{C2} is approximately 1.6×10^5 times bigger than i_{C1}. (Remember that a one decade of current change in a BJT corresponds to approximately a 60-mV change in v_{BE}, so a factor of 10^5 is precisely the change we expect for a ΔV_{BE} of 300 mV.) However, if v_{BE1} exceeds v_{BE2} by 300 mV, then i_{C1} will be 1.6×10^5 times larger than i_{C2}. Thus, the assumption that all the current from the source I_{EE} is switched from one side to the other appears justified for a few-hundred-millivolt difference in v_{BE}.

A useful expression for the normalized difference in collector currents can be derived from Eq. (10.1):

$$\frac{i_{C1} - i_{C2}}{i_{C1} + i_{C2}} = \frac{\exp\left(\dfrac{v_{BE1}}{V_T}\right) - \exp\left(\dfrac{v_{BE2}}{V_T}\right)}{\exp\left(\dfrac{v_{BE1}}{V_T}\right) + \exp\left(\dfrac{v_{BE2}}{V_T}\right)} = \tanh\left(\frac{v_{BE1} - v_{BE2}}{2V_T}\right) \tag{10.3}$$

Using Kirchhoff's current law at the emitter node yields

$$i_{E1} + i_{E2} = I_{EE} \tag{10.4}$$

For the forward-active region, $i_C = \alpha_F i_E$, and assuming matched devices with identical current gains, Eq. (10.4) can be rewritten as

$$i_{C1} + i_{C2} = \alpha_F I_{EE} \tag{10.5}$$

Combining Eqs. (10.3) and (10.5) gives the desired result for the collector current difference in terms of the difference in base-emitter voltages:

$$i_{C1} - i_{C2} = \alpha_F I_{EE} \tanh\left(\frac{v_{BE1} - v_{BE2}}{2V_T}\right) = \alpha_F I_{EE} \tanh\left(\frac{\Delta v_{BE}}{2V_T}\right) \tag{10.6}$$

Figure 10.3 plots a graph of Eq. (10.6) in normalized form, showing that only a small voltage change is required to switch the current from one collector to the other. Ninety-nine percent of the current switches for $|\Delta v_{BE}| > 4.6V_T$ (130 mV)! We see that a relatively small voltage change is required to completely switch the current from one side to the other in the current switch. This small voltage change directly contributes to the high speed of ECL logic gates.

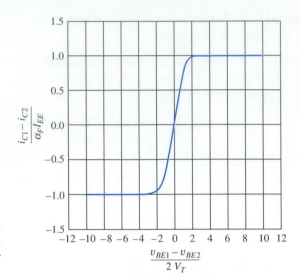

Figure 10.3 Normalized collector current difference versus $\Delta v_{BE}/2V_T$ for the bipolar current switch.

EXERCISE: Calculate the ratio i_{C2}/i_{C1} for $(v_{BE2} - v_{BE1}) = 0.2$ V and 0.4 V.

ANSWERS: 2.98×10^3; 8.89×10^6

Current Switch Analysis for $v_I > V_{REF}$

Now let us explore the actual current switch circuit for the case of $v_I = V_{REF} + 0.3$ V $= -0.7$ V, as in Fig. 10.4. From Fig. 10.3 we expect 0.3 V to be more than enough to fully switch the current. In this design, V_{REF} has been selected to be -1.0 V (the reasons for this choice will become clear shortly). Because $v_I > V_{REF}$, we assume that Q_2 is off ($i_{C2} = 0$) and Q_1 is conducting in the forward-active region, with $V_{BE1} = 0.7$ V. Applying Kirchhoff's voltage law to the circuit in Fig. 10.4:

$$v_I - v_{BE1} + v_{BE2} - V_{REF} = 0 \tag{10.7}$$

$$(V_{REF} + 0.3 \text{ V}) - (0.7) + v_{BE2} - V_{REF} = 0$$

$$v_{BE2} = 0.4 \text{ V}$$

The base-emitter voltage difference is given by $v_{BE1} - v_{BE2} = 300$ mV, so essentially all the current I_{EE} switches to the emitter of Q_1, and Q_2 is nearly cut off. [However, Q_2 is actually still in the forward-active region by our strict definition of the regions of operation for the bipolar transistor ($v_{BE} \geq 0$, $v_{BC} \leq 0$)].

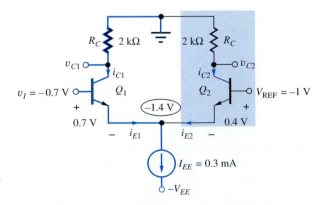

Figure 10.4 Current switch circuit with $v_I > V_{REF}$. Q_1 is conducting; Q_2 is "off."

Kirchhoff's current law at the emitter node requires

$$i_{E1} + i_{E2} = I_{EE}$$

and

$$i_{E1} \approx I_{EE} \qquad \text{because } i_{E2} \approx 0$$

The output voltages v_{C1} and v_{C2} at the two collectors are given by

$$v_{C1} = -i_{C1}R_C = -\alpha_F i_{E1} R_C \approx -\alpha_F I_{EE} R_C \qquad (10.8)$$

and

$$v_{C2} = -i_{C2}R_C = -\alpha_F i_{E2} R_C \approx 0 \qquad (10.9)$$

in which $i_C = \alpha_F i_E$ in the forward-active region. For $\alpha_F \approx 1$, the two output voltages become

$$v_{C1} = -i_{C1}R_C \approx -I_{EE}R_C \qquad \text{and} \qquad v_{C2} = -i_{C2}R_C = 0 \qquad (10.10)$$

For the circuit in Fig. 10.4, $I_{EE} = 0.3$ mA and $R_C = 2$ kΩ, and

$$v_{C1} = -(0.3 \text{ mA})(2 \text{ k}\Omega) = -0.6 \text{ V} \qquad \text{and} \qquad v_{C2} = 0 \text{ V} \qquad (10.11)$$

Check of Forward-Active Region Assumptions

Now we can check our assumptions concerning the forward-active region of operation. For Q_1, $v_{BC1} = v_{B1} - v_{C1} = -0.7 \text{ V} - (-0.6 \text{ V}) = -0.1 \text{ V}$, and the collector-base junction is indeed reverse-biased. We assumed that the emitter-base junction was forward-biased, so the assumption of forward-active region is consistent with our circuit analysis. For Q_2, $V_{BC2} = -1.0 \text{ V} - (0 \text{ V}) = -1.0 \text{ V}$ and $v_{BE2} = 0.4 \text{ V}$, so Q_2 is also in the forward-active region although it is conducting a negligibly small current.

Current Switch Analysis for $v_I < V_{REF}$

The second logic state occurs for $v_I = V_{REF} - 0.3 \text{ V} = -1.3 \text{ V}$, as in Fig. 10.5. Because $v_I < V_{REF}$, we assume that Q_2 is conducting in the forward-active region, with $v_{BE2} = 0.7 \text{ V}$. Kirchhoff's voltage law again requires

$$v_I - v_{BE1} + v_{BE2} - V_{REF} = 0$$

which yields

$$(V_{REF} - 0.3 \text{ V}) - v_{BE1} + (0.7) - V_{REF} = 0$$

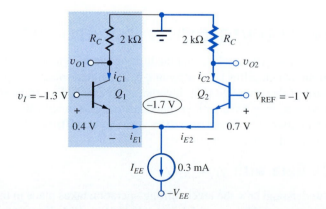

Figure 10.5 Current switch circuit with $v_I < V_{REF}$. Q_2 is conducting; Q_1 is "off."

and

$$v_{BE1} = 0.4 \text{ V}$$

v_{BE1} is much less than v_{BE2}, so now $i_{E1} \approx 0$. Kirchhoff's current law requires

$$i_{E1} + i_{E2} = I_{EE}$$

and therefore

$$i_{E2} \approx I_{EE} \qquad \text{because } i_{E1} \approx 0$$

For this case, the output voltages at v_{C1} and v_{C2} are given by

$$v_{C1} = -i_{C1}R_C = -\alpha_F i_{E1}R_C \approx 0 \tag{10.12a}$$

and $$v_{C2} = -i_{C2}R_C = -\alpha_F i_{E2}R_C \approx -\alpha_F I_{EE}R_C \tag{10.12b}$$

For $\alpha_F \approx 1$, the two output voltages become

$$v_{C1} = -i_{C1}R_C = 0 \qquad \text{and} \qquad v_{C2} = -I_{EE}R_C = -0.6 \text{ V} \tag{10.13}$$

The results from Eqs. (10.11) and (10.13) are combined in Table 10.1. We see there are two discrete voltage levels at the two outputs, 0 V and -0.6 V, that can correspond to a logic 1 and a logic 0, respectively. Note, however, that the voltages at the outputs of the current switch do not match the input voltages used at v_I. This current switch circuit fails to meet one of the important criteria for logic gates set forth in Sec. 6.2: The logic levels must be restored as the signal goes through the gate. That is, the voltage levels at the output of a logic gate must be compatible with the levels used at the input of the gate.

> **EXERCISE:** Redesign the circuit in Fig. 10.4 to reduce the power by a factor of 5 while maintaining the voltage levels the same.
>
> **ANSWER:** $R_C = 10 \text{ k}\Omega$, $I_{EE} = 60 \text{ μA}$

T a b l e 10.1		
Current Switch Voltage Levels		
v_I ($V_{\text{REF}} = -0.1$ V)	v_{C1}	v_{C2}
$V_{\text{REF}} + 0.3$ V $= -0.7$ V	-0.6 V	0 V
$V_{\text{REF}} - 0.3$ V $= -1.3$ V	0 V	-0.6 V

10.2 THE EMITTER-COUPLED LOGIC (ECL) GATE

We observe in Table 10.1 that the high and low logic levels at the input and output of the current switch differ by exactly one base-emitter voltage drop (0.7 V), which leads to the circuit of the complete ECL inverter in Fig. 10.6. Two transistors, Q_3 and Q_4, have been added, and their base-emitter junctions are used to shift the output voltages down by one base-emitter drop. These transistors act as **level shifters** in the circuit and are usually called emitter followers.

ECL Gate with $v_I = V_{OH}$

To understand how the level-shifting operation takes place in the ECL circuit, consider the case for $v_I = V_{OH} = -0.7$ V indicated in Fig. 10.6. Equations for the output voltages v_{O1}

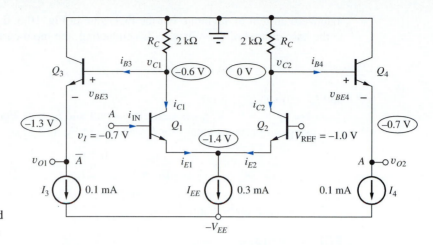

Figure 10.6 Emitter-coupled logic circuit with $v_I = V_{OH}$.

and v_{O2} can be written as

$$v_{O1} = -(i_{C1} + i_{B3})R_C - v_{BE3} \qquad \text{and} \qquad v_{O2} = -(i_{C2} + i_{B4})R_C - v_{BE4} \quad (10.14)$$

The base currents are given by

$$i_{B3} = \frac{I_3}{\beta_F + 1} \qquad \text{and} \qquad i_{B4} = \frac{I_4}{\beta_F + 1}$$

In a typical digital IC technology, $\beta_F \geq 20$ and $i_B R_C \ll v_{BE}$. Then

$$v_{O1} \approx -i_{C1} R_C - v_{BE3} = -0.6 - 0.7 = -1.3 \text{ V}$$

and   (10.15)

$$v_{O2} \approx -i_{C2} R_C - v_{BE4} = 0 - 0.7 = -0.7 \text{ V}$$

For sufficiently large β_F, the addition of Q_3 and Q_4 does not change the voltage at v_{C1} or v_{C2}.

The base-collector voltages of Q_3 and Q_4 will be -0.6 V and 0 V, respectively, and the two current sources, I_3 and I_4, force a current of 0.1 mA in the emitters of Q_3 and Q_4. Thus, both Q_3 and Q_4 are in the forward-active region, so $v_{BE3} = v_{BE4} = 0.7$ V has been used.

> **EXERCISE:** What are the base currents i_{B3} and i_{B4} in Fig. 10.6 if $\beta_F = 20$? Compare $i_B R_C$ to V_{BE}.
>
> **ANSWERS:** 4.76 μA, 9.52 mV $\ll$ 0.7 V

ECL Gate with $v_I = V_{OL}$

For $v_I = V_{OL} = -1.3$ V, the outputs change state, and

$$v_{O1} \approx -i_{C1} R_C - v_{BE3} = 0 - 0.7 = -0.7 \text{ V}$$

and   (10.16)

$$v_{O2} \approx -i_{C2} R_C - v_{BE4} = -0.6 - 0.7 = -1.3 \text{ V}$$

Input Current of the ECL Gate

In NMOS and CMOS logic circuits, the inputs are normally connected to FET gates, and the static input current to the logic gate is zero. In bipolar logic circuits, however, there is a nonzero current in the input. For the ECL gate in Fig. 10.6, the input current i_{in} is equal to the base current of Q_1. When Q_1 is conducting, the input current is given by

$$i_{in} = i_{B1} = \frac{i_{E1}}{\beta_F + 1} \tag{10.17}$$

and $i_{in} \approx 0$ when Q_1 is off.

For $v_I = -1.3$ V, i_{E1} is negligibly small and $i_{in} \approx 0$. For $v_I = -0.7$ V, $i_{E1} = I_{EE}$ and, using our previous values for I_{EE} and β_F in Eq. (10.17),

$$i_{in} = \frac{i_{EE}}{\beta_F + 1} = \frac{0.3 \text{ mA}}{21} = 14.3 \text{ } \mu\text{A}$$

Thus, a circuit that is providing an input to an ECL gate must be capable of supplying 14.3 µA to each input that it drives.

ECL Summary

Table 10.2 summarizes the behavior of the basic ECL inverter in Fig. 10.6. The requirement for level compatibility between the input and output voltages is now met. For this ECL gate design,

$$V_{OH} = -0.7 \text{ V}$$
$$V_{OL} = -1.3 \text{ V} \tag{10.18}$$
$$\Delta V = V_{OH} - V_{OL} = 0.6 \text{ V}$$

To provide symmetrical noise margins, the reference voltage V_{REF} is normally centered midway between the two logic levels:

$$V_{REF} = \frac{V_{OH} + V_{OL}}{2} = -1.0 \text{ V} \tag{10.19}$$

In the design in Fig. 10.6, the logic signal swings symmetrically above and below V_{REF} by one-half the logic swing, or 0.3 V. Note that the logic swing ΔV is just equal to the voltage drop developed across the load resistor R_C:

$$\Delta V = I_{EE} R_C \tag{10.20}$$

Two important observations should be made at this point. If the input at v_I is now defined as the logic variable A, then the output at v_{O1} corresponds to $\overline{A}$ but the output at v_{O2} corresponds to A! A complete ECL gate generates both true and complement outputs for a given logic function. Having both true and complement outputs available can often reduce the total number of logic gates required to implement a given logic function.

The second observation relates to the speed of emitter-coupled logic. As seen in the analysis, the transistors remain in the forward-active region at all times. The off transistor is actually conducting current but at a very low level, and it is ready to switch rapidly into high

T a b l e 10.2

ECL Voltage Levels and Input Current

v_I	v_{O1}	v_{O2}	i_{in}
$V_{REF} + 0.3$ V $= -0.7$ V	-1.3 V	-0.7 V	$+14.3$ µA
$V_{REF} - 0.3$ V $= -1.3$ V	-0.7 V	-1.3 V	0

conduction for a base-emitter voltage change of only a few tenths of a volt. The transistors avoid the saturation region, which substantially slows down the switching speed of the bipolar transistor. (A detailed discussion of this problem is in Sec. 10.11.) The reduced logic swing of ECL contributes to its high speed, and the small ΔV reduces the dynamic power required to charge and discharge the load capacitances.

> **EXERCISE:** Find V_{OH}, V_{OL}, V_{REF}, and ΔV for the ECL gate in Fig. 10.6 if I_{EE} is changed to 0.2 mA.
>
> **ANSWERS:** -0.7 V, -1.1 V, -0.9 V, 0.4 V

10.3 V_{IH}, V_{IL}, AND NOISE MARGIN ANALYSIS FOR THE ECL GATE

The simulated VTC for the ECL gate is given in Fig. 10.7, in which both outputs switch between the two logic levels specified in Table 10.2. The two outputs remain constant until the input comes within approximately 100 mV of the reference voltage, and then they rapidly change states as the input voltage changes by an additional 200 mV. The approach to finding the values of V_{IH} and V_{IL} and the noise margins is similar to that used for NMOS and CMOS circuits, but the algebra is simpler.

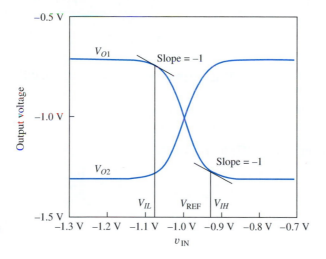

Figure 10.7 SPICE simulation results for ECL voltage transfer function.

V_{IL} and V_{IH}

V_{IH} and V_{IL} are defined by the points at which $\partial v_{O1}/\partial v_I = -1$ for the inverting output or $\partial v_{O2}/\partial v_I = +1$ for the noninverting output. Writing the expression for v_{O1} in Fig. 10.6 yields

$$v_{O1} = v_{C1} - v_{BE3} = -(i_{C1} + i_{B3})R_C - v_{BE3} \qquad (10.21)$$

and taking the derivative with respect to v_I gives

$$\frac{\partial v_{O1}}{\partial v_I} = -R_C \frac{\partial i_{C1}}{\partial v_I} \qquad (10.22)$$

The base current and base-emitter voltage of Q_3 are constant because $i_{E3} = I_3$, a constant current. An expression for i_{C1} in terms of v_I can be obtained using the same procedure as that used to derive Eqs. (10.2) and (10.3):

$$\frac{i_{C1}}{i_{C1} + i_{C2}} = \frac{1}{1 + \exp\left(\dfrac{v_{BE2} - v_{BE1}}{V_T}\right)} \quad \text{and} \quad i_{C1} = \frac{\alpha_F I_{EE}}{1 + \exp\left(\dfrac{v_{BE2} - v_{BE1}}{V_T}\right)}$$

(10.23)

because $i_{C1} + i_{C2} = \alpha_F I_{EE}$. Equation (10.7) can be rearranged to yield a relationship between the input voltage and the base-emitter voltages:

$$(v_{BE2} - v_{BE1}) = V_{\text{REF}} - v_I$$

(10.24)

Rewriting i_{C1} from Eq. (10.23):

$$i_{C1} = \frac{\alpha_F I_{EE}}{1 + \exp\left(\dfrac{V_{\text{REF}} - v_I}{V_T}\right)}$$

(10.25)

Taking the derivative and substituting the result in Eq. (10.22) yields

$$\frac{\partial v_{O1}}{\partial v_I} = -R_C \frac{(-\alpha_F I_{EE}) \exp\left(\dfrac{V_{\text{REF}} - v_I}{V_T}\right)\left(\dfrac{-1}{V_T}\right)}{\left[1 + \exp\left(\dfrac{V_{\text{REF}} - v_I}{V_T}\right)\right]^2} = \frac{-\left(\dfrac{1}{V_T}\right) i_{C1} R_C}{\left[1 + \exp\left(\dfrac{v_I - V_{\text{REF}}}{V_T}\right)\right]}$$

(10.26)

At $v_I = V_{IL}$, $v_I < V_{\text{REF}}$, $\exp[(v_I - V_{\text{REF}})/V_T] \ll 1$, and Eq. (10.26) simplifies to

$$\frac{\partial v_{O1}}{\partial v_I} \approx -\left(\frac{1}{V_T}\right) i_{C1} R_C = -1$$

(10.27)

Solving Eq. (10.27) for i_{C1} yields

$$i_{C1} = \frac{V_T}{R_C}$$

and using Eq. (10.2),

$$V_{\text{REF}} - V_{IL} = V_T \ \ln\left(\frac{I_{EE} - i_{C1}}{i_{C1}}\right) = V_T \ \ln\left(\frac{I_{EE} - \dfrac{V_T}{R_C}}{\dfrac{V_T}{R_C}}\right)$$

(10.28)

Solving for V_{IL} yields

$$V_{IL} = V_{\text{REF}} - V_T \ \ln\left(\frac{I_{EE} R_C}{V_T} - 1\right) = V_{\text{REF}} - V_T \ \ln\left(\frac{\Delta V}{V_T} - 1\right)$$

(10.29)

Then, using symmetry, or a similar analysis, the value of V_{IH} is

$$V_{IH} = V_{\text{REF}} + V_T \ \ln\left(\frac{I_{EE} R_C}{V_T} - 1\right) = V_{\text{REF}} + V_T \ \ln\left(\frac{\Delta V}{V_T} - 1\right)$$

(10.30)

Noise Margins

The noise margins are found using Eqs. (10.29) and (10.30):

$$NM_L = V_{IL} - V_{OL} = V_{REF} - V_T \ln\left(\frac{I_{EE}R_C}{V_T} - 1\right) - V_{REF} + \frac{\Delta V}{2}$$

and   (10.31)

$$NM_H = V_{OH} - V_{IH} = V_{REF} + \frac{\Delta V}{2} - V_{REF} - V_T \ln\left(\frac{I_{EE}R_C}{V_T} - 1\right)$$

or

$$NM_L = V_T\left[\frac{I_{EE}R_C}{2V_T} - \ln\left(\frac{I_{EE}R_C}{V_T} - 1\right)\right]$$

and   (10.32)

$$NM_H = V_T\left[\frac{I_{EE}R_C}{2V_T} - \ln\left(\frac{I_{EE}R_C}{V_T} - 1\right)\right]$$

Using the values from Fig. 10.6, we find

$$V_{REF} - V_{IL} = 78.5 \text{ mV} = V_{IH} - V_{REF}$$

$$NM_L = 0.22 \text{ V} = NM_H$$

V_{IL} occurs at an input voltage approximately 78 mV below V_{REF}, and V_{IH} occurs at an input voltage approximately 78 mV above V_{REF}. These numbers are in excellent agreement with the circuit simulation results in Fig. 10.7, and the high and low state noise margins are both equal to 0.22 V.

> **EXERCISE:** What are the noise margins for the circuit in Fig. 10.6 if I_{EE} is changed to 0.2 mA?
>
> **ANSWER:** 0.132 V

10.4 CURRENT SOURCE IMPLEMENTATION

Bias for the ECL gate in Fig. 10.6 is usually not provided by current sources. This is particularly true of the sources that bias emitter-follower transistors Q_3 and Q_4. The simplest elements that can be used to set the currents in Q_3 and Q_4 are the resistors R, indicated in Fig. 10.8. The currents are no longer equal in Q_3 and Q_4 because the voltages across the

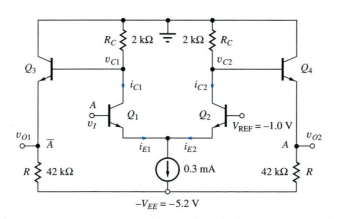

Figure 10.8 Resistor bias for the level-shifting transistors.

two resistors are slightly different. However, the same value resistor is used on both sides, and the average emitter current is designed to be equal to I_3 and I_4.

For example, suppose that $v_{O1} = V_{OH}$ and $v_{O2} = V_{OL}$. Then,

$$i_{E3} = \frac{v_{O1} - (-V_{EE})}{R} = \frac{V_{OH} + V_{EE}}{R} \quad \text{and} \quad i_{E4} = \frac{v_{O2} - (-V_{EE})}{R} = \frac{V_{OL} + V_{EE}}{R}$$

$$(10.33)$$

The average value of the two emitter currents is given by

$$\frac{i_{E3} + i_{E4}}{2} = \frac{2V_{EE} + v_{OH} + v_{OL}}{2R} = \left(V_{EE} + \frac{v_{OH} + v_{OL}}{2}\right)\frac{1}{R} \quad (10.34)$$

R can be found using the values calculated for the original ECL gate:

$$R = \frac{\left(V_{EE} + \dfrac{v_{OH} + v_{OL}}{2}\right)}{\dfrac{i_{E3} + i_{E4}}{2}} = \frac{\left(5.2 + \dfrac{-0.7 - 1.3}{2}\right) \text{V}}{0.1 \text{ mA}} = 42 \text{ k}\Omega \quad (10.35)$$

Using Eq. (10.33), we see that the individual currents for this ECL circuit are

$$i_{E3} = \frac{-0.7 + 5.2}{42 \text{ k}\Omega} = 0.107 \text{ mA} \quad \text{and} \quad i_{E4} = \frac{-1.3 + 5.2}{42 \text{ k}\Omega} = 0.093 \text{ mA} \quad (10.36)$$

As is to be expected, one current is slightly above the average design value and one is slightly below the design value. The larger the value of V_{EE}, the smaller the difference between the two currents.

Current Source I_{EE}

Source I_{EE} can also be replaced by a resistor, as in Fig. 10.9. For $v_I = -1.3$ V, the voltage at the emitters of Q_1 and Q_2 is the same as that in Fig. 10.5, -1.7 V, and the value of R_{EE} required to set the emitter current i_{E2} to 0.3 mA is

$$R_{EE} = \frac{[-1.7 - (-5.2)] \text{ V}}{0.3 \text{ mA}} = 11.7 \text{ k}\Omega$$

The use of resistor R_{EE} is usually accompanied by a slight modification in the value of the resistor connected to the collector of Q_1. Referring to Fig. 10.10 for the case of

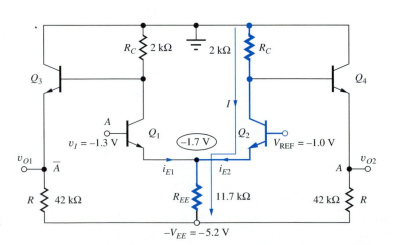

Figure 10.9 ECL gate with current source I_{EE} replaced by a resistor.

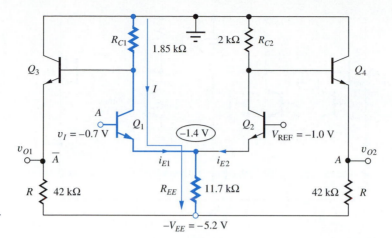

Figure 10.10 Modification of one of the collector-load resistors.

$v_I = -0.7$ V, we find that the voltage at the emitters of Q_1 and Q_2 is -1.4 V, and hence the emitter current has changed slightly due to the voltage change across resistor R_{EE}:

$$i_E = \frac{[-1.4 - (-5.2)] \text{ V}}{11.7 \text{ k}\Omega} = 0.325 \text{ mA}$$

Because the emitter current increases, the value of R_{C1} must be decreased to maintain a constant logic swing ΔV. The new value of the resistor R_{C1} in the collector of Q_1 is

$$R_{C1} = \frac{0.6 \text{ V}}{0.325 \text{ mA}} = 1.85 \text{ k}\Omega$$

The corrected design values appear in the circuit in Fig. 10.10.

> **EXERCISE:** What are the new values of R_{EE} and R_{C1} for the circuit in Fig. 10.10 if I_{EE} is changed to 0.2 mA and $R_{C2} = 2 \text{ k}\Omega$?
>
> **ANSWERS:** 18.0 kΩ, 1.89 kΩ

10.5 THE ECL OR-NOR GATE

The ECL inverter becomes an OR-NOR gate through the addition of transistors in parallel with the original input transistor of the inverter, as in Fig. 10.11(a). If any one of the inputs (A or B or C) is at a high input level ($v_I > V_{REF}$), then the current from source I_{EE} will be switched into collector node v_{C1}. Output Y_1 will drop to a low level, and output Y_2 will rise to a high level. Y_1 therefore represents a NOR output, and Y_2 is an OR output:

$$Y_1 = \overline{A + B + C} \qquad \text{and} \qquad Y_2 = A + B + C$$

The logic symbol in Fig. 10.11(b) is used for the dual output OR-NOR gate. The NOR output is marked by the small circle, which indicates the complemented or inverted output.

The full ECL gate produces both true and complemented outputs. However, not every gate need be implemented this way. For example, the three-input logic gate in Fig. 10.12 has been designed with only the NOR output available; the two-input gate in Fig. 10.13 provides only the OR function. Note that the resistor in the collector of Q_2 is not needed in Fig. 10.12 and has been eliminated. Similarly, the left-hand collector resistor is eliminated from the circuit in Fig. 10.13.

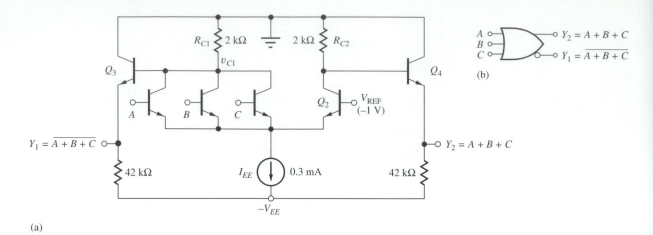

Figure 10.11 (a) Three-input ECL OR-NOR gate and (b) logic symbol.

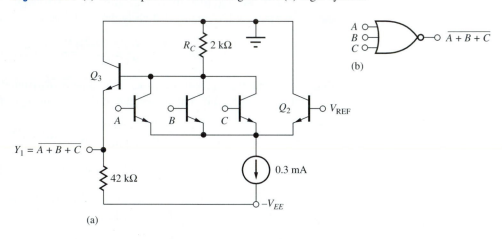

Figure 10.12 (a) Three-input ECL NOR gate and (b) logic symbol.

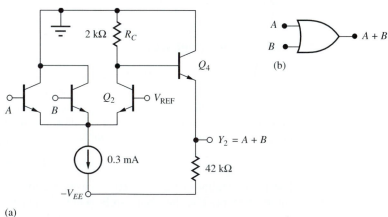

Figure 10.13 (a) Two-input ECL OR gate and (b) logic symbol.

EXERCISES: What are the new values of R_{C1} and R_{C2} for the circuit in Fig. 10.11 if I_{EE} is replaced by a 11.7-kΩ resistor? Assume $V_{REF} = -1$ V and $V_{EE} = -5.2$ V. What is the new value of R_C for the circuit in Fig. 10.12 if I_{EE} is replaced by a 11.7-kΩ resistor? Assume $V_{REF} = -1$ V and $V_{EE} = -5.2$ V.

ANSWERS: 1.85 kΩ, 2.00 kΩ; 1.85 kΩ

EXERCISE: What is the new value of R_C for the circuit in Fig. 10.13 if I_{EE} is replaced by a 11.7-kΩ resistor? Assume $V_{\text{REF}} = -1$ V and $V_{EE} = -5.2$ V.

ANSWER: 2.00 kΩ

10.6 THE EMITTER FOLLOWER

Let us now look in more detail at the operation of the emitter followers that provide the level-shifting function in the ECL gate. An emitter follower is shown biased by an ideal current source in Fig. 10.14(a). For $v_I \le V_{CC}$, Q_1 operates in the forward-active region because its base-collector voltage is negative, and the current source is forcing a current out of the emitter. The behavior of the emitter follower can be better understood by replacing Q_1 with its model for the forward-active region, as in Fig. 10.14(b).

Using Kirchhoff's voltage law:

$$v_O = v_I - v_{BE} \tag{10.37}$$

For the forward-active region, the transport equations yield

$$i_E \approx \frac{I_S}{\alpha_F}\left[\exp\left(\frac{v_{BE}}{V_T}\right) - 1\right] \tag{10.38}$$

Because the emitter current is constant, v_{BE} is also constant, and v_O is approximately

$$v_O = v_I - v_{BE} \approx v_I - 0.7 \text{ V} \tag{10.39}$$

The difference between the input and output voltages is fixed. Thus, the voltage at the emitter "follows" the voltage at the input, but with a fixed offset equal to one base-emitter diode voltage. This is also clearly evident in Fig. 10.14(b), in which the base and emitter terminals are connected together through the base-emitter diode.

The voltage transfer characteristic for the emitter follower appears in Fig. 10.15. The output voltage v_O at the emitter follows the input voltage with a slope of $+1$ and a fixed offset voltage equal to $V_{BE} \approx 0.7$ V. For positive inputs, the output follows the input voltage until the BJT begins to enter saturation at the point when $v_I > V_{CC}$. The maximum output voltage occurs when the transistor saturates with $v_O = V_{CC} - V_{\text{CESAT}}$ and $v_I = V_{CC} - v_{\text{CESAT}} + v_{BE}$. At this point, the input voltage is approximately one diode-drop above V_{CC}! Any further increase in v_I will destroy the bipolar transistor.

The minimum output voltage is set by the characteristics of the current source. An ideal current source would continue to operate with $v_O < -V_{EE}$, but most electronic current sources require $v_O \ge -V_{EE}$. Thus, the minimum value of the input voltage is one diode drop greater than $-V_{EE}$: $v_I = -V_{EE} + v_{BE}$. For v_I less than this value, Q_1 begins to cut off.

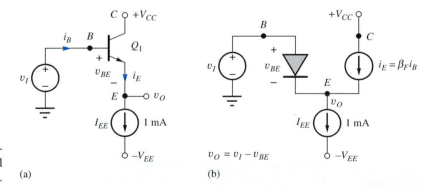

Figure 10.14 (a) Emitter follower and (b) transport model for the forward-active region.

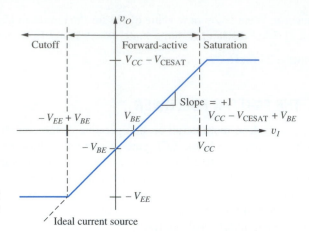

Figure 10.15 Voltage transfer characteristic for the emitter follower.

Emitter Follower with Resistor Bias

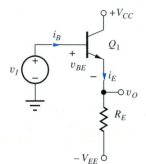

Figure 10.16 Emitter follower biased by resistor R_E.

Simple resistor bias was used for the **emitter followers** in the final ECL gate design in a manner similar to that shown in Fig. 10.16. However, for resistor bias, the emitter current of the transistor changes as the output voltage changes:

$$i_E = \frac{v_O - (-V_{EE})}{R_E} = \frac{v_O + V_{EE}}{R_E} \qquad (10.40)$$

Although the current changes, v_{BE} does not change significantly because of the logarithmic dependence of v_{BE} on i_E, as obtained from Eq. (10.1):

$$v_{BE} = V_T \ln\left(\frac{\alpha_F i_E}{I_S}\right) \qquad (10.41)$$

Remember that a change in i_E at room temperature equal to a factor of 10 requires only a 60-mV change in v_{BE}. So, the relationship between the input and output voltages remains

$$v_O = v_I - v_{BE} \approx v_I - 0.7 \text{ V}$$

Figure 10.17 is a comparison of the emitter currents in the transistors in Figs. 10.14 and 10.16. For the current source case, the emitter current remains fixed at the current I_{EE}. For resistor bias, the output voltage v_O follows v_I down until the current in the resistor becomes zero at $v_O = -V_{EE}$. For $v_I > (-V_{EE} + v_{BE})$, the emitter current increases in direct proportion to the input voltage, as predicted by Eq. (10.40).

EXERCISE: What value of R_E is required to set $i_E = 0.3$ mA for $v_I = 0$ in the emitter follower in Fig. 10.16 if $-V_{EE} = -5.2$ V?

ANSWER: 15.0 kΩ

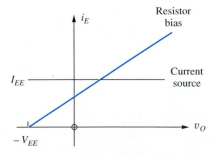

Figure 10.17 Emitter-follower current versus output voltage.

Emitter Follower with a Load Resistor

An external load resistor is often connected to an **emitter follower,** as shown by R_L in Fig. 10.18(a). The addition of R_L sets a new limit V_{MIN} on the negative output swing of the emitter follower. V_{MIN} represents the Thévenin equivalent voltage at v_O for $i_E = 0$, as in Fig. 10.18(b):

$$V_{MIN} = \frac{R_L}{R_L + R_E}(-V_{EE}) \tag{10.42}$$

For $V_I > V_{MIN} + v_{BE}$, the behavior of the emitter follower is the same as discussed previously. However, for v_O to drop below V_{MIN}, emitter current i_E has to be negative, which is impossible in this circuit. The modified VTC for the emitter follower is shown in Fig. 10.18(c), in which the minimum output voltage is now V_{MIN}.

> **EXERCISE:** If $R_E = 15\ \text{k}\Omega$, $V_{CC} = 0\ \text{V}$, and $-V_{EE} = -5.2\ \text{V}$, what is the minimum output voltage of the emitter follower in Fig. 10.18(a) if $R_L = \infty$? If $R_L = 10\ \text{k}\Omega$?
>
> **ANSWERS:** $-5.20\ \text{V}$; $-2.08\ \text{V}$
>
> **EXERCISE:** (a) If $R_L = 10\ \text{k}\Omega$, $V_{CC} = 5\ \text{V}$, and $-V_{EE} = -5.2\ \text{V}$, what value of R_E is required to achieve $V_{MIN} = -4\ \text{V}$? (b) What is the value of i_E for $v_O = 0\ \text{V}$, $-4\ \text{V}$, and $+4\ \text{V}$?
>
> **ANSWERS:** $3.00\ \text{k}\Omega$; $1.73\ \text{mA}$, $0\ \text{A}$, $3.47\ \text{mA}$

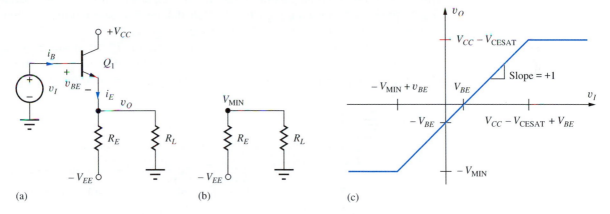

Figure 10.18 (a) Emitter follower with load resistor R_L added; (b) circuit with Q_1 cut off; (c) voltage transfer function for emitter follower with load resistor.

10.7 "EMITTER DOTTING" OR "WIRED-OR" LOGIC

In most logic circuits including NMOS, CMOS, and TTL, the outputs of two logic gates cannot be directly connected together. (See Prob. 8.10.) However, it is possible to tie the outputs of emitter followers together, and this capability provides a powerful enhancement to the logic function of ECL.

Parallel Connection of Emitter-Follower Outputs

Consider the circuit of Fig. 10.19, with the input voltages as shown. The output follows the most positive input voltage (minus the 0.7-V base-emitter offset), and the transistor

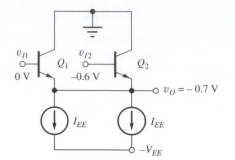

Figure 10.19 Parallel connection of two emitter followers.

with the lower input voltage operates near cutoff. For the specific example in Fig. 10.19, the input voltage to Q_2 is at -0.6 V. If Q_2 were conducting, then its emitter would be one diode drop below its base at -1.3 V. However, the input to Q_1 is 0 V, and its emitter can only drop down to -0.7 V. Thus, the output is at -0.7 V. The base-emitter voltage of transistor Q_2 is forced to become -0.1 V, and Q_2 is cut off. Note that because Q_2 is cut off, the emitter of Q_1 must now supply the current of both current sources, $i_{E1} = 2I_{EE}$.

The Wired-OR Logic Function

Now, suppose that one emitter-follower input corresponds to the logic variable A, and the second input corresponds to logic variable B, as in Fig. 10.20. The output will be high if either A or B is high, whereas the output will be low only if both A and B are low. This corresponds to the OR function: $Y = A + B$. The logical OR function can be obtained by simply connecting the outputs of two ECL gates together. This is a powerful additional feature provided by the ECL logic family. Note that the two base-emitter junctions behave in a manner similar to the diode OR gate discussed in Sec. 6.5.

A simple example is provided in the logic circuit in Fig. 10.21, in which the outputs of two ECL gates are connected together to provide the logic function $Y_1 = \overline{(A + B + C)} + \overline{(D + E)}$. The upper gate also provides a second output, $Y_2 = A + B + C$.

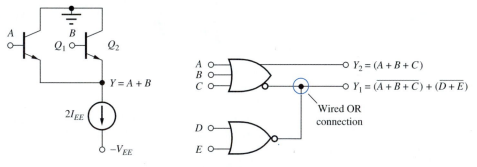

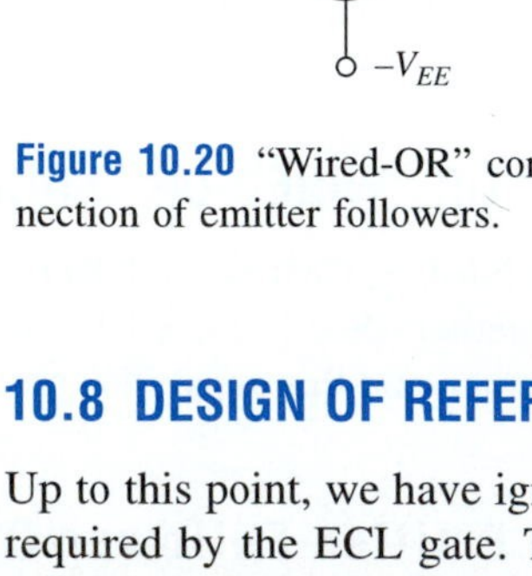

Figure 10.20 "Wired-OR" connection of emitter followers.

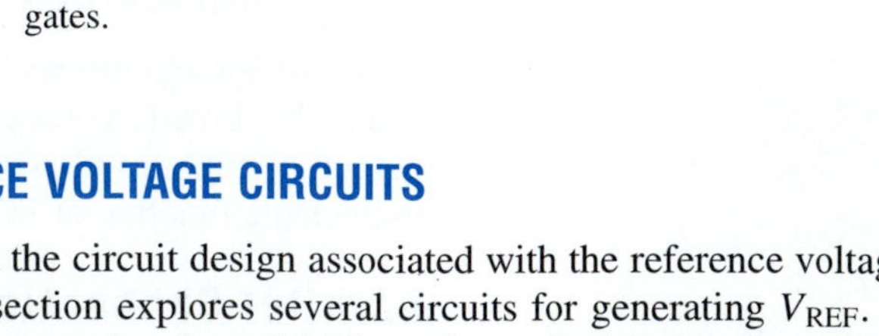

Figure 10.21 "Wired-OR" connection of two ECL logic gates.

10.8 DESIGN OF REFERENCE VOLTAGE CIRCUITS

Up to this point, we have ignored the circuit design associated with the reference voltage required by the ECL gate. This section explores several circuits for generating V_{REF}. A resistive voltage divider between ground and a -5.2-V supply, as depicted in Fig. 10.22, is a simple realization of the reference supply. Resistors R_1 and R_2 in the voltage divider

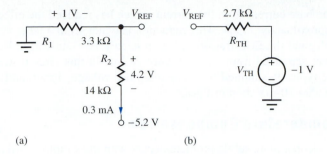

Figure 10.22 (a) Resistor voltage divider and (b) its Thévenin equivalent.

(a)　　　　　　　　　　(b)

are chosen to set the current in the reference circuit to 0.3 mA. (The reason for this choice will be made clear shortly.) The sum of the resistors is then given by

$$R_1 + R_2 = \frac{5.2 \text{ V}}{0.3 \text{ mA}} = 17.3 \text{ k}\Omega$$

and R_1 is chosen to provide a voltage drop of 1 V:

$$R_1 = \frac{1 \text{ V}}{0.3 \text{ mA}} = 3.3 \text{ k}\Omega$$

The resulting circuit is shown in Fig. 10.22 along with its Thévenin equivalent circuit, a -1-V source in series with a 2.7-kΩ resistor.

Figure 10.23 shows this reference circuit connected to the current switch from Fig. 10.5. The equivalent output resistance R_{TH} of the reference circuit can cause a problem with proper operation of the ECL circuit because the base current i_{B2} causes a voltage drop in the 2.7-kΩ resistor and a reduction in the effective reference voltage that appears at the base of Q_2.

For example, suppose $\beta_F = 30$. The voltage at the base of Q_2 is

$$v_{B2} = -1 - (2.7 \text{ k}\Omega)i_{B2}$$

$$= -1 - (2.7 \text{ k}\Omega)\left(\frac{i_{E2}}{\beta_F + 1}\right)$$

$$= -1 - (2.7 \text{ k}\Omega)\left(\frac{0.3 \text{ mA}}{31}\right)$$

$$= -0.97 \text{ V}$$

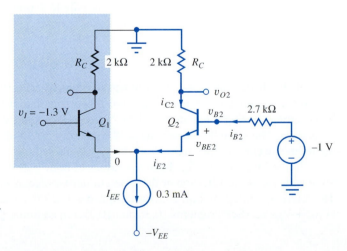

Figure 10.23 Thévenin equivalent of V_{REF} connected to current switch.

The base current from the current switch has reduced the effective reference potential by approximately 30 mV. This reduction may not seem a large amount, but it is greater than $1V_T$, and the ECL transition region is only $10V_T$ in width. Remember that V_{IH} and V_{IL} were separated from V_{REF} by only 78 mV in this circuit. In addition, many ECL gates are typically supplied from one reference voltage circuit, and each added gate will cause another 30-mV drop in V_{REF}.

Temperature Compensation

A second, more subtle problem occurs with the simple resistive voltage divider reference circuit when current source I_{EE} is replaced by a resistor, as in Fig. 10.24. The emitter current in Q_2 is

$$i_{E2} = \frac{v_{B2} - v_{BE2} - (-V_{EE})}{R_{EE}} \tag{10.43}$$

We know from Sec. 3.5 that the base-emitter voltage has a negative temperature coefficient and changes with temperature by approximately -1.8 mV/K. If the -1-V source is fixed, then the emitter current, and hence the value of V_{OL} at v_{O2}, will change with temperature. It can be seen from Eqs. (10.31) that a change in V_{OL} changes the value of NM_L, and the logic swing is no longer symmetrical about V_{REF}.

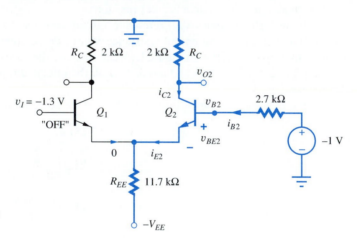

Figure 10.24 Current switch with emitter resistor.

The reference circuit in Fig. 10.25 adds a diode to provide **temperature compensation** for the reference voltage. Neglecting base current i_{B2}, the voltage at the emitter of Q_2 is now given by

$$v_{E2} = -1.7 + v_{D1} - v_{BE2} \tag{10.44}$$

If the diode voltage v_{D1} is designed to be identical to v_{BE2}, then v_{E2} will be equal to -1.7 V regardless of temperature. For v_{D1} to accurately match v_{BE2}, the diode must be constructed using a bipolar transistor, as described shortly in Sec. 10.9, and the diode current must be set to the same value as the emitter current of Q_2. This was why we chose the reference current to be 0.3 mA.

In the ECL gate in Fig. 10.6, the values of both V_{OH} and V_{OL} change with temperature because of the variation of the base-emitter voltage of emitter-followers Q_3 and Q_4. The reference voltage in Fig. 10.26 is designed to track this variation and maintain $V_{REF} \approx (V_{OH} + V_{OL})/2$. (See Problems 10.36 and 10.37.) In addition, Q_5 buffers the -0.3-V node,

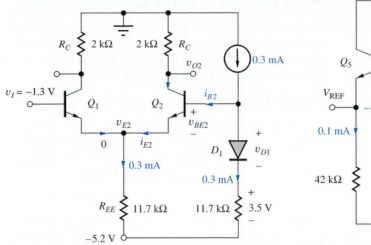

Figure 10.25 Reference divider with diode for temperature compensation.

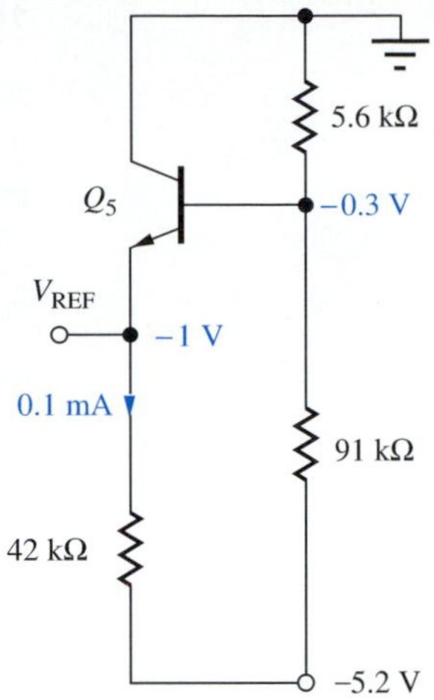

Figure 10.26 Temperature-compensated buffered reference.

and the base currents of a large number of ECL gates can be supplied from the emitter of Q_5. Only the base current of Q_5 remains to disturb the voltage at the -0.3-V node.

> **EXERCISE:** How much does V_{REF} change in the circuit in Fig. 10.26 if T increases by 40°C and the temperature coefficient of the base-emitter junction is -1.8 mV/°C? What is the new value of V_{REF}? Assume the current gain of Q_5 is very large.
>
> **ANSWERS:** $+72.0$ mV, -0.928 V

10.9 DIODES IN BIPOLAR INTEGRATED CIRCUITS

In integrated circuits, we often want the characteristics of a diode to match those of the BJT as closely as possible. In addition, it takes about the same amount of area to fabricate a diode as a full bipolar transistor. For these reasons, a diode is usually formed by connecting the base and collector terminals of a bipolar transistor, as shown in Fig. 10.27. This connection forces $v_{BC} = 0$.

Using the Gummel-Poon equations for BJT with this boundary condition yields an expression for the terminal current of the "diode":

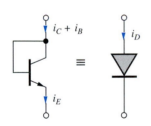

Figure 10.27 Diode-connected transistor.

$$i_D = i_E = (i_C + i_B) = \left(I_S + \frac{I_S}{\beta_F}\right)\left[\exp\left(\frac{v_{BE}}{V_T}\right) - 1\right] = \frac{I_S}{\alpha_F}\left[\exp\left(\frac{v_D}{V_T}\right) - 1\right] \quad (10.45)$$

The terminal current has an i-v characteristic corresponding to that of a diode with a reverse saturation current that is determined by the BJT parameters. The diodes in Figs. 10.25 and 10.26 would be implemented in this manner. This technique is often used in both analog and digital circuit design; we will see many examples of its use in the analog designs in Part III.

> **EXERCISE:** What is the equivalent saturation current of the diode in Fig. 10.27 if the transistor is described by $I_S = 2 \times 10^{-14}$ A and $\alpha_F = 0.95$?
>
> **ANSWER:** 21 fA

10.10 ECL POWER-DELAY CHARACTERISTICS

As pointed out in the chapters on MOS logic design, the power-delay product (PDP) is an important figure of merit for comparing logic families. In this section, we first explore the power dissipation of the ECL gate and then characterize its delay at low power. The results are then combined to form the power-delay product.

Power Dissipation

The static power dissipation of the ECL gate is easily calculated based on our original inverter circuit, shown in Fig. 10.28. The total current I in the inverter is independent of the logic state within the gate: $I = I_{EE} + I_3 + I_4$. Thus, the average ECL power dissipation $\langle P \rangle$ is independent of logic state and is equal to

$$\langle P \rangle = V_{EE}(I_{EE} + I_3 + I_4) \tag{10.46}$$

For the values given in Fig. 10.28, the power dissipation is 2.6 mW.

For the circuit using resistor bias, in Fig. 10.29, the power is very similar. Referring back to Sec. 10.3 and Figs. 10.10 and 10.11, we remember that the sum $i_3 + i_4 = 0.2$ mA is a constant regardless of input state, and the average value of the current I_{EE} is

$$\langle I_{EE} \rangle = \frac{0.300 + 0.325}{2} \text{ mA} = 0.313 \text{ mA} \tag{10.47}$$

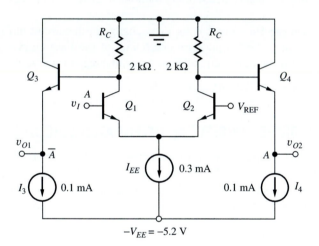

Figure 10.28 ECL inverter.

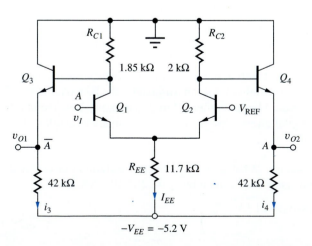

Figure 10.29 ECL gate with resistor biasing.

based on a 50 percent logic state duty cycle. Thus, the average power dissipation is $\langle P \rangle = (5.2\ \text{V})(0.200 + 0.313\ \text{mA}) = 2.7\ \text{mW}$—essentially the same as for the circuit in Fig. 10.28.

> **EXERCISE:** Scale the resistors in the ECL gate in Fig. 10.29 to reduce the power by a factor of 10.
>
> **ANSWERS:** 20 kΩ, 18.5 kΩ, 117 kΩ, 420 kΩ

Power Reduction

Note that 40 percent of the power in the circuits in Figs. 10.28 and 10.29 dissipates in the emitter-follower stages. Two techniques have been used to reduce the power consumption in more advanced ECL gates. The first is to simply return the emitter-follower resistors to a second, less negative power supply such as the −2-V supply in Fig. 10.30. The resistors in the emitters of Q_3 and Q_4 have been changed to 10 kΩ to keep the currents in Q_3 and Q_4 equal to 0.1 mA. The power dissipation in this circuit is reduced by 33 percent to

$$P = 5.2(0.313) + 2(0.1) = 1.8\ \text{mW} \qquad (10.48)$$

This method, however, requires the cost of another power supply and its associated wiring for power distribution.

Another power-reduction technique is illustrated in Fig. 10.31, in which the resistors that supply current to the emitter followers are now connected between each input and

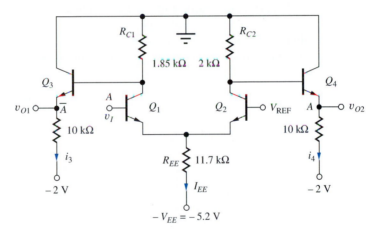

Figure 10.30 ECL circuit with reduced power in the emitter followers.

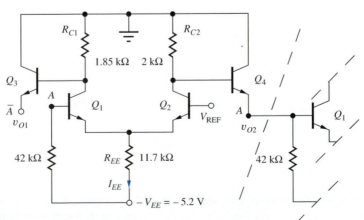

Figure 10.31 Repartitioned ECL gate.

the −5.2-V supply. In Fig. 10.19 we saw that one emitter follower would have to supply the current of multiple current sources when the wired-OR function was used. Using the repartitioned circuit in Fig. 10.31, the emitter follower current is always equal to the current of only one of the original emitter followers. This redesign significantly reduces the overall power consumption in large logic networks. However, any output that does not drive the input of another logic gate needs to have an external termination resistor connected from its output to the negative power supply.

Gate Delay

The capacitances that dominate the delay of the ECL inverter at low power levels have been added to the circuit in Fig. 10.32. The symbol C_{CB} represents the capacitance of the reverse-biased collector-base junction, and C_{CS} represents the capacitance between the collector and the substrate of the transistor. Transistors Q_1 and Q_2 switch the current I_{EE} back and forth very rapidly in response to the input v_I. The emitter followers can supply large amounts of current to quickly charge any load capacitances connected to the two outputs.

At low power, the speed of the ECL gate is dominated by the $R_C − C_L$ time constant at the collectors of Q_1 and Q_2, and the response of the inverter can be modeled by the simple RC circuit in Fig. 10.33, in which R_C is the collector-load resistance and C_L is the effective load capacitance at the collector node of Q_2, given by:

$$C_L = C_{CS2} + C_{CB2} + C_{CB4} \tag{10.49}$$

The load capacitance consists of the base-collector capacitances of Q_2 and Q_4 plus the collector-substrate capacitance of Q_2.

For the negative-going transient, the capacitor is initially discharged, and current $−I_{EE}$ is switched into the node at $t = 0$. The voltage at node v_{C2} is described by

$$v_{C2}(t) = -I_{EE}R_C\left[1 - \exp\left(-\frac{t}{R_C C_L}\right)\right] \tag{10.50}$$

The collector-node voltage exponentially approaches the final value of $−I_{EE}R_C$. The actual output voltage at v_O is level-shifted down by one 0.7-V drop by the emitter follower.

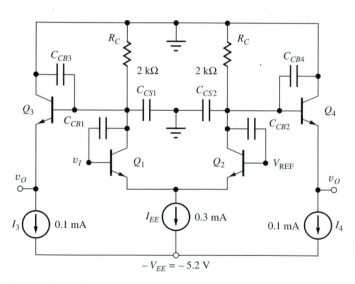

Figure 10.32 ECL inverter with capacitances at the collector nodes of the current switch.

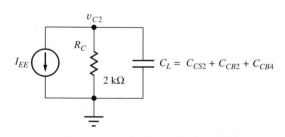

Figure 10.33 Simplified model for the dynamic response of an ECL gate.

The propagation-delay time is the time required for the output to make 50 percent of its transition:

$$v_{C2}(\tau_{PHL}) = -\frac{I_{EE}R_C}{2} \quad \text{and} \quad \tau_{PHL} = 0.69R_C C_L \tag{10.51}$$

For the positive-going transition, the capacitor is initially charged to the negative voltage $-I_{EE}R_C$. At $t = 0$, the current source is switched off, and the capacitor simply discharges through R_C:

$$v_{C2}(t) = -I_{EE}R_C \exp\left(-\frac{t}{R_C C_L}\right) \tag{10.52}$$

For this case, the propagation delay is

$$v_{C2}(\tau_{PLH}) = -\frac{I_{EE}R_C}{2} \quad \text{with } \tau_{PLH} = 0.69R_C C_L \tag{10.53}$$

Using Eqs. (10.51) and (10.53), the average propagation delay of the ECL gate is

$$\tau_P = \frac{\tau_{PHL} + \tau_{PLH}}{2} = 0.69R_C C_L \tag{10.54}$$

Figure 10.34 shows the results of simulation of the switching behavior of the ECL gate in Fig. 10.32. In this case, the transistor capacitances are $C_{CB} = 0.5$ pF and $C_{CS} = 1.0$ pF. For $R_C = 2$ kΩ, the two propagation-delay times from Eqs. (10.51) and (10.53) are estimated to be 2.8 ns. This prediction agrees very well with the waveforms in Fig. 10.34.

Note the two transient "spikes" (circled in Fig. 10.34) that show up on the $\overline{v_O}$ output coinciding with the switching points on the input waveform. These spikes do not show up on the v_O output. The transients are in the same direction as the input signal change and result from the coupling of the input waveform directly through capacitance C_{BC1} to the inverting output. A similar path to the noninverting output does not exist. This is another good illustration of detailed simulation results that one should always try to understand.

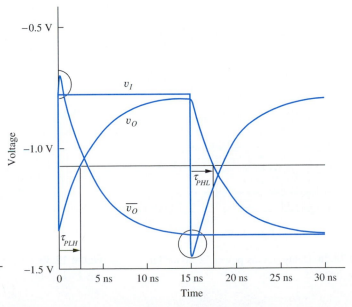

Figure 10.34 Simulated switching waveforms for the ECL inverter of Fig. 10.32.

Such unusual observations should be studied to determine if they are real effects or some artifact of the simulation tool as well as to understand how they might affect the performance of the circuit.

Power-Delay Product

Using the values calculated from Eqs. (10.46) and (10.54) for the gate in Fig. 10.32, the power-delay product is 2.6 mW $\times$ 2.8 ns, or 7.3 pJ. From Eq. (10.54), we see that the propagation delay of the inverter for a given capacitance is directly proportional to the choice of R_C, and we know R_C is related to the logic swing and the current source I_{EE} by $R_C = \Delta V / I_{EE}$. Assuming that we want to keep the logic swing and the noise margins constant, then we can reduce R_C only if we increase the current I_{EE} and hence the power of the gate. This illustrates the direct power-delay trade-off involved in gate design because I_{EE} accounts for most of the power in the ECL logic gate.

The analysis presented in the previous section was valid for operation in the region of constant power-delay product. However, as power is increased, the effect of charge storage in the BJT (discussed in detail in the next section) becomes more and more important, and the delay of the ECL gate enters a region in which it becomes independent of power. Finally, at even higher power levels, the delay starts to degrade as the f_T of the BJT falls. These three regions are shown in Fig. 10.35.

Figure 10.36 summarizes the power-delay characteristics of a number of commercial ECL unit logic gates as well as the requirements for high-performance circuits for use in high-density IC chips. The more recent ECL unit logic families offer subnanosecond performance but consume relatively large amounts of power in order to reliably drive the large off-chip capacitances associated with printed circuit board mounting and interconnect. The large power-delay products are not usable for VLSI circuit densities. Much lower power-delay products are associated with state-of-the-art on-chip logic circuits that benefit from smaller capacitive loads as well as significantly improved bipolar device technology.

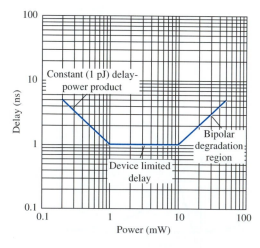

Figure 10.35 Delay versus power behavior for bipolar logic.

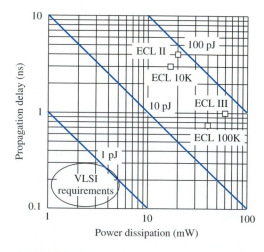

Figure 10.36 Power-delay characteristics for various ECL gates.

EXERCISE: What will be the delay and power-delay product for the ECL gate in Fig. 10.32 if I_{EE} is changed to 0.5 mA but the logic swing is maintained the same?

ANSWERS: 1.4 ns, 5.0 pJ

10.11 THE SATURATING BIPOLAR INVERTER

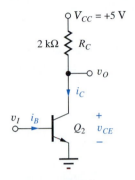

Figure 10.37 Single transistor bipolar inverter and device parameters.

At the heart of many bipolar logic gates is the simple saturating bipolar inverter circuit in Fig. 10.37, which uses a single BJT switching device Q_2 to pull v_O down to V_{OL} and a resistor load element to pull the output up to the power supply V_{CC}. The input voltage v_I and the base current i_B supplied to the base of the bipolar transistor will be designed to switch Q_2 between the saturation and nonconducting states.

For analysis and design of saturating BJT circuits, we use the transistor parameters in Table 10.3. The base-emitter or base-collector voltages in the forward- or reverse-active regions are assumed to be 0.7 V. However, when a transistor saturates, its base-emitter voltage increases slightly, and 0.8 V will be used for the base-emitter voltage of a saturated transistor. Our BJT circuits will be designed to have a worst case $V_{CESAT} = 0.15$ V. Transistors in most logic technologies are optimized for speed, and current gain is often compromised, as indicated by the relatively low value of β_F in Table 10.3. β_R typically ranges between 0.1 and 2 in TTL technology. Up to now, we have not found a use for the reverse-active region of operation, but as we shall see in Sec. 10.12, it plays a very important role in TTL circuits.

T a b l e 10.3	
BJT Parameters	
I_S	10^{-15} A
β_F	40
β_R	0.25
V_{BE}	0.70 V
V_{BESAT}	0.80 V
V_{CESAT}	0.15 V

Static Inverter Characteristics

Writing the equation for the output voltage of the inverter in Fig. 10.37, we find

$$v_O = v_{CE} = V_{CC} - i_C R_C \tag{10.55}$$

If the base-emitter voltage ($v_{BE} = v_I$) is several hundred millivolts less than the normal turn-on voltage of the base-emitter junction (0.6 to 0.7 V), then Q_2 will be nearly cut off, with $i_C \approx 0$. Equivalently, if the input base current i_B is zero, then Q_2 will also be near cutoff. For either case,

$$v_O = V_{OH} \approx V_{CC} \tag{10.56}$$

In this particular logic circuit, the value of V_{OH} is set by the power supply voltage: $V_{OH} = 5$ V.

The low-state output level is set by the saturation voltage of the bipolar transistor, $V_{OL} = V_{CESAT}$. To ensure saturation, we require that

$$i_B > \frac{i_{CMAX}}{\beta_F} \quad \text{where } i_{CMAX} = \frac{V_{CC} - V_{CESAT}}{R_C} \approx \frac{V_{CC}}{R_C} \tag{10.57}$$

as discussed in Sec. 5.12. For the circuit in Fig. 10.37, $i_{CMAX} = 2.43$ mA, assuming $V_{CESAT} = 0.15$ V. Using $\beta_F = 40$, the transistor will be saturated for

$$i_B > \frac{2.43 \text{ mA}}{40} = 60.8 \text{ μA}$$

EXERCISE: Estimate the static power dissipation of the inverter in Fig. 10.37 for $v_O = V_{OH}$ and $v_O = V_{OL}$. What value of R_C is required to reduce the power dissipation by a factor of 10?

ANSWERS: 0, 12.1 mW; 20 kΩ

Saturation Voltage of the Bipolar Transistor

An expression for the **saturation voltage** of the BJT in terms of its base and collector currents was derived in Eq. (5.46) and is repeated here:

$$V_{CESAT} = V_T \ln\left(\frac{1}{\alpha_R}\right) \frac{1 + \dfrac{i_C}{(\beta_R + 1)i_B}}{1 - \dfrac{i_C}{\beta_F i_B}} \quad \text{for } i_B > \frac{i_C}{\beta_F} \tag{10.58}$$

Recall that the ratio i_C/i_B is the forced beta β_{FOR} and that $i_C/i_B = \beta_F$ is true only for the forward-active region. Note that Eq. (10.58) becomes infinite for $i_C/i_B = \beta_F$. Equation (10.58) can be rewritten in terms of β_{FOR} as

$$V_{CESAT} = V_T \ln\left(\frac{1}{\alpha_R}\right) \frac{1 + \dfrac{\beta_{FOR}}{(\beta_R + 1)}}{1 - \dfrac{\beta_{FOR}}{\beta_F}} \tag{10.59}$$

Equation (10.59) is plotted as a function of $\beta_{FOR} = i_C/i_B$ in Fig. 10.38. As i_B becomes very large or i_C becomes very small, β_{FOR} approaches zero, and V_{CESAT} reaches its minimum value:

$$V_{CESAT}^{MIN} = V_T \ln\left(\frac{1}{\alpha_R}\right) \tag{10.60}$$

The minimum value of V_{CESAT} is approximately 40 mV for the transistor depicted in Fig. 10.38.

For the more general case, i_{CMAX} is known from Eq. (10.57), and Eq. (10.58) can be used to ensure that our circuit design supplies enough base current to saturate the transistor to the desired level. As assumed earlier, $V_{CESAT} \le 0.15$ V. Solving Eq. (10.58) for i_C/i_B,

$$\frac{i_C}{i_B} \le \beta_F \left[\frac{1 - \dfrac{1}{\alpha_R \Gamma}}{1 + \dfrac{\beta_F}{\beta_R \Gamma}}\right] \quad \text{where } \Gamma = \exp\left(V_{CESAT}/V_T\right) \tag{10.61}$$

Using Eq. (10.61) with $i_C = 2.43$ mA and the values from Table 10.3, reaching $V_{CESAT} = 0.15$ V requires $i_C/i_B \le 28.3$ or $i_B \ge 86$ μA.

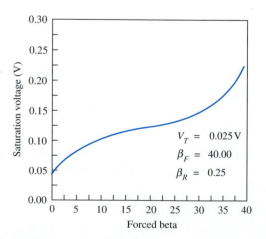

$$V_T = 0.025 \text{ V}$$
$$\beta_F = 40.00$$
$$\beta_R = 0.25$$

Figure 10.38 Saturation voltage V_{CESAT} versus forced beta i_C/i_B.

Load-Line Visualization

As presented in Chapter 7, an important way of visualizing inverter operation is to look at the load line, Eq. (10.55), drawn on the BJT transistor output characteristics, as in Fig. 10.39. The BJT switches between the two operating points on the load line (indicated by the circles in Fig. 10.39). At the right-hand end of the load line, the BJT is cut off, with $i_C = 0$ and $v_{CE} = 5$ V. At the Q-point near the left end of the load line, the BJT represents a low resistance in the saturation region, with $v_O = V_{CESAT}$. Note that the current in saturation is limited primarily by the load resistance and is nearly independent of the base current.

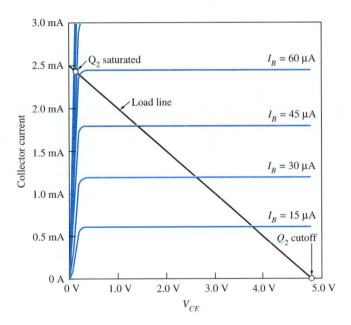

Figure 10.39 BJT output characteristics and load line.

EXERCISE: A transistor must reach a saturation voltage ≤ 0.1 V with $I_C = 10$ mA. What are the maximum value of β_{FOR} and the minimum value of the base current? Use the transistor parameters from Table 10.3.

ANSWERS: 9.24, 1.08 mA

Switching Characteristics of the Saturated BJT

A very important change occurs in the switching characteristics of bipolar transistors when they saturate. The excess base current that drives the transistor into saturation causes additional charge storage in the base region of the transistor. This charge must be removed before the transistor can turn off, and an extra delay time, termed the **storage time t_S,** appears in the switching characteristic of the saturated BJT.

We illustrate the problem through the circuit simulation results presented in Fig. 10.41 for the inverter circuit in Fig. 10.40, in which the BJT is driven by a current source that forces current I_{BF} into the base to turn the transistor on and pulls current I_{BR} out of the base to turn the transistor back off. Negative base current can only occur in the *npn* transistor during the transient that removes charge from the base. Diode D_1 is added to the circuit to provide a steady-state path for the negative source current because we know that the *npn* transistor cannot support a large negative steady-state base current without junction breakdown.

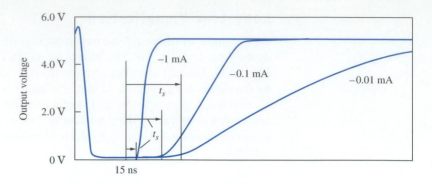

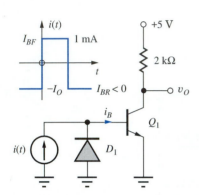

Figure 10.40 Bipolar inverter with current source drive.

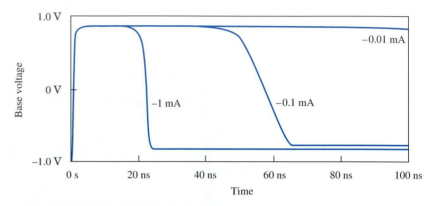

Figure 10.41 Switching behavior for the BJT inverter for three values of reverse base current: $I_{BR} = -1$ mA, -0.1 mA, and -0.01 mA.

Referring to Figs. 10.40 and 10.41 at $t = 0$, we see that the current source forces a base current $I_{BF} = 1$ mA into the transistor, rapidly charging the base-emitter capacitance and supplying charge to the base. The BJT turns on and saturates within approximately 5 ns. At $t = 15$ ns, the direction of the current source reverses, and simulation results are shown for three different values of reverse current. For a small reverse current (0.01 mA), electron–hole recombination in the base is the only mechanism available to remove the excess base charge. The transistor turns off very slowly because of the slow decay of the charge stored on the base-emitter junction capacitance. As the reverse base current is increased, both storage time and rise time are substantially reduced.

Observe the behavior of the voltage at the base of the transistor. The base voltage remains constant at $+0.85$ V until the excess **stored base charge** has been removed from the base. Then the base voltage can drop and the transistor turns off. Note that the base voltage is still above 0.8 V at $t = 100$ ns for the smallest reverse base current! The storage time t_S can be calculated from the following formula [1]:

$$t_S = \tau_S \ \ln\left(\frac{I_{BF} - I_{BR}}{\dfrac{i_{\text{CMAX}}}{\beta_F} - I_{BR}} \right) \tag{10.62}$$

in which the **storage time constant τ_s** is given by

$$\tau_s = \frac{\alpha_F(\tau_F + \alpha_R \tau_R)}{1 - \alpha_F \alpha_R} \tag{10.63}$$

I_{BF} and I_{BR} are the forward and reverse base currents defined in Fig. 10.40, and α_F and α_R are the forward and reverse common-base current gains. Note that the value of I_{BR} is negative.

The constants τ_F and τ_R are called the **forward** and **reverse transit times** for the transistor and determine the amount of charge stored in the base in the forward- and reverse-active modes of operation—Q_F and Q_R, respectively:

$$Q_F = i_F \tau_F \qquad \text{and} \qquad Q_R = i_R \tau_R \qquad (10.64)$$

In Eq. (10.64), i_F and i_R are the forward and reverse current components from the Gummel-Poon model.

The storage time constant quantifies the amount of excess charge, over and above that needed to support the actual collector current, stored in the base when the bipolar transistor enters saturation:

$$Q_{XS} = \tau_S \left(i_B - \frac{i_{\text{CMAX}}}{\beta_F} \right) \qquad (10.65)$$

The storage time t_S represents a significant degradation in the speed of the BJT when it tries to come out of saturation, as can be seen in Fig. 10.41 and Example 10.1.

EXAMPLE 10.1: Calculate the storage time constant and storage times for the three currents used in Figs. 10.40 and 10.41 if $\alpha_F = 0.976$, $\alpha_R = 0.20$, $\tau_F = 0.25$ ns, and $\tau_R = 25$ ns.

SOLUTION: The resulting value of τ_S is

$$\tau_S = \frac{0.976(0.25 \text{ ns} + .20(25 \text{ ns}))}{1 - 0.976(0.20)} = 6.4 \text{ ns}$$

Using Eq. (10.57) with this value of τ_S and $I_{BF} = 1$ mA:

I_{BR}	t_S
-0.01 mA	16.9 ns
-0.10 mA	12.3 ns
-1.0 mA	4.0 ns

These values agree well with the storage times that can be observed in Fig. 10.41. ◆

EXERCISE: For Example 10.1, calculate the excess charge stored in the base and compare to Q_F.

ANSWERS: 6.01 pC, 0.625 pC, $Q_{XS} \gg Q_F$

10.12 A TRANSISTOR-TRANSISTOR LOGIC (TTL) PROTOTYPE

Figure 10.42 is the prototype for a low power TTL inverter. Transistor Q_1 has been added to the inverter of Fig. 10.37 to control the supply of base current to Q_2. Input voltage v_I causes the current i_{B1} to switch between either the base-emitter diode or the base-collector

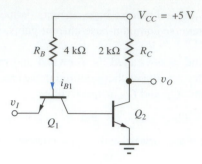

Figure 10.42 TTL inverter prototype.

diode of Q_1. We first explore circuit behavior for $v_I = V_{OL}$, find V_{OH}, and then use it to study the circuit for $v_I = V_{OH}$.

TTL Inverter for $v_I = V_{OL}$

The input to the TTL gate in Fig. 10.43 is set to $V_{OL} = V_{CESAT} = 0.15$. The +5-V supply tends to force current i_{B1} down through the 4-kΩ resistor and into the base of Q_1, turning on the base-emitter diode of Q_1. Transistor Q_1 attempts to pull a collector current $i_{C1} = \beta_F i_{B1}$ out of the base of Q_2, but only leakage currents can flow in the reverse direction out of this base. Therefore, $i_{C1} \approx 0$. Because Q_1 is operating with $\beta_F i_B > i_C$, it saturates, with both junctions being forward-biased. Thus the voltage at the base of Q_2 is given by

$$v_{BE2} = v_I + V_{CESAT1} = 0.15 + 0.04 = 0.19 \text{ V} \tag{10.66}$$

where $V_{CESAT1} = 0.04$ V has been used because $i_{C1} = 0$. Because v_{BE2} is only 0.19 V, Q_2 does not conduct any substantial collector current (although it technically remains in the forward-active region—see Prob. 10.55), and the output voltage will be $v_O = V_{CC} = 5$ V. Base current i_{B1} is given by

$$i_{B1} = \frac{5 - v_{B1}}{4 \text{ k}\Omega} \qquad \text{where } v_{B1} = v_1 + V_{BESAT} = 0.95 \text{ V for } V_{BESAT} = 0.8 \text{ V} \tag{10.67}$$

For the gate in Fig. 10.43, we find that $i_{B1} = 1.01$ mA. This current enters the base and exits the emitter of Q_1 because $i_{C1} \approx 0$. For this TTL gate, the input current for the low input state is $i_{IL} = -i_{E1}$, or

$$-i_{IL} = i_{E1} = (i_{B1} + i_{C1}) \approx i_{B1} = \frac{5 - v_{B1}}{4 \text{ k}\Omega} = \frac{5 - 0.95}{4 \text{ k}\Omega} = 1.01 \text{ mA} \tag{10.68}$$

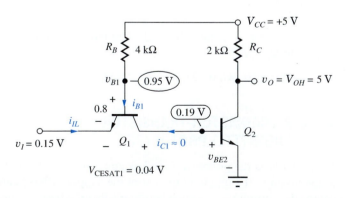

Figure 10.43 TTL gate with input $v_I = V_{OL}$.

This is a logic gate characteristic that we have not seen before. In TTL, there is a relatively large current that the input signal source v_I must absorb. We shall see shortly how this current limits the fanout of the TTL gate.

> **Exercise:** What would be the values of V_{BE2} and i_{IL} in Fig. 10.43 if $\beta_{R1} = 2$?
>
> **Answers:** 0.19 V, −1.01 mA

TTL Inverter for $v_I = V_{OH}$

$V_{OH} = 5$ V is applied as the input to the inverter in Fig. 10.44. Because the emitter of Q_1 is at 5 V, base current i_{B1} cannot enter the base-emitter diode; it instead forward-biases the base-collector diode. Transistor Q_1 enters the reverse-active region with the base-collector junction forward-biased and the base-emitter junction reverse-biased. Base current i_{B1} causes a current $(\beta_R + 1)i_{B1}$ to *exit* the collector terminal, and this current becomes the base current of Q_2:

$$i_{B2} = (\beta_R + 1)i_{B1} \tag{10.69}$$

In addition, a current $\beta_R i_{B1}$ *enters* the emitter terminal, and this current represents the input current i_{IH} for the input high state:

$$i_{IH} = +\beta_R i_{B1} \tag{10.70}$$

A small value of β_R is desired to keep i_{IH} low.

For proper circuit operation, $i_{B2} = (\beta_R + 1)i_{B1}$ is designed to be much greater than i_{C2}/β_F, Q_2 saturates, and its base-emitter voltage becomes 0.8 V. The voltage $v_{B1} = v_{BC1} + V_{BESAT2} = 0.7 + 0.8 = 1.5$ V. The base current of Q_1 is now

$$i_{B1} = \frac{(5 - 1.5)\ \text{V}}{4\ \text{k}\Omega} = 0.875\ \text{mA}$$

and $\tag{10.71}$

$$i_{IH} = \beta_R i_{B1} = 0.25(0.875\ \text{mA}) = 0.219\ \text{mA}$$

Evaluating Eq. (10.69), we find that the base current of Q_2 is

$$i_{B2} = (\beta_R + 1)i_{B1} = (1.25)0.875\ \text{mA} = 1.09\ \text{mA} \tag{10.72}$$

Current i_{B2} is much greater than the 86 μA required to saturate Q_2, as we calculated immediately following Eq. (10.61). The forced beta in this circuit is $\beta_{FOR} = 2.43\ \text{mA}/1.09\ \text{mA} = 2.22$, and Eq. (10.59) indicates that Q_2 actually has $V_{CESAT2} = 67$ mV. The additional base current calculated above is needed to ensure that the V_{CESAT} specification is met when the inverter must drive a large fanout.

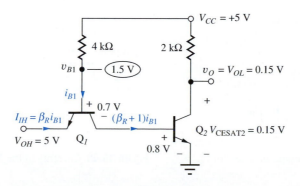

Figure 10.44 TTL gate with input $v_I = V_{OH}$.

EXERCISE: What would be the values of v_{BE2} and i_{IH} in Fig. 10.44 if $\beta_{R1} = 2$?

ANSWERS: 0.80 V, 1.75 mA

Power in the Prototype TTL Gate

Now we explore the power dissipation in the TTL gate for the two logic states. For $v_I = 5$ V and $v_O = V_{OL}$, as in Fig. 10.45, the total power being consumed by the gate is

$$P_{OL} = V_{CC}i_{CC} + v_I i_{IH} = V_{CC}(i_{C2} + i_{B1}) + v_I i_{IH} \tag{10.73}$$

For the circuit in Fig. 10.45,

$$P_{OL} = 5 \text{ V}(2.4 \text{ mA} + 0.88 \text{ mA} + 0.22 \text{ mA}) = 17.6 \text{ mW}$$

For $v_I = V_{OL}$ and $v_O = V_{OH}$, as in Fig. 10.46, the power being consumed by the gate is

$$P_{OH} = V_{CC}i_{CC} + v_I i_{IL} = V_{CC}i_{B1} + v_I i_{IL} \tag{10.74}$$

For the values in Fig. 10.46,

$$P_{OH} = 5 \text{ V}(1.0 \text{ mA}) + 0.15 \text{ V}(-1.0 \text{ mA}) = 4.85 \text{ mW}$$

Assuming that the gate spends 50 percent of the time in each state (a 50 percent duty cycle), the average power dissipation $\langle P \rangle$ is

$$\langle P \rangle = \frac{17.6 + 4.85}{2} \text{ mW} = 11.2 \text{ mW}$$

V_{IH}, V_{IL}, and Noise Margins for the TTL Prototype

Figure 10.47 shows the results of circuit simulation of the VTC for the TTL inverter of Figs. 10.42 to 10.44. As expected, V_{OH} is equal to V_{CC}. For $v_O = V_{OL}$, the output transistor is heavily saturated, with $V_{OL} < 0.1$ V. The transition region between V_{OH} and V_{OL} is quite narrow, which is a result of the exponential characteristics of the BJT.

As can be observed in the VTC, the difference between V_{IH} and V_{IL} is only slightly larger than 0.1 V (although large enough to change i_C by a factor of more than 50!). Calculating the exact input voltages for which the slope of the VTC equals -1 is complex, but a simplified analysis of the circuit in Fig. 10.48 yields the approximate location of the V_{IH} and V_{IL} transition points.

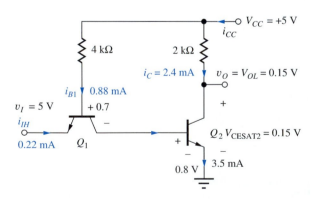

Figure 10.45 Currents in the prototype inverter for $v_O = V_{OL}$.

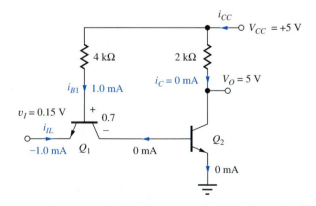

Figure 10.46 Currents in the TTL gate for $v_I = V_{OL}$.

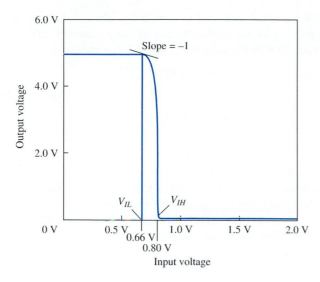

Figure 10.47 SPICE simulation of the VTC of the prototype TTL gate.

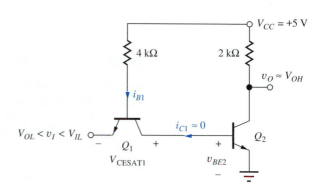

Figure 10.48 TTL gate with input v_I below V_{IL}.

For an input voltage near V_{OL}, Q_1 is saturated and the voltage at the base of Q_2 is given by

$$v_{BE2} = v_I + V_{\text{CESAT1}} = v_I + 0.04 \text{ V} \tag{10.75}$$

using the actual value of saturation voltage from Fig. 10.38 for $i_{C1} = 0$. Because of the exponential turn-on of the transistor, the slope of the VTC changes rapidly at the point at which Q_2 just begins to conduct as v_{BE2} reaches 0.7 V, and this point marks V_{IL}:

$$V_{IL} \approx 0.7 - V_{\text{CESAT1}} = 0.66 \text{ V} \tag{10.76}$$

Similar arguments yield an approximate value of V_{IH}. In Fig. 10.49, the input voltage is above V_{IH}, and the base-emitter voltage of Q_2 is given by $V_{\text{BESAT2}} = 0.8$ V. As the input decreases, the output remains at V_{CESAT} until current begins to be diverted away from the base of Q_2. This occurs approximately as the base-emitter and base-collector voltages of Q_1 become equal, or $v_I = 0.8$ V (see Prob. 10.57). Thus, we expect V_{IH} to be given approximately by

$$V_{IH} \approx V_{\text{BESAT2}} = 0.8 \text{ V} \tag{10.77}$$

These approximate values for V_{IH} and V_{IL}, based on Eqs. (10.76) and (10.77), agree well with the simulation results in Fig. 10.47. These estimates are accurate because of the

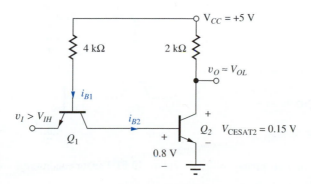

Figure 10.49 TTL gate with input V_I above V_{IH}.

exponential behavior of the BJT. Less than a 60-mV change in v_{BE} changes i_C by a factor of 10, so the estimates of V_{IH} and V_{IL} should not be in error by more than ± 60 mV.

Using Eqs. (10.76) and (10.77) with the values of V_{OH} and V_{OL} yields

$$\text{NM}_L = 0.66 - 0.15 = 0.51 \text{ V}$$

and   (10.78)

$$\text{NM}_H = 5.0 - 0.8 = 4.2 \text{ V}$$

Prototype Inverter Summary

Figure 10.50 is a summary of the static characteristics of the prototype TTL inverter. V_{OH} is equal to the power supply voltage of 5 V, and an input of this value produces an output low state of $V_{OL} \leq 0.15$ V. The highly asymmetrical noise margins are $\text{NM}_L = 0.51$ V and $\text{NM}_H = 4.2$ V. When the input is high, a current of 0.22 mA enters the TTL input, and when the input is low, a current of 1.0 mA exits from the input.

Fanout Limitations of the TTL Prototype

For NMOS, CMOS, and ECL logic, fanout restrictions were not investigated in detail because the input current to the various logic gates was zero, as for the case of NMOS and CMOS, or was a very small base current, as for the case of ECL. However, a substantial current exists in the input terminal of the TTL inverter for both input states, as summarized in Fig. 10.50. This input current limits the number of gates that can be connected to the output of an individual TTL logic gate. Both logic states must be checked to see which set of conditions actually limits the fanout of the gate.

Fanout Limit for $v_O = V_{OL}$

N inverters are shown connected to the output of one TTL inverter in Fig. 10.51. The maximum value of N is termed the **fanout** capability of the TTL gate. N can be determined from the conditions required to maintain Q_2 in saturation with $V_{\text{CESAT2}} \leq 0.15$ V.

Referring to Fig. 10.51, the collector current of Q_2 is given by

$$i_C = i_R + N(1.01 \text{ mA}) = 2.43 \text{ mA} + N(1.01 \text{ mA})$$ (10.79)

In Sec. 10.11 we found that a forced beta $\beta_{\text{FOR}} \leq 28.3$ was required to maintain $V_{\text{CESAT}} \leq 0.15$ V. Also, the base current of Q_2 was previously found to be 1.09 mA for $v_I = 5$ V, so

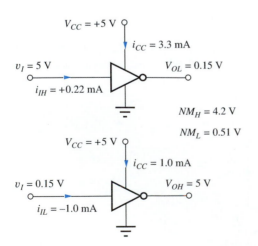

Figure 10.50 Summary of TTL prototype inverter characteristics.

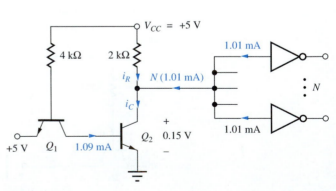

Figure 10.51 Fanout conditions for $v_O = V_{OL}$.

the collector current must satisfy

$$i_C \leq 28.3 i_B = 28.3 \times 1.09 \text{ mA} = 30.8 \text{ mA}$$

or (10.80)

$$2.43 \text{ mA} + N(1.01 \text{ mA}) \leq 30.8 \text{ mA} \quad \text{and} \quad N \leq 28.1$$

Because the number of gates must be an integer, the fanout capability of this gate is $N = 28$ for the output in the low state. Twenty-eight similar gates can be driven by one logic gate and still maintain the design value of V_{OL}. $N = 28$ still represents a relatively large value for fanout.

Fanout Limit for $v_O = V_{OH}$

The circuit conditions for $v_I = 0.15$ V and $v_O = V_{OH}$ are given in Fig. 10.52. At the output node, the collector current of Q_2 is zero, but the input currents of the N inverters must be supplied through the 2-kΩ load resistor. The resulting expression for v_O becomes:

$$v_O = 5 - 2000 i_R = 5 - N(2000 \ \Omega)(0.22 \text{ mA}) = 5 - N(0.44) \text{ V} \quad (10.81)$$

Each added fanout connection causes the output voltage to drop an additional 0.44 V below 5 V.

To determine N, we must understand how far v_O can drop without having a detrimental effect on the inverters connected to the output. The inverter circuit with $v_I \approx V_{IH}$ is redrawn in Fig. 10.53. Q_1 is operating in the reverse-active region, and its collector current, $i_C = -(\beta_R + 1)i_{B1}$, will be independent of the base-emitter voltage as long as the base-emitter junction is reverse-biased. Therefore, the base current of Q_2 will be constant as long as

$$v_{BE1} = (v_{B1} - v_I) \leq 0 \quad (10.82)$$

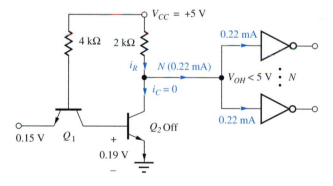

Figure 10.52 Fanout conditions for $v_O = V_{OH}$.

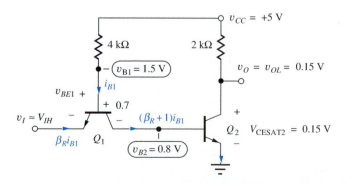

Figure 10.53 Circuit for determining V_{OH} limitations.

which requires that $v_I \geq 1.5$ V. Combining Eq. (10.82) with Eq. (10.81) allows us to determine the fanout N:

$$5 - N(2000 \ \Omega)(0.22 \ \text{mA}) \geq 1.5 \quad \text{or} \quad N \leq 7.95 \qquad (10.83)$$

For the output voltage in the high state, the fanout N must not exceed 7.95. Because N must once again be an integer, the maximum fanout is limited to 7. Further, because the overall fanout specification for the TTL gate must be the smallest N that works properly regardless of logic state, the fanout for the prototype TTL inverter must be specified as $N = 7$.

> **EXERCISE:** What is the fanout limit if V_{CESAT2} is required to be less than 0.1 V? What would be the input current i_{IH} and fanout limit for $v_I = V_{OH}$ for the TTL prototype inverter circuit if $\beta_{R1} = 2$?
>
> **ANSWERS:** 7; 1.75 mA, 1

10.13 STANDARD TTL

The TTL gate described thus far has been a prototype for understanding the more complex gate that forms standard TTL logic. This basic circuit is also useful for low-level on-chip applications. However, with an overdriven transistor Q_2 to pull the output down, but only the 2-kΩ load resistor to pull the output up, the dynamic response of this gate will be highly asymmetric, as was the case for NMOS logic. In addition, we found in the last section that the prototype circuit has a limited fanout capability and is quite sensitive to the value of β_R.

The circuit for the classical TTL inverter shown in Fig. 10.54 solves these problems. This circuit is typically found in TTL unit logic in which several identical gates are packaged together in a single **dual-in-line package,** or **DIP.** Input transistor Q_1 operates in exactly the same manner as Q_1 in the prototype gate, and Q_2 forces the output low to V_{CESAT2}. The load resistor is replaced with an **active pull-up circuit** formed by transistor Q_4 and diode D_1. Q_3 and D_1 are required to ensure that Q_4 is turned off when Q_2 is turned on and vice versa.

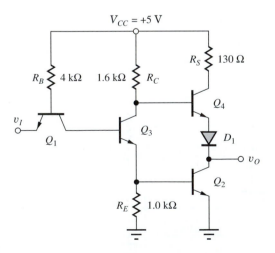

Figure 10.54 Standard TTL inverter.

Analysis for $v_I = V_{OL}$

Figure 10.55 is the full TTL circuit with an input voltage of 0.15 V. Base current i_{B1} causes Q_1 to saturate, with $i_{C1} \approx 0$ and $V_{CESAT1} = 0.04$ V. The emitter current is equal to the base current given by

$$i_{E1} \approx i_{B1} = \frac{(5 - 0.8 - 0.15)\ \text{V}}{4\ \text{k}\Omega} = 1.0\ \text{mA} \tag{10.84}$$

The voltage v_{B3} at the base of Q_3 is approximately $0.15\ \text{V} + 0.04\ \text{V} = 0.19$ V, which keeps both Q_2 and Q_3 off because 0.19 V is less than one base-emitter voltage drop, and two are required to turn on both Q_2 and $Q_3 (v_{BE2} + v_{BE3} = 1.4$ V).

Because Q_2 and Q_3 are off with i_{C2} and i_{C3} approximately zero, the output portion of the gate may be simplified to the circuit of Fig. 10.56. In this circuit, base current is supplied to Q_4 through resistor R_C, and the output reaches

$$v_O = 5 - i_{B4}R_C - v_{BE4} - v_{D1} \tag{10.85}$$

For normal values of load current i_L, modeled by the current source in Fig. 10.56, the voltage drop in R_C is usually negligible, and the nominal value of V_{OH} is

$$V_{OH} \approx 5 - v_{BE4} - v_{D1} = 5 - 0.7 - 0.7 = 3.6\ \text{V} \tag{10.86}$$

The 130-Ω resistor R_S is added to the circuit to protect transistor Q_4 from accidental short circuits to ground. Resistor R_S allows Q_4 to saturate and limits the power dissipation in the transistor. For example, if v_O is connected directly to ground, then the current through Q_4 and D_1 will be limited to approximately

$$i_{C4} = \frac{V_{CC} - V_{CESAT4} - V_{D1}}{R_S}$$

and

$$i_{C4} \le \frac{(5 - 0 - 0.7)\ \text{V}}{130\ \Omega} = 33.1\ \text{mA} \tag{10.87}$$

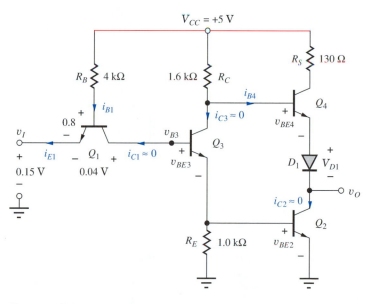

Figure 10.55 Standard TTL inverter with $v_I = 0.15$ V.

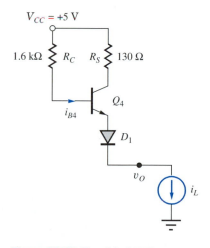

Figure 10.56 Simplified TTL output stage for $v_O = V_{OH}$.

EXERCISES: What would i_{C4} be if Q_4 remains in the forward-active region when v_O is shorted to ground? Use $\beta_F = 40$.
What is the maximum value of i_L for which $v_O \geq 3$ V if $\beta_{F4} = 40$? Is Q_4 in the forward-active region at this value of i_C?

ANSWERS: 92.3 mA; 15.4 mA, yes

Analysis for $v_I = V_{OH}$

V_{OH} is now applied as the input to the TTL circuit in Fig. 10.57. This input level exceeds the voltage required at the base of Q_3 to turn on both Q_2 and Q_3, $(v_{B3} \geq v_{BE3} + v_{BE2})$, and the base current to Q_3 becomes

$$i_{B3} = (\beta_R + 1)i_{B1} = (\beta_R + 1)\frac{V_{CC} - v_{BC1} - v_{BESAT3} - v_{BESAT2}}{R_B}$$

or   (10.88)

$$i_{B3} = (0.25 + 1)\frac{(5 - 0.7 - 0.8 - 0.8) \text{ V}}{4 \text{ k}\Omega} = 0.84 \text{ mA}$$

Both Q_2 and Q_3 are designed to saturate, so both base-emitter voltages are assumed to be 0.8 V in Eq.(10.86). For this case, the input current entering the emitter is

$$i_{IH} = -i_{E1} = \beta_R i_{B1} = 0.25(0.68 \text{ mA}) = 0.17 \text{ mA} \tag{10.89}$$

The base current of Q_2 ultimately determines the fanout limit of this TTL gate; it is given by

$$i_{B2} = i_{E3} - i_{RE} = i_{C3} + i_{B3} - i_{RE} \tag{10.90}$$

Currents i_{RE} and i_{C3} are given by

$$i_{RE} = \frac{V_{BESAT2}}{R_E} = \frac{0.8 \text{ V}}{1.0 \text{ K}} = 0.80 \text{ mA}$$

(10.91)

$$i_{C3} = \frac{5 - V_{CESAT3} - V_{BESAT2}}{1.6 \text{ K}} = \frac{5 - 0.15 - 0.8}{1.6 \text{ K}} = 2.53 \text{ mA}$$

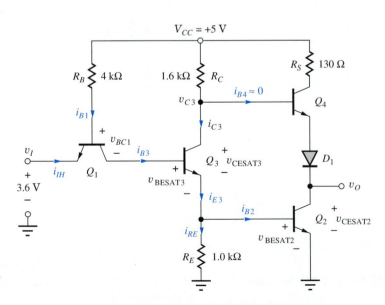

Figure 10.57 Standard TTL inverter with $v_I = V_{OH}$.

and

$$i_{B2} = (2.53 + 0.84 - 0.80)\ \text{mA} = 2.57\ \text{mA} \tag{10.92}$$

in which it has been assumed that Q_4 is off with $i_{B4} = 0$.

The assumption that Q_4 is off can be checked by calculating the voltage $v_{C3} - v_O$:

$$v_{C3} - v_O = (V_{\text{CESAT3}} + V_{\text{BESAT2}}) - (V_{\text{CESAT2}}) \tag{10.93}$$

$$= 0.80 + 0.15 - 0.15 = 0.80\ \text{V}$$

This voltage, 0.8 V, must be shared by the base-emitter junction of Q_4 and diode D_1, but it is not sufficient to turn on the series combination of the two. However, if D_1 were not present, the full 0.8 V would appear across the base-emitter junction of Q_4, and it would saturate. Thus, D_1 must be added to the circuit to ensure that Q_4 is off when Q_2 and Q_3 are saturated.

Power Consumption

Figure 10.58 summarizes the voltages and currents in the TTL gate. Assuming a 50 percent duty cycle, the average power consumed by the TTL gate is

$$\langle P \rangle = \frac{P_{OL} + P_{OH}}{2} \tag{10.94}$$

$$\langle P \rangle = \frac{[5\ \text{V}(0.92\ \text{mA}) + 3.6\ \text{V}(0.17\ \text{mA})] + [5\ \text{V}(1.0\ \text{mA}) + 0.15\ \text{V}(-1.0\ \text{mA})]}{2}$$

$$\langle P \rangle = 5.03\ \text{mW}$$

TTL Propagation Delay and Power-Delay Product

Analysis of the propagation delay of the TTL inverter is fairly complex because several saturating transistors are involved. Therefore, we investigate the behavior by looking at the results of simulation of the full TTL inverter. From Fig. 10.59, the average propagation

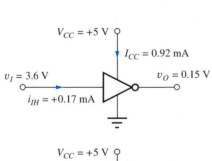

$V_{CC} = +5$ V
$I_{CC} = 0.92$ mA
$v_I = 3.6$ V
$v_O = 0.15$ V
$i_{IH} = +0.17$ mA

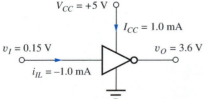

$V_{CC} = +5$ V
$I_{CC} = 1.0$ mA
$v_I = 0.15$ V
$v_O = 3.6$ V
$i_{IL} = -1.0$ mA

Figure 10.58 Voltage and current summary for standard TTL.

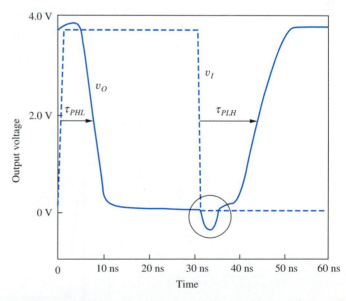

Figure 10.59 SPICE simulation of the full TTL inverter propagation delay.

delay is approximately

$$\tau_P = \frac{\tau_{PHL} + \tau_{PLH}}{2} = \frac{6 + 14}{2}\ \text{ns} = 10\ \text{ns} \tag{10.95}$$

This value represents the nominal delay of standard TTL.

On the high-to-low transition, transistor Q_1 must come out of saturation and enter the reverse-active mode, while Q_2 and Q_3 must go from near cutoff to saturation. For the low-to-high transition, Q_2 and Q_3 must both come out of saturation. Thus, we may expect one storage time delay for the first case and two storage time delays for the second. Thus, τ_{PLH} should be greater than τ_{PHL}, as in the simulation results.

Using these simulation results and the power calculated from Eq. (10.94), we estimate the power-delay product for the standard TTL gate to be

$$\text{PDP} = (5.0\ \text{mW})(10\ \text{ns}) = 50\ \text{pJ} \tag{10.96}$$

a rather large value.

TTL Voltage Transfer Characteristic and Noise Margins

Figure 10.60 gives the results of simulation of the VTC for the TTL inverter. The various break points in the characteristic can be easily identified in a manner similar to that used for the TTL prototype gate. As the input voltage increases to become equal to 0.7 V, base current begins to enter Q_3. The emitter voltage of Q_3 starts to rise, and its collector voltage begins to fall. Q_4 functions as an emitter follower, and the output drops as the collector voltage of Q_3 falls. As Q_3 turns on, the slope changes abruptly, giving $V_{IL} \approx 0.7$ V.

As the input voltage (and the voltage at v_{B3}) approaches 1.5 V, there is enough voltage to both saturate Q_3 and turn on Q_2. As Q_2 turns on and Q_3 saturates, turning off Q_4, the output voltage drops more abruptly, causing break point V_2 in the curve. In Fig. 10.60 it can be seen that $V_{IH} \approx 1.8$ V, which is slightly larger than $V_{\text{BESAT3}} + V_{\text{BESAT2}}$, the voltage at v_{B3} for which both Q_2 and Q_3 are heavily saturated. For this voltage, Q_1 is coming out of heavy saturation and starting to operate in the reverse-active mode.

Using $V_{IL} = 0.7$ V, $V_{OL} = 0.15$ V, $V_{IH} = 1.8$ V, and $V_{OH} = 3.6$ V yields

$$\text{NM}_L = 0.7\ \text{V} - 0.15\ \text{V} = 0.55\ \text{V}$$

and

$$\text{NM}_H = 3.6\ \text{V} - 1.8\ \text{V} = 1.8\ \text{V} \tag{10.97}$$

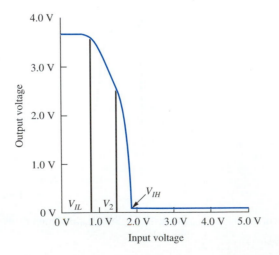

Figure 10.60 SPICE simulation of the VTC for the TTL gate in Fig. 10.54.

Fanout Limitations of Standard TTL

The active pull-up circuit can supply relatively large amounts of current with the output changing very little (see Probs. 10.79 to 10.81), so the fanout becomes limited by the current sinking capability of Q_2. For $v_O = V_{OL}$, Q_4 and D_1 are off, and the collector current of Q_2 is equal to the input currents of the N gates connected to the output, as shown in Fig. 10.61:

$$Ni_{IL} \leq \beta_{FOR}i_{B2} \tag{10.98}$$

or

$$N(1 \text{ mA}) \leq 28.3(2.57 \text{ mA}) \quad \text{and} \quad N \leq 72.7$$

Using the transistor parameters in Table 10.3 with this circuit yields a fanout limit of 72. However, from Eq. (10.90), we see that the fanout is sensitive to the actual values of β_R, R_B, and R_E. The parameters of the transistors in the standard TTL IC process are somewhat different from those in Table 10.3, and the specifications must be guaranteed over a wide range of temperature, supply voltages, and IC process variations. Thus, the fanout of standard TTL is actually specified to be $N \leq 10$.

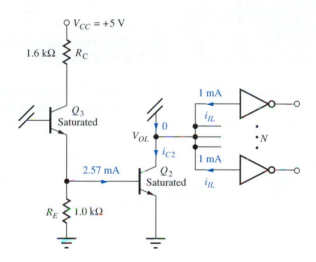

Figure 10.61 Fanout conditions for $v_O = V_{OL}$.

10.14   LOGIC FUNCTIONS IN TTL

The TTL inverter becomes a two-input gate with the addition of a second transistor in parallel with transistor Q_1, as drawn in the prototype TTL schematic in Fig. 10.62. If either the emitter of Q_{1A} or the emitter of Q_{1B} is in a low state, then base current i_B will be diverted out of the corresponding emitter terminal, the base current of Q_2 will be negligibly small, and the output will be high. Base current will be supplied to Q_2, and the output will

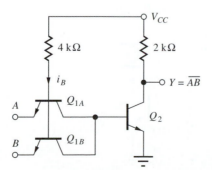

Figure 10.62 Two-input TTL NAND gate: $Y = \overline{AB}$.

be low, only if both inputs A and B are high. Table 10.4 is the truth table for this gate, which corresponds to a two-input NAND gate.

Standard TTL logic families provide gates with eight or more inputs. An eight-input gate conceptually has eight transistors in parallel. However, because the input transistors all have common base and collector connections, these devices are actually implemented as a single multi-emitter transistor, which is usually drawn as shown in the three-input NAND gate diagram in Fig. 10.63.

T a b l e 10.4		
Two-Input NAND Gate Truth Table		
A	**B**	**$Y = \overline{AB}$**
0	0	1
0	1	1
1	0	1
1	1	0

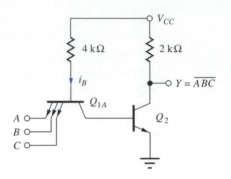

Figure 10.63 Multi-emitter realization of the three-input NAND gate.

The concept of the merged structure for a multi-emitter transistor appears in Fig. 10.64, in which the three-emitter transistor with merged base and collector regions takes up far less area than three individual transistors would require.

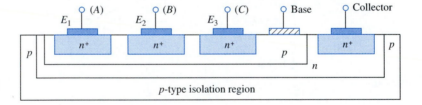

Figure 10.64 Merged structure for three-emitter bipolar transistor.

A complete standard three-input TTL NAND gate is shown in the schematic in Fig. 10.65. If any one of the three input emitters is low, then the base current to transistor

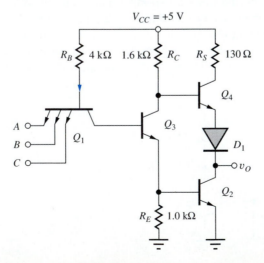

Figure 10.65 Standard TTL three-input NAND gate.

Q_3 will be zero and the output will be high, yielding $Y = \overline{ABC}$. The behavior of the rest of the gate is identical to that described in the discussion of Figs. 10.54 to 10.58.

Although the basic TTL gate provides the NAND function, other logic operations can be implemented with the addition of more transistors. One example is shown in Fig. 10.66, in which the input circuitry of Q_1 and Q_3 is replicated to provide the **AND-OR-Invert,** or **AOI,** logic function (a complemented sum-of-products function). This five-input gate provides the logic function $Y = \overline{ABC + DE}$.

TTL also has several power options, including standard, high-power, and low-power versions, in which the resistor values are modified to change the power level and hence the gate delay. **Low-power TTL** has a delay of approximately 30 ns, and the **high-power TTL** series (54H/74H) has a delay of approximately 7 ns. An example of the circuit for the 54L/74L series of low-power TTL is given in Fig. 10.67. Here the resistors have been scaled to reduce the power consumption by a factor of 5, and the delay increases by a factor of approximately 3.

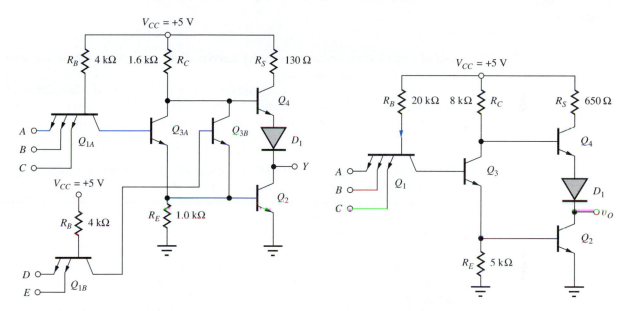

Figure 10.66 TTL AND-OR-Invert (AOI) gate: $Y = \overline{ABC + DE}$.

Figure 10.67 Low-power TTL NAND gate.

Input Clamping Diodes

In Fig. 10.59, we observe a negative-going transient on the output signal near $t = 15$ ns, which resulted from the rapid input signal transition. Another source of such transients is "ringing," which results from high-speed signals exciting the distributed L-C interconnection network between logic gates, as diagrammed in Fig. 6.4. To prevent large excursions of the inputs below ground level, which can destroy the TTL input transistors, a diode is usually added to each input to clamp the input signal to no more than one diode-drop below ground potential. These input clamping diodes are added to the TTL NAND gate schematic in Fig. 10.68.

10.15 SCHOTTKY-CLAMPED TTL

As discussed in Sec. 10.13, saturation of the transistors in TTL logic substantially slows down the dynamic response of the logic gates. The **Schottky-clamped transistor** drawn in Fig. 10.69 was developed to solve this problem. The Schottky-clamped transistor con-

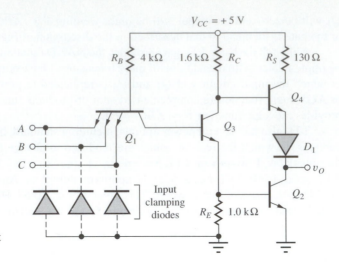

Figure 10.68 TTL NAND gate with clamping diodes at the input.

sists of a metal semiconductor **Schottky barrier diode** in parallel with the collector-base junction of the bipolar transistor.

When conducting, the forward voltage drop of the Schottky diode is designed to be approximately 0.45 V, so it will turn on before the collector-base diode of the bipolar transistor becomes strongly forward-biased. Referring to Fig. 10.69, we see that

$$v_{CE} = v_{BE} - v_{SD} = 0.70 - 0.45 = 0.25 \text{ V} \qquad (10.99)$$

The Schottky diode prevents the BJT from going into deep saturation by diverting excess base current through the Schottky diode and around the BJT. Because the BJT is prevented from entering heavy saturation, 0.7 V has been used for the value of v_{BE} in Eq. (10.99).

A cross section of the structure used to fabricate the Schottky transistor is given in Fig. 10.70. Conceptually, an aluminum base contact overlaps the collector-base junction, forming an ohmic contact to the p-type base region and a Schottky diode to the more lightly doped n-type collector region. (Remember that aluminum is a p-type dopant in silicon.) This is another example of the novel merged structures that can be fabricated using IC technology.

In Fig. 10.71, both transistors in the TTL inverter have been replaced with Schottky-clamped transistors, and the resulting gate is the prototype for a **Schottky TTL inverter.** With a high-input level applied to the gate, as in Fig. 10.72, a base current of $i_{B2} = (\beta_R + 1)i_{B1}$ attempts to saturate Q_2. The Schottky diode prevents Q_2 from heavily saturating, and v_{CE} is limited to 0.25 V, as given by Eq. (10.99). Thus, $V_{OL} = 0.25$ V for this inverter.

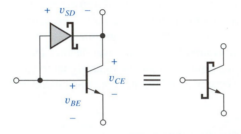

Figure 10.69 Schottky-clamped transistor.

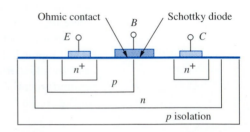

Figure 10.70 Cross section of the merged Schottky diode and bipolar transistor structure.

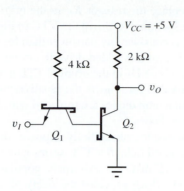

Figure 10.71 Prototype TTL inverter with Schottky-clamped transistors.

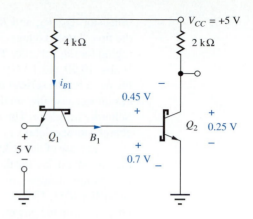

Figure 10.72 Prototype Schottky TTL gate with input at V_{OH}.

Figure 10.73 shows the Schottky inverter with input $v_I = V_{OL} = 0.25$ V. The current through the 4-kΩ resistor causes Q_1 to saturate, with its v_{CE} clamped to 0.25 V by the Schottky diode. The resulting base-emitter voltage of Q_2 is 0.5 V, which is 200 mV below the voltage required to turn on Q_2. Thus, Q_2 is off and $V_{OH} = 5$ V.

Invention of this circuit required a good understanding of the exponential dependence of the BJT collector current on base-emitter voltage as well as knowledge of the differences between Schottky and *pn* junction diodes. Successful manufacture of the circuit relies on tight process control to maintain the desired difference between the forward drops of the base-emitter and Schottky diodes.

Figure 10.74 is the schematic for a full three-input Schottky TTL NAND gate. Each saturating transistor in the original gate—Q_1, Q_2, and Q_3—is replaced with a Schottky

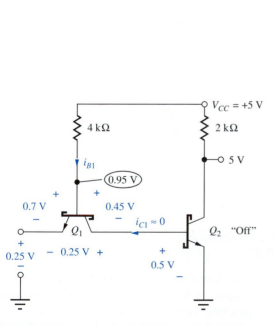

Figure 10.73 Prototype Schottky TTL gate with input at V_{OL}.

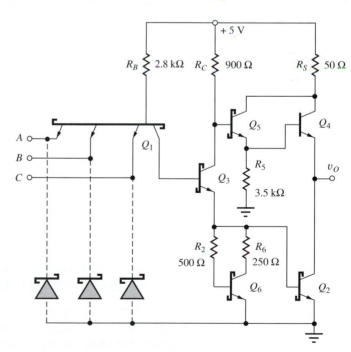

Figure 10.74 Schottky TTL NAND gate.

transistor. Q_6, R_2, and R_6 replace the resistor R_E in the original TTL gate and eliminate the first "knee" voltage corresponding to V_{IL} in the VTC in Fig. 10.60. Thus, the transition region for the Schottky TTL is considerably narrower than for the original TTL circuit (see Probs. 10.99 and 10.101). Q_5 provides added drive to emitter follower Q_4 and eliminates the need for the series output diode D_1 in the original TTL gate. Q_4 cannot saturate in this circuit because the smallest value for v_{CB4} is the positive voltage V_{CESAT5}, so it is not a Schottky transistor. The input clamp diodes are replaced with Schottky diodes to eliminate charge storage delays in these diodes.

The use of Schottky transistors substantially improves the speed of the gate, reducing the nominal delay for the standard Schottky TTL series gate (54S/74S) to 3 ns at a power dissipation of approximately 15 mW. An extremely popular TTL family is **low-power Schottky TTL** (54LS/74LS), which provides the delay of standard TTL (10 ns) but at only one-fifth the power. This gate is shown in Fig. 10.75. The resistor values are increased to decrease the power, but speed is maintained at lower power by eliminating the storage times associated with saturating transistors. This family is widely used to replace standard TTL because it offers the same delay at substantially less power.

As IC technology has continued to improve, the complexity and performance of TTL has also continued to increase. The advanced Schottky logic (ALS) and advanced low-power Schottky logic families were introduced with improved power-delay characteristics. The increasing complexity is apparent in the 54ALS/74ALS circuit in Fig. 10.76. Note the use of *pnp* transistors at the input.

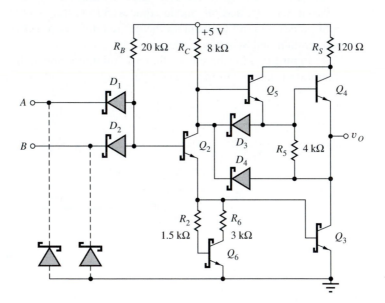

Figure 10.75 Low-power Schottky TTL NAND gate.

10.16 COMPARISON OF THE POWER-DELAY PRODUCTS OF ECL AND TTL

Figure 10.77 is a comparison of the power versus delay characteristics of a number of the ECL and TTL unit-logic families that have been produced. ECL, with its nonsaturating transistors and low logic swing, is generally faster than TTL, although one can see the performance overlap between generations that occurred for ECL II versus Schottky TTL, for example. A new generation of IC technology and better circuit techniques achieve

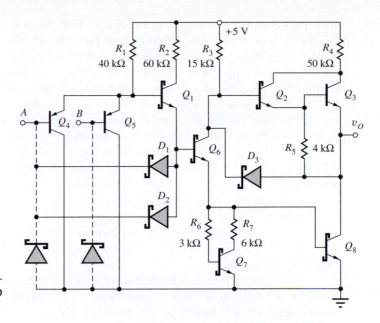

Figure 10.76 Advanced low-power Schottky TTL NAND gate.

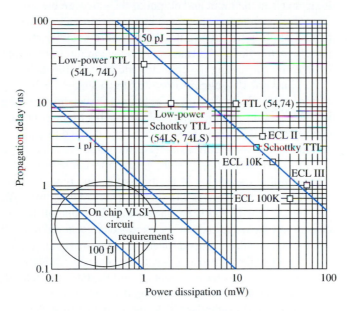

Figure 10.77 Power-delay products for various commercial unit-logic families.

higher speed circuits for a given power level. However, for high-density integrated circuits, significant improvements in power and power-delay products are required, as indicated by the circle in the lower left-hand corner of Fig. 10.77.

SUMMARY

This chapter introduced the two commercially most important forms of bipolar logic: emitter-coupled logic (ECL) and transistor-transistor logic (TTL or T^2L). Simple prototype circuits were introduced for the ECL and TTL gates, and then the full gate structures were analyzed. The voltage transfer characteristics for ECL and TTL were investigated, and values of V_{IH}, V_{IL}, and the noise margins were determined for these two circuit families. It was found that ECL logic gates generate both true and complement outputs, and the basic ECL gate provides the OR-NOR logic functions. On the other hand, basic TTL gates realize multi-input NAND functions. Standard ECL unit-logic families provide delays in the 0.5- to 5-ns range, with a power-delay product of approximately 50 pJ, whereas the various TTL families achieve delays of 3 to 30 ns, with similar power-delay products.

The ECL gate introduced two new circuit techniques: the current switch and the emitter-follower circuit. The current switch consists of two matched BJTs and a current source. This circuit rapidly switches the bias current back and forth between the two transistors, based on a comparison of the logic input signal with a reference voltage. In the ECL gate, the transistors actually switch between two points in the forward-active region, which is one reason why ECL is the highest speed form of bipolar logic. A second factor is the relatively small logic swing, typically in the 0.4- to 0.8-V range. The low ECL logic swing results in noise margins of only a few tenths of a volt. ECL is somewhat unusual compared to the other logic families that have been studied in that it is typically designed to operate from a single negative power supply, historically -5.2 V, and V_{OH} and V_{OL} are both negative voltages.

In the emitter-follower circuit, the output signal replicates the input signal except for a fixed offset equal to one base-emitter diode voltage, approximately 0.7 V. In ECL, this fixed-voltage offset is used to provide the level-shifting function needed to ensure that the logic levels at the input and output of the gates are the same.

Temperature-compensated reference circuits are used to provide the reference voltage required in the ECL gate. Temperature compensation is achieved using diodes that closely match the bipolar transistors in the circuit. In integrated circuits, diodes are usually realized by connecting the collector and base terminals of a transistor together.

Classical TTL circuits operate from a single $+5$-V supply and provide a logic swing of approximately 3.5 V, with noise margins exceeding 1 V. During operation, the transistors in TTL circuits become saturated. The collector-emitter saturation voltage of the BJT is controlled by the value of the forced beta, defined as $\beta_{\text{FOR}} = i_C/i_B$. The transistor enters saturation if the base current exceeds the value needed to support the collector current (that is, $i_B > i_C/\beta_F$ so that $\beta_{\text{FOR}} < \beta_F$). An undesirable result of saturation is storage of excess charge in the base region of the transistor. The time needed to remove the excess charge can cause the BJT to turn off slowly. This delayed turn-off response is characterized by the storage time t_S and is proportional to the value of the storage time constant τ_S, which determines the magnitude of the excess charge stored in the base during saturation.

The Schottky-clamped transistor merges a standard bipolar transistor with a Schottky diode and was developed as a way to prevent saturation in bipolar transistors. The Schottky diode diverts excess base current around the base-collector diode of the BJT and prevents heavy saturation of the device. Schottky TTL circuits offer considerable improvement in speed compared to standard TTL for a given power dissipation because the storage time delays are eliminated.

It was found that the TTL input transistors operate in the reverse-active mode when the input is in the high state. This is the only actual use of this mode that we encounter in this text. In addition, the TTL gate has relatively large input currents for both high- and low-input voltages. The input current is positive for high-input levels and negative for low-input levels. This input current limits the fanout capability of the gate. The fanout capability of TTL was analyzed in detail. At the output of the TTL gate, another emitter follower can be found. The emitter follower provides high current drive needed to support large fanouts as well as to rapidly pull up the output.

TTL gates come in many forms, including standard, low-power, high-power, Schottky, low-power Schottky, advanced Schottky, and advanced low-power Schottky versions. Standard TTL has essentially been replaced by low-power Schottky (54LS/74LS) TTL, which provides similar delay but at reduced power. Schottky TTL (54S/74S) provides a high-speed alternative for circuits with critical speed requirements.

The standard ECL and TTL unit-logic families have relatively large power-delay products (20 to 100 pJ), which are not suitable for high-density VLSI chip designs. VLSI circuit densities require subpicojoule power-delay products; simplified circuit designs with much lower values of power-delay product are required for VLSI applications.

Key Terms

Active pull-up circuit
AND-OR-Invert (AOI) logic
Base-emitter saturation voltage (V_{BESAT})
Collector-emitter saturation voltage (V_{CESAT})
Clamp diodes
Current switch circuit
Dual-in-line package (DIP)
Emitter-coupled logic (ECL)
Emitter-coupled pair
Emitter dotting
Emitter follower

Fanout
Forward-active region
Forward transit time
High-power TTL
Level shifter
Low-power TTL
Low-power Schottky TTL
Merged transistor structure
Reference voltage
Reverse-active region
Reverse transit time
Saturation region
Saturation voltage

Schottky barrier diode
Schottky-clamped transistor
Schottky TTL inverter
Stored base charge
Storage time t_S
Storage time constant τ_S
Sum-of-products logic function
Temperature compensation
Transistor-transistor logic (TTL, T^2L)
Wired-OR logic

Reference

Hodges, D. A. and H. G. Jackson, *Analysis and Design of Digital Integrated Circuits,* 2d ed. McGraw-Hill, New York 1988.

Additional Reading

Haznedar, H. *Digital Microelectronics.* Benjamin/Cummings, Redwood City, CA: 1991.

Glasford, G. M. *Digital Electronic Circuits.* Prentice-Hall, Englewood Cliffs, NJ: 1988.

Sedra, A. S. and K. C. Smith. *Microelectronic Circuits.* 3d ed. Saunders, Philadelphia, PA: 1990.

PSPICE Simulation Data *FIGURE 10.7 ECL inverter VTC

```
VIN 2 0 DC -1.3
VREF 4 0 -1.0
VEE 8 0 -5.2
Q1 1 2 3 NBJT
Q2 5 4 3 NBJT
Q3 0 1 6 NBJT
Q4 0 5 7 NBJT
IEE 3 8 .0003
I4 7 8 .0001
I3 6 8 .0001
RC1 0 1 2K
RC2 0 5 2K
.DC VIN -1.3 -0.7 .01
.MODEL NBJT NPN
.PROBE V(2) V(1) V(5) V(6) V(7)
.END
```

*FIGURE 10.34 ECL inverter delay

```
VIN 2 0 PULSE(-1.36 -0.78 0 .01NS .01NS 15NS)
VREF 4 0 -1.07
VEE 8 0 -5.2
Q1 1 2 3 NBJT
Q2 5 4 3 NBJT
Q3 0 1 6 NBJT
Q4 0 5 7 NBJT
IEE 3 8 .0003
I4 7 8 .0001
I3 6 8 .0001
RC1 0 1 2K
RC2 0 5 2K
.TRAN 0.1N 30N
.MODEL NBJT NPN BF=40 BR=0.25 IS=1E-17 TF =0.15NS TR=15NS
+CJC=0.5PF CJE=.25PF CJS=1.0PF RB=100 RC=5 RE=1
.PROBE V(2) V(1) V(5) V(6) V(7)
.END
```

*FIGURE 10.39 BJT load line

```
II 0 1 DC 0
VCC 2 0 5
Q1 2 1 0 NBJT
.DC VCC 0 5 .1 II 0 105U 15U
.MODEL NBJT NPN BF=40 BR=.25 IS=1E-17
.PROBE I(VCC)
.END
```

*FIGURE 10.41 BJT inverter delay

```
II1 0 2 PULSE(-.00001 .001 0 .2NS .2NS 15NS)
II2 0 5 PULSE(-.001 .001 0 .2NS .2NS 15NS)
II3 0 4 PULSE(-.0001 .001 0 .2NS .2NS 15NS)
VCC 8 0 5
Q1 3 2 0 NBJT
D1 0 2 DN
RC1 8 3 2K
Q2 6 5 0 NBJT
D2 0 5 DN
RC2 8 6 2K
Q3 7 4 0 NBJT
D3 0 4 DN
RC3 8 7 2K
.TRAN .1NS 100NS
.MODEL NBJT NPN BF=40 BR=0.25 IS=1E-17 TF =0.25NS TR=25NS
+CJC=0.6PF CJE=.6PF
.MODEL DN D IS=1E-17
.PROBE V(2) V(3) V(4) V(5) V(6) V(7)
.END
```

*Figure 10.47 Prototype TTL inverter VTC

```
VI 1 0 DC 0
VCC 5 0 DC 5
Q1 3 2 1 NBJT
Q2 4 3 0 NBJT
RB 5 2 4K
RC 5 4 2K
.DC VI 0 5 .01
.MODEL NBJT NPN BF=40 BR=.25 IS=1E-17
.PROBE V(1) V(2) V(3) V(4)
.END
```

*Figure 10.59 TTL inverter delay

```
VI 1 0 PULSE(0 3.7 0 .5NS .5NS 30NS)
VCC 9 0 5
Q1 2 8 1 NBJT
Q2 6 2 3 NBJT
Q3 4 3 0 NBJT
Q4 7 6 5 NBJT
D1 5 4 DN
RB 9 8 4K
RC 9 6 1.6K
RE 3 0 1.0K
RS 9 7 130
RL 4 0 100K
.TRAN .1NS 60NS
.MODEL NBJT NPN BF=40 BR=0.35 IS=1E-17 TF =0.6NS TR=50NS
+CJC=1.0PF CJE=1.0PF CJS=2.0PF RB=100 RC=5 RE=1
.MODEL DN D
.PROBE V(1) V(2) V(3) V(4) V(5) V(6)
.END
```

*Figure 10.60 Full TTL inverter VTC

```
VI 1 0 DC 0
VCC 9 0 DC 5
Q1 2 8 1 NBJT
Q2 6 2 3 NBJT
Q3 4 3 0 NBJT
Q4 7 6 5 NBJT
D1 5 4 DN
RB 9 8 4K
RC 9 6 1.6K
RE 3 0 1.0K
RS 9 7 130
RL 4 0 100K
.DC VI 0 5 .01
.MODEL NBJT NPN BF=40 BR=0.25 IS=1E-17 TF =0.25NS TR=25NS
+CJC=0.6PF CJE=.6PF CJS=1.25PF RB=100 RC=5 RE=1
.MODEL DN D
.PROBE V(1) V(2) V(3) V(4) V(5) V(6)
.END
```

Problems

For SPICE simulations, use the device parameters in Appendix B. For hand calculations use the values in Table 9.3 on page 417.

10.1 The Current Switch (Emitter-Coupled Pair)

10.1. (a) What value of v_I is required in Fig. P10.1 to switch 99.5 percent of the current I_{EE} into transistor Q_1 if $V_{REF} = -1.25$ V? What value of v_I will switch 99.5 percent of I_{EE} into transistor Q_2? (b) Repeat part (a) if $V_{REF} = -2$ V.

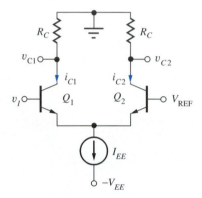

Figure P10.1

10.2. What are the voltages at v_{C1} and v_{C2} in the circuit in Fig. P10.1 for $v_I = -1.6$ V if $I_{EE} = 2.0$ mA, $R_C = 350$ Ω, and $V_{REF} = -1.25$ V?

10.3. What are the voltages at v_{C1} and v_{C2} in the circuit in Fig. P10.1 for $v_I = -1.6$ V, $I_{EE} = 5.0$ mA, $R_C = 350$ Ω, and $V_{REF} = -2$ V?

10.4. What are the voltages at v_{C1} and v_{C2} in the circuit in Fig. P10.4 for $v_I = -1.7$ V, $I_{EE} = 0.3$ mA, $R_1 = 3.33$ kΩ, $R_C = 2$ kΩ, and $V_{REF} = -2$ V?

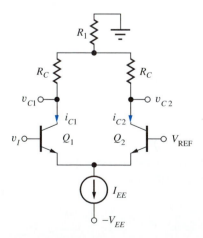

Figure P10.4

*10.5. A bipolar transistor is operating with $v_{BE} = +0.7$ V and $v_{BC} = +0.3$ V. By the strict definitions given in the chapter on bipolar transistors, this transistor is operating in the saturation region. Use the transport equations to demonstrate that it actually behaves as if it is still in the forward-active region. Discuss this result. (You may use $I_S = 10^{-15}$ A, $\alpha_F = 0.98$, and $\alpha_R = 0.2$.)

**10.6. A low-voltage current switch is shown Fig. P10.6. (a) What are the voltage levels corresponding to V_{OH} and V_{OL} at v_{O2}? (b) Do these voltage levels appear to be compatible with the levels needed at the input v_I? Why? (c) What is the value of R? (d) For $v_I = V_{OH}$ from part (a), what are the regions of operation of transistors Q_1 and Q_2? (e) For $v_I = V_{OL}$ from part (a), what are the regions of operation of transistors Q_1 and Q_2? (f) Your answers in parts (c) and (d) should have involved regions other than the forward-active region. Discuss whether this appears to represent a problem in this circuit.

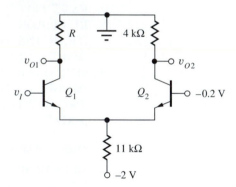

Figure P10.6

10.2 The Emitter-Coupled Logic (ECL) Gate

10.7. The values of I_{EE} and R_C in Fig. 10.6 are changed to 5 mA and 200 Ω, respectively. What are the new values of V_{OH}, V_{OL}, V_{REF}, and ΔV?

10.8. Redesign the values of resistors and current sources in Fig. 10.6 to increase the power consumption by a factor of 5. The values of V_{OH} and V_{OL} should remain constant.

*10.9. Redesign the circuit of Fig. 10.6 to have a logic swing of 0.8 V. Use the same currents. (a) What are the new values of V_{OH}, V_{OL}, V_{REF}, and the resistors? (b) What are the values of the noise margins? (c) What is the minimum value of V_{CB} for Q_1 and Q_2? Do the values of V_{CB} represent a problem?

10.10. Emitter followers are added to the outputs of the circuit in Fig. P10.4 in the same manner as in Fig. 10.6. (a) Draw the new circuit. (b) If $I_{EE} = 0.3$ mA, $R_1 = 3.33$ kΩ, $R_C = 2$ kΩ, and $V_{REF} = -2$ V, what are the values of V_{OH}, V_{OL}, and the logic swing ΔV? (c) Are the input and output levels of this gate compatible with each other?

10.11. Emitter followers are added to the outputs of the circuit in Fig. P10.4 in the same manner as in Fig. 10.6. (a) Draw the new circuit. (b) What are the values of R_C, V_{OH}, V_{OL}, and V_{REF} if $I_{EE} = 2$ mA, $R_1 = 600$ Ω, and $\Delta V = 0.4$ V?

**10.12. Calculate the fanout for the ECL inverter in Fig. 10.6 at room temperature for $\beta_F = 35$. Define the fanout N to be equal to the number of inverters for which the V_{OH} level deteriorates by no more than one V_T. (Hint: At v_{O2}, $\Delta V_{OH} = \Delta V_{BE4} + \Delta i_{B4} R_C$.) Do we need to consider the case for $v_O = V_{OL}$? Why?

10.3–10.4 V_{IH}, V_{IL}, and Noise Margin Analysis for the ECL Gate and Current Source Implementation

10.13. Redesign the values of resistors and current sources in Fig. 10.10 to increase the power consumption by a factor of 10. The values of V_{OH} and V_{OL} should remain constant.

10.14. What are the values of V_{OH}, V_{OL}, V_{REF}, ΔV, the noise margins, and the average power dissipation for the circuit in Fig. P10.14?

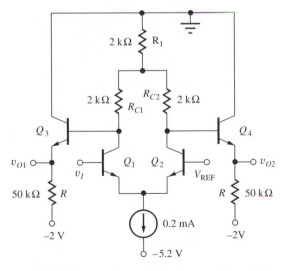

Figure P10.14

10.15. What is the minimum logic swing ΔV required for an ECL gate to have a noise margin of 0.1 V at room temperature?

*10.16. Suppose the values of resistors in Fig. 10.8 all increase in value by 20%. (a) How do the values of V_{OH}, V_{OL}, and the noise margins change? (b) Repeat part (a) for the circuit of Fig. 10.10.

10.17. Change the values of resistors and current sources in Fig. 10.10 to reduce the power consumption by a factor of 10. The values of V_{OH} and V_{OL} should remain constant.

10.18. Redesign the circuit of Fig. 10.10 to have a logic swing of 0.8 V. Use the same currents. (a) What are the new values of V_{OH}, V_{OL}, V_{REF}, and the resistors? (b) What are the values of the noise margins? (c) What is the minimum value of V_{CB} for Q_1 and Q_2? Do the values of V_{CB} represent a problem?

**10.19. Suppose that an ECL gate is to be designed to operate over the $-55°C$ to $+75°C$ temperature range and must maintain a minimum noise margin of 0.1 V over that full range. What must be the value of the logic swing of this ECL gate at room temperature?

10.20. Replace the current source in Fig. P10.14 with a resistor. Assume $V_{REF} = -1.3$ V. Do any of the three collector resistors need to be changed? If so, what are the new values?

*10.21. The current source for a current switch is implemented with a transistor and three resistors, as in Fig. P10.21. What is the current I_{EE}? What is the minimum permissible value of V_{REF} if transistor Q_S is to remain in the forward-active region? Assume that β_F is large. (See Section 5.13).

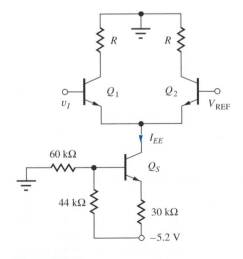

Figure P10.21

10.22. Change the values of resistors and current sources in Fig. 10.10 to reduce the power consumption by a factor of 5. The values of V_{OH} and V_{OL} should remain constant.

10.5 The ECL OR-NOR Gate

10.23. Draw the schematic of a five-input ECL OR gate.

10.24. Draw the schematic of a four-input ECL NOR gate.

10.25. $V_{CC} = +1.3$ V and $V_{EE} = -3.2$ V in the ECL gate in Fig. P10.25. (a) Find V_{OH} and V_{OL} at the emitter of Q_5. (b) What is the value of R required to give the same voltage levels at the emitter of Q_1?

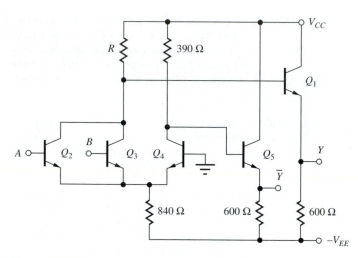

Figure P10.25

10.26. $V_{CC} = +1$ V and $V_{EE} = -2.5$ V in the ECL gate in Fig. P10.25. (a) Find V_{OH} and V_{OL} at the emitter of Q_5. (b) What is the value of R required to give the same voltage levels at the emitter of Q_1?

10.27. (a) Only the OR output is needed in the circuit of Fig. P10.25. Redraw the circuit, eliminating the unneeded components. Use $V_{CC} = +1.3$ V and $V_{EE} = -3.2$ V. (b) Repeat part (a) if only the NOR output is needed.

10.6 The Emitter Follower

10.28. In the circuit in Fig. P10.28, $\beta_F = 50$, $V_{CC} = +5$ V, $-V_{EE} = -5$ V, $I_{EE} = 2.5$ mA, and $R_L = 1.2$ kΩ. What is the minimum voltage at v_O? What are the emitter, base, and collector currents if $v_I = +4$ V?

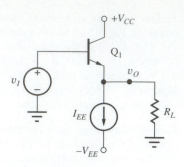

Figure P10.28

10.29. In the circuit in Fig. P10.29, $R_L = 2$ kΩ, $V_{CC} = 15$ V, and $-V_{EE} = -15$ V. (a) What is the maximum value of R_E that can be used if v_O is to reach -12 V? (b) What is the emitter current of Q_1 when $v_O = +12$ V?

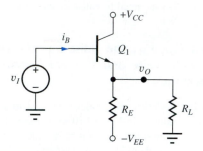

Figure P10.29

10.7 "Emitter Dotting" or "Wired-OR" Logic

10.30. The two outputs of the inverter in Fig. 10.6 are accidentally connected together. What will be the output voltage for $v_I = -0.7$ V? For $v_I = -1.3$ V? What will be the currents in transistors Q_3 and Q_4 for each case?

10.31. What are the logic functions for Y and Z in Fig. P10.31?

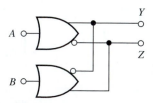

Figure P10.31

*10.32. Draw the full circuit schematic for an ECL implementation of the logic function $Y = A + B + \overline{(C + D)}$ using a wired-OR connection of two ECL gates.

10.8 Design of Reference Voltage Circuits

*10.33. Derive an equation similar to Eq. (10.44) for the voltage at the emitter node of the current switch circuit when the circuit of Fig. 10.26 is used to provide the reference voltage. Assume β_F is large. How much does the emitter current change if T increases by 50 K?

*10.34. Suppose the temperature-compensated reference circuit in Fig. 10.26 is used to supply V_{REF} to the ECL inverter in Fig. 10.10, but the values of all resistors in the circuit increase in value by 5%. What are the new values of V_{OH}, V_{OL}, and the noise margins for this circuit?

10.35. The reference circuit in Fig. 10.26 has $V_{REF} = -1.0$ V at $T = 25°C$. (a) What is the output value of V_{REF} at $T = 85°C$ if the base-emitter and diode voltages have temperature coefficients of -1.8 mV/°C. (b) What is the value of V_{REF} at $-55°C$?

10.36. Simulate the voltage transfer characteristic of the ECL inverter in Fig. 10.10 at $T = -55°C, 25°C$, and 85°C. Use a constant voltage source for V_{REF}. What are V_{OH}, V_{OL}, and the noise margins at the three temperatures?

*10.37. Simulate the current switch in Fig. 10.4 with the reference voltage provided by the circuit in Fig. 10.26 at $T = -55°C, 25°C$, and 85°C. What are V_{OH}, V_{OL}, and the noise margins at each temperature?

10.38. Design the reference circuit in Fig. 10.26 to supply $V_{REF} = -2$ V while keeping the currents the same.

*10.39. What are all possible effective values of V_{REF} at the base of Q_2 in Fig. 10.23 if three identical inverters are connected to node v_{B2}?

*10.40. What are all possible effective values of V_{REF} at the base of Q_2 in Fig. 10.25 if four identical inverters are connected to the anode of diode D_1?

10.9 Diodes in Bipolar Integrated Circuits

*10.41. Derive the result in Eq. (10.41) by applying the circuit constraints to the transport equations.

10.42. What is the reverse saturation current of the diode in Fig. 10.27 if the transistor is described by $I_S = 10^{-15}$ A, $\alpha_R = 0.20$, and $\alpha_F = 0.98$?

10.43. The two transistors in Fig. P10.43 are identical. What is the collector current of Q_2 if $I = 25$ μA and $\beta_F = 25$?

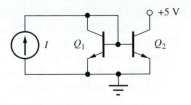

Figure P10.43

10.10 ECL Power-Delay Characteristics

10.44. Suppose the ECL inverter in Figs. 10.32 and 10.34 must operate at a power of 20 μW. If the current sources are scaled by the same factor, and the capacitances and voltage levels remain the same, what will be the new propagation delay of the inverter?

10.45. The logic swing in the inverter in Fig. 10.32 is reduced by a factor of 2 by reducing the value of R_C and changing V_{REF}. What is the new value of V_{REF}? What is the new value of the power-delay product?

10.46. The logic swing in the inverter in Fig. 10.32 is reduced by a factor of 2 by reducing the value of all the current sources by a factor of 2 and changing V_{REF}. What is the new value of V_{REF}? What is the new value of the power-delay product?

*10.47. (a) The logic circuit in Fig. P10.47 represents an alternate form of an ECL gate. If $V_{EE} = -3.3$ V, $V_{REF} = -1.0$ V, $R_B = 3.2$ kΩ, and $R_E = 1.6$ kΩ, find the values of V_{OL}, V_{OH}, and the power consumption in the gate. What are the values of R_{C1} and R_{C2}? (b) What are the logic function descriptions for the two outputs? (c) Compare the number of transistors in this gate with a standard ECL gate providing the same logic function.

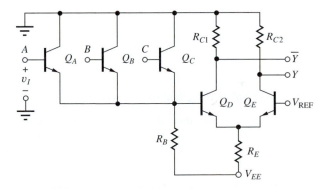

Figure P10.47

**10.48. Assume that you need 0.6 V across R_E to properly stabilize the current in the modified ECL gate in Fig. P10.47. Design the resistors in the gate for a logic swing of 0.4 V and an average current of 1 mA through R_B and R_E. What are the minimum values of V_{EE} and the value of V_{REF}?

10.49. Use SPICE and the values in Prob. 10.47 to find the propagation delay of the gate in Fig. P10.47.

10.50. Redesign the ECL inverter in Fig. 10.29 to change the average power dissipation to 1 mW. Scale the power in the current switch and the emitter followers by the same factor.

10.51. The power supply $-V_{EE}$ in Fig. 10.30 is changed to -2 V. What are the new values of R_{EE} and R_{C1} required to keep the logic levels and logic swing unchanged? What is the new power dissipation?

*10.52. What type of logic gate is the circuit in Fig. P10.52? What logic function is provided at the output Y?

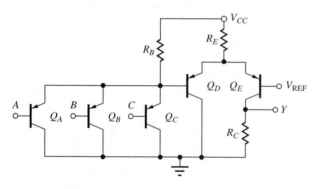

Figure P10.52

*10.53. Design the circuit in Fig. P10.52 to provide a logic swing of 0.6 V from a power supply of $+3$ V. The power consumption should average 1 mW, with 90% of the power consumed by Q_D and Q_E.

10.54. (a) Use SPICE to find the propagation delay of the gate in Prob. 10.53. (b) In Prob. 10.4. (c) In Fig. P10.14.

10.11 The Saturating Bipolar Inverter

10.55. Calculate the collector and base currents in a bipolar transistor operation with $v_{BE} = 0.20$ V and $v_{BC} = -4.8$ V. Use the BJT parameters from Table 10.3.

10.56. What is the value of V_{CESAT} of transistor Q_1 in Fig. 10.44 based on Eq. (10.58) and the BJT parameters from Table 10.3.

10.57. (a) What is the ratio i_C/i_E in Fig. P10.57 for $v_I = 0.8$ V? If needed, you may use the parameters in Table 10.3. (b) For $v_I = 0.6$ V? (c) For $v_I = 1.0$ V? (d) What is the dc input voltage v_I required for $i_C/i_E = -1$?

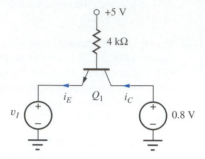

Figure P10.57

10.58. Calculate the storage time for the inverter in Fig. 10.40 if $I_{BF} = 2$ mA, $I_{BR} = -0.5$ mA, $\tau_F = 0.4$ ns, and $\tau_R = 12$ ns. Use Table 10.3.

10.59. (a) What is the base-emitter voltage in the circuit in Fig. P10.59? Use the transport equations and the transistor parameters from Table 10.3. (b) What is the base-emitter voltage if $\beta_F = 80$? (c) What is V_{BE} if I_B is increased to 1 mA and $\beta_F = 40$?

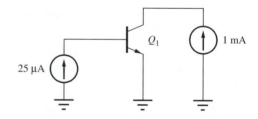

Figure P10.59

10.60. Calculate the value of v_{CE} for the two circuits in Fig. P10.60.

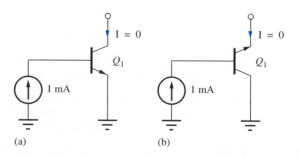

Figure P10.60

10.12 A Transistor-Transistor Logic (TTL) Prototype

*10.61. Suppose the TTL circuit in Fig. 10.42 is operated with $V_{CC} = +3$ V. What are the new values of V_{OH}, V_{OL}, V_{IH}, V_{IL}, and fanout for this gate?

10.62. What are the worst-case minimum and maximum values of the power consumed by the gate in Fig. 10.42 if the 2-kΩ and 4-kΩ resistors have a tolerance of $\pm 20\%$?

**10.63. A fixed value for V_{OL} was assumed in the analysis of the prototype TTL gate in Fig. 10.44. However, an exact value can be found by the simultaneous solution of Eqs. (10.55) and (10.58) if we assume that $i_{B2} = 1.09$ mA is constant. Find the actual V_{OL} level for the circuit in Fig. 10.44 using an iterative numerical solution of these two equations.

10.64. A low-power TTL gate is shown in Fig. P10.64. Find V_{OH}, V_{OL}, V_{IL}, V_{IH}, and the noise margins for this circuit.

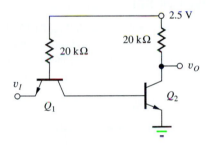

Figure P10.64

*10.65. A low-power TTL gate similar to the gate in Fig. P10.64 is needed for a VLSI design. The following supply voltages are being considered: 0.5, 1.0, 1.5, 2.0, and 2.5 V. Which of these voltages represents the minimum supply needed for the circuit to operate properly? Why?

*10.66. The TTL prototype in Fig. 10.42 is operated from $V_{DD} = 3.0$ V. (a) Based on the results in Fig. 10.47, draw the new VTC. (b) What are approximate values of the new V_{IL} and V_{IH}? (c) What are the new values of the noise margins?

10.67. Scale the resistors in the TTL prototype in Fig. 10.42 to change the power of the gate to 1.0 mW.

10.68. (a) Use SPICE to determine the average propagation delay for the TTL prototype of Fig. 10.42. (b) Repeat for the scaled gate design from Prob. 10.67.

*10.69. The inverter in Fig. P10.69(a) is a member of the diode-transistor logic (DTL) family that was used

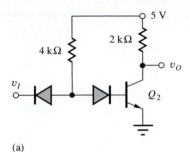

(a)

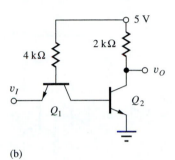

(b)

Figure P10.69

prior to the invention of TTL. (a) Find V_{OH} and V_{OL} for the circuit in Fig. P10.69(a). What are the input currents in the two logic states? (b) What is the fanout limit for the DTL inverter? (c) Compare the values from parts (a) and (b) to those for the circuit in Fig. P10.69(b).

*10.70. The inverter in Fig. P10.69(a) is a member of the diode-transistor logic (DTL) family that was used prior to the invention of TTL. Sketch the VTC and compare to the VTC for the circuit in Fig. P10.69(b).

*10.71. The inverter in Fig. P10.69(a) is a member of the diode-transistor logic (DTL) family that was used before the introduction of TTL. Simulate the VTC of the DTL inverter and compare to that of the circuit in Fig. P10.69(b). Discuss the location of the break points in the characteristic.

*10.72. Simulate the propagation delay of the two inverters in Fig. P10.69. Discuss the reasons for any differences that are observed. (*Hint:* Calculate the values of I_{BR} available to bring Q_2 out of saturation and calculate the storage times in the two inverters.)

**10.73. The circuits in Fig. P10.73 are members of the diode-transistor logic (DTL) family that was used before the invention of TTL. (a) Simulate the propagation delay of the two DTL inverters in Fig. P10.73. Discuss the reasons for any differences that are observed. What is the function of the

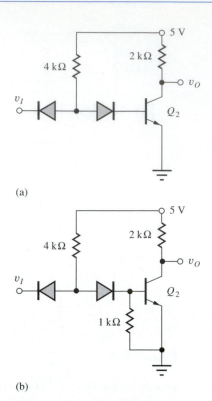

(a)

(b)

Figure P10.73

1-kΩ resistor in Fig. P10.73(b), and why is it important? (*Hint:* Calculate the values of I_{BR} available to bring Q_2 out of saturation and calculate the storage times in the two inverters.)

*10.74. Sketch the VTC for the simplified TTL gate in Fig. P10.74. Discuss the relationship between the observed break points in the VTC to the switching points of the various transistors. Estimate the noise margins.

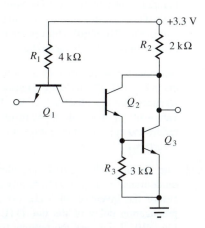

Figure P10.74

10.75. Simulate the VTC for the simplified TTL gate in Fig. P10.74. Discuss the relationship between the observed break points in the VTC to the switching points of the various transistors. What are the noise margins?

Fanout Limitations of the TTL Prototype

10.76. A fabrication process control problem causes $\beta_F = 25$ and $\beta_R = 1$ in the transistors used in the TTL circuit in Fig. 10.42. What is the new value of the fanout?

*10.77. What is the minimum value of the fanout specification for the gate in Fig. 10.42 if the 2-kΩ and 4-kΩ resistors have a tolerance of ±20%? Assume the resistors in each gate track each other.

10.78. The fanout for the circuit in Fig. 10.42 was calculated to be 7. Redesign the value of R_B to increase the fanout to 10.

10.13 Standard TTL

10.79. Suppose the output in Fig. P10.79 is accidentally shorted to ground. (a) Calculate the emitter current in the circuit if $R_S = 0$ and $\beta_F = 100$. (b) Repeat for $R_S = 130\ \Omega$.

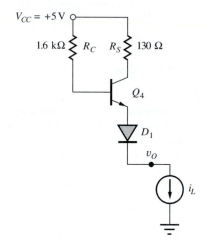

Figure P10.79

10.80. Calculate the power dissipation in the circuit in both parts of Prob. 10.79.

10.81. Use SPICE to plot v_O versus I_L for the circuit in Fig. P10.79.

*10.82. Simulate the voltage transfer characteristic for the modified TTL gate in Fig. P10.82. Discuss why the first "knee" voltage at V_2 in Fig. 10.60 has been eliminated.

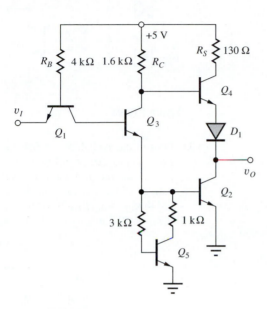

Figure P10.82

10.83. Calculate the currents in Q_1 to Q_4 in the low-power TTL gate in Fig. 10.67 for (a) $v_I = V_{OH}$ and (b) $v_I = V_{OL}$.

10.84. Simulate the voltage transfer characteristic for the low-power TTL gate in Fig. 10.67.

10.85. Simulate the voltage transfer characteristic for the low-power TTL gate in Fig. 10.67 for $T = -55°C$, $+25°C$, and $+85°C$.

Fanout Limitations of Standard TTL

*10.86. Calculate the fanout limit for $v_O = V_{OH}$ for the standard TTL gate in Fig. 10.65. Assume that V_{OH} must not drop below 2.4 V.

*10.87. Calculate the fanout limit for the standard TTL gate in Fig. 10.65 if $R_B = 5$ kΩ, $R_C = 2$ kΩ, $R_E = 1.25$ kΩ, $\beta_R = 0.05$, and $\beta_F = 20$. Assume that V_{OH} must not drop below 2.4 V.

*10.88. Plot the fanout of the standard TTL gate of Fig. 10.65 versus β_R for β_R ranging between 0 and 5.

*10.89. (a) Calculate V_{OH} and V_{OL} for the inverter in Fig. P10.89. (b) What are the input currents in the two logic states? (c) What is the fanout capability of the gate?

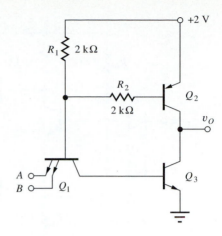

Figure P10.89

*10.90. (a) Calculate V_{OH} and V_{OL} for the inverter in Fig. P10.90. (b) What are the input currents in the two logic states? (c) What is the fanout capability of the gate?

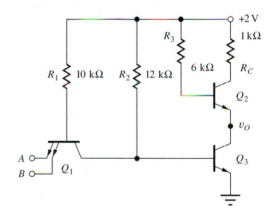

Figure P10.90

10.14 Logic Functions in TTL

*10.91. The circuit in Fig. P10.91 on p. 452 can be considered a member of the diode-transistor logic (DTL) family. (a) What is the logic function of this gate? (b) Calculate V_{OH} and V_{OL} for this DTL inverter. (c) What are the input currents in the two logic states? (d) Sketch the VTC and compare to the VTC for the standard TTL circuit.

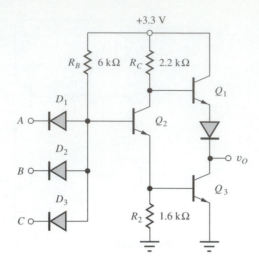

Figure P10.91

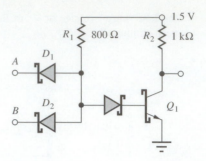

Figure P10.93

10.94. Prior to the availability of Schottky diodes, the *Baker clamp* circuit in Fig. P10.94 was used to prevent saturation. What is the collector-emitter voltage of the transistor in this circuit assuming that $i_B > i_C/\beta_F$? What are i_{D1}, i_{D2}, and i_C if $i_{BB} = 250\ \mu\text{A}$, $i_{CC} = 1\ \text{mA}$, $\beta_F = 20$, and $\beta_R = 2$?

*10.92. For the circuit in Fig. P10.92, $R_1 = 4\ \text{k}\Omega$, $R_2 = 4\ \text{k}\Omega$, $R_3 = 4.3\ \text{k}\Omega$, $R_4 = 10\ \text{k}\Omega$, $R_5 = 5\ \text{k}\Omega$, and $R_6 = 5\ \text{K}$. (a) What is the logic function Y? (b) What are the values of V_{OL} and V_{OH}? (c) What are the input currents in the high- and low-input states?

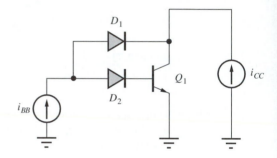

Figure P10.94

10.95. Calculate the values of i_{B1}, i_{B2}, and i_{IN} for the Schottky TTL inverter in Fig. 10.72.

10.96. Calculate the values of i_{B1}, i_{B2}, and i_{IN} for the Schottky TTL inverter in Fig. 10.73.

*10.97. Calculate the fanout N for the Schottky TTL inverter in Fig. 10.71.

*10.98. Calculate the currents in Q_1 to Q_6 in the Schottky TTL gate in Fig. 10.74 for (a) all inputs at V_{OH} and (b) all inputs at V_{OL}.

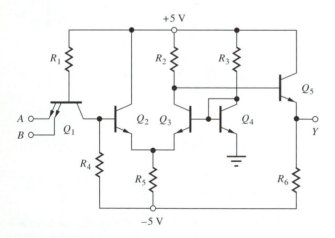

Figure P10.92

10.15 Schottky-Clamped TTL

10.93. (a) Find V_{OH} and V_{OL} for the Schottky DTL gate in Fig. P10.93. (b) What are the input currents in the two logic states? (c) What is the fanout of the gate?

 10.99. Simulate the voltage transfer characteristic and propagation delay for the Schottky TTL gate in Fig. 10.74.

*10.100. Calculate the currents in Q_2 to Q_6 in the low-power Schottky TTL gate in Fig. 10.75 for (a) all inputs at V_{OH} and (b) all inputs at V_{OL}.

 *10.101. Simulate the voltage transfer characteristic and propagation delay for the low-power Schottky

TTL gate in Fig. 10.75 for (a) $T = -55°C$, (b) for $+25°C$, and (c) for $+85°C$.

*10.102. Simulate the voltage transfer characteristic and propagation delay for the advanced low-power Schottky TTL gate in Fig. 10.75 for (a) $T = -55°C$, (b) for $+25°C$, and (c) for $+85°C$.

*10.103. What is the logic function of the gate in Fig. P10.103. Find V_{OH}, V_{OL}, and V_{REF} for the circuit, assuming $V_{EE} = -3$ V, $R_C = 0.54$ kΩ, and $R_E = 0.75$ kΩ. Assume $V_{BE} = 0.7$ and $V_D = 0.4$ V for the Schottky diode.

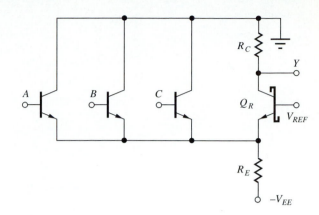

Figure P10.104

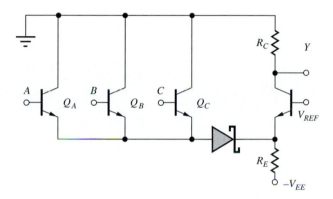

Figure P10.103

10.104. What is the logic function of the gate in Fig. P10.104. Find V_{OH}, V_{OL}, and V_{REF} for the circuit, assuming $V_{EE} = -3$ V, $R_C = 3.3$ kΩ, and $R_E = 2.4$ kΩ. Assume $V_{BE} = 0.7$ and $V_D = 0.4$ V for the Schottky diode.

10.105. Estimate i_B and i_C of the Schottky transistor in Fig. P10.105 if the external collector terminal is open. Assume the forward voltage of the Schottky diode is 0.45 V.

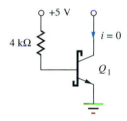

Figure P10.105

PART III

Analog Circuit
Design

C H A P T E R　1 1

Analog Systems

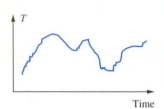

Figure 11.1 Temperature vs. time—a continuous analog signal.

Part II of this book discussed the analysis and design of circuits used to manipulate information in discrete form—that is, binary data. However, most physical information appears in continuous or analog form. Physical variables in the natural world, such as temperature, humidity, pressure, light intensity, or sound may take on any value within some continuous range and can be represented by the analog signal in Fig. 11.1. In electrical form, these signals may be the output of transducers that measure pressure, temperature, or flow rate, or could be the audio output of a microphone or cassette tape player. The characteristics of these signals are most often manipulated using linear amplifiers, which change the amplitude and/or phase of a signal without affecting its spectral content.

Chapter 11 begins our study of the circuits used for analog electronic signal processing. The chapter discusses the concepts of linear amplification and the quantities used to measure the performance of analog amplifiers, including voltage gain, current gain, and power gain; input and output resistance; upper- and lower-cutoff frequencies; and bandwidth. The magnitudes of amplifier gains are often expressed in terms of a logarithmic decibel (dB) scale.

Linear amplifiers can be conveniently modeled using two-port representations. We use *g*-, *h*-, *y*-, and *z*-parameters found in two-port analysis to describe these amplifiers. In this chapter, we also review basic amplifier transfer functions and Bode plots. Amplifiers are classified into categories in terms of their frequency domain characteristics: low-pass, high-pass, band-pass, all-pass, and band-rejection amplifiers.

11.1 AN EXAMPLE OF AN ANALOG ELECTRONIC SYSTEM

We begin exploring some of the uses for analog amplifiers by examining a familiar electronic system, the FM stereo receiver, shown schematically in Fig. 11.2. At the receiving antenna are complex **very high frequency,** or **VHF,**[1] radio signals in the 88- to 108-MHz range that contain the information for at least two channels of stereo music. These signals may have amplitudes as small as 1 μV and often reach the receiver input through a 75-Ω coaxial cable. At the output of the receiver are audio amplifiers that develop the voltage and current necessary to deliver 100 W of power to the 8-Ω speakers in the 50- to 15,000-Hz audio frequency range.

---

[1] The radio spectrum is traditionally divided into different frequency bands: RF, or radio frequency (0.5–50 MHz); VHF, or very high frequency (50–150 MHz); UHF, or ultra high frequencies (150–1000 MHz); and so on.

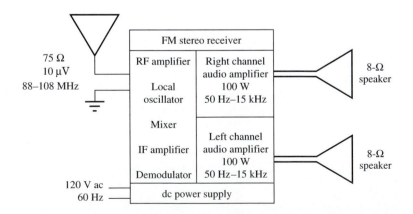

Figure 11.2 FM stereo receiver.

T a b l e 11.1	
FM Stereo Receiver	
Linear Circuit Functions	**Nonlinear Circuit Functions**
Radio frequency amplification Audio frequency amplification Frequency selection (tuning) Impedance matching (75-Ω input) Tailoring audio frequency response Local oscillator	dc power supply (rectification) Frequency conversion (mixing) Detection/demodulation

This receiver is a complex analog system that provides many forms of analog signal processing, some linear and some nonlinear. For example, the amplitude of the signal must be increased at VHF frequencies as well as at **radio** and **audio frequencies** (**RF** and **AF,** respectively). Large overall voltage, current, and power gains are required to go from the very small VHF signal received from the antenna to the 100-W audio signal delivered to the speaker. The input of the receiver is often designed to match the 75-Ω impedance of the coaxial transmission line coming from the antenna.

In addition, we usually want only one station to be heard at a time. The desired signal must be selected from the multitude of signals appearing at the antenna, and the receiver requires circuits with high frequency selectivity at its input. An adjustable frequency signal source, called the *local oscillator,* is also needed to tune the receiver. The electronic implementations of all these functions are based on **linear amplifiers.**

In most receivers, the incoming VHF signal frequency is changed, through a process called *mixing,* to a lower **intermediate frequency (IF)**[2], where the audio information can be readily separated from the RF carrier through a process called *demodulation.* Mixing and demodulation are two basic examples of nonlinear analog signal processing. But even these nonlinear circuits are based on linear amplifier designs. Finally, the dc voltages needed to power the system are obtained using the nonlinear rectifier circuits described in Chapter 3.

11.2 AMPLIFICATION

Linear amplifiers are an extremely important class of circuits, and most of Part III discusses various aspects of their analysis and design. As an introduction to amplification, let us concentrate on one of the channels of the audio portion of the FM receiver in Fig. 11.3. In this figure, the input to the stereo amplifier channel is represented by the Thévenin equivalent source v_s and source resistor $R_S = 5\ \text{k}\Omega$. The speaker at the output is modeled by an 8-Ω resistor.

Based on Fourier analysis, we know that a complex signal v_s can be represented as the sum of many individual sine waves:

$$v_s = \sum_{i=1}^{\infty} V_i \sin(\omega_i t + \phi_i) \tag{11.1}$$

[2] Common IF frequencies are 11.7 MHz, 455 kHz, and 262 kHz.

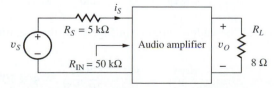

Figure 11.3 Audio amplifier channel from FM receiver.

where V_i = amplitude of ith component of signal
 $\quad\quad\quad \omega_i$ = radian frequency
 $\quad\quad\quad \phi_i$ = phase

If the amplifier is linear, the principle of superposition applies, so that each signal component can be treated individually and the results summed to find the complete signal. For simplicity in our analysis, we will consider only one component of the signal, with frequency ω_s and amplitude V_s:

$$v_S = V_s \sin \omega_s t \tag{11.2}$$

For this example, we assume $V_s = 0.001$ V, 1 mV. Because this signal serves as our reference input, we can assume $\phi_S = 0$ without loss of generality.

The output of the linear amplifier is a sinusoidal signal at the same frequency but with a different amplitude V_O and phase θ:

$$v_O = V_o \sin(\omega_s t + \theta) \tag{11.3}$$

The amplifier output power is

$$P_o = \left(\frac{V_o}{\sqrt{2}}\right)^2 \frac{1}{R_L} \tag{11.4}$$

(Remember from circuit theory that the quantity $V_O/\sqrt{2}$ in this equation represents the rms value of the sinusoidal voltage signal.) For an amplifier delivering 100 W to the 8-Ω load, the amplitude of the output voltage is

$$V_o = \sqrt{2 P_o R_L} = \sqrt{2 \times 100 \times 8} = 40 \text{ V} \tag{11.5}$$

This output power level also requires an output current

$$i_o = I_o \sin(\omega_s t + \theta) \tag{11.6}$$

with an amplitude

$$I_o = \frac{V_o}{R_L} = \frac{40 \text{ V}}{8 \ \Omega} = 5 \text{ A} \tag{11.7}$$

Note that because the load element is a resistor, i_o and v_o have the same phase.

Voltage Gain

For sinusoidal signals, the **voltage gain A_V** of an amplifier is defined in terms of the **phasor representations** of the input and output voltages. Using $\sin \omega t = Im[\varepsilon^{j\omega t}]$ as our reference, the phasor representation of v_s is $v_s = V_s \angle 0°$ and that for v_O is $v_o = V_o \angle \theta$. Similarly, $i_s = I_s \angle 0°$ and $i_o = I_o \angle \theta$. The voltage gain is then expressed by the phasor ratio:

$$A_V = \frac{v_o}{v_s} = \frac{V_o \angle \theta}{V_s \angle 0} = \frac{V_o}{V_s} \angle \theta \tag{11.8}$$

The magnitude and phase of A_V are given by

$$|A_V| = \frac{V_o}{V_s} \quad \text{and} \quad \angle A_V = \theta \tag{11.9}$$

respectively. For the audio amplifier in Fig. 11.3, the magnitude of the required voltage gain is

$$|A_V| = \frac{V_o}{V_s} = \frac{40 \text{ V}}{10^{-3} \text{ V}} = 4 \times 10^4 \tag{11.10}$$

We will find in subsequent chapters that achieving this level of voltage gain usually requires several stages of amplification. Be sure to note that the magnitude of the gain is defined by the amplitudes of the signals and is a constant; it is *not* a function of time! For the rest of this section, we concentrate on the magnitudes of the gains, saving a more detailed consideration of amplifier phase for Sec. 11.6.

Current Gain

The audio amplifier in the example requires a substantial increase in current level as well. The input current is determined by the **source resistance R_S** and the **input resistance R_{IN}** of the amplifier. When we write the input current as $i_s = I_s \sin \omega_s t$, the amplitude of the current is

$$I_s = \frac{V_s}{R_S + R_{IN}} = \frac{10^{-3} \text{ V}}{5 \text{ k}\Omega + 50 \text{ k}\Omega} = 1.82 \times 10^{-8} \text{ A} \tag{11.11}$$

The phase $\phi = 0$ because of the circuit is purely resistive.

The **current gain** is defined as the ratio of the phasor representations of i_o and i_s:

$$A_I = \frac{i_o}{i_s} = \frac{I_o \angle \theta}{I_s \angle 0} = \frac{I_o}{I_s} \angle \theta \tag{11.12}$$

The magnitude of the overall current gain is equal to the ratio of the amplitudes of the output and input currents:

$$|A_I| = \frac{I_o}{I_s} = \frac{5 \text{ A}}{1.82 \times 10^{-8} \text{ A}} = 2.75 \times 10^8 \tag{11.13}$$

This level of current gain also requires several stages of amplification.

Power Gain

The power delivered to the amplifier input is quite small, whereas the power delivered to the speaker is substantial. Thus, the amplifier also exhibits a very large power gain. **Power gain A_P** is defined as the ratio of the output power P_o delivered to the load to the power P_s delivered from the source:

$$A_P = \frac{P_o}{P_s} = \frac{\dfrac{V_o}{\sqrt{2}}\dfrac{I_o}{\sqrt{2}}}{\dfrac{V_s}{\sqrt{2}}\dfrac{I_s}{\sqrt{2}}} = \frac{V_o I_o}{V_s I_s} = |A_V||A_I| \tag{11.14}$$

Note from Eq. (11.14) that either rms or peak values of voltage and current may be used to define power gain as long as the choice is applied consistently at the input and output of the amplifier. (This is also true for A_V and A_I.) For our ongoing example,

$$A_P = \frac{40 \times 5}{10^{-3} \times 1.82 \times 10^{-8}} = 1.10 \times 10^{13} \tag{11.15}$$

a very large number.

> **EXERCISE:** (a) Verify that $|A_P| = |A_V||A_I|$ in Eq. (11.15). (b) An amplifier must deliver 20 W to a 16-Ω speaker. The sinusoidal input signal source can be represented as a 5-mV source in series with a 10-kΩ resistor. If the input resistance of the amplifier is 20 kΩ, what are the voltage, current, and power gains required of the overall amplifier?
>
> **ANSWERS:** 5060, 9.49×10^6, 4.80×10^{10}

The Decibel Scale

The various gain expressions often involve some rather large numbers, and it is customary to express the values of voltage, current, and power gain in terms of the **decibel,** or **dB** (one-tenth of a Bel):

$$A_{PdB} = 10 \log A_P$$

$$A_{VdB} = 20 \log |A_V|$$

$$A_{IdB} = 20 \log |A_I|$$

(11.16)

The number of decibels is 10 times the base 10 logarithm of the arithmetic power ratio, and decibels are added and subtracted just like logarithms to represent multiplication and division. Because power is proportional to the square of both voltage and current, a factor of 20 appears in the expressions for A_{VdB} and A_{IdB}.

Table 11.2 has a number of useful examples. From this table, we can see that an increase in voltage or current gain by a factor of 10 corresponds to a change of 20 dB, whereas a factor of 10 increase in power gain corresponds to a change of 10 dB. A factor of 2 corresponds to a 6-dB change in voltage or current gain or a 3-dB change in power gain. In the chapters that follow, the various gains routinely are expressed interchangeably in terms of arithmetic values or dB, so it is important to become comfortable with the conversions in Eqs. (11.16) and Table 11.2.

T a b l e 11.2

Expressing Gain in Decibels

$|$Gain$|$	A_{VdB} or A_{IdB}	A_{PdB}
1000	60 dB	30 dB
500	54 dB	27 dB
300	50 dB	25 dB
100	40 dB	20 dB
20	26 dB	13 dB
10	20 dB	10 dB
$\sqrt{10} = 3.16$	10 dB	5 dB
2	6 dB	3 dB
1	0 dB	0 dB
0.5	−6 dB	−3 dB
0.1	−20 dB	−10 dB

EXERCISE: Express the voltage gain, current gain, and power gain in the previous exercise in dB.

ANSWERS: 74.1 dB, 140 dB, 107 dB

EXERCISE: Express the voltage gain, current gain, and power gain in Eqs. (11.10), (11.13), and (11.15) in dB.

ANSWERS: 92.0 dB, 169 dB, 130 dB.

11.3 AMPLIFIER BIASING FOR LINEAR OPERATION

The amplifiers we discuss in subsequent chapters are constructed from solid-state devices that we know from our study of the large-signal models in Chapters 3 to 6 to be highly nonlinear. In addition, the output voltage range of a real amplifier is limited by its power supply voltages. Amplifiers must be carefully biased to ensure linear operation.

As an example, consider the voltage transfer characteristic of the particular amplifier in Fig. 11.4. In this amplifier, the output voltage is restricted to $2\text{ V} \leq v_O \leq 16\text{ V}$. In addition, the input-output relationship is linear only over certain portions of the characteristic. For the amplifier to provide linear amplification of a time-varying signal v_i, the total input signal to the amplifier must be **biased** by the dc voltage V_I into the desired region of the characteristic. Using our standard notation, described in Chapter 1, the total input voltage v_I is represented as the sum of two components:

$$v_I = V_I + v_i \tag{11.17}$$

in which V_I represents the dc value of v_I and v_i is the time-varying component of the input signal.

The voltage gain A_V of an amplifier describes the relation between changes in the output signal voltage

$$v_O = V_O + v_o \tag{11.18}$$

and changes in the input signal v_I and is defined by the slope of the amplifier's VTC, evaluated for an input voltage equal to the dc bias voltage V_I:

$$A_V = \left. \frac{\partial v_O}{\partial v_I} \right|_{v_I = V_I} \tag{11.19}$$

The slope of the VTC in Fig. 11.4 is everywhere ≥ 0, so the amplifier input and output are in phase; this amplifier is a **noninverting amplifier.** If the slope had been negative, then the input and output signals would be 180° out of phase, and the amplifier would be characterized as an **inverting amplifier.**

The voltage gain of the amplifier in Fig. 11.4 depends on the bias point. If the amplifier input is biased at $V_I = 0.45$ V, for example, the voltage gain will be $+60$ for input signals v_i, satisfying $|v_i| \leq 0.05$ V. If the input signal exceeds this value, then the output signal will be distorted due to the change in amplifier slope. The amplifier could also be biased with $V_I = 0.3$ V, for which the voltage gain is $+10$. Note that $V_I = 0.4$ should not

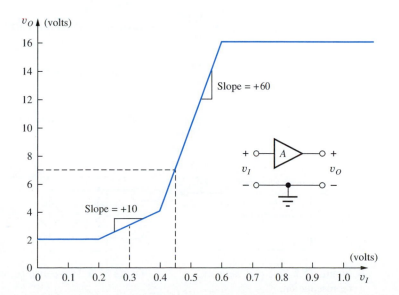

Figure 11.4 Voltage transfer characteristic and two possible bias points for the amplifier: $V_I = 0.3$ V and $V_I = 0.45$ V.

be chosen as a bias point for this amplifier because the gain is different for positive and negative values of v_i, and the output signal would be a distorted version of the input signal.

> **EXERCISE:** (a) What bias point should be chosen for the amplifier in Fig. 11.4 to provide the maximum possible linear input signal magnitude? What is the maximum input signal amplitude? (b) What is the voltage gain if the amplifier is biased at $V_I = 0.8$ V?
>
> **ANSWERS:** 0.5 V, $|v_i| \leq 0.1$ V; 0

11.4 TWO-PORT MODELS FOR AMPLIFIERS

The **two-port network** in Fig. 11.5 is very useful for modeling the behavior of amplifiers in complex systems. From network theory, we know that two-port networks can be represented in terms of **two-port parameters.** Four of these sets are used as models for amplifiers in this text: the g-, h-, y-, and z-parameters; the s- and $abcd$-parameters are not required. Note in these two-port representations that (v_1, i_1) and (v_2, i_2) represent the signal components of the voltages and currents at the two ports of the network.

The g-parameters

The g-parameter description is one of the most commonly used representations for a voltage amplifier:

$$\mathbf{i_1} = g_{11}\mathbf{v_1} + g_{12}\mathbf{i_2}$$
$$\mathbf{v_2} = g_{21}\mathbf{v_1} + g_{22}\mathbf{i_2}$$

(11.20)

Figure 11.6 is a network representation of these equations.

The g-parameters are determined from a given network using a combination of **open-circuit** ($i = 0$) and **short-circuit** ($v = 0$) **termination** conditions by applying the following parameter definitions:

$$g_{11} = \left.\frac{\mathbf{i_1}}{\mathbf{v_1}}\right|_{\mathbf{i_2}=0} = \text{open-circuit input conductance}$$

$$g_{12} = \left.\frac{\mathbf{i_1}}{\mathbf{i_2}}\right|_{\mathbf{v_1}=0} = \text{reverse short-circuit current gain}$$

$$g_{21} = \left.\frac{\mathbf{v_2}}{\mathbf{v_1}}\right|_{\mathbf{i_2}=0} = \text{forward open-circuit voltage gain}$$

(11.21)

$$g_{22} = \left.\frac{\mathbf{v_2}}{\mathbf{i_2}}\right|_{\mathbf{v_1}=0} = \text{short-circuit output resistance}$$

Figure 11.5 Two-port network representation.

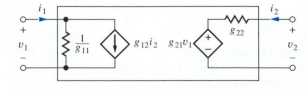

Figure 11.6 Two-port g-parameter representation.

The Hybrid or *h*-parameters

The **h-parameter** description is also widely used in electronic circuits and is one convenient model for a current amplifier:

$$\mathbf{v_1} = h_{11}\mathbf{i_1} + h_{12}\mathbf{v_2}$$
$$\mathbf{i_2} = h_{21}\mathbf{i_1} + h_{22}\mathbf{v_2}$$

(11.22)

Figure 11.7 is the network representation of these equations.

As with the *g*-parameters, the *h*-parameters are determined from a given network using a combination of open- and short-circuit measurement conditions:

$$h_{11} = \left.\frac{\mathbf{v_1}}{\mathbf{i_1}}\right|_{\mathbf{v_2}=0} = \text{short-circuit input resistance}$$

$$h_{12} = \left.\frac{\mathbf{v_1}}{\mathbf{v_2}}\right|_{\mathbf{i_1}=0} = \text{reverse open-circuit voltage gain}$$

(11.23)

$$h_{21} = \left.\frac{\mathbf{i_2}}{\mathbf{i_1}}\right|_{\mathbf{v_2}=0} = \text{forward short-circuit current gain}$$

$$h_{22} = \left.\frac{\mathbf{i_2}}{\mathbf{v_2}}\right|_{\mathbf{i_1}=0} = \text{open-circuit output conductance}$$

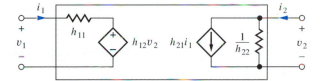

Figure 11.7 Two-port *h*-parameter representation.

The Admittance or *y*-parameters

The admittance, or *y*-parameter, description will be used during the analysis of feedback amplifiers in Chapter 18,

$$\mathbf{i_1} = y_{11}\mathbf{v_1} + y_{12}\mathbf{v_2}$$
$$\mathbf{i_2} = y_{21}\mathbf{v_1} + y_{22}\mathbf{v_2}$$

(11.24)

Figure 11.8 is a network representation of these equations.

The *y*-parameters are often referred to as the short-circuit parameters because they are determined from a given network using only short-circuit terminations:

$$y_{11} = \left.\frac{\mathbf{i_1}}{\mathbf{v_1}}\right|_{\mathbf{v_2}=0} = \text{short-circuit input conductance}$$

$$y_{12} = \left.\frac{\mathbf{i_1}}{\mathbf{v_2}}\right|_{\mathbf{v_1}=0} = \text{reverse short-circuit transconductance}$$

(11.25)

$$y_{21} = \left.\frac{\mathbf{i_2}}{\mathbf{v_1}}\right|_{\mathbf{v_2}=0} = \text{forward short-circuit transconductance}$$

$$y_{22} = \left.\frac{\mathbf{i_2}}{\mathbf{v_2}}\right|_{\mathbf{v_1}=0} = \text{short-circuit output conductance}$$

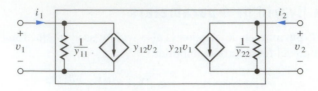

Figure 11.8 Two-port y-parameter representation.

The Impedance or z-parameters

The impedance, or z-**parameters,** will also be used for analysis of feedback amplifiers in Chapter 18,

$$\mathbf{v_1} = z_{11}\mathbf{i_1} + z_{12}\mathbf{i_2}$$
$$\mathbf{v_2} = z_{21}\mathbf{i_1} + z_{22}\mathbf{i_2}$$

(11.26)

Figure 11.9 is a network representation of Eq. (11.26). The z-parameters are determined from a given network using open-circuit measurement conditions and are often referred to as the open-circuit parameters:

$$z_{11} = \frac{\mathbf{v_1}}{\mathbf{i_1}}\bigg|_{\mathbf{i_2}=0} = \text{open-circuit input resistance}$$

$$z_{12} = \frac{\mathbf{v_1}}{\mathbf{i_2}}\bigg|_{\mathbf{i_1}=0} = \text{reverse open-circuit transresistance}$$

(11.27)

$$z_{21} = \frac{\mathbf{v_2}}{\mathbf{i_1}}\bigg|_{\mathbf{i_2}=0} = \text{forward open-circuit transresistance}$$

$$z_{22} = \frac{\mathbf{v_2}}{\mathbf{i_2}}\bigg|_{\mathbf{i_1}=0} = \text{open-circuit output resistance}$$

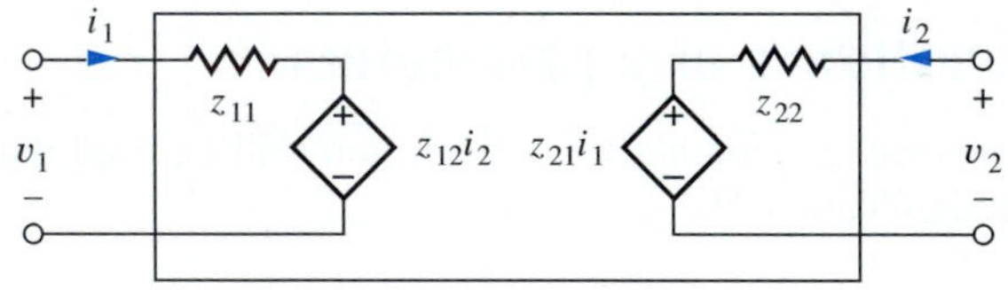

Figure 11.9 Two-port z-parameter representation.

11.5 MISMATCHED SOURCE AND LOAD RESISTANCES

In most amplifiers, it is desired that the forward voltage gain, current gain, transconductance, or transresistance be much larger than the corresponding parameter in the reverse direction. In the rest of this book, we assume that $g_{21} \gg g_{12}$, $h_{21} \gg h_{12}$, and so on unless otherwise defined, and we use two-port representations in which the 1–2 parameter is assumed to be zero. For example, voltage amplifiers are conveniently represented by the g-parameter description in Fig. 11.10, in which the parameters have been relabeled

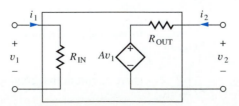

Figure 11.10 Two-port (g-parameter) representation of a voltage amplifier ($g_{12} = 0$).

as input resistance $R_{\text{IN}} = (1/g_{11})$, open-circuit voltage gain $A = g_{21}$, output resistance $R_{\text{OUT}} = g_{22}$, and $g_{12} = 0$.

In introductory circuit theory, the maximum power transfer theorem is usually discussed. Maximum power transfer occurs when the source and load resistances are matched (equal in value). In most voltage and current amplifier applications, however, the opposite situation is desired. A completely mismatched condition is used at both the input and output ports of the amplifier.

Voltage Amplifiers

To understand this statement, consider the **voltage amplifier** in Fig. 11.11. The input to the two-port is a Thévenin equivalent representation of the input source, and the output is connected to a load represented by resistor R_L. To find the voltage gain, voltage division is applied to each loop:

$$\mathbf{v_o} = A\mathbf{v_1}\frac{R_L}{R_{\text{OUT}} + R_L} \qquad \text{and} \qquad \mathbf{v_1} = \mathbf{v_s}\frac{R_{\text{IN}}}{R_S + R_{\text{IN}}} \tag{11.28}$$

Combining these two equations yields an expression for the magnitude of the voltage gain A_V:

$$|A_V| = \frac{V_o}{V_s} = A\frac{R_{\text{IN}}}{R_S + R_{\text{IN}}}\frac{R_L}{R_{\text{OUT}} + R_L} \tag{11.29}$$

To achieve maximum voltage gain, the resistors should satisfy

$$R_{\text{IN}} \gg R_S \qquad \text{and} \qquad R_{\text{OUT}} \ll R_L \tag{11.30}$$

For this case,

$$|A_V| = A \tag{11.31}$$

The situation described by these two equations is a totally mismatched condition at both the input and the output ports. An **ideal voltage amplifier** satisfies Eq. (11.30) by having $R_{\text{IN}} = \infty$ and $R_{\text{OUT}} = 0$.

The magnitude of the current gain of the amplifier in Fig. 11.11 can be expressed as

$$|A_I| = \frac{I_o}{I_1} = \frac{\dfrac{V_o}{R_L}}{\dfrac{V_s}{R_S + R_{\text{IN}}}} = \frac{V_o}{V_s}\frac{R_S + R_{\text{IN}}}{R_L} \tag{11.32}$$

which can be rewritten in terms of the voltage gain as

$$|A_I| = |A_V|\frac{R_S + R_{\text{IN}}}{R_L} \tag{11.33}$$

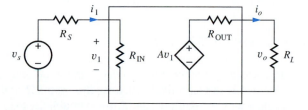

Figure 11.11 Two-port representation of an amplifier with source and load connected.

Current Amplifiers

A similar argument can be made for an ideal current amplifier based on the h-parameter representation in Fig. 11.12 (with $h_{12} = 0$). In this case, the input source is represented by

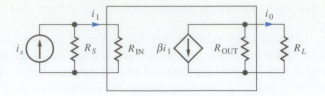

Figure 11.12 Current amplifier with source and load connected.

its Norton equivalent, and the output is connected to a load represented by resistor R_L. The input resistance of the amplifier is $R_{IN} = h_{11}$, the output resistance is $R_{OUT} = (1/h_{22})$, and the short-circuit current gain $\beta = h_{21}$.

To find the overall current gain of the amplifier, current division is used at the input and output ports:

$$\mathbf{i_o} = -\beta \mathbf{i_1} \frac{R_{OUT}}{R_{OUT} + R_L} \qquad \text{and} \qquad \mathbf{i_1} = \mathbf{i_s} \frac{R_S}{R_S + R_{IN}} \qquad (11.34)$$

Combining these two expressions yields an expression for the magnitude of the current gain[3] A_I:

$$|A_I| = \frac{I_o}{I_s} = \beta \frac{R_S}{R_S + R_{IN}} \frac{R_{OUT}}{R_{OUT} + R_L} \qquad (11.35)$$

Maximum current gain is achieved for

$$R_S \gg R_{IN} \qquad \text{and} \qquad R_{OUT} \gg R_L \qquad (11.36)$$

for which

$$|A_I| = \beta \qquad (11.37)$$

An **ideal current amplifier** meets the requirements of Eq. (11.36) with

$$R_{IN} = 0 \qquad \text{and} \qquad R_{OUT} = \infty \qquad (11.38)$$

EXERCISE: Write an expression for the power gain of the amplifier in Fig. 11.11 in terms of the voltage gain.

ANSWER: $A_P = A^2 \dfrac{R_S + R_{IN}}{R_L}$

EXERCISE: Suppose the audio amplifier in Fig. 11.3 can be modeled by $R_{IN} = 50 \text{ k}\Omega$ and $R_{OUT} = 0.5 \ \Omega$. What value of open-circuit gain A is required to achieve an output power of 100 W if $v_s = 0.001 \sin 2000 \pi t$? How much power is being dissipated in R_{OUT}? What is the current gain?

ANSWERS: 46,800, 6.25 W, 2.75×10^8

EXERCISE: Repeat the preceding exercise if the input and output ports are matched to the source and load respectively (that is, $R_{IN} = 5 \text{ k}\Omega$ and $R_{OUT} = 8 \ \Omega$). (It should become clear why we don't design R_{OUT} to match the load resistance.)

ANSWERS: 160,000, 100 W

---

[3] For this case, $A_I = |A_I| \angle 180°$.

11.6 AMPLIFIER TRANSFER FUNCTIONS AND FREQUENCY RESPONSE

The gain expressions evaluated thus far have been constants. However, real amplifiers cannot provide uniform amplification at all frequencies. As frequency increases, shunt capacitances between all circuit elements and the ground node always cause the gain to decrease to zero at very high frequencies. At low frequencies, any series capacitors in the circuit limit the amplifier's ability to provide gain, and special circuits, called *dc-coupled amplifiers,* must be used if amplification is to be provided at dc. Because of these differences, amplifiers are classified into several general categories including low-pass, high-pass, band-pass, band-reject, and all-pass, based on the characteristics of their **transfer functions** in the frequency domain.

The frequency-dependent voltage gain of an amplifier is characterized by the voltage transfer function $A_V(s)$, which is the ratio of the Laplace transforms $V_o(s)$ and $V_s(s)$ of the input and output voltages of the amplifier, where $s = \sigma + j\omega$ is the complex frequency variable and $j = \sqrt{-1}$:

$$A_V(s) = \frac{V_o(s)}{V_s(s)} \tag{11.39}$$

The frequency-dependent current gain is characterized in a similar manner by its transfer function $A_I(s)$:

$$A_I(s) = \frac{I_o(s)}{I_s(s)} \tag{11.40}$$

The circuits we study will be modeled entirely by lumped circuit elements (R, L, C, and so on), and the numerator $N(s)$ and denominator $D(s)$ of the transfer functions will be polynomials in s

$$A_V(s) = \frac{N(s)}{D(s)} = \frac{a_m s^m + \cdots + a_1 s + a_o}{b_n s^n + \cdots + b_1 s + b_o} \tag{11.41}$$

which can be represented in factored form as

$$A_V(s) = \frac{N(s)}{D(s)} = K \frac{(s + z_1)(s + z_2) \cdots (s + z_m)}{(s + p_1)(s + p_2) \cdots (s + p_n)} \tag{11.42}$$

The frequencies $(-z_1, -z_2, \ldots, -z_m)$, for which the transfer function becomes zero are called the *zeros* of the transfer function, and the frequencies $(-p_1, -p_2, \ldots, -p_n)$, for which the transfer function becomes infinite are called the *poles* of the transfer function. In general, the values of the poles and zeros are complex numbers, although the majority of amplifiers we study will have only real values for the poles and zeros. Some of the zeros of the transfer function may also be at infinite frequency.

EXERCISE: What are the poles and zeros of the voltage transfer function

$$A_v(s) = \frac{300s}{s^2 + 5100s + 500000}$$

ANSWERS: Poles: -100, -5000; zeros: 0 (and ∞)

Bode Plots

Transfer functions of general amplifiers can be quite complicated, having many poles and zeros, but their overall behavior can be broken down into the categories mentioned in the introduction: low-pass, high-pass, band-pass, band-reject, and all-pass amplifiers. The basic forms of each category are discussed in the next several subsections.

When we explore the characteristics of amplifiers, we are usually interested in the behavior of the transfer function for physical frequencies ω—that is, for $s = j\omega$. The transfer function can then be represented in polar form by its **magnitude** $|A_V(j\omega)|$ and **phase angle** $\angle A_V(j\omega)$, which are both functions of frequency:

$$A_V(j\omega) = |A_V(j\omega)| \angle A_V(j\omega) \tag{11.43}$$

It is often convenient to display this information separately in a graphical form called a **Bode plot.** The Bode plot displays the magnitude of the transfer function in dB and the phase in degrees (or radians) versus a logarithmic frequency scale. Examples will be given as the various amplifier types are discussed.

The Low-Pass Amplifier

A single-pole[4] low-pass amplifier is described by the transfer function

$$A_V(s) = \frac{A_o\omega_H}{s + \omega_H} = \frac{A_o}{1 + \dfrac{s}{\omega_H}} \tag{11.44}$$

in which A_o is the low-frequency gain and ω_H represents the cutoff frequency of this low-pass amplifier. Let us first explore the behavior of the magnitude of $A_V(s)$ and then look at the phase response.

Magnitude Response

Substituting $s = j\omega$ into Eq. (11.44) and finding the magnitude of the function $A_V(j\omega)$ yields

$$|A_V(j\omega)| = \left| \frac{A_o\omega_H}{j\omega + \omega_H} \right| = \frac{|A_o\omega_H|}{\sqrt{\omega^2 + \omega_H^2}} \tag{11.45}$$

The Bode magnitude plot is given in terms of dB:

$$|A_V(j\omega)|_{dB} = 20\log|A_o\omega_H| - 20\log\sqrt{\omega^2 + \omega_H^2} \tag{11.46}$$

For a given set of numeric values, Eq. (11.45) can easily be evaluated and plotted using a package such as MATLAB or a spreadsheet, and results in the graph in Fig. 11.13.

For the general case, the graph is conveniently plotted in terms of its asymptotic behavior at low and high frequencies. For low frequencies, $\omega \ll \omega_H$, the magnitude is

---

[4] A general low-pass amplifier may have many poles. The single-pole version is the simplest approximation to the ideal low-pass characteristic described in Chapter 1.

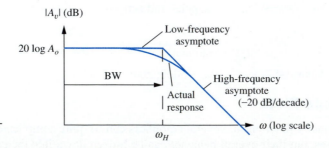

Figure 11.13 Low-pass amplifier: BW $= \omega_H$.

approximately

$$\left.\frac{A_o\omega_H}{\sqrt{\omega^2 + \omega_H^2}}\right|_{\omega \ll \omega_H} \approx \frac{A_o\omega_H}{\sqrt{\omega_H^2}} = A_o \qquad \text{or} \qquad (20\log A_o)\,\text{dB} \qquad (11.47)$$

At frequencies well below ω_H, the gain of the amplifier is constant and equal to A_o, which corresponds to the horizontal asymptote in Fig. 11.13. Signals at frequencies below ω_H are amplified by the gain A_o. In fact, the gain of this amplifier is constant down to dc ($\omega = 0$)! A_o represents the low-frequency gain of this amplifier but is also called the **midband gain** A_{mid} of the amplifier.

However, as ω exceeds ω_H, the gain of the amplifier begins to decrease (high-frequency roll-off). For sufficiently high frequencies, $\omega \gg \omega_H$, the magnitude can be approximated by

$$\left.\frac{A_o\omega_H}{\sqrt{\omega^2 + \omega_H^2}}\right|_{\omega \gg \omega_H} \approx \frac{A_o\omega_H}{\sqrt{\omega^2}} = \frac{A_o\omega_H}{\omega} \qquad (11.48)$$

and converting Eq. (11.48) to dB yields

$$|A_V(j\omega)|_{\text{dB}} \approx \left(20\log A_o - 20\log\frac{\omega}{\omega_H}\right)\text{dB} \qquad (11.49)$$

For frequencies much greater than ω_H, the transfer function decreases at a rate of 20 dB per decade increase in frequency, as indicated by the high-frequency asymptote in Fig. 11.13. Obviously, ω_H plays an important role in characterizing the amplifier; this critical frequency is called the **upper-cutoff frequency** of the amplifier. At $\omega = \omega_H$, the gain of the amplifier is

$$|A_V(j\omega_H)| = \frac{A_o\omega_H}{\sqrt{\omega_H^2 + \omega_H^2}} = \frac{A_o}{\sqrt{2}} \qquad \text{or} \qquad [(20\log A_o) - 3]\,\text{dB} \qquad (11.50)$$

and ω_H is sometimes referred to as the **upper $-$3-dB frequency** of the amplifier. ω_H is also often termed the **upper half-power point** of the amplifier because the output power of the amplifier, which is proportional to the square of the voltage, is reduced by a factor of 2 at $\omega = \omega_H$. Note that when the expressions for the two asymptotes given in Eqs. (11.47) and (11.48) are equated, they intersect precisely at $\omega = \omega_H$.

Bandwidth

The gain of the amplifier in Fig. 11.12 is approximately uniform (it varies by less than 3 dB) for all frequencies below ω_H. This is called a **low-pass amplifier.** The **bandwidth (BW)** of an amplifier is defined by the range of frequencies in which the amplification is approximately constant; it is expressed in either radians/second or Hz. For the low-pass amplifier,

$$\text{BW} = \omega_H(\text{rad/s}) \qquad \text{or} \qquad \text{BW} = f_H = \frac{\omega_H}{2\pi}\,\text{Hz} \qquad (11.51)$$

> **EXERCISE:** Find the midband gain, cutoff frequency, and bandwidth of the low-pass amplifier with the following transfer function:
>
> $$A_V(s) = -\frac{2\pi \times 10^6}{(s + 5000\pi)}$$
>
> **ANSWERS:** -400, 2.5 kHz, 2.5 kHz

Phase Response

The phase behavior versus frequency is also of interest in many applications and later will be found to be of great importance to the stability of feedback amplifiers. Again substituting $s = j\omega$ in Eq. (11.44), the phase response of the low-pass amplifier is found to be

$$\angle A_V(j\omega) = \angle \frac{A_o}{1 + j\dfrac{\omega}{\omega_H}} = \angle A_o - \tan^{-1}\left(\frac{\omega}{\omega_H}\right) \tag{11.52}$$

The phase angle of A_o is $0°$ if A_o is positive and $180°$ if A_o is negative.

The frequency-dependent phase term associated with each pole or zero in a transfer function involves the evaluation of the inverse tangent function. Important values appear in Table 11.3, and a graph of the complete inverse tangent function is given in Fig. 11.14. At the pole or zero frequency indicated by critical frequency ω_C, the magnitude of the phase shift is $45°$. One decade below ω_C, the phase is $5.7°$, and one decade above ω_C, the phase is $84.3°$. Two decades away from ω_C, the phase approaches its asymptotic limits of $0°$ and $90°$. Note that the phase response can also be approximated by the three straight-line segments in Fig. 11.14, in a manner similar to the asymptotes of the magnitude response.

The phase of more complex transfer functions with multiple poles and zeros is simply given by the appropriate sum and differences of inverse tangent functions. However, they are most easily evaluated with a computer or calculator.

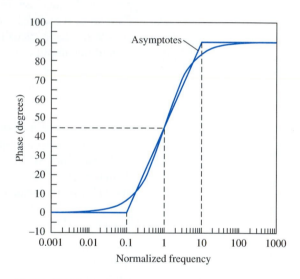

<table>
<tr><th colspan="2">T a b l e 11.3</th></tr>
<tr><th colspan="2">Inverse Tangent</th></tr>
<tr><th>ω</th><th>$\tan^{-1} \dfrac{\omega}{\omega_C}$</th></tr>
<tr><td>$0.01\,\omega_C$</td><td>$0.057°$</td></tr>
<tr><td>$0.1\,\omega_C$</td><td>$5.7°$</td></tr>
<tr><td>ω_C</td><td>$45°$</td></tr>
<tr><td>$10\,\omega_C$</td><td>$84.3°$</td></tr>
<tr><td>$100\,\omega_C$</td><td>$89.4°$</td></tr>
</table>

Figure 11.14 Phase versus normalized frequency (ω/ω_C) resulting from a single inverse tangent term $+\tan^{-1}(\omega/\omega_C)$. The straight-line approximation is also given.

EXERCISE: Find the magnitude and phase of the following transfer function for $\omega = 0.95$, 1.0, and 1.10.

$$A_V(s) = 20\frac{s^2 + 1}{s^2 + 0.1s + 1}$$

ANSWERS: 14.3, $-44.3°$; 0, $-90°$; 17.7, $+27.6°$

EXERCISE: Make a Bode plot of the following $A_V(s)$ using MATLAB:

$$A_V(s) = -\frac{2\pi \times 10^6}{(s + 5000\pi)}$$

ANSWER: $w = \text{logspace}(2, 6, 100)$

$\text{bode}(2*\text{pi}*1\text{e}6,[1\ 5000*\text{pi}],w)$

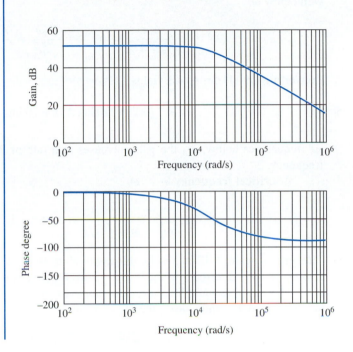

The High-Pass Amplifier

The transfer function for a single-pole **high-pass amplifier** can be written as

$$A_V(s) = \frac{A_o s}{s + \omega_L} \qquad (11.53)$$

and the magnitude of Eq. (11.53) is

$$|A_V(j\omega)| = \left|\frac{A_o j\omega}{j\omega + \omega_L}\right| = \frac{A_o \omega}{\sqrt{\omega^2 + \omega_L^2}} \qquad (11.54)$$

The Bode magnitude plot for this function is depicted in Fig. 11.15. In this case, the gain of the amplifier is constant for all frequencies above the **lower-cutoff frequency** ω_L. At

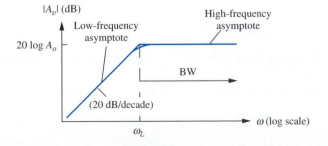

Figure 11.15 High-pass amplifier.

frequencies high enough to satisfy $\omega \gg \omega_L$, the magnitude can be approximated by

$$\frac{A_o\omega}{\sqrt{\omega^2 + \omega_L^2}}\bigg|_{\omega \gg \omega_L} \approx \frac{A_o\omega}{\sqrt{\omega^2}} = A_o \qquad \text{or} \qquad (20\log A_o)\,\text{dB} \qquad (11.55)$$

For ω exceeding ω_L, the gain is constant at the midband gain $A_{\text{mid}} = A_o$. At frequencies well below ω_L,

$$\frac{A_o\omega}{\sqrt{\omega^2 + \omega_L^2}}\bigg|_{\omega \ll \omega_L} \approx \frac{A_o\omega}{\sqrt{\omega_L^2}} = \frac{A_o\omega}{\omega_L} \qquad (11.56)$$

Converting Eq. (11.56) to dB yields

$$|A_V(j\omega)| \approx (20\log A_o) + 20\log\frac{\omega}{\omega_L} \qquad (11.57)$$

At frequencies below ω_L, the gain increases at a rate of 20 dB per decade increase in frequency.

At **critical frequency** $\omega = \omega_L$,

$$|A_V(j\omega_L)| = \frac{A_o\omega_L}{\sqrt{\omega_L^2 + \omega_L^2}} = \frac{A_o}{\sqrt{2}} \qquad \text{or} \qquad [(20\log A_o) - 3]\,\text{dB} \qquad (11.58)$$

The gain is again 3 dB below its midband value. Besides being called the lower-cutoff frequency, ω_L is referred to as the **lower $-$3-dB frequency** or the **lower half-power point.**

The high-pass amplifier provides approximately uniform gain at all frequencies above ω_L, and its bandwidth is therefore infinite:

$$\text{BW} = \infty - \omega_L = \infty \qquad (11.59)$$

The phase dependence of the high-pass amplifier is found by evaluating the phase of $A_V(j\omega)$ from Eq. (11.54):

$$\text{and} \qquad \angle A_V(j\omega) = \angle \frac{A_o j\omega}{j\omega + \omega_L} = \angle A_o + 90° - \tan^{-1}\left(\frac{\omega}{\omega_L}\right) \qquad (11.60)$$

This phase expression is similar to that of the low-pass amplifier, except for a $+90°$ shift due to the s term in the numerator.

EXERCISE: Find the midband gain, cutoff frequency, and bandwidth of the amplifier with the following transfer function:

$$A_V(s) = \frac{250s}{(s + 250\pi)}$$

ANSWERS: 250, 125 Hz, ∞

EXERCISE: Use MATLAB to produce a Bode plot of this transfer function.

ANSWER: $w = \text{logspace}(1,5,100)$

```
bode([250 0],[1 250*pi],w)
```

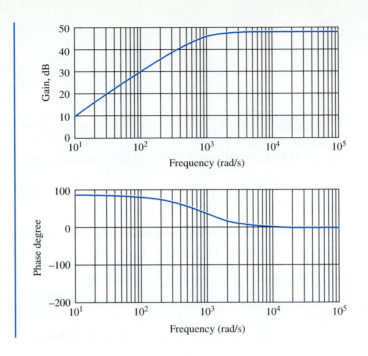

Band-Pass Amplifiers

The transfer function for a basic **band-pass amplifier** can be constructed from the product of the low-pass and high-pass transfer functions from Eqs. (11.44) and (11.53):

$$A_V(s) = \frac{A_o s \omega_H}{(s + \omega_L)(s + \omega_H)} = A_o \frac{s}{(s + \omega_L)} \frac{1}{\left(\dfrac{s}{\omega_H} + 1\right)} \tag{11.61}$$

Figure 11.16 is a graph of the magnitude of this transfer function. The concept of midband gain should be much clearer in this figure. The midband range of frequencies is defined by $\omega_L \leq \omega \leq \omega_H$, for which

$$\left|A_V(j\omega)\right| \approx A_o \tag{11.62}$$

A_o represents the gain in this midband region: $A_{\mathrm{mid}} = A_o$.

The mathematical expression for the magnitude of $A_V(j\omega)$ is

$$\left|A_V(j\omega)\right| = \left|\frac{A_o j\omega\,\omega_H}{(j\omega + \omega_L)(j\omega + \omega_H)}\right| = \frac{A_o\,\omega\,\omega_H}{\sqrt{(\omega^2 + \omega_L^2)(\omega^2 + \omega_H^2)}} \tag{11.63a}$$

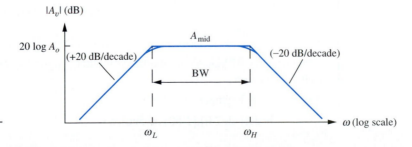

Figure 11.16 Band-pass amplifier.

or

$$|A_V(j\omega)| = \frac{A_o}{\sqrt{\left(1 + \frac{\omega_L^2}{\omega^2}\right)\left(1 + \frac{\omega^2}{\omega_H^2}\right)}} \tag{11.63b}$$

The expression in Eq. (11.63b) has been written in a form that exposes the gain in the midband region.

At both ω_L and ω_H, it is easy to show, assuming $\omega_L \ll \omega_H$, that

$$|A_V(j\omega_L)| = \frac{A_o}{\sqrt{2}} = |A(j\omega_H)| \quad \text{or} \quad [(20\log A_o) - 3]\text{ dB} \tag{11.64}$$

The gain is 3 dB below the midband gain at both critical frequencies. The region of approximately uniform gain (that is, the region of less than 3 dB variation) extends from ω_L to ω_H (f_L to f_H), and hence the bandwidth of the band-pass amplifier is

$$\text{BW} = f_H - f_L = \frac{\omega_H - \omega_L}{2\pi} \tag{11.65}$$

Evaluating the phase of $A_V(j\omega)$ from Eq. (11.60),

$$\angle A_V(j\omega) = \angle A_o + 90° - \tan^{-1}\left(\frac{\omega}{\omega_L}\right) - \tan^{-1}\left(\frac{\omega}{\omega_H}\right) \tag{11.66}$$

An example of this phase response is in the next exercise.

The graph in Fig. 11.16 is a representative of a relatively wide-band amplifier. In this figure, $f_H \gg f_L$, and

$$\text{BW} \approx f_H \tag{11.67}$$

The next section explores transfer functions for band-pass amplifiers with much narrower bandwidths.

EXERCISE: Find the midband gain, lower- and upper-cutoff frequencies, and bandwidth of the amplifier with the following transfer function:

$$A_V(s) = -\frac{2 \times 10^7 s}{(s + 100)(s + 50000)}$$

ANSWERS: 52 dB, 15.9 Hz, 7.96 kHz, 7.94 kHz

EXERCISE: Write an expression for the phase of this transfer function. What is the phase shift for $w = 0, 100, 50{,}000$, and ∞?

ANSWERS: $\angle A_V(j\omega) = -90° - \tan^{-1}\left(\frac{\omega}{100}\right) - \tan^{-1}\left(\frac{\omega}{50000}\right)$;

$-90°, -135°, -225°, -270°$

EXERCISE: Use MATLAB or another computer program to produce a Bode plot of this transfer function.

ANSWER: $w = $ logspace(0, 7, 150)

bode([-2e7 0],[1 50100 5e6],w)

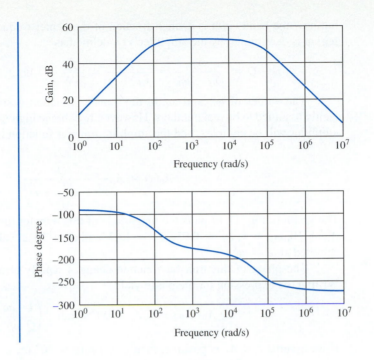

Narrow-Band or High-Q Bandpass Amplifiers

In Fig. 11.16 and the last exercise, the values of ω_H and ω_L were widely separated—that is, $\omega_H \gg \omega_L$. In applications such as the radio frequency (RF) amplifiers mentioned in Sec. 11.1, for example, a bandpass amplifier with a very narrow bandwidth is desired, as depicted in Fig. 11.17. The maximum gain A_o occurs at the **center frequency ω_o** of the amplifier and decreases rapidly by 3 dB at ω_H and ω_L. The bandwidth is again defined by

$$\text{BW} = f_H - f_L = \frac{\omega_H - \omega_L}{2\pi} \tag{11.68}$$

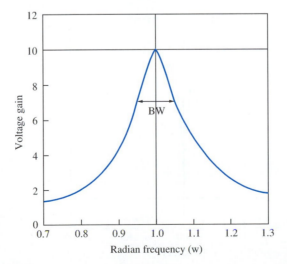

Figure 11.17 Band-pass amplifier with a high Q. For this graph, $A_o = 10$, $\omega_o = 1$, $\omega_L = 0.95$, $\omega_H = 1.05$, and $Q = 10$. Note the use of linear scales on both axes.

but now the bandwidth is a small fraction of the center frequency ω_o. The width of this region is determined by the amplifier's **Q,** defined as

$$Q = \frac{\omega_o}{\omega_H - \omega_L} = \frac{f_o}{f_H - f_L} = \frac{f_o}{\text{BW}} \quad \text{or} \quad \text{BW} = \frac{f_o}{Q} \quad (11.69)$$

The values of ω_H and ω_L in the transfer function described by Eq. (11.61) were tacitly assumed to be real numbers. However, to achieve high Q, the poles of the band-pass amplifier will be complex, and the amplifier transfer function is described by

$$A_v(s) = A_o \frac{s \dfrac{\omega_o}{Q}}{s^2 + s \dfrac{\omega_o}{Q} + \omega_o^2} \quad (11.70)$$

The graph in Fig. 11.17 plots the magnitude of this transfer function versus frequency for $A_o = 10$, $\omega_o = 1$, $\omega_L = 0.95$, $\omega_H = 1.05$, and $Q = 10$ and clearly exhibits a sharp peak centered at $\omega = \omega_o$.

The phase of this transfer function changes rapidly near the center frequency ω_o. Writing the expression for the phase yields

$$\angle A_V(j\omega) = \angle A_o + 90° - \tan^{-1}\left(\frac{1}{Q} \frac{\omega \, \omega_o}{\omega_o^2 - \omega^2}\right) \quad (11.71)$$

If we assume that A_o is positive, then $\angle A_V(j\omega) = 90°$ for $\omega \ll \omega_o$. The phase is 0° at $\omega = \omega_o$, and reaches $-90°$ for $\omega \gg \omega_o$.

> **EXERCISE:** Find the midband gain, center frequency, bandwidth, and Q of the amplifier with the following transfer function:
>
> $$A_V(s) = \frac{6 \times 10^{13} s}{s^2 + 2 \times 10^5 s + 10^{14}}$$
>
> **ANSWERS:** 30, 1.59 MHz, 50, 31.8 kHz

Band-Rejection Amplifiers

In some cases, we need an amplifier that can reject a narrow band of frequencies, as depicted in Fig. 11.18. This transfer function is also referred to as a **notch filter** and exhibits

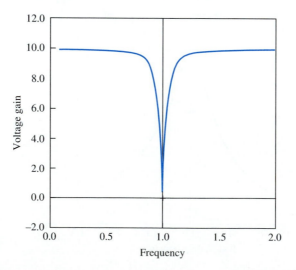

Figure 11.18 Band-rejection transfer function for $A_o = 10$, $\omega_o = 1$, and $Q = 10$. Note the use of linear scales on both axes.

a sharp null at the center frequency ω_o. At frequencies well removed from ω_o, the gain approaches A_o. To achieve a sharp null, the transfer function has a pair of zeros on the $j\omega$ axis at the notch frequency ω_o, and the poles of the amplifier are complex:

$$A_v(s) = A_o \frac{s^2 + \omega_o^2}{s^2 + s\dfrac{\omega_o}{Q} + \omega_o^2} \tag{11.72}$$

Figure 11.18 is the Bode plot for Eq. (11.72) for the case $A_o = 10$, $\omega_o = 1$, and $Q = 10$. Note the sharp null at $\omega = \omega_o$. Details of the phase response of this transfer function are left for the next exercise. However, it will be discovered to change abruptly by 180° near $\omega = \omega_o$.

> **EXERCISE:** Write the equation for the transfer function for the notch filter in Fig. 11.17.
>
> **ANSWER:** $A_V(s) = 10 \dfrac{s^2 + 1}{s^2 + 0.1s + 1}$
>
> **EXERCISE:** Write expressions for the magnitude and phase of Eq. (11.72). Plot a graph of the phase versus frequency.
>
> **ANSWERS:**
> $$|A_V(j\omega)| = |A_o| \frac{\left| 1 - \left(\dfrac{\omega}{\omega_o}\right)^2 \right|}{\sqrt{\left(1 - \left(\dfrac{\omega}{\omega_o}\right)^2\right)^2 + \left(\dfrac{\omega}{Q\,\omega_o}\right)^2}}$$
>
> $$\angle A_V(j\omega) = \angle A_o + \angle(\omega_o^2 - \omega^2) - \tan^{-1}\left(\frac{1}{Q}\frac{\omega\,\omega_o}{\omega_o^2 - \omega^2}\right)$$

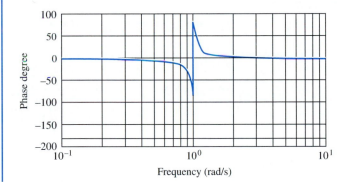

Frequency (rad/s)

The All-Pass Function

As may be inferred from the name, an all-pass transfer function has a uniform magnitude response at all frequencies. This unusual function can be used to tailor the phase characteristics of a signal. A simple example of the all-pass transfer function is

$$A_V(s) = A_o \frac{s - \omega_o}{s + \omega_o} \tag{11.73}$$

For positive A_o,

$$|A_V(j\omega)| = A_o \quad \text{and} \quad \angle A_V(j\omega) = -2\tan^{-1}\frac{\omega}{\omega_o} \tag{11.74}$$

| **EXERCISE:** Verify the results in Eq. (11.74).

More Complex Transfer Functions

Most amplifiers have much more complex transfer functions than those indicated in Figs. 11.13 to 11.18, but these can be built up as products of the basic functions given in earlier sections. An example of an amplifier with four poles and four zeros (two at infinity) is

$$A_V(s) = \frac{Ks(s + \omega_2)}{(s + \omega_1)(s + \omega_3)(s + \omega_4)(s + \omega_5)}$$

$$= \frac{A_{\text{mid}}s(s + \omega_2)}{(s + \omega_1)(s + \omega_3)\left(\dfrac{s}{\omega_4} + 1\right)\left(\dfrac{s}{\omega_5} + 1\right)} \tag{11.75}$$

which has the Bode plot in Fig. 11.19.

As can be observed, this amplifier has two frequency ranges in which the gain is approximately constant. The midband region is always defined as the region of highest gain, and the cutoff frequencies are defined in terms of the midband gain:

$$|A_v(j\omega_L)| = \frac{A_{\text{mid}}}{\sqrt{2}} = |A_v(j\omega_H)| \tag{11.76}$$

In Fig. 11.19, the poles and zeros are widely spaced, so $\omega_L \approx \omega_3$, $\omega_H \approx \omega_4$, and the bandwidth is BW $\approx f_4 - f_3 = (\omega_4 - \omega_3)/2\pi$.

If the critical frequencies are not widely spaced, then the poles and zeros interact and the process for determining the upper- and lower-cutoff frequencies can become substantially more complicated. As a simple example, consider a low pass transfer function with two identical poles:

$$A_V(s) = \frac{A_o\omega_1^2}{(s + \omega_1)^2} \qquad \text{for which } A_V(0) = A_o \tag{11.77}$$

The upper-cutoff frequency is defined by

$$|A_V(j\omega_H)| = \frac{A_o}{\sqrt{2}} \qquad \text{or} \qquad \frac{A_o}{\left[\sqrt{1 + \left(\dfrac{\omega_H}{\omega_1}\right)^2}\right]^2} = \frac{A_o}{\sqrt{2}} \tag{11.78}$$

Solving for ω_H yields

$$\omega_H = 0.644\omega_1 \tag{11.79}$$

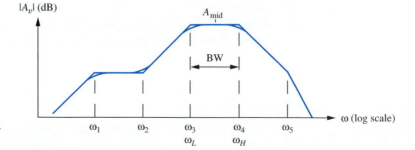

Figure 11.19 An amplifier transfer function with multiple poles and zeros.

The cutoff frequency of the two-pole transfer function is only 64 percent that of the single-pole function. This "bandwidth shrinkage" in multipole amplifiers is discussed in more detail in Chapter 12. Approximation techniques for finding ω_L and ω_H in more complex cases are discussed in Chapter 17.

> **EXERCISE:** Find the midband gain, lower- and upper-cutoff frequencies, and bandwidth of the amplifier with the following transfer function:
>
> $$A_v(s) = \frac{6.4 \times 10^{12} \, \pi^2}{(s + 200\pi)(s + 80000\pi)^2}$$
>
> **ANSWERS:** 1000, 100 Hz, 25.6 kHz, 25.5 kHz

SUMMARY

This chapter introduced analog amplification. Important amplifier characteristics including voltage gain, current gain, power gain, input resistance, and output resistance were all discussed. Gains are expressed in terms of the phasor representations of sinusoidal signals or as transfer functions using Laplace transforms. The magnitudes of the gains are often expressed in terms of the logarithmic decibel or dB scale.

It was demonstrated that bias must be provided to an amplifier to ensure that it operates in its linear region. The choice of bias point of the amplifier, its Q-point, can affect both the gain of the amplifier and the size of the input signal range for which linear amplification will occur. Improper choice of bias point can lead to nonlinear operation of an amplifier and distortion of the signal.

Linear amplifiers can be conveniently modeled using two-port representations. The g-, h-, y-, and z-parameters are of particular interest for describing amplifiers in this text. In most of the amplifiers we consider, the 1–2 parameter will be neglected. It was noted that the g-parameter description is highly useful for representing voltage amplifiers. The current amplifier can be conveniently represented by an h-parameter description. These networks were recast in terms of input resistance, R_{IN}, output resistance R_{OUT}, open-circuit voltage gain A, and short-circuit current gain β. Ideal voltage amplifiers have $R_{IN} = \infty$ and $R_{OUT} = 0$, whereas $R_{IN} = 0$ and $R_{OUT} = \infty$ for ideal current amplifiers.

Linear amplifiers can be used to tailor the magnitude and/or phase of sinusoidal signals and are often characterized by their frequency response. Low-pass, high-pass, band-pass, band-reject (or notch), and all-pass characteristics were discussed. The characteristics of these amplifiers are conveniently displayed in graphical form as a Bode plot, which presents the magnitude (in dB) and phase (in degrees) of a transfer function versus a logarithmic frequency scale. Bode plots can be created easily using MATLAB.

In an amplifier, the midband gain A_{mid} represents the maximum gain of the amplifier. At the upper- and lower-cutoff frequencies—f_H and f_L, respectively—the voltage gain is equal to $A_{mid}/\sqrt{2}$ and is 3 dB below its midband value ($20 \log |A_{mid}|$). The bandwidth of the amplifier extends from f_L to f_H and is defined as $BW = f_H - f_L$. Narrow band-pass amplifiers are characterized in terms of $Q = f_o/BW$, in which f_o is the center frequency.

Key Terms

All-pass network	Band-reject amplifier	Bode plot
Audio frequency (AF)	Bandwidth (BW)	Center frequency
Band-pass amplifier	Bias	Critical frequency

Current amplifier
Current gain
Decibel (dB)
High-pass amplifier
Ideal current amplifier
Ideal voltage amplifier
Input resistance (R_{IN})
Intermediate frequency (IF)
Inverting amplifier
Linear amplifier
Low-pass amplifier
Lower-cutoff frequency
Lower half-power point
Lower −3 dB frequency
Magnitude

Midband gain
Noninverting amplifier
Notch filter
Null frequency
Open-circuit termination
Open-circuit voltage gain
Output resistance
Phase angle
Phasor representation
Power gain (A_P)
Q
Radio frequency (RF)
Short-circuit current gain
Short-circuit termination
Source resistance (R_S)

Transfer function
Two-port network
Two-port parameters
  g-parameters
  h-parameters
  y-parameters
  z-parameters
Upper-cutoff frequency
Upper half-power point
Upper −3-dB frequency
Very high frequency (VHF)
Voltage amplifier
Voltage gain

Problems

11.1 An Example of an Analog Electronic System

11.1. In addition to those given in the introduction, list 15 physical variables in your everyday life that can be represented as continuous analog signals.

11.2 Amplification

11.2. Convert the following to decibels: (a) voltage gains of 125, −50, 50,000, −100,000, 0.85; (b) current gains of 600, 3000, −10^6, 200,000, 0.95; (c) power gains of 2×10^9, 4×10^5, 6×10^8, 10^{10}.

11.3. Suppose the input and output voltages of an amplifier are given by

$$v_S = 1\sin(1000\pi t) + 0.333\sin(3000\pi t)$$
$$+ 0.200\sin(5000\pi t) \text{ V}$$

and

$$v_O = 2\sin\left(1000\pi t + \frac{\pi}{6}\right)$$
$$+ \sin\left(3000\pi t + \frac{\pi}{6}\right)$$
$$+ \sin\left(5000\pi t + \frac{\pi}{6}\right) \text{ V}$$

(a) Plot the input and output voltage waveforms of v_S and v_O for $0 \le t \le 4$ ms. (b) What are the amplitudes, frequencies, and phases of the individual signal components in v_S? (c) What are the amplitudes, frequencies, and phases of the individual signal components in v_O? (d) What are the voltage gains at the three frequencies? (e) Is this a linear amplifier?

11.4. What are the voltage gain, current gain, and power gain required of the amplifier in Fig. 11.3 if $V_s = 5$ mV and the desired output power is 40 W?

11.3 Amplifier Biasing for Linear Operation

11.5. The circuit inside the box in Fig. P11.5 contains only resistors and diodes. The terminal V_O is connected to some point in the circuit inside the box. (a) Is the largest possible value of V_O most nearly 0 V, −6 V, +6 V, or +15 V? Why? (b) Is the smallest possible value of V_O most nearly 0 V, −9 V, +6 V, or +15 V? Why?

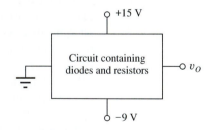

Figure P11.5

11.6. The input voltage applied to the amplifier in Fig. P11.6 is $v_I = V_B + V_M \sin 1000t$. What is the voltage gain of the amplifier for small values of V_M if $V_B = 0.6$ V? What is the maximum value of V_M that can be used and still have an undistorted sinusoidal signal at v_O?

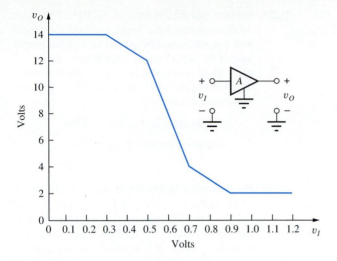

Figure P11.6

11.7. Repeat Prob. 11.6 for $V_B = 0.8$ V.

11.8. Repeat Prob. 11.6 for $V_B = 0.5$ V.

11.9. The input voltage applied to the amplifier in Fig. P11.6 is $v_I = (0.6 + 0.1 \sin 1000t)$ V. (a) Write expressions for the output voltage. (b) Draw a graph of two cycles of the output voltage. (c) Calculate the first five spectral components of this signal. You may use MATLAB or other computer analysis tools.

*11.10. The input voltage applied to the amplifier in Fig. P11.6 is $v_I = (0.5 + 0.1 \sin 1000t)$ V. (a) Write expressions for the output voltage. (b) Draw a graph of two cycles of the output voltage. (c) Calculate the first five spectral components of this signal. You may use MATLAB or other computer analysis tools.

11.4 Two-Port Models for Amplifiers

11.11. Calculate the g-parameters in terms of the y-parameters in Fig. 11.8. What are the expressions for the g-parameters if $y_{12} = 0$?

11.12. Calculate the h-parameters in terms of the y-parameters in Fig. 11.8. What are the expressions for the h-parameters if $y_{12} = 0$?

11.13. Calculate the h-parameters in terms of the g-parameters in Fig. 11.6. What are the values of the h-parameters if $g_{12} = 0$?

11.14. Calculate the g-parameters in terms of the z-parameters in Fig. 11.9. What are the values of the g-parameters if $z_{12} = 0$?

11.15. (a) Redraw the h-parameter, two-port network and rewrite the equations that describe the network if

$h_{12} = 0$. Express R_{IN}, R_{OUT}, and A of the network in Fig. P11.15 in terms of the h-parameters (with $h_{12} = 0$). (b) Repeat this problem for the y-parameters with $y_{12} = 0$. (c) Repeat this problem for the z-parameters with $z_{12} = 0$.

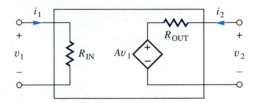

Figure P11.15

11.16. Calculate the g-parameters for the circuit in Fig. P11.16.

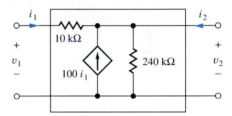

Figure P11.16

11.17. Calculate the h-parameters for the circuit in Fig. P11.16.

11.18. Calculate the y-parameters for the circuit in Fig. P11.16.

11.19. Calculate the z-parameters for the circuit in Fig. P11.16.

11.20. Calculate the g-parameters for the circuit in Fig. P11.20.

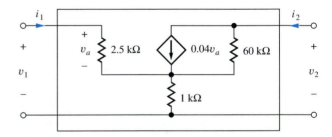

Figure P11.20

11.21. Calculate the h-parameters for the circuit in Fig. P11.20.

11.22. Calculate the y-parameters for the circuit in Fig. P11.20.

11.23. Calculate the z-parameters for the circuit in Fig. P11.20.

11.24. Calculate the g-parameters for the circuit in Fig. P11.24.

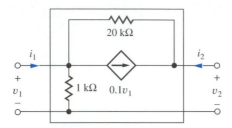

Figure P11.24

11.25. Calculate the h-parameters for the circuit in Fig. P11.24.

11.26. Calculate the y-parameters for the circuit in Fig. P11.24.

11.27. Calculate the z-parameters for the circuit in Fig. P11.24.

11.5 Mismatched Source and Load Resistances

11.28. An amplifier connected in the circuit in Fig. P11.28 has the two-port parameters listed below, with $R_S = 1$ kΩ and $R_L = 16$ Ω. (a) Find the overall voltage gain A_V, current gain A_I, and power gain A_P for the amplifier and express the results in dB. (b) What is the amplitude V_s of the sinusoidal input signal v_S needed to deliver 1 W to the 16-Ω load resistor? (c) How much power is dissipated in the amplifier when 1 W is delivered to the load resistor?

$$\text{Input resistance } R_{\text{IN}} = 1 \text{ M}\Omega$$

$$\text{Output resistance } R_{\text{OUT}} = 0.5 \text{ }\Omega$$

$$A = 54 \text{ dB}$$

$$v_S = V_s \sin \omega t$$

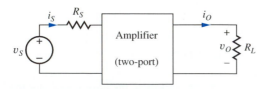

Figure P11.28

11.29. Suppose that the amplifier of Fig. P11.28 has been designed to match the source and load resistances with the parameters below. (a) What is the amplitude of the input signal v_S needed to deliver 1 W to the 16-Ω load resistor? (b) How much power is dissipated in the amplifier when 1 W is delivered to the load resistor?

$$\text{Input resistance } R_{\text{IN}} = 1 \text{ k}\Omega$$

$$\text{Output resistance } R_{\text{OUT}} = 16 \text{ }\Omega$$

$$A = 54 \text{ dB}$$

11.30. For the circuit in Fig. 11.11, $R_S = 1$ kΩ, $R_L = 16$ Ω, and $A = -1000$. What values of R_{IN} and R_{OUT} will produce maximum power in the load resistor R_L? What is the maximum power that can be delivered to R_L if v_s is a sine wave with an amplitude of 10 mV? What is the power gain of this amplifier?

11.31. For the circuit in Fig. 11.11, $R_S = 2$ kΩ, $R_{\text{IN}} = 20$ kΩ, $R_{\text{OUT}} = 100$ Ω, and $R_L = 2$ kΩ. What value of A is required to produce a voltage gain of 77 dB if the amplifier is to be an inverting amplifier ($\theta = 180°$)?

11.32. For the circuit in Fig. 11.12, $R_S = 200$ kΩ, $R_{\text{IN}} = 20$ kΩ, $R_{\text{OUT}} = 300$ kΩ, and $R_L = 50$ kΩ. What value of β is required to produce a current gain of 200?

11.33. For the circuit in Fig. 11.12, $R_S = 100$ kΩ, $R_L = 10$ kΩ, and $\beta = 5000$. What values of R_{IN} and R_{OUT} will produce maximum power in the load resistor R_L? What is the maximum power that can be delivered to R_L if i_s is a sine wave with an amplitude of 1 μA? What is the power gain of this amplifier?

11.34. Two amplifiers are connected in series, or cascaded, in the circuit in Fig. P11.34. If $R_S = 1$ kΩ, $R_{\text{IN}} = 5$ kΩ, $R_{\text{OUT}} = 250$ Ω, $R_L = 100$ Ω, and $A = -1000$, what are the voltage gain, current gain, and power gain of the overall amplifier?

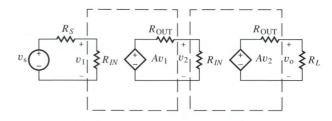

Figure P11.34

*11.35. For the circuit in Fig. 11.11, show that

$$A_{PdB} = A_{VdB} - 10\log\left(\frac{R_L}{R_S + R_{IN}}\right)$$

and

$$A_{PdB} = A_{IdB} + 10\log\left(\frac{R_L}{R_S + R_{IN}}\right)$$

11.6 Amplifier Transfer Functions and Frequency Response

11.36. Find the poles and zeros of the following transfer functions:

(a) $A_I(s) =$

$$-\frac{3 \times 10^9 s^2}{(s^2 + 51s + 50)(s^2 + 13,000s + 3 \times 10^7)}$$

*(b) $A_V(s) =$

$$-\frac{10^5(s^2 + 51s + 50)}{s^5 + 1000s^4 + 50,000s^3 + 20,000s^2 + 13,000s + 3 \times 10^7}$$

11.37. What are A_{mid} in dB, f_H, f_L, and the BW in Hz for the amplifier described by

$$A_V(s) = \frac{2\pi \times 10^7 s}{(s + 20\pi)(s + 2\pi \times 10^4)}$$

What type of amplifier is this?

11.38. What are A_{mid} in dB, f_H, f_L, and the BW in Hz for the amplifier described by

$$A_V(s) = \frac{2\pi \times 10^6}{s + 20\pi}$$

What type of amplifier is this?

11.39. What are A_{mid} in dB, f_H, f_L, and the BW in Hz for the amplifier described by

$$A_V(s) = \frac{10^4 s}{s + 100\pi}$$

What type of amplifier is this?

11.40. What are A_{mid} in dB, f_H, f_L, the BW in Hz, and the Q for the amplifier described by

$$A_V(s) = -\frac{10^7 s}{s^2 + 10^5 s + 10^{14}}$$

What type of amplifier is this?

11.41. What are A_{mid} in dB, f_H, f_L, and the BW in Hz for the amplifier described by

$$A_V(s) = -20\frac{s^2 + 10^{12}}{s^2 + 10^4 s + 10^{12}}$$

What type of amplifier is this?

*11.42. What are A_{mid} in dB, f_H, f_L, and the BW in Hz for the amplifier described by

$$A_V(s) =$$

$$\frac{4\pi^2 \times 10^{14} s^2}{(s + 20\pi)(s + 50\pi)(s + 2\pi \times 10^5)(s + 2\pi \times 10^6)}$$

What type of amplifier is this?

11.43. Use MATLAB, a spreadsheet, or other computer program to generate a Bode plot of the magnitude and phase of the transfer function in Prob. 11.37.

11.44. Use MATLAB, a spreadsheet, or other computer program to generate a Bode plot of the magnitude and phase of the transfer function in Prob. 11.38.

11.45. Use MATLAB, a spreadsheet, or other computer program to generate a Bode plot of the magnitude and phase of the transfer function in Prob. 11.39.

11.46. Use MATLAB, a spreadsheet, or other computer program to generate a Bode plot of the magnitude and phase of the transfer function in Prob. 11.40.

11.47. Use MATLAB, a spreadsheet, or other computer program to generate a Bode plot of the magnitude and phase of the transfer function in Prob. 11.41.

11.48. Use MATLAB, a spreadsheet, or other computer program to generate a Bode plot of the magnitude and phase of the transfer function in Prob. 11.42.

11.49. The voltage gain of an amplifier is described by the transfer function in Prob. 11.37 and has an input $v_s = 0.001\sin\omega t$ V. Write an expression for the amplifier's output voltage at a frequency of (a) 5 Hz, (b) 500 Hz, (c) 50 kHz.

11.50. The voltage gain of an amplifier is described by the transfer function in Prob. 11.38 and has an input $v_s = 10\sin\omega t$ µV. Write an expression for the amplifier's output voltage at a frequency of (a) 2 Hz, (b) 2 kHz, (c) 200 kHz.

11.51. The voltage gain of an amplifier is described by the transfer function in Prob. 11.39 and has an input $v_s = 0.3\sin\omega t$ mV. Write an expression for the amplifier's output voltage at a frequency of (a) 1 Hz, (b) 50 Hz, (c) 5 kHz.

11.52. The voltage gain of an amplifier is described by the transfer function in Prob. 11.42 and has an input $v_s = 0.001\sin\omega t$ V. Write an expression for the amplifier's output voltage at a frequency of (a) 5 Hz, (b) 500 Hz, (c) 50 kHz.

11.53. The voltage gain of an amplifier is described by the transfer function in Prob. 11.40 and has an input $v_s = 0.005\sin\omega t$ V. Write an expression for the amplifier's output voltage at a frequency of (a) 1.59 MHz, (b) 1 MHz, (c) 5 MHz.

11.54. The voltage gain of an amplifier is described by the transfer function in Prob. 11.41 and has an input $v_s = 0.025 \sin \omega t$ V. Write an expression for the amplifier's output voltage at a frequency of (a) 159 kHz, (b) 50 kHz, (c) 200 kHz.

11.55. (a) Write an expression for the transfer function of a low-pass voltage amplifier with a gain of 20 dB and $f_H = 5$ MHz. (b) Repeat if the amplifier exhibits a phase shift of 180° at $f = 0$.

11.56. (a) Write an expression for the transfer function of a voltage amplifier with a gain of 40 dB, $f_L = 100$ Hz, and $f_H = 100$ kHz. (b) Repeat if the amplifier exhibits a phase shift of 180° at $f = 0$.

 11.57. Make a Bode plot of the transfer function in Eq. (11.77) if $A_o = -1000$ and $\omega_1 = 50,000\pi$. What are A_{mid} and ω_H? What is the slope of the magnitude plot for $\omega \gg \omega_H$?

11.58. (a) What is the bandwidth of the low-pass amplifier described by

$$A_V(s) = A_o \left(\frac{\omega_1}{s + \omega_1} \right)^3$$

if $A_o = -2500$ and $\omega_1 = 50,000\pi$. (b) Make a Bode plot of this transfer function. What is the slope of the magnitude plot for $\omega \gg \omega_H$?

*11.59. The input to an all-pass amplifier with a gain of 10 is

$$v_S = 1 \sin(1000\pi t) + 0.333 \sin(3000\pi t)$$
$$+ 0.200 \sin(5000\pi t) \text{ V}$$

(a) If the phase shift of the amplifier at 500 Hz is 10°, what must be the phase shift at the other two frequencies if the shape of the output waveform is to be the same as that of the input waveform? Write an expression for the output signal. (b) Use the computer to check your answer by plotting the input and output waveforms.

CHAPTER 12

Operational Amplifiers

The **operational amplifier,** or **op amp,** is a fundamental building block of analog circuit design. The name "operational amplifier" originates from the use of this type of amplifier to perform specific electronic circuit functions or operations, such as scaling, summation, and integration, in analog computers.

Integrated circuit operational amplifiers evolved rapidly following development of the first bipolar integrated circuit processes in the 1960s. Early IC amplifier designs offered performance improvements over tube-type designs and discrete semiconductor realizations but were somewhat "delicate." The μA-709, introduced by Fairchild Semiconductor in 1965, was one of the first widely used general-purpose IC operational amplifiers. IC op amp circuits improved quickly, and the now-classic Fairchild μA-741 amplifier design, which appeared in the late 1960s, is a robust amplifier with excellent characteristics for most general-purpose applications. The internal circuit design of these op amps used 20 to 50 bipolar transistors. Later designs improved performance in most specification areas. Today there is an almost overwhelming array of operational amplifiers from which to choose.

This chapter introduces the important performance specifications of operational amplifiers and provides a general overview to help users choose an amplifier from among the array of available components. The chapter begins by exploring the characteristics of the ideal operational amplifier. A number of basic circuit applications are discussed, including inverting and noninverting amplifiers, the summing and instrumentation amplifiers, the integrator, and a basic low-pass filter. Limitations caused by the nonideal behavior of the operational amplifier are also discussed. These limitations include finite gain, bandwidth and input and output resistances, common-mode rejection, offset voltage, and bias current.

The frequency response of circuits containing operational amplifiers is analyzed, including both single-stage and cascaded amplifiers. A multistage design example is explored using computer analysis via a spreadsheet. A macro model for simulation of op-amp frequency response is presented, and large-signal response limitations, including slew rate considerations and full-power bandwidth, are discussed. Continuous-time active filters and discrete-time switched capacitor circuits are also introduced. The chapter concludes with several examples of operational amplifier use in nonlinear circuit applications, including precision rectifiers and positive-feedback multivibrator circuits.

12.1 THE DIFFERENTIAL AMPLIFIER

The basic **differential amplifier** is shown in schematic form in Fig. 12.1. The amplifier has two inputs, to which the input signals v_+ and v_- are connected, and a single output v_O, all referenced to the common (ground) terminal between the two power supplies V_{CC} and V_{EE}. In most applications, $V_{CC} \geq 0$ and $-V_{EE} \leq 0$, and the voltages are often symmetric—that is, ± 5 V, ± 12 V, ± 15 V, ± 18 V, ± 22 V, and so on. These power supply voltages limit the output voltage range: $-V_{EE} \leq v_O \leq V_{CC}$.

For simplicity, the amplifier is most often drawn without explicitly showing the power supplies, as in Fig. 12.2(a), or the ground connection, as in Fig. 12.2(b)—but we must remember that the power and ground terminals are always present in the implementation of a real circuit.

For purposes of signal analysis, the differential amplifier can be represented by its input resistance R_{ID}, output resistance R_O, and controlled voltage source Av_{id}, as in Fig. 12.3. This is the simplified g-parameter two-port representation from Chap. 11 with $g_{12} = 0$.

$$A = \text{voltage gain (open-circuit voltage gain)}$$

$$v_{id} = (v_+ - v_-) = \text{differential input signal voltage}$$

$$R_{ID} = \text{amplifier input resistance} \tag{12.1}$$

$$R_O = \text{amplifier output resistance}$$

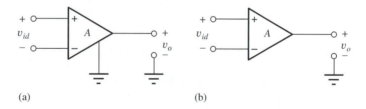

Figure 12.1 The differential amplifier, including power supplies.

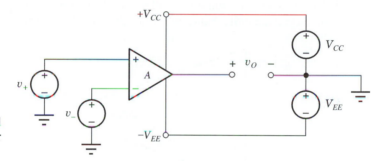

Figure 12.2 (a) Amplifier without power supplies explicitly included. (b) Differential amplifier with implied ground connection.

(a)   (b)

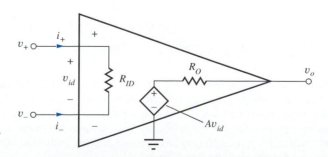

Figure 12.3 Differential amplifier.

The signal voltage developed at the output of the amplifier is in phase with the voltage applied to the + input terminal and 180° out of phase with the signal applied to the − input terminal. The v_+ and v_- terminals are therefore referred to as the **noninverting input** and **inverting input,** respectively.

In a typical application, the amplifier is driven by a signal source having a Thévenin equivalent voltage v_S and resistance R_S and is connected to a load represented by the resistor R_L, as in Fig. 12.4. For this simple circuit, the output voltage can be written in terms of the dependent source as

$$\mathbf{v_o}^* = A\mathbf{v_{id}}\frac{R_L}{R_O + R_L} \tag{12.2}$$

and the voltage $\mathbf{v_{id}}$ is

$$\mathbf{v_{id}} = \mathbf{v_s}\frac{R_{ID}}{R_{ID} + R_S} \tag{12.3}$$

Combining Eqs. (12.2) and (12.3) yields an expression for the overall voltage gain of the amplifier circuit in Fig. 12.4 for arbitrary values of R_S and R_L:

$$A_V = \frac{\mathbf{v_o}}{\mathbf{v_s}} = A\frac{R_{ID}}{R_S + R_{ID}}\frac{R_L}{R_O + R_L} \tag{12.4}$$

Operational-amplifier circuits are most often **dc-coupled amplifiers,** and the signals v_o and v_s may in fact have a dc component that represents a dc shift of the input away from the Q-point. The op amp amplifies not only the ac components of the signal but also this dc component. We must remember that the ratio needed to find A_V, as indicated in Eq. (12.4), is determined by the amplitude and phase of the individual signal components and is not a time-varying quantity, but $\omega = 0$ is a valid signal frequency!

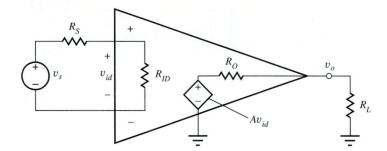

Figure 12.4 Amplifier with source and load attached.

EXAMPLE 12.1: Calculate the voltage gain for an amplifier with the following parameters: $A = 100$, $R_{ID} = 100$ kΩ, and $R_O = 100$ Ω, with $R_S = 10$ kΩ and $R_L = 1000$ Ω. Express the result in dB.

SOLUTION: Using Eq. (12.4)

$$A_V = 100\left(\frac{100\text{ k}\Omega}{10\text{ k}\Omega + 100\text{ k}\Omega}\right)\left(\frac{1000\ \Omega}{100\ \Omega + 1000\ \Omega}\right) = 82.6$$

$$A_{V\text{dB}} = 20\log|A_V| = 20\log|82.6| = 38.3\text{ dB}$$

Author's note: Recall from Chapters 1 and 11 that v_s, v_o, i_2 and so on represent our signal voltages and currents and are generally functions of time: $v_s(t)$, $v_o(t)$, $i_2(t)$. But whenever we do algebraic calculations of voltage gain, current gain, input resistance, output resistance, and so on, we must use **phasor** representations of the individual signal components in our calculations: $\mathbf{v_s}$, $\mathbf{v_o}$, $\mathbf{i_2}$. Note that the signals $v_s(t)$, $v_o(t)$, $i_2(t)$ may be composed of many individual signal components, one of which may be a dc shift away from the Q-point value.

DISCUSSION: The amplifier's internal voltage gain capability is $A = 100$, but an overall gain of only 82.6 is being realized because a portion of the signal source voltage (≈ 9 percent) is being dropped across R_S and part of the internal amplifier voltage (Av_{id}) (also ≈ 9 percent) is being lost across R_O. ◆

The Ideal Differential Amplifier

An ideal differential amplifier would produce an output that depends only on the voltage difference v_{id} between its two input terminals, and this voltage would be independent of source and load resistances. Referring to Eq. (12.4), we see that this behavior can be achieved if the input resistance of the amplifier is infinite and the output resistance is zero (as pointed out previously in Sec. 11.5). For this case, Eq. (12.4) reduces to

$$\mathbf{v_o} = A\mathbf{v_{id}} \qquad \text{or} \qquad A_V = \frac{\mathbf{v_o}}{\mathbf{v_{id}}} = A \tag{12.5}$$

and the full amplifier gain is realized. A is referred to as either the **open-circuit voltage gain** or **open-loop gain** of the amplifier and represents the maximum voltage gain available from the device.

As also mentioned in Chapter 11, we often want to achieve the fully mismatched resistance condition in voltage amplifier applications ($R_{ID} \gg R_S$ and $R_O \ll R_L$), so that maximum voltage gain in Eq. (12.5) can be achieved. For the mismatched case, the overall amplifier gain is independent of the source and load resistances, and multiple amplifier stages can be cascaded without concern for interaction between stages.

12.2 THE IDEAL OPERATIONAL AMPLIFIER

As noted earlier, the term "operational amplifier" grew from use of these high-performance amplifiers to perform specific electronic circuit functions or operations, such as scaling, summation, and integration, in analog computers. The operational amplifier used in these applications is an ideal differential amplifier with an additional property: infinite voltage gain. Although it is impossible to realize the **ideal operational amplifier,** its conceptual use allows us to understand the basic performance to be expected from a given analog circuit and serves as a model to help in circuit design. Once the properties of the ideal amplifier and its use in basic circuits are understood, then various ideal assumptions can be removed in order to understand their effect on circuit performance.

The ideal operational amplifier is a special case of the ideal difference amplifier in Fig. 12.3, in which $R_{ID} = \infty$, $R_O = 0$, and, most importantly, voltage gain $A = \infty$. Infinite gain leads to the first of two assumptions used to analyze circuits containing ideal op amps. Solving for $\mathbf{v_{id}}$ in Eq. (12.5),

$$\mathbf{v_{id}} = \frac{\mathbf{v_o}}{A} \qquad \text{and} \qquad \lim_{A \to \infty} \mathbf{v_{id}} = 0 \tag{12.6}$$

If A is infinite, then the input voltage v_{id} will be zero for any finite output voltage. We will refer to this condition as Assumption 1 for ideal op-amp circuit analysis.

An infinite value for the input resistance R_{ID} forces the two input currents i_+ and i_- to be zero, which will be Assumption 2 for analysis of ideal op-amp circuits. These two results, combined with Kirchhoff's voltage and current laws, form the basis for analysis of all ideal op-amp circuits.

Assumptions for Ideal Operational-Amplifier Analysis

1. Input voltage difference is zero: $v_{id} = 0$

2. Input currents are zero: $i_+ = 0$ and $i_- = 0$

(12.7)

Infinite gain and infinite input resistance are the explicit characteristics that lead to Assumptions 1 and 2. However, the ideal operational amplifier actually has quite a number of additional implicit properties, but these assumptions are seldom clearly stated. They are

- Infinite common-mode rejection
- Infinite power supply rejection
- Infinite output voltage range (not limited by $-V_{EE} \le v_O \le V_{CC}$)
- Infinite output current capability
- Infinite open-loop bandwidth
- Infinite slew rate
- Zero output resistance
- Zero input-bias currents and offset current
- Zero input-offset voltage

These terms may be unfamiliar at this point, but they are all defined and discussed in detail later in this chapter. Following presentation of a number of examples of circuits using the ideal operational amplifier, we discuss the effect on circuit performance of removing these ideal assumptions.

12.3 ANALYSIS OF CIRCUITS CONTAINING IDEAL OPERATIONAL AMPLIFIERS

This section describes a number of classic operational-amplifier circuits, including the basic inverting and noninverting amplifiers; the unity-gain buffer, or voltage follower; the summing, difference, and instrumentation amplifiers; the low-pass filter; and the integrator. Analysis of these various circuits demonstrates use of the two ideal op-amp assumptions in combination with Kirchhoff's voltage and current laws (KVL and KCL, respectively).

The Inverting Amplifier

An **inverting-amplifier** circuit is built by grounding the positive input of the operational amplifier and connecting resistors R_1 and R_2, called the **feedback network,** between the inverting input and the signal source and amplifier output node, respectively, as in Fig. 12.5. We wish to find a set of two-port parameters that characterize the overall circuit, including the open-circuit voltage gain $\mathbf{A_v}$, input resistance R_{IN}, and output resistance R_{OUT}. We assume that the reverse-transfer parameter is negligibly small.

We begin by determining the voltage gain. To find A_V, we need a relationship between $\mathbf{v_s}$ and $\mathbf{v_o}$, which we can find by writing an equation for the single loop shown in Fig. 12.6.

$$\mathbf{v_s} - \mathbf{i_s}R_1 - \mathbf{i_2}R_2 - \mathbf{v_o} = 0 \tag{12.8}$$

Applying KCL at the inverting input to the amplifier yields a relationship between $\mathbf{i_s}$ and $\mathbf{i_2}$

$$\mathbf{i_s} = \mathbf{i_-} + \mathbf{i_2} \tag{12.9}$$

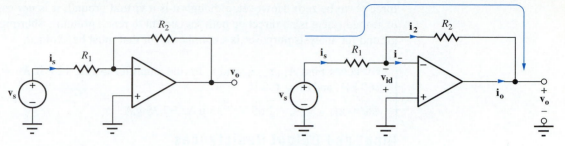

Figure 12.5 Inverting-amplifier circuit.   **Figure 12.6** Inverting-amplifier circuit.

which can be simplified because Assumption 2 states that $\mathbf{i}_-$ must be zero:

$$\mathbf{i_s} = \mathbf{i_2} \tag{12.10}$$

Equation (12.8) then becomes

$$\mathbf{v_s} - \mathbf{i_s} R_1 - \mathbf{i_s} R_2 - \mathbf{v_o} = 0 \tag{12.11}$$

Current $\mathbf{i_s}$ can be written in terms of $\mathbf{v_s}$ as

$$\mathbf{i_s} = \frac{\mathbf{v_s} - \mathbf{v_-}}{R_1} \tag{12.12}$$

where $\mathbf{v_-}$ is the voltage at the inverting input (negative input) of the op amp. But, Assumption 1 states that the input voltage $\mathbf{v_{id}}$ must be zero, so $\mathbf{v_-}$ must also be zero because the positive input is grounded:

$$\mathbf{v_{id}} = \mathbf{v_+} - \mathbf{v_-} = 0 \quad \text{but} \quad \mathbf{v_+} = 0 \text{ so } \mathbf{v_-} = 0$$

Because $\mathbf{v_-} = 0$,

$$\mathbf{i_s} = \frac{\mathbf{v_s}}{R_1} \tag{12.13}$$

and Eq. (12.11) reduces to

$$-\mathbf{v_s}\frac{R_2}{R_1} - \mathbf{v_o} = 0 \quad \text{or} \quad \mathbf{v_o} = -\mathbf{v_s}\frac{R_2}{R_1} \tag{12.14}$$

The voltage gain is given by

$$A_V = \frac{\mathbf{v_o}}{\mathbf{v_s}} = -\frac{R_2}{R_1} \tag{12.15}$$

An alternate approach to the same result is to use Eqs. (12.10) and (12.13), writing an expression similar to Eq. (12.13) for $\mathbf{i_2}$:

$$\mathbf{i_2} = \frac{\mathbf{v_-} - \mathbf{v_o}}{R_2} = -\frac{\mathbf{v_o}}{R_2} \tag{12.16}$$

Substituting Eqs. (12.13) and (12.16) into Eq. (12.10) results in

$$\frac{\mathbf{v_s}}{R_1} = -\frac{\mathbf{v_o}}{R_2} \tag{12.17}$$

which yields the same expression for the voltage gain, as does Eq. (12.15).

Referring to Eq. (12.15), we should note several things. The voltage gain is negative, indicative of an inverting amplifier with a 180° phase shift between dc or sinusoidal input and output signals. In addition, the gain can be greater than or equal to 1 if $R_2 \geq R_1$ (the most common case), but it can also be less than 1 for $R_1 > R_2$.

In the amplifier circuit in Figs. 12.5 and 12.6, the inverting-input terminal of the operational amplifier is at ground potential, 0 V, and is referred to as a **virtual ground.** The ideal operational amplifier adjusts its output to whatever voltage is necessary to force v_- to be zero. However, although it is a virtual ground, it is *not* connected directly to ground (there is no direct dc path for current to reach ground). Shorting this terminal to ground for analysis purposes is a common error that must be avoided.

> **EXERCISE:** Find A_V, v_o, i_s, and i_o for the amplifier in Fig. 12.6 if $R_1 = 68$ kΩ, $R_2 = 360$ kΩ, and $v_s = 0.5$ V.
>
> **ANSWERS:** -5.29, -2.65 V, 7.35 μA, -7.35 μA

Input and Output Resistances of the Ideal Inverting Amplifier

The input resistance R_{IN} of the overall amplifier is found directly from Eq. (12.13) to be

$$R_{\text{IN}} = \frac{\mathbf{v_s}}{\mathbf{i_i}} = R_1 \tag{12.18}$$

The output resistance R_{OUT} is the Thévenin equivalent resistance; it is found by applying a test signal current (or voltage) source to the output of the amplifier circuit and determining the voltage (or current), as in Fig. 12.7. All other *independent* voltage and current sources in the circuit must be turned off, and v_s is set to zero in Fig. 12.7.

The output resistance of the overall amplifier is defined by

$$R_{\text{OUT}} = \frac{\mathbf{v_x}}{\mathbf{i_x}} \tag{12.19}$$

Writing a single-loop equation for Fig. 12.7 gives

$$\mathbf{v_x} = \mathbf{i_2} R_2 + \mathbf{i_1} R_1 \tag{12.20}$$

but $\mathbf{i_1} = \mathbf{i_2}$ because $\mathbf{i_-} = 0$ based on op-amp Assumption 2. Therefore,

$$\mathbf{v_x} = \mathbf{i_1}(R_2 + R_1) \tag{12.21}$$

However, $\mathbf{i_1}$ must be zero because Assumption 1 tells us that $\mathbf{v_-} = 0$. Thus, $\mathbf{v_x} = 0$ independent of the value of $\mathbf{i_x}$, and

$$R_{\text{OUT}} = 0 \tag{12.22}$$

> **EXERCISE:** Design an inverting amplifier (choose R_1 and R_2) with an input resistance of 20 kΩ and a gain of 40 dB.
>
> **EXERCISE:** If $V_S = 2$ V, $R_1 = 4.7$ kΩ, and $R_2 = 24$ kΩ, find I_S, I_2, and V_O in Fig. 12.6. Why is the symbol V_S being used instead of v_s, and so on?
>
> **ANSWERS:** 20 kΩ, 2 MΩ; 0.426 mA, 0.426 mA, -10.2 V; the problem is stated specifically in terms of dc values.

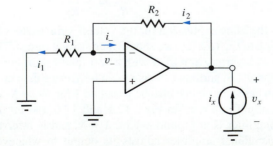

Figure 12.7 Test current applied to the amplifier to determine the output resistance: $R_{\text{OUT}} = \mathbf{v_x}/\mathbf{i_x}$.

The Noninverting Amplifier

The operational amplifier can also be used to construct a **noninverting amplifier** with the circuit indicated in the schematic in Fig. 12.8. The input signal is applied to the positive or (noninverting) input terminal of the operational amplifier, and a portion of the output signal is fed back to the negative input terminal. Analysis of the circuit is performed by relating the voltage at v_1 to both the input voltage v_s and the output voltage v_o.

Because Assumption 2 states that the input current i_- is zero, v_1 can be related to the output voltage through the voltage divider formed by R_1 and R_2:

$$\mathbf{v_1} = \mathbf{v_o}\frac{R_1}{R_1 + R_2} \tag{12.23}$$

and writing an equation around the loop including v_s, v_{id}, and v_1 yields a relation between $\mathbf{v_1}$ and $\mathbf{v_s}$:

$$\mathbf{v_s} - \mathbf{v_{id}} = \mathbf{v_1} \tag{12.24}$$

However, Assumption 1 requires that $\mathbf{v_{id}} = 0$, so

$$\mathbf{v_s} = \mathbf{v_1} \tag{12.25}$$

Combining Eqs. (12.23) and (12.25) and solving for $\mathbf{v_o}$ in terms of $\mathbf{v_s}$ gives

$$\mathbf{v_o} = \mathbf{v_s}\frac{R_1 + R_2}{R_1} \tag{12.26}$$

which yields an expression for the voltage gain of the noninverting amplifier:

$$A_V = \frac{\mathbf{v_o}}{\mathbf{v_s}} = \frac{R_1 + R_2}{R_1} = 1 + \frac{R_2}{R_1} \tag{12.27}$$

Note that the gain is positive and must be greater than or equal to 1 because R_1 and R_2 are positive numbers for real resistors.

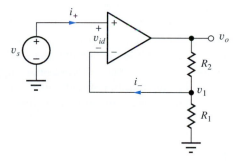

Figure 12.8 Noninverting amplifier configuration.

Input and Output Resistances of the Noninverting Amplifier

Using Assumption 2, we find that the input resistance of the noninverting amplifier is given by

$$R_{\text{IN}} = \frac{\mathbf{v_s}}{\mathbf{i_+}} = \infty \qquad \text{because } \mathbf{i_+} = 0 \tag{12.28}$$

To find the output resistance, a test current is applied to the output terminal and the source v_s is set to 0 V. The resulting circuit is identical to that in Fig. 12.7, so the output resistance of the noninverting amplifier is also zero.

EXERCISE: Draw the circuit used to determine the output resistance of the noninverting amplifier and convince yourself that it is indeed the same as Fig. 12.7.

EXERCISE: What are the voltage gain in dB and the input resistance of the amplifier shown here? If $v_s = 0.25$ V, what are the values of v_o and i_o?

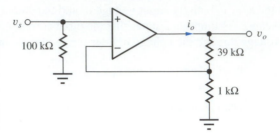

ANSWERS: 32.0 dB, 100 kΩ; +10.0 V, 0.250 mA

EXERCISE: Design a noninverting amplifier (choose R_1 and R_2 from Appendix C) to have a gain of 54 dB. The current $i_o \leq 0.1$ mA when $v_o = 10$ V.

ANSWERS: Two possibilities of many: (220 Ω and 110 kΩ) or (200 Ω and 100 kΩ)

The Unity-Gain Buffer, or Voltage Follower

A special case of the noninverting amplifier, known as the **unity-gain buffer,** or **voltage follower,** is shown in Fig. 12.9, in which the value of R_1 is infinite and that of R_2 is zero. Substituting these values in Eq. (12.27) yields $A_V = 1$. An alternative derivation can be obtained by writing a single-loop equation for Fig. 12.9:

$$\mathbf{v_s} - \mathbf{v_{id}} = \mathbf{v_o} \qquad \text{or} \qquad \mathbf{v_o} = \mathbf{v_s} \text{ and } A_V = 1 \qquad (12.29)$$

because the ideal operational amplifier forces $\mathbf{v_{id}}$ to be zero.

Why is such an amplifier useful? The ideal unity-gain buffer provides a gain of 1 with infinite input resistance and zero output resistance and therefore provides a tremendous impedance-level transformation while maintaining the level of the signal voltage. Many transducers represent high-source impedances and cannot supply any significant current to drive a load. The ideal unity-gain buffer, however, does not require any input current, yet can drive any desired load resistance without loss of signal voltage. Thus, the unity-gain buffer is found in many sensor and data acquisition applications.

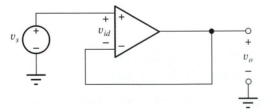

Figure 12.9 Unity-gain buffer (voltage follower).

Summary of Ideal Inverting and Noninverting Amplifier Characteristics

Table 12.1 summarizes the properties of the ideal inverting and noninverting amplifiers; the properties are recapitulated here. The gain of the noninverting amplifier must be greater

	Inverting Amplifier	Noninverting Amplifier
Table 12.1 Summary of the Ideal Inverting and Noninverting Amplifier		
Voltage gain A_V	$-\dfrac{R_2}{R_1}$	$1 + \dfrac{R_2}{R_1}$
Input resistance R_{IN}	R_1	∞
Output resistance R_{OUT}	0	0

than or equal to 1, whereas the inverting amplifier can be designed with a gain magnitude greater than or less than unity (as well as exactly 1). The gain of the inverting amplifier is negative, indicating a 180° phase inversion between input and output voltages.

The input resistance represents an additional major difference between the two amplifiers. R_{IN} is extremely large for the noninverting amplifier but is relatively low for the inverting amplifier, limited by the value of R_1. The output resistance of both ideal amplifiers is zero.

EXAMPLE 12.2: Let us explore these differences more fully with a numeric analysis of the two amplifiers. Each amplifier is designed to have a gain of 40 dB.

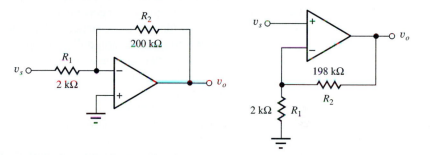

SOLUTIONS: Inverting amplifier: $A_V = -\dfrac{200 \text{ k}\Omega}{2 \text{ k}\Omega} = -100$ or 40 dB

$$R_{IN} = 2 \text{ k}\Omega \quad \text{and} \quad R_{OUT} = 0 \ \Omega$$

Noninverting amplifier: $A_V = 1 + \dfrac{198 \text{ k}\Omega}{2 \text{ k}\Omega} = +100$ or 40 dB

$$R_{IN} = \infty \quad \text{and} \quad R_{OUT} = 0 \ \Omega$$

COMMENTS: Table 12.2 (next page) compares the characteristics of the two amplifier designs. In addition to the sign inversion in the gain of the two amplifiers, we see that the input resistance of the inverting amplifier is only 2 kΩ, whereas that of the noninverting amplifier is infinite. Note that the noninverting amplifier achieves our ideal voltage amplifier goals. ◆

The Summing Amplifier

Operational amplifiers can also be used to combine signals using the **summing-amplifier** circuit depicted in Fig. 12.10. Here, two input sources v_1 and v_2 are connected to the

	Inverting Amplifier	Noninverting Amplifier
Table 12.2 Numeric Comparison of the Ideal Inverting and Noninverting Amplifier		
Voltage gain A_V	-100 (40 dB)	$+100$ (40 dB)
Input resistance R_{IN}	$2\ k\Omega$	∞
Output resistance R_{OUT}	0	0

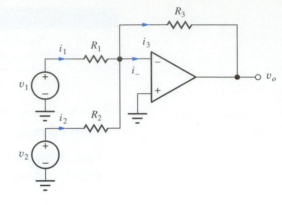

Figure 12.10 The summing amplifier.

inverting input of the amplifier through resistors R_1 and R_2. Because the negative amplifier input represents a virtual ground,

$$\mathbf{i_1} = \frac{\mathbf{v_1}}{R_1} \qquad \mathbf{i_2} = \frac{\mathbf{v_2}}{R_2} \qquad \mathbf{i_3} = -\frac{\mathbf{v_o}}{R_3} \tag{12.30}$$

Because $\mathbf{i_-} = \mathbf{0}$, $\mathbf{i_3} = \mathbf{i_1} + \mathbf{i_2}$, and substituting Eq. (12.30) into this expression yields

$$\mathbf{v_o} = -\frac{R_3}{R_1}\mathbf{v_1} - \frac{R_3}{R_2}\mathbf{v_2} \tag{12.31}$$

The output voltage sums the scaled replicas of the two input voltages, and the scale factors for the two inputs may be independently adjusted through the choice of resistors R_1 and R_2. These two inputs can be scaled independently because of the virtual ground maintained at the inverting-input terminal of the op amp.

The inverting-amplifier input node is also commonly called the **summing junction** because the currents i_1 and i_2 are "summed" at this node and forced through the feedback resistor R_3. Although the amplifier in Fig. 12.10 has only two inputs, any number of inputs can be connected to the summing junction through additional resistors. A simple digital-to-analog converter can be formed in this way (see Probs. 12.25 to 12.29).

> **EXERCISE:** What is the summing-amplifier output voltage v_o in Fig. 12.10 if $v_1 = 2\sin 1000\pi t$ V, $v_2 = 4\sin 2000\pi t$ V, $R_1 = 1$ kΩ, $R_2 = 2$ kΩ, and $R_3 = 3$ kΩ? What are the input resistances presented to sources v_1 and v_2? What is the current supplied by the op-amp output terminal?
>
> **ANSWERS:** $(-6\sin 1000\pi t - 6\sin 2000\pi t)$ V; 1 kΩ, 2 kΩ; $(-2\sin 1000\pi t - 2\sin 2000\pi t)$ mA

The Difference Amplifier

Except for the summing amplifier, all the circuits thus far have had a single input. However, the operational amplifier may itself be used in a **difference amplifier** configuration, which amplifies the difference between two input signals as shown schematically in Fig. 12.11. Our analysis begins by relating the output voltage to the voltage at v_- as

$$\mathbf{v_o} = \mathbf{v_-} - \mathbf{i_2}R_2 = \mathbf{v_-} - \mathbf{i_1}R_2 \tag{12.32}$$

because $\mathbf{i_2} = \mathbf{i_1}$ since $\mathbf{i_-}$ must be zero. The current $\mathbf{i_1}$ can be written as

$$\mathbf{i_1} = \frac{\mathbf{v_1} - \mathbf{v_-}}{R_1} \tag{12.33}$$

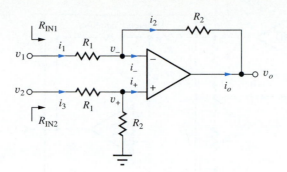

Figure 12.11 Circuit for the difference amplifier.

Combining Eqs. (12.32) and (12.33) yields

$$\mathbf{v_o} = \mathbf{v_-} - \frac{R_2}{R_1}(\mathbf{v_1} - \mathbf{v_-}) = \left(\frac{R_1 + R_2}{R_1}\right)\mathbf{v_-} - \frac{R_2}{R_1}\mathbf{v_1} \qquad (12.34)$$

Because the voltage between the op-amp input terminals must be zero, $\mathbf{v_-} = \mathbf{v_+}$, and the current $\mathbf{i_+}$ is also zero, $\mathbf{v_+}$ can be written as

$$\mathbf{v_+} = \frac{R_2}{R_1 + R_2}\mathbf{v_2} \qquad (12.35)$$

using the voltage division formula. Substituting Eq. (12.35) into Eq. (12.34) yields the final result

$$\mathbf{v_o} = \left(-\frac{R_2}{R_1}\right)(\mathbf{v_1} - \mathbf{v_2}) \qquad (12.36)$$

Thus, the circuit in Fig. 12.11 amplifies the difference between v_1 and v_2 by a factor that is determined by the ratio of resistors R_2 and R_1. For $R_2 = R_1$,

$$\mathbf{v_o} = -(\mathbf{v_1} - \mathbf{v_2}) \qquad (12.37)$$

This particular circuit is sometimes called a **differential subtractor.**

The input resistance of this circuit, however, is limited by resistors R_2 and R_1. Input resistance R_{IN2}, presented to source v_2, is simply the series combination of R_2 and R_1 because i_+ is zero. For $v_2 = 0$, input resistance R_{IN1} equals R_1 because the circuit reduces to the inverting amplifier under this condition. However, for the general case, the input current i_1 is a function of both v_1 and v_2.

> **EXERCISE:** Suppose $V_1 = 5$ V, $V_2 = 3$ V, $R_1 = 10$ kΩ, and $R_2 = 100$ kΩ in Fig. 12.11. What are the values of V_O, V_+, V_-, I_1, I_2, I_3, and I_O?
>
> **ANSWERS:** -20 V, 2.73 V, 2.73 V, 227 μA, 227 μA, 27.3 μA, -227 μA

The Instrumentation-Amplifier Configuration

We often need to amplify the difference in two signals but cannot use the difference amplifier in Fig. 12.11 because its input resistance is too low. In such a case, we can combine two noninverting amplifiers with a difference amplifier to form the high-performance composite **instrumentation amplifier** depicted in Fig. 12.12.

In this circuit, op amp 3, with resistors R_3 and R_4, forms a difference amplifier. Using Eq. (12.36), the output voltage $\mathbf{v_o}$ is

$$\mathbf{v_o} = \left(-\frac{R_4}{R_3}\right)(\mathbf{v_a} - \mathbf{v_b}) \qquad (12.38)$$

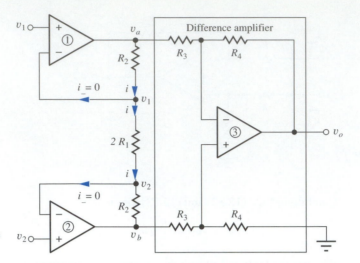

Figure 12.12 Circuit for the instrumentation amplifier.

in which voltages $\mathbf{v_a}$ and $\mathbf{v_b}$ are the outputs of the first two amplifiers. Because the $\mathbf{i_-}$ input currents to amplifiers 1 and 2 must be zero, voltages $\mathbf{v_a}$ and $\mathbf{v_b}$ are related to each other by

$$\mathbf{v_a} - \mathbf{i}R_2 - \mathbf{i}(2R_1) - \mathbf{i}R_2 = \mathbf{v_b} \tag{12.39}$$

or

$$\mathbf{v_a} - \mathbf{v_b} = 2\mathbf{i}(R_1 + R_2) \tag{12.40}$$

Because the voltage across the inputs of both op amps 1 and 2 must also be zero, the voltage difference $(\mathbf{v_1} - \mathbf{v_2})$ appears directly across the resistor $2R_1$, and

$$\mathbf{i} = \frac{\mathbf{v_1} - \mathbf{v_2}}{2R_1} \tag{12.41}$$

Combining Eqs. (12.38), (12.40), and (12.41) yields a final expression for the output voltage of the instrumentation amplifier:

$$\mathbf{v_o} = -\frac{R_4}{R_3}\left(1 + \frac{R_2}{R_1}\right)(\mathbf{v_1} - \mathbf{v_2}) \tag{12.42}$$

The ideal instrumentation amplifier amplifies the difference in the two input signals and provides a gain that is equivalent to the product of the gains of the noninverting and difference amplifiers. The input resistance presented to both input sources is infinite because the input current to both op amps is zero, and the output resistance is forced to zero by the difference amplifier.

Exercise: Suppose $V_1 = 5.001$ V, $V_2 = 4.999$ V, $R_1 = 1$ kΩ, $R_2 = 49$ kΩ, $R_3 = 10$ kΩ, and $R_4 = 10$ kΩ in Fig. 12.12. Write expressions for V_A and V_B. What are the values of V_O, V_A, V_B, and I?

Answers: $V_A = V_1 + IR_2$, $V_B = V_2 - IR_2$; -0.100 V, 5.05 V, 4.95 V, 1.00 μA

A Low-Pass Filter

Although the operational-amplifier circuit examples thus far have used only resistors in the feedback network, other passive elements or even solid-state devices can be part of the feedback path. The general case of the inverting configuration with passive feedback is shown in Fig. 12.13, in which resistors R_1 and R_2 have been replaced by general impedances $Z_1(s)$

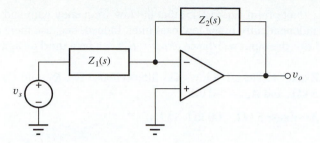

Figure 12.13 Generalized inverting-amplifier configuration.

and $Z_2(s)$, which may now be a function of frequency. (Note that resistive feedback is just one special case of the amplifier in Fig. 12.13.)

The gain of the amplifier in this figure is obtained in a manner identical to that in the resistive-feedback case. Replacing R_1 by Z_1 and R_2 by Z_2 in Eq. (12.15) yields the transfer function $A_V(s)$:

$$A_V(s) = \frac{\mathbf{V_o}(s)}{\mathbf{V_s}(s)} = -\frac{Z_2(s)}{Z_1(s)} \qquad (12.43)$$

One useful circuit involving frequency-dependent feedback is the single-pole, **low-pass filter** in Fig. 12.14, for which

$$Z_1(s) = R_1 \qquad \text{and} \qquad Z_2(s) = \frac{R_2 \dfrac{1}{sC}}{R_2 + \dfrac{1}{sC}} = \frac{R_2}{sCR_2 + 1} \qquad (12.44)$$

Substituting the results from Eq. (12.44) into Eq. (12.43) yields an expression for the voltage transfer function for the amplifier in Fig. 12.14.

$$A_V(s) = -\frac{R_2}{R_1}\frac{1}{sCR_2 + 1} = -\frac{R_2}{R_1}\frac{1}{\dfrac{s}{\omega_H} + 1} \qquad \text{where } \omega_H = 2\pi f_H = \frac{1}{R_2 C} \qquad (12.45)$$

Figure 12.15 is the asymptotic Bode plot of the magnitude of the gain in Eq. (12.45). The transfer function exhibits a low-pass characteristic with a single pole at frequency ω_H, the upper-cutoff frequency (-3 dB point) of the low-pass filter. At frequencies below ω_H, the amplifier behaves as an inverting amplifier with gain set by the ratio of resistors R_2 and R_1; at frequencies above ω_H, the amplifier response rolls off at a rate of -20 dB/decade.

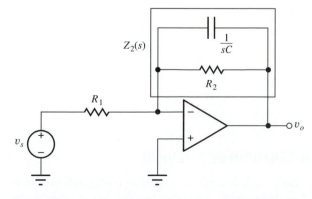

Figure 12.14 Inverting amplifier with frequency-dependent feedback.

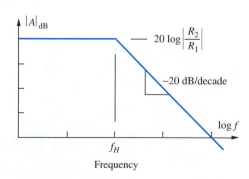

Figure 12.15 Bode plot of the voltage gain of the low-pass filter.

Note from Eq. (12.45) that the low-frequency gain and the cutoff frequency can be set independently in the low-pass filter. Indeed, because there are three elements—R_1, R_2, and C—the input resistance ($R_{IN} = R_1$) can be a third design parameter.

> **EXERCISE:** Design a low-pass filter (choose R_1, R_2, and C) with $f_H = 2$ kHz, $R_{IN} = 5$ kΩ, and $A_V = 40$ dB.
>
> **ANSWERS:** 5 kΩ, 500 kΩ, 159 pF

Integrator

The **integrator** is another highly useful building block formed from an operational amplifier with frequency-dependent feedback. In the integrator circuit, feedback-resistor R_2 is replaced by capacitor C, as in Fig. 12.16. This circuit provides an opportunity to explore op-amp circuit analysis in the time domain (for frequency-domain analysis, see Prob. 12.71). Because the inverting-input terminal represents a virtual ground,

$$i_s = \frac{v_s}{R} \qquad \text{and} \qquad i_c = -C\frac{dv_o}{dt} \qquad (12.46)$$

For an ideal op amp, $i_- = 0$, so i_c must equal i_s. Equating the two expressions in Eq. (12.46) and integrating both sides of the result yields

$$\int dv_o = \int -\frac{1}{RC}v_s\, d\tau \qquad \text{or} \qquad v_o(t) = -\frac{1}{RC}\int_0^t v_s(\tau)\, d\tau + v_o(0) \qquad (12.47)$$

in which the initial value of the output voltage is determined by the voltage on the capacitor at $t = 0$: $v_o(0) = V_C(0)$. Thus the voltage at the output of this circuit at any time t represents the initial capacitor voltage plus the integral of the input signal from the start of the integration interval, chosen in this case to be $t = 0$.

> **EXERCISE:** Suppose the input voltage $v_s(t)$ to an integrator is a 500-Hz square wave with a peak-to-peak amplitude of 10 V and 0 dc value. Choose the values of R and C in the integrator so that the peak output voltage will be 10 V and $R_{IN} = 10$ kΩ.
>
> **ANSWERS:** 10 kΩ, 0.05 μF

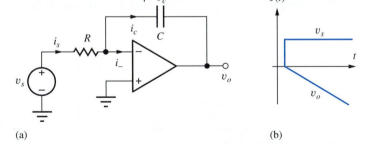

Figure 12.16 (a) The integrator circuit. (b) Output voltage for a step-function input with $v_C(0) = 0$.

(a) (b)

12.4 AMPLIFIER TERMINOLOGY REVIEW

Now that we have analyzed a number of amplifier configurations, let us step back and review the terminology being used. Amplifier terminology is often a source of confusion because the portion of the circuit that is being called an *amplifier* must often be determined from the context of the discussion.

In Fig. 12.17 for example, an overall amplifier (the three-stage amplifier) is formed from the cascade connection of three inverting amplifiers (A, B, C), and each inverting amplifier has been implemented using an operational amplifier (op amp 1, 2, 3). Thus, we can identify at least seven different "amplifiers" in Fig. 12.17: operational amplifiers 1, 2, 3; inverting amplifiers A, B, C; and the composite three-stage amplifier ABC.

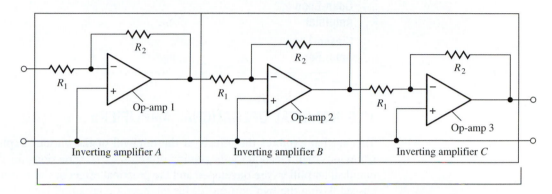

Figure 12.17 Three-stage amplifier cascade.

Two-Port Representations

At each level in Fig. 12.17, we can represent the "amplifier" as a **two-port model** with a value of voltage gain, input resistance, and output resistance, defined as in Fig. 12.18. Each amplifier stage—A, B, and C—is built using an operational amplifier that has a gain A, input resistance R_{ID}, and output resistance R_O. These quantities are usually called the open-loop parameters of the operational amplifier: *open-loop gain, open-loop input resistance,* and *open-loop output resistance*. They describe the op amp as a two-port by itself with no external elements connected.

Each single-stage amplifier built from an operational amplifier and the feedback network consisting of R_1 and R_2 is termed a **closed-loop amplifier.** We use A_V, R_{IN}, and R_{OUT} for each closed-loop amplifier, as well as for the overall composite amplifier. Table 12.3 on the following page summarizes this terminology.

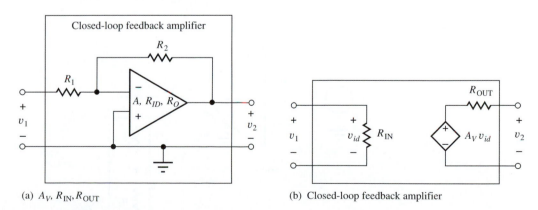

(a) A_V, R_{IN}, R_{OUT}

(b) Closed-loop feedback amplifier

Figure 12.18 (a) Inverting amplifier using an operational amplifier. (b) Two-port representation of the overall amplifier.

Feedback-Amplifier Terminology Comparison

	Voltage Gain	Input Resistance	Output Resistance
Open-Loop Amplifier	A	R_{ID}	R_O
Closed-Loop Amplifier	A_V	R_{IN}	R_{OUT}

12.5 NONIDEAL OPERATIONAL AMPLIFIERS

This section explores the effects of the removal of the various explicit and implicit assumptions mentioned at the beginning of Sec. 12.2. Expressions for the characteristics of nonideal amplifiers are developed and the practical effect of the various error terms is discussed. Using the two-port model for the operational amplifier in Fig. 12.18, we explore the effects of one nonideal parameter at a time.

Finite Open-Loop Gain

A real operational amplifier provides a large but noninfinite gain. Op amps are commercially available with minimum open-loop gains of 80 dB (10,000) to over 120 dB (1,000,000). The finite open-loop gain contributes to deviations of the **closed-loop gain,** input resistance, and output resistance from those presented for the ideal amplifier in Table 12.1.

Evaluation of the closed-loop gain for the noninverting amplifier of Fig. 12.19 provides our first example of amplifier calculations involving nonideal amplifiers. In Fig. 12.19, the output voltage of the amplifier is given by

$$\mathbf{v_o} = A\mathbf{v_{id}} \qquad \text{where } \mathbf{v_{id}} = \mathbf{v_s} - \mathbf{v_1} \qquad (12.48)$$

Because $i_- = 0$ by Assumption 2, v_1 is set by the voltage divider formed by resistors R_1 and R_2:

$$\mathbf{v_1} = \frac{R_1}{R_1 + R_2}\mathbf{v_o} = \beta\mathbf{v_o} \qquad \text{where } \beta = \frac{R_1}{R_1 + R_2} \qquad (12.49)$$

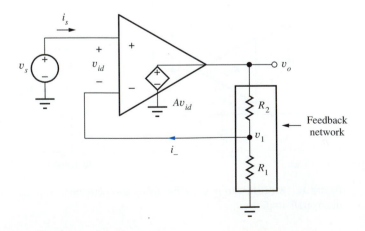

Figure 12.19 Operational amplifier with finite open-loop gain A.

The parameter β is called the **feedback factor** and represents the fraction of the output voltage that is fed back from the output to the input.

Combining Eqs. (12.48) and (12.49) gives

$$\mathbf{v_o} = A(\mathbf{v_s} - \beta\mathbf{v_o}) \tag{12.50}$$

and solving for $\mathbf{v_o}$ yields the classic **feedback amplifier** voltage-gain formula in Eq. (12.51).

$$A_V = \frac{\mathbf{v_o}}{\mathbf{v_s}} = \frac{A}{1+A\beta} \tag{12.51}$$

The product $A\beta$ is called the **loop gain** (or **loop transmission T**) and plays an important role in feedback amplifiers. For $A\beta \gg 1$, A_V approaches the ideal gain expression found previously:

$$A_{\text{ideal}} = \frac{1}{\beta} = 1 + \frac{R_2}{R_1} \tag{12.52}$$

The meaning of the loop gain is explored more fully in Chapter 18, which is dedicated to the study of feedback systems.

The voltage $\mathbf{v_{id}}$ across the input is given by

$$\mathbf{v_{id}} = \mathbf{v_s} - \mathbf{v_1} = \mathbf{v_s} - \beta\mathbf{v_o} = \mathbf{v_s} - \frac{A\beta}{1+A\beta}\mathbf{v_s} = \frac{\mathbf{v_s}}{1+A\beta} \tag{12.53}$$

Although $\mathbf{v_{id}}$ is no longer zero, it is small for large values of $A\beta$.

EXERCISE: Suppose $A = 10^5$, $\beta = 1/100$, and $v_S = 100$ mV. What are v_o and v_{id}?

ANSWERS: 10.0 V, 0.100 mV (v_{id} is small but nonzero)

Gain Error

In many applications it is important to know, or to control by design, just how far the actual gain in Eq. (12.51) deviates from the ideal gain expression in Eq. (12.52). The **gain error (GE)** is defined as the difference between the ideal gain and the actual gain:

$$\text{GE} = (\text{ideal gain}) - (\text{actual gain}) \tag{12.54}$$

This error is more often expressed as a fractional error or percentage error, and the **fractional gain error (FGE)** is defined as

$$\text{FGE} = \frac{(\text{ideal gain}) - (\text{actual gain})}{(\text{ideal gain})} \tag{12.55}$$

For the noninverting amplifier in Fig. 12.19, the gain error is given by

$$\text{GE} = \frac{1}{\beta} - \frac{A}{1+A\beta} = \frac{1}{\beta(1+A\beta)} \tag{12.56}$$

and

$$\text{FGE} = \frac{\dfrac{1}{\beta} - \dfrac{A}{1+A\beta}}{\dfrac{1}{\beta}} = \frac{1}{1+A\beta} \approx \frac{1}{A\beta} \quad \text{for } A\beta \gg 1 \tag{12.57}$$

For $A\beta \gg 1$, we see that the value of the FGE is determined by the reciprocal of the loop gain $A\beta$.

EXAMPLE 12.3: Suppose a noninverting amplifier is designed to have a gain of 200 (46 dB) and is built using an operational amplifier with an open-loop gain of 80 dB. What are the values of the ideal gain, the actual gain, and the gain error in percent?

SOLUTION: First, we need to clarify the meaning of some terminology. We normally design an amplifier to produce a given value of ideal gain, and then determine the deviations to be expected from the ideal case. So, when it is said that this amplifier is designed to have a gain of 200, we set $\beta = \frac{1}{200}$. We do not normally try to adjust the design values of R_1 and R_2 to try to compensate for the finite open-loop gain of the amplifier. One reason is that we do not know the exact value of the gain A but generally have only a lower bound. Also, the resistors we use have tolerances, and their exact values are also unknown.

Hence, for this example, the ideal gain = 200. The actual gain and FGE are given by

$$A_v = \frac{A}{1 + A\beta} = \frac{10^4}{1 + \frac{10^4}{200}} = 196 \qquad \text{and} \qquad \text{FGE} = \frac{200 - 196}{200} = 0.02 \text{ or } 2\%$$

COMMENTS: The actual gain is 196, representing a 2 percent error from the ideal design gain of 200. Note that this gain error expression does not include the effects of resistor tolerances, which are an additional source of gain error in an actual circuit. If the gain must be more precise, a higher-gain op amp must be used, or the resistors can be replaced by a potentiometer so the gain can be adjusted manually.   ◆

Nonzero Output Resistance

The next effect we explore is the influence of a nonzero output resistance on the characteristics of the inverting and noninverting closed-loop amplifiers. In this case, we assume that the op amp has a nonzero output resistance R_O as well as a finite open-loop gain A. (As we shall see, finite gain must also be assumed; otherwise, we would get the same output resistance as for the ideal case.)

To determine the (Thévenin equivalent) output resistances of the two amplifiers in Fig. 12.20, each output terminal is driven with a test signal source v_x (a current source could also be used), and the current i_x is calculated; all other independent sources in the network must be turned off. The output resistance is then given by

$$R_{\text{OUT}} = \frac{\mathbf{v_x}}{\mathbf{i_x}} \tag{12.58}$$

From Fig. 12.20 we observe that the two amplifier circuits are identical for the output resistance calculation. Thus, analysis of the circuit in Fig. 12.21 gives the expression for R_{OUT} for both the inverting and noninverting amplifiers.

Analysis begins by expressing current $\mathbf{i_x}$ as

$$\mathbf{i_x} = \mathbf{i_o} + \mathbf{i_2} \tag{12.59}$$

and $\mathbf{i_o}$ can be related to $\mathbf{v_x}$ by

$$\mathbf{i_o} = \frac{\mathbf{v_x} - A\mathbf{v_{id}}}{R_O} \tag{12.60}$$

The current $\mathbf{i_2}$ can be found from

$$\mathbf{v_x} = \mathbf{i_2}R_2 + \mathbf{i_1}R_1 = \mathbf{i_2}(R_1 + R_2) \qquad \text{or} \qquad \mathbf{i_2} = \frac{\mathbf{v_x}}{R_1 + R_2} \tag{12.61}$$

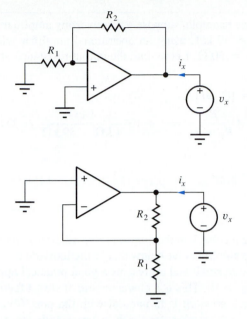

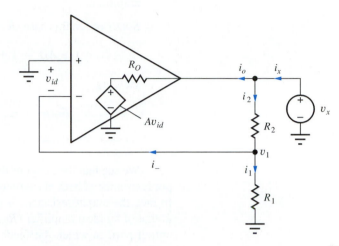

Figure 12.20 Circuits for determining output resistances of the inverting and noninverting amplifiers.

Figure 12.21 Circuit explicitly showing amplifier with A and R_O.

because $\mathbf{i_1} = \mathbf{i_2}$ due to op-amp Assumption 2: $\mathbf{i_-} = 0$. The input voltage $\mathbf{v_{id}}$ is equal to $-\mathbf{v_1}$, and because $\mathbf{i_-} = 0$,

$$\mathbf{v_1} = \frac{R_1}{R_1 + R_2}\mathbf{v_x} = \beta\mathbf{v_x} \tag{12.62}$$

Combining Eqs. (12.59) through (12.62) yields

$$\frac{1}{R_{\text{OUT}}} = \frac{\mathbf{i_x}}{\mathbf{v_x}} = \frac{1 + A\beta}{R_O} + \frac{1}{R_1 + R_2} \tag{12.63}$$

Equation (12.63) represents the output conductance of the amplifier and corresponds to the sum of the conductances of two parallel resistors. Thus the output resistance can be expressed as

$$R_{\text{OUT}} = \frac{R_O}{1 + A\beta}\|(R_1 + R_2) \tag{12.64}$$

The output resistance in Eq. (12.63) represents the series combination of R_1 and R_2 in parallel with a resistance $R_O/(1 + A\beta)$ that represents the output resistance of the operational amplifier including the effects of feedback. In almost every practical situation, the value of $R_O/(1 + A\beta)$ is much less than that of $(R_1 + R_2)$, and the output resistance expression in Eq. (12.64) simplifies to

$$R_{\text{OUT}} \approx \frac{R_O}{1 + A\beta} \tag{12.65}$$

An example of the degree of dominance of the resistance term in Eq. (12.64) is given in Example 12.4.

Note that the output resistance would be zero if A were assumed to be infinite in Eqs. (12.64) or (12.65). This is the reason why the analysis must simultaneously account for both finite A and nonzero R_O.

EXAMPLE 12.4: As a numeric example, suppose a noninverting amplifier is designed with $R_1 = 1$ kΩ and $R_2 = 39$ kΩ, using an operational amplifier with an open-loop gain of 80 dB and $R_O = 50$ Ω. Let us find the output resistance of the overall amplifier.

SOLUTION: In this case, $A = 10^4$ and

$$1 + A\beta = 1 + A\frac{R_1}{R_1 + R_2} = 1 + 10^4 \frac{1 \text{ kΩ}}{1 \text{ kΩ} + 39 \text{ kΩ}} = 251$$

yielding

$$R_{\text{OUT}} = \frac{50 \text{ Ω}}{251} \,\|\, (40 \text{ kΩ}) = 0.199 \text{ Ω} \,\|\, 40 \text{ kΩ} = 0.198 \text{ Ω}$$

◆

We see that the effect of the feedback in the circuit in Fig. 12.20 is to reduce the output resistance of both closed-loop amplifiers far below that of the individual op amp itself. In fact, the output resistance is quite small and represents a good practical approximation to that of an ideal amplifier ($R_{\text{OUT}} = 0$). This is a characteristic of **shunt feedback** at the output port, in which the feedback network is in parallel with the port. Shunt feedback tends to lower the resistance at a port, whereas feedback in series with a port, termed **series feedback,** tends to raise the resistance at that port. The properties of series and shunt feedback are explored in greater detail in Chapter 18.

EXERCISE: What is the gain error (in percent) for the amplifier in the previous example?

ANSWER: 0.40 percent

EXERCISE: Suppose the resistors both have 5 percent tolerances. What are the worst-case (highest and lowest) values of gain that can be expected if the open-loop gain were infinite? What is the gain error for each of these two cases?

ANSWERS: 44.1, 36.3, +10.3 percent, −9.25 percent

EXERCISE: A noninverting amplifier must have a closed-loop gain of 40 dB and an output resistance of less than 0.1 Ω. The only op amp available has an output resistance of 200 Ω. What is the minimum open-loop gain of the op amp that will meet the requirements?

ANSWER: 106 dB

Finite Input Resistance

Next we explore the effect of the finite input resistance of the operational amplifier on the open-loop input resistances of the noninverting and inverting amplifier configurations. In this case, we shall find that the results are greatly different for the two amplifiers.

Let us first consider the noninverting amplifier circuit in Fig. 12.22, in which test source $\mathbf{v_x}$ is applied to the input. To find R_{IN}, we must calculate the current $\mathbf{i_x}$ given by

$$\mathbf{i_x} = \frac{\mathbf{v_x} - \mathbf{v_1}}{R_{ID}} \tag{12.66}$$

The voltage $\mathbf{v_1}$ is equal to

$$\mathbf{v_1} = \mathbf{i_1}R_1 = (\mathbf{i_2} - \mathbf{i_-})R_1 \approx \mathbf{i_2}R_1 \tag{12.67}$$

which has been simplified by assuming that the input current $\mathbf{i_-}$ to the op amp can still be neglected with respect to $\mathbf{i_2}$. We will check this assumption shortly. The assumption is

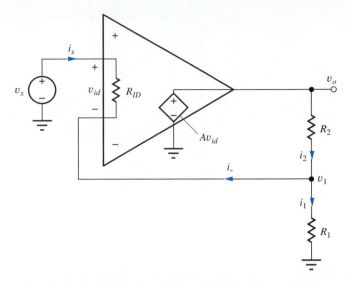

Figure 12.22 Input resistance of the noninverting amplifier.

equivalent to saying that $i_1 \approx i_2$ and permits the voltage v_1 to again be written in terms of the resistive voltage divider as

$$\mathbf{v_1} \approx \frac{R_1}{R_1 + R_2}\mathbf{v_o} = \beta\mathbf{v_o} = \beta(A\mathbf{v_{id}}) = A\beta(\mathbf{v_x} - \mathbf{v_1}) \qquad (12.68)$$

Solving for $\mathbf{v_1}$ in terms of $\mathbf{v_x}$ yields

$$\mathbf{v_1} = \frac{A\beta}{1 + A\beta}\mathbf{v_x} \qquad (12.69)$$

and substituting this result into Eq. (12.66) yields an expression for R_{IN}

$$\mathbf{i_x} = \frac{\mathbf{v_x} - \dfrac{A\beta}{1 + A\beta}\mathbf{v_x}}{R_{ID}} = \frac{\mathbf{v_x}}{(1 + A\beta)R_{ID}} \qquad \text{and} \qquad R_{IN} = R_{ID}(1 + A\beta) \quad (12.70)$$

Note from Eq. (12.70) that the input resistance can be very large—much larger than that of the op amp itself. R_{ID} is often large (1 MΩ to 1 TΩ) to start with, and it is multiplied by the loop gain $A\beta$, which is typically designed to be much greater than 1.

> **EXERCISE:** Suppose a noninverting amplifier has $R_{ID} = 1$ MΩ, with $R_1 = 10$ kΩ and $R_2 = 390$ kΩ, and the open-loop gain is 80 dB. What is the input resistance of the overall amplifier? What are the currents I_- and I_1 for a dc input voltage $V_S = 1$ V? Is $I_- \ll I_1$?
>
> **ANSWERS:** 251 MΩ; -3.98 nA, 100 μA; yes

For the numbers in the preceding exercise, it is easy to see that the current $\mathbf{i_-}$, which equals $-\mathbf{i_x}$, is small compared to the current through R_2 and R_1 (see Prob. 12.34). Thus, our simplifying assumption that led to Eqs. (12.67) and (12.68) is well justified.

Input Resistance for the Inverting-Amplifier Configuration

The input resistance of the inverting amplifier can be determined using the circuit in Fig. 12.23(a). The input resistance is

$$R_{IN} = \frac{\mathbf{v_x}}{\mathbf{i_x}} \qquad (12.71)$$

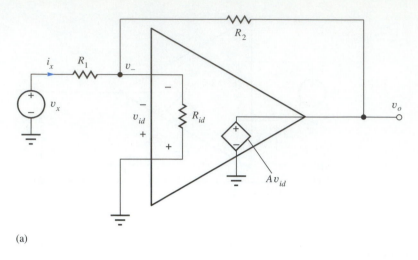

(a)

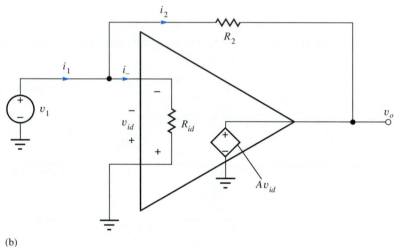

Figure 12.23 Inverting amplifier input-resistance calculation: (a) complete amplifier, (b) amplifier with R_1 removed.

(b)

where the test signal $\mathbf{v_x}$ can be expressed as

$$\mathbf{v_x} = \mathbf{i_x}R_1 + \mathbf{v_-} \qquad \text{and} \qquad R_{\text{IN}} = R_1 + \frac{\mathbf{v_-}}{\mathbf{i_x}} \tag{12.72}$$

The total input resistance R_{IN} is equal to R_1 plus the resistance looking into the inverting terminal of the operational amplifier, which can be found using the circuit in Fig. 12.23(b). The input current in Fig. 12.23(b) is

$$\mathbf{i_1} = \mathbf{i_-} + \mathbf{i_2} = \frac{\mathbf{v_1}}{R_{ID}} + \frac{\mathbf{v_1} - \mathbf{v_o}}{R_2} = \frac{\mathbf{v_1}}{R_{ID}} + \frac{\mathbf{v_1} + A\mathbf{v_1}}{R_2} \tag{12.73}$$

Using this result, the input conductance can be written as

$$G_1 = \frac{\mathbf{i_1}}{\mathbf{v_1}} = \frac{1}{R_{ID}} + \frac{1+A}{R_2} \tag{12.74}$$

which represents the sum of two conductances. Thus, the equivalent resistance looking into the inverting-input terminal is the parallel combination of two resistors,

$$R_{ID} \left\| \left(\frac{R_2}{1+A} \right) \right. \tag{12.75}$$

and the overall input resistance of the inverting amplifier becomes

$$R_{\text{IN}} = R_1 + R_{ID} \left\| \left(\frac{R_2}{1 + A} \right) \right. \tag{12.76}$$

Normally, R_{ID} will be large and Eq. (12.76) can be approximated by

$$R_{\text{IN}} \approx R_1 + \left(\frac{R_2}{1 + A} \right) \tag{12.77}$$

For large A and common values of R_2, the input resistance approaches the ideal result $R_{\text{IN}} \approx R_1$. In other words, we see that the input resistance is usually dominated by R_1 connected to the quasi virtual ground at the op-amp input. (Remember, v_{id} is no longer zero for a finite-gain amplifier.)

> **EXERCISE:** Find the input resistance R_{IN} of an inverting amplifier that has $R_1 = 1\ \text{k}\Omega$, $R_2 = 100\ \text{k}\Omega$, $R_{ID} = 1\ \text{M}\Omega$, and $A = 100\ \text{dB}$. What is the deviation of R_{IN} from its ideal value?
>
> **ANSWERS:** $1001\ \Omega$; $1\ \Omega$ out of $1000\ \Omega$ or 0.1 percent

Summary of Nonideal Inverting and Noninverting Amplifiers

Table 12.4 is a summary of the simplified expressions for the closed-loop voltage gain, input resistance, and output resistance of the inverting and noninverting amplifiers. These equations are most often used in the design of these basic amplifier circuits.

T a b l e 12.4		
Inverting and Noninverting Amplifier Summary		
$\beta = \dfrac{R_1}{R_1 + R_2}$	**Inverting Amplifier**	**Noninverting Amplifier**
Voltage Gain A_V	$-\dfrac{R_2}{R_1}\left(\dfrac{A\beta}{1+A\beta}\right) \approx -\dfrac{R_2}{R_1}$	$\dfrac{A}{1+A\beta} \approx \dfrac{1}{\beta} = 1 + \dfrac{R_2}{R_1}$
Input Resistance R_{IN}	$R_1 + R_{ID}\left\|\dfrac{R_2}{1+A}\right. \approx R_1$	$R_{ID}(1+A\beta) \approx R_{ID}A\beta$
Output Resistance R_{OUT}	$\dfrac{R_O}{1+A\beta} \approx \dfrac{R_O}{A\beta}$	$\dfrac{R_O}{1+A\beta} \approx \dfrac{R_O}{A\beta}$

Finite Common-Mode Rejection Ratio

Unfortunately, the output voltage of the real amplifier in Fig. 12.24 (p. 512) contains components in addition to the scaled replica of the input voltage (Av_{id}). In particular, a real amplifier also responds to the signal that is in common to both inputs, called the **common-mode input voltage v_{ic}** defined as

$$v_{ic} = \left(\frac{v_1 + v_2}{2} \right) \tag{12.78}$$

The common-mode input signal is amplified by the **common-mode gain** A_{cm} to give an overall output voltage expressed by

$$v_o = A(v_1 - v_2) + A_{cm}\left(\frac{v_1 + v_2}{2}\right) \tag{12.79}$$

Equation (12.79) is often written as

$$v_o = A(v_{id}) + A_{cm}(v_{ic}) \tag{12.80}$$

where A (or A_{dm}) = **differential-mode gain**
A_{cm} = common-mode gain
$v_{id} = (v_1 - v_2)$ = differential-mode input voltage
$v_{ic} = \left(\dfrac{v_1 + v_2}{2}\right)$ = common-mode input voltage

Simultaneous solution of these last two equations allows voltages v_1 and v_2 to be expressed in terms of v_{ic} and v_{id} as

$$v_1 = v_{ic} + \frac{v_{id}}{2} \qquad \text{and} \qquad v_2 = v_{ic} - \frac{v_{id}}{2} \tag{12.81}$$

and the amplifier in Fig. 12.24 can be redrawn in terms of v_{ic} and v_{id}, as in Fig. 12.25.

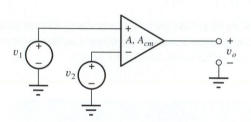

Figure 12.24 Operational amplifier with inputs v_1 and v_2.

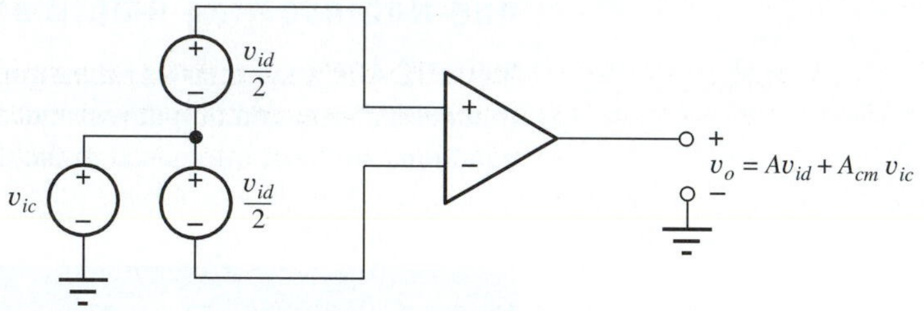

Figure 12.25 Operational amplifier with common-mode and differential-mode inputs shown explicitly.

An ideal amplifier would amplify the **differential-mode input voltage** v_{id} and totally reject the common-mode input signal ($A_{cm} = 0$), as has been tacitly assumed thus far. However, an actual amplifier has a nonzero value of A_{cm}, and Eq. (12.80) is often rewritten in a slightly different form by factoring out A:

$$v_o = A\left[v_{id} + \frac{A_{cm}v_{ic}}{A}\right] = A\left[v_{id} + \frac{v_{ic}}{\text{CMRR}}\right] \tag{12.82}$$

In this equation, **CMRR** is the **common-mode rejection ratio,** defined by the ratio of A and A_{cm}

$$\text{CMRR} = \left|\frac{A}{A_{cm}}\right| \tag{12.83}$$

CMRR is often expressed in dB as

$$\text{CMRR}_{\text{dB}} = 20\log\left|\frac{A}{A_{cm}}\right| \text{ dB} \tag{12.84}$$

An ideal amplifier has $A_{cm} = 0$ and therefore infinite CMRR. Actual amplifiers usually have $A \gg A_{cm}$, and the CMRR typically falls in the range

$$60 \text{ dB} \le \text{CMRR}_{\text{dB}} \le 120 \text{ dB}$$

A value of 60 dB is a relatively poor level of common-mode rejection, whereas achieving 120 dB (or even higher) is possible but difficult. Generally, the sign of A_{cm} is unknown ahead of time. In addition, CMRR specifications represent a lower bound. An illustration of the problems that can be caused by ignorance of errors caused by finite common-mode rejection is given in Example 12.5.

EXAMPLE 12.5: Suppose the amplifier in Fig. 12.24 has a differential-mode gain of 250 and a CMRR of 80 dB. What is the output voltage if $v_1 = 5.001$ V and $v_2 = 4.999$ V? What is the error introduced by the finite CMRR?

SOLUTION: A CMRR specification of 80 dB corresponds to CMRR $= \pm 10^4$. Let us assume CMRR $= +10^4$ for this example. The differential- and common-mode input voltages are

$$v_{id} = 5.001 \text{ V} - 4.999 \text{ V} = 0.002 \text{ V}$$

and
$$v_{ic} = \frac{5.001 + 4.999}{2} = 5.000 \text{ V}$$

$$v_o = A\left[v_{id} + \frac{v_{ic}}{\text{CMRR}}\right] = 250\left[0.002 + \frac{5.000}{10^4}\right] \text{ V}$$

$$= 250[0.002 + 0.0005] \text{ V} = 0.625 \text{ V}$$

An ideal amplifier would amplify only v_{id} and produce an output voltage of 0.500 V. For this particular situation, the output voltage is in error by 25 percent due to the finite common-mode rejection of the amplifier. Common-mode rejection is often important in measurements of small voltage differences in the presence of large common-mode voltages, as in the example shown here.

$$\text{(Note in this case that } A_{cm} = \frac{A}{\text{CMRR}} = \frac{250}{10^4} = 0.025, -32 \text{ dB.)}$$

EXERCISE: The CMRR specification of 80 dB in Example 12.5 actually corresponds to $-10^4 \leq \text{CMRR} \leq +10^4$. What range of output voltages may occur?

ANSWER: $0.375 \text{ V} \leq v_o \leq 0.625 \text{ V}$

Voltage-Follower Gain Error Due to CMRR

Finite CMRR can also play an important role in determining the gain error in the voltage-follower circuit in Fig. 12.26, for which

$$\mathbf{v_{id}} = \mathbf{v_s} - \mathbf{v_o} \qquad \text{and} \qquad \mathbf{v_{ic}} = \frac{\mathbf{v_s} + \mathbf{v_o}}{2}$$

Using Eq. (12.84)

$$\mathbf{v_o} = A\left[(\mathbf{v_s} - \mathbf{v_o}) + \frac{\mathbf{v_s} + \mathbf{v_o}}{2 \text{ CMRR}}\right] \tag{12.85}$$

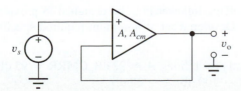

Figure 12.26 CMRR error in the voltage follower.

Solving this equation for $\mathbf{v_o}$ yields

$$A_V = \frac{\mathbf{v_o}}{\mathbf{v_s}} = \frac{A\left[1 + \dfrac{1}{2\,\text{CMRR}}\right]}{1 + A\left[1 - \dfrac{1}{2\,\text{CMRR}}\right]} \tag{12.86}$$

The ideal gain for the voltage follower is unity, so the gain error is equal to

$$\text{GE} = 1 - \frac{A\left[1 + \dfrac{1}{2\,\text{CMRR}}\right]}{1 + A\left[1 - \dfrac{1}{2\,\text{CMRR}}\right]} = \frac{1 - \dfrac{A}{\text{CMRR}}}{1 + A\left[1 - \dfrac{1}{2\,\text{CMRR}}\right]} \tag{12.87}$$

Normally, both A and CMRR will be $\gg 1$, so that Eq. (12.87) can be reduced to

$$\text{GE} \approx \frac{1}{A} - \frac{1}{\text{CMRR}} \tag{12.88}$$

The first term in Eq. (12.88) is the error due to the finite gain of the amplifier, as discussed earlier in this chapter, but the second term shows that CMRR may introduce an error of even greater import in the voltage follower.

EXAMPLE 12.6: Calculate the gain error for a voltage follower that is built using an op amp with $A = 80$ dB and CMRR $= 60$ dB.

SOLUTION: Equation (12.88) gives a gain error of

$$\text{GE} \approx \frac{1}{10^4} - \frac{1}{10^3} = -9.00 \times 10^{-4} \text{ or } 0.090\%$$

COMMENT: In this calculation, the error due to finite CMRR is ten times larger than that due to finite gain. Note that the gain error is negative, which corresponds to a gain greater than 1! Finite open-loop gain alone always causes A_V to be slightly less than 1.

$$A_V = \frac{A\left[1 + \dfrac{1}{2\,\text{CMRR}}\right]}{1 + A\left[1 - \dfrac{1}{2\,\text{CMRR}}\right]} = \frac{10^4\left[1 + \dfrac{1}{2(1000)}\right]}{1 + 10^4\left[1 - \dfrac{1}{2(1000)}\right]} = 1.001$$

We must be aware of errors related to CMRR whenever we are trying to perform precision amplification and measurement.   ◆

Discussion of CMRR often focuses on amplifier behavior at dc. However, CMRR can be an even greater problem at higher frequencies. **Common-mode rejection** decreases rapidly as frequency increases, typically with a slope of at least -20 dB/decade increase in frequency. This roll-off of the CMRR can begin at frequencies below 100 Hz. Thus, common-mode rejection at 60 or 120 Hz can be much worse than that specified for dc.

EXERCISE: A voltage follower is to be designed to provide a gain error of less than 0.005 percent. Develop a set of minimum required specifications on open-loop gain and CMRR.

ANSWER: Several possibilities: $A = 92$ dB, CMRR $= 92$ dB; $A = 100$ dB, CMRR $= 88$ dB; CMRR $= 100$ dB, $A = 88$ dB.

Power Supply Rejection Ratio

A parameter closely related to CMRR is the **power supply rejection ratio,** or **PSRR.** When power supply voltages change due to long-term drift or the existence of noise on the supplies, the equivalent input-offset voltage (see p. 516) changes slightly. PSRR is a measure of the ability of the amplifier to reject these power supply variations. PSRR values are similar to those of CMRR, with typical values in the range of 60 to 120 dB.

Common-Mode Input Resistance

Up to now, the discussion of the input resistance of an op amp has been limited to the resistance R_{ID}, which is actually the approximate resistance presented to a purely differential-mode input voltage v_{id}. In Fig. 12.27, two new resistors with value $2 R_{IC}$ have been added to the circuit to model the finite common-mode input resistance of the amplifier.

When a purely common-mode signal v_{ic} is applied to the input of this amplifier, as depicted in Fig. 12.28, with $v_{id} = 0$, the input current is nonzero even though R_{ID} is shorted out. In this situation, the total resistance presented to source v_{ic} is the parallel combination of the two resistors with value $2R_{IC}$, which thus equals R_{IC}. Therefore, R_{IC} is the equivalent resistance presented to the common-mode source; it is called the **common-mode input resistance** of the op amp. The value of R_{IC} is often much greater than that of the **differential-mode input resistance** R_{ID}, typically in excess of 10^9 Ω (1 GΩ).

From Fig. 12.29, we see that a purely differential-mode input signal actually sees an input resistance equivalent to

$$R_{\text{IN}} = R_{ID} \| 4R_{IC} \tag{12.89}$$

As mentioned, however, R_{IC} is typically much greater than R_{ID}, and the differential-mode input resistance is approximately equal to R_{ID}.

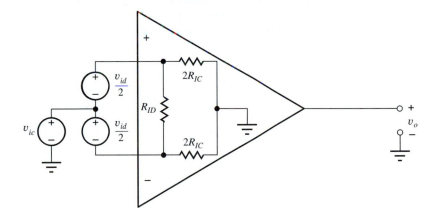

Figure 12.27 Op amp with common-mode input resistances added.

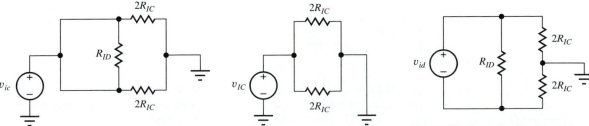

Figure 12.28 Amplifier with only a common-mode input signal present.

Figure 12.29 Amplifier input for a purely differential-mode input.

DC Error Sources

A second class of error sources results from the need to bias the internal circuits that form the operational amplifier and from mismatches between pairs of solid-state devices in these circuits. These dc error sources include the input-offset voltage V_{OS}, the input-bias currents I_{B1} and I_{B2}, and the input-offset current I_{OS}.

Input-Offset Voltage

When the inputs of the amplifier in Fig. 12.30 are both zero, the output of the amplifier is not truly zero but is resting at some dc voltage level. A small dc voltage seems to have been applied to the input of the amplifier, which is being amplified by the gain. The equivalent dc **input-offset voltage** V_{OS} is defined as

$$V_{OS} = \frac{V_O}{A} \tag{12.90}$$

Equation (12.82) can be modified to include the effects of this offset voltage by adding the V_{OS} term:

$$v_O = A\left[v_{id} + \frac{v_{ic}}{\text{CMRR}} + V_{OS}\right] \tag{12.91}$$

The first term in brackets represents the desired differential input signal to the amplifier, whereas the second and third terms represent the common-mode and offset-voltage error sources that corrupt the input signal.

As in the case of CMRR, the actual sign of the offset voltage is not known, and only the magnitude of the worst-case offset voltage is specified. Most commercial operational amplifiers have offset-voltage specifications of less than 10 mV, and op amps can easily be purchased with V_{OS} specified to be less than a few mV. For additional cost, internally trimmed op amps are available with $V_{OS} < 0.25$ mV.

In Example 12.7, the effect of offset voltage on circuit performance is found using the model in Fig. 12.31, in which the offset voltage is represented by a source in series with the input to an otherwise ideal amplifier. V_{OS} is amplified just as any input signal source, and the dc output voltage of the amplifier in Fig. 12.31 is

$$V_O = \left(1 + \frac{R_2}{R_1}\right)V_{OS} \tag{12.92}$$

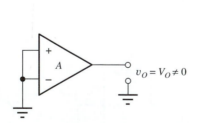

Figure 12.30 Amplifier with zero input voltage but nonzero output voltage. (*Note:* The offset voltage cannot be measured in this manner.)

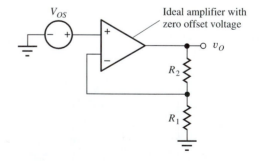

Figure 12.31 Offset voltage can be modeled by a voltage source V_{OS} in series with the amplifier input.

EXAMPLE 12.7: Suppose the amplifier in Fig. 12.31 has $|V_{OS}| \leq 3$ mV and R_2 and R_1 are 99 kΩ and 1.2 kΩ, respectively. What is the quiescent dc voltage at the amplifier output?

SOLUTION: Using Eq. (12.92), we find that the output voltage is

$$|V_O| \leq \left(1 + \frac{99 \text{ k}\Omega}{1.2 \text{ k}\Omega}\right)(0.003) = 0.25 \text{ V}$$

Because we do not actually know the sign of V_{OS}, and the V_{OS} specification represents an upper bound, we actually have

$$-0.25 \text{ V} \leq V_O \leq 0.25 \text{ V}$$

Offset-Voltage Adjustment

Addition of a potentiometer allows the **offset voltage** of most IC op amps to be manually adjusted to zero. Commercial amplifiers typically provide two terminals to which the potentiometer can be connected, as in Fig. 12.32. The third terminal of the potentiometer is connected to the positive or negative power supply voltage. The potentiometer value depends on the internal design of the amplifier.

Input-Bias and Offset Currents

For the transistors that form the operational amplifier to operate, a small but nonzero dc bias current must be supplied to each input terminal of the amplifier. These currents represent base currents in an amplifier built with bipolar transistors or gate currents in one designed with MOSFETs or JFETs. This dc current, although small, is an additional source of error, as we shall see.

The bias currents can be modeled by two current sources I_{B1} and I_{B2} connected to the noninverting and inverting inputs of the amplifier, as in Fig. 12.33. The values of I_{B1} and I_{B2} are similar but not identical, and the actual direction of the currents depends on the details of the internal amplifier circuit (NPN, PNP, NMOS, PMOS, and so on). The difference between the two bias currents is called the **offset current I_{OS}.**

$$I_{OS} = I_{B1} - I_{B2} \tag{12.93}$$

The offset-current specification for an op amp is normally expressed as an upper bound on the magnitude of I_{OS}:

$$|I_{OS}| \leq I_{MAX} \tag{12.94}$$

and the actual sign of I_{OS} for a given op amp is not known.

In an operational amplifier circuit, the **input-bias currents** produce an undesired voltage at the amplifier output. Consider the inverting amplifier in Fig. 12.34 as an example.

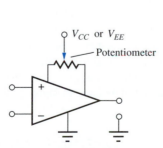

Figure 12.32 Offset-voltage adjustment of an operational amplifier.

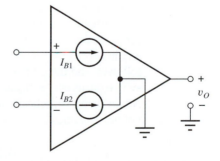

Figure 12.33 Operational amplifier with input-bias currents modeled by current sources I_{B1} and I_{B2}.

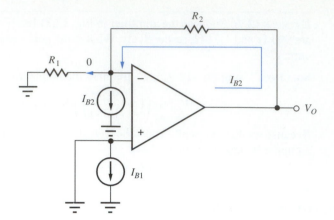

Figure 12.34 Inverting amplifier with input-bias currents modeled by current sources I_{B1} and I_{B2}.

In this circuit, I_{B1} is shorted out by the direct connection of the noninverting input to ground and does not affect the circuit. However, because the inverting input represents a virtual ground, the current in R_1 must be zero, forcing I_{B2} to be supplied by the amplifier output through R_2. Thus, the dc output voltage is equal to

$$V_O = I_{B2}R_2 \qquad (12.95)$$

The output-voltage error in Eq. (12.95) can be reduced by placing a **bias current compensation resistor** R_B in series with the noninverting input of the amplifier, as in Fig. 12.35. Using analysis by superposition, the output due to I_{B1} acting alone is

$$V_O = -I_{B1}R_B\left(1 + \frac{R_2}{R_1}\right) \qquad (12.96)$$

The total output voltage is the sum of Eqs. (12.95) and (12.96):

$$V_O^T = I_{B2}R_2 - I_{B1}R_B\left(1 + \frac{R_2}{R_1}\right) \qquad (12.97)$$

If R_B is set equal to the parallel combination of R_1 and R_2,

$$R_B = \frac{R_1 R_2}{R_1 + R_2} \qquad (12.98)$$

then the expression for the output-voltage error reduces to

$$V_O^T = (I_{B2} - I_{B1})R_2 = -I_{OS}R_2 \qquad (12.99)$$

The value of the offset current is typically a factor of 10 smaller than either of the individual bias currents, so the dc output-voltage error can be substantially reduced by using bias current compensation techniques.

Another example of the problems associated with offset-voltage and bias currents occurs in the integrator circuit in Fig. 12.36. A reset switch has been added to the integrator and is kept closed for $t < 0$. With the switch closed, the circuit is equivalent to a voltage follower, and the output voltage v_O is equal to the offset voltage V_{OS}. However, when the switch opens at $t = 0$, the circuit begins to integrate its own offset-voltage and bias current. Again using superposition analysis, it is easy to show (see Prob. 12.50) that the output voltage becomes

$$v_O(t) = V_{OS} + \frac{V_{OS}}{RC}t + \frac{I_{B2}}{C}t \qquad \text{for } t \geq 0 \qquad (12.100)$$

The output voltage becomes a ramp with a constant slope determined by the values of V_{OS} and I_{B2}. Eventually, the integrator output saturates at a limit set by one of the two power

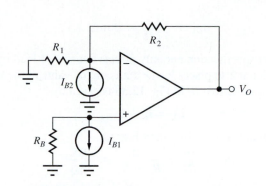

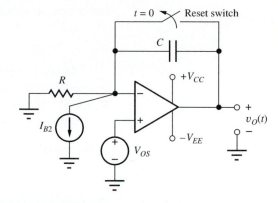

Figure 12.35 Inverting amplifier with bias current compensation resistor R_B.

Figure 12.36 Example of dc offset-voltage and bias current errors in an integrator.

supplies, as discussed in more detail in the next section. If an integrator is built in the laboratory without a reset switch, the output is normally found to be resting near one of the power supply voltages.

> **EXERCISE:** An integrator has $R = 10\,\text{k}\Omega$, $C = 100\,\text{pF}$, $V_{OS} = 1.5\,\text{mV}$, and $I_{B2} = 100$ nA. How long will it take v_O to saturate (reach V_{CC} or V_{EE}) after the power supplies are turned on if $V_{CC} = V_{EE} = 15\,\text{V}$?
>
> **ANSWER:** $t = 6.0\,\text{ms}$

Output Voltage and Current Limits

An actual operational amplifier has a limited range of voltage and current capability at its output. For example, the voltage at the output of the amplifier in Fig. 12.37 cannot exceed V_{CC} or be more negative than $-V_{EE}$. In fact, for many amplifier designs, the output-voltage range is limited to several volts less than the power supply span. For example, the output-voltage limits for a particular op amp might be specified as

$$-(V_{EE} - 1)\,\text{V} \leq v_O \leq (V_{CC} - 2)\,\text{V} \tag{12.101}$$

Commercial operational amplifiers also contain circuits that restrict the magnitude of the current in the output terminal in order to limit power dissipation in the amplifier and to protect the amplifier from accidental short circuits. The current-limit specification is often given in terms of the minimum load resistance that an amplifier can drive with a given voltage swing. For example, an amplifier may be guaranteed to deliver an output of $\pm 10\,\text{V}$ only for a total load resistance $\geq 5\,\text{k}\Omega$. This is equivalent to saying that the total

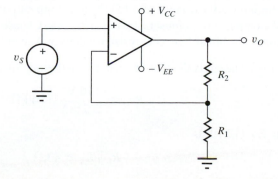

Figure 12.37 Amplifier with power supply voltages indicated.

output current i_O is limited to

$$|i_O| \leq \frac{10\ \text{V}}{5\ \text{k}\Omega} = 2\ \text{mA} \qquad (12.102)$$

The output-current specification not only affects the size of load resistor that can be connected to the amplifier, it also places lower limits on the value of the feedback resistors R_1 and R_2. The total output current i_O in Fig. 12.38 is given by

$$\mathbf{i_O} = \mathbf{i_L} + \mathbf{i_F} \qquad (12.103)$$

or, because the current into the inverting input is zero,

$$\mathbf{i_O} = \frac{\mathbf{v_O}}{R_L} + \frac{\mathbf{v_O}}{R_2 + R_1} = \frac{\mathbf{v_O}}{R_{\text{EQ}}} \qquad (12.104)$$

The amplifier output must supply current not only to the load but also to its own feedback network! From Eq. (12.104), we see that the resistance that the noninverting amplifier must drive is equivalent to the parallel combination of the load resistance and the series combination of R_1 and R_2:

$$R_{\text{EQ}} = R_L \,\|\, (R_1 + R_2) \qquad (12.105)$$

For the case of the inverting amplifier in Fig. 12.39, R_{EQ} is given by

$$R_{\text{EQ}} = R_L \,\|\, R_2 \qquad (12.106)$$

because the inverting-input terminal of the amplifier represents a virtual ground.

The output-current constraint represented by Eqs. (12.105) and (12.106) often helps us choose the size of the feedback resistors during the design process.

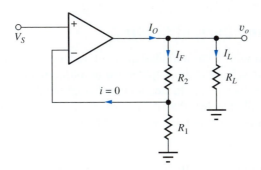

Figure 12.38 Output-current limit in the non-inverting amplifier.

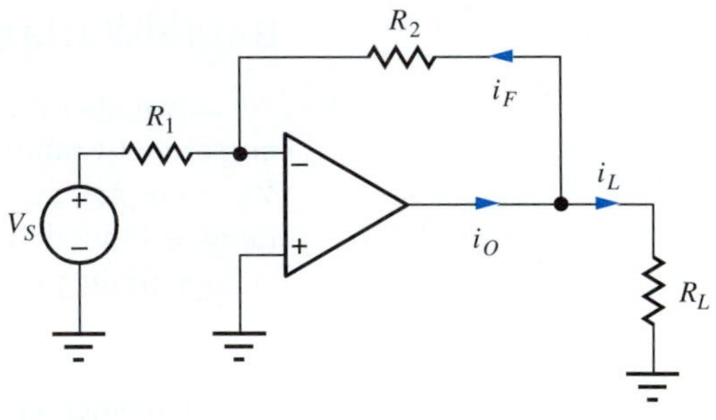

Figure 12.39 Output-current limit in the inverting-amplifier circuit.

EXAMPLE 12.8: Suppose the amplifier in Fig. 12.39 is to be designed to have a gain of 20 dB and must develop a peak output voltage of at least 10 V when connected to a minimum load resistance of 5 kΩ. The op-amp output current specification states that the output current must be less than 2.5 mA. Choose acceptable values of R_1 and R_2 from the table of 5 percent resistor values in Appendix C.

SOLUTION: The equivalent load resistance on the amplifier must be greater than 4 kΩ:

$$R_{\text{EQ}} \geq \frac{10\ \text{V}}{2.5\ \text{mA}} = 4\ \text{k}\Omega$$

Using Eq. (12.106),

$$R_L \,\|\, R_2 \geq 4\ \text{k}\Omega$$

Because the minimum value of R_L is 5 kΩ, the feedback resistor R_2 must satisfy

$$R_2 \geq 20 \text{ k}\Omega$$

We also have

$$\frac{R_2}{R_1} = 10$$

because the gain was specified as 20 dB. We should allow some safety margin in the value of R_2. For example, a 27-kΩ resistor with a 5 percent tolerance will have a minimum value of 25.6 kΩ and would be satisfactory. A 22-kΩ resistor would have a minimum value of 20.9 kΩ and would also just barely meet the specification. A wide range of choices still exists for R_1 and R_2. Several acceptable choices would be

$$R_2 = 22 \text{ k}\Omega \text{ and } R_1 = 2.2 \text{ k}\Omega$$

$$R_2 = 27 \text{ k}\Omega \text{ and } R_1 = 2.7 \text{ k}\Omega$$

$$R_2 = 47 \text{ k}\Omega \text{ and } R_1 = 4.7 \text{ k}\Omega$$

$$R_2 = 100 \text{ k}\Omega \text{ and } R_1 = 10 \text{ k}\Omega$$

◆

EXERCISE: Design a noninverting amplifier to have a gain of 20 dB and to develop a peak output voltage of at least 20 V when connected to a load resistance of at least 5 kΩ. The op-amp output current specification states that the output current must be less than 5 mA. Choose acceptable values of R_1 and R_2 from the table of 5 percent resistor values in Appendix C.

ANSWER: Some possibilities: 27 kΩ and 3 kΩ; 270 kΩ and 30 kΩ; 180 kΩ and 20 kΩ; *but not* 18 kΩ and 2 kΩ because of tolerances.

12.6 FREQUENCY RESPONSE AND BANDWIDTH OF OPERATIONAL AMPLIFIERS

Most general-purpose operational amplifiers are low-pass amplifiers designed to have high gain at dc and a **single-pole frequency response** described by

$$A(s) = \frac{A_o \omega_B}{s + \omega_B} = \frac{\omega_T}{s + \omega_B} \tag{12.107}$$

in which A_o is the open-loop gain at dc, ω_B is the open-loop bandwidth of the op amp, and ω_T is called the **unity-gain frequency,** the frequency at which $|A(j\omega)| = 1$ (0 dB). The magnitude of Eq. (12.107) versus frequency can be expressed as

$$|A(j\omega)| = \frac{A_o \omega_B}{\sqrt{\omega^2 + \omega_B^2}} = \frac{A_o}{\sqrt{1 + \dfrac{\omega^2}{\omega_B^2}}} \tag{12.108}$$

An example is depicted graphically in the Bode plot in Fig. 12.40. For $\omega \ll \omega_B$, the gain is constant at the dc value A_o. The bandwidth of the open-loop amplifier, the frequency at which the gain is 3 dB below A_o, is ω_B (or $f_B = \omega_B/2\pi$). In Fig. 12.40, $A_o = 10,000$ (80 dB) and $\omega_B = 1000$ rad/s (159 Hz).

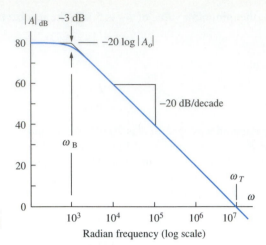

Figure 12.40 Voltage gain vs. frequency for an operational amplifier.

At high frequencies, $\omega \gg \omega_B$, the transfer function can be approximated by

$$\left|A(j\omega)\right| \approx \frac{A_o \omega_B}{\omega} = \frac{\omega_T}{\omega} \tag{12.109}$$

Using Eq. (12.109), we see that the magnitude of the gain is indeed unity at $\omega = \omega_T$:

$$\left|A(j\omega)\right| = \frac{\omega_T}{\omega} = 1 \qquad \text{for } \omega = \omega_t \tag{12.110}$$

Rewriting the result in Eq. (12.110),

$$\left|A(j\omega)\right|\omega \approx \omega_T \qquad \text{and dividing by } 2\pi \qquad \left|A(j\omega)\right|f \approx f_T \tag{12.111}$$

The amplifier in Fig. 12.40 has $\omega_t = 10^7$ rad/s.

Equation (12.111) states that, for any frequency $\omega \gg \omega_B$, the product of the magnitude of amplifier gain and frequency has a constant value equal to the unity-gain frequency ω_T. For this reason, the parameter ω_T (or f_T) is often referred to as the **gain-bandwidth product (GBW)** of the amplifier. The important result in Eq. (12.111) is a property of *single-pole* amplifiers that can be represented by transfer functions of the form of Eq. (12.107).

> **EXERCISE:** An op amp has a gain of 100 dB at dc and a unity-gain frequency of 5 MHz. What is f_B? Write the transfer function for the gain of the op amp.
>
> **ANSWER:** 50 Hz; $A(s) = \dfrac{10^7 \pi}{s + 100\pi}$

Frequency Response of the Noninverting Amplifier

We now use the frequency-dependent op-amp gain expression to study the closed-loop frequency response of the noninverting and inverting amplifiers. The closed-loop gain for the noninverting amplifier was found previously to be

$$A_V = \frac{A}{1 + A\beta} \qquad \text{where } \beta = \frac{R_1}{R_1 + R_2} \tag{12.112}$$

The algebraic derivation of this gain expression actually placed no restrictions on the functional form of A. Up to now, we have assumed A to be a constant, but we can explore the frequency response of the closed-loop feedback amplifier by replacing A in Eq. (12.112) by the frequency-dependent voltage-gain expression for the op amp, Eq. (12.107):

$$A_V(s) = \frac{A(s)}{1 + A(s)\beta} = \frac{\dfrac{A_o\omega_B}{s + \omega_B}}{1 + \dfrac{A_o\omega_B}{s + \omega_B}\beta} = \frac{A_o\omega_B}{s + \omega_B(1 + A_o\beta)} \tag{12.113}$$

Dividing by the factor $(1 + A_o\beta)\omega_B$, Eq. (12.113) can be written as

$$A_V(s) = \frac{\dfrac{A_o}{1 + A_o\beta}}{\dfrac{s}{(1 + A_o\beta)\omega_B} + 1} = \frac{A_V(0)}{\dfrac{s}{\omega_H} + 1} \tag{12.114}$$

where the upper-cutoff frequency is

$$\omega_H = \omega_B(1 + A_o\beta) = \omega_T\frac{(1 + A_o\beta)}{A_o} = \frac{\omega_T}{A_V(0)} \tag{12.115}$$

The closed-loop amplifier also has a single-pole response of the same form as Eq. (12.107), but its dc gain and bandwidth are given by

$$A_V(0) = \frac{A_o}{1 + A_o\beta} \qquad \text{and} \qquad \omega_H = \frac{\omega_T}{A_V(0)} \tag{12.116}$$

For $A_o\beta \gg 1$, Eq. (12.115) reduces to

$$A_V(0) \approx \frac{1}{\beta} \qquad \text{and} \qquad \omega_H \approx \beta\omega_T \tag{12.117}$$

Note that the gain-bandwidth product of the closed-loop amplifier is constant:

$$A_V(0)\,\omega_H = \omega_T$$

From Eq. (12.116), we see that the gain must be reduced in order to increase ω_H, or vice versa. We will explore this in more detail shortly.

The loop gain $A(s)\beta$ is now also a function of frequency. At frequencies for which $|A(j\omega)\beta| \gg 1$, Eq. (12.113) reduces to $1/\beta$, the constant value derived previously for low frequencies. At frequencies for which $|A(j\omega)\beta| \ll 1$, Eq. (12.113) becomes $A_V \approx A(j\omega)$. At low frequencies, the gain is set by the feedback, but at high frequencies we find that the gain must follow the gain of the amplifier. We should not expect a (negative) feedback amplifier to produce more gain than is available from the open-loop operational amplifier by itself.

These results are indicated graphically by the bold lines in Fig. 12.41 on the following page for an amplifier with $1/\beta = 35$ dB. The loop gain can be expressed as

$$A\beta = \frac{A}{\left(\dfrac{1}{\beta}\right)} \qquad \text{and (in dB)} \qquad |A\beta|_{\text{dB}} = |A|_{\text{dB}} - \left|\frac{1}{\beta}\right|_{\text{dB}} \tag{12.118}$$

At any given frequency, the magnitude of the loop gain is equal to the difference between A_{dB} and $(1/\beta)_{\text{dB}}$ on the graph. The upper half-power frequency $\omega_H = \beta\omega_t$ corresponds to the frequency at which $(1/\beta)$ intersects $|A(j\omega)|$ corresponding to $|A\beta| = 1$ (actually $A\beta \approx -j1 = 1\underline{/-90°}$). For the case in Fig. 12.41, $\beta = 0.0178$ (-35 dB) and $\omega_H = 0.0178 \times 10^7 = 178 \times 10^3$ rad/s.

EXERCISE: An op amp has a dc gain of 100 dB and a unity-gain frequency of 10 MHz. What is the cutoff frequency of the op amp? If the op amp is used to build a non-inverting amplifier with a closed-loop gain of 60 dB, what is the bandwidth of the feedback amplifier? Write an expression for the transfer function of the op amp. Write an expression for the transfer function of the noninverting amplifier.

ANSWERS: 100 Hz; 10 kHz; $A(s) = \dfrac{2\pi \times 10^7}{s + 200\pi}$; $A(s) = \dfrac{2\pi \times 10^7}{s + 2\pi \times 10^4}$

EXERCISE: Show that $A\beta \approx -j1$ at the frequency at which $(1/\beta)$ intersects $|A(j\omega)|$.

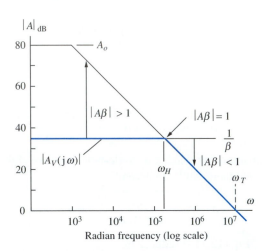

Figure 12.41 Graphical interpretation of operational amplifier with feedback.

Inverting Amplifier Frequency Response

The frequency response for the inverting-amplifier configuration can be found in a manner similar to that for the noninverting case by substituting the frequency-dependent op-amp gain expression, Eq. (12.107), into the equation for the closed-loop gain of the inverting amplifier.

$$A_V = \left(-\frac{R_2}{R_1}\right) \frac{A(s)\beta}{1 + A(s)\beta} \qquad \text{where } \beta = \frac{R_1}{R_1 + R_2}$$

or $$A_V = \left(-\frac{R_2}{R_1}\right) \frac{\dfrac{A_o\omega_B}{s + \omega_B}\beta}{1 + \dfrac{A_o\omega_B}{s + \omega_B}\beta} = \frac{\left(-\dfrac{R_2}{R_1}\right) \dfrac{A_o\beta}{(1 + A_o\beta)}}{\dfrac{s}{\omega_B(1 + A_o\beta)} + 1} \qquad (12.119)$$

For $A_o\beta \gg 1$, these equations reduce to

$$A_V = \frac{\left(-\dfrac{R_2}{R_1}\right)\dfrac{A_o\beta}{(1 + A_o\beta)}}{\dfrac{s}{\omega_H} + 1} \approx \frac{\left(-\dfrac{R_2}{R_1}\right)}{\dfrac{s}{\omega_H} + 1} \qquad \text{and} \qquad \omega_H = \frac{\omega_t}{\dfrac{A_o}{(1 + A_o\beta)}} \approx \beta\omega_T \qquad (12.120)$$

where the approximate values hold for $A_o\beta \gg 1$. This expression again represents a single-pole transfer function. The gain at low frequencies, $A_V(0)$, is set by the resistor ratio $(-R_2/R_1)$, and the bandwidth expression is identical to that of the noninverting amplifier, $\omega_H = \beta\omega_T$.

The frequency response characteristics of the inverting and noninverting amplifiers are summarized in Table 12.5, in which the expressions have been recast in terms of the

T a b l e 12.5		
Inverting and Noninverting Amplifier Frequency Response Comparison		
$\beta = \dfrac{R_1}{R_1 + R_2}$	**Noninverting Amplifier**	**Inverting Amplifier**
dc gain	$A_V(0) = 1 + \dfrac{R_2}{R_1}$	$A_V(0) = -\dfrac{R_2}{R_1}$
Feedback factor	$\beta = \dfrac{1}{A_V(0)}$	$\beta = \dfrac{1}{1 + |A_V(0)|}$
Bandwidth	$f_B = \beta f_T$	$f_B = \beta f_T$
Input resistance	$R_{IC} \| R_{ID}(1 + A\beta)$	R_1
Output resistance	$\dfrac{R_O}{1 + A\beta}$	$\dfrac{R_O}{1 + A\beta}$

ideal value of the gain at low frequencies. The expressions are quite similar. However, for a given value of dc gain, the noninverting amplifier will have slightly greater bandwidth than the inverting amplifier because of the difference in the relation between β and $A_V(0)$. The difference is significant only for amplifier stages designed with low values of closed-loop gain.

> **EXERCISE:** An op amp has a dc gain of 100 dB and a unity-gain frequency of 10 MHz. What is the cutoff frequency of the op amp? If the op amp is used to build an inverting amplifier with a closed-loop gain of 60 dB, what is the bandwidth of the feedback amplifier? Write an expression for the transfer function of the op amp. Write an expression for the transfer function of the inverting amplifier.
>
> **ANSWERS:** 100 Hz; 10 kHz; $A(s) = \dfrac{2\pi \times 10^7}{s + 200\pi}$; $A(s) = \dfrac{2\pi \times 10^7}{s + 2\pi \times 10^4}$
>
> **EXERCISE:** If the amplifier in the preceding exercise is used in a voltage follower, what is its bandwidth? If the amplifier is used in an inverting amplifier with $A_V = -1$, what is its bandwidth?
>
> **ANSWERS:** 10 MHz; 5 MHz

Frequency Response of Cascaded Amplifiers

When several amplifiers are connected in cascade, as in Fig. 12.42 for example, the overall transfer function can be written as the product of the transfer functions of the individual

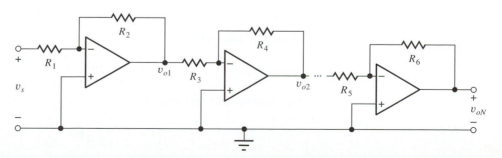

Figure 12.42 Multistage amplifier cascade.

stages:

$$A_V(s) = \frac{\mathbf{V_{oN}(s)}}{\mathbf{V_s(s)}} = \frac{\mathbf{V_{o1}}}{\mathbf{V_s}} \frac{\mathbf{V_{o2}}}{\mathbf{V_{o1}}} \cdots \frac{\mathbf{V_{oN}}}{\mathbf{V_{o(N-1)}}} = A_{V1}(s) A_{V2}(s) \cdots A_{VN}(s) \quad (12.121)$$

It is extremely important to remember that this product representation implicitly assumes that the stages do not interact with each other, which can be achieved with $R_{OUT} = 0$ or $R_{IN} = \infty$ (that is, the interconnection of the various amplifiers must not alter the transfer function of any of the amplifiers).

In the general case, each amplifier has a different value of dc gain and bandwidth, and the overall transfer function becomes

$$A_V(s) = \frac{A_{V1}(0)}{\left(1 + \dfrac{s}{\omega_{H1}}\right)} \frac{A_{V2}(0)}{\left(1 + \dfrac{s}{\omega_{H2}}\right)} \cdots \frac{A_{VN}(0)}{\left(1 + \dfrac{s}{\omega_{HN}}\right)} \quad (12.122)$$

The gain at low frequencies ($s = 0$) is

$$A_V(0) = A_{V1}(0) A_{V2}(0) \cdots A_{VN}(0) \quad (12.123)$$

The overall bandwidth of the cascade amplifier is defined to be the frequency at which the voltage gain is reduced by a factor of $1/\sqrt{2}$ (-3 dB) from its low-frequency value or, stated mathematically,

$$|A_V(j\omega_H)| = \frac{|A_{V1}(0) A_{V2}(0) \cdots A_{VN}(0)|}{\sqrt{2}} \quad (12.124)$$

In the general case, hand calculation of ω_H based on Eq. (12.124) can be quite tedious, and approximate techniques for estimating ω_H will be developed in Chapter 17. With the aid of a computer or calculator, solver routines or iterative trial-and-error can be used directly to find ω_H. Example 12.9 uses direct algebraic evaluation of Eq. (12.124) for the case of two amplifiers.

EXAMPLE 12.9: Suppose two amplifiers with transfer functions $A_{V1}(s)$ and $A_{V2}(s)$ are connected in cascade. What are the dc gain and bandwidth of the overall two-stage amplifier?

$$A_{V1}(s) = \frac{500}{1 + \dfrac{s}{2000}} \qquad \text{and} \qquad A_{V2}(s) = \frac{250}{1 + \dfrac{s}{4000}}$$

SOLUTION: The overall dc gain is the product of the dc gains of the two amplifiers:

$$A_V = 500 \times 250 = 1.25 \times 10^5 = 102 \text{ dB}$$

The magnitude of the frequency response is given by

$$|A_V(j\omega)| = \frac{1.25 \times 10^5}{\sqrt{1 + \dfrac{\omega^2}{2000^2}} \sqrt{1 + \dfrac{\omega^2}{4000^2}}}$$

and ω_H is defined by

$$|A_V(j\omega_H)| = \frac{1.25 \times 10^5}{\sqrt{2}}$$

Equating the denominators of these two equations and squaring both sides yields

$$\left(1 + \frac{\omega_H^2}{2000^2}\right)\left(1 + \frac{\omega_H^2}{4000^2}\right) = 2$$

which can be rearranged into the following quadratic equation in terms of ω_H^2:

$$(\omega_H^2)^2 + 2.00 \times 10^7 (\omega_H^2) - 6.40 \times 10^{13} = 0$$

Using the quadratic formula or our calculator's root-finding routine gives the following values for ω_H^2

$$\omega_H^2 = 2.81 \times 10^6 \qquad -4.56 \times 10^7$$

The value of ω_H must be real, so the only acceptable answer is

$$\omega_H = 1.68 \times 10^3 \qquad \text{or} \qquad f_H = 267 \text{ Hz}$$

COMMENT: As should be expected, the bandwidth of the overall amplifier is less than that of each individual amplifier:

$$f_{H1} = \frac{2000}{2\pi} = 318 \text{ Hz} \qquad \text{and} \qquad f_{H2} = \frac{4000}{2\pi} = 637 \text{ Hz}$$

◆

EXERCISE: An amplifier is formed by cascading two amplifiers with the following transfer functions. What is the gain at low frequencies? What is the gain at f_H? What is f_H?

$$A_{V1}(s) = \frac{50}{1 + \dfrac{s}{10,000\pi}} \qquad \text{and} \qquad A_{V2}(s) = \frac{25}{1 + \dfrac{s}{20,000\pi}}$$

ANSWERS: 1250; 884; 8380 Hz

EXERCISE: An amplifier is formed by cascading three amplifiers with the following transfer functions. What is the gain at low frequencies? What is the gain at f_H? What is f_H?

$$A_{V1}(s) = \frac{-100}{1 + \dfrac{s}{10,000\pi}}, \qquad A_{V2}(s) = \frac{66.7}{1 + \dfrac{s}{15,000\pi}}, \qquad A_{V3}(s) = \frac{50}{1 + \dfrac{s}{20,000\pi}}$$

ANSWERS: -3.33×10^5; -2.36×10^5; 6900 Hz

Cascade of Identical Amplifier Stages

For the special case in which a cascade-amplifier configuration is composed of identical amplifiers, then a simple result can be obtained for the bandwidth of the overall amplifier. For N identical stages,

$$A_V(s) = \left[\frac{A_{V1}(0)}{1 + \dfrac{s}{\omega_{H1}}}\right]^N = \frac{[A_{V1}(0)]^N}{\left(1 + \dfrac{s}{\omega_{H1}}\right)^N} \qquad (12.125)$$

and

$$A_V(0) = [A_{V1}(0)]^N \qquad (12.126)$$

in which $A_{V1}(0)$ and ω_{H1} are the closed-loop gain and bandwidth of each individual amplifier stage.

The bandwidth ω_H of the overall cascade amplifier is determined from

$$|A_V(j\omega_H)| = \frac{[A_{V1}(0)]^N}{\left(\sqrt{1 + \frac{\omega_H^2}{\omega_{H1}^2}}\right)^N} = \frac{[A_{V1}(0)]^N}{\sqrt{2}} \tag{12.127}$$

Solving for ω_H in terms of ω_{H1} for the cascaded-amplifier bandwidth yields

$$\omega_H = \omega_{H1}\sqrt{2^{1/N} - 1} \quad \text{or} \quad f_H = f_{H1}\sqrt{2^{1/N} - 1} \tag{12.128}$$

Sample values of the **bandwidth shrinkage factor** $\sqrt{2^{1/N} - 1}$ are given in Table 12.6. (The $N = 2$ case was already encountered in Chapter 11.)

Although most amplifier designs do not actually cascade identical amplifiers, Eq. (12.128) can be used to help guide the design of a multistage amplifier or, in some cases, to estimate the bandwidth of a portion of a more complex amplifier. (An additional useful result is in Prob. 12.80.)

Table 12.6

Bandwidth Shrinkage Factor

N	$\sqrt{2^{1/N} - 1}$
1	1
2	0.644
3	0.510
4	0.435
5	0.386
6	0.350
7	0.323

An Amplifier Design Example

EXAMPLE 12.10: We now use a spreadsheet to explore the design of a multistage amplifier to meet the following specifications:

$$A_V \geq 100 \text{ dB}$$

$$\text{Bandwidth} \geq 50 \text{ kHz}$$

$$R_{\text{OUT}} \leq 0.1 \ \Omega$$

$$R_{\text{IN}} \geq 20 \text{ k}\Omega$$

using an operational amplifier with the following specifications:

$$A_o = 100 \text{ dB}$$

$$f_t = 1 \text{ MHz}$$

$$R_{ID} = 1 \text{ G}\Omega$$

$$R_O = 50 \ \Omega$$

The design must have the minimum number of stages required to meet the specifications in order to achieve minimum cost.

SOLUTION: Because the required value of R_{IN} is relatively low and can be met by a resistor, both the inverting and noninverting amplifier stages should be considered. More than one stage will be required because the op amp by itself cannot simultaneously meet the specifications for A_V, f_H, and R_{OUT}. For example, if we were to use the open-loop op amp by itself, it would provide a gain of 100 dB (10^5) but have a bandwidth of only $f_t/10^5 = 10$ Hz. Thus, we must reduce the gain of each stage in order to increase the bandwidth.

For simplicity in the design, we assume that the amplifier will be built from a cascade of N identical amplifier stages. The design formulas will be set up in a logical order so that we can choose one design variable, and the rest of the equations can then be evaluated based on that single design choice. For this particular design, the gain and bandwidth are the most difficult specifications to achieve, whereas the required input and output resistance specifications are easily met. We can initially force our design to meet either the gain or the bandwidth specification and then find the number of stages that will be required to achieve the other specifications.

In this example, we force the cascade amplifier to meet the gain specification, and then find the number of stages needed to meet the bandwidth by repeated trial and error.

To meet the gain specification, we set the gain of each stage to

$$A_V(0) = \sqrt[N]{10^5}$$

Based on this choice, we can then calculate the other characteristics of the amplifier using the following process:

1. Choose N.
2. Calculate the gain required of each stage $A_V(0) = \sqrt[N]{10^5}$.
3. Find β using the numerical result from step 2.
4. Calculate the bandwidth f_{H1} of each stage.
5. Calculate the bandwidth of N stages using Eq. (12.128).
6. Using $A\beta$, calculate R_{OUT} and R_{IN}.
7. See if specifications are met. If not, go back to step 1 and try a new value of N.

The formulas for the noninverting and inverting amplifiers are slightly different, as summarized in Table 12.7. These formulas have been used for the results tabulated in the spreadsheet in Table 12.8 on the next page.

From Table 12.8, we see that a cascade of six noninverting amplifiers meets all the specifications, but seven inverting amplifier stages are required. This occurs because the inverting amplifier has a slightly smaller bandwidth than the noninverting amplifier for a given value of closed-loop gain. We are usually interested in the

T a b l e 12.7

N-Stage Cascades of Noninverting and Inverting Amplifiers

$\beta = \dfrac{R_1}{R_1 + R_2}$	Noninverting Amplifier	Inverting Amplifier
2. Single-stage gain $A_V(0) = \sqrt[N]{10^5}$	$A_V(0) = 1 + \dfrac{R_2}{R_1}$	$A_V(0) = -\dfrac{R_2}{R_1}$
3. Feedback factor	$\beta = \dfrac{1}{A_V(0)}$	$\beta = \dfrac{1}{1 + |A_V(0)|}$
4. Bandwidth of each stage	$f_{H1} = \dfrac{f_T}{\dfrac{A_o}{1 + A_o\beta}}$	$f_{H1} = \dfrac{f_T}{\dfrac{A_o}{1 + A_o\beta}}$
5. N-stage bandwidth	$f_H = f_{H1}\sqrt{2^{1/N} - 1}$	$f_B = f_{H1}\sqrt{2^{1/N} - 1}$
6. Input resistance	$R_{ID}(1 + A_o\beta)$	R_1
Output resistance	$\dfrac{R_O}{1 + A_o\beta}$	$\dfrac{R_O}{1 + A_o\beta}$

	Table 12.8				

Design of Cascade of *N* Identical Operational Amplifier Stages

Cascade of Identical Noninverting Amplifiers

# of Stages	$A_V(0)$ Gain per Stage $1/\beta$	f_{H1} Single Stage $\beta \times f_T$	f_H *N* Stages	R_{IN}	R_{OUT}
1	1.00E + 05	1.00E + 01	1.000E + 01	2.00E + 09	2.50E + 01
2	3.16E + 02	3.16E + 03	2.035E + 03	3.17E + 11	1.58E − 01
3	4.64E + 01	2.15E + 04	1.098E + 04	2.16E + 12	2.32E − 02
4	1.78E + 01	5.62E + 04	2.446E + 04	5.62E + 12	8.89E − 03
5	1.00E + 01	1.00E + 05	3.856E + 04	1.00E + 13	5.00E − 03
6	**6.81E + 00**	**1.47E + 05**	**5.137E + 04**	**1.47E + 13**	**3.41E − 03**
7	5.18E + 00	1.93E + 05	6.229E + 04	1.93E + 13	2.59E − 03
8	4.22E + 00	2.37E + 05	7.134E + 04	2.37E + 13	2.11E − 03
9	3.59E + 00	2.78E + 05	7.873E + 04	2.78E + 13	1.80E − 03
10	3.16E + 00	3.16E + 05	8.472E + 04	3.16E + 13	1.58E − 03
11	2.85E + 00	3.51E + 05	8.955E + 04	3.51E + 13	1.42E − 03
12	2.61E + 00	3.83E + 05	9.342E + 04	3.83E + 13	1.31E − 03
13	2.42E + 00	4.12E + 05	9.653E + 04	4.12E + 13	1.21E − 03
14	2.28E + 00	4.39E + 05	9.899E + 04	4.39E + 13	1.14E − 03
15	2.15E + 00	4.64E + 05	1.009E + 05	4.64E + 13	1.08E − 03
17	1.97E + 00	5.08E + 05	1.036E + 05	5.08E + 13	9.84E − 04
20	1.78E + 00	5.62E + 05	1.056E + 05	5.62E + 13	8.89E − 04
22	1.69E + 00	5.93E + 05	1.060E + 05	5.93E + 13	8.44E − 04
24	1.62E + 00	6.19E + 05	1.060E + 05	6.19E + 13	8.08E − 04
25	1.58E + 00	6.31E + 05	1.058E + 05	6.31E + 13	7.92E − 04

Cascade of Identical Inverting Amplifiers

# of Stages	$A_V(0)$ $(1/\beta) - 1$	f_{H1} Single Stage	f_H *N* Stages	R_{IN}	R_{OUT}
1	1.00E + 05	1.00E + 01	1.00E + 01	R_1	2.50E + 01
2	3.16E + 02	3.15E + 03	2.03E + 03	R_1	1.58E − 01
3	4.64E + 01	2.11E + 04	1.08E + 04	R_1	2.32E − 02
4	1.78E + 01	5.32E + 04	2.32E + 04	R_1	8.89E − 03
5	1.00E + 01	9.09E + 04	3.51E + 04	R_1	5.00E − 03
6	6.81E + 00	1.28E + 05	4.48E + 04	R_1	3.41E − 03
7	**5.18E + 00**	**1.62E + 05**	**5.22E + 04**	R_1	**2.59E − 03**
8	4.22E + 00	1.92E + 05	5.77E + 04	R_1	2.11E − 03
9	3.59E + 00	2.18E + 05	6.16E + 04	R_1	1.80E − 03
10	3.16E + 00	2.40E + 06	6.44E + 04	R_1	1.58E − 03

most economical design, so the six-stage amplifier will be chosen. Note that the R_{OUT} requirement is met with $N > 2$ for both amplifiers.

To complete the design, we must choose values for R_1 and R_2. From Table 12.8, the gain of each stage must be at least 6.81, requiring the resistor ratio R_2/R_1 to be 5.81. Because we will probably not be able to find two 5 percent resistors that give a ratio of exactly 5.81, we need to explore the acceptable range for the ratio now that we know we need six stages. In Table 12.9, a spreadsheet is again used to study six-stage amplifier designs having gains ranging from 6.81 to 7.01. As the single-stage

Table 12.9

Cascade of Six Identical Noninverting Amplifiers

# of Stages	$A_V(0)$ Gain per Stage $1/\beta$	N Stage Gain	f_{H1} Single Stage $\beta \times f_T$	f_H N Stages	R_{IN}	R_{OUT}
6	6.81E + 00	1.00E + 05	1.47E + 05	5.137E + 04	1.47E + 13	3.41E − 03
6	6.83E + 00	1.02E + 05	1.46E + 05	5.121E + 04	1.46E + 13	3.42E − 03
6	6.85E + 00	1.04E + 05	1.46E + 05	5.107E + 04	1.46E + 13	3.43E − 03
6	6.87E + 00	1.05E + 05	1.45E + 05	5.092E + 04	1.46E + 13	3.44E − 03
6	6.89E + 00	1.07E + 05	1.45E + 05	5.077E + 04	1.45E + 13	3.45E − 03
6	6.91E + 00	1.09E + 05	1.45E + 05	5.062E + 04	1.45E + 13	3.46E − 03
6	6.93E + 00	1.11E + 05	1.44E + 05	5.048E + 04	1.44E + 13	3.47E − 03
6	6.95E + 00	1.13E + 05	1.44E + 05	5.033E + 04	1.44E + 13	3.48E − 03
6	6.97E + 00	1.15E + 05	1.43E + 05	5.019E + 04	1.43E + 13	3.49E − 03
6	6.99E + 00	1.17E + 05	1.43E + 05	5.004E + 04	1.43E + 13	3.50E − 03
6	7.01E + 00	1.19E + 05	1.43E + 05	4.990E + 04	1.43E + 13	3.51E − 03

gain is increased, the overall bandwidth decreases. From Table 12.9, we see that the specifications will be met for resistor ratios falling between 5.81 and 5.99.

Many acceptable resistor ratios can be found in the table of 5 percent resistors in Appendix C. Picking $A_V(0) = 6.91$, a value near the center of the range of acceptable gain and bandwidth, two possible resistor sets are

$$R_1 = 22 \text{ k}\Omega, R_2 = 130 \text{ k}\Omega$$

with $\quad 1 + \dfrac{R_2}{R_1} = 6.91, \; A = 101 \text{ dB}, \; f_H = 50.6 \text{ kHz}, \; R_{OUT} = 0.035 \; \Omega$

and for $\quad\quad\quad R_1 = 5.6 \text{ k}\Omega, \; R_2 = 33 \text{ k}\Omega$

with $\quad 1 + \dfrac{R_2}{R_1} = 6.89, \; A = 101 \text{ dB}, \; f_H = 50.8 \text{ kHz}, \; R_{OUT} = 0.035 \; \Omega$

The overall size of these resistors has been chosen so that the feedback resistors do not heavily load the output of the op amp. For example, the resistors $R_1 = 220 \; \Omega$ and $R_2 = 1.3 \text{ k}\Omega$ or $R_1 = 56 \; \Omega$ and $R_2 = 330 \; \Omega$, although providing acceptable resistor ratios, would not be desirable choices for a final design. ◆

The Influence of Tolerances on Design

Now that we have completed Example 12.10, let us explore the effects of the resistor tolerances on our design. We have chosen resistors that have 5 percent tolerances; Table 12.10

Table 12.10

Cascade of Six Identical Noninverting Amplifiers—Worse-Case Analysis

R Values	One-Stage Gain	Six-Stage Gain	f_{H1}	f_H	R_{IN}	R_{OUT}
Nominal	6.91E + 00	1.09E + 05	1.45E + 05	5.065E + 04	1.45E + 13	3.45E−03
High	7.53E + 00	1.82E + 05	1.33E + 05	**4.647E + 04**	1.33E + 13	3.77E−03
Low	6.35E + 00	**6.53E + 04**	1.58E + 05	5.514E + 04	1.58E + 13	3.17E−03

presents the results of calculating the worst-case specifications, in which

$$A_{VNOM} = 1 + \frac{130 \text{ k}\Omega}{22 \text{ k}\Omega} = 6.91$$

$$A_{VHI} = 1 + \frac{130 \text{ k}\Omega(1.05)}{22 \text{ k}\Omega(0.95)} = 7.53$$

$$A_{VLO} = 1 + \frac{130 \text{ k}\Omega(0.95)}{22 \text{ k}\Omega(1.05)} = 6.35$$

The nominal design values easily meet both specifications, with a margin of 9 percent for the gain but only 1.3 percent for the bandwidth. When the resistor tolerances are set to give the largest gain per stage, the gain specification is easily met, but the bandwidth shrinks below the specification limit. At the opposite extreme, the gain of the six stages fails to meet the required specification. This analysis gives us an indication that there may be a problem with the design. Of course, assuming that all the amplifiers reach the worst-case gain and bandwidth limits at the same time is an extreme conclusion. Nevertheless, the nominal bandwidth does not exceed the specification limit by very much.

A Monte Carlo analysis would be much more representative of the actual design results. Such an analysis for 10,000 cases of our six-stage amplifier indicates that if this circuit is built with 5 percent resistors, more than 30 percent of the amplifiers will fail to meet either the gain or bandwidth specification. (The details of this calculation and exact results are left for Prob. 12.79.)

12.7 LARGE-SIGNAL LIMITATIONS—SLEW RATE AND FULL-POWER BANDWIDTH

Up to this point, we have tacitly assumed that the internal circuits that form the operational amplifier can respond instantaneously to changes in the input signal. However, the internal amplifier nodes all have an equivalent capacitance to ground, and only a finite amount of current is available to charge these capacitances. Thus there will be some limit to the rate of change of voltage on the various nodes. This limit is described by the **slew-rate (SR)** specification of the operational amplifier. The slew rate defines the maximum rate of change of voltage at the output of the operational amplifier. Typical values of slew rate for general-purpose op amps fall into the range

$$0.1 \text{ V/}\mu\text{s} \le \text{SR} \le 10 \text{ V/}\mu\text{s}$$

although much higher values are possible in special designs. An example of a slew-rate limited signal at an amplifier output is shown schematically in Fig. 12.43.

For a given frequency, the slew rate limits the maximum amplitude of a signal that can amplified without distortion. Consider a sinusoidal output signal for example:

$$v_o = V_M \sin \omega t \qquad (12.129)$$

The maximum rate of change of this signal occurs at the zero crossings and is given by

$$\left. \frac{dv_O}{dt} \right|_{\text{max}} = V_M \omega \cos \omega t \big|_{\text{max}} = V_M \omega \qquad (12.130)$$

For no signal distortion, this maximum rate of change must be less than the slew rate:

$$V_M \omega \le \text{SR} \qquad \text{or} \qquad V_M \le \frac{\text{SR}}{\omega} \qquad (12.131)$$

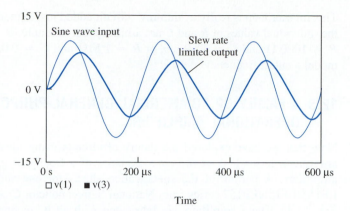

Figure 12.43 An example of a slew-rate limited output signal.

The **full-power bandwidth** f_M is the highest frequency at which a full-scale signal can be developed. Denoting the amplitude of the full-scale output signal by V_{FS}, the full-power bandwidth can be written as

$$f_M \leq \frac{\text{SR}}{2\pi V_{FS}} \qquad (12.132)$$

> **EXERCISE:** Suppose that an op amp has a slew rate of 0.5 V/μs. What is the largest sinusoidal signal amplitude that can be reproduced without distortion at a frequency of 20 kHz? If the amplifier must deliver a signal with a 10-V maximum amplitude, what is the full-power bandwidth corresponding to this signal?
>
> **ANSWERS:** 3.98 V; 7.96 kHz

12.8 MACRO MODEL FOR THE OPERATIONAL AMPLIFIER FREQUENCY RESPONSE

The actual internal circuit of an operational amplifier may contain from 20 to 100 bipolar and/or field-effect transistors. If the actual circuits were used for each op amp, simulations of complex circuits containing many op amps would be very slow. Simplified circuit representations, called **macro models,** have been developed to model the terminal behavior of the op amp. The two-port model that we used in this chapter is one simple form of macro model. This section introduces a model that can be used for SPICE simulation of the frequency response of circuits utilizing operational amplifiers.

To model the single-pole roll-off, an auxiliary loop consisting of the voltage-controlled voltage source with value v_1 in series with R and C is added to the interior of the original two-port, as depicted in Fig. 12.44. The product of R and C is chosen to give the desired -3 dB point for the open-loop amplifier. If a voltage source is applied to the input, then the open-circuit voltage gain ($R_L = \infty$) is

$$A_V(s) = \frac{\mathbf{V_o}(s)}{\mathbf{V_1}(s)} = \frac{A_o \omega_B}{s + \omega_B} \qquad \text{where } \omega_B = \frac{1}{RC} \qquad (12.133)$$

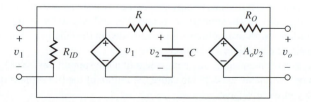

Figure 12.44 Macro model for operational amplifier.

This interior loop is really a "dummy" circuit added just to model the frequency response; the individual values of R and C are arbitrary. For example, $R = 1\ \Omega$ and $C = 0.0159$ F, $R = 1000\ \Omega$ and $C = 15.9\ \mu$F, or $R = 1\ M\Omega$ and $C = 0.0159\ \mu$F may all be used to model a cutoff frequency of 10 Hz.

12.9 A FAMILY OF COMMERCIAL GENERAL-PURPOSE OPERATIONAL AMPLIFIERS

Now that we have explored the theory of circuits using ideal and nonideal operational amplifiers, let us look at the characteristics of a family of general-purpose operational amplifiers. A portion of the specification sheets for one such commercial family, the LF155/LF156/LF157 series from National Semiconductor Corporation,* is reproduced in Fig. 12.45. These amplifiers are fabricated with an IC technology that has both bipolar transistors and JFETs.

Note that many of the specifications are stated in terms of typical values plus either upper or lower bounds. For example, the voltage gain at $T = 25°C$ with ±15-V power supplies is typically 200,000 but has a minimum value of 50,000 and no upper bound. The offset voltage is typically 3 mV with an upper bound of 5 mV, but the LF155A version is also available with a typical offset voltage of 1 mV and an upper bound of 2.5 mV. The input stage of this amplifier contains JFETs, so the input-bias current is very small, and the nominal input resistance is very large.

The minimum common-mode rejection ratio (at dc) is 85 dB, and PSRR and CMRR specifications are the same. With ±15-V power supplies, the amplifier can handle input signals with a common-mode range of at least ±11 V, and the amplifier is guaranteed to develop an output-voltage swing of ±10 V with a 2-kΩ load resistance.

The LF-156A has a minimum gain-bandwidth product (unity-gain frequency f_T) of 4 MHz, and a minimum slew rate of 10 V/μs. The LF-157 is a special wide-band version of the amplifier that is designed to be used only at closed-loop gains of 5 or larger. Considerable additional information is included concerning the performance of the amplifier family over a large range of power supply voltages and temperatures.

12.10 ACTIVE FILTERS

A wealth of knowledge exists on basic *RLC* filter design (see the Additional Reading section at the end of the chapter). However, the inductors needed to realize *RLC* filters for frequencies in the audio range can be quite bulky and heavy. IC technology fostered the development of high-performance low-cost op amps, and *RC* active-filter circuits were developed in which inductors are replaced with capacitors and op amps employing positive feedback.

---

* LIFE SUPPORT POLICY

  NATIONAL'S PRODUCTS ARE NOT AUTHORIZED FOR USE AS CRITICAL COMPONENTS IN LIFE SUPPORT DEVICES OR SYSTEMS WITHOUT THE EXPRESS WRITTEN APPROVAL OF THE PRESIDENT OF NATIONAL SEMICONDUCTOR CORPORATION.
  As used herein:

  1. Life support devices or systems are devices or systems which, (a) are intended for surgical implant into the body, or (b) support or sustain life, and whose failure to perform, when properly used in accordance with instructions for use provided in the labelling, can be reasonably expected to result in a significant injury to the user.
  2. A critical component is any component of a life support device or system whose failure to perform can be reasonably expected to cause the failure of the life support device or system, or to affect its safety or effectiveness.

Semiconductor

LF155/LF156/LF157 Series Monolithic JFET Input Operational Amplifiers

General Description

These are the first monolithic JFET input operational amplifiers to incorporate well matched, high voltage JFETs on the same chip with standard bipolar transistors (BI-FET™ Technology). These amplifiers feature low input bias and offset currents/low offset voltage and offset voltage drift, coupled with offset adjust which does not degrade drift or common-mode rejection. The devices are also designed for high slew rate, wide bandwidth, extremely fast settling time, low voltage and current noise and a low 1/f noise corner.

Advantages

- Replace expensive hybrid and module FET op amps
- Rugged JFETs allow blow-out free handling compared with MOSFET input devices
- Excellent for low noise applications using either high or low source impedance—very low 1/f corner
- Offset adjust does not degrade drift or common-mode rejection as in most monolithic amplifiers
- New output stage allows use of large capacitive loads (5,000 pF) without stability problems
- Internal compensation and large differential input voltage capability

Applications

- Precision high speed integrators
- Fast D/A and A/D converters
- High impedance buffers
- Wideband, low noise, low drift amplifiers
- Logarithmic amplifiers
- Photocell amplifiers
- Sample and Hold circuits

Common Features

(LF155A, LF156A, LF157A)

- Low input bias current   30 pA
- Low Input Offset Current   3 pA
- High input impedance $10^{12}\,\Omega$
- Low input offset voltage   1 mV
- Low input offset voltage temp. drift   3 μV/°C
- Low input noise current   0.01 pA/$\sqrt{\text{Hz}}$
- High common-mode rejection ratio   100 dB
- Large dc voltage gain   106 dB

Uncommon Features

	LF155A	LF156A	LF157A (A$_V$=5)	Units
Extremely fast settling time to 0.01%	4	1.5	1.5	μs
Fast slew rate	5	12	50	V/μs
Wide gain bandwidth	2.5	5	20	MHz
Low input noise voltage	20	12	12	nV/$\sqrt{\text{Hz}}$

Simplified Schematic

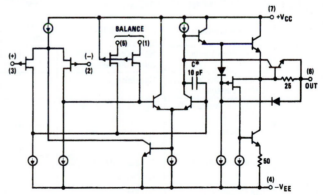

*3 pF in LF157 series.

TL/H/5646–1

Figure 12.45 Specification sheets for the LF155/LF156/LF157 series of operational amplifiers. (*Reprinted with permission of National Semiconductor Corporation.*)

LF155/LF156/LF157

Absolute Maximum Ratings

If Military/Aerospace specified devices are required, contact the National Semiconductor Sales Office/Distributors for availability and specifications.
(Note 8)

	LF155A/6A/7A	LF155/6/7	LF355B/6B/7B LF255/6/7	LF355/6/7 LF355A/6A/7A
Supply Voltage	±22V	±22V	±22V	±18V
Differential Input Voltage	±40V	±40V	±40V	±30V
Input Voltage Range (Note 2)	±20V	±20V	±20V	±16V
Output Short Circuit Duration	Continuous	Continuous	Continuous	Continuous
T_{jMAX}				
H-Package	150°C	150°C	115°C	115°C
N-Package			100°C	100°C
M-Package			100°C	100°C
Power Dissipation at $T_A = 25°C$ (Notes 1 and 9)				
H-Package (Still Air)	560 mW	560 mW	400 mW	400 mW
H-Package (400 LF/Min Air Flow)	1200 mW	1200 mW	1000 mW	1000 mW
N-Package			670 mW	670 mW
M-Package			380 mW	380 mW
Thermal Resistance (Typical) θ_{JA}				
H-Package (Still Air)	160°C/W	160°C/W	160°C/W	160°C/W
H-Package (400 LF/Min Air Flow)	65°C/W	65°C/W	65°C/W	65°C/W
N-Package			130°C/W	130°C/W
M-Package			195°C/W	195°C/W
(Typical) θ_{JC}				
H-Package	23°C/W	23°C/W	23°C/W	23°C/W
Storage Temperature Range	−65°C to +150°C	−65°C to +150°C	−65°C to +150°C	−65°C to +150°C
Soldering Information (Lead Temp.)				
Metal Can Package				
Soldering (10 sec.)	300°C	300°C	300°C	300°C
Dual-In-Line Package				
Soldering (10 sec.)		260°C	260°C	260°C
Small Outline Package				
Vapor Phase (60 sec.)			215°C	215°C
Infrared (15 sec.)			220°C	220°C

See AN-450 "Surface Mounting Methods and Their Effect on Product Reliability" for other methods of soldering surface mount devices.

ESD tolerance				
(100 pF discharged through 1.5 kΩ)	1200V	1200V	1200V	1200V

DC Electrical Characteristics (Note 3) $T_A = T_j = 25°C$

Symbol	Parameter	Conditions	LF155A/6A/7A			LF355A/6A/7A			Units
			Min	Typ	Max	Min	Typ	Max	
V_{OS}	Input Offset Voltage	$R_S = 50Ω$, $T_A = 25°C$		1	2		1	2	mV
		Over Temperature			2.5			2.3	mV
$\Delta V_{OS}/\Delta T$	Average TC of Input Offset Voltage	$R_S = 50Ω$		3	5		3	5	μV/°C
$\Delta TC/\Delta V_{OS}$	Change in Average TC with V_{OS} Adjust	$R_S = 50Ω$, (Note 4)		0.5			0.5		μV/°C per mV
I_{OS}	Input Offset Current	$T_j = 25°C$, (Notes 3, 5)		3	10		3	10	pA
		$T_j \le T_{HIGH}$			10			1	nA
I_B	Input Bias Current	$T_j = 25°C$, (Notes 3, 5)		30	50		30	50	pA
		$T_j \le T_{HIGH}$			25			5	nA
R_{IN}	Input Resistance	$T_j = 25°C$		10^{12}			10^{12}		Ω
A_{VOL}	Large Signal Voltage Gain	$V_S = ±15V$, $T_A = 25°C$ $V_O = ±10V$, $R_L = 2k$	50	200		50	200		V/mV
		Over Temperature	25			25			V/mV
V_O	Output Voltage Swing	$V_S = ±15V$, $R_L = 10k$	±12	±13		±12	±13		V
		$V_S = ±15V$, $R_L = 2k$	±10	±12		±10	±12		V

Figure 12.45 (*cont'd.*) Specification sheets for the LF155/LF156/LF157 series of operational amplifiers.

DC Electrical Characteristics (Note 3) $T_A = T_j = 25°C$ (Continued)

Symbol	Parameter	Conditions	LF155A/6A/7A			LF355A/6A/7A			Units
			Min	Typ	Max	Min	Typ	Max	
V_{CM}	Input Common-Mode Voltage Range	$V_S = \pm15V$	±11	$+15.1$ -12		±11	$+15.1$ -12		V V
CMRR	Common-Mode Rejection Ratio		85	100		85	100		dB
PSRR	Supply Voltage Rejection Ratio	(Note 6)	85	100		85	100		dB

AC Electrical Characteristics $T_A = T_j = 25°C$, $V_S = \pm15V$

Symbol	Parameter	Conditions	LF155A/355A			LF156A/356A			LF157A/357A			Units
			Min	Typ	Max	Min	Typ	Max	Min	Typ	Max	
SR	Slew Rate	LF155A/6A; $A_V = 1$, LF157A; $A_V = 5$	3	5		10	12		40	50		V/μs V/μs
GBW	Gain Bandwidth Product			2.5		4	4.5		15	20		MHz
t_s	Settling Time to 0.01%	(Note 7)		4			1.5			1.5		μs
e_n	Equivalent Input Noise Voltage	$R_S = 100Ω$ $f = 100$ Hz $f = 1000$ Hz		25 20			15 12			15 12		nV/√Hz nV/√Hz
i_n	Equivalent Input Noise Current	$f = 100$ Hz $f = 1000$ Hz		0.01 0.01			0.01 0.01			0.01 0.01		pA/√Hz pA/√Hz
C_{IN}	Input Capacitance			3			3			3		pF

DC Electrical Characteristics (Note 3)

Symbol	Parameter	Conditions	LF155/6/7			LF255/6/7 LF355B/6B/7B			LF355/6/7			Units
			Min	Typ	Max	Min	Typ	Max	Min	Typ	Max	
V_{OS}	Input Offset Voltage	$R_S = 50Ω$, $T_A = 25°C$ Over Temperature		3	5 7		3	5 6.5		3	10 13	mV mV
$\Delta V_{OS}/\Delta T$	Average TC of Input Offset Voltage	$R_S = 50Ω$		5			5			5		μV/°C
$\Delta TC/\Delta V_{OS}$	Change in Average TC with V_{OS} Adjust	$R_S = 50Ω$, (Note 4)		0.5			0.5			0.5		μV/°C per mV
I_{OS}	Input Offset Current	$T_j = 25°C$, (Notes 3, 5) $T_j \leq T_{HIGH}$		3	20 20		3	20 1		3	50 2	pA nA
I_B	Input Bias Current	$T_j = 25°C$, (Notes 3, 5) $T_j \leq T_{HIGH}$		30	100 50		30	100 5		30	200 8	pA nA
R_{IN}	Input Resistance	$T_j = 25°C$		10^{12}			10^{12}			10^{12}		Ω
A_{VOL}	Large Signal Voltage Gain	$V_S = \pm15V$, $T_A = 25°C$ $V_O = \pm10V$, $R_L = 2k$ Over Temperature	50 25	200		50 25	200		25 15	200		V/mV V/mV
V_O	Output Voltage Swing	$V_S = \pm15V$, $R_L = 10k$ $V_S = \pm15V$, $R_L = 2k$	±12 ±10	±13 ±12		±12 ±10	±13 ±12		±12 ±10	±13 ±12		V V
V_{CM}	Input Common-Mode Voltage Range	$V_S = \pm15V$	±11	$+15.1$ -12		±11	±15.1 -12		$+10$	$+15.1$ -12		V V
CMRR	Common-Mode Rejection Ratio		85	100		85	100		80	100		dB
PSRR	Supply Voltage Rejection Ratio	(Note 6)	85	100		85	100		80	100		dB

Figure 12.45 (*cont'd.*) Specification sheets for the LF155/LF156/LF157 series of operational amplifiers.

LF155/LF156/LF157

DC Electrical Characteristics $T_A = T_j = 25°C$, $V_S = \pm 15V$

Parameter	LF155A/155, LF255, LF355A/355B		LF355		LF156A/156, LF256/356B		LF356A/356		LF157A/157 LF257/357B		LF357A/357		Units
	Typ	Max	Typ	Max	Typ	Max	Typ	Max	Typ	Max	Typ	Max	
Supply Current	2	4	2	4	5	7	5	10	5	7	5	10	mA

AC Electrical Characteristics $T_A = T_j = 25°C$, $V_S = \pm 15V$

Symbol	Parameter	Conditions	LF155/255/ 355/355B	LF156/256, LF356B	LF156/256/ 356/356B	LF157/257, LF357B	LF157/257/ 357/357B	Units
			Typ	Min	Typ	Min	Typ	
SR	Slew Rate	LF155/6: $A_V = 1$, LF157: $A_V = 5$	5	7.5	12	30	50	$V/\mu s$ $V/\mu s$
GBW	Gain Bandwidth Product		2.5		5		20	MHz
t_s	Settling Time to 0.01%	(Note 7)	4		1.5		1.5	μs
e_n	Equivalent Input Noise Voltage	$R_S = 100\Omega$ $f = 100$ Hz $f = 1000$ Hz	25 20		15 12		15 12	$nV/\sqrt{Hz}$ $nV/\sqrt{Hz}$
i_n	Equivalent Input Current Noise	$f = 100$ Hz $f = 1000$ Hz	0.01 0.01		0.01 0.01		0.01 0.01	$pA/\sqrt{Hz}$ $pA/\sqrt{Hz}$
C_{IN}	Input Capacitance		3		3		3	pF

Notes for Electrical Characteristics

Note 1: The maximum power dissipation for these devices must be derated at elevated temperatures and is dictated by T_{jMAX}, θ_{jA}, and the ambient temperature, T_A. The maximum available power dissipation at any temperature is $P_d = (T_{jMAX} - T_A)/\theta_{jA}$ or the 25°C P_{dMAX}, whichever is less.

Note 2: Unless otherwise specified the absolute maximum negative input voltage is equal to the negative power supply voltage.

Note 3: Unless otherwise stated, these test conditions apply:

	LF155A/6A/7A LF155//6/7	LF255//6/7	LF355A/6A/7A	LF355B/6B/7B	LF355//6/7
Supply Voltage, V_S	$\pm 15V \leq V_S \leq \pm 20V$	$\pm 15V \leq V_S \leq \pm 20V$	$\pm 15V \leq V_S \leq \pm 18V$	$\pm 15V \leq V_S \pm 20V$	$V_S = \pm 15V$
T_A	$-55°C \leq T_A \leq +125°C$	$-25°C \leq T_A \leq +85°C$	$0°C \leq T_A \leq +70°C$	$0°C \leq T_A \leq +70°C$	$0°C \leq T_A \leq +70°C$
T_{HIGH}	$+125°C$	$+85°C$	$+70°C$	$+70°C$	$+70°C$

and V_{OS}, I_B and I_{OS} are measured at $V_{CM} = 0$.

Note 4: The Temperature Coefficient of the adjusted input offset voltage changes only a small amount (0.5μV/°C typically) for each mV of adjustment from its original unadjusted value. Common-mode rejection and open loop voltage gain are also unaffected by offset adjustment.

Note 5: The input bias currents are junction leakage currents which approximately double for every 10°C increase in the junction temperature, T_J. Due to limited production test time, the input bias currents measured are correlated to junction temperature. In normal operation the junction temperature rises above the ambient temperature as a result of internal power dissipation, Pd. $T_J = T_A + \theta_{jA}$ Pd where θ_{jA} is the thermal resistance from junction to ambient. Use of a heat sink is recommended if input bias current is to be kept to a minimum.

Note 6: Supply Voltage Rejection is measured for both supply magnitudes increasing or decreasing simultaneously, in accordance with common practice.

Note 7: Settling time is defined here, for a unity gain inverter connection using 2 kΩ resistors for the LF155/6. It is the time required for the error voltage (the voltage at the inverting input pin on the amplifier) to settle to within 0.01% of its final value from the time a 10V step input is applied to the inverter. For the LF157, $A_V = -5$, the feedback resistor from output to input is 2 kΩ and the output step is 10V (See Settling Time Test Circuit).

Note 8: Refer to RETS155AX for LF155A, RETS155X for LF155, RETS156AX for LF156A, RETS156X for LF156, RETS157A for LF157A and RETS157X for LF157 military specifications.

Note 9: Max. Power Dissipation is defined by the package characteristics. Operating the part near the Max. Power Dissipation may cause the part to operate outside guaranteed limits.

Figure 12.45 (*cont'd.*) Specification sheets for the LF155/LF156/LF157 series of operational amplifiers.

This section introduces basic low-pass, high-pass, and band-pass **active filters.** A simple low-pass filter was discussed in Sec. 12.3, but this circuit produced only a single pole. Many of the filters described in this section are more efficient in the sense that the circuits achieve two poles of filtering per op amp. The interested reader can explore the material further in many texts that deal exclusively with active-filter design.

Low-Pass Filter

A basic two-pole low-pass filter configuration is shown in Fig. 12.46 and is formed from an op amp with two resistors and two capacitors. In this particular circuit the op amp is operated as a voltage follower, which provides unity gain over a wide range of frequencies. The filter uses positive feedback through C_1 at frequencies above dc to realize complex poles without the need for inductors.

Let us now find the transfer function describing the voltage gain of this filter. The ideal op-amp forces $\mathbf{V_o}(s) = \mathbf{V_2}(s)$, so there are only two independent nodes in the circuit. Writing nodal equations for $\mathbf{V_1}(s)$ and $\mathbf{V_2}(s)$ yields

$$\begin{bmatrix} G_1 \mathbf{V_s}(s) \\ 0 \end{bmatrix} = \begin{bmatrix} sC_1 + G_1 + G_2 & -(sC_1 + G_2) \\ -G_2 & sC_2 + G_2 \end{bmatrix} \begin{bmatrix} \mathbf{V_1}(s) \\ \mathbf{V_2}(s) \end{bmatrix} \tag{12.134}$$

and the determinant of this system of equations is

$$\Delta = s^2 C_1 C_2 + sC_2(G_1 + G_2) + G_1 G_2 \tag{12.135}$$

Solving for $\mathbf{V_2}(s)$ and remembering that $\mathbf{V_o}(s) = \mathbf{V_2}(s)$ yields

$$\mathbf{V_o}(s) = \mathbf{V_2}(s) = \frac{G_1 G_2}{\Delta} \mathbf{V_s}(s) \tag{12.136}$$

and

$$A_{LP}(s) = \frac{\mathbf{V_o}(s)}{\mathbf{V_s}(s)} = \frac{\dfrac{G_1 G_2}{C_1 C_2}}{s^2 + s\dfrac{G_1 + G_2}{C_1} + \dfrac{G_1 G_2}{C_1 C_2}} \tag{12.137}$$

$$= \frac{\dfrac{1}{R_1 R_2 C_1 C_2}}{s^2 + s\dfrac{1}{C_1}\left(\dfrac{1}{R_1} + \dfrac{1}{R_2}\right) + \dfrac{1}{R_1 R_2 C_1 C_2}}$$

Equation (12.140) is most often written in standard form as

$$A_V(s) = \frac{\omega_o^2}{s^2 + s\dfrac{\omega_o}{Q} + \omega_o^2} \tag{12.138}$$

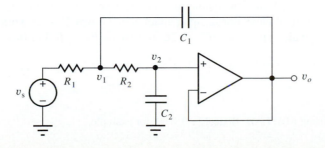

Figure 12.46 A two-pole low-pass filter.

in which

$$\omega_o = \frac{1}{\sqrt{R_1 R_2 C_1 C_2}} \quad \text{and} \quad Q = \sqrt{\frac{C_1}{C_2}} \frac{\sqrt{R_1 R_2}}{R_1 + R_2} \tag{12.139}$$

The frequency ω_o is referred to as the cutoff frequency of the filter, although the exact value of the cutoff frequency, based on the strict definition of ω_H, is equal to ω_o only for $Q = 1/\sqrt{2}$. At low frequencies—that is, $\omega \ll \omega_o$—the filter has unity gain, but for frequencies well above ω_o, the filter response exhibits a two-pole roll-off, falling at a rate of 40 dB/decade. At $\omega = \omega_o$, the gain of the filter is equal to Q.

Figure 12.47 shows the response of the filter for $\omega_o = 1$ and four values of Q: 0.25, $1/\sqrt{2}$, 2, and 10. $Q = 1/\sqrt{2}$ corresponds to the maximally flat magnitude response of a **Butterworth filter,** which gives the maximum bandwidth without a peaked response. For a Q larger than $1/\sqrt{2}$, the filter response exhibits a peaked response that is usually undesirable, whereas a Q below $1/\sqrt{2}$ does not take maximum advantage of the filter's bandwidth capability. Because the voltage follower must accurately provide a gain of 1, ω_o should be designed to be one to two decades below the unity-gain frequency of the op amp.

From a practical point of view, a much wider selection of resistor values than capacitor values exists, and the filters are often designed with $C_1 = C_2 = C$. Then ω_o and Q are adjusted by choosing different values of R_1 and R_2. For the equal capacitor design,

$$\omega_o = \frac{1}{C\sqrt{R_1 R_2}} \quad \text{and} \quad Q = \frac{\sqrt{R_1 R_2}}{R_1 + R_2} \tag{12.140}$$

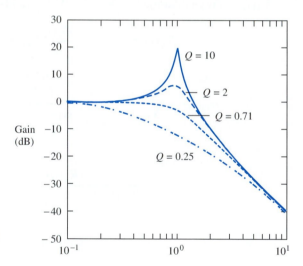

Figure 12.47 Low-pass filter response[1] for $\omega_o = 1$ and four values of Q.

EXAMPLE 12.11: Design a low-pass filter using the circuit in Fig. 12.46 with $f_o = 5$ kHz and a maximally flat response.

SOLUTION: The maximally flat response is achieved for $Q = 1/\sqrt{2}$. Unfortunately, the equal capacitor design cannot achieve this Q. One workable choice for the element values is $C_1 = 2C_2 = 2C$ and $R_1 = R_2 = R$. For these values,

$$R = \frac{1}{\sqrt{2}\omega_o C} \quad \text{and} \quad Q = \frac{1}{\sqrt{2}}$$

---

[1]Using MATLAB: Bode(1,[1 0.1 1]), for example.

but we still have two values to select and only one constraint. We must call upon our engineering judgment to make the design choice.

Note that $1/\omega_o C$ represents the reactance of C at the frequency ω_o, and R is 30 percent smaller than this value. Thus, the impedance level of the filter is set by the choice of C (or R). If the impedance level is too low, the op amp is not able to supply the current needed to drive the feedback network.

At 5 kHz, a 0.01-μF capacitor has a reactance of 3.18 kΩ:

$$\frac{1}{\omega_o C} = \frac{1}{10^4 \pi (10^{-8})} = 3180 \ \Omega$$

This is a readily available value of capacitance, and so

$$R = \frac{3180 \ \Omega}{\sqrt{2}} = 2250 \ \Omega$$

Referring to the precision resistor table in Appendix C, we find that the nearest 1 percent resistor value is 2260 Ω. The completed design values are

$$R_1 = R_2 = 2.26 \ \text{k}\Omega, \ C_1 = 0.02 \ \mu\text{F}, \ C_2 = 0.01 \ \mu\text{F}$$

Using these values yields $f_o = 4980$ Hz and $Q = 0.707$. ◆

EXERCISE: Starting with Eq. (12.138), show that $|(A_V(j\omega_o)| = Q$.

EXERCISE: Change the cutoff frequency of this filter to 2 kHz by changing the values of R_1 and R_2. Do not change the Q.

ANSWER: $R_1 = R_2 = 5.62$ kΩ

EXERCISE: Use the Q expression in Eq. (12.140) to show that $Q = 1/\sqrt{2}$ cannot be realized using the equal capacitance design. What is the maximum Q for $C_1 = C_2$?

ANSWER: 0.5

Sensitivity

An important concern in the design of active filters is the **sensitivity** of ω_o and Q to changes in passive element values and op-amp parameters. The sensitivity of design parameter P to changes in circuit parameter Z is defined mathematically as

$$S_Z^P = \frac{\dfrac{\partial P}{P}}{\dfrac{\partial Z}{Z}} = \frac{Z}{P}\frac{\partial P}{\partial Z} = \frac{\partial \ln(P)}{\partial \ln(Z)} \tag{12.141}$$

Sensitivity S represents the fractional change in parameter P due to a given fractional change in the value of Z. For example, evaluating the sensitivity of ω_o with respect to the values of R and C using Eq. (12.139) yields

$$S_R^{\omega_o} = S_C^{\omega_o} = -\frac{1}{2} \tag{12.142}$$

A 2 percent increase in the value of R or C will cause a 1 percent decrease in the frequency ω_o.

EXERCISE: Calculate $S_{C_1}^Q$ and $S_{R_2}^Q$ for the low-pass filter using Eq. (12.139) and the values in the example.

ANSWERS: $-0.5, 0$

High-Pass Filter with Gain

A **high-pass filter** can be achieved with the same topology as Fig. 12.46 by interchanging the position of the resistors and capacitors, as shown in Fig. 12.48. In many applications, filters with gain in the midband region are preferred; the voltage follower in the low-pass filter has been replaced with a noninverting amplifier with a gain of K in the filter of Fig. 12.48. Gain K provides an additional degree of freedom in the design of the filter elements. The analysis is virtually identical to that of the low-pass filter. Nodes v_1 and v_2 are the only independent nodes because $v_o = +Kv_2$, and writing the two nodal equations yields the following system of equations:

$$\begin{bmatrix} sC_1\mathbf{V_s}(s) \\ 0 \end{bmatrix} = \begin{bmatrix} s(C_1 + C_2) + G_1 & -(sC_2 + KG_1) \\ -sC_2 & sC_2 + G_2 \end{bmatrix}\begin{bmatrix} \mathbf{V_1}(s) \\ \mathbf{V_2}(s) \end{bmatrix} \tag{12.143}$$

The system determinant is

$$\Delta = s^2C_1C_2 + s(C_1 + C_2)G_2 + sC_2G_1(1 - K) + G_1G_2 \tag{12.144}$$

and the output voltage is

$$\mathbf{V_o}(s) = K\mathbf{V_2}(s) = K\frac{s^2C_1C_2\mathbf{V_s}(s)}{\Delta} \tag{12.145}$$

Combining Eqs. (12.144) and (12.145) yields the filter transfer function

$$A_{HP}(s) = \frac{\mathbf{V_o}(s)}{\mathbf{V_s}(s)} = \frac{+Ks^2}{s^2 + s\left[\dfrac{1}{R_2}\left(\dfrac{1}{C_1} + \dfrac{1}{C_2}\right) + \dfrac{1 - K}{R_1C_1}\right] + \dfrac{1}{R_1R_2C_1C_2}} \tag{12.146}$$

which can be written in standard form as

$$A_{HP}(s) = K\frac{s^2}{s^2 + s\dfrac{\omega_o}{Q} + \omega_o^2} \tag{12.147}$$

in which

$$\omega_o = \frac{1}{\sqrt{R_1R_2C_1C_2}} \qquad \text{and} \qquad Q = \left[\sqrt{\frac{R_1}{R_2}}\frac{C_1 + C_2}{\sqrt{C_1C_2}} + (1 - K)\sqrt{\frac{R_2C_2}{R_1C_1}}\right]^{-1} \tag{12.148}$$

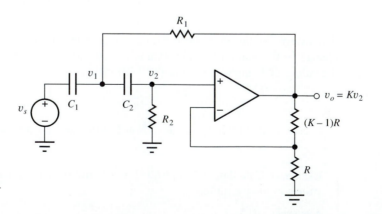

Figure 12.48 A high-pass filter with gain.

For the case $R_1 = R_2 = R$ and $C_1 = C_2 = C$, Eqs. (12.147) and (12.148) can be simplified to

$$A_{HP}(s) = K \frac{s^2}{s^2 + s\dfrac{3-K}{RC} + \dfrac{1}{R^2C^2}}$$

$$\omega_o = \frac{1}{RC} \qquad \text{and} \qquad Q = \frac{1}{3-K} \qquad\qquad (12.149)$$

For this design choice, ω_o and Q can be adjusted independently.

Figure 12.49 shows the high-pass filter responses for a filter with $\omega_o = 1$ and four values of Q. The parameter ω_o corresponds approximately to the lower-cutoff frequency of the filter, and $Q = 1/\sqrt{2}$ again represents the maximally flat, or Butterworth filter, response.

The noninverting amplifier circuit in Fig. 12.48 must have $K \geq 1$. Note in Eq. (12.149) that $K = 3$ corresponds to infinite Q. This situation corresponds to the poles of the filter being exactly on the imaginary axis at $s = j\omega_o$ and results in sinusoidal oscillation. (Oscillators are discussed in detail in Chapter 18.) For $K > 3$, the filter poles will be in the right-half plane, and values of $K \geq 3$ correspond to unstable filters. Therefore, $1 \leq K < 3$.

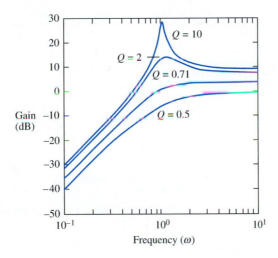

Figure 12.49 High-pass filter response[2] for $\omega_o = 1$ and four values of Q.

EXERCISE: What is the gain at $\omega = \omega_o$ for the filter described by Eq. (12.149)?

ANSWER: $\dfrac{K}{3-K}$

EXERCISE: The high-pass filter in Fig. 12.48 has been designed with $C_1 = 0.001 \ \mu F$, $C_2 = 0.0047 \ \mu F$, $R_1 = 10 \ k\Omega$, and $R_2 = 20 \ k\Omega$, and the amplifier gain is 2. What are f_o and Q for this filter?

ANSWERS: 5.19 kHz, 1.21

[2]Using MATLAB: Bode([(3-sqrt(2)) 0 0],[1 sqrt(2) 1]), for example.

EXERCISE: Derive an expression for the sensitivity of Q with respect to the closed-loop gain K for the high-pass filter in Fig. 12.48. What is the value of sensitivity if $Q = 1/\sqrt{2}$?

ANSWERS: $S_K^Q = Q(3 - Q)$; 1.62

Band-Pass Filter

A **band-pass filter** can be realized by combining the low-pass and high-pass characteristics of the previous two filters. Figure 12.50 is one possible circuit for such a band-pass filter. In this case, the op amp is used in its inverting configuration; this circuit is sometimes called an "infinite-gain" filter because the full open-loop gain of the op amp, ideally infinity, is utilized.

Analysis of the circuit in Fig. 12.50 can be reduced to a one-node problem by using op-amp theory to relate $\mathbf{V_o}(s)$ directly to $\mathbf{V_1}(s)$:

$$sC_2\mathbf{V_1}(s) = -\frac{\mathbf{V_o}(s)}{R_2} \quad \text{or} \quad \mathbf{V_1}(s) = -\frac{\mathbf{V_o}(s)}{sC_2R_2} \tag{12.150}$$

Using KCL at node v_1,

$$G_1\mathbf{V_s} = [s(C_1 + C_2) + G_1]\mathbf{V_1}(s) - sC_1\mathbf{V_o}(s) \tag{12.151}$$

Combining Eqs. (12.150) and (12.151) yields

$$A_{BP}(s) = \frac{\mathbf{V_o}(s)}{\mathbf{V_s}(s)} = \frac{-\dfrac{s}{R_1C_1}}{s^2 + s\dfrac{1}{R_2}\left(\dfrac{1}{C_1} + \dfrac{1}{C_2}\right) + \dfrac{1}{R_1R_2C_1C_2}} \tag{12.152}$$

which can be expressed as

$$A_{BP}(s) = -\frac{\dfrac{s}{R_1C_1}}{s^2 + s\dfrac{\omega_o}{Q} + \omega_o^2} = -\sqrt{\frac{R_2C_2}{R_1C_1}}\frac{s\omega_o}{s^2 + s\dfrac{\omega_o}{Q} + \omega_o^2} \tag{12.153}$$

with

$$\omega_o = \frac{1}{\sqrt{R_1R_2C_1C_2}} \quad \text{and} \quad Q = \sqrt{\frac{R_2}{R_1}}\frac{\sqrt{C_1C_2}}{C_1 + C_2} \tag{12.154}$$

If C_1 is set equal to $C_2 = C$, the expressions for center frequency and Q become

$$\omega_o = \frac{1}{C\sqrt{R_1R_2}} \qquad Q = \frac{1}{2}\sqrt{\frac{R_2}{R_1}} \qquad A_{BP}(s) = -2Q\frac{s\omega_o}{s^2 + s\dfrac{\omega_o}{Q} + \omega_o^2} \tag{12.155}$$

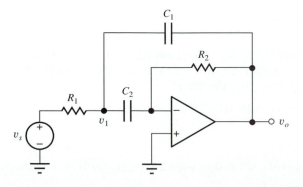

Figure 12.50 Band-pass filter using inverting op-amp configuration.

The response of the band-pass filter is shown in Fig. 12.51 for $\omega_o = 1$, $C_1 = C_2$, and three values of Q. Parameter ω_o now represents the center frequency of the band-pass filter. The response peaks at ω_o, and the gain at the center frequency is equal to $2Q^2$. At frequencies much less than or much greater than ω_o, the filter response corresponds to a single-pole high- or low-pass filter, changing at a rate of 20 dB/decade.

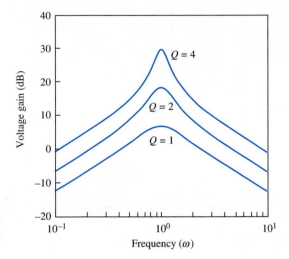

Figure 12.51 Band-pass filter response[3] for $\omega_o = 1$ and three values of Q assuming $C_1 = C_2$.

EXERCISE: The filter in Fig. 12.50 is designed with $C_1 = C_2 = 0.02\ \mu\text{F}$, $R_1 = 1\ \text{k}\Omega$, and $R_2 = 82\ \text{k}\Omega$. What are the values of f_o and Q?

ANSWERS: 879 Hz, 4.5

The Tow-Thomas Biquad

The three single-amplifier filters just discussed do not permit independent design of ω_o, Q, and midband gain. Multi-amplifier filters trade increased component cost for ease of design and low sensitivity and can be used to realize the general biquadratic transfer function defined by

$$T(s) = \frac{a_2 s^2 + a_1 s + a_0}{s^2 + \dfrac{\omega_o}{Q}s + \omega_o^2} \tag{12.156}$$

Low-pass, high-pass, band-pass, all-pass, and notch filters can all be represented by this transfer function with appropriate choices of the numerator coefficients. Compare Eq. (12.156) with Eqs. (12.153), (12.147), and (12.138). One example is the **Tow-Thomas biquad** in Fig. 12.52(a). The Tow-Thomas biquad inherently produces band-pass and low-pass outputs at v_{bp} and v_{lp}, respectively, but the other filter functions can easily be obtained with the addition of a few passive components, as in Fig. 12.52(b).

The filter response can be found by treating the first op amp as a multi-input integrator and noting that the third op amp simply forms an inverter with $V_o(s) = -V_{lp}(s)$. Using superposition, the output of the first integrator can be written as

$$\mathbf{V_{bp}}(s) = -\frac{1}{sR_1 C}\mathbf{V_s}(s) - \frac{1}{sRC}[-\mathbf{V_{lp}}(s)] - \frac{1}{sR_2 C}\mathbf{V_{bp}}(s) \tag{12.157}$$

[3]Using MATLAB: Bode([4 0],[1 .5 1]), for example.

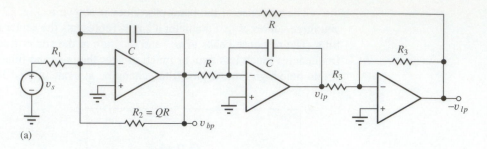

(a)

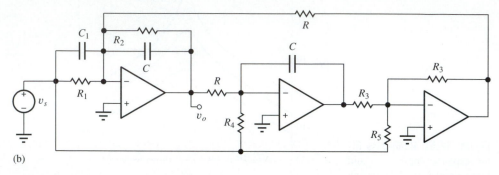

(b)

Figure 12.52 (a) Tow-Thomas filter with band-pass and low-pass outputs. (b) Full Tow-Thomas biquad.

$\mathbf{V_{lp}}(s)$ and $\mathbf{V_{bp}}(s)$ are related to each other by the second integrator:

$$\mathbf{V_{lp}}(s) = -\frac{1}{sRC}\mathbf{V_{bp}}(s) \tag{12.158}$$

Combining Eqs. (12.157) and (12.158) and solving for $\mathbf{V_{bp}}(s)$ gives

$$A_{BP}(s) = \frac{\mathbf{V_{bp}}(s)}{\mathbf{V_s}(s)} = -\frac{\dfrac{s}{R_1 C}}{s^2 + s\dfrac{1}{R_2 C} + \dfrac{1}{R^2 C^2}} = -\frac{\left(\dfrac{R}{R_1}\right)\dfrac{s}{RC}}{s^2 + s\left(\dfrac{R}{R_2}\right)\dfrac{1}{RC} + \dfrac{1}{R^2 C^2}} \tag{12.159}$$

or

$$A_{BP}(s) = -K\frac{s\omega_o}{s^2 + s\dfrac{\omega_o}{Q} + \omega_o^2} \tag{12.160}$$

in which

$$\omega_o = \frac{1}{RC} \qquad K = \left(\frac{R}{R_1}\right) \qquad Q = \frac{R_2}{R} \tag{12.161}$$

The low-pass output is obtained using Eqs. (12.158) and (12.160):

$$A_{LP}(s) = K\frac{\dfrac{1}{R^2 C^2}}{s^2 + s\dfrac{1}{R_2 C} + \dfrac{1}{R^2 C^2}} = K\frac{\omega_o^2}{s^2 + s\dfrac{\omega_o}{Q} + \omega_o^2} \tag{12.162}$$

In Eq. (12.161), it can be observed that the center frequency ω_o, Q, and gain K of the filter are each controlled by separate element values and can all be adjusted independently.

Figure 12.52(b) shows the addition of the components needed to achieve other forms of the biquadratic transfer function. If v_O is defined as the output of the first amplifier, then

$$A_V(s) = \frac{\mathbf{V_o}(s)}{\mathbf{V_s}(s)} = -\frac{s^2\left(\dfrac{C_1}{C}\right) + \dfrac{s}{C}\left(\dfrac{1}{R_1} - \dfrac{R_3}{RR_5}\right) + \dfrac{1}{RR_4C^2}}{s^2 + s\left(\dfrac{R}{R_2}\right)\dfrac{1}{RC} + \dfrac{1}{R^2C^2}} \qquad (12.163)$$

Magnitude and Frequency Scaling

The values of resistance and capacitance calculated for a given filter design may not always be convenient, or the values may not correspond closely to the standard values that are available. Magnitude scaling can be used to transform the values of the impedances of a filter without changing its frequency response. Frequency scaling, however, allows us to transform a filter design from one value of ω_o to another without changing the Q of the filter.

Magnitude Scaling

The magnitude of impedances of a filter may all be increased or decreased by a **magnitude scaling** factor K_M without changing ω_o or Q of the filter. To scale the magnitude of the impedance of the filter elements, the value of each resistor[4] is multiplied by K_M and the value of the capacitor is divided by K_M:

$$R' = K_M R \quad \text{and} \quad C' = \frac{C}{K_M} \quad \text{so that} \quad |Z'_C| = \frac{1}{\omega C'} = \frac{K_M}{\omega C} = K_M|Z_C| \qquad (12.164)$$

In all the filters discussed in Sec. 12.10, Q is determined by ratios of capacitor values and/or resistor values whereas ω_o always has the form $\omega_o = 1/\sqrt{R_1R_2C_1C_2}$. Applying magnitude scaling to the low-pass filter described by Eq. (12.139) yields

$$\omega'_o = \frac{1}{\sqrt{K_M R_1(K_M R_2)\dfrac{C_1}{K_M}\dfrac{C_2}{K_M}}} = \frac{1}{\sqrt{R_1R_2C_1C_2}} = \omega_o$$

and $\qquad\qquad\qquad\qquad\qquad\qquad\qquad\qquad\qquad\qquad\qquad\qquad\qquad\qquad (12.165)$

$$Q' = \sqrt{\frac{\dfrac{C_1}{K_M}}{\dfrac{C_2}{K_M}}}\frac{\sqrt{K_M R_1(K_M R_2)}}{K_M R_1 + K_M R_2} = \sqrt{\frac{C_1}{C_2}}\frac{K_M\sqrt{R_1R_2}}{K_M(R_1 + R_2)} = \sqrt{\frac{C_1}{C_2}}\frac{\sqrt{R_1R_2}}{R_1 + R_2} = Q$$

Thus, both Q and ω_o are independent of the magnitude scaling factor K_M.

> **EXERCISE:** The filter in Fig. 12.50 is designed with $R_1 = R_2 = 2.26$ kΩ, $C_1 = 0.02$ μF, and $C_2 = 0.01$ μF. What are the new values of C_1, C_2, R_1, R_2, f_o, and Q if the impedance magnitude is scaled by a factor of (a) 5 and (b) 0.885?
>
> **ANSWERS:** 0.004 μF, 0.002 μF, 11.3 kΩ, 11.3 kΩ, 4980 Hz, 0.707; 0.0226 μF, 0.0113 μF, 2.00 kΩ, 2.00 kΩ, 4980 Hz, 0.707

---

[4] In *RLC* filters, each inductor value is also increased by K_M: $L' = K_M L$ so $|Z'_L| = K_M|Z_L|$.

Frequency Scaling

The cutoff or center frequencies of a filter may be scaled by a **frequency scaling** factor K_F without changing the Q of the filter if each capacitor value is divided by K_F, and the resistor values are left unchanged.

$$R' = R \qquad \text{and} \qquad C' = \frac{C}{K_F}$$

Once again, using the low-pass filter as an example yields:

$$\omega_o' = \frac{1}{\sqrt{R_1 R_2 \dfrac{C_1}{K_F} \dfrac{C_2}{K_F}}} = \frac{K_F}{\sqrt{R_1 R_2 C_1 C_2}} = K_F \omega_o$$

and

$$Q' = \sqrt{\frac{\dfrac{C_1}{K_F}}{\dfrac{C_2}{K_F}}} \frac{\sqrt{R_1 R_2}}{R_1 + R_2} = \sqrt{\frac{C_1}{C_2}} \frac{\sqrt{R_1 R_2}}{R_1 + R_2} = Q \tag{12.166}$$

In this case, we see that the value of ω_o is increased by the factor K_F, but Q remains unaffected.

> **EXERCISE:** The filter in Fig. 12.50 is designed with $C_1 = C_2 = 0.02\ \mu\text{F}$, $R_1 = 1\ \text{k}\Omega$, and $R_2 = 82\ \text{k}\Omega$. (a) What are the values of f_o and Q? (b) What are the new values of C_1, C_2, R_1, R_2, f_o, and Q if the frequency is scaled by a factor of 4?
>
> **ANSWERS:** 880 Hz, 4.5; 0.005 μF, 0.005 μF, 1 kΩ, 82 kΩ, 3.5 kHz, 4.5.

12.11 SWITCHED-CAPACITOR CIRCUITS

As discussed in some detail in Chapter 7, resistors occupy inordinately large amounts of area in integrated circuits, particularly compared to MOS transistors. **Switched-capacitor (SC) circuits** are an elegant way to eliminate the resistors required in filters by replacing those elements with capacitors and switches. The filters become the discrete-time or sampled-data equivalents of the continuous-time filters discussed in Sec. 12.10, and the circuits then become compatible with high-density MOS IC processes.

A basic building block of SC circuits is the **switched-capacitor integrator** in Fig. 12.53. Resistor R of the continuous-time integrator in Fig. 12.53(a) is replaced by capacitor C_1 and MOSFET switches S_1 and S_2 in Fig. 12.53(b). The switches are driven by the **two-phase nonoverlapping clock** depicted in Fig. 12.53(c). When phase Φ_1 is high, switch S_1 is on and S_2 is off, and when phase Φ_2 is high, switch S_2 is on and S_1 is off, assuming the switches are implemented using NMOS transistors.

Figure 12.54 gives the (piecewise linear) equivalent circuits that can be used to analyze the circuit during the two individual phases of the clock. During phase 1, capacitor C_1 charges up to the value of source voltage v_S through switch S_1. At the same time, switch S_2 is open and the output voltage v_O stored on C_2 remains constant. During phase 2, capacitor C_1 becomes completely discharged because the op amp maintains a virtual ground at its input, and the charge stored on C_1 during the first phase is transferred directly to capacitor C_2 by the current that discharges C_1.

The charge stored on C_1 while phase 1 is positive (S_1 on) is

$$Q_1 = C_1 V_S \tag{12.167}$$

where $V_S = v_S[(n-1)T]$ is the voltage stored on C_1 when the switch opens at the end of the sampling interval. The change in charge stored on C_2 during phase 2 is

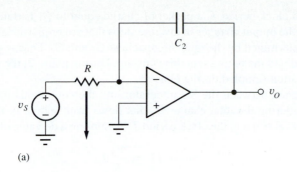

(a)

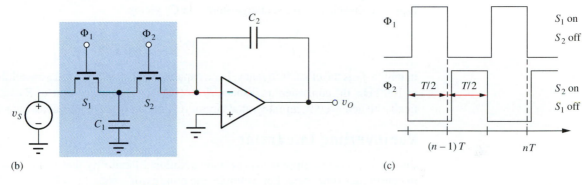

(b)   (c)

Figure 12.53 (a) Continuous-time integrator. (b) Switched-capacitor integrator. (c) Two-phase nonoverlapping clock controls the switches of the SC circuit.

Figure 12.54 Equivalent circuits during (a) phase 1 and (b) phase 2.

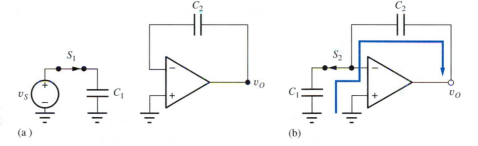

(a)   (b)

$$\Delta Q_2 = -C_2\,\Delta v_O \tag{12.168}$$

Equating these two equations yields

$$\Delta v_O = -\frac{C_1}{C_2}V_S \tag{12.169}$$

The output voltage at the end of the nth clock cycle can be written as

$$v_O[nT] = v_O[(n-1)T] - \frac{C_1}{C_2}v_S[(n-1)T]^{\,5} \tag{12.170}$$

[5]Using z-transform notation, Eq. (12.170) can be written as

$$V_O(z) = z^{-1}V_O(z) - \frac{C_1}{C_2}z^{-1}V_S(z)$$

and the transfer function for the integrator is

$$T(z) = \frac{V_O(z)}{V_S(z)} = -\frac{C_1}{C_2}\frac{1}{z-1}$$

During each clock period T, a packet of charge equal to Q_1 is transferred to storage capacitor C_2, and the output changes in discrete steps that are proportional to the input voltage with a gain determined by the ratio of capacitors C_1 and C_2. During phase 1, the input voltage is sampled and the output remains constant. During phase 2, the output changes to reflect the information sampled during phase 1.

An equivalence between the SC integrator and the continuous time integrator can be found by considering the total charge Q_S that flows from source v_S through resistor R during a time interval equal to the clock period T. Assuming a dc value of v_S for simplicity,

$$Q_S = IT = \frac{V_S}{R}T \qquad (12.171)$$

Equating this charge to the charge stored on C_1 yields

$$\frac{V_S}{R}T = C_1 V_S \qquad \text{and} \qquad R = \frac{T}{C_1} = \frac{1}{f_C C_1} \qquad (12.172)$$

in which f_C is the clock frequency. For a capacitance $C_1 = 1$ pF and a switching frequency of 100 kHz, the equivalent resistance $R = 10$ MΩ. This large value of R could not realistically be achieved in an integrated circuit realization of the continuous-time integrator.

Noninverting Integrator

Switched-capacitor circuits also provide additional flexibility that is not readily available in continuous-time form. For example, the polarity of a signal can be inverted without the use of an amplifier. In Fig. 12.55, four switches and a floating capacitor are used to realize a **noninverting integrator.**

The circuits valid during the two individual phases appear in Fig. 12.56. During phase 1, switches S_1 are closed, a charge proportional to V_S is stored on C_1, and v_O remains constant. During phase 2, switches S_2 are closed, and a charge packet equal to $C_1 V_S$ is removed from C_2 instead of being added to C_2 as in the circuit in Fig. 12.51. For the circuit in Fig. 12.55, the output-voltage change at the end of one switch cycle change is

$$\Delta v_O = +\frac{C_1}{C_2}V_S \qquad (12.173)$$

The capacitances on the source-drain nodes of the MOSFET switches in Fig. 12.53 can cause undesirable errors in the inverting SC integrator circuit. By changing the phasing of the switches, as indicated in Fig. 12.57, the noninverting integrator of Fig. 12.56 can be changed to an inverting integrator. During phase 1 in Fig. 12.58(a), the source is connected through C_1 to the summing junction of the op amp, a charge equivalent to $C_1 V_S$ is delivered to C_2, and the output-voltage change is given by Eq. (12.169). During phase 2, Fig. 12.58(b), the source is disconnected, v_O remains constant, and capacitor C_1 is completely discharged in preparation for the next cycle.

During phase 1, node 1 is driven by voltage source v_S and node 2 is maintained at zero by the virtual ground at the op-amp input. During phase 2, both terminals of capacitor

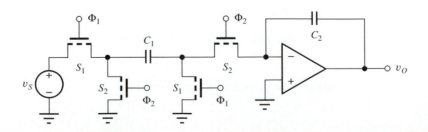

Figure 12.55 Noninverting SC integrator. (All transistors are NMOS devices.)

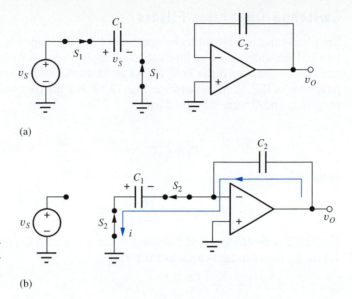

Figure 12.56 Equivalent circuits for the noninverting integrator during (a) phase 1 and (b) phase 2.

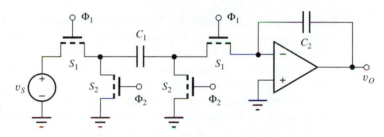

Figure 12.57 Inverting integrator achieved by changing clock phases of the switches.

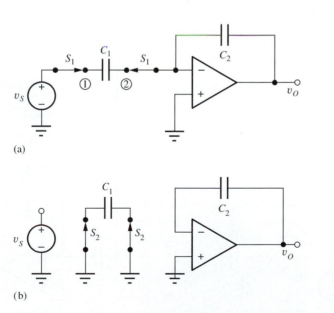

Figure 12.58 (a) Phase 1 of the stray-insensitive inverting integrator. (b) Phase 2 of the stray-insensitive inverting integrator.

C_1 are forced to zero. Thus, any stray capacitances present at node 1 or 2 do not introduce errors into the charge transfer process. A similar set of conditions is true for the noninverting integrator. These two circuits are referred to as **stray-insensitive circuits** and are preferred for use in actual SC circuit implementations.

Switched-Capacitor Filters

Switched-capacitor circuit techniques have been developed to a high level of sophistication and are widely used as filters in audio applications as well as in digital-to-analog and analog-to-digital converter designs. As an example, the SC implementation of the band-pass filter in Fig. 12.50 is shown in Fig. 12.59. For the continuous-time circuit, the center frequency and Q were described by

$$\omega_o = \frac{1}{\sqrt{R_1 R_2 C_1 C_2}} \quad \text{and} \quad Q = \sqrt{\frac{R_2}{R_1}} \frac{\sqrt{C_1 C_2}}{(C_1 + C_2)} \qquad (12.174)$$

In the SC version,

$$R_1 = \frac{T}{C_3} \quad \text{and} \quad R_2 = \frac{T}{C_4} \qquad (12.175)$$

in which T is the clock period. Substituting these values in Eq. (12.174) gives the equivalent values for the **switched-capacitor filter:**

$$\omega_o = \frac{1}{T} \sqrt{\frac{C_3 C_4}{C_1 C_2}} = f_C \sqrt{\frac{C_3 C_4}{C_1 C_2}} \quad \text{and} \quad Q = \sqrt{\frac{C_3}{C_4}} \frac{\sqrt{C_1 C_2}}{(C_1 + C_2)} \qquad (12.176)$$

Note that the center frequency of this filter is tunable just by changing the clock frequency f_C, whereas the Q is independent of frequency. This property can be extremely useful in applications requiring tunable filters. However, since switched-capacitor filters are sampled-data systems, we must remember that the filter's input signal spectrum is limited to $f \leq f_C/2$ by the sampling theorem.

A more complex example appears in the SC implementation of the Tow-Thomas biquad in Fig. 12.52 given in Fig. 12.60. In this case, the ability to change polarities allows the elimination of one complete operational amplifier in the SC implementation.

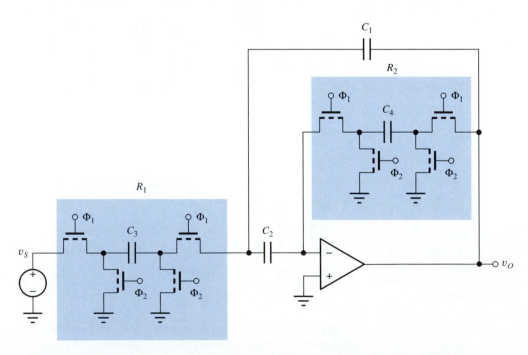

Figure 12.59 Switched-capacitor implementation of the second-order band-pass filter in Fig. 12.50.

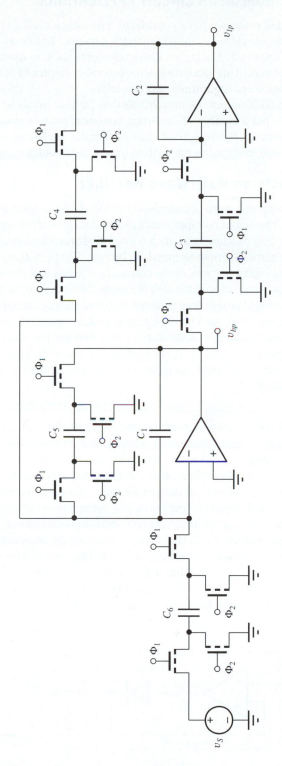

Figure 12.60 Switched-capacitor implementation of the Tow-Thomas biquad.

12.12 NONLINEAR CIRCUIT APPLICATIONS

Up to this point, we have considered only operational-amplifier circuits that use passive linear-circuit elements in the feedback network. But many interesting and useful circuits can be constructed using nonlinear elements such as diodes and transistors in the feedback network. This section explores several examples of such circuits, including precision rectification and logarithmic amplification.

In addition, our op-amp circuits thus far have involved only negative feedback configurations, but a number of important nonlinear circuits employ positive feedback. Section 12.13 looks at this important class of circuits, including op-amp implementations of the astable and monostable multivibrators and the Schmitt trigger circuit.

A Precision Half-Wave Rectifier

An op amp and diode are combined in Fig. 12.61 to form a **precision half-wave rectifier** circuit. The output v_O represents a rectified replica of the input signal v_S without loss of the voltage drop encountered with a normal diode rectifier circuit. The op amp tries to force the voltage across its input terminals to be zero. For $v_S > 0$, v_O equals v_S, and $i > 0$. Because current i_- must be zero, diode current i_D is equal to i, diode D is forward-biased, and the feedback loop is closed through the diode. However, for negative output voltages, currents i and i_D would be less than zero, but negative current cannot go through D_1. Thus, the diode cuts off ($i_D = 0$), the feedback loop is broken (inactive), and $v_O = 0$ because $i = 0$.

The resulting voltage transfer function for the precision rectifier is shown in Fig. 12.62. For $v_S \geq 0$, $v_O = v_S$, and for $v_S \leq 0$, $v_O = 0$. The rectification is precise; for $v_S \geq 0$, the operational amplifier adjusts its output v_1 to exactly absorb the forward voltage drop of the diode:

$$v_1 = v_O + v_D = v_S + v_D \tag{12.177}$$

This circuit provides accurate rectification even for very small input voltages and is sometimes called a **superdiode.** The primary sources of error are gain error due to the finite gain of the op amp, as well as an offset error due to the offset voltage of the amplifier.

A practical problem occurs in this circuit for negative input voltages. Although the output voltage is zero, as desired for the rectifier, the voltage across the op-amp input terminals is now negative, and the output voltage v_1 is saturated at the negative supply limit. Most modern op amps provide input voltage protection and will not be damaged by a large voltage across the input. However, unprotected op amps can be destroyed if the magnitude of the input voltage is larger than 1 or 2 V. The saturated output of the op amp is not usually harmful to the amplifier, but it does take time for the internal circuits to recover from the saturated condition, thus slowing down the response time of the circuit. It is preferable to prevent the op amp from saturating, if possible.

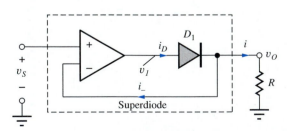

Figure 12.61 Precision half-wave rectifier circuit (or "superdiode").

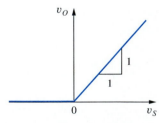

Figure 12.62 Voltage transfer characteristic for the precision rectifier.

Nonsaturating Precision-Rectifier Circuit

The saturation problem can be solved using the circuit given in Fig. 12.63. An inverting-amplifier configuration is used instead of the noninverting configuration, and diode D_2 is added to keep the feedback loop closed when the output of the rectifier is zero.

For positive input voltages, as depicted in Fig. 12.64(a), the op-amp output voltage v_1 becomes negative, forward-biasing diode D_2 so that current i_S passes through diode D_2 and into the output of the op amp. The inverting input is at virtual ground, the current in R_2 is zero, and the output remains at zero. Diode D_1 is reverse-biased.

For $v_S < 0$ in Fig. 12.64(b), diode D_1 turns on and supplies source current i_S and load current i, and D_2 is off. The circuit behaves as an inverting amplifier with gain equal to $-R_2/R_1$. Thus, the overall voltage transfer characteristic can be described by

$$v_O = 0 \text{ for } v_S \geq 0 \quad \text{and} \quad v_O = -\frac{R_2}{R_1}v_S \quad \text{for } v_S \leq 0 \quad (12.178)$$

as shown in Fig. 12.64(c). The output voltage of the op amp itself, v_1, is one diode-drop below zero for positive input voltages and one diode above the output voltage for negative input voltages. The inverting input is a virtual ground in both cases, and the negative feedback loop is always active: through D_1 and R_2 for $v_S < 0$ and through D_2 for $v_S > 0$.

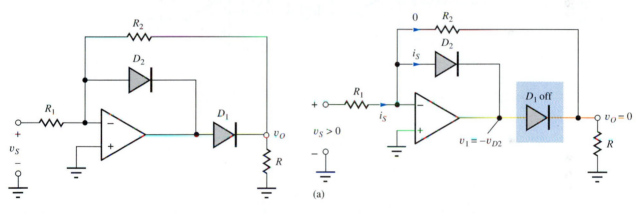

Figure 12.63 Nonsaturating precision-rectifier circuit.

Figure 12.64a (a) Active feedback elements for $v_s \geq 0$.

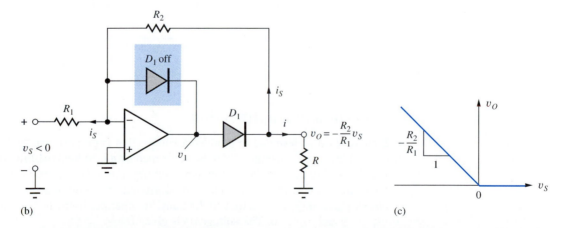

Figure 12.64 (b) Active feedback elements for $v_S < 0$. (c) Improved rectifier voltage transfer characteristic.

An AC Voltmeter

The half-wave rectifier circuit can be combined with a low-pass filter to form a basic ac voltmeter circuit, as in Fig. 12.65. For a sinusoidal input signal with an amplitude V_M at a frequency ω_o, the output voltage v_1 is a rectified sine wave that can be described by its Fourier series as:

$$v_1(t) = -\left(\frac{R_2}{R_1}\right)\left(\frac{V_M}{\pi}\right)\left[1 + \frac{\pi}{2}\sin\omega_o t - \sum_{n=2}^{\infty}\frac{1+\cos n\pi}{(n^2-1)}\cos n\omega_o t\right] \quad (12.179)$$

If the cutoff frequency of the low-pass filter is chosen such that $\omega_C \ll \omega_o$, then the output voltage v_O will consist primarily of the dc voltage component (see Prob. 12.121) given by

$$v_O = \frac{R_4}{R_3}\left[\frac{R_2}{R_1}\frac{V_M}{\pi}\right] \quad (12.180)$$

The voltmeter range (scale factor) can be adjusted through the choice of the four resistors.

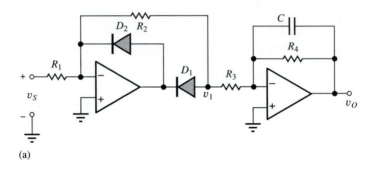

(a)

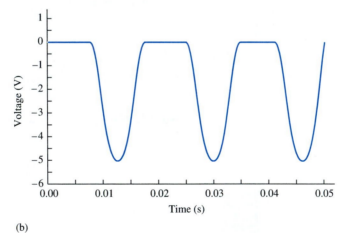

(b)

Figure 12.65 (a) AC voltmeter circuit consisting of a half-wave rectifier and low-pass filter. (b) Voltage waveform at rectifier output v_1 for $v_S = (-5\sin 120\pi t)$ V and $R_2 = R_1$.

Logarithmic Amplification

Sometimes it is desirable to produce a voltage that is proportional to the logarithm of another signal. This "operation" can be performed using the **logarithmic-amplifier** circuit in Fig. 12.66. For $v_S > 0$, the operational amplifier forces the collector current i_C of transistor Q_1 to be equal to current i_S. The virtual ground at the op-amp input sets the collector-base voltage of Q_1 to be zero, and the transistor operates in the forward-active region, with $v_{BC} = 0$ and $v_{BE} > 0$. The voltage v_O is given by

$$v_O = -v_{BE} = -V_T\ln\left[1 + \frac{i_S}{I_S}\right] \approx -V_T\ln\left[\frac{v_S}{I_S R}\right] \qquad \text{for } v_S > 0 \quad (12.181)$$

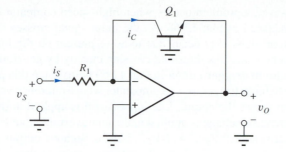

Figure 12.66 Basic logarithmic-amplifier circuit.

where the thermal voltage $V_T = kT/q$ and I_S is the saturation current of the bipolar transistor.

For $v_O > 0$, the base-emitter junction of the transistor is reverse-biased, the feedback loop is broken, and v_O saturates at the positive amplifier output level. (Note that this voltage is probably large enough to cause emitter-base junction breakdown.) This simple circuit provides an output voltage that is proportional to the logarithm of the input voltage, but circuit operation is restricted to positive input signals. We also see that output voltage is very sensitive to temperature, remembering that $V_T = kT/q$ and the BJT saturation current I_S. More sophisticated versions of this circuit can be found in the books listed in the Additional Reading section at the end of the chapter.

12.13 CIRCUITS USING POSITIVE FEEDBACK

Up to now, all our circuits except the active filters have used negative feedback: A voltage or current proportional to the output signal was returned to the inverting-input terminal of the operational amplifier. However, positive feedback can also be used to perform a number of useful nonlinear functions, and we investigate several possibilities in this final section, including the comparator, Schmitt trigger, and several multivibrator circuits.

The Comparator and Schmitt Trigger

It is often useful to compare a voltage to a known reference level. This can be done electronically using the **comparator** circuit in Fig. 12.67. We want the output of the comparator be a logic 1 when the input signal exceeds the reference level and a logic 0 when the input is less than the reference level. The basic comparator is simply a very high gain amplifier without feedback, as indicated in Fig. 12.67. For input signals exceeding the reference voltage V_{REF}, the output saturates at V_{CC}; for input signals less than V_{REF}, the output saturates at $-V_{EE}$, as indicated in the voltage transfer characteristic in Fig. 12.67.[6] Amplifiers built for use as comparators are specifically designed to be able to saturate at the two voltage extremes without incurring excessive internal time delays.

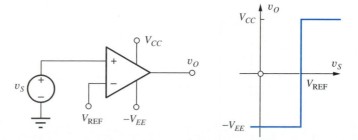

Figure 12.67 Comparator circuit using an infinite-gain amplifier.

---

[6] In this section, we assume that the output can reach the supply voltages.

However, a problem occurs when high-speed comparators are used with noisy signals, as indicated in Fig. 12.68. As the input signal crosses through the reference level, multiple transitions may occur due to noise present on the input. In digital systems, we often want to detect this threshold crossing cleanly by generating only a single transition, and the **Schmitt-trigger** circuit in Fig. 12.69 helps solve this problem.

The Schmitt trigger uses a comparator whose reference voltage is derived from a voltage divider across the output. The input signal is applied to the inverting-input terminal, and the reference voltage is applied to the noninverting input (positive feedback). For positive output voltages, $V_{REF} = \beta V_{CC}$, but for negative output voltages, $V_{REF} = -\beta V_{EE}$, where $\beta = R_1/(R_1 + R_2)$. Thus, the reference voltage changes when the output switches state.

Consider the case for an input voltage increasing from below V_{REF}, as in Fig. 12.70. The output is at V_{CC} and $V_{REF} = \beta V_{CC}$. As the input voltage crosses through V_{REF}, the output switches state to $-V_{EE}$, and the reference voltage simultaneously drops, reinforcing the voltage across the comparator input. In order to cause the comparator to switch states a second time, the input must now drop below $V_{REF} = -\beta V_{EE}$, as depicted in Fig. 12.71.

Now consider the situation as v_S decreases from a high level, as in the voltage transfer characteristic in Fig. 12.71. The output is at $-V_{EE}$ and $V_{REF} = -\beta V_{EE}$. As the input voltage crosses through V_{REF}, the output switches state to V_{CC} and the reference voltage simultaneously increases, again reinforcing the voltage across the comparator input.

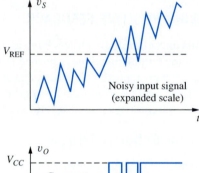

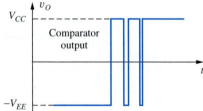

Figure 12.68 Comparator response to noisy input signal.

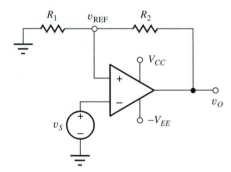

Figure 12.69 Schmitt-trigger circuit.

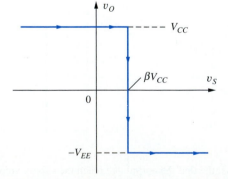

Figure 12.70 Voltage transfer characteristic for the Schmitt trigger as v_S increases from below $V_{REF} = +\beta V_{CC}$.

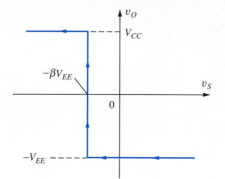

Figure 12.71 Voltage transfer characteristic for the Schmitt trigger as v_S decreases from above $V_{REF} = -\beta V_{EE}$.

The voltage transfer characteristics from Figs. 12.70 and 12.71 are combined to yield the overall voltage transfer characteristic for the Schmitt trigger given in Fig. 12.72. The arrows indicate the portion of the characteristic that is traversed for increasing and decreasing values of the input signal. The Schmitt trigger is said to exhibit hysteresis in its VTC, and will not respond to input noise that has a magnitude V_N smaller than the difference between the two threshold voltages:

$$V_N < \beta[V_{CC} - (-V_{EE})] = \beta(V_{CC} + V_{EE}) \qquad (12.182)$$

The Schmitt trigger with positive feedback is an example of a circuit with two stable states: a **bistable circuit,** or **bistable multivibrator.** Another example of a bistable circuit is the digital storage element usually called the flip-flop (see Chapter 9).

> **EXERCISE:** If $V_{CC} = +10$ V $= V_{EE}$, $R_1 = 1$ kΩ, and $R_2 = 9.1$ kΩ, what are the values of the switching thresholds for the Schmitt-trigger circuit in Figs. 12.69 through 12.72 and the magnitude of the hysteresis?
>
> **ANSWERS:** +0.99 V, −0.99 V, 1.98 V

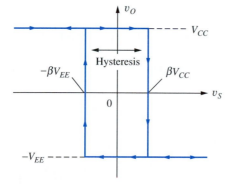

Figure 12.72 Complete voltage transfer characteristic for the Schmitt trigger.

The Astable Multivibrator

Another type of multivibrator circuit employs a combination of positive and negative feedback and is designed to oscillate and generate a rectangular output waveform. The output of the circuit in Fig. 12.73 has no stable state and is referred to as an **astable circuit,** or **astable multivibrator.**

Operation of the astable-multivibrator circuit can best be understood by referring to the waveforms in Fig. 12.74. The output voltage switches periodically (oscillates) between

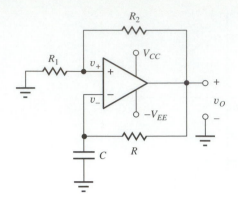

Figure 12.73 Operational amplifier in an astable-multivibrator circuit.

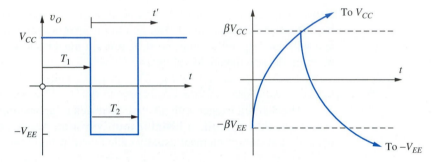

Figure 12.74 Waveforms for the astable multivibrator.

the two output voltages V_{CC} and $-V_{EE}$. Let us assume that the output has just switched to $v_O = V_{CC}$ at $t = 0$. The voltage at the inverting-input terminal of the op amp charges exponentially toward a final value of V_{CC} with a time constant $\tau = RC$. The voltage on the capacitor at the time of the output transition is $v_C = -\beta V_{EE}$. Thus, the expression for the voltage on the capacitor can be written as

$$v_C(t) = V_{CC} - (V_{CC} + \beta V_{EE}) \exp\left(-\frac{t}{RC}\right) \tag{12.183}$$

The comparator changes state again at time T_1 when $v_C(t)$ just reaches βV_{CC}:

$$\beta V_{CC} = V_{CC} - (V_{CC} + \beta V_{EE}) \exp\left(-\frac{T_1}{RC}\right) \tag{12.184}$$

Solving for time T_1 yields

$$T_1 = RC \ln \frac{1 + \beta \left(\dfrac{V_{EE}}{V_{CC}}\right)}{1 - \beta} \tag{12.185}$$

During time interval T_2, the output is low and the capacitor discharges from an initial voltage of βV_{CC} toward a final voltage of $-V_{EE}$. For this case, the capacitor voltage can be expressed as

$$v_C(t') = -V_{EE} + (V_{EE} + \beta V_{CC}) \exp\left(-\frac{t'}{RC}\right) \tag{12.186}$$

in which $t' = 0$ at the beginning of the T_2 interval. At $t' = T_2$, $v_C = -\beta V_{EE}$,

$$-\beta V_{EE} = -V_{EE} + (V_{EE} + \beta V_{CC}) \exp\left(-\frac{T_2}{RC}\right) \qquad (12.187)$$

and T_2 is equal to

$$T_2 = RC \ln \frac{1 + \beta \left(\dfrac{V_{CC}}{V_{EE}}\right)}{1 - \beta} \qquad (12.188)$$

For the common case of symmetrical power supply voltages, $V_{CC} = V_{EE}$, and the output of the astable multivibrator represents a square wave with a period T given by

$$T = T_1 + T_2 = 2RC \ln \frac{1 + \beta}{1 - \beta} \qquad (12.189)$$

The astable-multivibrator circuit has been used as the basis of inexpensive function generators that provide square, triangle, and sine wave outputs at frequencies up to a few MHz, as shown in Fig. 12.75. The frequency of the oscillator is varied by changing either R_3 or C_3. C_3 is often changed in decade steps; R_3 may be varied continuously using a potentiometer. The output of the astable multivibrator drives an op-amp integrator circuit to produce a triangular waveform. The output of the integrator can then be passed through a low-pass filter or piecewise linear shaping circuit to produce a low-distortion sine wave.

EXERCISE: What is the frequency of oscillation of the circuit in Fig. 12.73 if $V_{CC} = +5$ V, $-V_{EE} = -5$ V, $R_1 = 6.8$ kΩ, $R_2 = 6.8$ kΩ, $R = 10$ kΩ, and $C = 0.001$ μF?

ANSWER: 45.5 kHz

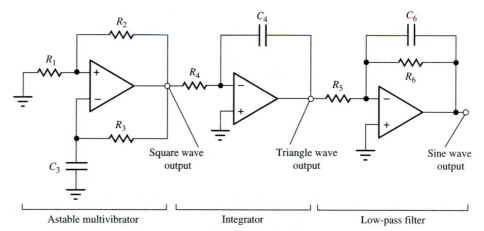

Figure 12.75 Simple function generator using an astable multivibrator, integrator, and low-pass filter.

The Monostable Multivibrator or One Shot

A third type of multivibrator operates with one stable state and is used to generate a single pulse of known duration following application of a trigger signal. The circuit rests quiescently in its stable state, but can be "triggered" to generate a single transient pulse of fixed duration T. Once the time T is past, the circuit returns to the stable state to await another **triggering** pulse. This **monostable circuit** is variously called a **monostable multivibrator**, a **single shot,** or a **one shot.**

An example of a comparator-based monostable multivibrator circuit is given in Fig. 12.76. Diode D_1 has been added to the astable multivibrator in Fig. 12.73 to couple the triggering signal v_T into the circuit, and clamping diode D_2 has been added to limit the negative voltage excursion on capacitor C.

The circuit rests in its quiescent state with $v_O = -V_{EE}$. If the trigger signal voltage v_T is less than the voltage at node 2,

$$v_T < -\frac{R_1}{R_1 + R_2}V_{EE} = -\beta V_{EE} \qquad (12.190)$$

diode D_1 is cut off. Capacitor C discharges through R until diode D_2 turns on, clamping the capacitor voltage at one diode-drop V_D below ground potential. In this condition, the differential-input voltage v_{ID} to the comparator is given by

$$v_{ID} = -\beta V_{EE} - (-V_D) = -\beta V_{EE} + V_D \qquad (12.191)$$

As long as the value of the voltage divider is chosen so that

$$v_{ID} < 0 \text{ or } \beta V_{EE} > V_D \qquad \text{where } \beta = \frac{R_1}{R_1 + R_2} \qquad (12.192)$$

then the output of the circuit will have one stable state.

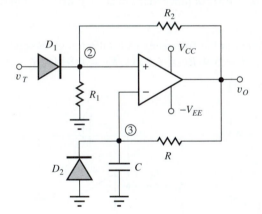

Figure 12.76 Example of an operational-amplifier monostable-multivibrator circuit.

Triggering the Monostable Multivibrator

The monostable multivibrator can be triggered by applying a positive pulse to the trigger input v_t, as shown in the waveforms in Fig. 12.77. As the trigger pulse level exceeds a voltage of $-\beta V_{EE}$, diode D_1 turns on and subsequently pulls the voltage at node 2 above that at node 3. At this point, the comparator output changes state, and the voltage at the noninverting-input terminal rises abruptly to a voltage equal to $+\beta V_{CC}$. Diode D_1 cuts off, isolating the comparator from any further changes on the trigger input.

The voltage on the capacitor now begins to charge from its initial voltage $-V_D$ toward a final voltage of V_{CC} and can be expressed mathematically as

$$v_C(t) = V_{CC} - (V_{CC} + V_D)\exp\left(-\frac{t}{RC}\right) \qquad (12.193)$$

where the time origin ($t = 0$) coincides with the start of the trigger pulse. However, the comparator changes state again when the capacitor voltage reaches $+\beta V_{CC}$. Thus, the

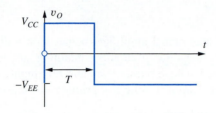

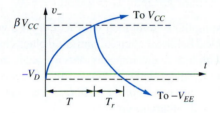

Figure 12.77 Monostable multivibrator waveforms.

pulse width T is given by

$$\beta V_{CC} = V_{CC} - (V_{CC} + V_D)\exp\left(-\frac{T}{RC}\right) \tag{12.194}$$

or

$$T = RC\ln\frac{1 + \left(\dfrac{V_D}{V_{CC}}\right)}{1 - \beta} \tag{12.195}$$

The output of the circuit consists of a positive pulse with a fixed duration T set by the values of R_1, R_2, R, and C.

For a well-defined pulse width to be generated, this circuit should not be retriggered until the voltages on the various nodes have all returned to their quiescent steady-state values. Following the return of the output to $-V_{EE}$, the capacitor voltage charges from a value of βV_{CC} toward $-V_{EE}$, but reaches steady state when diode D_2 begins to conduct. Thus, the recovery time can be calculated from

$$-V_D = -V_{EE} + (V_{EE} + \beta V_{CC})\exp\left(-\frac{T_r}{RC}\right) \tag{12.196}$$

and

$$T_r = RC\ln\frac{1 + \beta\left(\dfrac{V_{CC}}{V_{EE}}\right)}{1 - \left(\dfrac{V_D}{V_{EE}}\right)} \tag{12.197}$$

EXERCISE: For the monostable multivibrator circuit in Fig. 12.76, $V_{CC} = +5$ V $= V_{EE}$, $R_1 = 22$ kΩ, $R_2 = 18$ kΩ, $R = 11$ kΩ, and $C = 0.002$ μF. What is the pulse width of the one shot? What is the minimum time between trigger pulses for this circuit?

ANSWER: 20.4 μs; 33.4 μs.

SUMMARY

Our introduction to operational amplifiers began with a discussion of the ideal op amp and then explored the behavior of circuits containing nonideal op amps. Ideal operational amplifiers are assumed to have infinite gain and zero input current, and circuits containing these amplifiers were analyzed using two primary assumptions:

1. The differential input voltage is zero: $v_{id} = 0$.
2. The input currents are zero: $i_+ = 0$ and $i_- = 0$.

These two assumptions, combined with Kirchhoff's voltage and current laws, were used to analyze the ideal behavior of circuit building blocks based on operational amplifiers. Constant feedback with resistive voltage dividers is used in the inverting- and noninverting-amplifier configurations, the voltage follower, the difference amplifier, the summing amplifier, and the instrumentation amplifier, whereas frequency-dependent feedback is used in the low-pass filter and integrator circuits.

Infinite gain and input resistance are the explicit characteristics that lead to properties 1 and 2 just mentioned. However, many additional properties are implicit characteristics of ideal operational amplifiers; these assumptions are seldom clearly stated, though. They are

- Infinite common-mode rejection
- Infinite power supply rejection
- Infinite output voltage range
- Infinite output current capability
- Infinite open-loop bandwidth
- Infinite slew rate
- Zero output resistance
- Zero input-bias currents
- Zero input-offset voltage

The effect of removing the various ideal operational amplifier assumptions was explored in detail. Expressions were developed for the gain, gain error, input resistance, and output resistance of the closed-loop inverting and noninverting amplifiers, and it was found that the loop gain $A\beta$ plays an important role in determining the value of these closed-loop amplifier parameters. Analysis of the effects of the dc error sources, including offset voltage, bias current, and offset current was also discussed. Real op amps also have limited output voltage and current ranges as well as a finite rate of change of the output voltage called the slew rate. Circuit constraints due to these factors were also discussed.

The frequency response of basic single-pole operational amplifiers is characterized by two parameters: the open-loop gain A_o and the gain-bandwidth product ω_T. Analysis of the gain and bandwidth of the inverting and noninverting amplifier configurations demonstrated the direct tradeoff between the closed-loop gain and closed-loop bandwidth of these amplifiers. The gain-bandwidth product is constant, and the closed-loop gain must be reduced in order to increase the bandwidth, or vice versa. The bandwidth of multistage amplifiers was also discussed. An expression was developed for the bandwidth of a cascade of N identical amplifiers and was cast in terms of the bandwidth shrinkage factor. Simplified macro models are often used for simulation of the frequency response, as well as other characteristics, of circuits containing op amps.

A comprehensive example of the design of a multistage amplifier was presented in which a computer spreadsheet was used to explore the design space. The influence of resistor tolerances on this design was also discussed.

Active RC filters including low-pass, high-pass, and band-pass circuits were introduced. These designs use RC feedback networks and operational amplifiers to replace bulky inductors that would normally be required in RLC filters designed for the audio range. Single-amplifier active filters employ a combination of negative and positive feedback to realize second-order low-pass, high-pass, and band-pass transfer functions. The sensitivity of filter characteristics to passive component and op-amp parameter values was also defined. Magnitude and frequency scaling can be used to change the impedance level and ω_o of a filter without affecting its Q. Multiple op-amp filters offer low sensitivity and ease of design, compared to their single op-amp counterparts.

Switched-capacitor (SC) circuits use a combination of capacitors and switches to replace resistors in integrated circuit filter designs. These filters represent the sampled-data or discrete-time equivalents of the continuous-time RC filters and are fully compatible with MOS IC technology. Inverting and noninverting SC integrators and implementations of two SC active filters were presented.

Nonlinear circuit applications of operational amplifiers were also introduced, including precision-rectifier circuits and a logarithmic amplifier. Multivibrator circuits were discussed, including the comparator; the bistable Schmitt-trigger circuit, which is often used in place of the comparator in noisy environments; the monostable multivibrator or one shot used to generate a single pulse of known duration; and the astable multivibrator, which has no stable state but oscillates continuously, producing a square wave output.

Key Terms

Active filters
All-pass filter
Astable circuit
Astable multivibrator
Band-pass filter
Bandwidth shrinkage factor
Bias current compensation
   register
Bistable circuit
Bistable multivibrator
Butterworth filter
Closed-loop amplifier
Closed-loop gain
Common-mode gain
Common-mode input resistance
Common-mode input voltage
Common-mode rejection

Common-mode rejection ratio
   (CMRR)
Comparator
dc-Coupled amplifier
Difference amplifier
Differential amplifier
Differential-mode input
   voltage
Differential subtractor
Feedback amplifier
Feedback factor (β)
Feedback network
Fractional gain error
   (FGE)
Frequency scaling
Full-power bandwidth
Gain-bandwidth product (GBW)

Gain error (GE)
High-pass filter
Ideal operational amplifier
Input-bias current
Instrumentation amplifier
Integrator
Inverting amplifier
Inverting input
Inverting integrator
Logarithmic amplifier
Loop gain ($A\beta$) (Loop
   transmission T)
Low-pass filter
Macro model
Magnitude scaling
Monostable circuit
Monostable multivibrator

Noninverting amplifier	Precision half-wave rectifier	Switched-capacitor
Noninverting input	Schmitt trigger	(SC) circuits
Noninverting integrator	Sensitivity	Switched-capacitor filters
Notch filter	Series feedback	Switched-capacitor integrator
Offset current	Shunt feedback	Tow-Thomas biquad
Offset voltage	Single-pole frequency	Triggering
One shot	response	Two-phase nonoverlapping
Open-circuit voltage gain	Single shot	clock
Open-loop gain (A_o)	Slew rate (SR)	Two-port model
Operational amplifier	Stray-insensitive circuits	Unity-gain buffer
(op amp)	Summing amplifier	Unity-gain frequency (f_T)
Power supply rejection	Summing junction	Virtual ground
ratio (PSRR)	Superdiode	Voltage follower

Additional Reading

Connelly, J. A., and P. Choi. *Macromodeling with SPICE.* Prentice-Hall, Englewood Cliffs, NJ: 1992.

Franco, S. *Design with Operational Amplifiers and Analog Integrated Circuits.* McGraw-Hill, New York: 1988.

Ghausi, M. S., and K. R. Laker. *Modern Filter Design—Active RC and Switched Capacitor.* Prentice-Hall, Englewood Cliffs, NJ: 1981.

Gray, P. R., and R. G. Meyer. *Analysis and Design of Analog Integrated Circuits.* 3d ed. Wiley, New York: 1993.

Huelsman, L. P., and P. E. Allen. *Introduction to Theory and Design of Active Filters.* McGraw-Hill, New York: 1980.

Kennedy, E. J. *Operational Amplifier Circuits—Theory and Applications.* Holt, Rinehart and Winston, New York: 1988.

Roberge, James K. *Operational Amplifiers—Theory and Practice.* Wiley, New York: 1975.

Problems

12.1 The Differential Amplifier

12.1. A differential amplifier connected in the circuit in Fig. P12.1 has the parameters listed below with $R_S = 5$ kΩ and $R_L = 1$kΩ. (a) Find the overall voltage gain A_V, current gain A_I, and power gain A_P for the amplifier, and express the results in dB. (b) What is the amplitude V_S of the sinusoidal input signal needed to develop a 10-V peak-to-peak signal at v_o?

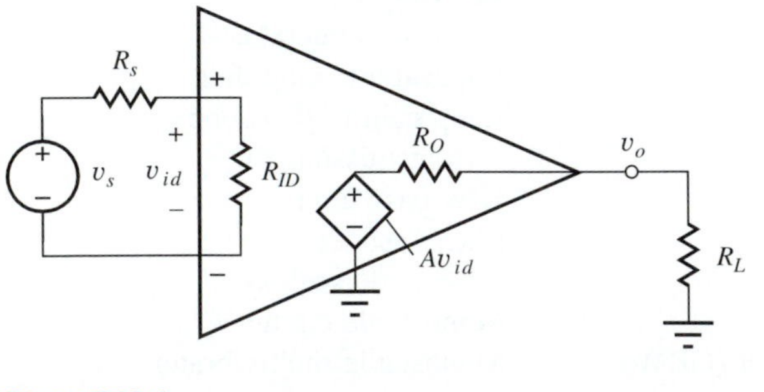

$$\text{Input resistance } R_{ID} = 1 \text{ M}\Omega$$
$$\text{Output resistance } R_O = 0.5 \text{ }\Omega$$
$$A = 60 \text{ dB}$$
$$v_S = V_S \sin \omega t$$

12.2. Suppose that the amplifier in Fig. P12.1 has been designed to match the source and load resistances in Prob. 12.1 with the parameters below. (a) What is the amplitude of the input signal v_s needed to develop a 20-V peak-to-peak signal at

Figure P12.1

v_o? (b) How much power is dissipated in the amplifier when 0.5 W is delivered to the load resistor?

$$\text{Input resistance } R_{ID} = 5 \text{ k}\Omega$$
$$\text{Output resistance } R_O = 1 \text{ k}\Omega$$
$$A = 30 \text{ dB}$$

12.3. The input to an amplifier comes from a transducer that can be represented by a 1-mV voltage source in series with a 50-kΩ resistor. What input resistance is required of the amplifier for $v_{ID} \geq 0.99$ mV?

12.4. An amplifier has a sinusoidal output signal and is delivering 100 W to a 50-Ω load resistor. What output resistance is required if the amplifier is to dissipate no more than 5 W in its own output resistance?

12.2 The Ideal Operational Amplifier

12.5. An almost ideal op amp has an open-circuit output voltage $v_o = 10$ V and a gain $A = 100$ dB. What is the input voltage v_{id}? How large must the voltage gain be to make $v_{id} \leq 1 \ \mu$V?

12.6. Suppose a differential amplifier has $A = 120$ dB, and it is operating in a circuit with an open-circuit output voltage $v_o = 15$ V. What is the input voltage v_{id}? How large must the voltage gain be to make $v_{id} \leq 1 \ \mu$V? What is the input current i_+ if $R_{ID} = 1$ MΩ?

12.3 Analysis of Circuits Containing Ideal Operational Amplifiers

12.7. What are the voltage gain, input resistance, and output resistance of the amplifier in Fig. P12.7 if $R_1 = 4.7$ kΩ and $R_2 = 220$ kΩ? Express the voltage gain in dB.

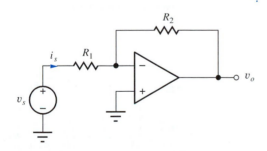

Figure P12.7

12.8. Write an expression for the output voltage $v_o(t)$ of the circuit in Fig. P12.7 if $R_1 = 910 \ \Omega$, $R_2 =$

8.2 kΩ, and $v_s(t) = (0.05 \sin 4638t)$ V. Write an expression for the current $i_S(t)$.

12.9. What are the voltage gain, input resistance, and output resistance of the amplifier in Fig. P12.9 if $R_1 = 8.2$ kΩ and $R_2 = 680$ kΩ? Express the voltage gain in dB.

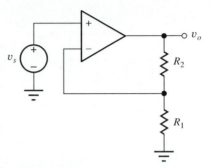

Figure P12.9

12.10. Write an expression for the output voltage $v_o(t)$ of the circuit in Fig. P12.9 if $R_1 = 910 \ \Omega$, $R_2 = 8.2$ kΩ, and $v_s(t) = (0.05 \sin 9125t)$ V.

12.11. Write an expression for the output voltage $v_o(t)$ of the circuit in Fig. P12.11 if $R_1 = 1$ kΩ, $R_2 = 2$ kΩ, $R_3 = 51$ kΩ, $v_1(t) = (0.01 \sin 3770t)$ V, and $v_2(t) = (0.04 \sin 10000t)$ V. Write an expression for the voltage appearing at the summing junction (v_-).

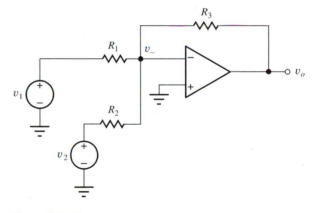

Figure P12.11

*12.12. (a) What are the gain, input resistance, and output resistance of the amplifier in Fig. P12.12 if $R_1 = 180 \ \Omega$ and $R_2 = 47$ kΩ? Express the gain in dB. (b) If the resistors have 10 percent tolerances, what are the worst-case values (highest and lowest) of gain that could occur? (c) What are the resulting positive and negative tolerances on the voltage gain with respect to the ideal value? (d) What is the ratio of the largest to the smallest voltage gain? (e) Perform a 500-case Monte Carlo analysis of this circuit. What percentage of the circuits has a gain within ± 5 percent of the nominal design value?

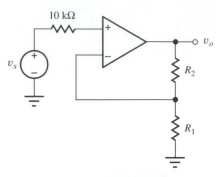

Figure P12.12

12.13. (a) What is the gain of the circuit in Fig. P12.13 if $A_V = \mathbf{v_o}/(\mathbf{v_1} - \mathbf{v_2})$ and $R = 10 \text{ k}\Omega$? (b) What is the input resistance presented to v_2? What is the input resistance at terminal v_1?

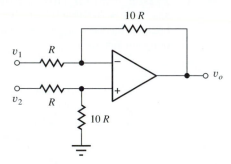

Figure P12.13

12.14. Find an expression for the output voltage in Fig. P12.14.

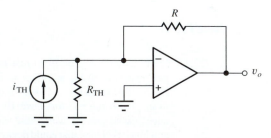

Figure P12.14

12.15. Find expressions for the gain and input resistance in the three circuits in Fig. P12.15.

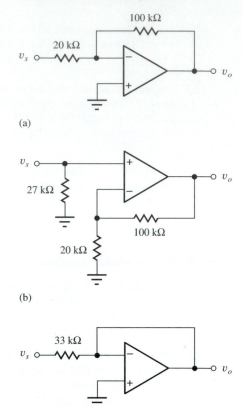

(a)

(b)

(c)

Figure P12.15

*12.16. (a) What is the output current I_O in the circuit of Fig. P12.16 if $-V_{EE} = -10$ V and $R = 10 \ \Omega$? Assume that the MOSFET is saturated. (b) What is the minimum voltage V_{DD} needed to saturate the MOSFET if $V_{TN} = 2.5$ V and $K_n = 0.25$ A/V^2. (c) What must be the power dissipation rating of resistor R?

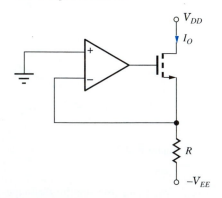

Figure P12.16

*12.17. (a) What is the output current I_O in the circuit in Fig. P12.17 if $-V_{EE} = -15$ V and $R = 30$ Ω? Assume that the BJT is in the forward-active region and $\beta_F = 30$. (b) What is the voltage at the output of the operational amplifier if the saturation current I_S of the BJT is 10^{-13} A? (c) What is the minimum voltage V_{CC} needed for forward-active region operation of the bipolar transistor? (d) What must be the power dissipation rating of the resistor R? How much power is dissipated in the transistor if $V_{CC} = 15$ V?

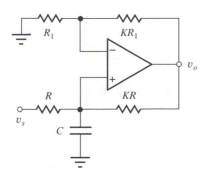

Figure P12.17

**12.18. What is the transfer function for the circuit in Fig. P12.18?

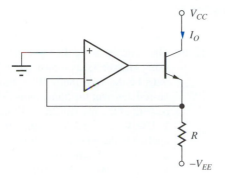

Figure P12.18

12.19. The circuit in Fig. P12.19 represents a current source that forces a current through the floating load impedance Z_L. (a) Find the relationship between the current i_o and the input voltages v_1 and v_2. (b) What is the output impedance of the current source as seen at the terminals of Z_L? (c) What is the output impedance of the current source as seen at the terminals of Z_L if both operational amplifiers have finite open-loop gain A?

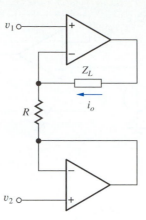

Figure P12.19

*12.20. The circuit in Fig. P12.20 is a current source that operates with a grounded load Z_L. (a) Find the relationship between the current i_o and the input voltages v_1 and v_2 if $R_1 = R_2 = R_3 = R_4$. (b) What is the output impedance of the current source as seen at the terminals of Z_L for $R_1 = R_2 = R_3 = R_4$?

*12.21. Find the five node voltages and output current for the current source circuit in Fig. P12.20 if $v_1 = 4$ V, $v_2 = 6$ V, $R = 10$ kΩ, $R_1 = 5$ kΩ, $R_2 = 5$ kΩ, $R_3 = 5.01$ kΩ, $R_4 = 4.99$ kΩ, and $Z_L = 10$ kΩ. (b) What is the output resistance of the current source?

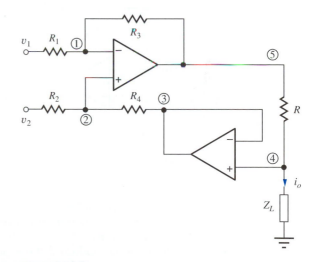

Figure P12.20

12.22. Derive an expression for the current I_L in terms of I_S, R_1, and R_2 for the circuit in Fig. P12.22. Calculate the input and output resistance of this circuit if the op amp is ideal.

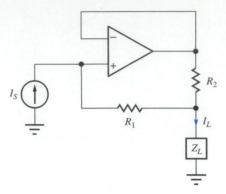

Figure P12.22

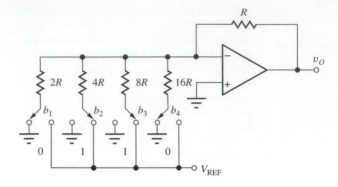

Figure P12.25

12.23. What are the input and output resistances of the circuit in Fig. P12.22 if $R_1 = 10$ kΩ, $R_2 = 1$ kΩ, and $Z_L = 3.6$ kΩ?

12.24. Find expressions for the voltage v_{o1} and v_{o2} in terms of v_s, R_1, R_2, and R_3 for the circuit in Fig. P12.24. The op amps are ideal.

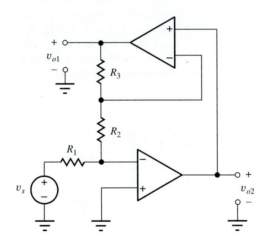

Figure P12.24

12.25. The summing amplifier can be used to form a simple 4-bit digital-to-analog converter (DAC) using the circuit in Fig. P12.25. The individual bits of the binary input word (b_1 b_2 b_3 b_4) are used to control the position of the switches, with the resistor connected to 0 V if $b_i = 0$ and connected to V_{REF} if $b_i = 1$. (a) What is the output voltage for the DAC as shown with input data of 0110 if $V_{REF} = 3.2$ V? (b) Suppose the input data changes to 1001. What will be the new output voltage? (c) Make a table giving the output voltages for all 16 possible input data combinations.

*12.26. The switches in Fig. P12.25 can be implemented using MOSFETs, as shown in Fig. P12.26. What must be the W/L ratios of the transistors if the on-resistance of the transistor is to be less than 1 percent of the resistor $2R = 10$ kΩ when $b_3 = 1$. Use $V_{REF} = 3.2$ V. Assume that the voltage applied to the gate of the MOSFET is 5 V when $b_3 = 1$ and 0 V when $b_3 = 0$. For the MOSFET, $V_{TN} = 1$ V, $K'_n = 50$ μA/V^2, $2\phi_F = 0.6$ V and $\gamma = 0.5 \sqrt{V}$.

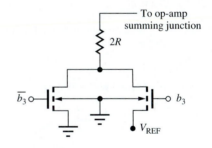

Figure P12.26

**12.27. The output voltage of the DAC in Fig. P12.25 must have an error of no more than 5 percent of V_{REF} for any input combination. What can be the tolerances on the resistors R, $2R$, $4R$, $8R$, and $16R$ if each resistor is allowed to contribute approximately the same error to the output voltage?

12.28. A circuit similar to that in Fig. P12.25 is to be used to realize a 10-bit DAC. How many resistors are needed? What is the ratio of the largest resistor to the smallest resistor? Does this seem to represent a problem?

*12.29. The circuit in Fig. P12.29 uses a "R-2R ladder" network that requires only two different resistor values to form a 4-bit DAC. The individual bits of the binary input word (b_1 b_2 b_3 b_4) are used to control the position of the switches, with the resistor connected to 0 V if $b_i = 0$ and connected to V_{REF} if $b_i = 1$. Find the output voltage for the four input combinations 0001, 0010, 0100, and 1000 if $V_{REF} = 4.8$ V.

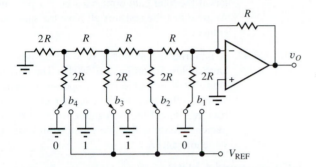

Figure P12.29

12.4 Amplifier Terminology Review

12.30. Seven amplifiers were identified in Fig. 12.17. Find two more possibilities.

12.31. An amplifier is formed by cascading two operational-amplifier stages, as shown in Fig. P12.31. (a) Replace each amplifier stage with

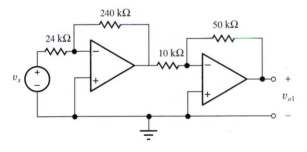

Figure P12.31

its two-port representation. (b) Use the circuit model from part (a) to find the overall two-port representation (A_V, R_{IN}, R_{OUT}) for the complete two-stage amplifier. (c) Draw the circuit of the two-port corresponding to the complete two-stage amplifier.

12.32. An amplifier is formed by cascading three identical operational-amplifier stages, as shown in Fig. P12.32. (a) Replace each op-amp circuit with its two-port representation. (b) Use the circuit model from part (a) to find the overall two-port representation (A_V, R_{IN}, R_{OUT}) for the complete three-stage amplifier. (c) Draw the circuit of two-port corresponding to the complete three-stage amplifier.

12.5 Nonideal Operational Amplifiers
Finite Gain, Input Resistance, and Output Resistance

12.33. (a) Repeat the derivation of the output resistance in Fig. 12.21 using a test current source rather than a test voltage source. (b) Why was a current source used in the derivation associated with Fig. 12.7?

12.34. Calculate the currents i_1, i_2, and i_- for the amplifier in Fig. 12.22 if $v_x = 0.1$ V, $R_1 = 1$ kΩ, $R_2 = 47$ kΩ, $R_{ID} = 1$ MΩ, and $A = 10^5$.

12.35. What are the actual values of the two input resistances R_{IN1} and R_{IN2} and the output resistance R_{OUT} of the instrumentation amplifier in Fig. 12.12 if it is constructed using operational amplifiers with $A = 4 \times 10^4$, $R_{ID} = 500$ kΩ, and $R_O = 75$ Ω? Assume $R_2 = 49$ R_1 and $R_3 = R_4 = 10$ kΩ.

 12.36. A voltage follower is built using an operational amplifier and must have a gain error ≤0.01 percent. What is the minimum open-loop gain specification for the op amp?

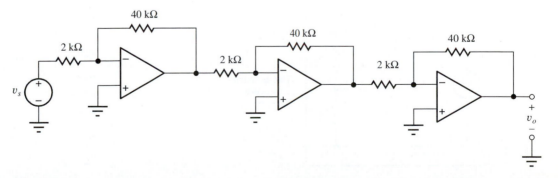

Figure P12.32

12.37. An op amp has $R_{ID} = 500$ kΩ, $R_O = 35$ Ω, and $A = 5 \times 10^4$. You must decide if a single-stage amplifier can be built that meets all of the specifications below. (a) Which configuration (inverting or noninverting) must be used and why? (b) Assume that the gain specification must be met and show which of the other specifications can or cannot be met.

$$|A_V| = 200 \quad R_{IN} \geq 2 \times 10^8 \ \Omega \quad R_{OUT} \leq 0.2 \ \Omega$$

12.38. An op amp has $R_{ID} = 1$ MΩ, $R_O = 100$ Ω, and $A = 1 \times 10^4$. Can a single-stage amplifier be built with this op amp that meets all of the following specifications? Show which specifications can be met and which cannot.

$$|A_V| = 200 \quad R_{IN} \geq 10^8 \ \Omega \quad R_{OUT} \leq 0.2 \ \Omega$$

12.39. The overall amplifier circuit in Fig. P12.39 is a two-terminal network. $R_1 = 6.8$ kΩ and $R_2 = 110$ kΩ. What is its Thévenin equivalent circuit if the operational amplifier has $A = 5 \times 10^4$, $R_{ID} = 1$ MΩ, and $R_O = 250$ Ω?

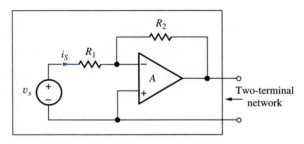

Figure P12.39

12.40. The circuit in Fig. P12.40 is a two-terminal network. $R_1 = 390$ Ω and $R_2 = 56$ kΩ. What is its Thévenin equivalent circuit if the operational

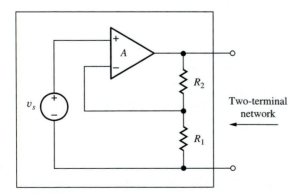

Figure P12.40

amplifier has $A = 1 \times 10^4$, $R_{ID} = 100$ kΩ, and $R_O = 200$ Ω?

*12.41. An inverting amplifier is to be designed to have a closed-loop gain of 60 dB. The only op amp that is available has an open-loop gain of 106 dB. What must be the tolerance of the feedback resistors if the total gain error must be ≤ 1 percent? Assume that the resistors all have the same tolerances.

*12.42. A noninverting amplifier is to be designed to have a closed-loop gain of 54 dB. The only op amp that is available has an open-loop gain of 40,000. What must be the tolerance of the feedback resistors if the total gain error must be ≤ 2 percent? Assume that the resistors all have the same tolerances.

DC Errors and CMRR

12.43. The common-mode rejection ratio of the difference amplifier in Fig. P12.43 is most often limited by the mismatch in the resistor pairs and not by the CMRR of the amplifier itself. Suppose that the nominal value of R is 10 kΩ and its tolerance is 0.05 percent. What is the worst-case value of the CMRR in dB?

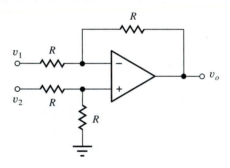

Figure P12.43

12.44. The multimeter in Fig. P12.44 has a common-mode rejection specification of 80 dB. What pos-

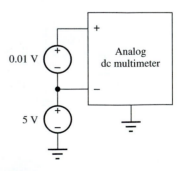

Figure P12.44

sible range of voltages can be indicated by the meter?

*12.45. The op amp in the amplifier circuit in Fig. P12.45 is ideal and

$$v_1 = (10 \sin 120\pi t + 0.25 \sin 5000\pi t) \text{ V}$$

$$v_2 = (10 \sin 120\pi t - 0.25 \sin 5000\pi t) \text{ V}$$

(a) What are the differential-mode and common-mode input voltages to this amplifier? (b) What are the differential-mode and common-mode gains of this amplifier? (c) What is the common-mode rejection ratio of this amplifier? (d) Find v_o.

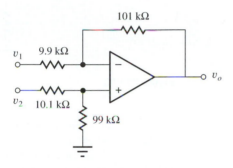

Figure P12.45

12.46. What are the actual values of the two input resistances R_{IN1} and R_{IN2} and the output resistance R_{OUT} of the instrumentation amplifier in Fig. 12.12 if it is constructed using operational amplifiers with $A = 7.5 \times 10^4$, $R_{ID} = 1 \text{ M}\Omega$, $R_{IC} = 500 \text{ M}\Omega$, and $R_O = 100 \text{ }\Omega$? Assume $R_1 = 1 \text{ k}\Omega$, $R_2 = 24 \text{ k}\Omega$, and $R_3 = R_4 = 10 \text{ k}\Omega$.

12.47. Calculate the worst-case output voltage for the circuit in Fig. P12.47 if $V_{OS} = 1 \text{ mV}$, $I_{B1} = 100 \text{ nA}$, and $I_{B2} = 95 \text{ nA}$. What would the ideal

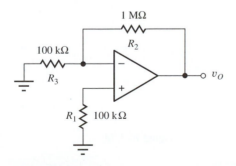

Figure P12.47

output voltage be? What is the total error in this circuit? Is there a better choice for the value of R_1? If so, what is the value?

12.48. The voltage transfer characteristic for an operational amplifier is given in Fig. P12.48. What are the values of gain and offset voltage for this op amp?

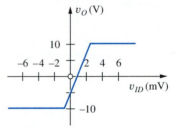

Figure P12.48

12.49. Plot voltage gain A versus v_{ID} for the amplifier voltage transfer characteristic given in Fig. P12.48.

12.50. Use superposition to derive the result in Eq. (12.100).

12.51. The amplifier in Fig. P12.51 is to be designed to have a gain of 40 dB. What values of R_1 and R_2 should be used in order to meet the gain specification and minimize the effects of bias current errors?

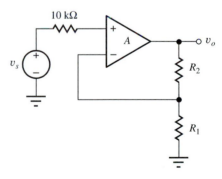

Figure P12.51

12.52. In the instrumentation amplifier in Fig. P12.52, $v_A = 4.99 \text{ V}$ and $v_B = 5.01 \text{ V}$. Find the values of node voltages $v_1, v_2, v_3, v_4, v_5, v_6, v_O$, and currents i_1, i_2, and i_3. What are the values of the common-mode gain, differential-mode gain, and CMRR of the amplifier? The op amps are ideal.

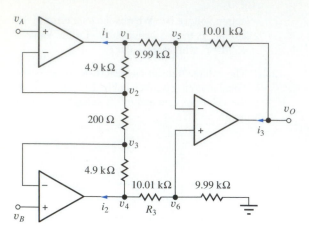

Figure P12.52

*12.53. The op amp in the circuit of Fig. P12.53 has an open-loop gain of 10,000, an offset voltage of 1 mV, and an input-bias current of 100 nA. (a) What would be the output voltage for an ideal op amp? (b) What is the actual output voltage for the worst-case polarity of offset voltage? (c) What is the percentage error in the output voltage compared to the ideal output voltage?

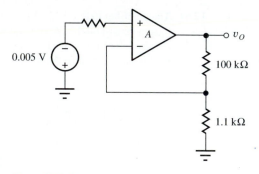

Figure P12.53

Voltage and Current Limits

12.54. The output-voltage range of the op amp in Fig. P12.54 is equal to the power supply voltages.

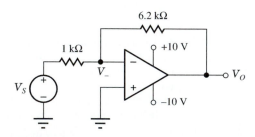

Figure P12.54

What are the values of V_O and V_- for the amplifier if the dc input V_S is (a) 1 V and (b) −3 V?

12.55. What are the voltages V_O and V_{ID} in the op-amp circuit in Fig. P12.55 for dc input voltages of (a) V_S = 250 mV and (b) V_S = 500 mV if the output-voltage range of the op amp is limited to the power supply voltages.

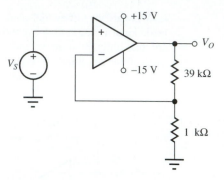

Figure P12.55

 12.56. Design a noninverting amplifier with A_V = 40 dB that can deliver a ±10-V signal to a 10-kΩ load resistor. Your op amp can supply only 1.5 mA of output current. Use standard resistor 5 percent values in your design.

 12.57. Design an inverting amplifier with A_V = 46 dB that can deliver ±15 V to a 5-kΩ load resistor. Your op amp can supply only 4 mA of output current. Use standard resistor 5 percent values in your design.

12.58. What is the minimum value of R in the circuit in Fig. P12.58 if the maximum op-amp output current is 5 mA and the current gain of the transistor is $\beta_F \geq 50$?

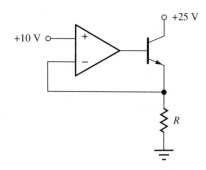

Figure P12.58

12.59. (a) Design a single-stage inverting amplifier with a gain of 46 dB using an operational amplifier. The input resistance should be as low as possible while achieving the op-amp output drive capability mentioned below. The amplifier must be able to produce the signal $v_O = (10 \sin 1000t)$ V at its output when an external load resistance $R_L \geq 5$ kΩ is connected to the output of the amplifier. You have an operational amplifier available whose output is guaranteed to deliver ± 10 V into a 4-kΩ load resistance. Otherwise, the amplifier is ideal. (b) If the amplifier input signal is $v_S = V \sin 1000t$, what is the largest acceptable value for the input signal amplitude V? (c) What is the input resistance of your amplifier?

Cascaded Amplifiers

12.60. An amplifier is formed by cascading two operational amplifier stages, as shown in Fig. P12.31. For the op amps, $A = 10^5$, $R_{ID} = 500$ kΩ, and $R_O = 100$ Ω. (a) Replace each amplifier stage circuit with its two-port representation. (b) Use the circuit model from part (a) to find the overall two-port representation (A_V, R_{IN}, R_{OUT}) for the complete two-stage amplifier. (c) Draw the circuit of the two-port corresponding to the complete two-stage amplifier. (d) How do the element values compare with the ideal case in Prob. 12.31.

12.61. An amplifier is formed by cascading three identical operational amplifier stages, as shown in Fig. P12.32. Assume $A = 10^5$, $R_{ID} = 250$ kΩ, and $R_O = 200$ Ω for each op amp. (a) Replace each op-amp circuit with its two-port representation. (b) Use the circuit model from part (a) to find the overall two-port representation (A_V, R_{IN}, R_{OUT}) for the complete three-stage amplifier. (c) Draw the circuit of two-port corresponding to the complete three-stage amplifier. (d) How do the element values compare with the ideal case in Prob. 12.32.

**12.62. A cascade amplifier is to be designed to meet the following specifications:

$$A_V = 5000 \quad R_{IN} \geq 10 \text{ M}\Omega \quad R_{OUT} \leq 0.1 \ \Omega$$

How many amplifier stages will be required if the stages must use an op amp below? Because of bandwidth requirements, assume that no individual stage can have a gain greater than 50.

$$\text{Op-amp specifications:} \quad A = 85 \text{ dB}$$
$$R_{ID} = 1 \text{ M}\Omega$$
$$R_O = 100 \ \Omega$$
$$R_{IC} \geq 1 \text{ G}\Omega$$

12.6 Frequency Response and Bandwidth of Operational Amplifiers

12.63. What is the transfer function for the voltage gain of the amplifier in Fig. P12.63?

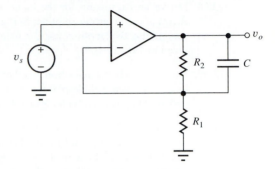

Figure P12.63

*12.64. The low-pass filter in Fig. P12.64 has $R_1 = 10$ kΩ, $R_2 = 330$ kΩ, and $C = 100$ pF. If the tolerances of the resistors are ± 10 percent and that of the capacitor is $+20$ percent$/-50$ percent, what are the nominal and worst-case values of the low-frequency gain and cutoff frequency?

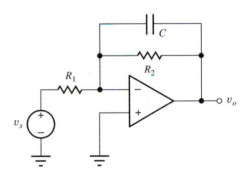

Figure P12.64 Low-pass filter

*12.65. Design a multistage low-pass filter to have a gain of 1000, a bandwidth of 20 kHz, and a response that rolls off at high frequencies at a rate of -60 dB/decade. Each stage should use the circuit in Fig. P12.64. (Questions to ask: How many stages are required? What are the gain and bandwidth required of each stage? What is the bandwidth shrinkage factor?)

*12.66. Derive an expression for the output impedance $Z_{OUT}(s)$ of the inverting and noninverting amplifiers in Fig. 12.20, assuming that the op amp has a transfer function given by Eq. (12.107).

*12.67. Use MATLAB, a spreadsheet, or other computer tool to plot the output impedance in Prob. 12.66 as a function of frequency if $R_1 = 10\text{ k}\Omega$, $R_2 = 100\text{ k}\Omega$, and the op amp has an open-loop gain $A_o = 100$ dB, $R_o = 100\ \Omega$, and $f_T = 1$ MHz.

*12.68. Derive an expression for the input impedance $Z_{IN}(s)$ of the inverting amplifier in Fig. 12.5, assuming that the amplifier has a transfer function given by Eq. (12.107).

12.69. Use MATLAB, a spreadsheet, or other computer tool to produce a Bode plot for $A_{V1}(s)$, $A_{V2}(s)$, and the composite $A_V(s)$ for Example 12.9.

12.70. Use MATLAB, a spreadsheet, or other computer tool to draw a Bode plot for the low-pass filter circuit in Fig. 12.14 with $R_1 = 4.3\text{ k}\Omega$, $R_2 = 82\text{ k}\Omega$, and $C = 200$ pF if the op amp is not ideal but has an open-loop gain $A_o = 100$ dB and $f_T = 5$ MHz.

*12.71. (a) Derive an expression for the transfer function of the ideal integrator in Fig. 12.16 in the frequency domain. (b) Repeat if the transfer function of the op amp is given by Eq. (12.107).

12.72. Use MATLAB, a spreadsheet, or other computer tool to draw a Bode plot for the integrator circuit in Fig. 12.16 with $R_1 = 10\text{ k}\Omega$, and $C = 470$ pF if the op amp is not ideal but has an open-loop gain $A_o = 100$ dB and $f_T = 5$ MHz.

12.73. Design a single-pole low-pass filter with a dc gain of 20 dB, $f_H = 1$ kHz, and $R_{IN} = 20\text{ k}\Omega$, using the circuit in Fig. 12.14.

12.74. (a) What are the gain and bandwidth of the individual amplifier stages in Fig. P12.74 below if the op amps have $A_o = 10^5$ and $f_T = 3$ MHz? (b) What are the overall gain and bandwidth of the three-stage amplifier?

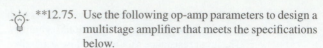

12.75. Use the following op-amp parameters to design a multistage amplifier that meets the specifications below.

$$A_V = 86\text{ dB} \pm 1\text{ dB} \qquad R_{IN} \geq 10\text{ k}\Omega$$

$$R_{OUT} \leq 0.01\ \Omega \qquad f_H \geq 75\text{ kHz}$$

The amplifier should use the minimum number of op-amp stages that will meet the requirements. (A spreadsheet or simple computer program will be helpful in finding the solution.)

$$\text{Op-amp specifications:} \quad \begin{aligned} A_o &= 10^5 \\ R_{ID} &= 10^9\ \Omega \\ R_o &= 50\ \Omega \\ GBW &= 1\text{ MHz} \end{aligned}$$

12.76. (a) Design the amplifier in Prob. 12.75, including values for the feedback resistors in each stage. (b) What is the bandwidth of your amplifier if the op amps have $f_T = 5$ MHz?

12.77. A cascade amplifier is to be designed to meet the following specifications:

$$A_V = 60\text{ dB} \pm 1\text{ dB} \qquad R_{IN} = 27\text{ k}\Omega$$

$$R_{OUT} \leq 0.1\ \Omega \qquad \text{Bandwidth} = 20\text{ kHz}$$

How many amplifier stages will be required if the stages must use the following op-amp specifications?

$$\text{Op-amp specifications:} \quad \begin{aligned} A_o &= 85\text{ dB} \\ f_T &= 5\text{ MHz} \\ R_O &= 100\ \Omega \\ R_{ID} &= 1\text{ M}\Omega \\ R_{IC} &\geq 1\text{ G}\Omega \end{aligned}$$

12.78. Design the amplifier in Prob. 12.77, including values for the feedback resistors in each stage.

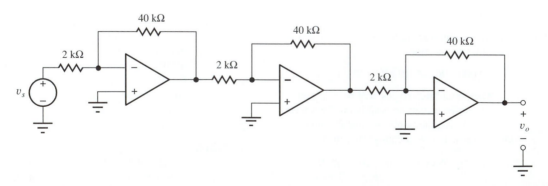

Figure P12.74

**12.79. (a) Perform a Monte Carlo analysis of the six-stage cascade amplifier design resulting from the example in Tables 12.8 and 12.9, and determine the fraction of the amplifiers that will not meet either the gain or bandwidth specifications. Assume the resistors are uniformly distributed between their limits.

$$A_V \geq 100 \text{ dB} \qquad \text{and} \qquad f_H \geq 50 \text{ kHz}$$

(b) What tolerance must be used to ensure that less than 0.1 percent of the amplifiers fail to meet both specifications?

The following equation can be used to estimate the location of the half-power frequency for N closely spaced poles, where $\overline{f_{H1}}$ is the average of the individual cutoff frequencies of the N stages and f_{H1}^i is the cutoff frequency of the ith individual stage.

$$f_H = \overline{f_{H1}} \sqrt{2^{1/N} - 1}$$

where $\overline{f_{H1}} = \dfrac{1}{N} \sum_{i=1}^{N} f_{H1}^i$

**12.80. (a) Show that the number of stages that optimizes the bandwidth of a cascade of identical noninverting amplifier stages having a total gain G is given by

$$N = \cfrac{\ln 2}{\ln \left[\cfrac{\ln G}{\ln G - \ln \sqrt{2}} \right]}$$

(b) Calculate N for the amplifier in Example 12.10.

12.81. What are the gain and bandwidth of the amplifier in Fig. P12.81 for the nominal and worst-case values of the feedback resistors if $A = 50{,}000$ and $f_T = 1$ MHz?

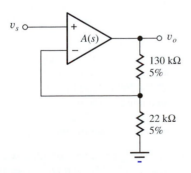

Figure P12.81

**12.82. Perform a Monte Carlo analysis of the circuit in Fig. P12.81. (a) What are the three sigma limits on the gain and bandwidth of the amplifier if $A_o = 50{,}000$ and $f_T = 1$ MHz? (b) Repeat if A_o is uniformly distributed in the interval $[5 \times 10^4, 1.5 \times 10^5]$ and f_T is uniformly distributed in the interval $[10^6, 3 \times 10^6]$.

12.7 Large Signal Limitations—Slew Rate and Full-Power Bandwidth

12.83. An audio amplifier is to be designed to develop a 30-V peak-to-peak sinusoidal signal at a frequency of 20 kHz. What must be the slew-rate specification of the amplifier?

12.84. An amplifier has a slew rate of 10 V/μs. What is the full-power bandwidth for signals having an amplitude of 10 V?

12.85. An amplifier must reproduce the output waveform in Fig. P12.85. What must be its slew rate?

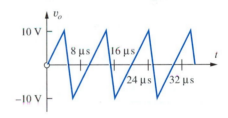

Figure P12.85

12.8 Macro Model for the Operational Amplifier Frequency Response

12.86. A single-pole op amp has the following specifications:

$$A_o = 80{,}000 \qquad f_T = 5 \text{ MHz}$$

$$R_{ID} = 250 \text{ k}\Omega \qquad R_O = 50 \text{ }\Omega$$

(a) Draw the circuit of a macro model for this operational amplifier. (b) Draw the circuit of a macro model for this operational amplifier if the op amp also has $R_{IC} = 500$ MΩ.

12.87. Draw a macro model for the amplifier in Prob. 12.86, including the additional elements necessary to model $R_{IC} = 100$ MΩ, $I_{B1} = 105$ nA, $I_{B2} = 95$ nA, and $V_{OS} = 1$ mV.

*12.88. A two-pole operational amplifier can be represented by the transfer function

$$A(s) = \frac{A_o \omega_1 \omega_2}{(s + \omega_1)(s + \omega_2)}$$

where
$A_o = 80{,}000$
$f_1 = 1 \text{ kHz}$
$f_2 = 100 \text{ kHz}$
$R_{ID} = 400 \text{ k}\Omega$
$R_O = 75 \Omega$

Create a macro model for this amplifier. (*Hint:* Consider using two "dummy" loops.)

 12.89. Simulate the frequency response of the nominal design of the six-stage cascade amplifier from Table 12.10. Use the macro model in Fig. 12.44 to represent the op amp.

 *12.90. Use the Monte Carlo analysis capability in PSPICE to simulate 1000 cases of the behavior of the six-stage amplifier in Table 12.10. Assume that all resistors and capacitors have 5 percent tolerances and the open-loop gain and bandwidth of the op amps each has a 50 percent tolerance. Use uniform statistical distributions. What are the lowest and highest observed values of gain and bandwidth for the amplifier?

12.9 Commercial General-Purpose Operational Amplifiers

12.91. (a) What are the element values for the macro model in Fig. 12.44 for the LF-155 op amp described in specification sheets in Fig. 12.45? Use $R = 1 \text{ k}\Omega$ and the nominal specifications.

12.92. What are the worst-case values (minimum or maximum, as appropriate) of the following parameters of the LF-357 op amp described in specification sheets in Fig. 12.45: open-loop gain, CMRR, PSRR, $V_{OS}, I_{B1}, I_{B2}, I_{OS}, R_{ID}$, slew rate, gain-bandwidth product, and power supply voltages?

12.10 Active Filters

12.93. (a) Repeat the design example for a maximally flat second-order low-pass filter with $f_o = 20$ kHz, using the circuit in Fig. 12.46. Assume $C = 0.005 \ \mu\text{F}$. What is the filter bandwidth? (b) Use frequency scaling to change f_o to 40 kHz.

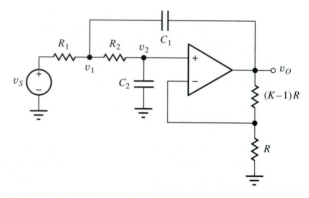 *12.94. (a) Use MATLAB or other computer tool to make a Bode plot for the response of the filter in Prob. 12.93, assuming the op amp is ideal. (b) Use SPICE to simulate the characteristics of the filter in Prob. 12.93 using a single-pole op amp with

$A_o = 100$ dB, $R_{ID} = \infty$, $R_O = 0$, and $f_T = 1$ MHz. (c) Discuss any disagreement between the SPICE results and the ideal response.

*12.95. Derive an expression for the input impedance of the filter in Fig. 12.46.

 12.96. Use MATLAB or another computer tool to plot the input impedance of the low-pass filter in Fig. 12.46 versus frequency for $R_1 = R_2 = 2.26 \text{ k}\Omega$, $C_1 = 0.02 \ \mu\text{F}$, and $C_2 = 0.01 \ \mu\text{F}$.

*12.97. (a) What is the transfer function for the low-pass filter in Fig. P12.97? (b) What is S_K^Q for this filter if $R_1 = R_2$ and $C_1 = C_2$?

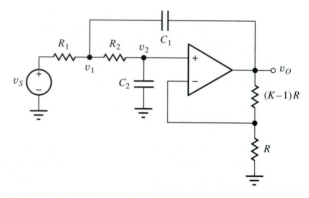

Figure P12.97

12.98. What are the expressions for $S_{R_1}^{\omega_o}$ and $S_{C_1}^{\omega_o}$ for the high-pass filter of Fig. 12.48?

12.99. What is $S_Q^{\omega_o}$ for the band-pass filter of Fig. 12.50 for $C_1 = C_2$? What is the value for $f_o = 10 \text{ kHz}$ and $Q = 10$?

 12.100. Design a maximally flat second-order low-pass filter with a bandwidth of 1 kHz using the circuit in Fig. 12.46.

 12.101. Design a high-pass filter with a lower-half power frequency of 20 kHz and $Q = 1$ using the circuit in Fig. 12.48.

12.102. (a) Calculate f_o, Q, and the bandwidth for the band-pass filter in Fig. 12.50 if $R_1 = 1 \text{ k}\Omega$, $R_2 = 200 \text{ k}\Omega$, and $C_1 = C_2 = 220 \text{ pF}$. (b) Use magnitude scaling to change the element values so that $R_1 = 3.3 \text{ k}\Omega$. (c) Use frequency scaling to double f_o for the filter in part (a).

 12.103. (a) Design a band-pass filter with a center frequency of 1 kHz and $Q = 5$ using the circuit in Fig. 12.50. What is the filter bandwidth? (b) Use frequency scaling to change f_o to 2.25 kHz.

*12.104. (a) Use MATLAB or another computer tool to make a Bode plot for the response of the filter in Prob. 12.102(a), assuming the op amp is ideal. (b) Use SPICE to simulate the characteristics of the filter in Prob. 12.102(a) using a single-pole op amp with $A_o = 94$ dB, $R_{ID} = \infty$, $R_O = 0$, and $f_T = 1$ MHz. (c) Discuss any disagreement between the SPICE results and the ideal response.

12.105. (a) Two identical band-pass filters having $\omega_o = 1$ and $Q = 3$ are designed using the circuit in Fig. 12.50 with $C_1 = C_2$. If the filters are cascaded, what are the center frequency Q and bandwidth of the overall filter? (b) Write the transfer function for the composite filter.

12.106. Use MATLAB or other computer tool to produce a Bode plot for the two-stage filter in Prob. 12.105.

*12.107. The first stage of a two-stage filter consists of a band-pass filter with $f_o = 5$ kHz and $Q = 5$. The second stage is also a band-pass filter, but it has $f_o = 6$ kHz and $Q = 5$. If the filters use Fig. 12.50 with $C_1 = C_2$, what are the center frequency, Q, and bandwidth of the overall filter?

12.108. Use MATLAB or another computer tool to produce a Bode plot for the two-stage filter in Prob. 12.107.

12.109. Design a band-pass filter with 20 dB gain at $f_o = 600$ Hz, $Q = 5$, and $R_{IN} = 10$ kΩ using the Tow-Thomas biquad in Fig. 12.52.

12.110. Calculate S_C^Q for the Tow-Thomas biquad in Fig. 12.52.

12.11 Switched-Capacitor Circuits

12.111. Draw a graph of the output voltage for the SC integrator in Fig. 12.55 for five clock periods if $C_1 = 4C_2$, $v_s = 1$ V, and $v_O(0) = 0$.

12.112. Draw a graph of the output voltage for the SC integrator in Fig. 12.57 for five clock periods if $C_1 = 4C_2$, $v_s = 1$ V, and $v_O(0) = 0$.

12.113. (a) Draw a graph of the output voltage for the SC integrator in Fig. 12.55 for five clock periods if $C_1 = 4C_2$ and v_s is the signal in Fig. P12.113. **(b) Repeat for the integrator in Fig. 12.57.

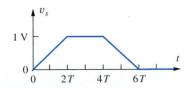

Figure P12.113

12.114. (a) What is the output voltage at the end of one clock cycle of the SC integrator in Fig. 12.53 if $C_1 = 1$ pF, $C_2 = 0.2$ pF, $v_s = 1$ V, and there is a stray capacitance $C_s = 0.1$ pF between each end of capacitor C_1 and ground? What are the gain and gain error of this circuit? (b) Repeat for the integrator in Fig. 12.57.

*12.115. (a) Simulate two clock cycles of the integrator of Prob. 12.114(a) using NMOS transistors with $W/L = 2/1$ and 100-kHz clock signals with rise and fall times of 0.5 μs. (b) Repeat for Prob. 12.114(b).

12.116. What are the center frequency, Q, and bandwidth of the switched capacitor band-pass filter in Fig. 12.59 if $C_1 = 0.4$ pF, $C_2 = 0.4$ pF, $C_3 = 1$ pF, $C_4 = 0.1$ pF, and $f_c = 100$ kHz?

12.117. Draw the circuit for a switched-capacitor implementation of the low-pass filter in Fig. 12.46.

12.12 Nonlinear Circuit Applications Nonlinear Feedback

*12.118. Write an expression for the output voltage in terms of the input voltage for the circuit in Fig. P12.118 on p. 580. Diode D is formed from a diode-connected transistor, and all three transistors are identical.

12.119. Draw the output voltage waveform for the circuit in Fig. P12.119 on p. 580 for the triangular input waveform shown.

*12.120. The signal v_S in Fig. P12.119 is used as the input voltage to the circuit in Fig. 12.65. What will be the dc component of the voltage waveform at v_O if $R_1 = 2.7$ kΩ, $R_2 = 8.2$ kΩ, $R_3 = 10$ kΩ, $R_4 = 10$ kΩ, $C = 0.22$ μF, and $T = 1$ ms?

**12.121. What must be the cutoff frequency of the low-pass filter in Fig. 12.65 if the rms value of the total ac component in the output voltage must be less than 1 percent of the dc voltage? Assume $R_1 = R_2$ and $v_S = -5 \sin 120\pi t$ V.

12.122. The triangular waveform in Fig. P12.119 is applied to the circuit in Fig. P12.122 on p. 580. Draw the corresponding output waveform.

12.123. The triangular waveform in Fig. P12.119 is applied to the circuit in Fig. P12.123 on p. 581. Draw the corresponding output waveform.

12.124. Simulate the circuit in Prob. 12.122 using $R_1 = 10$ kΩ, $R_2 = 10$ kΩ, $R_3 = 10$ kΩ, and $R_4 = 10$ kΩ. Use op amps with $A_o = 100$ dB.

12.125. Simulate the circuit in Prob. 12.123 for $R = 10$ kΩ. Use op amps with $A_o = 100$ dB.

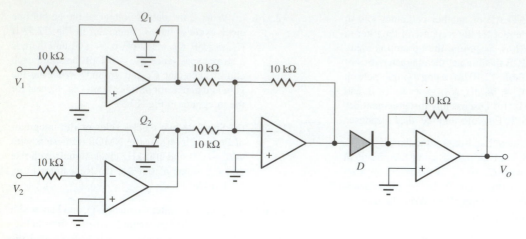

Figure P12.118

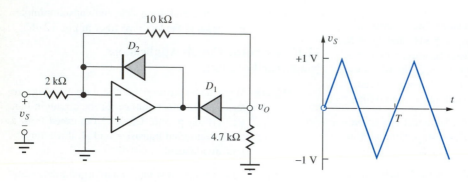

Figure P12.119

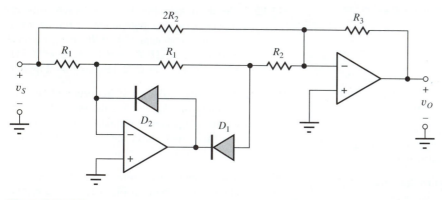

Figure P12.122

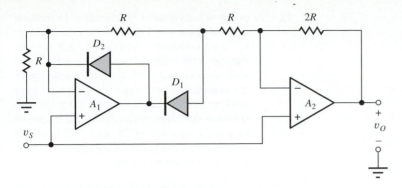

Figure P12.123

12.13 Circuits Using Positive Feedback

12.126. What are the values of the two switching thresholds and hysteresis in the Schmitt-trigger circuit in Fig. P12.126?

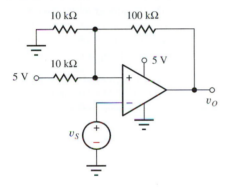

Figure P12.126

12.127. What are the switching thresholds and hysteresis for the Schmitt-trigger circuit in Fig. P12.127?

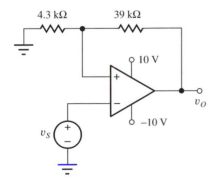

Figure P12.127

12.128. What are the switching thresholds and hysteresis for the Schmitt-trigger circuit in Fig. P12.128?

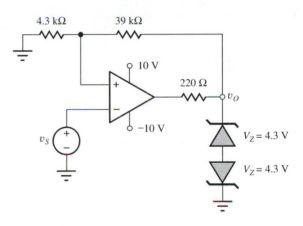

Figure P12.128

12.129. Design a Schmitt trigger to have its switching thresholds centered at 1 V with a hysteresis of ± 0.05 V, using the circuit topology in Fig. P12.126.

12.130. What is the frequency of oscillation of the astable multivibrator in Fig. P12.130 on p. 582?

**12.131. Draw the waveforms for the astable multivibrator in Fig. P12.131. What is its frequency of oscillation? (Be careful—think before you calculate!)

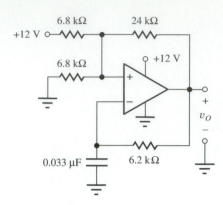

Figure P12.130

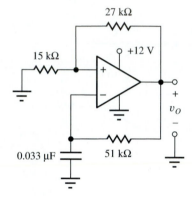

Figure P12.131

 12.132. (a) Design an astable multivibrator to oscillate at a frequency of 1 kHz. Use the circuit in Fig. 12.73 with symmetric supplies of ±5 V. Assume that the total current from the op-amp output must never exceed 1 mA. (b) If the resistors have ±5 percent tolerances and the capacitors have ±10 percent tolerances, what are the worst-case values of oscillation frequency? (c) If the power supplies are actually +4.75 and −5.25 V, what is the oscillation frequency for the nominal resistor and capacitor design values?

**12.133. The circuit in Fig. 12.75 has been designed to generate a sine wave output voltage with an amplitude of 5 V at a frequency of 1 kHz. The low-pass filter has been designed to have a low-frequency gain of −1 and a cutoff frequency of 1.5 kHz. What are the magnitudes of the undesired frequency components in the output waveform at frequencies of 2 kHz, 3 kHz, and 5 kHz?

12.134. Two diodes are added to the circuit in Fig. P12.131 to convert it to a monostable multivibrator similar to the circuit in Fig. 12.76, and the power supplies are changed to ±10 V. What are the pulse width and recovery time of the monostable circuit?

12.135. Design a monostable multivibrator to have a pulse width of 10 μs and a recovery time of 5 μs. Use the circuit in Fig. 12.76 with ±5 V supplies.

Small-Signal Modeling and Linear Amplification

Chapter 13 begins our study of basic amplifier circuits that are used in the design of more complex analog components and systems, such as high-performance operational amplifiers, analog-to-digital and digital-to-analog converters, stereo radio equipment, compact disk players, communication receivers, cellular telephones, and so on. The chapter introduces the general behavior of individual transistors as amplifiers and then studies in detail the operation of the common-emitter bipolar transistor circuit. This is followed by analysis of common-source amplifiers employing MOS and junction FETs. Circuits containing these devices are compared, and expressions are developed for the voltage gain and input and output resistances of the various amplifiers. The advantages and disadvantages of each are discussed in detail.

To simplify the analysis and design processes, superposition is used, whereby the circuits are split into two parts: a dc equivalent circuit used to find the Q-point of the transistor and an ac equivalent circuit used for analysis of the circuit's response to signal sources. As a by-product of this approach, we discover how capacitors and inductors are used to change the ac and dc circuit topologies.

The use of superposition is based on linearity, and our ac analysis requires the use of "small-signal" models that exhibit a linear relation between their terminal voltages and currents. The concept of a small signal is developed, and small-signal models for the diode, bipolar transistor, MOSFET, and JFET are all discussed in detail.

Several examples of the complete analysis of common-emitter and common-source amplifiers are included in this chapter. The relationship between the choice of operating point and the small-signal characteristics of the amplifier are fully developed, as is the relationship between Q-point design and output signal voltage swing.

13.1 THE TRANSISTOR AS AN AMPLIFIER

As discussed in Part I, the bipolar junction transistor is a good amplifier when it is biased in the forward-active region of operation; field-effect transistors should be operated in the saturation or pinch-off regions in order to be used as amplifiers. In these regions of operation, the transistors have the capacity to provide high voltage, current, and power gains. This chapter focuses on determining voltage gain, input resistance, and output resistance. Evaluation of current gain and power gain are addressed in later chapters.

We provide bias to the transistor in order to stabilize the operating point in the desired region of operation. Once the dc operating point has been established, we can use the transistor as an amplifier. The Q-point—whatever is chosen—controls many other amplifier characteristics, including:

- Small-signal parameters of the transistor
- Voltage gain, input resistance, and output resistance
- Maximum input and output signal amplitudes
- Power consumption

The BJT Amplifier

To get a clearer understanding of how a transistor can provide linear amplification, let us assume that a bipolar transistor is biased in the forward-active region by the dc voltage source V_{BE} shown in Fig. 13.1. For this particular transistor, the fixed base-emitter voltage of 0.700 V sets the Q-point to be $(I_C, V_{CE}) = (1.5\,\text{mA}, 5\,\text{V})$ with $I_B = 15\,\mu\text{A}$, as indicated in Fig. 13.2. Both I_B and V_{BE} have been shown as parameters on the output characteristics in Fig. 13.2 (usually only I_B is given).

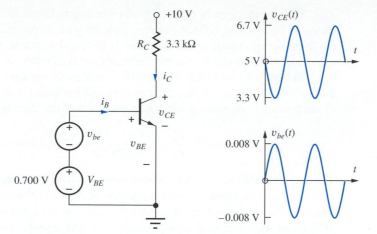

Figure 13.1 BJT biased in the forward-active region by the voltage source V_{BE}. A small sinusoidal signal voltage v_{be} is applied in series with V_{BE} and generates a similar waveform at the collector.

To provide amplification, a signal must be injected into the circuit in a manner that causes the transistor voltages and currents to vary with the applied signal. For the circuit in Fig. 13.1, the base-emitter voltage is forced to vary about its Q-point value by the signal source v_{be} placed in series with V_{BE}, so the total base-emitter voltage becomes

$$v_{BE} = V_{BE} + v_{be} \qquad (13.1)$$

In Fig. 13.2, we see that the 8-mV peak change in base-emitter voltage produces a 5-μA change in base current and a 0.5-mA change in collector current.

The collector-emitter voltage of the BJT can be expressed as

$$v_{CE} = 10 - i_C R_C \qquad (13.2)$$

Equation (13.2) should be recognized as the equation for the load line for this transistor. The change in collector current develops a time-varying voltage across the load resistor R_C and at the collector terminal of the transistor. The 0.5-mA change in collector current develops a 1.65-V change in collector-emitter voltage.

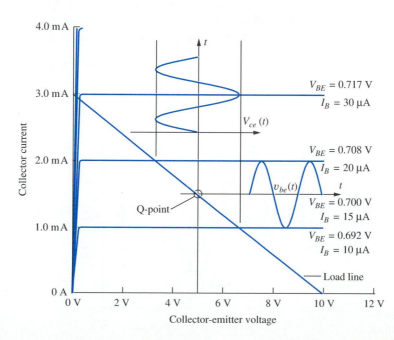

Figure 13.2 Load-line Q-point and signals for circuit of Fig. 13.1.

If these changes in operating currents and voltages are all small enough, then the collector current and collector-emitter voltage waveforms will be undistorted replicas of the input signal. Small-signal operation is device-dependent; it is precisely defined when the small-signal model for the bipolar transistor is introduced.

In Figs. 13.1 and 13.2, we see that a small input voltage change at the base is causing a large voltage change at the collector. The voltage gain for this circuit is defined in terms of the frequency domain (phasor) representation of the signals:

$$A_V = \frac{\mathbf{v_{ce}}}{\mathbf{v_{be}}} = \frac{1.65\angle 180}{0.008\angle 0} = 206\angle 180 = -206 \tag{13.3}$$

The magnitude of the collector-emitter voltage is 206 times larger than the base-emitter signal amplitude; this represents a voltage gain of 206. It is also important to note in Figs. 13.1 and 13.2 that the output signal voltage decreases as the input signal increases, indicating a 180° phase shift between the input and the output signals. This 180° phase shift is represented by the minus sign in Eq. (13.3).

EXERCISE: The common-emitter current gain β_F of the bipolar transistor is defined by $\beta_F = I_C/I_B$. (a) What is the value of β_F for the transistor in Fig. 13.2? (b) The dc collector current of the BJT in the forward-active region is given by $I_C = I_S \exp V_{BE}/V_T$. Use the Q-point data to find the saturation current I_S of the transistor in Fig. 13.2. (Remember $V_T = 0.025$ V.) (c) The ratio of $\mathbf{v_{be}}/\mathbf{i_b}$ represents the small-signal input resistance R_{IN} of the BJT. What is its value for the transistor in Fig. 13.2? (d) Does the BJT remain in the forward-active region during the full range of signal voltages at the collector?

ANSWERS: $\beta_F = 100$; $I_S = 1.04 \times 10^{-15}$ A; $R_{IN} = 1.6$ kΩ; yes

---

The MOSFET Amplifier

The amplifier circuit using a MOSFET in Figs. 13.3 and 13.4 is directly analogous to the BJT amplifier circuit in Figs. 13.1 and 13.2. Here the gate-to-source voltage is forced to vary about its Q-point value ($V_{GS} = 3$ V) by signal source v_{gs} placed in series with the dc bias source V_{GS}. In this case, the total gate-source voltage is

$$v_{GS} = V_{GS} + v_{gs}$$

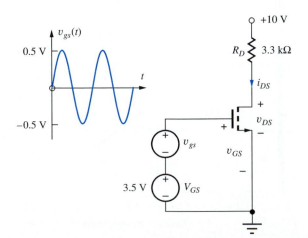

Figure 13.3 A MOSFET common-source amplifier.

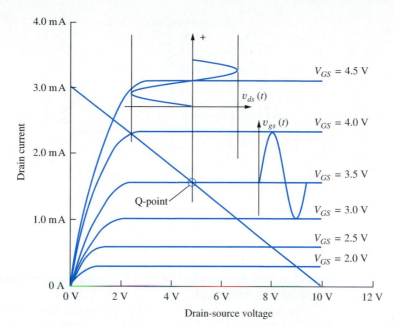

Figure 13.4 Q-point, load line, and signals for the circuit of Fig. 13.3.

The resulting signal voltages are superimposed on the MOSFET output characteristics in Fig. 13.4. $V_{GS} = 3.5$ V sets the Q-point (I_{DS}, V_{DS}) at (1.56 mA, 4.8 V), and the 1-V p-p change in v_{GS} causes a 1.25-mA p-p change in i_D and a 4-V p-p change in v_{DS}.

> **EXERCISE:** (a) Write an expression for the drain-source voltage (the load-line equation) for the MOSFET in Fig. 13.3. (b) What is the approximate voltage gain for the amplifier in Fig. 13.4? (c) Does the MOSFET in Fig. 13.4 remain in the saturation region of operation during the full-output signal swing? (d) If the dc drain current of the MOSFET in saturation is given by $I_{DS} = (K_n/2)(V_{GS} - V_{TN})^2$, what are the values of the parameter K_n and threshold voltage V_{TN} for the transistor in Fig. 13.4?
>
> **ANSWERS:** $v_{DS} = 10 - 3300 i_D$; $A_V = -4$; no, not near the positive peak of v_{GS}, corresponding to the peak negative excursion of v_{DS}; $K_n = 5 \times 10^4$ A/V^2, $V_{TN} = 1$ V

13.2 COUPLING AND BYPASS CAPACITORS

The constant base-emitter or gate-source voltage biasing techniques used in Figs. 13.1 and 13.3 are not very desirable methods of establishing the Q-point for a bipolar transistor or FET because the operating point is highly dependent on the transistor parameters. As discussed in detail in Chapter 4, bias circuits, such as the four-resistor network in Fig. 13.5, are much preferred for establishing a stable Q-point for the transistor.

To use the transistor as an amplifier, ac signals need to be introduced into the circuit, but application of these ac signals must not disturb the dc Q-point that has been established by the bias network. One method of injecting an input signal and extracting an output signal without disturbing the Q-point is to use **ac coupling** through capacitors. The values of these capacitors are chosen to have negligible impedances in the frequency range of interest, but at the same time the capacitors provide open circuits at dc so the Q-point is not disturbed. When power is first applied to the amplifier circuit, transient currents charge the capacitors, but the final steady-state operating point is not affected.

Figure 13.6 is an example of the use of capacitors; the transistor is biased by the same four-resistor network shown in Fig. 13.5. An input signal v_s is *coupled* onto the base node of the transistor through capacitor C_1, and the signal developed at the collector is coupled to

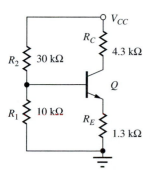

Figure 13.5 Transistor biased in the forward-active region using the four-resistor bias network (see Sec. 5.14 for an example).

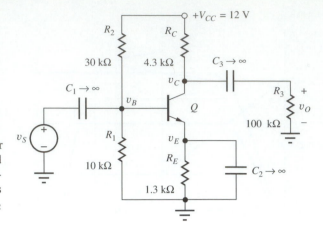

Figure 13.6 Common-emitter amplifier stage built around the four-resistor bias network. C_1 and C_3 function as coupling capacitors, and C_2 is a bypass capacitor.

the load resistor R_3 through capacitor C_3. C_1 and C_3 are referred to as **coupling capacitors, or dc blocking capacitors.**

For now, the values of C_1 and C_3 are assumed to be very large, so their reactance $(1/\omega C)$ at the signal frequency ω will be negligible. This assumption is indicated in the figure by $C \to \infty$. Calculation of more exact values of the capacitors is left until the discussion of amplifier frequency response in Chapter 17.

Figure 13.6 also shows the use of capacitor C_2, called a **bypass capacitor.** In many circuits, we want to force signal currents to go around elements of the bias network. Capacitor C_2 provides a low impedance path for ac current from the emitter to ground, bypassing emitter resistor R_E. Thus R_E, which is required for good Q-point stability, can be effectively removed from the circuit when ac signals are considered.

Simulation results of the behavior of this circuit are shown in Fig. 13.7. A 5-mV sine wave signal at a frequency of 1 kHz is applied to the base terminal of transistor Q through

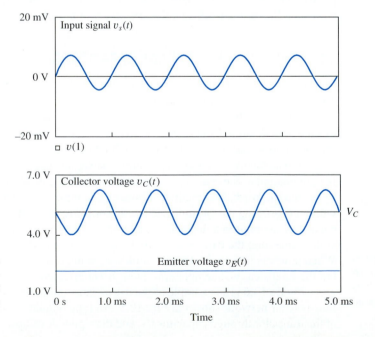

Figure 13.7 SPICE simulation results for v_s, v_C, and v_E for the amplifier in Fig. 13.5 with $v_s = 0.005 \sin 2000\pi t$ V.

coupling capacitor C_1; this signal produces a sinusoidal signal at the collector node with an amplitude of approximately 1.1 V, centered on the Q-point value of $V_C \approx 5$ V. Note once again that there is a 180° phase shift between the input and output voltage signals. These values indicate that the amplifier is providing a voltage gain of

$$A_V = \frac{\mathbf{v_c}}{\mathbf{v_s}} = \frac{-1.1 \text{ V}}{+0.005 \text{ V}} = -220 \tag{13.4}$$

In Fig. 13.7, we should also observe that the voltage at the emitter node remains constant at its Q-point value of slightly more than 2 V. The very low impedance of the bypass capacitor prevents any signal voltage from being developed at the emitter. The bypass capacitor maintains an "ac ground" at the emitter terminal. In other words, zero signal voltage appears at the emitter, and the emitter voltage remains constant at its dc Q-point value.

> **EXERCISE:** Calculate the Q-point for the bipolar transistor in Fig. 13.5. Use $\beta_F = 100$, $V_{BE} = 0.7$ V, and $V_A = \infty$.
>
> **ANSWER:** (1.66 mA, 2.68 V)
>
> **EXERCISE:** Write expressions for $v_C(t)$, $v_E(t)$, and $i_c(t)$ based upon the waveforms shown in Fig. 13.7.
>
> **ANSWERS:** $v_C(t) = (5.1 - 1.1 \sin 2000\pi t)$ V, $v_E(t) = 2.1$ V, $i_c(t) = -2.6 \sin 2000\pi t$ mA
>
> **EXERCISE:** Suppose capacitor C_2 is 500 μF. What is its reactance at a frequency of 1000 Hz?
>
> **ANSWER:** 0.318 Ω

13.3 CIRCUIT ANALYSIS USING dc AND ac EQUIVALENT CIRCUITS

To simplify the circuit analysis and design tasks, we shall invoke superposition and break the amplifier into two parts, performing separate dc and ac circuit analyses. We find the Q-point of the circuit using the **dc equivalent circuit**—the circuit that is appropriate for steady-state dc analysis. To construct the dc equivalent circuit, we assume that capacitors are open circuits and inductors are short circuits.

Once we have found the Q-point, we determine the response of the circuit to the ac signals using an **ac equivalent circuit.** In constructing the ac equivalent circuit, we assume that the reactance of the coupling and bypass capacitors is negligible at the operating frequency ($|Z_C| = 1/\omega C = 0$), and we replace the capacitors by short circuits. Similarly, we assume the impedance of any inductors in the circuit is extremely large ($|Z_L| = \omega L \to \infty$), so we replace inductors by open circuits. Because the voltage at a node connected to a dc voltage source cannot change, these points represent grounds in the ac equivalent circuit (no ac voltage can appear at such a node: $v_{ac} = 0$). Furthermore, the current through a dc current source does not change even if the voltage across the source changes ($i_{ac} = 0$), so we replace dc current sources with open circuits in the ac equivalent circuit.

We emphasize again that this two-part analysis is analysis by superposition. To carry it out, we must use linear models for the ac behavior of the transistor, referred to as *small-signal models.* We will soon develop small-signal models for the diode, BJT, MOSFET, and JFET.

Menu for dc and ac Analysis

To summarize, our analysis of amplifier circuits is performed using the two-part process listed here:

dc Analysis

1. Find the dc equivalent circuit by replacing all capacitors with open circuits and inductors by short circuits.
2. Find the Q-point from the dc equivalent circuit using the appropriate large-signal model for the transistor.

ac Analysis

3. Find the ac equivalent circuit by replacing all capacitors by short circuits and all inductors by open circuits. dc voltage sources are replaced by ground connections, and dc current sources are replaced by open circuits in the ac equivalent circuit.
4. Replace the transistor by its small-signal model.
5. Analyze the ac characteristics of the amplifier using the small-signal ac equivalent circuit from step 4.
6. Combine the results from steps 2 and 5 to yield the total voltages and currents in the network.

Step 6 is the conclusion of the **analysis by superposition.** However, because we are most often interested in determining the ac behavior of the circuit, we seldom actually perform this final step of combining the dc and ac results.

EXAMPLE 13.1: Let us draw the dc and ac equivalent circuits (steps 1 and 3) for the amplifier in Fig. 13.8(a). The circuit is similar to that in Fig. 13.6 except that a source resistor R_S has been added.

SOLUTION: The dc equivalent circuit is found by removing all the capacitors from the circuit. We find that the resulting dc equivalent circuit in Fig. 13.8(b) is identical to the four-resistor bias circuit of Fig. 13.5. Opening capacitors C_1 and C_2 disconnects v_s, R_S and R_3 from the circuit.

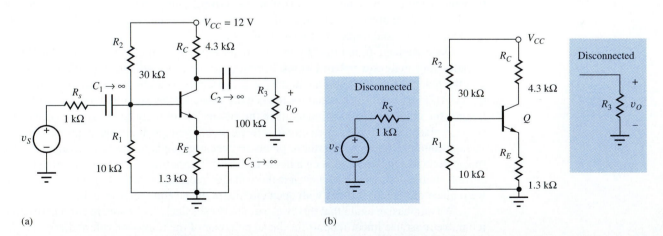

(a)   (b)

Figure 13.8 (a) Complete ac-coupled amplifier circuit. (b) Simplified equivalent circuit for dc analysis.

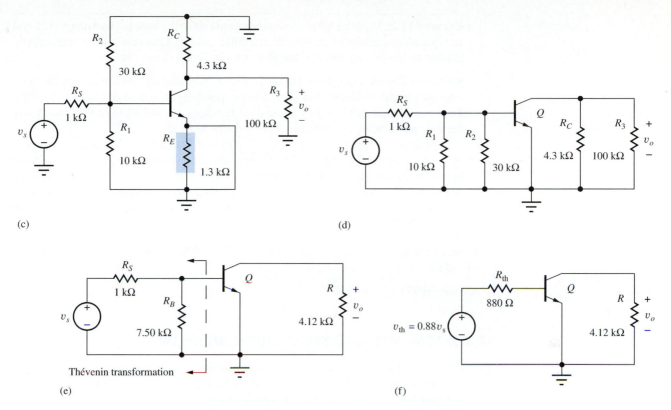

(c)

(d)

(e)

(f)

Figure 13.8 (*Continued*) (c) Circuit after step 3. Note that the input and output are now v_s and v_o. (d) Redrawn version of Fig. 13.8(c). (e) Continued simplification of the ac circuit. (f) Standard form obtained using a Thévenin transformation.

To construct the ac equivalent circuit, we replace the capacitors by short circuits. Also, the dc voltage source becomes an ac ground in Fig. 13.8(c). In the ac equivalent circuit, the source resistance is now connected directly to the base node, and the external load resistor R_3 is connected directly to the collector node. Note that resistor R_E is shorted out by the presence of bypass capacitor C_3.

Figure 13.8(d) is redrawn from Fig. 13.8(c). Because the power supply represents an ac ground, bias resistors R_1 and R_2 appear in parallel between the base node and ground, and R_C and R_3 are in parallel at the collector. The emitter is connected directly to ground.

In Fig. 13.8(e), R_1 and R_2 have been combined into the resistor R_B, and R_C and R_3 have been combined into the resistor R:

$$R_B = R_1 \,\|\, R_2 = 10 \text{ k}\Omega \,\|\, 30 \text{ k}\Omega \qquad \text{and} \qquad R = R_C \,\|\, R_3 = 4.3 \text{ k}\Omega \,\|\, 100 \text{ k}\Omega$$

A final simplification is achieved by taking a Thévenin transformation of the network consisting of v_s, R_S, and R_B; this yields the circuit in Fig. 13.8(f). We refer to Fig. 13.8(f) as our "standard form" for amplifier analysis. In this network, the circuit is reduced to an equivalent signal source and source resistance, the transistor, and an equivalent load resistance R.

Notice again how the capacitors have been used to modify the circuit topology for ac signals. In particular, capacitor C_3 causes the emitter to be connected directly to ground, effectively removing R_E from the ac circuit. ◆

EXAMPLE 13.2:   Figure 13.9 is a second example showing how to construct the dc and ac equivalent circuits of an overall amplifier circuit. This case uses a split-supply biasing technique; an inductor has also been included in the circuit.

SOLUTION: The dc equivalent circuit is found by replacing the capacitors by open circuits and the inductor by a short circuit, resulting in the circuit in Fig. 13.9(b). The open capacitors C_1 and C_2 again disconnect v_s, R_S, and R_3 from the circuit, and the shorted inductor connects the drain directly to V_{DD}.

The ac equivalent circuit in Fig. 13.9(c) is obtained by replacing the capacitors by short circuits and the inductor by an open circuit. Figure 13.9(c) has been redrawn in simplified form in Fig. 13.9(d), and transformed to our standard form for analysis in Fig. 13.9(e). Again, the designer has used the capacitors and inductor to achieve very different circuit topologies for the dc and ac equivalent circuits.   ◆

EXERCISE: What are the values of v_{th} and R_{th} in Fig. 13.9(e) if $R_S = 20 \text{ k}\Omega$, and $R_G = 470 \text{ k}\Omega$?

ANSWER: 0.959 v_S, 19.2 kΩ

13.4 INTRODUCTION TO SMALL-SIGNAL MODELING

As mentioned earlier, separation of the dc and ac analyses represents analysis by superposition. For this approach to be valid, the signal currents and voltages must be small enough to ensure that the ac circuit behaves in a linear manner. Thus, we must assume that the time-varying signal components are **small signals.** The amplitudes that are considered to be small signals are device-dependent; we will define these as we develop the small-signal models for each device. Our study of **small-signal models** begins with the diode and then proceeds to the bipolar junction transistor and the field-effect transistor.

Small-Signal Model for the Diode

We are interested in the relationship between variations in the diode voltage and current around the Q-point values. The total terminal voltage and current for the diode in Fig. 13.10 (p. 594) can be written as

$$v_D = V_D + v_d \qquad \text{and} \qquad i_D = I_D + i_d \tag{13.5}$$

A relationship between the ac and dc quantities can be developed directly from the diode equation:

$$i_D = I_S \left[\exp\left(\frac{v_D}{V_T}\right) - 1 \right] \tag{13.6}$$

Substituting Eq. (13.5) into (13.6) yields

$$I_D + i_d = I_S \left[\exp\left(\frac{V_D + v_d}{V_T}\right) - 1 \right] = I_S \left[\exp\left(\frac{V_D}{V_T}\right) \exp\left(\frac{v_d}{V_T}\right) - 1 \right] \tag{13.7}$$

and expanding the second exponential using Maclaurin's series:

$$I_D + i_d = I_S \left\{ \left[\exp\left(\frac{V_D}{V_T}\right) \right] \left[1 + \frac{v_d}{V_T} + \frac{1}{2}\left(\frac{v_d}{V_T}\right)^2 + \frac{1}{6}\left(\frac{v_d}{V_T}\right)^3 + \cdots \right] - 1 \right\} \tag{13.8}$$

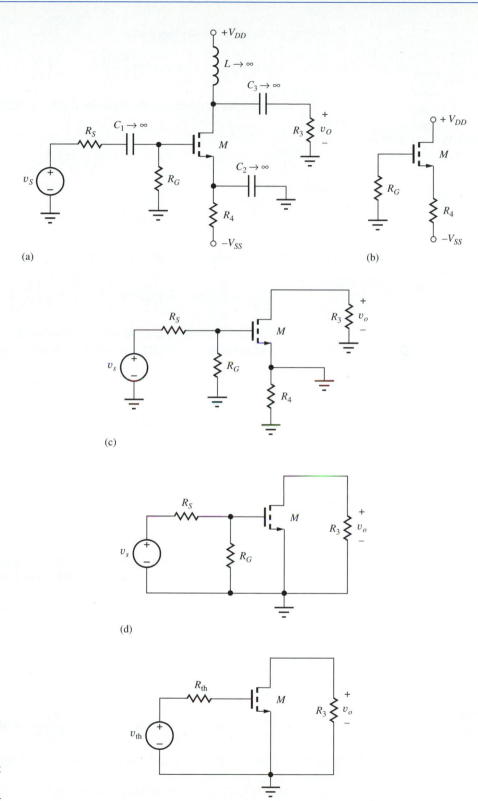

Figure 13.9 (a) An amplifier biased by two power supplies. (b) dc Equivalent circuit for Q-point analysis. (c) First step in generating the ac equivalent circuit. (d) Simplified ac equivalent circuit. (e) ac Equivalent circuit after Thévenin transformation.

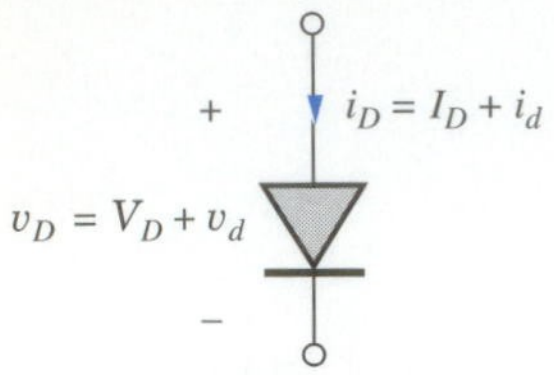

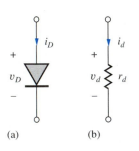

Figure 13.10 Total diode terminal voltage and current.

Collecting the dc and ac terms together,

$$I_D + i_d = I_S\left[\exp\left(\frac{V_D}{V_T}\right) - 1\right] + I_S \exp\left(\frac{V_D}{V_T}\right)\left[\frac{v_d}{V_T} + \frac{1}{2}\left(\frac{v_d}{V_T}\right)^2 + \frac{1}{6}\left(\frac{v_d}{V_T}\right)^3 + \cdots\right] \quad (13.9)$$

We recognize the first term on the right-hand side of Eq. (13.9) as the dc diode current I_D:

$$I_D = I_S\left[\exp\left(\frac{V_D}{V_T}\right) - 1\right]$$

and also   (13.10)

$$I_S \exp\left(\frac{V_D}{V_T}\right) = I_D + I_S$$

Subtracting I_D from both sides of the equation yields an expression for i_d in terms of v_d:

$$i_d = (I_D + I_S)\left[\frac{v_d}{V_T} + \frac{1}{2}\left(\frac{v_d}{V_T}\right)^2 + \frac{1}{6}\left(\frac{v_d}{V_T}\right)^3 + \cdots\right] \quad (13.11)$$

We want the signal current i_d to be a linear function of the signal voltage v_d. Using only the first two terms of Eq. (13.11), we find that linearity requires

$$\frac{v_d}{V_T} \gg \frac{1}{2}\left(\frac{v_d}{V_T}\right)^2 \qquad \text{or} \qquad v_d \ll 2V_T = 0.05 \text{ V} \quad (13.12)$$

If the relationship in Eq. (13.12) is met, then Eq. (13.11) can be written as

$$i_d = (I_D + I_S)\left(\frac{v_d}{V_T}\right) \qquad \text{or} \qquad i_d = g_d v_d \quad (13.13)$$

in which g_d is called the **small-signal conductance** of the diode. The total diode current can now be represented as

$$i_D = I_D + g_d v_d \quad (13.14)$$

Equation (13.14) states that the total diode current is the dc current I_D (at the Q-point) plus a small change in current ($i_d = g_d v_d$) that is linearly related to the small voltage change v_d across the diode.

The values of the **diode conductance g_d**, or the equivalent **diode resistance r_d**, are determined by the operating point of the diode:

$$g_d = \frac{I_D + I_S}{V_T} \qquad \text{and} \qquad r_d = \frac{1}{g_d} \quad (13.15)$$

For forward bias with $I_D \gg I_S$,

$$g_d \approx \frac{I_D}{V_T} \qquad \text{or} \qquad g_d \approx \frac{I_D}{0.025 \text{ V}} = 40 I_D \quad (13.16)$$

at room temperature. The diode and its corresponding small-signal model, represented by resistor r_d, are given in Fig. 13.11.

Equation (13.12) defines the requirement for small-signal operation of the diode. The shift in diode voltage away from the Q-point value must be much less than 50 mV. Choosing a factor of 10 as adequate to satisfy the inequality yields $v_d \leq 0.005$ V for small-signal operation. This is indeed a small voltage change.

(a)   (b)

Figure 13.11 (a) The diode. (b) Small-signal model for the diode.

Graphical Interpretation of the Small-Signal Behavior of the Diode

As depicted graphically in Fig. 13.12, diode conductance g_d actually represents the slope of the diode characteristic evaluated at the Q-point. Stated mathematically, g_d can be written as

$$g_d = \left.\frac{\partial i_D}{\partial v_D}\right|_{Q\text{-point}} = \left.\frac{\partial}{\partial v_d}\left\{I_S\left[\exp\left(\frac{v_D}{V_T}\right) - 1\right]\right\}\right|_{Q\text{-point}} \tag{13.17}$$

or

$$g_d = \left.\frac{I_S}{V_T}\exp\left(\frac{v_D}{V_T}\right)\right|_{Q\text{-point}} = \frac{I_S}{V_T}\exp\left(\frac{V_D}{V_T}\right) = \frac{I_D + I_S}{V_T} \tag{13.18}$$

which is identical to the result obtained in Eq. (13.15). Note that g_d is small but not zero for $I_D = 0$ because the slope of the diode equation is nonzero at the origin, as depicted in Fig. 13.13.

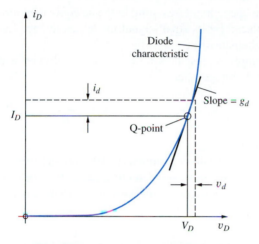

Figure 13.12 The relationship between small increases in voltage and current above the diode operating point (I_D, V_D). For small changes $i_d = g_d v_d$.

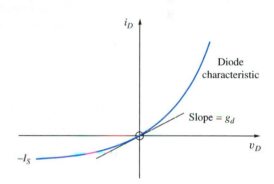

Figure 13.13 The diode conductance is not zero for $I_D = 0$.

> **EXERCISE:** Calculate the values of the diode resistance r_d for a diode with $I_S = 1$ fA operating at $I_D = 0, 50\ \mu A, 2$ mA, and 3 A.
>
> **ANSWERS:** 25.0 TΩ, 500 Ω, 12.5 Ω, 8.33 mΩ
>
> **EXERCISE:** What is the small-signal diode resistance r_d at room temperature for $I_D = 1.5$ mA? What is the small-signal resistance of this diode at $T = 100°C$?
>
> **ANSWERS:** 16.7 Ω, 21.4 Ω

The Current-Controlled Attenuator

As an example of the use of the small-signal diode model, let us analyze the behavior of the current-controlled attenuator circuit in Fig. 13.14. In this circuit, the magnitude of the ac signal voltage v_o developed across the diode can be controlled by the value of dc bias current supplied to the diode. This circuit provides an excellent example of how the choice

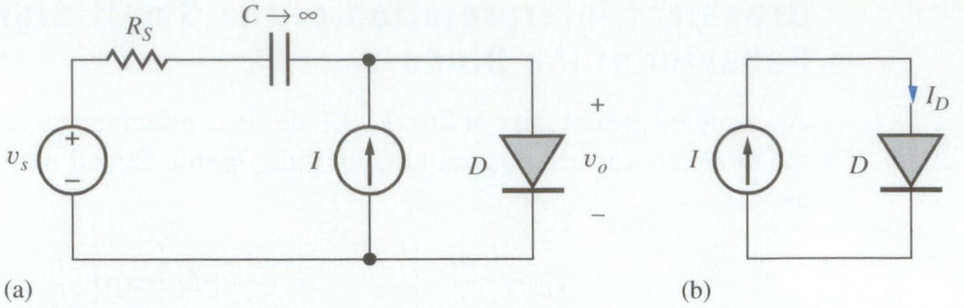

Figure 13.14 (a) Current-controlled attenuator circuit. (b) Equivalent circuit for dc analysis.

of (dc) Q-point affects the ac behavior of a circuit, and it provides more practice creating dc and ac equivalent circuits for analysis.

We begin the analysis by drawing the dc equivalent circuit and finding the diode Q-point. Replacing the coupling capacitor C by an open circuit yields the simplified dc equivalent circuit in Fig. 13.14(b). The dc diode current I_D is simply equal to the source current I: $I_D = I$.

To form the ac equivalent circuit, capacitor C is replaced by a short circuit and the dc current source by an open circuit, resulting in the ac equivalent circuit in Fig. 13.15(a). Next, the diode is replaced by its small-signal model, as in Fig. 13.15(b). Now we can analyze the circuit mathematically.

The ac circuit simply represents a resistive voltage divider across the input signal source; the output signal voltage $\mathbf{v_o}$ is

$$\mathbf{v_o} = \mathbf{v_s}\frac{r_d}{r_d + R_S} = \mathbf{v_s}\frac{1}{1 + \dfrac{R_S}{r_d}} \tag{13.19}$$

The signal appearing across the diode terminals is determined by the ratio R_S/r_d. However, from Eqs. (13.15) and (13.16), we know that the value of r_d is determined by the Q-point current of the diode, which is equal to dc current source I. Using Eq. (13.15), we can rewrite the voltage $\mathbf{v_o}$ as

$$\mathbf{v_o} = \mathbf{v_s}\frac{1}{1 + \dfrac{R_S}{r_d}} = \mathbf{v_s}\frac{1}{1 + \dfrac{(I + I_S)R_S}{V_T}} \tag{13.20}$$

The results of evaluating Eq. (13.20) for $R_S = 1\text{ k}\Omega$ and various values of I are in Table 13.1 for a diode at room temperature having $I_S = 10^{-15}$ A.

The output voltage v_o ranges from v_s down to $0.024v_s$ as the dc current is changed from zero to 1 mA. The fourth column gives the maximum value of input voltage v_s

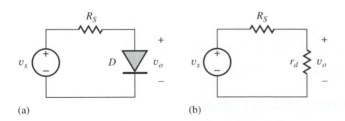

(a)   (b)

Figure 13.15 (a) Equivalent circuit for ac analysis of the current-controlled attenuator. (b) Diode replaced by its small-signal model.

Table 13.1			
Diode Attenuator Characteristics			
I	r_d	V_o	$V_{s\ max}$
0	$25 \times 10^{12}\ \Omega$	$1.00v_s$	5.0 mV
1 μA	25.0 kΩ	$0.96v_s$	5.2 mV
10 μA	2.5 kΩ	$0.71v_s$	7.0 mV
100 μA	250.0 Ω	$0.20v_s$	25 mV
1 mA	25.0 Ω	$0.024v_s$	205 mV

that can be applied to the circuit and still satisfy the small-signal requirement that $v_d \leq$ 0.005 V. When $I = 0$ and $v_o = v_s$, then the magnitude of v_s is limited to only 5 mV! However, for $I = 100\ \mu A$, the input signal is attenuated by a factor of 5, so v_s can have an amplitude of 25 mV and still meet the small-signal requirement. Note carefully that it is the signal voltage directly across the diode terminals that determines the small-signal limit.

13.5 SMALL-SIGNAL MODELS FOR BIPOLAR JUNCTION TRANSISTORS

Now that the concept of small-signal modeling has been introduced, we shall develop the small-signal model for the more complicated bipolar transistor. The BJT is a three-terminal device, and its small-signal model is based on the two-port y-parameter network shown in Fig. 13.16. We express the relationships between the port voltages and currents using the y-parameters:

$$\mathbf{i_1} = y_{11}\mathbf{v_1} + y_{12}\mathbf{v_2}$$
$$\mathbf{i_2} = y_{21}\mathbf{v_1} + y_{22}\mathbf{v_2}$$

(13.21)

Viewing the BJT as the two-port network in Fig. 13.17, the input port variables are $v_1 = v_{be}$ and $i_1 = i_b$, and the output port variables are $v_2 = v_{ce}$ and $i_2 = i_c$. Rewriting Eq. (13.21) in terms of these variables yields

$$\mathbf{i_b} = y_{11}\mathbf{v_{be}} + y_{12}\mathbf{v_{ce}}$$
$$\mathbf{i_c} = y_{21}\mathbf{v_{be}} + y_{22}\mathbf{v_{ce}}$$

(13.22)

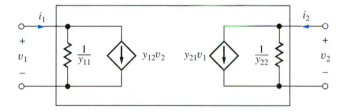

Figure 13.16 y-Parameter representation for a two-port network.

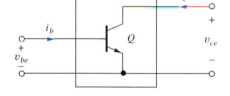

Figure 13.17 Two-port representation of the npn transistor.

The port variables in Fig. 13.17 can be considered to represent either the time-varying portion of the total voltages and currents or small changes in the total quantities away from the Q-point values.

$$v_{BE} = V_{BE} + v_{be} \qquad v_{CE} = V_{CE} + v_{ce}$$
$$i_B = I_B + i_b \qquad i_C = I_C + i_c$$

or

(13.23)

$$v_{be} = \Delta v_{BE} = v_{BE} - V_{BE} \qquad v_{ce} = \Delta v_{CE} = v_{CE} - V_{CE}$$
$$i_b = \Delta i_B = i_B - I_B \qquad i_c = \Delta i_C = i_C - I_C$$

We can write the y-parameters in terms of small-signal voltages and currents or in terms of derivatives of the complete port variables, as in Eq. (13.24):

$$y_{11} = \left. \frac{\mathbf{i_b}}{\mathbf{v_{be}}} \right|_{\mathbf{v_{ce}}=0} = \left. \frac{\partial i_B}{\partial v_{BE}} \right|_{\text{Q-point}}$$

$$y_{12} = \left. \frac{\mathbf{i_b}}{\mathbf{v_{ce}}} \right|_{\mathbf{v_{be}}=0} = \left. \frac{\partial i_B}{\partial v_{CE}} \right|_{\text{Q-point}}$$

$$y_{21} = \left. \frac{\mathbf{i_c}}{\mathbf{v_{be}}} \right|_{\mathbf{v_{ce}}=0} = \left. \frac{\partial i_C}{\partial v_{BE}} \right|_{\text{Q-point}} \qquad (13.24)$$

$$y_{22} = \left. \frac{\mathbf{i_c}}{\mathbf{v_{ce}}} \right|_{\mathbf{v_{be}}=0} = \left. \frac{\partial i_C}{\partial v_{CE}} \right|_{\text{Q-point}}$$

Because we have the transport model, Eq. (5.47), which expresses the BJT terminal currents in terms of the terminal voltages, as repeated in Eq. (13.25) for the forward-active region, we use the derivative formulation to determine the y-parameters for the transistor:

$$i_C = I_S \left[\exp\left(\frac{v_{BE}}{V_T}\right) \right] \left[1 + \frac{v_{CE}}{V_A} \right]$$

$$\beta_F = \beta_{FO} \left[1 + \frac{v_{CE}}{V_A} \right] \qquad (13.25)$$

$$i_B = \frac{i_C}{\beta_F} = \frac{I_S}{\beta_{FO}} \left[\exp\left(\frac{v_{BE}}{V_T}\right) \right]$$

Evaluating the various derivatives[1] of Eqs. (13.25) yields the y-parameters for the BJT:

$$y_{12} = \left. \frac{\partial i_B}{\partial v_{CE}} \right|_{\text{Q-point}} = 0$$

$$y_{21} = \left. \frac{\partial i_C}{\partial v_{BE}} \right|_{\text{Q-point}} = \left. \frac{I_S}{V_T} \left[\exp\left(\frac{v_{BE}}{V_T}\right) \right] \left[1 + \frac{v_{CE}}{V_A} \right] \right|_{\text{Q-point}}$$

$$y_{21} = \frac{I_S}{V_T} \left[\exp\left(\frac{V_{BE}}{V_T}\right) \right] \left[1 + \frac{V_{CE}}{V_A} \right] = \frac{I_C}{V_T} \qquad (13.26)$$

$$y_{22} = \left. \frac{\partial i_C}{\partial v_{CE}} \right|_{\text{Q-point}} = \left. \frac{I_S}{V_A} \left[\exp\left(\frac{v_{BE}}{V_T}\right) \right] \right|_{\text{Q-point}}$$

$$y_{22} = \frac{I_S}{V_A} \left[\exp\left(\frac{V_{BE}}{V_T}\right) \right] = \frac{I_C}{V_A + V_{CE}}$$

Calculation of y_{11} has been saved until last because it requires a bit more effort and the use of some new information. The current gain of a BJT is actually operating point-dependent, and this dependence should be included when evaluating the derivative needed for y_{11}:

$$y_{11} = \left. \frac{\partial i_B}{\partial v_{BE}} \right|_{\text{Q-point}} = \left[\frac{1}{\beta_F} \frac{\partial i_C}{\partial v_{BE}} - \frac{i_C}{\beta_F^2} \frac{\partial \beta_F}{\partial v_{BE}} \right]_{\text{Q-point}} \qquad (13.27)$$

Expanding the second term using the chain rule yields

$$y_{11} = \left[\frac{1}{\beta_F} \frac{\partial i_C}{\partial v_{BE}} - \frac{i_C}{\beta_F^2} \frac{\partial \beta_F}{\partial i_C} \frac{\partial i_C}{\partial v_{BE}} \right]_{\text{Q-point}} \qquad (13.28)$$

---

[1] We could equally well have taken the direct approach used in analysis of the diode.

and factoring out the first term:

$$y_{11} = \frac{1}{\beta_F} \frac{\partial i_C}{\partial v_{BE}} \left[1 - \frac{i_C}{\beta_F} \frac{\partial \beta_F}{\partial i_C} \right]_{\text{Q-point}} = \frac{I_C}{\beta_F V_T} \left[1 - \left(\frac{i_C}{\beta_F} \frac{\partial \beta_F}{\partial i_C} \right)_{\text{Q-point}} \right] \quad (13.29)$$

Finally, Eq. (13.29) can be simplified by defining a new parameter β_o:

$$y_{11} = \frac{I_C}{\beta_o V_T} \qquad \text{where } \beta_o = \frac{\beta_F}{\left[1 - I_C \left(\frac{1}{\beta_F} \frac{\partial \beta_F}{\partial i_C} \right)_{\text{Q-point}} \right]} \quad (13.30)$$

β_o represents the **small-signal common-emitter current gain** of the bipolar transistor.

The parameters in Eqs. (13.26) and (13.30) historically have been represented by special symbols in the small-signal model of the BJT, as defined in Eq. (13.31):

$$\textbf{Transconductance:} \qquad g_m = y_{21} = \frac{I_C}{V_T} \approx 40 I_C$$

$$\textbf{Input resistance:} \qquad r_\pi = \frac{1}{y_{11}} = \frac{\beta_o V_T}{I_C} = \frac{\beta_o}{g_m} \qquad (13.31)$$

$$\textbf{Output resistance:} \qquad r_o = \frac{1}{y_{22}} = \frac{V_A + V_{CE}}{I_C}$$

The two-port representation in Fig. 13.18 using these symbols shows the intrinsic low-frequency **hybrid-pi small-signal model** for the bipolar transistor. Additional elements will be added to model frequency dependencies in Chapter 17.

From Eq. (13.31), we see that the values of the small-signal parameters are controlled explicitly by our choice of Q-point. Transconductance g_m is directly proportional to the collector current of the bipolar transistor, whereas input resistance r_π and output resistance r_o are both inversely proportional to the collector current. The output resistance exhibits a weak dependence on collector-emitter voltage (generally $V_{CE} \ll V_A$). Note that these parameters are independent of the geometry of the BJT. For example, small high-frequency transistors or large-geometry power devices all have the same value of g_m for a given collector current.

Table 13.2 displays examples of the variation in values of the parameters with operating point. The values of g_m, r_π, and r_o can each be varied over many orders of magnitude by changing the value of the dc collector current corresponding to the Q-point. (The last column is the amplification factor μ_F, to be introduced shortly.)

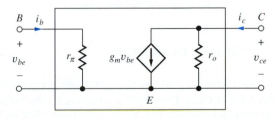

Figure 13.18 Hybrid-pi small-signal model for the intrinsic bipolar transistor.

Table 13.2				
BJT Small-Signal Parameters versus Current: $\beta_o = 100$, $V_A = 75$ V, $V_{CE} = 10$ V				
I_C	g_m	r_π	r_o	μ_f
1 μA	4×10^{-5} S	2.5 MΩ	85 MΩ	3400
10 μA	4×10^{-4} S	250.0 kΩ	8.5 MΩ	3400
100 μA	0.004 S	25.0 kΩ	850 kΩ	3400
1 mA	0.04 S	2.5 kΩ	85 kΩ	3400
10 mA	0.40 S	250.0 Ω	8.5 kΩ	3400

Small-Signal Current Gain

Two important auxiliary relationships also exist between the small-signal parameters. It can be seen in Eq. (13.31) that the parameters g_m and r_π are related by the small-signal current gain β_o:

$$\beta_o = g_m r_\pi \tag{13.32}$$

As mentioned before, the dc current gain in a real transistor is not constant but is a function of operating current, as indicated in Fig. 13.19. From this figure, we see that

$$\frac{\partial \beta_F}{\partial i_C} > 0 \text{ for } i_C < I_M \qquad \text{and} \qquad \frac{\partial \beta_F}{\partial i_C} < 0 \text{ for } i_C > I_M$$

where I_M is the collector current at which β_F is maximum. Thus, for the **small-signal current gain** defined by

$$\beta_o = \frac{\beta_F}{\left[1 - I_C \left(\frac{1}{\beta_F} \frac{\partial \beta_F}{\partial i_C}\right)_{\text{Q-point}}\right]} \tag{13.33}$$

$\beta_o > \beta_F$ for $i_C < I_M$, and $\beta_o < \beta_F$ for $i_C > I_M$. That is, the ac current gain β_o exceeds the dc current gain β_F when the collector current is below I_M and is smaller than β_F when I_C exceeds I_M.

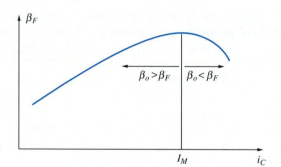

Figure 13.19 dc Current gain versus current for the BJT.

The Amplification Factor

The second important auxiliary relationship is given by the **amplification factor** μ_f, which is equal to the product of g_m and r_o:

$$\mu_f = g_m r_o = \frac{I_C}{V_T} \frac{V_A + V_{CE}}{I_C} = \frac{V_A + V_{CE}}{V_T} \tag{13.34}$$

From Eq. (13.34), the amplification factor can be seen to be almost independent of operating point for $V_{CE} \ll V_A$:

$$\mu_f \approx \frac{V_A}{V_T} \approx 40 V_A \qquad \text{for } V_{CE} \ll V_A \tag{13.35}$$

We shall find that the amplification factor μ_f plays an important role in circuit design. It appears often in the analysis of amplifier circuits. Parameter μ_f represents the maximum voltage gain that the individual transistor can provide. For V_A ranging from 25 V to 100 V, μ_f ranges from 1000 to 4000. Note in Table 13.2 that μ_f does not change with the choice of operating point. As we see later in this chapter, this is a very significant difference between the BJT and FET.

It is important to realize that although we developed the small-signal model of the BJT based on analysis of the transistor oriented in the common-emitter configuration in Fig. 13.17, the resulting hybrid-pi model can actually be used in the analysis of any circuit topology. This point becomes clearer in the next chapter.

EXERCISE: Calculate the values of g_m, r_π, r_o, and μ_f for a bipolar transistor with $\beta_o = 75$ and $V_A = 60$ V operating at a Q-point of (50 μA, 5 V).

ANSWERS: 2.00 mS, 37.5 kΩ, 1.30 MΩ, 2600

EXERCISE: Calculate the values of g_m, r_π, r_o, and μ_f for a bipolar transistor with $\beta_o = 50$ and $V_A = 75$ V operating at a Q-point of (250 μA, 15 V).

ANSWERS: 10.0 mS, 5.00 kΩ, 360 kΩ, 3600

EXERCISE: Use graphical analysis to find values of β_{FO}, g_m, β_o, and r_o at the Q-point for the transistor in Fig. 13.2. Calculate the value of r_π.

ANSWERS: 100, 62.5 mS, 100, ∞; 1.60 kΩ

Equivalent Forms of the Small-Signal Model

The small-signal model in Fig. 13.18 includes the voltage-controlled current source $g_m v_{be}$. It is often useful in circuit analysis to transform this model into a current-controlled source.

Recognizing that the voltage $\mathbf{v_{be}}$ in Fig. 13.20 can be written in terms of the current $\mathbf{i_b}$ as

$$\mathbf{v_{be}} = \mathbf{i_b} r_\pi \tag{13.36}$$

the current-controlled source can be rewritten as

$$g_m \mathbf{v_{be}} = g_m r_\pi \mathbf{i_b} = \beta_o \mathbf{i_b} \tag{13.37}$$

Figure 13.20(a) and (b) shows the two equivalent forms of the small-signal BJT model. The model in Fig. 13.20(a) recognizes the fundamental voltage-controlled current source nature of the transistor that is explicit in the transport model. From the second model, Fig. 13.20(b), we see that

$$\mathbf{i_c} = \beta_o \mathbf{i_b} + \frac{\mathbf{v_{ce}}}{r_o} \approx \beta_o \mathbf{i_b} \tag{13.38}$$

which demonstrates the auxiliary relationship that $\mathbf{i_c} \approx \beta_o \mathbf{i_b}$ in the forward-active region of operation. For the most typical case, $\mathbf{v_{ce}}/r_o \ll \beta_o \mathbf{i_b}$. Thus, the basic relationship $i_C = \beta i_B$ is useful for both ac and dc analysis when the BJT is operating in the forward-active region. We will find that sometimes circuit analysis is more easily performed using the model in Fig. 13.20(a), and at other times more easily performed using the model in Fig. 13.20(b).[2]

Figure 13.20 Two equivalent forms of the BJT small-signal model: (a) voltage-controlled current source model, and (b) current-controlled current source model.

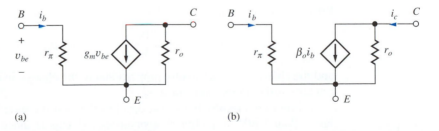

(a)   (b)

---

[2] An alternative model, called the T-model, is in Prob. 13.50.

Definition of a Small Signal for the Bipolar Transistor

For small-signal operation, we want the relationship between changes in voltages and currents to be linear. We can find the constraints on the BJT corresponding to small-signal operation using the simplified transport model for the total collector current of the transistor in the forward-active region:

$$i_C = I_S \left[\exp \left(\frac{v_{BE}}{V_T} \right) \right] = I_S \left[\exp \left(\frac{V_{BE} + v_{be}}{V_T} \right) \right] \tag{13.39}$$

Rewriting the exponential as a product,

$$i_C = I_C + i_c = \left[I_S \exp \left(\frac{V_{BE}}{V_T} \right) \right] \left[\exp \left(\frac{v_{be}}{V_T} \right) \right] = I_C \left[\exp \left(\frac{v_{be}}{V_T} \right) \right] \tag{13.40}$$

in which it has been recognized that

$$I_S \exp \left(\frac{V_{BE}}{V_T} \right) \tag{13.41}$$

represents the dc collector current I_C. Now, expanding the remaining exponential in Eq. (13.40), its Maclaurin's series yields

$$i_C = I_C \left[1 + \frac{v_{be}}{V_T} + \frac{1}{2} \left(\frac{v_{be}}{V_T} \right)^2 + \frac{1}{6} \left(\frac{v_{be}}{V_T} \right)^3 + \cdots \right] \tag{13.42}$$

Recognizing

$$i_c = i_C - I_C \tag{13.43}$$

yields

$$i_C = I_C \left[\frac{v_{be}}{V_T} + \frac{1}{2} \left(\frac{v_{be}}{V_T} \right)^2 + \frac{1}{6} \left(\frac{v_{be}}{V_T} \right)^3 + \cdots \right] \tag{13.44}$$

Linearity requires that i_c be proportional to v_{be}, so we must have

$$\frac{1}{2} \left(\frac{v_{be}}{V_T} \right)^2 \ll \frac{v_{be}}{V_T} \qquad \text{or} \qquad v_{be} \ll 2V_T \tag{13.45}$$

From Eq. (13.45), we see that small-signal operation requires the signal applied to the base-emitter junction to be much less than twice the thermal voltage, which is 50 mV at room temperature. In this book, we assume that a factor of 10 satisfies the condition in Eq. (13.45), and

$$|v_{be}| \le 0.005 \text{ V} \tag{13.46}$$

is our definition of a small signal *for the BJT.* If the condition in Eq. (13.45) is met, then Eq. (13.42) can be approximated as

$$i_C \approx I_C \left[1 + \frac{v_{be}}{V_T} \right] = I_C + \frac{I_C}{V_T} v_{be} = I_C + g_m v_{be} \tag{13.47}$$

and the change in i_C is directly proportional to the change in v_{be}. The constant of proportionality is the transconductance g_m.

From Eq. (13.46), the signal developed across the base-emitter junction must be no larger than 5 mV to qualify as a small signal! This is indeed small. But *note well:* We must not infer that signals at other points in the circuit need be small. Referring back to Fig. 13.2, we can see that a 16-mV *p-p* signal v_{be} generates a 3.3-V *p-p* signal at the collector. This is fortunate because we often want linear amplifiers to develop signals that are many volts in amplitude.

Let us now explore the change in collector current i_c that corresponds to small-signal operation. Using Eq. (13.47),

$$\frac{i_c}{I_C} = \frac{i_C - I_C}{I_C} = \frac{g_m}{I_C} v_{be} = \frac{v_{be}}{V_T} \leq \frac{0.005}{0.025} = 0.200 \qquad (13.48)$$

A 5-mV change in v_{BE} corresponds to a 20 percent deviation in i_C from its Q-point value as well as a 20 percent change in i_E because $\alpha_F \approx 1$. Some authors prefer to permit $|v_{be}| \leq 10$ mV, which corresponds to a 40 percent change in i_C from the Q-point value. In either case, relatively large changes in voltage can occur at the collector and/or emitter terminals of the transistor when the signal currents i_c and i_e flow through resistors external to the transistor.

> **EXERCISE:** Does the amplitude of the signal in Figs. 13.1 and 13.2 satisfy the requirements for small-signal operation?
>
> **ANSWER:** No, $v_{be} = 8$ mV exceeds our definition of a small signal.

Small-Signal Model for the *pnp* Transistor

The small-signal model for the *pnp* transistor is identical to that of the *npn* transistor. At first glance, this fact is surprising to most people because the dc currents flow in opposite directions. The circuits in Fig. 13.21 will be used to help explain this situation.

In Fig. 13.21, the *npn* and *pnp* transistors are each biased by dc current source I_B, establishing the Q-point current $I_C = \beta_F I_B$. In each case a signal current i_b is also injected *into* the base. For the *npn* transistor, the total base and collector currents are (for $\beta_o = \beta_F$):

$$i_B = I_B + i_b \qquad \text{and} \qquad i_C = I_C + i_c = \beta_F I_B + \beta_F i_b \qquad (13.49)$$

An increase in base current of the *npn* transistor causes an increase in current entering the collector terminal.

For the *pnp* transistor,

$$i_B = I_B - i_b \qquad \text{and} \qquad i_C = I_C - i_c = \beta_F I_B - \beta_F i_b \qquad (13.50)$$

The signal current injected into the base of the *pnp* transistor causes a decrease in the total collector current, which is again equivalent to an increase in the signal current entering the

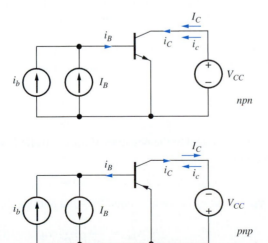

Figure 13.21 dc Bias and signal currents for *npn* and *pnp* transistors.

collector. Thus, for both the *npn* and *pnp* transistors, a signal current injected into the base causes a signal current to enter the collector, and the polarities of the current-controlled source in the small-signal model are identical, as in Fig. 13.22.

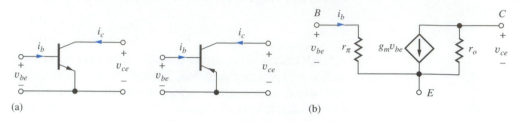

(a)   (b)

Figure 13.22   (a) Two-port notations for *npn* and *pnp* transistors. (b) The small-signal models are identical.

13.6 THE BJT COMMON-EMITTER (C-E) AMPLIFIER

Now we are in a position to analyze the small-signal characteristics of the complete **common-emitter (C-E) amplifier** shown in Fig. 13.23(a). The ac equivalent circuit of Fig. 13.23(b) was constructed earlier (Example 13.1) by assuming that the capacitors all have zero impedance at the signal frequency and the dc voltage source represents an ac ground. For simplicity, we assume that we have found the Q-point and know the values of I_C and V_{CE}. Several examples of complete amplifier analysis appear later in this chapter. In Fig. 13.23(c), the circuit has been simplified using a Thévenin source transformation:

$$\mathbf{v_{th}} = \frac{R_B}{R_B + R_S}\mathbf{v_s} \quad \text{and} \quad R_{th} = \frac{R_B R_S}{R_B + R_S} \quad \text{where } R_B = R_1 \| R_2 \quad (13.51)$$

The transistor is next replaced by its small-signal model in Fig. 13.23(d). A final simplification appears in Fig. 13.23(e), in which the resistor R_L represents the total equivalent load resistance on the transistor: the parallel combination of R_C, R_3, and the output resistance r_o of the transistor itself.

$$R_L = r_o \| R_C \| R_3 \quad (13.52)$$

In Fig. 13.23(b) through (e), the reason why this amplifier configuration is called a common-emitter amplifier is apparent. The emitter terminal represents the common connection between the amplifier input and output ports. The input signal is applied to the transistor's base, the output signal appears at the collector, and both the input and output signals are referenced to the (common) emitter terminal.

Now we are ready to develop an expression for the voltage gain A_v between the signal source v_s and the output v_o in Fig. 13.23(a). We first write the voltage gain in terms of v_{th} in Fig. 13.23(e), and then express it in terms of v_s using Eq. (13.51) for v_{th}. Starting with the circuit in Fig. 13.23(e),

$$A_{Vth} = \frac{\mathbf{v_o}}{\mathbf{v_{th}}} \quad (13.53)$$

The output voltage is equal to the negative of the controlled-source current times the value of the load resistor

$$\mathbf{v_o} = -g_m\mathbf{v_{be}}R_L \quad (13.54)$$

The voltage $\mathbf{v_{be}}$ across r_π is readily found by voltage division:

$$\mathbf{v_{be}} = \frac{r_\pi}{r_\pi + R_{th}}\mathbf{v_{th}} \quad (13.55)$$

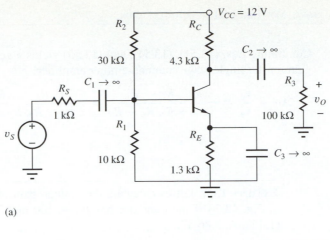

(a)

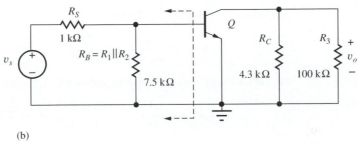

(b)

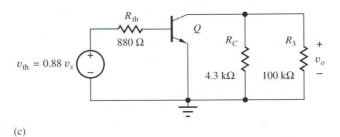

(c)

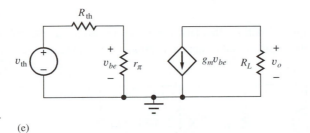

(d)

Figure 13.23 (a) Common-emitter amplifier circuit employing a bipolar transistor. (b) ac Equivalent circuit for the common-emitter amplifier in part (a). The common-emitter connection should now be evident. (c) Simplified ac equivalent circuit. (d) ac Equivalent circuit with the bipolar transistor replaced by its small-signal model. (e) Final equivalent circuit for ac analysis of the common-emitter amplifier.

(e)

Combining Eqs. (13.51), (13.54), and (13.55) yields a general expression for the voltage gain for the single-stage common-emitter amplifier:

$$A_V = \frac{\mathbf{v_o}}{\mathbf{v_s}} = -\frac{g_m r_\pi R_L}{r_\pi + R_{\text{th}}} \frac{R_B}{R_B + R_S} = -\frac{\beta_o R_L}{r_\pi + R_{\text{th}}} \frac{R_B}{R_B + R_S} = -\frac{g_m R_L}{1 + \dfrac{R_{\text{th}}}{r_\pi}} \frac{1}{1 + \dfrac{R_S}{R_B}}$$

(13.56)

EXAMPLE 13.3: Let us calculate the voltage gain of the common-emitter amplifier in Fig. 13.23 if the transistor has $\beta_o = 100$ and $V_A = 75$ V, and the Q-point is (1.45 mA, 3.86 V).

SOLUTION: To evaluate Eq. (13.56),

$$A_V = -\frac{\beta_o R_L}{r_\pi + R_{\text{th}}} \frac{R_B}{R_B + R_S} \qquad \text{and} \qquad R_B = R_1 \| R_2$$

the values of the various resistors and small-signal model parameters are required:

$$r_\pi = \frac{\beta_o V_T}{I_C} = \frac{100\,(0.025\text{ V})}{1.45\text{ mA}} = 1.72\text{ k}\Omega$$

$$r_o = \frac{V_A + V_{CE}}{I_C} = \frac{75\text{ V} + 3.86\text{ V}}{1.45\text{ mA}} = 54.4\text{ k}\Omega$$

$$R_B = R_1 \| R_2 = 7.50\text{ k}\Omega \qquad R_{\text{th}} = R_S \| R_B = 882\ \Omega$$

$$R_L = R_C \| R_3 \| r_o = 3.83\text{ k}\Omega$$

Using these values,

$$A_V = \frac{100 \times 3.83\text{ k}\Omega}{1.72\text{ k}\Omega + 0.882\text{ k}\Omega} \frac{7.50\text{ k}\Omega}{7.50\text{ k}\Omega + 1.00\text{ k}\Omega} = -130$$

Thus, the common-emitter amplifier in Fig. 13.23 provides a small-signal voltage gain $A_V = -130$ or 42.3 dB. ◆

Model Simplifications

We now explore the limits to the voltage gain of the common-emitter amplifier using a number of model simplifications. If we assume that the source resistance is small enough that $R_S \ll R_B$ and $R_{\text{th}} \ll r_\pi$, then Eq. (13.56) can be reduced to

$$A_V = -\frac{\beta_o R_L}{r_\pi} = -g_m R_L = -g_m(r_o \| R_C \| R_3)$$

(13.57)

The approximations that lead from Eq. (13.56) to Eq. (13.57) are equivalent to saying that the total input signal v_s appears across r_π as shown in Fig. 13.24. Equation (13.57) states

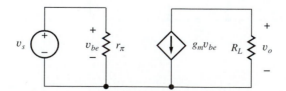

Figure 13.24 Simplified circuit corresponding to Eq. (13.57).

that the **intrinsic voltage gain** of the common-emitter stage is equal to the product of the transistor transconductance g_m and the total load resistance R_L. The total load resistance consists of the output resistance r_o in parallel with the collector resistance R_C and the external load resistor R_3. Remember that the minus signs in Eqs. (13.56) and (13.57) indicate that the output voltage is "inverted," or 180° out of phase with respect to the input.

Achieving the gain in Eq. (13.57) requires the input resistance of the transistor amplifier to be much greater than the Thévenin equivalent source resistance, as well as requiring $R_B \gg R_S$. This mismatched condition was previously discussed in Chapter 11, and is a condition that we often strive to achieve in voltage amplifier designs.

A Design Guide for the Common-Emitter Amplifier with Resistive Load

When a resistor is used as the load on the common-emitter amplifier, its value is generally much smaller than that of the transistor output resistance r_o. In addition, during design of the amplifier, we often try to achieve $R_3 \gg R_C$. For these conditions, the total load resistance on the collector of the transistor is approximately equal to R_C, and Eq. (13.57) can be reduced to

$$A_V \approx -g_m R_C = -\frac{I_C R_C}{V_T} \tag{13.58}$$

The $I_C R_C$ product represents the dc voltage dropped across the collector resistor R_C. This voltage must be less than the power supply voltage and typically ranges between one-fourth and three-fourths of V_{CC}. Assuming $I_C R_C = \zeta V_{CC}$ with $0 \le \zeta \le 1$, and remembering that the reciprocal of V_T is 40 V^{-1}, Eq. (13.58) can be rewritten as

$$A_V = -\frac{I_C R_C}{V_T} \approx -40\zeta V_{cc} \qquad \text{with } 0 \le \zeta \le 1 \tag{13.59}$$

In this book we assume $\zeta = 0.25$ ($I_C R_C = V_{CC}/4$). Using a value at the low end of the range helps account for various approximations that led to Eq. (13.59) and yields

$$A_V = -\frac{I_C R_C}{V_T} \approx -40\left(\frac{V_{CC}}{4}\right) = -10 V_{CC} \ ^3 \tag{13.60}$$

Equation (13.60) is a basic rule of thumb for the design of the resistively loaded common-emitter amplifier: The magnitude of the voltage gain is approximately 10 times the power supply voltage. For a C-E amplifier operating from a 15-V power supply, we estimate the gain to be −150; a 10-V supply is expected to produce a gain of approximately −100. Equation (13.60) is a first-order estimate of the gain of the resistively loaded amplifier stage. That is, we only need to know the power supply voltage to make a prediction of the gain of the common-emitter amplifier.

Common-Emitter Voltage Gain Upper Bound

In more complex circuits, which are introduced in later chapters, it is possible to force the effective value of R_L to approach r_o. In this case, the voltage gain of the common-emitter stage is limited by the gain of the transistor. Letting R_C and $R_3 \to \infty$ in Eq. (13.57) yields

$$A_V = -g_m r_o = -\mu_f \tag{13.61}$$

---

[3]For dual power supplies, the corresponding estimate would be $A_V = -10(V_{CC} + V_{EE})$.

Equation (13.61) demonstrates that the voltage gain of the common-emitter stage cannot exceed the amplification factor μ_f of the transistor itself! In this case, the only load on the transistor is its own output resistance r_o. Parameter μ_f represents an upper bound on voltage gain of a single-transistor amplifier.

Note that a resistively loaded BJT amplifier does not make very effective use of the voltage gain capability of the transistor. Our "10 V_{CC}" rule of thumb is typically in the range of a few hundred, whereas μ_f is often several thousand.

> **EXERCISE:** The common-emitter amplifier in Fig. 13.23 is operating from a single $+20$-V power supply. The BJT has $\beta_F = 100$ and $V_A = 50$ V, and is operating at a Q-point of (100 μA, 10 V). The amplifier has $R_{\text{th}} = 5$ kΩ, $R_C = 100$ kΩ, and $R_3 = \infty$. What is the voltage gain predicted using our rule of thumb estimate? What is the actual voltage gain? What is the value of μ_f for this transistor?
>
> **ANSWERS:** -200; -286; 2400

13.7 SMALL-SIGNAL MODELS FOR FIELD-EFFECT TRANSISTORS

We now develop a small-signal model for the field-effect transistor and then use it in the next section to analyze the behavior of the common-source amplifier stage, which is the FET version of the common-emitter amplifier. First we consider the MOSFET as a three-terminal device; we then explore the changes necessary when the MOSFET is operated as a four-terminal device. At the end of the section, the model for the JFET is discussed.

The small-signal model of the MOSFET is based on the y-parameter two-port network in Fig. 13.16. The MOSFET can be represented by the two port in Fig. 13.25 with the input port variables defined as $v_1 = v_{gs}$ and $i_1 = i_g$ and the output port variables defined as $v_2 = v_{ds}$ and $i_2 = i_{ds}$. Rewriting Eq. (13.21) in terms of these variables yields

$$\mathbf{i_g} = y_{11}\mathbf{v_{gs}} + y_{12}\mathbf{v_{ds}}$$
$$\mathbf{i_{ds}} = y_{21}\mathbf{v_{gs}} + y_{22}\mathbf{v_{ds}}$$
(13.62)

Remember that the port variables in Fig. 13.25 can be considered to represent either the time-varying portion of the total voltages and currents or small changes in the total quantities.

$$v_{GS} = V_{GS} + v_{gs} \qquad v_{DS} = V_{DS} + v_{ds}$$
$$i_G = I_G + i_g \qquad i_{DS} = I_{DS} + i_{ds}$$
$$v_{gs} = \Delta v_{GS} \quad v_{ds} = \Delta v_{DS} \qquad i_g = \Delta i_G \quad i_{ds} = \Delta i_{DS}$$
(13.63)

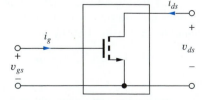

Figure 13.25 The MOSFET represented as a two-port network.

The y-parameters can be written in terms of the small-signal variations or in terms of derivatives of the complete port variables, as in Eq. (13.64):

$$y_{11} = \left.\frac{\mathbf{i_g}}{\mathbf{v_{gs}}}\right|_{\mathbf{v_{ce}}=0} = \left.\frac{\partial i_G}{\partial v_{GS}}\right|_{\text{Q-point}} \qquad y_{12} = \left.\frac{\mathbf{i_g}}{\mathbf{v_{ds}}}\right|_{\mathbf{v_{be}}=0} = \left.\frac{\partial i_G}{\partial v_{DS}}\right|_{\text{Q-point}}$$

$$y_{21} = \left.\frac{\mathbf{i_{ds}}}{\mathbf{v_{gs}}}\right|_{\mathbf{v_{ce}}=0} = \left.\frac{\partial i_{DS}}{\partial v_{GS}}\right|_{\text{Q-point}} \qquad y_{22} = \left.\frac{\mathbf{i_{ds}}}{\mathbf{v_{ds}}}\right|_{\mathbf{v_{be}}=0} = \left.\frac{\partial i_{DS}}{\partial v_{DS}}\right|_{\text{Q-point}} \tag{13.64}$$

We evaluate these parameters by taking appropriate derivatives of the large-signal model equations for the drain current of the saturated MOS transistor, as developed in Chapter 4, and repeated here in Eq. (13.65).

$$i_{DS} = \frac{K_n}{2}(v_{GS} - V_{TN})^2(1 + \lambda v_{DS}) \tag{13.65}$$

where $K_n = \mu_n C_{\text{ox}}(W/L)$ for $v_{DS} \geq v_{GS} - V_{TN}$ and $i_G = 0$.

$$y_{11} = \left.\frac{\partial i_G}{\partial v_{GS}}\right|_{v_{DS}} = 0$$

$$y_{12} = \left.\frac{\partial i_G}{\partial v_{DS}}\right|_{v_{GS}} = 0$$

$$y_{21} = \left.\frac{\partial i_{DS}}{\partial v_{GS}}\right|_{\text{Q-point}} = K_n(V_{GS} - V_{TN})(1 + \lambda V_{DS}) = \frac{2I_D}{V_{GS} - V_{TN}}$$

$$y_{22} = \left.\frac{\partial i_{DS}}{\partial v_{DS}}\right|_{\text{Q-point}} = i_D = \lambda\frac{K_n}{2}(V_{GS} - V_{TN})^2 = \frac{\lambda I_D}{1 + \lambda V_{DS}} = \frac{I_D}{\dfrac{1}{\lambda} + V_{DS}}$$

$$\tag{13.66}$$

Because i_G is always zero and therefore independent of v_{GS} and v_{DS}, y_{11} and y_{12} are both zero. Remembering that the gate terminal is insulated from the channel by the gate oxide, we can reasonably expect that the input resistance $1/y_{11}$ of the transistor is infinite.

As for the bipolar transistor, y_{21} is called the transconductance, and $1/y_{22}$ represents the output resistance of the transistor.

$$\text{Transconductance:} \quad g_m = y_{21} = \frac{I_{DS}}{\dfrac{V_{GS} - V_{TN}}{2}}$$

$$\tag{13.67}$$

$$\text{Output resistance:} \quad r_o = \frac{1}{y_{22}} = \frac{\dfrac{1}{\lambda} + V_{DS}}{I_{DS}}$$

The small-signal circuit model for the MOSFET resulting from Eqs. (13.66) and (13.67) is illustrated in Fig. 13.26.

From Eq. (13.67), we again see that the values of the small-signal parameters are directly controlled by the design of the Q-point. The form of the equations for g_m and r_o of the MOSFET directly mirrors that of the BJT. However, one-half the internal gate drive $(V_{GS} - V_{TN})/2$ replaces the thermal voltage V_T in the transconductance expression, and $1/\lambda$ replaces the Early voltage in the output resistance expression. The value of $V_{GS} - V_{TN}$ is often a volt or more in MOSFET circuits, whereas $V_T = 0.025$ V at room temperature.

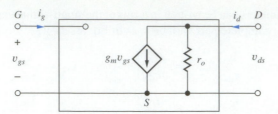

Figure 13.26 Small-signal model for the three-terminal MOSFET.

Thus, for a given operating current, the MOSFET can be expected to have a much smaller transconductance than the BJT. However, the value of $1/\lambda$ is similar to V_A, so the output resistances are similar for a given operating point $(I_{DS}, V_{DS}) = (I_C, V_{CE})$.

The actual dependence of transconductance g_m on current is not shown explicitly by Eq. (13.67) because I_{DS} is a function of $(V_{GS} - V_{TN})$. Rewriting the expression for $g_m = y_{21}$ from Eq. (13.66) yields

$$g_m = K_n(V_{GS} - V_{TN})(1 + \lambda V_{DS}) = \sqrt{2K_n I_{DS}(1 + \lambda V_{DS})} \qquad (13.68)$$

which can be simplified for $\lambda V_{DS} \ll 1$ to

$$g_m \approx K_n(V_{GS} - V_{TN}) \qquad \text{or} \qquad g_m \approx \sqrt{2K_n I_{DS}} \qquad (13.69)$$

Here we see two other important differences between the MOSFET and BJT. The MOSFET transconductance increases only as the square root of drain current, whereas the BJT transconductance is directly proportional to collector current. In addition, the MOSFET transconductance is dependent on the geometry of the transistor because $K \propto W/L$, whereas the transconductance of the BJT is geometry-independent. It is also worth noting that the current gain of the MOSFET is infinite. Because the value of $r_\pi = (1/y_{11})$ is infinite for the MOSFET, the product $g_m r_\pi$ equals infinity as well.

Amplification Factor

Another important difference between the BJT and MOSFET is the variation of the amplification factor μ_f with operating point. Using Eqs. (13.67) for g_m and r_o, we find that the amplification factor becomes

$$\mu_f = g_m r_o = \frac{I_{DS}}{\dfrac{V_{GS} - V_{TN}}{2}} \cdot \frac{\dfrac{1}{\lambda} + V_{DS}}{I_{DS}} = \frac{\dfrac{1}{\lambda} + V_{DS}}{\left(\dfrac{V_{GS} - V_{TN}}{2}\right)} \qquad (13.70)$$

or writing it in terms of the drain current using Eq. (13.68) yields

$$\mu_f = g_m r_o = \sqrt{2K_n I_{DS}(1 + \lambda V_{DS})} \frac{\dfrac{1}{\lambda} + V_{DS}}{I_{DS}} = \left(\frac{1}{\lambda} + V_{DS}\right)\sqrt{\frac{2K_n}{I_{DS}}(1 + \lambda V_{DS})}$$

For $\lambda V_{DS} \ll 1$,

$$\mu_f \approx \frac{1}{\lambda}\sqrt{\frac{2K_n}{I_{DS}}} \approx \frac{2}{\lambda(V_{GS} - V_{TN})} \qquad (13.71)$$

The amplification factor of the MOSFET decreases as the operating current increases. Thus the larger the operating current of the MOSFET, the smaller its voltage gain capability becomes. In contrast, the amplification factor of the BJT is independent of operating point.

This is an extremely important difference to keep in mind, particularly during the design process.

Table 13.3 displays examples of the values of the MOSFET small-signal parameters for a variety of operating points. Just as for the bipolar transistor, the values of g_m and r_o can each be varied over many orders of magnitude through the choice of Q-point. By comparing the results in Tables 13.2 and 13.3, we see that g_m, r_o, and μ_f of the MOSFET are all similar to those of the bipolar transistor at low currents. However, as the drain current increases, the value of g_m of the MOSFET does not grow as rapidly as for the bipolar transistor, and μ_F drops significantly. This particular MOSFET has a significantly lower amplification factor than the BJT for currents greater than a few tens of microamperes.

> **EXERCISES:** (a) Calculate the values of g_m, r_o, and μ_f for a MOSFET transistor with $K_n = 1$ mA/V^2 and $\lambda = 0.02$ V^{-1} operating at Q-points of (250 μA, 5 V) and (5 mA, 10 V). (b) Use graphical analysis to find values of g_m and r_o at the Q-point for the transistor in Fig. 13.4.
>
> **ANSWERS:** 7.42×10^{-4} S, 220 kΩ, 163; 3.46×10^{-3} S, 12.0 kΩ, 40.0; 1.3×10^{-3} S, ∞

T a b l e 13.3				
MOSFET Small-Signal Parameters versus Current: $K_n = 1$ mA/V^2, $\lambda = 0.0133$ V^{-1}, $V_{DS} = 10$ V				
I_D	g_m	r_π	r_0	μ_f
1 μA	4.76×10^{-5} S	∞	85.20 MΩ	4060
10 μA	1.51×10^{-4} S	∞	8.52 MΩ	1280
100 μA	4.76×10^{-4} S	∞	852.0 kΩ	406
1 mA	1.51×10^{-3} S	∞	85.2 kΩ	128
10 mA	4.76×10^{-3} S	∞	8.52 kΩ	40.0

Definition of Small-Signal Operation for the MOSFET

The limits of linear operation of the MOSFET can be explored using the simplified drain-current expression ($\lambda = 0$) for the MOSFET repeated here from Eq. (7.11):

$$i_{DS} = \frac{K_n}{2}(v_{GS} - V_{TN})^2 \qquad \text{for } v_{DS} \geq v_{GS} - V_{TN} \tag{13.72}$$

Expanding this expression using $v_{GS} = V_{GS} + v_{gs}$ and $i_{DS} = I_{DS} + i_{ds}$ gives

$$i_{DS} = \frac{K_n}{2}[V_{GS} + v_{gs} - V_{TN}]^2 \tag{13.73}$$

or

$$I_{DS} + i_{ds} = \frac{K_n}{2}[(V_{GS} - V_{TN})^2 + 2v_{gs}(V_{GS} - V_{TN}) + v_{gs}^2] \tag{13.74}$$

Recognizing that the dc drain current is equal to

$$I_{DS} = \frac{K_n}{2}(V_{GS} - V_{TN})^2 \tag{13.75}$$

and subtracting this term from both sides of Eq. (13.74) yields an expression for the signal current i_{ds}:

$$i_{ds} = \frac{K_n}{2}[2v_{gs}(V_{GS} - V_{TN}) + v_{gs}^2] \tag{13.76}$$

For linearity, i_{ds} must be directly proportional to v_{gs}, which is achieved for

$$v_{gs}^2 \ll 2v_{gs}(V_{GS} - V_{TN}) \tag{13.77}$$

Finally, dividing by v_{gs}, we find that small-signal operation of the MOSFET requires

$$v_{gs} \ll 2(V_{GS} - V_{TN}) \qquad \text{or} \qquad v_{gs} = 0.2(V_{GS} - V_{TN}) \tag{13.78}$$

using a factor of 10 as satisfying the inequality.

Because the MOSFET can easily be biased with $(V_{GS} - V_{TN})$ equal to several volts, we see that it can handle much larger values of v_{gs} than the values of v_{be} corresponding to the bipolar transistor. This is another fundamental difference between the MOSFET and BJT and can be very important in circuit design, particularly in RF amplifier design for example.

Now let us explore the change in drain current that corresponds to small-signal operation. Using Eq. (13.78),

$$\frac{i_{ds}}{I_{DS}} = \frac{g_m v_{gs}}{I_{DS}} = \frac{0.2(V_{GS} - V_{TN})}{\dfrac{V_{GS} - V_{TN}}{2}} \le 0.4 \tag{13.79}$$

A change of $0.2\,(V_{GS} - V_{TN})$ in v_{GS} corresponds to a 40 percent deviation in the drain and source currents from their Q-point values.

> **Exercise:** A MOSFET transistor with $K_n = 2.0$ mA/V^2 and $\lambda = 0$ is operating at a Q-point of (25 mA, 10 V). What is the largest value of v_{gs} that corresponds to a small signal? If a BJT is biased at the same Q-point, what is the largest value of v_{be} that corresponds to a small signal?
>
> **Answers:** 1 V; 0.005 V

Body Effect in the Four-Terminal MOSFET

When the body terminal of the MOSFET is not connected to the source terminal, as in Fig. 13.27, an additional controlled source must be introduced into the small-signal model. Referring to the simplified drain-current expression for the MOSFET from Sec. 4.8:

$$i_{DS} = \frac{K_n}{2}(v_{GS} - V_{TN})^2 \tag{13.80}$$

$$V_{TN} = V_{TO} + \gamma(\sqrt{v_{SB} + 2\phi_F} - \sqrt{2\phi_F})$$

we recognize that the drain current is dependent on the threshold voltage, and the threshold voltage changes as v_{SB} changes. Thus, a **back-gate transconductance** can be defined:

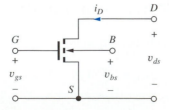

Figure 13.27 MOSFET as a four-terminal device.

$$g_{mb} = \left.\frac{\partial i_{DS}}{\partial v_{BS}}\right|_{\text{Q-point}} = -\left.\frac{\partial i_{DS}}{\partial v_{SB}}\right|_{\text{Q-point}} = -\left.\left(\frac{\partial i_{DS}}{\partial V_{TN}}\right)\left(\frac{\partial V_{TN}}{\partial v_{SB}}\right)\right|_{\text{Q-point}} \tag{13.81}$$

Evaluating the first-derivative term in brackets,

$$\left.\frac{\partial i_{DS}}{\partial V_{TN}}\right|_{\text{Q-point}} = -K_n(V_{GS} - V_{TN}) = -g_m \tag{13.82}$$

and the derivative term in the second set of brackets is

$$\left.\frac{\partial V_{TN}}{\partial v_{SB}}\right|_{\text{Q-point}} = \frac{\gamma}{2\sqrt{V_{SB} + 2\phi_F}} = \eta \tag{13.83}$$

in which η represents the **back-gate transconductance parameter.** Combining Eqs. (13.82) and (13.83) yields

$$g_{mb} = -(-g_m)\eta \qquad \text{or} \qquad g_{mb} = +\eta g_m \tag{13.84}$$

For typical values of γ and V_{SB},

$$0 \le \eta \le 1 \tag{13.85}$$

We also need to explore the question of whether there is a conductance connected from the bulk terminal to the other terminals. However, the bulk terminal represents a reverse-biased diode between the bulk and channel. Using our small-signal model for the diode, Eq. (13.15), we see that

$$\left.\frac{\partial i_B}{\partial v_{BS}}\right|_{\text{Q-point}} = \frac{I_{DS} + I_S}{V_T} \approx 0 \tag{13.86}$$

because $I_{DS} \approx -I_S$ for the reverse-biased diode. Thus there is no conductance indicated between the bulk and source or drain terminals in the small-signal model.

The resulting small-signal model for the four-terminal MOSFET is given in Fig. 13.28, in which a second voltage-controlled current source has been added to model the back-gate transconductance g_{mb}.

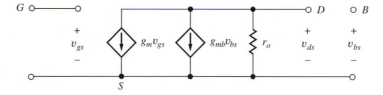

Figure 13.28 Small-signal model for the four-terminal MOSFET.

EXERCISE: Calculate the values of g_{mb} for a MOSFET transistor with $\gamma = 0.75$ V$^{0.5}$ and $2\phi_F = 0.6$ V for $V_{SB} = 0$ and $V_{SB} = 3$ V.

ANSWERS: 0.48, 0.20

Small-Signal Model for the PMOS Transistor

Just as was the case for the *pnp* and *npn* transistors, the small-signal model for the PMOS transistor is identical to that of the NMOS device. The circuits in Fig. 13.29 should help reinforce this result.

In Fig. 13.29, the NMOS and PMOS transistors are each biased by the dc voltage source V_{GG}, establishing the Q-point current I_{DS}. In each case, a signal voltage v_{gg} is added in series with V_{GG} so that a positive value of v_{gg} causes the gate-to-source voltage of each transistor to increase. For the NMOS transistor, the total gate-to-source voltage and drain

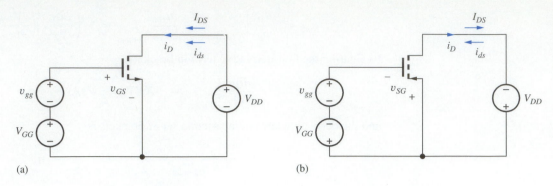

Figure 13.29 dc Bias and signal currents for (a) NMOS and (b) PMOS transistors.

current are

$$v_{GS} = V_{GG} + v_{gg} \qquad \text{and} \qquad i_{DS} = I_{DS} + i_{ds} \tag{13.87}$$

and an increase in v_{gg} causes an increase in current into the drain terminal. For the PMOS transistor,

$$v_{SG} = V_{GG} - v_{gg} \qquad \text{and} \qquad i_{Ds} = I_{Ds} - i_{ds} \tag{13.88}$$

A positive signal voltage v_{gg} reduces the source-to-gate voltage of the PMOS transistor and causes a decrease in the total current exiting the drain terminal. This reduction in total current is equivalent to an increase in the signal current entering the drain.

Thus, for both the NMOS and PMOS transistors, an increase in the value of v_{GS} causes an increase in current into the drain, and the polarities of the voltage-controlled current source in the small-signal model are identical, as depicted in Fig. 13.30.

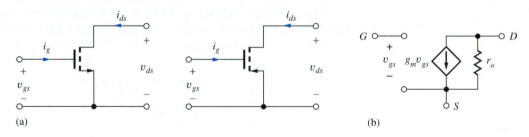

Figure 13.30 (a) NMOS and PMOS transistors. (b) The small-signal models are identical.

Small-Signal Model for the Junction Field-Effect Transistor

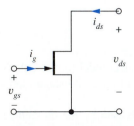

Figure 13.31 The JFET as a two-port network.

The drain-current expressions for the JFET and MOSFET can be written in essentially identical form (see Prob. 13.73), so we should not be surprised that the small-signal models also have the same form. For small-signal analysis, we represent the JFET as the two-port network in Fig. 13.31. The small-signal parameters can be determined from the large-signal model given in Chapter 4 for the drain current of the JFET operating in the pinch-off region:

$$i_{DS} = I_{DSS} \left[1 - \frac{v_{GS}}{V_P} \right]^2 [1 + \lambda v_{DS}] \qquad \text{for } v_{DS} \geq v_{GS} - V_P \tag{13.89}$$

The total gate current i_G represents the current of the gate-to-channel diode, which we express in terms of the gate-to-source voltage v_{GS} and saturation current I_{SG}:

$$i_G = I_{SG}\left[\exp\left(\frac{v_{GS}}{V_T}\right) - 1\right]$$ (13.90)

Once again using the derivative formulation from Eq. (13.64):

$$\frac{1}{r_g} = y_{11} = \left.\frac{\partial i_G}{\partial v_{GS}}\right|_{\text{Q-point}} = \frac{I_G + I_{SG}}{V_T}$$

$$y_{12} = \left.\frac{\partial i_G}{\partial v_{DS}}\right|_{\text{Q-point}} = 0$$

$$g_m = y_{21} = \left.\frac{\partial i_{DS}}{\partial v_{GS}}\right|_{\text{Q-point}} = 2\frac{I_{DSS}}{-V_P}\left[1 - \frac{V_{GS}}{V_P}\right][1 + \lambda V_{DS}] = \frac{I_{DS}}{\dfrac{V_{GS} - V_P}{2}}$$

$$g_m = \frac{2}{|V_P|}\sqrt{I_{DSS}I_{DS}(1 + \lambda V_{DS})} \approx \frac{2}{|V_P|}\sqrt{I_{DSS}I_{DS}} \approx 2\frac{I_{DSS}}{V_P^2}[V_{GS} - V_P]$$ (13.91)

$$\frac{1}{r_o} = y_{22} = \left.\frac{\partial i_{DS}}{\partial v_{DS}}\right|_{\text{Q-point}} = \lambda I_{DSS}\left[1 - \frac{V_{GS}}{V_P}\right]^2 = \frac{\lambda I_{DS}}{1 + \lambda V_{DS}} = \frac{I_{DS}}{\dfrac{1}{\lambda} + V_{DS}}$$

Because the JFET is normally operated with the gate junction reverse-biased,

$$I_G = -I_{GS} \quad\text{and}\quad r_g = \infty$$ (13.92)

Thus, the small-signal model for the JFET in Fig. 13.32 is identical to that of the MOSFET, including the formulas used to express g_m and r_o when V_{TN} is replaced by V_P.

As a result, the definition of a small signal and the expression for the amplification factor μ_F are also similar to those of the MOSFET:

$$v_{gs} \leq 0.2(V_{GS} - V_P)$$

and

$$\mu_F = g_m r_o = 2\frac{\dfrac{1}{\lambda} + V_{DS}}{V_{GS} - V_P} = \frac{2}{\lambda|V_P|}\sqrt{\frac{I_{DSS}}{I_{DS}}(1 + \lambda V_{DS})}$$ (13.93)

$$\mu_F \approx \frac{2}{\lambda|V_P|}\sqrt{\frac{I_{DSS}}{I_{DS}}}$$

EXERCISES: Calculate the values of g_m, r_o, and μ_f for a JFET with $I_{DSS} = 5$ mA, $V_P = -2$ V, and $\lambda = 0.02$ V^{-1} if it is operating at a Q-point of (2 mA, 5 V). What is the largest value of v_{gs} that can be considered to be a small signal?

ANSWERS: 3.32×10^{-3} S, 27.5 kΩ, 91; 0.24 V

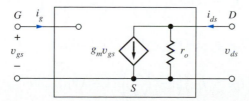

Figure 13.32 Small-signal model for the JFET.

13.8 SUMMARY AND COMPARISON OF THE SMALL-SIGNAL MODELS OF THE BJT AND FET

Table 13.4 is a succinct comparison of the small-signal models of the bipolar junction transistor and the field-effect transistor; the table has been constructed to highlight the similarities and differences between the two types of devices.

The transconductance of the BJT is directly proportional to operating current, whereas that of the FET increases only with the square root of current. Both can be represented as the drain current divided by a characteristic voltage: V_T for the BJT, $(V_{GS} - V_{TN})/2$ for the MOSFET, and $(V_{GS} - V_P)/2$ for the JFET.

T a b l e 13.4

Small-Signal Parameter Comparison

Parameter	Bipolar Transistor	MOSFET	JFET
Trans-conductance g_m	$\dfrac{I_C}{V_T}$	$\dfrac{I_{DS}}{\left[\dfrac{V_{GS} - V_{TN}}{2}\right]}$ $K_n(V_{GS} - V_{TN})(1 + \lambda V_{DS})$ $\sqrt{2K_n I_{DS}(1 + \lambda V_{DS})}$	$\dfrac{I_{DS}}{\left[\dfrac{V_{GS} - V_P}{2}\right]}$ $2\dfrac{I_{DSS}}{V_P^2}(V_{GS} - V_P)(1 + \lambda V_{DS})$ $\dfrac{2}{|V_P|}\sqrt{I_{DSS} I_{DS}(1 + \lambda V_{DS})}$
Input resistance	$r_\pi = \dfrac{\beta_o}{g_m} = \dfrac{\beta_o V_T}{I_C}$	∞	∞
Output resistance r_o	$\dfrac{V_A + V_{CE}}{I_C}$	$\dfrac{\dfrac{1}{\lambda} + V_{DS}}{I_{DS}}$	$\dfrac{\dfrac{1}{\lambda} + V_{DS}}{I_{DS}}$
Amplification factor μ_f	$\dfrac{V_A + V_{CE}}{V_T}$	$\dfrac{\dfrac{1}{\lambda} + V_{DS}}{\dfrac{V_{GS} - V_{TN}}{2}}$ $\approx \dfrac{1}{\lambda}\sqrt{\dfrac{2K_n}{I_{DS}}} = \dfrac{2}{\lambda(V_{GS} - V_{TN})}$	$\dfrac{\dfrac{1}{\lambda} + V_{DS}}{\dfrac{V_{GS} - V_P}{2}}$ $\approx \dfrac{2}{\lambda|V_P|}\sqrt{\dfrac{I_{DSS}}{I_{DS}}}$
Small-signal requirement	$v_{be} \leq 0.005$ V	$v_{gs} \leq 0.2(V_{GS} - V_{TN})$	$v_{gs} \leq 0.2(V_{GS} - V_P)$

dc i-v expressions for use with Table 13.4

$$I_C = I_S\left[\exp\left(\frac{V_{BE}}{V_T}\right) - 1\right]\left[1 + \frac{V_{CE}}{V_A}\right] \qquad V_T = \frac{kT}{q}$$

$$I_{DS} = \frac{K_n}{2}(V_{GS} - V_{TN})^2(1 + \lambda V_{DS}) \qquad K_n = \mu_n C_{ox}\frac{W}{L}$$

$$I_{DS} = I_{DSS}\left(1 - \frac{V_{GS}}{V_P}\right)^2(1 + \lambda V_{DS})$$

The input resistance of the bipolar transistor is set by the value of r_π, which is inversely proportional to the Q-point current and can be quite small at even moderate currents (1 to 10 mA). On the other hand, the input resistance of the FETs is extremely high, approaching infinity.

The expressions for the output resistances of the transistors are almost identical, with the parameter $1/\lambda$ in the FET taking the place of the Early voltage V_A of the BJT. The value of $1/\lambda$ is similar to V_A, so the output resistances can be expected to be similar in value for comparable operating currents.

The amplification factor of the BJT is essentially independent of operating current and has a typical value of several thousand at room temperature. In contrast, μ_f of the FET is inversely proportional to the square root of operating current and decreases as the Q-point current is raised. At very low currents, μ_f of the FET can be similar to that of the BJT, but in normal operation it is often much smaller and can even fall below 1 for high currents (see Prob. 13.67).

Small-signal operation is dependent on the size of the base-emitter voltage of the BJT or gate-source voltage of the field-effect transistor. The magnitude of voltage that corresponds to small-signal operation can be significantly different for these two devices. For the BJT, v_{be} must be less than 5 mV. This value is indeed small, and it is independent of Q-point. In contrast, the FET requirement is $v_{gs} \le 0.2(V_{GS} - V_{TN})$ or $0.2(V_{GS} - V_P)$, which is dependent on bias point and can be designed to be as much as a volt or more.

This discussion highlighted the similarities and differences between the bipolar and field-effect transistors. An understanding of Table 13.4 is extremely important to the design of analog circuits. As we study single and multistage amplifier design in the coming sections and chapters, we will note the effect of these differences and relate them to our circuit designs.

13.9 THE COMMON-SOURCE AMPLIFIER

Now we are in a position to analyze the small-signal characteristics of the **common-source (C-S) amplifier** shown in Fig. 13.33(a), which uses an enhancement-mode n-channel MOSFET ($V_{TN} > 0$) in a four-resistor bias network. The ac equivalent circuit of Fig. 13.33(b) is constructed by assuming that the capacitors all have zero impedance at the signal frequency and that the dc voltage sources represent ac grounds. Bias resistors R_1 and R_2 appear in parallel and are combined into gate resistor R_G. For simplicity at this point, we assume that we have found the Q-point and know the values of I_{DS} and V_{DS}.

In Fig. 13.33(c), v_s, R_S, and R_G have been replaced by their Thévenin equivalents

$$\mathbf{v_{th}} = \frac{R_G}{R_G + R_S}\mathbf{v_s} \qquad \text{and} \qquad R_{th} = \frac{R_G R_S}{R_G + R_S} \qquad (13.94)$$

and the transistor has been replaced by its small-signal model in Fig. 13.33(d). A final simplification appears in Fig. 13.33(e), in which resistor R_L represents the total equivalent load resistance on the transistor: the parallel combination of R_C, R_3, and the output resistance r_o of the transistor itself.

$$R_L = r_o \parallel R_D \parallel R_3 \qquad (13.95)$$

In Fig. 13.33(b) and (c), the common-source nature of this amplifier should be apparent. The input signal is applied to the transistor's gate terminal, the output signal appears at the drain, and both the input and output signals are referenced to the (common) source terminal. Note that the small-signal models for the MOSFET and BJT are virtually identical at this step, except that r_π is replaced by an open circuit for the MOSFET.

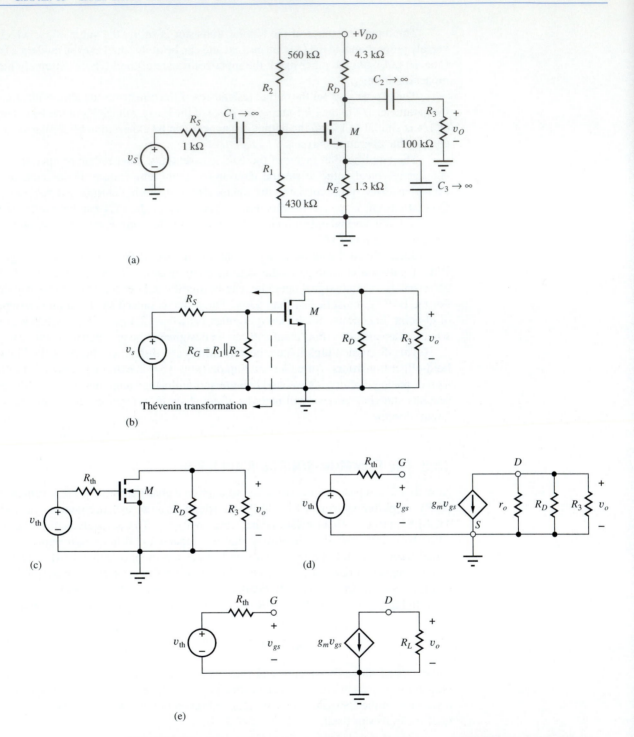

Figure 13.33 (a) Common-source amplifier circuit employing a MOSFET. (b) ac Equivalent circuit for common-source amplifier in part (a). The common-source connection should now be apparent. (c) Simplified ac equivalent circuit. (d) ac Equivalent circuit with the MOSFET replaced by its small-signal model. (e) Final equivalent circuit for ac analysis of the common-source amplifier.

Our goal is to develop an expression for the voltage gain A_V of the circuit in Fig. 13.33(a) from the source v_s to the output v_o. The voltage gain is first written in terms of v_{th} in Fig. 13.33(e) and then expressed in terms of v_s using Eq. (13.94) for v_{th}. For the circuit in Fig. 13.33(e),

$$A_{V\text{th}} = \frac{\mathbf{v_o}}{\mathbf{v_{\text{th}}}} \qquad (13.96)$$

The output voltage is equal to the negative of the controlled-source current times the load resistor,

$$\mathbf{v_o} = -g_m \mathbf{v_{gs}} R_L \qquad (13.97)$$

Because of the infinite input resistance of the MOSFET itself, the full value of $\mathbf{v_{\text{th}}}$ appears across $\mathbf{v_{gs}}$:

$$\mathbf{v_{gs}} = \mathbf{v_{\text{th}}} \qquad (13.98)$$

Combining Eqs. (13.94), (13.97), and (13.98) yields a general expression for the voltage gain of the common-source stage:

$$A_V = \frac{\mathbf{v_o}}{\mathbf{v_s}} = (-g_m R_L)\left(\frac{R_G}{R_G + R_S}\right) \qquad (13.99)$$

If $R_G \gg R_S$ as is often the case, the full signal voltage v_s appears across the gate-to-source terminals of the MOSFET, and Eq. (13.99) can be reduced to

$$A_V = -g_m R_L = -g_m(r_o \| R_D \| R_3) \qquad (13.100)$$

Based on our discussion of the BJT amplifier, we recognize that the expression $(-g_m R_L)$ represents the intrinsic voltage gain of both the common-emitter and common-source amplifiers. In its most fundamental form, the gain of the common-source amplifier is equal to the product of the transistor transconductance and the effective load resistance on the transistor. For $R_G \gg R_S$, the common-source amplifier stage in Fig. 13.33(b) reduces to that shown in Fig. 13.34. The total load resistance R_L consists of output resistance r_o in parallel with drain-bias resistor R_D and external load resistor R_3. Note that the minus signs in Eqs. (13.99) and (13.100) again indicate that the output voltage is "inverted," or 180° out of phase with the input voltage.

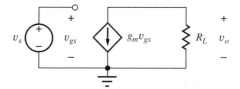

Figure 13.34 Simplified circuit corresponding to the resulting Eq. (13.100) for $R_G \gg R_S$.

EXERCISE: Calculate the Q-point for the MOSFET in Fig. 13.33 for $V_{DD} = 12$ V if $K_n = 0.500$ mA/V², $V_{TN} = 1$ V, and $\lambda = 0.0133$ V⁻¹.

ANSWER: (1.45 mA, 3.86 V)

EXAMPLE 13.4: Calculate the gain of the common-source amplifier in Fig. 13.33 if the transistor has $K_n = 0.500$ mA/V², $V_{TN} = 1$ V, and $\lambda = 0.0133$ V⁻¹, and the Q-point is (1.45 mA, 3.86 V).

SOLUTION: We need to evaluate Eq. (13.99):

$$A_V = (-g_m R_L)\left(\frac{R_G}{R_G + R_S}\right)$$

Calculating the values of the various resistors and small-signal model parameters yields

$$g_m = \sqrt{2K_n I_{DS}(1 + \lambda V_{DS})}$$

$$g_m = \sqrt{2\left(5 \times 10^{-4}\,\frac{A}{V^2}\right)(1.45 \times 10^{-3}\,A)\left(1 + \frac{0.0133}{V}3.88\,V\right)} = 1.23\,mS$$

$$r_o = \frac{\frac{1}{\lambda} + V_{CE}}{I_{DS}} = \frac{\left(\frac{1}{0.0133} + 3.86\right)V}{1.45 \times 10^{-3}\,A} = 54.5\,k\Omega$$

$$R_G = R_1 \| R_2 = 243\,k\Omega \qquad R_{th} = R_S \| R_G = 1\,k\Omega$$

$$R_L = R_D \| R_3 \| r_o = 3.83\,k\Omega$$

$$A_V = -(1.23 \times 10^{-3}\,S \times 3.83 \times 10^3\,\Omega)\left(\frac{243\,k\Omega}{243\,k\Omega + 1\,k\Omega}\right) = -4.69$$

Thus the common-source amplifier in Fig. 13.34 provides a small-signal voltage gain $A_V = -4.69$ or 13.4 dB.

DISCUSSION: Note that this C-S amplifier has been designed to operate at the same Q-point as the C-E amplifier in Fig. 13.23, but the gain is more than 25 times smaller. For these cases, the total load resistances are similar, but the gain of the C-S stage is limited by the relatively low transconductance of the MOSFET.   ◆

A Rule of Thumb for the Common-Source Amplifier with Resistive Load

When a resistive load is used with the common-source amplifier, its value is generally much smaller than that of the transistor output resistance r_o. In addition, we often try to achieve $R_3 \gg R_D$ in many designs. For these conditions, the total load resistance on the collector of the transistor is approximately equal to R_D, and Eq. (13.100) can be reduced to

$$A_v \approx -g_m R_D \tag{13.101}$$

Substituting the expression for g_m from Eq. (13.67), we can express the voltage gain as

$$A_V \approx -\frac{I_D R_D}{\left(\frac{V_{GS} - V_{TN}}{2}\right)} \tag{13.102}$$

The product $I_D R_D$ represents the dc voltage drop across the drain resistor R_D. This voltage is usually in the range of one-fourth to three-fourths the power supply voltage V_{DD}. Assuming $I_D R_D = V_{DD}/2$ and $V_{GS} - V_{TN} = 1$ V, we can rewrite Eq. (13.102) as

$$A_V \approx -\frac{V_{DD}}{V_{GS} - V_{TN}} \approx -V_{DD} \tag{13.103}$$

Equation (13.103) is a basic rule of thumb for the design of the resistively loaded common-source amplifier; its form is very similar to that for the BJT in Eq. (13.59). The magnitude of the gain is approximately the power supply voltage divided by the internal gate drive ($V_{GS} - V_{TN}$) of the MOSFET. For a common-source amplifier operating from a 12-V power supply, Eq. (13.103) predicts the voltage gain to be -12.

Note that this estimate is an order of magnitude smaller than the gain for the BJT operating from the same power supply. Equation (13.102) should be carefully compared to the corresponding expression for the BJT, Eq. (13.58). Except in special circumstances, the denominator term ($V_{GS} - V_{TN}$)/2 in Eq. (13.102) for the MOSFET is much greater than the corresponding term $V_T = 0.025$ V for the BJT, and the MOSFET voltage gain should be expected to be correspondingly lower.

Common-Source Voltage Gain Upper Bound

As in the common-emitter case, more complex circuits can be used to force the effective value of ($R_D \parallel R_3$) to be much greater than r_o. Letting R_D and $R_3 \to \infty$ in Eq. (13.100) yields

$$A_V = -g_m r_o = -\mu_f \qquad (13.104)$$

Here again we see that the voltage gain of the common-source stage cannot exceed the amplification factor μ_f of the transistor itself. In this case, the only load on the transistor is its own output resistance r_o; parameter μ_f again represents an upper bound on the voltage gain of the single-transistor amplifier.

EXAMPLE 13.5: For the C-S amplifier in Fig. 13.34, compare the rule-of-thumb estimate for the gain to the actual gain and to the amplification factor of the transistor.

SOLUTION: Our rule-of-thumb estimate for the voltage gain is

$$A_V \approx -\frac{V_{DD}}{V_{GS} - V_{TN}}$$

For the given Q-point,

$$V_{GS} - V_{TN} \approx \sqrt{\frac{2I_{DS}}{K_n}} = \sqrt{\frac{2 \times 1.45 \times 10^{-3}\ \text{A}}{5 \times 10^{-4}\ \dfrac{\text{A}}{\text{V}^2}}} = 2.41\ \text{V}$$

and

$$A_V \approx -\frac{12}{2.41} = -4.98$$

which clearly represents a very good first-order estimate of the actual gain (-4.69) of the amplifier calculated in the previous example. (Actually it is surprisingly close.)

The amplification factor of the MOSFET is equal to

$$\mu_F = \frac{\dfrac{1}{\lambda} + V_{DS}}{\dfrac{V_{GS} - V_{TN}}{2}} = \frac{(75 + 3.86)\ \text{V}}{1.20\ \text{V}} = 65.7$$

DISCUSSION: The rule of thumb produces a good estimate for the gain of this amplifier. Although the amplification factor for this MOSFET is much smaller than that for the BJT, the gain of this resistively loaded amplifier circuit is still not limited by μ_f. ◆

13.10 INPUT AND OUTPUT RESISTANCES OF THE COMMON-EMITTER AND COMMON-SOURCE AMPLIFIERS

If the voltage gain of the MOSFET amplifier is generally much lower than that of the BJT, there must be other reasons for using the MOSFET. One of the reasons was mentioned earlier: A small signal can be much larger for the MOSFET than for the BJT. Another important difference is in the relative size of the input impedance of the amplifiers. This section explores the input and output resistances of both the common-emitter and common-source amplifiers.

The input resistance $R_{\rm IN}$ to the common-emitter and common-source amplifiers is defined in Fig. 13.35(a) and (b) to be the total resistance looking into the amplifier at coupling capacitor C_1. $R_{\rm IN}$ represents the total resistance presented to the signal source. The input resistance definition is repeated in Fig. 13.36, in which the amplifiers have been reduced to their ac equivalent circuits.

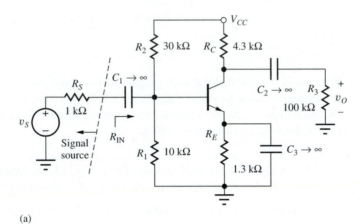

(a)

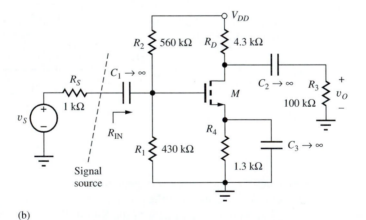

(b)

Figure 13.35 (a) Input resistance definition for the common-emitter amplifier. (b) Input resistance definition for the common-source amplifier.

C-E Input Resistance

Let us first calculate the input resistance for the common-emitter stage. In Fig. 13.37, the BJT has been replaced by its small-signal model, and the input resistance is found to be

$$\mathbf{v_x} = \mathbf{i_x}(R_B \parallel r_\pi) \qquad \text{and} \qquad R_{\rm IN} = \frac{\mathbf{v_x}}{\mathbf{i_x}} = R_B \parallel r_\pi = R_1 \parallel R_2 \parallel r_\pi \quad (13.105)$$

$R_{\rm IN}$ is equal to the parallel combination of r_π and the two base-bias resistors R_1 and R_2.

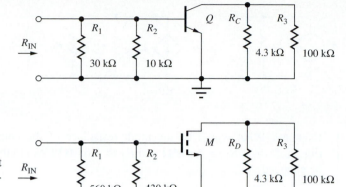

Figure 13.36 ac Equivalent circuits for the input resistance for the common-emitter and common-source amplifiers of Fig. 13.35.

EXAMPLE 13.6: Let us calculate R_{IN} for the amplifier in Fig. 13.37 assuming that the Q-point = (1.45 mA, 3.86 V).

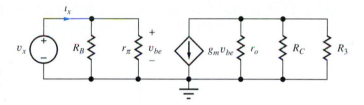

Figure 13.37 Input resistance for the common-emitter amplifier.

SOLUTION: The value of $R_B = 30 \text{ k}\Omega \parallel 10 \text{ k}\Omega = 7.5 \text{ k}\Omega$, r_π is given by

$$r_\pi = \frac{\beta_o V_T}{I_C} = \frac{100\,(0.025\text{ V})}{1.45\text{ mA}} = 1.72 \text{ k}\Omega$$

and

$$R_{IN} = 7.5 \text{ k}\Omega \parallel 1.72 \text{ k}\Omega = 1.40 \text{ k}\Omega$$

DISCUSSION: The input resistance to this amplifier, 1.40 kΩ, is actually quite low. We will see in Chapter 14 that we can give up some of the voltage gain of the BJT amplifier in order to raise its input resistance.   ◆

C-S Input Resistance

Now let compare the input resistance of the common-source amplifier to that of the common-emitter stage. In Fig. 13.38, the MOSFET in Fig. 13.36 has been replaced by its small-signal model. This circuit is similar to that in Fig. 13.37 except that $r_\pi \to \infty$. Because the gate terminal of the MOSFET itself represents an open circuit, the input resistance of the circuit is simply limited by our design of the value of R_G:

$$\mathbf{v_x} = \mathbf{i_x} R_G \qquad \text{and} \qquad R_{IN} = R_G \qquad\qquad (13.106)$$

In the C-S amplifier in Figs. 13.35 and 13.38, $R_G = (560 \text{ k}\Omega \parallel 430 \text{ k}\Omega) = 243 \text{ k}\Omega$, so $R_{IN} = 243 \text{ k}\Omega$. We see that the input resistance of the C-S amplifier can easily be much larger than that of the corresponding C-E stage.

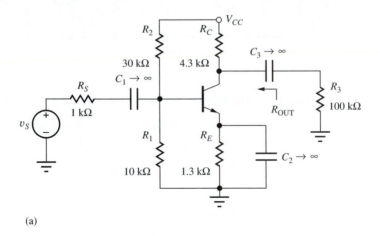

Figure 13.38 Input resistance for the common-source amplifier.

EXERCISE: What would be the input resistance of the common-source amplifier in Fig. 13.35(b) if $R_1 = 4.3\ \text{M}\Omega$ and $R_2 = 5.6\ \text{M}\Omega$? Would the Q-point of the amplifier be changed?

ANSWERS: 2.43 MΩ; no, the Q-point remains the same because $I_G = 0$ and the dc voltage at the gate is unchanged.

In a manner similar to that for the input resistances, the output resistances of the C-E and C-S amplifiers are defined in Fig. 13.39(a) and (b) as the total equivalent resistance looking into the output of the amplifier at coupling capacitor C_3. The definition of the output resistance is repeated in Fig. 13.40, in which the two amplifiers have been reduced to their ac equivalent circuits. For the output resistance calculation, the input source v_S is set to zero. In Fig. 13.41, the transistors are replaced by their small-signal models, and test source v_x is applied to the output for calculation of the resistance.

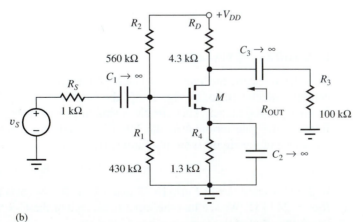

(a)

(b)

Figure 13.39 (a) Output resistance definition for the common-emitter amplifier. (b) Output resistance definition for the common-source amplifier.

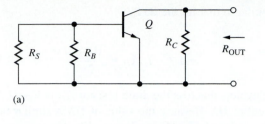

(a)

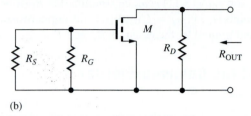

(b)

Figure 13.40 Output resistance definition for (a) common-emitter and (b) common-source amplifiers.

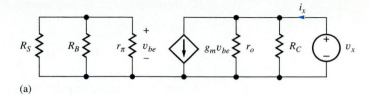

(a)

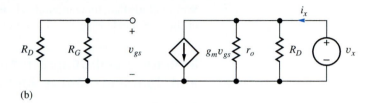

(b)

Figure 13.41 (a) C-E and (b) C-S amplifier output resistances.

C-E Output Resistance

For the BJT in Fig. 13.41(a), the current from test source v_x is equal to

$$\mathbf{i_x} = \frac{\mathbf{v_x}}{R_C} + \frac{\mathbf{v_x}}{r_o} + g_m\mathbf{v_{be}} \tag{13.107}$$

However, there is no excitation at the base node:

$$\frac{\mathbf{v_{be}}}{R_S} + \frac{\mathbf{v_{be}}}{R_B} + \frac{\mathbf{v_{be}}}{r_\pi} = 0 \qquad \text{and} \qquad \mathbf{v_{be}} = 0 \tag{13.108}$$

Thus, $g_m\mathbf{v_{be}} = 0$, and the output resistance is given by

$$R_{\text{OUT}} = \frac{\mathbf{v_x}}{\mathbf{i_x}} = r_o \parallel R_C \tag{13.109}$$

which is equivalent to the parallel combination of R_C and r_o.

Let us compare the values of r_o and R_C by multiplying each by I_C:

$$I_C r_o = I_C \frac{V_A + V_{CE}}{I_C} \approx V_A \qquad \text{and} \qquad I_C R_C \approx \frac{V_{CC}}{2} \tag{13.110}$$

As discussed previously, the voltage developed across the collector resistor R_C is typically 0.25 to $0.75V_{CC}$, but the apparent voltage across r_o is the Early voltage V_A. Thus, from the relations in Eq. (13.110), we expect $r_o \gg R_C$, and Eq. (13.109) yields $R_{\text{OUT}} \approx R_C$.

C-S Output Resistance

For the MOSFET in Fig. 13.41(b), the analysis is the same. The voltage $\mathbf{v_{gs}}$ will be zero, and R_{OUT} is equal to the parallel combination of r_o and R_D:

$$R_{\text{OUT}} = \frac{\mathbf{v_x}}{\mathbf{i_x}} = r_o \parallel R_D \tag{13.111}$$

Comparing r_o and R_D in a manner similar to that for the BJT,

$$I_D r_o = I_D \frac{\frac{1}{\lambda} + V_{DS}}{I_D} \approx \frac{1}{\lambda} \quad \text{and} \quad I_D R_D \approx \frac{V_{DD}}{2} \qquad (13.112)$$

where it is assumed that the voltage developed across the drain resistor R_D is $V_{DD}/2$. The effective voltage across r_o is equivalent to $1/\lambda$. Because the value of $1/\lambda$ is similar to the Early voltage V_A, we expect $r_o \gg R_D$, and Eq. (13.111) can be simplified to $R_{\text{OUT}} \approx R_D$. We conclude that, for comparable bias points $(I_C, V_{CE}) = (I_{DS}, V_{DS})$, the output resistances of the C-E and C-S stages are similar and limited by the resistors R_C and R_D.

Summary and Comparison of the Common-Emitter and Common-Source Amplifiers

Table 13.5 is a comparison of the basic characteristics of the common-emitter and common-source amplifier stages. The voltage gain expressions are similar, but the value of g_m for the BJT is usually much larger than that of the FET. Thus A_V is much larger for the BJT case, as predicted by our rule-of-thumb estimates. The input resistance of the C-S stages is limited only by the design value of R_G and can be quite large, whereas the values of R_B and r_π are usually much smaller for the case of the BJT. The output resistances of the C-E and C-S stages are similar for similar choices of operating points because R_{OUT} is limited by the collector or drain-bias resistors R_C or R_D.

T a b l e   13.5

Common-Emitter/Common-Source Amplifier Comparison

	Common-Emitter Amplifier	Common-Source Amplifier
Voltage Gain $A_V = \dfrac{v_o}{v_s}$	$-\dfrac{\beta_o R_L}{r_\pi + R_{\text{th}}} \dfrac{R_B}{R_B + R_S}$ $-\dfrac{g_m R_L}{1 + \dfrac{R_{\text{th}}}{r_\pi}} \dfrac{R_B}{R_B + R_S}$ $\approx -g_m R_L \approx -10 V_{CC}$	$(-g_m R_L)\left(\dfrac{R_G}{R_G + R_S}\right)$ $\approx -g_m R_L \approx -V_{DD}$
Input Resistance	$R_B \parallel r_\pi$	R_G
Output Resistance	$R_C \parallel r_o \approx R_C$	$R_D \parallel r_o \approx R_D$

13.11 EXAMPLES OF COMMON-EMITTER AND COMMON-SOURCE AMPLIFIERS

This section presents several examples of analysis of common-emitter and common-source amplifiers. Each example uses a different form of dc bias network in order to provide additional examples of the many methods used to establish the transistor Q-point.

A Common-Emitter Amplifier

We begin with analysis of the common-emitter stage, shown schematically in Fig. 13.42, in which the amplifier is biased by symmetrical positive and negative 5-V power supplies. The use of the second supply permits elimination of one of the bias resistors in the base circuit. The remaining 100-kΩ resistor is required to isolate the base node from ground so that an input-signal voltage can be applied to the base. To analyze the circuit, we first draw the dc equivalent circuit and find the Q-point. We then develop the ac equivalent circuit, find the small-signal model parameters, and characterize the small-signal properties of the amplifier.

Q-Point Analysis

The first step is to draw the dc equivalent circuit. Opening the three capacitors in Fig. 13.42 yields the simplified circuit in Fig. 13.43. The Q-point can be found by finding the base current, then the collector current, and finally the collector-emitter voltage. For the input loop containing the base-emitter junction and $I_E = (\beta_F + 1)I_B$,

$$10^5 I_B + V_{BE} + (\beta_F + 1)I_B(1.6 \times 10^4) = 5 \tag{13.113}$$

or

$$10^5 I_B + 0.7 + 66 I_B(1.6 \times 10^4) = 5 \tag{13.114}$$

Solving for the base current yields

$$I_B = \frac{(5 - 0.7)\ \text{V}}{10^5\ \Omega + 1.06 \times 10^6\ \Omega} = 3.71\ \mu\text{A} \tag{13.115}$$

$$I_C = 65 I_B = 241\ \mu\text{A}$$

$$I_E = 66 I_B = 245\ \mu\text{A}$$

Writing an equation for the output loop containing V_{CE},

$$5 - 10^4 I_C - V_{CE} - 1.6 \times 10^4 I_E - (-5) = 0 \tag{13.116}$$

and solving for V_{CE} yields:

$$V_{CE} = 10 - 10^4 I_C - 1.6 \times 10^4 I_E = 10 - 2.41 - 3.92 = 3.67\ \text{V} \tag{13.117}$$

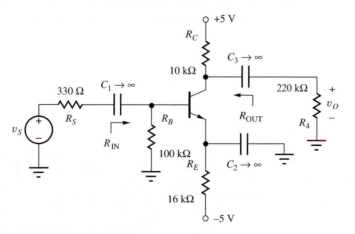

Figure 13.42 A common-emitter amplifier biased by two supplies. The BJT parameters are $\beta_F = 65$ and $V_A = 50$ V.

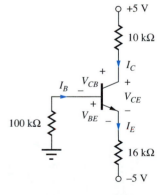

Figure 13.43 dc Equivalent circuit for Fig. 13.42. For Q-point analysis, use $\beta_F = 65$ and $V_A = \infty$.

In writing Eqs. (13.113) and (13.116), we tacitly assumed that the transistor is in the forward-active region of operation, and the dc analysis is not complete until we check this assumption. Writing an expression for V_{CB},

$$5 - 10^4 I_C - V_{CB} + 10^5 I_B = 0 \tag{13.118}$$

and

$$V_{CB} = 5 - 2.41 + 0.371 = 2.22 > 0 \;\checkmark \tag{13.119}$$

Because $V_{CB} > 0$ ($V_{BC} < 0$), the transistor is indeed in the forward-active region and the Q-point is

$$(I_C, V_{CE}) = (0.241 \text{ mA}, 3.67 \text{ V}) \tag{13.120}$$

It is important to note in this dc analysis that we used the simplified form of the transport model, in which $V_A = \infty$. As discussed in previous chapters, we want to use the lowest complexity model that provides reasonable answers. Using V_{CE} from our analysis, we see that

$$\frac{V_{CE}}{V_A} = \frac{3.67 \text{ V}}{50 \text{ V}} = 0.0734 \tag{13.121}$$

Including the Early voltage term would change our answers by less than 10 percent but would considerably complicate the dc analysis. This is confirmed by SPICE simulation of the circuit, which yields a Q-point of (0.248 mA, 3.50 V). Note that the bias circuit stabilizes the Q-point with respect to variations in device parameters, and the changes in Q-point are actually even less than predicted by Eq. (13.121). In addition, these differences in Q-point values are much smaller than the uncertainty in either the bias resistor values or the device parameter values for a real circuit, so neglecting V_A does not introduce significant additional uncertainty.

ac Analysis

The next step is to draw the ac equivalent circuit and simplify it before beginning the detailed analysis. For the ac analysis, we replace all capacitors by short circuits and the dc voltage sources with ground connections. This step appears in Fig. 13.44.

The circuit in Fig. 13.44 is redrawn in simplified form in Fig. 13.45, in which the 16-kΩ resistor has been removed because it is "shorted out" by ground connections at both ends, and the parallel connection of the two resistors attached to the collector is

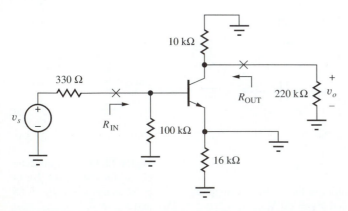

Figure 13.44 First step in construction of the ac equivalent circuit.

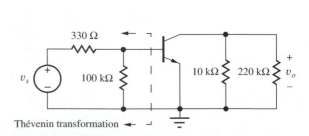

Figure 13.45 Redrawn circuit of Fig. 13.44.

shown more explicitly. Once we become skilled with this process, we can skip directly to Fig. 13.45 without the intermediate step in Fig. 13.44.

With two further simplifications, the C-E amplifier circuit can be redrawn in the standard form for analysis, Fig. 13.46. The input source $\mathbf{v_s}$ and the 330-Ω and 100-kΩ resistors are replaced by their Thévenin equivalent circuit,

$$\mathbf{v_{th}} = \mathbf{v_s} \frac{100 \text{ k}\Omega}{330 \ \Omega + 100 \text{ k}\Omega} = 0.997 \ \mathbf{v_s}$$

and

$$R_{th} = 330 \ \Omega \parallel 100 \text{ k}\Omega = 329 \ \Omega$$

and the two parallel resistors at the output have been combined into one equivalent resistor.

Small-Signal Analysis

The final step prior to mathematical analysis is to replace the transistor symbol by its small-signal model. Using the Q-point values,

$$g_m = 40I_C = \frac{40}{V}(2.41 \times 10^{-4} \text{ A}) = 9.64 \times 10^{-3} \text{ S}$$

$$r_\pi = \frac{\beta_o V_T}{I_C} = \frac{65(0.025 \text{ V})}{2.41 \times 10^{-4} \text{ A}} = 6.64 \text{ k}\Omega \tag{13.122}$$

$$r_o = \frac{V_A + V_{CE}}{I_C} = \frac{(50 + 3.67) \text{ V}}{2.41 \times 10^{-4} \text{ A}} = 223 \text{ k}\Omega$$

Figure 13.47 is drawn using these small-signal parameter values, and we now can use this circuit to determine the voltage gain of the common-emitter amplifier.

The output voltage v_o is

$$\mathbf{v_o} = -g_m \mathbf{v_{be}}(r_o \parallel 9.57 \text{ k}\Omega) = -9.64 \times 10^{-3} \text{ S}(223 \text{ k}\Omega \parallel 9.57 \text{ k}\Omega)\mathbf{v_{be}} \tag{13.123}$$

$$= -88.5 \mathbf{v_{be}}$$

and

$$\mathbf{v_{be}} = 0.997 \mathbf{v_s} \frac{6.64 \text{ k}\Omega}{6.64 \text{ k}\Omega + 0.329 \text{ k}\Omega} = 0.950 \mathbf{v_s} \tag{13.124}$$

Combining Eqs. (13.123) and (13.124) yields the value of the voltage gain:

$$A_V = \frac{\mathbf{v_o}}{\mathbf{v_s}} = -88.5 \times 0.950 = -84.1 \tag{13.125}$$

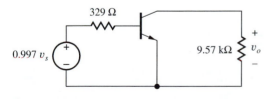

Figure 13.46 Standard form for the ac equivalent circuit.

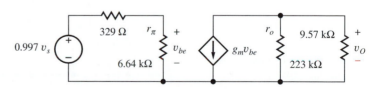

Figure 13.47 ac Equivalent circuit, including the small-signal model.

EXERCISE: What is the amplification factor of the BJT characterized by the parameters in Fig. 13.47? How does A_V compare to μ_f?

ANSWERS: 2150; $A_V \ll \mu_f$

> **EXERCISE:** What is the largest value of v_s that corresponds to a small signal for the BJT amplifier in Fig. 13.47? What is the largest value of v_o that corresponds to a small signal in this amplifier?
>
> **ANSWERS:** 5.26 mV; 0.442 V

Input Resistance

Because we are often interested in the input and output resistances of the amplifier, we shall now calculate these values. The input resistance is defined looking into the amplifier at the position of coupling capacitor C_1 in Figs. 13.42 and 13.44. The simplified ac model used to calculate R_{IN} appears in Fig. 13.48, and the transistor is replaced by its small-signal model in Fig. 13.49. From Fig. 13.49, the input resistance is easily found to be

$$R_{IN} = 100 \text{ k}\Omega \parallel r_\pi = 100 \text{ k}\Omega \parallel 6.64 \text{ k}\Omega = 6.23 \text{ k}\Omega \qquad (13.126)$$

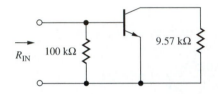

Figure 13.48 ac Model for calculating R_{IN}.

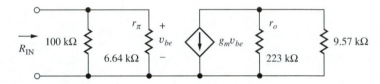

Figure 13.49 Small-signal model for calculating R_{IN}.

Output Resistance

The output resistance is defined looking back into the location of coupling capacitor C_3 in Figs. 13.42 and 13.44. The simplified ac equivalent circuit for determining R_{OUT} is given in Fig. 13.50, and the small-signal model is given in Fig. 13.51.

Because there is no source driving the left-hand node of this circuit, $\mathbf{v_{be}}$ must be zero, as proved rigorously in Eq. (13.108). Because $g_m \mathbf{v_{be}} = 0$, the output resistance is simply the parallel combination of r_o and R_C:

$$R_{OUT} = r_o \parallel R_C = 223 \text{ k}\Omega \parallel 10 \text{ k}\Omega = 9.57 \text{ k}\Omega \qquad (13.127)$$

In summary, the BJT amplifier of Fig. 13.42 has the following characteristics:

$$A_V = -84.1 \qquad R_{IN} = 6.23 \text{ k}\Omega \qquad R_{OUT} = 9.57 \text{ k}\Omega$$

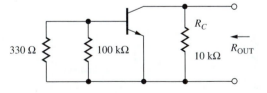

Figure 13.50 ac Circuit model for calculating R_{OUT}.

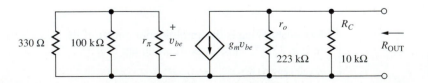

Figure 13.51 Small-signal model for calculating R_{OUT}.

A MOSFET Common-Source Amplifier

A MOSFET in the common-source configuration is shown in Fig. 13.52. Gate-to-source bias is derived from a voltage divider connected to the drain (R_{G3}, R_{G2}, R_{G1}). Capacitors C_1 and C_3 couple the ac signal into and out of the amplifier, respectively. Bypass capacitor C_2 provides an ac ground between resistors R_{G2} and R_{G3} to prevent feedback of ac signals from the drain to the gate.

dc Analysis

Analysis begins by constructing the dc equivalent circuit in Fig. 13.53, which is obtained by replacing the capacitors by open circuits. To find the Q-point, we first find V_{DS} and then V_{GS} and I_{DS}. We start by writing an expression for the drain-source voltage of the MOSFET:

$$V_{DS} = 10 - 2 \times 10^4 (I_{DS} + I_1) \tag{13.128}$$

The drain current of the MOSFET is described by

$$I_{DS} = \frac{K_n}{2}(V_{GS} - V_{TN})^2 \quad \text{for } V_{DS} \ge V_{GS} - V_{TN} \tag{13.129}$$

Note here again that the $(1 + \lambda V_{DS})$ correction term is not used in the dc analysis. Because the gate current $I_G = 0$, current I_1 is equal to

$$I_1 = \frac{V_{DS}}{R_{G3} + R_{G2} + R_{G1}} = \frac{V_{DS}}{5 \times 10^6} \tag{13.130}$$

Because $I_G = 0$, the gate-source voltage is set by V_{DS} and the resistive voltage divider is formed by R_{G1}, R_{G2}, and R_{G3}:

$$V_{GS} = V_{DS}\frac{R_{G1}}{R_{G1} + R_{G2} + R_{G3}} = V_{DS}\frac{2\text{ M}\Omega}{(2+2+1)\text{ M}\Omega} = 0.4V_{DS} \tag{13.131}$$

Substituting Eqs. (13.129) through (13.131) into (13.128),

$$V_{DS} = 10 - 2 \times 10^4 \left[\frac{5 \times 10^{-4}}{2}(0.4V_{DS} - V_{TN})^2 + 2 \times 10^{-7}V_{DS} \right] \tag{13.132}$$

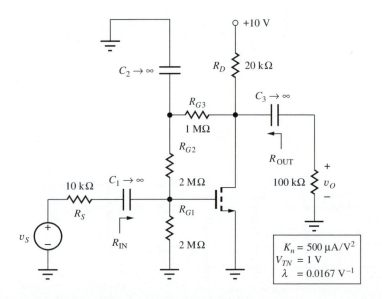

Figure 13.52 MOSFET common-source amplifier.

$$K_n = 500 \text{ μA/V}^2$$
$$V_{TN} = 1 \text{ V}$$
$$\lambda = 0.0167 \text{ V}^{-1}$$

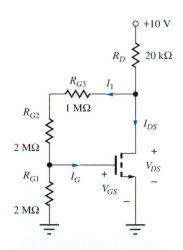

Figure 13.53 Equivalent circuit for Q-point analysis of the amplifier in Fig. 13.52.

and collecting terms yields the following quadratic equation for V_{DS}:

$$0.8V_{DS}^2 - 3.00V_{DS} - 5 = 0 \tag{13.133}$$

Solving for V_{DS} gives

$$V_{DS} = +5 \text{ V}, -1.25 \text{ V} \tag{13.134}$$

V_{DS} must equal 5 V because V_{DS} cannot be negative in this circuit. Using this value in Eqs. (13.131) and (13.129) gives

$$V_{GS} = 2 \text{ V} \quad \text{and} \quad I_{DS} = 250 \text{ μA}$$

The use of Eq. (13.129) presupposes saturation region operation, so we must check to see if the following equation is satisfied:

$$V_{DS} \geq V_{GS} - V_{TN} \quad \text{and} \quad 5 > 1 \text{✔}$$

The conditions for saturation are met, so the Q-point in this circuit is

$$(I_{DS}, V_{DS}) = (250 \text{ μA}, 5 \text{ V}) \tag{13.135}$$

ac Analysis

The next step is to develop the equivalent circuit needed for ac analysis. Replacing the capacitors in Fig. 13.52 by short circuits and grounding the dc voltage source node results in the circuit in Fig. 13.54(a), which is redrawn in clearer form in Fig. 13.54(b).

Figure 13.54(b) can be simplified to our standard form by taking the Thévenin equivalent of the circuit attached to the MOSFET gate and replacing the three parallel resistors attached to the drain by a single equivalent resistor. The resulting circuit is in Fig. 13.55.

The final step is to replace the transistor by its small-signal model, yielding the circuit in Fig. 13.56. The small-signal parameters are evaluated using the Q-point values:

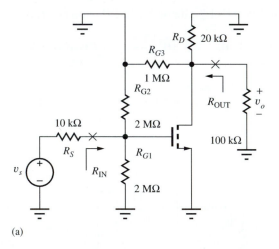

(a)

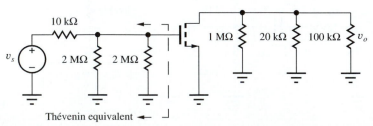

(b)

Figure 13.54 (a) Initial step in constructing the ac equivalent circuit. (b) Redrawn equivalent of circuit in (a).

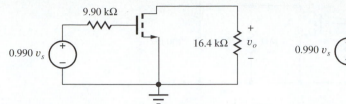

Figure 13.55 Simplification of the circuit in Fig. 13.54.

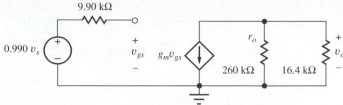

Figure 13.56 Small-signal model for the MOSFET amplifier.

$$g_m = \sqrt{2K_n I_{DS}(1 + \lambda V_{DS})}$$

$$= \sqrt{2\left(5 \times 10^{-4} \frac{A}{V^2}\right)(2.50 \times 10^{-4}\ A)\left(1 + \frac{0.0167}{V} 5\ V\right)} = 5.20 \times 10^{-4}\ S$$

$$r_o = \frac{\left(\dfrac{1}{\lambda}\right) + V_{DS}}{I_D} = \frac{(60 + 5)\ V}{2.50 \times 10^{-4}\ A} = 260\ k\Omega \qquad (13.136)$$

The amplifier voltage gain can now be calculated using the model in Fig. 13.56. The output voltage and gate-source voltages are

$$\mathbf{v_o} = -g_m \mathbf{v_{gs}}(r_o \parallel 16.4\ k\Omega) = -5.20 \times 10^{-4}\ S(260\ k\Omega \parallel 16.4\ k\Omega)\mathbf{v_{gs}} \qquad (13.137)$$

$$= -8.02\mathbf{v_{gs}} \qquad \text{and} \qquad \mathbf{v_{gs}} = 0.990\mathbf{v_s}$$

Combining the last two results gives the overall voltage gain of the amplifier:

$$A_V = \frac{\mathbf{v_o}}{\mathbf{v_s}} = -8.02 \times 0.990 = -7.94 \qquad (13.138)$$

EXERCISE: What is the amplification factor of the MOSFET characterized by the parameters in Fig. 13.56? How does A_V compare to μ_f?

ANSWERS: 135; $A_V \ll \mu_f$

EXERCISE: What is the largest value of v_s that corresponds to a small signal for the amplifier in Fig. 13.52? What is the largest value of v_o that corresponds to a small signal in this amplifier?

ANSWERS: 202 mV; 1.60 V

Input Resistance

The input resistance is defined as the Thévenin equivalent resistance of the amplifier looking into the position of coupling capacitor C_1 in Figs. 13.52 and 13.54. The equivalent circuits used to find R_{IN}, deduced from these figures, are shown in Fig. 13.57. Because the impedance looking into the MOSFET gate is infinite, R_{IN} is limited by the gate-bias resistors:

$$R_{IN} = R_G = 1\ M\Omega \qquad (13.139)$$

Output Resistance

The output resistance of this amplifier is the Thévenin equivalent resistance of the amplifier looking into coupling capacitor C_3 in Fig. 13.52. The equivalent circuit for R_{OUT} can

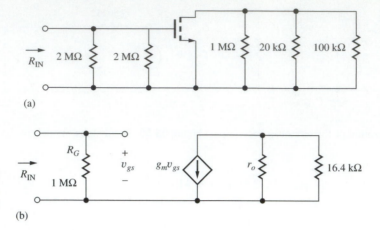

(a)

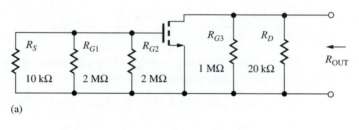

(b)

Figure 13.57 (a) Equivalent circuit for calculating R_{IN}. (b) Small-signal equivalent for the circuit in (a).

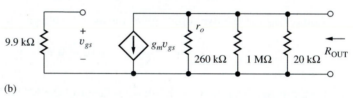

(a)

(b)

Figure 13.58 (a) Simplified circuit for output resistance calculation. (b) Small-signal model for output resistance calculation.

be found from Fig. 13.54 and is drawn in Fig. 13.58(a). When the source is turned off, three resistors appear between the MOSFET gate and ground: the 10-kΩ source resistance and two 2-MΩ gate-bias resistors, R_{G1} and R_{G2}. At the drain terminal, R_D and R_{G3} appear in parallel connected to ground.

The transistor is replaced by its small-signal model in Fig. 13.58(b). In this circuit, $v_{gs} = 0$ so R_{OUT} is equal to the parallel combination of the 20-kΩ, 1-MΩ, and 260-kΩ resistors:

$$R_{\text{OUT}} = 20 \text{ k}\Omega \parallel 1 \text{ M}\Omega \parallel 260 \text{ k}\Omega = 18.2 \text{ k}\Omega \tag{13.140}$$

In summary, the MOSFET amplifier in Fig. 13.52 has the following characteristics:

$$A_V = -7.94 \qquad R_{\text{IN}} = 1 \text{ M}\Omega \qquad R_{\text{OUT}} = 18.2 \text{ k}\Omega$$

A Common-Source Amplifier Using a JFET

Our final example is the common-source amplifier using an n-channel JFET, depicted in Fig. 13.59. Capacitors C_1 and C_3 are used to couple the signal into and out of the amplifier, and bypass capacitor C_2 provides an ac ground at the source of the JFET. The JFET is inherently a depletion-mode device; it requires only three resistors for proper biasing: R_G, R_4, and R_D.

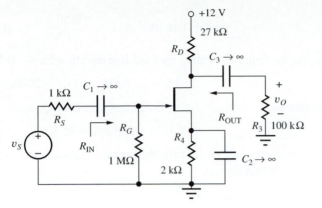

Figure 13.59 Common-source amplifier using a junction field-effect transistor. For the JFET, $I_{DSS} = 1$ mA, $V_P = -1$ V, $\lambda = 0.02$ V^{-1}.

dc Analysis

The dc equivalent circuit, obtained from Fig. 13.59 by opening the capacitors, appears in Fig. 13.60. Assuming operation in the pinch-off region, the drain current of the JFET is expressed as

$$I_{DS} = I_{DSS}\left[1 - \frac{V_{GS}}{V_P}\right]^2 \tag{13.141}$$

in which λ is assumed to be zero for dc analysis. The gate-source voltage may be related to the drain current by writing a loop equation including V_{GS}:

$$I_G(10^6) + V_{GS} + I_S(2000) = 0 \tag{13.142}$$

However, the gate current is zero, so $I_S = I_D$ and $V_{GS} = -2000I_D = -2000I_{DS}$. Substituting this result and the device parameters into Eq. (13.141) yields a quadratic equation for V_{GS}:

$$V_{GS} = -(2 \times 10^3)(1 \times 10^{-3})\left(1 - \frac{V_{GS}}{(-1)}\right)^2 \tag{13.143}$$

Rearranging Eq. (13.143),

$$2V_{GS}^2 + 5V_{GS} + 2 = 0 \tag{13.144}$$

and solving for V_{GS} yields

$$V_{GS} = -0.50 \text{ V}, -2.0 \text{ V} \tag{13.145}$$

V_{GS} must be negative but less negative than the pinch-off voltage of the n-channel JFET, so the -0.50-V result must be the correct choice. The corresponding value of I_{DS} becomes

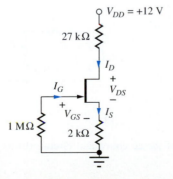

Figure 13.60 Circuit for determining the Q-point of the JFET.

$$I_{DS} = 1 \times 10^{-3} \text{ A} \left[1 - \frac{-0.50 \text{ V}}{-1 \text{ V}}\right]^2 = 0.250 \text{ mA} \qquad (13.146)$$

V_{DS} can be found by writing the load-line equation for the JFET,

$$12 = 27,000 I_D + V_{DS} + 2000 I_S \qquad (13.147)$$

Substituting $I_S = I_D = I_{Ds} = 0.250$ mA gives the Q-point:

$$(250 \text{ } \mu\text{A}, 4.75 \text{ V}) \qquad (13.148)$$

As always, we must check the region of operation to be sure our original assumption of pinch-off was correct:

$$V_{DS} \geq V_{GS} - V_P \qquad 4.75 > -0.50 - (-1) \qquad 4.75 > 0.50 \text{ ✔}$$

ac Analysis

As in the previous examples, we begin by finding the circuit to be used in the ac analysis. In Fig. 13.61(a), the capacitors in Fig. 13.59 have been replaced with short circuits, and the dc voltage source has been replaced with a ground connection. The ac equivalent circuit is redrawn in Fig. 13.61(b), eliminating resistor R_4 and indicating the parallel connection of R_D and R_3. The source of the JFET is clearly the terminal in common between the input and output ports.

The small-signal model for the JFET is substituted for the transistor in the circuit in Fig. 13.62. The parallel 27-kΩ and 100-kΩ resistors have been replaced by a single 21.3-kΩ resistor, and v_s, R_S, and R_G have been replaced by their Thévenin equivalent circuit:

$$\mathbf{v_{th}} = \mathbf{v_s} \frac{R_G}{R_G + R_S} = \mathbf{v_s} \frac{1 \text{ M}\Omega}{1.001 \text{ M}\Omega} = 0.999 \mathbf{v_s}$$

$$R_{th} = \frac{R_G R_S}{R_G + R_S} = \frac{(1 \text{ M}\Omega)(1 \text{ k}\Omega)}{1 \text{ M}\Omega + 1 \text{ k}\Omega} = 999 \text{ }\Omega \qquad (13.149)$$

The output voltage in the circuit in Fig. 13.62 is given by

$$\mathbf{v_o} = -g_m(r_o \parallel 21.3 \text{ k}\Omega)\mathbf{v_{gs}} \qquad \text{and} \qquad \mathbf{v_{gs}} = 0.999\mathbf{v_s} \qquad (13.150)$$

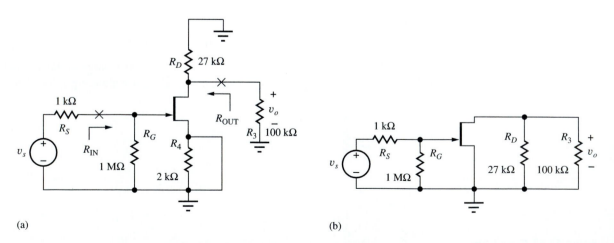

(a)

(b)

Figure 13.61 (a) Construction of the ac equivalent circuit. (b) Redrawn version of the circuit in (a).

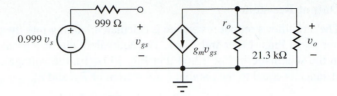

Figure 13.62 Simplified ac equivalent circuit.

To evaluate Eq. (13.150), the values of the small-signal parameters are needed:

$$g_m = \frac{2}{|V_P|}\sqrt{I_{DSS}I_{DS}(1 + \lambda V_{DS})} \approx \frac{2}{|-1\text{ V}|}\sqrt{(0.001\text{ A})(0.00025\text{ A})\left(1 + \frac{0.02}{V}4.75\text{V}\right)}$$

$$= 1.05\text{ mS}$$

$$r_o = \frac{\dfrac{1}{\lambda} + V_{DS}}{I_{DS}} = \frac{(50 + 4.75)\text{ V}}{0.25 \times 10^{-3}\text{ A}} = 219\text{ k}\Omega \tag{13.151}$$

Substituting these values into Eq. (13.150) and solving for the voltage gain gives:

$$A_V = \frac{\mathbf{v_o}}{\mathbf{v_s}} = -0.999(1.05 \times 10^{-3}\text{ S})(219\text{ k}\Omega \parallel 21.3\text{ k}\Omega) = -20.4 \tag{13.152}$$

Thus, this particular common-source JFET amplifier is an inverting amplifier with a voltage gain of -20.4 or 26.2 dB.

> **EXERCISE:** What is the amplification factor of the JFET characterized by the parameters in Eq. (13.151)? How does A_V compare to μ_f?
>
> **ANSWERS:** 230; $A_V \ll \mu_f$

> **EXERCISE:** What is the largest value of v_s that corresponds to a small signal for the JFET amplifier? What is the largest value of v_o that corresponds to a small signal in this amplifier?
>
> **ANSWERS:** 100 mV; 2.04 V

Input Resistance

The amplifier's input resistance is calculated looking into the position of coupling capacitor C_1 in Figs. 13.59 and 13.61, and the equivalent circuit for finding R_{IN} is redrawn in Fig. 13.63. In Fig. 13.63(b), we see that the input resistance is set by the gate-bias resistor R_G, because the input resistance of the JFET itself is infinite.

$$R_{IN} = R_G = 1\text{ M}\Omega \tag{13.153}$$

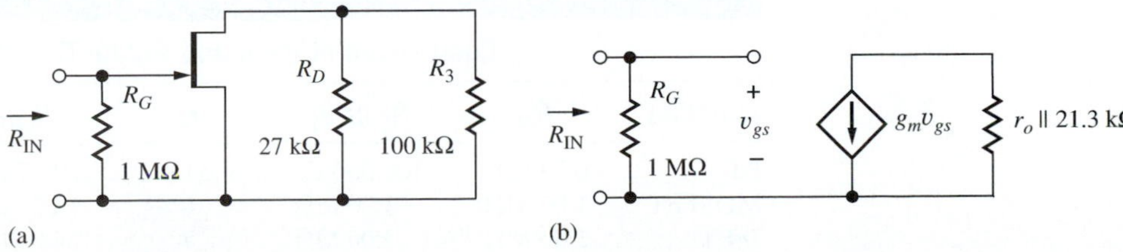

Figure 13.63 (a) ac Equivalent circuit for determining R_{IN}. (b) Small-signal model for the circuit in part (a).

(a)

(b)

Output Resistance

The amplifier's output resistance is calculated looking into the position of coupling capacitor C_3 in Figs. 13.59 and 13.61. The equivalent circuit for calculating R_{OUT} is presented in the schematic in Fig. 13.64. For Fig. 13.64(b), the voltage $v_{gs} = 0$, and the output resistance is equal to the parallel combination of R_D and r_o:

$$R_{OUT} = R_D \| r_o = 27 \text{ k}\Omega \| 219 \text{ k}\Omega = 24.0 \text{ k}\Omega \qquad (13.154)$$

In summary, our JFET amplifier provides the following characteristics:

$$A_v = -20.4 \qquad R_{IN} = 1.00 \text{ M}\Omega \qquad R_{OUT} = 24.0 \text{ k}\Omega$$

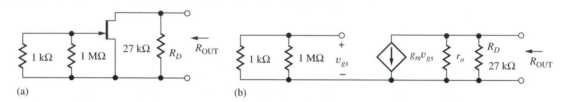

(a)   (b)

Figure 13.64 (a) ac Equivalent circuit for determining R_{OUT}. (b) Small-signal model for circuit in (a).

Comparison of the Amplifier Examples

Tables 13.6 and 13.7 compare the numerical results for the amplifiers analyzed in the previous three examples. Table 13.5 summarized the theoretical expressions. The three amplifiers have all been designed to have similar Q-points, as indicated in Table 13.6. In this table, we see that the BJT yields a much higher voltage gain than either of the FET circuits. However, all the voltage gains are well below the value of the amplification factor, which is characteristic of amplifiers with resistive loads in which the gain is limited by the external resistors (that is, in which $r_o \gg R_C$ or R_D).

T a b l e 13.6				
Comparison of Three Amplifier Voltage Gains				
Amplifier	**Q-point**	**A_V**	**μ_f**	**Rule-of-thumb Estimates**
BJT	(241 µA, 3.67 V)	−84.1	2150	−100
MOSFET	(250 µA, 5.00 V)	−7.94	135	−10
JFET	(250 µA, 4.75 V)	−20.4	230	−24

T a b l e 13.7						
Comparison of Input and Output Resistances						
Amplifier	**R_{IN}**	**R_B or R_G**	**r_π**	**R_{OUT}**	**R_C or R_D**	**r_o**
BJT	6.23 kΩ	100.00 kΩ	6.64 kΩ	9.57 kΩ	10 kΩ	223 kΩ
MOSFET	1.00 MΩ	1.00 MΩ	∞	18.2 kΩ	20 kΩ	260 kΩ
JFET	1.00 MΩ	1.00 MΩ	∞	24.0 kΩ	27 kΩ	219 kΩ

Let us compare the amplifier gains to the rule-of-thumb estimates. For the three cases,

$$\text{BJT:} \qquad A_V \approx -10 V_{CC} = -10(10) = -100$$

$$\text{MOSFET:} \quad A_V \approx -\frac{V_{DD}}{V_{GS} - V_{TN}} = -\frac{10}{2 - 1} = -10 \qquad (13.155)$$

$$\text{JFET:} \qquad A_V \approx -\frac{V_{DD}}{V_{GS} - V_P} = -\frac{12}{-0.5 - (-1)} = -24$$

We see that the estimates are within approximately 20 percent of the full calculations and represent good first-order estimates of the voltage gain.

Table 13.7 compares the input and output resistances. We see that the bipolar input resistance, in this case dominated by the value of r_π, is orders of magnitude smaller than that of the FETs. On the other hand, R_{IN} of the FET stages is limited by the choice of gate-bias resistor R_G. All the output resistances are limited by the external resistors and are of similar magnitude.

Guidelines for Neglecting the Transistor Output Resistance

In all these amplifier examples, we found that the transistor's own output impedance did not greatly affect the results of the various calculations. The following question naturally arises: Why not just neglect r_o altogether, which will simplify the analysis? The answer is: The resistance r_o must be included whenever it makes a difference. We use the following rule: The transistor output resistance r_o can be neglected in voltage gain calculations as long as the computed value of $A_V \ll \mu_f$. However, in Thévenin equivalent resistance calculations r_o can play a very important role and one must be careful not to overlook limitations due to r_o. If r_o is neglected, and an input or output resistance is calculated that is similar to or much larger than r_o, then the calculation should be rechecked with r_o included in the circuit. At this point, this procedure may sound mysterious, but in the next several chapters we shall find circuits in which r_o is very important.

13.12   AMPLIFIER POWER AND SIGNAL RANGE

We explored a number of examples showing how the selection of Q-point affects the value of the small-signal parameters of the transistors and hence affects the voltage gain, input resistance, and output resistance of common-emitter and common-source amplifiers. For the FET, the choice of Q-point also determines the value of v_{gs}, which corresponds to small-signal operation. Two additional characteristics that are set by Q-point design are discussed in this section. The choice of operating point determines the level of power dissipation in the transistor and overall circuit, and it also determines the maximum linear signal range at the output of the amplifier.

Power Dissipation

The static power dissipation of the amplifiers can be determined from the dc equivalent circuits used earlier. The power that is supplied by the dc sources is dissipated in both the resistors and transistors. For the amplifier in Fig. 13.65(a), for example, the power P_D dissipated in the transistor is the sum of the power dissipation in the collector-base and emitter-base junctions:

$$P_D = V_{CB} I_C + V_{BE}(I_B + I_C) = (V_{CB} + V_{BE}) I_C + V_{BE} I_B \qquad (13.156)$$

or $\qquad P_D = V_{CE} I_C + V_{BE} I_B \qquad$ where $V_{CE} = V_{CB} + V_{BE}$

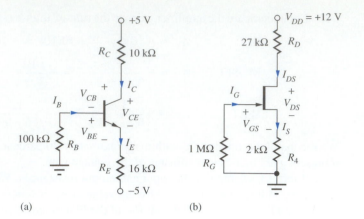

Figure 13.65 dc Equivalent circuits for the (a) BJT and (b) JFET amplifiers from Figs. 13.42 and 13.59.

The total power P_S supplied to the amplifier is determined by the currents in the two power supplies:

$$P_S = V_{CC}I_C + V_{EE}I_E \tag{13.157}$$

Similarly for the JFET circuit in Fig. 13.65(b), the power dissipated in the transistor is given by

$$P_D = V_{DS}I_{DS} + V_{GS}I_G = V_{DS}I_{DS} \tag{13.158}$$

because the gate current is zero. The total power being supplied to the amplifier is equal to:

$$P_S = V_{DD}I_{DS} \tag{13.159}$$

> **EXERCISE:** What power is being dissipated by the bipolar transistor in Fig. 13.65(a)? Assume $\beta_F = 65$. What is the total power being supplied to the amplifier? Use the Q-point information already calculated.
>
> **ANSWERS:** 873 μW; 2.48 mW

> **EXERCISE:** What power is being dissipated by the JFET in Fig. 13.65(b)? What is the total power being supplied to the amplifier? Use the Q-point information already calculated.
>
> **ANSWERS:** 1.19 mW, 3.00 mW

Signal Range

We next discuss the relationship between the Q-point and the amplitude of the signals that can be developed at the output of the amplifier. Let us reconsider the amplifier from Fig. 13.6, which is reproduced in Fig. 13.66 with $V_{CC} = 12$ V, and the corresponding waveforms, which are given in Fig. 13.67. The collector and emitter voltages at the operating point are 5.12 V and 2.10 V, respectively, and hence the value of V_{CE} at the Q-point is 3.02 V.

Because the bypass capacitor at the emitter forces the emitter voltage to remain constant, the total collector-emitter voltage can be expressed as

$$v_{CE} = V_{CE} - V_M \sin \omega t \tag{13.160}$$

in which $V_M \sin \omega t$ is the signal voltage being developed at the collector. The bipolar transistor must remain in the forward-active region at all times, which requires that the

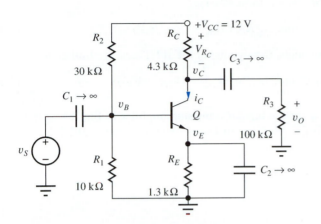

Figure 13.66 Common-emitter amplifier stage from Fig. 13.6.

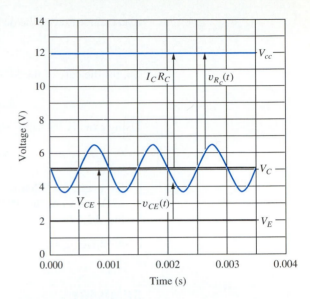

Figure 13.67 Waveforms for the amplifier in Fig. 13.66.

collector-emitter voltage remain larger than base-emitter voltage V_{BE}:

$$v_{CE} \geq V_{BE} \quad \text{or} \quad v_{CE} \geq 0.7 \text{ V} \tag{13.161}$$

Thus the amplitude of the signal at the collector must satisfy

$$V_M \leq V_{CE} - V_{BE} \tag{13.162}$$

The positive power supply presents an additional limit to the signal swing. Writing an expression for the voltage across resistor R_C,

$$v_{R_c}(t) = I_C R_C + V_M \sin \omega t \geq 0 \tag{13.163}$$

In this circuit, the voltage across the resistor cannot become negative; that is, the voltage V_C at the transistor collector cannot exceed the power supply voltage V_{CC}. Equation (13.163) indicates that the amplitude V_M of the ac signal developed at the collector must be smaller than the voltage drop across R_C at the Q-point:

$$V_M \leq I_C R_C \tag{13.164}$$

Thus, the signal swing at the collector is limited by the smaller of the two limits expressed in Eqs. (13.162) or (13.164):

$$V_M \leq \min[I_C R_C, (V_{CE} - V_{BE})] \tag{13.165}$$

A similar expression can be developed for field-effect transistor circuits. Referring to the circuit simulation results in Fig. 13.4, we see that the MOSFET is actually not operating in the saturation region at the negative peak of the signal swing at the drain. This causes distortion in the output waveform. We must require that the MOSFET remain saturated, or v_{DS} must always remain larger than $v_{GS} - V_{TN}$.

$$v_{DS} = V_{DS} - V_M \sin \omega t \geq v_{GS} - V_{TN} \approx V_{GS} - V_{TN} \tag{13.166}$$

in which it has been assumed that $v_{gs} \ll V_{GS}$, and a sinusoidal signal is used as an example. In direct analogy to Eq. (13.164) for a BJT circuit, the signal amplitude in the FET case also cannot exceed the dc voltage drop across R_D:

$$V_M \leq I_{DS}R_D \tag{13.167}$$

So, for the case of the MOSFET, V_M must satisfy:

$$V_M \leq \min[I_{DS}R_D, (V_{DS} - (V_{GS} - V_{TN}))] \tag{13.168}$$

Using exactly the same arguments, the signals for the JFET case are limited to

$$V_M \leq \min[I_{DS}R_D, (V_{DS} - (V_{GS} - V_P))] \tag{13.169}$$

EXERCISE: (a) What is V_M for the bipolar transistor amplifier in Fig. 13.42 if $V_{CC} = 12$ V? (b) For the MOSFET amplifier in Fig. 13.52? (c) For the JFET amplifier in Fig. 13.59?

ANSWERS: 2.41 V; 4.00 V; 4.25 V

SUMMARY

Chapter 13 initiated our study of the basic amplifier circuits used in the design of more complex analog components and systems such as operational amplifiers, audio amplifiers, and RF communications equipment. The chapter began with an introduction to the use of the transistor as an amplifier, and then explored the detailed operation of the BJT common-emitter (C-E) and FET common-source (C-S) amplifiers. Expressions were developed for the voltage gain and input and output resistances of these amplifiers. The common-emitter amplifier can provide good voltage gain but often has only a low-to-moderate input resistance. In contrast, the FET stages can have very high input resistance, but typically provide relatively modest values of voltage gain. The output resistances of both circuits tend to be determined by the resistors in the bias network and are similar for comparable operating points.

The superposition principle is used to simplify the analysis and design of amplifiers. Circuits are split into two parts: a dc equivalent circuit used to find the Q-point of the transistor and an ac equivalent circuit used for analysis of the response of the circuit to signal sources. The design engineer often must respond to competing goals in the design of the dc and ac characteristics of the amplifier, and coupling capacitors, bypass capacitors, and inductors are used to change the ac and dc circuit topologies.

The use of superposition requires linearity, and the ac analyses were all based on linear small-signal models for the transistors. The small-signal models for the diode, bipolar transistor (the hybrid-pi model), MOSFET, and JFET were all discussed in detail. The small-signal model for the diode is simply a resistor that has a value given by $r_d = V_T/I_D$. The results in Table 13.4 for the three-terminal devices are extremely important. The structure of the models is similar. The expressions relating the transconductance g_m, output resistance r_o, and input resistance r_π to the Q-point were all found by evaluating derivatives of the large-signal model equations developed in earlier chapters. The transconductance of the BJT is directly proportional to current, whereas that of the FET increases only in proportion to the square root of current. The resistances r_π and r_o are inversely proportional to Q-point current. The resistor r_π is infinite for the case of the FET, so it does not actually appear in the small-signal model.

The small-signal current gain of the BJT was defined as $\beta_o = g_m r_\pi$, and its value generally differs from that of the large-signal current gain β_F. Because r_π for the FET is infinite, the FET exhibits an infinite small-signal current gain.

The amplification factor, defined as $\mu_f = g_m r_o$, represents the maximum gain available from the transistor in the C-E and C-S amplifiers. Expressions were evaluated for the amplification factors of the BJT and FETs. Parameter μ_f was found to be independent of Q-point for the BJT, but for the FET, the amplification factor decreases as operating current increases. For usual operating points, μ_f for the BJT will be several thousand whereas that for the FET ranges between tens and hundreds. It was discovered that each device pair, the npn and pnp BJTs, the NMOS and PMOS FETs, and the n- and p-channel JFETs, has the same small-signal model.

The definition of a small signal was found to be device-dependent. The signal voltage v_d developed across the diode must be less than 5 mV in order to satisfy the requirements of a small signal. Similarly, the base-emitter signal voltage v_{be} of the BJT must be less than 5 mV for small-signal operation. However, FETs can amplify much larger signals without distortion. For the MOSFET and JFET, $v_{gs} \leq 0.2(V_{GS} - V_{TN})$ and $v_{gs} \leq 0.2(V_{GS} - V_P)$ represent the small-signal limits, respectively.

The common-emitter and common-source amplifiers were analyzed in detail. Table 13.5 is another extremely important table. It summarizes the overall characteristics of these two amplifiers. The rule-of-thumb estimates in Table 13.5 were developed to provide quick predictions of the voltage gain of the C-E and C-S stages. Several examples of the complete analysis of common-emitter and common-source amplifiers were included near the end of the chapter.

The relationship between Q-point design and the small-signal characteristics of the amplifier was fully developed. The chapter closed with a discussion of the relationship between operating point design and the power dissipation and output signal swing of the amplifiers. The amplitude of the signal voltage at the output of the amplifier is limited by the smaller of the Q-point value of the collector-base or drain-gate voltage of the transistor, and by the Q-point value of the voltage across the collector or drain-bias resistors R_C or R_D.

Key Terms

ac Coupling
ac Equivalent circuit
Amplification factor
Analysis by superposition
Back-gate transconductance
Bypass capacitor
Common-emitter (C-E) amplifier
Common-source (C-S) amplifier

Coupling capacitor
dc Blocking capacitor
dc Equivalent circuit
Diode conductance
Diode resistance
Hybrid-pi small-signal model
Input resistance
Intrinsic voltage gain

Output resistance
Small signal
Small-signal common-emitter current gain
Small-signal conductance
Small-signal current gain
Small-signal models
Transconductance

PSPICE Simulation Data *Figure 13.1 npn Load Line

```
*
IB 0 1 DC .001
VCE 2 0 DC 5
Q1 2 1 0 0 NBJT
. OP
. DC VCE 0 10 .025 IB 10U 50U 10U
. MODEL NBJT nNPN IS=1E-15 BF=100 BR=1
. PROBE V(1) I(VCE)
.END
```

*Figure 13.3 NMOSFET Load Line

```
*
VGS 1 0 DC 1
VDS 2 0 DC 5
M1 2 1 0 0 NMOSFET
. OP
. DC VDS 0 10 .025 VGS 2 4.5 .5
. MODEL NMOSFET NMOS KP=5E-4 VTO =1
. PROBE V(1) I(VDS)
. END
```

*Figure 13.7 Common-Emitter Amplifier

```
*
VCC 5 0 DC 12
VS 1 0 SIN(0 .005 1000)
C1 1 2 5U
CE 3 0 500U
R1 2 0 10K
R2 2 5 30K
RC 4 5 4.3K
RE 3 0 1.3K
Q1 4 2 3 NBJT
. OP
. OPTIONS RELTOL=1E-6
. MODEL NBJT NPN BF=100 VA=60
. TRAN 0.1US 5MS
. PROBE V(1) V(2) V(3) V(4) V(5)
. END
```

*Figure 13.43 Common-Emitter Amplifier Biased From Two Supplies

```
*
VCC 5 0 DC 5
VSS 4 0 DC -5
RC 5 3 10K
RB 2 0 100K
RE 1 4 16K
Q1 3 2 1 NBJT
. OP
. MODEL NBJT NPN BF=65 VA=50 IS=9.3E-15
. PROBE V(1) V(2) V(3) V(4) V(5)
.END
```

Problems

Figures P13.1 through P13.10 are used in a variety of problems in this chapter. Assume all capacitors and inductors have infinite value unless otherwise noted. Assume $V_{BE} = 0.7$ V and $\beta_F = \beta_o$ unless otherwise specified.

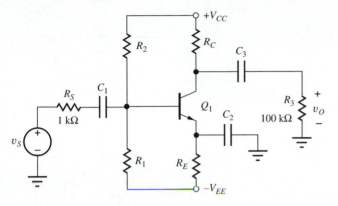

Figure P13.1

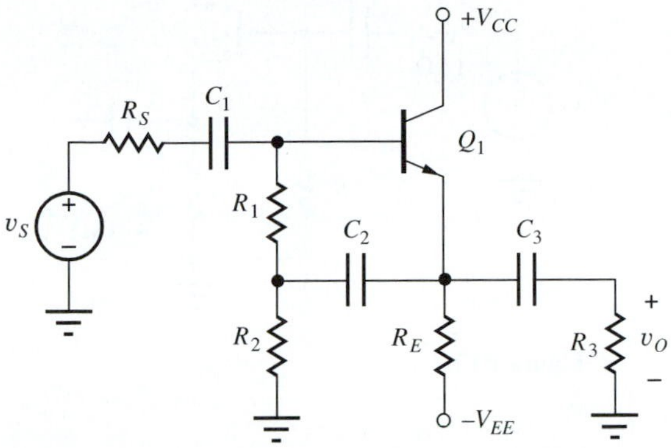

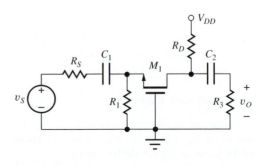

Figure P13.2

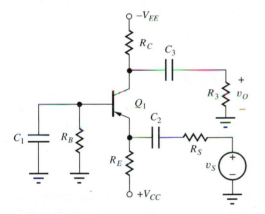

Figure P13.3

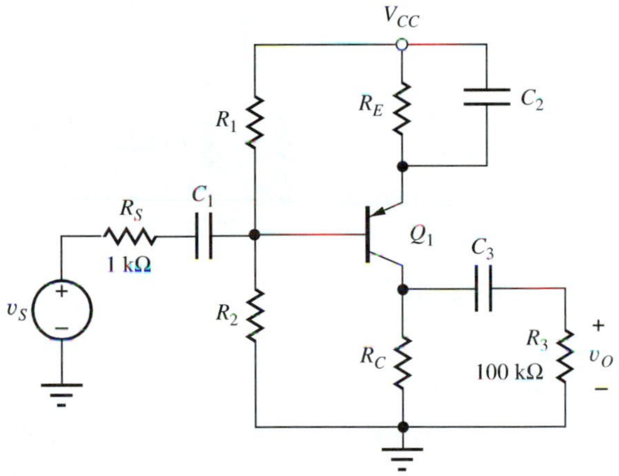

Figure P13.4

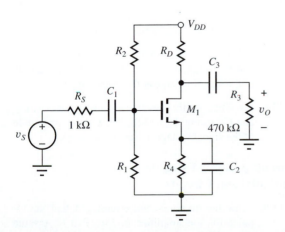

Figure P13.5

Figure P13.6

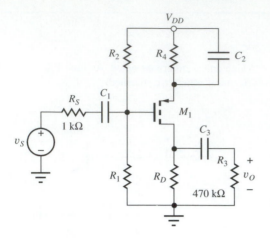

Figure P13.7

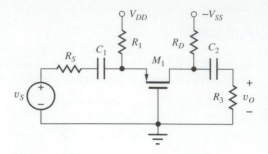

Figure P13.8

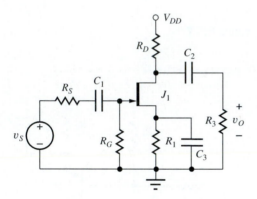

Figure P13.9

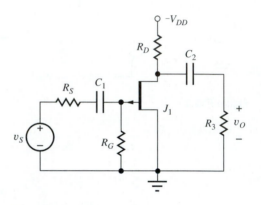

Figure P13.10

13.1 The Transistor as an Amplifier

13.1. (a) Suppose $v_{be}(t) = 0.005 \sin 2000\pi t$ V in the bipolar amplifier in Figs. 13.1 and 13.2. Write expressions for $v_{BE}(t)$, $v_{ce}(t)$, and $v_{CE}(t)$. (b) What is the maximum value of I_C that corresponds to the forward-active region of operation?

13.2. (a) Suppose $v_{gs}(t) = 0.25 \sin 2000\pi t$ V in the MOSFET amplifier in Figs. 13.3 and 13.4. Write expressions for $v_{GS}(t)$, $v_{ds}(t)$, and $v_{DS}(t)$. (b) What is the maximum value of I_{DS} that corresponds to the saturation region of operation?

13.2 Coupling and Bypass Capacitors

13.3. (a) What are the functions of capacitors C_1, C_2, and C_3 in Fig. P13.3? (b) What is the magnitude of the signal voltage at the base of Q_1?

13.4. (a) What are the functions of capacitors C_1, C_2, and C_3 in Fig. P13.4? (b) What is the magnitude of the signal voltage at the emitter of Q_1?

13.5. (a) What are the functions of capacitors C_1, C_2, and C_3 in Fig. P13.5? (b) What is the magnitude of the signal voltage at the source of M_1?

13.6. (a) What are the functions of capacitors C_1 and C_2 in Fig. P13.6? (b) What are the functions of capacitors C_1 and C_2 in Fig. P13.9?

13.7. (a) What are the functions of capacitors C_1, C_2, and C_3 in Fig. P13.7? (b) What is the magnitude of the signal voltage at the source of M_1?

13.8. (a) What are the functions of capacitors C_1, C_2, and C_3, in Fig. P13.1? (b) What is the magnitude of the signal voltage at the emitter of Q_1?

13.3 Circuit Analysis Using dc and ac Equivalent Circuits

13.9. Draw the dc equivalent circuit and find the Q-point for the amplifier in Fig. P13.1. Assume $\beta_F = 75$, $V_{CC} = 12$ V, $-V_{EE} = -12$ V, $R_S =$

1 kΩ, $R_1 = 5$ kΩ, $R_2 = 10$ kΩ, $R_3 = 24$ kΩ, $R_E = 4$ kΩ, and $R_C = 6$ kΩ.

13.10. Use SPICE to find the Q-point for the circuit in Fig. P13.1. Compare the results to the hand calculations in Prob. 13.9.

13.11. Draw the dc equivalent circuit and find the Q-point for the amplifier in Fig. P13.2. Assume $\beta_F = 100$, $V_{CC} = 9$ V, $-V_{EE} = -9$ V, $R_S = 1$ kΩ, $R_1 = 43$ kΩ, $R_2 = 43$ kΩ, $R_3 = 24$ kΩ, and $R_E = 82$ kΩ.

13.12. Use SPICE to find the Q-point for the circuit in Fig. P13.2. Compare the results to the hand calculations in Prob. 13.11.

13.13. Draw the dc equivalent circuit and find the Q-point for the amplifier in Fig. P13.3. Assume $\beta_F = 65$, $V_{CC} = 7.5$ V, $-V_{EE} = -7.5$ V, $R_S = 0.47$ kΩ, $R_B = 3$ kΩ, $R_C = 33$ kΩ, $R_E = 68$ kΩ, and $R_3 = 120$ kΩ.

13.14. Use SPICE to find the Q-point for the circuit in Fig. P13.3. Compare the results to the hand calculations in Prob. 13.13.

13.15. Draw the dc equivalent circuit and find the Q-point for the amplifier in Fig. P13.4. Assume $\beta_F = 135$ and $V_{CC} = 9$ V, $R_1 = 20$ kΩ, $R_2 = 62$ kΩ, $R_C = 13$ kΩ, and $R_E = 3.9$ kΩ.

13.16. Use SPICE to find the Q-point for the circuit in Fig. P13.4. Compare the results to the hand calculations in Prob. 13.15.

13.17. Draw the dc equivalent circuit and find the Q-point for the amplifier in Fig. P13.5. Assume $K_n = 250$ μA/V^2, $V_{TN} = 1$ V, $V_{DD} = 15$ V, $R_S = 1$ kΩ, $R_1 = 1$ MΩ, $R_2 = 2.7$ MΩ, $R_D = 82$ kΩ, and $R_4 = 27$ kΩ.

13.18. Use SPICE to find the Q-point for the circuit in Fig. P13.5. Compare the results to the hand calculations in Prob. 13.17.

13.19. Draw the dc equivalent circuit and find the Q-point for the amplifier in Fig. P13.6. Assume $K_n = 500$ μA/V^2, $V_{TN} = -2$ V, $V_{DD} = 15$ V, $R_S = 1$ kΩ, $R_1 = 3.9$ kΩ, $R_D = 4.3$ kΩ, and $R_3 = 51$ kΩ.

13.20. Use SPICE to find the Q-point for the circuit in Fig. P13.6. Compare the results to the hand calculations in Prob. 13.19.

13.21. Draw the dc equivalent circuit and find the Q-point for the amplifier in Fig. P13.7. Assume $K_p = 400$ μA/V^2, $V_{TP} = -1$ V, $V_{DD} = 18$ V, $R_1 = 3.3$ MΩ, $R_2 = 3.3$ MΩ, $R_D = 24$ kΩ, and $R_4 = 22$ kΩ.

13.22. Use SPICE to find the Q-point for the circuit in Fig. P13.7. Compare the results to the hand calculations in Prob. 13.21.

13.23. Draw the dc equivalent circuit and find the Q-point for the amplifier in Fig. P13.8. Assume $K_p = 200$ μA/V^2, $V_{TP} = +1$ V, $V_{DD} = 12$ V, $-V_{SS} = -12$ V, $R_1 = 33$ kΩ, $R_D = 22$ kΩ, $R_S = 500$ Ω, and $R_3 = 100$ kΩ.

13.24. Use SPICE to find the Q-point for the circuit in Fig. P13.8. Compare the results to the hand calculations in Prob. 13.23.

13.25. Draw the dc equivalent circuit and find the Q-point for the amplifier in Fig. P13.9. Assume $I_{DSS} = 5$ mA, $V_P = -5$ V, $V_{DD} = 18$ V, $R_G = 10$ MΩ, $R_D = 3.9$ kΩ, $R_S = 10$ kΩ, $R_1 = 2$ kΩ, and $R_3 = 36$ kΩ.

13.26. Use SPICE to find the Q-point for the circuit in Fig. P13.9. Compare the results to the hand calculations in Prob. 13.25.

13.27. Draw the dc equivalent circuit and find the Q-point for the amplifier in Fig. P13.10. Assume $I_{DSS} = 1$ mA, $V_P = 3$ V, $-V_{DD} = -15$ V, $R_G = 2.2$ MΩ, $R_D = 7.5$ kΩ, $R_S = 10$ kΩ, and $R_3 = 220$ kΩ.

13.28. Use SPICE to find the Q-point for the circuit in Fig. P13.10. Compare the results to the hand calculations in Prob. 13.27.

13.29. (a) Draw the equivalent circuit used for ac analysis of the circuit in Fig. P13.1. (Use transistor symbols for this part.) Assume all capacitors have infinite value. (b) Redraw the ac equivalent circuit, replacing the transistor with its small-signal model. (c) Identify the function of each capacitor in the circuit (bypass or coupling).

13.30. (a) Repeat Prob. 13.29 for the circuit in Fig. P13.2. (b) Repeat Prob. 13.29 for the circuit in Fig. P13.3.

13.31. (a) Repeat Prob. 13.29 for the circuit in Fig. P13.4. (b) Repeat Prob. 13.29 for the circuit in Fig. P13.5.

13.32. (a) Repeat Prob. 13.29 for the circuit in Fig. P13.6. (b) Repeat Prob. 13.29 for the circuit in Fig. P13.7.

13.33. (a) Repeat Prob. 13.29 for the circuit in Fig. P13.8. (b) Repeat Prob. 13.29 for the circuit in Fig. P13.9.

13.34. Repeat Prob. 13.29 for the circuit in Fig. P13.10.

13.35. Describe the function of each of the resistors in the circuit in Fig. P13.4.

13.36. Describe the function of each of the resistors in the circuit in Fig. P13.5.

13.37. Describe the function of each of the resistors in the circuit in Fig. P13.7.

13.4 Introduction to Small-Signal Modeling

13.38. (a) Calculate r_d for a diode with $V_D = 0.6$ V if $I_S = 10$ fA. (b) What is the value of r_d for $V_D = 0$ V? (c) At what voltage does r_d exceed 10^{15} Ω?

13.39. What is the value of the small-signal diode resistance r_d of a diode operating at a dc current of 1 mA at temperatures of (a) 75 K, (b) 100 K, (c) 200 K, (d) 300 K, and (e) 400 K.

13.40. What bias current I is required for the attenuator in Fig. 13.14 to provide an attenuation of 20 dB if $R_S = 20$ kΩ? What is the largest permissible magnitude of v_s for small-signal operation at this bias current?

13.41. (a) Compare $[\exp(v_d/V_T) - 1]$ to v_d/V_T for $v_d = +5$ mV and -5 mV? How much error exists between the linear approximation and the exponential? (b) Repeat for $v_d = \pm10$ mV.

13.5 Small-Signal Models for Bipolar Junction Transistors

13.42. What collector current is required for a bipolar transistor to achieve a transconductance of 30 mS?

13.43. At what Q-point current will $r_\pi = 10$ kΩ for a bipolar transistor with $\beta_o = 75$? What are the approximate values of g_m and r_o if $V_A = 100$ V?

13.44. The following table contains the small-signal parameters for a bipolar transistor. What are the values of β_F and V_A? Fill in the values of the missing entries in the table if $V_{CE} = 10$ V.

Bipolar Transistor Small-Signal Parameters

I_C (A)	g_m (S)	r_π (Ω)	r_o (Ω)	μ_f
0.002			40,000	
	0.12	500		
		480,000		

13.45. (a) Compare $[\exp(v_{be}/V_T) - 1]$ to v_{be}/V_T for $v_{be} = +5$ mV and -5 mV? How much error exists between the linear approximation and the exponential? (b) Repeat for $v_{be} = \pm7.5$ mV. (c) Repeat for $v_{be} = \pm2.5$ mV.

13.46. At what Q-point current will $r_\pi = 1$ MΩ for a bipolar transistor with $\beta_o = 75$? What are the values of g_m and r_o if $V_A = 100$ V?

13.47. The output characteristics of a bipolar transistor appear in Fig. P13.145. (a) What are the values of β_F and β_o at $I_B = 4$ μA and $V_{CE} = 10$ V? (b) What are the values of β_F and β_o at $I_B = 8$ μA and $V_{CE} = 10$ V?

**13.48. (a) Suppose that a BJT is operating with a total collector current given by

$$i_C(t) = 0.001 \exp\left(\frac{v_{be}(t)}{V_T}\right)$$

and $v_{be}(t) = V_M \sin 2000\pi t$ with $V_M = 5$ mV. What is the value of the dc collector current? Plot the collector current using MATLAB. Use FFT capability of MATLAB to find the amplitude of i_c at 1000 Hz? At 2000 Hz? At 3000 Hz? (b) Repeat for $V_M = 50$ mV.

13.49. (a) Use SPICE to find the Q-point of the circuit in Fig. P13.1 using the element values in Prob. 13.9. Include the .OP statement. Use the Q-point information from SPICE to calculate the values of the small-signal parameters of transistor Q_1. Compare the values with those printed out by SPICE and discuss the source of any discrepancies. (b) Repeat part (a) for the circuit in Fig. P13.4 with the element values from Prob. P13.15.

*13.50. Another small-signal model, the T-model in Fig. P13.50, is of historical interest and quite useful in certain situations. Show that this model is equivalent to the hybrid-pi model if the emitter resistance $r_e = r_\pi/(\beta_o + 1) = \alpha_o/g_m = V_T/I_E$. (Hint: Calculate the short-circuit input admittance y_{11} for both models assuming $\beta_F = \beta_o$.)

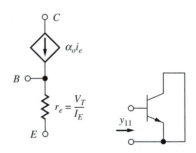

Figure P13.50

13.6 The BJT Common-Emitter (C-E) Amplifier

13.51. A C-E amplifier is operating from a single 12-V supply. Estimate its voltage gain.

*13.52. A C-E amplifier is operating from symmetrical ±15-V power supplies. Estimate its voltage gain.

13.53. A battery-powered amplifier must be designed to provide a gain of 50. Can a single-stage amplifier be designed to meet this goal if it must operate from two ±1.5-V batteries?

13.54. A battery-powered C-E amplifier is operating from a single 1.5-V battery. Estimate its voltage gain. What will the gain be if the battery voltage drops to 1 V?

*13.55. The common-emitter amplifier in Fig. P13.55 must develop a 10-V peak-to-peak sinusoidal signal across the 10-kΩ load resistor R_L. (a) What is the minimum collector current I_C that will satisfy the requirements of small-signal operation of the transistor? (b) What is the minimum power supply voltage V_{CC}?

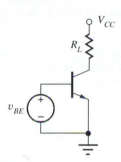

Figure P13.55

*13.56. A common-emitter amplifier has an intrinsic voltage gain of 40 dB. What is the amplitude of the largest output signal voltage at the collector that corresponds to small-signal operation?

13.57. (a) What is the voltage gain of the common-emitter amplifier in Fig. P13.1? (b) What is the voltage gain of the common-emitter amplifier in Fig. P13.4? Assume $\beta_F = 135$, $V_{CC} = V_{EE} = 9$ V, $R_1 = 20$ kΩ, $R_2 = 62$ kΩ, $R_C = 13$ kΩ, and $R_E = 3.9$ kΩ for part (a) and $V_{CC} = 18$ V for part (b).

*13.58. A common-emitter amplifier has a gain of 50 dB and is developing a 15-V peak-to-peak ac signal at its output. Is this amplifier operating within its small-signal region? If the input signal to this amplifier is a sine wave, do you expect the output to be distorted? Why or why not?

13.59. The ac equivalent circuit for an amplifier is shown in Fig. P13.59. Assume the capacitors have infinite value, $R_S = 750$ Ω, $R_B = 100$ kΩ, $R_C = 100$ kΩ, and $R_3 = 100$ kΩ. Calculate the voltage gain for the amplifier if the BJT Q-point is (50 μA, 10 V). Assume $\beta_o = 100$ and $V_A = 75$ V.

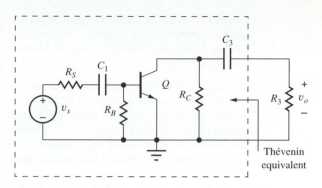

Figure P13.59

13.60. What are the worst-case values of voltage gain for the amplifier in Prob. 13.59 if β_o can range from 60 to 100? Assume that the Q-point is fixed.

13.61. The ac equivalent circuit for an amplifier is shown in Fig. P13.59. Assume the capacitors have infinite value, $R_S = 50$ Ω, $R_B = 4.7$ kΩ, $R_C = 4.3$ kΩ, and $R_3 = 10$ kΩ. Calculate the voltage gain for the amplifier if the BJT Q-point is (2.5 mA, 7.5 V). Assume $\beta_o = 75$ and $V_A = 50$ V.

13.62. The ac equivalent circuit for an amplifier is shown in Fig. P13.62. Assume the capacitors have infinite value, $R_S = 10$ kΩ, $R_B = 5$ MΩ, $R_C = 1.5$ MΩ and $R_3 = 3.3$ MΩ. Calculate the voltage gain for the amplifier if the BJT Q-point is (1 μA, 1.5 V). Assume $\beta_o = 40$ and $V_A = 50$ V.

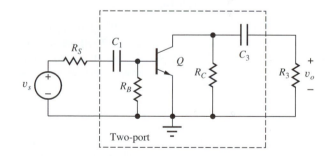

Figure P13.62

13.63. Simulate the behavior of the BJT common-emitter amplifier in Fig. 13.23 and compare the results to the calculations in the example. Use 100 μF for all capacitor values and perform the ac analysis at a frequency of 1000 Hz.

*13.64. An amplifier is required with a voltage gain of 20,000 and will be designed using a cascade of several C-E amplifier stages operating from a single 10-V power supply. Estimate the minimum number of amplifier stages that will be required to achieve this gain.

 13.65. (a) Use SPICE to simulate the dc and ac characteristics of the amplifier in Prob. 13.15. What is the Q-point? What is the value of the small-signal voltage gain? Use 100 μF for all capacitor values and perform the ac analysis at a frequency of 1000 Hz. (b) Compare the results to hand calculations.

13.7 Small-Signal Models for Field-Effect Transistors

13.66. The following table contains the small-signal parameters for a MOS transistor. What are the values of K_n and λ? Fill in the values of the missing entries in the table if $V_{DS} = 6$ V and $V_{TN} = 1$ V.

MOSFET Small-Signal Parameters

I_{DS}	g_m (S)	r_0 (Ω)	μ_f	Small-Signal Limit v_{gs} (V)
0.8 mA		40,000		
50 μA	0.0002			
10 mA				

13.67. An n-channel MOSFET has $K_n = 250$ μA/V^2, $V_{TN} = 1$ V, and $\lambda = 0.02$ V^{-1}. At what drain current will the MOSFET no longer be able to provide any voltage gain (that is, $\mu_F \le 1$)?

13.68. Compare $[1+v_{gs}/(V_{GS}-V_{TN})]^2-1$ to $[2v_{gs}/(V_{GS}-V_{TN})]$ for $v_{gs} = 0.2\,(V_{GS} - V_{TN})$. How much error exists between the linear approximation and the quadratic expression? Repeat for $v_{gs} = 0.4\,(V_{GS} - V_{TN})$.

 13.69. Use SPICE to find the Q-point of the circuit in Fig. P13.5 for the element values in Prob. 13.17. Include the .OP statement. Use the Q-point information from SPICE to calculate the values of the small-signal parameters of transistor M_1. Compare the values with those printed out by SPICE and discuss the source of any discrepancies.

 13.70. Repeat Prob. 13.69 for the circuit in Fig. P13.7 with the element values from Prob. 13.21.

 *13.71. At approximately what Q-point can we achieve an input resistance of $R_{\text{IN}} = 2$ MΩ in a common-source amplifier if the transistor has $K_n =$

500 μA/V^2, $V_{TN} = 1$ V, $\lambda = 0.02$ V^{-1}, and the power supply is 18 V?

 13.72. At approximately what Q-point will $R_{\text{OUT}} = 50$ kΩ in a common-source amplifier if the transistor has $\lambda = 0.02$ V^{-1} and the power supply is 18 V?

13.73. Show that the drain-current expression for the JFET can be represented in exactly the same form as that of the MOSFET using the substitutions $V_P = V_{TN}$ and $K_n = 2I_{DSS}/V_P^2$.

**13.74. (a) Suppose that a JFET is operating with $i_D = 0.005[1 - (v_{gs}/V_{GS} - V_P)]^2$, $V_{GS} - V_P = 2$ V, and $v_{gs} = V_M \sin \omega_o t$ with $V_M = 0.4$ V. Plot the drain current using MATLAB. Use the FFT capability of MATLAB to find the amplitude of i_{ds} at 1000 Hz. At 2000 Hz. At 3000 Hz. (b) Repeat for $V_M = 1$ V.

13.75. The following table contains the small-signal parameters for a JFET. What are the values of I_{DSS} and λ? Fill in the values of the missing entries in the table if $V_{DS} = 6$ V and $V_P = -2.5$ V.

JFET Small-Signal Parameters

I_{DS}	g_m (S)	r_0 (Ω)	μ_f	Small-Signal Limit v_{gs} (V)
1 mA				
50 μA	0.0005			
10 mA		15,000		

 13.76. Use SPICE to find the Q-point of the circuit in Fig. P13.9 for the element values in Prob. 13.25. Include the .OP statement. Use the Q-point information from SPICE to calculate the values of the small-signal parameters of transistor J_1. Compare the values with those printed out by SPICE and discuss the source of any discrepancies.

 13.77. Repeat Prob. 13.76 for the circuit in Fig. P13.10 with the element values from Prob. 13.27.

**13.78. Figure P13.78 gives the device characteristics and schematic of an amplifier circuit including a "new"[4] electronic device called a *triode* vacuum tube. (a) Write the equation for the load line for the circuit. (b) What is the Q-point (I_P, V_{PK})? Assume $i_G = 0$. (c) Using the following definitions, find the values of g_m,

---

[4]New to us at least.

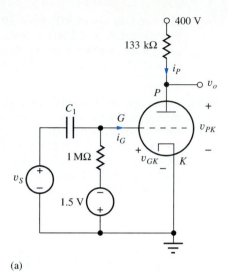

(a)

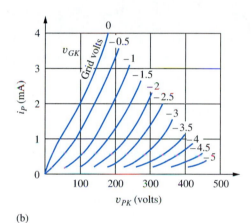

(b)

Figure P13.78 (a) "New" electron device—the triode vacuum tube. (b) Triode output characteristics: G = grid, P = plate, K = cathode.

r_o, and μ_f. (d) What is the voltage gain of the circuit?

$$g_m = \left.\frac{\Delta i_P}{\Delta v_{GK}}\right|_{\text{Q-point}}$$

$$r_o = \left(\left.\frac{\Delta i_P}{\Delta v_{PK}}\right|_{\text{Q-point}}\right)^{-1} \qquad \mu_f = g_m r_o$$

13.8 Summary and Comparison of the Small-Signal Models of the BJT and FET

13.79. A circuit requires the use of a transistor with a transconductance of 0.5 S. A bipolar transistor with $\beta_F = 60$ and a MOSFET with $K_n =$

25 mA/V^2 are available. Which transistor would be preferred and why?

13.80. A circuit is to be biased at a current of 10 mA and achieve an input resistance of at least 1 MΩ. Should a BJT or FET be chosen for this circuit and why?

13.81. A BJT has $V_A = 25$ V and a MOSFET has $K_n = 25$ mA/V^2 and $\lambda = 0.02$ V^{-1}. At what current level is the amplification factor of the MOSFET equal to that of the BJT if $V_{DS} = V_{CE} = 10$ V? What is μ_f for the BJT?

13.82. An amplifier circuit is needed with an input resistance of 75 Ω. Should a BJT or MOSFET be chosen for this circuit? Discuss.

13.9 The Common-Source Amplifier

13.83. A C-S amplifier is operating from a single 12-V supply with $V_{GS} - V_{TN} = 1$ V. Estimate its voltage gain.

13.84. A common-source amplifier has a gain of 15 dB and is developing a 15-V peak-to-peak ac signal at its output. Is this amplifier operating within its small-signal region? Discuss.

13.85. A C-S amplifier is operating from a single 15-V supply. The MOSFET has $K_n = 1$ mA/V^2. What is the Q-point current required for a voltage gain of 30?

13.86. A C-S amplifier is operating from a single 9-V supply. What is the maximum value of $V_{GS} - V_{TN}$ that can be used if the amplifier must have a gain of at least 30?

13.87. A MOSFET common-source amplifier must amplify a sinusoidal ac signal with a peak amplitude of 0.5 V. What is the minimum value of $V_{GS} - V_{TN}$ for the transistor? If a voltage gain of 20 dB is required, what is the minimum power supply voltage?

13.88. A MOSFET common-source amplifier must amplify a sinusoidal ac signal with a peak amplitude of 0.1 V. What is the minimum value of $V_{GS} - V_{TN}$ for the transistor? If a voltage gain of 35 dB is required, what is the minimum power supply voltage?

13.89. An amplifier is required with a voltage gain of 1000 and will be designed using a cascade of several C-S amplifier stages operating from a single 10-V power supply. Estimate the minimum number of amplifier stages required to achieve this gain.

13.90. The amplifier in Fig. P13.90 is the MOSFET amplifier of Fig. 13.33 with the currents decreased by a factor of approximately 10. What is the voltage gain of this amplifier? Assume $K_n = 0.500$ mA/V^2, $V_{TN} = 1$ V, and $\lambda = 0.0133$ V^{-1}. Compare the results to those in Fig. 13.33 and discuss the reasons for any difference in gain.

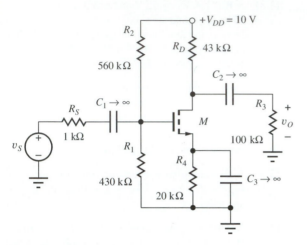

Figure P13.90

13.91. The ac equivalent circuit for an amplifier is shown in Fig. P13.91. Assume the capacitors have infinite value, $R_S = 100$ kΩ, $R_G = 6.8$ MΩ, $R_D = 50$ kΩ, and $R_3 = 120$ kΩ. Calculate the voltage gain for the amplifier if the MOSFET Q-point is (100 μA, 5 V). Assume $K_n = 500$ μA/V^2 and $\lambda = 0.02$ V^{-1}.

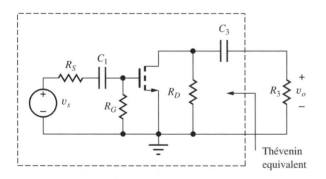

Figure P13.91

13.92. What are the worst-case values of voltage gain for the amplifier in Prob. 13.91 if K_n can range from 300 μA/V^2 to 700 μA/V^2? Assume the Q-point is fixed.

13.93. The ac equivalent circuit for an amplifier is shown in Fig. P13.91. Assume the capacitors have infi-

nite value, $R_S = 100$ kΩ, $R_G = 10$ MΩ, $R_D = 560$ kΩ, and $R_3 = 2.2$ MΩ. Calculate the voltage gain for the amplifier if the MOSFET Q-point is (10 μA, 5 V). Assume $K_n = 100$ μA/V^2 and $\lambda = 0.02$ V^{-1}.

13.94. The ac equivalent circuit for an amplifier is shown in Fig. P13.94. Assume the capacitors have infinite value, $R_S = 10$ kΩ, $R_G = 1$ MΩ, $R_D = 3.9$ kΩ, and $R_3 = 270$ kΩ. Calculate the voltage gain for the amplifier if the MOSFET Q-point is (2 mA, 7.5 V). Assume $K_n = 1$ mA/V^2 and $\lambda = 0.015$ V^{-1}.

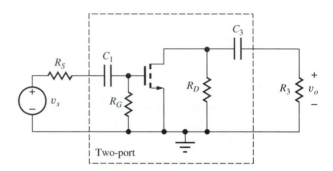

Figure P13.94

13.95. Use SPICE to simulate the dc and ac characteristics of the amplifier in Fig. P13.5 using the parameters in Prob. 13.17. What is the Q-point? What are the values of the small-signal voltage gain, input resistance, and output resistance of the amplifier? Use 100 μF for all capacitor values and perform the ac analysis at a frequency of 1000 Hz.

13.96. Use SPICE to simulate the dc and ac characteristics of the amplifier in Fig. P13.7 using the parameters in Prob. 13.21. What is the Q-point? What are the values of the small-signal voltage gain, input resistance, and output resistance of the amplifier? Use 100 μF for all capacitor values and perform the ac analysis at a frequency of 1000 Hz.

13.97. Use SPICE to simulate the dc and ac characteristics of the amplifier in Fig. P13.9 using the parameters in Prob. 13.25. What is the Q-point? What are the values of the small-signal voltage gain, input resistance, and output resistance of the amplifier? Use 100 μF for all capacitor values and perform the ac analysis at a frequency of 1000 Hz.

13.98. Use SPICE to simulate the dc and ac characteristics of the amplifier in Fig. P13.10 using the parameters in Prob. 13.27. What is the Q-point? What are the values of the small-signal voltage gain, input resistance, and output resistance of the amplifier? Use 100 μF for all capacitor values and perform the ac analysis at a frequency of 1000 Hz.

13.99. The JFET amplifier in Fig. P13.99 must develop a 10-V peak-to-peak sinusoidal signal across the 15-kΩ load resistor R_D. What is the minimum drain current I_D that will satisfy the requirements for small-signal operation of the transistor?

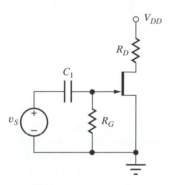

Figure P13.99

13.100. The ac equivalent circuit for an amplifier is shown in Fig. P13.100. Assume the capacitors have infinite value, $R_S = 10\ \text{k}\Omega$, $R_G = 1\ \text{M}\Omega$, $R_D = 7.5\ \text{k}\Omega$, and $R_3 = 160\ \text{k}\Omega$. Calculate the voltage gain for the amplifier if the JFET Q-point is (1 mA, 9 V). Assume $I_{DSS} = 1$ mA, $V_P = -3$ V, and $\lambda = 0.015\ \text{V}^{-1}$.

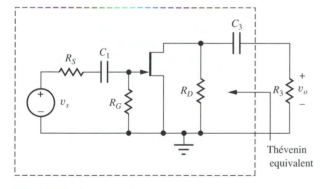

Figure P13.100

13.10 Input and Output Resistances of the Common-Emitter and Common-Source Amplifiers

13.101. The ac equivalent circuit for an amplifier is shown in Fig. P13.59. Assume the capacitors have infinite value, $R_S = 750\ \Omega$, $R_B = 100\ \text{k}\Omega$, $R_C = 100\ \text{k}\Omega$, and $R_3 = 100\ \text{k}\Omega$. Calculate the

input resistance and output resistance for the amplifier if the BJT Q-point is (50 μA, 10 V). Assume $\beta_o = 100$ and $V_A = 75$ V.

13.102. What are the worst-case values of input resistance and output resistance for the amplifier in Prob. 13.59 if β_o can range from 60 to 100? Assume that the Q-point is fixed.

13.103. The ac equivalent circuit for an amplifier is shown in Fig. P13.59. Assume the capacitors have infinite value, $R_S = 50\ \Omega$, $R_B = 4.7\ \text{k}\Omega$, $R_C = 4.3\ \text{k}\Omega$, and $R_3 = 10\ \text{k}\Omega$. Calculate the input resistance and output resistance for the amplifier if the BJT Q-point is (2.5 mA, 7.5 V). Assume $\beta_o = 75$ and $V_A = 50$ V.

13.104. The ac equivalent circuit for an amplifier is shown in Fig. P13.62. Assume the capacitors have infinite value, $R_S = 10\ \text{k}\Omega$, $R_B = 5\ \text{M}\Omega$, $R_C = 1.5\ \text{M}\Omega$, and $R_3 = 3.3\ \text{M}\Omega$. Calculate the input resistance and output resistance for the amplifier if the BJT Q-point is (1 μA, 1.5 V). Assume $\beta_o = 40$ and $V_A = 50$ V.

*13.105. Calculate the z-parameters for the two-port indicated in Prob. 13.62.

*13.106. Calculate the z-parameters for the two-port indicated in Prob. 13.94.

13.107. What are the input resistance and output resistance of the amplifier in Prob. P13.90? Compare the results to those in Fig. 13.33 and discuss the reasons for any difference in voltage gain.

13.108. Calculate the input and output resistances for the amplifier in Prob. 13.91.

13.109. What are the worst-case values of the input and output resistances for the amplifier in Prob. 13.91 if K_n can range from 300 μA/V² to 700 μA/V²? Assume the Q-point is fixed.

13.110. Calculate the input and output resistances for the amplifier in Prob. 13.93.

13.111. Calculate the input and output resistances for the amplifier in Prob. 13.94.

13.112. Calculate the input and output resistances for the amplifier in Prob. 13.100.

13.113. Calculate the Thévenin equivalent representation for the amplifier in Prob. 13.59.

13.114. Calculate the Thévenin equivalent representation for the amplifier in Prob. 13.61.

13.115. Calculate the Thévenin equivalent representation for the amplifier in Prob. 13.91.

13.116. Calculate the Thévenin equivalent representation for the amplifier in Prob. 13.93.

13.117. Calculate the Thévenin equivalent representation for the amplifier in Prob. 13.100.

13.11 Examples of Common-Emitter and Common-Source Amplifiers

 13.118. Simulate the behavior of the BJT common-emitter amplifier in Fig. 13.42 and compare the results to the calculations in the example. Use 100 μF for all capacitor values and perform the ac analysis at a frequency of 1000 Hz.

13.119. The amplifier in Fig. P13.119 is the bipolar amplifier in Fig. 13.42 with currents increased by a factor of approximately 10. What are the voltage gain and input resistance and output resistance of this C-E stage? Compare the gain to that of Fig. 13.42. Did you expect this result? Why? Assume $\beta_F = 65$ and $V_A = 50$ V.

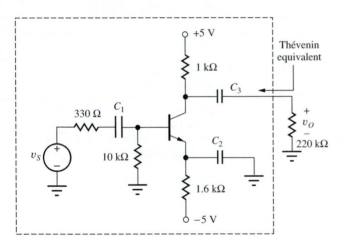

Figure P13.119

 13.120. Simulate the behavior of the BJT common-emitter amplifier in Fig. P13.119 and compare the results to the calculations in Prob. 13.119. Use 100 μF for all capacitor values and perform the ac analysis at a frequency of 10,000 Hz.

13.121. The amplifier in Fig. P13.121 is the bipolar amplifier in Fig. 13.42 with currents reduced by a factor of approximately 10. What are the voltage gain and input resistance and output resistance of this amplifier? Compare to that in Fig. 13.42, and discuss the reasons for any differences in gain.

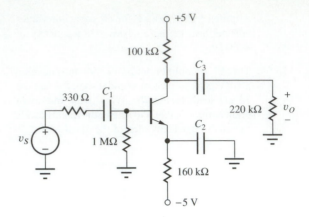

Figure P13.121

 13.122. Simulate the behavior of the BJT common-emitter amplifier in Fig. P13.121 and compare the results to the calculations in Prob. 13.121. Use 100 μF for all capacitor values and perform the ac analysis at a frequency of 1000 Hz.

 *13.123. The gain in the C-S amplifier in Fig. 13.52 can be increased without changing the Q-point by picking a new MOSFET with a larger value K_n (that is, a MOSFET with a larger W/L ratio) and changing the value of R_{G1}. What value of K_n is needed to increase the gain by a factor of 10? What are the new values of $V_{GS} - V_{TN}$ and R_{G1}?

 13.124. (a) Recalculate the Q-point for the transistor in Fig. 13.42 using $V_A = 50$ V. How do these values compare to the result given in Eq. (13.120)? (b) Use PSPICE to perform a 500-case Monte Carlo analysis to find the spread of the Q-point values about the nominal values if the resistors all have tolerances of 10%. Does neglecting V_A in the hand bias calculations appear to make sense? Discuss.

 *13.125. Perform a 250-case Monte Carlo analysis of the ac gain of the common-emitter amplifier in Fig. 13.42. Assume 10% resistor tolerances, β_F is uniformly distributed between 40 and 100, and V_A is uniformly distributed between 50 V and 80 V. The power supplies have a 5% tolerance. What are the mean and standard deviation of the gain? What are the 3σ limits on the gain? Use 100 μF for all capacitor values and perform the ac analysis at a frequency of 1000 Hz.

 13.126. Use SPICE to simulate the behavior of the MOSFET common-source amplifier in Fig. 13.52 and compare the results to the calculations in the example. Use 100 μF for all capacitor values and perform the ac analysis at a frequency of 1000 Hz.

13.127. Use SPICE to simulate the voltage gain and input resistance and output resistance of the amplifier in Prob. P13.90. Use 100 μF for all capacitor values and perform the ac analysis at a frequency of 1000 Hz.

13.128. Simulate the behavior of the JFET common-source amplifier in Fig. 13.59 and compare the results to the calculations in the example. Use 100 μF for all capacitor values and perform the ac analysis at a frequency of 1000 Hz.

13.12 Amplifier Power and Signal Range

13.129. Calculate the dc power dissipation in each element in the circuit in Fig. 13.65(a) if $\beta_F = 65$. Compare the result to the total power delivered by the sources.

13.130. Calculate the dc power dissipation in each element in the circuit in Fig. 13.65(b). Compare the result to the total power delivered by the sources.

13.131. Calculate the dc power dissipation in each element in the circuit in Problem 13.9. Compare the result to the total power delivered by the sources.

13.132. Repeat Prob. 13.131 for the circuit in Prob. 13.13.

13.133. Repeat Prob. 13.131 for the circuit in Prob. 13.17.

13.134. Repeat Prob. 13.131 for the circuit in Prob. 13.21.

13.135. Repeat Prob. 13.131 for the circuit in Prob. 13.25.

*13.136. A common bias point for a transistor is shown in Fig. P13.136. What is the maximum amplitude

signal that can be developed at the collector terminal that will satisfy the small-signal assumptions (in terms of V_{CC})?

*13.137. The MOSFET in Fig. P13.137 has $K_n = 500$ μA/V² and $V_{TN} = -1.5$ V. What is the largest permissible signal voltage at the drain that will satisfy the requirements for small-signal operation if $R_D = 15$ kΩ? What is the minimum value of V_{DD}?

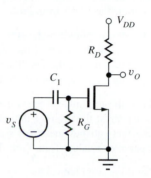

Figure P13.137

*13.138. The simple C-E amplifier in Fig. P13.138 is biased with $V_{CE} = V_{CC}/2$. Assume that the transistor can saturate with $V_{CESAT} = 0$ V and still be operating linearly. What is the amplitude of the largest sine wave that can appear at the output? What is the ac signal power P_{ac} being dissipated in the load resistor R_L? What is the total dc power P_S being supplied from the power supply? What is the efficiency ε of this amplifier if ε is defined as $\varepsilon = 100\% \times P_{ac}/P_S$?

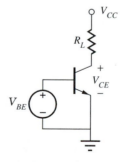

Figure P13.138

13.139. What is the amplitude of the largest ac signal that can appear at the collector of the transistor in

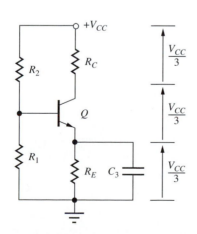

Figure P13.136

Fig. P13.1 that satisfies the small-signal limit? Use the parameter values from Prob. 13.9.

13.140. What is the amplitude of the largest ac signal that can appear at the collector of the transistor in Fig. P13.4 that satisfies the small-signal limit? Use the parameter values from Prob. 13.15.

13.141. What is the amplitude of the largest ac signal that can appear at the drain of the transistor in Fig. P13.5 that satisfies the small-signal limit? Use the parameter values from Prob. 13.17.

13.142. What is the amplitude of the largest ac signal that can appear at the drain of the transistor in Fig. P13.7 that satisfies the small-signal limit? Use the parameter values from Prob. 13.21.

13.143. What is the amplitude of the largest ac signal that can appear at the drain of the transistor in Fig. P13.9 that satisfies the small-signal limit? Use the parameter values from Prob. 13.25.

13.144. What is the amplitude of the largest ac signal that can appear at the drain of the transistor in Fig. P13.10 that satisfies the small-signal limit? Use the parameter values from Prob. 13.27.

13.145. Draw the load line for the circuit in Fig. 13.1 on the output characteristics in Fig. P13.145 for $V_{CC} = 20$ V and $R_C = 20$ kΩ. Locate the Q-point for $I_B = 2$ μA. Estimate the maximum output voltage swing from the characteristics. Repeat for $I_B = 5$ μA.

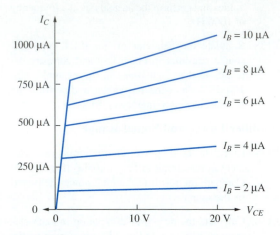

Figure P13.145

Single-Transistor Amplifiers

Chapter 13 introduced the common-emitter and common-source amplifiers, in which the input signal was applied to the base and gate terminals of the BJT and MOSFET, and the output signal was taken from the collector and drain. However, bipolar and field-effect transistors are three-terminal devices, and this chapter explores the use of all the terminals for signal input and output. Three useful amplifier configurations are identified, each using a different terminal as the common or reference terminal. When implemented using bipolar transistors, these are called the common-emitter, common-collector, and common-base amplifiers; the corresponding names for the FET implementations are the common-source, common-drain, and common-gate amplifiers. Each amplifier category provides a unique set of characteristics in terms of voltage gain, input resistance, output resistance, and current gain.

The chapter looks in depth at the characteristics of each amplifier configuration, focusing on the limits solid-state devices place on individual amplifier performance. Expressions are developed for the properties of each amplifier, and their similarities and differences are discussed in detail in order to build the understanding needed for the circuit design process. The transistor-level results are used throughout this book to analyze and design more complex single- and multistage amplifiers.

Much discussion is devoted to single-transistor amplifiers because they are the heart of analog design. These single-stage amplifiers are an important part of the basic "tool set" of analog circuit designers, and a good understanding of their similarities and differences is a prerequisite for more complex amplifier design.

14.1 AMPLIFIER CLASSIFICATION

In Chapter 13, the input signal was applied to the base or gate of the transistor, and the output signal was taken from the collector or drain. However, the transistor has three separate terminals that may possibly be used to inject a signal for amplification: the base, emitter, and collector for the BJT; the gate, source, and drain for the FET. We will see shortly that only the base and emitter or gate and source are useful as signal insertion points; the collector and emitter or drain and source are useful points for signal removal. The examples we use in this chapter of the various amplifier configurations all use the same four-resistor bias circuits shown in Fig. 14.1. Coupling and bypass capacitors are then used to change the signal injection and extraction points and modify the ac characteristics of the amplifiers.

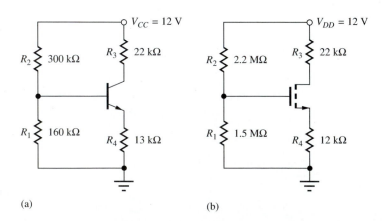

Figure 14.1 Four-resistor bias circuits for the (a) BJT and (b) MOSFET.

(a)   (b)

Signal Injection and Extraction—The BJT

For the BJT in Fig. 14.1(a), the large-signal transport model provides guidance for proper location of the input signal. In the forward-active region of the BJT,

$$i_C = I_S \left[\exp\left(\frac{v_{BE}}{V_T}\right) \right]$$

$$i_B = \frac{i_C}{\beta_F} = \frac{I_S}{\beta_{FO}} \left[\exp\left(\frac{v_{BE}}{V_T}\right) \right] \qquad (14.1)$$

$$i_E = \frac{I_S}{\alpha_F} \left[\exp\left(\frac{v_{BE}}{V_T}\right) \right]$$

To cause i_C, i_E, and i_B to vary significantly, we need to change the base-emitter voltage v_{BE}, which appears in the exponential term. Because v_{BE} is equivalent to

$$v_{BE} = v_B - v_E \qquad (14.2)$$

an input signal voltage can be injected into the circuit to vary the voltage at either the base or the emitter of the transistor. Note that the Early voltage has been omitted from Eq. (14.1), which indicates that varying the collector voltage has no effect on the terminal currents. Thus the collector terminal is not an appropriate terminal for signal injection. Even for finite values of Early voltage, current variations with collector voltage are small, especially when compared to the exponential dependence of the currents on v_{BE}—again, the collector is not used as a signal injection point.

Substantial changes in the collector and emitter currents can create large voltage signals across the collector and emitter resistors R_3 and R_4 in Fig. 14.1. Thus, signals can be removed from the amplifier at the collector or emitter terminals. However, because the base current i_B is a factor of β_F smaller than either i_C or i_E, the base terminal is not normally used as an output terminal.

Signal Injection and Extraction—The FET

A similar set of arguments can be used for the FET in Fig. 14.1(b), based on the expression for the n-channel MOSFET drain current in saturation:

$$i_S = i_D = i_{DS} = \frac{K_n}{2}(v_{GS} - V_{TN})^2 \qquad \text{and} \qquad i_G = 0 \qquad (14.3)$$

To cause i_D and i_S to vary significantly, we need to change the gate-source voltage v_{GS}. Because v_{GS} is equivalent to

$$v_{GS} = v_G - v_S \qquad (14.4)$$

an input signal voltage can be injected so as to vary either the gate or source voltage of the FET. Varying the drain voltage has only a minor effect (for $\lambda \neq 0$) on the terminal currents, so the drain terminal is not an appropriate terminal for signal injection. As for the BJT, substantial changes in the drain or source currents can develop large voltage signals across resistors R_3 and R_4 in Fig. 14.1(b). However, the gate terminal is not used as an output terminal because the gate current is always zero. An identical set of arguments holds for the JFET.

In summary, effective amplification requires a signal to be injected into either the base/emitter or gate/source terminals of the transistors in Fig. 14.1; the output signal can be taken from the collector/emitter or drain/source terminals. We do not inject a signal into the collector or drain or extract a signal from the base or gate terminals. These constraints yield three families of amplifiers: the **common-emitter/common-source (C-E/C-S)** circuits, the **common-base/common-gate (C-B/C-G)** circuits, and the **common-collector/common-drain (C-C/C-D)** circuits.

These amplifiers are classified in terms of the structure of the ac equivalent circuit; each is discussed in detail in the next several sections. As noted earlier, the circuit examples all use the same four-resistor bias circuits in Fig. 14.1 in order to establish the Q-point of the various amplifiers. Coupling and bypass capacitors are then used to change the ac equivalent circuits. We will find that the ac characteristics of the various amplifiers are significantly different.

> **EXERCISE:** Find the Q-points for the transistors in Fig. 14.1 and calculate the small-signal model parameters for the BJT and MOSFET. Use $\beta_F = 100$, $V_A = 50$ V, $K_n = 500$ μA/V^2, $V_{TN} = 1$ V, and $\lambda = 0.02$ V^{-1}. What are the values of μ_f? What is the value of $V_{GS} - V_{TN}$ for the MOSFET?
>
> **ANSWERS:**

	I_C/I_{DS}	V_{CE}/V_{DS}	$V_{GS} - V_{TN}$	g_m	r_π	r_o	μ_f
BJT	245 μA	3.64 V	...	9.80 mS	10.2 kΩ	219 kΩ	2150
FET	241 μA	3.81 V	0.982 V	0.491 mS	∞	223 kΩ	110

Generalized Common-Emitter (C-E) and Common-Source (C-S) Amplifiers

The circuits in Fig. 14.2 are generalized versions of the common-emitter and common-source amplifiers introduced in Chapter 13. In these circuits, resistor R_4 in Fig. 14.1 has been split into two parts, R_5 and R_6, with only resistor R_6 bypassed by capacitor C_2. In the C-E circuit in Fig. 14.2(a), the signal is injected into the base and taken out of the collector of the BJT. The emitter is the common terminal between the input and output ports. In the C-S circuit in Fig. 14.2(b), the signal is injected into the gate and taken out of the drain of the MOSFET; the source is the common terminal between the input and output ports.

The simplified ac equivalent circuits for these amplifiers appear in Figs. 14.2(c) and (d). We see that these network topologies are identical. Resistor R_5, connected between the emitter or source and ground, represents the unbypassed portion of the original bias resistor R_4. The presence of R_5 in the ac equivalent circuits gives an added degree of freedom to the designer, and allows gain to be traded for increased input resistance, output resistance, and input signal range. Our comparative analysis will show that the C-E and C-S circuits can provide moderate-to-high values of voltage, current gain, input resistance, and output resistance.

> **EXERCISE:** Construct the ac equivalent circuit for the C-E and C-S amplifiers in Fig. 14.2, and show that the ac models are correct. What are the values of v_{th}, R_{th}, R_5, and R_L?
>
> **ANSWERS:** $0.981v_s$, 1.96 kΩ, 3.00 kΩ, 18.0 kΩ; $0.998v_s$, 2.00 kΩ, 2.00 kΩ, 18.0 kΩ

Common-Collector (C-C) and Common-Drain (C-D) Topologies

The C-C and C-D circuits are shown in Fig. 14.3. Here the signal is injected into the base [Fig. 14.3(a)] and gate [Fig. 14.3(b)] and extracted from the emitter and source of the

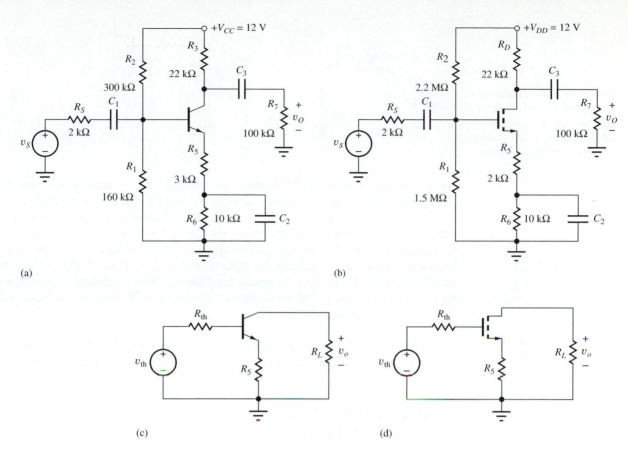

(a)

(b)

(c)

(d)

Figure 14.2 Generalized versions of the (a) common-emitter (C-E) and (b) common-source (C-S) amplifiers. (c) Simplified ac equivalent circuit of the C-E amplifier in (a). (d) Simplified ac equivalent circuit of the C-S amplifier in (b).

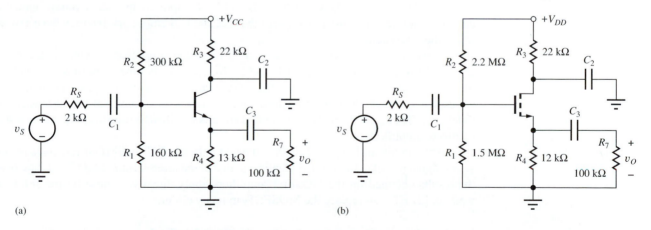

(a)

(b)

Figure 14.3 (a) Common-collector (C-C) amplifier. (b) Common-drain (C-D) amplifier.

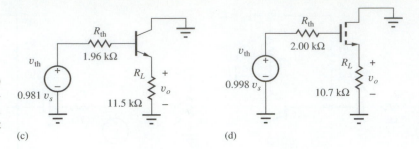

Figure 14.3 (Continued) (c) Simplified ac equivalent circuit for the C-C amplifier. (d) Simplified ac equivalent circuit for the C-D amplifier.

transistors. The collector and drain are bypassed directly to ground by the capacitors C_2 and represent the common terminals between the input and output ports. Once again, the ac equivalent circuits in Figs. 14.3(c) and (d) are identical in structure; the only differences are the resistor and transistor parameter values. Analysis will show that the C-C and C-D amplifiers provide a voltage gain of approximately 1, a high input resistance and a low output resistance. In addition, the input signals to the C-C and C-D amplifiers can be quite large without exceeding the small-signal limits. These amplifiers, often called emitter or source followers, are the single-transistor equivalents of the op-amp voltage-follower circuit that we studied in Chapter 12.

EXERCISE: Construct the ac equivalent circuit for the C-C and C-D amplifiers in Fig. 14.3, and show that the ac models are correct. Verify the values of v_{th}, R_{th}, and R_L.

Common-Base (C-B) and Common-Gate (C-G) Amplifiers

The third class of amplifiers contains the C-B and C-G circuits in Fig. 14.4. ac Signals are injected into the emitter and source and extracted from the collector and drain of the transistor. The base and gate terminals are connected to signal ground through bypass capacitors C_2; these terminals are the common connections between the input and output ports. The resulting ac equivalent circuits in Figs. 14.4(c) and (d) are again identical in structure. Analysis will show that the C-B and C-G amplifiers provide a voltage gain and output resistance very similar to those of the C-E and C-S amplifiers, but they have a much lower input resistance.

Analyses in the next several sections involve the simplified ac equivalent circuits given in Figs. 14.2(c), (d), 14.3(c), (d), and 14.4(c), (d). We assume for purposes of analysis that the circuits have been reduced to these "standard amplifier prototypes." These circuits are used to delineate the limits that the devices place on performance of the various circuit topologies. The results from these simplified circuits will then be used to analyze and design complete amplifiers.

The circuits in Figs. 14.2 to 14.4 showed only the BJT and MOSFET. Because the small-signal model of the JFET is identical to that of the three-terminal MOSFET, however, the results obtained for the MOSFET amplifiers apply directly to those for the JFETs as well, and JFETs can replace the MOSFETs in many circuits.

EXERCISE: Construct the ac equivalent circuit for the C-B and C-G amplifiers in Fig. 14.4, and show that the ac models are correct. What are the values of v_{th}, R_{th}, and R_L?

ANSWERS: $0.867v_s$, 1.73 kΩ, 18.0 kΩ; $0.857v_s$, 1.71 kΩ, 18.0 kΩ

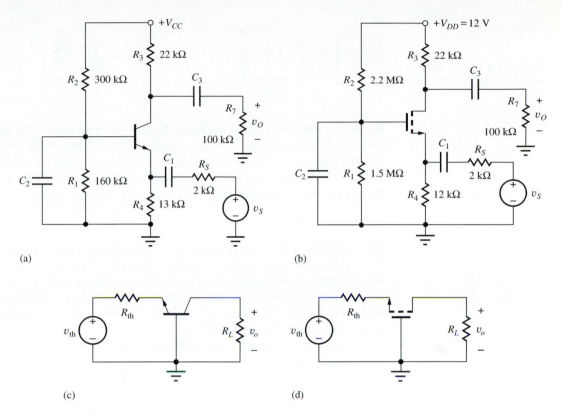

Figure 14.4 (a) Common-base (C-B) amplifier. (b) Common-gate (C-G) amplifier. (c) Simplified ac equivalent circuit for the C-B amplifier. (d) Simplified ac equivalent circuit for the C-G amplifier.

14.2 INVERTING AMPLIFIERS—COMMON-EMITTER AND COMMON-SOURCE CIRCUITS

We begin our comparative analysis of the various amplifier families with the common-emitter and common-source amplifiers, whose ac equivalent circuits are repeated in Fig. 14.5. Here again we note that the topologies are identical. Performance differences arise because of the differences in the parameters of the transistors used in the circuit.

The small-signal models for the BJT and MOSFET are in Fig. 14.6. Again, we observe that the topologies are very similar, except for the finite value of r_π for the BJT.

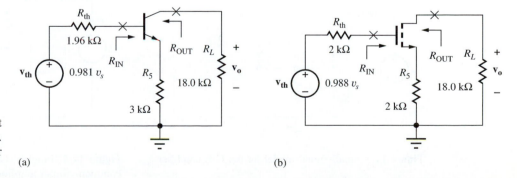

Figure 14.5 (a) ac Equivalent circuit for the C-E amplifier. (b) ac Equivalent circuit for the C-S amplifier.

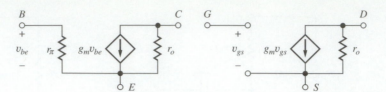

Figure 14.6 Small-signal models for the BJT and MOS-FET.

Because of these similarities, we begin the analyses with that for the bipolar transistor because it has the more general small-signal model; we obtain results for the FET cases from the BJT expressions by taking limits as r_π and $\beta_o = g_m r_\pi$ approach infinity. Expressions for the voltage gain, input resistance, output resistance, and current gain are developed for each of the single-transistor amplifiers.

Voltage Gain

We will begin by deriving an expression for the voltage gain. The BJT in Fig. 14.5(a) has been replaced by its small-signal model in Fig. 14.7. To simplify the analysis, we use our rule of thumb from Chapter 13 and assume that r_o can be neglected during analysis of the voltage gain of resistively loaded amplifiers. Figure 14.8 shows the simplified small-signal equivalent circuit with r_o removed. Note also that the small-signal model has been changed to its current-controlled representation.

Beginning the analysis, the **voltage gain** A_{Vth}, defined from the Thévenin source v_{th} to the output v_o, is

$$A_{Vth} = \frac{\mathbf{v_o}}{\mathbf{v_{th}}} \tag{14.5}$$

where the output voltage is expressed as

$$\mathbf{v_o} = -\beta_o \mathbf{i} R_L \tag{14.6}$$

An equation for $\mathbf{i}$ in terms of $\mathbf{v_{th}}$ can be found from loop 1:

$$\mathbf{v_{th}} = \mathbf{i} R_{th} + \mathbf{i} r_\pi + (\beta_o + 1)\mathbf{i} R_5 = \mathbf{i}(R_{th} + r_\pi + (\beta_o + 1)R_5) \tag{14.7}$$

Combining Eqs. (14.5) through (14.7) yields the gain expression for the common-emitter amplifier:

$$A_{Vth}^{CE} = -\frac{\beta_o R_L}{R_{th} + r_\pi + (\beta_o + 1)R_5} = -\frac{R_L}{\dfrac{R_{th} + r_\pi + R_5}{\beta_o} + R_5} \tag{14.8}$$

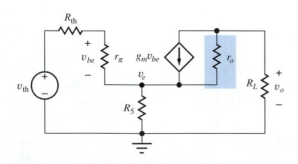

Figure 14.7 Small-signal model for the C-E amplifier.

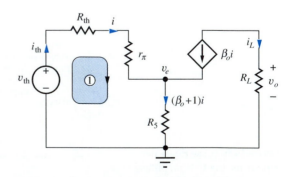

Figure 14.8 Simplified small-signal model for the common-emitter amplifier in which r_o is neglected.

To find the gain for the common-source amplifier, we factor r_π out of the denominator to yield (remembering that $\beta_o = g_m r_\pi$):

$$A_{Vth}^{CE} = -\frac{\beta_o R_L}{r_\pi\left(1 + g_m R_5 + \dfrac{R_{th} + R_5}{r_\pi}\right)} = -\frac{g_m R_L}{1 + g_m\left(R_5 + \dfrac{R_{th} + R_5}{\beta_o}\right)} \quad (14.9)$$

If the limit in Eq. (14.9) is taken as $\beta_o \to \infty$, the last term in the denominator goes to zero, and the gain of the C-S amplifier becomes

$$A_{Vth}^{CS} = -\frac{g_m R_L}{1 + g_m R_5} \quad (14.10)$$

The results in Eqs. (14.9) and (14.10) are very similar. The only difference is the last term in the denominator in Eq. (14.9), which results from the finite current gain of the bipolar transistor. In most cases, $R_5 \gg (R_{th} + R_5)/\beta_o$, and

$$A_{Vth}^{CE} \approx A_{Vth}^{CS} = -\frac{g_m R_L}{1 + g_m R_5} = -\frac{R_L}{\dfrac{1}{g_m} + R_5} \quad (14.11)$$

Note the minus signs in Eqs. (14.8) through (14.11), indicating that these amplifiers invert the signal; there is a 180° phase difference between the input and output signals.

EXAMPLE 14.1: Calculate the voltage gain A_{Vth} of the BJT and MOSFET amplifiers using Eqs. (14.8) and (14.10). Use the parameter values tabulated below.

SOLUTION: The transistor parameter values were calculated in the first exercise in this chapter and are repeated here:

	I_C/I_{DS}	V_{CE}/V_{DS}	$V_{GS} - V_{TN}$	g_m	r_π	r_o	μ_f
BJT	245 μA	3.64 V	...	9.80 mS	10.2 kΩ	219 kΩ	2150
FET	241 μA	3.81 V	0.982 V	0.491 mS	∞	223 kΩ	110

For the C-E amplifier,

$$A_{Vth}^{CE} = -\frac{\beta_o R_L}{R_{th} + r_\pi + (\beta_o + 1)R_5}$$

$$= -\frac{100\,(18.0\text{ k}\Omega)}{1.96\text{ k}\Omega + 10.2\text{ k}\Omega + (101)3.00\text{ k}\Omega} = -5.71$$

For the MOSFET amplifier,

$$A_{Vth}^{CS} = -\frac{g_m R_L}{1 + g_m R_5} = -\frac{(0.491\text{ mS})(18.0 \times \text{k}\Omega)}{1 + (0.491\text{ mS})(2.00 \times \text{k}\Omega)} = -4.46 \quad \blacklozenge$$

Important Limits

Equations (14.8) to (14.11) give the results for the gain of the C-E and C-S amplifiers for general values of the circuit element parameters, but it is also important to understand the bounds and limitations of these expressions.

Zero Resistance in the Emitter or Source

The upper bound is achieved if R_5 is set to zero in Eqs. (14.9) and (14.10), which should correspond to the C-E and C-S amplifiers that were analyzed in detail in Chapter 13:

$$A_{V\text{th}}^{CE} = -\frac{g_m R_L}{1 + \dfrac{R_{\text{th}}}{r_\pi}} \approx -g_m R_L \qquad \text{and} \qquad A_{V\text{th}}^{CS} = -g_m R_L \qquad (14.12)$$

The magnitude of the gain of both amplifiers approaches the $(g_m R_L)$ product (also discussed in detail in Chapter 13), and this value represents the maximum gain that can be achieved with generalized inverting amplifiers. Thus, the $(10\ V_{CC})$ rule-of-thumb estimate for the BJT, and the $V_{DD}/(V_{GS} - V_{TN})$ estimate for the FET apply as upper bounds here.

Limit for Large R_5

For any nonzero value of R_5, the denominator of Eqs. (14.9) and (14.10) increases, and the voltage gain must be smaller than the limits in Eq. (14.12). If R_5 in Eq. (14.11) becomes large enough to satisfy

$$g_m R_5 \gg 1 \qquad (14.13)$$

then the gain expressions can be simplified to

$$A_{V\text{th}}^{CE} = A_{V\text{th}}^{CS} = -\frac{R_L}{R_5} \qquad (14.14)$$

For both cases, the gain is set by the ratio of the effective load resistor R_L to the unbypassed resistor R_5 in the emitter or source. This is an extremely useful result because the gain is now independent of transistor characteristics, which can vary widely from device to device.

Summarizing the results in Eqs. (14.11) and (14.13) for the common-emitter and common-source amplifiers:

$$A_{V\text{th}}^{CE} = -\frac{\beta_o R_L}{R_{\text{th}} + r_\pi + (\beta_o + 1)R_5} \qquad A_{V\text{th}}^{CS} = -\frac{g_m R_L}{1 + g_m R_5}$$

$$A_{V\text{th}}^{CE} \approx A_{V\text{th}}^{CS} = -\frac{g_m R_L}{1 + g_m R_5} \qquad (14.15)$$

$$|A_{V\text{th}}| \leq \min\left(\frac{R_L}{R_5}, g_m R_L\right)$$

The voltage gains in Eq. (14.15) are all much less than the amplification factor μ_f, so neglecting r_o in the small-signal model of Fig. 14.8 is a valid simplification.

Including an unbypassed resistor R_5 in the C-E/C-S amplifiers reduces the gain below the $g_m R_L$ limit, but this loss of gain is actually a tradeoff for a number of benefits. As noted, the voltage gain can be made substantially independent of device parameter variations, and as we demonstrate next, the input and output resistances and input signal range can all be increased significantly.

> **EXERCISE:** Evaluate $-g_m R_L$ and $-R_L/R_5$ for the C-E and C-S amplifiers in Fig. 14.5, and compare the magnitudes to the exact calculations in Example 14.1.
>
> **ANSWERS:** -176, -6.00; -8.84, -9.00; $5.71 < 6.00$; $4.46 < 8.84$

Input Resistance

An expression for the resistance looking into the base of the transistor can be formulated from Fig. 14.9 in a manner identical to that used to develop Eq. (14.7). The voltage applied to the base node is written in terms of the current entering the transistor:

$$\mathbf{v_x} = \mathbf{i_x} r_\pi + (\beta_o + 1)\mathbf{i_x} R_5 = \mathbf{i_x}[r_\pi + (\beta_o + 1)R_5] \tag{14.16}$$

and

$$R_{IN}^{CE} = \frac{\mathbf{v_x}}{\mathbf{i_x}} = r_\pi + (\beta_o + 1)R_5 \tag{14.17a}$$

which can also be written for $\beta_o \gg 1$ as

$$R_{IN}^{CE} \approx r_\pi(1 + g_m R_5) \tag{14.17b}$$

The **input resistance** to the common-emitter amplifier is equal to the transistor input resistance r_π plus the resistor in the emitter amplified by the base-to-emitter current gain $(\beta_o + 1)$. For the BJT, the emitter resistor R_5 can be used to significantly increase R_{IN}.

For the FET case, both r_π and β_o are infinite, so the input resistance for this case is independent of R_5 and given by

$$R_{IN}^{CS} = \infty \tag{14.18}$$

It is instructive to rederive the expression for the output voltage v_o of the C-E amplifier using the input resistance expression in Eq. (14.17). Referring back to Fig. 14.8, we see that the current i that enters the base from the Thévenin source v_{th} is equal to the voltage v_{th} divided by the total resistance in series with the source, $R_{th} + R_{IN}^{CE}$:

$$\mathbf{i} = \frac{\mathbf{v_{th}}}{R_{th} + R_{IN}^{CE}} = \frac{\mathbf{v_{th}}}{R_{th} + r_\pi + (\beta_o + 1)R_5} \tag{14.19}$$

The current i is then amplified by the current gain β_o and develops the output voltage v_o across load resistor R_L:

$$\mathbf{v_o} = -\mathbf{i}\beta_o R_L = \mathbf{v_{th}}\frac{-\beta_o R_L}{R_{th} + R_{IN}^{CE}} = -\mathbf{v_{th}}\frac{\beta_o R_L}{R_{th} + r_\pi + (\beta_o + 1)R_5} \tag{14.20}$$

Dividing by $\mathbf{v_{th}}$ yields the voltage gain expression in Eq. (14.8).

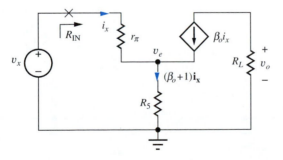

Figure 14.9 Input resistance of the common-emitter amplifier.

EXERCISE: Calculate R_{IN} for the C-E and C-S amplifiers in Fig. 14.5. How does R_{IN}^{CE} compare to r_π?

ANSWERS: 313 k$\Omega \approx \beta_o R_5$, ∞; $R_{IN}^{CE} \gg r_\pi$

> **EXERCISE:** Draw the small-signal model used to calculate the input resistance for the common-source amplifier. Calculate R_{IN} directly and verify the result given in Eq. (14.18).

Output Resistance

Calculation of **output resistance** begins with the simplified small-signal model in Fig. 14.10(b). R_{OUT} equals the ratio of $\mathbf{v_x}$ to $\mathbf{i_x}$, where $\mathbf{i_x}$ represents the current through the dependent source:

$$\mathbf{i_x} = \beta_o \mathbf{i} \tag{14.21}$$

To find $\mathbf{i}$, we write an expression for $\mathbf{v_e}$:

$$\mathbf{v_e} = (\beta_o + 1)\mathbf{i}R_5 \tag{14.22}$$

and realize that the current $\mathbf{i}$ can also be written directly in terms of $\mathbf{v_e}$:

$$\mathbf{i} = -\frac{\mathbf{v_e}}{R_{th} + r_\pi} \tag{14.23}$$

Combining Eqs. (14.22) and (14.23) yields Eq. (14.24):

$$\mathbf{v_e}\left[1 + \frac{(\beta_o + 1)R_5}{r_\pi + R_{th}}\right] = 0 \quad \text{and} \quad \mathbf{v_e} = 0 \tag{14.24}$$

Because $\mathbf{v_e} = 0$, Eq. (14.23) requires that $\mathbf{i}$ equal zero as well. Hence, $\mathbf{i_x} = 0$, and the output resistance of this circuit is infinite!

On the surface, this result may seem acceptable. However, a red flag should go up. We know from Chapter 13 that $R_{OUT} = r_o$ when $R_5 = 0$, not infinity. We must be suspicious of the result in Eq. (14.24) because it does not approach the correct limit as $R_5 \to 0$. Using the simplified circuit model in Fig. 14.10(b), in which r_o is neglected, has led to an unreasonable result.

We improve our analysis by moving to the next level of model complexity, as shown in Fig. 14.11. For this analysis, the circuit is driven by the test current i_x, and the voltage v_x must be determined in order to find R_{OUT}.[1]

Writing an equation around loop 1 and applying KCL at the output node,

$$\mathbf{v_x} = \mathbf{v_r} + \mathbf{v_e} = (\mathbf{i_x} - \beta_o\mathbf{i})r_o + \mathbf{v_e} \tag{14.25}$$

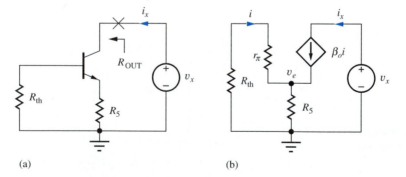

Figure 14.10 Circuits for calculating output resistance of the C-E amplifier.

(a)   (b)

---

[1] The following sequence of equations has been developed by the author as an "easy" way to derive this result; this approach is not expected to be obvious. Alternatively, the circuit in Fig. 14.11 can be formulated as a two-node problem by combining R_{th} and r_π and analyzed directly using nodal analysis (see Prob. 14.11).

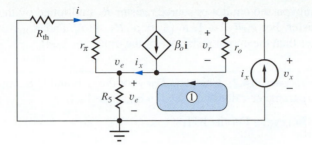

Figure 14.11 Output resistance of the C-E amplifier with r_o included.

The current i_x is forced through the parallel combination of $(R_{th} + r_\pi)$ and R_5, so that v_e can be expressed as

$$\mathbf{v_e} = \mathbf{i_x}[(R_{th} + r_\pi)\|R_5] = \mathbf{i_x}\frac{(R_{th} + r_\pi)R_5}{R_{th} + r_\pi + R_5} \tag{14.26}$$

At the emitter node, current division can be used to find $\mathbf{i}$ in terms of $\mathbf{i_x}$:

$$\mathbf{i} = -\mathbf{i_x}\frac{R_5}{R_{th} + r_\pi + R_5} \tag{14.27}$$

Combining Eqs. (14.25) through (14.27) yields a somewhat messy expression for the output resistance of the C-E amplifier:

$$R_{OUT} = r_o\left(1 + \frac{\beta_o R_5}{R_{th} + r_\pi + R_5}\right) + (R_{th} + r_\pi)\|R_5 \tag{14.28}$$

To help simplify Eq. (14.28), it is useful to factor r_π out of the numerator and denominator of the second term in parentheses:

$$R_{OUT} = r_o\left(1 + \frac{g_m R_5}{1 + \dfrac{R_{th} + R_5}{r_\pi}}\right) + (R_{th} + r_\pi)\|R_5 \tag{14.29}$$

The last term in Eq. (14.29) cannot exceed R_5, but we know from Chapter 13 that r_o is much larger than the external bias resistor R_5, and neglecting the third term relative to r_o yields

$$R_{OUT} \approx r_o\left(1 + \frac{g_m R_5}{1 + \dfrac{R_{th} + R_5}{r_\pi}}\right) = r_o\left(1 + \frac{\beta_o R_5}{R_{th} + r_\pi + R_5}\right) \tag{14.30}$$

If we now assume that $r_\pi \gg (R_{th} + R_5)$, we achieve the basic result that should be remembered:

$$R_{OUT} \approx r_o(1 + g_m R_5) = r_o + \mu_f R_5 \approx \mu_f R_5 \qquad \text{for } g_m R_5 \gg 1 \tag{14.31}$$

Note that the assumption that leads from Eq. (14.30) to Eq. (14.31) is exact for the FET case in which $r_\pi \to \infty$. Note as well that Eqs. (14.30) and (14.31) simplify to the expected result when $R_5 = 0$—that is, when $R_{OUT} = r_o$. Now we can feel comfortable that our level of modeling is sufficient to produce a meaningful result.

Equation (14.31) tells us that the output resistance of both the common-emitter and common-source amplifiers is equal to the output resistance r_o of the transistor itself plus the unbypassed emitter or source resistor R_5 multiplied by the amplification factor of the transistor. For $g_m R_5 \gg 1$, $R_{\text{OUT}} \approx \mu_f R_5 \gg r_o$, and R_{OUT} can be designed to be much greater than the output resistance of the transistor itself.

EXAMPLE 14.2: Calculate R_{OUT} for the C-E and C-S amplifiers in Fig. 14.5. Use the parameter values tabulated in Example 14.1.

SOLUTION: For the BJT,

$$R_{\text{OUT}} \approx r_o \left[1 + \frac{g_m R_5}{1 + \dfrac{R_{\text{th}} + R_5}{r_\pi}} \right]$$

$$\approx 219 \text{ k}\Omega \left[1 + \frac{9.8 \times 10^{-3} \text{ S}(3 \times 10^3 \ \Omega)}{1 + \dfrac{1.96 \times 10^3 \ \Omega + 3 \times 10^3 \ \Omega}{1.02 \times 10^4 \ \Omega}} \right] = 4.55 \text{ M}\Omega$$

For the MOSFET,

$$R_{\text{OUT}} \approx r_o [1 + g_m R_5]$$

$$\approx 223 \text{ k}\Omega [1 + 4.91 \times 10^{-4} \times 2 \times 10^3] = 442 \text{ k}\Omega$$

DISCUSSION: Note that the estimate of R_{OUT} for the BJT case,

$$R_{\text{OUT}}^{CE} \approx \mu_f R_5 = 6.44 \text{ M}\Omega$$

is somewhat high because the denominator in Eq. (14.30) is greater than 1, and that for the MOSFET,

$$R_{\text{OUT}}^{CS} \approx \mu_f R_5 = 219 \text{ k}\Omega$$

is too low because $g_m R_5 \gg 1$ is not satisfied. The much lower value of μ_f for the FET causes $R_{\text{OUT}}^{CS} \ll R_{\text{OUT}}^{CE}$. ◆

EXERCISE: Draw the small-signal model for the common-source amplifier and directly derive the result in Eq. (14.31) for the case of the FET.

EXERCISE: Show that the maximum output resistance for the common-emitter amplifier is $R_{\text{OUT}} \approx (\beta_o + 1)r_o$ by taking the limit as $R_5 \to \infty$ in Eq. (14.30).

Increased Signal Range

An important additional benefit of adding resistor R_5 to the circuit is to increase the allowed size of the input signal v_{th}. For small-signal operation, the magnitude of the base-emitter voltage v_{be}, developed across r_π in the small-signal model, must be less than 5 mV (you may wish to review Sec. 13.5). This voltage can be found using the input current $\mathbf{i}$ from Eq. (14.19):

$$\mathbf{v_{be}} = \mathbf{i} r_\pi = \mathbf{v_{th}} \frac{r_\pi}{R_{\text{th}} + r_\pi + (\beta_o + 1)R_5} = \frac{\mathbf{v_{th}}}{1 + g_m R_5 + \dfrac{R_{\text{th}} + R_5}{r_\pi}} \qquad (14.32)$$

Requiring $|v_{be}|$ in Eq. (14.32) to be less than 5 mV gives

$$|v_{\text{th}}| \leq 0.005\left[1 + g_m R_5\left(1 + \frac{R_{\text{th}} + R_5}{\beta_o}\right)\right] \approx 0.005(1 + g_m R_5) \text{ V} \qquad (14.33)$$

If $g_m R_5 \gg 1$, then v_{th} can also be increased well beyond the 5-mV limit.

For the case of the FET, the magnitude of the gate-source voltage v_{gs} must be less than $0.2(V_{GS} - V_{TN})$, and the expression corresponding to Eq. (14.32) is

$$|v_{gs}| = \frac{|v_{\text{th}}|}{1 + g_m R_5} \leq 0.2(V_{GS} - V_{TN}) \qquad (14.34)$$

and

$$|v_{\text{th}}| \leq 0.2(V_{GS} - V_{TN})(1 + g_m R_5) \qquad (14.35)$$

The presence of R_5 also increases the permissible value of v_{th}.

> **EXERCISE:** What are the largest values of v_{th} and v_s that correspond to small-signal operation of the amplifiers in Fig. 14.5(a) and 14.5(b)?
>
> **ANSWERS:** 155 mV, 159 mV; 293 mV, 297 mV

Satisfying the Condition $g_m R_5 \gg 1$

Achieving the simplified gain expressions in Eq. (14.14) and the output resistance expression in Eq. (14.31) requires $g_m R_5 \gg 1$. This condition is desirable because it can be used to stabilize the amplifier voltage gain, to achieve high levels of input and output resistance, and to increase the input signal range. Let us explore the conditions required to satisfy $g_m R_5 \gg 1$ using the expressions for g_m of the BJT and MOSFET. For the BJT:

$$g_m R_5 = \frac{I_C R_5}{V_T} = \alpha_F \frac{I_E R_5}{V_T} \approx \frac{I_E R_5}{V_T} \qquad \frac{I_E R_5}{V_T} \gg 1 \text{ requires } I_E R_5 \gg V_T = 0.025 \text{ V}$$

$$(14.36)$$

and for the MOSFET:

$$g_m R_5 = \frac{I_{DS} R_5}{\dfrac{V_{GS} - V_{TN}}{2}} = \frac{2 I_{DS} R_5}{V_{GS} - V_{TN}} \qquad \frac{2 I_{DS} R_5}{V_{GS} - V_{TN}} \gg 1 \text{ requires } I_{DS} R_5 \gg \frac{V_{GS} - V_{TN}}{2}$$

For the bipolar transistor, $I_E R_5$ represents the dc voltage drop across emitter resistor R_5 and must be much greater than 25 mV—for example, it might be 250 mV, which is easily achieved. For the MOSFET, the voltage across the resistor in the source must be much greater than $V_{GS} - V_{TN}/2$. With careful design, this condition can be satisfied with $I_{DS} R_5$ equal to a few volts.

Current Gain

The **current gain** $A_{I\text{th}}$ is defined as the ratio of the current delivered to the load resistor R_L to the current being supplied from the Thévenin source. For the C-E amplifier in Fig. 14.12, the current in R_L is equal to i_{th} amplified by the current gain β_o and yielding a current gain equal to $-\beta_o$. For the FET, r_π is infinite, i_{th} is zero, and the current gain is infinite. Summarizing these results,

$$A_{I\text{th}}^{CE} = -\beta_o \qquad \text{and} \qquad A_{i\text{th}}^{CS} = \infty \qquad (14.37)$$

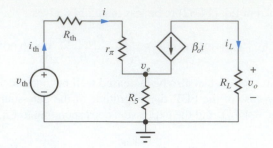

Figure 14.12 Circuit for calculating C-E/C-S current gain.

C-E/C-S Amplifier Summary

Table 14.1 summarizes the results derived thus far for the common-emitter and common-source amplifiers in Fig. 14.13. Note that the FET results can always be obtained from the BJT results by letting r_π and $\beta_o \to \infty$. The rule-of-thumb estimates for the $g_m R_L$ product (from Chapter 13) are included in the table.

T a b l e 14.1

Common-Emitter/Common-Source Amplifier Summary

	C-E Amplifier	**C-S Amplifier**
Voltage Gain $A_{V\text{th}} = \dfrac{v_o}{v_{\text{th}}}$ $\|A_{V\text{th}}\| \le \min\left(\dfrac{R_L}{R_5},\ g_m R_L\right)$	$-\dfrac{\beta_o R_L}{R_{\text{th}} + r_\pi + (\beta_o + 1)R_5}$ $\approx -\dfrac{g_m R_L}{1 + g_m R_5}$ $g_m R_L \approx 10 V_{CC}$	$-\dfrac{g_m R_L}{1 + g_m R_5} = -\dfrac{R_L}{1/g_m + R_5}$ $g_m R_L \approx \dfrac{V_{DD}}{V_{GS} - V_{TN}}$ $g_m R_L \approx V_{DD}$
Input Resistance	$r_\pi + (\beta_o + 1)R_5 \approx r_\pi(1 + g_m R_5)$	∞
Output Resistance	$r_o(1 + g_m R_5) = r_o + \mu_f R_5$	$r_o(1 + g_m R_5) = r_o + \mu_f R_5$
Input Signal Range	$\approx 0.005(1 + g_m R_5)$	$0.2(V_{GS} - V_{TN})(1 + g_m R_5)$
Current Gain	$-\beta_o$	∞

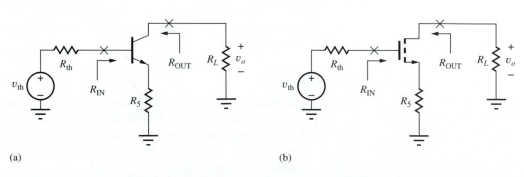

(a)　　　　　　　　　　　　(b)

Figure 14.13 (a) Common-emitter and (b) common-source amplifiers for use with Table 14.1.

The numeric results for the two specific amplifier cases are collected together in Table 14.2. The common-emitter and common-source amplifiers have similar voltage gains. The C-E amplifier approaches the R_L/R_5 limit (-6) more closely because $g_m R_5 = 29.4$ for the BJT case, but only 0.982 for the MOSFET. The C-S amplifier provides extremely high input resistance, but that of the BJT amplifier is also substantial due to the $\mu_f R_5$ term. The output resistance of the C-E amplifier is also much higher than the C-S amplifier because μ_f is much larger for the BJT than for the FET. The input signal levels have been increased above the $R_5 = 0$ case—again by a substantial amount in the BJT case. The current gains are identical to those of the individual transistors.

	T a b l e 14.2	
Common-Emitter/Common-Source Amplifier Comparison		
	C-E Amplifier	**C-S Amplifier**
Voltage Gain	-5.71	-4.46
Input Resistance	313 kΩ	∞
Output Resistance	4.55 MΩ	442 kΩ
Input Signal Range	159 mV	297 mV
Current Gain	-100	∞

14.3 FOLLOWER CIRCUITS—COMMON-COLLECTOR AND COMMON-DRAIN AMPLIFIERS

We now consider a second class of amplifiers, the common-collector (C-C) and common-drain (C-D) amplifiers, as represented by the ac equivalent circuits in Fig. 14.14. As in Sec. 14.2, the BJT circuit in Fig. 14.14(a) is analyzed first, and then the MOSFET circuit in Fig. 14.14(b) is treated as a special case with $r_\pi \to \infty$.

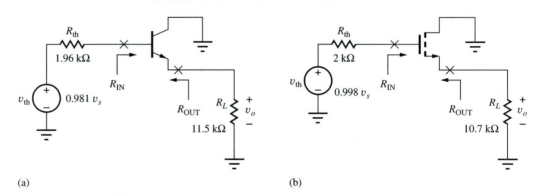

(a)   (b)

Figure 14.14 (a) ac Equivalent circuit for the C-C amplifier. (b) ac Equivalent circuit for the C-D amplifier.

Voltage Gain

The bipolar transistor in Fig. 14.14(a) is replaced by its small-signal model in Fig. 14.15 (r_o is again neglected). The output voltage v_o now appears across load resistor R_L connected

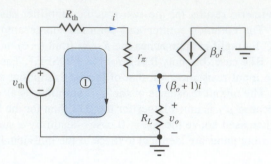

Figure   14.15 Small-signal model for the C-C amplifier.

to the emitter of the transistor and is equal to

$$\mathbf{v_o} = +(\beta_o + 1)\mathbf{i}R_L \tag{14.38}$$

Current i is found from an expression similar to Eq. (14.7):

$$\mathbf{v_{th}} = \mathbf{i}R_{th} + \mathbf{i}r_\pi + (\beta_o + 1)\mathbf{i}R_L = \mathbf{i}[R_{th} + r_\pi + (\beta_o + 1)R_L] \tag{14.39}$$

Combining Eqs. (14.38) and (14.39) yields an expression for the voltage gain of the C-C amplifier:

$$A_{Vth}^{CC} = +\frac{(\beta_o + 1)R_L}{R_{th} + r_\pi + (\beta_o + 1)R_L} = +\frac{g_m R_L}{\alpha_o + g_m\left(R_L + \dfrac{R_{th}}{\beta_o + 1}\right)} \approx \frac{g_m R_L}{1 + g_m R_L} \tag{14.40}$$

where the last approximation holds for large β_o. For $g_m R_L \gg 1$, which is usually the case,

$$A_{Vth}^{CC} \approx +1 \tag{14.41}$$

Letting $\beta_o \to \infty$ (and $\alpha_o \to 1$) in Eq. (14.40) yields the corresponding gain for the single FET amplifier:

$$A_{Vth}^{CD} = +\frac{g_m R_L}{1 + g_m R_L} \tag{14.42}$$

which again reduces to

$$A_{Vth}^{CD} \approx 1 \tag{14.43}$$

for $g_m R_L \gg 1$.

The C-C and C-D amplifiers both have a gain that approaches 1. That is, the output voltage follows the input voltage, and the C-C and C-D amplifiers are often called **emitter followers** and **source followers,** respectively. In most cases, the BJT does a better job of achieving $g_m R_L \gg 1$ than does the FET, and the BJT gain is closer to unity than that of the FET. However, in both cases the value of voltage gain typically falls in the range of

$$0.75 \le A_{Vth} \le 1 \tag{14.44}$$

Obviously, the gain in Eq. (14.43) is much less than the amplification factor μ_f, so neglecting r_o in the model of Fig. 14.15 is valid, unless the FET is operating at very high currents.

EXAMPLE 14.3: Calculate the gain of the C-C and C-D amplifiers using Eqs. (14.40) and (14.42) and the parameter values from Example 14.1.

SOLUTION: For the C-C amplifier,

$$A_{Vth}^{CC} = \frac{(\beta_o + 1)R_L}{R_{th} + r_\pi + (\beta_o + 1)R_L}$$

$$= \frac{101(1.15 \times 10^4 \ \Omega)}{1.96 \times 10^3 \ \Omega + 1.02 \times 10^4 \ \Omega + (101)1.15 \times 10^4 \ \Omega} = 0.990 \approx 1$$

For the C-D amplifier,

$$A_{Vth}^{CD} = -\frac{g_m R_L}{1 + g_m R_L}$$

$$= \frac{(4.91 \times 10^{-4} \ \text{S})(1.07 \times 10^4 \ \Omega)}{1 + (4.91 \times 10^{-4} \ \text{S})(1.07 \times 10^4 \ \Omega)} = 0.840$$

DISCUSSION: The C-C amplifier has a gain much closer to 1 because $g_m R_L$ is again much larger than it is for the C-D case.   ◆

EXERCISE: Compare the values of $g_m R_L$ for the C-C and C-D amplifiers in Example 14.3.

ANSWER: $113 \gg 5.25$

Follower Signal Range

Because the emitter- and source-follower circuits have a gain approaching unity, only a small portion of the input signal actually appears across the base-emitter or gate-source terminals. Thus these circuits can be used with relatively large input signals without violating their respective small-signal limits. Again, the voltage developed across r_π in the small-signal model must be less than 5 mV for small-signal operation of the BJT. An expression for v_{be} is found in a manner identical to that used to derive Eq. (14.32):

$$\mathbf{v_{be}} = \mathbf{i}r_\pi = \mathbf{v_{th}}\frac{r_\pi}{R_{th} + r_\pi + (\beta_o + 1)R_L} = \frac{\mathbf{v_{th}}}{1 + g_m R_L + \dfrac{R_{th} + R_L}{r_\pi}} \qquad (14.45)$$

Requiring the amplitude of voltage v_{be} to be less than 5 mV gives

$$|v_{th}| \leq 0.005 \ \text{V}\left[1 + g_m\left(R_L + \frac{R_{th} + R_L}{\beta_o}\right)\right] \approx 0.005(1 + g_m R_L) \ \text{V} \qquad (14.46)$$

for large β_o. Normally, $g_m R_L \gg 1$, and the magnitude of v_{th} can be increased well beyond the 5-mV limit.

For the case of the FET (letting $r_\pi \to \infty$), the corresponding expression becomes

$$|v_{gs}| = \frac{|v_{th}|}{1 + g_m R_L} \leq 0.2(V_{GS} - V_{TN}) \qquad (14.47)$$

and

$$|v_{th}| \leq 0.2(V_{GS} - V_{TN})(1 + g_m R_L) \qquad (14.48)$$

which also increases the permissible range for v_{th}.

EXERCISE: What are the largest values of v_{th} that correspond to small-signal operation of the amplifiers in Fig. 14.14?

ANSWERS: 0.575 V, 1.23 V

Input Resistance

The resistances looking into either of the transistors in Fig. 14.14 are exactly the same as for the C-E or C-S amplifiers. In the small-signal model in Fig. 14.16, R_{IN} is equal to r_π plus the amplified reflection of R_L for the BJT case, and equal to ∞ for the FET.

$$R_{IN}^{CC} = \frac{\mathbf{v_x}}{\mathbf{i}} = r_\pi + (\beta_o + 1)R_L \qquad \text{and} \qquad R_{IN}^{CD} = \infty \qquad (14.49)$$

EXERCISE: Calculate the input resistances of the C-C and C-D amplifiers above.

ANSWERS: 1.17 MΩ, ∞

EXERCISE: Derive the expression for the input resistance of the C-C amplifier including r_o. What is the upper bound of this expression for very large R_L?

ANSWERS: $R_{IN}^{CC} = r_\pi + (\beta_o + 1)(R_L \| r_o); \approx \beta_o r_o$

As for the C-E case, the input resistance expression can used to find the voltage gain. In Fig. 14.15, the current i that enters the base can be written as

$$\mathbf{i} = \frac{\mathbf{v_{th}}}{R_{th} + R_{IN}^{CE}} = \frac{\mathbf{v_{th}}}{R_{th} + r_\pi + (\beta_o + 1)R_L} \qquad (14.50)$$

This input current is amplified by the current gain $(\beta_o + 1)$, and the output voltage developed across the load resistor is

$$\mathbf{v_o} = +(\beta_o + 1)\mathbf{i}R_L = +\frac{\mathbf{v_{th}}}{R_{th} + r_\pi + (\beta_o + 1)R_L}(\beta_o + 1)R_L \qquad (14.51)$$

Dividing by $\mathbf{v_{th}}$ yields the voltage gain expression in Eq. (14.40).

Output Resistance

The resistance looking into the output of the C-C circuit can be calculated based on the circuit in Fig. 14.17, in which the test source v_x is applied directly to the emitter terminal. Using KCL at the emitter node yields

$$\mathbf{i_x} = -\mathbf{i} - \beta_o\mathbf{i} = \frac{\mathbf{v_x}}{r_\pi + R_{th}} - \beta_o\mathbf{i} = \frac{\mathbf{v_x}}{r_\pi + R_{th}} - \beta_o\left(-\frac{\mathbf{v_x}}{r_\pi + R_{th}}\right) \qquad (14.52)$$

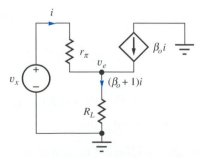

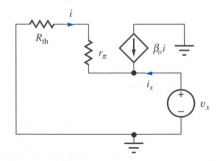

Figure 14.16 Input resistance for the C-C amplifier.

Figure 14.17 C-C/C-D output resistance calculation.

Collecting terms and rearranging gives

$$R_{OUT}^{CC} = \frac{r_\pi + R_{th}}{\beta_o + 1} \tag{14.53}$$

Expanding Eq. (14.53) yields

$$R_{OUT}^{CC} = \frac{r_\pi}{\beta_o + 1} + \frac{R_{th}}{\beta_o + 1} = \frac{\alpha_o}{g_m} + \frac{R_{th}}{\beta_o + 1} \approx \frac{1}{g_m} + \frac{R_{th}}{\beta_o + 1} \tag{14.54}$$

Because the current gain is infinite for the FET,

$$R_{OUT}^{CD} = \frac{1}{g_m} \tag{14.55}$$

From Eqs. (14.54) and (14.55), it can be observed that the output resistance is primarily determined by the reciprocal of the transconductance of the transistor. This is an extremely important result to remember. For the BJT case, an additional term is added, but it is usually small, unless R_{th} is very large. The value of R_{OUT} for the C-C and C-D circuits can be quite low. For instance, at a current of 5 mA, the g_m of the bipolar transistor is $40 \times 0.005 = 0.2$ S, and $1/g_m$ is only 5 Ω.

EXAMPLE 14.4:   Calculate the output resistances of the C-C and C-D amplifiers above using the parameter values from Example 14.1.

SOLUTION: For the C-C amplifier,

$$R_{OUT}^{CC} = \frac{\alpha_o}{g_m} + \frac{R_{th}}{\beta_o + 1}$$

$$= \frac{0.99}{9.8 \times 10^{-3} \text{ S}} + \frac{1.96 \times 10^3 \, \Omega}{101} = (101 + 19.4) \, \Omega = 120 \, \Omega$$

and for the C-D case,

$$R_{OUT}^{CD} = \frac{1}{g_m} = \frac{1}{4.91 \times 10^{-4} \text{ S}} = 2.04 \text{ k}\Omega$$

DISCUSSION: The output resistance of the C-C amplifier is much lower because of its larger transconductance at the given Q-point. Note that the term due to R_{th} increases the output resistance of the C-C amplifier by 19 percent in this example.   ◆

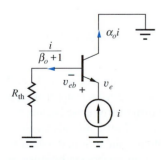

Figure 14.18 Circuit to aid in interpreting Eq. (14.56).

Let us further interpret the two terms in Eq. (14.54) by injecting a current into the emitter of the BJT, as in Fig. 14.18. Multiplying **i** by the input resistance gives the voltage that must be developed at the emitter:

$$\mathbf{v_e} = \frac{\alpha_o \mathbf{i}}{g_m} + \frac{\mathbf{i}}{\beta_o + 1} R_{th} \tag{14.56}$$

Current ($\alpha_o\mathbf{i}$) comes out of the collector and must be supported by the emitter-base voltage $\mathbf{v_{eb}} = \alpha_o\mathbf{i}/g_m$, represented by the first term in Eq. (14.56). Base current $\mathbf{i_b} = -\mathbf{i}/\beta_o + 1$ creates a voltage drop in resistance R_{th} and yields the second term. In the FET case, only the first term exists because $\alpha_o = 1$ and $\beta_o = \infty$ (that is, $i_g = 0$).

EXERCISE: Drive the emitter node in Fig. 14.17 with a test current source i_x, and verify the output resistance results in Eq. (14.54).

Current Gain

Current gain A_{Ith} is the ratio of the current delivered to the load element to the current being supplied from the Thévenin source. In Fig. 14.19, the current i_{th} plus its amplified replica ($\beta_o i_{th}$) are combined in load resistor R_L, yielding a current gain equal to ($\beta_o + 1$). For the FET, r_π is infinite, i_{th} is zero, and the current gain is infinite. Thus, for the C-C/C-D amplifiers,

$$A_{Ith}^{CC} = \frac{i_l}{i_{th}} = \beta_o + 1 \quad \text{and} \quad A_{Ith}^{CD} = \infty \tag{14.57}$$

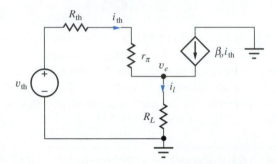

Figure 14.19 Circuit for calculating C-C/C-D current gain.

C-C/C-D Amplifier Summary

Table 14.3 summarizes the results that have been derived for the common-collector and common-drain amplifier in Fig. 14.20. As before, the FET results in the table can always be obtained from the BJT results by letting r_π and $\beta_o \to \infty$. The numeric results from the two specific amplifiers in Fig. 14.14 are gathered together in Table 14.4.

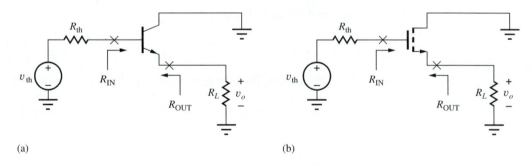

(a)   (b)

Figure 14.20 (a) Common-collector and (b) common-drain amplifiers for use with Table 14.3.

In Tables 14.3 and 14.4, the similarity between the characteristics of the C-C and C-D amplifiers should be readily apparent. Both amplifiers provide a gain approaching unity, a high input resistance, and a low output resistance. The differences arise because of the finite value of r_π and β_o of the BJT. The FET can more easily achieve very high values of input resistance because of the infinite resistance looking into its gate terminal, whereas the C-C amplifier can more easily reach very low levels of output resistance because of its higher transconductance for a given operating current. Both amplifiers can be designed to handle relatively large input signal levels. The current gain of the FET is inherently infinite, whereas that of the BJT is limited by its finite value of β_o.

	C-C Amplifier	C-D Amplifier
Table 14.3		
Common-Collector/Common-Drain Amplifier Summary		

	C-C Amplifier	**C-D Amplifier**
Voltage Gain $A_{Vth} = \dfrac{v_o}{v_{th}}$	$\dfrac{(\beta_o + 1)R_L}{R_{th} + r_\pi + (\beta_o + 1)R_L}$ $\approx \dfrac{g_m R_L}{1 + g_m R_L} \approx +1$	$\dfrac{g_m R_L}{1 + g_m R_L} = \dfrac{R_L}{(1/g_m) + R_L}$ $\approx +1$
Input Resistance	$r_\pi + (\beta_o + 1)R_L$	∞
Output Resistance	$\dfrac{\alpha_o}{g_m} + \dfrac{R_{th}}{\beta_o + 1} \approx \dfrac{1}{g_m}$	$\dfrac{1}{g_m}$
Input Signal Range	$\approx 0.005(1 + g_m R_L)$	$0.2(V_{GS} - V_{TN})(1 + g_m R_L)$
Current Gain	$\beta_o + 1$	∞

Table 14.4

Common-Collector/Common-Drain Amplifier Comparison

	C-C Amplifier	**C-D Amplifier**
Voltage Gain	0.980	0.840
Input Resistance	1.17 MΩ	∞
Output Resistance	121 Ω	2.04 kΩ
Input Signal Range	0.575 V	1.23 V
Current Gain	101	∞

14.4 NONINVERTING AMPLIFIERS—COMMON-BASE AND COMMON-GATE CIRCUITS

The final class of amplifiers to be analyzed consists of the common-base and common-gate amplifiers represented by the two ac equivalent circuits in Fig. 14.21. As in Secs. 14.2 and 14.3, we analyze the BJT circuit first and treat the MOSFET in Fig. 14.21(b) as a special case of Fig. 14.21(a).

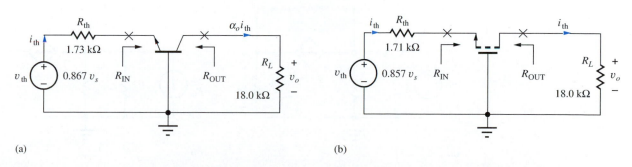

(a) (b)

Figure 14.21 ac Equivalent circuits for the (a) C-B and (b) C-G amplifiers.

Voltage Gain

The bipolar transistor is replaced by its small-signal model in Fig. 14.22(a). Because the amplifier has a resistor load, the circuit model is simplified by neglecting r_o, as redrawn in Fig. 14.22(b). In addition, the polarities of v_{be} and the dependent current source $g_m v_{be}$ have both been reversed, and the signal source has been transformed to its Norton equivalent circuit.

For the common-base circuit, output voltage v_o appears at the collector across resistor R_L and is equal to

$$\mathbf{v_o} = +g_m \mathbf{v_{eb}} R_L \tag{14.58}$$

The voltage $\mathbf{v_{eb}}$ can be found using KCL at the emitter node:

$$\frac{\mathbf{v_{th}}}{R_{th}} - g_m \mathbf{v_{eb}} = \frac{\mathbf{v_{eb}}}{R_{th}} + \frac{\mathbf{v_{eb}}}{r_\pi} \tag{14.59}$$

Solving for $\mathbf{v_{eb}}$ yields

$$\mathbf{v_{eb}} = \mathbf{v_{th}} \left(\frac{1}{1 + \dfrac{R_{th}}{r_\pi} + g_m R_{th}} \right) = \mathbf{v_{th}} \left(\frac{r_\pi}{r_\pi + (\beta_o + 1)R_{th}} \right) \tag{14.60}$$

Combining Eqs. (14.58) and (14.60) produces an expression for the voltage gain of the common-base amplifier:

$$A_{V\text{th}}^{CB} = +\frac{\beta_o R_L}{r_\pi + (\beta_o + 1)R_{th}} \tag{14.61}$$

Dividing the numerator and denominator by r_π and recognizing that $\alpha_o = \beta_o / \beta_o + 1$ yields

$$A_{V\text{th}}^{CB} = +\frac{g_m R_L}{1 + \dfrac{g_m R_{th}}{\alpha_o}} \approx +\frac{g_m R_L}{1 + g_m R_{th}} \tag{14.62}$$

for $\alpha_o \approx 1$. For the FET, $\alpha_o = 1$, and the final result in Eq. (14.62) is exact:

$$A_{V\text{th}}^{CG} = +\frac{g_m R_L}{1 + g_m R_{th}} \tag{14.63}$$

Note that the gain expressions in Eqs. (14.62) and (14.63) are positive, indicating that the output signal is in phase with the input signal. Thus, the C-B and C-G amplifiers are classified as noninverting amplifiers.

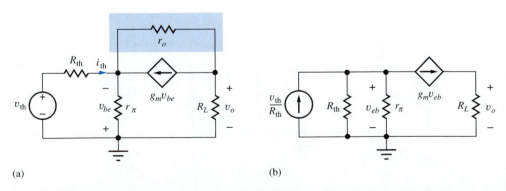

(a)   (b)

Figure 14.22 (a) Small-signal model for the common-base amplifier. (b) Simplified model neglecting r_o and reversing the direction of the controlled source.

EXAMPLE 14.5: Calculate the gain of the C-B and C-G amplifiers using Eqs. (14.62) and (14.63) and the parameters in Example 14.1.

SOLUTION: For the C-B amplifier,

$$A_{V\text{th}}^{CB} = \frac{g_m R_L}{1 + \dfrac{g_m R_{\text{th}}}{\alpha_o}} = \frac{9.80 \times 10^{-3}\ \text{S}(1.80 \times 10^4\ \Omega)}{1 + \dfrac{9.80 \times 10^{-3}\ \text{S}(1.73 \times 10^3\ \Omega)}{0.990}} = +9.73$$

For the C-G amplifier,

$$A_{V\text{th}}^{CG} = \frac{g_m R_L}{1 + g_m R_{\text{th}}} = \frac{4.91 \times 10^{-4}\ \text{S}(1.80 \times 10^4\ \Omega)}{1 + (4.91 \times 10^{-4}\ \text{S})(1.80 \times 10^4\ \Omega)} = +4.80$$

◆

EXERCISE: Calculate the gain of the C-B amplifier in Example 14.5, assuming $\alpha_o = 1$. How much error is introduced by this approximation?

ANSWERS: 9.83, 1.03 percent

Important Limits

As for the C-E/C-S amplifiers, two limiting conditions are of particular importance (see Prob. 14.36). The upper bound occurs for $g_m R_{\text{th}} \ll 1$, for which Eqs. (14.61) and (14.62) reduce to

$$A_{V\text{th}}^{CB} \approx +g_m R_L \qquad \text{and} \qquad A_{V\text{th}}^{CG} \approx +g_m R_L \qquad (14.64)$$

Equation (14.64) represents the upper bound on the gain of the C-B/C-G amplifiers and is the same as that for the C-E/C-S amplifiers, except the gain is noninverting.

However, if $g_m R_{\text{th}} \gg 1$, then Eqs. (14.62) and (14.63) both reduce to

$$A_{V\text{th}}^{CB} = A_{V\text{th}}^{CG} \approx +\frac{R_L}{R_{\text{th}}} \qquad (14.65)$$

For this case, the C-B and C-G amplifiers both have a gain that approaches the ratio of the value of the load resistor to that of the Thévenin source resistance and is independent of the transistor parameters. For both the common-base and common-gate amplifiers, the voltage gain is limited by

$$A_{V\text{th}} \leq \min\left(\frac{R_L}{R_{\text{th}}},\ g_m R_L\right) \qquad (14.66)$$

For resistor loads, the limit in Eq. (14.66) is much less than the amplification factor μ_f, so neglecting r_o is valid.

EXERCISE: Compare the gains of the C-B and C-G amplifiers calculated in Example 14.5 to the two limits just developed.

ANSWERS: $9.73 < 10.4 < 176$; $4.80 < 8.84 < 10.5$

Input Signal Range

The relationship between v_{eb} and v_{th}, which was found in Eq. (14.60), can be rearranged to give

$$v_{\text{th}} = v_{eb}\left(1 + g_m R_{\text{th}} + \frac{R_{\text{th}}}{r_\pi}\right) \qquad (14.67)$$

and the small-signal limit requires

$$|v_{th}| \leq 0.005 \left(1 + g_m R_{th} + \frac{R_{th}}{r_\pi}\right) \text{ V} \qquad (14.68)$$

For the FET case, letting $r_\pi \to \infty$ and replacing $\mathbf{v_{eb}}$ by $\mathbf{v_{sg}}$ yields

$$\mathbf{v_{th}} = \mathbf{v_{sg}}(1 + g_m R_{th}) \qquad (14.69)$$

and

$$|v_{th}| \leq 0.2(V_{GS} - V_{TN})(1 + g_m R_{th}) \qquad (14.70)$$

The relative size of R_{th} and g_m will determine the signal-handling limits.

> **EXERCISE:** Calculate the maximum values of v_{th} for the C-B and C-G amplifiers in Fig. 14.21 based on Eqs. (14.68) and (14.70).
>
> **ANSWERS:** 90.6 mV, 362 mV

Input Resistance

To determine the input resistance of the common-base amplifier, a test voltage is applied directly to the emitter of the BJT in Fig. 14.23(a). The small-signal model is included in Fig. 14.23(b), where r_o is neglected. An expression for the input resistance is easily found by applying KCL at the emitter:

$$\mathbf{i_x} + g_m \mathbf{v_{be}} = -\frac{\mathbf{v_{be}}}{r_\pi} \qquad (14.71)$$

But, $\mathbf{v_{be}} = -\mathbf{v_x}$, and

$$\mathbf{i_x} - g_m \mathbf{v_x} = \frac{\mathbf{v_x}}{r_\pi} \qquad (14.72)$$

Solving for $\mathbf{v_x}$ in terms of $\mathbf{i_x}$ yields

$$\mathbf{v_x} = \frac{\mathbf{i_x}}{g_m + \dfrac{1}{r_\pi}} \qquad (14.73)$$

Multiplying numerator and denominator by r_π and simplifying yields:

$$R_{IN}^{CB} = \frac{r_\pi}{\beta_o + 1} = \frac{\beta_o}{\beta_o + 1}\frac{r_\pi}{\beta_o} = \frac{\alpha_o}{g_m} \approx \frac{1}{g_m} \qquad (14.74)$$

The corresponding expression for the FET is obtained by recognizing that $\alpha_o = 1$; the right-hand side of Eq. (14.74) represents an equality for the FET. Thus,

$$R_{IN}^{CB} \approx \frac{1}{g_m} \qquad \text{and} \qquad R_{IN}^{CG} = \frac{1}{g_m} \qquad (14.75)$$

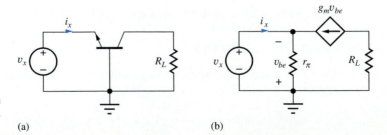

Figure 14.23 Input resistance of the common-base amplifier.

(a)   (b)

At this point, it is important to observe that input resistances for the C-B/C-G amplifiers are very similar to the output resistances found for the C-C/C-D amplifiers. Figure 14.23(a) is redrawn in Fig. (b) to show its similarity to Fig. 14.17, except R_{th}^{CC} is missing from Fig. 14.24(a). The load resistance R_L shown in Fig. 14.24(a) is isolated from v_x by the dependent current source [see Fig. 14.23(b)], so it does not influence the resistance calculation. Thus, the input resistance of the C-B/C-G amplifiers is equivalent to the output resistance of the C-C/C-D amplifiers with R_{th}^{CC} set to zero.

As has been done with the other amplifier configurations, the voltage gain can be calculated using input resistance information. Referring back to Fig. 14.21(a),

$$\mathbf{i_{th}} = \frac{\mathbf{v_{th}}}{R_{\text{th}} + R_{\text{IN}}^{CB}} \tag{14.76}$$

This current is amplified by the common-base current gain α_o and generates the output voltage v_o:

$$\mathbf{v_o} = \alpha_o \mathbf{i_{th}} R_L = \alpha_o \frac{\mathbf{v_{th}}}{R_{\text{th}} + R_{\text{IN}}^{CB}} R_L \tag{14.77}$$

Using Eq. (14.71), assuming $\alpha_o \approx 1$ and dividing by $\mathbf{v_{th}}$ yields the gain

$$A_{V\text{th}} \approx \frac{R_L}{R_{\text{th}} + \dfrac{1}{g_m}} = \frac{g_m R_L}{1 + g_m R_{\text{th}}} \tag{14.78}$$

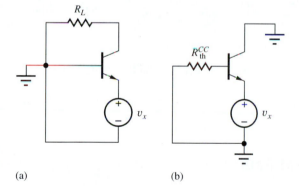

(a)   (b)

Figure 14.24 Rearrangement of (a) the C-B amplifier and (b) the C-C amplifier.

EXERCISE: Calculate the input resistances of the C-B and C-G amplifiers. Compare these values to R_{OUT}^{CC} and R_{OUT}^{CD}.

ANSWERS: 102 Ω; 2.04 kΩ; 102 Ω ≈ 121 Ω; 2.04 kΩ = 2.04 kΩ

Output Resistance

The output resistance of the C-B/C-G amplifiers can be calculated for the circuit in Fig. 14.25, in which a test source v_x is applied to the collector terminal. The desired resistance is that looking into the collector with the base grounded and resistor R_{th} in the emitter. If the circuit is redrawn as shown in Fig. 14.25(b), we should recognize it to be the same as the C-E circuit in Fig. 14.10, repeated in Fig. 14.25(c), except that the resistance R_{th}^{CE} in the base is zero and resistor R_5 has been relabeled R_{th}.

Thus, the output resistance for the C-B amplifier can be found using the results from the common-emitter amplifier, Eq. (14.30), without further detailed calculation, by

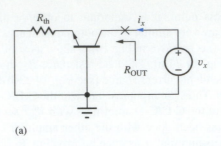

(a)

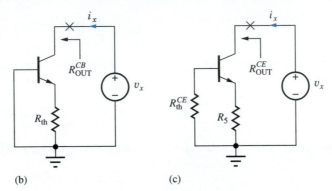

Figure 14.25 (a) Circuit for calculating the C-B output resistance. (b) Redrawn version of the circuit in (a). (c) Circuit used in common-emitter analysis (see Fig. 14.10).

(b)   (c)

substituting $R_{th}^{CE} = 0$ and replacing R_5 with R_{th}:

$$R_{OUT}^{CE} = r_o\left(1 + \frac{\beta_o R_5}{R_{th}^{CE} + r_\pi + R_5}\right) \quad \text{and} \quad R_{OUT}^{CB} = r_o\left(1 + \frac{\beta_o R_{th}}{R_{th} + r_\pi}\right) \quad (14.79)$$

For $r_\pi \gg R_{th}$,

$$R_{OUT}^{CB} = R_{OUT}^{CG} \approx r_o(1 + g_m R_{th}) = r_o + \mu_f R_{th} \approx \mu_f R_{th} \quad (14.80)$$

EXERCISE: Calculate the output resistances of the C-B and C-G amplifiers.

ANSWERS: 3.93 MΩ; 410 kΩ

Current Gain

The current gain A_{Ith} is the ratio of the current through the load resistor to the current being supplied from the Thévenin source. If a current i_{th} is injected into the emitter of the C-B transistor in Fig. 14.26, then the current $i_l = \alpha_o i_{th}$ comes out of the collector. Thus the common-base current gain is simply α_o.

For the FET, α_o is exactly 1, and we have

$$A_{Ith}^{CB} = \frac{\mathbf{i_l}}{\mathbf{i_{th}}} = +\alpha_o \approx +1 \quad \text{and} \quad A_{Ith}^{CG} = +1 \quad (14.81)$$

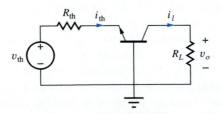

Figure 14.26 Common-base current gain.

C-B/C-G Amplifier Summary

Table 14.5 summarizes the results derived for the common-base and common-gate amplifiers in Fig. 14.27, and the numeric results for the specific amplifiers in Fig. 14.21 are collected together in Table 14.6. Table 14.5 again displays the symmetry between the various characteristics of the common-base and common-gate amplifiers. The voltage gain

	T a b l e 14.5	
	Common-Base/Common-Gate Amplifier Summary	
	C-B Amplifier	**C-G Amplifier**
Voltage Gain $A_{V\text{th}} = \dfrac{v_o}{v_{\text{th}}}$ $A_{V\text{th}} \leq \min\left(\dfrac{R_L}{R_{\text{th}}},\, g_m R_L\right)$	$+\dfrac{R_L}{(1/g_m)+(R_{\text{th}}/\alpha_0)}$ $\approx \dfrac{g_m R_L}{1+g_m R_{\text{th}}}$ $g_m R_L \approx 10 V_{CC}$	$\dfrac{g_m R_L}{1+g_m R_{\text{th}}}$ $g_m R_L \approx \dfrac{V_{DD}}{V_{GS}-V_{TN}}$ $g_m R_L \approx V_{DD}$
Input Resistance	$\dfrac{\alpha_o}{g_m} \approx \dfrac{1}{g_m}$	$\dfrac{1}{g_m}$
Output Resistance	$r_o(1+g_m R_{\text{th}}) = r_o + \mu_f R_{\text{th}}$	$r_o(1+g_m R_{\text{th}}) = r_o + \mu_f R_{\text{th}}$
Input Signal Range	$0.005(1+g_m R_{\text{th}})$	$0.2(V_{GS}-V_{TN})(1+g_m R_{\text{th}})$
Current Gain	$\alpha_o \approx +1$	$+1$

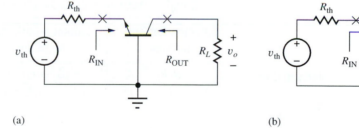

Figure 14.27 Circuits for use with summary Table 14.5. (a) Common-base amplifier, (b) common-gate amplifier.

	T a b l e 14.6	
	Common-Base/Common-Gate Amplifier Comparison	
	C-B Amplifier	**C-G Amplifier**
Voltage Gain	+10.4	+4.80
Input Resistance	102 Ω	2.04 kΩ
Output Resistance	3.93 MΩ	410 kΩ
Input Signal Range	90.6 mV	362 mV
Current Gain	1	1

and current gain are very similar. Numeric differences occur because of differences in the parameter values of the BJT and FET at similar operating points.

Both amplifiers can provide significant voltage gain, low input resistance, and high output resistance. The higher amplification factor of the BJT gives it an advantage in achieving high output resistance; the C-B amplifier can more easily reach very low levels of input resistance because of the BJT's higher transconductance for a given operating current. The FET amplifier can inherently handle larger signal levels.

14.5 AMPLIFIER PROTOTYPE REVIEW AND COMPARISON

Sections 14.2 to 14.4 compared the three individual classes of BJT and FET circuits: the C-E/C-S, C-C/C-D, and C-B/C-G amplifiers. In this section we review these results and compare the three BJT and FET amplifier configurations.

The BJT Amplifiers

Table 14.7 collects the results of analysis of the three BJT amplifiers in Fig. 14.28; Table 14.8 gives approximate results.

For reasonable values of current gain β_o, the voltage gain of all three amplifiers can be expressed as

$$|A_{Vth}| \approx \frac{g_m R_L}{1 + g_m R_E} = \frac{R_L}{\frac{1}{g_m} + R_E} \tag{14.82}$$

Table 14.7

Single-Transistor Bipolar Amplifiers

	Common-Emitter Amplifier	Common-Collector Amplifier	Common-Base Amplifier
Voltage Gain $A_{Vth} = \frac{v_o}{v_{th}}$ $g_m R_L \approx 10 V_{CC}$	$\frac{-\beta_o R_L}{R_{th} + r_\pi + (\beta_o + 1)R_5}$ $\approx -\frac{g_m R_L}{1 + g_m R_5}$	$\frac{(\beta_o + 1)R_L}{R_{th} + r_\pi + (\beta_o + 1)R_L}$ $\approx \frac{g_m R_L}{1 + g_m R_L} \approx +1$	$\frac{g_m R_L}{1 + (g_m/\alpha_o)R_{th}}$ $\approx \frac{g_m R_L}{1 + g_m R_{th}}$
Input Resistance	$r_\pi + (\beta_o + 1)R_5$ $\approx r_\pi + \beta_o R_5$ $\approx r_\pi(1 + g_m R_5)$	$r_\pi + (\beta_o + 1)R_L$ $\approx r_\pi + \beta_o R_L$ $\approx r_\pi(1 + g_m R_L)$	$\frac{\alpha_o}{g_m} \approx \frac{1}{g_m}$
Output Resistance	$r_o + \mu_F R_5$ $= r_o(1 + g_m R_5)$	$\frac{\alpha_o}{g_m} + \frac{R_{th}}{\beta_o + 1}$	$r_o + \mu_F R_{th}$ $= r_o(1 + g_m R_{th})$
Input Signal Range	$\approx 0.005(1 + g_m R_5)$	$\approx 0.005(1 + g_m R_L)$	$\approx 0.005(1 + g_m R_{th})$
Current Gain	$-\beta_o$	$\beta_o + 1$	$\alpha_o \approx +1$

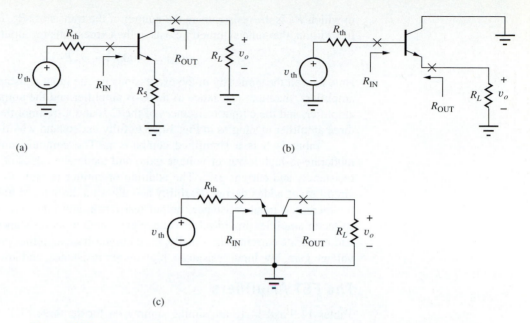

Figure 14.28 The three BJT amplifier configurations: (a) common-emitter amplifier, (b) common-collector amplifier, and (c) common-base amplifier.

Table 14.8

Simplified Characteristics of Single BJT Amplifiers

	Common-Emitter ($R_5 = 0$)	Common-Emitter with Emitter Resistor R_5	Common-Collector	Common-Base
Voltage Gain $A_{Vth} = \dfrac{v_o}{v_{th}}$	$-g_m R_L$ $\approx -10V_{CC}$ (high)	$-\dfrac{R_L}{R_5}$ (moderate)	1 (low)	$+g_m R_L$ $\approx +10V_{CC}$ (high)
Input Resistance	r_π (moderate)	$\beta_o R_5$ (high)	$\beta_o R_L$ (high)	$1/g_m$ (low)
Output Resistance	r_o (moderate)	$\mu_f R_5$ (high)	$1/g_m$ (low)	$\mu_f R_{th}$ (high)
Current Gain	$-\beta_o$ (moderate)	$-\beta_o$ (moderate)	$\beta_o + 1$ (moderate)	1 (low)

in which R_E is the resistance in the emitter of the transistor (R_5, R_L, or R_{th}, respectively). In addition, the same symmetry exists in the expressions for input signal range:

$$|v_{be}| \leq 0.005(1 + g_m R_E) \text{ V} \tag{14.83}$$

Note as well the similarity in the expressions for the input resistances of the C-E and C-C amplifiers, the input resistance of the C-B amplifier and the output resistance of the C-C amplifier, and the output resistances of the C-E and C-B amplifiers. Carefully review the three amplifier topologies in Fig. 14.28 to fully understand why these symmetries occur.

Table 14.8 is a simplified comparison. The common-emitter amplifier provides moderate-to-high levels of voltage gain, and moderate values of input resistance, output resistance, and current gain. The addition of emitter resistor R_5 to the common-emitter circuit gives added design flexibility and allows a designer to trade reduced voltage gain for increased input resistance, output resistance, and input signal range. The common-collector amplifier provides low voltage gain, high input resistance, low output resistance, and moderate current gain. Finally, the common-base amplifier provides moderate to high voltage gain, low input resistance, high output resistance, and low current gain.

The FET Amplifiers

Tables 14.9 and 14.10 are similar summaries for the three FET amplifiers shown in Fig. 14.29. The voltage gain and signal range of all three amplifiers can again be expressed, in this case exactly, as

$$|A_{Vth}| = \frac{g_m R_L}{1 + g_m R_{SS}} \tag{14.84}$$

and

$$|v_{gs}| \leq 0.2(V_{GS} - V_{TN})(1 + g_m R_{SS}) \text{ V} \tag{14.85}$$

Table 14.9

Single-Transistor FET Amplifiers

	Common-Source Amplifier	Common-Drain Amplifier	Common-Gate Amplifier
Voltage Gain $A_{Vth} = \dfrac{v_o}{v_{th}}$	$= -\dfrac{g_m R_L}{1 + g_m R_5}$ $g_m R_L \approx \dfrac{V_{DD}}{V_{GS} - V_{TN}}$	$= \dfrac{g_m R_L}{1 + g_m R_L} \approx +1$	$= \dfrac{g_m R_L}{1 + g_m R_{th}}$ $g_m R_L \approx \dfrac{V_{DD}}{V_{GS} - V_{TN}}$
Input Resistance	∞	∞	$1/g_m$
Output Resistance	$r_o(1 + g_m R_5) \approx \mu_f R_5$	$1/g_m$	$r_o(1 + g_m R_{th}) \approx \mu_f R_{th}$
Input Signal Range	$0.2(V_{GS} - V_{TN})(1 + g_m R_5)$	$0.2(V_{GS} - V_{TN})(1 + g_m R_L)$	$0.2(V_{GS} - V_{TN})(1 + g_m R_{th})$
Current Gain	∞	∞	$+1$

	T a b l e 14.10			
	Simplified Characteristics of Single FET Amplifiers			
	Common-Source ($R_5 = 0$)	Common-Source with Source Resistor R_5	Common-Drain	Common-Gate
Voltage Gain $A_{Vth} = \dfrac{v_0}{v_{th}}$	$-g_m R_L$ $\approx -V_{DD}$ (moderate)	$-\dfrac{R_L}{R_5}$ (moderate)	1 (low)	$+g_m R_L$ $\approx -V_{DD}$ (moderate)
Input Resistance	∞ (high)	∞ (high)	∞ (high)	$1/g_m$ (low)
Output Resistance	r_o (moderate)	$\mu_f R_5$ (high)	$1/g_m$ (low)	$\mu_f R_{th}$ (high)
Current Gain	∞ (high)	∞ (high)	∞ (high)	1 (low)

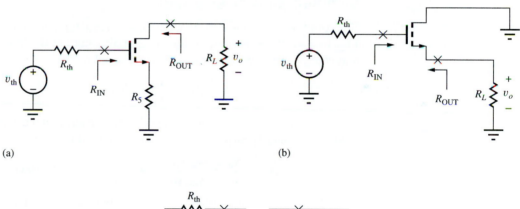

(a) (b) (c)

Figure 14.29 The three FET amplifier configurations: (a) common-source, (b) common-drain, and (c) common-gate.

in which R_{SS} is the resistance in the source of the transistor (R_5, R_L, or R_{th}, respectively). Note the symmetry between the output resistances of the C-S and C-G amplifiers. Also, the input resistance of the C-G amplifier and output resistance of the C-D amplifier are identical. Review the three amplifier topologies in Fig. 14.29 carefully to fully understand why these symmetries occur. The addition of resistor R_5 to the common-source circuit allows the designer to trade reduced voltage gain for increased output resistance and input signal range.

Table 14.10 is a final relative comparison of the FET amplifiers. The common-source amplifier provides moderate voltage gain and output resistance but high values of input resistance and current gain. The common-drain amplifier provides low voltage gain and output resistance, and high input resistance and current gain. Finally, the common-gate amplifier provides moderate voltage gain, high output resistance, and low input resistance and current gain. Tables 14.7 to 14.10 are very useful in the initial phase of amplifier design, when the engineer must make a basic choice of amplifier configuration to meet the design specifications.

14.6 OVERALL AMPLIFIER PERFORMANCE

Now that we have an understanding of the basic performance and limitations of the three prototype amplifier configurations, we are in a position to use these results to characterize the overall performance of the complete amplifiers in Figs. 14.2 to 14.4. We start with the amplifiers in Fig. 14.2 and then proceed to those in Figs. 14.3 and 14.4.

Common-Emitter Amplifier

Figure 14.30 gives the full ac equivalent circuit for the common-emitter amplifier in Fig. 14.2(a). We want to determine the overall values of the input and output resistances and voltage and current gains of the overall amplifier:

$$A_V = \frac{v_o}{v_s} \quad \text{and} \quad A_I = \frac{i_o}{i_s} \tag{14.86}$$

The overall voltage gain A_V can be written in terms of the gain A_{Vth} and the Thévenin equivalent voltage source v_{th}, which were found in Fig. 14.3:

$$A_V = \frac{v_o}{v_s} = \frac{v_o}{v_{th}} \frac{v_{th}}{v_s} = A_{Vth} \frac{v_{th}}{v_s} = -5.71(0.981) = -5.60 \tag{14.87}$$

The overall input resistance of the amplifier can be found from Fig. 14.31, at the point indicated in Fig. 14.30, by writing an expression for the current i_x:

$$i_x = i_r + i_b \tag{14.88}$$

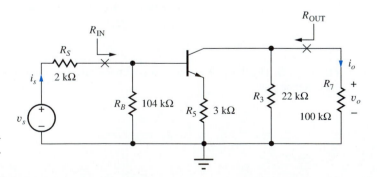

Figure 14.30 Full ac equivalent circuit for the C-E amplifier in Fig. 14.2(a).

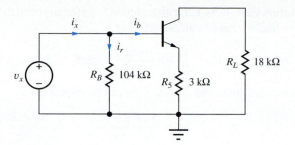

Figure 14.31 Circuit for calculating the overall input resistance of the amplifier.

In Eq. (14.88), the current $\mathbf{i_r}$ is simply $\mathbf{v_x}/R_B$; we already found that $\mathbf{i_b} = \mathbf{v_x}/R_{\mathrm{IN}}^{CE}$. Therefore,

$$\mathbf{i_x} = \frac{\mathbf{v_x}}{R_B} + \frac{\mathbf{v_x}}{R_{\mathrm{IN}}^{CE}} \tag{14.89}$$

Solving for the ratio of $\mathbf{v_x}$ to $\mathbf{i_x}$ yields an expression for R_{IN}:

$$R_{\mathrm{IN}} = \frac{\mathbf{v_x}}{\mathbf{i_x}} = \frac{R_B R_{\mathrm{IN}}^{CE}}{R_B + R_{\mathrm{IN}}^{CE}} = R_B \| R_{\mathrm{IN}}^{CE} \tag{14.90}$$

Equations (14.89) and (14.90) indicate that the input resistance of the overall amplifier is equal to the base bias resistance R_B in parallel with the equivalent input resistance of the transistor in the C-E configuration. For this particular circuit,

$$R_{\mathrm{IN}} = 104\ \mathrm{k\Omega} \| 313\ \mathrm{k\Omega} = 78.1\ \mathrm{k\Omega} \tag{14.91}$$

The overall output resistance of the amplifier can be found in a similar manner from Fig. 14.32 by writing an expression for current i_x.

$$\mathbf{i_x} = \mathbf{i_r} + \mathbf{i_c} = \frac{\mathbf{v_x}}{R_3} + \frac{\mathbf{v_x}}{R_{\mathrm{OUT}}^{CE}} \tag{14.92}$$

and

$$R_{\mathrm{OUT}} = \frac{\mathbf{v_x}}{\mathbf{i_x}} = R_3 \| R_{\mathrm{OUT}}^{CE} \tag{14.93}$$

The output resistance of the overall amplifier is equal to the collector bias resistance R_3 in parallel with the output resistance of the transistor in the C-E configuration. For this particular circuit,

$$R_{\mathrm{OUT}} = 22\ \mathrm{k\Omega} \| 4.55\ \mathrm{M\Omega} = 21.9\ \mathrm{k\Omega} \tag{14.94}$$

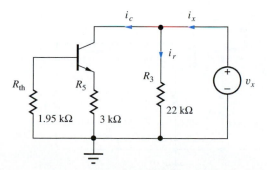

Figure 14.32 Circuit for calculating the overall output resistance of the amplifier.

Current gain $A_I = \mathbf{i_o}/\mathbf{i_s}$ can be found by referring back to Fig. 14.30. The two currents needed to find A_I can be calculated from

$$\mathbf{i_o} = \frac{\mathbf{v_o}}{R_7} = \frac{A_V \mathbf{v_s}}{R_7} \quad \text{and} \quad \mathbf{i_s} = \frac{\mathbf{v_s}}{R_S + R_{\text{IN}}} \tag{14.95}$$

Using these equations, the current gain can be expressed as

$$A_I = \frac{\mathbf{v_o}}{\mathbf{v_s}} \frac{R_S + R_{\text{IN}}}{R_7} = A_V \frac{R_S + R_{\text{IN}}}{R_7} \tag{14.96}$$

and for the C-E amplifier in Fig. 14.2,

$$A_I = -5.60\frac{(78.1 + 2)\text{ k}\Omega}{100\text{ k}\Omega} = -4.48 \tag{14.97}$$

The maximum input signal for this amplifier was presented in Table 14.2 and was 159 mV.

Up to this point, we have not discussed the **power gain.** However, referring back to Chapter 11, we can calculate the power gain from

$$A_P = |A_V||A_I| = (5.60)(4.48) = 25.1 \text{ or } 14 \text{ dB} \tag{14.98}$$

Common-Source Amplifier

Repeating this analysis for the common-source amplifier in Fig. 14.33 yields:

$$A_V = A_{V\text{th}}\frac{\mathbf{v_{th}}}{\mathbf{v_s}} = -4.46(0.998) = -4.45$$

$$R_{\text{IN}} = R_G\|R_{\text{IN}}^{CS} = 892 \text{ K}\Omega\|\infty = 892 \text{ K}\Omega$$

$$R_{\text{OUT}} = R_3\|R_{\text{OUT}}^{CS} = 22 \text{ K}\Omega\|442 \text{ K}\Omega = 21.5 \text{ K}\Omega \tag{14.99}$$

$$A_I = A_V\frac{R_S + R_{\text{IN}}}{R_7} = -4.45\frac{894 \text{ k}\Omega}{100 \text{ k}\Omega} = -39.8$$

$$|v_s| \leq 297 \text{ mV} \qquad \text{from Table 14.2}$$

$$A_P = |A_V||A_I| = (4.45)(39.8) = 177 \text{ or } 22.5 \text{ dB}$$

Table 14.11 is a final comparison of the numeric results for the common-emitter and common-source amplifiers. Now that the effects of the bias resistors have been fully included, the voltage gain and output resistance of the amplifiers are very similar. However, the infinite input resistance and current gain of the FET still translate into a higher overall amplifier input resistance as well as a higher current gain. The output resistances are both limited by the bias elements, not the transistors. The high input resistance of the FET helps it achieve a power gain that is an order of magnitude better.

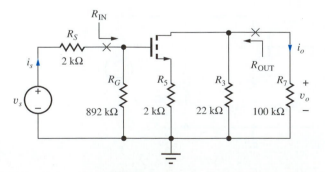

Figure 14.33 Full ac equivalent circuit for the C-S amplifier in Fig. 14.2(b).

T a b l e 14.11

Common-Emitter/Common-Source Amplifier Comparison

	C-E Amplifier	C-S Amplifier
Voltage Gain	−5.60	−4.45
Input Resistance	78.1 kΩ	892 kΩ
Output Resistance	21.9 kΩ	21.5 kΩ
Current Gain	−4.48	−39.8
Input Signal Range	159 mV	297 mV
Power Gain	25.1	177

EXERCISE: Change the value of R_5 so the voltage gain of the C-S amplifier is identical to that of the C-E amplifier in Fig. 14.2. A new value of R_6 must be used so the Q-point is not changed. What is the new value of R_6?

ANSWERS: 1.17 kΩ, 10.8 kΩ

EXERCISE: Using current division, show that the output current i_o and current gain A_I for the C-E amplifier can be written as

$$\mathbf{i_o} = -\mathbf{i_s}\frac{R_B}{R_B + R_{IN}^{CE}}\beta_o\frac{R_3}{R_3 + R_7} \quad \text{and} \quad A_I = -\frac{R_B}{R_B + R_{IN}^{CE}}\beta_o\frac{R_3}{R_3 + R_7}$$

EXERCISE: Evaluate the preceding expression for the current gain and show that it gives the same result as Eq. (14.97).

EXERCISE: Use circuit simulation to verify the results in Table 14.11. Assume $I_S = 5 \times 10^{-16}$ A for the BJT, $C_1 = 10$ μF, $C_2 = 4.7$ μF, $C_3 = 47$ μF, and $f = 5000$ Hz.

Common-Collector Amplifier

Next, we use the transistor-level results to characterize the common-collector amplifier in Fig. 14.3, whose ac equivalent circuit appears in Fig. 14.34. A_V can again be written in terms of the gain A_{Vth} and the Thévenin equivalent voltage source v_{th}, which were

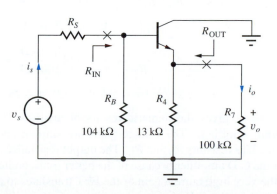

Figure 14.34 Full ac equivalent circuit for the C-C amplifier in Fig. 14.3(a).

calculated in Fig. 14.5:

$$A_V = \frac{\mathbf{v_o}}{\mathbf{v_s}} = \frac{\mathbf{v_o}}{\mathbf{v_{th}}}\frac{\mathbf{v_{th}}}{\mathbf{v_s}} = A_{Vth}\frac{\mathbf{v_{th}}}{\mathbf{v_s}} = 0.980(0.981) = 0.961 \qquad (14.100)$$

In a manner similar to that used to derive Eq. (14.90), the overall input resistance of the amplifier can be written as the base bias resistance R_B in parallel with the input resistance of the transistor in the C-C configuration. For this particular circuit,

$$R_{IN} = R_B \| R_{IN}^{CC} = 104 \text{ k}\Omega \| 1.17 \text{ M}\Omega = 92.8 \text{ k}\Omega \qquad (14.101)$$

The overall output resistance of the amplifier is found in a manner analogous to that used to derive Eq. (14.93), yielding

$$R_{OUT} = R_4 \| R_{OUT}^{CC} = 13 \text{ k}\Omega \| 121 \text{ }\Omega = 120 \text{ }\Omega \qquad (14.102)$$

The output resistance of the overall amplifier is equal to the emitter bias resistance R_4 in parallel with the output resistance of the transistor in the C-C configuration. Note that R_{OUT} is still dominated by R_{OUT}^{CC}.

The currents needed to find the gain $A_I = \mathbf{i_o}/\mathbf{i_s}$ can be found with reference to Fig. 14.34,

$$\mathbf{i_o} = \frac{\mathbf{v_o}}{R_7} = \frac{A_v \mathbf{v_s}}{R_7} \qquad \text{and} \qquad \mathbf{i_s} = \frac{\mathbf{v_s}}{R_S + R_{IN}} \qquad (14.103)$$

and the current gain is

$$A_I = \frac{\mathbf{i_o}}{\mathbf{i_s}} = \frac{\mathbf{v_o}}{\mathbf{v_s}}\frac{R_S + R_{IN}}{R_7} = A_V \frac{R_S + R_{IN}}{R_7} = 0.961\frac{94.8 \text{ k}\Omega}{100 \text{ k}\Omega} = 0.911 \qquad (14.104)$$

Using the results of Eqs. (14.100) and (14.104), the power gain is

$$A_P = |A_V \| A_I| = 0.961(0.911) = 0.875 \qquad (14.105)$$

> **EXERCISE:** Rigorously derive the results given in Eqs. (14.101) and (14.102). Follow the derivation in Eqs. (14.88) to (14.94).

Common-Drain Amplifier

Figure 14.35 is the ac model for the common-drain amplifier in Fig. 14.3(b). Following the same analysis we used for the common-collector amplifier,

$$A_V = A_{Vth}\frac{\mathbf{v_{th}}}{\mathbf{v_s}} = 0.840(0.998) = 0.838$$

$$R_{IN} = R_G \| R_{IN}^{CD} = 892 \text{ k}\Omega \| \infty = 892 \text{ k}\Omega$$

$$R_{OUT} = R_4 \| R_{OUT}^{CD} = 12 \text{ k}\Omega \| 2.04 \text{ k}\Omega = 1.74 \text{ k}\Omega \qquad (14.106)$$

$$A_I = A_V \frac{R_S + R_{IN}}{R_7} = 0.838\frac{894 \text{ k}\Omega}{100 \text{ k}\Omega} = 7.49$$

$$A_P = |A_V \| A_I| = 0.838(7.49) = 6.28$$

Table 14.12 gives the numeric results of analysis of the common-collector and common-drain amplifiers. The voltage gains are similar, and both input resistances are limited by the bias resistors R_B and R_G. The output resistance of the C-B amplifier is lower than that of the C-D amplifier because of the better transconductance exhibited by the BJT. However, the very high current gain of the FET translates to a higher overall current gain and power gain for the C-D circuit.

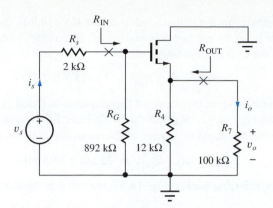

Figure 14.35 Full ac equivalent circuit for the C-D amplifier in Fig. 14.3(b).

	T a b l e 14.12		
	Common-Collector/Common-Drain Amplifier Comparison		
		C-C Amplifier	**C-D Amplifier**
Voltage Gain		0.961	0.838
Input Resistance		92.8 kΩ	892 kΩ
Output Resistance		120 Ω	1.74 kΩ
Current Gain		0.911	7.49
Power Gain		0.875	6.28

EXERCISE: Use circuit simulation to verify the results in Table 14.12. Assume $I_S = 5 \times 10^{-16}$ A for the BJT, $C_1 = 10$ μF, $C_2 = 4.7$ μF, $C_3 = 47$ μF, and $f = 5000$ Hz.

Common-Base Amplifier

The final pair of amplifiers to be evaluated consists of the common-base and common-gate amplifiers in Fig. 14.4. The ac equivalent circuit for the common-base amplifier in Fig. 14.4(a) is drawn in Fig. 14.36. A_V is again written in terms of the gain A_{Vth} and the Thévenin equivalent voltage source v_{th}, which were already calculated:

$$A_V = \frac{\mathbf{v_o}}{\mathbf{v_s}} = \frac{\mathbf{v_o}}{\mathbf{v_{th}}} \frac{\mathbf{v_{th}}}{\mathbf{v_s}} = A_{Vth} \frac{\mathbf{v_{th}}}{\mathbf{v_s}} = 10.4(0.867) = 9.02 \qquad (14.107)$$

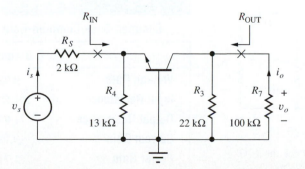

Figure 14.36 Full ac equivalent circuit for the C-B amplifier in Fig. 14.4(a).

In a manner similar to that used to derive Eq. (14.90), the overall input resistance of the amplifier is set by emitter bias resistor R_4 in parallel with the input resistance of the transistor in the C-B configuration:

$$R_{IN} = R_4 \parallel R_{IN}^{CB} = 13 \text{ k}\Omega \parallel 102 \ \Omega = 101 \ \Omega \tag{14.108}$$

The overall output resistance of the amplifier is found in a manner analogous to that used to derive Eq. (14.93). R_{OUT} of the overall amplifier is the collector bias resistance R_3 in parallel with the output resistance of the transistor in the C-B configuration.

$$R_{OUT} = R_3 \parallel R_{OUT}^{CB} = 22 \text{ k}\Omega \parallel 3.93 \text{ M}\Omega = 21.9 \text{ k}\Omega \tag{14.109}$$

Finally, referring back to Fig. 14.32, we see that the current gain is

$$A_I = \frac{i_o}{i_s} = A_V \frac{R_S + R_{IN}}{R_7} = 9.02 \frac{2.10 \text{ k}\Omega}{100 \text{ k}\Omega} = 0.189 \tag{14.110}$$

From the results of Eqs. (14.107) and (14.110), the power gain is

$$A_P = |A_V \parallel A_I| = 9.02(0.189) = 1.71 \tag{14.111}$$

Common-Gate Amplifier

Figure 14.37 is the ac equivalent circuit for the common-gate amplifier in Fig. 14.4(b). Following the same analysis we used for the common-base amplifier,

$$A_V = A_{Vth} \frac{v_{th}}{v_s} = 4.80(0.857) = 4.11$$

$$R_{IN} = R_4 \parallel R_{IN}^{CG} = 12 \text{ k}\Omega \parallel 2.04 \text{ k}\Omega = 2.04 \text{ k}\Omega$$

$$R_{OUT} = R_3 \parallel R_{OUT}^{CG} = 22 \text{ k}\Omega \parallel 410 \text{ k}\Omega = 20.9 \text{ k}\Omega \tag{14.112}$$

$$A_I = A_V \frac{R_S + R_{IN}}{R_7} = 4.11 \frac{4.04 \text{ k}\Omega}{100 \text{ k}\Omega} = 0.166$$

$$A_P = |A_V \parallel A_I| = 4.11(0.166) = 0.682$$

Table 14.13 shows the numeric results for the common-base and common-gate amplifiers. The voltage gain and input resistance of the BJT amplifier reflect the higher transconductance of the bipolar transistor. The output resistances are both limited by the bias elements in the complete circuit. Both current gains must be less than unity in these configurations.

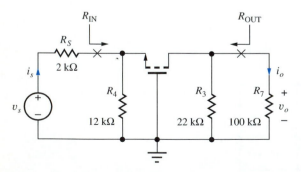

Figure 14.37 Full ac equivalent circuit for the C-G amplifier in Fig. 14.4(b).

	T a b l e 14.13	
	Common-Base/Common-Gate Amplifier Comparison	
	C-B Amplifier	**C-G Amplifier**
Voltage Gain	9.02	4.11
Input Resistance	101 Ω	2.04 kΩ
Output Resistance	21.9 kΩ	20.9 kΩ
Current Gain	0.189	0.166
Power Gain	1.71	0.682

EXERCISE: Using current division, show that the output current i_o and current gain A_i for the C-B amplifier can be written as

$$\mathbf{i_o} = \mathbf{i_s}\frac{R_4}{R_4 + R_{\text{IN}}^{CB}}\alpha_o\frac{R_3}{R_3 + R_7} \quad \text{and} \quad A_I = \frac{R_4}{R_4 + R_{\text{IN}}^{CB}}\alpha_o\frac{R_3}{R_3 + R_7}$$

EXERCISE: Evaluate the preceding expression for the current gain, and show that it gives the same result as Eq. (14.112).

EXERCISE: Use circuit simulation to verify the results in Table 14.13. Assume $I_S = 5 \times 10^{-16}$ A for the BJT, $C_1 = 10$ μF, $C_2 = 4.7$ μF, $C_3 = 47$ μF, and $f = 5000$ Hz.

14.7 AMPLIFIER DESIGN EXAMPLES

Now that we have become "experts" in the characteristics of single-amplifier amplifiers, we will use this knowledge to tackle several amplifier design problems. We should emphasize that no "cookbook" exists for design. Every design is a new, creative experience. Each design has its own unique set of constraints, and there may be more than one way to achieve the desired results. The examples presented here further illustrate the approach to design; they also underscore the interaction between the designer's choice of Q-point and the small-signal properties of the amplifiers.

EXAMPLE 14.6: A COMMON-COLLECTOR/COMMON DRAIN AMPLIFIER

For our first design example, an amplifier is required to meet the specifications in the following problem statement:

> Design a follower with an input resistance $R_{\text{IN}} \geq 20$ MΩ and a gain of at least 0.95 when driving an external load of at least 3 kΩ.

Although a follower circuit is specified, we must still choose between the emitter-follower (C-C) and source-follower (C-D) configurations. Reviewing Tables 14.8 and 14.10, we find that the input resistance of the C-D amplifier prototype is infinite, whereas that of the C-C amplifier is limited to $\beta_o R_L$. For a load resistance of 3 kΩ, a current gain β_o in excess of 6600 is required to meet the input-resistance specification. This current gain is beyond the range of normal bipolar transistors, so here we rule out the C-C amplifier. (However, be sure to watch for the Darlington circuit in the next chapter.)

Figure 14.38 is a basic source-follower circuit. In this amplifier, we recognize that R_{IN} is set simply by the value of R_G, and we can pick $R_G = 22$ MΩ (± 5 percent) to meet the specification. The 22-MΩ value is chosen to ensure that the design specifications are met when the effect of the tolerance is included. The choices of source resistor R_S and power supply voltages are related to the voltage gain requirement:

$$\frac{g_m R_L}{1 + g_m R_L} \geq 0.95 \quad \text{or} \quad g_m R_L \geq 19 \tag{14.113}$$

The $g_m R_L$ product can be related to the drain current and device parameter K_n by using $g_m = \sqrt{2K_n I_{DS}}$, and from Eq. (14.113),

$$\sqrt{2K_n I_{DS}}\, R_L \geq 19 \quad \text{or} \quad \sqrt{K_n I_{DS}} \geq \frac{19}{\sqrt{2}\, R_L} \tag{14.114}$$

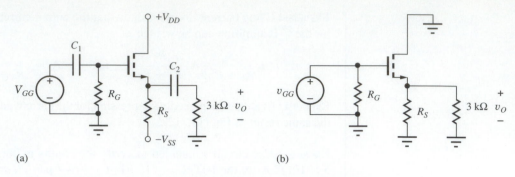

Figure 14.38 (a) Common-drain amplifier and (b) ac equivalent circuit.

In Fig. 14.38(b), the equivalent load resistor $R_L = R_S \parallel 3\,\text{k}\Omega \le 3\,\text{k}\Omega$. Let us choose $R_L \ge 1.5\,\text{k}\Omega$ (that is, $R_S \ge 3\,\text{k}\Omega$). Substituting this value into Eq. (14.114) yields

$$\sqrt{K_n I_{DS}} \ge \frac{19}{\sqrt{2}(1.5 \times 10^3)} = 8.96\,\text{mA} \qquad (14.115)$$

Equation (14.115) indicates that the geometric mean between K_n and I_{DS} must be at least 9 mA. Thus, R_S will be in the 0.5- to 5-kΩ range for reasonable values of V_{SS}.

We must now select a FET. Substituting the drain-current expression for the MOSFET,

$$I_{DS} = \frac{K_n}{2}(V_{GS} - V_{TN})^2 \qquad (14.116)$$

into Eq. (14.115) gives an expression for K_n:

$$K_n \ge \frac{\sqrt{2}}{(V_{GS} - V_{TN})} 8.96\,\text{mA} \qquad (14.117)$$

As is often the case in design, one equation—here, Eq. (14.117)—contains two unknowns. We must make a design decision. Table 14.14 presents some possible solution pairs for Eq. (14.117).

Let us assume we have looked through our device catalogs and found a MOSFET with $V_{TN} = 1.5\,\text{V}$ and $K_n = 20\,\text{mA/V}^2$. Evaluating Eq. (14.115) for this FET gives

$$I_{DS} \ge \frac{(8.96\,\text{mA})^2}{20\,\text{mA}} = 4.01\,\text{mA} \qquad (14.118)$$

Let us choose $I_{DS} = 5\,\text{mA}$, to try to provide some design margin. Then,

$$V_{GS} = V_{\text{TH}} + \sqrt{\frac{2 I_{DS}}{K_n}} = 1.5 + \sqrt{\frac{2(0.005)}{0.02}} = 2.21\,\text{V} \qquad (14.119)$$

Now we are finally in a position to find R_S. A relationship among I_{DS}, R_S, and V_{SS} can be found using the dc equivalent circuit in Fig. 14.39.

Because $I_G = 0$,

$$V_{GS} + I_{DS} R_S - V_{SS} = 0 \quad \text{or} \quad R_S = \frac{V_{SS} - V_{GS}}{I_D} = \frac{V_{SS} - 2.21}{0.005} \qquad (14.120)$$

Values have been selected for V_{GS} and I_{DS}, but Eq. (14.120) is another equation with two unknowns. Table 14.15 presents several possible solution pairs from which to make a design selection. Earlier in the design discussion, we assumed that $R_S \ge 3\,\text{k}\Omega$, so one acceptable choice is $V_{SS} = 20\,\text{V}$, $R_S = 3.56\,\text{k}\Omega$.

T a b l e 14.14	
Possible Solutions to Eq. (14.117)	
$V_{GS} - V_{TN}$ (V)	K_n (mA/V^2)
1.0	12.7
1.5	8.19
2.0	6.14
2.5	5.07

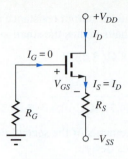

Figure 14.39 dc Equivalent circuit for the C-D amplifier.

T a b l e 14.15	
Possible Solutions to Eq. (14.120)	
V_{SS}	R_S
10 V	1.56 kΩ
15 V	2.56 kΩ
20 V	3.56 kΩ
25 V	4.56 kΩ

The final design decision is the choice of V_{DD}, which must be large enough to ensure that the MOSFET operates in the saturation region under all signal conditions:

$$v_{DS} \geq v_{GS} - V_{TN} \qquad (14.121)$$

and

$$v_{DS} = v_D - v_S = V_{DD} - (V_S + v_s) = V_{DD} + V_{GS} - v_s \qquad (14.122)$$

for $v_S = V_S + v_s$ and $V_S = -V_{GS}$. Combining these last two equations yields

$$V_{DD} + V_{GS} - v_s \geq V_{GS} - V_{TN} \qquad \text{or} \qquad V_{DD} \geq v_s - V_{TN} = v_s - 1.5 \text{ V} \qquad (14.123)$$

The largest amplitude signal v_s at the source that satisfies the small-signal requirements is

$$|v_s| \leq 0.2(V_{GS} - V_{TN})(1 + g_m R_L)\left(\frac{g_m R_L}{1 + g_m R_L}\right) = 0.2(0.71)(19) = 2.70 \text{ V} \qquad (14.124)$$

Thus, if we choose a V_{DD} of at least 1.2 V, then the MOSFET remains saturated for all signals that satisfy the small-signal criteria. The final design (except for the capacitor values, which must wait until a later chapter) is in Fig. 14.40, in which the nearest 5 percent values have been used for the resistors and V_{DD} has been chosen to be a common power supply value of +5 V. ◆

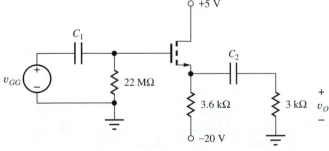

Figure 14.40 Completed source-follower design.

EXERCISE: Find the actual Q-point, input resistance, and voltage gain for the circuit in Fig. 14.40. ($K_n = 20$ mA/V^2, $V_{TN} = 1.5$ V)

ANSWERS: (4.94 mA, 7.20 V), 22 MΩ, +0.959

EXERCISE: Find the output resistance of the amplifier in Fig. 14.40. What is the largest value of v_{gg} that satisfies the small-signal constraints?

ANSWERS: 69.8 Ω, 3.43 V

EXAMPLE 14.7: A COMMON-BASE/COMMON-GATE AMPLIFIER

The requirements of the second design problem are even less specific than those in the previous design:

> Design an amplifier to match a 75-Ω source resistance (for example, a coaxial transmission line) and to provide a voltage gain of 34 dB.

Our first problem is to select a circuit configuration and transistor type. From the various examples in this and previous chapters, we realize that $A_v = 50$ (34 dB) is a reasonably high value of gain. At the same time, the required input resistance of 75 Ω is relatively low. Looking through our amplifier comparison charts in Tables 14.8 and 14.10, we find that the common-base and common-gate amplifiers most nearly meet these two requirements: high gain and low input resistance. From past examples, we should recognize that it will probably be easier to achieve a gain of 50 with a BJT than with a FET. Thus the common-base amplifier is the one that seems to most nearly meet the problem specifications.

For simplicity, let us use the dual supply-bias circuit in Fig. 14.41, which requires only two bias resistors. In addition, to get some practice analyzing circuits using pnp devices, we have arbitrarily selected a pnp transistor. We happen to have a pnp transistor available with $\beta_F = 80$ and $V_A = 50$ V.

Next, we select the power supplies V_{CC} and V_{EE}. Remembering our rule of thumb from Chapter 13, $A_v = 10\,(V_{CC} + V_{EE})$. The matched input resistance situation causes a factor of 2 voltage loss between the signal source v_s and the emitter-base junction. Thus, an overall gain of 50 requires a value of $g_m R_L = 100$, and we estimate that a total supply voltage of 10 V is required. Using symmetrical supplies, we have $V_{CC} = V_{EE} = 5$ V.

Figure 14.42(a) and (b) are the dc and ac equivalent circuits needed to analyze the behavior of the amplifier in Fig. 14.41. Resistor R_E and the Q-point of the transistor can now be determined from the input resistance requirement. From Fig. 14.42(b), we recognize that the input resistance of the amplifier is equal to resistor R_E in parallel with the input resistance of the common-base transistor. From Table 14.5, $R_{IN}^{CB} = \alpha_o/g_m$:

$$R_{IN} = R_E \parallel R_{IN}^{CB} \approx R_E \left\| \frac{\alpha_o}{g_m} \right. \tag{14.125}$$

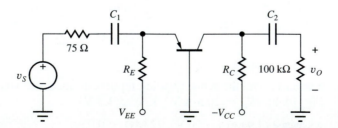

Figure 14.41 Common-base circuit topology.

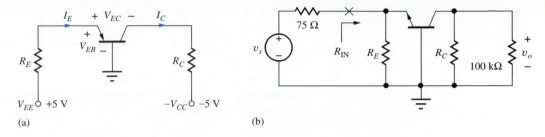

Figure 14.42 (a) dc and (b) ac equivalent circuits for the common-base amplifier.

Expanding Eq. (14.125) and using the expression for g_m yields

$$R_{IN} = \frac{\dfrac{\alpha_o}{g_m}R_E}{\dfrac{\alpha_o}{g_m} + R_E} = \frac{R_E}{1 + \dfrac{g_m R_E}{\alpha_o}} = \frac{R_E}{1 + \dfrac{40 I_C R_E}{\alpha_o}} \approx \frac{R_E}{1 + 40 I_E R_E} \quad (14.126)$$

In Eq. (14.126), the $I_E R_E$ product represents the dc voltage developed across the resistor R_E. Here again we see the direct coupling between the small-signal input resistance and the dc Q-point values. From the dc equivalent circuit in Fig. 14.39(a) and assuming $V_{EB} = 0.7$ V,

$$I_E R_E = V_{EE} - V_{EB} = 5 - 0.7 = 4.3 \text{ V} \quad (14.127)$$

Combining Eqs. (14.126) and (14.127) with the input resistance specification,

$$75 = \frac{R_E}{1 + 40(4.3)} \quad \text{and} \quad R_E = 13.0 \text{ k}\Omega \quad (14.128)$$

I_C can now be found using Eq. (14.128):

$$I_C = \alpha_o I_E = \frac{80}{81}\frac{4.3}{13.0 \times 10^3} = 327 \text{ }\mu\text{A} \quad (14.129)$$

It is interesting to note that once V_{EE} was chosen for this circuit, R_E and I_C were both indirectly fixed.

The next step in the design is to choose the collector resistor R_C. The circuit in Fig. 14.41 is redrawn in prototype form in Fig. 14.43, for which the gain is

$$A_{Vth}^{CB} = \frac{g_m R_L}{1 + \dfrac{g_m}{\alpha_o}R_{th}} \quad (14.130)$$

For our circuit,

$$R_{th} = 75 \text{ }\Omega \parallel R_E = 75 \text{ }\Omega \parallel 13.0 \text{ k}\Omega = 74.6 \text{ }\Omega$$
$$g_m = 40 I_C = 40(327 \text{ }\mu\text{A}) = 13.1 \text{ mS}$$
$$R_L = R_C \parallel 100 \text{ k}\Omega \quad (14.131)$$
$$\mathbf{v_{th}} = \frac{R_E}{75 + R_E}\mathbf{v_s} = \frac{13,000}{75 + 13,000}\mathbf{v_s} = 0.994\mathbf{v_s}$$

Solving for R_L in Eq. (14.130) yields

$$A_V = 0.994\frac{g_m R_L}{1 + \dfrac{g_m}{\alpha_o}R_{th}}$$

and
$$R_L = \frac{50}{0.994}\left(\frac{1 + \dfrac{0.0131\text{ S}}{0.988}(74.6\ \Omega)}{0.0131\text{ S}}\right) = 7.64\text{ k}\Omega \qquad (14.132)$$

Because $R_L = R_C \parallel 100\text{ k}\Omega$, $R_C = 8.27\text{ k}\Omega$.

The final step is to finish checking the Q-point of the transistor by calculating V_{EC}. Using the circuit in Fig. 14.39(a),

$$V_{EB} = V_{EC} + I_C R_C - 5 \qquad (14.133)$$

and solving for V_{EC} yields

$$V_{EC} = 5 + V_{EB} - I_C R_C = 5 + 0.6 - (0.327\text{ mA})(8.27\text{ k}\Omega) = +2.90\text{ V} \ \checkmark \qquad (14.134)$$

V_{EC} is positive and greater than 0.7 V, so the *pnp* transistor is operating in the forward-active region, as required.

The completed design (except for C_1 and C_2) is shown in Fig. 14.44, in which the nearest 5 percent values have been used for the resistors. This amplifier provides a gain of approximately 50 and an input resistance of approximately 75 Ω.

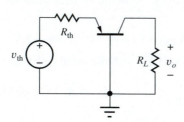

Figure 14.43 ac Circuit in proto-type form.

Figure 14.44 Final design for amplifier with $R_{IN} = 75\ \Omega$ and $A_V = 50$.

One limitation of this amplifier design is its signal-handling ability. Only 5 mV can appear across the emitter-base junction, which sets a limit on the signal v_s:

$$\mathbf{v_{eb}} = \mathbf{v_s}\frac{R_{IN}^{CB}}{R_S + R_{IN}^{CB}} = \mathbf{v_s}\frac{75}{75 + 75} = \frac{\mathbf{v_s}}{2} \qquad (14.135)$$

Thus, for small-signal operation to be valid, the magnitude of the input signal v_s must not exceed 10 mV.

In this design we were lucky that we remembered to account for the factor of 2 loss in Eq. (14.137) due to the matched resistance condition at the input. Otherwise, our initial choice of power supplies might not have been sufficient to meet the gain specification, and a second design iteration could have been required. ◆

EXERCISE: Draw the *npn* analog of the circuit in Fig. 14.44. Use the same circuit element values but change polarities as needed.

EXERCISE: What are the actual values of input resistance and gain for the amplifier in Fig. 14.44?

ANSWERS: 73.4 Ω, +50.4

EXERCISE: What is the largest sinusoidal signal voltage that can appear at the output of the amplifier in Fig. 14.44? What is the largest output signal consistent with the requirements for small-signal operation?

ANSWERS: $(2.90 \text{ V} - V_{EB}) \approx 2.20 \text{ V}, 0.490 \text{ V}$

EXERCISE: Suppose that both V_{EE} and V_{CC} were changed to 7.5 V. What are the new values of I_C, V_{EC}, R_E, and R_C required to meet the same specifications?

ANSWERS: 327 µA, 4.10 V, 20.8 kΩ, 8.27 kΩ

EXERCISE: Suppose the resistors and power supplies in the circuit in Fig. 14.44 all have 5 percent tolerances. Will the BJT remain in the forward-active region in the worst-case situation? Repeat for tolerances of 10 percent. Do the values of current gain β_F or V_A have any significant effect on the design? Discuss.

ANSWERS: Yes; yes; no, not unless they become very small.

Monte Carlo Evaluation of the Common-Base Amplifier Design

Before going on to the third design example, we carry out a statistical evaluation of the common-base design to see if it is a viable design for the mass production of large numbers of amplifiers. We use a spreadsheet analysis here although we could easily evaluate the same equation set using a simple computer program written in any high-level language or using the Monte Carlo option in some circuit simulation programs.

To perform a Monte Carlo analysis of the circuit in Fig. 14.44, we assign random values to V_{CC}, V_{EE}, R_C, R_E, and β_F; we then use these values to determine I_C and V_{EC}, R_{IN}, and A_v. Referring back to Eq. (5.86) in Chapter 5, we write each parameter in the form

$$P = P_{NOM}(1 + 2\varepsilon (\text{RAND()} - 0.5)) \tag{14.136}$$

where P_{NOM} = nominal value of parameter
          ε = parameter tolerance
     RAND() = random-number generator in spreadsheet

For the design in Fig. 14.44, we assume that the resistors and power supplies have 5 percent tolerances and the current gain has a ±25 percent tolerance. As mentioned in Chapter 5, it is important that each variable invoke a separate evaluation of the random-number generator so that the random values are independent of each other. The random-element values are then used to characterize the Q-point, R_{IN}, and A_v. The expressions for the Monte Carlo analysis are presented in a logical sequence for evaluation in Eqs. (14.137):

1. $V_{CC} = 5(1 + 0.1(\text{RAND()} - 0.5))$

2. $V_{EE} = 5(1 + 0.1(\text{RAND()} - 0.5))$

3. $R_E = 13{,}000(1 + 0.1(\text{RAND()} - 0.5))$

4. $R_C = 8200(1 + 0.1(\text{RAND()} - 0.5))$

5. $\beta_F = 80(1 + 0.5(\text{RAND()} - 0.5))$

6. $I_C = \dfrac{V_{EE} - 0.7}{R_E}$ (14.37)

7. $\quad V_{EC} = 0.7 + V_{CC} - I_C R_C$

8. $\quad g_m = 40 I_C$

9. $\quad R_{IN} = R_E \left\| \dfrac{\alpha_o}{g_m}\right.$

10. $\quad A_v = g_m R_L \dfrac{R_{IN}}{R_S + R_{IN}} \qquad$ where $R_L = R_C \parallel 100\ \text{k}\Omega$

Table 14.16 summarizes the results of a 1000-case analysis. The transistor is always in the forward-active region. The mean collector current of 331 μA corresponds closely to the nominal values of the standard 5 percent resistors that were selected for the final circuit. The mean values of R_{IN} and A_V are 74.3 Ω and 49.9, respectively, and are also quite close to the design value. The 3σ limit corresponds to only slightly more than 10 percent deviation from the nominal design specification, and even the worst observed cases of R_{IN} will yield acceptable values of SWR (standing wave ratio) on the transmission line that the amplifier was designed to match. Overall, we should be able to mass produce this design and have few problems meeting the specifications.

T a b l e 14.16
Monte Carlo analysis of the common-base amplifier design

Case #	VCC (1)	VEE (2)	RE (3)	RC (4)	BF (5)	IC (6)	VEC (7)	gm(8)	RIN(9)	Av (10)
1	4.932	5.090	13602	8461	96.02	3.23E-04	2.902	1.29E-02	76.2	50.8
2	4.951	5.209	12844	8208	93.01	3.51E-04	2.769	1.40E-02	70.1	51.4
3	4.844	4.759	13418	8440	98.33	3.03E-04	2.990	1.21E-02	81.3	49.0
4	4.787	5.162	13193	8294	72.82	3.38E-04	2.682	1.35E-02	72.5	50.9
5	5.073	5.181	12358	8542	79.30	3.63E-04	2.676	1.45E-02	67.7	54.2
6	5.224	5.234	13025	8483	84.54	3.48E-04	2.971	1.39E-02	70.6	52.8
7	4.901	5.174	13166	8316	89.93	3.40E-04	2.775	1.36E-02	72.4	51.2
8	5.202	4.910	12631	8116	89.23	3.33E-04	3.197	1.33E-02	73.7	49.6
9	4.926	4.842	12861	7971	77.42	3.22E-04	3.058	1.29E-02	76.2	47.9
10	5.075	5.074	13612	8198	91.55	3.21E-04	3.141	1.29E-02	76.5	49.2
990	4.947	5.238	12688	8346	63.63	3.58E-04	2.662	1.43E-02	68.4	52.6
991	4.835	5.130	13639	8116	72.96	3.25E-04	2.899	1.30E-02	75.5	48.9
992	5.241	5.100	12917	7879	88.92	3.41E-04	3.257	1.36E-02	72.2	48.8
993	4.867	4.893	13051	8516	69.79	3.21E-04	2.831	1.28E-02	76.3	50.8
994	5.058	4.985	12671	8599	88.17	3.38E-04	2.850	1.35E-02	72.7	52.7
995	5.125	4.841	12672	8472	81.48	3.27E-04	3.057	1.31E-02	75.1	51.1
996	4.863	5.058	12453	8134	68.56	3.50E-04	2.716	1.40E-02	70.0	50.8
997	5.157	5.016	12945	8225	98.03	3.33E-04	3.115	1.33E-02	73.8	50.3
998	4.932	5.183	12458	8211	78.17	3.60E-04	2.677	1.44E-02	68.2	52.0
999	5.034	4.940	13444	7969	76.71	3.15E-04	3.221	1.26E-02	77.8	47.4
1000	5.119	5.002	12948	7892	95.25	3.32E-04	3.196	1.33E-02	74.0	48.3
Mean	5.006	4.997	12992	8205	79.95	3.31E-04	2.990	1.32E-02	74.29	49.88
std. dev.	0.143	0.146	381	239	11.27	1.44E-05	0.199	5.75E-04	3.22	1.74
min.	4.750	4.751	12351	7792	60.04	2.97E-04	2.409	1.19E-02	66.85	45.36
max.	5.248	5.250	13650	8609	99.98	3.67E-04	3.613	1.47E-02	82.54	54.63

(X) = equation number in text

EXAMPLE 14.8: A COMMON-EMITTER/COMMON-SOURCE DESIGN

As a third example, let us try to meet the requirements of the previous design using a C-E/C-S design. Although the input resistance of the C-E and C-S amplifiers is usually considered in the moderate to high range, we can always limit it by reducing the size of the resistors in the bias network. Consider the common-source amplifier in Fig. 14.45. If the gate-bias resistor R_G is reduced to 75 Ω, then the input resistance of the amplifier will also be 75 Ω. (This design technique is sometimes referred to as **swamping** of the impedance level.) A BJT could also be used, but the JFET has been chosen because it offers the potential of a higher signal-handling capability. (A MOSFET would serve equally well.)

Because resistor R_5 is fully bypassed, this amplifier yields the full gain $-g_m R_L$, but the matched input causes a loss of input signal by a factor of 2:

$$\mathbf{v_{th}} = \mathbf{v_s}\frac{75}{75 + 75} = \frac{\mathbf{v_s}}{2} \tag{14.138}$$

Thus the prototype amplifier must deliver a gain of 100 for the overall amplifier to have a gain of 50. (This was actually the case for the C-B amplifier as well.) Referring back to Table 14.9, we find that our design guide for the voltage gain of the JFET common-source amplifier is

$$A_V = \frac{V_{DD}}{V_{GS} - V_P} \tag{14.139}$$

Here again we have a single constraint equation with two variables; Table 14.17 presents some possible design choices. Let us choose the 20 V/0.2 V option.

Because $V_{GS} - V_P$ must be small in order to achieve high gain, a JFET with a relatively large value of I_{DSS} (or a MOSFET with a large K_n or K_p) must be chosen if I_{DS} is to be a reasonable current. We assume that we have found a JFET with $I_{DSS} = 20$ mA and $V_P = -2$ V in our parts catalog. With these parameters, the JFET drain current is then

$$I_{DS} = I_{DSS}\left(1 - \frac{V_{GS}}{V_P}\right)^2 = (20\text{ mA})\left(1 - \frac{-2 + 0.2}{-2}\right)^2 = 0.2\text{ mA} \tag{14.140}$$

Note that I_{DS} is only 1 percent of I_{DSS} because of the small value of $V_{GS} - V_P$ required to satisfy Eq. (14.139).

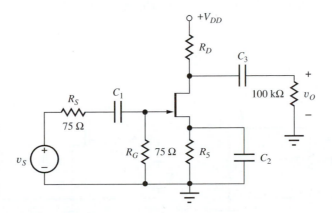

Figure 14.45 Common-source amplifier.

Table 14.17	
Possibilities for $A_v = 100$	
V_{DD}	$V_{GS} - V_P$
20 V	0.2 V
25 V	0.25 V
30 V	0.3 V

With reference to the dc equivalent circuit in Fig. 14.46(a), we can now calculate the value of R_5. Because the gate current is zero for the FET, the voltage developed across R_5 equals $-V_{GS}$:

$$R_5 = \frac{-V_{GS}}{I_{DS}} = \frac{-(V_P + 0.2 \text{ V})}{0.2 \text{ mA}} = \frac{1.8 \text{ V}}{0.2 \text{ mA}} = 9.00 \text{ k}\Omega \qquad (14.141)$$

The gain of the amplifier is

$$A_V = \frac{\mathbf{v_{th}}}{\mathbf{v_s}}(-g_m R_L) = \frac{-g_m R_L}{2} \qquad \text{where } R_L = R_D \parallel 100 \text{ k}\Omega \quad (14.142)$$

Setting Eq. (14.142) equal to 50 and solving for R_L yields

$$R_L = \frac{2A_V}{g_m} = \frac{A_V(V_{GS} - V_P)}{I_D} = \frac{50(0.2 \text{ V})}{0.2 \text{ mA}} = 50 \text{ k}\Omega \qquad (14.143)$$

For $R_L = 50$ kΩ, R_D must be 100 kΩ.

Now we have encountered a problem. A drain current of 0.2 mA in $R_D = 100$ kΩ requires a voltage drop equal to the total power supply voltage of 20 V. Thus, the power supply voltage must be increased. For pinch-off region operation, $V_{DS} \geq V_{GS} - V_P$, where

$$V_{DS} = V_{DD} - I_{DS}R_D - I_{DS}R_5 \qquad (14.144)$$

Therefore,

$$V_{DD} - 20 - 1.8 \geq (-1.8) - (-2) \qquad \text{or} \qquad V_{DD} \geq 22 \text{ V} \quad (14.145)$$

is sufficient to ensure pinch-off operation. Let us choose $V_{DD} = 25$ V to provide additional design margin and room for additional signal voltage swing at the drain. The circuit corresponding to the final amplifier design is in Fig. 14.47, where standard 5 percent resistor values have once again been selected.

The designs in Examples 14.7 and 14.8 demonstrate that usually more than one, often very different, design approaches can meet the specifications for a given problem. Choosing one design over another depends on many factors. For example, one criterion could be the use of power supply voltages that are already available in the rest of the system. Total power consumption might be an important issue. Our common-base design uses a power of approximately 3.3 mW and uses two power supplies, whereas the common-source design consumes 5 mW from a single 25-V supply.

Another important factor could be amplifier cost. The core of the JFET amplifier requires three resistors, R_D, R_G, and R_5; bypass capacitor C_2; and the JFET. The

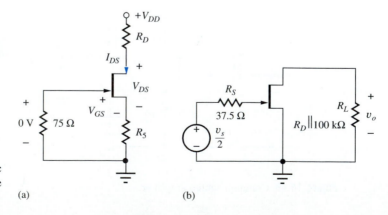

Figure 14.46 (a) dc and (b) ac equivalent circuits for the common-source amplifier.

(a)

(b)

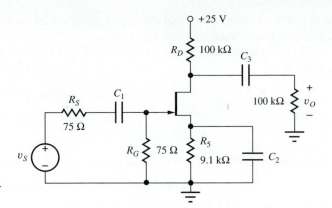

Figure 14.47 Final common-source amplifier design.

common-base amplifier core requires resistors R_E and R_C and the BJT. The cost of the additional parts, plus the expense of inserting them into a printed circuit board (often more expensive than the parts cost!), will probably tilt the economic decision away from the C-S design toward the C-B amplifier. However, the maximum input signal capability of the JFET amplifier, $|v_s| = 2 \times 0.2(V_{GS} - V_P) = 0.08$ V can be of overriding importance in certain applications. Obviously, the final decision will involve many factors. ◆

14.8 THE INFLUENCE OF BODY EFFECT ON AMPLIFIER PERFORMANCE

Up to now we have considered only three-terminal MOSFETs in our analog circuits. However, in many circuits, the body of the MOS transistor cannot be connected to its source. This is particularly true in the implementation of analog and digital circuits in integrated form. In this section we analyze the characteristics of the FET amplifiers using MOSFETs in a four-terminal configuration, and we modify the expressions from Table 14.9 to include the influence of **body effect** on the performance of the prototype amplifier circuits.

Common-Source Amplifier

The common-source amplifier in Figs. 14.48 and 14.49 is the first example of analysis of an analog circuit that includes the body effect. The small-signal model in Fig. 14.49 includes

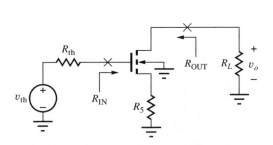

Figure 14.48 Common-source amplifier employing MOSFET in the four-terminal configuration.

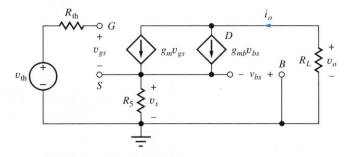

Figure 14.49 Small-signal model for the common-source amplifier of Fig. 14.48.

the dependent current source that models the effects of the back-gate transconductance g_{mb}. Remember from Chapter 13 that $g_{mb} = \eta g_m$.

To find the voltage gain of the circuit in Fig. 14.46, we must find the output current $\mathbf{i_o}$ given by

$$\mathbf{i_o} = g_m \mathbf{v_{gs}} + g_{mb} \mathbf{v_{bs}} \tag{14.146}$$

in which

$$\mathbf{v_{gs}} = \mathbf{v_{th}} - \mathbf{v_s} \quad \text{and} \quad \mathbf{v_{bs}} = -\mathbf{v_s} \tag{14.147}$$

The voltage at the MOSFET source can also be written in terms of $\mathbf{i_o}$:

$$\mathbf{v_s} = (g_m \mathbf{v_{gs}} + g_{mb} \mathbf{v_{bs}}) R_5 = \mathbf{i_o} R_5 \tag{14.148}$$

Substituting Eqs. (14.147) into (14.148) and solving for $\mathbf{v_s}$ yields

$$\mathbf{v_s} = \frac{g_m R_5}{1 + (g_m + g_{mb}) R_5} \mathbf{v_{th}} = \frac{g_m R_5}{1 + g_m(1 + \eta) R_5} \mathbf{v_{th}} \tag{14.149}$$

and substituting Eqs. (14.149) and (14.147) into (14.146) gives an expression for $\mathbf{i_o}$ (after some algebra):

$$\mathbf{i_o} = \frac{g_m}{1 + g_m(1 + \eta) R_5} \mathbf{v_{th}} \tag{14.150}$$

The output voltage is expressed as $\mathbf{v_o} = -\mathbf{i_o} R_L$, and the voltage gain is found using Eq. (14.150):

$$A_{V\text{th}} = \frac{\mathbf{v_o}}{\mathbf{v_{th}}} = -\frac{g_m R_L}{1 + g_m(1 + \eta) R_5} \tag{14.151}$$

This expression is the same as that derived earlier for the common-source amplifier, except for the addition of the $(1 + \eta)$ factor in the denominator. If $\eta = 0$, this expression reduces to Eq. (14.10), as it should.

Because the gate current i_g is zero in Figs. 14.48 and 14.49, the input resistance (and current gain) will be infinite and not changed by existence of the four-terminal connection. The output resistance can be calculated based on the circuit model in Fig. 14.50. Here we see that v_{bs} is identical to v_{gs}, so the two dependent current sources can be combined into one source:

$$\mathbf{i} = g_m \mathbf{v_{gs}} + g_{mb} \mathbf{v_{bs}} = (g_m + g_{mb}) \mathbf{v_{gs}} = g_m(1 + \eta) \mathbf{v_{gs}} \tag{14.152}$$

With this transformation, the circuit model becomes identical to that used to find the output resistance for the three-terminal BJT and FET case (Fig. 14.11), and we can use the results from Eq. (14.31) with g_m replaced by $g_m(1 + \eta)$:

$$R_{\text{OUT}}^{CS} = r_o[1 + g_m(1 + \eta) R_5] \tag{14.153}$$

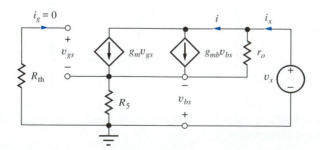

Figure 14.50 Small-signal model for finding the output resistance of the common-source amplifier.

Common-Drain Amplifier

Analysis of the common-drain amplifier in Fig. 14.51 is very similar to that for the common-source amplifier in Figs. 14.48 and 14.49, except that the output is taken across the resistor in the source. The output current has exactly the same form as Eq. (14.150):

$$\mathbf{i_o} = \frac{g_m}{1 + g_m(1 + \eta)R_L}\mathbf{v_{th}} \tag{14.154}$$

The output voltage is expressed as $\mathbf{v_o} = +\mathbf{i_o}R_L$, and the voltage gain is

$$A_{V\text{th}} = \frac{\mathbf{v_o}}{\mathbf{v_{th}}} = \frac{g_m R_L}{1 + g_m(1 + \eta)R_L} \tag{14.155}$$

Again it can be observed in Fig. 14.51 that R_{IN} is defined looking directly into the gate of the FET. Because i_g is zero, R_{IN} and $A_{I\text{th}}$ are both infinite. The output resistance can be found with the aid of the circuit diagram in Fig. 14.52. Because $i_g = 0$, the circuit connection again forces v_{bs} to be equal to v_{gs}. Thus, the two parallel current generators can be combined into one source, and we can simply modify the output resistance results for the FET from Eq. (14.55):

$$R_{\text{OUT}}^{CD} = \frac{1}{g_m(1 + \eta)} \tag{14.156}$$

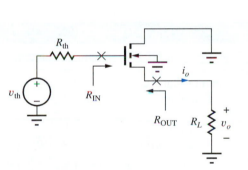

Figure 14.51 Common-drain amplifier including body effect.

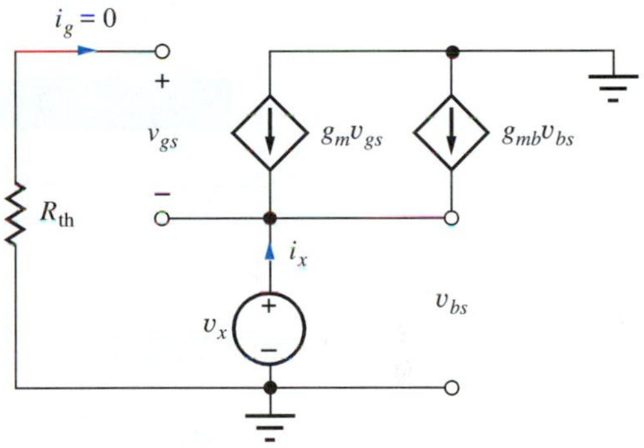

Figure 14.52 Circuit for finding the common-drain output resistance.

Common-Gate Amplifier

Finally, the schematic diagram for the common-gate amplifier is given in Fig. 14.53. Here, we observe that the circuit forces $v_{bs} = v_{gs}$ to always be true, and the FET results from

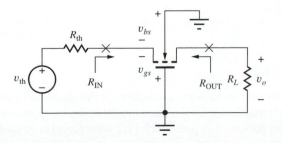

Figure 14.53 Common-gate amplifier with four-terminal MOSFET.

Sec. 14.4 can all be used directly by replacing g_m with $g_m(1 + \eta)$:

$$A_{V\text{th}}^{CG} = \frac{g_m(1 + \eta)R_L}{1 + g_m(1 + \eta)R_\text{th}}$$

$$R_{\text{IN}}^{CG} = \frac{1}{g_m(1 + \eta)} \tag{14.157}$$

$$R_{\text{OUT}}^{CG} = r_o[1 + g_m(1 + \eta)R_\text{th}]$$

> **EXERCISE:** Draw the small-signal model for the circuit in Fig. 14.50 and use it to directly derive the results presented in Eqs. (14.157).

Table 14.18 gives the results of the preceding analyses as well as results for the signal limits. Including the body effect through the parameter η, a positive number, improves some of the characteristics of the amplifiers and degrades others. The gain of the common-gate amplifier more closely approaches the R_L/R_th limit, but the gain of the source follower is degraded. Body effect tends to lower the input resistance and output resistance of the common-gate and the common-drain amplifiers, respectively, and raises the output resistance of both the common-source and common-gate amplifiers; η also increases the input signal range. The improvements may come as a surprise because body effect usually degrades the performance of digital circuits. However, we will find, in later chapters, that body effect indeed causes additional problems, particularly with Q-point design in CMOS analog circuits.

Table 14.18

Four-Terminal MOSFET Amplifier Summary

	Common-Source Amplifier	Common-Drain Amplifier	Common-Gate Amplifier
Voltage Gain $A_{V\text{th}} = \dfrac{v_o}{v_\text{th}}$	$-\dfrac{g_m R_L}{1 + g_m(1 + \eta)R_S}$	$\dfrac{g_m R_L}{1 + g_m(1 + \eta)R_L}$ $\approx +1$	$+\dfrac{g_m(1 + \eta)R_L}{1 + g_m(1 + \eta)R_\text{th}}$
Input Resistance	∞	∞	$\dfrac{1}{g_m(1 + \eta)}$
Output Resistance	$r_o + \mu_f R_S(1 + \eta)$	$\dfrac{1}{g_m(1 + \eta)}$	$r_o + \mu_f R_\text{th}(1 + \eta)$
Input Signal Range	$0.2(V_{GS} - V_{TN}) \cdot$ $(1 + g_m(1 + \eta)R_S)$	$0.2(V_{GS} - V_{TN}) \cdot$ $(1 + g_m(1 + \eta)R_L)$	$0.2(V_{GS} - V_{TN}) \cdot$ $(1 + g_m(1 + \eta)R_\text{th})$
Current Gain	∞	∞	$+1$

SUMMARY

This chapter was an in-depth evaluation of the characteristics of amplifiers implemented using single transistors. Of the three available device terminals, only the base or emitter of the BJT and the source or gate of the FET were found to be useful as signal input terminals, and the collector or emitter and drain or source were found acceptable as output terminals. The collector and drain are not used as input terminals, and the base and gate are not used as output terminals. These restrictions led to three basic classifications of amplifiers: the inverting amplifiers—the common-emitter and common-source amplifiers; the followers—the common-collector and common-drain amplifiers (also known as emitter followers or source followers); and the noninverting common-base and common-gate amplifiers.

Detailed analyses of these three amplifier classes were performed using the small-signal models for the transistors. These analyses produced expressions for the voltage gain, current gain, input resistance, output resistance, and input signal range, which are summarized in a group of important tables:

The results summarized in these tables form the basic toolkit of the analog circuit designer. A thorough understanding of these results is a prerequisite for design and for the analysis of more complex analog circuits.

Table 14.19 is a relative comparison of these three amplifier classes. The inverting amplifiers (C-E and C-S amplifiers) can provide significant voltage and current gain as well as high input and output resistance. If a resistor is included in the emitter or source of the transistor, the voltage gain is reduced but can be made relatively independent of the individual transistor characteristics. However, this reduction in gain is a tradeoff for increases in input resistance, output resistance, and input signal range. Because of its higher transconductance, the BJT more easily achieves high values of voltage gain than the FET, whereas the infinite input resistance of the FET gives it the advantage in achieving high input resistance amplifiers. The FET also typically has a larger input signal range than the BJT.

The emitter and source followers (C-C and C-D amplifiers) provide a voltage gain of approximately 1, high input resistance, and low output resistance. The followers provide moderate levels of current gain and achieve the highest input signal range. These C-C and C-D amplifiers are the single-transistor equivalents of the voltage-follower operational-amplifier configuration introduced in Chapter 12.

Table 14.19		
Relative Comparison of Single-Transistor Amplifiers		
	Inverting Amplifiers (C-E and C-S)	Followers (C-C and C-D)	Noninverting Amplifiers (C-B and C-G)
Voltage Gain	Moderate	Low (≈ 1)	Moderate
Input Resistance	Moderate to high	High	Low
Output Resistance	Moderate to high	Low	High
Input Signal Range	Low to moderate	High	Low to moderate
Current Gain	Moderate	Moderate	Low (≈ 1)

The noninverting amplifiers (C-B and C-G amplifiers) provide voltage gain, signal range, and output resistances very similar to those of the inverting amplifiers but have relatively low input resistance and current gain less than 1. All the amplifier classes provide at least moderate levels of either voltage gain or current gain (or both) and are therefore capable, with proper design, of providing significant power gain.

Design examples were presented for amplifiers using the inverting, noninverting, and follower configurations, and an example using Monte Carlo analysis to evaluate the effects of element tolerances on circuit performance was also given.

The chapter concluded with analysis of amplifier circuits containing field-effect transistors operating as four-terminal devices; Table 14.18 summarized the results of these analyses.

Key Terms

Body effect
Common-base (C-B) amplifier
Common-collector (C-C) amplifier
Common-emitter (C-E) amplifier
Common-drain (C-D) amplifier
Common-gate (C-G) amplifier

Common-source (C-S) amplifier
Current gain
Emitter follower
Power gain
Input resistance
Output resistance

Signal range
Source follower
Swamping
Voltage gain

Additional Reading

Gray, P. R., and R. G. Meyer. *Analysis and Design of Analog Integrated Circuits.* 3d ed. Wiley, New York: 1993.

Horenstein, M. N. *Microelectronic Circuits and Devices.* Prentice-Hall, Englewood Cliffs, NJ: 1990.

Savant, C. J., M. S. Rodeen, and G. L. Carpenter. *Electronic Design—Circuits and Systems.* 2d ed. Benjamin/Cummings, Redwood City, CA: 1991.

Sedra, A. S., and K. C. Smith. *Microelectronic Circuits.* 3d ed. Saunders, Philadelphia: 1991.

PSPICE Simulation Data

```
*Common-Emitter Amplifier
*
VCC 5 0 DC 12
R1 3 0 160K
R2 5 3 300K
R3 5 4 22K
R5 2 1 3K
R6 1 0 10K
R7 8 0 100K
Q1 4 3 2 NBJT
VS 6 0 AC 1
RS 6 7 2K
C1 7 3 10UF
C2 4 8 4.7UF
C3 1 0 47UF
```

```
.MODEL NBJT NPN IS=5E-16 BF=100 VA=50
.OP
.AC LIN 1 5000 5000
.PRINT AC VM(8) VP(8) IM(VS) IP(VS)
.END


*Common-Collector Amplifier
*
C1 7 3 10UF
C2 2 8 4.7UF
C3 4 0 47UF


*Common-Base Amplifier
*
C1 7 2 10UF
C2 4 8 4.7UF
C3 3 0 47UF


*Common-Source Amplifier
*
VCC 5 0 DC 12
R1 3 0 1.5MEG
R2 5 3 2.2MEG
R3 5 4 22K
R5 2 1 2K
R6 1 0 10K
R7 8 0 100K
M1 4 3 2 2 NMOSFET
VS 6 0 AC 1
RS 6 7 2K
C1 7 3 10UF
C2 4 8 4.7UF
C3 1 0 47UF
.MODEL NMOSFET NMOS KP=5E-4 VTO=1 LAMBDA=.02
.OP
.AC LIN 1 5000 5000
.PRINT AC VM(8) VP(8) IM(VS) IP(VS)
.END


*Common-Drain Amplifier
*
C1 7 3 10UF
C2 2 8 4.7UF
C3 4 0 47UF


*Common-Gate Amplifier
*
C1 7 2 10UF
C2 4 8 4.7UF
C3 3 0 47UF
```

Problems

Assume all capacitors and inductors have infinite value unless otherwise indicated

14.1 Amplifier Classification

14.1. Draw the ac equivalent circuits for, and classify (that is, as C-S, C-G, C-D, C-E, C-B, C-C, and not useful), the amplifiers in Figs. P14.1(a) to (o).

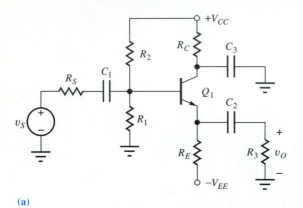

(a)

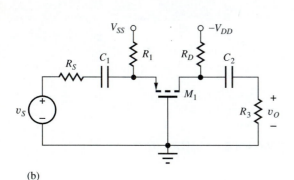

(b)

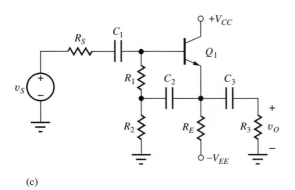

(c)

Figure P14.1(a), (b), (c)

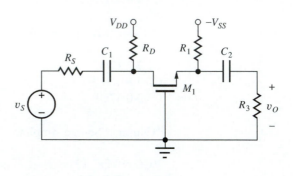

(d)

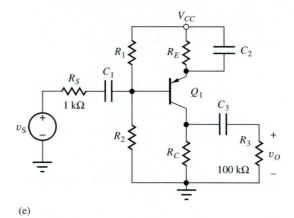

(e)

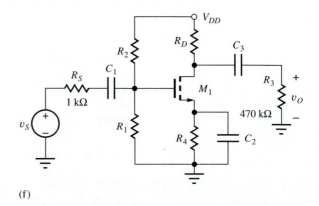

(f)

Figure P14.1(d), (e), (f)

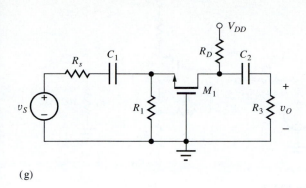

(g)

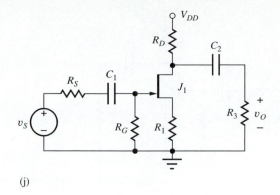

(j)

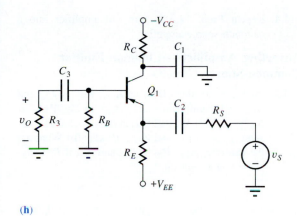

(h)

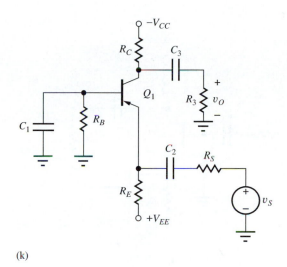

(k)

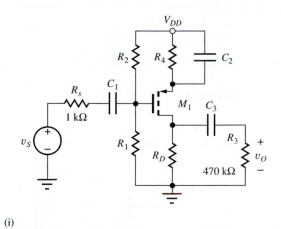

(i)

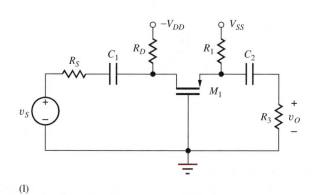

(l)

Figure P14.1(g), (h), (i)

Figure P14.1(j), (k), (l)

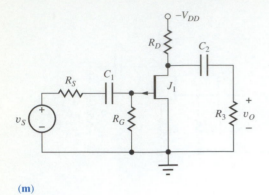

(m)

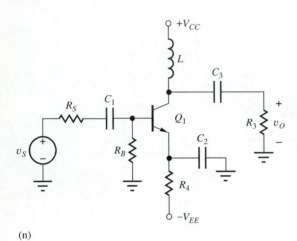

(n)

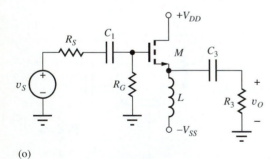

(o)

Figure P14.1(m), (n), (o)

14.2. A PMOS transistor is biased by the circuit in Fig. P14.2. Using the external source and load configurations in the figure, add coupling and bypass capacitors to the circuit to turn the amplifier into a common-gate amplifier.

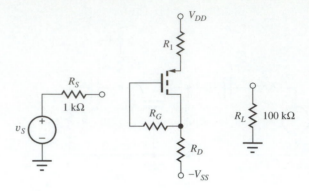

Figure P14.2

14.3. Repeat Prob. 14.2 to turn the amplifier into a common-drain amplifier.

14.4. Repeat Prob. 14.2 to turn the amplifier into a common-source amplifier.

14.2 Inverting Amplifiers—Common-Emitter and Common-Source Circuits

14.5. (a) What are the values of A_{Vth}, R_{IN}, R_{OUT}, and A_{Ith} for the common-source stage in Fig. P14.5 if $R_{th} = 75\ \text{k}\Omega$, $R_L = 2\ \text{k}\Omega$, and $R_5 = 200\ \Omega$? Assume $g_m = 5\ \text{mS}$ and $r_o = 10\ \text{k}\Omega$. (b) What are the values of A_{Vth}, R_{IN}, R_{OUT}, and A_{Ith} if R_5 is bypassed by a capacitor?

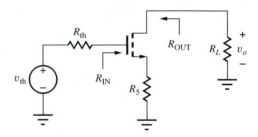

Figure P14.5

14.6. (a) What are the values of A_{Vth}, R_{IN}, R_{OUT}, and A_{Ith} for the common-emitter stage in Fig. P14.6 if $g_m = $

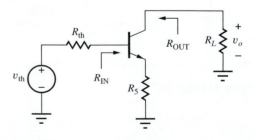

Figure P14.6

20 mS, $\beta_o = 75$, $r_o = 100$ kΩ, $R_{\text{th}} = 500$ Ω, $R_L = 12$ kΩ, and $R_5 = 200$ Ω? (b) What are the values if R_5 is changed to 560 Ω?

14.7. **(a)** Estimate the voltage gain of the inverting amplifier in Fig. P14.7. (b) Place a bypass capacitor in the circuit to change the gain to approximately -10. (c) Where should the bypass capacitor be placed to change the gain to approximately -20? (d) Where should the bypass capacitor be placed to achieve maximum gain? **(e)** Estimate this gain?

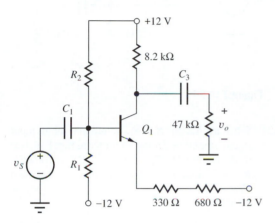

Figure P14.7

14.8. What values of R_5 and R_L are required in the ac equivalent circuit in Fig. P14.8 to achieve $A_{V\text{th}} = -10$ and $R_{\text{IN}} = 500$ kΩ? Assume $\beta_o = 75$.

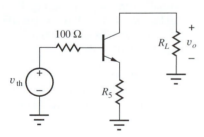

Figure P14.8

14.9. Assume that $R_5 = 0$ in Fig. P14.8. What values of R_L and I_C are required to achieve $A_{V\text{th}} = -10$ and $R_{\text{IN}} = 500$ kΩ? Assume $\beta_o = 75$.

14.10. Use nodal analysis to rederive the output resistance of the common-source circuit in Fig. P14.10, as expressed in Eq. (14.31).

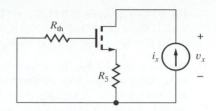

Figure P14.10

**14.11. Use nodal analysis to find the output resistance of the common-emitter circuit in Fig. 14.11 as redrawn in Fig. P14.11.

$$R_1 = R_{\text{th}} + r_\pi; \quad g'_m = g_m \frac{r_\pi}{R_{\text{th}} + r_\pi} = \frac{\beta_o}{R_{\text{th}} + r_\pi}$$

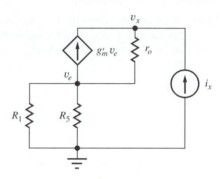

Figure P14.11

14.12. What are A_V, A_I, R_{IN}, R_{OUT}, and the maximum amplitude of the signal source for the amplifier in Fig. P14.1(e) if $R_1 = 20$ kΩ, $R_2 = 62$ kΩ, $R_E = 3.9$ kΩ, $R_C = 8.2$ kΩ, and $V_{CC} = 12$ V? Use $\beta_F = 75$. Compare A_V to our rule-of-thumb estimate and discuss the reasons for any discrepancy.

14.13. What are A_V, A_I, R_{IN}, R_{OUT}, and the maximum amplitude of the signal source for the amplifier in Fig. P14.1(f) if $R_1 = 500$ kΩ, $R_2 = 1.4$ MΩ, $R_4 = 27$ kΩ, $R_D = 75$ kΩ, and $V_{DD} = 18$ V? Use $K_n = 250$ μA/V^2 and $V_{TN} = 1$ V. Compare A_V to our rule-of-thumb estimate and discuss the reasons for any discrepancy.

14.14. What are A_V, A_I, R_{IN}, R_{OUT}, and the maximum amplitude of the signal source for the amplifier in Fig. P14.1(i) if $R_1 = 2.2$ MΩ, $R_2 = 2.2$ MΩ, $R_4 = 22$ kΩ, $R_D = 18$ kΩ, and $V_{DD} = 18$ V? Use $K_p = 400$ μA/V^2 and $V_{TP} = -1$ V.

14.15. What are A_V, A_I, R_{IN}, R_{OUT}, and the maximum amplitude of the signal source for the amplifier in

Fig. P14.1(j) if $R_S = 500\ \Omega$, $R_1 = 11\ \text{k}\Omega$, $R_G = 1\ \text{M}\Omega$, $R_3 = 500\ \text{k}\Omega$, $R_D = 39\ \text{k}\Omega$, and $V_{DD} = 20\ \text{V}$? Use $I_{DSS} = 20\ \text{mA}$ and $V_P = -4\ \text{V}$.

14.16. What are A_V, A_I, R_{IN}, R_{OUT}, and the maximum value of the source voltage for the amplifier in Fig. P14.1(m) if $R_S = 5\ \text{k}\Omega$, $R_G = 10\ \text{M}\Omega$, $R_3 = 36\ \text{k}\Omega$, $R_D = 1.8\ \text{k}\Omega$, and $V_{DD} = 16\ \text{V}$? Use $I_{DSS} = 5\ \text{mA}$ and $V_P = -5\ \text{V}$.

14.17. What are A_V, A_I, R_{IN}, R_{OUT}, and the maximum value of the source voltage for the amplifier in Fig. P14.1(n) if $R_S = 250\ \Omega$, $R_B = 20\ \text{k}\Omega$, $R_3 = 1\ \text{M}\Omega$, $R_4 = 9.1\ \text{k}\Omega$, $V_{CC} = 10\ \text{V}$, and $V_{EE} = 10\ \text{V}$? Use $\beta_F = 80$ and $V_A = 100\ \text{V}$.

14.3 Follower Circuits—Common-Collector and Common-Drain Amplifiers

14.18. What are the values of $A_{V\text{th}}$, R_{IN}, R_{OUT}, and $A_{I\text{th}}$ for the common-collector stage in Fig. P14.18 if $R_{\text{th}} = 47\ \text{k}\Omega$, $R_L = 1\ \text{k}\Omega$, $\beta_o = 80$, and $g_m = 0.4\ \text{S}$?

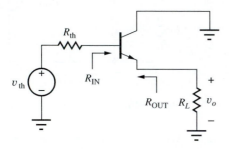

Figure P14.18

14.19. What are the values of $A_{V\text{th}}$, R_{IN}, R_{OUT}, and $A_{I\text{th}}$ for the common-drain stage in Fig. P14.19 if $R_{\text{th}} = 100\ \text{k}\Omega$, $R_L = 1\ \text{k}\Omega$, and $g_m = 10\ \text{mS}$?

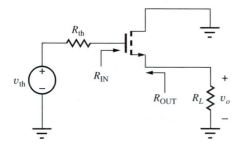

Figure P14.19

*14.20. The gate resistor R_G in Fig. P14.20 is said to be "bootstrapped" by the action of the source fol-

lower. (a) Assume that the FET is operating with $g_m = 3.54\ \text{mS}$ and r_o can be neglected. Draw the small-signal model and find A_V, R_{IN}, and R_{OUT} for the amplifier. (b) What would R_{IN} be if A_V were exactly $+1$?

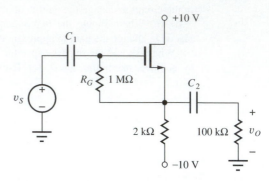

Figure P14.20

14.21. What are A_V, A_I, R_{IN}, R_{OUT}, and maximum input signal amplitude for the amplifier in Fig. P14.1(a) if $R_S = 500\ \Omega$, $R_1 = 51\ \text{k}\Omega$, $R_2 = 100\ \text{k}\Omega$, $R_3 = 24\ \text{k}\Omega$, $R_E = 4.7\ \text{k}\Omega$, $R_C = 2\ \text{k}\Omega$, and $V_{CC} = V_{EE} = 18\ \text{V}$? Use $\beta_F = 125$ and $V_A = 50\ \text{V}$.

14.22. What are A_V, A_I, R_{IN}, R_{OUT}, and the maximum input signal amplitude for the amplifier in Fig. P14.1(c) if $R_S = 500\ \Omega$, $R_1 = 500\ \text{k}\Omega$, $R_2 = 500\ \text{k}\Omega$, $R_3 = 500\ \text{k}\Omega$, $R_E = 430\ \text{k}\Omega$, and $V_{CC} = V_{EE} = 5\ \text{V}$? Use $\beta_F = 100$ and $V_A = 60\ \text{V}$.

14.23. What are A_V, A_I, R_{IN}, R_{OUT}, and maximum input signal for the amplifier in Fig. P14.1(o) if $R_S = 10\ \text{k}\Omega$, $R_G = 1\ \text{M}\Omega$, $R_3 = 100\ \text{k}\Omega$, and $V_{DD} = V_{SS} = 5\ \text{V}$? Use $K_n = 400\ \mu\text{A/V}^2$, $V_{TN} = 1\ \text{V}$, and $\lambda = 0.02\ \text{V}^{-1}$.

14.24. Rework Prob. 14.20(a) by using the formulas for the bipolar transistor by "pretending" that R_G makes the JFET equivalent to a BJT with $r_\pi = R_G$.

*14.25. Recast the signal-range formula for the common-collector amplifier in Table 14.3 in terms of the dc voltage developed across the emitter resistor R_4 in Fig. 14.3(a). Assume $R_7 = \infty$.

*14.26. The input to a common-collector amplifier is a triangular input signal with a peak-to-peak amplitude of 10 V. (a) What is the minimum gain required of the C-C amplifier to meet the small-signal limit? (b) What is the minimum dc voltage required across the emitter resistor in this amplifier to satisfy the limit in (a)?

*14.27. Design the emitter-follower circuit in Fig. P14.27 to meet the small-signal requirements when $v_o = 7.5 \sin 2000\pi t$ V. Assume $C_1 = C_2 = \infty$ and $\beta_F = 50$.

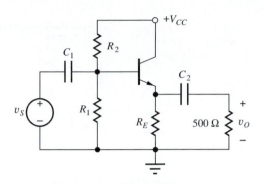

Figure P14.27

14.4 Noninverting Amplifiers—Common-Base and Common-Gate Circuits

14.28. What are the values of A_{Vth}, R_{IN}, R_{OUT}, and A_{Ith} for the common-gate stage in Fig. P14.28 operating with $g_m = 0.5$ mS, $R_{th} = 50$ Ω, and $R_L = 100$ kΩ? (b) What are the values if R_{th} is changed to 5 kΩ?

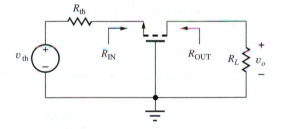

Figure P14.28

14.29. What are the values of A_{Vth}, R_{IN}, R_{OUT}, and A_{Ith} for the common-base stage in Fig. P14.29 operating with $I_C = 12.5$ μA, $\beta_o = 100$, $V_A = 60$ V, $R_{th} = 50$ Ω, and $R_L = 100$ kΩ? (b) What are the values if R_{th} is changed to 2.2 kΩ?

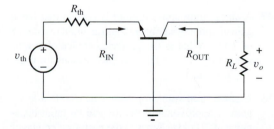

Figure P14.29

14.30. Estimate the voltage gain of the amplifier in Fig. P14.30. Explain your answer.

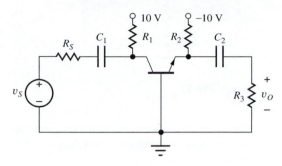

Figure P14.30

14.31. What are A_V, A_I, R_{IN}, R_{OUT}, and the maximum input signal amplitude for the amplifier in Fig. P14.1(b) if $R_S = 500$ Ω, $R_1 = 33$ kΩ, $R_3 = 100$ kΩ, $R_D = 24$ kΩ, and $V_{DD} = V_{SS} = 12$ V? Use $K_p = 200$ μA/V^2 and $V_{TP} = -1$ V.

14.32. What are A_V, A_I, R_{IN}, R_{OUT}, and the maximum input signal for the amplifier in Fig. P14.1(g) if $R_S = 1$ kΩ, $R_1 = 3.9$ kΩ, $R_3 = 51$ kΩ, $R_D = 20$ kΩ, and $V_{DD} = 15$ V? Use $K_n = 500$ μA/V^2 and $V_{TN} = -2$ V.

14.33. What are A_V, A_I, R_{IN}, R_{OUT}, and the maximum input signal for the amplifier in Fig. P14.1(k) if $R_S = 500$ Ω, $R_B = 100$ kΩ, $R_3 = 100$ kΩ, $R_E = 82$ kΩ, $R_C = 39$ kΩ, and $V_{EE} = V_{CC} = 9$ V? Use $\beta_F = 50$ and $V_A = 50$ V.

14.34. What are A_V, A_I, R_{IN}, R_{OUT}, and the maximum input signal for the amplifier in Fig. P14.1(k) if $R_S = 5$ kΩ, $R_B = 1$ MΩ, $R_3 = 1$ MΩ, $R_E = 820$ kΩ, $R_C = 390$ kΩ, and $V_{EE} = V_{CC} = 9$ V? Use $\beta_F = 50$ and $V_A = 50$ V.

14.35. What are A_V, A_I, R_{IN}, R_{OUT}, and the maximum input signal for the amplifier in Fig. P14.1(b) if $R_S = 250$ Ω, $R_1 = 68$ kΩ, $R_3 = 200$ kΩ, $R_D = 43$ kΩ, and $V_{DD} = V_{SS} = 15$ V? Use $K_p = 200$ μA/V^2 and $V_{TP} = -1$ V.

14.36. The gain of the common-gate and common-base stages can be written as $A_{vth} = R_L/[(1/g_m) + R_{th}]$. When $R_{th} \ll 1/g_m$, the circuit is said to be "voltage driven," and when $R_{th} \gg 1/g_m$, the circuit is said to be "current driven." What are the approximate voltage gain expressions for these two conditions? Discuss the reason for the use of these adjectives to describe the two circuit limits.

14.37. What is the input resistance to the common-base stage in Fig. P14.37 if $I_C = 1$ mA and $\beta_F = 75$?

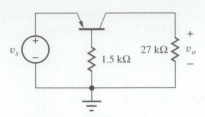

Figure P14.37

14.38. What is the input resistance to the common-gate stage in Fig. P14.38 if $I_{DS} = 1$ mA, $I_{DSS} = 5$ mA, and $V_P = -2$ V?

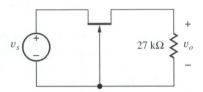

Figure P14.38

14.39. What is the input resistance to the common-gate stage in Fig. P14.39 if $I_{DS} = 1$ mA, $K_p = 1.25$ mA/V^2, and $V_{TP} = 2$ V?

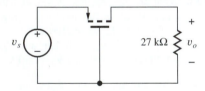

Figure P14.39

14.40. (a) Estimate the output resistance looking into the collector of the transistor in Fig. P14.40 if $R_E = 143$ kΩ, $V_A = 50$ V, $\beta_F = 100$, and $V_{EE} = 15$ V? (b) What is the minimum value of V_{CC} required to ensure that Q_1 is operating in the forward-active region? (c) Repeat parts (a) and (b) if $R_E = 15$ kΩ.

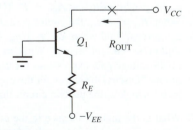

Figure P14.40

*14.41. What is the resistance looking into the collector terminal in Fig. P14.41 if $I_E = 50\,\mu$A, $\beta_o = 125$, $V_A = 50$ V, and $V_{CC} = 10$ V? (*Hint: r_o must be considered in this circuit. Otherwise $R_{OUT} = \infty$.*)

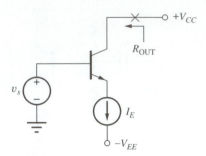

Figure P14.41

14.5 Amplifier Prototype Review and Comparison

14.42. A single-transistor amplifier is needed that has a gain of 30 dB and an input resistance of 5 MΩ. What is the preferred choice of amplifier configuration, and why did you make this selection?

14.43. A single-transistor amplifier is needed that has a gain of 52 dB and an input resistance of 1 MΩ. What is the preferred choice of amplifier configuration? Discuss your reasons for making this selection.

14.44. A single-transistor amplifier is needed that has a gain of −100 and an input resistance of 5 Ω. What is the preferred choice of amplifier configuration? Discuss your reasons for making this selection.

14.45. A single-transistor amplifier is needed that has a gain of approximately 0 dB and an input resistance of 25 MΩ with a load resistor of 10 kΩ. What is the preferred choice of amplifier configuration, and why did you make this selection?

14.46. A follower is needed that has a gain of at least 0.98 and an input resistance of at least 250 kΩ with a load resistance of 5 kΩ. What is the preferred choice of amplifier configuration? Discuss your reasons for making this selection.

14.47. A single-transistor amplifier is needed that has a gain of approximately +10 and an input resistance of 2 kΩ. What is the preferred choice of amplifier configuration? Discuss your reasons for making this selection.

14.48. A single-transistor amplifier is needed that has a gain of approximately 80 dB and an input resistance of 100 kΩ. What is the preferred choice of amplifier configuration, and why did you make this selection?

14.49. A common-collector amplifier is being driven from a source having a resistance of 250 Ω. What is the minimum output resistance of this amplifier if the transistor has $\beta_o = 150$?

14.6 Overall Amplifier Performance

**14.50. Show that the emitter resistor R_E in Fig. P14.50 can be absorbed into the transistor by redefining the small-signal parameters of the transistor to be

$$g_m' \cong \frac{g_m}{1 + g_m R_E} \qquad r_\pi' \cong r_\pi(1 + g_m R_E)$$

$$r_o' \cong r_o(1 + g_m R_E)$$

What is the expression for the common-emitter small-signal current gain β_o' for the new transistor? What is the expression for the amplification factor μ_f' for the new transistor?

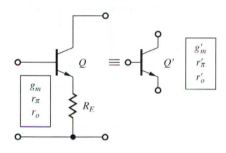

Figure P14.50

*14.51. Perform a transient simulation of the behavior of the common-emitter amplifier in Fig. P14.51 for sinusoidal input voltages of 5 mV, 10 mV, and 15 mV at a frequency of 1 kHz. Use the Fourier

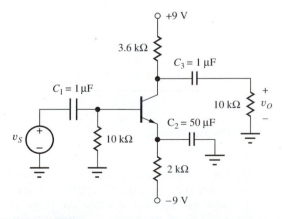

Figure P14.51

analysis capability of SPICE to analyze the output waveforms. Compare the amplitudes of the 2-kHz and 3-kHz harmonics to the amplitude of the desired signal at 1 kHz. Assume $\beta_F = 100$ and $V_A = 70$ V.

14.52. In the circuits in Fig. P14.52, $I_B = 10$ μA. Use SPICE to determine the output resistances of the two circuits by sweeping the voltage V_{CC} from 10 to 20 V. Use $\beta_F = 60$ and $V_A = 20$ V. Compare results to hand calculations using the small-signal parameter values from SPICE.

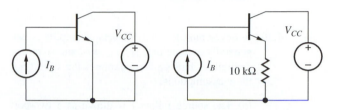

Figure P14.52

14.53. What is the Thévenin equivalent representation for the amplifier in Fig. P14.53?

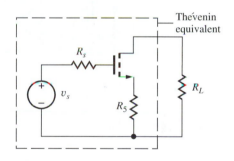

Figure P14.53

14.54. What is the Thévenin equivalent representation for the amplifier in Fig. P14.54?

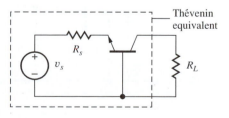

Figure P14.54

14.55. What is the Thévenin equivalent representation for the amplifier in Fig. P14.55?

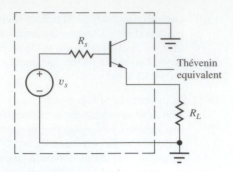

Figure P14.55

 14.56. In developing two-port models of amplifiers, we generally assume that y_{12}, z_{12}, h_{12}, and so on are negligible. This problem explores the validity of these assumptions.

(a) The source follower is drawn as a two-port in Fig. P14.56(a). Calculate y_{21} and y_{12} for this amplifier in terms of the small-signal parameters. Compare the two results.

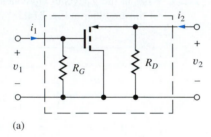

(a)

Figure P14.56(a)

(b) The emitter follower is drawn as a two-port in Fig. P14.56(b). Calculate y_{21} and y_{12} for this amplifier in terms of the small-signal parameters. Compare the two results.

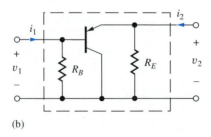

(b)

Figure P14.56(b)

(c) The common-base amplifier is drawn as a two-port in Fig. P14.56(c). Calculate y_{21} and

y_{12} for this amplifier in terms of the small-signal parameters. Compare the two results.

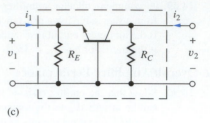

(c)

Figure P14.56(c)

(d) The common-gate amplifier is drawn as a two-port in Fig. P14.56(d). Calculate y_{21} and y_{12} for this amplifier in terms of the small-signal parameters. Compare the two results.

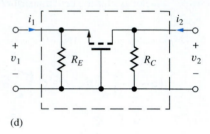

(d)

Figure P14.56(d)

(e) The common-emitter amplifier is drawn as a two-port in Fig. P14.56(e). Calculate y_{21} and y_{12} for this amplifier in terms of the small-signal parameters. Compare the two results.

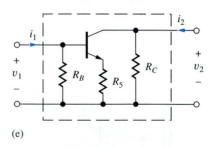

(e)

Figure P14.56(e)

(f) The common-source amplifier is drawn as a two-port in Fig. P14.56(f). Calculate y_{21} and y_{12} for this amplifier in terms of the small-signal parameters. Compare the two results.

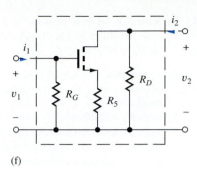

(f)

Figure P14.56(f)

14.57. Our calculation of the input resistance of the common-gate and common-base amplifiers neglected r_o in the calculation. Calculate an improved estimate for R_{IN} for the common-gate stage in Fig. P14.57.

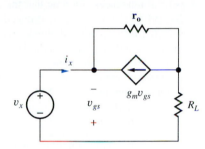

Figure P14.57

14.58. The circuit in Fig. P14.58 is called a phase inverter. Calculate the two gains $A_{V1} = \mathbf{v_{o1}}/\mathbf{v_s}$ and $A_{V2} = \mathbf{v_{o2}}/\mathbf{v_s}$. What is the largest ac signal that can be developed at output v_{o1} in this particular circuit? Assume $\beta_F = 100$.

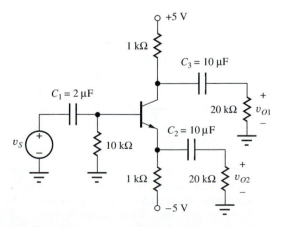

Figure P14.58

14.59. (a) Calculate the values of A_V, R_{IN}, and R_{OUT} for the amplifier in Fig. P14.1(a) if $R_S = 500\ \Omega$, $R_1 = 51\ \text{k}\Omega$, $R_2 = 100\ \text{k}\Omega$, $R_3 = 24\ \text{k}\Omega$, $R_E = 4.7\ \text{k}\Omega$, $R_C = 2\ \text{k}\Omega$, and $V_{CC} = V_{EE} = 18\ \text{V}$. Use $\beta_F = 125$ and $V_A = 50\ \text{V}$. (b) Use SPICE to verify the results of your hand calculations. Assume $f = 10\ \text{kHz}$ and $C_1 = 10\ \mu\text{F}$, $C_2 = 47\ \mu\text{F}$, $C_3 = 10\ \mu\text{F}$.

14.60. (a) Calculate the values of A_V, R_{IN}, and R_{OUT} for the amplifier in Fig. P14.1(b) if $R_S = 500\ \Omega$, $R_1 = 33\ \text{k}\Omega$, $R_3 = 100\ \text{k}\Omega$, $R_D = 24\ \text{k}\Omega$, and $V_{DD} = V_{SS} = 12\ \text{V}$. Use $K_p = 200\ \mu\text{A/V}^2$, $V_{TP} = -1\ \text{V}$, and $\lambda = 0.02\ \text{V}^{-1}$. (b) Use SPICE to verify the results of your hand calculations. Assume $f = 50\ \text{kHz}$, $C_1 = 10\ \mu\text{F}$, and $C_2 = 47\ \mu\text{F}$.

14.61. (a) Calculate the values of A_V, R_{IN}, and R_{OUT} for the amplifier in Fig. P14.1(c) if $R_S = 500\ \Omega$, $R_1 = 500\ \text{k}\Omega$, $R_2 = 500\ \text{k}\Omega$, $R_3 = 500\ \text{k}\Omega$, $R_E = 430\ \text{k}\Omega$, and $V_{CC} = V_{EE} = 5\ \text{V}$. Use $\beta_F = 100$ and $V_A = 60\ \text{V}$. (b) Use SPICE to verify the results of your hand calculations. Assume $f = 10\ \text{kHz}$ and $C_1 = 10\ \mu\text{F}$, $C_2 = 47\ \mu\text{F}$, $C_3 = 10\ \mu\text{F}$.

14.62. (a) Calculate the values of A_V, R_{IN}, and R_{OUT} for the amplifier in Fig. P14.1(e) if $R_1 = 20\ \text{k}\Omega$, $R_2 = 62\ \text{k}\Omega$, $R_E = 3.9\ \text{k}\Omega$, $R_C = 8.2\ \text{k}\Omega$, and $V_{CC} = 12\ \text{V}$. Use $\beta_F = 75$ and $V_A = 60\ \text{V}$. (b) Use SPICE to verify the results of your hand calculations. Assume $f = 5\ \text{kHz}$ and $C_1 = 2.2\ \mu\text{F}$, $C_2 = 47\ \mu\text{F}$, $C_3 = 10\ \mu\text{F}$.

14.63. (a) Calculate the values of A_V, R_{IN}, and R_{OUT} for the amplifier in Fig. P14.1(f) if $R_1 = 500\ \text{k}\Omega$, $R_2 = 1.4\ \text{M}\Omega$, $R_4 = 27\ \text{k}\Omega$, $R_D = 75\ \text{k}\Omega$, and $V_{DD} = 18\ \text{V}$. Use $K_n = 250\ \mu\text{A/V}^2$, $\lambda = 0.02\ \text{V}^{-1}$, and $V_{TN} = 1\ \text{V}$. (b) Use SPICE to verify the results of your hand calculations. Assume $f = 5\ \text{kHz}$ and $C_1 = 2.2\ \mu\text{F}$, $C_2 = 47\ \mu\text{F}$, $C_3 = 10\ \mu\text{F}$.

14.64. (a) Calculate the values of A_V, R_{IN}, and R_{OUT} for the amplifier in Fig. P14.1(g) if $R_S = 1\ \text{k}\Omega$, $R_1 = 3.9\ \text{k}\Omega$, $R_3 = 51\ \text{k}\Omega$, $R_D = 20\ \text{k}\Omega$, and $V_{DD} = 15\ \text{V}$. Use $K_n = 500\ \mu\text{A/V}^2$, $\lambda = 0.02\ \text{V}^{-1}$, and $V_{TN} = -2\ \text{V}$. (b) Use SPICE to verify the results of your hand calculations. Assume $f = 20\ \text{kHz}$ and $C_1 = 2.2\ \mu\text{F}$, $C_2 = 47\ \mu\text{F}$, $C_3 = 10\ \mu\text{F}$.

14.65. (a) Calculate the values of A_V, R_{IN}, and R_{OUT} for the amplifier in Fig. P14.1(i) if $R_1 = 2.2\ \text{M}\Omega$, $R_2 = 2.2\ \text{M}\Omega$, $R_4 = 22\ \text{k}\Omega$, $R_D = 18\ \text{k}\Omega$, and $V_{DD} = 18\ \text{V}$. Use $K_p = 400\ \mu\text{A/V}^2$, $\lambda = 0.02\ \text{V}^{-1}$, and $V_{TP} = -1\ \text{V}$. (b) Use SPICE to verify the results of your hand calculations. Assume

$f = 7500$ Hz and $C_1 = 2.2$ μF, $C_2 = 47$ μF, $C_3 = 10$ μF.

14.66. (a) Calculate the values of A_V, R_{IN}, and R_{OUT} for the amplifier in Fig. P14.1(j) if $R_S = 500$ Ω, $R_1 = 11$ kΩ, $R_G = 1$ MΩ, $R_3 = 500$ kΩ, $R_D = 39$ kΩ, and $V_{DD} = 20$ V. Use $I_{DSS} = 20$ mA, $\lambda = 0.02$ V^{-1}, and $V_P = -4$ V. (b) Use SPICE to verify the results of your hand calculations. Assume $f = 4000$ Hz and $C_1 = 2.2$ μF, $C_2 = 47$ μF.

14.67. (a) Calculate the values of A_V, R_{IN}, and R_{OUT} for the amplifier in Fig. P14.1(k) if $R_S = 500$ Ω, $R_B = 100$ kΩ, $R_3 = 100$ kΩ, $R_E = 82$ kΩ, $R_C = 39$ kΩ, and $V_{EE} = V_{CC} = 9$ V. Use $\beta_F = 50$ and $V_A = 50$ V. (b) Use SPICE to verify the results of your hand calculations. Assume $f = 12$ kHz and $C_1 = 4.7$ μF, $C_2 = 47$ μF, $C_3 = 10$ μF.

14.68. (a) Calculate the values of A_V, R_{IN}, and R_{OUT} for the amplifier in Fig. P14.1(m) if $R_S = 5$ kΩ, $R_G = 10$ MΩ, $R_3 = 36$ kΩ, $R_D = 1.8$ kΩ, and $V_{DD} = 16$ V. Use $I_{DSS} = 5$ mA, $V_P = 5$ V, and $\lambda = 0.02$ V^{-1}. (b) Use SPICE to verify the results of your hand calculations. Assume $f = 3000$ Hz and $C_1 = 2.2$ μF, $C_2 = 10$ μF.

14.69. (a) Calculate the values of A_V, R_{IN}, and R_{OUT} for the amplifier in Fig. P14.1(n) if $R_S = 250$ Ω, $R_B = 20$ kΩ, $R_3 = 1$ MΩ, $R_4 = 9.1$ kΩ, $V_{CC} = 10$ V, and $V_{EE} = 10$ V. Use $\beta_F = 80$ and $V_A = 100$ V. (b) Use SPICE to verify the results of your hand calculations. Assume $f = 500$ kHz and $C_1 = 4.7$ μF, $C_2 = 100$ μF, $C_3 = 1$ μF, and $L = 1$ H.

14.70. (a) Calculate the values of A_V, R_{IN}, and R_{OUT} for the amplifier in Fig. P14.1(o) if $R_S = 10$ kΩ, $R_G = 1$ MΩ, $R_3 = 100$ kΩ, and $V_{DD} = V_{SS} = 5$ V. Use $K_n = 400$ μA/V^2, $V_{TN} = 1$ V, and $\lambda = 0.02$ V^{-1}. (b) Use SPICE to verify the results of your hand calculations. Assume $f = 100$ kHz and $C_1 = 2.2$ μF, $C_3 = 4.7$ μF, and $L = 100$ mH.

14.7 Amplifier Design Examples

14.71. Repeat the source-follower design in Example 14.6 for a MOSFET with $K_n = 30$ mA/V^2 and $V_{TN} = 2$ V. Assume $V_{GS} - V_{TN} = 0.5$ V.

14.72. A common-base amplifier was used in the design problem in Example 14.7 to match the 75-Ω input resistance. One could conceivably match the input resistance with a common-emitter stage (with $R_5 = 0$). What collector current is required to set $R_{IN} = 75$ Ω for a BJT with $\beta_o = 100$?

*14.73. Redesign the bias network so that the common-base amplifier in Fig. 14.44 can operate from a single +10-V supply.

14.74. A common-gate amplifier is needed with an input resistance of 10 Ω. Two n-channel MOSFETs are available: one with $K_n = 5$ mA/V^2 and the other with $K_n = 500$ mA/V^2. Both are capable of providing the desired value of R_{IN}. Which one would be preferred and why? (*Hint:* Find the required Q-point current for each transistor.)

*14.75. (a) Calculate worst-case estimates of the gain of the common-base amplifier in Fig. 14.44 if the resistors and power supplies all have 5 percent tolerances. (b) Compare your answers to the Monte Carlo results in Table 14.16.

**14.76. Use PSPICE to perform a 1000-case Monte Carlo analysis of the common-base amplifier in Fig. 14.44 if the resistors and power supplies have 5 percent tolerances. Assume that the current gain β_F and V_A are uniformly distributed in the intervals [60, 100] and [50, 70], respectively. What are the mean and 3σ limits on the voltage gain predicted by these simulations? Compare the 3σ values to the worst-case calculations in Prob. 14.75. Compare your answers to the Monte Carlo results in Table 14.16. Use $C_1 = 47$ μF, $C_2 = 4.7$ μF, and $f = 10$ kHz.

**14.77. The common-base amplifier in Fig. P14.77 is the implementation of the design from Example 14.7 using the nearest 1 percent resistor values. (a) What are the worst-case values of gain and input resistance if the power supplies have ± 2 percent tolerances? (b) Use a computer program or spreadsheet to perform a 1000-case Monte Carlo analysis to find the mean and 3σ limits on the gain and input resistances. Compare these values to the worst-case estimates from part (a).

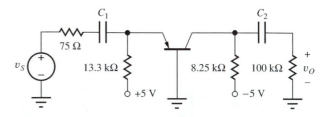

Figure P14.77

**14.78. Use PSPICE to perform a 1000-case Monte Carlo analysis of the circuit in Fig. P14.77 assuming the resistors have 1 percent tolerances and the power supplies have ± 2 percent tolerances. Find the mean and 3σ limits on the gain and input resistance at a frequency of 10 kHz. Assume that the current gain β_F and V_A are uniformly distributed in the intervals (60, 100) and (50, 70), respectively. Use $C_1 = 100\ \mu\text{F}$, $C_2 = 1\ \mu\text{F}$, and $f = 10\ \text{kHz}$.

 14.79. Suppose that we forgot about the factor of 2 loss in signal that occurs at the input of the common-base stage in Example 14.7 and selected $V_{CC} = V_{EE} = 2.5\ \text{V}$. Repeat the design to see if the specifications can be met using these power supply values.

 **14.80. (a) Use a spreadsheet or other computer tool to perform a Monte Carlo analysis of the design in Fig. 14.40. The resistors and power supplies have 5 percent tolerances. V_{TN} is uniformly distributed in the interval [1 V, 2 V], and K_n is uniformly distributed in the interval [10 mA/V², 30 mA/V²]. (b) Use the Monte Carlo option in PSPICE to perform the same analysis at a frequency of 10 kHz for $C_1 = 4.7\ \mu\text{F}$ and $C_2 = 68\ \mu\text{F}$. Compare the results.

14.8 The Influence of Body Effect on Amplifier Performance

14.81. (a) What are the values of $A_{V\text{th}}$, R_{IN}, R_{OUT}, and $A_{I\text{th}}$ for the common-drain stage in Fig. P14.81 if $R_{\text{th}} = 100\ \text{k}\Omega$, $R_L = 1\ \text{k}\Omega$, $g_m = 10\ \text{mS}$, and $\eta = 0.5$? (b) Compare your results to those of Prob. 14.19.

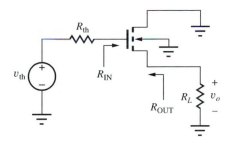

Figure P14.81

14.82. (a) What are the values of $A_{V\text{th}}$, R_{IN}, R_{OUT}, and $A_{I\text{th}}$ for the common-source stage in Fig. P14.82 if $R_{\text{th}} = 75\ \text{k}\Omega$, $R_L = 2\ \text{k}\Omega$, and $R_5 = 200\ \Omega$? Assume $g_m = 10\ \text{mS}$, $r_o = 10\ \text{k}\Omega$, and $\eta = 0.75$. (b) Compare your results to those of Prob. 14.5.

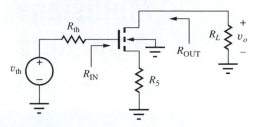

Figure P14.82

14.83. (a) What are the values of $A_{V\text{th}}$, R_{IN}, R_{OUT}, and $A_{I\text{th}}$ for the common-gate stage in Fig. P14.83 operating $g_m = 0.5\ \text{mS}$, $\eta = 1$, $R_{\text{th}} = 50\ \Omega$, and $R_L = 100\ \text{k}\Omega$? (b) Compare your results to those of Prob. 14.28.

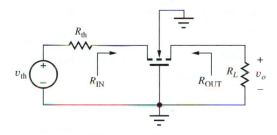

Figure P14.83

Multistage Amplifiers

In most situations, a single-transistor amplifier cannot meet all the given specifications. The required voltage gain often exceeds the amplification factor of a single transistor, or the combination of voltage gain, input resistance, and output resistance cannot be met simultaneously. For example, consider the specifications of a good general-purpose operational amplifier. Such an amplifier has an input resistance exceeding 1 MΩ, a voltage gain of 100,000, and an output resistance of less than 100 Ω. It should be clear from our investigation of amplifiers in Chapters 13 and 14 that these requirements cannot all be met simultaneously with a single-transistor amplifier. A number of stages must be cascaded in order to create an amplifier that can meet all these requirements.

Chapter 15 begins our study of combining single-transistor amplifier stages to achieve higher levels of overall performance. Several examples of multistage amplifiers are presented, and important two-transistor configurations, including the Darlington and cascode circuits, are introduced. In our work in Chapter 12, most of the operational amplifier circuits provided amplification of dc signals. To realize amplifiers of this type, coupling capacitors that block dc signal flow through the amplifier must be eliminated, which leads to the concept of direct-coupled or dc-coupled amplifiers that can satisfy the requirement for dc amplification.

The most important dc-coupled amplifier is the symmetric two-transistor differential amplifier. Not only is the differential amplifier a key circuit in the design of operational amplifiers, it is also a fundamental building block in all analog IC design. In this chapter, we present the transistor-level implementation of BJT and FET differential amplifiers and explore how the differential-mode and common-mode gains, common-mode rejection ratio, differential-mode and common-mode input resistances, and output resistance of the amplifier are all related to transistor parameters.

Subsequently, a second gain stage and an output stage are added to the differential amplifier, creating the prototype for a basic operational amplifier. The definitions of class-A, class-B and class-AB amplifiers are introduced, and the basic op-amp design is further improved by adding class-B and class-AB output stages. In audio applications, these output stages often use transformer coupling.

Bias for analog circuits is most often provided by current sources. An ideal current source provides a fixed output current, independent of the voltage across the source; that is, the current source has an infinite output resistance. Electronic current sources cannot achieve infinite output resistance, but very high values are possible, and a number of basic current source circuits and techniques for achieving high output resistance are introduced and compared. Analysis of the various current sources uses the single-stage amplifier results from Chapters 13 and 14.

15.1 MULTISTAGE ac-COUPLED AMPLIFIERS

Our study of multistage amplifiers begins with analysis of the three-stage, **ac-coupled amplifier** in Fig. 15.1. The function of the various stages can more readily be seen in the ac equivalent circuit for this amplifier in Fig. 15.2(a). MOSFET M_1, operating in the common-source configuration, provides a high input resistance with modest voltage gain. Bipolar transistor Q_2 in the common-emitter configuration provides a second stage with high voltage gain. Q_3, an emitter follower, provides a low output resistance and buffers the high gain stage, Q_2, from the relatively low load resistance (250 Ω). In Fig. 15.2, the base bias resistors have been replaced by $R_{B2} = R_1 \| R_2$ and $R_{B3} = R_3 \| R_4$.

In the amplifier in Fig. 15.1, the input and output of the overall amplifier are ac-coupled through capacitors C_1 and C_6. Bypass capacitors C_2 and C_4 are used to obtain maximum voltage gain from the two inverting amplifiers. Interstage coupling capacitors

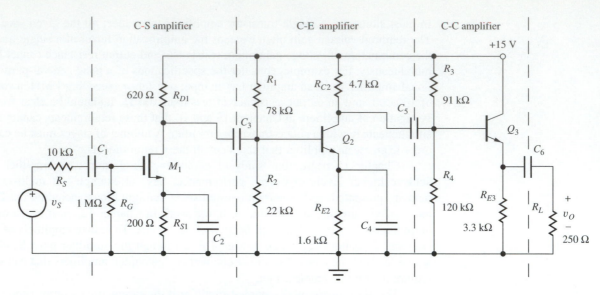

Figure 15.1 Three-stage ac-coupled amplifier.

C_3 and C_5 transfer the ac signals between the amplifiers but provide isolation at dc. Thus, the individual Q-points of the transistors are not affected by connecting the stages together. Figure 15.2(b) gives the dc equivalent circuit for the amplifier in which the capacitors have all been removed. The isolation of the three individual transistor amplifier stages is apparent in this figure.

We want to characterize this amplifier by determining its voltage, input and output resistances, current and power gains, and input signal range using the transistor parameters in Table 15.1. First, the Q-points of the three transistors must be found. Each transistor stage in Fig. 15.2(b) is independently biased, and, for expediency, we assume that the Q-points listed in Table 15.2 have already been found using the dc analysis procedures developed in previous chapters. The details of these dc calculations are left for the following exercise.

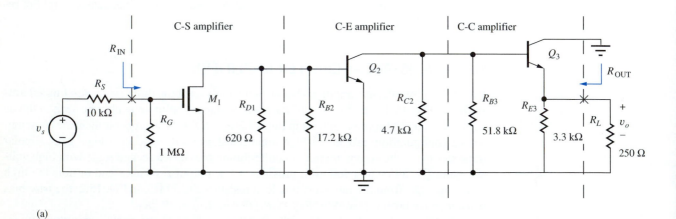

(a)

Figure 15.2 (a) Equivalent circuit for ac analysis.

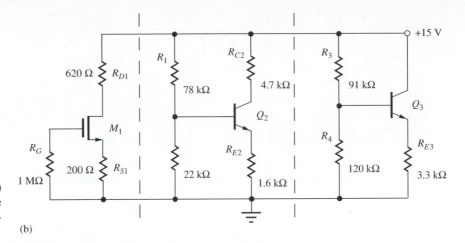

Figure 15.2 (Continued) (b) dc Equivalent circuit for the three-stage ac-coupled amplifier.

(b)

T a b l e   15.1
Transistor Parameters for Figs. 1–11

M_1	$K_n = 10\ \text{mA/V}^2,\ V_{TN} = -2\ \text{V},\ \lambda = 0.02\ \text{V}^{-1}$
Q_2	$\beta_F = 150,\ V_A = 80\ \text{V},\ V_{BE} = 0.6\ \text{V}$
Q_3	$\beta_F = 80,\ V_A = 60\ \text{V},\ V_{BE} = 0.6\ \text{V}$

T a b l e   15.2
Q-Points and Small-Signal Parameters for the Transistors in Fig. 15.1

	Q-Point Values	**Small-Signal Parameters**
M_1	(5.00 mA, 10.9 V)	$g_{m1} = 10.0\ \text{mS},\ r_{o1} = 12.2\ \text{k}\Omega$
Q_2	(1.57 mA, 5.09 V)	$g_{m2} = 62.8\ \text{mS},\ r_{\pi 2} = 2.39\ \text{k}\Omega,$ $r_{o2} = 54.2\ \text{k}\Omega$
Q_3	(1.99 mA, 8.36 V)	$g_{m3} = 79.6\ \text{mS},\ r_{\pi 3} = 1.00\ \text{k}\Omega,$ $r_{o3} = 34.4\ \text{k}\Omega$

EXERCISE: Verify the values of the Q-points and small-signal parameters in Table 15.2.

EXERCISE: Why can't a single transistor amplifier meet the op-amp specifications mentioned in the introduction to this chapter?

Voltage Gain

The ac equivalent circuit for the three-stage amplifier example has been redrawn and is shown in simplified form in Fig. 15.3, in which v_s, R_S, and R_G have been replaced by a Thévenin equivalent circuit, and the three sets of parallel resistors have been combined into the following: $R_{I1} = 620\ \Omega \| 17.2\ \text{k}\Omega = 598\ \Omega$, $R_{I2} = 4.7\ \text{k}\Omega \| 51.8\ \text{k}\Omega = 4.31\ \text{k}\Omega$,

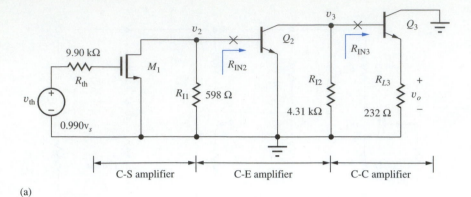

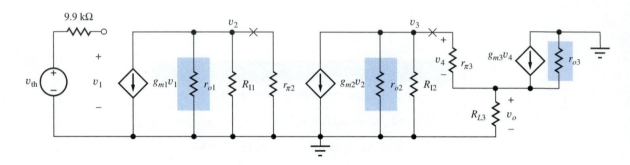

(a)

(b)

Figure 15.3 (a) Simplified ac equivalent circuit for the three-stage amplifier. (b) Small-signal equivalent circuit for the three-stage amplifier.

and $R_{L3} = 3.3\ \text{k}\Omega\|250\ \Omega = 232\ \Omega$. The voltage gain of the overall amplifier can be expressed as

$$A_V = \frac{\mathbf{v_o}}{\mathbf{v_s}} = \frac{\mathbf{v_o}}{\mathbf{v_{th}}}\frac{\mathbf{v_{th}}}{\mathbf{v_s}} = A_{V\text{th}}\frac{\mathbf{v_{th}}}{\mathbf{v_o}} \qquad (15.1)$$

and

$$A_{V\text{th}} = \frac{\mathbf{v_o}}{\mathbf{v_{th}}} = \frac{\mathbf{v_2}}{\mathbf{v_{th}}}\frac{\mathbf{v_3}}{\mathbf{v_2}}\frac{\mathbf{v_o}}{\mathbf{v_3}} = A_{V1}A_{V2}A_{V3} \qquad (15.2)$$

We see that the overall voltage gain is equal to the product of the gains of the individual single-transistor amplifier stages.

We use our knowledge of single-transistor amplifiers, gained in Chapters 13 and 14, to determine expressions for the three voltage gains. The first stage is a common-source amplifier with a gain

$$A_{V1} = \frac{\mathbf{v_2}}{\mathbf{v_{th}}} = -g_{m1}R_{L1} \qquad (15.3)$$

in which R_{L1} represents the total load resistance[1] connected to the drain of M_1. From the ac circuit in Fig. 15.3(a) and the small-signal version in (b), we can see that R_{L1} is equal to the parallel combination of R_{I1} and R_{IN2}, the input resistance at the base of Q_2. Because

---

[1] The output resistances r_{o1}, r_{o2}, and r_{o3} are neglected because each amplifier has an external resistor as a load, and we expect $|A_V| \ll \mu_f$ for each stage.

Q_2 is a common-emitter stage, $R_{IN2} = r_{\pi 2}$,

$$R_{L1} = 598\ \Omega \| r_{\pi 2} = 598\ \Omega \| 2390\ \Omega = 478\ \Omega \tag{15.4}$$

and the gain of the first stage is

$$A_{V1} = \frac{\mathbf{v_2}}{\mathbf{v_{th}}} = -0.01\ \text{S} \times 478\ \Omega = -4.78 \tag{15.5}$$

The gain of the second stage is that of a common-emitter amplifier:

$$A_{V2} = \frac{\mathbf{v_3}}{\mathbf{v_2}} = -g_{m2} R_{L2} \tag{15.6}$$

in which R_{L2} represents the total load resistance connected to the collector of Q_2. In Fig. 15.3, R_{L2} is equal to the parallel combination of R_{I2} and R_{IN3}, where R_{IN3} represents the input resistance of Q_3.

Q_3 is an emitter follower with $R_{IN3} = r_{\pi 3} + (\beta_{o3} + 1)R_{L3}$. Thus, R_{L2} is equal to

$$R_{L2} = R_{I2} \| [r_{\pi 3} + (\beta_{o3} + 1)R_{L3}] = 4310\ \Omega \| [1000\ \Omega + (81)232\ \Omega] = 3.54\ \text{k}\Omega \tag{15.7}$$

and the gain of the second stage is

$$A_{V2} = -62.8\ \text{mS} \times 3.54\ \text{k}\Omega = -222 \tag{15.8}$$

Finally, the gain of the emitter follower stage is

$$A_{V3} = \frac{\mathbf{v_o}}{\mathbf{v_3}} = \frac{(\beta_{o3} + 1)R_{L3}}{r_{\pi 3} + (\beta_{o3} + 1)R_{L3}} = \frac{(81)232\ \Omega}{1000\ \Omega + (81)232\ \Omega} = 0.950 \tag{15.9}$$

Substituting the voltage gains for the individual stages into Eq. (15.2) gives the gain for the overall amplifier:

$$A_V = A_{V1} A_{V2} A_{V3} \frac{\mathbf{v_{th}}}{\mathbf{v_s}} = (-4.78)(-222)(0.950)(0.990) = +998 \tag{15.10}$$

The three-stage amplifier circuit realizes a noninverting amplifier with a gain of approximately 60 dB.

> **EXERCISE:** Recalculate A_V, including the influence of r_{o1}, r_{o2}, and r_{o3}.
>
> **ANSWER:** 903 (59.1 dB)

> **EXERCISE:** Estimate the gain of the amplifier in Fig. 15.1 using our simple design estimates from Chapter 14 if M_1 has $V_{GS} - V_{TN} = 1$ V. What is the origin of the discrepancy?
>
> **ANSWERS:** $(-15)(-150)(1) = 2250$; only 3 V is dropped across R_{D1}, whereas the estimate assumes $V_{DD}/2 = 7.5$ V. Taking this difference into account, $(2250)(3/7.5) = 900$.

> **EXERCISE:** What would be the value of A_V if the interstage resistances R_{I1} and R_{I2} could be eliminated (made ∞)? Would r_{o1}, r_{o2}, and r_{o3} be required in this case?
>
> **ANSWERS:** 28,200; r_{o2} would need to be included.

Input and Output Resistances

The input and output resistances of this amplifier can be determined by referring to Figs. 15.2 to 15.5. Because the gate current i_g in Fig. 15.4 must be zero, we see that the input

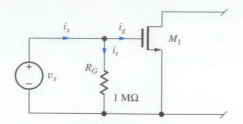

Figure 15.4 Input resistance of the three-stage amplifier.

resistance is simply $R_{\text{IN}} = R_G = 1$ MΩ and is independent of the circuitry connected to the drain of M_1.

From Fig. 15.5, we see that the output resistance of the overall amplifier is determined by the output resistance of the emitter follower in parallel with the 3300-Ω resistor. Writing this mathematically gives,

$$i_x = i_r + i_e = \frac{v_x}{3300} + \frac{v_x}{R_{\text{OUT3}}} \tag{15.11}$$

Using the results from Table 14.3, we find that the overall output resistance is

$$R_{\text{OUT}} = \frac{v_x}{i_x} = 3300\|R_{\text{OUT3}} = 3300\left\|\left(\frac{\alpha_{o3}}{g_{m3}} + \frac{R_{\text{th}3}}{\beta_{o3} + 1}\right)\right. \tag{15.12}$$

in which the Thévenin equivalent source resistance of stage 3, $R_{\text{th}3}$, must be found.

$R_{\text{th}3}$ can be determined with the aid of Fig. 15.6. The third stage Q_3 is removed, and test voltage v_x is applied to node v_3. Current i_x from the test source v_x is equal to

$$i_x = \frac{v_x}{R_{I2}} + i_2 = \frac{v_x}{R_{I2}} + \frac{v_x}{R_{\text{OUT}}^{CE}} \quad \text{or} \quad R_{\text{th}3} = \frac{v_x}{i_x} = R_{I2}\|R_{\text{OUT}}^{CE} = R_{I2}\|r_{o2} \tag{15.13}$$

$R_{\text{th}3}$ is equal to the parallel combination of interstage resistance R_{I2} and the output resistance of Q_2, which we know is just equal to r_{o2}:

$$R_{\text{th}3} = R_{I2}\|r_{o2} = 4310\ \Omega\|54{,}200\ \Omega = 3990\ \Omega \tag{15.14}$$

Evaluating Eq. (15.12) for the output resistance of the overall amplifier yields

$$R_{\text{OUT}} = 3300\ \Omega\left\|\left(\frac{\alpha_{o3}}{g_{m3}} + \frac{R_{\text{th}3}}{\beta_{o3} + 1}\right)\right. = 3300\ \Omega\left\|\left(\frac{0.988}{0.0796\ \text{S}} + \frac{3990\ \Omega}{81}\right)\right. = 60.5\ \Omega \tag{15.15}$$

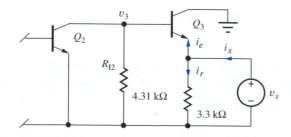

Figure 15.5 Output resistance of the three-stage amplifier.

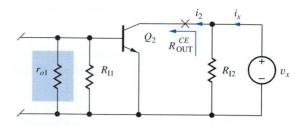

Figure 15.6 Thévenin equivalent source resistance for stage 3.

Current and Power Gain

The input current delivered to the amplifier from source v_s in Fig. 15.2 is given by

$$i_s = \frac{v_s}{R_s + R_{IN}} = \frac{v_s}{10^4 + 10^6} = 9.90 \times 10^{-7} v_s \qquad (15.16)$$

and the current delivered to the load from the amplifier is

$$i_o = \frac{v_o}{250} = \frac{A_V v_s}{250} = \frac{998 v_s}{250} = 3.99 v_s \qquad (15.17)$$

Combining Eqs. (15.16) and (15.17) gives the current gain

$$A_I = \frac{i_o}{i_s} = \frac{3.99 v_s}{9.90 \times 10^{-7} v_s} = 4.03 \times 10^6 \qquad (15.18)$$

Combining Eqs. (15.1) and (15.18) with the power gain expression from Chapter 11 yields a value for overall power gain of the amplifier:

$$A_P = \frac{P_o}{P_s} = \left| \frac{v_o i_o}{v_s i_s} \right| = |A_V A_I| = 998 \times 4.03 \times 10^6 = 4.02 \times 10^9 \qquad (15.19)$$

Because input resistance to the common-source stage is large, only a small input current is required to develop a large output current. Thus current gain is large. In addition, the voltage gain of the amplifier is significant, and combining a large voltage gain with a large current gain yields a very substantial power gain.

Input Signal Range

Our final step in characterizing this amplifier is to determine the largest input signal that can be applied to the amplifier. In a multistage amplifier, the small-signal assumptions must not be violated anywhere in the amplifier chain. The first stage of the amplifier in Figs. 15.2 and 15.3 is easy to check. Voltage source v_{th} appears directly across the gate-source terminals of the MOSFET, and to satisfy the small-signal limit, v_{th} $(= 0.990 v_s)$ must satisfy

$$|v_{th}| \le 0.2(V_{GS1} - V_{TN}) \qquad \text{or} \qquad |v_s| \le \frac{0.2(-1+2)}{0.990} = 0.202 \text{ V} \qquad (15.20)$$

The first stage limits the input signal to 202 mV.

To satisfy the small-signal requirements, the base-emitter voltage of Q_2 must also be less than 5 mV. In this amplifier, $v_{be2} = v_2$. Because

$$|v_2| = |A_{V1} v_{th}| \le 5 \text{ mV}$$

$$|v_{th}| \le \frac{5 \text{ mV}}{A_{V1}} = \frac{0.005}{4.78} = 1.05 \text{ mV} \qquad (15.21)$$

and

$$|v_s| \le \frac{1.05 \text{ mV}}{0.990} = 1.06 \text{ mV}$$

In this design, the small-signal requirements are violated at Q_2 if the amplitude of the input signal v_s exceeds 1.06 mV.

Finally, using Eq. (14.32) for the emitter-follower output stage (with $R_{th} = 0$),

$$v_{be3} \approx \frac{v_3}{1 + g_{m3} R_{L3}} = \frac{A_{V1} A_{V2} v_{th}}{1 + g_{m3} R_{L3}} = \frac{A_{V1} A_{V2}(0.990 v_s)}{1 + g_{m3} R_{L3}} \qquad (15.22)$$

and requiring $|v_{be3}| \leq 5$ mV yields

$$|v_s| \leq \frac{1 + g_{m3}R_{L3}}{A_{V1}A_{V2}(0.990)}0.005 = \frac{1 + 0.0796 \text{ S}(232 \text{ }\Omega)}{(-4.78)(-222)(0.99)}0.005 \text{ V} = 92.7 \text{ }\mu\text{V} \quad (15.23)$$

To satisfy all the small-signal limitations, the maximum amplitude of the input signal to the amplifier must be no greater than the smallest of the three values computed in Eqs. (15.20), (15.21), and (15.23):

$$|v_s| \leq \min(202 \text{ mV}, 1.06 \text{ mV}, 92.7 \text{ }\mu\text{V}) = 92.7 \text{ }\mu\text{V} \quad (15.24)$$

In this design, output stage linearity limits the input signal amplitude to less than 93 μV. Note that the maximum output voltage that satisfies the small-signal limit is only

$$|v_o| \leq A_V(92.7 \text{ }\mu\text{V}) = 998(92.7 \text{ }\mu\text{V}) = 92.5 \text{ mV} \quad (15.25)$$

Table 15.3 summarizes the characteristics calculated for the three-stage amplifier in Fig. 15.1. The amplifier provides a noninverting voltage gain of approximately 60 dB, a high input resistance, and a low output resistance. The current and power gains are both quite large. The input signal must be kept below 92.7 μV in order to satisfy the small-signal limitations of the transistors.

T a b l e 15.3	
Three-Stage Amplifier Summary	
Voltage Gain	+998
Input Signal Range	92.7 μV
Input Resistance	1 MΩ
Output Resistance	60.5 Ω
Current Gain	$+4.03 \times 10^6$
Power Gain	4.02×10^9

Improving Amplifier Voltage Gain

We know that the gain of the C-S amplifier is inversely proportional to the square root of drain current. In this amplifier, there is no need to operate the first stage at a 5-mA bias current level, and the voltage gain of the amplifier could be increased by reducing I_{DS1} while maintaining a constant voltage drop across R_{D1}. It should be possible to improve the signal range by increasing the current in the output stage and the voltage drop across R_{E3}. Another possibility is to replace Q_3 with a FET. Some gain loss might again occur in the third stage because the gain of a common-drain amplifier is typically less than that of a common-collector stage, but this could be made up by improving the gain of the first and second stages (see Probs. 15.3 and 15.6).

> **EXERCISE:** (a) What would be the voltage gain of the amplifier if I_{DS1} is reduced to 1 mA and R_{D1} is increased to 3 kΩ so that V_D is maintained constant? (b) The FET g_m decreases by $\sqrt{5}$. Why did the gain not increase by a factor of $\sqrt{5}$?
>
> **ANSWERS:** 1840; although R_{D1} increases by a factor of 5, the total load resistance at the drain of M_1 does not.

The Common-Emitter Cascade

The three-stage amplifier in Fig. 15.1 uses a common-source stage in cascade with a common-emitter stage. However, we know from Chapters 13 and 14 that common-emitter stages typically offer more voltage gain than common-source stages, and, to achieve the highest possible voltage gain, several common-emitter stages are often cascaded, as indicated by the ac equivalent circuit for an n-stage amplifier in Fig. 15.7. The gain can be written as the product of the gains of the individual stages;

$$A_V = \frac{\mathbf{v_1}}{\mathbf{v_s}}\frac{\mathbf{v_2}}{\mathbf{v_1}}\cdots\frac{\mathbf{v_o}}{\mathbf{v_{n-1}}} = A_{V1}A_{V2}\cdots A_{Vn} \qquad (15.26)$$

For all but the final stage, the gain is given by

$$A_{Vi} = -g_{mi}(R_{Ii}\|r_{\pi i+1}) \qquad (15.27)$$

where g_{mi} = transconductance of transistor i
R_{Ii} = ith interstage resistance
$r_{\pi i+1}$ = input resistance of transistor $i + 1$

The gain of the last stage is $A_{vn} = -g_{mn}R_L \approx -10V_{CC}$, where V_{CC} is the power supply voltage.

Two limits are of particular interest. If the gain is limited by the interstage resistances, then each stage has a gain of approximately $-10V_{CC}$, and the overall gain of the n-stage amplifier is

$$A_{Vn} = (-10V_{CC})^n \qquad (15.28)$$

For the second case, the gain is assumed to be limited by the input resistance of the transistors, and the gain becomes

$$A_{Vn} = (-1)^n\frac{I_{C1}}{I_{Cn}}\beta_{o2}\beta_{o3}\cdots\beta_{on}(10V_{CC}) \qquad (15.29)$$

Normally, $I_{Cn} \geq I_{C1}$ because the signal and power levels usually increase in each successive stage of most amplifiers. Because β_o is often less than $10V_{CC}$, Eq. (15.29) is often the actual limiting case.

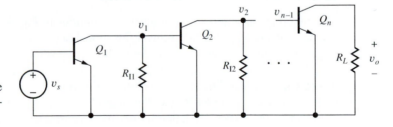

Figure 15.7 n-Stage cascade of common-emitter amplifiers.

The origin of Eq. (15.29) can be more readily understood from the three-stage example in Fig. 15.8, in which the interstage resistors are assumed infinite in value. The output signal current from the first stage is $-g_{m1}v_s$. This current is amplified by the current gain of the next two stages and produces an output current of

$$\mathbf{i_{c3}} = \beta_{o3}\beta_{o2}g_{m1}\mathbf{v_s} \qquad (15.30)$$

which develops the output voltage across load resistance R_L:

$$\mathbf{v_o} = -\beta_{o3}\beta_{o2}g_{m1}R_L\mathbf{v_s} \qquad (15.31)$$

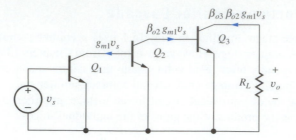

Figure 15.8 Ideal common-emitter cascade.

The voltage gain of the overall cascade is then

$$A_{V3} = \frac{\mathbf{v_o}}{\mathbf{v_s}} = -\beta_{o3}\beta_{o2}g_{m1}R_L = -\frac{g_{m1}}{g_{m3}}\beta_{o3}\beta_{o2}(g_{m3}R_L) \tag{15.32}$$

Writing the transconductances in terms of their respective collector currents yields an equation in the form of Eq. (15.29):

$$A_{V3} = -\frac{g_{m1}}{g_{m3}}\beta_{o3}\beta_{o2}(g_{m3}R_L) = -\frac{I_{c1}}{I_{c3}}\beta_{o2}\beta_{o3}(10V_{CC}) \tag{15.33}$$

For a cascade of n identical stages ($I_{Cn} = I_{C1}$), Eq. (15.33) becomes

$$A_{Vn} = (-1)^n(\beta_o)^{n-1}(10V_{CC}) \tag{15.34}$$

Except for the last stage, the voltage gain of each stage defined by Eq. (15.34) is equal to the current gain β_o, which may be less than $10V_{CC}$.

> **EXERCISE:** An amplifier is required with a gain of 140 dB. Estimate the minimum number of amplifier stages that will be required if the design must use a 15-V supply and transistors with $\beta_o = 75$.
>
> **ANSWER:** Five stages; although Eq. (15.28) yields an estimate of four stages, Eq. (15.34) yields an estimate of five. ($\beta_o < 10V_{CC}$.)

15.2 DIRECT-COUPLED AMPLIFIERS

The coupling capacitors in the multistage amplifier in Fig. 15.1 limit the low frequency response of the amplifier and prevent its application as a dc amplifier. For the amplifier to provide gain at dc or very low frequencies, capacitors in series with the signal path (C_1, C_3, C_5, and C_6) must be eliminated. Such an amplifier is called a **dc-coupled,** or **direct-coupled, amplifier.** Using a direct-coupled design can also eliminate the additional resistors that are required to bias the individual stages in an ac-coupled amplifier, thus producing a less expensive amplifier design. Bypass capacitors C_2 and C_4 also affect the gain at low frequencies and cause the amplifier to have a high-pass response. However, they do not inherently prevent the amplifier from operating at dc.

Figure 15.9 is a direct-coupled version of the three-stage amplifier in Fig. 15.1. In this particular example, the interior amplifier uses a direct-coupled design. The dc levels at the various nodes in Fig. 15.9 have been designed to permit direct connections between the stages, and coupling capacitors C_3 and C_5 have been eliminated between M_1 and Q_2, and between Q_2 and Q_3, respectively. In the design, C_1 is still used to isolate the input source from the amplifier, and C_6 is required to prevent the dc level at the output of the emitter follower from being applied to the load resistance R_L. Also, the amplifier in Fig. 15.9 still includes bypass capacitors to enhance the ac performance (see Prob. 15.2). An amplifier

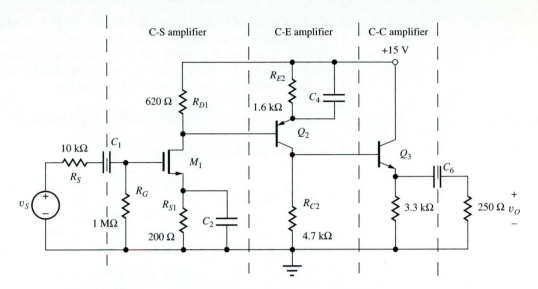

Figure 15.9 A direct-coupled version of the three-stage amplifier in Fig. 15.1.

truly designed for dc amplification will eliminate all capacitors, and the basic differential and operational amplifier circuits to be discussed later in this chapter do completely eliminate the need for both coupling and bypass capacitors.

   npn Transistor Q_2 in Fig. 15.1 has been replaced by a pnp transistor in Fig. 15.9. Alternating npn or n-channel with pnp or p-channel transistors from stage to stage is common in dc-coupled designs. This is a technique developed to take maximum advantage of the available power supply voltage.

dc Analysis

In the dc equivalent circuit in Fig. 15.10, the voltage at the drain of M_1 provides bias voltage to the base of Q_2, and the voltage developed at the collector of Q_2 establishes the base bias for Q_3. For amplifiers, the transistors should be operating in the saturation region (MOSFET) or the forward-active region (BJT). Thus, the current in M_1 is independent of the voltage at its drain and therefore independent of the fact that the base of Q_2 happens to be connected to its drain. Similarly, the collector current of Q_2 is not be affected by the

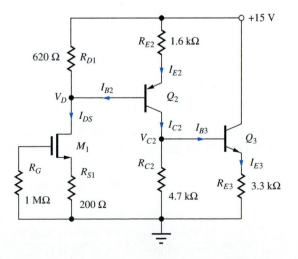

Figure 15.10 dc Equivalent circuit for direct-coupled amplifier.

presence of Q_3 attached to its collector. Because of this lack of interaction, the dc analysis can proceed through the circuit from left to right, from M_1 to Q_2 to Q_3.

Note from the circuit symbols and from the values in Table 15.1 that a depletion-mode MOSFET is used to simplify the bias circuit of the input stage. Assuming saturation and zero gate current, the drain current of M_1 is given by

$$I_{DS} = \frac{K_n}{2}(V_{GS} - V_{TN})^2 = \frac{0.01}{2}(-200I_{DS} + 2)^2 \tag{15.35}$$

and collecting terms yields a quadratic equation for I_D:

$$10^4 I_{DS}^2 - 250I_{DS} + 1 = 0 \tag{15.36}$$

The solutions to Eq. (15.36) are $I_{DS} = 5.00$ mA or $I_{DS} = 20.0$ mA. A 20-mA drain-source current will produce a voltage drop of 4 V across R_{S1} and cut off the FET. Thus, the drain current must be $I_{DS} = 5.00$ mA, and the voltage at the source of M_1 is $V_S = +1$ V.

Applying KCL at the drain node, the drain voltage of M_1 can be expressed as

$$V_D = 15 - 620(I_{DS} - I_{B2}) \tag{15.37}$$

If we assume that $I_{B2} \ll I_{DS}$, then

$$V_D \approx 15 - 620I_{DS} = 15 - 620 \, \Omega(0.005 \text{ A}) = 11.9 \text{ V} \tag{15.38}$$

and the drain-source voltage of M_1 is $V_{DS} = 11.9 - 1 = 10.9$ V, which is indeed sufficient to saturate M_1.

The Q-point of bipolar transistor Q_2 is controlled by the voltage at its base, which is equal to the drain voltage of M_1. Assuming forward-active region operation,

$$15 - 1600I_{E2} - V_{EB2} = V_D \tag{15.39}$$

and solving Eq. (15.39) for I_{E2} gives

$$I_{E2} = \frac{15 - V_D - V_{EB2}}{1600} = \frac{15 \text{ V} - 11.9 \text{ V} - 0.7 \text{ V}}{1600 \, \Omega} = 1.50 \text{ mA} \tag{15.40}$$

Based on the current gain $\beta_{F2} = 150$ from Table 15.1,

$$I_{C2} = 1.50 \text{ mA} \quad \text{and} \quad I_{B2} = 10.0 \, \mu\text{A} \tag{15.41}$$

The results in Eq. (15.41) justify the assumption $I_{B2} \ll I_{DS}$ used in Eq. (15.38).

The voltage V_{C2} at the collector of Q_2 can be expressed as

$$V_{C2} = 4700(I_{C2} - I_{B3}) \tag{15.42}$$

Assuming that $I_{B3} \ll I_{C2}$,

$$V_{C2} \approx 4700I_{C2} = 4700 \, \Omega(0.00150 \text{ A}) = 7.05 \text{ V} \tag{15.43}$$

Checking the collector-emitter voltage of Q_2,

$$V_{EC2} = V_{E2} - V_{C2} = V_{D1} + V_{EB2} - V_{C2} = 11.9 + 0.7 - 7.05 = 5.55 \text{ V} \tag{15.44}$$

which is greater than 0.7 V. This confirms that Q_2 is operating in the forward-active region.

Just as is the case for Q_2, the Q-point of Q_3 is also controlled by the voltage at its base:

$$V_{C2} - V_{BE3} = 3300I_{E3} \tag{15.45}$$

and

$$I_{E3} = \frac{V_{C2} - V_{BE3}}{3300} = \frac{(7.05 - 0.700) \text{ V}}{3300 \, \Omega} = 1.92 \text{ mA} \tag{15.46}$$

Using the current gain $\beta_{F3} = 80$,

$$I_{C3} = 1.90 \text{ mA} \quad \text{and} \quad I_{B3} = 23.8 \text{ μA} \tag{15.47}$$

I_{B3} is less than 2 percent of I_{C2}, so neglecting I_{B3} in the calculation of V_{C2} in Eq. (15.43) was a reasonable assumption.

Finally, the collector-emitter voltage of Q_3 is

$$V_{CE3} = 15 - V_{E3} = 15 - 3.3 \text{ kΩ}(1.90 \text{ mA}) = 8.73 \text{ V} \tag{15.48}$$

which verifies that Q_3 is operating in the forward-active region.

Calculation of the Q-points of the three transistors is complete. The Q-point values have been used to determine the values of the small-signal parameters, as summarized in Table 15.4. (Be sure to compare the Q-point values in Table 15.4 to those in Table 15.2.)

T a b l e 15.4		
Q-Points and Small-Signal Parameters for the Transistors in Fig. 15.9		
	Q-Point Values	**Small-Signal Parameters**
M_1	(5.00 mA, 10.9 V)	$g_m = 0.01$ S, $r_o = 12.2$ kΩ
Q_2	(1.50 mA, 5.55 V)	$g_m = 60.0$ mS, $r_\pi = 2.50$ kΩ, $r_o = 57.0$ kΩ
Q_3	(1.90 mA, 8.73 V)	$g_m = 76.0$ mS, $r_\pi = 1.05$ kΩ, $r_o = 36.2$ kΩ

EXERCISE: Verify that the values of the small-signal parameters in Table 15.4 are correct.

EXERCISE: What is the minimum value of V_{DS} needed to saturate M_1? Find I_{E2} and V_{D1} if $\beta_{F2} = 10$. (Assume I_{B2} no longer satisfies $I_{B2} \ll I_{D1}$.) Use these values to find I_{C3} and V_{C2} if $\beta_{F3} = 10$. (Assume I_{B3} no longer satisfies $I_{B3} \ll I_{C2}$.)

ANSWERS: +1 V; 1.37 mA, 12.0 V; 1.42 mA, 5.77 V

ac Analysis

The ac equivalent circuit for the amplifier in Fig. 15.9 is drawn in Fig. 15.11, and is very similar to that in Fig. 15.3. The values of the interstage resistors have increased slightly in value due to the absence of bias resistors $R_1 - R_4$ in Fig. 15.1. Because the Q-points

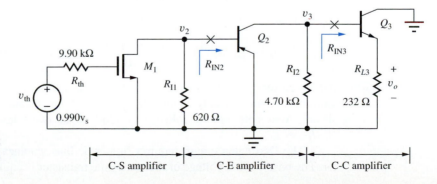

Figure 15.11 ac Equivalent circuit valid for small-signal analysis.

and small-signal parameters of the transistors are also almost identical to those in the ac-coupled amplifier, the overall characteristics of the amplifier should be quite similar to those of Fig. 15.1, and indeed they are: $A_V = 1100$, $R_{IN} = 1$ MΩ, and $R_{OUT} = 70.5$ Ω. Details of these calculations mirror those done in Sec. 15.1 and are left as the next exercise.

Thus, in this case we can achieve the same amplifier performance with either an ac- or dc-coupled design. dc Coupling requires fewer components, but the Q-points of the various stages become interdependent. If the Q-point of one stage shifts, the Q-points of all the stages may also shift (see Prob. 15.13).

EXERCISE: Calculate the actual voltage gain, input resistance, and output resistance of the direct-coupled amplifier in Fig. 15.9.

ANSWERS: 1100, 1 MΩ, 70.5 Ω

The Darlington Circuit

In many circuits, it would be advantageous to have a bipolar transistor with a much higher current gain than that of a single BJT (Recall Example 14.6, for instance). An FET may not be usable because it cannot provide the required amplification factor, or a bipolar IC technology that does not realize FETs may be in use. The circuit depicted in Fig. 15.12, called the **Darlington configuration,** or **Darlington circuit,** is an important two-stage direct-coupled amplifier that attempts to solve this problem. The Darlington circuit behaves in a manner similar to that of a single transistor but with a current gain equal to the product of the current gains of the individual transistors. The dc and ac behavior of the Darlington circuit are discussed in the next two sections.

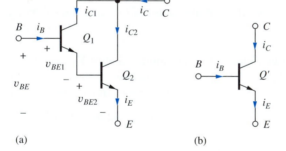

Figure 15.12 (a) Darlington connection of two bipolar transistors. (b) Representation as a single composite transistor Q'.

dc Analysis

Writing an expression for the dc collector current I_C at the output of the composite transistor in Fig. 15.12(a) in terms of the input base current I_B,

$$I_C = I_{C1} + I_{C2} = \beta_{F1}I_B + \beta_{F2}I_{E1} = \beta_{F1}I_B + \beta_{F2}(\beta_{F1} + 1)I_B \qquad (15.49)$$

and factoring $\beta_{F1}\beta_{F2}$ from Eq. (15.49) gives

$$I_C = \beta_{F1}\beta_{F2}\left[1 + \frac{1}{\beta_{F1}} + \frac{1}{\beta_{F2}}\right]I_B \approx \beta_{F1}\beta_{F2}I_B \quad \text{for } \beta_{F1}, \beta_{F2} \gg 1 \qquad (15.50)$$

If both current gains are much larger than 1, then the composite transistor has a current gain that is approximately equal to the product of the current gains of the individual transistors. Also, note that the collector currents of the two transistors are related by $I_{C2} \approx \beta_{F2}I_{C1} \approx I_C$.

The Darlington circuit requires higher dc bias voltages than does a single transistor. The base-emitter voltage of the composite transistor is equivalent to two diode voltage drops

$$V_{BE} = V_{BE1} + V_{BE2} \approx 1.4 \text{ V} \tag{15.51}$$

and to keep the collector-base junction of Q_1 reverse-biased, V_{CE} must also be greater than $(V_{BE1} + V_{BE2})$.

ac Analysis

The ac behavior of the Darlington circuit can be explored by treating the configuration as the two-port in Fig. 15.13 and calculating its y-parameters:

$$\begin{aligned} \mathbf{i_1} &= y_{11}\mathbf{v_1} + y_{12}\mathbf{v_2} \\ \mathbf{i_2} &= y_{21}\mathbf{v_1} + y_{22}\mathbf{v_2} \end{aligned} \tag{15.52}$$

These parameters are easily found by replacing the transistors in Fig. 15.13 by their small-signal models and applying the definitions of the parameters to the resulting network. Because of the relationship between I_{C1} and I_{C2}, the small-signal parameters of the two transistors are also related to each other by the expressions given with the circuit in Fig. 15.13. The results of this analysis are presented in Eq. (15.53), although the detailed calculations are left for Prob. 15.22.

$$\begin{aligned} r_\pi' &= (y_{11})^{-1} = r_{\pi1} + (\beta_{o1} + 1)r_{\pi2} \approx 2\beta_{o1}r_{\pi2} \\[2mm] y_{12} &\approx -\frac{1}{(\beta_{o1} + 1)r_{o1}} \approx 0 \\[2mm] g_m' &= y_{21} = \frac{g_{m1}}{2} + \frac{g_{m2}}{2} \approx \frac{g_{m2}}{2} \\[2mm] r_o' &= (y_{22})^{-1} \approx r_{o2} \left\| \left(2\frac{r_{o1}}{\beta_{o2}}\right) \approx \frac{2}{3}r_{o2} \right. \end{aligned} \tag{15.53}$$

The ac current gain β_o' and amplification factor μ_f' for the composite Darlington transistor are

$$\begin{aligned} \beta_o' &= \left.\frac{y_{21}}{y_{11}}\right|_{v_2=0} = g_m'r_\pi' \approx \beta_{o1}\beta_{o2} \\[2mm] \mu_f' &= \left.\frac{\mathbf{v_2}}{\mathbf{v_1}}\right|_{i_2=0} = g_m'r_o' = \frac{g_{m2}}{2}2\frac{r_{o2}}{3} = \frac{\mu_{f2}}{3} \end{aligned} \tag{15.54}$$

From Eqs. (15.53) and (15.54), we can see that the Darlington configuration behaves as a single composite transistor operating with a very high, effective current gain, $\beta_{o1}\beta_{o2}$, but with a transconductance equal to one-half that of a single BJT operating at the collector current I_C. The high current gain results in a high input resistance; however, the amplification factor of the composite device has been reduced by a factor of 4.

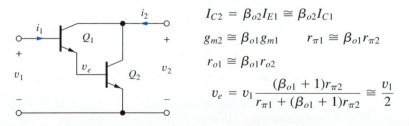

Figure 15.13 Darlington circuit as a two-port.

$$I_{C2} = \beta_{o2}I_{E1} \cong \beta_{o2}I_{C1}$$

$$g_{m2} \cong \beta_{o1}g_{m1} \qquad r_{\pi1} \cong \beta_{o1}r_{\pi2}$$

$$r_{o1} \cong \beta_{o1}r_{o2}$$

$$v_e = v_1\frac{(\beta_{o1} + 1)r_{\pi2}}{r_{\pi1} + (\beta_{o1} + 1)r_{\pi2}} \cong \frac{v_1}{2}$$

> **EXERCISE:** What is the current gain of a Darlington transistor if $\beta_{F1} = 50$, $V_{A1} = 75$ V, $\beta_{F2} = 80$, and $V_{A2} = 60$ V? If the operating current of the composite transistor is 500 μA and $V_{CE} = 10$, what are the values of r'_π, g'_m, r'_o, and μ'_f?
>
> **ANSWERS:** 4000; 400 kΩ, 0.01 S, 70 kΩ, 700

The Cascode Amplifier—A C-E/C-B Cascade

Another very important direct-coupled two-transistor amplifier configuration is the cascade connection of the common-emitter and common-base amplifiers. This special amplifier configuration is referred to as the **cascode amplifier.** Although this section focuses on the C-E/C-B version of the cascode amplifier, it can be made with any combination of C-E/C-S and C-B/C-G stages (that is, with C-E/C-B, C-E/C-G, C-S/C-G, or C-S/C-B)—(see Probs. 15.24, 15.26, 15.28, 15.29).

dc Considerations

In Fig. 15.14, we can see that the collector current of Q_1 is the emitter current of Q_2, and so $I_{C2} = \alpha_F I_{C1}$. For typical transistors with reasonably high current gain, $I_{C2} \approx I_{C1}$. The base of Q_2 must be biased by a voltage source V_{BB} that is large enough to ensure that Q_1 is operating in the forward-active region. The minimum value of V_{BB} is

$$V_{CE1} = V_{BB} - V_{BE2} \geq V_{BE1} \quad \text{or} \quad V_{BB} \geq 2V_{BE} \tag{15.55}$$

which must be equal to at least $2V_{BE}$, or approximately 1.4 V.

ac Analysis

The ac behavior of the cascode circuit can also be explored by treating the configuration as the two-port in Fig. 15.15 and calculating its y-parameters. As with the Darlington circuit, these parameters can be found by replacing the transistors in Fig. 15.15 by their small-signal models, recognizing that the transistor parameters are related through $I_{C2} = \alpha_{F2}I_{C1}$. The results are given in Eq. (15.56), but the detailed calculations are left for Prob. 15.23.

$$
\begin{aligned}
r'_\pi &= (y_{11})^{-1} = r_{\pi1} \\
y_{12} &\approx 0 \\
g'_m &= y_{21} = \alpha_{o2}g_{m1} \approx g_{m2} \\
r'_o &= (y_{22})^{-1} \approx r_{o2}(1 + g_{m2}(r_{\pi2}\|r_{o1})) \approx \beta_{o2}r_{o2}
\end{aligned}
\tag{15.56}
$$

The current gain β'_o and amplification factor μ'_f for the composite cascode transistor are

$$\beta'_o = \left.\frac{y_{21}}{y_{11}}\right|_{v_2=0} = \beta_{o1}\alpha_{o2} \approx \beta_{o1}$$

$$\mu'_f = \left.\frac{\mathbf{v_2}}{\mathbf{v_1}}\right|_{i_2=0} = \beta_{o2}\mu_{f2}$$

$$\tag{15.57}$$

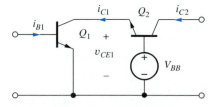

Figure 15.14 Cascode circuit with dc bias source V_{BB}.

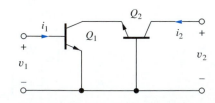

Figure 15.15 Cascode circuit as a two-port.

From Eqs. (15.56) and (15.57), we can see that the cascode configuration behaves as a single composite common-emitter transistor operating at a collector current $I_C \approx I_{C2}$, but having an extremely high amplification factor of $\beta_{o2}\mu_{f2}$. The cascode stage is often found in high-performance differential and operational amplifiers, where it can afford very high voltage gain and common-mode rejection. It can also be used to realize current sources with very high output resistances. In Chapter 17, we shall find that cascode amplifiers also offer much better bandwidth than the corresponding single-transistor C-E or C-S stages.

> **EXERCISE:** Calculate the two-port parameters of the cascode amplifier in Fig. 15.15 if the transistors are identical and Q_2 has $I_{C2} = 100$ μA. Use $\beta_F = \beta_o = 100$, $V_A = 75$ V, and $V_{CE2} = 10$. What are the current gain and amplification factor for the cascode configuration? What would be the values of r_π, g_m, r_o, and μ_f for a single transistor operating with $I_C = 100$ μA and $V_{CE} = 10$ V?
>
> **ANSWERS:** 24.8 kΩ, 0, 0.004 S, 85 MΩ; 99.2, 340,000; 25.0 kΩ, 0.004 S, 85 kΩ, 3000

15.3 DIFFERENTIAL AMPLIFIERS

The direct-coupled amplifier design in Sec. 15.2 still uses internal bypass capacitors to achieve high ac gain as well as external coupling capacitors at the input and output. The dc-coupled **differential amplifiers** in Fig. 15.16 can be used to eliminate these capacitors in most designs. Sometimes considered the C-C/C-B cascade, the differential amplifier is one of the most important additions to our "toolkit" of basic building blocks for analog design. This circuit forms the heart of operational amplifier design as well as of most dc-coupled analog circuits. Although the differential amplifier contains two transistors in a symmetrical configuration, it is usually thought of as a single-stage amplifier, and our analyses will show that it has characteristics similar to those of common-emitter or common-source amplifiers.

Figure 15.16 shows bipolar and MOS versions of the differential amplifier. Each circuit has two input terminals, v_1 and v_2, and the **differential-mode output voltage** v_{OD} is defined by the voltage difference between the collectors or drains of the two transistors. Ground-referenced outputs can also be taken between either collector or drain—v_{C1}, v_{C2}, v_{D1}, or v_{D2}—and ground.

The symmetrical nature of the amplifier provides useful dc and ac properties. However, ideal performance is obtained from the differential amplifier only when it is perfectly symmetrical, and the best versions are built using IC technology in which the transistor characteristics can be closely matched. Two transistors are said to be **matched** if they have

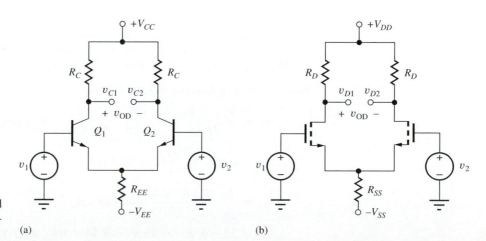

Figure 15.16 (a) Bipolar and (b) MOS differential amplifiers.

(a)

(b)

identical characteristics and parameter values; that is, the parameter sets (I_S, β_{FO}, V_A) or $(K_n, V_{TN},$ and $\lambda)$, Q-points, and temperatures of the two transistors are identical.

dc Analysis of the Bipolar Differential Amplifier

The quiescent operating points of the transistors in the bipolar differential amplifier can be found by setting both input signal voltages to zero, as in Fig. 15.17. In this circuit, both bases are grounded and the two emitters are connected together. Therefore, $V_{BE1} = V_{BE2} = V_{BE}$. If bipolar transistors Q_1 and Q_2 are assumed to be matched, then the symmetry of the circuit also forces $V_{C1} = V_{C2} = V_C$, and the terminal currents of the two transistors are identical: $I_{C1} = I_{C2} = I_C$, $I_{E1} = I_{E2} = I_E$, and $I_{B1} = I_{B2} = I_B$.

The emitter currents can be found by writing a loop equation starting at the base of Q_1:

$$V_{BE} + 2I_E R_{EE} - V_{EE} = 0 \tag{15.58}$$

Therefore

$$I_E = \frac{V_{EE} - V_{BE}}{2R_{EE}} \qquad I_C = \alpha_F I_E \qquad I_B = \frac{I_C}{\beta_F} \tag{15.59}$$

The voltages at the two collectors are equal to

$$V_{C1} = V_{C2} = V_{CC} - I_C R_C \tag{15.60}$$

and $V_{CE1} = V_{CE2}$. For the symmetrical amplifier, the dc output voltage is zero:

$$V_{OD} = V_{C1} - V_{C2} = 0 \text{ V} \tag{15.61}$$

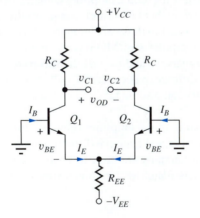

Figure 15.17 Circuit for dc analysis of the bipolar differential amplifier.

Example 15.1: Find the Q-points, V_C, and I_B for the differential amplifier in Fig. 15.16 if $V_{CC} = V_{EE} = 15$ V, $R_{EE} = 75$ kΩ, $R_C = 75$ kΩ, and $\beta_F = 100$.

Solution: Using Eqs. (15.59) and (15.60):

$$I_E = \frac{V_{EE} - V_{BE}}{2R_{EE}} = \frac{(15 - 0.7) \text{ V}}{2(75 \times 10^3 \ \Omega)} = 95.3 \ \mu A$$

$$I_C = \alpha_F I_E = \frac{100}{101}I_E = 94.4 \ \mu A$$

$$I_B = \frac{I_C}{\beta_F} = \frac{94.4 \ \mu A}{100} = 0.944 \ \mu A$$

$$V_C = 15 - I_C R_C = 15 \text{ V} - (9.44 \times 10^{-5} \text{ A})(7.5 \times 10^4 \ \Omega) = 7.92 \text{ V}$$

and

$$V_{CE} = V_C - V_E = 7.92 \text{ V} - (-0.7 \text{ V}) = 8.62 \text{ V}$$

Both transistors in the differential amplifier are biased at a Q-point of (94.4 μA, 8.62 V) with $I_B = 0.944$ μA and $V_C = 7.92$ V.

Note, that for $V_{EE} \gg V_{BE}$, I_E can approximated by

$$I_E \approx \frac{V_{EE}}{2R_{EE}} = \frac{15 \text{ V}}{150 \text{ k}\Omega} = 100 \text{ μA}$$

This estimate represents only a 6 percent error compared to the more accurate calculation. ◆

EXERCISE: Draw a *pnp* version of the *npn* differential amplifier in Fig. 15.16(a).

ANSWER: See Fig. P15.43.

ac Analysis of the Bipolar Differential Amplifier

The ac analysis of the differential amplifier can be simplified by breaking input sources v_1 and v_2 into their equivalent differential-mode input (v_{id}) and common-mode input (v_{ic}) signal components, shown in Fig. 15.18, and defined by

$$v_{id} = v_1 - v_2 \qquad \text{and} \qquad v_{ic} = \frac{v_1 + v_2}{2} \tag{15.62}$$

The input voltages can be written in terms of v_{ic} and v_{id} as

$$v_1 = v_{ic} + \frac{v_{id}}{2} \qquad \text{and} \qquad v_2 = v_{ic} - \frac{v_{id}}{2} \tag{15.63}$$

Circuit analysis can then be performed using superposition of the differential-mode and common-mode input signal components. This technique was originally used in our study of operational amplifiers in Chapter 12.

The differential-mode and common-mode output voltages, v_{od} and v_{oc}, are defined in a similar manner:

$$v_{od} = v_{c1} - v_{c2} \qquad \text{and} \qquad v_{oc} = \frac{v_{c1} + v_{c2}}{2} \tag{15.64}$$

For the general amplifier case, the voltages v_{od} and v_{oc} will be functions of both v_{id} and v_{ic} and can be written as

$$\begin{bmatrix} v_{od} \\ v_{oc} \end{bmatrix} = \begin{bmatrix} A_{dd} & A_{cd} \\ A_{dc} & A_{cc} \end{bmatrix} = \begin{bmatrix} v_{id} \\ v_{ic} \end{bmatrix} \tag{15.65}$$

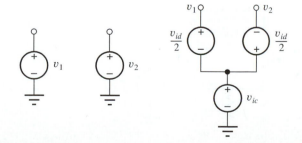

Figure 15.18 Definition of the differential-mode (v_{id}) and common-mode (v_{ic}) input voltages.

in which four gains are defined:

$$A_{dd} = \textbf{differential-mode gain}$$

$$A_{cd} = \textbf{common-mode (to differential-mode) conversion gain}$$

$$A_{cc} = \textbf{common-mode gain}$$

$$A_{dc} = \textbf{differential-mode (to common-mode) conversion gain}$$

For an ideal symmetrical amplifier with matched transistors, A_{cd} and A_{dc} are zero, and Eq. (15.65) reduces to

$$\begin{bmatrix} v_{od} \\ v_{oc} \end{bmatrix} = \begin{bmatrix} A_{dd} & 0 \\ 0 & A_{cc} \end{bmatrix} \begin{bmatrix} v_{id} \\ v_{ic} \end{bmatrix} \qquad (15.66)$$

In this case, a differential-mode input signal produces a purely differential-mode output signal, and a purely common-mode input produces only a common-mode output.

However, when the differential amplifier is not completely balanced because of transistor mismatches, or when an unbalanced output is taken from one side, A_{dc} or A_{cd} may no longer be zero. In the following discussions, we assume that the transistors are identical unless stated otherwise.

> **EXERCISE:** Measurement of a differential amplifier yielded the following sets of values:
>
> $$v_{od} = 2.2 \text{ V and } v_{oc} = 1.002 \text{ V} \qquad \text{for } v_1 = 1.01 \text{ V and } v_2 = 0.990 \text{ V}$$
>
> $$v_{od} = 0 \text{ V and } v_{oc} = 5.001 \text{ V} \qquad \text{for } v_1 = 4.995 \text{ V and } v_2 = 5.005 \text{ V}$$
>
> What are v_{id} and v_{ic} for the two cases? What are the values of A_{dd}, A_{cd}, A_{cd}, and A_{cc} for the amplifier?
>
> **ANSWERS:** 0.02 V, 1.00 V; −0.01 V, 5.00 V; 100, 0.200, 0.100, 1.00

Differential-Mode Input Signals

The purely differential-mode input signals are applied to the differential amplifier in Fig. 15.19, and the two transistors are replaced with their small-signal models in Fig. 15.20. We want to find the gain for both differential and single-ended outputs as well as the input and output resistances. Because the transistors have resistor loads, the output resistances will be neglected in the calculations.

Summing currents at the emitter node in Fig. 15.20:

$$g_{\pi}\mathbf{v_3} + g_m\mathbf{v_3} + g_m\mathbf{v_4} + g_{\pi}\mathbf{v_4} = G_{EE}\mathbf{v_e} \qquad (15.67)$$

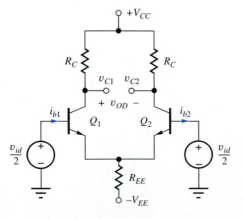

Figure 15.19 Differential amplifier with a differential-mode input signal.

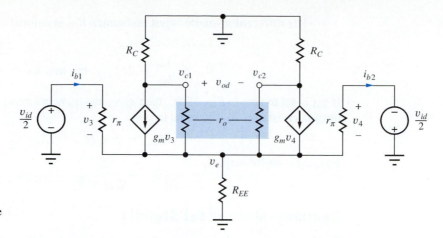

Figure 15.20 Small-signal model for differential-mode inputs.

or
$$(g_m + g_\pi)(\mathbf{v_3} + \mathbf{v_4}) = G_{EE}\mathbf{v_e} \qquad (15.68)$$

These equations have been simplified by representing resistances r_π and R_{EE} by their equivalent conductances g_π and G_{EE}. The base-emitter voltages are

$$\mathbf{v_3} = \frac{\mathbf{v_{id}}}{2} - \mathbf{v_e} \qquad \text{and} \qquad \mathbf{v_4} = -\frac{\mathbf{v_{id}}}{2} - \mathbf{v_e} \qquad (15.69)$$

giving $\mathbf{v_3} + \mathbf{v_4} = -2\mathbf{v_e}$. Combining Eq. (15.69) with Eq. (15.68) yields

$$\mathbf{v_e}(G_{EE} + 2g_\pi + 2g_m) = 0 \qquad (15.70)$$

which requires $\mathbf{v_e} = 0$.

For a purely differential-mode input voltage, the voltage at the emitter node is identically zero. This is an extremely important result. *The emitter node in the differential amplifier represents a **virtual ground** for differential-mode input signals.*

Because the voltage at the emitter node is zero, Eq. (15.69) yields

$$\mathbf{v_3} = \frac{\mathbf{v_{id}}}{2} \qquad \text{and} \qquad \mathbf{v_4} = -\frac{\mathbf{v_{id}}}{2} \qquad (15.71)$$

and the output signal voltages are

$$\mathbf{v_{c1}} = -g_m R_C \frac{\mathbf{v_{id}}}{2} \qquad \mathbf{v_{c2}} = +g_m R_C \frac{\mathbf{v_{id}}}{2} \qquad \mathbf{v_{od}} = -g_m R_C \mathbf{v_{dm}} \qquad (15.72)$$

The differential-mode gain A_{dd} for a **balanced output, $\mathbf{v_{od}} = \mathbf{v_{c1}} - \mathbf{v_{c2}}$,** is

$$A_{dd} = \left.\frac{\mathbf{v_{od}}}{\mathbf{v_{id}}}\right|_{\mathbf{v_{ic}}=0} = -g_m R_C \qquad (15.73)$$

If either $\mathbf{v_{c1}}$ or $\mathbf{v_{c2}}$ alone is used as the output, referred to as **single-ended** (or ground-referenced) **outputs,** then

$$A_{dd1} = \left.\frac{\mathbf{v_{c1}}}{\mathbf{v_{id}}}\right|_{\mathbf{v_{ic}}=0} = -\frac{g_m R_C}{2} = -\frac{A_{dd}}{2} \qquad \text{or} \qquad A_{dd2} = \left.\frac{\mathbf{v_{c2}}}{\mathbf{v_{id}}}\right|_{\mathbf{v_{ic}}=0} = +\frac{g_m R_C}{2} = \frac{A_{dd}}{2}$$
$$(15.74)$$

depending on which output is selected.

The virtual ground condition at the emitter node causes the amplifier to behave as a single-stage common-emitter amplifier. The balanced differential output provides the full gain of a common-emitter stage, whereas the output at either collector provides a gain equal to one-half that of the C-E stage.

The **differential-mode input resistance R_{ID}** is defined as

$$R_{ID} = \frac{v_{id}}{i_{b1}} = 2r_\pi \qquad \text{because } i_{b1} = \frac{\dfrac{v_{id}}{2}}{r_\pi} \tag{15.75}$$

If v_{id} is set to zero in Fig. 15.20, then $g_m v_3$ and $g_m v_4$ are zero, and the **differential-mode output resistance R_{OD}** is equal to

$$R_{OD} = 2(R_C \| r_o) \approx 2R_C \tag{15.76}$$

For single-ended outputs,

$$R_{OD} \approx R_C \tag{15.77}$$

Common-Mode Input Signals

Purely common-mode input signals are applied to the differential amplifier in Fig. 15.21. For this case, both sides of the amplifier are completely symmetrical. Thus the two base currents, the emitter currents, the collector currents, and the two collector voltages must be equal. Using this symmetry as a basis, the output voltage can be developed by writing a loop equation including either base-emitter junction.

For the small-signal model in Fig. 15.22,

$$v_{ic} = i_b r_\pi + v_e = i_b[r_\pi + 2(\beta_o + 1)R_{EE}] \tag{15.78}$$

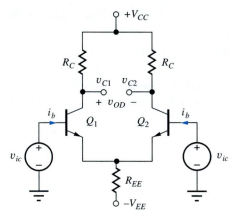

Figure 15.21 Differential amplifier with purely common-mode input.

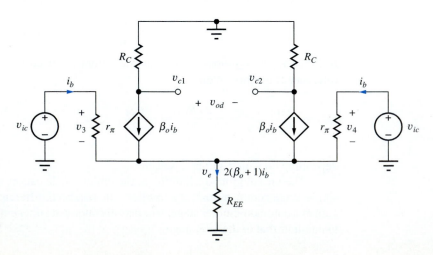

Figure 15.22 Small-signal model with common-mode input.

and solving for $\mathbf{i_b}$

$$\mathbf{i_b} = \frac{\mathbf{v_{ic}}}{r_\pi + 2(\beta_o + 1)R_{EE}} \tag{15.79}$$

The output voltage at either collector is given by

$$\mathbf{v_{c1}} = \mathbf{v_{c2}} = -\beta_o\mathbf{i_b}R_C = \frac{-\beta_o R_C}{r_\pi + 2(\beta_o + 1)R_{EE}}\mathbf{v_{ic}} \tag{15.80}$$

and the voltage at the emitter is

$$\mathbf{v_e} = 2(\beta_o + 1)\mathbf{i_b}R_{EE} = \frac{2(\beta_o + 1)R_{EE}}{r_\pi + 2(\beta_o + 1)R_{EE}}\mathbf{v_{ic}} \approx \mathbf{v_{ic}} \tag{15.81}$$

The differential output voltage $\mathbf{v_{od}}$ is identically zero because the voltages are equal at the two collectors:

$$\mathbf{v_{od}} = \mathbf{v_{c1}} - \mathbf{v_{c2}} = 0 \tag{15.82}$$

The common-mode conversion gain for a differential output is also 0:

$$A_{cd} = \left.\frac{\mathbf{v_{od}}}{\mathbf{v_{ic}}}\right|_{\mathbf{v_{id}}=0} = 0 \tag{15.83}$$

If the output is taken from one collector, then A_{cd} is no longer zero:

$$A_{cd} = A_{cc} = \left.\frac{\mathbf{v_c}}{\mathbf{v_{ic}}}\right|_{\mathbf{v_{id}}=0} = -\frac{\beta_o R_C}{r_\pi + 2(\beta_o + 1)R_{EE}} \approx -\frac{\alpha_o R_C}{2R_{EE}} \tag{15.84}$$

By multiplying and dividing Eq. (15.84) by the collector current, the expression can be rewritten as

$$A_{cd} \approx \frac{\alpha_o R_C}{2R_{EE}} = -\frac{I_C R_C}{2\dfrac{I_C}{\alpha_F}R_{EE}} = \frac{\dfrac{V_{CC}}{2}}{2I_E R_{EE}} = \frac{V_{CC}}{2(V_{EE} - V_{BE})} \approx \frac{V_{CC}}{2V_{EE}} \tag{15.85}$$

where it is assumed that $\alpha_F = \alpha_o$ and $I_C R_C = V_{CC}/2$. For single-ended outputs, we find that the common-mode conversion gain is determined by the ratio of the two power supply voltages, and for symmetrical power supply voltages, $A_{cd} \approx 0.5$.

Common-Mode Input Resistance

The **common-mode input resistance** can be calculated using Eq. (15.78):

$$R_{IC} = \frac{\mathbf{v_{ic}}}{2\mathbf{i_b}} = \frac{r_\pi + 2(\beta_o + 1)R_{EE}}{2} = \frac{r_\pi}{2} + (\beta_o + 1)R_{EE} \tag{15.86}$$

Equations (15.79), (15.80), (15.81), and the numerator of Eq. (15.86) should be recognized as those of a common-emitter amplifier with a resistor of value $2R_{EE}$ in the emitter. This observation is discussed in detail shortly.

Common-Mode Rejection Ratio (CMRR)

As defined in Chapter 12, the **common-mode rejection ratio,** or **CMRR,** characterizes the ability of an amplifier to amplify the desired differential-mode input signal and reject the undesired common-mode input signal. For a general differential amplifier stage characterized by Eq. (12.65), CMRR is defined as

$$\text{CMRR} = \left| \frac{A_{dm}}{A_{cm}} \right| \tag{15.87}$$

where A_{dm} and A_{cm} are the overall differential-mode and common-mode gains.

For the differential amplifier, CMRR is dependent on the designer's choice of output voltage. For a differential output v_{od}, the common-mode conversion gain A_{cd} of the balanced amplifier is zero, and the CMRR is infinite. However, if the output is taken from either collector,

$$\text{CMRR} = \left| \frac{A_{dd1}}{A_{cd}} \right| = \left| \frac{-\dfrac{g_m R_C}{2}}{-\dfrac{\alpha_o R_C}{2R_{EE}}} \right| = \frac{g_m R_{EE}}{\alpha_o} \approx g_m R_{EE} \tag{15.88}$$

For high CMRR, we see that a large value of R_{EE} is desired.

Let us explore Eq. (15.88) a bit further by writing g_m in terms of the collector current.

$$\text{CMRR} = \frac{40 I_C R_{EE}}{\alpha_o} = 20(2 I_E R_{EE}) = 20(V_{EE} - V_{BE}) \approx 20 V_{EE} \tag{15.89}$$

For the differential amplifier biased by resistor R_{EE}, CMRR is limited by the available negative power supply voltage V_{EE}. Also observe that the differential-mode gain will be determined by the positive power supply voltage:

$$A_{dd} = -g_m R_C = -40(I_C R_C) \approx -10 V_{CC} \tag{15.90}$$

using our design estimate from Chapter 13 with $I_C R_C = V_{CC}/4$.

> **EXERCISE:** Estimate the differential-mode gain, common-mode gain, and CMRR for a differential amplifier with V_{EE} and $V_{CC} = 15$ V if the differential output is used. If the output v_{C2} is used.
>
> **ANSWERS:** $-150, 0, \infty$; $+75, -0.5, 43.5$ dB

Effects of Mismatches

Although the CMRR for an ideal differential amplifier with differential output is infinite, an actual amplifier will not be perfectly symmetrical because of mismatches in the transistors, and the two conversion gains A_{cd} and A_{dc} will not be zero. For this case, many of the errors will still be proportional to the result in Eq. (15.88) and will be of the form [1]:

$$\text{CMRR} \propto g_m R_{EE} \left(\frac{\Delta g}{g} \right) \tag{15.91}$$

in which the $\Delta g/g = 2(g_1 - g_2)/(g_1 + g_2)$ factor represents the fractional mismatch between the small-signal device parameters on the two sides of the differential amplifier (see Probs. 15.48 and 15.50). Therefore, maximizing the $g_m R_{EE}$ product is equally important to improving the performance of differential amplifiers with differential outputs.

Analysis Using Half-Circuits

We noted that the differential amplifier behaves much as the single-transistor common-emitter amplifier. The analogy can be carried even further using the **half-circuit** method of analysis, in which the symmetry of the differential amplifier is used to simplify the circuit analysis by splitting the circuit into **differential-mode** and **common-mode half-circuits.**

The half-circuits are constructed by first drawing the differential amplifier in a fully symmetric form, as in Fig. 15.23. To achieve full symmetry, the power supplies have been

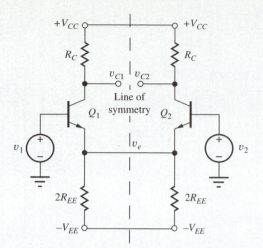

Figure 15.23 Circuit emphasizing symmetry of the differential amplifier.

split into two equal value sources in parallel, and the emitter resistor R_{EE} has been separated into two equal parallel resistors, each of value $2R_{EE}$. It is important to recognize from Fig. 15.23 that these modifications have not changed any of the currents or voltages in the circuit.

Once the circuit is drawn in symmetrical form, two basic rules are used to construct the half-circuits: one for differential-mode signal analysis and one for common-mode signal analysis:

Rules for Constructing Half-Circuits

Differential-mode signals	Points on the line of symmetry represent virtual grounds and can be connected to ground for ac analysis. (For example, remember that we found that $v_e = 0$ for differential-mode signals.)
Common-mode signals	Points on the line of symmetry can be replaced by open circuits. (No current flows through these connections.)

Differential-Mode Half Circuits

Applying the first rule to the circuit in Fig. 15.23 for differential-mode signals yields the circuit in Fig. 15.24. The two power supply lines and the emitter node all become ac grounds. (Of course, the power supply lines would become ac grounds in any case.) Simplifying the circuit yields the two differential-mode half-circuits in Fig. 15.25, each of which represents a common-emitter amplifier stage. The differential-mode behavior of the circuit, as described by Eqs. (15.72) to (15.77), can easily be found by direct analysis of the half-circuits:

$$\mathbf{v_{c1}} = -g_m R_C \frac{\mathbf{v_{id}}}{2} \qquad \mathbf{v_{c2}} = +g_m R_C \frac{\mathbf{v_{id}}}{2} \qquad \mathbf{v_o} = \mathbf{v_{c1}} - \mathbf{v_{c2}} = -g_m R_C \mathbf{v_{id}}$$

and   (15.92)

$$R_{ID} = \frac{\mathbf{v_{id}}}{\mathbf{i_b}} = 2r_\pi \qquad \text{and} \qquad R_{OD} = 2(R_C \| r_o)$$

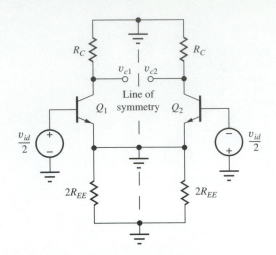

Figure 15.24 ac Grounds for differential-mode inputs.

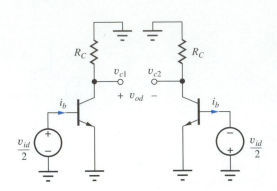

Figure 15.25 Differential-mode half-circuits.

Common-Mode Half-Circuits

If the second rule is applied to the circuit in Fig. 15.23, all points on the line of symmetry become open circuits, and we obtain the circuit in Fig. 15.26. The common-mode half-circuits obtained from Fig. 15.26 are redrawn in Fig. 15.27. The dc circuit with V_{IC} set to zero in Fig. 15.27(a) is used to find the Q-point of the amplifier. The circuit in Fig. 15.27(b) should be used to find the operating point when a large dc common-mode input is applied, and the ac circuit of (c) is used for common-mode signal analysis.

The common-mode half-circuit in Fig. 15.27(c) simply represents the common-emitter amplifier with an emitter resistor $2R_{EE}$, which was studied in great detail in Chapter 14. In addition, Eqs. (15.84), (15.86), and (15.88) could have been written down directly using the results of our analysis from Chapter 14.

We can see that use of the differential-mode and common-mode half-circuits can greatly simplify the analysis of symmetric circuits. Half-circuit techniques are used shortly to analyze the MOS differential amplifier from Fig. 15.16.

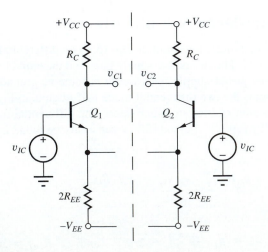

Figure 15.26 Construction of the common-mode half-circuit.

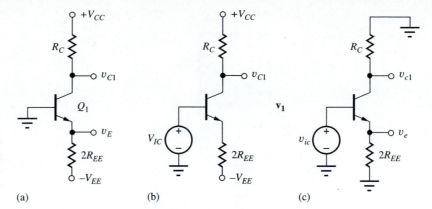

Figure 15.27 Common-mode half-circuits for (a) Q-point analysis, (b) dc common-mode input, and (c) common-mode signal analysis.

Common-Mode Input Voltage Range

Common-mode input voltage range is another important consideration in the design of differential amplifiers. The upper limit to the dc common-mode input voltage V_{IC} in the circuit in Fig. 15.27(b) is set by the requirement that Q_1 remain in the forward-active region of operation. Writing an expression for the collector-base voltage of Q_1,

$$V_{CB} = V_{CC} - I_C R_C - V_{IC} \geq 0$$

or
$$V_{IC} \leq V_{CC} - I_C R_C \qquad (15.93)$$

in which

$$I_C = \alpha_F \frac{V_{IC} - V_{BE} + V_{EE}}{2R_{EE}} \qquad (15.94)$$

Solving the preceding two equations for V_{IC} yields

$$V_{IC} \leq V_{CC} \frac{1 - \alpha_F \dfrac{R_C}{2R_{EE}} \dfrac{(V_{EE} - V_{BE})}{V_{CC}}}{1 + \alpha_F \dfrac{R_C}{2R_{EE}}} \qquad (15.95)$$

For symmetrical power supplies, $V_{EE} \gg V_{BE}$ and $R_C = R_{EE}$, and Eq. (15.95) yields $V_{IC} \leq V_{CC}/3$.

Note from Eq. (15.94) that I_C changes as V_{IC} changes. The upper limit on V_{IC} is set by Eq. (15.95) and by the allowable shift in Q-point current as V_{IC} changes.

> **EXERCISE:** Find the positive common-mode input voltage range for the differential amplifier in Fig. 15.21 if $V_{CC} = V_{EE} = 15$ V and $R_C = R_{EE}$.
>
> **ANSWER:** ≈ 5.20 V

FET Differential Amplifiers

Differential amplifiers can be designed equally well using FETs. The MOS version of the differential amplifier from Fig. 15.16 is reproduced in Fig. 15.28 along with a new current source biasing technique in which biasing resistor R_{SS} has been replaced by the current source I_{SS}, which directly controls the source currents of the two MOSFETs.

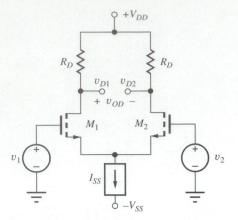

Figure 15.28 Differential amplifier employing MOS-FETs and electronic current source bias.

The rectangular symbol in Figs. 15.28 and 15.29 denotes an electronic current source with a finite output resistance, as shown graphically in the *i-v* characteristic in Fig. 15.30. The electronic source has a Q-point current equal to I_{SS} and an output resistance equal to R_{SS}.

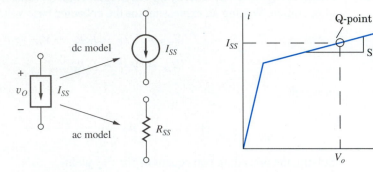

Figure 15.29 Electronic current source and models.

Figure 15.30 *i-v* Characteristic for an electronic current source.

dc Analysis

We use the MOSFET amplifier as our first direct application of half-circuit analysis; the amplifier is redrawn in symmetrical form in Fig. 15.31(a). If the connections on the line

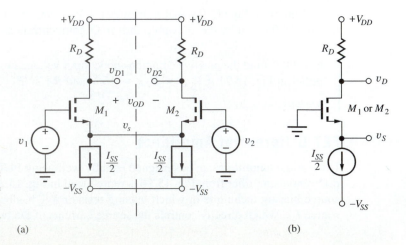

Figure 15.31 (a) Symmetric circuit representation of the MOS differential amplifier. (b) Half-circuit for dc analysis.

(a)

(b)

of symmetry are replaced with open circuits and the two input voltages are set to zero, we obtain in Fig. 15.31(b) the half-circuit needed for dc analysis.

It is immediately obvious from the dc half-circuit that the current in the source of the NMOS transistor must be equal to one-half bias current I_{SS}:

$$I_S = \frac{I_{SS}}{2} \tag{15.96}$$

The gate-source voltage of the MOSFET can be determined directly from the drain-current expression for the transistor:

$$I_{DS} = \frac{K_n}{2}(V_{GS} - V_{TN})^2 \tag{15.97}$$

$$V_{GS} = V_{TN} + \sqrt{\frac{2I_{DS}}{K_n}} = V_{TN} + \sqrt{\frac{I_{SS}}{K_n}} \tag{15.98}$$

Note that

$$V_S = -V_{GS} \tag{15.99}$$

The voltages at both MOSFET drains are

$$V_{D1} = V_{D2} = V_{DD} - I_{DS}R_D \qquad \text{and} \qquad V_O = 0 \tag{15.100}$$

The drain-source voltage is

$$V_{DS} = V_{DD} - I_{DS}R_D + V_{GS} \tag{15.101}$$

EXAMPLE 15.2: Find the Q-points for the MOSFETs in the differential amplifier in Fig. 15.28 if $V_{DD} = V_{SS} = 12$ V, $I_{SS} = 200$ μA, $R_D = 62$ kΩ, $K_n = 5$ mA/V^2, and $V_{TN} = 1$ V. What is the maximum V_{IC} for which M_1 remains saturated?

SOLUTION: Using Eqs. (15.94) through (15.97):

$$I_{DS} = \frac{I_{SS}}{2} = 100 \text{ μA}$$

$$V_{GS} = V_{TN} + \sqrt{\frac{I_{SS}}{K_n}} = 1 \text{ V} + \sqrt{\frac{2 \times 10^{-4} \text{ A}}{5 \times 10^{-3} \frac{\text{A}}{\text{V}^2}}} = 1.2 \text{ V}$$

$$V_{DS} = V_{DD} - I_{DS}R_D + V_{GS} = 12 - (10^{-4} \text{ A})(6.2 \times 10^4 \text{ Ω}) + 1.2 = 7.00 \text{ V}$$

Checking for saturation, $V_{GS} - V_{TN} = 0.2$ V and $V_{DS} \geq 0.2$. ✔ Thus, both transistors in the differential amplifier are biased at a Q-point of (100 μA, 7.00 V).

Requiring saturation of M_1 for nonzero V_{IC},

$$V_{GD} = V_{IC} - (V_{DD} - I_{DS}R_D) \leq V_{TN}$$

$$V_{IC} \leq V_{DD} - I_D R_D + V_{TN} = 12 \text{ V} - 10^{-4} \text{ A}(6.2 \times 10^4 \text{ Ω}) + 1 \text{ V} = 6.8 \text{ V} \qquad \blacklozenge$$

EXERCISE: Draw a PMOS version of the NMOS differential amplifier in Fig. 15.28.

ANSWER: See Figs. P15.63 and P15.65.

EXERCISE: Replace the MOSFET in Example 15.2 by a four-terminal device with its substrate connected to $V_{SS} = -12$ V, and find the new Q-point for the transistor. Assume $V_{TO} = 1$ V, $\gamma = 0.75 \sqrt{\text{V}}$, and $2\phi_F = 0.6$ V. What is the new value of V_{TN}?

ANSWERS: (100 μA, 8.75 V); 2.75 V

ac Analysis

The differential-mode and common-mode half-circuits for the differential amplifier in Fig. 15.31 are given in Fig. 15.32. In the differential-mode half-circuit, the MOSFET sources represent a virtual ground. In the common-mode circuit, the electronic current source has been modeled by twice its small-signal output resistance R_{SS} representing the finite output resistance of the current source.

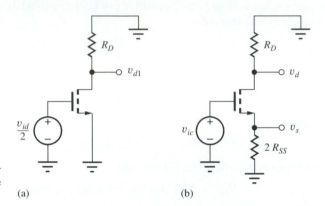

Figure 15.32 (a) Differential-mode and (b) common-mode half-circuits.

(a)   (b)

Differential-Mode Input Signals

The differential-mode half-circuit represents a common-source amplifier, and the output voltages are given by

$$\mathbf{v_{d1}} = -g_m R_D \frac{\mathbf{v_{id}}}{2} \qquad \mathbf{v_{d2}} = +g_m R_D \frac{\mathbf{v_{id}}}{2} \qquad \mathbf{v_{od}} = -g_m R_D \mathbf{v_{id}} \qquad (15.102)$$

The differential-mode gain is

$$A_{dd} = \left. \frac{\mathbf{v_{od}}}{\mathbf{v_{id}}} \right|_{\mathbf{v_{ic}} = 0} = -g_m R_D \qquad (15.103)$$

whereas taking the single-ended output between either drain and ground provides a gain of one-half A_{dd}:

$$A_{dd1} = \left. \frac{\mathbf{v_{d1}}}{\mathbf{v_{id}}} \right|_{\mathbf{v_{ic}} = 0} = -\frac{g_m R_D}{2} = -\frac{A_{dd}}{2}$$

and

$$A_{dd2} = \left. \frac{\mathbf{v_{d2}}}{\mathbf{v_{id}}} \right|_{\mathbf{v_{ic}} = 0} = +\frac{g_m R_D}{2} = +\frac{A_{dd}}{2} \qquad (15.104)$$

The differential-mode input and output resistances are infinite and $2R_D$, respectively:

$$R_{ID} = \infty \quad \text{and} \quad R_{OD} = 2R_D \qquad (15.105)$$

The virtual ground at the source node causes the amplifier to again behave as a single-stage inverting amplifier. A differential output provides the full gain of the common-source stage, whereas using the single-ended output at either drain reduces the gain by a factor of 2.

> **EXERCISE:** In a manner similar to the analysis in Fig. 15.20, derive directly from the full small-signal model the expressions for the differential-mode voltage gains of the MOS differential amplifier.

Common-Mode Input Signals

The common-mode half-circuit is that of an inverting amplifier with a source resistor equal to $2R_{SS}$. Using the results from Chapter 14,

$$\mathbf{v_{d1}} = \mathbf{v_{d2}} = \frac{-g_m R_D}{1 + 2g_m R_{SS}} \mathbf{v_{ic}} \tag{15.106}$$

and the signal voltage at the source is

$$\mathbf{v_s} = \frac{2g_m R_{SS}}{1 + 2g_m R_{SS}} \mathbf{v_{ic}} \approx \mathbf{v_{ic}} \tag{15.107}$$

The differential output voltage is zero because the voltages are equal at the two drains:

$$\mathbf{v_{od}} = \mathbf{v_{d1}} - \mathbf{v_{d2}} = 0 \tag{15.108}$$

Thus, the common-mode conversion gain for a differential output is zero:

$$A_{cd} = \frac{\mathbf{v_{od}}}{\mathbf{v_{ic}}} = 0 \tag{15.109}$$

If the output is taken from one drain, then the gain A_{cd} is

$$A_{cd} = \frac{\mathbf{v_{d1}}}{\mathbf{v_{ic}}} = -\frac{g_m R_D}{1 + 2g_m R_{SS}} \approx -\frac{R_D}{2R_{SS}} \tag{15.110}$$

The common-mode input source is connected directly to the MOSFET gate. Thus, the input current is zero and

$$R_{IC} = \infty \tag{15.111}$$

Common-Mode Rejection Ratio (CMRR)

For a purely common-mode input signal, the output voltage of the balanced MOS amplifier is zero, and the CMRR is infinite. If a single-ended output is taken from either drain, however,

$$\text{CMRR} = \left| \frac{A_{dd1}}{A_{cd}} \right| = \left| \frac{-\dfrac{g_m R_D}{2}}{-\dfrac{R_D}{2R_{SS}}} \right| = g_m R_{SS} \tag{15.112}$$

For high CMRR, a large value of R_{SS} is again desired. In Fig. 15.32, R_{SS} represents the output resistance of the current source in Fig. 15.28, and its value is much greater than resistor R_{EE}, which is used to bias the amplifier in Fig. 15.16. For this reason, as well as for Q-point stability, most differential amplifiers are biased by a current source, as in Fig. 15.28.

To compare the MOS amplifier more directly to the BJT analysis, however, let us assume for the moment that the MOS amplifier is biased by a resistor of value

$$R_{SS} = \frac{V_{SS} - V_{GS}}{I_{SS}} \tag{15.113}$$

Then Eq. (15.112) can be rewritten in terms of the circuit voltages, as was done for Eq. (15.89):

$$\text{CMRR} = \frac{2I_D R_{SS}}{V_{GS} - V_{TN}} = \frac{I_{SS} R_{SS}}{V_{GS} - V_{TN}} = \frac{(V_{SS} - V_{GS})}{V_{GS} - V_{TN}} \tag{15.114}$$

Using the numbers from the example,

$$\text{CMRR} = \frac{(V_{SS} - V_{GS})}{V_{GS} - V_{TN}} = \frac{(12 - 1.2)}{0.20} = 54 \qquad (15.115)$$

—a paltry 35 dB. This is almost 10 dB worse than the result for the BJT amplifier. Because of the low values of CMRR in both the BJT and FET circuits, the use of current sources with much higher effective values of R_{SS} or R_{EE} is common in all differential amplifiers.

15.4 EVOLUTION TO BASIC OPERATIONAL AMPLIFIERS

One extremely important application of differential amplifiers is as the input stage of operational amplifiers. Differential amplifiers provide the desired differential input and common-mode rejection capabilities, and a ground-referenced signal is available at the output. However, an op amp usually requires higher voltage gain than is available from a single differential amplifier stage, and most op amps use two stages of gain.

A Two-Stage Prototype for an Operational Amplifier

To achieve a higher gain, a *pnp* common-emitter amplifier Q_3 has been connected to the output of a differential amplifier, Q_1–Q_2, to form the simple two-stage op amp depicted in Fig. 15.33. Bias is provided by current source I_1.

dc Analysis

The dc equivalent circuit for the op amp is shown in Fig. 15.34 and will be used to find the Q-points of the three transistors. The emitter currents of Q_1 and Q_2 are each equal to one-half the bias current I_1:

$$I_{E1} = I_{E2} = \frac{I_1}{2} \qquad (15.116)$$

The voltage at the collector of Q_1 is equal to

$$V_{C1} = V_{CC} - I_{C1}R_C = V_{CC} - \alpha_{F1}\frac{I_1}{2}R_C \qquad (15.117)$$

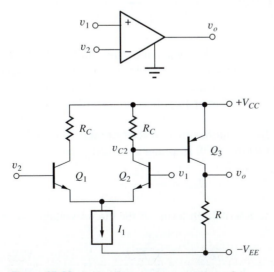

Figure 15.33 A simple two-stage prototype for an operational amplifier.

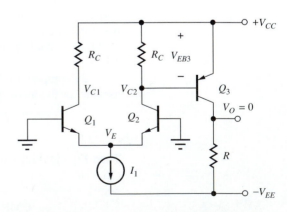

Figure 15.34 dc Equivalent circuit for the two-stage amplifier.

and that at the collector of Q_2 is

$$V_{C2} = V_{CC} - (I_{C2} - I_{B3})R_C = V_{CC} - \left(\alpha_{F2}\frac{I_1}{2} - I_{B3}\right)R_C \qquad (15.118)$$

If the base current of Q_3 can be neglected, and the common-base current gains are approximately 1, then Eqs. (15.117) and (15.118) become

$$V_{C1} \approx V_{C2} \approx V_{CC} - \frac{I_1 R_C}{2} \qquad (15.119)$$

and because $V_E = -V_{BE}$,

$$V_{CE1} \approx V_{CE2} \approx V_{CC} - \frac{I_1 R_C}{2} + V_{BE} \qquad (15.120)$$

In this particular circuit, it is important to note that the voltage drop across R_C is constrained to be equal to the emitter-base voltage V_{EB3} of Q_3, or approximately 0.7 V.

The value of the collector current of Q_3 can be found by remembering that this circuit is going to represent an operational amplifier, and because both inputs in Fig. 15.34 are zero, V_O should also be zero. This is the situation that exists when the circuit is used in any of the negative feedback circuits discussed in Chapter 12.
Thus, I_{C3} must satisfy

$$I_{C3} = \frac{V_{EE}}{R} \qquad (15.121)$$

Also, because $V_O = 0$,

$$V_{EC3} = V_{CC} \qquad (15.122)$$

We also know that V_{EB3} and I_{C3} are intimately related through the transport model relationship,

$$V_{EB3} = V_T \ln\left(1 + \frac{I_{C3}}{I_{S3}}\right) \qquad (15.123)$$

in which I_{S3} is the saturation current of Q_3. For the offset voltage of this amplifier to be zero, the value of R_C must be carefully selected, based on Eqs. (15.119) and (15.121):

$$R_C = \frac{V_T}{\left(\alpha_{F2}\dfrac{I_1}{2} - I_{B3}\right)} \ln\left(1 + \frac{I_{C3}}{I_{S3}}\right) = \frac{V_T}{\left(\alpha_{F2}\dfrac{I_1}{2} - \dfrac{I_{C3}}{\beta_{F3}}\right)} \ln\left(1 + \frac{I_{C3}}{I_{S3}}\right) \qquad (15.124)$$

> **EXERCISE:** Find the Q-points for the transistors in the amplifier in Fig. 15.34 if $V_{CC} = V_{EE} = 15$ V, $I_1 = 150$ μA, $R_C = 10$ kΩ, $R = 20$ kΩ, and $\beta_F = 100$. What must be the value of I_{S3} if the output voltage is to be zero?
>
> **ANSWERS:** (74.3 μA, 14.9 V), (74.3 μA, 15.01 V), (750 μA, 15.0 V); 1.90×10^{-15} A

ac Analysis

The ac equivalent circuit for the two-stage op amp is shown in Fig. 15.35, in which the bias source I_1 has been replaced by its equivalent ac resistance R_1. Analysis of the differential-mode behavior of the op amp can be determined from the simplified equivalent circuit in Fig. 15.36 based on the differential-mode half-circuit for the input stage.

It is important to realize that the overall two-stage amplifier no longer represents a symmetrical circuit. Thus, half-circuit analysis is not theoretically justified. However,

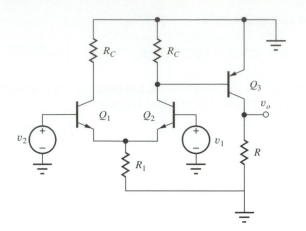 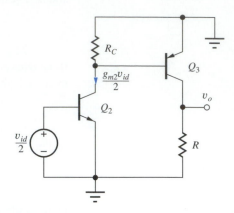

Figure 15.35 ac Equivalent circuit for the two-stage op amp.

Figure 15.36 Simplified model using differential-mode half-circuit.

we know that voltage variations at the collector of Q_2 (or at the drain of an FET) do not substantially alter the current in the transistor when it is operating in the forward-active region (or saturation region for the FET). Thus, continuing to represent the differential amplifier by its half-circuit is a highly useful engineering approximation.

The small-signal model corresponding to Fig. 15.36 appears in Fig. 15.37. In the following analysis, output resistances r_{o2} and r_{o3} are neglected because they are in parallel with external resistors R_C and R. From Fig. 15.37, the overall differential-mode gain A_{dm} of this two-stage operational amplifier can be expressed as

$$A_{dm} = \frac{\mathbf{v_o}}{\mathbf{v_{id}}} = \frac{\mathbf{v_{c2}}}{\mathbf{v_{id}}} \frac{\mathbf{v_o}}{\mathbf{v_{c2}}} = A_{V1}A_{V2} \tag{15.125}$$

and A_{V1} and A_{V2} can be found from analysis of the circuit in the figure.

The first stage is a differential amplifier with the output taken from the inverting side,

$$A_{V1} = \frac{\mathbf{v_{c2}}}{\mathbf{v_{id}}} = -\frac{g_{m2}}{2}R_{L1} = -\frac{g_{m2}}{2}\frac{R_C r_{\pi3}}{R_C + r_{\pi3}} \tag{15.126}$$

in which the load resistance R_{L1} is equal to the collector resistor R_C in parallel with the input resistance $r_{\pi3}$ of the second stage.

The second stage is also a resistively loaded common-emitter amplifier with gain

$$A_{V2} = \frac{\mathbf{v_o}}{\mathbf{v_{C2}}} = -g_{m3}R \tag{15.127}$$

Combining Eqs. (15.125) to (15.127) yields the overall voltage gain for the two-stage amplifier:

$$A_{dm} = A_{V1}A_{V2} = \left(-\frac{g_{m2}}{2}\frac{R_C r_{\pi3}}{R_C + r_{\pi3}}\right)(-g_{m3}R) = \frac{g_{m2}R_C}{2}\frac{\beta_{o3}R}{R_C + r_{\pi3}} \tag{15.128}$$

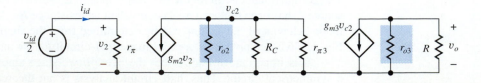

Figure 15.37 Small-signal model for Fig. 15.36.

Equation (15.128) appears to contain quite a number of parameters and is difficult to interpret. However, some thought and manipulation will help reduce this expression to its basic design parameters. Multiplying the numerator and denominator of Eq. (15.128) by g_{m3} yields

$$A_{dm} = \frac{1}{2} \frac{(g_{m2} R_C) \beta_{o3} (g_{m3} R)}{g_{m3} R_C + \beta_{o3}} \tag{15.129}$$

and expanding the transconductances in terms of the collector currents yields

$$A_{dm} = \frac{1}{2} \frac{(40 I_{C2} R_C) \beta_{o3} (40 I_{C3} R)}{40 I_{C3} R_C + \beta_{o3}} = \frac{1}{2} \frac{(40 I_{C2} R_C) \beta_{o3} (40 I_{C3} R)}{40 \dfrac{I_{C3}}{I_{C2}} I_{C2} R_C + \beta_{o3}} \tag{15.130}$$

If the base current of Q_3 is neglected, then $I_{C2} R_C = V_{BE3} \approx 0.7$ V, and $I_{C3} R = V_{EE}$, as pointed out during the dc analysis. Substituting these results into Eq. (15.130) yields

$$A_{dm} = \frac{1}{2} \frac{(28) \beta_{o3} (40 V_{EE})}{28 \left(\dfrac{I_{C3}}{I_{C2}} \right) + \beta_{o3}} = \frac{560 V_{EE}}{1 + \dfrac{56}{\beta_{o3}} \left(\dfrac{I_{C3}}{I_1} \right)} \tag{15.131}$$

In the final result in Eq. (15.131), A_{dm} is reduced to its basics. Once the power supply voltage V_{EE} and transistor Q_3 (that is, β_{o3}) are chosen, the only remaining design parameter is the ratio of the collector currents in the first and second stages. An upper limit on I_{C2} and I_1 is usually set by the permissible dc bias current, I_{B1}, at the input of the amplifier, whereas the minimum value of I_{C3} is determined by the current needed to drive the total load impedance connected to the output node. Generally, I_{C3} is several times larger than I_{C1}.

Figure 15.38 is a graph of Eq. (15.131), showing the variation of amplifier gain versus the collector current ratio. Observe that the gain starts to drop rapidly as I_{C3}/I_{C2} exceeds approximately 5. Such a graph is very useful as an aid in choosing the operating point during the design of the basic two-stage operational amplifier.

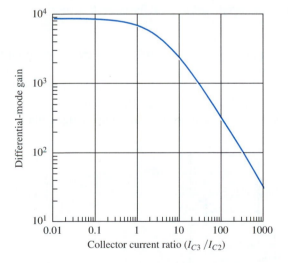

Figure 15.38 Differential-mode gain versus collector current ratio for $V_{EE} = 15$ V and $\beta_{o3} = 100$.

EXERCISE: What is the maximum possible gain of the amplifier described by Eq. (15.131) for $V_{CC} = V_{EE} = 15$ V, $\beta_{o1} = 50$, and $\beta_{o3} = 100$? What is the maximum voltage gain for the amplifier if the input bias current to the amplifier must not exceed 1 μA, and $I_{C3} = 500$ μA. Repeat if $I_{C3} = 5$ mA.

ANSWERS: 8400; 2210; 290

EXERCISE: What is the maximum possible gain of the amplifier described by Eq. (15.131) if $V_{CC} = V_{EE} = 1.5$ V?

ANSWER: 840

Input and Output Resistances

From the ac model of the amplifier in Figs. 15.36 and 15.37, the differential-mode input resistance R_{ID} of the simple op amp is equal to the input resistance of the differential amplifier given by

$$R_{ID} = \frac{v_{id}}{i_{id}} = 2r_{\pi 2} \qquad R_{ID} = 2r_{\pi 2} = 2r_{\pi 1} \qquad (15.132)$$

and the output resistance is given by

$$R_{OUT} = R \| r_{o3} \approx R \qquad (15.133)$$

EXERCISE: What are the input and output resistances for the two amplifier designs in the previous exercise?

ANSWER: 50 kΩ, 30 kΩ; 50 kΩ, 3 kΩ

Before proceeding, we need to understand how the coupling and bypass capacitors have been eliminated from the two-stage op-amp prototype. The virtual ground at the emitters of the differential amplifier allows the input stage to achieve the full inverting amplifier gain without the need for an emitter bypass capacitor. Use of the *pnp* transistor permits direct coupling between the first and second stages and allows the emitter of the *pnp* to be connected to an ac ground point. In addition, the *pnp* provides the voltage **level shift** required to bring the output back to 0 V. Thus, the need for any bypass or coupling capacitors is entirely eliminated, and $v_o = 0$ for $v_1 = 0 = v_2$.

CMRR

The common-mode gain and CMRR of the two-stage amplifier can be determined from the ac circuit model with common-mode input that is shown in Fig. 15.39, in which the half-circuit has again been used to represent the differential input stage. If Fig. 15.39 is compared to Fig. 15.36, we see that the circuitry beyond the collector of Q_2 is identical in both figures. The only difference in output voltage is therefore due to the difference in the

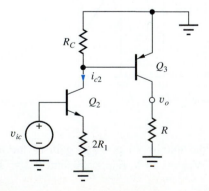

Figure 15.39 ac Equivalent circuit for common-mode inputs.

value of the collector current i_{c2}. In Fig. 15.39, i_{c2} is the collector current of a C-E stage with emitter resistor $2R_1$:

$$\mathbf{i_{c2}} = \frac{\beta_{o2}\mathbf{v_{ic}}}{r_{\pi2} + 2(\beta_{o2} + 1)R_1} = \frac{g_{m2}\mathbf{v_{ic}}}{1 + 2\dfrac{g_{m2}}{\alpha_{o2}}R_1} \approx \frac{g_{m2}\mathbf{v_{ic}}}{1 + 2g_{m2}R_1} \tag{15.134}$$

whereas i_{c2} in Fig. 15.36 was

$$\mathbf{i_{c2}} = \frac{g_{m2}}{2}\mathbf{v_{id}} \tag{15.135}$$

Thus the common-mode gain A_{cm} of the op amp is found from Eq. (15.128) by replacing the quantity $g_{m2}/2$ by $g_{m2}/(1 + 2g_{m2}R_1)$:

$$A_{cm} = \frac{g_{m2}R_C}{1 + 2g_{m2}R_1}\frac{\beta_{o3}R}{R_C + r_{\pi3}} = \frac{2A_{dm}}{1 + 2g_{m2}R_1} \tag{15.136}$$

From Eq. (15.136), the CMRR of the simple op amp is

$$\text{CMRR} = \left|\frac{A_{dm}}{A_{cm}}\right| = \frac{1 + 2g_{m2}R_1}{2} \approx g_{m2}R_1 \tag{15.137}$$

which is identical to the CMRR of the differential input stage alone.

> **EXERCISE:** What is the CMRR of the amplifier in Fig. 15.33 if $I_1 = 100\ \mu\text{A}$ and $R_1 = 750\ \text{k}\Omega$?
>
> **ANSWER:** 63.5 dB

Improving the Op-Amp Voltage Gain

From the previous several exercises, we can see that the prototype op amp has a relatively low overall voltage gain and a higher output resistance than is normally associated with a true operational amplifier. This section explores the use of an additional current source to improve the voltage gain; the next section adds an emitter follower to reduce the output resistance.

Figure 15.38 indicates that the overall amplifier gain decreases rapidly as the quiescent current of the second stage increases. In the exercise, the overall gain is quite low when $I_{C3} = 5\ \text{mA}$. One technique that can be used to improve the voltage gain is to replace resistor R by a second current source, as shown in Fig. 15.40. The modified ac model is in Fig. 15.41. The small-signal model is the same as Fig. 15.37 except R is replaced by output resistance R_2 of current source I_2. The load on Q_3 is now the output resistance R_2 of the current source in parallel with the output resistance of Q_3 itself. In Sec. 15.6, we shall discover that it is possible to design a current source with $R_2 \gg r_{o3}$, and, by neglecting R_2, the differential-mode gain expression for the overall amplifier becomes

$$A_{dm} = A_{V1}A_{V2} = \left(-\frac{g_{m2}}{2}\frac{R_C r_{\pi3}}{R_C + r_{\pi3}}\right)(-g_{m3}r_{o3}) \tag{15.138}$$

We can reduce Eq. (15.138) to

$$A_{dm} = \frac{14\mu_{f3}}{1 + \dfrac{28}{\beta_{o3}}\left(\dfrac{I_{C3}}{I_{C2}}\right)} \approx \frac{560V_{A3}}{1 + \dfrac{56}{\beta_{o3}}\left(\dfrac{I_{C3}}{I_1}\right)} \tag{15.139}$$

using the same steps that led to Eq. (15.131). This expression is similar to Eq. (15.131) except that power supply voltage V_{EE} has been replaced by the Early voltage of Q_3. For

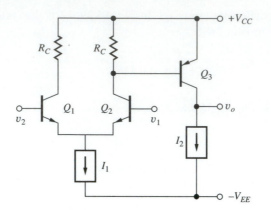

Figure 15.40 Amplifier with improved voltage gain.

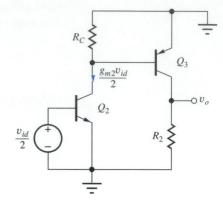

Figure 15.41 ac Differential-mode equivalent representation of Fig. 15.33.

low values of the collector current ratio, excellent voltage gains, approaching $560V_{A3}$, are possible from this simple two-stage amplifier. Also, note that the amplifier gain is no longer directly dependent on the choice of V_{CC} and V_{EE}.

Although adding the current source has improved the voltage gain, it also has degraded the output resistance. The output resistance of the amplifier is now determined by the characteristics of current source I_2 and transistor Q_3:

$$R_{\text{OUT}} = R_2 \| r_{o3} \approx r_{o3} \tag{15.140}$$

Because of the relatively high output resistance, this amplifier more nearly represents a transconductance amplifier with a current output ($A_{TC} = \mathbf{i_o}/\mathbf{v_{id}}$) rather than a true low-output resistance voltage amplifier.

> **EXERCISE:** Start with Eq. (15.138) and show that Eq. (15.139) is correct.
>
> **EXERCISE:** What is the maximum possible voltage gain for the amplifier described by Eq. (15.139) for $V_{CC} = 15$ V, $V_{EE} = 15$ V, $V_{A3} = 75$ V, $\beta_{o1} = 50$, and $\beta_{o3} = 100$? What is the voltage gain if the input bias current to the amplifier must not exceed 1 μA, and $I_{C3} = 500$ μA? Repeat if $I_{C3} = 5$ mA.
>
> **ANSWERS:** 42,000; 11,000; 1450
>
> **EXERCISE:** What are the input and output resistances for the last two amplifier designs?
>
> **ANSWER:** 50 kΩ, 180 kΩ; 50 kΩ, 18 kΩ

Output Resistance Reduction

As mentioned earlier, the two-stage op-amp prototype at this point more nearly represents a high-output resistance transconductance amplifier than a voltage amplifier with a low output resistance. A third stage, which maintains the amplifier voltage gain but provides a low output resistance, needs to be added to the amplifier. This sounds like the description of a follower circuit—unity voltage gain and low output resistance!

An emitter-follower (C-C) stage is added to the prototype amplifier in Fig. 15.42. In this case, the C-C amplifier is biased by a third current source I_3, and an external load resistance R_L has been connected to the output of the amplifier. The ac equivalent circuit is drawn in Fig. 15.43, in which the output resistances of I_2 and I_3 are assumed to be very large and will be neglected in the analysis. Based on the equivalent circuit model in

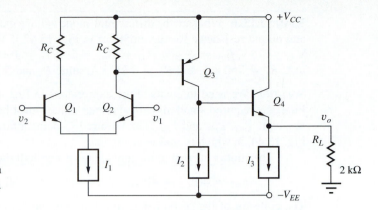

Figure 15.42 Amplifier with common-collector stage Q_4 added.

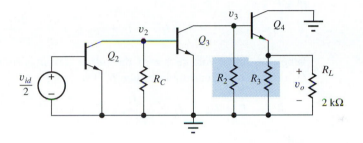

Figure 15.43 Simplified ac equivalent circuit for the three-stage op amp.

Fig. 15.43, the overall gain of the three-stage operational amplifier can be expressed as

$$A_{dm} = \frac{\mathbf{v_2}}{\mathbf{v_{id}}} \frac{\mathbf{v_3}}{\mathbf{v_2}} \frac{\mathbf{v_o}}{\mathbf{v_3}} = A_{V1}A_{V2}A_{V3} \qquad (15.141)$$

The gain of the first stage is equal to the gain of the differential input pair (neglecting r_{o2}):

$$A_{V1} = -\frac{g_{m2}}{2}(R_C \| r_{\pi3}) \qquad (15.142)$$

The second stage is a common-emitter amplifier with a load resistance equal to the output resistance of Q_3 in parallel with the input resistance of the emitter follower:

$$A_{V2} = -g_{m3}(r_{o3} \| R_{\mathrm{IN}}^{CC}) \qquad \text{where } R_{\mathrm{IN}}^{CC} = r_{\pi4} + (\beta_{o4} + 1)R_L \qquad (15.143)$$

Finally, the gain of emitter follower Q_4 is (neglecting r_{o4}):

$$A_{V3} = \frac{(\beta_{o4} + 1)R_L}{r_{\pi4} + (\beta_{o4} + 1)R_L} \approx 1 \qquad (15.144)$$

The input resistance is set by the differential pair:

$$R_{ID} = 2r_{\pi2} \qquad (15.145)$$

and the output resistance of the amplifier is now determined by the resistance looking back into the emitter of Q_4:

$$R_{\mathrm{OUT}} = \frac{1}{g_{m4}} + \frac{R_{\mathrm{th4}}}{\beta_{o4} + 1} \qquad (15.146)$$

In this case, there is a relatively large Thévenin equivalent source resistance at the base of Q_4, $R_{\mathrm{th4}} \approx r_{o3}$, and the overall output resistance is

$$R_{\mathrm{OUT}} = \frac{1}{g_{m4}} + \frac{r_{o3}}{\beta_{o4} + 1} = \frac{1}{g_{m4}}\left[1 + \frac{\mu_{f3}}{\beta_{o4} + 1}\frac{I_{C4}}{I_{C3}}\right] \qquad (15.147)$$

EXAMPLE 15.3: What are the differential-mode voltage gain, CMRR, input resistance, and output resistance for the amplifier in Fig. 15.42 if $V_{CC} = 15$ V, $V_{EE} = 15$ V, $V_{A3} = 75$ V, $\beta_{o1} = \beta_{o2} = \beta_{o3} = \beta_{o4} = 100$, $I_1 = 100\ \mu$A, $I_2 = 500\ \mu$A, $I_3 = 5$ mA, $R_1 = 750$ kΩ, and $R_L = 2$ kΩ? Assume R_2 and $R_3 = \infty$.

SOLUTION: We need to evaluate the expressions in Eqs. (15.141) through (15.147). First, the required small-signal parameter values must be evaluated, including g_{m2}, $r_{\pi2}$, $r_{\pi3}$, g_{m3}, r_{o3}, and $r_{\pi4}$. The required Q-point information can be found from Fig. 15.44, in which v_1 and v_2 equal zero.

The emitter current in the input stage is one-half the bias current source I_1 and

$$g_{m2} = 40I_{C2} = 40(\alpha_{F2}I_{E2}) = 40(0.99 \times 50\ \mu\text{A}) = 1.98\ \text{mS}$$

The collector of the second stage must supply the current I_2 plus the base current of Q_4:

$$I_{C3} = I_2 + I_{B4} = I_2 + \frac{I_{E4}}{\beta_{F4} + 1}$$

When the output voltage is zero, the output current is zero, and the emitter current of Q_4 is equal to the current in source I_3. Therefore,

$$I_{C3} = I_2 + I_{B4} = I_2 + \frac{I_3}{\beta_{F4} + 1} = 5 \times 10^{-4}\ \text{A} + \frac{5 \times 10^{-3}\ \text{A}}{101} = 550\ \mu\text{A}$$

and

$$g_{m3} = 40I_{C3} = \frac{40}{\text{V}}(5.5 \times 10^{-4}\ \text{A}) = 2.20 \times 10^{-2}\ \text{S}$$

$$r_{\pi3} = \frac{\beta_{o3}}{g_{m3}} = \frac{100}{2.20 \times 10^{-2}\ \text{S}} = 4.55\ \text{k}\Omega$$

To find the output resistance of Q_3, V_{EC3} is needed. When properly designed, the dc output voltage of the amplifier will be zero when the input voltages are zero. Hence, the voltage at node 3 is one base-emitter voltage drop above zero, or $+0.7$ V, and $V_{EC3} = 15 - 0.7 = 14.3$ V. The output resistance of Q_3 is

$$r_{o3} = \frac{V_{A3} + V_{EC3}}{I_{C3}} = \frac{(75 + 14.3)\ \text{V}}{5.50 \times 10^{-4}\ \text{A}} = 162\ \text{k}\Omega$$

Remembering that $I_{E4} = I_3$,

$$I_{C4} = \alpha_{F4}I_{E4} = 0.990 \times 5\ \text{mA} = 4.95\ \text{mA}$$

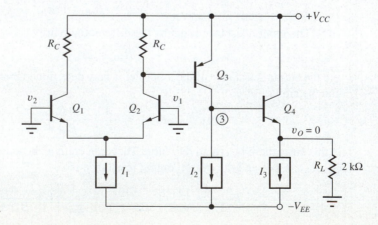

Figure 15.44 Operational amplifier with $v_1 = 0 = v_2$.

and

$$r_{\pi 4} = \frac{\beta_{o4}V_T}{I_{C4}} = \frac{100 \times 0.025 \text{ V}}{4.95 \times 10^{-3} \text{ A}} = 505 \text{ }\Omega$$

Finally, the value of R_C is needed:

$$R_C = \frac{V_{EB3}}{I_{C2} - I_{B3}} = \frac{V_{EB3}}{I_{C2} - \dfrac{I_{C3}}{\beta_{F3}}} = \frac{0.7 \text{ V}}{\left(49.5 - \dfrac{550}{100}\right) \times 10^{-6} \text{ A}} = 15.9 \text{ k}\Omega$$

Now, the characteristics of the amplifier can be evaluated:

$$A_{V1} = -\frac{g_{m2}(R_C \| r_{\pi 3})}{2} = -\frac{(1.98 \text{ mS})(15.9 \text{ k}\Omega \| 4.55 \text{ k}\Omega)}{2} = -3.50$$

$$A_{V2} = -g_{m3}[r_{o3} \| (r_{\pi 4} + (\beta_{o4} + 1)R_L)] = -(22.0 \text{ mS})(162 \text{ k}\Omega \| 203 \text{ k}\Omega)$$

$$= -1980!$$

$$A_{V3} = \frac{(\beta_{o4} + 1)R_L}{(r_{\pi 4} + (\beta_{o4} + 1)R_L)} = \frac{101(2000 \text{ }\Omega)}{505 \text{ }\Omega + 101(2000 \text{ }\Omega)} = 0.998 \approx 1$$

$$A_{dm} = A_{V1}A_{V2}A_{V3} = -3.50 \times -1980 \times 0.998 = 6920$$

$$R_{ID} = 2r_{\pi 2} = 2\frac{\beta_{o2}}{g_{m2}} = 2\frac{100}{\dfrac{40}{\text{V}}(4.95 \times 10^{-5} \text{ A})} = 101 \text{ k}\Omega$$

$$R_{\text{OUT}} = \frac{1}{g_{m4}} + \frac{r_{o3}}{\beta_{o4} + 1} = \frac{1}{\dfrac{40}{\text{V}}(4.95 \times 10^{-3} \text{ A})} + \frac{162 \text{ k}\Omega}{101} = 1.61 \text{ k}\Omega$$

$$\text{CMRR} = g_{m2}R_1 = \left(\frac{40}{\text{V}}5 \times 10^{-5} \text{ A}\right)(7.5 \times 10^5 \text{ }\Omega) = 1500 = 63.5 \text{ dB}$$

DISCUSSION: This amplifier achieves a reasonable set of op-amp characteristics for a simple circuit: $A_V = 6920$, $R_{ID} = 101$ kΩ, and $R_{\text{OUT}} = 1.61$ kΩ. Note that the second stage, loaded by current source I_2 and buffered from R_L by the emitter follower, is achieving a gain that is a substantial fraction of Q_3's amplification factor. However, even with the emitter follower, the reflected load resistance $(\beta_{o4} + 1)R_L$ is similar to the value of r_{o3} and is reducing the overall voltage gain by a factor of almost 2. Also, note that the output resistance is dominated by r_{o3} and not by the reciprocal of g_{m4}. ◆

EXERCISE: The op amp in Example 15.3 is operated as a voltage follower. What are the closed-loop gain, input resistance, and output resistance?

ANSWERS: +0.99986, 699 MΩ, 0.233 Ω

A CMOS Operational-Amplifier Prototype

Similar circuit design ideas have been used to develop the basic CMOS operational amplifier depicted in Fig. 15.45(a). A differential amplifier, formed by transistors M_1 and M_2, is followed by common-source stage M_3 and source follower M_4. Current sources are again used to bias the differential input and source-follower stages and as a load for M_3. Referring to the ac equivalent circuit in Fig. 15.45(b), we see that the differential-mode gain is

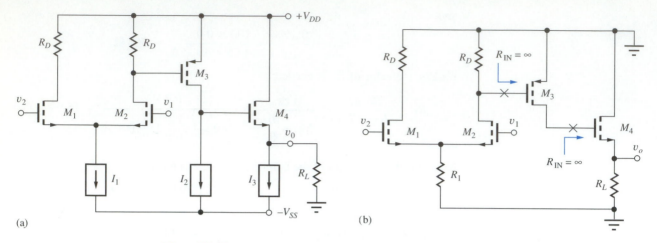

Figure 15.45 (a) A CMOS operational amplifier prototype. (b) ac Equivalent circuit for the CMOS amplifier, in which the output resistances of current sources I_2 and I_3 have been neglected.

given by

$$A_{dm} = A_{V1}A_{V2}A_{V3} = \left(-\frac{g_{m2}}{2}R_D\right)(-g_{m3}r_{o3})\left(\frac{g_{m4}R_L}{1+g_{m4}R_L}\right) \qquad (15.148a)$$

$$= \mu_{f3}\left(\frac{g_{m2}}{2}R_D\right)\left(\frac{g_{m4}R_L}{1+g_{m4}R_L}\right) \qquad (15.148b)$$

Equation (15.148) is relatively easy to construct using our single-stage amplifier formulas because the input resistance of each FET is infinite and the gain of one stage is not altered by the presence of the next.

Expanding g_{m2}, realizing that the product $I_{DS2}R_D$ represents the voltage across R_D, which must equal V_{GS3}, and assuming that the source follower has a gain of nearly 1 yields

$$A_{dm} = A_{V1}A_{V2}(1) = \mu_{f3}\left(\frac{V_{SG3}}{V_{GS2}-V_{TN2}}\right) \qquad (15.149)$$

The overall differential-mode gain is approximately equal to the product of the voltage gain of the first stage and the amplification factor of the second stage.

Although Eq. (15.149) is a simple expression, we often prefer to have the gain expressed in terms of the various bias currents, and expanding μ_{f3}, V_{GS2}, and V_{SG3} yields

$$A_{dm} = \frac{1}{\lambda_3}\sqrt{\frac{K_{n2}}{I_{DS2}}\frac{K_{p3}}{I_{DS3}}}\left[\sqrt{\frac{2I_{DS3}}{K_{p3}}} - V_{TP3}\right] \qquad (15.150)$$

Because of the Q-point dependence of μ_f, there are more degrees of freedom in Eq. (15.150) than in the corresponding expression for the bipolar amplifier, Eq. (15.139). This is particularly true in the case of integrated circuits, in which the values of K_n and K_p can be easily changed by modifying the W/L ratios of the various transistors. However, the benefit of operating both gain stages of the amplifier at low currents is obvious from Eq. (15.150), and picking a transistor with a small value of λ for M_3 is also clearly important.

It is worth noting that because the gate currents of the MOS devices are zero, input-bias current does not place a restriction on I_{DS1}, whereas it does place a practical upper bound on I_{C1} in the case of the bipolar amplifier. The input and output resistances of the op amp are determined by M_2 and M_4. From our knowledge of single-stage amplifiers,

$$R_{ID} = \infty \qquad \text{and} \qquad R_{OUT} = \frac{1}{g_{m4}} \qquad (15.151)$$

CMRR is once again determined by the differential input stage:

$$\text{CMRR} = g_{m2}R_1 \tag{15.152}$$

in which R_1 is the output resistance of current source I_1.

> **EXERCISE:** For the CMOS amplifier in Fig. 15.45(a), $\lambda_3 = 0.01$ V, $K_{n1} = K_{n4} = 5.0$ mA/V^2, $K_{p3} = 2.5$ mA/V^2, $I_1 = 200$ μA, $I_2 = 500$ μA, $I_3 = 5$ mA, $R_1 = 375$ kΩ, and $V_{TP3} = -1$ V. What is the actual gain of the source follower if $R_L = 2$ kΩ? What are the voltage gain, CMRR, input resistance, and output resistance of the amplifier?
>
> **ANSWERS:** 0.934; 2410, 51.5 dB, ∞, 141 Ω
>
> **EXERCISE:** What is the quiescent power consumption of this op amp if $V_{DD} = V_{SS} = 12$ V?
>
> **ANSWER:** 137 mW

15.5 OUTPUT STAGES

The basic operational-amplifier circuits discussed in Sec. 15.4 used followers for the output stages. The final stage of these amplifiers is designed to provide a low-output resistance as well as a relatively high current drive capability. However, because of this last requirement, the output stages of the amplifiers in the previous section consume approximately 90 percent of the total power.

Followers are **class-A amplifiers,** defined as circuits in which the transistors conduct during the full 360° of the signal waveform. The class-A amplifier is said to have a **conduction angle $\theta_C = 360°$.** Unfortunately, the maximum efficiency of the class-A stage is only 25 percent. Because the output stage must often deliver relatively large powers to the amplifier load, this low efficiency can cause high power dissipation in the amplifier. This section analyzes the efficiency of the class-A amplifier and then introduces the concept of the **class-B push-pull output stage.** The class-B push-pull stage uses two transistors, each of which conducts during only one-half, or 180°, of the signal waveform ($\theta_C = 180°$) and can achieve much higher efficiency than the class-A stage. Characteristics of the class-A and class-B stages can also be combined into a third category, the class-AB amplifier, which forms the output stage of most operational amplifiers.

The Source Follower—Class-A Output Stage

We analyzed the large- and small-signal behavior of follower circuits in detail and found that they provide high input resistance, low output resistance, and a voltage gain of approximately 1. The large-signal operation of the emitter follower, biased by the **ideal current source,** was discussed in Chapter 10, so here we focus on the source-follower circuit in Fig. 15.46.

For $v_I \le V_{DD} + V_{TN}$, M_1 will be operating in the saturation region (be sure to prove this to yourself). The current source forces a constant current I_{SS} to flow out of the source. Using Kirchhoff's voltage law:

$$v_O = v_I - v_{GS} \tag{15.153}$$

Because the source current is constant, v_{GS} is also constant, and the v_O is

$$v_O = v_I - V_{GS} = v_I - \left(V_{TN} + \sqrt{\frac{2I_{SS}}{K_n}}\right) \tag{15.154}$$

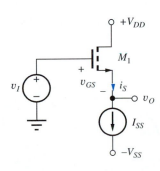

Figure 15.46 Source-follower circuit.

The difference between the input and output voltages is fixed. Thus, from a large-signal perspective (as well as from a small-signal perspective), we expect the source follower to provide a gain of approximately 1.

The voltage transfer characteristic for the source follower appears in Fig. 15.47. The output voltage at the source follows the input voltage with a slope of $+1$ and a fixed offset voltage equal to V_{GS}. For positive inputs, M_1 remains in saturation until $v_I = V_{DD} + V_{TN}$. The maximum output voltage is $v_o = V_{DD}$ for $v_I = V_{DD} + V_{GS}$. Note that to actually reach this output, the input voltage must exceed V_{DD}.

The minimum output voltage is set by the characteristics of the current source. An ideal current source will continue to operate even with $v_o < -V_{SS}$, but most electronic current sources require $v_o \geq -V_{SS}$. Thus, the minimum value of the input voltage is $v_I = -V_{SS} + V_{GS}$.

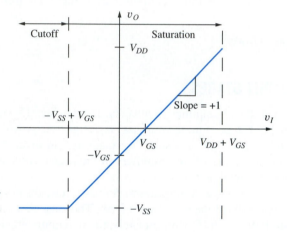

Figure 15.47 Voltage transfer characteristic for the source follower.

Source Follower with External Load Resistor

When a load resistor R_L is connected to the output, as in Fig. 15.48, the output voltage range is restricted by a new limit. The total source current of M_1 is equal to

$$i_S = I_{SS} + \frac{v_O}{R_L} \tag{15.155}$$

and must be greater than zero. In this circuit, current cannot go back into the MOSFET source, and the minimum output voltage occurs at the point at which transistor M_1 cuts off. In this situation, $i_S = 0$ and $v_{\text{MIN}} = -I_{SS}R_L$. M_1 cuts off when the input voltage falls to one threshold voltage drop above V_{MIN}: $v_I = -I_{SS}R_L + V_{TN}$.

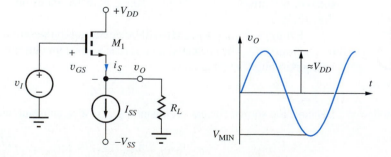

Figure 15.48 Source follower with external load resistor R_L.

Efficiency of Class-A Amplifiers

Now consider the emitter follower in Fig. 15.48 biased with $I_{SS} = V_{SS}/R_L$ and using symmetrical power supplies $V_{DD} = V_{SS}$. Assuming that V_{GS} is much less than the amplitude of v_I, then a sinusoidal output signal can be developed with an amplitude approximately equal to V_{DD},

$$v_O \approx V_{DD} \sin \omega t \tag{15.156}$$

The efficiency ζ of the amplifier is defined as the power delivered to the load at the signal frequency ω, divided by the average power supplied to the amplifier:

$$\zeta = \frac{P_{ac}}{P_{av}} \tag{15.157}$$

The average power P_{av} supplied to the source follower is

$$P_{av} = \frac{1}{T} \int_0^T \left[I_{SS}(V_{DD} + V_{SS}) + \left(\frac{V_{DD} \sin \omega t}{R_L} \right) V_{DD} \right] dt \tag{15.158}$$

$$= I_{SS}(V_{DD} + V_{SS}) = 2 I_{SS} V_{DD}$$

where T is the period of the sine wave. The first term in brackets in Eq. (15.158) is the power dissipation due to the dc current source; the second term results from the ac drain current of the transistor. The last simplification assumes symmetrical power supply voltages.

Because the output voltage is a sine wave, the power delivered to the load at the signal frequency is

$$P_{ac} = \frac{\left(\frac{V_{DD}}{\sqrt{2}} \right)^2}{R_L} = \frac{V_{DD}^2}{2 R_L} \tag{15.159}$$

Combining Eqs. (15.157) through (15.159) yields

$$\zeta = \frac{\frac{V_{DD}^2}{2 R_L}}{2 I_{SS} V_{DD}} = \frac{1}{4} \quad \text{or} \quad 25\% \tag{15.160}$$

because $I_{SS} R_L = V_{SS} = V_{DD}$. Thus a follower, operating as a class-A amplifier, can achieve an efficiency of only 25 percent, at most, for sinusoidal signals (see Probs. 15.111 to 15.113). Equation (15.158) indicates that the low efficiency is caused by the Q-point current I_{SS} that flows continuously between the two power supplies. The average of the sine wave current is zero, and the sinusoidal current does not contribute to the value of the integral in Eq. (15.158).

Class-B Push-Pull Output Stage

Class-B amplifiers improve the efficiency by operating the transistors at zero Q-point current, eliminating the quiescent power dissipation. A **complementary push-pull** (class-B) **output stage** using CMOS transistors is shown in Fig. 15.49, and the voltage and current waveforms for the composite output stage appear in Fig. 15.50. NMOS transistor M_1 operates as a source follower for positive input signals, and PMOS transistor M_2 operates as a source follower for negative inputs.

Consider the sinusoidal input in Fig. 15.50, for example. As the input voltage v_I swings positive, M_1 turns on supplying current to the load, and the output follows the input

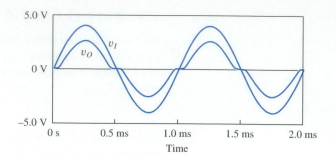

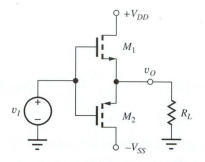

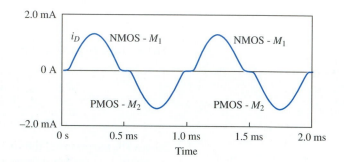

Figure 15.49 Complementary MOS class-B amplifier.

Figure 15.50 Cross-over distortion and drain currents in the class-B amplifier.

on the positive swing. When the input becomes negative, M_2 turns on sinking current from the load, and the output follows the input on the negative swing.

Each transistor conducts current for approximately 180° of the signal waveform, as shown in Fig. 15.50. Because the n- and p-channel gate-source voltages are equal in Fig. 15.49, only one of the two transistors can be on at a time. Also, the Q-point current for $v_O = 0$ is zero, and the efficiency can be high.

However, although the efficiency is high, a distortion problem occurs in the class-B stage. Because V_{GS1} must exceed threshold voltage V_{TN} to turn on M_1, and V_{GS2} must be less than V_{TP} to turn on M_2, a "dead zone" appears in the push-pull class-B voltage transfer characteristic, shown in Fig. 15.51. Neither transistor is conducting for

$$V_{TP} \le v_{GS} \le V_{TN} \qquad (-1 \text{ V} \le v_{GS} \le 1 \text{ V in Fig. 15.51}) \qquad (15.161)$$

This **dead zone,** or **cross-over region,** causes distortion of the output waveform, as shown in the simulation results in Fig. 15.50. As the sinusoidal input waveform crosses through zero, the output voltage waveform becomes distorted. The waveform distortion in Fig. 15.50 is called **cross-over distortion.**

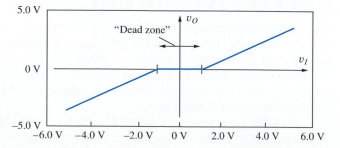

Figure 15.51 SPICE simulation of the voltage transfer characteristic for the complementary class-B amplifier.

Class-B Efficiency

Simulation results for the currents in the two transistors are also included in Fig. 15.51. If cross-over distortion is neglected, then the current flowing in each transistor can be approximated by a half-wave rectified sinusoid with an amplitude of approximately V_{DD}/R_L. Assuming $V_{DD} = V_{SS}$, the average power dissipated from each power supply is

$$P_{\text{av}} = \frac{1}{T} \int_0^{T/2} V_{DD} \frac{V_{DD}}{R_L} \sin \frac{2\pi}{T} t \, dt = \frac{V_{DD}^2}{\pi R_L} \tag{15.162}$$

The total ac power delivered to the load is still given by Eq. (15.159), and ζ for the class-B output stage is

$$\zeta = \frac{\dfrac{V_{DD}^2}{2R_L}}{2\dfrac{V_{DD}^2}{\pi R_L}} = \frac{\pi}{4} \approx 0.785 \tag{15.163}$$

By eliminating the quiescent bias current, the class-B amplifier can achieve an efficiency of 78.5 percent!

In closed-loop feedback amplifier applications such as those introduced in Chapter 12, the effects of cross-over distortion are reduced by the loop gain $A\beta$. However, an even better solution is to eliminate the cross-over region by operating the output stage with a small nonzero quiescent current.

Class-AB Amplifiers

The benefits of the class-B amplifier can be maintained, and cross-over distortion can be minimized by biasing the transistors into conduction but at a relatively low quiescent current level. The basic technique is shown in Fig. 15.52. A bias voltage V_{GG} is used to establish a small quiescent current in both output transistors. This current is chosen to be much smaller than the peak ac current that will be delivered to the load. In Fig. 15.52, the bias source is split into two symmetrical parts so that $v_O = 0$ for $v_I = 0$.

Because both transistors are conducting for $v_I = 0$, the cross-over distortion can be eliminated, but the additional power dissipation can be kept small enough that the efficiency is not substantially degraded. The amplifier in Fig. 15.52 is classified as a **class-AB amplifier.** Each transistor conducts for more than the 180° of the class-B amplifier but less than the full 360° of the class-A amplifier.

Figure 15.53 shows the results of circuit simulation of the voltage transfer characteristic of the class-AB output stage in Fig. 15.52 with a quiescent bias current of approx-

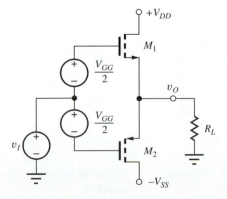

Figure 15.52 Complementary output stage biased for class-AB operation.

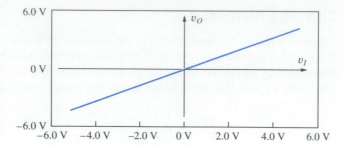

imately 60 μA. The distorted cross-over region has been eliminated, even for this small quiescent bias current.

Figure 15.54 shows one method for generating the needed bias voltage that is consistent with the CMOS operational amplifier circuit of Fig. 15.45. Bias current I_G develops the required bias voltage for the output stage across resistor R_G. If we assume that $K_p = K_n$ and $V_{TN} = -V_{TP}$ for the MOSFETs and $v_O = 0$, then the bias voltage splits equally between the gate-source terminals of the two transistors. The drain currents of the two transistors are both

$$I_{DS} = \frac{K_n}{2} \left(\frac{V_{GG}}{2} - V_{TN} \right)^2 \tag{15.164}$$

The bipolar version of the class-AB push-pull output stage employs complementary *npn* and *pnp* transistors, as shown in Fig. 15.55. The principle of operation of the bipolar circuit is the same as that for the MOS case. Transistors Q_1 and Q_2 operate as emitter followers for the positive and negative excursions of the output signal, respectively. Current source I_B develops a bias voltage V_{BB} across resistor R_B, which is shared between the base-emitter junctions of the two BJTs.

For class-AB operation, voltage V_{BB} is designed to be approximately $2V_{BE} \approx 1.4$ V, so both transistors are conducting a small collector current. If we assume the saturation currents of the two transistors are equal, then the bias voltage V_{BB} splits equally between the base-emitter junctions of the two transistors, and the two collector currents are

$$I_C = I_S \exp \left(\frac{I_B R_B}{2V_T} \right) \tag{15.165}$$

Each transistor is biased into conduction at a low level to eliminate cross-over distortion.

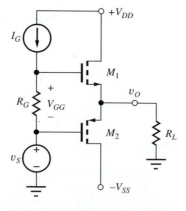

Figure 15.54 Method for biasing the class-AB amplifier.

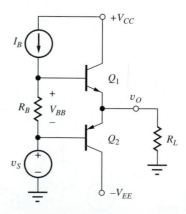

Figure 15.55 Bipolar class-AB amplifier.

A class-B version of the bipolar push-pull output stage is obtained by setting V_{BB} to zero. For this case, the output stage exhibits cross-over distortion for an input voltage range of approximately $2V_{BE}$.

> **EXERCISE:** Find the bias current in the transistors in Fig. 15.54 for $v_O = 0$ if $K_n = K_p = 25$ mA/V^2, $V_{TN} = 1$ V, and $V_{TP} = -1$ V, $I_G = 500$ μA, and $R_G = 4.4$ kΩ.
>
> **ANSWER:** 125 μA
>
> **EXERCISE:** Find the bias current in the transistors in Fig. 15.55 for $v_O = 0$ if $I_S = 10$ fA, $I_B = 500$ μA, and $R_B = 2.4$ kΩ.
>
> **ANSWER:** 265 μA

Class-AB Output Stages for Operational Amplifiers

In Figs. 15.56(a) and (b), the follower output stages of the prototype CMOS and bipolar op amps have been replaced with complementary class-AB output stages. Current source I_2, which originally provided a high impedance load to transistors Q_3 and M_3, is now also used to develop the dc bias voltage necessary for class-AB operation. The signal current

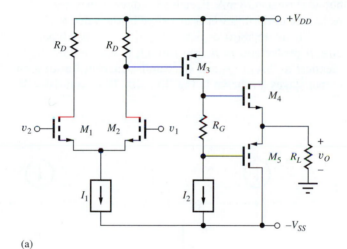

(a)

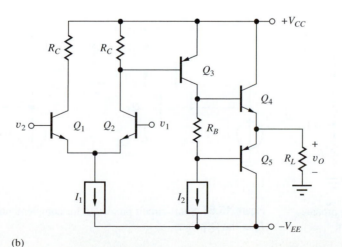

(b)

Figure 15.56 Class-AB output stages added to the (a) CMOS and (b) bipolar operational amplifiers.

is supplied by transistor M_3 or Q_3, respectively. The total quiescent power dissipation is greatly reduced in both these amplifiers.

Short-Circuit Protection

If the output of a follower circuit is accidentally shorted to ground, the transistor can be destroyed due to high current and high power dissipation, or, through direct destruction of the base-emitter junction of the BJT, from overvoltage operation. To make op amps as "robust" as possible, circuitry is often added to the output stage to provide protection from short circuits.

In Fig. 15.57, transistor Q_2 has been added to protect emitter follower Q_1. Under normal operating conditions, the voltage developed across R is less than 0.7 V, transistor Q_2 is cut off, and Q_1 functions as a normal follower. However, if emitter current I_{E1} exceeds a value of

$$I_{E1} = \frac{V_{BE2}}{R} = \frac{0.7 \text{ V}}{R} \tag{15.166}$$

then transistor Q_2 turns on and shunts any additional current from R_1 down through the collector of Q_2 and away from the base of Q_1. Thus the output current is limited to approximately the value in Eq. (15.166). For example, $R = 25 \ \Omega$ will limit the maximum output current to 28 mA. Because R is directly in series with the output, however, the output resistance of the follower is increased by the value of R.

Figure 15.58(a) depicts the complementary bipolar output stage including **short-circuit protection**. *pnp* Transistor Q_4 is used to limit the base current of Q_3 in a manner identical to that of Q_2 and Q_1. Similar **current-limiting circuits** can be applied to FET output stages, as shown in Fig. 15.58(b). Here, transistor M_2 steals the current needed to

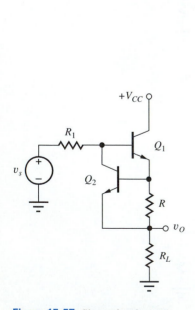

Figure 15.57 Short-circuit protection for an emitter follower.

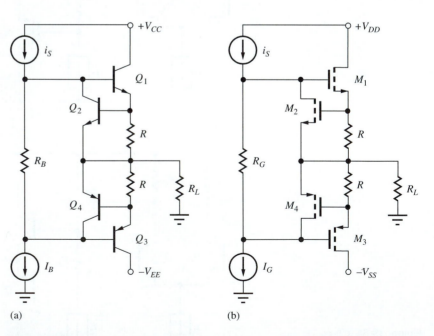

(a)   (b)

Figure 15.58 Short-circuit protection for complementary output stages. ($i_S = I_B$ or I_G at the Q-point.)

develop gate drive for M_1, and the output current is limited to

$$I_{S1} = \frac{V_{GS2}}{R} = \frac{V_{TN2} + \sqrt{\dfrac{2I_G}{K_{n2}}}}{R} \qquad (15.167)$$

Transistor M_4 provides similar protection to M_3.

Transformer Coupling

Designing amplifiers to deliver power to low impedance loads can be difficult. For example, loudspeakers typically have only an 8- or 16-Ω impedance. To achieve good voltage gain and efficiency in this situation, the output resistance of the amplifier needs to be quite low. One approach would be to use a feedback amplifier to achieve a low output resistance, as discussed in Chapter 12. An alternate approach to the problem is to use **transformer coupling.**

In Fig. 15.59, a follower circuit is coupled to the load resistance R_L through an ideal transformer with a turns ratio of $n{:}1$. In this circuit, a coupling capacitor C is required to block the dc path through the primary of the transformer. (See Prob. 15.140 for an alternate approach.)

As defined in network theory, the terminal voltages and currents of the ideal transformer are related by

$$\mathbf{v_1} = n\mathbf{v_2} \qquad \mathbf{i_2} = n\mathbf{i_1} \qquad \frac{\mathbf{v_1}}{\mathbf{i_1}} = n^2\frac{\mathbf{v_2}}{\mathbf{i_2}} \qquad \text{or} \qquad Z_1 = n^2 Z_L \qquad (15.168)$$

The transformer provides an impedance transformation by the factor n^2. Based on these equations, the transformer and load resistor can be represented by the ac equivalent circuit in Fig. 15.60, in which the resistor has been moved to the primary side of the transformer and the secondary is now an open circuit. The effective resistance that the transistor must drive is increased to

$$R_{\text{EQ}} = n^2 R_L \qquad (15.169)$$

and the voltage at the transformer output is

$$\mathbf{v_o} = \frac{\mathbf{v_1}}{n} \qquad (15.170)$$

Transformer coupling can reduce the problems associated with driving very low impedance loads. However, it is obviously restricted by the transformer to frequencies above dc.

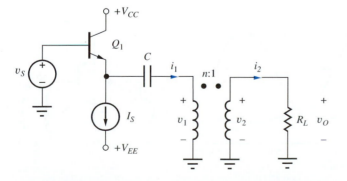

Figure 15.59 Follower circuit using transformer coupling.

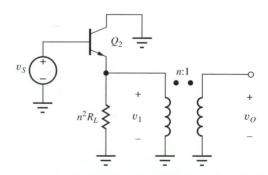

Figure 15.60 ac Equivalent circuit representation for the follower.

Figure 15.61 is a second example of the use of a transformer, in which an inverting amplifier stage is coupled to the load R_L through the ideal transformer. The dc and ac equivalent circuits appear in Figs. 15.61(b) and (c), respectively. At dc, the transformer represents a short circuit, the full dc power supply voltage appears across the transistor, and the quiescent operating current of the transistor is supplied through the primary of the transformer. At the signal frequency, a load resistance equal to $n^2 R_L$ is presented to the transistor.

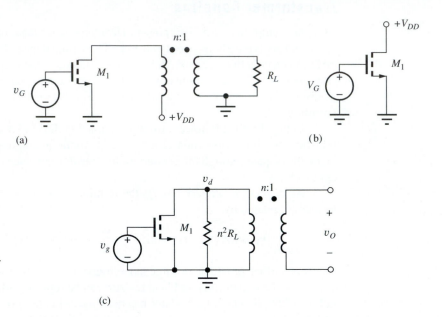

(a)

(b)

(c)

Figure 15.61 (a) Transformer-coupled inverting amplifier. (b) dc Equivalent circuit. (c) ac Equivalent circuit.

Results of simulation of the circuit in Fig. 15.61 are in Fig. 15.62 for the case $R_L = 8\ \Omega$, $V_{DD} = 10$ V, and $n = 10$. The behavior of this circuit is different from most that we have studied. The quiescent voltage at the drain of the MOSFET is equal to the full power supply voltage V_{DD}. The presence of the inductance of the transformer permits the signal voltage to swing symmetrically above and below V_{DD}, and the peak-to-peak amplitude of the signal at the drain can approach $2V_{DD}$.

Figure 15.63 is a final circuit example, which shows a transformer-coupled class-B output stage. Because the quiescent operating current in Q_1 and Q_2 are zero, the emitters may be connected directly to the primary of the transformer.

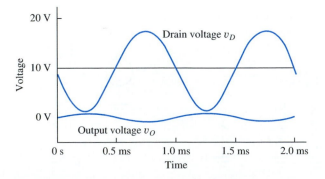

Figure 15.62 SPICE simulation of the transformer-coupled inverting amplifier stage for $n = 10$ with $V_{DD} = 10$ V.

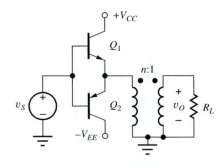

Figure 15.63 Transformer-coupled class-B output stage.

EXERCISE: Find the small-signal voltage gains

$$A_{V1} = \frac{\mathbf{v_d}}{\mathbf{v_g}} \quad \text{and} \quad A_{VO} = \frac{\mathbf{v_o}}{\mathbf{v_g}}$$

for the circuit in Fig. 15.61 if $V_{TN} = 1$ V, $K_n = 50$ mA/V^2, $V_G = 2$ V, $V_{DD} = 10$ V, $R_L = 8$ Ω, and $n = 10$. What are the largest values of v_g, v_d, and v_o that satisfy the small-signal limitations?

ANSWERS: -40, -4; 0.2 V, 8 V, 0.8 V

15.6 ELECTRONIC CURRENT SOURCES

The dc current source is clearly a fundamental and highly useful circuit component. In Sec. 15.4 we found that multiple current sources could be used to provide bias to the BJT and MOS op-amp prototypes as well as to improve their ac performance. This section explores the circuits used to realize basic electronic versions of ideal current sources. Chapter 16 explores current source design in more depth by looking at techniques specifically applicable to the design of integrated circuits.

In Fig. 15.64, the current-voltage characteristics of an ideal current source are compared with those of a resistor and a transistor current source. The current I_O through the ideal source is independent of the voltage appearing across the source, and the output resistance of the ideal source is infinite, as indicated by the zero slope of the current source i-v characteristic.

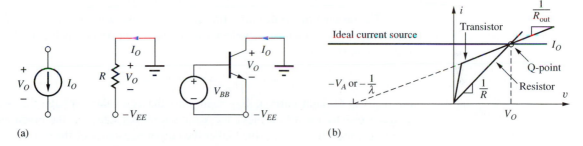

Figure 15.64 (a) Ideal, resistor, and BJT current sources. (b) i-v Characteristics of the three current sources.

For the ideal source, the voltage across the source can be positive or negative, and the current remains the same. However, **electronic current sources** must be implemented with resistors and transistors, and their operation is usually restricted to only one quadrant of the total i-v space. In addition, electronic sources have a finite output resistance, as indicated by the nonzero slope of the i-v characteristic. We will find that the output resistance of the transistor is much greater than a resistor for an equivalent Q-point.

In normal use, the circuit elements in Fig. 15.64 will actually be *sinking* current from the rest of the network, and some authors prefer to call these elements **current sinks.** The distinction between current sinks and current sources is indicated more clearly in Fig. 15.65. The source delivers current to the network, whereas the sink absorbs current from the network. In this book we use the generic term *current source* to refer to both sinks and sources.

The simplest forms of electronic current sources are shown in Fig. 15.66. A resistor is often used to establish bias currents in many circuits—differential amplifiers, for

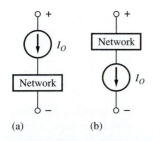

Figure 15.65 (a) Current source and (b) current sink.

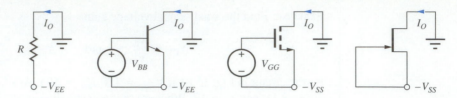

Figure 15.66 Simple electronic current source circuits.

example—but it represents our poorest approximation to an ideal current source. Individual transistor implementations of current sources generally operate in only one quadrant because the transistors must be biased in the forward-active, saturation, or pinch-off regions in order to maintain high impedance operation. However, the transistor source can realize very high values of output resistance.

For simplicity, the transistors in Fig. 15.66 are biased into conduction by the sources V_{BB} and V_{GG}. Remember that the JFET is a depletion-mode device and operates properly with $I_D = I_{DSS}$ for $V_{GS} = 0$. In these circuits, we assume that the collector-emitter and drain-source voltages are large enough to ensure operation in the forward-active, saturation, or pinch-off regions, as appropriate for each device.

Figure of Merit for Current Sources

Resistor R in Fig. 15.66 will be used as a reference for comparing current sources. (See Table 15.5.) The resistor provides an output current and output resistance of

$$I_O = \frac{V_{EE}}{R} \quad \text{and} \quad R_{\text{OUT}} = R \quad (15.171)$$

The product of the dc current I_O and output resistance R_{OUT} is the effective voltage V_{CS} across the current source, and we will use it as a **figure of merit (FOM)** for comparing various current sources:

$$V_{CS} = I_O R_{\text{OUT}} \quad (15.172)$$

For a given Q-point current, V_{CS} represents the equivalent voltage that will be needed across a resistor for it to achieve the same output resistance as the given current source. The larger the value of V_{CS}, the higher the output resistance of the source. For the resistor itself, V_{CS} is simply equal to the power supply voltage V_{EE}.

If ac models are drawn for each source in Fig. 15.66, the base, emitter, gate, and source of each transistor will be connected to ground, and each transistor will be considered operating in either the common-source or common-emitter configuration. The output resistance therefore will be equal to r_o in all cases, and the figures of merit for these sources will be

$$\text{BJT:} \quad V_{CS} = I_O R_{\text{OUT}} = I_C r_o = I_C \frac{V_A + V_{CE}}{I_C} = V_A + V_{CE} \approx V_A$$

$$(15.173)$$

$$\text{FET:} \quad V_{CS} = I_O R_{\text{OUT}} = I_D r_o = I_D \frac{\dfrac{1}{\lambda} + V_{DS}}{I_D} = \frac{1}{\lambda} + V_{DS} \approx \frac{1}{\lambda}$$

V_{CS} for the C-E/C-S transistor current sources is approximately equal to either the Early voltage V_A or $1/\lambda$. We can expect that both these values generally will be at least several times the available power supply voltage. Therefore, any of the single transistor sources will provide an output resistance that is greater than that of a resistor.

T a b l e 15.5			
Comparison of Simple Current Sources			
	I_o	R_{OUT}	V_{CS}
Resistor	$\dfrac{V_{EE}}{R}$	R	V_{EE}
BJT	$I_C = I_S \exp\left(\dfrac{V_{BB}}{V_T}\right)$	r_o	$V_A + V_{CE}$
MOSFET	$I_D = \dfrac{K_n}{2}(V_{GG} - V_{TN})^2$	r_o	$\dfrac{1}{\lambda} + V_{DS}$
JFET	$I_D = I_{DSS}$	r_o	$\dfrac{1}{\lambda} + V_{DS}$

Higher Output Resistance Sources

From our study of single-stage amplifiers in Chapter 14, we know that placing a resistor in series with the emitter or source of the transistor, as in Fig. 15.67, increases the output resistance. Referring back to Eqs. (14.30) and (14.31), we find that the output resistances for the circuits in Fig. 15.67 are

$$\text{BJT:} \quad R_{\text{OUT}} = r_o\left[1 + \frac{\beta_o}{1 + \dfrac{r_\pi + R_1\|R_2}{R_E}}\right] \leq (\beta_o + 1)r_o$$

and   (15.174)

$$\text{FET:} \quad R_{\text{OUT}} = r_o(1 + g_m R_S) \approx \mu_f R_S$$

The figures of merit are

$$\text{BJT: } V_{CS} \approx \beta_o(V_A + V_{CE}) \approx \beta_o V_A \qquad \text{and} \qquad \text{FET: } V_{CS} \approx \mu_f \frac{V_{SS}}{3} \quad (15.175)$$

where it has been assumed that $I_o R_S \approx V_{SS}/3$. Based on these figures of merit, the output resistance of the current sources in Fig. 15.67 can be expected to reach very high values, particularly at low current levels.[2] Table 15.6 compares V_{CS} for the various sources for typical device parameter values.

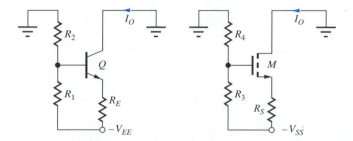

Figure 15.67 High-output resistance current sources.

---

[2] Because of its importance in analog circuit design, the $\beta_o V_A$ product is often used as a basic figure of merit for the bipolar transistor.

Table 15.6			
Comparison of the Basic Current Sources $\beta_o = 100$, $V_A = 1/\lambda = 50$ V, $\mu_{f_{FET}} = 100$			
Type of Source	**R_{OUT}**	**V_{CS}**	**Typical Values**
Resistor	R	V_{EE}	15 V
Single transistor	r_o	V_A or $\dfrac{1}{\lambda}$	50 V
BJT with emitter resistor R_E	$\beta_o r_o$	$\approx \beta_o V_A$	5000 V
FET with source resistor R_S ($V_{SS} = 15$ V)	$\mu_f R_S$	$\approx \mu_f \dfrac{V_{SS}}{3}$	500 V

Multiple Output Sources

The operational amplifiers in Figs. 15.42 and 15.45 both require three current sources, each having a different value. For economy of design, it is common to generate all these currents from a single voltage reference, as indicated by V_B in the bipolar circuit in Fig. 15.68. In this circuit, the three currents required for the bipolar op amp are available at the collectors of Q_1, Q_2, and Q_3. (Extension of the base directly through the transistor symbols indicates that the three bases are connected together.)

To find the output currents in Fig. 15.68, the circuit is redrawn in Fig. 15.69, in which R_1, R_2, and V_{EE} have been replaced by the Thévenin equivalents V_{BB} and R_{BB} referenced to the -15-V supply:

$$V_{BB} = \frac{R_1}{R_1 + R_2} V_{EE} = \frac{4.3 \text{ k}\Omega}{4.3 \text{ k}\Omega + 16 \text{ k}\Omega} 15 \text{ V} = 3.18 \text{ V}$$

$$(15.176)$$

$$R_{BB} = \frac{R_1 R_2}{R_1 + R_2} = \frac{4.3 \text{ k}\Omega (16 \text{ k}\Omega)}{4.3 \text{ k}\Omega + 16 \text{ k}\Omega} = 3.39 \text{ k}\Omega$$

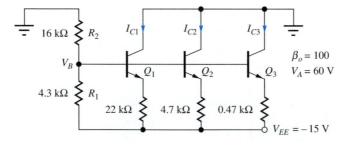

Figure 15.68 Multiple-output current source circuit.

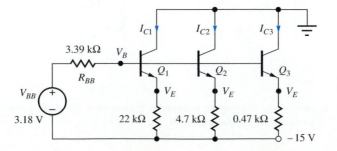

Figure 15.69 Multiple high-resistance current sources.

Writing an equation for the base voltage V_B,

$$V_B = -15 + 3.18 - (I_{B1} + I_{B2} + I_{B3})(3390) \tag{15.177}$$

The base currents can all be expressed in terms of the emitter voltage $V_E = V_B - V_{BE} = V_B - 0.7$ V, which is approximately the same for all three transistors:

$$I_{B1} = \frac{V_E + 15}{22 \text{ k}\Omega}\left(\frac{1}{\beta_{F1} + 1}\right)$$

$$I_{B2} = \frac{V_E + 15}{4.7 \text{ k}\Omega}\left(\frac{1}{\beta_{F2} + 1}\right) \tag{15.178}$$

$$I_{B3} = \frac{V_E + 15}{0.47 \text{ k}\Omega}\left(\frac{1}{\beta_{F3} + 1}\right)$$

Assuming that the transistors have the same values of current gain gives

$$I_{B1} + I_{B2} + I_{B3} = \frac{(V_B - 0.7) + 15}{\beta_F + 1}\left(\frac{1}{22 \text{ k}\Omega} + \frac{1}{4.7 \text{ k}\Omega} + \frac{1}{0.47 \text{ k}\Omega}\right) \tag{15.179}$$

Substituting Eq. (15.179) into (15.177) and solving for V_B with $\beta_o = 100$ yields

$$V_B = -12.0 \text{ V} \tag{15.180}$$

The three output currents can be determined from the base currents in Eq. (15.178):

$$V_E = -12.0 - 0.7 = -12.70 \text{ V}$$

$$I_{C1} = \beta_F I_{B1} = \alpha_F \frac{V_E + 15}{22 \text{ k}\Omega} = 0.99\frac{2.30 \text{ V}}{22 \text{ k}\Omega} = 103 \text{ }\mu\text{A}$$

$$I_{C2} = \beta_F I_{B2} = \alpha_F \frac{V_E + 15}{4.7 \text{ k}\Omega} = 0.99\frac{2.30 \text{ V}}{4.7 \text{ k}\Omega} = 484 \text{ }\mu\text{A} \tag{15.181}$$

$$I_{C3} = \beta_F I_{B3} = \alpha_F \frac{V_E + 15}{0.47 \text{ k}\Omega} = 0.99\frac{2.30 \text{ V}}{0.47 \text{ k}\Omega} = 4.84 \text{ mA}$$

These three currents are near the original design values used in the op-amp circuit example in Fig. 15.44. The output resistances of the three current sources ($V_A = 60$ V) are

$$R_{\text{OUT}} = r_o\left[1 + \frac{\beta_o}{1 + \frac{r_\pi + R_1\|R_2}{R_E}}\right] = \frac{72.7}{I_C}\left[1 + \frac{100}{1 + \frac{r_\pi + R_1\|R_2}{R_E}}\right]$$

$$R_{\text{OUT1}} = \frac{72.7 \text{ V}}{1.03 \times 10^{-4} \text{ A}}\left[1 + \frac{100}{1 + \frac{(24.3 + 3.39) \text{ k}\Omega}{22 \text{ k}\Omega}}\right] = 31.8 \text{ M}\Omega$$

$$R_{\text{OUT2}} = \frac{72.7 \text{ V}}{4.84 \times 10^{-4} \text{ A}}\left[1 + \frac{100}{1 + \frac{(5.16 + 3.39) \text{ k}\Omega}{4.7 \text{ k}\Omega}}\right] = 5.48 \text{ M}\Omega \tag{15.182}$$

$$R_{\text{OUT3}} = \frac{72.7 \text{ V}}{4.84 \times 10^{-3} \text{ A}}\left[1 + \frac{100}{1 + \frac{(0.489 + 3.39)}{0.47}}\right] = 177 \text{ k}\Omega$$

EXERCISE: R_{OUT2} was neglected in the analysis of the amplifier in Fig. 15.44. How does R_{OUT2} compare to r_{o3} and R_{IN4}.

ANSWER: 5.48 M$\Omega \gg$ (162 kΩ||203 kΩ) = 90.1 kΩ, so neglecting R_{OUT2} is valid.

EXERCISE: What is the CMRR of the amplifier in Fig. 15.44 using the current sources described by Eq. (15.182)?

ANSWER: 65,500 = 96.3 dB, an improvement of more than 30 dB!

EXERCISE: What would be the output resistances of the three current sources if the base node V_B were bypassed with a capacitor?

ANSWERS: 35.2 MΩ, 7.51 MΩ, 751 kΩ

EXERCISE: What are the values of $\beta_o r_o$ for the three current sources?

ANSWERS: 70.6 MΩ, 16.2 MΩ, 1.62 MΩ

Current Source Design Examples

This section provides examples of the design of current sources using the three-resistor bias circuits in Fig. 15.70. The computer (via a spreadsheet) is used to help explore the design space. The current source requirements are provided in the following design specifications.

Design Specifications

Design a current source using the circuits in Fig. 15.70 with a nominal output current of 200 μA and an output resistance greater than 10 MΩ using a single -15-V power supply. The source must also meet the following additional constraints.

Output voltage (compliance) range should be as large as possible while meeting the output resistance specification.

The total current used by the source should be less than 250 μA.

Bipolar transistors are available with (β_o, V_A) of (80, 100 V) or (150, 75 V). FETs are available with $\lambda = 0.01$ V^{-1}; K_n can be chosen as necessary.

When used in an actual application, the collector and drain of the current sources in Fig. 15.70 will be connected to some other point in the overall circuit, as indicated by the voltage $+V_O$ in the figure. For the current source to provide a high output resistance, the BJT must remain in the forward-active region, with the collector-base junction reverse-biased ($V_O \geq V_B$), or the FET must remain saturated ($V_O \geq V_G - V_{TN}$).

Specifications include the requirement that the output voltage range be as large as possible. Thus, the design goal is to achieve $I_o = 200$ μA and $R_{OUT} \geq 10$ MΩ with as low a voltage as possible at V_B or V_G. A range of designs is explored to see just how low a voltage can be used at V_B or V_G and still meet the I_o and R_{OUT} requirements. Investigating this design space is most easily done with the aid of the computer.

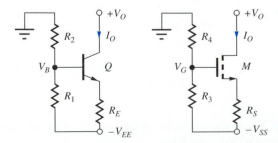

Figure 15.70 *npn* and NMOS current source circuits.

EXAMPLE 15.4: A BIPOLAR DESIGN

We start by designing a bipolar version of the current source, beginning with the expression for the output resistance of the bipolar source in Fig. 15.70. Because we will use a computer to help in the design, we use the most complete expression for the output resistance:

$$R_{\text{OUT}} = r_o \left[1 + \frac{\beta_o R_E}{R_E + r_\pi + R_1 \| R_2} \right] \approx r_o \left[1 + \frac{\beta_o}{1 + \frac{r_\pi + R_1 \| R_2}{R_E}} \right] \leq \beta_o r_o$$

(15.183)

The figure of merit for this source is

$$V_{CS} = I_o R_{\text{OUT}} \leq \beta_o V_A$$

(15.184)

and the design specifications require

$$\beta_o V_A = I_o R_{\text{OUT}} \geq (200 \ \mu\text{A})(10 \ \text{M}\Omega) = 2000$$

(15.185)

Although both the specified transistors easily meet the requirement of Eq. (15.185), the denominator of Eq. (15.183) can substantially reduce the output resistance below that predicted by the $\beta_o r_o$ limit (as was discovered in the last exercise). Thus, it will be judicious to select the transistor with the higher $\beta_o V_A$ product—that is, (150, 75 V).

Having made this decision, the equations relating the dc Q-point design to the output resistance of the source can be developed. In Fig. 15.71, the three-resistor bias circuit is simplified using a Thévenin transformation, for which:

$$V_{BB} = 15 \frac{R_1}{R_1 + R_2} = 15 \frac{R_{BB}}{R_2} \qquad \text{with } R_{BB} = \frac{R_1 R_2}{R_1 + R_2}$$

(15.186)

and the Q-point can be calculated using

$$I_B = \frac{V_{BB} - V_{BE}}{R_{BB} + (\beta_F + 1)R_E} \qquad I_o = I_C = \beta_F I_B$$

and

(15.187)

$$V_{CE} = V_O + V_{EE} - (V_{BB} - I_B R_{BB} - V_{BE})$$

The small-signal parameters required for evaluating Eq. (15.183) are given by their usual formulas:

$$r_o = \frac{V_A + V_{CE}}{I_C} \qquad \text{and} \qquad r_\pi = \frac{\beta_o V_T}{I_C}$$

(15.188)

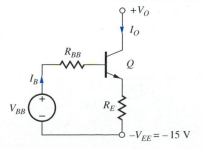

Figure 15.71 Equivalent circuit for the current source.

From Eq. (15.183), we can see that $R_{BB} = (R_1 \| R_2)$ should be made as small as possible in order to achieve maximum output resistance. From the design specifications, the complete current source must use no more than 250 μA. Because the output current is 200 μA, a maximum current of 50 μA can be used by the base bias network. To leave room for variations due to tolerances, let us pick a bias network current of 40 μA, which sets the sum of R_1 and R_2 to be

$$R_1 + R_2 = \frac{15 \text{ V}}{40 \text{ μA}} = 375 \text{ k}\Omega \tag{15.189}$$

Equations (15.183) to (15.189) provide the information necessary to explore the design space with the aid of a computer. These equations have been rearranged in order of evaluation in Eq. (15.190), with V_{BB} selected as the primary design variable.

Once V_{BB} is selected, R_1 and R_2 can be calculated. Then R_E and the Q-point can be determined, the small-signal parameters evaluated, and the output resistance determined from Eq. (15.177). $V_O = 0$ V is selected as a representative value.

$$R_1 = (R_1 + R_2)\frac{V_{BB}}{15} = 375 \text{ k}\Omega \left(\frac{V_{BB}}{15}\right)$$

$$R_2 = (R_1 + R_2) - R_1 = 375 \text{ k}\Omega - R_1$$

$$I_B = \frac{I_o}{\beta_F}$$

$$R_E = \alpha_F \left[\frac{V_{BB} - V_{BE} - I_B R_{BB}}{I_o}\right] \tag{15.190}$$

$$V_{CE} = V_{EE} - (V_{BB} - I_B R_{BB} - V_{BE})$$

$$r_o = \frac{V_A + V_{CE}}{I_o} \qquad r_\pi = \frac{\beta_o V_T}{I_o}$$

$$R_{OUT} = r_o\left[1 + \frac{\beta_o R_E}{R_E + r_\pi + R_{BB}}\right] = r_o\left[1 + \frac{\beta_o}{1 + \dfrac{r_\pi + R_{BB}}{R_E}}\right]$$

Table 15.7 presents the results of using a spreadsheet to assist in evaluating these equations for a range of V_{BB}. The smallest value of V_{BB} for which the output resistance exceeds 10 MΩ with some safety margin is 4.5 V. Note that this value of output resistance is achieved as

$$R_{OUT} = r_o\left[1 + \frac{\beta_o}{1 + \dfrac{r_\pi + R_1 \| R_2}{R_E}}\right]$$

$$= 432 \text{ k}\Omega\left[1 + \frac{150}{1 + \dfrac{(18.8 + 78.8) \text{ k}\Omega}{18.4 \text{ k}\Omega}}\right] = 432 \text{ k}\Omega\left[1 + \frac{150}{6.30}\right] = 10.7 \text{ M}\Omega$$

$$\tag{15.191}$$

Table 15.7

Spreadsheet Results for Current Source Design

V_{BB}	R_1	R_2	R_{BB}	R_E	r_o	R_{OUT}
1.0	2.50E + 04	3.50E + 05	2.33E + 04	1.34E + 03	4.49E + 05	2.52E + 06
1.5	3.75E + 04	3.38E + 05	3.38E + 04	3.75E + 03	4.46E + 05	4.91E + 06
2.0	5.00E + 04	3.25E + 05	4.33E + 04	6.17E + 03	4.44E + 05	6.46E + 06
2.5	6.25E + 04	3.13E + 05	5.21E + 04	8.60E + 03	4.41E + 05	7.61E + 06
3.0	7.50E + 04	3.00E + 05	6.00E + 04	1.10E + 04	4.39E + 05	8.52E + 06
3.5	8.75E + 04	2.88E + 05	6.71E + 04	1.35E + 04	4.36E + 05	9.31E + 06
4.0	1.00E + 05	2.75E + 05	7.33E + 04	1.59E + 04	4.34E + 05	1.00E + 07
4.5	**1.13E + 05**	**2.63E + 05**	**7.88E + 04**	**1.84E + 04**	**4.32E + 05**	**1.07E + 07**
5.0	1.25E + 05	2.50E + 05	8.33E + 04	2.08E + 04	4.29E + 05	1.13E + 07
5.5	1.38E + 05	2.38E + 05	8.71E + 04	2.33E + 04	4.27E + 05	1.20E + 07
6.0	1.50E + 05	2.25E + 05	9.00E + 04	2.57E + 04	4.24E + 05	1.26E + 07
6.5	1.63E + 05	2.13E + 05	9.21E + 04	2.82E + 04	4.22E + 05	1.32E + 07
7.0	1.75E + 05	2.00E + 05	9.33E + 04	3.07E + 04	4.19E + 05	1.39E + 07
7.5	1.88E + 05	1.88E + 05	9.38E + 04	3.32E + 04	4.17E + 05	1.46E + 07
8.0	2.00E + 05	1.75E + 05	9.33E + 04	3.56E + 04	4.14E + 05	1.54E + 07
8.5	2.13E + 05	1.63E + 05	9.21E + 04	3.81E + 04	4.12E + 05	1.62E + 07
9.0	2.25E + 05	1.50E + 05	9.00E + 04	4.06E + 04	4.09E + 05	1.71E + 07
9.5	2.38E + 05	1.38E + 05	8.71E + 04	4.31E + 04	4.07E + 05	1.81E + 07
10.0	2.50E + 05	1.25E + 05	8.33E + 04	4.56E + 04	4.04E + 05	1.91E + 07

For this design, the denominator in Eq. (15.191) reduces the output resistance by a factor of 6.3 below the $\beta_o r_o$ limit. So, it was a wise decision to choose the transistor with the largest $\beta_o V_A$ product. The final design appears in Fig. 15.72.

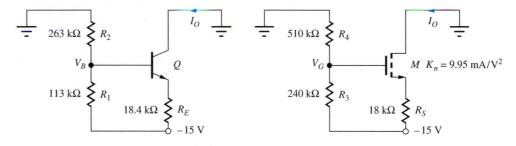

Figure 15.72 Final current source designs with $I_o = 200\ \mu A$ and $R_{OUT} \geq 10\ M\Omega$.

EXERCISE: What would be the output resistance of the bipolar current source if the base were bypassed to ground with a capacitor?

ANSWER: 32.5 MΩ

EXERCISE: The current source is to be implemented using the nearest 5 percent resistor values. What are the best values? Are resistors with a 1/4-W power dissipation rating adequate for use in this circuit? What are the actual output current and output resistance of your current source, based on these 5 percent resistor values?

ANSWERS: 110 kΩ, 270 kΩ, 18 kΩ; yes; 195 μA, 10.6 MΩ

EXAMPLE 15.5: A MOSFET IMPLEMENTATION

Next, we design a MOSFET version of the current source based on Fig. 15.73 to provide the same output resistance at a Q-point as that of the BJT. Because of the infinite current gain of the MOSFET, the expression for the output resistance of the current source in Fig. 15.73 is much less complex than that of the BJT source and is given by

$$R_{\text{OUT}} = r_o(1 + g_m R_S) \approx \mu_f R_S \qquad (15.192)$$

If values of R_S and V_S are selected that are the same as those of the BJT source, 18 kΩ and −11.5 V, respectively, then the MOSFET must have an amplification factor of

$$\mu_f \geq \frac{10 \text{ M}\Omega}{18 \text{ k}\Omega} = 556 \gg 1 \qquad (15.193)$$

The amplification factor of the MOSFET is given by

$$\mu_f = \frac{1}{\lambda}\sqrt{\frac{K_n}{2I_{DS}}}(1 + \lambda V_{DS}) \qquad (15.194)$$

and solving for K_n yields

$$K_n = 2I_{DS}\left(\frac{\lambda\mu_f}{1 + \lambda V_{DS}}\right)^2 = 400 \text{ μA}\left(\frac{\dfrac{0.01}{\text{V}}(556)}{1 + \dfrac{0.01}{\text{V}}(11.5 \text{ V})}\right)^2 = 9.95 \frac{\text{mA}}{\text{V}^2}$$

$$(15.195)$$

This is a relatively large value of K_n but is certainly achievable using either discrete components or integrated circuits.

In Fig. 15.73, the required gate voltage V_{GG} is

$$V_{GG} = I_{DS}R_S + V_{GS} = 3.60 + V_{TN} + \sqrt{\frac{2I_D}{K_n}}$$

$$= 3.60 \text{ V} + 1 \text{ V} + \sqrt{\frac{2(0.2 \text{ mA})}{9.95 \dfrac{\text{mA}}{\text{V}^2}}} = 4.80 \text{ V} \qquad (15.196)$$

If the current in the bias resistors is limited to 10 percent of the drain current, then

$$R_3 + R_4 = \frac{15 \text{ V}}{20 \text{ μA}} = 750 \text{ k}\Omega \qquad \text{and} \qquad R_4 = \frac{4.80 \text{ V}}{15 \text{ V}}750 \text{ k}\Omega = 240 \text{ k}\Omega$$

$$(15.197)$$

The final design appears in Fig. 15.72.

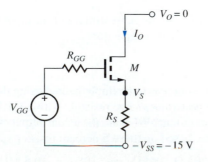

Figure 15.73 MOSFET current source.

EXERCISE: What is the minimum drain voltage for which the MOSFET source in Fig. 15.71 remains saturated?

ANSWER: -9.34 V

EXERCISE: What W/L ratio is required for the preceding FET if $K_n' = 25$ μA/V²?

ANSWER: 398/1

EXERCISE: What is the minimum collector voltage for which the BJT in Fig. 15.71 remains in the forward-active region?

ANSWER: -10.8 V

EXERCISE: The MOS current source is to be implemented using the nearest 5 percent resistor values. What are the best values? Are resistors with a 1/4-W power dissipation rating adequate for use in this circuit? What are the actual output current and output resistance of your current source based on these 5 percent resistor values?

ANSWERS: 510 kΩ, 240 kΩ, 18 kΩ; yes; 200 μA, 10.6 MΩ

SUMMARY

In most situations, the single-stage amplifiers discussed in Chapters 13 and 14 cannot meet all the requirements of the application. Therefore, we combine single-stage amplifiers in various ways to form multistage amplifiers that achieve higher levels of overall performance.

Both ac- and dc-coupling methods are used in multistage amplifiers depending on the application. ac Coupling allows the Q-point design of each stage to be done independently of the other stages. However, dc coupling can eliminate circuit elements, including both coupling capacitors and bias resistors, and represents a more economical approach to design. In addition, dc coupling is required to achieve a low-pass amplifier with gain at dc. Important two-transistor direct-coupled amplifiers include the Darlington configuration, which achieves very high current gain, and the cascode circuit, which exhibits a very high amplification factor.

Probably the most important dc-coupled amplifier is the symmetric two-transistor differential amplifier. Not only is the differential amplifier a key circuit in the design of operational amplifiers, it is a fundamental building block of all analog circuit design. In Chapter 15 we studied both BJT and MOS differential amplifiers in detail. Differential-mode gain, common-mode gain, common-mode rejection ratio (CMRR), and differential- and common-mode input resistances of the amplifier are all directly related to transistor parameters and hence Q-point design. Either a balanced or a single-ended output is available from the differential amplifier. The balanced output provides a voltage gain that is twice that of the single-ended output, and the CMRR of the balanced output is inherently much higher (that is, infinity for the ideal case).

One of the most important applications of differential amplifiers is to form the input stage of the operational amplifier. By adding a second gain stage plus an output stage to the differential amplifier, a basic op amp is created. The performance of differential and operational amplifiers can be greatly enhanced by the use of current sources.

An ideal current source provides a constant output current, independent of the voltage across the source; that is, the current source has an infinite output resistance. Although electronic current sources cannot achieve infinite output resistance, very high values are possible, and there are a number of basic current source circuits and techniques for achieving high output resistance. For a current source, the product of the source current and output resistance represents a figure of merit, V_{CS}, that can be used to compare current sources. A single-transistor current source can be built using the bipolar transistor in which V_{CS} can approach the $\beta_o V_A$ product of the BJT. For a very good bipolar transistor, this product can reach 10,000 V. For the FET case, V_{CS} can approach a significant fraction of $\mu_f V_{SS}$, in which V_{SS} represents the power supply voltage. Values as high as 1000 V are achievable with the FET source. Op-amp designs usually require a number of current sources, and, for economy of design, these multiple sources are often generated from a single-bias voltage.

Class-A, class-B, and class-AB amplifiers are defined in terms of their conduction angles: 360° for class-A, 180° for class-B, and between 180° and 360° for class-AB operation. The efficiency of the class-A amplifier cannot exceed 25 percent for sinusoidal signals, whereas that of the class-B amplifier has an upper limit of 78.5 percent. However, class-B amplifiers suffer from cross-over distortion caused by a dead zone in the transfer characteristic.

The class-AB amplifier trades a small increase in quiescent power dissipation and a small loss in efficiency for elimination of the cross-over distortion. The efficiency of the class-AB amplifier can approach that of the class-B amplifier when the quiescent operating point is properly chosen. The basic op-amp design can be further improved by replacing the class-A follower output stage with a class-AB output stage. Class-AB output stages are often used in operational amplifiers and are usually provided with short-circuit protection circuitry.

Amplifier stages may also employ transformer coupling. The impedance transformation properties of the transformer can be used to simplify the design of circuits that must drive low values of load resistances such as loudspeakers.

Key Terms

ac-Coupled amplifiers
Balanced output
Cascode amplifier
CE-CE cascade
Class-A, class-B, and class-AB amplifiers
Class-B push-pull output stage
Common-mode conversion gain
Common-mode gain
Common-mode half-circuit
Common-mode input resistance
Common-mode input voltage range
Common-mode rejection ratio (CMRR)
Complementary push-pull output stage

Conduction angle
Cross-over distortion
Cross-over region
Current-limiting circuit
Current sink
Darlington circuit
Darlington configuration
dc-Coupled (direct-coupled) amplifiers
Dead zone
Differential amplifier
Differential-mode conversion gain
Differential-mode gain
Differential-mode half-circuit
Differential-mode input resistance

Differential-mode output resistance
Differential output voltage
Electronic current source
Figure of merit (FOM)
Half-circuit analysis
Ideal current source
Level shift
Matched (devices)
Short-circuit protection
Single-ended output
Transformer coupling
Unbalanced output
Virtual ground

Reference

Thornton, R. D. et. al, *Multistage Transistor Circuits*, SEEC Volume 5, Wiley, New York: 1965.

Additional Reading

Jaeger, R. C. "A high output resistance current source." *IEEE JSSC,* vol. SC-9, pp. 192–194, August 1974.

Jaeger, R. C. "Common-mode rejection limitations of differential amplifiers." *IEEE JSSC,* vol. SC-11, pp. 411–417, June 1976.

Jaeger, R. C., and G. A. Hellwarth. "On the performance of the differential cascode amplifier." *IEEE JSSC,* vol. SC-8, pp. 169–174, April 1973.

PSPICE Simulation Data

*Figures 15.50, 15.51 Class B Amplifier

```
VI 1 0 DC 0 SIN(0 4 1000)
VDD 2 0 DC 15
VSS 3 0 DC -15
M1 2 1 4 4 N1 W=1000U L=2U
M2 3 1 4 4 P1 W=2500U L=2U
RL 4 0 2K
. MODEL N1 NMOS VTO=1 KP=25E-6
. MODEL P1 PMOS VTO=-1 KP=10E-6
. OP
. DC VI -5 5 .05
. TRAN 1U 2M
. PROBE V(1) V(4) I(VDD) I(VSS)
. END
```

*Figure 15.53 Class AB Amplifier

```
VI 1 0 DC 0
VDD 2 0 DC 15
VSS 3 0 DC -15
VGG1 5 1 DC 1.1
VGG2 6 1 DC -1.1
M1 2 5 4 4 N1 W=1000U L=2U
M2 3 6 4 4 P1 W=2500U L=2U
RL 4 0 2K
. MODEL N1 NMOS VTO=1 KP=25E-6
. MODEL P1 PMOS VTO=-1 KP=10E-6
. OP
. DC VI -5 5 .05
. PROBE V(1) V(4)
. END
```

*Figure 15.62 Transformer Coupled Inverting Amplifier

```
VGG 5 0 DC 2
VG 1 5 SIN(0 .2 1000)
VDD 3 0 DC 10
M1 2 1 0 0 NM
RL 4 0 8
LP 3 2 10H
LS 4 0 0.1H
KX LP LS 0.999
. OP
. TRAN 1U 2M
. MODEL NM NMOS VTO=1 KP=.05
. PROBE V(1) V(2) V(4)
. END
```

Problems

Unless otherwise specified, use $\beta_F = 100$, $V_A = 70$ V, $K_p = K_n = 1$ mA/V^2, $V_{TN} = -V_{TP} = 1$ V, and $\lambda = 0.02$ V^{-1}.

15.1 Multistage ac-Coupled Amplifiers

15.1. What are the voltage gain, input resistance, and output resistance of the amplifier in Fig. 15.1 if bypass capacitors C_2 and C_4 are removed from the circuit?

15.2. What is the gain of the amplifier in Fig. 15.9 if the bypass capacitors are removed from the circuit?

*15.3. Figure P15.3 is an "improved" version of the three-stage amplifier discussed in Sec. 15.1. Find the gain and input signal range for this amplifier. Was the performance actually improved?

15.4. Use SPICE to simulate the amplifier in Fig. P15.3 at a frequency of 2 kHz, and determine the voltage gain, input resistance, and output resistance. Assume the capacitors all have a value of 22 μF.

15.5. Use SPICE to determine the gain of the amplifier in Fig. P15.3 if C_2 and C_4 are removed from the circuit. Assume the capacitors all have a value of 22 μF.

*15.6. Figure P15.6 shows another "improved" design of the three-stage amplifier discussed in Sec. 15.1. Find the gain and input signal range for this amplifier. Was the performance improved?

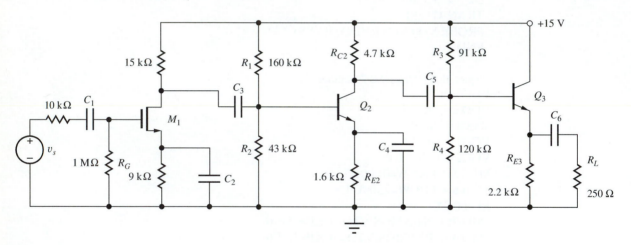

Figure P15.3

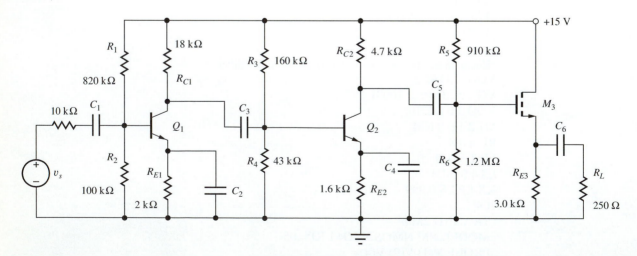

Figure P15.6

15.7. Use SPICE to simulate the amplifier in Fig. P15.6 at a frequency of 3 kHz and determine the voltage gain, input resistance, and output resistance. Assume the capacitors all have a value of 22 μF.

15.8. What is the gain of the amplifier in Fig. P15.6 if C_2 and C_4 are removed?

15.9. What are the midband voltage gain, input resistance, and output resistance of the amplifier in Fig. P15.9?

15.10. What are the voltage gain, input resistance, and output resistance of the amplifier in Fig. P15.9 if the bypass capacitors are removed?

15.11. Use SPICE to simulate the amplifier in Fig. P15.9 at a frequency of 5 kHz and determine the voltage gain, input resistance, and output resistance. Assume the capacitors all have a value of 10 μF.

15.12. What are the midband voltage gain, input resistance, and output resistance of the amplifier in Fig. P15.12 if $K_n = 50$ mA/V² and $V_{TN} = -2$ V?

15.13. (a) What are Q-points of the transistors of the circuit in Fig. 15.10 if $R_{D1} = 750\ \Omega$? (b) $R_{D1} = 910\ \Omega$?

15.2 Direct-Coupled Amplifiers

15.14. Find the Q-points of the transistors in Fig. P15.14. What is the midband voltage gain of the amplifier? Assume $\beta_F = 80$ for both transistors.

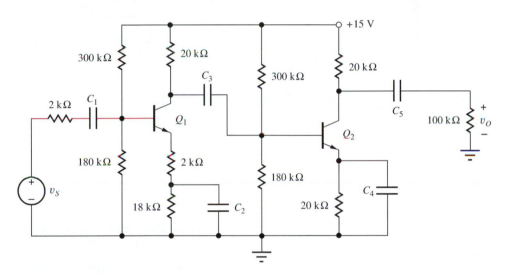

Figure P15.9

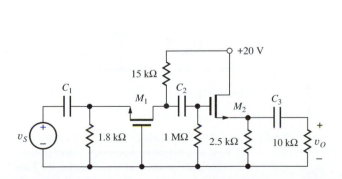

Figure P15.12

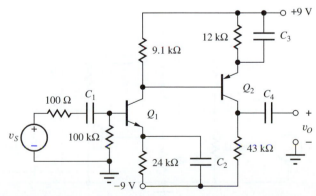

Figure P15.14

15.15. Use SPICE to simulate the amplifier in Fig. P15.14 at a frequency of 2.5 kHz and determine the voltage gain, input resistance, and output resistance. Assume the capacitors all have a value of 10 μF.

15.16. Find the Q-points of the transistors in Fig. P15.12 if C_2 is replaced with a short circuit, and the 1-MΩ resistor is removed from the circuit.

15.17. (a) Find the Q-points of the transistors in Fig. P15.17. What are the midband voltage gain, input resistance, and output resistance of the amplifier? Assume $\beta_F = 100$, $I_{DSS} = 5$ mA, and $V_P = -1$ V. (b) What is the gain if C_2 is removed?

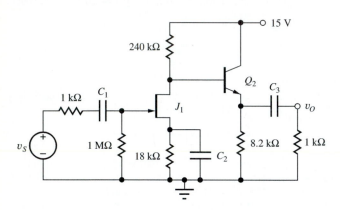

Figure P15.17

15.18. Use SPICE to simulate the amplifier in Fig. P15.17 at a frequency of 1 kHz, and determine the voltage gain, input resistance, and output resistance. Assume the capacitors all have a value of 33 μF.

15.19. (a) Find the Q-points of the transistors in Fig. P15.19. What are the midband voltage gain,

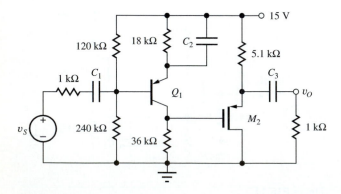

Figure P15.19

input resistance, and output resistance of the amplifier? Assume $\beta_F = 75$, $K_p = 4$ mA/V^2, and $V_{TP} = +4$ V. (b) What are the gain and input resistances if C_2 is removed?

15.20. Use SPICE to simulate the amplifier in Fig. P15.19 at a frequency of 2 kHz, and determine the voltage gain, input resistance, and output resistance. Assume the capacitors all have a value of 20 μF.

*15.21. (a) Find the Q-points of the transistors in Fig. P15.21 if $V_{CC} = 3$ V. Assume $\beta_F = \infty$, $R_C = 360$ kΩ, $R_E = 30$ kΩ, and $R_F = 300$ kΩ. (b) Repeat for $\beta_F = 75$.

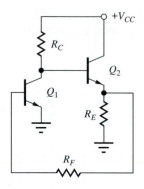

Figure P15.21

15.22. Derive the expressions for the y parameters of the Darlington configuration in Fig. 15.13.

15.23. Derive the expressions for the y parameters of the cascode configuration in Fig. 15.15.

15.24. Derive the expressions for the y parameters of the NMOS cascode configuration in Fig. P15.24. Assume dc coupling. How are I_{DS1} and I_{DS2} related to each other?

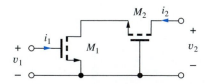

Figure P15.24

*15.25. The C-E/C-C cascade in Fig. P15.25 can be represented as a single two-port equivalent transistor in the same manner as was done for the Darlington and cascode configurations. Assume dc

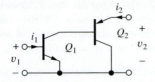

Figure P15.25

coupling. How are I_{C1} and I_{C2} related to each other? Find the values of r'_π, g'_m, r'_o, β'_o, and μ'_f.

15.26. The cascode amplifier of Fig. 15.15 is operated with an ideal current source as a load (that is, $R_L = \infty$). What is the voltage gain of the amplifier if $\beta_o = 100$ and $V_A = 75$ V?

15.27. The C-E/C-E cascade in Fig. P15.27 can be represented as a single two-port equivalent transistor in the same manner as was done for the Darlington and cascode configurations. Assume $I_{C2} = \beta_F I_{C1}$. Find the values of r_π, g'_m, r'_o, β'_o, and μ'_f.

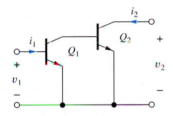

Figure P15.27

*15.28. For proper choice of the collector current of Q_1, the bipolar-JFET cascode amplifier in Fig. P15.28 does not require the bias source V_{BB} that was included in Fig. 15.14. For what range of values for I_{EE} is Q_1 in the forward-active region if $I_{DSS} = 1$ mA and $V_P = -4$ V?

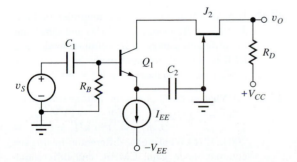

Figure P15.28

15.29. Find the Q-points of the transistors and voltage gain of the amplifier in Fig. P15.29. Draw the ac equivalent circuit and identify the type of amplifier represented by this circuit.

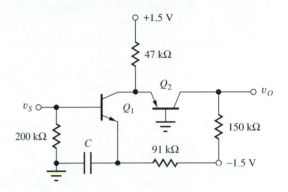

Figure P15.29

15.3 Differential Amplifiers
BJT Amplifiers

15.30. (a) What are the Q-points for the transistors in the amplifier in Fig. P15.30 if $V_{CC} = 12$ V, $V_{EE} = 12$ V, $R_{EE} = 270$ kΩ, $R_C = 330$ kΩ, and $\beta_F = 100$? (b) What are the differential-mode gain, and differential-mode input and output resistances? (c) What are the common-mode gain, CMRR, and common-mode input resistance for a single-ended output?

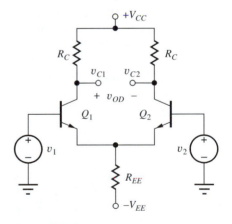

Figure P15.30

*15.31. (a) Use the common-mode gain to find voltages v_{C1}, v_{C2}, and v_{OD} for the differential amplifier in Fig. P15.30 if $V_{CC} = 12$ V, $V_{EE} = 12$ V, $R_{EE} = 270$ kΩ, $R_C = 390$ kΩ, $v_1 = 5.000$ V, and $v_2 = 5.000$ V. (b) Find the Q-points of the transistors directly with V_{IC} applied. Recalculate v_{c1} and v_{c2} and compare to the results in part (a). What is the origin of the discrepancy?

15.32. (a) What are the Q-points for the transistors in the amplifier in Fig. P15.30 if $V_{CC} = 1.5$ V, $V_{EE} = 1.5$ V, $\beta_F = 60$, $R_{EE} = 75$ kΩ, and $R_C = 100$ kΩ? (b) What are the differential-mode gain, common-mode gain, CMRR, and differential-mode and common-mode input and output resistances?

15.33. Use SPICE to simulate the amplifier in Prob. 15.30 at a frequency of 1 kHz, and determine the differential-mode gain, common-mode gain, CMRR, and differential-mode and common-mode input resistances.

15.34. (a) What are the Q-points for the transistors in the amplifier in Fig. P15.30 if $V_{CC} = 1.5$ V, $V_{EE} = 1.5$ V, $R_{EE} = 47$ kΩ, $R_C = 100$ kΩ, and $\beta_F = 100$? (b) What are the differential-mode gain, common-mode gain, CMRR, and differential-mode and common-mode input and output resistances?

15.35. Design a differential amplifier to have a differential gain of 46 dB and $R_{ID} = 1$ MΩ using the topology in Fig. P15.30, with $V_{CC} = V_{EE} = 12$ V and $\beta_F = 100$. (Be sure to check feasibility of the design using our rule-of-thumb estimates from Chapter 13 before you move deeper into the design calculations.)

15.36. Design a differential amplifier to have a differential gain of 58 dB and $R_{ID} = 100$ kΩ using the topology in Fig. P15.30, with $V_{CC} = V_{EE} = 9$ V and $\beta_F = 120$. (Be sure to check feasibility of the design using our rule-of-thumb estimates from Chapter 13 before you move deeper into the design calculations.)

15.37. (a) What are the Q-points for the transistors in the amplifier in Fig. P15.37 if $V_{CC} = 12$ V, $V_{EE} = 12$ V, $I_{EE} = 400$ μA, $\beta_F = 100$, $R_{EE} = 200$ kΩ, $R_C = 39$ kΩ, $V_A = \infty$, and $\beta_F =$

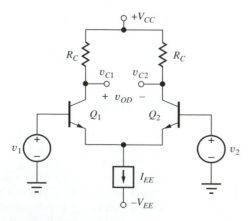

Figure P15.37

100? (b) What are the differential-mode gain, common-mode gain, CMRR, and differential-mode and common-mode input and output resistances? (c) Repeat part (b) for $V_A = 50$ V.

*15.38. What are the voltages v_{C1}, v_{C2}, and v_{OD} for the differential amplifier in Fig. P15.37 if $V_{CC} = 12$ V, $V_{EE} = 12$ V, $\beta_F = 75$, $I_{EE} = 400$ μA, $R_{EE} = 200$ kΩ, $R_C = 39$ kΩ, $v_1 = 2.005$ V, and $v_2 = 1.995$ V? What is the common-mode input range of this amplifier?

15.39. What is the value of the current I_{EE} required to achieve $R_{ID} = 5$ MΩ in the circuit in Fig. P15.37 if $\beta_o = 100$? What output resistance R_{EE} is required for CMRR = 100 dB?

15.40. For the amplifier in Fig. P15.40, $V_{CC} = 10$ V, $V_{EE} = 10$ V, $\beta_F = 100$, $I_{EE} = 20$ μA, and $R_C = 910$ kΩ. (a) What are the output voltages v_o and V_o for the amplifier for $v_s = 0$ V and $v_s = 2$ mV? (b) What is the maximum value of v_s?

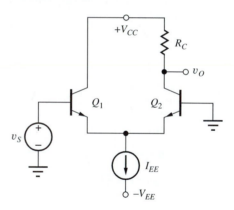

Figure P15.40

15.41. For the amplifier in Fig. P15.40, $V_{CC} = 12$ V, $V_{EE} = 12$ V, $\beta_F = 120$, $I_{EE} = 200$ μA, and $R_C = 110$ kΩ. (a) What are the output voltages V_O and v_o for the amplifier for $v_s = 0$ V and $v_s = 1$ mV? (b) What is the maximum value of v_s?

15.42. Use SPICE to simulate the amplifier in Prob. 15.41 at a frequency of 1 kHz, and determine the differential-mode gain, common-mode gain, CMRR, and differential-mode and common-mode input resistances. Use $V_A = 60$ V.

15.43. (a) What are the Q-points for the transistors in the amplifier in Fig. P15.43 if $V_{CC} = 15$ V, $V_{EE} = 15$ V, $\beta_F = 150$, $R_{EE} = 150$ kΩ, and $R_C = 200$ kΩ? (b) What are the differential-mode gain, common-mode gain, CMRR, and differential-mode and common-mode input resistances?

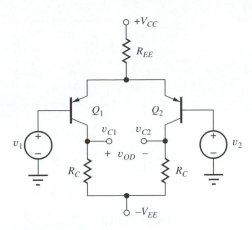

Figure P15.43

15.44. What are the voltages v_{C1}, v_{C2}, and v_{OD} for the differential amplifier in Fig. P15.43 if $V_{CC} = 10$ V, $V_{EE} = 10$ V, $\beta_F = 100$, $R_{EE} = 430$ kΩ, $R_C = 560$ kΩ, $v_1 = 1$ V, and $v_2 = 0.99$ V?

 15.45. Use SPICE to simulate the amplifier in Prob. 15.44 at a frequency of 5 kHz, and determine the differential-mode gain, common-mode gain, CMRR, and differential-mode and common-mode input resistances.

15.46. (a) What are the Q-points for the transistors in the amplifier in Fig. P15.46 if $V_{CC} = 3$ V, $V_{EE} = 3$ V, $\beta_F = 80$, $I_{EE} = 10$ μA, $R_{EE} = 5$ MΩ, and $R_C = 390$ kΩ? (b) What are the differential-mode gain, common-mode gain, CMRR, differential-mode and common-mode input resistances, and common-mode input range?

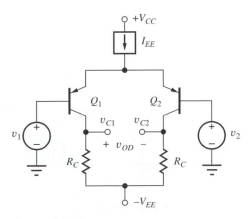

Figure P15.46

15.47. What are the voltages v_{C1}, v_{C2}, and v_{OD} for the differential amplifier in Fig. P15.46 if $V_{CC} = 22$ V, $V_{EE} = 22$ V, $\beta_F = 120$, $I_{EE} = 1$ mA,

$R_{EE} = 500$ kΩ, $R_C = 15$ kΩ, $v_1 = 0.01$ V, and $v_2 = 0$ V?

*15.48. The differential amplifier in Fig. P15.48 has mismatched collector resistors. Calculate A_{dd}, A_{cd}, and the CMRR of the amplifier if the output is the differential output voltage v_{od}, and $R = 100$ kΩ, $\Delta R/R = 0.01$, $V_{CC} = V_{EE} = 15$ V, $R_{EE} = 100$ kΩ, and $\beta_F = 100$.

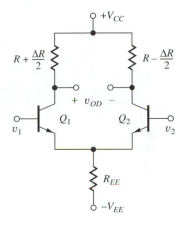

Figure P15.48

 15.49. Use SPICE to simulate the amplifier in Prob. 15.48 at a frequency of 100 Hz, and determine the differential-mode gain, common-mode gain, and CMRR.

**15.50. The transistors in the differential amplifier in Fig. P15.50 have mismatched transconductances. Calculate A_{dd}, A_{cd}, and the CMRR of the amplifier if the output is the differential output voltage v_{OD}, and $R = 100$ kΩ, $g_m = 3$ mS, $\Delta g_m/g_m = 0.01$, $V_{CC} = V_{EE} = 15$ V, and $R_{EE} = 100$ kΩ.

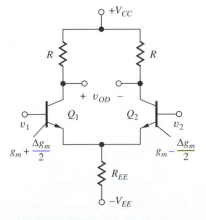

Figure P15.50

FET Differential Amplifiers

15.51. (a) What are the Q-points for the transistors in the amplifier in Fig. P15.51 if $V_{DD} = 15$ V, $V_{SS} = 15$ V, $R_{SS} = 62$ kΩ, and $R_D = 62$ kΩ? Assume $K_n = 400$ μA/V^2 and $V_{TN} = 1$ V. (b) What are the differential-mode gain, common-mode gain, CMRR, and differential-mode and common-mode input resistances?

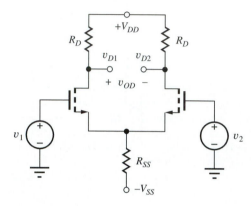

Figure P15.51

15.52. (a) What are the Q-points for the transistors in the amplifier in Fig. P15.51 if $V_{DD} = 12$ V, $V_{SS} = 12$ V, $R_{SS} = 220$ kΩ, and $R_D = 330$ kΩ? Assume $K_n = 400$ μA/V^2 and $V_{TN} = 1$ V. (b) What are the differential-mode gain, common-mode gain, CMRR, and differential-mode and common-mode input resistances?

15.53. Use SPICE to simulate the amplifier in Prob. 15.52 at a frequency of 1 kHz, and determine the differential-mode gain, common-mode gain, CMRR, and differential-mode and common-mode input resistances.

15.54. Design a differential amplifier to have a differential-mode output resistance of 5 kΩ and $A_{dm} = 20$ dB, using the circuit in Fig. P15.51 with $V_{DD} = V_{SS} = 5$ V. Assume $V_{TN} = 1$ V and $K_n = 25$ mA/V^2.

*15.55. (a) What are the Q-points for the transistors in the amplifier in Fig. P15.55 if $V_{DD} = 15$ V, $V_{SS} = 15$ V, $R_{SS} = 62$ kΩ, and $R_D = 62$ kΩ? Assume $K_n = 400$ μA/V^2, $\gamma = 0.75$ V$^{0.5}$, $2\phi_F = 0.6$ V, and $V_{TO} = 1$ V. (b) What are the differential-mode gain, common-mode gain, CMRR, and differential-mode and common-mode input resistances?

15.56. Use SPICE to simulate the amplifier in Prob. 15.55 at a frequency of 1 kHz, and determine the differential-mode gain, common-mode gain,

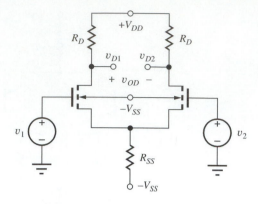

Figure P15.55

CMRR, and differential-mode and common-mode input resistances.

*15.57. (a) What are the Q-points for the transistors in the amplifier in Fig. P15.55 if $V_{DD} = 12$ V, $V_{SS} = 12$ V, $R_{SS} = 220$ kΩ, and $R_D = 330$ kΩ? Assume $K_n = 400$ μA/V^2, $\gamma = 0.75$ V$^{0.5}$, $2\phi_F = 0.6$ V, and $V_{TO} = 1$ V. (b) What are the differential-mode gain, common-mode gain, CMRR, and differential-mode and common-mode input resistances?

15.58. (a) What are the Q-points for the transistors in the amplifier in Fig. P15.58 if $V_{DD} = 15$ V, $V_{SS} = 15$ V, $I_{SS} = 300$ μA, $R_{SS} = 160$ kΩ, and $R_D = 75$ kΩ? Assume $K_n = 400$ μA/V^2 and $V_{TN} = 1$ V. (b) What are the differential-mode gain, common-mode gain, CMRR, and differential-mode and common-mode input resistances?

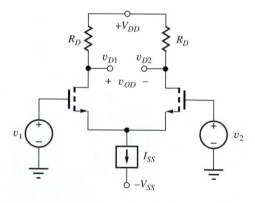

Figure P15.58

15.59. (a) What are the Q-points for the transistors in the amplifier in Fig. P15.58 if $V_{DD} = 9$ V, $V_{SS} = 9$ V, $I_{SS} = 40$ μA, $R_{SS} = 1.25$ MΩ, and $R_D = 300$ kΩ? Assume $K_n = 400$ μA/V^2 and $V_{TN} = 1$ V. (b) What are the differential-mode gain, common-mode gain, CMRR, and differential-mode and common-mode input resistances?

*15.60. (a) What are the Q-points for the transistors in the amplifier in Fig. P15.60 if $V_{DD} = 15$ V, $V_{SS} = 15$ V, $I_{SS} = 300\,\mu$A, $R_{SS} = 160$ kΩ, and $R_D = 75$ kΩ? Assume $K_n = 400\,\mu$A/V^2, $\gamma = 0.75$ V$^{0.5}$, $2\phi_F = 0.6$ V, and $V_{TO} = 1$ V. (b) What are the differential-mode gain, common-mode gain, CMRR, and differential-mode and common-mode input resistances?

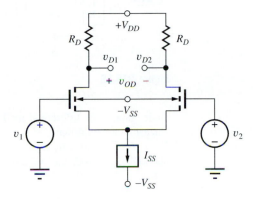

Figure P15.60

*15.61. (a) What are the Q-points for the transistors in the amplifier in Fig. P15.60 if $V_{DD} = 9$ V, $V_{SS} = 9$ V, $I_{SS} = 40\,\mu$A, $R_{SS} = 1.25$ MΩ, and $R_D = 300$ kΩ? Assume $K_n = 400\,\mu$A/V^2, $\gamma = 0.75$ V$^{0.5}$, $2\phi_F = 0.6$ V, and $V_{TO} = 1$ V. (b) What are the differential-mode gain, common-mode gain, CMRR, and differential-mode and common-mode input resistances?

15.62. Design a differential amplifier to have a differential-mode gain of 30 dB, using the circuit in Fig. P15.58 with $V_{DD} = V_{SS} = 7.5$ V. The circuit should have the maximum possible common-mode input range. Assume $V_{TN} = 1$ V and $K_n = 5$ mA/V^2.

15.63. (a) What are the Q-points for the transistors in the amplifier in Fig. P15.63 if $V_{DD} = 18$ V, $V_{SS} = 18$ V, $R_{SS} = 56$ kΩ, and $R_D = 91$ kΩ? Assume $K_n = 200\,\mu$A/V^2 and $V_{TP} = -1$ V. (b) What are the differential-mode gain, common-mode gain, CMRR, and differential-mode and common-mode input resistances?

15.64. Use SPICE to simulate the amplifier in Prob. 15.63 at a frequency of 3 kHz, and determine the differential-mode gain, common-mode gain, CMRR, and differential-mode and common-mode input resistances.

*15.65. (a) What are the Q-points for the transistors in the amplifier in Fig. P15.65 if $V_{DD} = 10$ V,

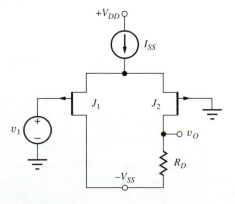

Figure P15.63

$V_{SS} = 10$ V, $I_{SS} = 40\,\mu$A, $R_{SS} = 1.25$ MΩ, and $R_D = 300$ kΩ? Assume $K_p = 200\,\mu$A/V^2, $\gamma = 0.6$ V$^{0.5}$, $2\phi_F = 0.6$ V, and $V_{TO} = -1$ V. (b) What are the differential-mode gain, common-mode gain, CMRR, and differential-mode and common-mode input resistances?

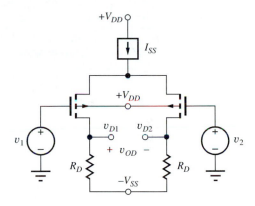

Figure P15.65

15.66. For the amplifier in Fig. P15.66, $V_{DD} = 12$ V, $V_{SS} = 12$ V, $I_{SS} = 20\,\mu$A, and $R_D = 820$ kΩ.

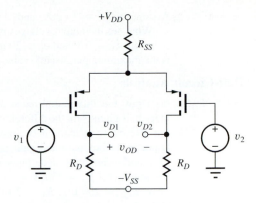

Figure P15.66

Assume $I_{DSS} = 1$ mA and $V_P = +2$ V.
(a) What are the output voltages v_O for the amplifier for $v_1 = 0$ V and $v_s = 20$ mV? (b) What is the maximum permissible value of v_s?

Half-Circuit Analysis

*15.67. (a) Draw the differential-mode and common-mode half-circuits for the differential amplifier in Fig. P15.67. (b) Use the half-circuits to find the Q-points, differential-mode gain, common-mode gain, and differential-mode input resistance for the amplifier if $\beta_o = 150$, $V_{CC} = 22$ V, $V_{EE} = 22$ V, $R_{EE} = 200$ kΩ, $R_1 = 2$ kΩ, and $R_C = 200$ kΩ.

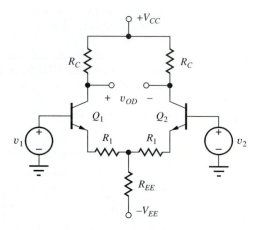

Figure P15.67

 15.68. Use SPICE to simulate the amplifier in Prob. 15.67 at a frequency of 1 kHz, and determine the differential-mode gain, common-mode gain, and differential-mode input resistances.

*15.69. (a) Draw the differential-mode and common-mode half-circuits for the differential amplifier in Fig. P15.69. (b) Use the half-circuits to find the Q-points, differential-mode gain, common-mode gain, and differential-mode input resistance for the amplifier if $\beta_o = 100$, $V_{CC} = 20$ V, $V_{EE} = 20$ V, $I_{EE} = 100$ μA, and $R_{EE} = 600$ kΩ?

 15.70. Use SPICE to simulate the amplifier in Fig. P15.69 at a frequency of 1 kHz, and determine the differential-mode gain, common-mode gain, and differential-mode input resistances.

*15.71. (a) Draw the differential-mode and common-mode half-circuits for the differential amplifier in Fig. P15.71. (b) Use the half-circuits to find the Q-points, differential-mode gain, common-

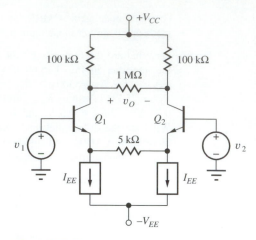

Figure P15.69

mode gain, and differential-mode input resistance for the amplifier if $V_{CC} = 15$ V, $V_{EE} = 15$ V, $I_{EE} = 100$ μA, $R_D = 75$ kΩ, $R_{EE} = 600$ kΩ, $\beta_o = 100$, $I_{DSS} = 200$ μA, and $V_P = -4$ V.

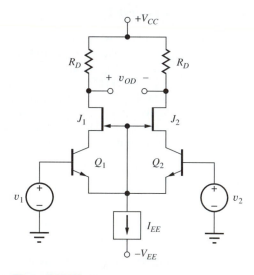

Figure P15.71

**15.72. (a) Draw the differential-mode and common-mode half-circuits for the differential amplifier in Fig. P15.72. (b) Use the half-circuits to find the Q-points, differential-mode gain, common-mode gain, and differential-mode input resistance for the amplifier if $K_n = 1000$ μA/V^2, $V_{TN} = 0.75$ V, $K_p = 500$ μA/V^2, $V_{TP} = -0.75$ V, $I_1 = 500$ μA, $I_2 = 400$ μA, $V_{DD} = 6$ V, $V_{SS} = 6$ V, and $R_D = 30$ kΩ.

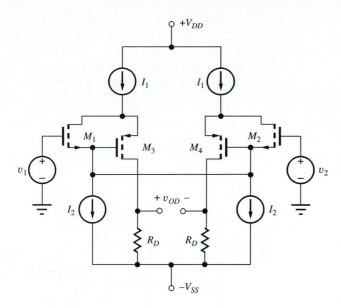

Figure P15.72

15.4 Evolution to Basic Operational Amplifiers

15.73. (a) What are the Q-points of the transistors in the amplifier in Fig. P15.73 if $V_{CC} = 12$ V, $V_{EE} = 12$ V, $I_1 = 50$ μA, $R = 24$ kΩ, $\beta_o = 100$, and $V_A = 60$ V? (b) What are the differential-mode voltage gain and input resistance? (c) What is the amplifier output resistance? (d) What is the common-mode input resistance? (e) Which terminal is the noninverting input?

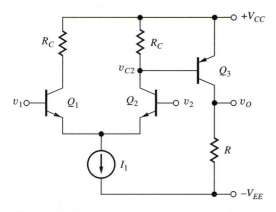

Figure P15.73

 15.74. Use SPICE to simulate the amplifier in Prob. 15.73 at a frequency of 1 kHz, and determine the differential-mode gain, CMRR, and differential-mode input resistance and output resistance.

15.75. (a) What are the Q-points of the transistors in the amplifier in Fig. P15.75 if $V_{CC} = 15$ V, $V_{EE} = 15$ V, $I_1 = 200$ μA, $R_E = 2.4$ kΩ, $R = 50$ kΩ, $\beta_o = 80$, and $V_A = 70$ V? (b) What are the

differential-mode voltage gain and input resistance? (c) What is the amplifier output resistance? (d) What is the common-mode input resistance? (e) Which terminal is the noninverting input?

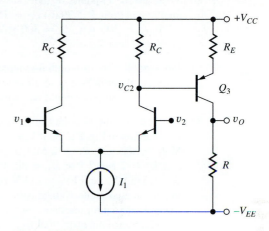

Figure P15.75

15.76. (a) What are the Q-points of the transistors in the amplifier in Fig. P15.75 if $V_{CC} = 15$ V, $V_{EE} = 15$ V, $I_1 = 200$ μA, $R_E = 0$, $R = 50$ kΩ, $\beta_o = 80$, and $V_A = 70$ V? (b) What are the differential-mode voltage gain and input resistance? (c) What is the common-mode input resistance?

*15.77. Plot a graph of the differential-mode voltage gain of the amplifier in Prob. P15.75 versus the value of R_E. (The computer might be a useful tool.)

15.78. Design an amplifier to have $R_{OUT} = 1$ kΩ and $A_{dm} = 2000$, using the circuit in Fig. P15.73. Use $V_{CC} = V_{EE} = 9$ V, and $\beta_F = 100$.

15.79. (a) What are the Q-points of the transistors in the amplifier in Fig. P15.79 if $V_{CC} = 15$ V,

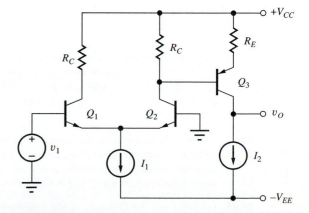

Figure P15.79

$V_{EE} = 15$ V, $I_1 = 200$ μA, $I_2 = 300$ μA, $R_E = 2.4$ kΩ, $\beta_o = 80$, and $V_A = 70$ V? (b) What are the differential-mode voltage gain, input resistance, and output resistance?

15.80. What are the Q-points of the transistors in the amplifier in Prob. P15.79 if $V_{CC} = 15$ V, $V_{EE} = 15$ V, $I_1 = 200$ μA, $I_2 = 300$ μA, $R_E = 0$, $\beta_o = 100$, and $V_A = 70$ V?

 *15.81. Plot a graph of the differential-mode voltage gain of the amplifier in Prob. P15.79 versus the value of R_E. (The computer might be a useful tool.)

15.82. (a) What are the Q-points of the transistors in the amplifier in Fig. P15.82 if $V_{CC} = V_{EE} = 15$ V, $I_1 = 500$ μA, $R_1 = 2$ MΩ, $I_2 = 500$ μA, and $R_2 = 2$ MΩ? Use $\beta_o = 80$, $V_A = 75$ V, $K_p = 5$ mA/V^2, and $V_{TP} = -1$ V. (b) What are the differential-mode voltage gain and input resistance and output resistance of the amplifier ? (c) Which terminal is the noninverting input? (d) Which terminal is the inverting input?

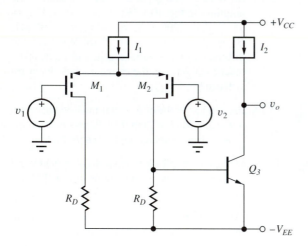

Figure P15.82

15.83. What is the voltage gain of the amplifier in Fig. P15.82 if $V_{CC} = V_{EE} = 5$ V, $I_1 = 500$ μA, $R_1 = 20$ MΩ, $I_2 = 100$ μA, $R_2 = 10$ MΩ, $\beta_o = 80$, $V_A = 75$ V, $K_p = 5$ mA/V^2, and $V_{TP} = -1$ V?

 *15.84. Use SPICE to simulate the amplifier in Prob. 15.82 at a frequency of 1 kHz, and determine the differential-mode gain, CMRR, and differential-mode input resistance and output resistance.

15.85. (a) What are the Q-points of the transistors in the amplifier in Fig. P15.85 if $I_1 = 500$ μA,

$R_1 = 1$ MΩ, $I_2 = 500$ μA, $R_2 = 1$ MΩ, and $V_{CC} = V_{EE} = 5$ V. Use $\beta_o = 80$, $V_A = 75$ V, $K_p = 5$ mA/V^2, and $V_{TP} = -1$ V. (b) What are the differential-mode voltage gain and input resistance and output resistance of the amplifier?

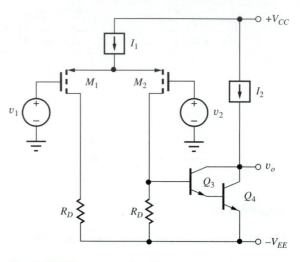

Figure P15.85

 *15.86. Use SPICE to simulate the amplifier in Prob. 15.85 at a frequency of 1 kHz, and determine the differential-mode gain, CMRR, and differential-mode input resistance and output resistance.

15.87. (a) What are the Q-points of the transistors in the amplifier in Fig. P15.87 if $V_{CC} = 15$ V, $V_{EE} = 15$ V, $I_1 = 100$ μA, $I_2 = 350$ μA, $I_3 = 1$ mA, $\beta_F = 100$, and $V_A = 50$ V? (b) What are the differential-mode voltage gain and input resistance? (c) What is the amplifier output resistance? (d) What is the common-mode input

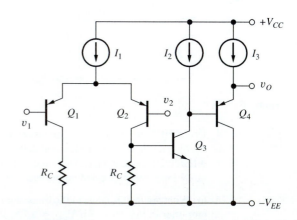

Figure P15.87

resistance? (e) Which terminal is the noninverting input?

 *15.88. Use SPICE to simulate the amplifier in Prob. 15.87 at a frequency of 1 kHz, and determine the differential-mode gain, CMRR, and differential-mode input resistance and output resistance.

15.89. (a) What are the Q-points of the transistors in the amplifier in Fig. P15.89 if $V_{DD} = 12$ V, $V_{SS} = 12$ V, $I_1 = 500$ μA, $I_2 = 2$ mA, $I_3 = 5$ mA, $K_n = 5$ mA/V², $V_{TN} = 0.75$ V, $\lambda_n = 0.02$ V⁻¹, $K_p = 2$ mA/V², $V_{TP} = -0.75$ V, and $\lambda_p = 0.015$ V⁻¹? (b) What are the differential-mode voltage gain and input resistance and output resistance of the amplifier?

5 V, $I_1 = 600$ μA, $I_2 = 500$ μA, $I_3 = 2$ mA, $K_n = 5$ mA/V², $V_{TN} = 0.70$ V, $\lambda_n = 0.02$ V⁻¹, $K_p = 2$ mA/V², $V_{TP} = -0.70$ V, and $\lambda_p = 0.015$ V⁻¹? (b) What are the differential-mode voltage gain and input resistance and output resistance of the amplifier?

15.92. (a) What are the Q-points of the transistors in the amplifier in Fig. P15.92 if $V_{CC} = 5$ V, $V_{EE} = 5$ V, $I_1 = 200$ μA, $I_2 = 500$ μA, $I_3 = 2$ mA, $R_E = 1$ kΩ, $R_L = 5$ kΩ, $\beta_o = 100$, $V_A = 50$ V, $I_{DSS} = 10$ mA, and $V_P = -5$ V? (b) What are the differential-mode voltage gain and input resistance and output resistance of the amplifier?

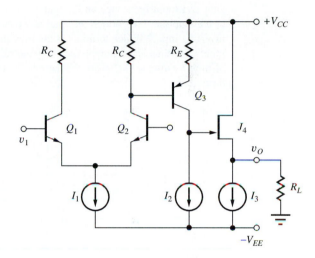

Figure P15.92

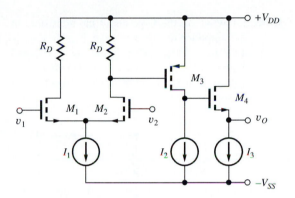

Figure P15.89

 *15.90. Use SPICE to simulate the amplifier in Prob. 15.89 at a frequency of 1 kHz, and determine the differential-mode gain, CMRR, and differential-mode input resistance and output resistance.

15.91. (a) What are the Q-points of the transistors in the amplifier in Fig. P15.91 if $V_{DD} = 5$ V, $V_{SS} = $

15.93. (a) What are the Q-points of the transistors in the amplifier in Fig. P15.93 if $V_{CC} = 5$ V, $V_{EE} = 5$ V, $I_1 = 200$ μA, $I_2 = 500$ μA, $I_3 = 2$ mA, $R_L = 2$ kΩ, $\beta_o = 100$, $V_A = 50$ V, $K_n = $

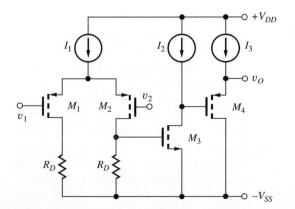

Figure P15.91

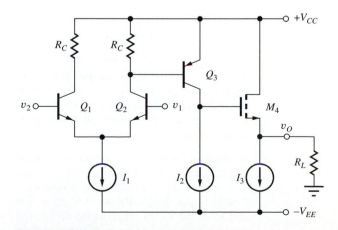

Figure P15.93

5 mA/V^2, and $V_{TN} = 0.70$ V? (b) What are the differential-mode voltage gain and input resistance and output resistance of the amplifier?

*15.94. Use SPICE to simulate the amplifier in Prob. 15.93 at a frequency of 2 kHz, and determine the differential-mode gain, CMRR, and differential-mode input resistance and output resistance.

*15.95. (a) What are the Q-points of the transistors in the amplifier in Fig. P15.95 if $V_{CC} = 3$ V, $V_{EE} = 3$ V, $I_1 = 10$ μA, $I_2 = 50$ μA, $I_3 = 250$ μA, $R_{C1} = 300$ kΩ, $R_{C2} = 78$ kΩ, $R_L = 5$ kΩ, $\beta_{on} = 100$, $V_{AN} = 50$ V, $\beta_{op} = 50$, and $V_{AP} = 70$ V? (b) What are the differential-mode voltage gain and input resistance and output resistance of the amplifier? (c) Which terminal is the non-inverting input? Which terminal is the inverting input? (d) What is the gain predicted by our rule-of-thumb estimate? What are the reasons for any discrepancy?

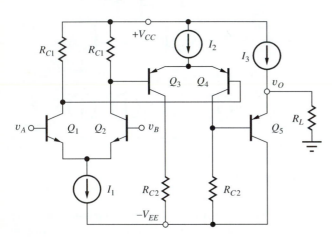

Figure P15.95

**15.96. (a) What are the Q-points of the transistors in the amplifier in Fig. P15.95 if $V_{CC} = V_{EE} = 18$ V, $I_1 = 100$ μA, $I_2 = 200$ μA, $I_3 = 750$ μA, $R_{C1} = 120$ kΩ, $R_{C2} = 170$ kΩ, $R_L = 2$ kΩ, $\beta_{on} = 100$, $V_{AN} = 50$ V, $\beta_{op} = 50$, and $V_{AP} = 70$ V? (b) What are the differential-mode voltage gain and input resistance and output resistance of the amplifier? (c) What is the common-mode input range? (d) Estimate the offset voltage of this amplifier.

*15.97. (a) What are the Q-points of the transistors in the amplifier in Fig. P15.97 if $V_{CC} = V_{EE} = 5$ V, $I_1 = 70$ μA, $R_1 = 25$ MΩ, $I_2 = 1$ mA, $R_2 = 5$ MΩ, $I_{DSS} = 5$ mA, $V_P = -5$ V, $\beta_o = 100$, and $V_A = 50$ V? (b) What are the differential-mode voltage gain and input resistance and output resistance of the amplifier?

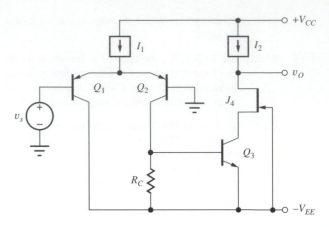

Figure P15.97

15.98. (a) What are the Q-points of the transistors in the amplifier in Fig. P15.98 if $V_{CC} = V_{EE} = 12$ V, $I_1 = 200$ μA, $R = 12$ kΩ, $\beta_F = 100$, and $V_A = 70$ V? (b) What are the differential-mode voltage gain and input resistance and output resistance of the amplifier?

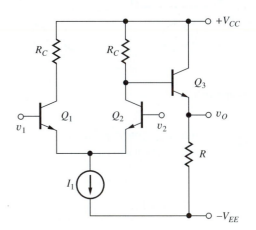

Figure P15.98

*15.99. Design an amplifier using the topology in Fig. P15.98 to have an input resistance of 300 kΩ and an output resistance of 100 Ω. Can these specifications all be met if $V_{CC} = V_{EE} = 12$ V, $\beta_{FO} = 100$, and $V_A = 60$ V? If so, what are the values of I_1, R_C, and R, and the voltage gain of the amplifier? If not, what needs to be changed?

*15.100. Design an amplifier using the topology in Fig. P15.98 to have an input resistance of 1 MΩ and an output resistance ≤2 Ω. Can these specifications all be met if $V_{CC} = V_{EE} = 9$ V, $\beta_{FO} = 100$, and $V_A = 60$ V? If so, what are the values of I_1, R_C, and R, and the voltage gain of the amplifier? If not, what needs to be changed?

**15.101. (a) What are the Q-points of the transistors in the amplifier in Fig. P15.101 if $V_{CC} = V_{EE} = 18$ V, $I_1 = 50$ μA, $I_2 = 500$ μA, $I_3 = 5$ mA, $\beta_{on} = 100$, $V_{AN} = 50$ V, $\beta_{op} = 50$, and $V_{AP} = 70$ V? (b) What are the differential-mode voltage gain and input resistance and output resistance of the amplifier?

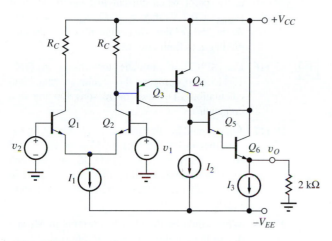

Figure P15.101

**15.102. (a) What are the Q-points of the transistors in the amplifier in Fig. P15.101 if $V_{CC} = V_{EE} = 22$ V, $I_1 = 50$ μA, $I_2 = 500$ μA, $I_3 = 5$ mA, $\beta_{on} = 100$, $V_{AN} = 50$ V, $\beta_{op} = 50$, and $V_{AP} = 70$ V? (b) What are the differential-mode voltage gain and input resistance and output resistance of the amplifier?

15.5 Output Stages

15.103. What is the quiescent current in the class-AB stage in Fig. P15.103 if $K_p = K_n = 600$ μA/V^2 and $V_{TN} = -V_{TP} = 0.75$ V?

*15.104. What is the quiescent current in the class-AB stage in Fig. P15.103 if $K_p = 400$ μA/V^2,

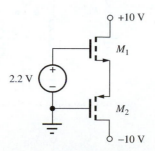

Figure P15.103

$K_n = 600$ μA/V^2, $V_{TP} = -0.8$ V, and $V_{TN} = 0.7$ V?

15.105. What is the quiescent current in the class-AB stage in Fig. P15.105 if both transistors have $I_S = 10^{-15}$ A?

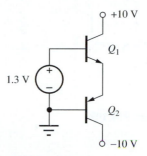

Figure P15.105

*15.106. What is the quiescent current in the class-AB stage in Fig. P15.105 if $I_S = 10^{-15}$ A for the *pnp* transistor and $I_S = 5 \times 10^{-15}$ A for the *npn* transistor?

15.107. Draw a sketch of the voltage transfer characteristic for the circuit in Fig. P15.107. Label important voltages on the characteristic.

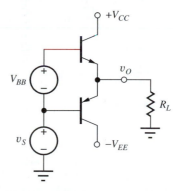

Figure P15.107

 15.108. Use SPICE to plot the voltage transfer characteristic for the class-AB stage in Fig. P15.107 if $I_S = 10^{-15}$ A and $\beta_F = 50$ for the *pnp* transistor, $I_S = 5 \times 10^{-15}$ A and $\beta_F = 60$ for the *npn* transistor, $V_{BB} = 1.3$ V, and $R_L = 1$ kΩ.

15.109. What is the quiescent current in the class-AB stage in Fig. P15.109 if I_S for the *npn* transistor is 10^{-15} A, I_S for the *pnp* transistor is 10^{-16} A, $I_B = 250$ μA, and $R_B = 5$ kΩ? Assume $\beta_F = \infty$ and $v_O = 0$.

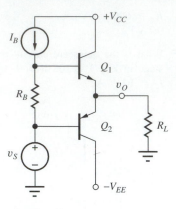

Figure P15.109

15.110. What is the quiescent current in the class-AB stage in Fig. P15.110 if $V_{TN} = 0.75$ V, $V_{TP} = -0.75$ V, $K_n = 500$ μA/V^2, $K_p = 200$ μA/V^2, $I_G = 500$ μA, and $R_G = 4$ kΩ?

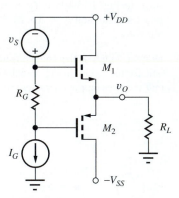

Figure P15.110

15.111. The source-follower in Fig. 15.48 has $V_{DD} = V_{SS} = 10$ V and $R_L = 1$ kΩ. If the amplifier is developing an output voltage of $5 \sin 2000\pi t$ V, what is the minimum value of I_{SS}? What are the maximum and minimum values of source current i_S that occur during the signal swing? What is the efficiency?

15.112. An ideal complementary class-B output stage is generating a square wave output signal across a 5-kΩ load resistor with a peak value of 5 V from ±5-V supplies. What is the efficiency of the amplifier?

*15.113. A complementary class-B output stage is generating a triangular output signal across a 100-kΩ load resistor with a peak value of 10 V from ±10-V supplies. What is the efficiency of the amplifier?

15.114. (a) Use the Fourier analysis capability of SPICE to find the amplitude of the first, second, third, fourth, and fifth harmonics of the input signal introduced by the cross-over region of the class-B amplifier in Fig. P15.107 if $V_{BB} = 0$, $V_{CC} = V_{EE} = 5$ V, $v_S = 4 \sin 2000\pi t$, and $R_L = 2$ kΩ. (b) Repeat for $V_{BB} = 1.3$ V.

Short-Circuit Protection

15.115. What is the current in the R_L circuit in Fig. 15.57 at the point when current just begins to limit ($V_{BE2} = 0.7$ V) if $R = 10$ Ω, $R_1 = 1$ kΩ, and $R_L = 250$ Ω? For what value of v_S does the output begin to limit current?

15.116. Use SPICE to simulate the circuit in Prob. 15.115, and compare the results to your hand calculations. Discuss the reasons for any discrepancies.

15.117. What would be the currents in Q_4 and Q_5 in the amplifier in Fig. 15.56(b) if $V_{CC} = V_{EE} = 15$ V, $I_2 = 500$ μA, $R_B = 2.4$ kΩ, $R_L = 2$ kΩ, and Q_3 is modeled by a voltage of $V_{CESAT} = 0.2$ V in series with a resistance of 50 Ω when it is saturated?

15.118. What would be the Q-point currents in M_4 and M_5 in the amplifier in Fig. 15.56(a) if $V_{DD} = V_{SS} = 15$ V, $I_2 = 250$ μA, $R_G = 7$ kΩ, $R_L = 2$ kΩ, and $V_{TN} = 0.75$ V, $V_{TP} = -0.75$ V, $K_n = 5$ mA/V^2, and $K_p = 2$ mA/V^2?

Transformer Coupling

15.119. Calculate the output resistance of the follower circuit (as seen at R_L) in Fig. 15.59 if $n = 10$ and $I_S = 10$ mA.

15.120. For the circuit in Fig. P15.120, $v_S = \sin 2000\pi t$, $R_E = 82$ kΩ, $R_B = 200$ kΩ, and $V_{CC} = V_{EE} = 9$ V. What value of n is required to deliver maximum power to R_L if $R_L = 10$ Ω? What is the power? Assume $C_1 = C_2 = \infty$.

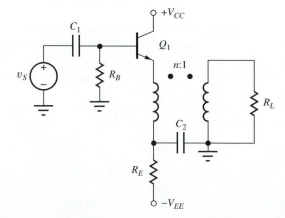

Figure P15.120

15.6 Electronic Current Sources

15.121. What are the output current and output resistance of the current source in Fig. P15.121 if $V_{EE} = 12$ V, $R_1 = 2$ MΩ, $R_2 = 2$ MΩ, $R_E = 220$ kΩ, $\beta_o = 100$, and $V_A = 50$ V?

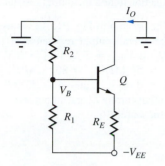

Figure P15.121

15.122. What are the output current and output resistance of the current source in Prob. 15.121 if the node V_B is bypassed to ground with a capacitor?

15.123. Design a current source to provide an output current of 1 mA using the topology of Fig. P15.121. The current source should use no more than 1.2 mA and have an output resistance of at least 500 kΩ. Assume $V_{EE} = 12$ V.

15.124. What are the output current and output resistance of the current source in Fig. P15.124 if $V_O = V_{DD} = 10$ V, $R_4 = 680$ kΩ, $R_3 = 330$ kΩ, $R_S = 30$ kΩ, $K_n = 500$ μA/V^2, $V_{TN} = 1$ V, and $\lambda = 0.01$ V^{-1}?

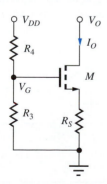

Figure P15.124

15.125. What are the output current and output resistance of the current source in Fig. P15.125 if $V_{CC} = 15$ V, $R_1 = 100$ kΩ, $R_2 = 200$ kΩ, $R_E = 43$ kΩ, $\beta_o = 75$, and $V_A = 50$ V?

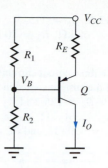

Figure P15.125

15.126. What are the output current and output resistance of the current source in Fig. P15.126 if $V_{DD} = 9$ V, $R_4 = 2$ MΩ, $R_3 = 1$ MΩ, $R_S = 100$ kΩ, $K_p = 750$ μA/V^2, $V_{TP} = -0.75$ V, and $\lambda = 0.01$ V^{-1}?

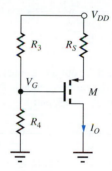

Figure P15.126

15.127. Design a current source to provide an output current of 175 μA using the topology in Fig. P15.126. The current source should use no more than 200 μA and have an output resistance of at least 2.5 MΩ. Assume $V_{DD} = 12$ V, $K_p = 200$ μA/V^2, $V_{TP} = -0.75$ V, and $\lambda = 0.02$ V^{-1}.

15.128. What are the two output currents and output resistances of the current source in Fig. P15.128

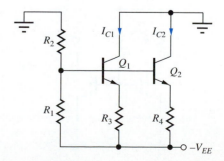

Figure P15.128

if $V_{EE} = 12$ V, $\beta_o = 125$, $V_A = 50$ V, $R_1 = 33$ kΩ, $R_2 = 68$ kΩ, $R_3 = 20$ kΩ, and $R_4 = 100$ kΩ?

*15.129. What are the three output currents and output resistances of the current source in Fig. P15.129 if $V_{EE} = 15$ V, $\beta_o = 125$, and $V_A = 50$ V, $R_1 = 100$ kΩ, $R_2 = 390$ kΩ, $R_3 = 27$ kΩ, $R_4 = 100$ kΩ, $R_5 = 330$ kΩ, and $R_6 = 100$ kΩ?

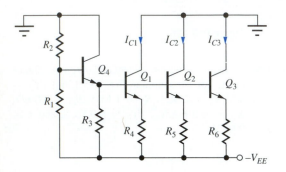

Figure P15.129

15.130. What are the three output currents and output resistances of the current source in Fig. P15.130 if $V_{EE} = 15$ V, $\beta_o = 75$, and $V_A = 60$ V?

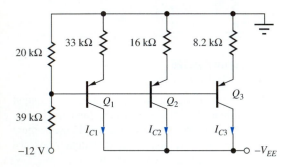

Figure P15.130

15.131. What are the two output currents and output resistances of the current sources in Fig. P15.131

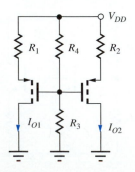

Figure P15.131

if $V_{DD} = 12$ V, $K_p = 250$ μA/V^2, $V_{TP} = -1$ V, $\lambda = 0.02$ V^{-1}, $R_1 = 100$ kΩ, $R_2 = 470$ kΩ, $R_3 = 2$ MΩ, and $R_4 = 2$ MΩ?

 15.132. Use SPICE to simulate the current source array in Prob. 15.131, and find the output currents and output resistances of the source. Use the .TF function to find the output resistances.

15.133. The op amp in Fig. P15.133 is used to increase the overall output resistance of current source M_1. If $V_{REF} = 5$ V, $V_{DD} = 0$ V, $V_{SS} = 15$ V, $R = 50$ kΩ, $K_n = 800$ μA/V^2, $V_{TN} = 0.8$ V, $\lambda = 0.02$ V^{-1}, and $A = 50,000$, what are the output current I_O and output resistance of the current source?

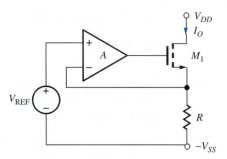

Figure P15.133

*15.134. The op amp in Fig. P15.134 is used in an attempt to increase the overall output resistance of the current source circuit. If $V_{REF} = 5$ V, $V_{CC} = 0$ V, $V_{EE} = 15$ V, $R = 50$ kΩ, $\beta_o = 120$, $V_A = 70$ V, and $A = 50,000$, what are the output current I_O and output resistance of the current source? Did the op amp help increase the output resistance? Explain why or why not.

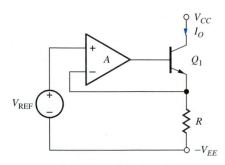

Figure P15.134

**15.135. How might the output resistance of the circuit in Fig. P15.134 be improved further using an additional bipolar transistor?

15.136. (a) What are the Q-points of the transistors in the amplifier in Fig. P15.136 if $\beta_o = 85$ and $V_A = 70$ V? (b) What are the differential-mode gain and CMRR of the amplifier?

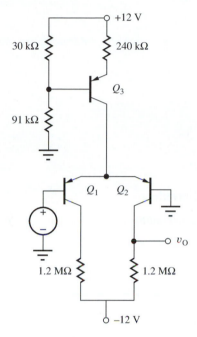

Figure P15.136

15.137. (a) What are the Q-points of the transistors in the amplifier in Fig. P15.137 if $K_n = 400$ μA/V^2, $V_{TN} = +1$ V, $\lambda = 0.02$ V^{-1}, $R_1 = 51$ kΩ, $R_2 = 100$ kΩ, $R_S = 7.5$ kΩ, and $R_D = 36$ kΩ? (b) What are the differential-mode gain and CMRR of the amplifier?

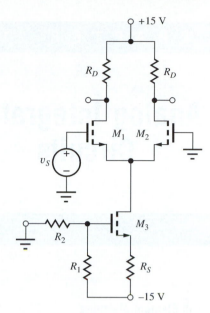

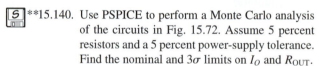

Figure P15.137

15.138. (a) A current source with $R_{OUT} = \beta_o r_o$ is used to bias a standard bipolar differential amplifier. What is an expression for the CMRR of this amplifier for single-ended outputs?

15.139. The output resistance of the MOS current source in Fig. P15.137 is given by $R_{OUT} = \mu_f R_S$. How much voltage must be developed across R_S to achieve an output resistance of 5 MΩ at a current of 100 μA if $K_n = 500$ μA/V^2 and $\lambda = 0.02$ V^{-1}?

15.140. Use PSPICE to perform a Monte Carlo analysis of the circuits in Fig. 15.72. Assume 5 percent resistors and a 5 percent power-supply tolerance. Find the nominal and 3σ limits on I_O and R_{OUT}.

Analog Integrated Circuits

Integrated circuit (IC) technology allows the realization of large numbers of virtually identical transistors. Although the absolute parameter tolerances of these devices are relatively poor, device characteristics can be matched to within 1 percent or less. The ability to build devices with nearly identical characteristics has led to the development of special circuit techniques that take advantage of the tight matching of the device characteristics.

Chapter 16 begins by exploring the use of matched transistors in the design of current sources, called *current mirrors,* in both MOS and bipolar technology. The cascode and Wilson current sources are subsequently added to our repertoire of high-output-resistance current source circuits. Circuit techniques that can be used to achieve power supply independent biasing are also introduced.

The current mirror is often used to bias analog circuits and to replace load resistors in differential and operational amplifiers. This active-load circuit can substantially enhance the voltage gain capability of many amplifiers, and a number of MOS and bipolar circuit examples are presented. The chapter then discusses circuit techniques used in IC operational amplifiers, including the classic 741 amplifier. This design provides a robust, high-performance, general-purpose operational amplifier with breakdown-voltage protection of the input stage and short-circuit protection of the output stage. The final two sections of the chapter present techniques for implementing digital-to-analog and analog-to-digital converters.

16.1 CIRCUIT ELEMENT MATCHING

Integrated circuit design is based directly on the ability to realize large numbers of transistors with nearly identical characteristics. Transistors are said to be **matched** when they have identical sets of device parameters: (I_S, β_{FO}, V_A) for the BJT, (V_{TN}, K', λ) for the MOSFET, or (I_{DSS}, V_P, λ) for the JFET. The planar geometry of the devices can easily be changed in integrated designs, and so the emitter area A_E of the BJT and the W/L ratio of the MOSFET become important circuit design parameters. (Remember from our study of MOS digital circuits in Part II that we found that W/L represents a fundamental circuit design parameter.)

In integrated circuits, absolute parameter values may vary widely from fabrication process run to process run, with ±25 to 30 percent tolerances not uncommon (see Table 16.1). However, the matching between nearby circuit elements on a given IC chip is typically within a fraction of a percent. Thus, IC design techniques have been invented

T a b l e 16.1

IC Tolerances and Matching [1]

	Absolute Tolerance, %	Mismatch, %
Diffused Resistors	30	≤ 2
Ion-Implanted Resistors	5	≤ 1
V_{BE}	10	≤ 1
I_S, β_F, V_A	30	≤ 1
V_{TN}, V_{TP}	15	≤ 1
K', λ	30	≤ 1

that rely heavily on **matched device** characteristics and resistor ratios rather than absolute parameter values. The circuits described in this chapter depend, for proper operation, on the tight device matching that can be realized through IC fabrication processes, and many will not operate correctly if built with mismatched discrete components. However, many of these circuits can be used in discrete circuit design if integrated transistor arrays are used in the implementation.

> **EXERCISE:** An IC resistor has a nominal value of 10 kΩ and a tolerance of ±30 percent. A particular process run has produced resistors with an average value 20 percent higher than the nominal value, and the resistors are found to be matched within 2 percent. What range of resistor values will occur in this process run?
>
> **ANSWER:** 11.88 kΩ–12.12 kΩ

16.2 CURRENT MIRRORS

Current mirror biasing is an extremely important technique in integrated circuit design. Not only is it heavily used in analog applications, it also appears routinely in digital circuit design as well. Figure 16.1 shows the circuits for basic MOS and bipolar current mirrors. In Fig. 16.1(a), MOSFETs M_1 and M_2 are assumed to have identical characteristics (V_{TN}, K_n', λ) and W/L ratios; in Fig. 16.1(b), the characteristics of Q_1 and Q_2 are assumed to be identical (I_S, β_{FO}, V_A). In both circuits, a reference current I_{REF} provides operating bias to the mirror, and the output current is represented by current I_O. These basic circuits are designed to have $I_O = I_{REF}$; that is, the output current mirrors the reference current—hence, the name "current mirror."

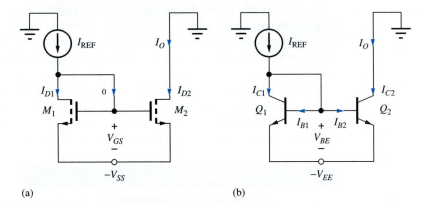

Figure 16.1 (a) MOS and (b) BJT current mirror circuits.

(a)   (b)

dc Analysis of the MOS Current Mirror

We begin with analysis of the MOS current mirror. Because the gate currents are zero for the MOSFETs, reference current I_{REF} must flow into the drain of M_1, which is forced to operate in saturation by the circuit connection because $V_{DS1} = V_{GS1} = V_{GS}$. V_{GS} must equal the value required for $I_{D1} = I_{REF}$. Assuming matched devices:[1]

$$I_{REF} = \frac{K_n}{2}(V_{GS1} - V_{TN})^2(1 + \lambda V_{DS1}) \quad \text{or} \quad V_{GS1} = V_{TN} + \sqrt{\frac{2I_{REF}}{K_{n1}(1 + \lambda V_{DS1})}}$$

$$(16.1)$$

---

[1] Matching between elements in the current mirror is very important; this is a case in which the $(1 + \lambda V_{DS})$ term is included in the dc, as well as ac, calculations.

Current I_O is equal to the drain current of M_2:

$$I_O = I_{D2} = \frac{K_n}{2}(V_{GS2} - V_{TN})^2(1 + \lambda V_{DS2}) \tag{16.2}$$

but the circuit connection forces $V_{GS2} = V_{GS1}$. Substituting Eq. (16.1) into Eq. (16.2) yields

$$I_O = I_{REF}\frac{(1 + \lambda V_{DS2})}{(1 + \lambda V_{DS1})} \approx I_{REF} \tag{16.3}$$

For equal values of V_{DS}, the output current is identical to the reference current (that is, the output mirrors the reference current). Unfortunately in most circuit applications, $V_{DS2} \neq V_{DS1}$, and there is a slight mismatch between the output current and the reference current, as demonstrated in Example 16.1.

EXAMPLE 16.1: Calculate the output current I_O for the MOS current mirror in Fig. 16.1(a) if $\lambda = 0.0133$ V^{-1}, $V_{SS} = 12$ V, $V_{TN} = 1$ V, $K_n = 150$ μA/V^2, and $I_{REF} = 50$ μA.

SOLUTION: We need to evaluate Eq. (16.3) and must find the value of V_{DS1} using Eq. (16.1)

$$V_{DS1} = V_{GS1} = V_{TN} + \sqrt{\frac{2I_{REF}}{K_n(1 + \lambda V_{DS1})}}$$

Solving iteratively for V_{DS1} from

$$V_{DS1} = 1\text{ V} + \sqrt{\frac{2(50\text{ μA})}{150\frac{\text{μA}}{\text{V}^2}\left(1 + \frac{0.0133}{\text{V}}V_{DS1}\right)}}$$

yields $V_{DS1} = 1.81$ V. Substituting this value and $V_{DS2} = 12$ V in Eq. (16.3):

$$I_o = (50\text{ μA})\frac{\left(1 + \frac{0.0133}{\text{V}}(12\text{ V})\right)}{\left(1 + \frac{0.0133}{\text{V}}(1.81\text{ V})\right)} = 56.6\text{ μA}$$

The ideal output current would be 50 μA, whereas the actual currents are mismatched by approximately 13 percent. ◆

EXERCISE: Based on the numbers in Example 16.1, what is the minimum value of the drain voltage required to keep M_2 saturated in Fig. 16.1(a)?

ANSWER: -11.2 V

dc Analysis of the Bipolar Current Mirror

Analysis of the BJT current mirror in Fig. 16.1(b) is similar to that of the FET. Applying KCL at the collector of "diode-connected" transistor Q_1 yields

$$I_{REF} = I_{C1} + I_{B1} + I_{B2} \quad \text{and} \quad I_O = I_{C2} \tag{16.4}$$

The currents needed to relate I_O to I_{REF} can be found using the transport model, noting that the circuit connection forces the two transistors to have the same base-emitter voltage V_{BE}:

$$I_{C1} = I_S \exp\left(\frac{V_{BE}}{V_T}\right)\left(1 + \frac{V_{CE1}}{V_A}\right) \qquad I_{C2} = I_S \exp\left(\frac{V_{BE}}{V_T}\right)\left(1 + \frac{V_{CE2}}{V_A}\right)$$

$$\beta_{F1} = \beta_{FO}\left(1 + \frac{V_{CE1}}{V_A}\right) \qquad\qquad \beta_{F2} = \beta_{FO}\left(1 + \frac{V_{CE2}}{V_A}\right) \qquad (16.5)$$

$$I_{B1} = \frac{I_S}{\beta_{FO}}\exp\left(\frac{V_{BE}}{V_T}\right) \qquad\qquad I_{B2} = \frac{I_S}{\beta_{FO}}\exp\left(\frac{V_{BE}}{V_T}\right)$$

Substituting Eq. (16.5) into Eq. (16.4) and solving for $I_O = I_{C2}$ yields

$$I_O = I_{\text{REF}}\frac{\left[1 + \dfrac{V_{CE2}}{V_A}\right]}{\left[1 + \dfrac{V_{CE1}}{V_A} + \dfrac{2}{\beta_{FO}}\right]} = I_{\text{REF}}\frac{\left[1 + \dfrac{V_{CE2}}{V_A}\right]}{\left[1 + \dfrac{V_{BE}}{V_A} + \dfrac{2}{\beta_{FO}}\right]} \qquad (16.6)$$

If the Early voltage were infinite, Eq. (16.6) would reduce to

$$I_O = I_{\text{REF}}\frac{1}{1 + \dfrac{2}{\beta_{FO}}} \qquad \text{or} \qquad \frac{I_O}{I_{\text{REF}}} = \frac{1}{1 + \dfrac{2}{\beta_{FO}}} \qquad (16.7)$$

and the output current would mirror the reference current, except for a small error due to the finite current gain of the BJT. For example, if $\beta_{FO} = 100$, the currents would match within 2 percent. As for the FET case, however, the collector-emitter voltage mismatch in Eq. (16.6) is generally more significant than the current gain defect term, as indicated in Example 16.2. We refer to the quantity I_O/I_{REF} as the **mirror ratio.**

EXAMPLE 16.2: Calculate the mirror ratio for the MOS and BJT current mirrors for $V_{GS} = 2$ V, $V_{DS} = 10$ V $= V_{CE}$, $V_{BE} = 0.7$ V, $\lambda = 0.02$ V^{-1}, $V_A = 50$ V, and $\beta_{FO} = 100$.

SOLUTION:

$$\text{FET:} \quad \frac{I_O}{I_{\text{REF}}} = \frac{(1 + \lambda V_{DS2})}{(1 + \lambda V_{DS1})} = \frac{\left(1 + \dfrac{0.02}{\text{V}}(10\text{ V})\right)}{\left(1 + \dfrac{0.02}{\text{V}}(2\text{ V})\right)} = 1.15$$

$$\text{BJT:} \quad \frac{I_O}{I_{\text{REF}}} = \frac{1 + \dfrac{V_{CE2}}{V_A}}{1 + \dfrac{2}{\beta_{FO}} + \dfrac{V_{CE1}}{V_A}} = \frac{1 + \dfrac{10\text{ V}}{50\text{ V}}}{1 + \dfrac{2}{100} + \dfrac{0.7\text{ V}}{50\text{ V}}} = 1.16$$

DISCUSSION: The FET and BJT mismatches are very similar—15 percent and 16 percent, respectively. The current gain error is a small contributor to the overall error in the BJT mirror ratio. ◆

EXERCISE: What is the actual value of V_{BE} in the bipolar current mirror in Example 16.2 if $I_S = 0.1$ fA and $I_{\text{REF}} = 100$ μA? What is the minimum value of the collector voltage required to maintain Q_2 in the forward-active region in Fig. 16.1(b)?

ANSWERS: 0.691 V; $-V_{EE} + 0.691$ V

Changing the MOS Mirror Ratio

The power of the current mirror is greatly increased if the mirror ratio can be changed from unity. For the MOS current mirror, the ratio can easily be modified by changing the W/L ratios of the two transistors forming the mirror. In Fig. 16.2, for example, remembering that $K_n = K_n'(W/L)$ for the MOSFET, the K_n values of the two transistors are given by

$$K_{n1} = K_n'\left(\frac{W}{L}\right)_1 \qquad \text{and} \qquad K_{n2} = K_n'\left(\frac{W}{L}\right)_2 \qquad (16.8)$$

Substituting these two different values of K_n in Eqs. (16.1) and (16.2) yields

$$I_o = I_{\text{REF}}\frac{K_{n2}(1 + \lambda V_{DS2})}{K_{n1}(1 + \lambda V_{DS1})} = I_{\text{REF}}\frac{\left(\dfrac{W}{L}\right)_2}{\left(\dfrac{W}{L}\right)_1}\frac{(1 + \lambda V_{DS2})}{(1 + \lambda V_{DS1})} \qquad (16.9)$$

For the particular values in Fig. 16.2, the nominal output current will be $I_O = 5I_{\text{REF}}$, ignoring the differences due to drain-source voltage mismatch. However, the differences in V_{DS} will again create an error in the mirror ratio.

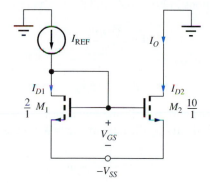

Figure 16.2 MOS current mirror with unequal (W/L) ratios.

EXERCISE: (a) Calculate the mirror ratio for the MOS current mirrors in the figure below for $\lambda = 0$. (b) For $\lambda = 0.02$ V^{-1} if $V_{TN} = 1$ V, $K_n' = 25$ μA/V^2, and $I_{\text{REF}} = 50$ μA.

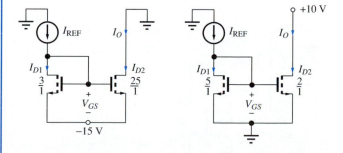

ANSWERS: 8.33, 0.400; 10.4, 0.462

Altering the BJT Current Mirror Ratio

In bipolar IC technology, the designer is free to modify the emitter area of the transistors, just as the W/L ratio can be chosen in MOS design. To alter the BJT mirror ratio, we use the fact that the saturation current of the bipolar transistor is proportional to its emitter area A_E and can be written as

$$I_S = I_{SO}\frac{A_E}{A} \tag{16.10}$$

In Eq. (16.10), I_{SO} represents the saturation current of a bipolar transistor with one unit of emitter area: $A_E = 1 \times A$. The actual dimensions associated with A are technology-dependent.

By changing the relative sizes of the emitters of the BJTs in the current mirror, the IC designer can modify the mirror ratio. For the modified mirror in Fig. 16.3,

$$I_{C1} = I_{SO}\frac{A_{E1}}{A}\exp\left(\frac{V_{BE}}{V_T}\right)\left(1 + \frac{V_{CE1}}{V_A}\right) \qquad I_{C2} = I_{SO}\frac{A_{E2}}{A}\exp\left(\frac{V_{BE}}{V_T}\right)\left(1 + \frac{V_{CE2}}{V_A}\right)$$

$$I_{B1} = \frac{I_{SO}}{\beta_{FO}}\frac{A_{E1}}{A}\exp\left(\frac{V_{BE}}{V_T}\right) \qquad\qquad I_{B2} = \frac{I_{SO}}{\beta_{FO}}\frac{A_{E2}}{A}\exp\left(\frac{V_{BE}}{V_T}\right) \tag{16.11}$$

Substituting these equations in Eq. (16.4) and then solving for I_O yields

$$I_O = nI_{\text{REF}}\frac{1 + \dfrac{V_{CE2}}{V_A}}{1 + \dfrac{V_{BE}}{V_A} + \dfrac{1+n}{\beta_{FO}}} \qquad \text{where } n = \frac{A_{E2}}{A_{E1}} \tag{16.12}$$

In the ideal case of infinite current gain and identical collector-emitter voltages, the mirror ratio would be determined only by the ratio of the two emitter areas:

$$\frac{I_O}{I_{\text{REF}}} = n \tag{16.13}$$

However, for finite current gain,

$$\frac{I_O}{I_{\text{REF}}} = \frac{n}{1 + \dfrac{1+n}{\beta_{FO}}} \tag{16.14}$$

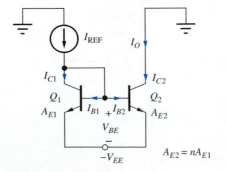

Figure 16.3 BJT current mirror with unequal emitter area.

Suppose $A_{E2}/A_{E1} = 10$ and $\beta_{FO} = 100$; then Eq. (16.14) becomes

$$\frac{I_O}{I_{REF}} = 10\frac{1}{1 + \dfrac{11}{100}} = 9.01 \tag{16.15}$$

A relatively large error (10 percent) is occurring even though the effect of collector-emitter voltage mismatch has been ignored. For high mirror ratios, the current gain error term can become quite important because the total number of units of base current increases directly with the mirror ratio.

> **EXERCISE:** (a) Calculate the ideal mirror ratio for the BJT current mirrors in the figure below if $V_A = \infty$ and $\beta_{FO} = \infty$. (b) If $V_A = \infty$ and $\beta_{FO} = 75$. (c) If $V_A = 60$ V, $\beta_{FO} = 75$, and $V_{BE} = 0.7$ V.

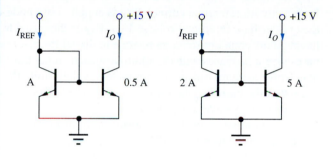

> **ANSWERS:** 0.500, 2.50; 0.490, 2.39; 0.606, 2.95

Multiple Current Sources

Analog circuits often require a number of different current sources to bias the various stages of the design. A single reference transistor, M_1 or Q_1, can be used to generate multiple output currents using the circuits in Figs. 16.4 and 16.5. In Fig. 16.4, the unusual connection of the gate terminals through the MOSFETs is being used as a "short-hand" method to indicate that all the gates are connected together. Circuit operation is similar to that of the basic current mirror. The reference current enters the **"diode-connected" transistor**—here, the MOSFET M_1—establishing gate-source voltage V_{GS}, which is then used to bias transistors M_2 through M_5, each having a different W/L ratio. Because there is no current

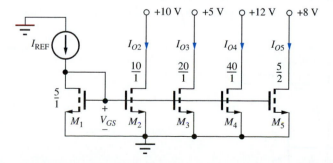

Figure 16.4 Multiple MOS current sources generated from one reference voltage.

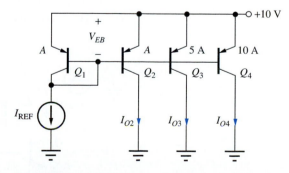

Figure 16.5 Multiple bipolar sources biased by one reference device.

gain defect in MOS technology, a large number of output transistors can be driven from one reference transistor.

> **EXERCISE:** What are the four output currents in the circuit in Fig. 16.4 if $I_{REF} = 100\ \mu A$ and $\lambda = 0$ for all the FETs?
>
> **ANSWERS:** 200 μA, 400 μA, 800 μA, 50.0 μA

> **EXERCISE:** Recalculate the four output currents in the circuit in Fig. 16.4 if $\lambda = 0.02$ for all the FETs. Assume $V_{GS} = 2$ V.
>
> **ANSWERS:** 231 μA, 423 μA, 954 μA, 55.8 μA

The situation is very similar in the *pnp* bipolar mirror in Fig. 16.5. Here again, the base terminals of the BJTs are extended through the transistors to simplify the drawing. In this circuit, reference current I_{REF} is supplied by diode-connected BJT Q_1 to establish the emitter-base reference voltage V_{EB}. V_{EB} is then used to bias transistors Q_2 to Q_4, each having a different emitter area relative to that of the reference transistor. Because the total base current increases with the addition of each output transistor, the base current error term gets worse as more transistors are added, which limits the number of outputs that can be used with the basic bipolar current mirror. The buffered current mirror in the next section was invented to solve this problem.

An expression for the output current from a given collector can be derived following the steps that led to Eq. (16.12):

$$I_{Oi} = n_i I_{REF} \frac{1 + \dfrac{V_{ECi}}{V_A}}{1 + \dfrac{V_{EB}}{V_A} + \dfrac{1 + \sum_{i=2}^{m} n_i}{\beta_{FO}}} \qquad \text{where } n_i = \frac{A_{Ei}}{A_{E1}} \qquad (16.16)$$

> **EXERCISE:** (a) What are the three output currents in the circuit in Fig. 16.5 if $I_{REF} = 10\ \mu A$, $\beta_{FO} = 50$, and $V_A = \infty$ for all the BJTs? (b) Repeat for $V_A = 50$ V and $V_{EB} = 0.7$ V. Use Eq. (16.16).
>
> **ANSWERS:** 7.46 μA, 37.3 μA, 74.6 μA; 8.86 μA, 44.3 μA, 88.6 μA

Buffered Current Mirror

The current gain defect in the bipolar current mirror can become substantial when a large mirror ratio is used or if many source currents are generated from one reference transistor. However, this error can be reduced greatly by using the circuit in Fig. 16.6, called

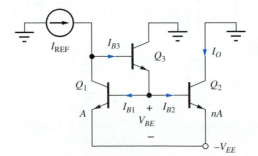

Figure 16.6 Buffered current mirror.

a **buffered current mirror.** The current gain of transistor Q_3 is used to reduce the base current that is subtracted from the reference current. Applying KCL at the collector of transistor Q_1, and assuming that $V_A = \infty$ for simplicity, I_{C1} is expressed as

$$I_C = I_{REF} - I_{B3} = I_{REF} - \frac{(1+n)\dfrac{I_C}{\beta_{FO1}}}{\beta_{FO3} + 1} \tag{16.17}$$

and solving for the collector current yields

$$I_O = nI_C = nI_{REF} \frac{1}{1 + \dfrac{(1+n)}{\beta_{FO1}(\beta_{FO3}+1)}} \tag{16.18}$$

The error term in the denominator has been reduced by a factor of $(\beta_{FO} + 1)$ from the error in Eq. (16.14).

> **EXERCISE:** What is the mirror ratio and the percent error for the buffered current mirror in Fig. 16.6 if $\beta_{FO} = 50$, $n = 10$, and $V_A = \infty$ for all the BJTs? (b) What is that value of V_{CE2} required to balance the mirror if $\beta_{FO} = \infty$?
>
> **ANSWERS:** 9.96, 0.430 percent; 1.4 V

Output Resistance of the Current Mirror

The output resistance of the basic current mirror can be found by referring to the ac model of Fig. 16.7. Diode-connected bipolar transistor Q_1 represents a simple two-terminal device, and its small-signal model is easily found using nodal analysis of Fig. 16.8:

$$\mathbf{i} = g_\pi \mathbf{v} + g_m \mathbf{v} + g_o \mathbf{v} = (g_m + g_\pi + g_o)\mathbf{v} \tag{16.19}$$

By factoring out g_m, an approximate result for the diode conductance is

$$\frac{\mathbf{i}}{\mathbf{v}} = g_m \left[1 + \frac{1}{\beta_o} + \frac{1}{\mu_f} \right] \approx g_m \qquad \text{and} \qquad R \approx \frac{1}{g_m} \tag{16.20}$$

for β_o and $\mu_f \gg 1$. The small-signal model for the diode-connected BJT is simply a resistor of value $1/g_m$. Note that this result is the same as the small-signal resistance r_d of an actual diode that was developed in Sec. 13.4, Chapter 13.

Using this diode model simplifies the ac model for the current mirror to that shown in Fig. 16.9. This circuit should be recognized as a common-emitter transistor with a Thévenin equivalent resistance $R_{th} = 1/g_m$ connected to its base; the output resistance just equals the output resistance r_{o2} of transistor Q_2.

The equation describing the small-signal model for the two-terminal "diode-connected" MOSFET is similar to that in Eq. (16.20) except that the current gain is infinite. Therefore, the two-terminal MOSFET is also represented by a resistor of value $1/g_m$, as in Fig. 16.10; the output resistance of the MOS current mirror is equal to r_{o2} of the MOSFET M_2.

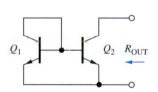

Figure 16.7 ac Model for the output resistance of the bipolar current mirror.

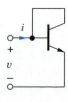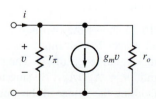

Figure 16.8 Model for "diode-connected" transistor.

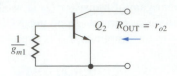

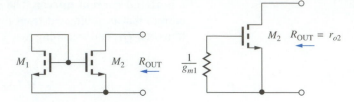

Figure 16.9 Simplified small-signal model for the bipolar current mirror.

Figure 16.10 Output resistance of the MOS current mirror.

Thus, the output resistance and figure of merit for the basic current mirror circuits are determined by output transistors Q_2 and M_2:

$$R_{OUT} = r_{o2} \quad \text{and} \quad V_{CS} \approx V_{A2} \quad \text{or} \quad \frac{1}{\lambda_2} \tag{16.21}$$

EXERCISE: What are the output resistances of sources I_{O2} and I_{O3} in Fig. 16.4 for $I_{REF} = 100\ \mu A$ and Fig. 16.5 for $I_{REF} = 10\ \mu A$ if $V_A = 1/\lambda = 50$ V?

ANSWERS: 260 kΩ, 130 kΩ; 6.77 MΩ, 1.35 MΩ

Two-Port Model for the Current Mirror

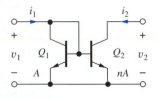

Figure 16.11 Current mirror as a two-port.

We shall see shortly that the current mirror can be used not only as a dc current source but, in more complex circuits, as a current amplifier and active load. It will be useful to understand the small-signal behavior of the current mirror, redrawn as a two-port in Fig. 16.11. Because the current mirror has a current input and current output, the h-parameters represent a convenient parameter set to model the current mirror:

$$\begin{aligned} \mathbf{v_1} &= h_{11}\mathbf{i_1} + h_{12}\mathbf{v_2} \\ \mathbf{i_2} &= h_{21}\mathbf{i_1} + h_{22}\mathbf{v_2} \end{aligned} \tag{16.22}$$

The small-signal model for the current mirror is in Fig. 16.12, in which diode-connected transistor Q_1 is represented in its simplified form by $1/g_{m1}$.

From the circuit in Fig. 16.12,

$$h_{11} = \left.\frac{\mathbf{v_1}}{\mathbf{i_1}}\right|_{\mathbf{v_2}=0} = \frac{1}{(g_{m1} + g_{\pi2} + g_{o1})} = \frac{1}{g_{m1}\left(1 + \dfrac{n}{\beta_{o2}} + \dfrac{1}{\mu_{f1}}\right)} \approx \frac{1}{g_{m1}}$$

$$h_{12} = \left.\frac{\mathbf{v_1}}{\mathbf{v_2}}\right|_{\mathbf{i_1}=0} = 0 \tag{16.23}$$

$$h_{21} = \left.\frac{\mathbf{i_2}}{\mathbf{i_1}}\right|_{\mathbf{v_2}=0} = \frac{g_{m2}r_{\pi2}}{1 + g_{m1}r_{\pi2} + g_{m1}g_{o1}} \cong \frac{\beta_{o2}}{1 + \dfrac{g_{m1}}{g_{m2}}\beta_{o2}} \approx \frac{g_{m2}}{g_{m1}} \approx \frac{I_{C2}}{I_{C1}} = n$$

$$h_{22} = \left.\frac{\mathbf{i_2}}{\mathbf{v_2}}\right|_{\mathbf{i_1}=0} = \frac{1}{r_{o2}}$$

Figure 16.13 shows the two-port model representation for these h-parameters. The bipolar current mirror has an input resistance of $1/g_{m1}$ determined by diode Q_1 and an output resistance equal to r_{o2} of Q_2. The current gain is determined approximately by the emitter-area ratio $n = A_{E2}/A_{E1}$. Be sure to remember to use the correct values of I_{C1} and I_{C2} when calculating the values of the small-signal parameters.

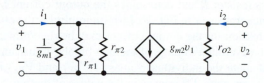

Figure 16.12 Small-signal model for the current mirror.

Figure 16.13 Simplified small-signal model for the current mirror.

Analysis of the MOS current mirror yields similar results [or by simply setting $\beta_{o2} = \infty$ in Eq. (16.23)]:

$$h_{11} = \frac{1}{g_{m1}} \qquad\qquad h_{12} = 0$$

$$h_{21} = \frac{g_{m2}}{g_{m1}} \approx \frac{\left(\dfrac{W}{L}\right)_2}{\left(\dfrac{W}{L}\right)_1} \approx n \qquad h_{22} = \frac{1}{r_{o2}} \qquad (16.24)$$

In this case, the current gain h_{21} is determined by the W/L ratios of the two FETs rather than by the bipolar emitter-area ratio.

> **EXERCISE:** What are the values of I_{C1} and I_{C2} and the small-signal parameters for the current mirror in Fig. 16.3 if $I_{REF} = 100 \ \mu A$, $\beta_{FO} = 50$, $V_A = 50 \ V$, $V_{BE} = 0.7 \ V$, $V_{CE2} = 10 \ V$, and $n = 5$?
>
> **ANSWERS:** 89.4 μA, 529 μA, 280 Ω, 0, 5.92, 113 kΩ

The Widlar Current Source

Resistor R in the **Widlar**[2] **current source** circuit shown in the schematic in Fig. 16.14 gives the designer an additional degree of freedom in adjusting the mirror ratio of the current mirror. In this circuit, the difference in the base-emitter voltages of transistors Q_1 and Q_2

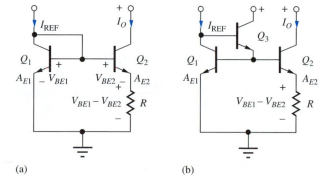

Figure 16.14 (a) Basic Widlar current source and (b) buffered Widlar source.

(a)   (b)

---

[2] Robert Widlar was a famous IC designer who made many lasting contributions to analog IC design. For examples, see references 2 and 3.

appears across resistor R and determines the output current I_O. Transistor Q_3 buffers the mirror reference transistor in Fig. 16.14(b) to minimize the effect of finite current gain.

An expression for the output current may be determined from the standard expressions for the base-emitter voltage of the two bipolar transistors. In this analysis, we must accurately calculate the individual values of V_{BE1} and V_{BE2} because the behavior of the circuit depends on small differences in the values of these two voltages.

Assuming high current gain,

$$V_{BE1} = V_T \ln\left(1 + \frac{I_{\text{REF}}}{I_{S1}}\right) \approx V_T \ln\frac{I_{\text{REF}}}{I_{S1}}$$

and   (16.25)

$$V_{BE2} = V_T \ln\left(1 + \frac{I_O}{I_{S2}}\right) \approx V_T \ln\frac{I_O}{I_{S2}}$$

The current in resistor R is equal to

$$I_{E2} = \frac{V_{BE1} - V_{BE2}}{R} = \frac{V_T}{R} \ln\left(\frac{I_{\text{REF}}}{I_O}\frac{I_{S2}}{I_{S1}}\right) \tag{16.26}$$

If the transistors are matched, then $I_{S1} = (A_{E1}/A)I_{SO}$ and $I_{S2} = (A_{E2}/A)I_{SO}$, and Eq. (16.26) can be rewritten as

$$I_O = \alpha_F I_{E2} \approx \frac{V_T}{R} \ln\left(\frac{I_{\text{REF}}}{I_O}\frac{A_{E2}}{A_{E1}}\right) \tag{16.27}$$

If I_{REF}, R, and the emitter-area ratio are all known, then Eq. (16.27) represents a transcendental equation that must be solved for I_O. The solution can be obtained by iterative trial and error or by using Newton's method.

Widlar Source Output Resistance

The ac model for the Widlar source in Fig. 16.14(a) represents a common-emitter transistor with resistor R in its emitter and a small value of R_{th} ($= 1/g_{m1}$) from diode Q_1 in its base, as indicated in Fig. 16.15. In normal operation, the voltage developed across resistor R is usually small ($\leq 10V_T$). Referring to Table 14.1, or by simplifying Eq. (15.174) for this case, we can reduce the output resistance of the source to

$$R_{\text{OUT}} \approx r_{o2}[1 + g_{m2}R] = r_{o2}\left[1 + \frac{I_O R}{V_T}\right] \tag{16.28}$$

in which $I_O R$ can be found from Eq. (16.27):

$$R_{\text{OUT}} \approx r_{o2}\left[1 + \ln\frac{I_{\text{REF}}}{I_O}\frac{A_{E2}}{A_{E1}}\right] = K r_{o2} \qquad \text{and} \qquad V_{CS} \approx K V_{A2} \tag{16.29}$$

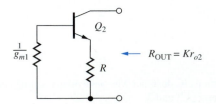

Figure 16.15 Widlar source output resistance − $K = 1 + \ln[(I_{\text{REF}}/I_{C2})(A_{E2}/A_{E1})]$

where
$$K = \left[1 + \ln \frac{I_{\text{REF}}}{I_O} \frac{A_{E2}}{A_{E1}}\right] \tag{16.30}$$

For typical values, $1 < K < 10$.

> **EXERCISE:** What value of R is required to set $I_O = 25\ \mu\text{A}$ if $I_{\text{REF}} = 100\ \mu\text{A}$ and $A_{E2}/A_{E1} = 5$? What are the values of output resistance and K in Eq. (16.29) for this source if $V_A + V_{CE} = 75$ V?
>
> **ANSWERS:** $3000\ \Omega$; $12\ \text{M}\Omega$, 4

> **EXERCISE:** Find the output current in the Widlar source if $I_{\text{REF}} = 100\ \mu\text{A}$, $R = 100\ \Omega$, and $A_{E2} = 10A_{E1}$. What are the values of output resistance and K in Eq. (16.29) for this source if $V_A + V_{CE} = 75$ V?
>
> **ANSWERS:** $301\ \mu\text{A}$; $551\ \text{k}\Omega$, 2.20

The MOS Analog of the Widlar Source

Figure 16.16 is the MOS version of the Widlar source. In this circuit, the difference between the gate-source voltages of transistors M_1 and M_2 appears across resistor R, and I_O can be expressed as

$$I_O = \frac{V_{GS1} - V_{GS2}}{R} = \frac{\sqrt{\dfrac{2I_{\text{REF}}}{K_{n1}}} - \sqrt{\dfrac{2I_O}{K_{n2}}}}{R}$$

or

$$I_O = \frac{1}{R}\sqrt{\frac{2I_{\text{REF}}}{K_{n1}}}\left(1 - \sqrt{\frac{I_O}{I_{\text{REF}}}\frac{(W/L)_1}{(W/L)_2}}\right) \tag{16.31}$$

or dividing through by I_{REF},

$$\frac{I_O}{I_{\text{REF}}} = \frac{1}{R}\sqrt{\frac{2}{K_{n1}I_{\text{REF}}}}\left(1 - \sqrt{\frac{I_O}{I_{\text{REF}}}\frac{(W/L)_1}{(W/L)_2}}\right) \tag{16.32}$$

If I_O is known, then I_{REF} can be calculated directly from Eq. (16.31). If I_{REF}, R, and the W/L ratios are known, then Eq. (16.32) can be written as a quadratic equation in terms

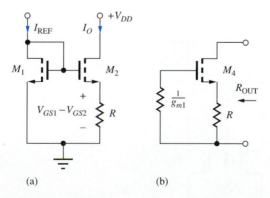

Figure 16.16 (a) MOS Widlar source and (b) small-signal model.

(a)   (b)

of $\sqrt{I_O/I_{\text{REF}}}$:

$$\left(\sqrt{\frac{I_O}{I_{\text{REF}}}}\right)^2 + \frac{1}{R}\sqrt{\frac{2}{K_{n1}I_{\text{REF}}}}\sqrt{\frac{(W/L)_1}{(W/L)_2}}\left(\sqrt{\frac{I_O}{I_{\text{REF}}}}\right) - \frac{1}{R}\sqrt{\frac{2}{K_{n1}I_{\text{REF}}}} = 0 \quad (16.33)$$

MOS Widlar Source Output Resistance

In Fig. 16.16(b), the small-signal model for the MOS Widlar source is recognized as a common-source stage with resistor R in its source. Therefore, from Table 14.1,

$$R_{\text{OUT}} = r_{o2}(1 + g_{m2}R) \quad (16.34)$$

> **EXERCISE:** (a) Find the output current in Fig. 16.16(a) if $I_{\text{REF}} = 200\ \mu\text{A}$, $R = 2\ \text{k}\Omega$, and $K_{n2} = 10K_{n1} = 250\ \mu\text{A/V}^2$. (b) What is R_{OUT} if $\lambda = 0.02/\text{V}$ and $V_{DS} = 10\ \text{V}$?
>
> **ANSWERS:** 764 μA; 176 kΩ

16.3 HIGH-OUTPUT-RESISTANCE CURRENT MIRRORS

In the discussion of differential amplifiers in Chapter 15, we found that current sources with very high output resistances are needed to achieve good CMRR. The basic current mirrors discussed in the previous sections have a figure of merit V_{CS} equal only to V_A or $1/\lambda$; that for the Widlar source is only a few times higher. This section continues our introduction to current mirrors by discussing two additional circuits, the Wilson current source and the cascode current source, which enhance the value of V_{CS} to the order of $\beta_o V_A$ or μ_f/λ.

The Wilson Source

The **Wilson current source** [4] depicted in Fig. 16.17 uses the same number of transistors as the buffered current mirror but achieves much higher output resistance; it is often used in applications requiring precisely matched current sources. The output current is taken from the drain of M_3, and M_1 and M_2 form a current mirror. During circuit operation, the three transistors are all saturated. Because the gate current of M_3 is zero, I_{D2} must equal reference current I_{REF}. If the transistors all have the same W/L ratios, then

$$V_{GS3} = V_{GS1} = V_{GS} \qquad \text{because } I_{D3} = I_{D1} \quad (16.35)$$

The current mirror requires

$$I_{D2} = I_{D1}\frac{1 + 2\lambda V_{GS}}{1 + \lambda V_{GS}} \quad (16.36)$$

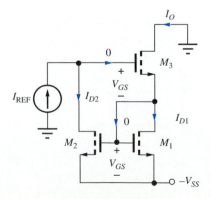

Figure 16.17 MOS Wilson current source.

and because $I_O = I_{D3}$ and $I_{D3} = I_{D1}$, the output current is given by

$$I_O = I_{REF}\frac{1 + \lambda V_{GS}}{1 + 2\lambda V_{GS}} \qquad \text{where } V_{GS} = V_{TN} + \sqrt{\frac{2I_{REF}}{K_n(1 + \lambda V_{GS})}} \qquad (16.37)$$

For small λ, $I_O \approx I_{REF}$. For example, if $\lambda = 0.02/V$ and $V_{GS} = 2$ V, then I_O and I_{REF} differ by 3.7 percent.

The Wilson source actually appeared first in bipolar form as drawn in Fig. 16.18. The circuit operates in a manner similar to the MOS source, except for the loss of current from I_{REF} to the base of Q_3 and the current gain error in the mirror formed by Q_1 and Q_2. Applying KCL at the base of Q_3,

$$I_{REF} = I_{C2} + I_{B3} \qquad (16.38)$$

in which I_{C2} and I_{B3} are related through the current mirror formed by Q_1 and Q_2:

$$I_{C2} = \frac{1 + \dfrac{2V_{BE}}{V_A}}{1 + \dfrac{V_{BE}}{V_A} + \dfrac{2}{\beta_{FO}}}I_{E3} = \frac{1 + \dfrac{2V_{BE}}{V_A}}{1 + \dfrac{V_{BE}}{V_A} + \dfrac{2}{\beta_{FO}}}(\beta_{FO} + 1)I_{B3} \qquad (16.39)$$

Note in Fig. 16.18 that $V_{CE1} = V_{BE}$ and $V_{CE2} = 2V_{BE}$.

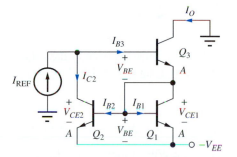

Figure 16.18 Original Wilson current source circuit using BJTs.

Directly combining Eqs. (16.38) and (16.39) yields a messy expression that is difficult to interpret. So, we will consider separately the errors due to finite current gain and Early voltage. First, let us assume that $V_A = \infty$. Combining the simplified forms of Eqs. (16.38) and (16.39) for $V_A = \infty$ yields

$$I_{REF} = \left[\frac{\beta_{FO}(\beta_{FO} + 1)}{\beta_{FO} + 2} + 1\right]I_{B3} \qquad I_O = \beta_{FO}I_{B3} \qquad (16.40)$$

and

$$I_O = \frac{I_{REF}}{1 + \dfrac{2}{\beta_{FO}(\beta_{FO} + 2)}} \qquad (16.41)$$

We can see from Eq. (16.41) that current gain errors are not significant. Q_3 buffers I_{REF} from the mirror transistor base currents in a manner similar to the buffered current mirror. For $\beta_{FO} = 50$, I_O and I_{REF} differ by only 0.1 percent.

For the second case, let us assume that $\beta_{FO} = \infty$. Again combining simplified forms of Eqs. (16.38) and (16.39) yields

$$I_O = I_{REF}\frac{1 + \dfrac{V_{BE}}{V_A}}{1 + \dfrac{2V_{BE}}{V_A}} \qquad (16.42)$$

For $V_{BE} = 0.7$ V and $V_A = 60$, $I_O = 0.989 I_{REF}$, representing approximately a 1 percent error.

The errors due to drain-source voltage mismatch in Fig. 16.17, or collector-emitter voltage mismatch in Fig. 16.18, may still be too large for use in precision circuits, but this problem can be significantly reduced by adding one more transistor to balance the circuit. In Fig. 16.19, transistor Q_4 reduces the collector-emitter voltage of Q_2 by one V_{BE} drop and balances the collector-emitter voltages of Q_1 and Q_2:

$$V_{CE2} = V_{BE1} + V_{BE2} - V_{BE4} = V_{BE} + V_{BE} - V_{BE} = V_{BE} \qquad (16.43)$$

All four transistors are operating at approximately the same value of collector current, and the values of V_{BE} are all the same if the devices are matched with equal emitter areas.

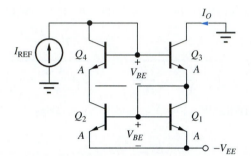

Figure 16.19 Wilson source using balanced collector-emitter voltages.

EXERCISE: Draw a voltage-balanced version of the MOS Wilson source by adding one additional transistor to the circuit in Fig. 16.17.

ANSWER: See Prob. 16.28

Output Resistance of the Wilson Source

The primary advantage of the Wilson source over the standard current mirror is its greatly increased output resistance. The small-signal model for the MOS version of the Wilson source is given in Fig. 16.20, in which test current i_x is applied to determine the output resistance.

The current mirror formed by transistors M_1 and M_2 is represented by its simplified two-port model assuming $n = 1$. The voltage v_x is determined from

$$\mathbf{v_x} = \mathbf{v_3} + \mathbf{v_1} = [\mathbf{i_x} - g_{m3}\mathbf{v_{gs}}]r_{o3} + \mathbf{v_1} \qquad (16.44)$$

where

$$\mathbf{v_{gs}} = \mathbf{v_2} - \mathbf{v_1} \qquad \text{with } \mathbf{v_1} = \frac{\mathbf{i_x}}{g_{m1}} \text{ and } \mathbf{v_2} = -\mu_{f2}\mathbf{v_1} \qquad (16.45)$$

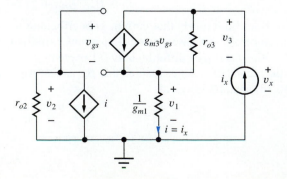

Figure 16.20 Small-signal model for the MOS version of the Wilson source.

Combining these equations, and recognizing that $g_{m1} = g_{m2}$ for $n = 1$ yields

$$R_{OUT} = \frac{\mathbf{v_x}}{\mathbf{i_x}} = r_{o3}\left[\mu_{f2} + 2 + \frac{1}{\mu_{f2}}\right] \approx \mu_{f2}r_{o3} \tag{16.46}$$

and

$$V_{CS} = I_{D3}\mu_{f2}\frac{1 + \lambda_3 V_{DS3}}{\lambda_3 I_{D3}} \approx \frac{\mu_{f2}}{\lambda_3} \tag{16.47}$$

Analysis of the bipolar source is somewhat more complex because of the finite current gain of the BJT and yields the following result:

$$R_{OUT} \approx \frac{\beta_{o3}r_{o3}}{2} \quad \text{and} \quad V_{CS} \approx \frac{\beta_o V_A}{2} \tag{16.48}$$

Derivation of this equation is left for Prob. 16.26.

> **EXERCISE:** Calculate R_{OUT} for the Wilson source in Fig. 16.18 if $\beta_F = 150$, $V_A = 50$ V, $V_{EE} = 15$ V, and $I_O = I_{REF} = 50\ \mu$A. What would be the output resistance of a standard current mirror operating at the same current?
>
> **ANSWER:** 96.6 MΩ versus 1.30 MΩ

Cascode Current Sources

We learned in Chapter 15 that the output resistance of the cascode connection (C-E/C-B cascade) of two transistors is very high, approaching $\mu_f r_o$ for the FET case and $\beta_o r_o$ for the BJT circuit. Figure 16.21 shows the implementation of the MOS and BJT **cascode current sources** using current mirrors.

In the MOS circuit in Fig. 16.21(a), $I_{D1} = I_{D3} = I_{REF}$. The current mirror formed by M_1 and M_2 forces the output current to be approximately equal to the reference current because $I_O = I_{D4} = I_{D2}$. Diode-connected transistor M_3 provides a dc bias voltage to the gate of M_4 and balances V_{DS1} and V_{DS2}. If all transistors are matched with the same W/L ratios, then the values of V_{GS} are all the same, and V_{DS2} equals V_{DS1}:

$$V_{DS2} = V_{GS1} + V_{GS3} - V_{GS4} = V_{GS} + V_{GS} - V_{GS} = V_{GS} = V_{DS1} \tag{16.49}$$

Thus the M_1-M_2 current mirror is precisely balanced, and $I_O = I_{REF}$.

The BJT source in Fig. 16.21(b) operates in the same manner. For $\beta_F = \infty$, $I_{REF} = I_{C3} = I_{C1}$ on the reference side of the source. Q_1 and Q_2 form a current mirror, which sets $I_O = I_{C4} = I_{C2} = I_{C1} = I_{REF}$. Diode Q_3 provides the bias voltage at the base of Q_4 needed to keep Q_2 in the forward-active region and balances the collector-emitter voltages of the current mirror:

$$V_{CE2} = V_{BE1} + V_{BE3} - V_{BE4} = 2V_{BE} - V_{BE} = V_{BE} = V_{CE1} \tag{16.50}$$

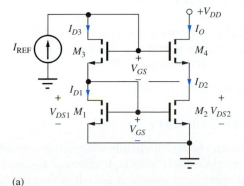

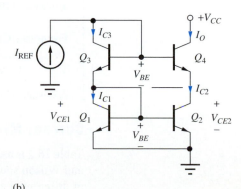

Figure 16.21 (a) MOS and (b) BJT cascode current sources.

(a)

(b)

Output Resistance of the Cascode Sources

Figure 16.22 shows the small-signal model for the MOS cascode source; the two-port model has been used for the current mirror formed of transistors M_1 and M_2. Because current i represents the gate current of M_4, which is zero, the circuit can be reduced to that in Fig. 16.22(b), which should be recognized as a common-emitter stage with resistor r_{o2} in its source. Thus, its output resistance is

$$R_{\text{OUT}} = r_{o4}(1 + g_{m4}r_{o2}) \approx \mu_{f4}r_{o2} \qquad \text{and} \qquad V_{CS} \approx \frac{\mu_{f4}}{\lambda_2} \approx \frac{\mu_{f4}}{\lambda_4} \quad (16.51)$$

Analysis of the output resistance of the BJT source in Fig. 16.23 is again more complex because of the finite current gain of the BJT. If the base of Q_4 were grounded, then the output resistance would be just equal to that of the cascode stage, $\beta_o r_o$. However, the base current i_b of Q_4 enters the current mirror, doubles the output current, and causes the overall output resistance to be reduced by a factor of 2:

$$R_{\text{OUT}} \approx \frac{\beta_{o4}r_{o4}}{2} \qquad \text{and} \qquad V_{CS} \approx \frac{\beta_{o4}V_{A4}}{2} \quad (16.52)$$

Detailed calculation of this result is left as Prob. 16.40.

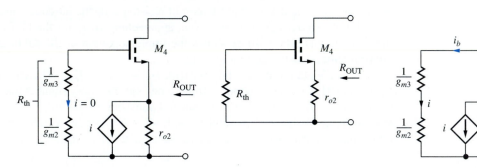

Figure 16.22 Small-signal model for the MOS cascode source.

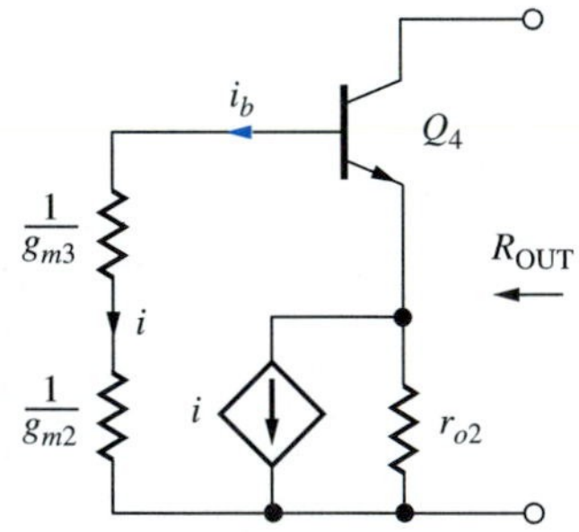

Figure 16.23 Small-signal model for the BJT cascode source.

EXERCISE: Calculate the output resistance of the MOS cascode current source in Fig. 16.21(a) and compare it to that of a standard current mirror if $I_O = I_{\text{REF}} = 50\ \mu\text{A}$, $V_{DD} = 15$ V, $K_n = 250\ \mu\text{A/V}^2$, $V_{TN} = 0.8$ V, and $\lambda = 0.015$ V^{-1}.

ANSWER: 379 MΩ versus 1.63 MΩ

EXERCISE: Calculate the output resistance of the BJT cascode current source in Fig. 16.21(b) and compare it to that of a standard current mirror if $I_O = I_{\text{REF}} = 50\ \mu\text{A}$, $V_{CC} = 15$ V, $\beta_o = 100$, and $V_A = 67$ V.

ANSWER: 81.3 MΩ versus 1.63 MΩ

Current Mirror Summary

Table 16.2 is a summary of the current mirror circuits discussed in this chapter. The cascode and Wilson sources can achieve very high values of V_{CS} and often find use in the design of differential and operational amplifiers as well as in many other analog circuits.

Table 16.2

Comparison of the Basic Current Mirrors

Type of Source	R_{OUT}	V_{CS}	Typical Values of V_{CS}
Resistor	R	V_{EE}	15 V
Two-transistor mirror	r_o	V_A or $\dfrac{1}{\lambda}$	50 V
Cascode BJT	$\dfrac{\beta_o r_o}{2}$	$\dfrac{\beta_o V_A}{2}$	2500 V
Cascode FET	$\mu_f r_o$	$\dfrac{\mu_f}{\lambda}$	5000 V
BJT Wilson	$\dfrac{\beta_o r_o}{2}$	$\dfrac{\beta_o V_A}{2}$	2500 V
FET Wilson	$\mu_f r_o$	$\dfrac{\mu_f}{\lambda}$	5000 V

16.4 REFERENCE CURRENT GENERATION

A **reference current** is required by all the current mirrors that have been discussed. The least complicated method for establishing this reference current is to use resistor R, as shown in Fig. 16.24(a).

However, the source's output current is directly proportional to the supply voltage V_{EE}:

$$I_{REF} = \frac{V_{EE} - V_{BE}}{R} \tag{16.53}$$

In MOS technology, the gate-source voltages of MOSFETs can be designed to be large, and several MOS devices can be connected in series between the power supplies to eliminate the need for large-value resistors. An example of this technique is given in Fig. 16.24(b), in which

$$V_{DD} + V_{SS} = V_{SG4} + V_{GS3} + V_{GS1} \tag{16.54}$$

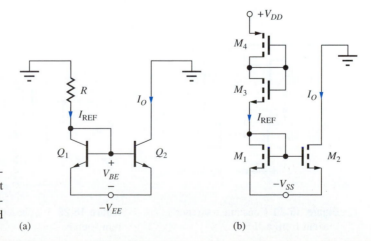

Figure 16.24 Reference current generation for current mirrors: (a) resistor reference and (b) series-connected MOSFETs.

(a)

(b)

and the drain currents must satisfy $I_{D1} = I_{D3} = I_{D4}$. However, any change in the supply voltages directly alters the values of the gate-source voltages of the three MOS transistors and again changes the reference current. Note that the series device technique is not usable in bipolar technology because of the small fixed voltage (≈ 0.7 V) developed across each diode.

In most cases, the supply voltage dependence of I_{REF} is undesirable. For example, we would like to fix the bias points of the devices in general-purpose op amps, even though they must operate from power supply voltages ranging from ± 3 V to ± 22 V. In addition, Eq. (16.53) indicates that relatively large values of resistance are required to achieve small operating currents, and these resistors use significant area in integrated circuits, as was discussed in detail in Sec. 7.1, Chapter 7. Thus, a number of circuit techniques that yield currents relatively independent of the power supply voltages have been invented.

> **EXERCISE:** What is the reference current in Fig. 16.24(a) if $R = 43$ kΩ and $V_{EE} = -5$ V? (b) If $V_{EE} = -7.5$ V?
>
> **ANSWERS:** 100 μA; 158 μA
>
> **EXERCISE:** What is the reference current in Fig. 16.24(b) if $K_n = K_p = 400$ μA/V^2, $V_{TN} = -V_{TP} = 1$ V, and $V_{SS} = -5$ V? (b) If $V_{SS} = -7.5$ V?
>
> **ANSWERS:** 88.9 μA; 450 μA. *Note:* the variation is worse than in the resistor bias case because of the square-law MOSFET characteristic.

Supply-Independent Biasing

Some bipolar technologies offer the capability of fabricating p-channel JFETs, which can be used to set a fixed reference current, as shown in Fig. 16.25. For this circuit, the JFET is operating with $V_{SG} = 0$, and therefore $I_D = I_{DSS}$, assuming that V_{SD} is large enough to pinch off the JFET. In MOS technology, depletion-mode devices can be used in a similar manner, if available. However, because both these circuit techniques require special IC processes and therefore lack generality, other methods are preferred.

A V_{BE}-Based Reference

One possibility is the **V_{BE}-based reference,** shown in Fig. 16.26, in which the output current is determined by the base-emitter voltage of Q_1. For high current gain, the collector current of Q_1 is equal to the current through resistor R_1,

$$I_{C1} = \frac{V_{EE} - V_{BE1} - V_{BE2}}{R_1} \approx \frac{V_{EE} - 1.4 \text{ V}}{R_1} \qquad (16.55)$$

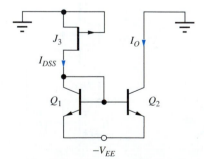

Figure 16.25 Constant reference current from a JFET.

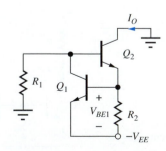

Figure 16.26 V_{BE}-based current source.

and the output current I_O is approximately equal to the current in R_2:

$$I_O = \alpha_{F2} I_{E2} = \alpha_{F2}\left(\frac{V_{BE1}}{R_2} + I_{B1}\right) \approx \frac{V_{BE1}}{R_2} \approx \frac{0.7\text{V}}{R_2} \tag{16.56}$$

Rewriting V_{BE1} in terms of V_{EE},

$$I_O \approx \frac{V_T}{R_2} \ln \frac{V_{EE} - 1.4 \text{ V}}{I_{S1} R_1} \tag{16.57}$$

A substantial degree of supply-voltage independence has been achieved because the output current is now only logarithmically dependent on changes in the supply voltage V_{EE}.

> **EXERCISE:** (a) Calculate I_O in Fig. 16.26 for $I_S = 10^{-16}$ A, $R_1 = 39\,\text{k}\Omega$, $R_2 = 6.8\,\text{k}\Omega$, and $V_{EE} = -5$ V. Assume infinite current gains. (b) Repeat for $V_{EE} = -7.5$ V.
>
> **ANSWERS:** 101 μA; 103 μA

The Widlar Source

Actually, we already discussed another source that achieves a similar independence from power supply voltage variations. The expression for the output current of the Widlar source given in Eq. (16.27) is

$$I_O = \alpha_F I_{E2} \approx \frac{V_T}{R} \ln\left(\frac{I_{\text{REF}}}{I_O} \frac{A_{E2}}{A_{E1}}\right) \tag{16.58}$$

Here again, the output current is only logarithmically dependent on the reference current I_{REF} (which may be proportional to V_{CC}).

Power-Supply Independent Bias Cell

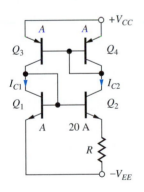

Figure 16.27 Power-supply independent bias circuit using the Widlar source and a current mirror.

Bias circuits with an even greater degree of power supply voltage independence can be obtained by combining the Widlar source with a standard current mirror, as indicated in the circuit in Fig. 16.27. Assuming high current gain, the *pnp* current mirror forces the currents on the two sides of the reference cell to be equal—that is, $I_{C1} = I_{C2}$. In addition, the emitter-area ratio of the Widlar source in Fig. 16.27 is equal to 20.

With these constraints, Eq. (16.58) can be satisfied by only one operating point:

$$I_{C2} \approx \frac{V_T}{R} \ln(20) = \frac{0.0749 \text{ V}}{R} \tag{16.59}$$

In this example, a fixed voltage of approximately 75 mV is developed across resistor R, and this voltage is independent of the power supply voltages. Resistor R can then be chosen to yield the desired operating current.

Obviously, a wide range of mirror ratios and emitter-area ratios can be used in the design of the circuit in Fig. 16.27. Although the current, once established, is independent of supply voltage, the actual value of I_C still depends on the absolute value of R and varies with run-to-run process variations.

Unfortunately, $I_{C1} = I_{C2} = 0$ is also a stable operating point for the circuit in Fig. 16.27. **Start-up circuits** must be included in IC realizations of this reference to see that the circuit reaches the desired operating point.

> **EXERCISE:** Find the output current in the current source in Fig. 16.27 if $A_{E3} = 10A_{E4}$, $A_{E2} = 10A_{E1}$, and $R = 1\,\text{k}\Omega$.
>
> **ANSWER:** 115 μA

Once the current has been established in the reference cell consisting of Q_1–Q_4 in Fig. 16.27, the base-emitter voltages of Q_1 and Q_4 can be used as reference voltages for other current mirrors, as shown in Fig. 16.28. In this figure, buffered current mirrors have been used in the reference cell to minimize errors associated with finite current gains of the *npn* and *pnp* transistors. Output currents are shown generated from basic mirror transistors Q_5 and Q_7 and from Widlar sources, Q_6 and Q_8.

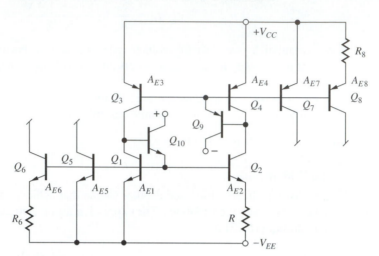

Figure 16.28 Multiple source currents generated from the supply-independent cell.

A Supply-Independent MOS Reference Cell

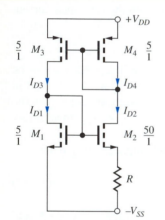

Figure 16.29 Supply-independent current source using MOS transistors.

The MOS analog of the circuit in Fig. 16.27 appears in Fig. 16.29. In this circuit, the PMOS current mirror forces a fixed relationship between drain currents I_{D3} and I_{D4}. For the particular case in Fig. 16.29, $I_{D3} = I_{D4}$, and so $I_{D1} = I_{D2}$. Substituting this constraint into Eq. (16.32) yields an equation for the value of R required to establish a given current I_{D2}:

$$R = \sqrt{\frac{2}{K_{n1}I_{D2}}}\left(1 - \sqrt{\frac{(W/L)_1}{(W/L)_2}}\right) \tag{16.60}$$

Based on Eq. (16.60), we see that the MOS source is independent of supply voltage but is a function of the absolute values of R and K'_n.

> **EXERCISE:** What value of R is required in the current source in Fig. 16.29 if I_{D2} is to be designed to be 100 μA and $K'_n = 25$ μA/V^2?
>
> **ANSWER:** 8.65 kΩ

Variation of Reference Cell Current with Power Supply Variations

Analysis of the bias circuits in this section has ignored the influence of the output resistance of the transistors, and the current is actually affected somewhat by changes in the power supply voltages. For small changes in supply voltages, the small-signal models of the circuit in Fig. 16.30(a) can be used to relate the changes in cell currents to the changes in power supply voltages. These two circuits are redrawn in simplified form in Fig. 16.30(b), in which resistor R has been absorbed into the model for transistor M_2 or Q_2 (see Prob. 16.119). Source v_x represents the total change in the supply voltages

$$v_x = \Delta V_{CC} + \Delta V_{EE} \qquad \text{or} \qquad v_x = \Delta V_{DD} + \Delta V_{SS} \tag{16.61}$$

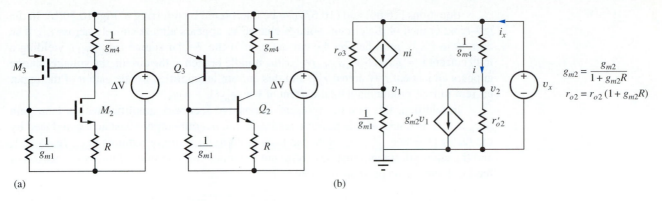

Figure 16.30 (a) Small-signal models for the reference cell current variations. (b) Simplified small-signal model.

and the current i_x is expressed as

$$\mathbf{i_x} = g_{m1}\mathbf{v_1} + g'_{m2}\mathbf{v_1} + g'_{o2}\mathbf{v_2} = (g_{m1} + g'_{m2})\mathbf{v_1} + g'_{o2}\mathbf{v_2} \qquad (16.62)$$

Node voltages $\mathbf{v_1}$ and $\mathbf{v_2}$ must both be found in order to determine $\mathbf{i_x}$.

Writing the nodal equations for the circuit using $i = g_{m4}(\mathbf{v_x} - \mathbf{v_2})$ and collecting terms,

$$(ng_{m4} + g_{o3})\mathbf{v_x} = (g_{m1} + g_{o3})\mathbf{v_1} + ng_{m4}\mathbf{v_2}$$
$$g_{m4}\mathbf{v_x} = g'_{m2}\mathbf{v_1} + (g_{m4} + g'_{o2})\mathbf{v_2} \qquad (16.63)$$

Calculating the determinant of this system of equations yields

$$\Delta = g_{m1}g_{m4}\left[1 - n\frac{g'_{m2}}{g_{m1}}\right] + O\left[\frac{g_m^2}{\mu_F}\right]^1 \qquad (16.64)$$

Solving Eq. (16.63) for $\mathbf{v_1}$ and $\mathbf{v_2}$ yields:

$$\mathbf{v_1} = \left[g_{m4}(g_{o3} + ng'_{o2}) + O\left(\frac{g_m g_o}{\mu_f}\right)\right]\frac{\mathbf{v_x}}{\Delta}$$
$$\mathbf{v_2} = \left[g_{m1}g_{m4}\left(1 - n\frac{g'_{m2}}{g_{m1}}\right) + O\left(\frac{g_m^2}{\mu_f}\right)\right]\frac{\mathbf{v_x}}{\Delta} \qquad (16.65)$$

Substituting the results from Eqs. (16.64) and (16.65) into Eq. (16.62) produces

$$\frac{\mathbf{i_x}}{\mathbf{v_x}} = \frac{g_{o3}\left(1 + \frac{g'_{m2}}{g_{m1}}\right) + g_{o2}(1 + n)}{1 - n\frac{g'_{m2}}{g_{m1}}} \qquad (16.66)$$

Equation (16.66) represents the sum of two conductance terms, and therefore the output resistance can be represented as the parallel combination of two equivalent resistances:

$$R_O = \left(\frac{r_{o3}}{1 + \frac{g'_{m2}}{g_{m1}}} \middle\| \frac{r'_{o2}}{1 + n}\right)\left(1 - n\frac{g'_{m2}}{g_{m1}}\right) \qquad \text{for } n\frac{g'_{m2}}{g_{m1}} < 1 \qquad (16.67)$$

[1]$O(x)$ = terms of the order of x.

Equations (16.66) and (16.67) can be interpreted by referring to Fig. 16.30(b). In the left-hand branch of the circuit, voltage change $\mathbf{v_x}$ appears almost entirely across r_{o3}. The current in r_{o3} is amplified by the current gain of the Widlar source (g'_{m2}/g_{m1}), yielding a total current $\mathbf{i} = g_{o3}(1 + g'_{m2}/g_{m1})\mathbf{v_x}$. In the middle branch of the circuit, the voltage change appears almost entirely across r'_{o2}, and this current is amplified by the gain n of the upper current mirror, producing a total current of $\mathbf{i} = g'_{o2}(1 + n)\mathbf{v_x}$.

In addition, this circuit represents a positive feedback amplifier with a loop gain $n(g'_{m2}/g_{m1})$. Because of this positive feedback, the overall output resistance is reduced by the factor $[1 - n(g'_{m2}/g_{m1})]$. Note carefully that circuit stability requires $n(g'_{m2}/g_{m1}) < 1$, and the circuit designer must be careful not to violate this condition. Further discussion of feedback circuits is postponed to Chapter 18.

EXERCISE: What is the output resistance of the source in Fig. 16.29 if $R = 8.65$ kΩ and $I_{D2} = 100$ μA? Assume $K'_n = 25$ μA/V^2, $K'_p = 10$ μA/V^2, $V_{TN} = -V_{TP} = 0.75$ V, and $1/\lambda = 80$ V.

ANSWER: 148 kΩ

EXERCISE: Simulate the circuit in Fig. 16.29 and determine I_{D2} and the output resistance of the source. (*Suggestion:* Make use of .TF)

ANSWER: 97.8 μA, 184 kΩ

Equation (16.67) indicates that the output resistances r'_{o2} and r_{o3} of the Widlar source and current mirror determine the resistance to power supply variations. R_O can be improved by increasing these two resistance values. Figure 16.31 shows improved versions of the supply-independent reference current cells in which cascode sources have been used to improve the output resistance of the Widlar portion of the cell, and Wilson sources have been used to improve the output resistance of the current mirrors.

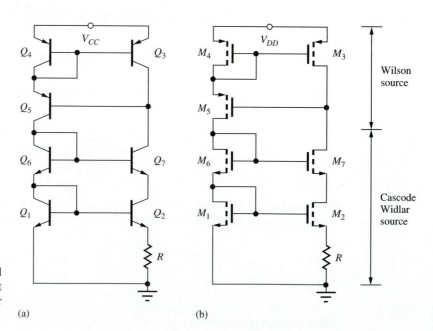

Figure 16.31 (a) Bipolar and (b) MOS reference current cells with improved power supply rejection.

16.5 THE CURRENT MIRROR AS AN ACTIVE LOAD

One of the most important applications of the current mirror is as a replacement for the load resistors of differential amplifier stages in IC operational amplifiers. This elegant application of the current mirror can greatly improve amplifier voltage gain while maintaining the operating-point balance necessary for good common-mode rejection and low offset voltage. When used in this manner, the current mirror is referred to as an **active load** because the passive load resistors have been replaced with active transistor circuit elements.

CMOS Differential Amplifier with Active Load

Figure 16.32 shows a CMOS differential amplifier with an active load; the load resistors have been replaced by a PMOS current mirror. Let us first study the quiescent operating point of this circuit and then look at its small-signal characteristics. Assume for the moment that the amplifier is balanced (in fact, it will turn out that it *is* balanced). Then bias current I_{SS} divides equally between transistors M_1 and M_2, and I_{D1} and I_{D2} are each equal to $I_{SS}/2$. Current I_{D3} must equal I_{D1} and is mirrored as I_{D4} at the output of the PMOS current mirror. Thus, I_{D3} and I_{D4} are also equal to $I_{SS}/2$, and the current in the drain of M_4 is exactly the current required to satisfy M_2.

The mirror ratio set by M_3 and M_4 is exactly unity when $V_{SD4} = V_{SD3}$ and hence $V_{DS1} = V_{DS2}$. Thus, the differential amplifier is completely balanced at dc when the quiescent output voltage is

$$V_O = V_{DD} - V_{SD4} = V_{DD} - V_{SG3} = V_{DD} - \left(\sqrt{\frac{I_{SS}}{K_p}} - V_{TP} \right) \qquad (16.68)$$

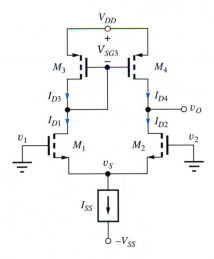

Figure 16.32 CMOS differential amplifier with PMOS active load.

Q-Points

The drain-source voltages of M_1 and M_2 are

$$V_{DS1} = V_O - V_S = V_{DD} - \left(\sqrt{\frac{I_{SS}}{K_p}} - V_{TP} \right) + \left(V_{TN} + \sqrt{\frac{I_{SS}}{K_n}} \right)$$

or

$$V_{DS1} = V_{DD} + V_{TN} + V_{TP} + \sqrt{\frac{I_{SS}}{K_n}} - \sqrt{\frac{I_{SS}}{K_p}} \approx V_{DD} \qquad (16.69)$$

and those of M_3 and M_4 are

$$V_{SD3} = V_{SG3} = \sqrt{\frac{I_{SS}}{K_p}} - V_{TP} \tag{16.70}$$

The drain currents of all the transistors are equal:

$$I_{DS1} = I_{DS2} = I_{SD3} = I_{SD4} = \frac{I_{SS}}{2} \tag{16.71}$$

(Remember that $V_{TP} < 0$ for p-channel enhancement-mode devices.)

Differential-Mode Signal Analysis

Analysis of the ac behavior of the differential amplifier begins with the differential-mode input applied in the ac circuit model in Fig. 16.33. The NMOS differential pair produces equal and opposite currents with amplitude $g_{m2}v_{id}/2$ at the drains of M_1 and M_2. Drain current i_{d1} is supplied by current mirror transistor M_3 and is replicated at the output of M_4. Thus the total current i_o in the load R_L is expressed as

$$\mathbf{i_o} = 2\frac{g_{m2}\mathbf{v_{id}}}{2} = g_{m2}\mathbf{v_{id}} \tag{16.72}$$

and the output voltage is

$$\mathbf{v_o} = \mathbf{i_o}R_L = (g_{m2}R_L)\mathbf{v_{id}} \quad \text{and} \quad A_{dd} = \frac{\mathbf{v_o}}{\mathbf{v_{id}}} = g_{m2}R_L \tag{16.73}$$

The current mirror provides a single-ended output but with a transconductance equivalent to the full value of the C-S amplifier!

The real power of this stage becomes apparent when R_L is replaced by another MOSFET connected to the output, such as transistor M_5 in the prototype op amp in Fig. 16.34. Here the only path for the total current $\mathbf{i_o}$ is back into output resistances r_{o2} and r_{o4} of M_2 and M_4. It will be shown in the next section that the resistance at node 1 is equivalent to the parallel combination of the output resistances of transistors M_2 and M_4:

$$R_{OD} = r_{o2} \parallel r_{o4} \tag{16.74}$$

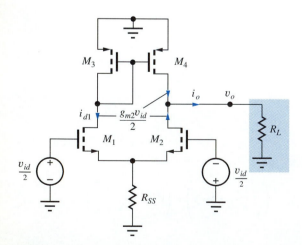

Figure 16.33 CMOS differential amplifier with differential-mode input.

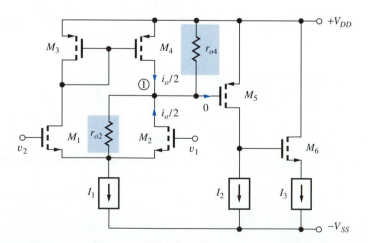

Figure 16.34 Simple CMOS op amp with active load in the first stage.

and the gain of the differential input stage becomes

$$A_{dd} = g_{m2}(r_{o2} \| r_{o4}) = \frac{\mu_{f2}}{1 + \dfrac{r_{o2}}{r_{o4}}} \approx \frac{\mu_{f2}}{2} \tag{16.75}$$

Equation (16.75) indicates that the gain of the input stage of the amplifier approaches one-half the amplification factor of the transistors forming the differential pair. We are now within a factor of 2 of the theoretical voltage gain limit. We will return to explore the characteristics of the overall operational amplifier in Fig. 16.34 in more detail in Sec. 16.6.

Output Resistance of the Differential Amplifier

The origin of the output resistance expression in Eq. (16.74) can be thought of conceptually in the following (although technically incorrect) manner. At node 1 in Fig. 16.34, r_{o4} is connected directly to ac ground at the positive power supply, whereas r_{o2} appears connected to virtual ground at the sources of M_2 and M_1. Thus r_{o2} and r_{o4} are effectively in parallel. Although this argument gives the correct answer, it is not precisely correct. Because the differential amplifier with active load no longer represents a truly symmetric circuit, the node at the sources of M_1 and M_2 *is not* truly a virtual ground.

Exact Analysis

A more precise analysis can be obtained from the circuit in Fig. 16.35. The output resistance r_{o4} of M_4 is indeed connected directly to ac ground and represents one component of the output resistance. However, the current from v_x due to r_{o2} is more complicated. The actual behavior can be determined from Fig. 16.35, in which R_{SS} is assumed to be negligible with respect to $1/g_{m1}$, $R_{SS} \gg 1/g_{m1}$.

Transistor M_2 is operating as a common-gate transistor with an effective resistance in its source of $R_S = 1/g_{m1}$. Based on the results in Table 14.1, the resistance looking into the drain of M_2 is

$$R_{O2} = r_{o2}(1 + g_{m2}R_S) = r_{o2}\left(1 + g_{m2}\frac{1}{g_{m1}}\right) = 2r_{o2} \tag{16.76}$$

Therefore, the drain current of M_2 is equal to $\mathbf{v_x}/2r_{o2}$. However, the current goes around the differential pair and into the input of the current mirror at M_3. The current is replicated by the mirror to become the drain current of M_4. The total current from source v_x becomes $2(\mathbf{v_x}/2r_{o2}) = \mathbf{v_x}/r_{o2}$. Combining this current with the current through r_{o4} yields a total

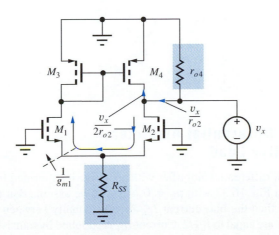

Figure 16.35 Output resistance component due to r_{o2}.

current of

$$i_x^T = \frac{v_x}{r_{o2}} + \frac{v_x}{r_{o4}} \qquad \text{and} \qquad R_{OD} = r_{o2} \parallel r_{o4} \tag{16.77}$$

The equivalent resistance at the output node is, in fact, exactly equal to the parallel combination of the output resistances of M_2 and M_4.

> **EXERCISE:** Find the Q-points of the transistors in Fig. 16.32 if $I_{SS} = 250$ μA, $K_n = 250$ μA/V², $K_p = 200$ μA/V², $V_{TN} = -V_{TP} = 0.75$ V, and $V_{DD} = V_{SS} = 5$ V. What are the transconductance, output resistance, and voltage gain of the amplifier if $\lambda = 0.0133$ V⁻¹?
>
> **ANSWERS:** (125 μA, 4.88 V), (125 μA, 1.87 V); 250 μS, 314 kΩ, 78.5

Common-Mode Input Signals

Figure 16.36 is the CMOS differential amplifier with a common-mode input signal. The common-mode input voltage causes a common-mode current i_{ic} in both sides of the differential pair consisting of M_1 and M_2:

$$i_{ic} = \frac{g_{m1}}{1 + 2g_{m1}R_{ss}} v_{ic} \approx \frac{v_{ic}}{2R_{ss}} \tag{16.78}$$

The current from M_1 is supplied by mirror reference transistor M_3, is replicated, and exits the drain of transistor M_4, thereby supplying exactly the common-mode signal current required by the drain of M_2. Thus, the output current i_o and voltage v_o are both zero, as is the common-mode conversion gain A_{cd}. Because the ideal common-mode gain is zero, the CMRR is infinite. In an actual amplifier, the common-mode conversion gain is determined by small imbalances in the transistors and overall symmetry of the amplifier and is nonzero.

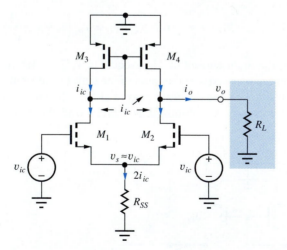

Figure 16.36 CMOS differential amplifier with common-mode input.

Bipolar Differential Amplifier with Active Load

The bipolar differential amplifier with an active load formed from a *pnp* current mirror is depicted in Fig. 16.37 with $v_1 = 0 = v_2$. If we assume that the circuit is balanced with $\beta_{FO} = \infty$, then the bias current I_{EE} divides equally between transistors Q_1 and Q_2, and I_{C1} and I_{C2} are equal to $I_{EE}/2$. Current I_{C1} is supplied by transistor Q_3 and is mirrored as I_{C4}

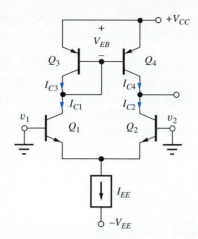

Figure 16.37 Bipolar differential amplifier with active load.

at the output of *pnp* transistor Q_4. Thus, I_{C3} and I_{C4} are both also equal to $I_{EE}/2$, and the dc current in the collector of Q_4 is exactly the current required to satisfy Q_2.

If β_{FO} is very large, then the current mirror ratio is exactly 1 when $V_{EC4} = V_{EC3} = V_{EB}$, and the differential amplifier is completely balanced when the quiescent output voltage is

$$V_O = V_{CC} - V_{EB} \tag{16.79}$$

Q-Points

The collector currents of all the transistors are equal:

$$I_{C1} = I_{C2} = I_{C3} = I_{C4} = \frac{I_{EE}}{2} \tag{16.80}$$

The collector-emitter voltages of Q_1 and Q_2 are

$$V_{CE1} = V_{CE2} = V_C - V_E = (V_{CC} - V_{EB}) - (-V_{BE}) \approx V_{CC} \tag{16.81}$$

and for Q_3 and Q_4,

$$V_{EC3} = V_{EC4} = V_{EB} \tag{16.82}$$

Finite Current Gain

The current gain defect in the current mirror upsets the dc balance of the circuit. However, as long as the transistors remain in the forward-active region, the collector current of Q_4 must equal the collector current of Q_2, and the collector-emitter voltage of Q_4 adjusts itself to make up for the current-gain defect of the current mirror. The required value of V_{EC4} can be found using the current mirror expression from Eq. (16.6):

$$I_{C4} = I_{C1} \frac{\left[1 + \dfrac{V_{EC4}}{V_A}\right]}{\left[1 + \dfrac{V_{EB}}{V_A} + \dfrac{2}{\beta_{FO4}}\right]} \tag{16.83}$$

However, because $I_{C4} = I_{C2}$ and $I_{C2} = I_{C1}$, the mirror ratio must be unity, which requires

$$V_{EC4} = V_{EB} + \frac{2V_A}{\beta_{FO4}} \tag{16.84}$$

For $\beta_{FO3} = 50$, $V_A = 60$ V, and $V_{EB} = 0.7$ V, $V_{EC4} = 3.10$ V.

This collector-emitter voltage difference represents a substantial offset at the amplifier output and translates to an equivalent input offset voltage of

$$V_{OS} = \frac{V_{EC4} - V_{EC3}}{A_{dd}} = \frac{V_{EC4} - V_{EB}}{A_{dd}} \qquad (16.85)$$

V_{OS} represents the input voltage needed to force the output voltage differential to be zero. For $A_{dd} = 100$, V_{OS} would be 24.0 mV. To eliminate this error, a buffered current mirror is usually used as the active load, as shown in Fig. 16.38.

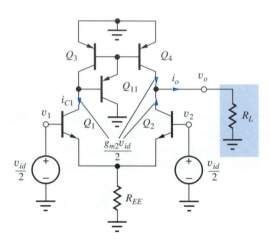

Figure 16.38 BJT differential amplifier with differential-mode input.

EXERCISE: Calculate the dc value of V_{EC4} if the circuit buffered current mirror replaces the active load in Fig. 16.37. What is V_{OS} if $A_{dd} = 100$?

ANSWERS: $V_{EC4} = 1.25$ V and $\Delta V_{EC} = 47$ mV; $V_{OS} = 0.47$ mV

It should be noted that Eq. (16.84) actually overestimates the value of V_{EC4} because the increase in V_{EC4} decreases V_{CE2} and thereby reduces I_{C2}.

Differential-Mode Signal Analysis

Analysis of the ac behavior of the differential amplifier begins with the differential-mode input applied in the ac circuit model in Fig. 16.38. The differential input pair produces equal and opposite currents with amplitude $g_{m2}v_{id}/2$ at the collectors of Q_1 and Q_2. Collector current i_{c1} is supplied by Q_3 and is replicated at the output of Q_4. Thus the total current i_o in the load R_L is equal to

$$\mathbf{i_o} = 2\frac{g_{m2}\mathbf{v_{id}}}{2} = g_{m2}\mathbf{v_{id}} \qquad (16.86)$$

The output voltage is

$$\mathbf{v_o} = \mathbf{i_o}R_L = (g_{m2}R_L)\mathbf{v_{id}} \qquad (16.87)$$

and

$$A_{dd} = \frac{\mathbf{v_o}}{\mathbf{v_{dm}}} = g_{m2}R_L \qquad (16.88)$$

The current mirror provides a single-ended output but with a voltage equal to the full gain of the C-E amplifier, just as for the FET case.

The power of the current mirror is again most apparent when additional stages are added, as in the prototype operational amplifier in Fig. 16.39. The resistance at the output of the differential input stage, node 1, is now equivalent to the parallel combination of the

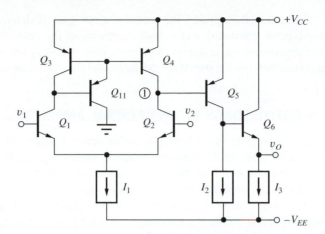

Figure 16.39 Bipolar op amp with active load in first stage.

output resistances of transistors Q_2 and Q_4 and the input resistance of Q_5:

$$R_{EQ} = r_{o2} \parallel r_{o4} \parallel r_{\pi 5} \approx r_{\pi 5} \tag{16.89}$$

and the gain of the differential input stage becomes

$$A_{dm} = g_{m2} R_{EQ} \approx g_{m2} r_{\pi 5} = \beta_{o5} \frac{I_{C2}}{I_{C5}} \tag{16.90}$$

> **EXERCISE:** What is the approximate differential-mode voltage gain of the amplifier in Fig. 16.39 if $\beta_{FO} = 150$, $V_A = 75$ V, and $I_{C5} = 3\, I_{C2}$?
>
> **ANSWER:** 50

Common-Mode Input Signals

Figure 16.40 is the bipolar differential amplifier with common-mode input signal. The common-mode input produces a common-mode current i_{ic} in each side of the differential pair consisting of Q_1 and Q_2:

$$\mathbf{i_{ic}} = \frac{g_{m2}}{1 + 2g_{m2} R_{EE}} \mathbf{v_{ic}} \approx \frac{\mathbf{v_{ic}}}{2R_{EE}} \tag{16.91}$$

The current from Q_1 is supplied by mirror reference transistor Q_3. This current is replicated by Q_4, which produces exactly the current required by the collector of Q_2. Thus, the output current, output voltage, and common-mode conversion gain A_{cd} are once again zero.

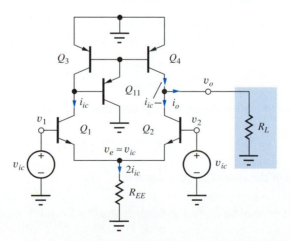

Figure 16.40 Bipolar differential amplifier with common-mode input.

In an actual amplifier, the common-mode gain is determined by small imbalances in the bipolar transistors and overall symmetry of the amplifier. In the bipolar case, one of these asymmetries is due to the current gain defect in the active load, which has been minimized through the use of the buffered current mirror, as depicted in Fig. 16.40.

16.6 ACTIVE LOADS IN OPERATIONAL AMPLIFIERS

Let us now explore more fully the use of active loads in MOS and bipolar operational amplifiers. Figure 16.41 shows a complete three-stage MOS operational amplifier. The input stage consists of NMOS differential pair M_1 and M_2 with PMOS current mirror load, M_3 and M_4, followed by a second common-source gain stage M_5 loaded by current source M_{10}. The output stage is a class-AB amplifier consisting of transistors M_6 and M_7. Bias currents I_1 and I_2 for the two gain stages are set by the current mirrors formed by transistors M_8, M_9, and M_{10}, and class-AB bias for the output stage is set by the voltage developed across resistor R_{GG}. At most, only two resistors are required: R_{GG} and one for the current mirror reference current.

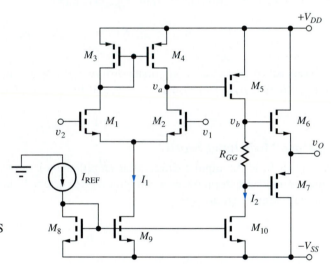

Figure 16.41 Complete CMOS op amp with current mirror bias.

CMOS Op-Amp Voltage Gain

Assuming that the gain of the output stage is approximately 1, then the overall differential-mode gain A_{dm} of the three-stage operational amplifier is equal to

$$A_{dm} = \frac{\mathbf{v_a}}{\mathbf{v_{id}}} \frac{\mathbf{v_b}}{\mathbf{v_a}} \frac{\mathbf{v_o}}{\mathbf{v_b}} = A_{V1} A_{V2}(1) \approx A_{V1} A_{V2} \tag{16.92}$$

As discussed earlier, the input stage provides a gain of

$$A_{V1} = g_{m2}(r_{o2} \parallel r_{o4}) \approx \frac{\mu_{f2}}{2} \tag{16.93}$$

The gain of the second stage is equal to

$$A_{V2} = g_{m5}(r_{o5} \parallel (R_{GG} + r_{o10})) \approx g_{m5}(r_{o5} \parallel r_{o10}) \approx g_{m5}(r_{o5} \parallel r_{o5}) = \frac{\mu_{f5}}{2} \tag{16.94}$$

assuming that the output resistances of M_5 and M_{10} are similar in value and $R_{GG} \ll r_{o10}$. Combining the three equations above yields

$$A_{dm} \approx \frac{\mu_{f2}\mu_{f5}}{4} \qquad (16.95)$$

The gain approaches one-quarter of the product of the amplification factors of the two gain stages.

The factor of 4 in the denominator of Eq. (16.95) can be eliminated by improved design. If a Wilson source is used in the first-stage active load, then the output resistance of the current mirror is much greater than r_{o2}, and A_{v1} becomes equal to μ_{f2}. The gain of the second stage can also be increased to the full amplification factor of M_5 if the current source M_{10} is replaced by a Wilson or cascode source. If both these circuit changes are used (see Prob. 16.64), then the gain of the op amp can be increased to

$$A_{dm} \approx \mu_{f2}\mu_{f5} \qquad (16.96)$$

This discussion has only scratched the surface of the many techniques available for increasing the gain of the CMOS op amp. Several examples are in the problems at the end of this chapter; further discussion can be found in the bibliography.

dc Design Considerations

When the circuit in Fig. 16.41 is operating in a closed-loop op-amp configuration, the drain current of M_5 must be equal to the output current I_2 of current source transistor M_{10}. For the amplifier to have a minimum offset voltage, the (W/L) ratio of M_5 must be carefully selected so the source-gate bias of M_5, $V_{SG5} = V_{SD4} = V_{SG3}$, is precisely the proper voltage to set $I_{D5} = I_2$. The W/L ratio of M_5 is also usually adjusted to account for V_{DS} and λ differences between M_5 and M_{10}. R_{GG} and the (W/L) ratios of M_6 and M_7 determine the quiescent current in the class-AB output stage.

Even resistor R_{GG} has been eliminated from the op amp in Fig. 16.42 by using the gate-source voltage of FET M_{11} to bias the output stage. The current in the class-AB stage is determined by the W/L ratios of the output transistors and the matching diode-connected MOSFET M_{11}.

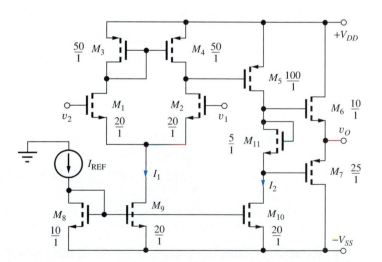

Figure 16.42 Op amp with current mirror bias of the class-AB output stage.

EXAMPLE 16.3: Find the voltage gain, input resistance, and output resistance of the amplifier in Fig. 16.42 if $K'_n = 25\,\mu A/V^2$, $K'_p = 10\,\mu A/V^2$, $V_{TN} = 0.75$ V, $V_{TP} = -0.75$ V, $V_{DD} = V_{SS} = 5$ V, $I_{REF} = 100\,\mu A$, and $\lambda = 0.0125\ V^{-1}$.

SOLUTION: The gain is calculated using Eq. (16.95).

$$A_{dm} \approx \frac{\mu_{f2}\mu_{f5}}{4} = \frac{1}{4}\left(\frac{1}{\lambda_2}\sqrt{\frac{2K_{n2}}{I_{D2}}}\right)\left(\frac{1}{\lambda_5}\sqrt{\frac{2K_{p5}}{I_{D5}}}\right)$$

For the amplifier in Fig. 16.42,

$$I_{D2} = \frac{I_1}{2} = \frac{2I_{REF}}{2} = 100\ \mu A \qquad I_{D5} = I_2 = 2I_{REF} = 200\ \mu A$$

$$K_{n2} = 20K'_n = 500\frac{\mu A}{V^2} \qquad\qquad K_{p5} = 100K'_p = 1000\frac{\mu A}{V^2}$$

and

$$A_{dm} \approx \frac{\mu_{f2}\mu_{f5}}{4} = \frac{1}{4}\left(\frac{1}{0.0125}\right)^2 V^2 \sqrt{\frac{2\left(500\frac{\mu A}{V^2}\right)}{100\ \mu A}}\sqrt{\frac{2\left(1000\frac{\mu A}{V^2}\right)}{200\ \mu A}} = 16,000$$

The input resistance is twice the input resistance of M_1, which is infinite:

$$R_{ID} = \infty$$

The output resistance is determined by the parallel combination of the output resistances of M_6 and M_7, which act as two source followers operating in parallel:

$$R_{OUT} = R_{O6} \parallel R_{o7} = \frac{1}{g_{m6}} \Bigg\| \frac{1}{g_{m7}} = \frac{1}{\sqrt{2K_{n6}I_{D6}}} \Bigg\| \frac{1}{\sqrt{2K_{p7}I_{D7}}}$$

To evaluate this expression, the current in the output stage must be found. The gate-source voltage of M_{11} is

$$V_{GS11} = V_{TN11} + \sqrt{\frac{2I_{D11}}{K_{n11}}} = 0.75\ V + \sqrt{\frac{2\,(200\ \mu A)}{125\left(\frac{\mu A}{V^2}\right)}} = 2.54\ V$$

In this design, $V_{TP} = -V_{TN}$ and the W/L ratios of M_6 and M_7 have been chosen so that $K_{p7} = K_{n6}$. Because I_{D6} must equal I_{D7}, then $V_{GS6} = V_{SG7}$. Thus, both V_{GS6} and V_{SG7} are equal to one-half V_{GS11}, and

$$I_{D7} = I_{D6} = \frac{250\ \mu A}{2\ V^2}(1.27\ V - 0.75\ V)^2 = 33.7\ \mu A$$

The transconductances of M_6 and M_7 are also equal,

$$g_{m7} = g_{m6} = \sqrt{2\left(2.50 \times 10^{-4}\frac{\mu A}{V^2}\right)(33.7 \times 10^{-6}\ \mu A)} = 1.30 \times 10^{-4}\ S$$

and the output resistance at the Q-point is $R_{OUT} = 3.85\ k\Omega$.   ◆

EXERCISE: Simulate the amplifier in Fig. 16.42 using SPICE and compare the results to the answers in Example 16.3. What are the offset voltage and CMRR? Which terminal is the noninverting input?

ANSWERS: 17,800, 3.63 $k\Omega$; 64 μV, 91 dB; v_1

Bipolar Operational Amplifiers

Active-load techniques can be applied equally well to bipolar op amps. In fact, most of the techniques discussed thus far were developed first for bipolar amplifiers and later applied to MOS circuits as NMOS and CMOS technologies matured. In the circuit in Fig. 16.43, a differential input stage with active load is formed by transistors Q_1 to Q_4. The first stage is followed by a high gain C-E amplifier formed of Q_5 and its current source load Q_8. Load resistance R_L is driven by the class-AB output stage, consisting of transistors Q_6 and Q_7 biased by current I_2 and diodes Q_{11} and Q_{12}. (The diodes will actually be implemented with BJTs, in this case with emitter areas five times those of Q_6 and Q_7.)

Based on our understanding of multistage amplifiers, the gain of this circuit is approximately $A_{dm} = A_{V1}A_{V2}A_{V3}$ and

$$A_{dm} \approx [g_{m2}r_{\pi 5}][g_{m5}(r_{o5} \parallel r_{o8} \parallel (\beta_{o6} + 1)R_L)][1] \approx \frac{g_{m2}}{g_{m5}}g_{m5}r_{\pi 5}g_{m5}\frac{r_{o5}}{2} = \frac{I_{C2}}{I_{C5}}\beta_{o5}\frac{\mu_{f5}}{2}$$

(16.97)

in which it has been assumed that the input resistance of the class-AB output stage is much larger than the parallel combination of r_{o5} and r_{o8}. Note that the upper limit to Eq. (16.97) is set by the $\beta_o V_A$ product of Q_5, because I_{C2} is typically less than or equal to I_{C5}.

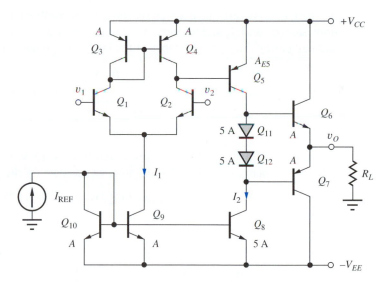

Figure 16.43 Complete bipolar operational amplifier.

EXERCISE: Estimate the voltage gain of the amplifier in Fig. 16.43 using Eq. (16.97) if $I_{REF} = 100\ \mu A$, $V_{A5} = 60\ V$, $\beta_{o1} = 150$, $\beta_{o5} = 50$, $R_L = 2\ M\Omega$, and $V_{CC} = V_{EE} = 15\ V$. What is the gain of the first stage? The second stage? What should be the emitter area of Q_5? What is R_{ID}? Which terminal is the inverting input?

ANSWERS: 7500; 5; 1500; 10 A; 150 kΩ; v_1

EXERCISE: Simulate the amplifier in the previous exercise using SPICE and determine the offset voltage, voltage gain, differential-mode input resistance, CMRR, and common-mode input resistance.

ANSWERS: 3.28 mV, 8440, 165 kΩ, 84.7 dB, 59.1 MΩ

An Amplifier with Improved Voltage Gain

To improve the gain of the amplifier in Fig. 16.43, Eq. (16.97) indicates that we need a transistor with an improved $\beta_o V_A$ product. We also see from the exercise that the first-stage gain is low because $r_{\pi 5}$ is small (the ratio I_{C2}/I_{C5} is too low). Mentally searching through our bag of basic circuit tools, we should discover the two-transistor Darlington circuit, which has a current gain of $\beta_{o1}\beta_{o2}$, an amplification factor of $\mu_{f2}/4$, an output resistance of $r_{o2}/2$, and an input resistance of $2\beta_{o1}r_{\pi 2}$. This configuration has been used to replace Q_5 in the circuit in Fig. 16.44. The *pnp* Darlington circuit requires an emitter-base bias of $2V_{EB}$, and the buffered current mirror provides proper dc balance at the collectors of Q_3 and Q_4.

Let us now determine an expression for the voltage gain of the amplifier in Fig. 16.44. Writing the voltage gain as a product of the gains of the individual stages and assuming the output stage has unity gain,

$$A_{dm} = \frac{\mathbf{v_a}}{\mathbf{v_{id}}} \frac{\mathbf{v_b}}{\mathbf{v_a}} \frac{\mathbf{v_o}}{\mathbf{v_b}} = A_{V1}A_{V2}(1) \approx A_{V1}A_{V2} \tag{16.98}$$

The input stage provides a gain of

$$A_{V1} = g_{m2}(r_{o2} \parallel r_{o4} \parallel 2\beta_{o6}r_{\pi 7}) \approx g_{m2}\left(\frac{r_{o2}}{2} \parallel 2\beta_{o6}r_{\pi 7}\right) \tag{16.99}$$

in which the load resistance represents the parallel combination of the output resistances of transistors Q_2 and Q_4 and the input resistance of the Darlington stage. We expect $r_{o4} \approx r_{o2}$, and comparing the input resistance of the Darlington stage to r_{o2} yields

$$\frac{2\beta_{o7}r_{\pi 8}}{r_{o2}} = \frac{2\beta_{o6}\dfrac{\beta_{o7}V_T}{I_{C7}}}{\dfrac{V_{A2} + V_{CE2}}{I_{C2}}} \approx \frac{I_1}{I_2}\frac{0.025\beta_{o6}\beta_{o7}}{V_{A2} + V_{CE2}} \tag{16.100}$$

Using $I_2 = 2I_1$, $\beta_o = 50$, $V_A = 60$ V, and $V_{CE} = 15$ V, we find that the value of Eq. (16.100) is approximately 0.42. Therefore, an estimate for the gain of the first stage is

$$A_{V1} \approx g_{m2}(0.5r_{o2} \parallel 0.42r_{o2}) = 0.23\mu_{f2} \tag{16.101}$$

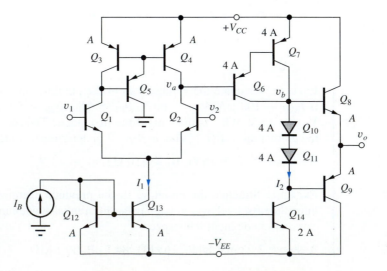

Figure 16.44 Op amp with buffered current mirror and second-stage Darlington circuit.

If we assume the resistance at node v_b is dominated by the output resistances of the Darlington stage and current source I_2, then the gain of the second stage is equal to

$$A_{V2} \approx \frac{g_{m7}}{2}\left(\frac{r_{o7}}{2} \parallel r_{o14}\right) \approx \frac{g_{m7}}{2}\left(\frac{r_{o7}}{2} \parallel r_{o7}\right) = \frac{g_{m7}}{2}\left(\frac{r_{o7}}{3}\right) = \frac{\mu_{f7}}{6} \qquad (16.102)$$

Combining Eqs. (16.98), (16.100), and (16.102) and assuming that the output stage provides a gain of unity yields a final estimate for the voltage gain of the amplifier in Fig. 16.44:

$$A_{dm} \approx \frac{\mu_{f2}\mu_{f7}}{26} = \frac{40\,(75)\,40\,(75)}{26} = 3.46 \times 10^5 \qquad (16.103)$$

> **EXERCISE:** Calculate the voltage gain of the circuit in Fig. 16.44 including the effect of a 2-kΩ load resistor on the output if the input resistance of the output stage is $(\beta_{o8}+1)R_L$. Assume $\beta_o = 100$, $V_A + V_{CE} = 75$ V, and $I_B = 100$ μA. Which terminal is the noninverting input?
>
> **ANSWERS:** 2.14×10^5; v_2

> **EXERCISE:** Use SPICE to determine the offset voltage, voltage gain, differential-mode input resistance, output resistance, CMRR, and common-mode input resistance of the amplifier in Fig. 16.44. Assume $\beta_{on} = 150$, $\beta_{op} = 50$, $V_A = 60$ V, $R_L = 2$ kΩ, and $I_B = 100$ μA.
>
> **ANSWERS:** 11.6 μV, 2.40×10^5, 128 kΩ, 822 Ω, 120 dB, 57.3 MΩ

We can come up with an almost endless array of circuit permutations to modify the various characteristics of the amplifier in Figs. 16.43 and 16.44. Cascode circuits can be used in the input stage and second stage. In BIMOS technology, FETs can be used to increase the input resistance at Q_5 as well as that of the output stages. A FET input stage will offer higher input resistance but lower voltage gain.

Input Stage Breakdown

Although the bipolar amplifier designs discussed thus far have provided excellent voltage gain, input resistance, and output resistance, the amplifiers all have a significant flaw. The input stage does not offer **overvoltage protection** and can easily be destroyed by the large input voltage differences that can occur, not only under fault conditions but also during unavoidable transients that occur during normal use of the amplifier. For example, the voltage across the input of an op amp can temporarily be equal to the total supply voltage span during slew-rate limited recovery.

Consider the worst-case fault condition applied to the differential pair in Fig. 16.45. Under the conditions shown, the base-emitter junction of Q_1 will be forward-biased, and that of Q_2 reverse-biased by a voltage of $(V_{CC} + V_{EE} - V_{BE1})$. If $V_{CC} = V_{EE} = 22$ V, the reverse voltage exceeds 41 V. Because of heavy doping in the emitter, the typical Zener breakdown voltage of the base-emitter junction of an *npn* transistor is only 5 to 7 V. Thus any voltage exceeding this value by more than one diode drop may destroy at least one of the transistors in the differential input pair.

Early IC op amps required circuit designers to add external diode protection across the input terminals, as shown Fig. 16.45(b). The diodes prevent the differential input voltage from exceeding approximately 1.4 V, but this technique adds extra components and cost to the design. The μA-741 described in the next section was the first commercial IC op amp to solve this problem by providing a fully protected input, as well as output, stage.

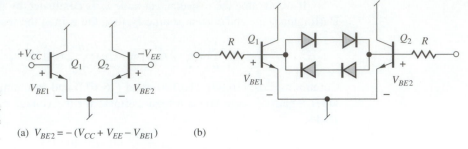

Figure 16.45 (a) Differential input stage voltages under a fault condition. (b) Simple diode input protection circuit.

(a) $V_{BE2} = -(V_{CC} + V_{EE} - V_{BE1})$ (b)

16.7 THE μA-741 OPERATIONAL AMPLIFIER

The now classic Fairchild **μA-741** operational-amplifier design was the first to provide a highly robust amplifier from the application engineer's point of view. The amplifier provides excellent overall characteristics (high gain, input resistance and CMRR, low output resistance, and good frequency response) while providing overvoltage protection for the input stage and short-circuit current limiting of the output stage. The 741 style of amplifier design quickly became the industry standard and spawned many related designs.

Figure 16.46 is a simplified schematic of the μA-741 operational amplifier. The three bias sources shown in symbolic form are discussed in more detail following a description of the overall circuit. The op amp has two stages of voltage gain followed by a class-AB output stage. In the first stage, transistors Q_1 to Q_4 form a differential amplifier with a buffered current mirror active load, Q_5 to Q_7. Practical operational amplifiers offer an offset voltage adjustment port, which is provided in the 741 through the addition of 1-kΩ resistors R_1 and R_2 and an external potentiometer R_{EXT}.

The second stage consists of emitter follower Q_{10} driving common-emitter amplifier Q_{11} with current source I_2 and transistor Q_{12} as load. Transistors Q_{13} to Q_{18} form a short-

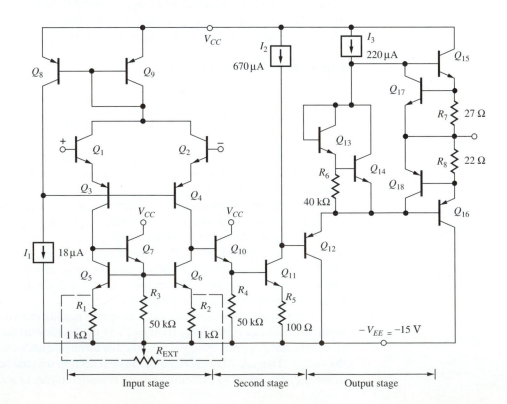

Figure 16.46 Overall schematic of the classic Fairchild μA-741 operational amplifier (the bias network appears in Fig. 16.47).

circuit protected class-AB push-pull output stage that is buffered from the second gain stage by emitter follower Q_{12}.

> **EXERCISE:** Reread this section and be sure you understand the function of each individual transistor in Fig. 16.46. Make a table listing the function of each transistor.

Bias Circuitry

The three current sources shown symbolically in Fig. 16.46 are generated by the bias circuitry in Fig. 16.47. The value of the current in the two diode-connected reference transistors Q_{20} and Q_{22} is determined by the power supply voltage and resistor R_5:

$$I_{\text{REF}} = \frac{V_{CC} + V_{EE} - 2V_{BE}}{R_5} = \frac{15 + 15 - 1.4}{39\text{ k}\Omega} = 0.733\text{ mA} \qquad (16.104)$$

assuming ± 15-V supplies. Current I_1 is derived from the Widlar source formed of Q_{20} and Q_{21}. The output current for this design is

$$I_1 = \frac{V_T}{5000}\ln\left[\frac{I_{\text{REF}}}{I_1}\right] \qquad (16.105)$$

Using the reference current calculated in Eq. (16.104) and iteratively solving for I_1 in Eq. (16.105) yields $I_1 = 18.4\ \mu\text{A}$.

The currents in mirror transistors Q_{23} and Q_{24} are related to the reference current I_{REF} by their emitter areas using Eq. (16.16). Assuming $V_O = 0$ and $V_{CC} = 15$ V, and neglecting the voltage drop across R_7 and R_8 in Fig. 16.46, $V_{EC23} = 15 + 1.4 = 16.4$ V and $V_{EC24} = 15 - 0.7 = 14.3$ V. Using these values with $\beta_F = 50$ and $V_A = 60$ V, the two source currents are

$$I_2 = 0.75(733\ \mu\text{A})\frac{1 + \dfrac{16.4\text{ V}}{60\text{ V}}}{1 + \dfrac{0.7\text{ V}}{60\text{ V}} + \dfrac{2}{50}} = 666\ \mu\text{A}$$

$$\qquad (16.106)$$

$$I_3 = 0.25(733\ \mu\text{A})\frac{1 + \dfrac{14.4\text{ V}}{60\text{ V}}}{1 + \dfrac{0.7\text{ V}}{60\text{ V}} + \dfrac{2}{50}} = 216\ \mu\text{A}$$

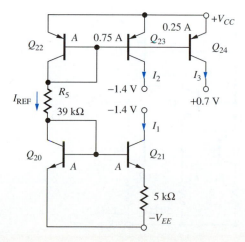

Figure 16.47 741 bias circuitry with voltages corresponding to $V_O = 0$ V.

and the two output resistances are

$$R_2 = \frac{V_{A23} + V_{EC23}}{I_2} = \frac{60 \text{ V} + 16.4 \text{ V}}{0.666 \text{ mA}} = 115 \text{ k}\Omega$$

$$R_3 = \frac{V_{A24} + V_{EC24}}{I_3} = \frac{60 \text{ V} + 14.3 \text{ V}}{0.216 \text{ mA}} = 344 \text{ k}\Omega$$

(16.107)

EXERCISE: What are the values of I_{REF}, I_1, I_2, and I_3 in the circuit in Fig. 16.47 for $V_{CC} = V_{EE} = 22$ V?

ANSWERS: 1.09 mA, 20.0 μA, 1.08 mA, 351 μA

EXERCISE: What is the output resistance of the Widlar source in Fig. 16.47 operating at 18.4 μA for $V_A = 60$ V and $V_{EE} = 15$ V?

ANSWER: 18.8 MΩ

dc Analysis of the 741 Input Stage

The input stage of the μA-741 amplifier is redrawn in the schematic in Fig. 16.48. As noted earlier, Q_1, Q_2, Q_3, and Q_4 form a differential input stage with an active load consisting of the buffered current mirror formed by Q_5, Q_6, and Q_7. In this input stage there are four base-emitter junctions between inputs v_1 and v_2, two from the *npn* transistors and, more importantly, two from the *pnp* transistors, and $(v_1 - v_2) = (V_{BE1} + V_{EB3} - V_{EB4} - V_{BE2})$.

In standard bipolar IC processes, *pnp* transistors are formed from lateral structures in which both junctions exhibit breakdown voltages equal to that of the collector-base junction of the *npn* transistor. This breakdown voltage typically exceeds 50 V. Because most general-purpose op-amp specifications limit the power supply voltages to less than ±22 V, the emitter-base junctions of Q_3 and Q_4 provide sufficient breakdown voltage to fully protect the input stage of the amplifier, even under a worst-case fault condition, such as that depicted in Fig. 16.45(a).

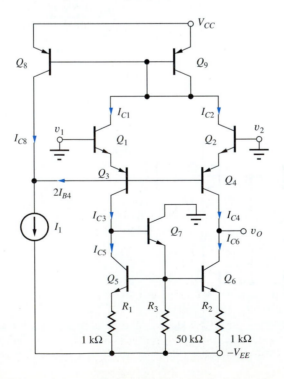

Figure 16.48 μA-741 input stage.

Q-Point Analysis

In the 741 input stage in Fig. 16.48, the current mirror formed by transistors Q_8 and Q_9 operates with transistors Q_1 to Q_4 to establish the bias currents for the input stage. Bias current I_1 represents the output of the Widlar source discussed previously (18 μA) and must be equal to the collector current of Q_8 plus the base currents of matched transistors Q_3 and Q_4:

$$I_1 = I_{C8} + I_{B3} + I_{B4} = I_{C8} + 2I_{B4} \qquad (16.108)$$

For high current gain, the base currents are small and $I_{C8} \approx I_1$.

The collector current of Q_8 mirrors the collector currents of Q_1 and Q_2, which are summed together in mirror reference transistor Q_9. Assuming high current gain and ignoring the collector-voltage mismatch between Q_7 and Q_8,

$$I_{C8} = I_{C1} + I_{C2} = 2I_{C2} \qquad (16.109)$$

Combining Eqs. (16.108) and (16.109) yields the ideal bias relationships for the input stage

$$I_{C1} = I_{C2} \approx \frac{I_1}{2} \qquad \text{and} \qquad I_{C3} = I_{C4} \approx \frac{I_1}{2} \qquad (16.110)$$

because the emitter currents of Q_1 and Q_3 and Q_2 and Q_4 must be equal. The collector current of Q_3 establishes a current equal to $I_1/2$ in current mirror transistors Q_5 and Q_6 as well. Thus, transistors Q_1 to Q_6 all operate at a nominal collector current equal to one-half the value of source I_1.

Now that we understand the basic ideas behind the input stage bias circuit, let us perform a more exact analysis. Expanding Eq. (16.108) using the current mirror expression from Eq. (16.6),

$$I_1 = 2I_{C2} \frac{1 + \dfrac{V_{EC8}}{V_{A8}}}{1 + \dfrac{2}{\beta_{FO8}} + \dfrac{V_{EB8}}{V_{A8}}} + 2I_{B4} \qquad (16.111)$$

I_{C2} is related to I_{B4} through the current gains of Q_2 and Q_4:

$$I_{C2} = \alpha_{F2}I_{E2} = \alpha_{F2}(\beta_{FO4} + 1)I_{B4} = \frac{\beta_{FO2}}{\beta_{FO2} + 1}(\beta_{FO4} + 1)I_{B4} \qquad (16.112)$$

Combining Eqs. (16.111) and (16.112) and solving for I_{C2} yields

$$I_{C2} = \frac{I_1}{2} \cfrac{1}{\cfrac{1 + \dfrac{V_{EC8}}{V_{A8}}}{1 + \dfrac{2}{\beta_{FO8}} + \dfrac{V_{EB8}}{V_{A8}}} + \cfrac{1}{\dfrac{\beta_{FO2}}{\beta_{FO2} + 1}(\beta_{FO4} + 1)}} \qquad (16.113)$$

which is equal to the ideal value of $I_1/2$ but reduced by the nonideal current mirror effects because of finite current gain and Early voltage.

The emitter current of Q_4 must equal the emitter current of Q_2, and so the collector current of Q_4 is

$$I_{C4} = \alpha_{F4}I_{E4} = \alpha_{F4}\frac{I_{C2}}{\alpha_{F2}} = \frac{\beta_{FO4}}{\beta_{FO4} + 1}\frac{\beta_{FO2} + 1}{\beta_{FO2}}I_{C2} \qquad (16.114)$$

The use of buffer transistor Q_9 essentially eliminates the current gain defect in the current mirror. Note from the full amplifier circuit in Fig. 16.46 that the base current of transistor Q_{10}, with its 50-kΩ emitter resistor R_4, is designed to be approximately equal to the base current of Q_7, and $V_{CE6} \approx V_{CE5}$ as well. Thus, the current mirror ratio is quite accurate and

$$I_{C5} = I_{C6} = I_{C3} \approx \frac{I_1}{2} \tag{16.115}$$

If 50-kΩ resistor R_3 were omitted, then the emitter current of Q_7 would be equal only to the sum of the base currents of transistors Q_5 and Q_6 and would be quite small. Because of the Q-point dependence of β_F, the current gain of Q_7 would be poor. R_3 increases the operating current of Q_7 to improve its current gain as well as to improve the dc balance and transient response of the amplifier. The value of R_3 is chosen to approximately match I_{B7} to I_{B10}.

To complete the Q-point analysis, the various collector-emitter voltages must be determined. The collectors of Q_1 and Q_2 are $1V_{EB}$ below the positive power supply, whereas the emitters are $1V_{BE}$ below ground potential. Hence,

$$V_{CE1} = V_{CE2} = V_{CC} - V_{EB9} + V_{BE2} \approx V_{CC} \tag{16.116}$$

The collector and emitter of Q_3 are approximately $2V_{BE}$ above the negative power supply voltage and $1V_{BE}$ below ground, respectively:

$$V_{EC3} = V_{E3} - V_{C3} = -0.7\text{V} - (-V_{EE} + 1.4 \text{ V}) = V_{EE} - 2.1 \text{ V} \tag{16.117}$$

The buffered current mirror effectively minimizes the error due to the finite current gain of the transistors, and $V_{CE6} = V_{CE5} \approx 2V_{BE} = 1.4$ V, neglecting the small voltage drop (<10 mV) across R_1 and R_2. Finally, the collector of Q_8 is $2V_{BE}$ below zero so that

$$V_{EC8} = V_{CC} + 1.4 \text{ V} \tag{16.118}$$

and the emitter of Q_7 is $1V_{BE}$ above $-V_{EE}$:

$$V_{CE7} = V_{EE} - 0.7 \text{ V} \tag{16.119}$$

EXAMPLE 16.4:   Calculate the bias currents in the 741 input stage if $I_1 = 18$ μA, $\beta_{FO2} = 150$, $\beta_{FO4} = 60$, $V_{A4} = 60$ V, and $V_{CC} = V_{EE} = 15$ V.

SOLUTION:

$$I_{C2} = \frac{18 \text{ }\mu\text{A}}{2} \cdot \cfrac{1}{\cfrac{1 + \cfrac{16.4 \text{ V}}{60 \text{ V}}}{1 + \cfrac{2}{50} + \cfrac{0.7 \text{ V}}{60 \text{ V}}} + \cfrac{1}{\cfrac{150}{150 + 1}(60 + 1)}}$$

$$= \frac{9.00 \text{ }\mu\text{A}}{\cfrac{1.27}{1.05} + 0.0165} = \frac{900 \text{ }\mu\text{A}}{1.23} = 7.32 \text{ }\mu\text{A}$$

$$I_{C3} = I_{C4} = \alpha_{F4}\frac{I_{C2}}{\alpha_{F2}} = \frac{\beta_{FO4}}{\beta_{FO4} + 1}\left(\frac{\beta_{FO2} + 1}{\beta_{FO2}}\right)I_{C2} = \frac{60}{61}\left(\frac{151}{150}\right)I_{C2} = 7.25 \text{ }\mu\text{A}$$

$$I_{C5} \approx I_{C3} = 7.25 \text{ }\mu\text{A} \qquad \text{and} \qquad I_{C6} = I_{C4} = 7.25 \text{ }\mu\text{A}$$

The actual bias currents are slightly greater than 7 μA, whereas the ideal value would be 9 μA. The dominant source of error arises from the collector-emitter voltage mismatch of the *pnp* current mirror.

Table 16.3 summarizes the Q-points based on these calculations and Eqs. (16.116) to (16.119) and compares them with SPICE simulation results.

Table 16.3		
Q-points of 741 Input Stage Transistors for $I_1 = 18\ \mu A$ and $V_{CC} = V_{EE} = 15\ V$		
Transistors	**Q-Point**	**SPICE Results**
Q_1 and Q_2	7.32 μA, 15 V	7.36 μA, 15.0 V
Q_3 and Q_4	7.25 μA, 12.9 V	7.28 μA, 13.0 V
Q_5 and Q_6	7.25 μA, 1.4 V	7.21 μA, 1.30 V
Q_7	12.2 μA, 14.3 V	13.1 μA, 14.3 V
Q_8	17.7 μA, 16.4 V	17.8 μA, 16.3 V
Q_9	14.0 μA, 0.7 V	14.1 μA, 0.66 V

EXERCISE: Suppose buffer transistor Q_7 and resistor R_3 are eliminated from the amplifier in Fig. 16.48 and Q_5 and Q_6 were connected as a standard current mirror. What would be the collector-emitter voltage of Q_6 if $V_{BE6} = 0.7$ V, $\beta_{FO6} = 100$, and $V_{A6} = 60$ V? Use Eq. (16.84).

ANSWER: 1.90 V

ac Analysis of the 741 Input Stage

The 741 input stage is redrawn in symmetric form in Fig. 16.49, with its active load temporarily replaced by two resistors. From Fig. 16.49, we see that the collectors of Q_1 and Q_2 as well as the bases of Q_3 and Q_4 lie on the line of symmetry of the amplifier and represent virtual grounds for differential-mode input signals.

The corresponding differential-mode half-circuit shown in Fig. 16.50 is a common-collector stage followed by a common-base stage, a C-C/C-B cascade. The characteristics

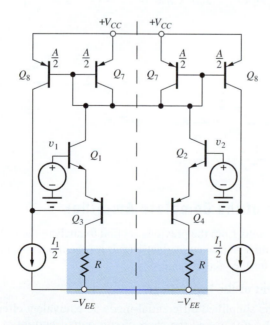

Figure 16.49 Symmetry in the 741 input stage.

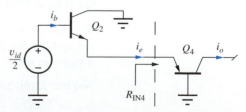

Figure 16.50 Differential-mode half-circuit for the 741 input stage.

of the C-C/C-B cascade can be determined from Fig. 16.50 and our knowledge of single-stage amplifiers.

The emitter current of Q_2 is equal to its base current i_b multiplied by $(\beta_{o2} + 1)$, and the collector current of Q_4 is α_{o4} times the emitter current. Thus, the output current can be written as

$$\mathbf{i_o} = \alpha_{o4}\mathbf{i_e} = \alpha_{o4}(\beta_{o2} + 1)\mathbf{i_b} \approx \beta_{o2}\mathbf{i_b} \tag{16.120}$$

The base current is determined by the input resistance to Q_2:

$$\mathbf{i_b} = \frac{\dfrac{\mathbf{v_{id}}}{2}}{r_{\pi 2} + (\beta_{o2} + 1)R_{\text{IN4}}} = \frac{\dfrac{\mathbf{v_{id}}}{2}}{r_{\pi 2} + (\beta_{o2} + 1)\left(\dfrac{r_{\pi 4}}{\beta_{o4} + 1}\right)} = \frac{\dfrac{\mathbf{v_{id}}}{2}}{r_{\pi 2} + r_{\pi 4}} \approx \frac{\mathbf{v_{id}}}{4r_{\pi 2}} \tag{16.121}$$

in which $R_{\text{IN4}} = r_{\pi 4}/(\beta_{o4} + 1)$ represents the input resistance of the common-base stage. Combining Eqs. (16.120) and (16.121) yields

$$\mathbf{i_o} \approx \beta_{o2}\frac{\mathbf{v_{id}}}{4r_{\pi 2}} = \frac{g_{m2}}{4}\mathbf{v_{id}} \tag{16.122}$$

Each side of the C-C/C-B input stage has a transconductance equal to one-half of the transconductance of the standard differential pair. From Eq. (16.121) we can also see that the differential-mode input resistance is twice the value of the corresponding C-E stage:

$$R_{ID} = \frac{\mathbf{v_{id}}}{\mathbf{i_b}} = 4r_{\pi 2} \tag{16.123}$$

From Fig. 16.51, we can see that the output resistance is equivalent to that of a common-base stage with a resistor of value $1/g_{m2}$ in its emitter:

$$R_{\text{OUT}} \approx r_{o4}(1 + g_{m4}R) = r_{o4}\left(1 + g_{m4}\frac{1}{g_{m2}}\right) = 2r_{o4} \tag{16.124}$$

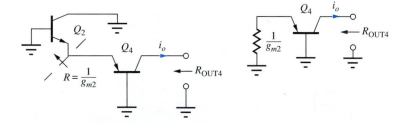

Figure 16.51 Output resistance of C-C/C-B cascade.

Voltage Gain of the Complete Amplifier

We now use the results from the previous section to analyze the overall ac performance of the op amp. We find a Norton equivalent circuit for the input stage and then couple it with a two-port model for the second stage.

Norton Equivalent of the Input Stage

Figure 16.52 is the simplified differential-mode ac equivalent circuit for the input stage. We use Figure 16.52(a) to find the short-circuit output current of the first stage. Based on our analysis of Fig. 16.50, the differential-mode input signal establishes equal and

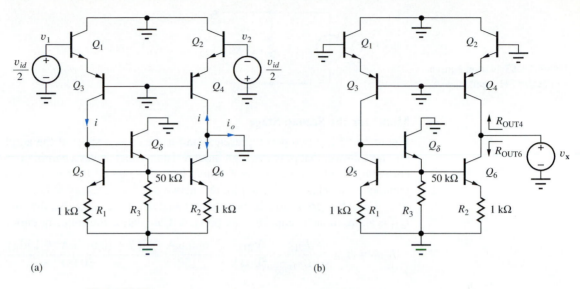

Figure 16.52 Circuits for finding the Norton equivalent of the input stage.

opposite currents in the two sides of the differential amplifier where $\mathbf{i} = (g_{m2}/4)\mathbf{v_{id}}$. Current i, exiting the collector of Q_3, is mirrored by the buffered current mirror so that a total signal current equal to $2i$ flows in the output terminal:

$$\mathbf{i_o} = -2\mathbf{i} = -\frac{g_{m2}\mathbf{v_{id}}}{2} = (-20I_{C2})\mathbf{v_{id}}$$

$$= -\left(\frac{20}{V}7.32 \times 10^{-6}\ \text{A}\right)\mathbf{v_{id}} = (-1.46 \times 10^{-4}\ \text{S})\mathbf{v_{id}} \tag{16.125}$$

The Thévenin equivalent resistance at the output is found using the circuit in Fig. 16.52(b) and is equal to

$$R_{\text{th}} = R_{\text{OUT6}} \| R_{\text{OUT4}} \tag{16.126}$$

Because only a small dc voltage is developed across R_2, the output resistance of Q_6 can be calculated from

$$R_{\text{OUT6}} \approx r_{o6}[1 + g_{m6}R_2] \approx r_{o6}\left[1 + \frac{I_{C6}R_2}{V_T}\right] = r_{o6}\left[1 + \frac{0.0073\ \text{V}}{0.025\ \text{V}}\right] = 1.3r_{o6} \tag{16.127}$$

The output resistance of Q_4 was already found in Eq. (16.124) to be $2r_{o4}$. Substituting the results from Eqs. (16.124) and (16.127) into Eq. (16.126),

$$R_{\text{th}} = 2r_{o4} \| 1.3r_{o6} = 0.79r_{o4} \approx 0.79\frac{60\ \text{V}}{7.25 \times 10^{-6}\ \text{A}} = 6.54\ \text{M}\Omega \tag{16.128}$$

in which $r_{o4} = r_{o2}$ has been assumed for simplicity with $V_A + V_{CE} = 60$ V.

The resulting Norton equivalent circuit for the input stage appears in Fig. 16.53. Based on the values in this figure, the open-circuit voltage gain of the first stage is -955. SPICE simulations yield values very similar to those in Fig. 16.53: $(1.40 \times 10^{-4}\ \text{S})\mathbf{v_{id}}$, 6.95 MΩ, and $A_{dm} = -973$.

> **EXERCISE:** Improve the estimate of R_{th} using the actual values of V_{CE6} and V_{CE4} if $V_{CC} = V_{EE} = 15$ V and $V_A = 60$ V. What are the values of R_{OUT4} and R_{OUT6}?
>
> **ANSWERS:** 7.12 MΩ; 20.2 MΩ, 11.0 MΩ

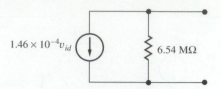

Figure 16.53 Norton equivalent of the 741 input stage.

$1.46 \times 10^{-4} v_{id}$ 6.54 MΩ

Model for the Second Stage

Figure 16.54 is a two-port representation for the second stage of the amplifier. Q_{10} is an emitter follower that provides high input resistance and drives a common-emitter amplifier consisting of Q_{11} and its current source load represented by output resistance R_2. A y-parameter model is constructed for this network.

From Fig. 16.46 and the bias current analysis, we can see that the collector current of Q_{11} is approximately equal to I_2 or 666 μA. Calculating the collector current of Q_{10} yields

$$I_{C10} \approx I_{E10} = \frac{I_{C11}}{\beta_{F11}} + \frac{V_{B11}}{50 \text{ k}\Omega} = \frac{666 \text{ μA}}{150} + \frac{0.7 + (0.67 \text{ mA})(0.1 \text{ k}\Omega)}{50 \text{ k}\Omega} = 19.8 \text{ μA} \tag{16.129}$$

Using these values to find the small-signal parameters with ($\beta_{on} = 150$) gives

$$r_{\pi 10} = \frac{\beta_{o10} V_T}{I_{C10}} = \frac{3.75 \text{ V}}{19.8 \text{ μA}} = 189 \text{ k}\Omega \quad \text{and} \quad r_{\pi 11} = \frac{3.75 \text{ V}}{0.666 \text{ mA}} = 5.63 \text{ k}\Omega \tag{16.130}$$

Parameters y_{11} and y_{21} are calculated by applying a voltage v_1 to the input port and setting $v_2 = 0$, as in Fig. 16.55. The input resistance to Q_{11} is that of a common-emitter stage with a 100-Ω emitter resistor:

$$R_{IN11} = r_{\pi 11} + (\beta_{o11} + 1)100 \approx 5630 + (151)100 = 20.7 \text{ k}\Omega \tag{16.131}$$

This value is used to simplify the circuit, as in Fig. 16.55(b), and the input resistance to Q_{10} is

$$[y_{11}]^{-1} = r_{\pi 10} + (\beta_{o10} + 1)(50 \text{ k}\Omega \parallel R_{IN11})$$
$$= 189 \text{ k}\Omega + (151)(50 \text{ k}\Omega \parallel 20.7 \text{ k}\Omega) = 2.40 \text{ M}\Omega \tag{16.132}$$

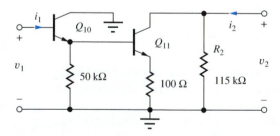

Figure 16.54 Two-port representation for the second stage.

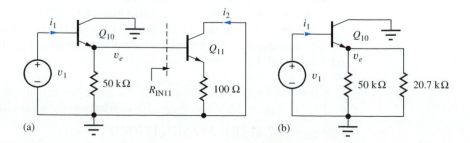

Figure 16.55 Network for finding y_{11} and y_{21}.

(a)

(b)

The gain of emitter follower Q_{10} is:

$$\mathbf{v_e} = \mathbf{v_1} \frac{(\beta_{o10} + 1)(50 \text{ k}\Omega \parallel R_{IN11})}{r_{\pi 10} + (\beta_{o10} + 1)(50 \text{ k}\Omega \parallel R_{IN11})} \tag{16.133}$$

$$= \frac{(151)(50 \text{ k}\Omega \parallel 20.7 \text{ k}\Omega)}{189 \text{ k}\Omega + (151)(50 \text{ k}\Omega \parallel 20.7 \text{ k}\Omega)} = 0.921\mathbf{v_1}$$

The output current $\mathbf{i_2}$ in Fig. 16.55(a) is given by

$$\mathbf{i_2} = \frac{\mathbf{v_e}}{\dfrac{1}{g_{m11}} + 100 \text{ }\Omega} = \frac{0.921\mathbf{v_1}}{\dfrac{1}{\dfrac{40}{\text{V}}(0.666 \text{ mA})} + 100 \text{ }\Omega} = 0.00670\mathbf{v_1} \tag{16.134}$$

yielding a forward transconductance of

$$y_{21} = 6.70 \text{ mS} \tag{16.135}$$

Parameters y_{12} and y_{22} can be found from the network in Fig. 16.56. We assume that the reverse transconductance y_{12} is negligible and reserve its calculation for Prob. 16.85. The output conductance y_{22} can be determined from Fig. 16.56(b).

$$[y_{22}]^{-1} = R_2 \parallel R_{OUT11} \tag{16.136}$$

where $R_2 = 115 \text{ k}\Omega$ was calculated during the analysis of the bias circuit.

Because the voltage drop across the 100-Ω resistor is small, the output resistance of Q_{11} is approximately

$$R_{OUT11} = r_{o11}[1 + g_{m11}R_E] = \frac{V_{A11} + V_{CE11}}{I_{C11}}\left[1 + \frac{I_{C11}R_E}{V_T}\right] \tag{16.137}$$

$$= \frac{60 \text{ V} + 13.6 \text{ V}}{0.666 \text{ mA}}\left[1 + \frac{0.067 \text{ V}}{0.025 \text{ V}}\right] = 407 \text{ k}\Omega$$

and

$$[y_{22}]^{-1} = 115 \text{ k}\Omega \parallel 407 \text{ k}\Omega = 89.1 \text{ k}\Omega \tag{16.138}$$

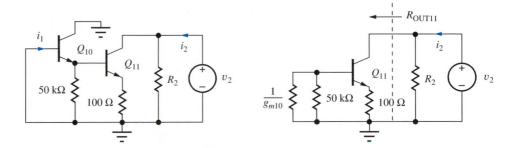

Figure 16.56 Network for finding y_{12} and y_{22}.

Figure 16.57 depicts the completed two-port model for the second stage, driven by the Norton equivalent of the input stage. Using this model, the open-circuit voltage gain for the first two stages of the amplifier is

$$\mathbf{v_2} = -0.00670(89.1 \text{ k}\Omega)\mathbf{v_1} = -597\mathbf{v_1}$$

$$\mathbf{v_1} = -1.46 \times 10^{-4}(6.54 \text{ M}\Omega \parallel 2.40 \text{ M}\Omega)\mathbf{v_{id}} = -256\mathbf{v_{id}} \tag{16.139}$$

$$\mathbf{v_2} = -597(-256\mathbf{v_{id}}) = 153{,}000\mathbf{v_{id}}$$

Figure 16.57 Combined model for first and second stages.

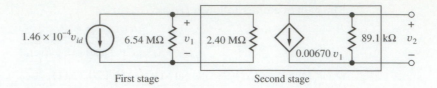

First stage   Second stage

Note from Eq. (16.138) that the 2.42-MΩ input resistance of Q_{10} reduces the voltage gain of the first stage by a factor of almost 4.

> **EXERCISE:** What would be the voltage gain of the input stage if transistor Q_{10} and its 50-kΩ emitter resistor were omitted so that the output of the first stage would be connected directly to the base of Q_{11}? Use the small-signal element values already calculated.
>
> **ANSWER:** -3.00

The 741 Output Stage

Figure 16.58 shows simplified models for the 741 output stage. Transistor Q_{12} is the emitter follower that buffers the high impedance node at the output of the second stage and drives the push-pull output stage composed of transistors Q_{15} and Q_{16}. Class-AB bias is provided by the sum of the base-emitter voltages of Q_{13} and Q_{14}, represented as diodes in Fig. 16.58(b). The 40-kΩ resistor is used to increase the value of I_{C13}. Without this resistor, I_{C13} would only be equal to the base current of Q_{14}. The short-circuit protection circuitry in Fig. 16.46 is not shown in Fig. 16.58 in order to simplify the diagram.

The input and output resistances of the class-AB output stage are actually complicated functions of the signal voltage because the operating current in Q_{15} and Q_{16} changes greatly as the output voltage changes. However, because only one transistor conducts strongly at any given time in the class-AB stage, separate circuit models can be used for positive and negative output signals. The model for positive signal voltages is shown in

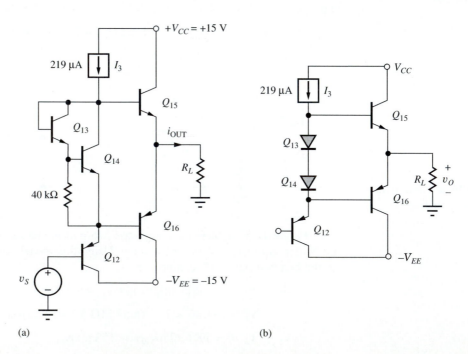

Figure 16.58 (a) 741 output stage without short-circuit protection. (b) Simplified output stage.

(a)   (b)

Fig. 16.59. (The model for negative signal swings is similar except *npn* transistor Q_{15} is replaced by *pnp* transistor Q_{16} connected to the emitter of Q_{12}.)

Let us first determine the input resistance of transistor Q_{12}. If R_{IN12} is much larger than the 89-kΩ output resistance of the two-port in Fig. 16.57, then it does not significantly affect the overall voltage gain of the amplifier. Using single-stage amplifier theory,

$$R_{IN12} = r_{\pi 12} + (\beta_{o12} + 1)R_{EQ1} \qquad (16.140)$$

where

$$R_{EQ1} = r_{d14} + r_{d13} + R_3 \parallel R_{EQ2} \qquad (16.141)$$

and

$$R_{EQ2} = r_{\pi 15} + (\beta_{o15} + 1)R_L \approx (\beta_{o15} + 1)R_L \qquad (16.142)$$

The value of R_3 (344 kΩ) was calculated in the bias circuit section. For $I_{C12} = 216\ \mu A$, and assuming a representative collector current in Q_{15} of 2 mA,

$$R_{EQ2} = r_{\pi 15} + (\beta_{o15} + 1)R_L = \frac{3.75\ V}{2\ mA} + (151)2\ k\Omega = 304\ k\Omega \qquad (16.143)$$

Note that the value of R_{EQ2} is dominated by the reflected load resistance $\beta_{o15}R_L$. Resistor $r_{\pi 15}$ represents a small part of R_{EQ2}, and knowing the exact value of I_{C15} is not critical.

$$R_{EQ1} = r_{d14} + r_{d13} + R_3 \parallel R_{EQ2} = 2\frac{0.025\ V}{0.216\ mA} + 344\ k\Omega \parallel 304\ k\Omega = 162\ k\Omega \qquad (16.144)$$

and

$$R_{IN12} = r_{\pi 12} + (\beta_{o12} + 1)R_{EQ1} = \frac{1.25\ V}{0.216\ mA} + (51)162\ k\Omega = 8.27\ M\Omega \qquad (16.145)$$

Because R_{IN12} is approximately 100 times the output resistance (y_{22}^{-1}) of the second stage, R_{IN12} has little effect on the gain of the second stage. Although the value of R_{IN12} changes for different values of load resistance, the overall op-amp gain is not affected because the value of R_{IN12} is so much larger than the value of y_{22}^{-1} in Fig. 16.59. Similar results are obtained for negative signal voltages. The values are slightly different because the current gain of the *pnp* transistor Q_{16} differs from that of the *npn* transistor Q_{15}.

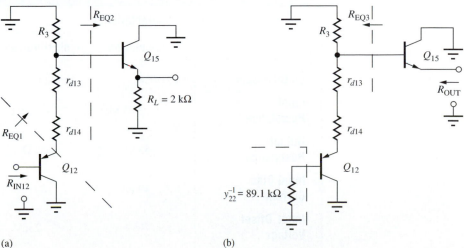

Figure 16.59 Circuits for determining input and output resistance of the output stage.

(a) (b)

Output Resistance

The output resistance of the amplifier for positive output voltages is determined by transistor Q_{15}

$$R_O = \frac{r_{\pi 15} + R_{EQ3}}{\beta_{o15} + 1} \tag{16.146}$$

in which

$$R_{EQ3} = R_3 \left\| \left[r_{d13} + r_{d14} + \frac{r_{\pi 12} + y_{22}^{-1}}{\beta_{o12} + 1} \right] \right.$$

$$= 304 \text{ k}\Omega \left\| \left[2\frac{0.025 \text{ V}}{0.219 \text{ mA}} + \frac{5.71 \text{ k}\Omega + 89.1 \text{ k}\Omega}{51} \right] = 2.08 \text{ k}\Omega \right. \tag{16.147}$$

Substituting the values from Eq. (16.147) into Eq. (16.146) yields

$$R_O = \frac{1.88 \text{ k}\Omega + 2.08 \text{ k}\Omega}{151} = 26.2 \text{ }\Omega \tag{16.148}$$

From Fig. 16.49, we can see that the 27-Ω resistor R_7, which determines the short-circuit current limit, adds directly to the overall output resistance of the amplifier so that actual op-amp output resistance is

$$R_{OUT} = R_O + R_7 = 53 \Omega \tag{16.149}$$

> **EXERCISE:** Repeat the calculation of R_{IN12} and R_{OUT} if pnp transistor Q_{16} has a current gain of 50, $I_{C16} = 2$ mA, and $I_{C15} = 0$. Be sure to draw the new equivalent circuit of the output stage for negative output voltages.
>
> **ANSWERS:** 3.94 MΩ ($\gg$ 89.1 kΩ), 53 Ω + 22 Ω = 75 Ω

Summary of the μA-741 Operational Amplifier Characteristics

Table 16.4 is a summary of the characteristics of the μA-741 operational amplifier. Column 2 gives our calculated values; column 3 presents values typically found in the actual

T a b l e 16.4

μA-741 Characteristics

	Calculation	Typical Values
Voltage Gain	153, 000	200, 000
Input Resistance	2.05 MΩ	2 MΩ
Output Resistance	53 Ω	75 Ω
Input Bias Current	49 nA	80 nA
Input Offset Voltage	—	2 mV

commercial product. The observed values depend on the exact values of current gain and Early voltage of the *npn* and *pnp* transistors and vary from process run to process run.

16.8 DIGITAL-TO-ANALOG CONVERSION

As described briefly in Chapter 1, the **digital-to-analog converter,** often referred to as a **D/A converter** or **DAC,** provides an interface between the discrete signals of the digital domain and the continuous signals of the analog world. The D/A converter takes digital information, most often in binary form, as an input and generates an output voltage or current that may then be used for electronic control or information display.

In the DAC in Fig. 16.60, an *n*-bit binary input word $(b_1, b_2, \ldots b_n)$ is combined with the **reference voltage V_{REF}** to set the output of the D/A converter. The digital input is treated as a binary fraction with the binary point located to the left of the word. Assuming a voltage output, the behavior of the DAC can be expressed mathematically as

$$V_O = V_{FS}(b_1 2^{-1} + b_2 2^{-2} + \cdots + b_n 2^{-n}) + V_{OS} \qquad \text{for } b_i \in \{1, 0\} \quad (16.150)$$

The DAC output may also be a current that can be represented as

$$I_O = I_{FS}(b_1 2^{-1} + b_2 2^{-2} + \cdots + b_n 2^{-n}) + I_{OS} \qquad \text{for } b_i \in \{1, 0\} \quad (16.151)$$

The **full-scale voltage V_{FS}** or **full-scale current I_{FS}** is related to the reference voltage V_{REF} of the converter by

$$V_{FS} = KV_{\text{REF}} \qquad \text{or} \qquad I_{FS} = GV_{\text{REF}} \qquad (16.152)$$

in which K and G determine the gain of the converter and are often set to a value of 1. Typical values of V_{FS} are 2.5, 5, 5.12, 10, and 10.24 V, whereas common values of I_{FS} are 2, 10 and 50 mA.

V_{OS} and I_{OS} represent the **offset voltage** or **offset current** of the converters, respectively, and characterize the converter output when the digital input code is equal to zero. The offset voltage is normally adjusted to zero, but the offset current of a current output DAC may be deliberately set to a nonzero value. For example, 2 to 10 mA and 10 to 50 mA ranges are used in some process control applications. For now, let us assume that the DAC output is a voltage.

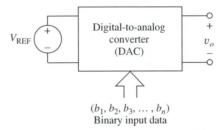

Figure 16.60 D/A converter with voltage output.

EXERCISE: What are the decimal values of the following 8-bit binary fractions? (a) 0.01100001 (b) 0.10001000.

ANSWERS: 0.37890625, 0.5312500

The smallest voltage change that can occur at the DAC output takes place when the **least significant bit (LSB) b_n** in the digital word changes from a 0 to a 1. This minimum voltage change is also referred to as the **resolution of the converter** and is given by

$$V_{\text{LSB}} = 2^{-n}V_{FS} \qquad (16.153)$$

At the other extreme, b_1 is referred to as the **most significant bit (MSB)** and has a weight of one-half V_{FS}.

For example, a 12-bit converter with a full-scale voltage of 10.24 V has an LSB or resolution of 2.500 mV. However, resolution can be stated in different ways. A 12-bit DAC may be said to have 12-bit resolution, a resolution of 0.025 percent of full scale, or a resolution of 1 part in 4096. DACs are available with resolutions ranging from as few as 6 bits to 18 or 20 bits. Resolutions of 8 to 12 bits are quite common and economical. Above 12 bits, DACs become more and more expensive, and great care must be taken to truly realize their full precision.

> **EXERCISE:** A 12-bit D/A converter has $V_{REF} = 5.12$ V. What is the output voltage for a binary input code of (101010101010)? What is V_{LSB}? What is the size of the MSB?
>
> **ANSWERS:** 3.41250 V, 1.25 mV, 2.56 V

D/A Converter Errors

Figure 16.61 and columns 1 and 2 in Table 16.5 present the relationship between the digital input code and the analog output voltage for an ideal three-bit DAC. The data points in the figure represent the eight possible output voltages, which range from 0 to $0.875 \times V_{FS}$. Note that the output voltage of the ideal DAC never reaches a value equal to V_{FS}. The maximum output is always 1 LSB smaller than V_{FS}. The ideal converter in Fig. 16.61 has been calibrated so that $V_{OS} = 0$ and 1 LSB is exactly $V_{FS}/8$. Figure 16.61 also shows the output of a converter with both gain and offset errors. The **gain error** of the D/A converter represents the deviation of the slope of the converter transfer function from that of the corresponding ideal DAC in Fig. 16.61, whereas the offset voltage is simply the output of the converter for a zero binary input code.

Although the outputs of both converters in Fig. 16.61 lie on a straight line, the output voltages of an actual DAC do not necessarily fall on a straight line. For example, the converter in Fig. 16.62 contains circuit mismatches that cause the output to no longer be perfectly linear. **Integral linearity error,** usually referred to as just **linearity error,** measures the deviation of the actual converter output from a straight line fitted to the converter output voltages. The error is usually specified as a fraction of an LSB or as a percentage of the full-scale voltage.

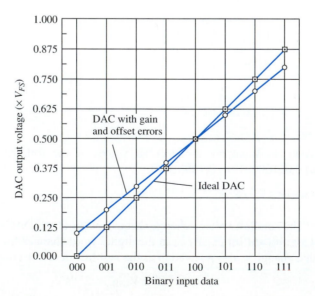

Figure 16.61 Transfer characteristic for an ideal DAC and a converter with both gain and offset errors.

T a b l e   16.5

D/A Converter Transfer Characteristics

Binary Input	Ideal DAC Output (x V_{FS})	DAC of Fig. 16.62 (x V_{FS})	Step Size (LSB)	Differential Linearity Error (LSB)	Integral Linearity Error (LSB)
000	0.0000	0.0000			0.00
001	0.1250	0.1000	0.80	−0.20	−0.20
010	0.2500	0.2500	1.20	+0.20	0.00
011	0.3750	0.3125	0.50	−0.50	−0.50
100	0.5000	0.5625	2.00	+1.00	+0.50
101	0.6250	0.6250	0.50	−0.50	0.00
110	0.7500	0.8000	1.40	+0.40	+0.40
111	0.8750	0.8750	0.60	−0.40	0.00

Table 16.5 lists the linearity errors for the nonlinear DAC in Fig. 16.62. This converter has linearity errors for input codes of 001, 011, 100, and 110. The overall linearity error for the DAC is specified as the magnitude of the largest error that occurs. Hence this converter will be specified as having a linearity error of either 0.5 LSB or 6.25 percent of full-scale voltage. A good converter exhibits a linearity error of less than 0.5 LSB.

A closely related measure of converter performance is the **differential linearity error.** When the binary input changes by 1 bit, the output voltage should change by 1 LSB. A converter's differential linearity error is the magnitude of the maximum difference between each output step of the converter and the ideal step size of 1 LSB. The size of each step and the differential linearity errors of the converter in Fig. 16.62 are also listed in Table 16.5. For instance, the DAC output changes by 0.8 LSB when the input code changes from 000 to 001. The differential linearity error represents the difference between this actual step size and 1 LSB. The integral linearity error for a given binary input represents the sum (integral) of the differential linearity errors for inputs up through the given input.

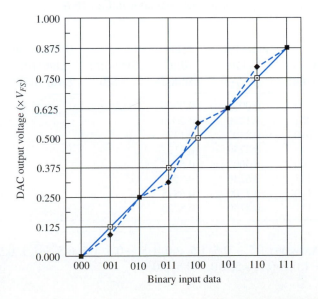

Figure 16.62 D/A converter with linearity errors.

Another specification that can be important in many applications is **monotonicity.** As the input code to a DAC is increased, the output should increase in a monotonic manner. If this does not happen, then the DAC is said to be nonmonotonic. In the nonmonotonic DAC in Fig. 16.63, the output decreases from $\frac{3}{16}V_{FS}$ to $\frac{1}{8}V_{FS}$ when the input code changes from 001 to 010. In a control system, this behavior represents an unwanted phase shift of 180° and can potentially lead to system instability.

In the upcoming exercise, we will find that this converter has a differential linearity error of 1.5 LSB, whereas the integral linearity error is 1 LSB. A tight linearity error specification does not necessarily guarantee good differential linearity. Although it is possible for a converter to have a differential linearity error of greater than 1 LSB and still be monotonic, a nonmonotonic converter always has a differential linearity error exceeding 1 LSB.

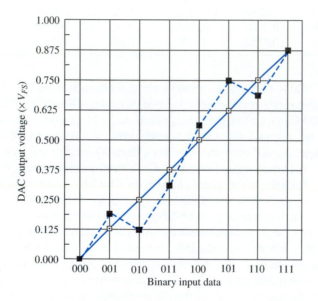

Figure 16.63 DAC with nonmonotonic output.

EXERCISE: Fill in the missing entries for step size, differential linearity error, and integral linearity error for the converter in Fig. 16.63.

Binary Input	Ideal DAC Output (x V_{FS})	Actual DAC Example	Step Size (LSB)	Differential Linearity Error (LSB)	Integral Linearity Error
000	0.0000	0.0000			0.00
001	0.1250	0.2000			
010	0.2500	0.1375			
011	0.3750	0.3125			
100	0.5000	0.5625			
101	0.6250	0.7500			
110	0.7500	0.6875			
111	0.8750	0.8750			0.00

ANSWERS: 1.5, −0.5, 1.5, 2.0, 1.5, −0.5, 1.5; 0.5, −1.5, 0.5, 1.0, 0.5, −1.5, 0.5; 0.5, −1.0, −0.5, 0.5, 1.0, −0.5, 0.0.

EXERCISE: What are the offset voltage and step size for the nonideal converter in Fig. 16.61 if the endpoints are at 0.100 and $0.800V_{FS}$?

ANSWERS: $0.100 \, V_{FS}$, $0.100 \, V_{FS}$

Digital-to-Analog Converter Circuits

We begin our discussion of the circuits used to realize DACs by considering MOS converters; we then explore bipolar designs. One of the simplest DAC circuits, the **weighted-resistor DAC,** shown in Fig. 16.64, uses the summing amplifier that we first encountered in Chapter 12, the reference voltage V_{REF}, and a weighted-resistor network. The binary input data controls the switches, with a logical 1 indicating that the switch is connected to V_{REF} and a logical 0 corresponding to a switch connected to ground. Successive resistors are weighted progressively by a factor of 2, thereby producing the desired binary weighted contributions to the output:

$$v_O = (b_1 2^{-1} + b_2 2^{-2} + \cdots + b_n 2^{-n})V_{\text{REF}} \qquad \text{for } b_i \in \{1, 0\} \qquad (16.154)$$

Differential and integral linearity errors and gain error occur when the resistor ratios are not perfectly maintained. Any op-amp offset voltage contributes directly to V_{OS} of the converter.

Several problems arise in building a DAC using the weighted-resistor approach. The primary difficulty is the need to maintain accurate resistor ratios over a very wide range of resistor values (for example, 4096 to 1 for a 12-bit DAC). In addition, because the switches are in series with the resistors, their on-resistance must be very low and they should have zero offset voltage. The designer can meet these last two requirements by using good MOSFETs or JFETs as switches, and the (W/L) ratios of the FETs can be scaled with bit position to equalize the resistance contributions of the switches. However, the wide range of resistor values is not suitable for monolithic converters of moderate to high resolution. We should also note that the current drawn from the voltage reference varies with the binary input pattern. This varying current causes a change in voltage drop in the Thévenin equivalent source resistance of the voltage reference and can lead to data-dependent errors sometimes called **superposition errors.**

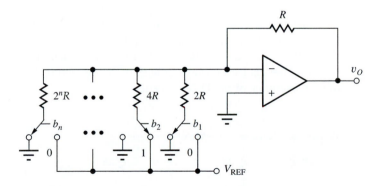

Figure 16.64 An n-bit weighted-resistor DAC.

EXERCISE: Suppose a 1-kΩ resistor is used for the MSB in an 8-bit converter similar to that in Fig. 16.64. What are the other resistor values?

ANSWERS: 2 kΩ, 4 kΩ, 8 kΩ, 16 kΩ, 32 kΩ, 64 kΩ, 128 kΩ, 500 Ω

The R-2R Ladder

The **R-2R ladder** in Fig. 16.65 avoids the problem of a wide range of resistor values. It is well-suited to integrated circuit realization because it requires matching of only two resistor values, R and $2R$. The value of R typically ranges from 2 kΩ to 10 kΩ. By forming successive Thévenin equivalents proceeding from left to right at each node in the ladder, we can show that the contribution of each bit is reduced by a factor of 2 going from the MSB to LSB. Like the weighted-resistor DAC, this network requires switches with low on-resistance and zero offset voltage, and the current drawn from the reference still varies with the input data pattern.

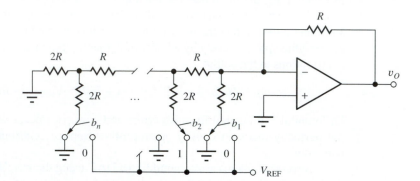

Figure 16.65 n-bit DAC using R-2R ladder.

Inverted R-2R Ladder

Because the currents in the resistor networks of the DACs in Figs. 16.64 and 16.65 change as the input data changes, power dissipation in the elements of the network changes, which can cause linearity errors in addition to superposition errors. Therefore some monolithic DACs use the configuration in Fig. 16.66, known as the **inverted R-2R ladder.** In this circuit, the currents in the ladder and reference are independent of the digital input because the input data cause the ladder currents to be switched either directly to ground or to the virtual ground input at the input of a current-to-voltage converter. Because both op-amp inputs are at ground potential, the ladder currents are independent of switch position. Note that complementary currents, I and $\bar{I}$, are available at the output of this DAC.

The inverted R-2R ladder is a popular DAC configuration, often implemented in CMOS technology. The switches still need to have low on-resistance to minimize errors within the converter. The R-2R ladder can be formed of diffused, implanted, or thin-film resistors; the choice depends on both the manufacturer's process technology and the required resolution of the D/A converter.

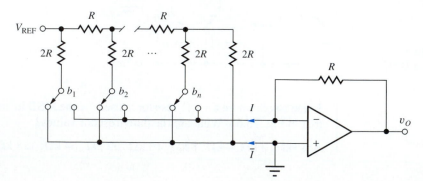

Figure 16.66 D/A converter using the inverted R-2R ladder.

An Inherently Monotonic DAC

MOS IC technology has facilitated some unusual approaches to D/A converter design. Figure 16.67 shows a DAC whose output is inherently monotonic. A long resistor string forms a multi-output voltage divider connected between the voltage reference and ground. An analog switch tree connects the desired tap to the input of an operational amplifier operating as a voltage follower. The appropriate switches are closed by a logic network that decodes the binary input data.

Each tap on the resistor network is forced to produce a voltage greater than or equal to that of the taps below it, and the output must therefore increase monotonically as the digital input code increases. An 8-bit version of this converter requires 256 equal-valued resistors and 510 switches, plus the additional decoding logic. This DAC can be fabricated in NMOS or CMOS technology, in which the large number of MOSFET switches and the complex decoding logic are easily realized.

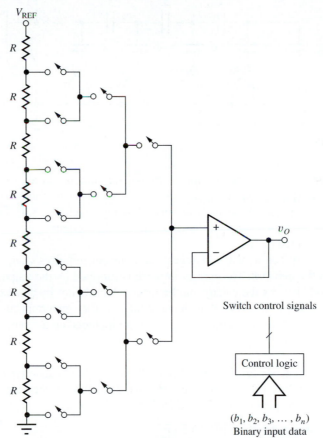

Figure 16.67 Inherently monotonic 3-bit D/A converter.

EXERCISE: How many resistors and switches are required to implement a 10-bit DAC using the technique in Fig. 16.67?

ANSWERS: 1024, 2046

Switched-Capacitor D/A Converters

D/A converters can be fabricated using only switches and capacitors (plus operational amplifiers). Figure 16.68(a) is a **weighted-capacitor DAC;** Fig. 16.68(b) is a **C-2C**

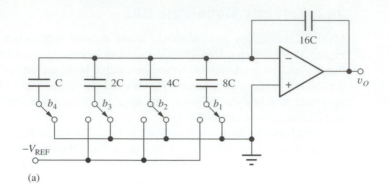

(a)

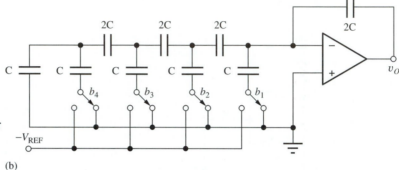

Figure 16.68 Switched-capacitor D/A converters. (a) Weighted-capacitor DAC; (b) C-2C DAC.

(b)

ladder DAC. Because these circuits are composed only of switches and capacitors, the only static power dissipation in these circuits occurs in the op amps. However, dynamic switching losses occur just as in CMOS logic (see Sec. 8.4). These circuits represent the direct switched-capacitor (S-C) analogs of the weighted-resistor and R-2R ladder techniques presented earlier.

When a switch changes state, current impulses charge or discharge the capacitors in the network. The current impulse is supplied by the output of the operational amplifier and changes the voltage on the feedback capacitor by an amount corresponding to the bit weight of the switch that changed state. These converters consume very little power, even when CMOS operational amplifiers are included on the same chip, and are widely used in VLSI systems.

> **EXERCISE:** (a) Suppose that an 8-bit weighted capacitor DAC is fabricated with the smallest unit of capacitance $C = 0.5$ pF. What is total capacitance the DAC requires? (b) Repeat for a C-2C ladder DAC.
>
> **ANSWERS:** 255.5 pF; 16.5 pF

Digital-to-Analog Converters in Bipolar Technology

Bipolar transistors do not perform well as voltage switches because of their inherent offset voltage in the saturation region of operation; however, they do make excellent current sources and current switches. Hence DACs realized with bipolar processes most often use some form of switched current source.

Figure 16.69 shows a DAC with binary-weighted current sources. Rather than turning the individual current sources off and on, the output of each source is switched selec-

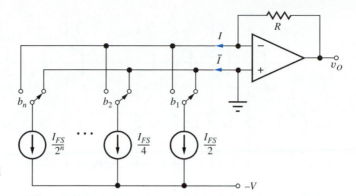

Figure 16.69 DAC using switching of binary-weighted current sources.

tively to ground or to the virtual ground at the input of a current-to-voltage converter. The currents switched into the summing junction are supplied through the feedback resistor R_F and determine the output voltage of the DAC.

Figure 16.70 is a simplified realization of a weighted-current source DAC, in which the current switches are implemented with bipolar transistors that operate in the same manner as in the emitter-coupled logic gates discussed in Chapter 10. If the voltage at b_1 exceeds V_{BB}, then the current of the first source is switched to the DAC output. If b_1 is less than V_{BB}, the current is switched to ground.

The base-emitter voltages of the current-source transistors in Fig. 16.70 must be identical for proper weighting of the current sources to occur, and this requires operation of the transistors at equal current densities. Thus, the area of each transistor is increased by a factor of 2 proceeding from the LSB to the MSB. At a resolution of 10 bits, 1023 unit-area transistors total are required. Furthermore, this type of converter requires the same wide range of resistor values as the weighted-resistor DAC previously discussed.

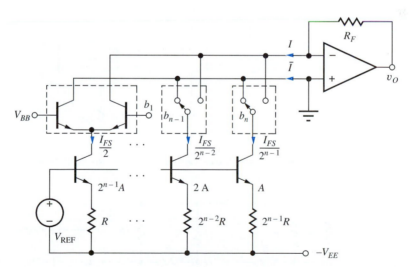

Figure 16.70 Weighted-current source DAC with current switches.

EXERCISE: If $I_{FS} = 2$ mA in an 8-bit DAC similar to Fig. 16.69, what is the current in the MSB? In the LSB? What is R_F of $V_{FS} = 5.00$ V at output v_O?

ANSWERS: 1 mA; 7.81 μA; 2.50 kΩ

There are a number of ways to overcome these problems. A direct solution is to split the current sources into groups; Fig. 16.71 is an example of an 8-bit DAC using two 4-bit

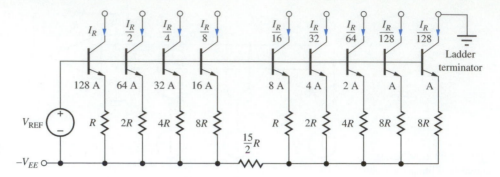

Figure 16.71 Eight-bit DAC using two 4-bit sections.

sections. For this case, the resistor and transistor area ratios are held to a more manageable range of 8 to 1. The two 4-bit sections are connected with a voltage-dropping resistor ($15R/2$) to correctly weight the current sources in the overall DAC. Proper operation requires an extra ladder-termination source with a current equal to that of the LSB. Multiple 4-bit sections of this type have been used in 8- and 12-bit converters.

The R-2R ladder may also be used to generate weighted current sources for a D/A converter, as shown in Fig. 16.72. Moving left to right from MSB to LSB, each transistor carries one-half the current of the preceding device. To maintain proper weighting of the current sources, however, the emitter areas of the transistors must still be scaled, and a ladder-termination source (Q_n) is required.

Figure 16.73 shows another method of using the R-2R ladder. An R-2R ladder is driven by equal-value current sources. This technique keeps total transistor area to a minimum and requires only one resistor value in the current source array. The outputs from the current sources are selectively switched into the various nodes of the ladder, which then provides the scaling by the proper power of 2.

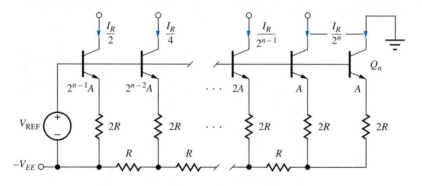

Figure 16.72 Weighted-current sources using an R-2R ladder.

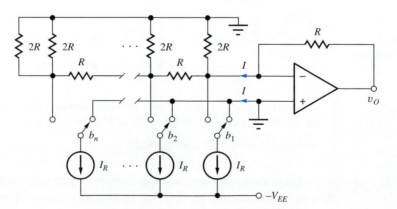

Figure 16.73 An alternate DAC circuit using an inverted R-2R ladder and equal-value current sources.

EXERCISE: If $I_R = 2$ mA and R $= 2.5$ kΩ in Fig. 16.73, calculate the output voltage if $b_2 = 1$ and the rest of the data bits are 0. What is V_{FS}?

ANSWERS: 2.5 V; 10.0 V

Reference Current Circuitry

The current sources in Figs. 16.69 to 16.73 all require a reference voltage or current; Fig. 16.74 shows three examples of circuitry used to establish the reference in the current-source D/A converters described in the preceding sections. In each case, an operational amplifier is used to set the current in a reference transistor Q_1. In the circuit in Fig. 16.74(a), the reference voltage appears directly across the leftmost $2R$ resistor and sets the emitter current of Q_1 to $V_{REF}/2R$. In (b) and (c), the collector current of Q_1 is forced to equal V_{REF}/R_{REF}. In all three cases, bipolar transistor and resistor ratio matching determine the currents in the rest of the current-source network.

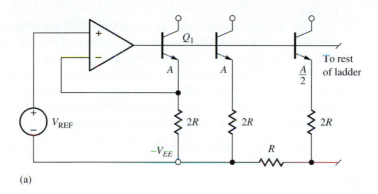

(a)

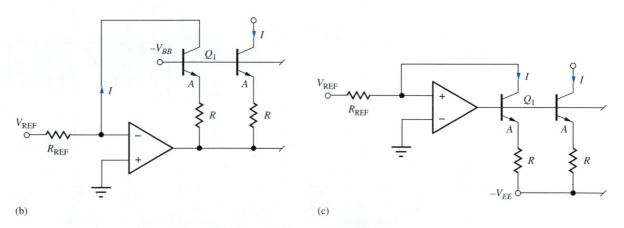

(b)   (c)

Figure 16.74 Several examples of D/A reference current circuits.

16.9 ANALOG-TO-DIGITAL CONVERSION

The **analog-to-digital converter,** also known as an **A/D converter** or **ADC,** is used to transform analog information in electrical form into digital data. The ADC in Fig. 16.75 takes an unknown continuous analog input signal, most often a voltage v_X, and converts it into an n-bit binary number that can be readily manipulated by a digital computer. The

Figure 16.75 Block diagram representation for an A/D converter.

n-bit number is a binary fraction representing the ratio between the unknown input voltage v_x and the converter's full-scale voltage $V_{FS} - KV_{REF}$.

Figure 16.76(a) is an example of the input-output relationship for an ideal 3-bit A/D converter. As the input increases from zero to full scale, the digital output code word stairsteps from 000 to 111. Except for 000 and 111, the output code is constant for an input voltage range equal to 1 LSB of the ADC, in this case $V_{FS}/8$. As the input voltage increases, the output code first underestimates the input voltage and then overestimates the input voltage. This error, called **quantization error,** is plotted against input voltage in Fig. 16.76(b).

For a given output code, we know only that the value of the input voltage v_X lies somewhere within a 1-LSB quantization interval. For example, if the output code of the 3-bit ADC is (100), then the input voltage can be anywhere between $\frac{7}{16}V_{FS}$ and $\frac{9}{16}V_{FS}$, a range of $V_{FS}/8$ V equivalent to 1 LSB of the 3-bit converter. From a mathematical point of view, the circuitry of an ideal ADC should be designed to pick the values of the bits in the binary word to minimize the magnitude of the quantization error v_ε between the unknown input voltage v_X and the nearest quantized voltage level:

$$v_\varepsilon = |v_X - (b_1 2^{-1} + b_2 2^{-2} + \cdots + b_n 2^{-n})V_{FS}| \qquad (16.155)$$

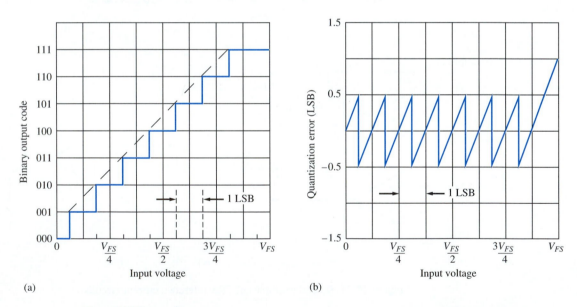

(a) (b)

Figure 16.76 Ideal 3-bit ADC: (a) input-output relationship and (b) quantization error.

EXERCISE: An 8-bit A/D converter has $V_{REF} = 5$ V. What is the binary output code word for an input of 1.2 V? What is the voltage range corresponding to 1 LSB of the converter?

ANSWERS: (00111101); 19.5 mV

Analog-to-Digital Converter Errors

As shown by the dashed line in Fig. 16.76(a), the code transition points of an ideal converter all fall on a straight line. However, an actual converter has integral and differential linearity errors similar to those of a digital-to-analog converter. Figure 16.77 is an example of the code transitions for a hypothetical nonideal converter. The converter is assumed to be calibrated so that the first and last code transitions occur at their ideal points.

In the ideal case, each code step, other than 000 and 111, would be the same width and should be equal to 1 LSB of the converter. Differential linearity error represents the difference between the actual code step width and 1 LSB, and integral linearity error is a measure of the deviation of the code transition points from their ideal positions. Table 16.6 lists the step size, differential linearity error, and integral linearity error for the converter in Fig. 16.77. Note that the ideal step sizes corresponding to codes 000 and 111 are 0.5 LSB and 1.5 LSB, respectively, because of the desired code transition points. As in D/A

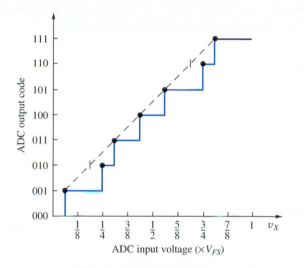

Figure 16.77 Example of code transitions in a non-ideal 3-bit ADC.

		T a b l e 16.6			
		A/D Converter Transfer Characteristics			
Binary Output Code	**Ideal ADC Transition Point ($\times V_{FS}$)**	**ADC of Fig. 16.77 ($\times V_{FS}$)**	**Step Size (LSB)**	**Differential Linearity Error (LSB)**	**Integral Linearity Error (LSB)**
000	0.0000	0.0000	0.5	0	0
001	0.0625	0.0625	1.5	0.50	0.5
010	0.1875	0.2500	0.5	−0.50	0
011	0.3125	0.3125	1.0	0	0
100	0.4375	0.4375	1.0	0	0
101	0.5625	0.5625	1.50	0.50	0.5
110	0.6875	0.7500	0.5	−0.50	0
111	0.8125	0.8125	1.5	0	0

converters, the integral linearity error should equal the sum of the differential linearity errors for the individual steps.

Figure 16.78 is an uncalibrated converter with both offset and gain errors. The first code transition occurs at a voltage that is 0.5 LSB too high, representing a converter **offset error** of 0.5 LSB. The slope of the fitted line does not give 1 LSB $= V_{FS}/8$, so the converter also exhibits a gain error.

A new type of error, which is specific to ADCs, can be observed in Fig. 16.78. The output code jumps directly from 101 to 111 as the input passes through $0.875V_{FS}$. The output code 110 never occurs, so this converter is said to have a **missing code.** A converter with a differential linearity error of less than 1 LSB does not exhibit missing codes in its input-output function. An ADC can also be **nonmonotonic.** If the output code decreases as the input voltage increases, the converter has a nonmonotonic input-output relationship.

All the above deviations from ideal A/D (or D/A) converter behavior are temperature-dependent; hence, converter specifications include temperature coefficients for gain, offset, and linearity. A good converter will be monotonic with less than 0.5 LSB linearity error and no missing codes over its full temperature range.

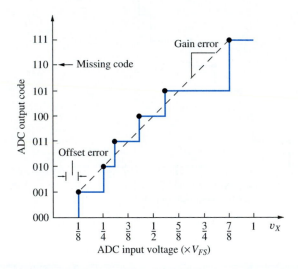

Figure 16.78 ADC with a missing code.

EXERCISE: An A/D converter is used in a digital multimeter (DVM) that displays 10 decimal digits. How many bits are required in the ADC?

ANSWER: 34 bits

EXERCISE: What are the minimum and maximum code step widths in Fig. 16.78? What are the differential and integral linearity errors for this ADC based on the dashed line in the figure?

ANSWERS: 0, 2.5 LSB; 1.5 LSB, 1 LSB

Basic Conversion Methods

Figure 16.79 shows the basic conversion scheme for a number of analog-to-digital converters. The unknown input voltage v_X is connected to one input of an analog comparator, and

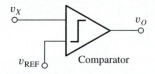

v_X

v_O

v_{REF} Comparator

Figure 16.79 Block diagram representation for a A/D converter.

a time-dependent reference voltage v_{REF} is connected to the other input of the comparator. (The transfer function for the comparator was originally discussed in Chapter 12. If input voltage v_X exceeds input v_{REF}, then the output voltage will be high, corresponding to a logic 1. If input v_X is less than v_{REF}, then the output voltage will be low, corresponding to a logic 0.)

In performing a conversion, the reference voltage is varied until the unknown input is determined within the quantization error of the converter. Ideally, the logic of the A/D converter will choose a set of binary coefficients b_i so that the difference between the unknown input voltage v_X and the final quantized value is less than or equal to 0.5 LSB. In other words, the b_i will be selected so that

$$\left| v_X - V_{FS} \sum_{i=1}^{n} b_i 2^{-i} \right| < \frac{V_{FS}}{2^{n+1}} \tag{16.156}$$

The basic difference among the operations of various converters is the strategy that is used to vary the reference signal V_{REF} to determine the set of binary coefficients $\{b_i, \ i = 1 \ldots n\}$.

Counting Converter

One of the simplest ways of generating the comparison voltage is to use a digital-to-analog converter. An n-bit DAC can be used to generate any one of 2^n discrete outputs simply by applying the appropriate digital input word. A direct way to determine the unknown input voltage v_X is to sequentially compare it to each possible DAC output. Connecting the digital input of the DAC to an n-bit binary counter enables a step-by-step comparison to the unknown input to be made, as shown in Fig. 16.80.

A/D conversion begins when a pulse resets the flip-flop and the counter output to zero. Each successive clock pulse increments the counter; the DAC output looks like a staircase during the conversion. When the output of the DAC exceeds the unknown input, the comparator output changes state, sets the flip-flop, and prevents any further clock pulses from reaching the counter. The change of state of the comparator output indicates that the conversion is complete. At this time, the contents of the binary counter represent the converted value of the input signal.

Several features of this converter should be noted. First, the length of the conversion cycle is variable and proportional to the unknown input voltage v_X. The maximum **conversion time** T_T occurs for a full-scale input signal and corresponds to 2^n clock periods or

$$T_T \leq \frac{2^n}{f_C} = 2^n T_C \tag{16.157}$$

where $f_C = 1/T_C$ is the clock frequency. Second, the binary value in the counter represents the smallest DAC voltage that is larger than the unknown input; this value is not necessarily the DAC output which is closest to the unknown input, as was originally desired. Also, the example in Fig. 16.80(b) shows the case for an input that is constant during the conversion period. If the input varies, the binary output will be an accurate representation of the value of the input signal at the instant the comparator changes state.

The advantage of the counting A/D converter is that it requires a minimum amount of hardware and is inexpensive to implement. Some of the least expensive A/D converters have used this technique. The main disadvantage is the relatively low conversion rate for a given D/A converter speed. An n-bit converter requires 2^n clock periods for its longest conversion.

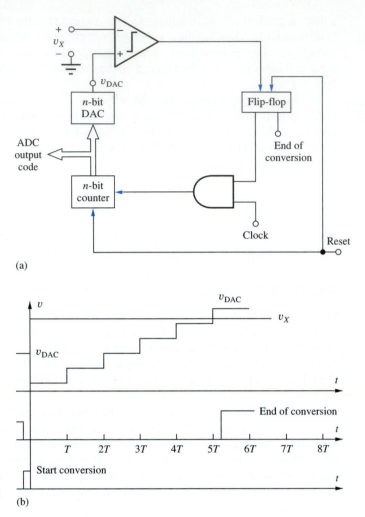

Figure 16.80 (a) Block diagram of the counting ADC. (b) Timing diagram.

EXERCISE: What is the maximum conversion time for an ADC using a 12-bit DAC and a 2-MHz clock frequency? What is the maximum possible number of conversions per second?

ANSWERS: 2.05 ms; 488 conversions/second

Successive Approximation Converter

The **successive approximation converter** uses a much more efficient strategy for varying the reference input to the comparator, one that results in a converter requiring only n clock periods to complete an n-bit conversion. Figure 16.81 is a schematic of the operation of a three-bit successive approximation converter. A "binary search" is used to determine the best approximation to v_X. After receiving a start signal, the successive approximation logic sets the DAC output to $(V_{FS}/2) - (V_{FS}/16)$ and, after waiting for the circuit to settle out, checks the comparator output. [The DAC output is offset by $(-\frac{1}{2}\text{LSB} = -V_{FS}/16)$ to yield the transfer function of Fig. 16.77.] At the next clock pulse, the DAC output is incremented by $V_{FS}/4$ if the comparator output was 1, and decremented by $V_{FS}/4$ if the comparator

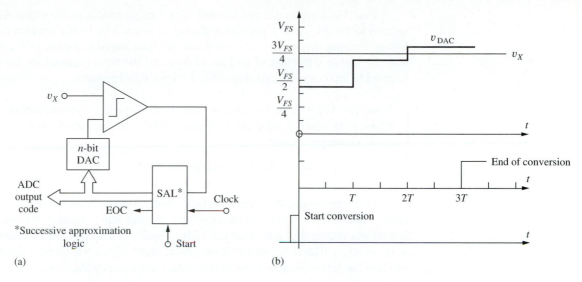

Figure 16.81 (a) Successive approximation ADC. (b) Timing diagram.

output was 0. The comparator output is again checked, and the next clock pulse causes the DAC output to be incremented or decremented by $V_{FS}/8$. A third comparison is made. The final binary output code remains unchanged if v_X is larger than the final DAC output or is decremented by 1 LSB if v_X is less than the DAC output. The conversion is completed following the logic decision at the end of the third clock period for the 3-bit converter, or at the end of n clock periods for an n-bit converter.

Figure 16.82 shows the possible code sequences for a 3-bit DAC and the sequence followed for the successive approximation conversion in Fig. 16.81. At the start of conversion, the DAC input is set to 100. At the end of the first clock period, the DAC voltage is found to be less than v_X, so the DAC code is increased to 110. At the end of the second clock period, the DAC voltage is still found to be too small, and the DAC code is increased to 111. After the third clock period, the DAC voltage is found to be too large, so the DAC code is decremented to yield a final converted value of 110.

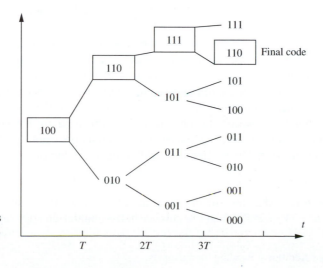

Figure 16.82 Code sequences for a 3-bit successive approximation ADC.

Fast conversion rates are possible with a successive approximation ADC. This conversion technique is very popular and used in many 8 to 16-bit converters. The primary factors limiting the speed of this ADC are the time required for the D/A converter output to settle within a fraction of an LSB of V_{FS} and the time required for the comparator to respond to input signals that may differ by very small amounts.

> **EXERCISE:** What is the conversion time for a successive approximation ADC using a 12-bit DAC and a 2-MHz clock frequency? What is the maximum possible number of conversions per second?
>
> **ANSWERS:** 6.00 μs; 167,000 conversions/second

In the discussion thus far, it has been tacitly assumed that the input remains constant during the full conversion period. A slowly varying input signal is acceptable as long as it does not change by more than 0.5 LSB ($V_{FS}/2^{n+1}$) during the conversion time ($T_T = n/f_C = nT_C$). The frequency of a sinusoidal input signal with a peak-to-peak amplitude equal to the full-scale voltage of the converter must satisfy the following inequality:

$$T_T \left\{ \max \left[\frac{d}{dt}(V_{FS} \sin \omega_o t) \right] \right\} \leq \frac{V_{FS}}{2^{n+1}} \quad \text{or} \quad \frac{n}{f_C}(V_{FS}\omega_o) \leq \frac{V_{FS}}{2^{n+1}} \quad (16.158)$$

and

$$f_O \leq \frac{f_C}{2^{n+2}n\pi}$$

For a 12-bit converter using a 1-MHz clock frequency, f_O must be less than 1.62 Hz. If the input changes by more than 0.5 LSB during the conversion process, the digital output of the converter does not bear a precise relation to the value of the unknown input voltage v_X. To avoid this frequency limitation, a high-speed **sample-and-hold circuit**[3] that samples the signal amplitude and then holds its value constant is usually used ahead of successive approximation ADCs.

Single-Ramp (Single-Slope) ADC

The discrete output of the D/A converter can be replaced by a continuously changing analog reference signal, as shown in Fig. 16.83. The reference voltage varies linearly with a well-defined slope from slightly below zero to above V_{FS}, and the converter is called a **single-ramp,** or **single-slope, ADC.** The length of time required for the reference signal to become equal to the unknown voltage is proportional to the unknown input.

Converter operation begins with a start conversion signal, which resets the binary counter and starts the ramp generator at a slightly negative voltage [see Fig. 16.83(b)]. As the ramp crosses through zero, the output of comparator 2 goes high and allows clock pulses to accumulate in the counter. The number in the counter increases until the ramp output voltage exceeds the unknown v_X. At this time, the output of comparator 1 goes high and prevents further clock pulses from reaching the counter. The number N in the counter at the end of the conversion is directly proportional to the input voltage because

$$v_X = KNT_C \quad (16.159)$$

where K is the slope of the ramp in volts/second. If the slope of the ramp is chosen to be $K = V_{FS}/2^n T_C$, then the number in the counter directly represents the binary fraction

[3] See Additional Reading for examples.

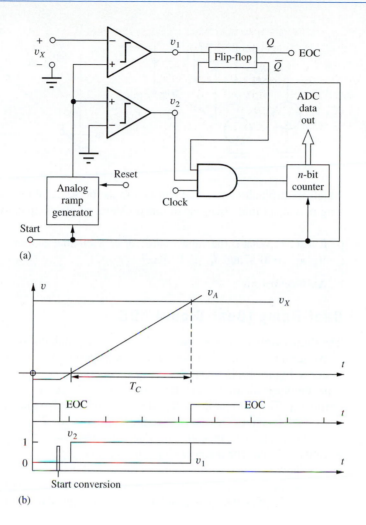

Figure 16.83 (a) Block diagram and (b) timing for a single-ramp ADC.

equal to v_X/V_{FS}:

$$\frac{v_X}{V_{FS}} = \frac{N}{2^n} \tag{16.160}$$

The conversion time T_T of the single-ramp converter is clearly variable and proportional to the unknown voltage v_X. Maximum conversion time occurs for $v_X = V_{FS}$, with

$$T_T \leq 2^n T_C \tag{16.161}$$

As is the case for the **counter-ramp converter,** the counter output represents the value of v_X at the time that the end-of-conversion signal occurs.

The ramp voltage is usually generated by an integrator connected to a constant reference voltage, as shown in Fig. 16.84. When the reset switch is opened, the output increases with a constant slope given by V_R/RC:

$$v_O(t) = -V_{OS} + \frac{1}{RC} \int_o^t V_R \, dt \tag{16.162}$$

The dependence of the ramp's slope on the RC product is one of the major limitations of the single-ramp A/D converter. The slope depends on the absolute values of R and C,

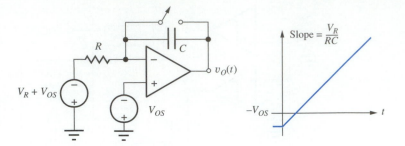

Figure 16.84 Ramp voltage generation using an integrator with constant input.

which are difficult to maintain constant in the presence of temperature variations and over long periods of time. Because of this problem, single-ramp converters are seldom used.

> **EXERCISE:** What is the value of RC for an 8-bit single-ramp ADC with $V_{FS} = 5.12$ V, $V_R = 2.000$ V, and $f_C = 1$ MHz?
>
> **ANSWER:** 0.1 ms

Dual-Ramp (Dual-Slope) ADC

The **dual-ramp,** or **dual-slope, ADC** solves the problems associated with the single-ramp converter and is commonly found in high-precision data acquisition and instrumentation systems. Figure 16.85 illustrates converter operation. The conversion cycle consists of two separate integration intervals. First, unknown voltage v_X is integrated for a known period of time T_1. The value of this integral is then compared to that of a known reference voltage V_{REF}, which is integrated for a variable length of time T_2.

At the start of conversion the counter is reset, and the integrator is reset to a slightly negative voltage. The unknown input v_X is connected to the integrator input through switch S_1. Unknown voltage v_X is integrated for a fixed period of time $T_1 = 2^n T_C$, which begins when the integrator output crosses through zero. At the end of time T_1, the counter overflows, causing S_1 to be opened and the reference input V_{REF} to be connected to the integrator

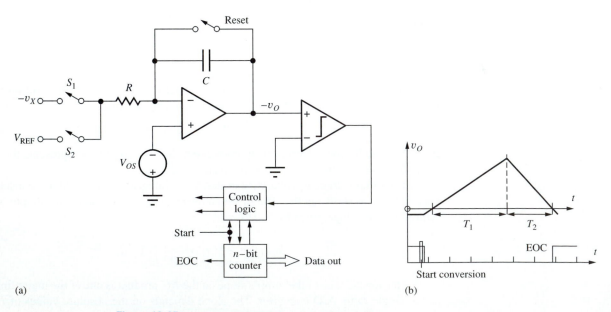

(a)

(b)

Figure 16.85 (a) Dual-ramp ADC and (b) timing diagram.

input through S_2. The integrator output then decreases until it crosses back through zero, and the comparator changes state, indicating the end of the conversion. The counter continues to accumulate pulses during the down ramp, and the final number in the counter represents the quantized value of the unknown voltage v_X.

Circuit operation forces the integrals over the two time periods to be equal:

$$\frac{1}{RC}\int_0^{T_1} v_X(t)\,dt = \frac{1}{RC}\int_{T_1}^{T_1+T_2} V_{\text{REF}}\,dt \qquad (16.163)$$

T_1 is set equal to $2^n T_C$ because the unknown voltage v_X was integrated over the amount of time needed for the n-bit counter to overflow. Time period T_2 is equal to NT_C, where N is the number accumulated in the counter during the second phase of operation.

Recalling the mean-value theorem from calculus,

$$\frac{1}{RC}\int_0^{T_1} v_X(t)\,dt = \frac{\langle v_X\rangle}{RC}T_1 \qquad (16.164)$$

and

$$\frac{1}{RC}\int_{T_1}^{T_1+T_2} V_{\text{REF}}(t)\,dt = \frac{V_{\text{REF}}}{RC}T_2 \qquad (16.165)$$

because V_{REF} is a constant. Substituting these two results into Eq. (16.163), we find the average value of the input $\langle v_x\rangle$ to be

$$\frac{\langle v_X\rangle}{V_{\text{REF}}} = \frac{T_2}{T_1} = \frac{N}{2^n} \qquad (16.166)$$

assuming that the RC product remains constant throughout the complete conversion cycle. The absolute values of R and C no longer enter directly into the relation between v_X and V_{FS}, and the long-term stability problem associated with the single-ramp converter is overcome. Furthermore, the digital output word represents the average value of v_X during the first integration phase. Thus, v_X can change during the conversion cycle of this converter without destroying the validity of the quantized output value.

The conversion time T_T requires 2^n clock periods for the first integration period, and N clock periods for the second integration period. Thus the conversion time is variable and

$$T_T = (2^n + N)T_C \le 2^{n+1}T_C \qquad (16.167)$$

because the maximum value of N is 2^n.

EXERCISE: What is the maximum conversion time for a 16-bit dual-ramp converter using a 1-MHz clock frequency? What is the maximum conversion rate?

ANSWERS: 0.131 s; 7.63 conversions/second

The dual ramp is a widely used converter. Although much slower than the successive approximation converter, the dual-ramp converter offers excellent differential and integral linearity. By combining its integrating properties with careful design, one can obtain accurate conversion at resolutions exceeding 20 bits, but at relatively low conversion rates. In a number of recent converters and instruments, the basic dual-ramp converter has been modified to include extra integration phases for automatic offset voltage elimination. These devices are often called *quad-slope* or *quad-phase converters*. Another converter, the triple ramp, uses coarse and fine down ramps to greatly improve the speed of the integrating converter (by a factor of $2^{n/2}$ for an n-bit converter).

Normal-Mode Rejection

As mentioned before, the quantized output of the dual-ramp converter represents the average of the input during the first integration phase. The integrator operates as a low-pass filter with the normalized transfer function shown in Fig. 16.86. Sinusoidal input signals, whose frequencies are exact multiples of the reciprocal of the integration time T_1, have integrals of zero value and do not appear at the integrator output. This property is used in many digital multimeters, which are equipped with dual-ramp converters having an integration time that is some multiple of the period of the 50- or 60-Hz power-line frequency. Noise sources with frequencies at multiples of the power-line frequency are therefore rejected by these integrating ADCs. This property is usually termed **normal-mode rejection.**

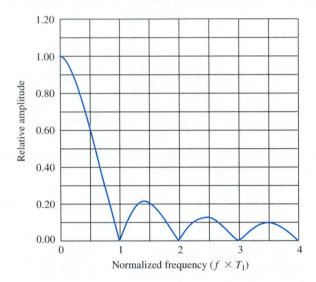

Figure 16.86 Normal-mode rejection for an integrating ADC.

The Parallel (Flash) Converter

The fastest converters employ substantially increased hardware complexity to perform a parallel rather than serial conversion. The term **flash converter** is sometimes used as the name of the parallel converter because of the device's inherent speed. Figure 16.87 shows a three-bit parallel converter in which the unknown input v_X is simultaneously compared to seven different reference voltages. The logic network encodes the comparator outputs directly into three binary bits representing the quantized value of the input voltage. The speed of this converter is very fast, limited only by the time delays of the comparators and logic network. Also, the output continuously reflects the input signal delayed by the comparator and logic network.

The parallel A/D converter is used when maximum speed is needed and is usually found in converters with resolutions of 10 bits or less because $2^n - 1$ comparators and reference voltages are needed for an n-bit converter. Thus the cost of implementing such a converter grows rapidly with resolution. However, converters with 6-, 8-, and 10-bit resolutions have been realized in monolithic IC technology. These converters achieve effective conversion rates as high as 10^8–10^9 conversions/second.

> **Exercise:** How many resistors and comparators are required to implement a 10-bit flash ADC?
>
> **Answers:** 1024 resistors; 1023 comparators

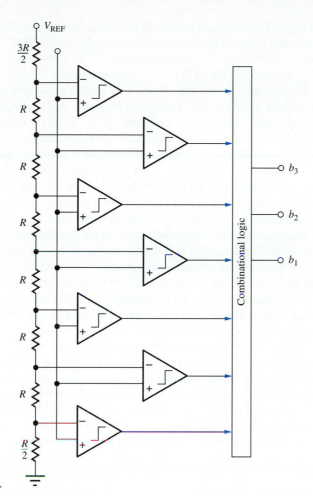

V_{REF}

$\dfrac{3R}{2}$

R

R

R

R

R

R

$\dfrac{R}{2}$

Combinational logic

b_3

b_2

b_1

Figure 16.87 3-bit flash ADC.

SUMMARY

Integrated circuit (IC) technology permits the realization of large numbers of virtually identical transistors. Although the absolute parameter tolerances of these devices are relatively poor, device characteristics can actually be matched to within less than 1 percent. The availability of large numbers of such closely matched devices has led to the development of special circuit techniques that depend on the similarity of device characteristics for proper operation. These matched circuit design techniques are used throughout analog circuit design and produce high-performance circuits that require very few resistors.

One of the most important of the IC techniques is the current mirror circuit, in which the output current replicates, or mirrors, the input current. Multiple copies of the replicated current can be generated, and the gain of the current mirror can be controlled by scaling the emitter areas of bipolar transistors or the W/L ratios of FETs. Errors in the mirror ratio of current mirrors are related directly to the finite output resistance and/or current gain of the transistors through the parameters λ, V_A and β_F.

In bipolar current mirrors, the finite current gain of the BJT causes an error in the mirror ratio, which the buffered current mirror circuit is designed to minimize. In both FET and BJT circuits, the ideal balance of the current mirror is disturbed by the mismatch in dc voltages between the input and output sections of the mirror. The degree of mismatch is determined by the output resistance of the current sources. The figure of merit V_{CS} for the basic current mirror is approximately equal to V_A for the BJT or $1/\lambda$ for the MOS version. However, the value of V_{CS} can be improved by up to two orders of magnitude through the use of either the cascode or Wilson current sources.

Current mirrors can also be used to generate currents that are independent of the power supply voltages. The V_{BE}-based reference and the Widlar reference produce currents that depend only on the logarithm of the supply voltage. By combining a Widlar source with a current mirror, a reference is realized that exhibits first-order independence of the power supply voltages. The only variation is due to the finite output resistance of the current mirror and Widlar source used in the supply-independent cell. Even this variation can be significantly reduced through the use of cascode and Wilson current mirror circuits within the reference cell. Once generated, the stabilized currents of the reference cell can be replicated using standard current mirror techniques.

An extremely important application of the current mirror is as a replacement for the load resistors in differential and operational amplifiers. This active-load circuit can substantially enhance the voltage gain capability of most amplifiers while maintaining the operating-point balance necessary for low offset voltage and good common-mode rejection. Amplifiers with active loads can achieve single-stage voltage gains that can approach the amplification factor of the transistor. Analysis of the ac behavior of circuits employing current mirrors can often be simplified using a two-port model for the mirror.

Active current mirror loads are often used to enhance the performance of both bipolar and MOS operational amplifiers. The now-classic μA-741 operational amplifier, introduced in the late 1960s, was the first highly robust design combining excellent overall amplifier performance with input-stage breakdown-voltage protection and short-circuit protection of the output stage. Active loads are used to achieve a voltage gain in excess of 100 dB in an amplifier with two stages of gain. This operational-amplifier design immediately became the industry standard op amp and spawned many similar designs.

Digital-to-analog (D/A) and analog-to-digital (A/D) converters provide the interface between the digital computer and the world of analog signals. Gain, offset, linearity, and differential linearity errors were all discussed. Simple MOS DACs can be formed using weighted-resistor, R-2R ladder and inverted R-2R ladder circuits, and MOS transistor switches. The inverted R-2R ladder configuration maintains a constant current within the ladder elements. Switched-capacitor techniques based on weighted-capacitor and C-2C ladder configurations are also widely used in VLSI ICs. In bipolar technology, DACs are usually based on multiple current sources and current switching. BJT matching is combined with weighted resistor and/or R-2R ladders to generate binary-weighted currents. Identical currents can also be switched into an R-2R ladder.

Basic ADC circuits compare the unknown voltage to a known time-varying reference signal. The reference signal is provided by a D/A converter in the counting and successive approximation converters. The counting converter sequentially compares the unknown to all possible outputs of the D/A converter; a conversion may take as many as 2^n clock periods to complete. The counting converter is simple but relatively slow. The successive approximation converter uses an efficient binary search algorithm to achieve a conversion in only n-clock periods and is a very popular conversion technique.

In the single- and dual-ramp ADCs, the reference voltage is an analog signal with a well-defined slope, usually generated by an integrator with a constant input voltage. The digital output of the single-ramp converter suffers from its dependence on the absolute values of the integrator time constant. The dual ramp greatly reduces this problem, and can achieve high differential and integral linearity, but with conversion rates of only a few conversions per second. The dual-ramp converter is widely used in high-precision instrumentation systems. Rejection of sinusoidal signals with periods that are integer multiples of the integration time, called normal-mode rejection, is an important feature of integrating converters.

The fastest A/D conversion technique is the parallel or "flash" converter, which simultaneously compares the unknown to all possible quantized values. Conversion speed is limited only by the speed of the comparators and logic network that form the converter. This high speed is achieved at a cost of high hardware complexity.

Key Terms

Active load
Analog-to-digital converter (ADC or A/D converter)
Buffered current mirror
C-2C ladder DAC
Cascode current source
Conversion time
Counter-ramp converter
Current gain defect
Current mirror
Differential linearity error
Digital-to-analog converter (DAC or D/A converter)
"Diode-connected" transistor
Dual-ramp (dual-slope) ADC
(Emitter) area scaling
Flash converter
Full-scale current
Full-scale voltage
Gain error

Integral linearity error
Inverted R-2R ladder
Least significant bit (LSB)
Linearity error
Matched devices
Matched transistors
μA-741
Mirror ratio
Missing code
Monotonicity
Most significant bit (MSB)
Multiple current mirrors
Nonmonotonic converter
Normal-mode rejection
Offset current
Offset error
Offset voltage
Overvoltage protection
Power-supply independent biasing

Power supply rejection
Quantization error
R-2R ladder
Reference current
Reference transistor
Reference voltage
Resolution of the converter
Sample-and-hold circuit
Short-circuit protection
Single-ramp (single-slope) ADC
Start-up circuit
Successive approximation converter
Superposition errors
V_{BE}-based reference
Weighted-capacitor DAC
Weighted-resistor DAC
Weighted-current source DAC
Widlar current source
Wilson current source

References

1. P. R. Gray and R. G. Meyer, *Analysis and Design of Analog Integrated Circuits,* 3rd ed., Wiley, New York: 1993.
2. R. J. Widlar, "Some circuit design techniques for linear integrated circuits," *IEEE Transactions on Circuit Theory,* vol. CT-12, no. 12, pp. 586–590, December 1965.
3. R. J. Widlar, "Design techniques for monolithic operational amplifiers," *IEEE Journal of Solid-State Circuits,* vol. SC-4, no. 4, pp. 184–191, August 1969.
4. G. R. Wilson, "A monolithic junction FET-NPN operational amplifier," *IEEE Journal of Solid-State Circuits,* vol. SC-3, no. 6, pp. 341–348, December 1968.
5. B. M. Gordon, "Linear electronic analog/digital conversion architectures," *IEEE Trans. Circuits and Systems,* vol. CAS-25, no. 7, pp. 391–418, July 1978.
6. S. K. Tewksbury et al., "Terminology related to the performance of S/H, A/D and D/A circuits," *IEEE Trans. Circuits and Systems,* vol. CAS-25, no. 7, pp. 419–426, July 1978.
7. R. C. Jaeger, "Tutorial: Analog data acquisition technology, parts I–IV," *IEEE Micro,* May–August 1982.

Additional Reading

Dooley, D. J. ed. *Data Conversion Integrated Circuits.* IEEE Press, New York: 1980.

Harrison, T. J. *Handbook of Industrial Control Computers.* Wiley, New York: 1972.

Hoeschele, D. F. *Analog-Digital and Digital-Analog Conversion Techniques.* Wiley, New York: 1968.

Schmid, H. *Electronic Analog/Digital Conversion.* Van Nostrand, New York: 1970.

Sheingold, D. H. ed. *Analog-Digital Conversion Notes.* Analog Devices, Norwood, Mass.: 1977.

PSPICE Simulation Data

Figure 16.29 MOS Reference

```
VDD 4 0 DC 5
M1 1 1 0 0 NM1 W = 10U L = 2U
M2 3 1 2 2 NM1 W = 100U L = 2U
M3 1 3 4 4 PM1 W = 10U L = 2U
M4 3 3 4 4 PM1 W = 10U L = 2U
R 2 0 8.65K
. MODEL NM1 NMOS KP = 25U VTO = 0.75 LAMBDA = .0125 GAMMA = 0.5
. MODEL PM1 PMOS KP = 10U VTO = −0.75 LAMBDA = .0125 GAMMA = 0.5
. OP
. TF I(VDD) VDD
. END
```

Figure 16.42 MOS Op Amp

```
VDM2 1 13 DC 64.17U
VDM1 3 13 DC 0
VCM 13 0 DC 0
VO 7 8 DC 0
VCC 12 0 DC 5
VEE 11 0 DC -5
M1 4 1 2 2 NM1 W = 40U L = 2U
M2 5 3 2 2 NM1 W = 40U L = 2U
M3 4 4 12 12 PM1 W = 100U L = 2U
M4 5 4 12 12 PM1 W = 100U L = 2U
M5 6 5 12 12 PM1 W = 200U L = 2U
M6 12 6 10 10 NM1 W = 20U L = 2U
M7 11 8 10 10 PM1 W = 50U L = 2U
M8 9 9 11 11 NM1 W = 20U L = 2U
M9 2 9 11 11 NM1 W = 40U L = 2U
M10 8 9 11 11 NM1 W = 40U L = 2U
M11 6 6 7 7 NM1 W = 10U L = 2U
RL 10 0 2000K
IREF 0 9 100U
. MODEL NM1 NMOS KP = 25U VTO = 0.75 LAMBDA = .0125
. MODEL PM1 PMOS KP = 10U VTO = -0.75 LAMBDA = .0125
. OP
. TF V(10) VDM1
. END
```

Figure 16.43 Bipolar Op Amp

```
VDM2 1 4 DC -3.28M
VDM1 5 4 DC 0
VCM 4 0 DC 0
VCC 12 0 DC 15
VEE 13 0 DC -15
Q1 3 1 2 N1
Q2 6 5 2 N1
Q3 3 3 12 P1
Q4 6 3 12 P1
Q5 7 6 12 P1 10
Q6 12 7 9 N1 5
Q7 13 8 9 P1
QD1 7 7 10 N1 5
QD2 8 8 10 P1 5
Q8 8 11 13 N1 5
Q9 2 11 13 N1
Q10 11 11 13 N1
RL 9 0 2000K
IREF 0 11 100U
. MODEL N1 NPN BF = 150 VAF = 60
.MODEL P1 PNP BF = 50 VAF = 60
. OP
. TF V(9) VDM
. END
```

Figure 16.44 Improved Bipolar Op Amp

```
VDM2 1 15 DC 11.6U
VDM1 5 15 DC 0
VCM 15 0 DC 0
VCC 12 0 DC 15
VEE 13 0 DC -15
Q1 3 1 2 N1
Q2 6 5 2 N1
Q3 3 4 12 P1
Q4 6 4 12 P1
Q5 0 3 4 P1
Q6 7 6 14 P1 4
Q7 7 14 12 P1 4
Q8 12 7 9 N1
Q9 13 10 9 P1
Q10 7 7 8 N1 4
Q11 10 10 8 P1 4
Q12 11 11 13 N1
Q13 2 11 13 N1
Q14 10 11 13 N1 2
RL 9 0 2K
IREF 0 11 100U
```

. MODEL N1 NPN BF = 150 VAF = 60
. MODEL P1 PNP BF = 50 VAF = 60
. OP
. TF V(9) VCM
. END

Figure 16.48 741 Input Stage

VDM2 1 15 DC .507M
VDM1 2 15 DC 0
VCM 15 0 DC 0
VCC 11 0 DC 15
VEE 13 0 DC -15
Q1 3 1 5 N1
Q2 3 2 4 N1
Q3 7 6 5 P1
Q4 8 6 4 P1
Q5 7 9 10 N1
Q6 8 9 12 N1
Q7 0 7 9 N1
Q8 6 3 11 P1
Q9 3 3 11 P1
R1 10 13 1K
R2 12 13 1K
R3 9 13 50K
IREF 6 0 18U
. MODEL N1 NPN BF = 150 VAF = 60
. MODEL P1 PNP BF = 50 VAF = 60
. OP
. TF V(8) VDM1
. END

Problems

16.1 Circuit Element Matching

16.1. An integrated circuit resistor has a nominal value of $3.64\ \text{k}\Omega$. A given process run has produced resistors with a mean value 15 percent higher than the nominal value, and the resistors are found to be matched within 3 percent. What are the maximum and minimum resistor values that will occur?

16.2. (a) The emitter areas of two bipolar transistors are mismatched by 10 percent. What will be the base-emitter voltage difference between these two transistors when their collector currents are identical? (Assume $V_A = \infty$.) (b) Repeat for a 20 percent area mismatch. (c) What degree of matching is required for a base-emitter voltage difference of less than 1 mV?

16.3. What is the worst-case fractional mismatch $\Delta I_D/I_D$ in drain currents in two MOSFETs if $K_n = 250\ \mu\text{A/V}^2 \pm 5$ percent and $V_{TN} = 1\ \text{V} \pm 25\ \text{mV}$ for (a) $V_{GS} = 2\ \text{V}$? (b) $V_{GS} = 4\ \text{V}$? Assume $I_{D1} = I_D + \Delta I_D/2$ and $I_{D2} = I_D - \Delta I_D/2$.

16.4. (a) A layout design error causes the W/L ratios of the two NMOSFETs in a differential amplifier to differ by 10 percent. What will be the gate-source voltage difference between these two transistors when their drain currents are identical if the nominal value of $(V_{GS} - V_{TN}) = 0.5\ \text{V}$? (Assume $V_{TN} = 1\ \text{V}$, $\lambda = 0$ and identical values of K'_n). (b) What degree of matching is required for a gate-source voltage difference of less than 3 mV?

*16.5. The collector currents of two BJTs are equal when the base-emitter voltages differ by 2 mV. What is the fractional mismatch $\Delta I_S/I_S$ in the saturation current of the two transistors if $I_{S1} = I_S + \Delta I_S/2$ and $I_{S2} = I_S - \Delta I_S/2$? Assume that the collector-emitter voltages and Early voltages are matched. If $\Delta \beta_{FO}/\beta_{FO} = 5$ percent, what are the values of I_{B1} and I_{B2} for the transistors at a Q-point of (100 μA, 10 V)? Assume $\beta_{FO} = 100$ and $V_A = 50$ V.

16.2 Current Mirrors

16.6. What are the output currents and output resistances for the current sources in Fig. P16.6 if $I_{REF} = 30$ μA, $K'_n = 25$ μA/V^2, $V_{TN} = 0.75$ V and $\lambda = 0.015$ V^{-1}?

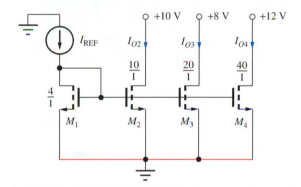

Figure P16.6

*16.7. What are the output currents and output resistances for the current sources in Fig. P16.7 if $R = 30$ kΩ, $K'_p = 15$ μA/V^2, $V_{TP} = -0.90$ V, and $\lambda = 0.01$ V^{-1}?

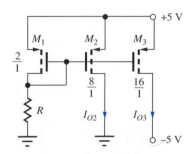

Figure P16.7

 16.8. Simulate the current source array in Fig. P16.6 and compare the results to the hand calculations in Prob. 16.6.

16.9. Simulate the current source array in Fig. P16.7 and compare the results to the hand calculations in Prob. 16.7.

 16.10. What value of R is required in Fig. P16.7 to have $I_{O2} = 35$ μA? Use device data from Prob. 16.7.

16.11. (a) What are the output currents and output resistances for the current sources in Fig. P16.11(a) if $R = 50$ kΩ, $\beta_{FO} = 50$, and $V_A = 60$ V? (b) Repeat for Fig. P16.11(b).

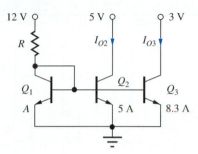

(a)

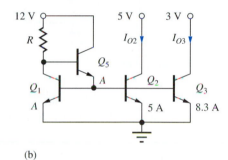

(b)

Figure P16.11

 16.12. Simulate the current source array in Fig. P16.11(a) and compare the results to the hand calculations in Prob. 16.11. (b) Repeat for Fig. 16.11(b).

 16.13. What value of R is required in Fig. P16.11(b) to have $I_{O3} = 166$ μA? What is the value of I_{O2}? Assume $\beta_{FO} = 50$ and $V_A = 60$ V.

16.14. What are the output currents and output resistances for the current sources in Fig. P16.14 if $R = 60$ kΩ, $\beta_{FO} = 50$, and $V_A = 60$ V?

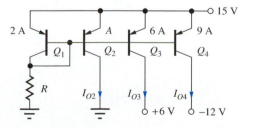

Figure P16.14

*16.15. Draw a buffered current mirror version of the source in Fig. P16.14 and find the value of R required to set $I_{REF} = 25\ \mu A$ if $\beta_{FO} = 50$ and $V_A = 60$ V. What are the values of the three output currents? What is the collector current of the additional transistor?

16.16. In Fig. P16.16, $R_2 = 5R_3$. What value of n is required to set I_{E3} to be equal to exactly $5I_{E2}$?

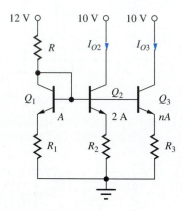

Figure P16.16

*16.17. What are the output currents and output resistances for the current sources in Fig. P16.16 if $R = 10$ kΩ, $R_1 = 10$ kΩ, $R_2 = 5$ kΩ, $R_3 = 2.5$ kΩ, $n = 4$, $\beta_{FO} = 75$, and $V_A = 60$ V?

 *16.18. What values of n and R_3 would be required in Prob. 16.17 so that $I_{O2} = 3I_{O3}$?

Widlar Sources

16.19. (a) What are the output current and output resistance for the Widlar current source I_{O2} in Fig. P16.19 if $R = R_2 = 10$ kΩ and $V_A = 60$ V? (b) For I_{O3} if $R_3 = 5$ kΩ and $n = 12$?

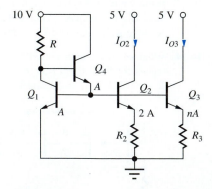

Figure P16.19

16.20. What value of R is required to set $I_{REF} = 75\ \mu A$ in Fig. P16.19? If $I_{REF} = 75\ \mu A$, what value of

R_2 is needed to set $I_{O2} = 5\ \mu A$? If $R_3 = 2$ kΩ, what value of n is required to set $I_{O3} = 10\ \mu A$?

 16.21. Simulate the source of Prob. 16.19 and compare the results to hand calculations.

16.22. (a) What are the output current and output resistance for the Widlar current source I_{O2} in Fig. P16.22 if $R = 40$ kΩ and $R_2 = 5$ kΩ? Use $V_A = 70$ V and $\beta_F = 100$. (b) For I_{O3} if $R_3 = 2.5$ kΩ and $n = 20$?

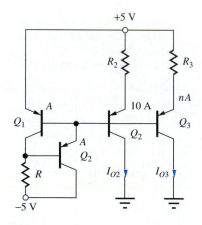

Figure P16.22

16.23. What value of R is required to set $I_{REF} = 50\ \mu A$ in Fig. P16.22. If $I_{REF} = 50\ \mu A$, what value of R_2 is needed to set $I_{O2} = 10\ \mu A$? If $R_3 = 2$ kΩ, what value of n is required to set $I_{O3} = 10\ \mu A$?

16.3 High Output Resistance Current Mirrors
Wilson Sources

16.24. $I_{REF} = 50\ \mu A$, $-V_{EE} = -5$ V, $\beta_{FO} = 125$, and $V_A = 40$ V in the Wilson source in Fig. P16.24. (a) What are the output current and output resistance for $n = 1$? (b) For $n = 3$? (c) What is the value of V_{CS} for the current source in (b)? (d) What is the minimum value of V_{EE}?

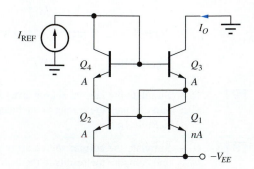

Figure P16.24

*16.25. Derive an expression for the output resistance of the Wilson source in Fig. P16.24 as a function of the area ratio n.

**16.26. Derive an expression for the output resistance of the BJT Wilson source in Fig. 16.18 and show that it can be reduced to Eq. (16.48). What assumptions were used in this simplification?

16.27. What is the minimum voltage that can be applied to the collector of Q_3 in Fig. P16.24 and have the transistor remain in the forward-active region if $I_{REF} = 15\,\mu A$, $n = 5$, $\beta_{FO} = 125$, and $I_{SO} = 3$ fA? Calculate an exact value based on the value of I_{SO}.

16.28. $R = 30\,k\Omega$ in the Wilson source in Fig. P16.28. (a) What is the output current if $(W/L)_1 = 5/1$, $(W/L)_2 = 20/1$, $(W/L)_3 = 20/1$, $K'_n = 25\,\mu A/V^2$, $V_{TN} = 0.75$ V, $\lambda = 0$ V^{-1}, and $V_{SS} = -5$ V. What value of $(W/L)_4$ is required to balance the drain voltages of M_1 and M_2? (*b) Repeat if $\lambda = 0.015$ V^{-1}. (c) Check your results in (b) with SPICE simulation.

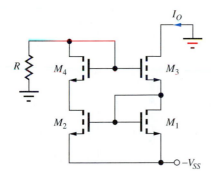

Figure P16.28

*16.29. Derive an expression for the output resistance of the Wilson source in Fig. P16.28 as a function of $(W/L)_1$, $(W/L)_2$, $(W/L)_3$, $(W/L)_4$, and the reference current I_{REF}. Assume $R = \infty$.

16.30. What is the minimum voltage required on the drain of M_3 to maintain it in saturation in the circuit in Fig. P16.28 if $I_{REF} = 150\,\mu A$, $(W/L)_1 = 5/1$, $(W/L)_2 = 20/1$, $(W/L)_3 = 20/1$, $K'_n = 25\,\mu A/V^2$, $V_{TN} = 0.75$ V, $\lambda = 0$ V^{-1}, and $-V_{SS} = -10$ V?

16.31. In Fig. P16.28, $(W/L)_3 = 5/1$, $(W/L)_4 = 5/1$, and $I_{REF} = 50\,\mu A$. What value of $(W/L)_2$ is required for $R_{OUT} = 250\,M\Omega$ if $K'_n = 25\,\mu A/V^2$, $V_{TN} = 0.75$ V, $\lambda = 0.0125$ V^{-1}. Assume $(W/L)_2 = (W/L)_1$, $R = \infty$, and $V_{SS} = 5$ V. Neglect V_{DS}.

**16.32. Redraw the equivalent circuit used to calculate the output resistance of the MOS Wilson source in Figs. 16.19 and 16.20 including a finite output resistance R_{REF} for the reference source. Based on this circuit, how large must R_{REF} be to keep from degrading the output resistance of the Wilson source? What type of current source could be use to implement I_{REF} to meet this requirement?

Cascode Current Sources

16.33. (a) What are the output current and output resistance for the cascode current source in Fig. P16.33 if $I_{REF} = 17.5\,\mu A$, $V_{DD} = 5$ V, $K_n = 75\,\mu A/V^2$, $V_{TN} = 0.75$ V, and $\lambda = 0.0125$ V^{-1}. (b) What is the value of V_{CS} for this current source? (c) What is the minimum value of V_{DD}?

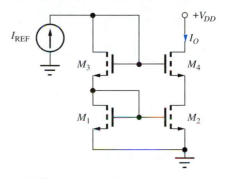

Figure P16.33

16.34. Use SPICE to simulate the current source in Prob. 16.33 and compare the results to your calculations.

16.35. (a) What are the output current and output resistance for the cascode current source in Fig. P16.35 if $I_{REF} = 17.5\,\mu A$, $\beta_{FO} = 110$, and $V_A = 50$ V? (b) What is the value of V_{CS} for this current source? (c) What is the minimum value of V_{CC}?

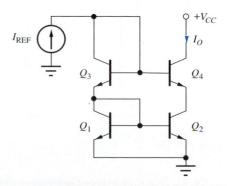

Figure P16.35

16.36. Simulate the current source in Prob. 16.35 and compare the results to your calculations.

16.37. In Fig. P16.33, $(W/L)_1 = 5/1$, $(W/L)_2 = 5/1$, $(W/L)_3 = 5/1$, and $I_{REF} = 50$ μA. What value of $(W/L)_4$ is required for $R_{OUT} = 250$ MΩ if $K'_n = 25$ μA/V^2, $V_{TN} = 0.75$ V, and $λ = 0.0125$ V^{-1}?

16.4 Reference Current Generation

16.38. Plot the variation of the output current vs. I_{REF} for the Widlar source in Fig. P16.38 for 50 μA $\leq I_{REF} \leq$ 5 mA if $R_2 = 4$ kΩ and $β_{FO} = 100$.

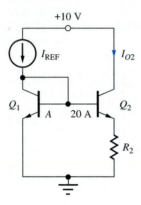

Figure P16.38

16.39. (a) What is the output current of the V_{BE}-based reference in Fig. P16.39(a) if $I_S = 10^{-15}$ A, $β_F = ∞$, $R_1 = 10$ kΩ, $R_2 = 2.2$ kΩ, and $V_{EE} = 15$ V? (b) For $V_{EE} = 3.3$ V? (c) What is the output current of the V_{BE}-based reference in Fig. P16.39(b) if $R_1 = 10$ kΩ, $R_2 = 10$ kΩ, and $V_{CC} = 5$ V?

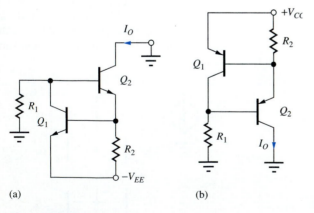

(a)   (b)

Figure P16.39

*16.40. Derive an expression for the output resistance of the cascode current source in Fig. 16.23.

*16.41. What is the output current of the NMOS reference in Fig. P16.41 if $R_1 = 10$ kΩ, $R_2 = 15$ kΩ, $K_n = 250$ μA/V^2, $V_{TN} = 0.75$ V, $λ = 0.017$ V^{-1}, and $V_{DD} = 10$ V?

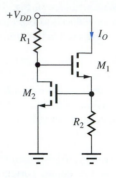

Figure P16.41

*16.42. What is the output current of the PMOS reference in Fig. P16.42 if $R_1 = 10$ kΩ, $R_2 = 18$ kΩ, $K_p = 100$ μA/V^2, $V_{TP} = -0.75$ V, $λ = 0.02$ V^{-1}, and $V_{DD} = 5$ V?

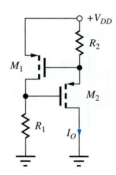

Figure P16.42

16.43. What are the collector currents in Q_1 and Q_2 in the reference in Fig. P16.43 if $V_{CC} = V_{EE} =$

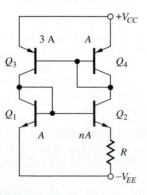

Figure P16.43

1.5 V, $n = 20$, and $R = 2.2$ kΩ? Assume $\beta_{FO} = \infty$ and $V_A = \infty$.

16.44. Simulate the reference in Fig. P16.43 using SPICE, assuming $\beta_{FO} = 100$ and $V_A = 50$ V. Compare the currents to hand calculations and discuss the source of any discrepancies. Use SPICE to determine the sensitivity of the reference currents to power supply voltage changes.

16.45. What are the drain currents in M_1 and M_2 in the reference in Fig. P16.45 if $R = 5.1$ kΩ and $V_{DD} = V_{SS} = 5$V? Use $K'_n = 25$ μA/V^2, $V_{TN} = 0.75$ V, $K'_p = 10$ μA/V^2, and $V_{TP} = -0.75$ V. Assume $\gamma = 0$ and $\lambda = 0$ for both transistor types.

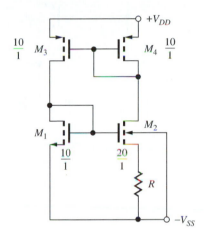

Figure P16.45

16.46. (a) Find the currents in both sides of the reference cell in Fig. P16.45 if $R = 10$ kΩ and $V_{DD} = V_{SS} = 5$ V, using $K'_n = 25$ μA/V^2, $V_{TON} = 0.75$ V, $K'_p = 10$ μA/V^2, $V_{TOP} = -0.75$ V, $\gamma_n = 0$ and $\gamma_p = 0$. Use $2\phi_F = 0.6$ V and $\lambda = 0$ for both transistor types. (b) Repeat for $\gamma_n = 0.5$ V$^{0.5}$ and $\gamma_p = 0.75$ V$^{0.5}$ and compare the results.

16.47. Simulate the references in Prob. 16.46(a) and (b) using SPICE with $\lambda = 0.017$ V^{-1}. Compare the currents to hand calculations (with $\gamma = 0$ and $\lambda = 0$) and discuss the source of any discrepancies. Use SPICE to determine the sensitivity of the reference currents to power supply voltage changes.

16.48. What are the collector currents in Q_1 to Q_8 in the reference in Fig. P16.48 if $V_{CC} = 0$ V, $V_{EE} = 3.3$ V, $R = 11$ kΩ, $R_6 = 3$ kΩ, $R_8 = 4$ kΩ, and $A_{E2} = 5$ A, $A_{E3} = 2$ A, $A_{E4} = A$, $A_{E5} = 2.5$ A, $A_{E6} = A$, $A_{E7} = 5$ A, and $A_{E8} = 3$ A?

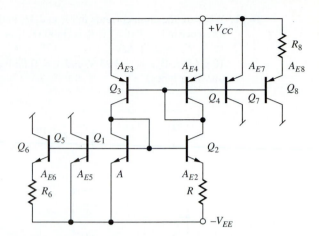

Figure P16.48

*16.49. What are the collector currents in Q_1 to Q_7 in the reference in Fig. P16.49 if $V_{CC} = 5$ V and $R = 4300$ Ω? Assume $\beta_F = \infty = V_A$.

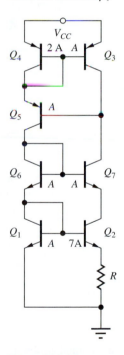

Figure P16.49

*16.50. (a) Simulate the reference in Prob. 16.49 using SPICE. Assume $\beta_{FOn} = 100$, $\beta_{FOp} = 50$, and both Early voltages $= 50$ V. Compare the currents to hand calculations and discuss the source of any discrepancies. Use SPICE to determine the sensitivity of the reference currents to power supply voltage changes. (b) Compare to simulations of the reference in Fig. 16.22 with $A_{E2} = 7$ A.

*16.51. What are the drain currents in M_1 and M_2 in the reference in Fig. P16.51 if $R = 3300\ \Omega$, $V_{DD} = 15$ V, $K'_n = 25\ \mu A/V^2$, $V_{TN} = 0.75$ V, $K'_p = 10\ \mu A/V^2$, $V_{TP} = -0.75$ V, and $\lambda = 0$ for both transistor types?

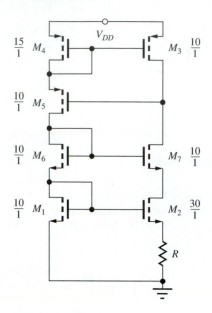

Figure P16.51

 16.52. Simulate the reference in Prob. 16.51 with SPICE using $\lambda = 0.017\ V^{-1}$ for both transistor types. Compare the currents to those in Prob. 16.51 and discuss the source of any discrepancies. Use SPICE to determine the sensitivity of the reference currents to power supply voltage changes.

16.5 The Current Mirror as an Active Load

*16.53. What are the values of A_{dd}, A_{cd}, and CMRR for the amplifier in Fig. 16.32 if $I_{SS} = 200\ \mu A$, $R_{SS} = 25\ M\Omega$, $K_n = K_p = 500\ \mu A/V^2$, $V_{TN} = 1$ V, and $V_{TP} = -1$ V and $\lambda = 0.02\ V^{-1}$ for both transistors?

 16.54. Use SPICE to simulate the amplifier in Prob. 16.53 and compare the results to the hand calculations.

**16.55. What are A_{dd} and A_{cd} for the bipolar differential amplifier in Fig. 16.37 ($R_L = \infty$) if $\beta_{op} = 70$, $\beta_{on} = 125$, $I_1 = 200\ \mu A$, $R_1 = 25\ M\Omega$, and the Early voltages for both transistors are 60 V? What is the CMRR for $v_{C1} = v_{C2}$?

 16.56. Use SPICE to calculate A_{dd} and A_{cd} for the differential amplifier in Prob. 16.55. Compare the results to hand calculations.

*16.57. (a) Find the Q-points of the transistors in the CMOS differential amplifier in Fig. P16.57 if $V_{DD} = V_{SS} = 10$ V and $I_{SS} = 200\ \mu A$. Assume $K'_n = 25\ \mu A/V^2$, $V_{TN} = 0.75$ V, $K'_p = 10\ \mu A/V^2$, $V_{TP} = -0.75$ V, and $\lambda = 0.017\ V^{-1}$ for both transistor types. (b) What is the voltage gain A_{dd} of the amplifier? (c) Compare this result to the gain of the amplifier in Fig. 16.32 if the Q-point and W/L ratios of M_1 to M_4 are the same.

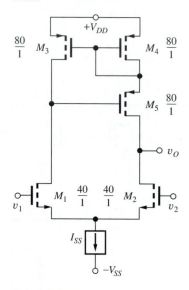

Figure P16.57

*16.58. Find the Q-points of the transistors in the folded-cascode CMOS differential amplifier in Fig. P16.58 if $V_{DD} = V_{SS} = 5$ V, $I_1 = $

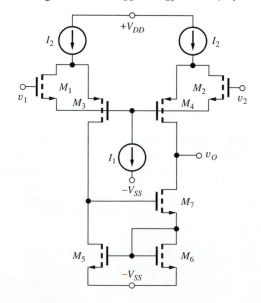

Figure P16.58

250 μA, $I_2 = 250$ μA, $(W/L) = 40/1$ for all transistors, $K'_n = 25$ μA/V^2, $V_{TN} = 0.75$ V, $K'_p = 10$ μA/V^2, $V_{TP} = -0.75$ V, and $\lambda = 0.017$ V^{-1} for both transistor types. Draw the differential-mode half-circuit for transistors M_1 to M_4 and show that the circuit is in fact a cascode amplifier. What is the differential-mode voltage gain of the amplifier?

*16.59. Design a current mirror bias network to supply the three currents needed by the amplifier in Fig. P16.58.

16.60. Use SPICE to simulate the amplifier in Prob. 16.58 and determine its voltage gain, output resistance, and CMRR. Compare to hand calculations.

Output Stages

16.61. What are the currents in Q_3 and Q_4 in the class-AB output stage in Fig. P16.61 if $R_1 = 20$ kΩ, $R_2 = 20$ kΩ, and $I_{S4} = I_{S3} = I_{S2} = 10^{-14}$ A. Assume $\beta_F = \infty$.

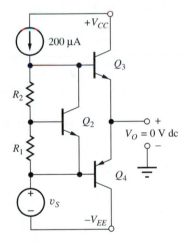

Figure P16.61

*16.62. Show that the currents in Q_3 and Q_4 in the class-AB output stage in Fig. P16.62 are equal to $I_o = I_2 \sqrt{(A_{E3}A_{E4})/(A_{E1}A_{E2})}$.

16.63. What are the currents in Q_3 and Q_4 in Fig. P16.62 if $A_{E1} = 3A_{E3}$, $A_{E2} = 3A_{E4}$, $I_2 = 300$ μA, $I_{SOpnp} = 4$ fA, and $I_{SOnpn} = 10$ fA?

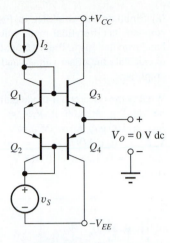

Figure P16.62

16.6 Active Loads in Operational Amplifiers

*16.64. (a) Find the Q-points of the transistors in Fig. P16.64 if $V_{DD} = V_{SS} = 10$ V, $I_{REF} = 250$ μA, $K'_n = 25$ μA/V^2, $V_{TN} = 0.75$ V, $K'_p = 10$ μA/V^2, and $V_{TP} = -0.75$ V. (b) What is the approximate value of the W/L ratio for M_6 of the CMOS op amp in order for the offset voltage to be zero? What is the differential-mode voltage gain of the op amp if $\lambda = 0.017$ V^{-1} for both transistor types?

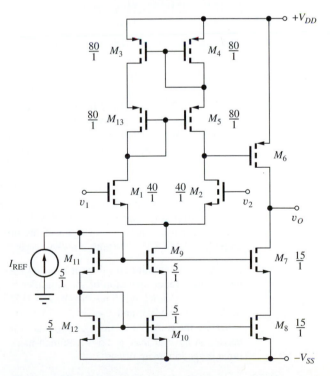

Figure P16.64

*16.65. (a) Simulate the amplifier in Prob. 16.64 and compare its differential-mode voltage gain to the hand calculations in Prob. 16.64. (b) Use SPICE to calculate the offset voltage and CMRR of the amplifier.

*16.66. What is the differential-mode gain of the amplifier in Fig. P16.66 if $V_{DD} = V_{SS} = 10$ V, $I_{REF} = 100$ μA, $K'_n = 25$ μA/V^2, $V_{TON} = 0.75$ V, $K'_p = 10$ μA/V^2, $V_{TOP} = -0.75$ V, $\gamma_n = 0$, and $\gamma_p = 0$. Use $\lambda = 0.017$ V^{-1} for both transistor types.

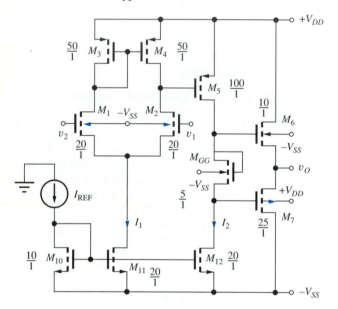

Figure P16.66

16.67. (a) Use SPICE to find the Q-points of the transistors of the amplifier in Prob. 16.66. (b) Repeat with $2\phi_F = 0.8$ V, $\gamma_n = 0.60$ V$^{0.5}$, and $\gamma_p = 0.75$ V$^{0.5}$, and compare the results to (a).

*16.68. Find the Q-points of the transistors in Fig. P16.66 if $V_{DD} = V_{SS} = 7.5$ V, $I_{REF} = 250$ μA, $(W/L)_{12} = 40/1$, $K'_n = 25$ μA/V^2, $V_{TN} = 0.75$ V, $K'_p = 10$ μA/V^2, and $V_{TP} = -0.75$ V. What is the differential-mode voltage gain of the op amp if $\lambda = 0.017$ V^{-1} for both transistor types?

*16.69. (a) Estimate the minimum values of V_{DD} and V_{SS} needed for proper operation of the amplifier in Prob. 16.66. Use $K'_n = 25$ μA/V^2, $V_{TN} = 0.75$ V, $K'_p = 10$ μA/V^2, and $V_{TP} = -0.75$ V. (b) What are the minimum values of V_{DD} and V_{SS} needed to have at least a ±5-V common-mode input range in the amplifier?

16.70. (a) Find the Q-points of the transistors in the CMOS op amp in Fig. 16.42 if $V_{DD} = V_{SS} = 5$ V, $I_{REF} = 250$ μA, $K'_n = 25$ μA/V^2, $V_{TN} = $

0.75 V, $K'_p = 10$ μA/V^2, and $V_{TP} = -0.75$ V. (b) What is the voltage gain of the op amp assuming the output stage has unity gain and $\lambda = 0.017$ V^{-1} for both transistor types? (c) What is the voltage gain if I_{REF} is changed to 500 μA?

16.71. Based on the example calculations and your knowledge of MOSFET characteristics, what will be the gain of the op amp in Example 16.3 if the I_{REF} is set to (a) 250 μA? (b) 20 μA? (*Note:* These should be short calculations.)

16.72. Based on the exercise answers and your knowledge of BJT characteristics, what will be the gain of the op amp in Fig. 16.43 if the I_{REF} is set to (a) 250 μA? (b) 50 μA? (*Note:* These should be short calculations.)

16.73. Draw the amplifier that represents the mirror image of Fig. 16.42 by interchanging NMOS and PMOS transistors. Choose the W/L ratios of the NMOS and PMOS transistors so the voltage gain of the new amplifier is the same as the gain of the amplifier in Fig. 16.42. Maintain the operating currents the same and use the device parameter values from the Example 16.3.

16.74. Draw the amplifier that represents the mirror image of Fig. 16.43 by interchanging *npn* and *pnp* transistors. If $\beta_{on} = 150$, $\beta_{op} = 60$, and $V_{AN} = V_{AP} = 60$ V, which of the two amplifiers will have the highest voltage gain? Why?

*16.75. What is the approximate emitter area of Q_{16} needed to achieve zero offset voltage in the amplifier in Fig. P16.75 if $I_B = 250$ μA and $V_{CC} = $

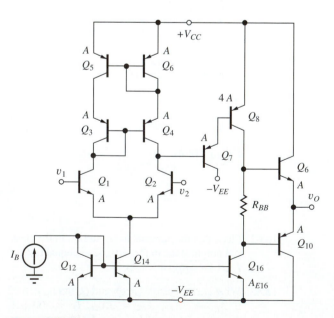

Figure P16.75

$V_{EE} = 5$ V? What is the value of R_{BB} needed to set the quiescent current in the output stage to 75 μA? What are the voltage gain and input resistance of this amplifier? Assume $\beta_{on} = 150$, $\beta_{op} = 60$, $V_{AN} = V_{AP} = 60$ V, and $I_{SOnpn} = I_{SOpnp} = 15$ fA.

 16.76. Use SPICE to simulate the characteristics of the amplifier in Prob. 16.75. Determine the offset voltage, voltage gain, input resistance, output resistance, and CMRR of the amplifier.

 16.77. (a) What are the minimum values of V_{CC} and V_{EE} needed for proper operation of the amplifier in Fig. P16.75? (b) What are the minimum values of V_{CC} and V_{EE} needed to have at least a ± 1-V common-mode input range in the amplifier?

16.7 The μA-741 Operational Amplifier

16.78. (a) What are the three bias currents in the source in Fig. P16.78 if $R_1 = 100$ kΩ, $R_2 = 4$ kΩ, and $V_{CC} = V_{EE} = 3$ V. (b) Repeat for $V_{CC} = V_{EE} = 22$ V. (c) Why is it important that I_1 in the μA-741 be independent of power supply voltage but it does not matter as much for I_2 and I_3?

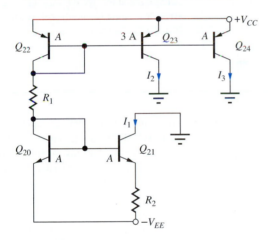

Figure P16.78

 16.79. Choose the values of R_1 and R_2 in Fig. P16.78 to set $I_2 = 250$ μA and $I_1 = 50$ μA if $V_{CC} = V_{EE} = 12$ V. What is I_3?

16.80. Choose the values of R_1 and R_2 in Fig. P16.78 to set $I_3 = 300$ μA and $I_1 = 75$ μA if $V_{CC} = V_{EE} = 15$ V. What is I_2?

*16.81. (a) Based on the schematic in Fig. 16.46, what are the minimum values of V_{CC} and V_{EE} needed for proper operation of μA-741 amplifier? (b) What are the minimum values of V_{CC} and V_{EE} needed to have at least a ± 1-V common-mode input range in the amplifier?

16.82. What are the values of the elements in the Norton equivalent circuit in Fig. 16.53 if I_1 in Fig. 16.46 is increased to 50 μA?

16.83. Suppose Q_{23} in Fig. 16.47 is replaced by a cascode current source. (a) What is the new value of output resistance R_2? (b) What are the new values of the y-parameters of Fig. 16.54? (c) What is the new value of A_{dm} for the op amp?

 16.84. Draw a schematic for the cascode current source in Prob. 16.83.

 16.85. Create a small-signal SPICE model for the circuit in Fig. 16.54 and verify the values of y_{11}, y_{21}, and y_{22}. What is the value of y_{12}?

**16.86. Figure P16.86 represents an op amp input stage that was developed following the introduction of the μA-741. (a) Find the Q-points for all the transistors in the differential amplifier in Fig. P16.86 if $V_{CC} = V_{EE} = 15$ V and $I_{REF} = 100$ μA. (b) Discuss how this bias network operates to establish the Q-points. (c) Label the inverting and noninverting input terminals. (d) What are the transconductance and output resistance of this amplifier? Use $V_A = 60$ V.

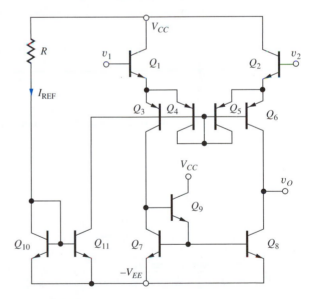

Figure P16.86

**16.87. Figure P16.87 represents an op-amp input stage that was developed following the introduction of the μA-741. Find the Q-points for all the transistors in the differential amplifier in Fig. P16.87 if $V_{CC} = V_{EE} = 15$ V and $I_{REF} = 100$ μA. (b) Discuss how this bias network operates to establish the Q-points. (c) Label the inverting and noninverting input terminals. (d) What are the

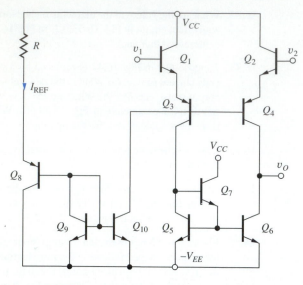

Figure P16.87

Binary Input	DAC Output Voltages	Step Size (LSB)	Differential Linearity Error (LSB)	Integral Linearity Error
000	0.0000			0.00
001	0.1000			
010	0.3000			
011	0.3500			
100	0.4750			
101	0.6300			
110	0.7250			
111	0.8750			0.00

transconductance and output resistance of this amplifier? Use $V_A = 60$ V.

16.8 Digital-to-Analog Conversion

16.88. Draw the transfer function, similar to Fig. 16.61, for a DAC with $V_{OS} = 0.5$ LSB and no gain error.

16.89. (a) What is the output voltage for the 4-bit DAC in Fig. P16.89, as shown with input data of 0110 if $V_{REF} = 3.0$ V? (b) Suppose the input data changes to 1001. What will be the new output voltage? (c) Make a table giving the output voltages for all 16 possible input data combinations.

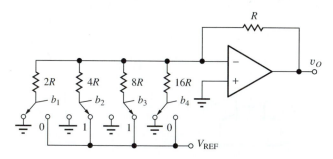

Figure P16.89

16.90. The op amp in Fig. P16.89 has an offset voltage of +5 mV and the feedback resistor has a value of $1.05R$ instead of R. What are the offset and gain errors of this DAC?

16.91. Fill in the missing entries for step size, differential linearity error, and integral linearity error for the DAC in the accompanying table.

*16.92. A 3-bit weighted-resistor DAC similar to Fig. 16.64 is made using standard 5 percent resistors with $R = 1$ kΩ, $2R = 2$ kΩ, $4R = 3.9$ kΩ, and $8R = 8.2$ kΩ. (a) Tabulate the nominal output values of this converter in a manner similar to Table 16.5. What are the values of differential linearity and integral linearity errors for the nominal resistor values? (b) What are the worst-case values of linearity error that can occur with the 5 percent resistors? (*Note:* this converter has a gain error. You must recalculate the "ideal" step size. It is not 0.1250 V.)

**16.93. Perform a 200-case Monte Carlo analysis of the DAC in Prob. 16.89 and find the worst-case differential and integral linearity errors for the DAC. Use 5% resistor tolerances.

*16.94. The switches in Fig. P16.89 can be implemented using MOSFETs, as shown in Fig. P16.94. What must be the W/L ratios of the transistors if the on-resistance of the transistor is to be less than 1 percent of the resistor $2R = 10$ kΩ? Use $V_{REF} = 3.0$ V. Assume that the voltage applied to the gate of the MOSFET is 5 V when $b_1 = 1$ and 0 V when $b_1 = 0$. For the MOSFET, $V_{TN} = 1$ V, $K_n' = 50$ μA/V², $2\phi_F = 0.6$ V, and $\gamma = 0.5 \sqrt{V}$.

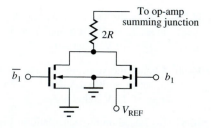

Figure P16.94

**16.95. The output voltage of a 3-bit weighted resistor DAC must have an error of no more than 5 percent of V_{REF} for any input combination. What can be the tolerances on the resistors R, $2R$, $4R$, and $8R$ if each resistor is allowed to contribute approximately the same error to the output voltage?

16.96. How many resistors are needed to realize a 10-bit weighted-resistor DAC? What is the ratio of the largest resistor to the smallest resistor?

16.97. Use Thévenin equivalent circuits for the R-2R ladder network in Fig. P16.97 to find the output voltage for the four input combinations 0001, 0010, 0100, and 1000 if $V_{REF} = 5.0$ V.

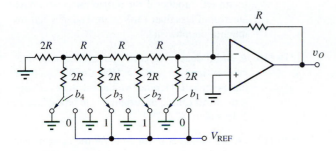

Figure P16.97

*16.98. Tabulate the output voltages for the eight binary input words for the 3-bit DAC in Fig. P16.98, and find the differential and integral linearity errors if $V_{REF} = 5.00$ V, $R_{REF} = 250$ Ω, and $R = 1.2188$ kΩ.

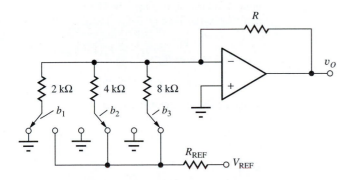

Figure P16.98

16.99. Suppose each switch in the DAC in Fig. P16.98 has an on-resistance of 200 Ω. (a) What value of R is required for zero gain error? (b) Find the differential and integral linearity errors if $V_{REF} = 5.00$ V, $R_{REF} = 0$ Ω. (c) Repeat for $R_{REF} = 250$ Ω.

*16.100. Show that $15R/2$ is the value of resistance required to maintain proper current source weighting in Fig. 16.71.

16.101. Design a two-section 6-bit current source array similar to that in Fig. 16.71. Use $V_{REF} = 3$ V, $-V_{EE} = -5$ V, and a LSB current of 25 μA.

16.102. (a) Derive a formula for the total capacitance in an n-bit weighted-capacitor DAC. (b) In an n-bit C-2C DAC.

16.103. Perform a transient simulation of the C-2C DAC in Fig. 16.68(b) when b_3 switches from a 0 to a 1 and then back to a 0. Use $C = 0.5$ pF with $V_{REF} = 5$ V, and model the switches with NMOS transistors with $W/L = 10/1$, as in Fig. P16.94.

16.104. A 4-bit weighted-current source array with $I_{FS} = 2$ mA is connected to the summing junction of the op amp in Fig. P16.104. (a) Make a table of the output voltages versus input code if $R = 5$ kΩ, $R_O = 1$ kΩ and $V_{REF} = 1$ V. (b) What is the equivalent offset current if the op amp has an offset voltage of +5 mV?

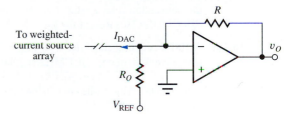

Figure P16.104

*16.105. A 3-bit inverted R-2R ladder with $R = 2.5$ kΩ and $V_{BB} = -2.5$ V is connected to the input of the op amp in Fig. P16.105. Draw the schematic of the complete D/A converter. Make a table of the output voltages versus input code if $R_1 = 5$ kΩ.

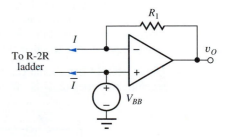

Figure P16.105

*16.106. Suppose a 10-bit DAC is built using the inherently monotonic circuit technique in Fig. 16.67. (a) If the resistor material has a sheet resistance of 50 Ω/square, and $R = 500$ Ω, estimate the number of squares that will be required for the resistor string. (b) If the minimum width of a resistor is 5 μm, what is the required length of the resistor string? Convert this length to inches.

16.9 Analog-to-Digital Conversion

16.107. A 14-bit ADC with $V_{FS} = 5.12$ V has an output code of 10101010110010. What is the possible range of input voltages?

16.108. A 20-bit ADC has $V_{FS} = 2$ V. (a) What is the value of the LSB? (b) What is the ADC output code for an input voltage of 1.630000 V? (c) What is the ADC output code for an input voltage of 0.997003 V?

16.109. Plot the transfer function and quantization error for an ideal 3-bit ADC that does not have the 0.5 LSB offset shown in Fig. 16.76. (that is, the first code transition occurs for $v_X = V_{FS}/8$). Why is the design in Fig. 16.76 preferred?

16.110. A 12-bit counting converter with $V_{FS} = 10$ V and $f_c = 1$ MHz has an input voltage $V_X = 3.760$ V. (a) What is the output code? What is the conversion time T_T for this value of V_X if $f_c = 1$ MHz? (b) Repeat for $V_X = 7.333$ V.

16.111. A 10-bit counting converter with $V_{FS} = 5.12$ V uses a clock frequency of 1 MHz and has an input voltage $v_X(t) = 5\cos 5000\pi t$ V. What is the output code? What is the conversion time T_T for this input voltage?

16.112. (a) A 12-bit successive approximation ADC with $V_{FS} = 2$ V is designed using the circuit in Fig. 16.81. What is the maximum permissible offset voltage of the comparator if this offset error is to be less than 0.1 LSB? (b) Repeat for a 20-bit ADC.

16.113. A 16-bit successive approximation ADC is be designed to operate at 50,000 conversions/second. What is the clock frequency? How rapidly must the unknown and reference voltage switches change state if the switch timing delay is to be equivalent to less than 0.1 LSB time?

*16.114. Figure P16.114 is the ramp generator for an integrating converter. (a) If the offset voltage of the

op amp is 10 mV and $V = 3$ V, what is the effective reference voltage of this converter? (b) The integrator is used in a single-slope converter with an integration time of 1/30 s and a full-scale voltage of 5.12 V. What is the RC time constant? If $R = 50$ kΩ, what is the value of C?

**16.115. A ramp generator using an op-amp integrator circuit is built using an operational amplifier with an open-loop gain $A_O = 5 \times 10^4$. A 5-V step function is applied to the input of the integrator at $t = 0$. Write an expression for the output of the integrator in the time domain. What is the minimum RC product if the output ramp is to have an error of less than 1 mV at the end of a 200-ms integration interval?

*16.116. A 20-bit dual-ramp converter is to have an integration time $T_1 = 0.2$ s. How rapidly must the unknown and reference voltage switches change state if this timing uncertainty is to be equivalent to less than 0.1 LSB?

**16.117. Derive the transfer function for the integrator in the dual-ramp converter, and show that it has the functional form of $|\sin x/x|$.

16.118. Write formulas for the number of resistors and number of comparators that are required to implement an n-bit flash converter.

Miscellaneous

16.119. Show that R_E can be absorbed into the common-emitter transistor in Fig. P16.119 to create an equivalent transistor Q' defined with

$$g'_m = \frac{g_m}{1 + g_m R_E} \qquad r'_\pi = r_\pi(1 + g_m R_E)$$

$$r'_o = r_o(1 + g_m R_E)$$

What are the values of β'_o and μ'_f?

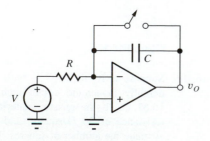

Figure P16.119

16.120. Show that Eq. (14.30), Chapter 14, reduces to $R_{OUT} = r_o(1 + g_m R_E)$ for small values of $I_E R_E$ ($R_5 = R_E$) with $R_{th} = 0$. How small must $I_E R_E$ be to satisfy the assumptions?

Figure P16.114

Frequency Response

Chapters 13 to 16 discussed analysis and design of the midband characteristics of amplifiers. Low-frequency response limitations due to coupling and bypass capacitors were ignored, and the internal capacitances of electronic devices, which limit the response at high frequencies, were also neglected. This chapter completes the discussion of basic amplifier design with the introduction of methods used to tailor the frequency response of analog circuits at both low and high frequencies. As part of this discussion, the internal device capacitances of bipolar and field-effect transistors are discussed, and frequency-dependent small-signal models of the transistors are introduced. The unity-gain bandwidth product of the devices is discussed and expressed in terms of the small-signal parameters.

The frequency responses of the single-stage inverting, noninverting, and follower configurations are each developed in detail. We show that the bandwidth of high-gain inverting and noninverting stages can be quite limited, whereas that of followers is normally very wide. Use of the cascode configuration is shown to significantly improve the frequency response of inverting amplifiers. Narrow-band (high-Q) bandpass amplifiers based on tuned circuits are also discussed.

Transfer functions for multistage amplifiers may have large numbers of poles and zeros, and direct circuit analysis, although possible, can be complex and unwieldy. Therefore, approximation techniques—the short-circuit and open-circuit time-constant methods—have been developed to estimate the upper- and lower-cutoff frequencies ω_H and ω_L. The Miller effect is introduced, and the relatively low bandwidth associated with inverting amplifiers is shown to be caused by Miller multiplication of the collector-base or gate-drain capacitance of the transistor in the amplifier. Internally compensated single-pole operational amplifiers use Miller multiplication to provide frequency compensation, and the resulting unity-gain frequencies can be directly related to amplifier slew rate.

17.1 AMPLIFIER FREQUENCY RESPONSE

Figure 17.1 is the Bode plot for the magnitude of the voltage gain of a hypothetical amplifier. Regardless of the number of poles and zeros, the voltage transfer function $A_v(s)$ can be written as the ratio of two polynomials in s:

$$A_V(s) = \frac{N(s)}{D(s)} = \frac{a_0 + a_1 s + a_2 s^2 + \cdots + a_m s^m}{b_0 + b_1 s + b_2 s^2 + \cdots + b_n s^n} = \qquad (17.1)$$

In principle, the numerator and denominator polynomials of Eq. (17.1) can be written in factored form, and the poles and zeros can be separated into two groups. Those associated with the low-frequency response below the midband region of the amplifier can be combined into a function $F_L(s)$, and those associated with the high-frequency response above

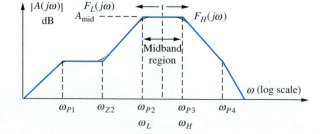

Figure 17.1 Bode plot for a general amplifier transfer function.

the midband region can be grouped into a function $F_H(s)$. Using F_L and F_H, $A(s)$ can be rewritten as

$$A(s) = A_{\text{mid}}F_L(s)F_H(s) \qquad (17.2)$$

in which A_{mid} is the **midband gain**[1] of the amplifier in the region between the **lower-** and **upper-cutoff frequencies** (ω_L and ω_H, respectively). For A_{mid} to appear explicitly as shown in Eq. (17.2), $F_H(s)$ and $F_L(s)$ must be written in the two particular standard forms defined by Eqs. (17.3) and (17.4):

$$F_L(s) = \frac{(s + \omega_{Z1}^L)(s + \omega_{Z2}^L) \cdots (s + \omega_{Zk}^L)}{(s + \omega_{P1}^L)(s + \omega_{P2}^L) \cdots (s + \omega_{Pk}^L)} \qquad (17.3)$$

$$F_H(s) = \frac{\left(1 + \dfrac{s}{\omega_{Z1}^H}\right)\left(1 + \dfrac{s}{\omega_{Z2}^H}\right) \cdots \left(1 + \dfrac{s}{\omega_{Zl}^H}\right)}{\left(1 + \dfrac{s}{\omega_{P1}^H}\right)\left(1 + \dfrac{s}{\omega_{P2}^H}\right) \cdots \left(1 + \dfrac{s}{\omega_{Pl}^H}\right)} \qquad (17.4)$$

The representation of $F_H(s)$ is chosen so that its magnitude approaches a value of 1 at frequencies well below the upper-cutoff frequency ω_H,

$$|F_H(j\omega)| \to 1 \qquad \text{for } \omega \ll \omega_{Zi}^H, \omega_{Pi}^H \text{ for } i = 1 \ldots l \qquad (17.5)$$

Thus, at low frequencies, the transfer function $A(s)$ becomes

$$A_L(s) \approx A_{\text{mid}}F_L(s) \qquad (17.6)$$

The form of $F_L(s)$ is chosen so its magnitude approaches a value of 1 at frequencies well above ω_L:

$$|F_L(j\omega)| \to 1 \qquad \text{for } \omega \gg \omega_{Zj}^L, \omega_{Pj}^L \text{ for } j = 1 \ldots k \qquad (17.7)$$

Thus, at high frequencies the transfer function $A(s)$ can be approximated by

$$A_H(s) \approx A_{\text{mid}}F_H(s) \qquad (17.8)$$

Low-Frequency Response

In many designs, the zeros of $F_L(s)$ can be placed at frequencies low enough to not influence the lower-cutoff frequency ω_L. In addition, one of the low-frequency poles in Fig. 17.1, say ω_{P2}, can be designed to be much larger than the others. For these conditions, the low-frequency portion of the transfer function can be written approximately as

$$F_L(s) \approx \frac{s}{s + \omega_{P2}} \qquad (17.9)$$

Pole ω_{P2} is referred to as the **dominant low-frequency pole** and the lower-cutoff frequency ω_L is approximately

$$\omega_L \approx \omega_{P2} \qquad (17.10)$$

The Bode plot in Fig. 17.2 is an example of a transfer function and its dominant pole approximation. The transfer function $A_L(s)$ for this figure has two poles and two zeros.

---

[1] You may wish to review some of the frequency response definitions in Chapter 11.

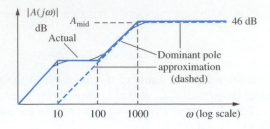

Figure 17.2 Bode plot for
the complete transfer function and its dominant pole
approximation.

EXAMPLE 17.1: Find A_{mid}, $F_L(s)$, and f_L for the transfer function in Fig. 17.2 expressed as

$$A_L(s) = 200\frac{s(s + 100)}{(s + 10)(s + 1000)}$$

SOLUTION:

$$A_{\text{mid}} = 200 = 46 \text{ dB} \qquad \text{and} \qquad F_L(s) = \frac{s(s + 100)}{(s + 10)(s + 1000)}$$

The poles occur for $s = -10$ and $s = -1000$. The zeros occur at $s = 0$ and $s = -100$. Because $1000 \gg (0, 10, 100)$, a dominant pole $(s = -1000)$ exists, and $A_V(s)$ can be represented by the approximation

$$A_L(s) \approx 200\frac{s}{(s + 1000)} \qquad\qquad F_L(s) \approx \frac{s}{(s + 1000)}$$

and

$$f_L = \frac{1000}{2\pi} = 159 \text{ Hz}$$

Figure 17.2 gives a plot of the two transfer functions. The dashed line represents the dominant pole approximation of the full transfer function (solid lines).   ◆

EXERCISE: For what range of frequencies does the approximation to $A_V(s)$ in Example 17.1 differ from the actual transfer function by less than 10 percent?

ANSWER: $\omega \geq 205$ rad/s

Estimating ω_L in the Absence of a Dominant Pole

If a dominant pole does not exist at low frequencies, then the poles and zeros interact to determine the lower-cutoff frequency, and a more complicated analysis must be used to find ω_L. As an example, consider the case of an amplifier having two zeros and two poles at low frequencies:

$$A_L(s) = A_{\text{mid}}F_L(s) = A_{\text{mid}}\frac{(s + \omega_{Z1})(s + \omega_{Z2})}{(s + \omega_{P1})(s + \omega_{P2})} \qquad (17.11)$$

For $s = j\omega$,

$$|A_L(j\omega)| = A_{\text{mid}}|F_L(j\omega)| = A_{\text{mid}}\sqrt{\frac{(\omega^2 + \omega_{Z1}^2)(\omega^2 + \omega_{Z2}^2)}{(\omega^2 + \omega_{P1}^2)(\omega^2 + \omega_{P2}^2)}} \qquad (17.12)$$

and remembering that ω_L is defined as the -3 dB frequency,

$$|A(j\omega_L)| = \frac{A_{\text{mid}}}{\sqrt{2}} \quad \text{and} \quad \frac{1}{\sqrt{2}} = \sqrt{\frac{(\omega_L^2 + \omega_{Z1}^2)(\omega_L^2 + \omega_{Z2}^2)}{(\omega_L^2 + \omega_{P1}^2)(\omega_L^2 + \omega_{P2}^2)}} \quad (17.13)$$

Squaring both sides and expanding Eq. (17.13),

$$\frac{1}{2} = \frac{\omega_L^4 + \omega_L^2(\omega_{Z1}^2 + \omega_{Z2}^2) + \omega_{Z1}^2\omega_{Z2}^2}{\omega_L^4 + \omega_L^2(\omega_{P1}^2 + \omega_{P2}^2) + \omega_{P1}^2\omega_{P2}^2} = \frac{1 + \dfrac{(\omega_{Z1}^2 + \omega_{Z2}^2)}{\omega_L^2} + \dfrac{\omega_{Z1}^2\omega_{Z2}^2}{\omega_L^4}}{1 + \dfrac{(\omega_{P1}^2 + \omega_{P2}^2)}{\omega_L^2} + \dfrac{\omega_{P1}^2\omega_{P2}^2}{\omega_L^4}} \quad (17.14)$$

If we assume that ω_L is larger than all the individual pole and zero frequencies, then the terms involving $1/\omega_L^4$ can be neglected and the lower-cutoff frequency can be estimated from

$$\omega_L \approx \sqrt{\omega_{P1}^2 + \omega_{P2}^2 - 2\omega_{Z1}^2 - 2\omega_{Z2}^2} \quad (17.15)$$

For the more general case of n poles and n zeros, a similar analysis yields

$$\omega_L \approx \sqrt{\sum_n \omega_{Pn}^2 - 2\sum_n \omega_{Zn}^2} \quad (17.16)$$

EXERCISE: Use Eq. (17.15) to estimate f_L for the transfer functions

$$A_V(s) = \frac{200s(s + 50)}{(s + 10)(s + 1000)} \quad \text{and} \quad A_V(s) = \frac{100s(s + 500)}{(s + 100)(s + 1000)}$$

ANSWERS: 159 Hz, 114 Hz

High-Frequency Response

In the region above midband, $A(s)$ can be represented by its high-frequency approximation:

$$A_H(s) \approx A_{\text{mid}}F_H(s) \quad (17.17)$$

Many of the zeros of $F_H(s)$ are often at infinite frequency, or high enough in frequency that they do not influence the value of $F_H(s)$ near ω_H. If, in addition, one of the pole frequencies—for example, ω_{P3} in Fig. 17.1—is much smaller than all the others, then a **dominant high-frequency pole** exists in the high-frequency response, and $F_H(s)$ can be represented by the approximation

$$F_H(s) \approx \frac{1}{1 + \dfrac{s}{\omega_{P3}}} \quad (17.18)$$

For the case of a dominant pole, the upper-cutoff frequency is given by $\omega_H \approx \omega_{P3}$. Figure 17.3 is an example of a Bode plot of a transfer function and its dominant-pole approximation.

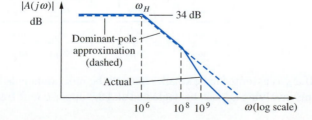

Figure 17.3 Bode plot for the complete transfer function and its dominant-pole approximation.

EXERCISE: The transfer function for the amplifier in Fig. 17.3 is

$$A_H(s) = 50 \frac{\left(1 + \dfrac{s}{10^9}\right)}{\left(1 + \dfrac{s}{10^6}\right)\left(1 + \dfrac{s}{10^8}\right)}$$

What are the locations of the poles and zeros of $A_H(s)$? What are A_{mid}, $F_H(s)$ for the dominant-pole approximation, and f_H?

ANSWERS: $\omega_{Z1} = 10^9$ rad/s, $\omega_{P1} = 10^6$ rad/s, $\omega_{P2} = 10^8$ rad/s; 50, $F_H(s) = \dfrac{1}{\left(1 + \dfrac{s}{10^6}\right)}$,

159 kHz

Estimating ω_H in the Absence of a Dominant Pole

If a dominant pole does not exist at high frequencies, then the poles and zeros interact to determine ω_H. An approximate expression for the upper-cutoff frequency can be found from the expression for F_H in a manner similar to that used to arrive at Eq. (17.16). Consider the case of an amplifier having two zeros and two poles at high frequencies:

$$A_H(s) = A_{mid}F_H(s) = A_{mid} \frac{\left(1 + \dfrac{s}{\omega_{Z1}}\right)\left(1 + \dfrac{s}{\omega_{Z2}}\right)}{\left(1 + \dfrac{s}{\omega_{P1}}\right)\left(1 + \dfrac{s}{\omega_{P2}}\right)}$$

and for $s = j\omega$,

$$|A_H(j\omega)| = A_{mid}|F_H(j\omega)| = A_{mid} \sqrt{\frac{\left(1 + \dfrac{\omega^2}{\omega_{Z1}^2}\right)\left(1 + \dfrac{\omega^2}{\omega_{Z2}^2}\right)}{\left(1 + \dfrac{\omega^2}{\omega_{P1}^2}\right)\left(1 + \dfrac{\omega^2}{\omega_{P2}^2}\right)}} \qquad (17.19)$$

At the upper-cutoff frequency $\omega = \omega_H$,

$$|A(j\omega_H)| = \frac{A_{mid}}{\sqrt{2}} \quad \text{and} \quad \frac{1}{\sqrt{2}} = \sqrt{\frac{\left(1 + \dfrac{\omega_H^2}{\omega_{Z1}^2}\right)\left(1 + \dfrac{\omega_H^2}{\omega_{Z2}^2}\right)}{\left(1 + \dfrac{\omega_H^2}{\omega_{P1}^2}\right)\left(1 + \dfrac{\omega_H^2}{\omega_{P2}^2}\right)}} \qquad (17.20)$$

Squaring both sides and expanding Eq. (17.20),

$$\frac{1}{2} = \frac{\left(1 + \dfrac{\omega_H^2}{\omega_{Z1}^2}\right)\left(1 + \dfrac{\omega_H^2}{\omega_{Z2}^2}\right)}{\left(1 + \dfrac{\omega_H^2}{\omega_{P1}^2}\right)\left(1 + \dfrac{\omega_H^2}{\omega_{P2}^2}\right)} = \frac{1 + \dfrac{\omega_H^2}{\omega_{Z1}^2} + \dfrac{\omega_H^2}{\omega_{Z2}^2} + \dfrac{\omega_H^4}{\omega_{Z1}^2\omega_{Z2}^2}}{1 + \dfrac{\omega_H^2}{\omega_{P1}^2} + \dfrac{\omega_H^2}{\omega_{P2}^2} + \dfrac{\omega_H^4}{\omega_{P1}^2\omega_{P2}^2}} \qquad (17.21)$$

If ω_H is assumed to be smaller than all the individual pole and zero frequencies, then the terms involving ω_H^4 can be neglected and the upper-cutoff frequency can be found from

$$\omega_H \approx \frac{1}{\sqrt{\dfrac{1}{\omega_{P1}^2} + \dfrac{1}{\omega_{P2}^2} - \dfrac{2}{\omega_{Z1}^2} - \dfrac{2}{\omega_{Z2}^2}}} \tag{17.22}$$

The expression for the general case of n poles and n zeros can be found in a manner similar to Eq. (17.22), and the resulting approximation for ω_H is

$$\omega_H \approx \frac{1}{\sqrt{\displaystyle\sum_n \frac{1}{\omega_{Pn}^2} - 2\sum_n \frac{1}{\omega_{zn}^2}}} \tag{17.23}$$

EXERCISE: Write the expression for the $A_H(s)$ below in standard form. What are the pole and zero frequencies? What are A_{mid}, $F_H(s)$, and f_H.

$$A_H(s) = \frac{2.5 \times 10^7 (s + 2 \times 10^5)}{(s + 10^5)(s + 5 \times 10^5)}$$

ANSWERS: $A_H(s) = 100\dfrac{\left(1 + \dfrac{s}{2 \times 10^5}\right)}{\left(1 + \dfrac{s}{10^5}\right)\left(1 + \dfrac{s}{5 \times 10^5}\right)};$ $10^5,\ 5 \times 10^5,\ 2 \times 10^5;\ \infty,$

40 dB, 21.7 kHz

17.2 DIRECT DETERMINATION OF THE LOW-FREQUENCY POLES AND ZEROS

To apply the theory in Sec. 17.1, we need to know the location of all the individual poles and zeros. In principle, the frequency response of an amplifier can always be calculated by direct analysis of the circuit in the frequency domain, so this section begins with an example of this form of analysis for the common-source amplifier. However, as circuit complexity grows, exact analysis by hand rapidly becomes intractable. Although SPICE analysis can always be used to study the characteristics of an amplifier for a given set of parameter values, a more general understanding of the factors that control the cutoff frequencies of the amplifier is needed for design. Because we are most often interested in the position of ω_L and ω_H, we subsequently develop approximation techniques that can be used to estimate ω_L and ω_H.

The circuit for the common-source amplifier from Chapter 13 is repeated in Fig. 17.4(a) along with its ac equivalent circuit in Fig. 17.4(b). At low frequencies below midband, the impedance of the capacitors can no longer be assumed to be negligible, and they must be retained in the ac equivalent circuit. To determine circuit behavior at low frequencies, we replace transistor Q_1 by its low-frequency small-signal model, as in Fig. 17.4(c). Because the stage has an external load resistor, r_o is neglected in the circuit model.

In the frequency domain, output voltage $\mathbf{V_o}(s)^2$ can be found by applying current division at the drain of the transistor:

$$\mathbf{V_o}(s) = \mathbf{I_o}(s)R_3 \qquad \text{where } \mathbf{I_o}(s) = -g_m\mathbf{V_{gs}}(s)\frac{R_D}{R_D + \dfrac{1}{sC_2} + R_3}$$

---

[2] $\mathbf{V_o}(s)$ represents the Laplace transform of $v_o(t)$.

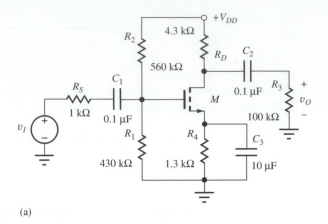

(a)

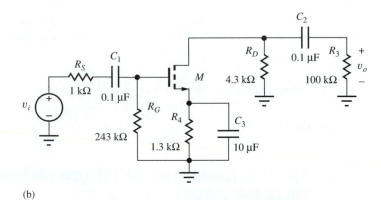

(b)

Figure 17.4 (a) A common-source amplifier, (b) low-frequency ac model, and (c) small-signal model.

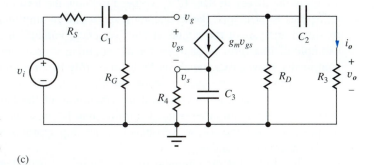

(c)

and

$$\mathbf{V_o}(s) = -g_m \mathbf{V_{gs}}(s) \frac{R_D}{R_D + \dfrac{1}{sC_2} + R_3} R_3 = -g_m(R_3 \| R_D) \frac{s}{s + \dfrac{1}{C_2(R_D + R_3)}} \mathbf{V_{gs}}(s)$$

(17.24)

Next, we must find $\mathbf{V_{gs}}(s) = \mathbf{V_g}(s) - \mathbf{V_s}(s)$. Because the gate terminal in Fig. 17.2(c) represents an open circuit, $\mathbf{V_g}(s)$ can be determined using voltage division:

$$\mathbf{V_g}(s) = \mathbf{V_i}(s) \frac{R_G}{R_s + \dfrac{1}{sC_1} + R_G} = \mathbf{V_i}(s) \frac{sC_1 R_G}{sC_1(R_s + R_G) + 1}$$

(17.25)

and the voltage at the source of the FET can be found by writing a nodal equation for $\mathbf{V_s}(s)$:

$$g_m(\mathbf{V_g} - \mathbf{V_s}) - G_4\mathbf{V_s} - sC_4\mathbf{V_s} = 0 \tag{17.26}$$

Solving Eq. (17.26) for $\mathbf{V_s}$ yields

$$\mathbf{V_s} = \frac{g_m}{sC_3 + g_m + G_4}\mathbf{V_g} \tag{17.27}$$

and

$$\mathbf{V_{gs}}(s) = (\mathbf{V_g} - \mathbf{V_s}) = \mathbf{V_g}\left[1 - \frac{g_m}{sC_3 + g_m + G_4}\right] = \frac{sC_3 + G_4}{sC_3 + g_m + G_4}\mathbf{V_g} \tag{17.28}$$

By dividing through by C_3, Eq. (17.28) can be rewritten as

$$(\mathbf{V_g} - \mathbf{V_s}) = \frac{s + \dfrac{1}{C_3 R_4}}{s + \dfrac{1}{C_3\left(\dfrac{1}{g_m}\middle\| R_4\right)}}\mathbf{V_g}(s) \tag{17.29}$$

Finally, combining Eqs. (17.24), (17.25), and (17.29) yields an overall expression for the voltage transfer function:

$$A_V(s) = \frac{\mathbf{V_O}(s)}{\mathbf{V_i}(s)} = A_{\text{mid}}F_L(s)$$

$$= \left[-g_m(R_3 \| R_D)\frac{R_G}{(R_S + R_G)}\right]\frac{s^2\left[s + \dfrac{1}{C_3 R_4}\right]}{\left[s + \dfrac{1}{C_1(R_s + R_G)}\right]\left[s + \dfrac{1}{C_3\left(\dfrac{1}{g_m}\middle\| R_4\right)}\right]\left[s + \dfrac{1}{C_2(R_D + R_3)}\right]} \tag{17.30}$$

In Eq. (17.30), $A(s)$ has been written in the form that directly exposes the midband gain and $F_L(s)$:

$$A(s) = A_{\text{mid}}F_L(s) \qquad \text{where } A_{\text{mid}} = -g_m(R_D \| R_4)\frac{R_G}{R_G + R_s} \tag{17.31}$$

A_{mid} should be recognized as the voltage gain of the circuit, with the capacitors all replaced by short circuits.

Although the analysis in Eqs. (17.24) to (17.31) may seem rather tedious, we nevertheless obtain a complete description of the frequency response. In this example, the poles and zeros of the transfer function appear in factored form in Eq. (17.30). Unfortunately, this is an artifact of this particular FET circuit and generally will not be the case. The infinite input resistance of the FET and absence of r_o in the circuit have decoupled the nodal equations for v_g, v_s, and v_o. In most cases, the mathematical analysis is even more complex. For example, if a bipolar transistor were used in which both r_π and r_o were included, the analysis would require the simultaneous solution of at least three equations in three unknowns.

> **EXERCISE:** Draw the midband ac equivalent circuit for the amplifier in Fig. 17.2 and derive the expression for A_{mid} directly from this circuit.
>
> **ANSWER:** Eq. (17.31)

Let us now explore the origin of the poles and zeros of the voltage transfer function. Eq. (17.30) has three poles and three zeros, *one pole and one zero for each independent capacitor* in the circuit. Two of the zeros are at $s = 0$ (dc), corresponding to series capacitors C_1 and C_2, each of which blocks the propagation of dc signals through the amplifier. The third zero occurs at the frequency for which the impedance of the parallel combination of R_4 and C_3 becomes infinite. At this frequency, propagation of signal current through the MOSFET is blocked, and the output voltage must be zero. Thus the three zero locations are

$$s = 0, 0, -\frac{1}{R_4 C_3} \qquad (17.32)$$

From the denominator of Eq. (17.30), the three poles are located at frequencies of

$$s = -\frac{1}{(R_S + R_G)C_1}, \; -\frac{1}{(R_D + R_3)C_2}, \; -\frac{1}{\left(R_4 \left\| \frac{1}{g_m} \right.\right)C_3} \qquad (17.33)$$

These pole frequencies are determined by the time constants associated with the three individual capacitors. Because the input resistance of the FET is infinite, the resistance present at the terminals of capacitor C_1 is simply the series combination of R_S and R_G, and because the output resistance r_o of the FET has been neglected, the resistance associated with capacitor C_2 is the series combination of R_3 and R_D. The effective resistance in parallel with capacitor C_3 is the equivalent resistance present at the source terminal of the FET, which is equal to the parallel combination of resistor R_4 and $1/g_m$. Section 17.3 has a more complete interpretation of these resistance expressions.

EXAMPLE 17.2: Find the locations of the poles and zeros of the MOSFET amplifier in Fig. 17.4. What is f_L? Assume $g_m = 1.23$ mS. Compare the results with SPICE simulation.

SOLUTION:

$$s = -\omega_{Z1} = 0 \qquad s = -\omega_{Z2} = 0$$

$$s = -\omega_{Z3} = -\frac{1}{(1.3 \text{ k}\Omega)(10 \text{ μF})} = -76.9 \text{ rad/s}$$

$$s = -\omega_{P1} = -\frac{1}{(1 \text{ k}\Omega + 243 \text{ k}\Omega)(0.1 \text{ μF})} = -41.0 \text{ rad/s}$$

$$s = -\omega_{P2} = -\frac{1}{(4.3 \text{ k}\Omega + 100 \text{ k}\Omega)(0.1 \text{ μF})} = -95.9 \text{ rad/s}$$

$$s = -\omega_{P3} = -\frac{1}{\left(1.3 \text{ k}\Omega \left\| \frac{1}{1.23 \text{ mS}} \right.\right)(10 \text{ μF})} = -200 \text{ rad/s}$$

$$f_L = \frac{1}{2\pi}\sqrt{200^2 + 95.9^2 + 41.0^2 - 2(76.9)^2 - 2(0)^2 - 2(0)^2}$$

$$= 31.5 \text{ Hz} \qquad \blacklozenge$$

Note the approximate pole-zero cancellation of ω_{P2} and ω_{Z3}, which leads to the 40-dB/decade slope in the accompanying simulation results. Also note the good agreement between the calculated and simulated values of f_L.

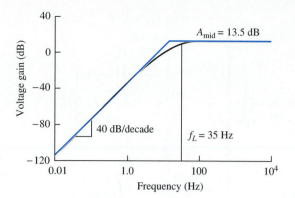

SPICE simulation results for the C-S amplifier in Fig. 17.4 (V_{DD} = 12 V).

17.3 ESTIMATION OF ω_L USING THE SHORT-CIRCUIT TIME-CONSTANT METHOD

To use Eq. (17.16) or Eq. (17.23), the location of all the poles and zeros of the amplifier must be known. In most cases, however, it is not easy to find the complete transfer function, let alone represent it in factored form. Fortunately, we are most often interested in the values of A_{mid}, and the upper- and lower-cutoff frequencies ω_H and ω_L that define the bandwidth of the amplifier, as indicated in Fig. 17.5. Knowledge of the exact position of all the poles and zeros is not necessary. Two techniques, the **short-circuit time-constant (SCTC) method** and the **open-circuit time-constant (OCTC) method**, have been developed; these produce good estimates of ω_L and ω_H, respectively, without having to find the complete transfer function.

It can be shown theoretically [1] that the lower-cutoff frequency for a network having n coupling and bypass capacitors can be estimated from Eq. (17.34)

$$\omega_L \approx \sum_{i=1}^{n} \frac{1}{R_{iS}C_i} \tag{17.34}$$

in which R_{iS} represents the resistance at the terminals of the ith capacitor C_i with all the other capacitors replaced by short circuits. The product $R_{iS}C_i$ represents the short-circuit time constant (SCTC) associated with capacitor C_i. We now use the SCTC method to find ω_L for the three classes of single-stage amplifiers.

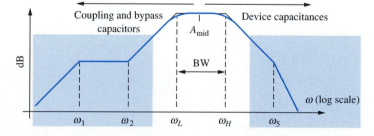

Figure 17.5 Midband region of primary interest in most amplifier transfer functions.

Estimate of ω_L for the Common-Emitter Amplifier

We use the C-E amplifier in Fig. 13.26, Chapter 13, as a first example of the SCTC method; this is redrawn in Fig. 17.6 and now includes finite values for the capacitors. The presence of r_π in the bipolar model causes direct calculation of the transfer function to be complex;

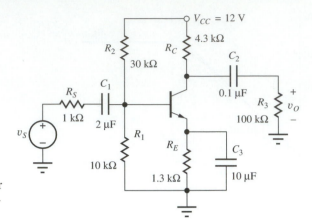

Figure 17.6 Common-emitter amplifier including finite capacitor values.

including r_o leads to even further difficulty. Thus, the circuit is a good example of applying the method of short-circuit time constants to a network.

The ac model for the C-E amplifier in Fig. 17.7 contains three capacitors, and three short-circuit time constants must be determined in order to apply Eq. (17.34). The three analyses rely on the expressions for the midband input and output resistances of the BJT amplifiers in Table 14.7.

R_{1S}

For C_1, R_{1S} is found by replacing C_2 and C_3 by short circuits, yielding the network in Fig. 17.8. R_{1S} represents the equivalent resistance present at the terminals of capacitor C_1. Based on Fig. 17.8,

$$R_{1S} = R_S + R_B \| R_{IN}^{CE} = R_2 + R_B \| r_\pi \qquad (17.35)$$

R_{1S} is equal to the source resistance R_S in series with the parallel combination of the base bias resistor R_B and the input resistance r_π of the BJT.

In Chapter 13 the Q-point for this amplifier was found to be (1.73 mA, 2.32 V), and for $\beta_o = 100$ and $V_A = 75$ V,

$$r_\pi = 1.45 \text{ k}\Omega \qquad \text{and} \qquad r_o = 44.7 \text{ k}\Omega$$

Using these values and those of the other circuit elements,

$$R_{1S} = 1000 \ \Omega + 7500 \ \Omega \| 1450 \ \Omega = 2220 \ \Omega$$

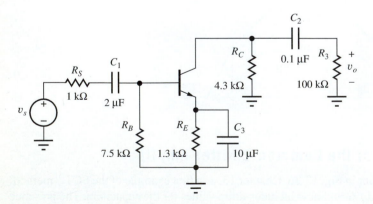

Figure 17.7 ac Model for the C-E amplifier in Fig. 17.6.

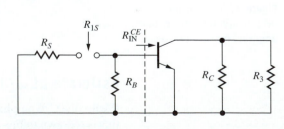

Figure 17.8 Circuit for finding R_{1S}.

and
$$\frac{1}{R_{1S}C_1} = \frac{1}{(2.22 \text{ k}\Omega)(2.00 \text{ }\mu\text{F})} = 225 \text{ rad/s} \qquad (17.36)$$

R_{2S}

The network used to find R_{2S} is constructed by shorting capacitors C_1 and C_3, as in Fig. 17.9. For this network,

$$R_{2S} = R_3 + R_C\|R_{OUT}^{CE} = R_3 + R_C\|r_o \approx R_3 + R_C \qquad (17.37)$$

R_{2S} represents the combination of load resistance R_3 in series with the parallel combination of collector resistor R_C and the output resistance r_o of the BJT. For the values in this particular circuit,

$$R_{2S} = R_3 + R_C\|r_o \approx 100 \text{ k}\Omega + 4.30 \text{ k}\Omega\|44.7 \text{ k}\Omega = 104 \text{ k}\Omega$$

and
$$\frac{1}{R_{2S}C_2} = \frac{1}{(104 \text{ k}\Omega)(0.100 \text{ }\mu\text{F})} = 96.1 \text{ rad/s} \qquad (17.38)$$

R_{3S}

Finally, the network used to find R_{3S} is constructed by shorting capacitors C_1 and C_2, as in Fig. 17.10, and

$$R_{3S} = R_E\|R_{OUT}^{CC} = R_E\|\frac{r_\pi + R_{th}}{\beta_o + 1} \qquad \text{where } R_{th} = R_S\|R_B \qquad (17.39)$$

R_{3S} represents the combination of emitter resistance R_E in parallel with the equivalent resistance at the emitter terminal of the BJT. For the values in this particular circuit,

$$R_{th} = R_S\|R_B = 1000 \text{ }\Omega\|7500 \text{ }\Omega = 882 \text{ }\Omega$$

$$R_{3S} = 1300 \text{ }\Omega\|\frac{1450 \text{ }\Omega + 882 \text{ }\Omega}{101} = 22.7 \text{ }\Omega$$

and
$$\frac{1}{R_{3S}C_3} = \frac{1}{(22.7 \text{ }\Omega)(10 \text{ }\mu\text{F})} = 4410 \text{ rad/s} \qquad (17.40)$$

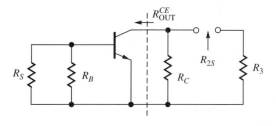

Figure 17.9 Circuit for finding R_{2S}.

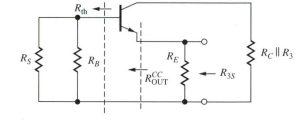

Figure 17.10 Circuit for finding R_{3S}.

The ω_L Estimate

Using the three time-constant values from Eqs. (17.36), (17.38), and (17.40) yields estimates for ω_L and f_L:

$$\omega_L \approx \sum_{i=1}^{3} \frac{1}{R_{iS}C_i} = 225 + 96.1 + 4410 = 4730 \text{ rad/s} \qquad (17.41)$$

and
$$f_L = \frac{\omega_L}{2\pi} = 753 \text{ Hz}$$

The lower-cutoff frequency of the amplifier is approximately 750 Hz.

Note in this example that the time constant associated with emitter bypass capacitor C_3 is dominant; that is, the value of $R_{3S}C_3$ is more than an order of magnitude larger than the other two time constants so that $\omega_L \approx 1/R_{3S}C_3$ ($f_L \approx 4410/2\pi = 702$ Hz). This is a common situation and a practical approach to the design of ω_L. Because the resistance presented at the emitter or source of the transistor is low, the time constant associated with an emitter or source bypass capacitor is often dominant and can be used to set ω_L. The other two time constants can easily be designed to be much larger.

EXAMPLE 17.3: Change the value of C_3 to set $f_L = 2000$ Hz for the circuit in Fig. 17.6. (Assume that C_1 and C_2 remain the same values.)

SOLUTION: For this case $\omega_L = 4000\pi = 12.6 \times 10^3$ is strongly dominated by the value of $R_{3S}C_3$. Therefore:

$$C_3 \approx \frac{1}{R_{3S}\omega_L} = \frac{1}{23.7(12.6 \times 10^3)} = 3.35 \ \mu\text{F}$$

◆

EXERCISE: Simulate the frequency response of the circuit in Fig. 17.6 using SPICE, and find the midband gain and lower-cutoff frequency. Use $\beta_o = 100$, $I_S = 1$ fA, and $V_A = 75$ V. What is the Q-point?

ANSWERS: 135, 635 Hz, (1.64 mA, 2.79 V)

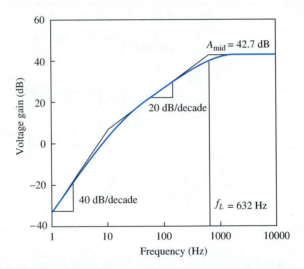

SPICE simulation results.

Estimate of ω_L for the Common-Source Amplifier

Equations (17.35), (17.37), and (17.39) can be applied directly to the C-S FET amplifier in Fig. 17.11 by substituting infinity for the values of the transistor's input resistance and current gain. These equations reduce directly to:

$$R_{1S} = R_S + R_G \| R_{IN}^{CS} = R_S + R_G$$

$$R_{2S} = R_3 + R_D \| R_{OUT}^{CS} = R_3 + R_D \| r_o \approx R_3 + R_D \tag{17.42}$$

$$R_{3S} = R_4 \| R_{OUT}^{CG} = R_4 \left\| \frac{1}{g_m} \right.$$

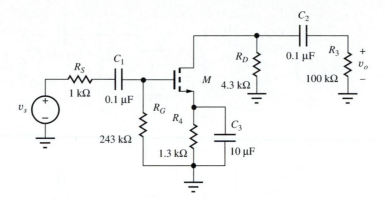

Figure 17.11 ac Model for common-source amplifier.

The three expressions in Eq. (17.42) represent the short-circuit time constants associated with the three capacitors in the circuit, as indicated in the ac circuit models in Figs. 17.12(a) to (c).

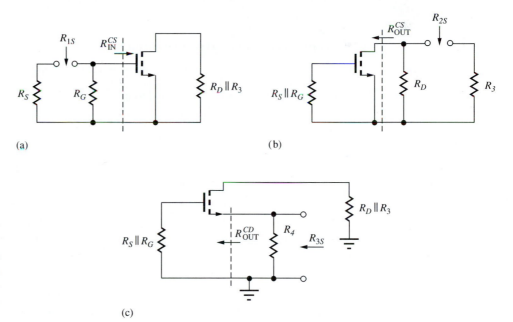

Figure 17.12 (a) Resistance R_{1S} at the terminals of C_1. (b) Resistance R_{2S} at the terminals of C_2. (c) Resistance R_{3S} at the terminals of C_3.

Estimate of ω_L for the Common-Base Amplifier

Next, we apply the short-circuit time-constant technique to the common-base amplifier in Fig. 17.13. The results are also directly applicable to the common-gate case if β_o and r_π are set equal to infinity. Figure 17.13(b) is the low-frequency ac equivalent circuit for the common-base amplifier. In this particular circuit, coupling capacitors C_1 and C_2 are the only capacitors present, and expressions for R_{1S} and R_{2S} are needed.

R_{1S}

R_{1S} is found by shorting capacitor C_2, as indicated in the circuit in Fig. 17.14. Based on this figure,

$$R_{1S} = R_S + R_E \| R_{IN}^{CB} \approx R_S + R_E \left\| \frac{1}{g_m} \right. \tag{17.43}$$

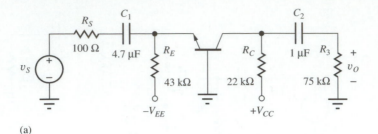

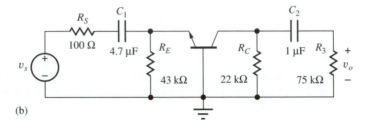

Figure 17.13 (a) Common-base amplifier. (b) Low-frequency ac equivalent circuit.

R_{2S}

Shorting capacitor C_1 yields the circuit in Fig. 17.15, and the expression for R_{2S} is

$$R_{2S} = R_3 + R_C \| R_{OUT}^{CB} \approx R_3 + R_C \tag{17.44}$$

because $R_{OUT}^{CB} \approx r_o(1 + g_m R_{th})$ is large.

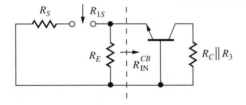

Figure 17.14 Equivalent circuit for determining R_{1S}.

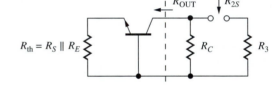

Figure 17.15 Equivalent circuit for determining R_{2S}.

> **EXERCISE:** Find the short-circuit time constants and f_L for the common-base amplifier in Fig. 17.13 if $\beta_o = 100$, $V_A = 70$ V, and the Q-point is (0.1 mA, 5 V). What is A_{mid}?
>
> **ANSWERS:** 1.64 ms, 97.0 ms, 98.7 Hz; 48.6

Estimate of ω_L for the Common-Gate Amplifier

The expressions for R_{1S} and R_{2S} for the common-gate amplifier in Fig. 17.16 are virtually identical to those of the common-base stage:

$$R_{1S} = R_S + R_4 \| R_{IN}^{CG} = R_S + R_4 \| \frac{1}{g_m}$$

$$R_{2S} = R_3 + R_D \| R_{OUT}^{CG} \approx R_3 + R_D \qquad \text{because } R_{OUT}^{CG} \approx \mu_f(R_4 \| R_S) \tag{17.45}$$

> **EXERCISE:** Draw the circuits used to find R_{1S} and R_{2S} for the common-gate amplifier in Fig. 17.16 and verify the results presented in Eq. (17.45).

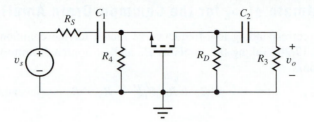

Figure 17.16 ac Circuit for common-gate amplifier.

Estimate of ω_L for the Common-Collector Amplifier

Figures 17.17(a) and (b) are schematics of an emitter follower and its corresponding low-frequency ac model, respectively. This circuit has two coupling capacitors, C_1 and C_2. The circuit for R_{1S} in Fig. 17.18 is constructed by shorting C_2, and the expression for R_{1S} is

$$R_{1S} = R_S + R_B \| R_{IN}^{CC} = R_S + R_B \| [r_\pi + (\beta_o + 1)(R_E \| R_3)] \tag{17.46}$$

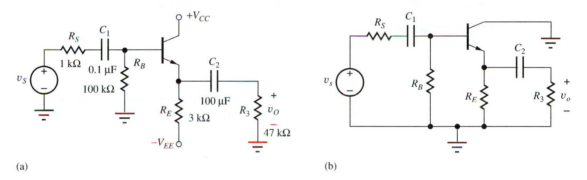

(a) (b)

Figure 17.17 (a) Common-collector amplifier. (b) Low-frequency ac model for the common-collector amplifier.

Similarly, the circuit used to find R_{2S} is found by shorting capacitor C_1, as in Fig. 17.19, and

$$R_{2S} = R_3 + R_E \| R_{OUT}^{CC} = R_3 + R_E \| \frac{R_{th} + r_\pi}{\beta_o + 1} \tag{17.47}$$

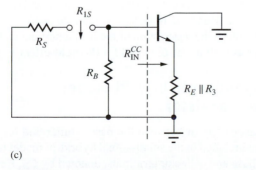

(c)

Figure 17.18 Circuit for finding R_{1S}.

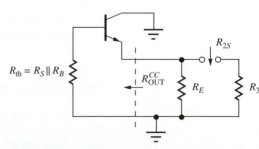

Figure 17.19 Circuit for finding R_{2S}.

Estimate of ω_L for the Common-Drain Amplifier

The corresponding low-frequency ac model for the common-drain amplifier appears in Fig. 17.20. Taking the limits as β_o and r_π approach infinity, Eqs. (17.46) and (17.47) become

$$R_{1S} = R_S + R_G\|R_{IN}^{CD} = R_S + R_G \qquad \text{because } R_{IN}^{CD} = \infty$$

and   (17.48)

$$R_{2S} = R_3 + R_4\|R_{OUT}^{CD} = R_3 + R_4\left\|\frac{1}{g_m}\right.$$

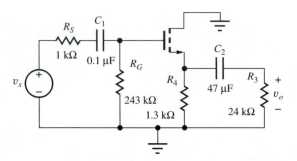

Figure 17.20 Low-frequency ac equivalent circuit for common-drain amplifier.

EXERCISE: Find the short-circuit time constants and f_L for the common-collector amplifier in Fig. 17.17(a) if $\beta_o = 100$, $V_A = 70$ V, and the Q-point $= (1$ mA, 5 V$)$. What is A_{mid}?

ANSWERS: 7.52 ms, 4.70 s, 21.2 Hz; 0.978

EXERCISE: Find the short-circuit time constants and f_L for the common-gate amplifier in Fig. 17.20 if $g_m = 1$ mS. What is A_{mid}?

ANSWERS: 43.1 ms, 1.16 s, 3.83 Hz; 0.551

17.4 TRANSISTOR MODELS AT HIGH FREQUENCIES

To explore the upper limits of amplifier frequency response, the high-frequency limitations of the transistors, which we have ignored thus far, must be taken into account. All electronic devices have capacitances between their various terminals, and these capacitances limit the range of frequencies for which the devices can provide useful voltage, current, or power gain. This section develops the description of the frequency-dependent hybrid-pi model for the bipolar transistor as well as the pi model for the field-effect transistor.

Frequency-Dependent Hybrid-Pi Model for the Bipolar Transistor

In the BJT, capacitances appear between the base-emitter and base-collector terminals of the transistor and are included in the small-signal hybrid-pi model in Fig. 17.21. The capacitance between the base and collector terminals, denoted by C_μ, represents the capacitance of the reverse-biased collector-base junction of the bipolar transistor and is related to the

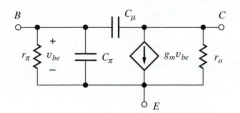

Figure 17.21 Capacitances in the hybrid-pi model of the BJT.

Q-point through an expression equivalent to Eq. (3.21), Chapter 3:

$$C_\mu = \frac{C_{\mu o}}{\sqrt{1 + \dfrac{V_{CB}}{\phi_{jc}}}} \qquad (17.49)$$

In Eq. (17.49), $C_{\mu o}$ represents the total collector-base junction capacitance at zero bias, and ϕ_j is the built-in potential of the collector-base junction, typically 0.6 to 1.0 V.

The internal capacitance between the base and emitter terminals, denoted by C_π, represents the diffusion capacitance associated with the forward-biased base-emitter junction of the transistor. C_π is related to the Q-point through Eq. (5.41):

$$C_\pi = g_m \tau_F \qquad (17.50)$$

in which τ_F is the forward transit-time of the bipolar transistor. In Fig. 17.21, C_π appears directly in parallel with r_π. For a given input signal current, the impedance of C_π causes the base-emitter voltage v_{be} to be reduced as frequency increases, thereby reducing the current in the controlled source at the output of the transistor.

Shunt capacitances such as C_π are always present in electronic devices and circuits. At low frequencies, the impedance of these capacitances is usually very large and so has negligible effect relative to the resistances such as r_π. However, as frequency increases, the impedance of C_π becomes smaller and smaller, and v_{be} eventually approaches zero. Thus, transistors cannot provide amplification at arbitrarily high frequencies.

Unity-Gain Frequency f_T

A quantitative description of the behavior of the transistor at high frequencies can be found by calculating the frequency-dependent short-circuit current gain $\beta(s)$ from the circuit in Fig. 17.22. For a current $\mathbf{I_b(s)}$ injected into the base, the collector current $\mathbf{I_c(s)}$ consists of two components:

$$\mathbf{I_c}(s) = g_m \mathbf{V_{be}}(s) - \mathbf{I_\mu}(s) \qquad (17.51)$$

Because the voltage at the collector is zero, v_{be} appears directly across C_μ and $\mathbf{I_\mu}(s) = sC_\mu \mathbf{V_{be}}(s)$. Therefore,

$$\mathbf{I_c}(s) = (g_m - sC_\mu)\mathbf{V_{be}}(s) \qquad (17.52)$$

Because the collector is connected directly to ground, C_π and C_μ appear in parallel in this circuit, and the base current flows through the parallel combination of r_π and $(C_\pi + C_\mu)$.

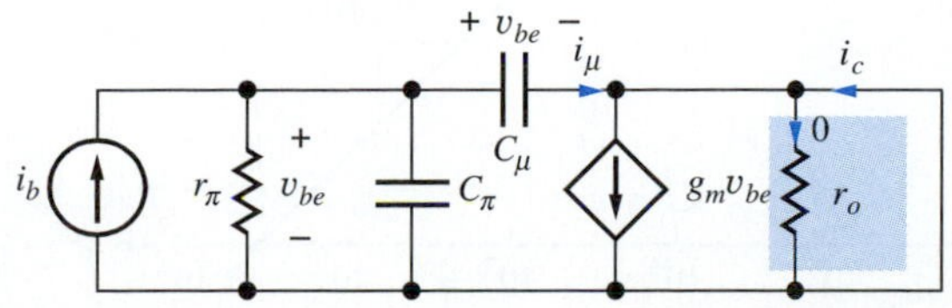

Figure 17.22 Finding the short-circuit current gain β of the BJT.

to develop the base-emitter voltage:

$$\mathbf{V_{be}}(s) = \mathbf{I_b}(s)\frac{r_\pi \dfrac{1}{s(C_\pi + C_\mu)}}{r_\pi + \dfrac{1}{s(C_\pi + C_\mu)}} = \mathbf{I_b}(s)\frac{r_\pi}{s(C_\pi + C_\mu)r_\pi + 1} \qquad (17.53)$$

Combining Eqs. (17.52) and (17.53),

$$\mathbf{I_c}(s) = (g_m - sC_\mu)\mathbf{I_b}(s)\frac{r_\pi \dfrac{1}{s(C_\pi + C_\mu)}}{r_\pi + \dfrac{1}{s(C_\pi + C_\mu)}} = \mathbf{I_b}(s)\frac{(g_m - sC_\mu)r_\pi}{s(C_\pi + C_\mu)r_\pi + 1} \qquad (17.54)$$

and the frequency-dependent current gain is

$$\beta(s) = \frac{\mathbf{I_c}(s)}{\mathbf{I_b}(s)} = \frac{\beta_o\left(1 - \dfrac{sC_\mu}{g_m}\right)}{s(C_\pi + C_\mu)r_\pi + 1} \qquad (17.55)$$

A right-half-plane transmission zero occurs in the current gain at an extremely high frequency,

$$s = +\omega_Z = +\frac{g_m}{C_\mu} \qquad (17.56)$$

and can almost always be neglected. Neglecting ω_Z results in the following simplified expression for $\beta(s)$:

$$\beta(s) \approx \frac{\beta_o}{s(C_\pi + C_\mu)r_\pi + 1} = \frac{\beta_o}{\dfrac{s}{\omega_\beta} + 1} \qquad (17.57)$$

in which ω_β represents the **beta-cutoff frequency**, defined by

$$\omega_\beta = \frac{1}{r_\pi(C_\pi + C_\mu)} \qquad \text{and} \qquad f_\beta = \frac{\omega_\beta}{2\pi} \qquad (17.58)$$

Figure 17.23 is a Bode plot for Eq. (17.57). From Eq. (17.57) and this graph, we see that the current gain has the value of $\beta_o = g_m r_\pi$ at low frequencies and exhibits a single-pole roll-off at frequencies above f_β, decreasing at a rate of 20 dB/decade and crossing

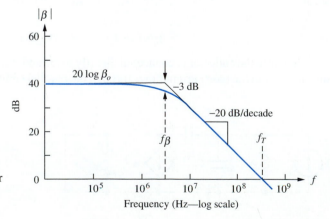

Figure 17.23 Common-emitter current gain versus frequency for the BJT.

through unity gain at $\omega = \omega_T = 2\pi f_T$. The magnitude of the current gain is 3 dB below its low-frequency value at the beta-cutoff frequency, f_β.

Equation (17.57) can be recast in terms of ω_T and ω_β as

$$\beta(s) = \frac{\beta_o \omega_\beta}{s + \omega_\beta} = \frac{\omega_T}{s + \omega_\beta} \tag{17.59}$$

where $\omega_T = \beta_o \omega_\beta$
$f_T = \omega_T / 2\pi$

The parameter f_T is referred to as the **unity gain-bandwidth product** of the transistor and characterizes one of the fundamental frequency limitations of the transistor. At frequencies above f_T, the transistor no longer offers any current gain and fails to be useful as an amplifier.

A relationship between the unity gain-bandwidth product and the small-signal parameters can be obtained from Eqs. (17.58) and (17.59):

$$\omega_T = \beta_o \omega_\beta = \frac{\beta_o}{r_\pi(C_\pi + C_\mu)} = \frac{g_m}{C_\pi + C_\mu} \tag{17.60}$$

Note that the transmission zero described by Eq. (17.56) occurs at a frequency beyond ω_T:

$$\omega_Z = \frac{g_m}{C_\mu} > \frac{g_m}{C_\pi + C_\mu} = \omega_T \tag{17.61}$$

To perform numeric calculations, we determine the values of f_T and C_μ from a transistor's specification sheet, and then calculate C_π by rearranging Eq. (17.60):

$$C_\pi = \frac{g_m}{\omega_T} - C_\mu \tag{17.62}$$

From Eq. (17.49) we can see that C_μ is only a weak function of operating point, and recasting g_m in Eq. (17.62) demonstrates that C_π is directly proportional to collector current:

$$C_\pi = \frac{40 I_C}{\omega_T} - C_\mu \tag{17.63}$$

> **EXERCISE:** A bipolar transistor has an $f_T = 500$ MHz and $C_{\mu o} = 2$ pF. What are the values of C_μ and C_π at Q-points of (100 μA, 8 V), (2 mA, 5 V), and (50 mA, 8 V)? Assume $V_{BE} = \phi_{jc} = 0.6$ V.
>
> **ANSWERS:** 0.551 pF, 0.722 pF; 0.700 pF, 24.8 pF; 0.551 pF, 636 pF

High-Frequency Model for the FET

To model the FET at high frequencies, gate-drain and gate-source capacitances C_{GD} and C_{GS} are added to the small-signal model, as shown in Fig. 17.24. For the MOSFET, these two capacitors represent the gate oxide and overlap capacitances discussed previously in Sec. 4.12; for the JFET, the two capacitors model the capacitance of the reverse-biased

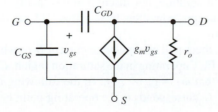

Figure 17.24 Pi model for the FET.

gate-channel junction. At high frequencies, currents through these two capacitors combine to form a current in the gate terminal, and the signal current i_g can no longer be assumed to be zero. Thus, even the FET has a finite current gain at high frequencies.

The short-circuit current gain for the FET can be calculated in the same manner as for the BJT, as in Fig. 17.25:

$$\mathbf{I_d}(s) = (g_m - sC_{GD})\mathbf{V_{gs}}(s) = \mathbf{I_g}(s)\frac{(g_m - sC_{GD})}{s(C_{GS} + C_{GD})} \tag{17.64}$$

and

$$\beta(s) = \frac{\mathbf{I_d}(s)}{\mathbf{I_g}(s)} = \frac{g_m\left(1 - \dfrac{sC_{GD}}{g_m}\right)}{s(C_{GS} + C_{GD})} = \frac{\omega_T}{s}\left(1 - \frac{s}{\omega_T\left(1 + \dfrac{C_{GS}}{C_{GD}}\right)}\right) \tag{17.65}$$

At dc, the current gain is infinite but falls at a rate of 20 dB/decade as frequency increases. The unity gain-bandwidth product ω_T of the FET is defined in a manner identical to that of the BJT,

$$\omega_T = \frac{g_m}{C_{GS} + C_{GD}} \tag{17.66}$$

and the FET current gain falls below 1 for frequencies in excess of ω_T, just as for the case of the bipolar transistor. The transmission zero now occurs at $\omega_Z = \omega_T(1 + C_{GS}/C_{GD})$, typically a few times ω_T.

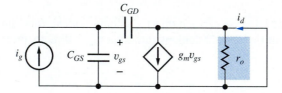

Figure 17.25 Circuit for calculating the short-circuit current gain of the FET.

EXERCISE: An NMOSFET has $f_T = 200$ MHz and $K_n = 10$ mA/V^2 and is operating at a drain current of 10 mA. Assume that $C_{GS} = 5C_{GD}$ and find the values of these two capacitors.

ANSWERS: $C_{GS} = 9.38$ pF, $C_{GD} = 1.88$ pF

Limitations of the High-Frequency Models

The pi-models of the transistor in Figs. 17.21 and 17.25 are good representations of the characteristics of the transistors for frequencies up to approximately $0.3f_T$. Above this frequency, the behavior of the simple pi-models begins to deviate significantly from that of the actual device. In addition, our discussion has tacitly assumed that ω_T is constant. However, this is only an approximation. In an actual BJT, ω_T depends on operating current, as shown in Fig. 17.26.

For a given BJT, there will be a collector current I_{CM}, which yields a maximum value of $f_T = f_{T_{max}}$. For the FET operating in the saturation region, C_{GS} and C_{GD} are independent of Q-point current so that $\omega_T \propto g_m \propto \sqrt{I_D}$. In the following discussions, we assume that the specified value of f_T corresponds to the operating point being used.

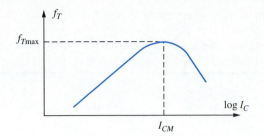

Figure 17.26 Current dependence of f_T.

> **EXERCISE:** As an example of the problem of using a constant value for the transistor f_T, repeat the calculation of C_π and C_μ for a Q-point of (20 μA, 8 V) if f_T = 500 MHz, $C_{\mu o}$ = 2 pF, and ϕ_{jc} = 0.6 V.
>
> **ANSWERS:** 0.551 pF, −0.296 pF. Impossible—C_π cannot have a negative value.

17.5 BASE RESISTANCE IN THE HYBRID-PI MODEL

One final circuit element, the base resistance r_x, completes the basic hybrid-pi description of the bipolar transistor. In the bipolar transistor cross section in Fig. 17.27, base current i_b enters the transistor through the external base contact and traverses a relatively high resistance region before actually entering the active area of the transistor. Circuit element r_x models the voltage drop between the base contact and the active region of the transistor and is included between the internal and external base nodes, B' and B, respectively, in the circuit model in Fig. 17.28. As discussed in the next section, the base resistance usually can be neglected at low frequencies. However, resistance r_x can represent an important limitation to the frequency response of the transistor in low-source resistance applications. Typical values of r_x range from a few hundred to a few thousand ohms.

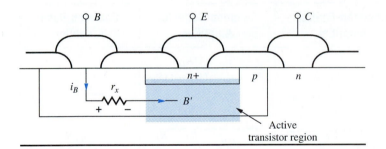

Figure 17.27 Base current flow in the BJT.

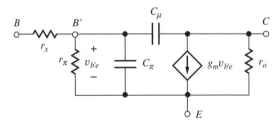

Figure 17.28 Completed hybrid-pi model, including the base resistance r_x.

Effect of Base Resistance on Midband Amplifiers

Before considering the high-frequency response of single and multistage amplifiers, we explore the effect of base resistance on the midband gain expressions for single-stage amplifiers. Although the model used in deriving the midband voltage gain expressions in Chapter 14 did not include the effect of base resistance, the expressions can be easily modified to include r_x. A simple approach is to use the circuit transformation shown in Fig. 17.29, in which r_x is absorbed into an equivalent pi model. The current generator in the model in Fig. 17.29(a) is controlled by the voltage developed across r_π, which is related to the total

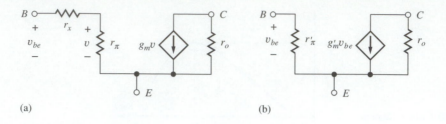

Figure 17.29 (a) Transistor model containing r_x. (b) Model transformation that "absorbs" r_x.

(a)   (b)

base-emitter voltage through voltage division by

$$\mathbf{v} = \mathbf{v_{be}}\frac{r_\pi}{r_x + r_\pi}$$ (17.67)

and the current in the controlled source is

$$\mathbf{i} = g_m\mathbf{v} = g_m\frac{r_\pi}{r_x + r_\pi}\mathbf{v_{be}} = g'_m\mathbf{v_{be}} \qquad \text{where } g'_m = \frac{\beta_o}{r_x + r_\pi}$$ (17.68)

Equations (17.67) and (17.68) lead to the model in Fig. 17.29(b), in which the base resistance has been absorbed into r'_π and g'_m of an equivalent transistor Q' defined by

$$g'_m = g_m\frac{r_\pi}{r_x + r_\pi} = \frac{\beta_o}{r_x + r_\pi} \qquad \text{and} \qquad r'_\pi = r_x + r_\pi$$ (17.69)

Note that current gain is conserved during the transformation: $\beta'_o = \beta_o$.

Based on Eq. (17.69), the original expressions from Table 14.7 can be transformed to those in Table 17.1 for the three classes of amplifiers in Fig. 17.30 by simply substituting

Table 17.1

Single-Stage Bipolar Amplifiers, Including Base Resistance

	Common-Emitter Amplifier	Common-Collector Amplifier	Common-Base Amplifier
Voltage Gain $A_{vth} = \dfrac{v_o}{v_{th}}$ $g'_m = \dfrac{\beta_o}{r_x + r_\pi}$ $r'_\pi = r_x + r_\pi$	$\dfrac{-\beta_o R_L}{R_{th} + r'_\pi + (\beta_o + 1)R_5}$ $\dfrac{-g'_m R_L}{1 + g'_m R_5 + \dfrac{R_{th} + R_5}{r'_\pi}}$	$\dfrac{(\beta_o + 1)R_L}{R_{th} + r'_\pi + (\beta_o + 1)R_L}$ $\dfrac{\left(\dfrac{1}{\alpha_o}\right)g'_m R_L}{1 + g'_m R_L + \dfrac{R_{th} + R_L}{r'_\pi}}$ $\approx +1$	$\dfrac{g'_m R_L}{1 + \dfrac{g_m}{\alpha_o}R_{th}}$ $\approx \dfrac{g'_m R_L}{1 + g'_m R_{th}}$
Input Resistance	$r'_\pi + (\beta_o + 1)R_5$	$r'_\pi + (\beta + 1)R_L$	$\dfrac{r'_\pi}{\beta_o + 1}$
Output Resistance	$r_o + \mu_f R_5$	$\dfrac{\alpha_o}{g'_m} + \dfrac{R_{th}}{\beta_o + 1}$	$r_o + \mu_f R_{th}$
Input Signal Range	$\approx 0.005(1 + g'_m R_5)$	$\approx 0.005(1 + g'_m R_L)$	$\approx 0.005(1 + g'_m R_{th})$
Current Gain	$-\beta_o$	$\beta_o + 1$	$\alpha_o \approx +1$

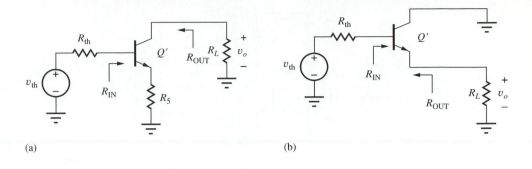

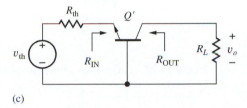

(c)

Figure 17.30 The three BJT amplifier configurations: (a) common-emitter; (b) common-collector; (c) common-base.

g'_m for g_m and r'_π for r_π. In many cases, particularly at bias points below a few hundred μA, $r_\pi \gg r_x$, and the expressions in Eq. (17.69) reduce to

$$g'_m \approx g_m \quad \text{and} \quad r'_\pi \approx r_\pi \qquad (17.70)$$

The expressions in Table 17.1 then become identical to those in Table 14.7.

17.6 HIGH-FREQUENCY LIMITATIONS OF SINGLE-STAGE AMPLIFIERS

Now that the complete hybrid-pi model has been described, we can explore the high-frequency limitations of the three basic single-stage amplifiers. This section begins with an example of direct analysis of the common-emitter amplifier; the approximation technique for estimating ω_H, the open-circuit time-constant method, is then presented.

Example of Direct High-Frequency Analysis

The common-emitter amplifier circuit discussed earlier in this chapter is redrawn in Fig. 17.31. At high frequencies, the impedance of the coupling and bypass capacitors are negligibly small, and the three capacitors can once again be considered short circuits, resulting in the high-frequency ac model in Fig. 17.31(b). In this figure, R_L represents the parallel combination of R_3 and R_C (100 kΩ∥4.3 kΩ), the emitter is connected directly to ground through bypass capacitor C_3, and base bias resistor R_B equals the parallel combination of R_1 and R_2 (30 kΩ∥10 kΩ).

Analysis of the circuit in Fig. 17.31 begins by replacing the transistor with its small-signal model, as in Fig. 17.32. In this figure, the signal source and associated resistors have been replaced by a Thévenin equivalent circuit in which

$$v_{\text{th}} = v_s \frac{R_B}{R_S + R_B} \quad \text{and} \quad R_{\text{th}} = \frac{R_S R_B}{R_S + R_B} \qquad (17.71)$$

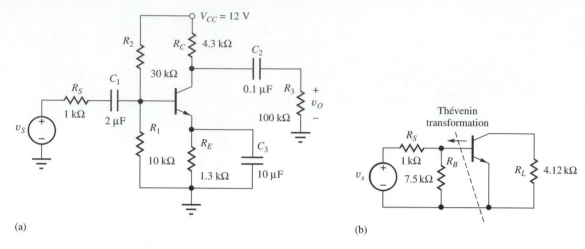

(a)

(b)

Figure 17.31 (a) Common-emitter amplifier. (b) High-frequency ac model for amplifier in Fig. 17.31(a).

Figure 17.32 ac Model for a common-emitter amplifier at high frequencies.

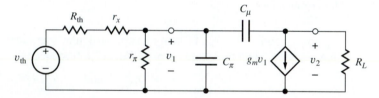

Direct analysis proceeds using nodal equations. The network in Fig. 17.32 can be reduced to a two-node problem by using a final Norton transformation of the resistors and voltage source attached to node v_1, as indicated in Fig. 17.33. The short-circuit current and Thévenin equivalent resistance for this network are expressed by

$$\mathbf{i_s} = \frac{\mathbf{V_{th}}}{R_{th} + r_x} \quad \text{and} \quad r_{\pi o} = r_\pi \| (R_{th} + r_x) \tag{17.72}$$

Figure 17.34 shows the common-emitter amplifier in final simplified form.

Writing and simplifying the nodal equations in the frequency domain for the circuit in Fig. 17.34 yields Eq. (17.73):

$$\begin{bmatrix} \mathbf{I_s}(s) \\ 0 \end{bmatrix} = \begin{bmatrix} s(C_\pi + C_\mu) + g_{\pi o} & -sC_\mu \\ -(sC_\mu - g_m) & sC_\mu + g_L \end{bmatrix} \begin{bmatrix} \mathbf{V_1}(s) \\ \mathbf{V_2}(s) \end{bmatrix} \tag{17.73}$$

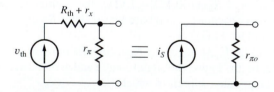

Figure 17.33 Norton source transformation for C-E amplifier.

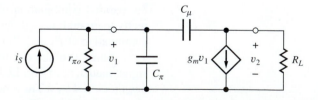

Figure 17.34 Simplified small-signal model for the high-frequency common-emitter amplifier.

An expression for the output voltage, node voltage $\mathbf{V}_2(s)$, can be found using Cramer's rule:

$$\mathbf{V}_2(s) = \mathbf{I}_s(s)\frac{(sC_\mu - g_m)}{\Delta} \tag{17.74}$$

in which Δ represents the determinant of the system of equations given by

$$\Delta = \big[s(C_\pi + C_\mu) + g_{\pi o}\big]\big[sC_\mu + g_L\big] - \big[-(sC_\mu - g_m)\big]\big[-sC_\mu\big]$$

or

$$\Delta = s^2 C_\pi C_\mu + s\big[C_\pi g_L + C_\mu(g_m + g_{\pi o} + g_L)\big] + g_L g_{\pi o} \tag{17.75}$$

From Eqs. (17.74) and (17.75), we see that the high-frequency response is characterized by two poles, one finite zero, and one zero at infinity. The finite zero appears in the right-half of the s-plane at a frequency

$$s = +\omega_Z = +\frac{g_m}{C_\mu} > \omega_T \tag{17.76}$$

The zero given by Eq. (17.76) can usually be neglected because it appears at a frequency above ω_T (for which the model itself is of questionable validity). Unfortunately, the denominator appears in unfactored polynomial form, and the positions of the poles are more difficult to find.

Approximate Polynomial Factorization

We estimate the pole locations based on a technique for approximate factorization of polynomials. Let us assume that the polynomial has two real roots a and b:

$$(s + a)(s + b) = s^2 + (a + b)s + ab = s^2 + A_1 s + A_0 \tag{17.77}$$

If we assume that a dominant root exists—that is, that $a \gg b$—then the two roots can be estimated directly from coefficients A_1 and A_0 using two approximations:

$$A_1 = a + b \approx a \qquad \text{and} \qquad \frac{A_0}{A_1} = \frac{ab}{a + b} \approx \frac{ab}{a} = b \tag{17.78}$$

$$a \approx A_1 \qquad \text{and} \qquad b \approx \frac{A_0}{A_1}$$

Note in Eq. (17.77) that the s^2 term is normalized to unity.

The approximate factorization technique exemplified by Eqs. (17.77) and (17.78) can be extended to polynomials having any number of widely spaced real roots. For a third-order polynomial, for example,

$$(s + a)(s + b)(s + c) = s^3 + A_2 s^2 + A_1 s + A_0$$

Assuming $c \ll b \ll a$, $\tag{17.79}$

$$c \approx A_0/A_1 \qquad b \approx A_1/A_2, \text{ and } a \approx A_2$$

Dominant Pole of the C-E Amplifier —The C_T Approximation

For the case of the common-emitter amplifier, the smallest root is the most important, because it is the one that limits the frequency response of the amplifier and determines ω_H. From Eq. (17.78) we see that the smaller root is given by the ratio of coefficients

A_0 and A_1:

$$\omega_{P1} \approx \frac{A_0}{A_1} = \frac{g_L g_{\pi o}}{C_\pi g_L + C_\mu(g_m + g_{\pi o} + g_L)} \left(\frac{C_\pi C_\mu}{C_\pi C_\mu}\right)$$

or

$$\omega_{P1} \approx \frac{1}{r_{\pi o}\left[C_\pi + C_\mu\left(1 + g_m R_L + \dfrac{R_L}{r_{\pi o}}\right)\right]} = \frac{1}{r_{\pi o} C_T} \tag{17.80}$$

The lower-frequency pole is determined by resistor $r_{\pi o}$ and the total effective capacitance C_T expressed by Eq. (17.81):

$$C_T = C_\pi + C_\mu\left(1 + g_m R_L + \frac{R_L}{r_{\pi o}}\right) \tag{17.81}$$

C_T consists of C_π plus C_μ multiplied by $(1 + g_m R_L + R_L/r_{\pi o})$. This factor can be quite large because $g_m R_L$ represents the intrinsic voltage gain of the common-emitter amplifier and can be expected to be of the order of 10–20 V_{CC}.

The location of the second pole of the amplifier is estimated from coefficient A_1 alone (in properly normalized form):

$$\omega_{P2} = \frac{C_\pi g_L + C_\mu(g_m + g_{\pi o} + g_L)}{C_\pi C_\mu} = \frac{1}{R_L C_\mu} + \frac{g_m + g_{\pi o} + g_L}{C_\pi}$$

$$= \frac{1}{R_L C_\mu} + \frac{g_m}{C_\pi}\left(1 + \frac{1}{g_m r_{\pi o}} + \frac{1}{g_m R_L}\right) \tag{17.82}$$

and

$$\omega_{P2} > \omega_T \qquad \text{because} \quad \frac{g_m}{C_\pi} > \omega_T \tag{17.83}$$

An overall expression for the gain of the common-emitter amplifier can be obtained by combining Eqs. (17.71) to (17.75), (17.80), and (17.82):

$$\mathbf{V_o}(s) = \frac{\mathbf{V_{th}}(s)}{R_{th} + r_x} \frac{(sC_\mu - g_m)}{g_L g_{\pi o}\left(1 + \dfrac{s}{\omega_{P1}}\right)\left(1 + \dfrac{s}{\omega_{P2}}\right)}$$

$$\tag{17.84}$$

and

$$\mathbf{V_o}(s) = \frac{\mathbf{V_{th}}(s)}{R_{th} + r_x}(-g_m R_L r_{\pi o})\frac{\left(1 - \dfrac{s}{\omega_Z}\right)}{\left(1 + \dfrac{s}{\omega_{P1}}\right)\left(1 + \dfrac{s}{\omega_{P2}}\right)}$$

Because ω_Z and ω_{P2} are both greater than ω_T, Eq. (17.84) can be approximated by

$$\mathbf{V_0}(s) \approx -\frac{\mathbf{V_{th}}(s)}{R_{th} + r_x}\frac{(g_m R_L r_{\pi o})}{\left(1 + \dfrac{s}{\omega_{P1}}\right)} \tag{17.85}$$

Recognizing that $r_{\pi o} = r_\pi(R_{th} + r_x)/(R_{th} + r_x + r_\pi)$ yields

$$A_{Vth}(s) = \frac{\mathbf{V_0}(s)}{\mathbf{V_{th}}(s)} \approx -\frac{\left(\dfrac{\beta_o R_L}{R_{th} + r_x + r_\pi}\right)}{\left(1 + \dfrac{s}{\omega_{P1}}\right)} \tag{17.86}$$

or

$$A_{Vth}(s) \approx \frac{A_{\text{mid}}}{\left(1 + \dfrac{s}{\omega_{P1}}\right)} \qquad (17.87)$$

in which

$$A_{\text{mid}} = -\frac{\beta_o R_L}{R_{\text{th}} + r_x + r_\pi} \qquad \text{and} \qquad \omega_{P1} = \frac{1}{r_{\pi o} C_T} \qquad (17.88)$$

Equation (17.87) indicates that the high-frequency behavior of the common-emitter amplifier can be modeled by a single **dominant pole**, as in the circuit in Fig. 17.35.

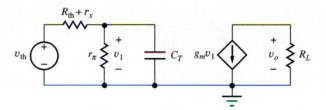

Figure 17.35 Dominant-pole model for the common-emitter amplifier at high frequencies.

EXAMPLE 17.4: Find the midband gain and the frequencies of all the poles and zeros of the common-emitter amplifier in Fig. 17.31, assuming $\beta_o = 100$, $f_T = 500\ \text{MHz}$, $C_\mu = 0.5\ \text{pF}$, $r_x = 250\ \Omega$, and a Q-point of (1.60 mA, 3.00 V).

SOLUTION: The common-emitter stage is characterized by Eqs. (17.80), (17.82), and (17.88).

$$A_{\text{mid}} = -\frac{\beta_o R_L}{R_{\text{th}} + r_x + r_\pi} \qquad\qquad \omega_Z = +\frac{g_m}{C_\mu}$$

$$\omega_{P1} = \frac{1}{r_{\pi o} C_T} \qquad\qquad \omega_{P2} = \frac{1}{R_L C_\mu} + \frac{g_m}{C_\pi}\left(1 + \frac{1}{g_m r_{\pi o}} + \frac{1}{g_m R_L}\right)$$

$$r_{\pi o} = r_\pi \| (R_{\text{th}} + r_x) \qquad\qquad C_T = C_\pi + C_\mu\left(1 + g_m R_L + \frac{R_L}{r_{\pi o}}\right)$$

The values of the various small-signal parameters must be found:

$$g_m = 40 I_C = 40(0.0016) = 64.0\ \text{mS} \qquad r_\pi = \frac{\beta_o}{g_m} = \frac{100}{0.064} = 1.56\ \text{k}\Omega$$

$$C_\pi = \frac{g_m}{2\pi f_T} - C_\mu = \frac{0.064}{2\pi(5 \times 10^8)} - 0.5 \times 10^{-12} = 19.9\ \text{pF}$$

$$R_L = R_C \| R_3 = 4.3\ \text{k}\Omega \| 100\ \text{k}\Omega = 4.12\ \text{k}\Omega$$

$$R_{\text{th}} = R_B \| R_s = 7.5\ \text{k}\Omega \| 1\ \text{k}\Omega = 882\ \Omega$$

$$r_{\pi o} = r_\pi \| (R_{\text{th}} + r_x) = 1.56\ \text{k}\Omega \| (882\ \Omega + 250\ \Omega) = 656\ \Omega$$

Substituting these values into the expression for C_T yields

$$C_T = C_\pi + C_\mu\left(1 + g_m R_L + \frac{R_L}{r_{\pi o}}\right)$$

$$= 19.9\text{ pF} + 0.5\text{ pF}\left[1 + 0.064(4120) + \frac{4120}{656}\right]$$

$$= 19.9\text{ pF} + 0.5\text{ pF}[1 + \underline{264} + 6.28]$$

$$= 19.9\text{ pF} + 136\text{ pF} = 156\text{ pF}$$

and

$$f_{P1} = \frac{1}{2\pi r_{\pi o} C_T} = \frac{1}{2\pi(656\text{ }\Omega)(156\text{ pF})} = 1.56\text{ MHz}$$

$$\omega_{P2} = \frac{1}{R_L C_\mu} + \frac{g_m}{C_\pi}\left(1 + \frac{1}{g_m r_{\pi o}} + \frac{1}{g_m R_L}\right)$$

$$= \frac{1}{(4.12\text{ k}\Omega)(0.5\text{ pF})} + \frac{0.064}{19.9\text{ pF}}\left(1 + \frac{1}{0.064(656)} + \frac{1}{0.064(4120)}\right)$$

$$f_{P2} = \frac{\omega_{P2}}{2\pi} = 603\text{ MHz}$$

$$f_Z = \frac{g_m}{2\pi C_\mu} = \frac{0.064}{2\pi(0.5\text{ pF})} = 20.4\text{ GHz}$$

$$A_{\text{mid}} = -\frac{\beta_o R_L}{R_{\text{th}} + r_x + r_\pi} = -\frac{100(4120)}{882 + 250 + 1560} = -153$$

DISCUSSION: The dominant pole is located at a frequency $f_{P1} = 1.56$ MHz, whereas f_{P2} and f_Z are estimated to be at frequencies above f_T. Thus, the upper-cutoff frequency f_H for this amplifier is determined solely by f_{P1} : $f_H \approx 1.56$ MHz. Note that this value of f_H is achieved using a transistor with $f_T = 500$ MHz; generally $f_H \ll f_T$ for a common-emitter amplifier. Note also that f_{P1} and f_{P2} are separated by a factor of almost 1000, clearly satisfying the requirement for widely spaced roots that was used in the approximate factorization.

It is important to keep in mind that the most important factor in determining the value of C_T is C_μ multiplied by the $g_m R_L$ product. To increase the upper-cutoff frequency f_H of this amplifier, the gain $(g_m R_L)$ must be reduced; a direct tradeoff must occur between amplifier gain and bandwidth. ◆

EXERCISE: Find the midband gain and the frequencies of the poles and zeros of the common-emitter amplifier in Example 17.4 if the transistor has $f_T = 500$ MHz, but $C_\mu = 1$ pF.

ANSWERS: -153, 835 kHz, 578 MHz, 10.2 GHz

Gain-Bandwidth Product Limitations of the C-E Amplifier

The important role of r_x in ultimately limiting the frequency response of the C-E amplifier should also not be overlooked. If the Thévenin equivalent source resistance R_{th} were reduced to zero in an attempt to increase the bandwidth, then $r_{\pi o}$ would not become zero but would be limited approximately to the value of r_x. Let us look at the asymptotic behavior of the gain-bandwidth product of the C-E amplifier,

$$\text{GBW} = |A_V \omega_H| \le \left(\frac{\beta_o R_L}{R_{\text{th}} + r_x + r_\pi}\right)\left(\frac{1}{r_{\pi o} C_T}\right) \tag{17.89}$$

using the following approximations:

$$R_{\text{th}} = 0, \ r_x \ll r_\pi \quad \text{so that } r_{\pi o} \approx r_x \text{ and } C_T \approx C_\mu (g_m R_L) \tag{17.90}$$

Substituting these values in Eq. (17.89) yields

$$\text{GBW} \le \frac{1}{r_x C_\mu} \tag{17.91}$$

The product of the base resistance r_x and the collector-base capacitance C_μ places an upper bound on the gain-bandwidth product of the C-E amplifier. From Eq. (17.91), we can see that one important consideration in the design of transistors for very high frequency operation is minimization of the $r_x C_\mu$ product.

> **Exercise:** Compare the gain-bandwidth product of the amplifier in Example 17.4 to the limit in Eq. (17.91) and to the f_T of the transistor.
>
> **Answers:** 239 MHz < 1.27 GHz, 239 MHz ≈ 500MHz/2

Dominant Pole for the Common-Source Amplifier

Analysis of the C-S amplifier in Fig. 17.36 mirrors that of the common-emitter amplifier. The small-signal model is similar to that for the C-E stage, except that both r_x and r_π are absent from the model. For Fig. 17.36(b),

$$R_{\text{th}} = R_S \| R_G \qquad R_L = R_D \| R_3 \qquad v_{\text{th}} = v_s \frac{R_G}{R_S + R_G} \tag{17.92}$$

The expressions for the finite zero and poles of the C-S amplifier can be found by comparing Fig. 17.36(b) to Fig. 17.34:

$$\omega_{P1} = \frac{1}{R_{\text{th}} C_T} \quad \text{and} \quad C_T = C_{GS} + C_{GD}\left(1 + g_m R_L + \frac{R_L}{R_{\text{th}}}\right)$$

$$\omega_{P2} = \frac{1}{R_L C_{GD}} + \frac{g_m}{C_{GS}}\left(1 + \frac{1}{g_m R_{\text{th}}} + \frac{1}{g_m R_L}\right) \qquad \omega_Z = \frac{g_m}{C_{GD}} \tag{17.93}$$

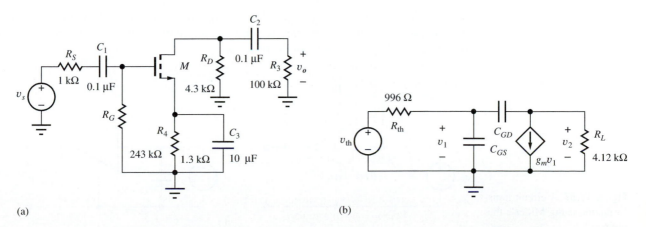

(a)   (b)

Figure 17.36 (a) Common-source amplifier. (b) The high-frequency small-signal model.

EXERCISE: What is the upper-cutoff frequency for the amplifier in Fig. 17.36 if $C_{GS} = 10$ pF, $C_{GD} = 2$ pF, and $g_m = 1.23$ mS? What are the positions of the second pole and the zero? What is the f_T of this transistor?

ANSWERS: 5.26 MHz; 58.7 MHz, 97.9 MHz; 16.3 MHz

17.7 MILLER MULTIPLICATION

The amplification of C_μ by the voltage gain of the C-E amplifier is an example of **Miller multiplication**. Miller originally derived an expression for the input admittance of the general amplifier shown in Fig. 17.37, in which capacitor C is connected between the input and output terminals of an inverting amplifier.

Let us calculate the input admittance of this amplifier. The output voltage v_o is equal to the negative gain times the input voltage v_s, and the input current to the amplifier is the admittance of the capacitor (sC) multiplied by the total voltage across the capacitor:

$$\mathbf{V_o}(s) = -A\mathbf{V_s}(s) \quad \text{and} \quad \mathbf{I_s}(s) = sC\,[\mathbf{V_s}(s) - \mathbf{V_o}(s)] \tag{17.94}$$

Combining these two equations yields an expression for the equivalent input admittance of the overall amplifier:

$$Y(s) = \frac{\mathbf{I_s}(s)}{\mathbf{V_s}(s)} = sC(1 + A) \tag{17.95}$$

Based on Eq. (17.95), the input admittance of the circuit of Fig. 17.37(a) can be represented by the equivalent circuit in Fig. 17.37(b). The total input capacitance is equal to capacitor C multiplied by the factor $(1 + A)$. This multiplication occurs because the total voltage across capacitor C in Fig. 17.37(a) is $v_c = v_s(1 + A)$ due to the inverting voltage gain of the amplifier, and hence the current drawn from the source is also increased by this same factor. The result in Eq. (17.95) is one example of the application of Miller's results, and the amplification of C by the factor $(1 + A)$ is often referred to as *Miller multiplication*.

Figure 17.38 is an equivalent representation of the common-emitter stage based on the concept of Miller multiplication. Capacitor C_π appears across the input of an amplifier with gain $A = -g_m R_L$, and C_μ is connected as a feedback element between the input and output of the amplifier. Using Miller's result, the total input capacitance will be

$$C_T = C_\pi + C_\mu(1 + A) = C_\pi + C_\mu(1 + g_m R_L) \tag{17.96}$$

which is similar to the result in Eq. (17.81), except for the missing $R_L/r_{\pi o}$ term. This term is absent because the Miller analysis does not directly include the effect of finite input and output resistances of the amplifier, which were implicitly included in the more complete result obtained by dominant root factorization.

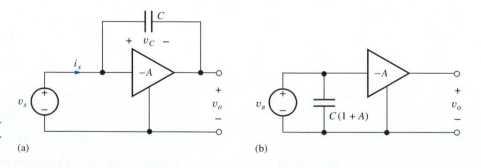

Figure 17.37 A circuit transformation using Miller's theorem.

(a)   (b)

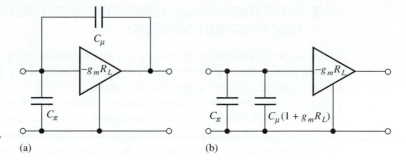

Figure 17.38 Miller's theorem applied to the common-emitter amplifier.

(a)   (b)

Miller Integrator

The integrator formed by a high-gain operational amplifier with feedback capacitor C in Fig. 17.39 is another important application of Miller multiplication and is often referred to as the **Miller integrator**. Later in this chapter, a technique called **Miller compensation** will be used to establish the unity gain-bandwidth product of single-pole operational amplifiers.

The output voltage $\mathbf{V_o}(s)$ of the circuit in Fig. 17.39 can be found by assuming there is no current in the input terminal of the amplifier:

$$\frac{\mathbf{V_s} - \mathbf{V_{in}}}{R} = sC(\mathbf{V_{in}} - \mathbf{V_o}) \qquad \text{and} \qquad \mathbf{V_o} = -A\mathbf{V_{in}} \qquad (17.97)$$

Solving for the voltage gain yields

$$A_V(s) = \frac{\mathbf{V_o}}{\mathbf{V_s}} = -\frac{\left(\dfrac{1}{RC}\right)\dfrac{A}{1+A}}{s + \dfrac{1}{RC(1+A)}} = -\frac{A\omega_o}{s + \omega_o} \qquad (17.98)$$

where $\omega_o = \dfrac{1}{RC(1+A)}$

For frequencies well above ω_o, ($\omega \gg \omega_o$), and assuming $A \gg 1$, Eq. (17.98) becomes

$$A_V(s) \approx -\frac{A\omega_o}{s} \approx -\frac{1}{sRC} \qquad (17.99)$$

which should be recognized as the transfer function for an integrator. The Miller multiplication of capacitor C is apparent in the numerator and denominator of Eq. (17.98) and the expression for ω_o.

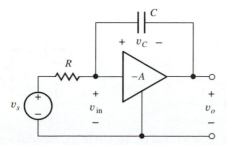

Figure 17.39 Integrator based on Miller multiplication.

17.8 ESTIMATION OF ω_H USING THE OPEN-CIRCUIT TIME-CONSTANT METHOD

A technique also exists for estimating ω_H that is similar to the short-circuit time-constant method used to find ω_L. However, the upper-cutoff frequency ω_H is found by calculating the open-circuit time-constants (OCTC) associated with the various device capacitances rather than the short-circuit time constants associated with the coupling and bypass capacitors. At high frequencies, the impedances of the coupling and bypass capacitors are negligibly small, and they effectively represent short circuits. The impedances of the device capacitances have now become small enough that they can no longer be neglected with respect to the internal resistances of the transistors. We will see shortly that the C_T approximation results derived directly in Sec. 17.6 actually can be found using the OCTC method.

Although again beyond the scope of this book, it can be shown theoretically[3] that the mathematical estimate for ω_H for a circuit having m capacitors is

$$\omega_H \approx \frac{1}{\sum_{i=1}^{m} R_{io} C_i} \qquad (17.100)$$

in which R_{io} represents the resistance measured at the terminals of capacitor C_i with the other capacitors open circuited. Because we already have results for the C-E stages, let us practice by applying the method to the high-frequency model for the C-E amplifier in Fig. 17.34.

Two capacitors, C_π and C_μ, are present in Fig. 17.34, and $R_{\pi o}$ and $R_{\mu o}$ will be needed to evaluate Eq. (17.100). $R_{\pi o}$ can easily be determined from the circuit in Fig. 17.40, in which C_μ is replaced by an open circuit, and we see that

$$R_{\pi o} = r_{\pi o} \qquad (17.101)$$

$R_{\mu o}$ can be determined from the circuit in Fig. 17.41, in which C_π is replaced by an open circuit. In this case, a bit more work is required. Test source i_x is applied to the network in Fig. 17.41(b), and v_x can be found by applying KVL around the outside loop:

$$\mathbf{v_x} = \mathbf{i_x} r_{\pi o} + \mathbf{i_L} R_L = \mathbf{i_x} r_{\pi o} + (\mathbf{i_x} + g_m \mathbf{v}) R_L \qquad (17.102)$$

However, voltage $\mathbf{v}$ is equal to $\mathbf{i_x} r_{\pi o}$, and substituting this result into Eq. (17.102) yields

$$R_{\mu o} = \frac{\mathbf{v_x}}{\mathbf{i_x}} = r_{\pi o} + (1 + g_m r_{\pi o}) R_L = r_{\pi o} \left[1 + g_m R_L + \frac{R_L}{r_{\pi o}} \right] \qquad (17.103)$$

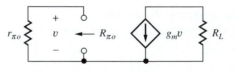

Figure 17.40 Circuit for finding $R_{\pi o}$.

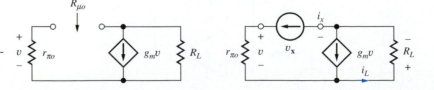

Figure 17.41 (a) Circuit defining $R_{\mu o}$. (b) Test source applied.

---

[3] See footnote 3 for ω_L, page 17. The OCTC and SCTC methods represent dominant root factorizations similar to Eq. (17.79).

which should look familiar [see Eq. (17.80)]. Substituting Eqs. (17.101) and (17.103) into Eq. (17.100) produces the estimate for ω_H:

$$\omega_H \approx \frac{1}{R_{\pi o}C_\pi + R_{\mu o}C_\mu} = \frac{1}{r_{\pi o}C_\pi + r_{\pi o}C_\mu\left(1 + g_m R_L + \dfrac{R_L}{r_{\pi o}}\right)} = \frac{1}{r_{\pi o}C_T} \qquad (17.104)$$

This is exactly the same result achieved from Eqs. (17.80) but with far less effort. (Remember, however, that this method does not produce an estimate for either the second pole or the zeros of the network.)

Gain-Bandwidth Tradeoff Using an Emitter Resistor

We know that the gain of the C-E stage can be decreased if an unbypassed emitter resistor is added to the high-frequency equivalent circuit, as in Fig. 17.42. For this stage, the midband gain is

$$A_{\mathrm{mid}} = -\frac{\beta_o R_L}{R_{\mathrm{th}} + r_x + r_\pi + (\beta_o + 1)R_E} \approx -\frac{g_m R_L}{1 + g_m R_E} \approx -\frac{R_L}{R_E} \qquad (17.105)$$

for $r_\pi \gg (R_{\mathrm{th}} + r_x)$ and $g_m R_E \gg 1$. The gain decreases as the value of R_E increases. From our knowledge of gain-bandwidth behavior, we should expect that the bandwidth of the stage will increase as A_{mid} decreases.

Let us find the bandwidth of the amplifier by applying the OCTC method to the small-signal model for the amplifier in Fig. 17.43. The two resistances, $R_{\pi o}$ and $R_{\mu o}$, must now be calculated for this new circuit configuration.

The circuit that determines $R_{\pi o}$ is given in Fig. 17.44(a). In this figure, r_π appears in parallel with the equivalent resistance R_{EQ} at the terminals of the test source in Fig. 17.44(b). The voltage developed across test source i_x is equal to

$$\mathbf{v_x} = \mathbf{i_x}(R_{\mathrm{th}} + r_x) + (\mathbf{i_x} - g_m\mathbf{v_x})R_E \qquad (17.106)$$

and solving for R_{EQ} and $R_{\pi o}$ yields

$$R_{\mathrm{EQ}} = \frac{\mathbf{v_x}}{\mathbf{i_x}} = \frac{R_{\mathrm{th}} + r_x + R_E}{1 + g_m R_E}$$

$$R_{\pi o} = r_\pi \| R_{\mathrm{EQ}} = r_\pi \| \frac{R_{\mathrm{th}} + r_x + R_E}{1 + g_m R_E} \approx \frac{R_{\mathrm{th}} + r_x + R_E}{1 + g_m R_E} \qquad (17.107)$$

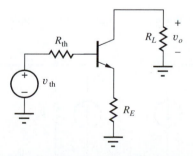

Figure 17.42 High-frequency ac equivalent circuit for the common-emitter amplifier with unbypassed emitter resistor.

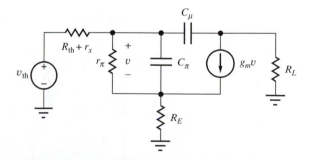

Figure 17.43 High-frequency small-signal model for the common-emitter amplifier.

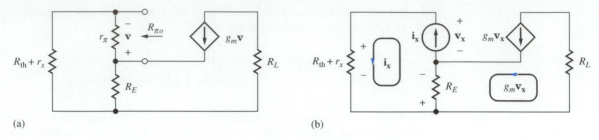

(a)   (b)

Figure 17.44 (a) Circuit for determining $R_{\pi o}$. (b) Simplified circuit with r_π removed.

$R_{\mu o}$ is found from analysis of the circuit in Fig. 17.45. To simplify the analysis, test source i_x is split into two equivalent sources as in Fig. 17.45(b). The voltage $v_x = (v_b - v_c)$ can then be found by superposition using the circuits in Figs. 17.46(a) and (b). For Fig. 17.46(a),

$$\mathbf{v_c} = -\mathbf{i_x} R_L \quad \text{and} \quad \mathbf{v_b} = 0 \tag{17.108}$$

and for (b),

$$\mathbf{v_b} = \mathbf{i_x}[(R_{th} + r_x)\|(r_\pi + (\beta_o + 1)R_E)] \quad \text{and} \quad \mathbf{v_c} = -\frac{\beta_o R_L}{r_\pi + (\beta_o + 1)R_E}\mathbf{v_b} \tag{17.109}$$

Combining the results from Eqs. (17.108) and (17.109) yields $R_{\mu o}$:

$$R_{\mu o} = \frac{\mathbf{v_x}}{\mathbf{i_x}} = \frac{\mathbf{v_b} - \mathbf{v_c}}{\mathbf{i_x}} = R_L + [(R_{th} + r_x)\|(r_\pi + (\beta_o + 1)R_E)]\left[1 + \frac{\beta_o R_L}{r_\pi + (\beta_o + 1)R_E}\right] \tag{17.110}$$

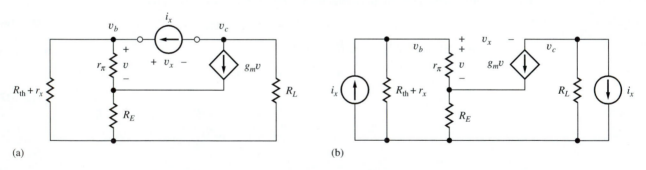

(a)   (b)

Figure 17.45 (a) Circuit for finding $R_{\mu o}$. (b) Equivalent two-source transformation.

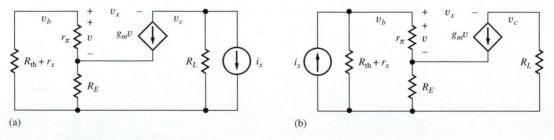

(a)   (b)

Figure 17.46 Two circuits for finding $v_x = (v_b - v_c)$ by superposition.

If it is assumed that $\beta_o \gg 1$ and $R_{th} + r_x \ll r_\pi + (\beta_o + 1)R_E$, then Eq. (17.110) can be simplified to:

$$R_{\mu o} \approx (R_{th} + r_x)\left(1 + \frac{g_m R_L}{1 + g_m R_E} + \frac{R_L}{R_{th} + r_x}\right) \tag{17.111}$$

Combining the results from Eqs. (17.107) and (17.111) yields the estimate for the upper-cutoff frequency of the generalized C-E stage as

$$\omega_H \approx \frac{1}{(R_{th} + r_x)\left[\dfrac{C_\pi}{1 + g_m R_E}\left(1 + \dfrac{R_E}{R_{th} + r_x}\right) + C_\mu\left(1 + \dfrac{g_m R_L}{1 + g_m R_E} + \dfrac{R_L}{R_{th} + r_x}\right)\right]} \tag{17.112}$$

If the total capacitance Eq. (17.112) is compared to the C_T approximation in Eq. (17.81), we can see that the most important terms, C_π and $C_\mu g_m R_L$, are both reduced by the factor $(1 + g_m R_E)$. Thus, although the midband gain in Eq. (17.105) is reduced by the factor $(1 + g_m R_E)$, the upper-cutoff frequency is simultaneously increased by approximately the same factor and the gain-bandwidth product remains approximately constant. Thus there is a direct design tradeoff between reduced gain and increased bandwidth.

EXAMPLE 17.5: Find the midband gain, f_H, and GBW product for the common-emitter amplifier in Fig. 17.31 if a 300-Ω portion of the emitter resistor is not bypassed. Assume $\beta_o = 100$, $f_T = 500$ MHz, $C_\mu = 0.5$ pF, $r_x = 250\ \Omega$, and the Q-point = (1.6 mA, 3.0 V).

SOLUTION: Using the values from the analysis of Fig. 17.31:

$$R_{th} + r_x = 882 + 250 = 1130\ \Omega$$

$$1 + g_m R_E = 1 + 0.064(300) = 20.2$$

$$\omega_H \approx \frac{1}{(R_{th} + r_x)\left[\dfrac{C_\pi}{1 + g_m R_E}\left(1 + \dfrac{R_E}{R_{th} + r_x}\right) + C_\mu\left(1 + \dfrac{g_m R_L}{1 + g_m R_E} + \dfrac{R_L}{R_{th} + r_x}\right)\right]}$$

$$\approx \frac{1}{1130\left[\dfrac{19.9\text{ pF}}{20.2}\left(1 + \dfrac{300}{1130}\right) + 0.5\text{ pF}\left(1 + \dfrac{264}{20.2} + \dfrac{4120}{1130}\right)\right]}$$

$$f_H \approx \frac{1}{2\pi}\frac{1}{1130\ \Omega[10.1\text{ pF}]} = 13.9\text{ MHz}$$

$$A_{Vth} = -\frac{\beta_o R_L}{R_{th} + r_x + r_\pi + (\beta_o + 1)R_E} = -\frac{100(4120)}{1130 + 1560 + (101)300} = -12.5$$

$$\mathbf{v_{th}} = \mathbf{v_s}\frac{7.5\text{ k}\Omega}{1.0\text{ k}\Omega + 7.5\text{ k}\Omega} = 0.882 v_s$$

$$A_{mid} = A_{Vth}\frac{\mathbf{v_{th}}}{\mathbf{v_s}} = 0.882(-12.8) = -11.0$$

$$\text{GBW} = 11.0 \times 13.9\text{ MHz} = 153\text{ MHz}$$

Remember, the original C-E stage had $A_{\text{mid}} = -153$ and $f_H = 1.56$ MHz for GBW $= 239$ MHz. Decreasing the gain has increased the bandwidth. The gain-bandwidth tradeoff is not exact, however, because of the terms in Eq. 17.112, which are not scaled by the $(1 + g_m R_E)$ factor. ◆

Dominant Pole for the Common-Base Amplifier

The OCTC approach is used in this section to find an estimate for the dominant pole of the common-base. The next section finds the similar expressions for the common-gate amplifiers. The common-base amplifier is represented by the high-frequency ac equivalent circuit in Fig. 17.47(a); the small-signal model for the BJT replaces the transistor symbol in Fig. 17.47(b). For Fig. 17.47(b),

$$R_{\text{th}} = R_E \| R_S \qquad \text{and} \qquad R_L = R_C \| R_3 \qquad (17.113)$$

The circuit used to determine $R_{\pi o}$ is given in Fig. 17.48(a). In this figure, r_π appears in parallel with the resistance at the terminals of the test source in Fig. 17.48(b). This circuit is very similar to that analyzed in the previous section. The voltage developed across

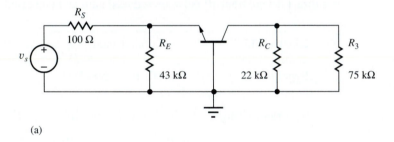

(a)

Figure 17.47 (a) High-frequency ac equivalent circuit for the common-base amplifier. (b) Small-signal model for the common-base amplifier.

(b)

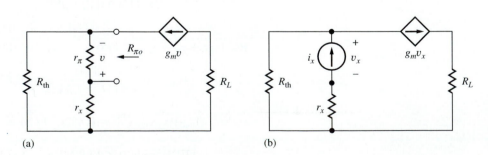

Figure 17.48 Circuits for finding $R_{\pi o}$.

(a)   (b)

the test source is

$$\mathbf{v_x} = (\mathbf{i_x} - g_m\mathbf{v_x})R_{\text{th}} + \mathbf{i_x}r_x$$

and solving for $\mathbf{v_x}/\mathbf{i_x}$

(17.114)

$$R_{\pi o} = r_\pi \left\| \frac{\mathbf{v_x}}{\mathbf{i_x}} = r_\pi \right\| \frac{R_{\text{th}} + r_x}{1 + g_m R_{\text{th}}} \approx \frac{R_{\text{th}} + r_x}{1 + g_m R_{\text{th}}}$$

$R_{\mu o}$ is found from analysis of the circuit in Fig. 17.49. To simplify the analysis, test source i_x is split into two equivalent sources, as in Fig. 17.49(b). The voltage $v_x = (v_b - v_c)$ can then be found by superposition using the circuits in Figs. 17.50(a) and (b). For Fig. 17.50(a),

$$\mathbf{v_c} = -\mathbf{i_x}R_L \qquad \text{and} \qquad \mathbf{v_b} = 0 \qquad (17.115)$$

and for Fig. 17.50(b),

$$\mathbf{v_b} = \mathbf{i_x}[r_x\|(r_\pi + (\beta_o + 1)R_{\text{th}})] \qquad \text{and} \qquad \mathbf{v_c} = -\frac{\beta_o R_L}{r_\pi + (\beta_o + 1)R_{\text{th}}}\mathbf{v_b} \quad (17.116)$$

Combining the results from Eqs. (17.115) and (17.116) yields $R_{\mu o}$:

$$R_{\mu o} = \frac{\mathbf{v_x}}{\mathbf{i_x}} = \frac{\mathbf{v_b} - \mathbf{v_c}}{\mathbf{i_x}} = R_L + \{r_x\|[r_\pi + (\beta_o + 1)R_{\text{th}}]\}\left(1 + \frac{\beta_o R_L}{r_\pi + (\beta_o + 1)R_{\text{th}}}\right)$$

(17.117)

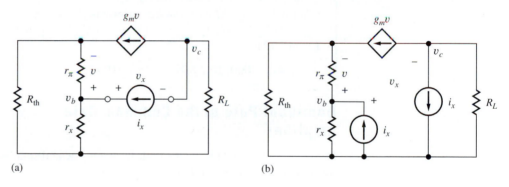

(a)   (b)

Figure 17.49 (a) Circuit for finding $R_{\mu o}$. (b) Split-source transformation.

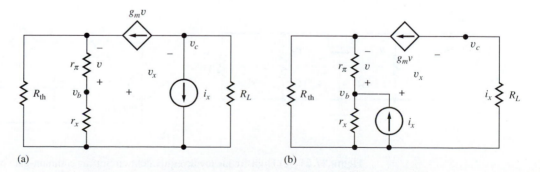

(a)   (b)

Figure 17.50 Circuits for finding $v_x = (v_b - v_c)$ by superposition.

If we assume that $\beta_o \gg 1$ and $r_x \ll r_\pi$, then Eq. (17.117) can be reduced to

$$R_{\mu o} = r_x\left(1 + \frac{g_m R_L}{1 + g_m R_{th}}\right) + R_L \tag{17.118}$$

Using the results from Eqs. (17.114) and (17.119) yields the estimate for the upper-cutoff frequency of the common-base stage as

$$\omega_H \approx \frac{1}{r_x\left[\dfrac{C_\pi}{1 + g_m R_{th}}\left(1 + \dfrac{R_{th}}{r_x}\right) + C_\mu\left(1 + \dfrac{g_m R_L}{1 + g_m R_{th}}\right)\right] + C_\mu R_L} \tag{17.119}$$

The first term in the denominator is typically of the order of $1/\omega_T$ and can be neglected. This simplification yields

$$\omega_H \approx \frac{1}{r_x C_\mu\left(1 + \dfrac{g_m R_L}{1 + g_m R_{th}}\right) + R_L C_\mu} \tag{17.120}$$

In many cases, the last term is dominant so that Eq. (17.120) can be further simplified to

$$\omega_H \approx \frac{1}{R_L C_\mu} \tag{17.121}$$

> **EXERCISE:** Find the midband gain and f_H using Eq. (17.119) for the common-base amplifier in Fig. 17.47 if the transistor has $\beta_o = 100$, $f_T = 500$ MHz, $r_x = 250\ \Omega$, $C_\mu = 0.5$ pF, and a Q-point (0.1 mA, 3.5 V). Compare the result to that predicted by Eq. (17.121).
>
> **ANSWERS:** $+48.0$; 10.7 MHz $<$ 18.7 MHz

Dominant Pole of the Common-Gate Amplifier

Figures 17.51(a) and (b) are the high-frequency ac and small-signal equivalent circuits for a common-gate amplifier. For Fig. 17.51(b),

$$R_{th} = R_4 \| R_s \quad \text{and} \quad R_L = R_D \| R_3 \tag{17.122}$$

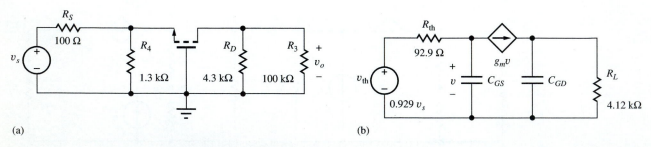

(a)   (b)

Figure 17.51 (a) High-frequency ac equivalent circuit for common-gate amplifier. (b) Corresponding small-signal model.

The results are similar to those for the common-base circuit except for $r_x = 0$ and the change in symbols in Eqs. (17.114), (17.118), and (17.120):

$$R_{GSo} = \frac{R_{th}}{1 + g_m R_{th}} = \frac{1}{G_{th} + g_m}$$

$$R_{GDo} = R_L \qquad (17.123)$$

$$\omega_H \approx \frac{1}{\dfrac{C_{GS}}{G_{th} + g_m} + R_L C_{GD}} \leq \frac{1}{R_L C_{GD}}$$

> **EXERCISE:** Find the midband gain and f_H for a common-gate amplifier if the transistor $C_{GS} = 10$ pF, $C_{GD} = 1$ pF, and $g_m = 3$ mS.
>
> **ANSWERS:** $+8.98$, 32.8 MHz

Dominant Pole for the Common-Collector Amplifier

The common-collector stage is represented by the high-frequency ac equivalent circuit in Fig. 17.52(a), and the small-signal model for the BJT replaces the transistor symbol in Fig. 17.52(b). In this circuit, the collector-base capacitance C_μ actually appears in parallel with the input of the transistor, as shown explicitly in the circuit rearrangement in Fig. 17.52(c).

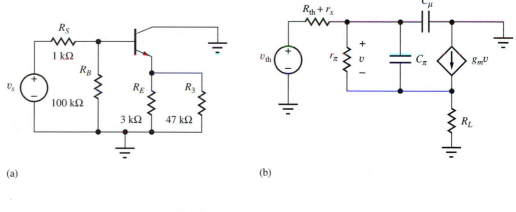

(a)   (b)

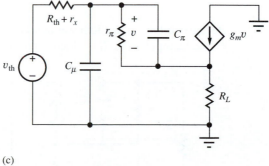

(c)

Figure 17.52 (a) High-frequency equivalent circuit for the C-C amplifier. (b) Small-signal model. (c) Rearrangement of the small-signal model.

For Fig. 17.52,

$$R_{th} = R_B \| R_S \qquad \text{and} \qquad R_L = R_E \| R_3 \qquad (17.124)$$

Once again, two resistances must be found in order to evaluate the open-circuit time constants. The circuit for determining $R_{\mu o}$ is drawn in Fig. 17.53, and $R_{\mu o}$ can be evaluated directly using our knowledge of single-transistor amplifiers:

$$R_{\mu o} = (R_{th} + r_x) \| R_{IN}^{CC} = (R_{th} + r_x) \| [r_\pi + (\beta_o + 1)R_L] \approx (R_{th} + r_x) \quad (17.125)$$

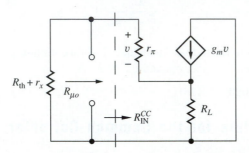

Figure 17.53 Circuit for finding $R_{\mu o}$.

Evaluation of $R_{\pi o}$ uses the circuits in Figs. 17.54 and 17.55. Based on Fig. 17.54, $R_{\pi o} = r_\pi \| R_{EQ}$, in which R_{EQ} is the resistance presented to the test current source i_x in Fig. 17.55. The voltage v_x can be found by applying KVL to the loop indicated in Fig. 17.55:

$$\mathbf{v_x} = \mathbf{i_x}(R_{th} + r_x) + \mathbf{i_L} R_L = \mathbf{i_x}(R_{th} + r_x) + (\mathbf{i_x} - g_m \mathbf{v_x})R_L \qquad (17.126)$$

and

$$R_{EQ} = \frac{\mathbf{v_x}}{\mathbf{i_x}} = \frac{R_{th} + r_x + R_L}{1 + g_m R_L} \qquad (17.127)$$

Using Eq. (17.127),

$$R_{\pi o} = r_\pi \left\| \frac{R_{th} + r_x + R_L}{1 + g_m R_L} \approx \frac{R_{th} + r_x + R_L}{1 + g_m R_L} \right. \qquad (17.128)$$

and

$$\omega_H \approx \frac{1}{(R_{th} + r_x + R_L)\dfrac{C_\pi}{1 + g_m R_L} + (R_{th} + r_x)C_\mu} \qquad (17.129)$$

Because of the emitter-follower action with a gain of nearly 1, the effect of C_π is reduced by the factor $(1 + g_m R_L)$, which is normally designed to be $\gg 1$.

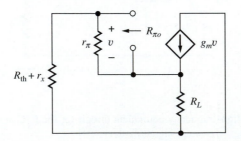

Figure 17.54 Circuit for finding $R_{\pi o}$.

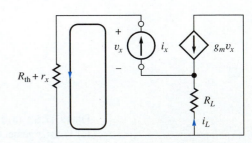

Figure 17.55 Network for finding R_{EQ}.

In the case of the emitter-follower, the OCTC technique underestimates ω_H. A better estimate is obtained if R_L is set to zero in the numerator of Eqs. (17.127) and (17.128) (see Prob. 17.52), which yields

$$\omega_H = \frac{1}{(R_{th} + r_x)\left[\dfrac{C_\pi}{1 + g_m R_L} + C_\mu\right]} \tag{17.130}$$

The upper-cutoff frequency of the emitter follower is very high. Thus the voltage gain of the emitter follower is essentially constant at a value of unity for all frequencies for which the hybrid-pi model is valid. Note that Eq. (17.130) also represents the GBW product of the emitter follower, and the limit for $R_{th} = 0$ and large R_L is

$$\text{GBW} = 1 \cdot (\omega_H) \le \frac{1}{r_x C_\mu} \tag{17.131}$$

which is the same upper bound as for the C-E amplifier stage.

> **EXERCISE:** Find A_{mid} and f_H for the common-collector amplifier in Fig. 17.52 if the Q-point is (1.5 mA, 5 V), $\beta_o = 100$, $r_x = 150\ \Omega$, $C_\mu = 0.5$ pF, and $f_T = 500$ MHz.
>
> **ANSWERS:** 0.980, 229 MHz

Dominant Pole for the Common-Drain Amplifier

The source follower in Fig. 17.56 offers behavior very similar to that of the emitter follower. Substituting $r_\pi = \infty$ and $r_x = 0$ in Eq. (17.129),

$$\omega_H = \frac{1}{\dfrac{R_{th}}{1 + g_m R_L}C_{GS} + R_{th}C_{GD}} = \frac{1}{R_{th}\left[\dfrac{C_{GS}}{1 + g_m R_L} + C_{GD}\right]} \tag{17.132}$$

in which

$$R_{th} = R_s \| R_G \qquad \text{and} \qquad R_L = R_4 \| R_3 \tag{17.133}$$

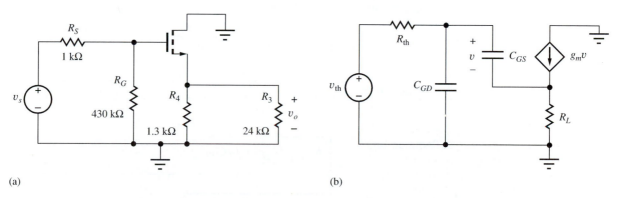

(a) (b)

Figure 17.56 (a) High-frequency ac equivalent circuit for a source follower. (b) Corresponding high-frequency small-signal model.

> **EXERCISE:** Find A_{mid} and f_H for the common-drain amplifier in Fig. 17.56 if $C_{GS} = 10$ pF, $C_{GD} = 1$ pF, and $g_m = 3$ mS.
>
> **ANSWERS:** 0.785, 51.0 MHz

Single-Stage Amplifier High-Frequency Response Summary

Table 17.2 collects the expressions for the dominant poles of the three classes of single-stage amplifiers. The inverting amplifiers provide high voltage gain but with the most limited bandwidth. The noninverting stages offer improved bandwidth with voltage gains similar to those of the inverting amplifiers. Remember, however, that the input resistance of the noninverting amplifiers is relatively low. The followers provide unity gain with very wide bandwidth.

It is also worth noting at this point that both the C-E and C-B (or C-S and C-G) stages have a bandwidth that is always less than that set by the time constant of R_L and C_μ (or C_{GD} and R_L) at the output node:

$$\omega_H < \frac{1}{R_L C_\mu} \qquad \text{or} \qquad \omega_H < \frac{1}{R_L C_{GD}} \tag{17.134}$$

Table 17.2

Upper-Cutoff Frequencies for the Single-Stage Amplifiers

	ω_H
Common-Emitter	$\dfrac{1}{r_{\pi o} C_T} = \dfrac{1}{r_{\pi o}\left[C_\pi + C_\mu\left(1 + g_m R_L + \dfrac{R_L}{r_{\pi o}}\right)\right]}$ $\qquad r_{\pi o} = r_\pi \| (R_{\text{th}} + r_x)$
Common-Source	$\dfrac{1}{R_{\text{th}} C_T} = \dfrac{1}{R_{\text{th}}\left[C_{GS} + C_{GD}\left(1 + g_m R_L + \dfrac{R_L}{R_{\text{th}}}\right)\right]}$
Common-Emitter with R_E	$\dfrac{1}{(R_{\text{th}} + r_x) C_{TB}}$ $C_{TB} = \dfrac{C_\pi}{1 + g_m R_E}\left(1 + \dfrac{R_E}{R_{\text{th}} + r_x}\right) + C_\mu\left(1 + \dfrac{g_m R_L}{1 + g_m R_E} + \dfrac{R_L}{R_{\text{th}} + r_x}\right)$
Common-Base	$\dfrac{1}{R_{\text{th}}\dfrac{C_\pi}{1 + g_m R_{\text{th}}}\left(1 + \dfrac{r_x}{R_{\text{th}}}\right) + C_\mu r_x\left(1 + \dfrac{g_m R_L}{1 + g_m R_{\text{th}}}\right) + C_\mu R_L}$
Common-Gate	$\dfrac{1}{R_{\text{th}}\dfrac{C_{GS}}{1 + g_m R_{\text{th}}} + R_L C_{GD}}$
Common-Collector	$\dfrac{1}{(R_{\text{th}} + r_x)\left[\dfrac{C_\pi}{1 + g_m R_L} + C_\mu\right]}$
Common-Drain	$\dfrac{1}{R_{\text{th}}\left[\dfrac{C_{GS}}{1 + g_m R_L} + C_{GD}\right]}$

17.9 FREQUENCY RESPONSE OF MULTISTAGE AMPLIFIERS

The open- and short-circuit time-constant methods are not limited to single-transistor amplifiers but are directly applicable to multistage circuits as well; the power of the technique becomes more obvious as circuit complexity grows. This section uses the OCTC techniques to estimate the frequency response of several important two-stage dc-coupled amplifiers, including the differential amplifier, the cascode stage, and the current mirror. Because these amplifiers are direct-coupled, they have low-pass characteristics and only the OCTC method is needed to determine f_H. Following is an example of analysis of a general three-stage amplifier in which f_L and f_H are found using the SCTC and OCTC approaches.

Differential Amplifier

As pointed out several times, the differential amplifier is a key building block of analog circuits, and hence it is important to understand the frequency response of the differential pair. An important element, C_{EE}, has been included in the differential amplifier circuit in Fig. 17.57(a). C_{EE} represents the total capacitance at the emitter node of the differential pair. Analysis of the frequency response of the symmetrical amplifier in Fig. 17.57(a) is greatly simplified through the use of the half-circuits in (b) and (c).

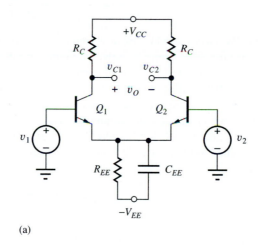

(a)

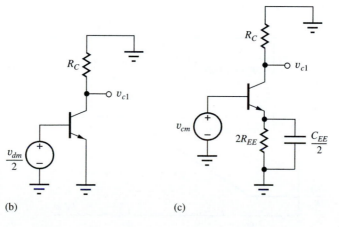

(b)   (c)

Figure 17.57 (a) Bipolar differential amplifier, (b) its differential-mode half-circuit, and (c) its common-mode half-circuit.

Differential-Mode Signals

We recognize the differential-mode half-circuit in Fig. 17.57(b) as being equivalent to the standard common-emitter stage. Thus the bandwidth for differential-mode signals is determined by the $r_{\pi o} C_T$ product that was developed in the analysis in Sec. 17.6, and we can expect amplifier gain-bandwidth products equal to a significant fraction of the f_T of the transistor. Because the emitter node is a virtual ground, C_{EE} has no effect on differential-mode signals.

Common-Mode Frequency Response

The important breakpoints in the Bode plot of the common-mode frequency response depicted in Fig. 17.58 can be determined from analysis of the common-mode half-circuit in Fig. 17.57(c). At very low frequencies, we know that the common-mode gain to either collector is small, given approximately by

$$|A_{cc}(0)| \approx \frac{R_C}{2R_{EE}} \ll 1 \tag{17.135}$$

However, capacitance C_{EE} in parallel with emitter resistor R_{EE} introduces a transmission zero in the common-mode frequency response at the frequency for which the impedance of the parallel combination of R_{EE} and C_{EE} becomes infinite. This zero is given by

$$s = -\omega_z = -\frac{1}{R_{EE}C_{EE}} \tag{17.136}$$

and typically occurs at relatively low frequencies. Although C_{EE} may be small, resistance R_{EE} is normally designed to be large, often the output resistance of a very high impedance current source. The presence of this zero causes the common-mode gain to increase at a rate of $+20$ dB/decade for frequencies above ω_Z. The common-mode gain continues to increase until the dominant pole of the pair is reached at relatively high frequencies.

The common-mode half-circuit is equivalent to a common-emitter stage with emitter resistor $2R_{EE}$; the OCTC for C_π and C_μ have already been found for this configuration in Sec. 16.8. The OCTC for $C_{EE}/2$ is just the resistance looking back into the emitter in Fig. 17.57(c):

$$R_{EEO} = 2R_{EE} \left\| \frac{r_x + r_\pi}{\beta_o + 1} \right. \approx \frac{1}{g_m} \tag{17.137}$$

Combining Eq. (17.137) with Eq. (17.112) for $R_{\text{th}} = 0$ yields the position of the pole in the common-mode response:

$$\omega_P \approx \frac{1}{r_x \left[\dfrac{C_\pi}{1 + 2g_m R_{EE}} \left(1 + \dfrac{2R_{EE}}{r_x} \right) + C_\mu \left(1 + \dfrac{g_m R_C}{1 + 2g_m R_{EE}} + \dfrac{R_C}{r_x} \right) \right] + \dfrac{C_{EE}}{2g_m}} \tag{17.138}$$

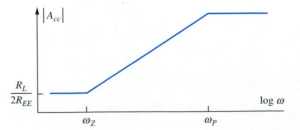

Figure 17.58 Bode plot for the common-mode gain of the differential pair.

Because R_{EE} is usually designed to be very large, Eq. (17.138) can be reduced to

$$\omega_P \approx \frac{1}{\dfrac{C_\pi + C_{EE}}{2g_m} + C_\mu(r_x + R_C)} \approx \frac{1}{C_\mu(r_x + R_C)} \qquad (17.139)$$

EXERCISE: Find f_Z and f_P for the common-mode response of the differential amplifier in Fig. 17.57 if $r_x = 250\ \Omega$, $C_\mu = 0.5$ pF, $R_{EE} = 25\ M\Omega$, $C_{EE} = 1$ pF, and $R_C = 50\ k\Omega$.

ANSWERS: 6.37 kHz, 6.34 MHz

The C-C/C-B Cascade

Figure 17.59(a) is an unbalanced version of the differential amplifier. This circuit can also be represented as the cascade of a common-collector and common-base amplifier, as in Fig. 17.59(b). The cutoff frequency of this two-stage amplifier is found by applying the OCTC approach, using the results of the previous single-stage amplifier analyses.

We assume the output resistance R_{EE} of the current source is very large and neglect it in the analysis because the resistances presented at the emitters of Q_1 and Q_2 in Fig. 17.60 are both small:

$$R_{OUT}^{CC1} = \frac{r_{x1} + r_{\pi 1}}{\beta_{o1} + 1} \approx \frac{1}{g_{m1}} \qquad \text{and} \qquad R_{IN}^{CB2} = \frac{r_{x2} + r_{\pi 2}}{\beta_{o2} + 1} \approx \frac{1}{g_{m2}} \qquad (17.140)$$

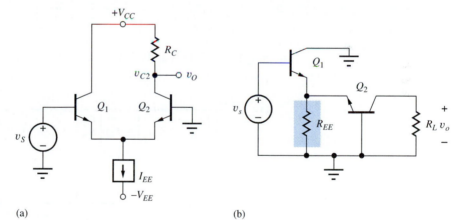

Figure 17.59 (a) The unbalanced differential amplifier and (b) its representation as a C-C/C-B cascade.

(a)

(b)

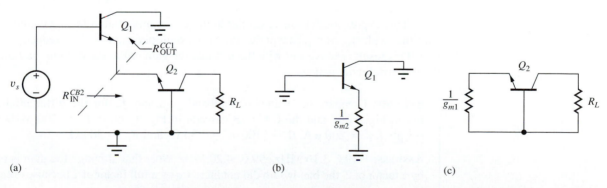

(a)

(b)

(c)

Figure 17.60 (a) Equivalent circuits for analysis of the OCTC of (b) Q_1 and (c) Q_2.

When using the open-circuit time-constant approach, the capacitances of Q_1 and Q_2 can be considered individually or grouped in pairs. By grouping the capacitors in pairs, $(C_{\pi 1}$ and $C_{\mu 1})$ and $(C_{\pi 2}$ and $C_{\mu 2})$, we can use the single-stage amplifier results in Table 17.3 (p. 952). During the analysis of the capacitances of Q_1, Q_2 can be replaced by R_{IN}^{CB2}, and during the analysis of the capacitances of Q_2, Q_1 can be replaced by R_{OUT}^{CC1}, as indicated in the two equivalent circuits in Fig. 17.60(b) and (c).

The circuit in Fig. 17.60(b) should be recognized as an emitter follower with a load resistor equal to $1/g_{m2}$, and using the results from Table 17.3, the sum of the two open-circuit time constants for transistor Q_1 is

$$r_{x1}\left[\frac{C_{\pi 1}}{1 + g_{m1}\dfrac{1}{g_{m2}}} + C_{\mu 1}\right] = r_{x1}\left[\frac{C_{\pi 1}}{2} + C_{\mu 1}\right] \qquad (17.141)$$

Similarly, the circuit in Fig. 17.60(c) should be recognized as a common-base stage with a source resistance equal to $1/g_{m1}$. Again using the results from Table 17.3, the sum of the OCTC for Q_2 is

$$r_{x2}\left[\frac{C_{\pi 2}}{1 + \dfrac{g_{m2}}{g_{m1}}}\left(1 + \frac{1}{g_{m1}r_{x2}}\right) + C_{\mu 2}\left(1 + \frac{g_m R_L}{1 + \dfrac{g_{m2}}{g_{m1}}}\right)\right] + C_{\mu 2}R_L \qquad (17.42)$$

$$\approx r_{x2}\left[\frac{C_{\pi 2}}{2} + C_{\mu 2}\left(1 + \frac{g_m R_L}{2} + \frac{R_L}{r_{x2}}\right)\right]$$

Combining Eqs. (17.141) and (17.142) and assuming the two transistors are matched yields

$$\omega_H = \frac{1}{r_{x1}\left[\dfrac{C_{\pi 1}}{2} + C_{\mu 1}\right] + r_{x2}\left[\dfrac{C_{\pi 2}}{2} + C_{\mu 2}\left(1 + \dfrac{g_m R_L}{2} + \dfrac{R_L}{r_{x2}}\right)\right]} \qquad (17.143)$$

or

$$\omega_H = \frac{1}{r_x\left[C_\pi + C_\mu\left(2 + \dfrac{g_m R_L}{2} + \dfrac{R_L}{r_x}\right)\right]} \qquad (17.144)$$

This expression for ω_H is similar to the C_T approximation for the common-emitter amplifier with $r_{\pi o} = r_{x1}$, except that the Miller multiplication of C_μ is reduced by a factor of 2. This result is consistent with the fact that the gain of the stage is one-half the gain of the full differential pair.

> **EXERCISE:** Compare the values of midband gain and f_H for the differential amplifier in Fig. 17.57 and the C-C/C-B cascade in Fig. 17.60 if $f_T = 500$ MHz, $C_\mu = 0.5$ pF, $I_{EE} = 200$ μA, $\beta_o = 100$, $r_x = 250$ Ω, and $R_L = 50$ kΩ.
>
> **ANSWERS:** -198, 3.16 MHz, 99.0, 4.20 MHz. Note that although the gain is reduced by a factor of 2, the bandwidth did not increase by a full factor of 2 because of the $R_L r_x$ term.

High-Frequency Response of the Cascode Amplifier

Chapter 16 introduced the cascade of the common-emitter and common-base stages in Fig. 17.61; this cascade is referred to as the **cascode amplifier**. The cascode stage offers a midband gain and input resistance equal to that of the common-emitter amplifier but with a much improved upper-cutoff frequency f_H, as will be demonstrated by the forthcoming analysis.

The bandwidth of the cascode stage can be determined using the OCTC approach. The time constants associated with $C_{\pi 1}$, $C_{\mu 1}$, $C_{\pi 2}$, and $C_{\mu 2}$ must be found; we can again simplify the analysis by grouping the capacitors in pairs to make maximum use of the results for the single-stage amplifiers.

The open-circuit time constants associated with $C_{\pi 1}$ and $C_{\mu 1}$ are calculated with $C_{\pi 2}$ and $C_{\mu 2}$ removed from the circuit. Thus, Q_2 can simply be replaced by its midband input resistance, $1/g_{m2}$, as shown in Fig. 17.62(a), and the time constants associated with Q_1 are given by the C_T approximation with a load resistor of value $1/g_{m2}$.

$$R_{\pi o1}C_{\pi 1} + R_{\mu o1}C_{\mu 1} = r_{\pi o1}C_{T1} = r_{\pi o1}\left[C_{\pi 1} + C_{\mu 1}\left(1 + \frac{g_{m1}}{g_{m2}} + \frac{1}{g_{m2}r_{\pi o1}}\right)\right] \quad (17.145)$$

Because $I_{C2} \approx I_{C1}$, $g_{m2} = g_{m1}$, and the intrinsic gain of the first stage is unity:

$$A_{V1} \approx -g_{m1}R_L \approx -g_{m1}\frac{1}{g_{m2}} = -1 \quad (17.146)$$

If we assume $g_{m2}r_{\pi o1} \gg 1$, then

$$r_{\pi o1}C_{T1} \approx r_{\pi o1}\left(C_{\pi 1} + 2C_{\mu 1}\right) \quad (17.147)$$

The term due to Miller multiplication has been reduced from a very large factor, 264 in the C-E example in Sec. 17.6, to only 2, and the $R_L/r_{\pi o}$ term has also been eliminated. These reductions can greatly increase the bandwidth of the overall amplifier.

The open-circuit time constants associated with $C_{\pi 2}$ and $C_{\mu 2}$ are calculated with $C_{\pi 1}$ and $C_{\mu 1}$ removed from the circuit and can be found using the circuit in Fig. 17.63, in which the first stage is replaced by r_{o1}. The time constants associated with Q_2 are those of

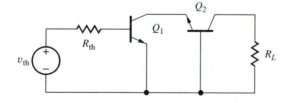

Figure 17.61 ac Model for the direct-coupled cascode amplifier.

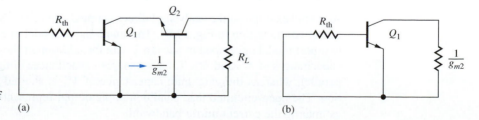

Figure 17.62 (a) Model for determining open-circuit time constants associated with the two capacitances of Q_1. (b) Simplified model.

(a)

(b)

a common-base stage with $R_{\text{th}} = r_{o1}$:

$$R_{\pi o2}C_{\pi 2} + R_{\mu o2}C_{\mu 2} = \frac{C_{\pi 2}}{1 + g_{m2}r_{o1}}(r_{o1} + r_x) + r_{x2}C_{\mu 2}\left(1 + \frac{g_{m2}R_L}{1 + g_{m2}r_{o1}} + \frac{R_L}{r_{x2}}\right)$$

$$R_{\pi o2}C_{\pi 2} + R_{\mu o2}C_{\mu 2} \approx \frac{C_{\pi 2}}{g_{m2}} + r_{x2}C_{\mu 2}\left(1 + \frac{R_L}{r_{o1}} + \frac{R_L}{r_{x2}}\right) \tag{17.148}$$

$$R_{\pi o2}C_{\pi 2} + R_{\mu o2}C_{\mu 2} \approx \frac{C_{\pi 2}}{g_{m2}} + (r_{x2} + R_L)C_{\mu 2} \qquad \text{for } r_{o1} \gg R_L \text{ and } \mu_F \gg 1$$

Combining Eqs. (17.147) and (17.148) yields an overall estimate for ω_H:

$$\omega_H = \frac{1}{R_{\pi o1}C_{\pi 1} + R_{\mu o1}C_{\mu 1} + R_{\pi o2}C_{\pi 2} + R_{\mu o2}C_{\mu 2}}$$

$$= \frac{1}{r_{\pi o1}(C_{\pi 1} + 2C_{\mu 1}) + \dfrac{C_{\pi 2}}{g_{m2}} + C_{\mu 2}(r_{x2} + R_L)} \tag{17.149a}$$

Assuming matched devices yields

$$\omega_H \approx \frac{1}{r_{\pi o1}C_{\pi} + C_{\mu}(2r_{\pi o1} + r_x + R_L)}$$

$$\approx \frac{1}{r_{\pi o1}[C_{\pi} + 2C_{\mu}] + (r_x + R_L)C_{\mu}} \tag{17.149b}$$

In many practical situations, Eq. (17.149) indicates that the overall bandwidth of the cascode amplifier is limited by the $R_L C_{\mu 2}$ time constant, which occurs at the output of the C-B stage.

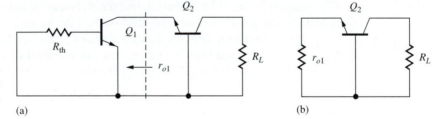

Figure 17.63 Model for determining open-circuit time constants associated with capacitances of Q_2.

(a)   (b)

EXERCISE: Find the midband value of $A_{V\text{th}}$ and upper-cutoff frequency of the cascode amplifier in Fig. 17.61 assuming $\beta_o = 100$, $f_T = 500$ MHz, $C_{\mu} = 0.5$ pF, $r_x = 250\ \Omega$, $R_{\text{th}} = 882\ \Omega$, $R_L = 4.12$ kΩ, and a Q-point of (1.60 mA, 3.00 V) for Q_2.

ANSWERS: -151, 10.0 MHz

Cutoff Frequency for the Current Mirror

As a final example of the analysis of direct-coupled amplifiers, let us find ω_H for the current mirror configuration in Fig. 17.64. The small-signal model in Fig. 17.64(b) represents the two-port model developed in Sec. 16.2 with the addition of the gate-source and gate-drain capacitances of M_1 and M_2. The gate-source capacitances of the two transistors appear in parallel, whereas the gate-drain capacitance of M_1 is shorted out by the circuit connection. The open-circuited load condition at the output represents a worst-case situation for estimating the current mirror bandwidth.

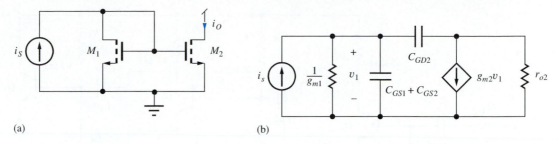

Figure 17.64 (a) MOS current mirror. (b) Small-signal model for the current mirror.

The circuit in Fig. 17.64(b) should be recognized as identical to the simplified model of the C-E stage in Fig. 17.34, and the results of the C_T approximation are directly applicable to the current mirror circuit with the following substitutions:

$$r_{\pi o} \rightarrow \frac{1}{g_{m1}} \qquad R_L \rightarrow r_{o2} \qquad C_\pi \rightarrow C_{GS1} + C_{GS2} \qquad C_\mu \rightarrow C_{GD2} \qquad (17.150)$$

Using the values from Eq. (17.150) in Eq. (17.80),

$$\omega_{P1} \approx \frac{1}{r_{\pi o} C_T} = \frac{1}{\dfrac{1}{g_{m1}} \left[C_{GS1} + C_{GS2} + C_{GD2} \left(1 + g_{m2} r_{o2} + \dfrac{r_{o2}}{\dfrac{1}{g_{m1}}} \right) \right]} \qquad (17.151)$$

and for matched transistors with equal W/L ratios,

$$\omega_{P1} \approx \frac{1}{\dfrac{2C_{GS1}}{g_{m1}} + 2C_{GD2} r_{o2}} \approx \frac{1}{2C_{GD2} r_{o2}} \qquad (17.152)$$

The result in Eq. (17.152) indicates that the bandwidth of the current mirror is controlled by the time constant at the output of the mirror due to the output resistance and gate-drain capacitance of M_2. Note that the value of Eq. (17.152) is directly proportional to the Q-point current through the dependence of r_{o2}.

> **EXERCISE:** (a) Find the bandwidth of the current mirror in Fig. 17.64 if $I_1 = 100$ μA, $C_{GD} = 1$ pF, and $\lambda = 0.02$ V^{-1}. (b) If $I_1 = 25$ μA.
>
> **ANSWERS:** 318 kHz; 79.6 kHz

Three-Stage Amplifier Example

As an example of a more complex analysis, let us estimate the upper- and lower-cutoff frequencies for the multistage amplifier in Fig. 17.65 that was introduced in Chapter 15. At low frequencies, the impedances of the internal device capacitances are very large and can be neglected. The coupling and bypass capacitors remain in the low-frequency High-frequency ac equivalent circuit in Fig. 17.66(b) (p. 953), and an estimate for ω_L is calculated using the SCTC approach.

The circuit has six independent coupling and bypass capacitors; Fig.17.66 gives the circuits for finding the six short-circuit time constants. The analysis proceeds using the small-signal parameters in Table 17.3. The low-frequency transistor parameter values in Table 17.3 are reproduced from Table 15.2.

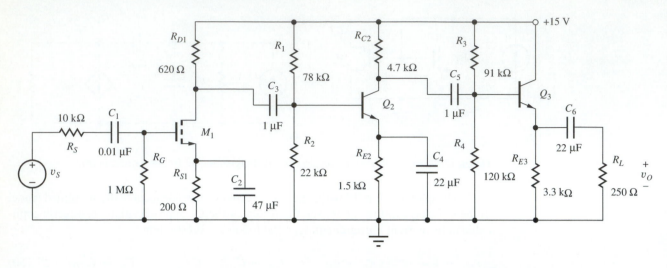

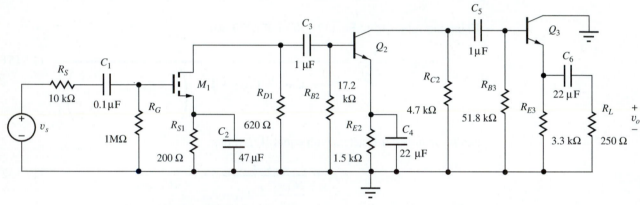

Figure 17.65 Three-stage amplifier and ac equivalent circuit.

<table>
<tr><td colspan="8" align="center">**T a b l e 17.3**</td></tr>
<tr><td colspan="8" align="center">**Transistor Parameters**</td></tr>
<tr><td></td><td>g_m</td><td>r_π</td><td>r_o</td><td>β_0</td><td>C_{GS}/C_π</td><td>C_{GD}/C_μ</td><td>r_x</td></tr>
<tr><td>**M_1**</td><td>10 mS</td><td>∞</td><td>12.2 kΩ</td><td>∞</td><td>5 pF</td><td>1 pF</td><td>0 Ω</td></tr>
<tr><td>**Q_2**</td><td>67.8 mS</td><td>2.39 kΩ</td><td>54.2 kΩ</td><td>150</td><td>39 pF</td><td>1 pf</td><td>250 Ω</td></tr>
<tr><td>**Q_3**</td><td>79.6 mS</td><td>1.00 kΩ</td><td>34.4 kΩ</td><td>80</td><td>50 pF</td><td>1 pF</td><td>250 Ω</td></tr>
</table>

R_{1S}

Because the input resistance to M_1 is infinite in Fig. 17.66(a), R_{1S} is given by

$$R_{1S} = R_S + R_G \| R_{\text{IN1}} = 10 \text{ k}\Omega + 1 \text{ M}\Omega \| \infty = 1.01 \text{ M}\Omega \qquad (17.153)$$

R_{2S}

R_{2S} represents the resistance present at the source terminal of M_1 in Fig. 17.66(b) and is equal to

$$R_{2S} = R_{S1} \left\| \frac{1}{g_{m1}} = 200 \text{ }\Omega \right\| \frac{1}{0.01 \text{ } S} = 66.7 \text{ }\Omega \qquad (17.154)$$

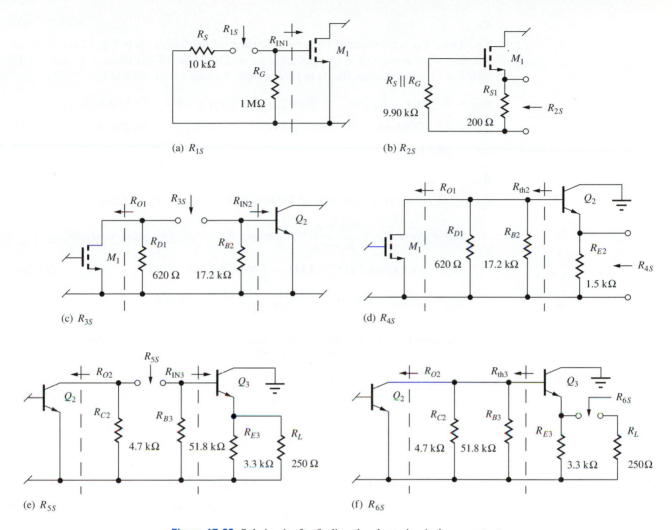

Figure 17.66 Subcircuits for finding the short-circuit time constants.

R_{3S}

Resistance R_{3S} is formed from a combination of four elements in Fig. 17.66(c). To the left, the output resistance of M_1 appears in parallel with the 620-Ω resistor R_{D1}, and on the right the 17.2-kΩ resistor R_{B2} is in parallel with the input resistance of Q_2:

$$R_{3S} = R_{D1} \| R_{O1} + R_{B2} \| R_{IN2} = R_{D1} \| r_{o1} + R_{B2} \| r_{\pi 2} \tag{17.155}$$
$$= 620\ \Omega \| 12.2\ \text{k}\Omega + 17.2\ \text{k}\Omega \| 2.39\ \text{k}\Omega = 2.69\ \text{k}\Omega$$

R_{4S}

R_{4S} represents the resistance present at the emitter terminal of Q_2 in Fig. 17.66(d) and is equal to

$$R_{4S} = R_{E2} \left\| \frac{R_{th2} + r_{\pi 2}}{(\beta_{o2} + 1)} \right. \qquad \text{where } R_{th2} = R_{B2} \| R_{D1} \| R_{O1} = R_{B2} \| R_{D1} \| r_{o1}$$

$$R_{th2} = R_{B2} \| R_{D1} \| r_{o1} = 17.2\ \text{k}\Omega \| 620\ \Omega \| 12.2\ \text{k}\Omega = 571\ \Omega \tag{17.156}$$

$$R_{4S} = 1500\ \Omega \left\| \frac{571\ \Omega + 2390\ \Omega}{(150 + 1)} \right. = 19.4\ \Omega$$

R_{5S}

Resistance R_{5S} is also formed from a combination of four elements in Fig. 17.66(e). To the left, the output resistance of Q_2 appears in parallel with the 4.7-kΩ resistor R_{C2}, and to the right the 51.8-kΩ resistor R_{B3} is in parallel with the input resistance of Q_3:

$$
\begin{aligned}
R_{5S} &= R_{C2}\|R_{O2} + R_{B3}\|R_{IN3} = R_{C2}\|r_{o2} + R_{B3}\|[r_{\pi3} + (\beta_{o3} + 1)(R_{E3}\|R_L)] \\
&= 4.7\ \text{k}\Omega\|54.2\ \text{k}\Omega + 51.8\ \text{k}\Omega\ \|[1.00\ \text{k}\Omega + (80 + 1)(3.3\ \text{k}\Omega\|250\ \Omega)] \qquad (17.157) \\
&= 18.4\ \text{k}\Omega
\end{aligned}
$$

R_{6S}

Finally, R_{6S} is the resistance present at the terminals of C_6 in Fig. 17.66(f):

$$
R_{6S} = R_L + R_{E3}\ \left\|\ \frac{R_{\text{th3}} + r_{\pi3}}{\beta_{o3} + 1}\right. \qquad \text{where } R_{\text{th3}} = R_{B3}\|R_{C2}\|R_{O2} = R_{B3}\|R_{C2}\|r_{o2}
$$

$$
R_{\text{th3}} = 51.8\ \text{k}\Omega\|4.7\ \text{k}\Omega\|54.2\ \text{k}\Omega = 3.99\ \text{k}\Omega \qquad (17.158)
$$

$$
R_{6S} = 250\ \Omega + 3.3\ \text{k}\Omega\ \left\|\ \frac{3.99\ \text{k}\Omega + 1.00\ \text{k}\Omega}{80 + 1}\right. = 311\ \Omega
$$

An estimate for ω_L can now be constructed using Eq. (17.34) and the resistance values calculated in Eqs. (17.153) to (17.158):

$$
\begin{aligned}
\omega_L &\approx \sum_{i=1}^{n} \frac{1}{R_{iS}C_i} = \frac{1}{R_{1S}C_1} + \frac{1}{R_{2S}C_2} + \frac{1}{R_{3S}C_3} + \frac{1}{R_{4S}C_4} + \frac{1}{R_{5S}C_5} + \frac{1}{R_{6S}C_6} \\
&\approx \frac{1}{(1.01\ \text{M}\Omega)(0.01\ \mu\text{F})} + \frac{1}{(66.7\ \Omega)(47\ \mu\text{F})} + \frac{1}{(2.69\ \text{k}\Omega)(1\ \mu\text{F})} \\
&\quad + \frac{1}{(19.4\ \Omega)(22\ \mu\text{F})} + \frac{1}{(18.4\ \text{k}\Omega)(1\ \mu\text{F})} + \frac{1}{(311\ \Omega)(22\ \mu\text{F})}) \\
&\approx 99.0 + 319 + 372 + \underline{2340} + 54.4 + 146 = 3330\ \text{rad/s} \qquad (17.159)
\end{aligned}
$$

$$
f_L = \frac{\omega_L}{2\pi} = 530\ \text{Hz} \qquad (17.160)
$$

The estimate of the lower-cutoff frequency is 530 Hz. The largest contributor is the fourth term, resulting from the time constant associated with emitter-bypass capacitor C_4.

> **EXERCISE:** Calculate the reactance of $C_{\pi2}$ at f_L and compare its value to $r_{\pi2}$. Calculate the reactance of $C_{\mu3}$ and compare it to $R_{B3}\|R_{IN3}$ in Fig. 17.66(e).
>
> **ANSWERS:** 7.7 M$\Omega \gg$ 2.39 kΩ; 300 M$\Omega \gg$ 14.3 kΩ

OCTC Estimate for the Upper-Cutoff Frequency ω_H

An estimate for the upper-cutoff frequency of the three-stage amplifier can be determined by applying the OCTC method to the high-frequency ac model of the amplifier in Fig. 17.67. At high frequencies, the impedances of the coupling and bypass capacitors are negligibly small, and we construct the circuit in Fig. 17.67 by replacing the coupling and bypass capacitors by short circuits. The high-frequency model of each transistor contains two capacitors, and if these are evaluated in pairs, then the OCTC constants can be evaluated with the aid of the results from the single-stage analyses in Table 17.3.

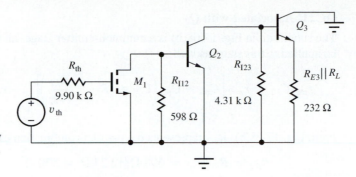

Figure 17.67 High-frequency ac model for three-stage amplifier in Fig. 17.65.

OCTC Associated with M_1

From the subcircuit for transistor M_1 in Fig. 17.68(a), we recognize this stage as a common-source stage. Using the C_T approximation from Table 17.3,

$$R_{th}C_{T1} = R_{th}\left[C_{GS1} + C_{GD1}\left(1 + g_{m1}R_{L1} + \frac{R_{L1}}{R_{th}}\right)\right] \tag{17.161}$$

In Eq. (17.161), the Thévenin source resistance is 9.90 kΩ, and the load resistance is the parallel combination of interstage resistance R_{I12} and $r_{\pi2}$:

$$R_{L1} = R_{I12}\|r_{\pi2} = 598\ \Omega\|2.39\ \text{k}\Omega = 478\ \Omega \tag{17.162}$$

Using these values, we see that the sum of the two OCTC associated with M_1 becomes

$$R_{th}C_{T1} = (9.90\ \text{k}\Omega)\left[5\ \text{pF} + 1\ \text{pF}\left(1 + 0.01\ \text{S}(478\ \Omega) + \frac{478\ \Omega}{9.9\ \text{k}\Omega}\right)\right] = 1.07 \times 10^{-7}\ \text{s} \tag{17.163}$$

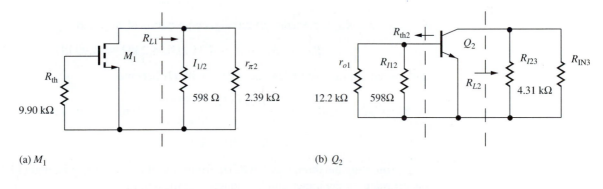

(a) M_1 (b) Q_2

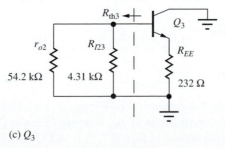

(c) Q_3

Figure 17.68 Subcircuits for evaluating the OCTC for each transistor.

OCTC Associated with Q_2

The subcircuit in Fig. 17.68(b) is a common-emitter stage, and the C_T approximation can be applied to this stage as well:

$$r_{\pi o2}C_{T2} = r_{\pi o2}\left[C_{\pi 2} + C_{\mu 2}\left(1 + g_{m2}R_{L2} + \frac{R_{L2}}{r_{\pi o2}}\right)\right] \qquad r_{\pi o2} = r_{\pi 2}\|(R_{th2} + r_{x2}) \tag{17.164}$$

From Fig. 17.68(b), R_{th2} represents the parallel combination of R_{I12} and r_{o1},

$$R_{th2} = R_{I12}\|r_{o1} = 598\ \Omega\|12.2\ \text{k}\Omega = 570\ \Omega \tag{17.165}$$

$$r_{\pi o2} = r_{\pi 2}\|(R_{th2} + r_{x2}) = 2.39\ \text{k}\Omega\|(570\ \Omega + 250\ \Omega) = 610\ \Omega$$

and R_L is the parallel combination of R_{I23} and R_{IN3}:

$$R_{L2} = R_{I23}\|R_{IN3} = R_{I23}\|[r_{\pi 3} + (\beta_{o3} + 1)(R_{E3}\|R_L)] \tag{17.166}$$

$$= 4.31\ \text{k}\Omega\|[1\ \text{k}\Omega + (80 + 1)(3.3\ \text{k}\Omega\|250\ \Omega)] = 3.54\ \text{k}\Omega$$

The sum of the two OCTC associated with Q_2 becomes

$$r_{\pi o2}C_{T2} = 610\ \Omega\left[39\ \text{pF} + 1\ \text{pF}\left(1 + 67.8\ \text{mS}(3.54\ \text{k}\Omega) + \frac{3.54\ \text{k}\Omega}{610\ \Omega}\right)\right] \tag{17.167}$$

$$= 1.74 \times 10^{-7}\ \text{s}$$

OCTC Associated with Q_3

The stage in Fig. 17.68(c) represents an emitter follower with OCTC again taken from Table 17.3:

$$R_{\pi 3O}C_{\pi 3} + R_{\mu 3O}C_{\mu 3} = \frac{(R_{th3} + r_{x3})}{1 + g_{m3}R_{EE}}C_{\pi 3} + (R_{th3} + r_{x3})C_{\mu 3} \tag{17.168}$$

For this case, R_{th3} represents the parallel combination of R_{I23} and r_{o2},

$$R_{th3} = R_{I23}\|r_{o2} = 4.31\ \text{k}\Omega\|54.2\ \text{k}\Omega = 3.99\ \text{k}\Omega \tag{17.169}$$

and the sum of the two OCTC associated with Q_3 becomes

$$R_{\pi 3O}C_{\pi 3} + R_{\mu 3O}C_{\mu 3} = \frac{(3.99\ \text{k}\Omega + 250\ \Omega)}{1 + 79.6\ \text{mS}(0.232\ \text{k}\Omega)}50\ \text{pF} + (3.99\ \text{k}\Omega + 250\ \Omega)\ 1\ \text{pF}$$

$$= 1.51 \times 10^{-8}\ \text{S} \tag{17.170}$$

Summing the three sets of OCTC from Eqs. (17.163), (17.167), and (17.170) yields the estimate for the upper-cutoff frequency of the amplifier:

$$\omega_H = \frac{1}{1.07 \times 10^{-7}\ \text{s} + 1.74 \times 10^{-7}\ \text{s} + 1.51 \times 10^{-8}\ \text{s}} = 3.38 \times 10^6\ \text{rad/s} \tag{17.171}$$

and

$$f_H = \frac{\omega_H}{2\pi} = 538\ \text{kHz} \tag{17.172}$$

Note that common-source stage M_1 and common-emitter stage Q_2 are both making substantial contributions to f_H, whereas follower Q_3 represents a negligible contribution. Based on the results in Eqs. (17.159) and (17.170), the midband region of the amplifier extends from $f_L = 530\ \text{Hz}$ to $f_H = 538\ \text{kHz}$ for a bandwidth BW = 537 kHz.

EXERCISE: Calculate the reactance of C_1, C_2, and C_3, in Fig. 17.65(b) at $f = f_H$, and compare the values to the midband resistances in the circuit at the terminals of the capacitors.

ANSWERS: 29.6 $\Omega \ll$ 1.01 MΩ; 6.29 m$\Omega \ll$ 66.7 Ω; 296 m$\Omega \ll$ 2.69 kΩ

EXERCISE: Use SPICE to simulate the amplifier in Fig. 17.65 and find A_{mid}, f_H, f_L, and the bandwidth.

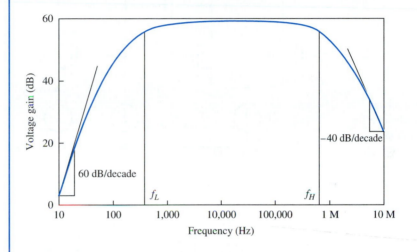

ANSWERS: 59.5 dB, 380 Hz, 650 kHz, 650 kHz. Note that the OCTC and SCTC methods provide only estimates of f_H and f_L, whereas the SPICE results are exact. It is not unusual for the estimates to differ by 25 percent from the actual values.

17.10 SINGLE-POLE OPERATIONAL-AMPLIFIER COMPENSATION

General-purpose operational amplifiers often use internal **frequency compensation,** which forces the overall amplifier to have a single-pole frequency response, as discussed in Chapter 12. The voltage transfer functions of these amplifiers can be represented by Eq. (17.173):

$$A_V(s) = \frac{A_o \omega_B}{s + \omega_B} = \frac{\omega_T}{s + \omega_B} \tag{17.173}$$

This form of transfer function can be obtained by connecting a compensation capacitor C_C around the second gain stage of the basic operational amplifier, as depicted in Fig. 17.69. This capacitor transforms the second gain stage, transistor M_5, into a Miller integrator. Figure 17.70 is a simplified representation for the three-stage op amp. The input stage is modeled by its Norton equivalent circuit, represented by current source $G_m v_{dm}$ and output resistance R_o. The second stage forms a Miller integrator with voltage gain $A_{V2} = g_{m5} r_{o5} = \mu_{f5}$, and the follower output stage is represented as a unity-gain buffer.

The circuit in Fig. 17.70 can be further simplified using the **Miller effect** relations. Feedback capacitor C_C is multiplied by the factor $(1 + A_{V2})$ and placed in parallel with the input of the second-stage amplifier, as in Fig. 17.71, and an expression for the output

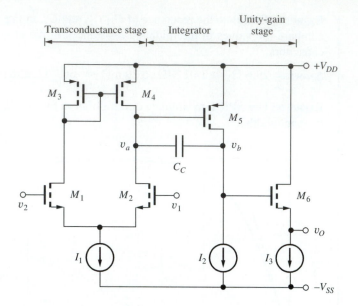

Figure 17.69 Frequency-compensation technique for single-pole operational amplifiers.

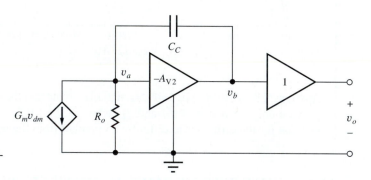

Figure 17.70 Simplified model for three-stage op amp.

voltage can now be obtained from analysis of this figure. The output voltage $\mathbf{V_o}(s)$ must equal $\mathbf{V_b}(s)$ because the output buffer has a gain of 1. Also, $\mathbf{V_b}(s)$ equals $-A_{V2}\mathbf{V_a}(s)$.

Writing the nodal equation for $\mathbf{V_a}(s)$ assuming $i = 0$,

$$-G_m\mathbf{V_{dm}}(s) = \mathbf{V_a}(s)[sC_C(1 + A_{V2}) + G_o] \qquad (17.174)$$

and

$$\frac{\mathbf{V_a}(s)}{\mathbf{V_{dm}}(s)} = \frac{-G_mR_o}{sR_oC_C(1 + A_{V2}) + 1} \qquad (17.175)$$

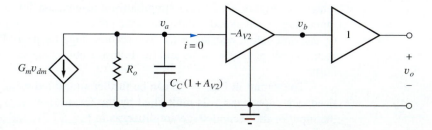

Figure 17.71 Equivalent circuit based on Miller multiplication.

Combining these results gives the overall gain of the op amp:

$$A_V(s) = \frac{\mathbf{V_o}(s)}{\mathbf{V_{dm}}(s)} = \frac{\mathbf{V_b}(s)}{\mathbf{V_{dm}}(s)} = \frac{-A_{V2}\mathbf{V_a}(s)}{\mathbf{V_{dm}}(s)} = \frac{G_m R_o A_{V2}}{1 + s R_o C_C (1 + A_{V2})} \quad (17.176)$$

Rewriting Eq. (17.176) in the form of (17.173) yields

$$A_V(s) = \frac{\dfrac{G_m A_{V2}}{C_C(1 + A_{V2})}}{s + \dfrac{1}{R_o C_C(1 + A_{V2})}} = \frac{\omega_T}{s + \omega_B} = \frac{A_o \omega_B}{s + \omega_B} \quad (17.177)$$

Figure 17.72 is a Bode plot for this transfer function. At low frequencies the gain is $A_o = G_m R_o A_{V2}$, and the gain rolls off at 20 dB/decade above the frequency ω_B. Comparing Eq. (17.177) to (17.173),

$$\omega_B = \frac{1}{R_o C_C(1 + A_{V2})} \quad \text{and} \quad \omega_T = \frac{G_m A_{V2}}{C_C(1 + A_{V2})} \quad (17.178)$$

For large A_{V2},

$$\omega_T \approx \frac{G_m}{C_C} \quad (17.179)$$

Equation (17.179) is an extremely useful result. The unity gain frequency of the operational amplifier is set by the designer's choice of the values of the input stage transconductance and **compensation capacitor C_C**.

The single pole of the amplifier is at a relatively low frequency, as determined by the large values of the output resistance of the first stage and the Miller input capacitance of the second stage.

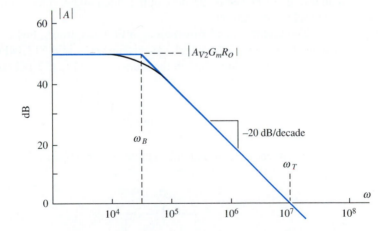

Figure 17.72 Gain magnitude plot for the ideal single-pole op amp.

EXERCISE: What are the approximate values of G_m, R_o, f_T, and f_B for the op amp in Fig. 17.69 if $K_{n2} = 1$ mA/V^2, $K_{p5} = 1$ mA/V^2, $C_C = 20$ pF, $\lambda = 0.02$ V^{-1}, $I_1 = 100$ μA, and $I_2 = 500$ μA?

ANSWERS: 0.316 mS, 500 kΩ, 2.52 MHz, 158 Hz

Transmission Zeros in FET Op Amps

Equation (17.179) presents an excellent method for controlling the frequency response of the operational amplifier with two gain stages. Unfortunately, however, we have overlooked a potential problem in the analysis of this amplifier: The simplified Miller approach does not take into account the finite transconductance of the second-stage amplifier.

The source of the problem can be understood by using the complete small-signal model for transistor M_5, as incorporated in Fig. 17.73. The previous analysis overlooked the zero that is determined by g_{m5} and the total feedback capacitance between the drain and gate of M_5. The circuit in Fig. 17.73 should once again look familiar. It is the same topology as the circuit for the simplified C-E amplifier, and we can use the results of the analysis in Eq. (17.84) by making the appropriate symbolic substitutions identified in Eq. (17.180):

$$r_{\pi o} \to R_o \qquad R_L \to r_{o5} \qquad C_\pi \to C_{GS5} \qquad C_\mu \to C_C + C_{GD5} \qquad (17.180)$$

With these transformations, Eq. (17.84) becomes

$$A_{vth}(s) = (-g_{m5}r_{o5})\frac{\left(1 - \dfrac{s}{\omega_Z}\right)}{\left(1 + \dfrac{s}{\omega_{P1}}\right)} \qquad \text{in which} \quad \omega_Z = \frac{g_{m5}}{C_C + C_{GD5}} = \omega_T\frac{g_{m5}}{g_{m2}}$$

and $\hspace{8cm}$ (17.181)

$$\omega_{P1} = \frac{1}{R_o C_T} \qquad \text{where} \quad C_T = C_{GS5} + (C_C + C_{GD5})\left(1 + \mu_{f5} + \frac{r_{o5}}{R_o}\right)$$

In the case of many FET amplifier designs, ω_Z cannot be neglected because of the relatively low ratio of transconductances between FET M_5 and M_2. In bipolar designs, ω_Z can usually be neglected because of the much higher transconductance that is achieved for a given Q-point current.

The problem can be overcome in FET amplifiers, however, through the addition of resistor R_Z in Fig. 17.74, which cancels the zero in Eq. (17.181). If we assume that $C_C \gg C_{GD}$, then the location of ω_Z in the numerator of Eq. (17.181) becomes

$$\omega_Z = \frac{\left(\dfrac{1}{g_{m5}}\right) - R_Z}{C_C} \qquad (17.182)$$

and the zero can be eliminated by setting $R_Z = 1/g_{m5}$.

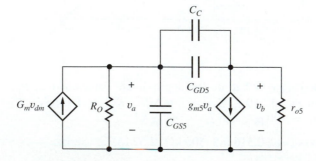

Figure 17.73 More complete model for op-amp compensation.

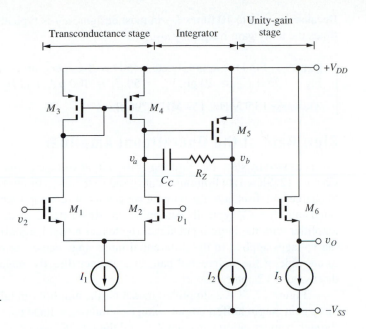

Figure 17.74 Zero cancellation using resistor R_Z.

EXERCISE: Find the approximate location of f_Z for the op amp in Fig. 17.74 using the values from the previous exercise. What value of R_Z is needed to eliminate f_Z?

ANSWERS: 7.96 MHz; 1 kΩ

Bipolar Amplifier Compensation

The bipolar op amp in Fig. 17.75 is compensated in the same manner as the MOS amplifier. However, because the transconductance of the BJT is generally much higher than that of a FET for a given operating current, the transmission zero occurs at such a high frequency that it does not cause a problem. Applying Eq. (17.179) to the circuit in Fig. 17.75 yields an expression for the unity gain frequency of the two-stage bipolar amplifier:

$$\omega_T = \frac{g_{m2}}{C_C} = \frac{40I_{C2}}{C_C} = \frac{20I_1}{C_C} \qquad \text{and} \qquad \omega_Z = \frac{g_{m5}}{C_C} = \omega_T\left(\frac{I_{C5}}{I_{C2}}\right) \quad (17.183)$$

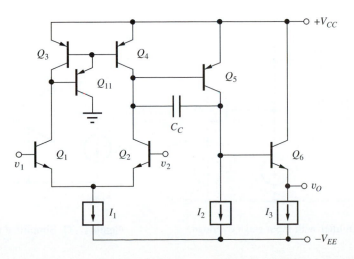

Figure 17.75 Frequency compensation of a bipolar op amp.

Because I_{C5} is 5 to 10 times I_{C2} in most designs, ω_Z is typically at a frequency of 5 to 10 times the unity gain frequency ω_T.

> **EXERCISE:** Find the approximate locations of ω_T, ω_Z, and ω_B for the bipolar op amp in Fig. 17.75 if $C_C = 20$ pF, $V_A = 50$, $I_1 = 100$ µA, and $I_2 = 500$ µA.
>
> **ANSWERS:** 15.9 MHz, 159 MHz, 796 Hz

Slew Rate of the Operational Amplifier

Errors caused by slew-rate limiting of the output voltage of the amplifier were discussed in Chapter 12. Slew-rate limiting occurs because there is a limited amount of current available to charge and discharge the internal capacitors of the amplifier. For an internally compensated amplifier, C_C typically determines the **slew rate.** Consider the example of the CMOS amplifier with the large input signal (no longer a small signal) in Fig. 17.76. In this case, the voltages applied to the differential input stage cause current I_1 to switch completely to one side of the differential pair, in a manner directly analogous to the current switch discussed in Chapter 10.

Figure 17.77 is a simplified model for the amplifier in this condition. Because of the unity gain output buffer, output voltage v_O follows voltage v_B. Current I_1 must be supplied through compensation capacitor C_C, and the rate of change of the v_B, and hence v_O, must satisfy

$$I_1 = C_C \frac{d(v_B(t) - v_A(t))}{dt} = C_C \frac{d\left(v_B(t) + \dfrac{v_B(t)}{A_{V2}}\right)}{dt} \tag{17.184}$$

If A_{V2} is assumed to be very large, then the amplifier will behave in a manner similar to an ideal integrator; that is, node voltage v_A represents a virtual ground and Eq. (17.184) becomes

$$I_1 \approx C_C \frac{dv_B(t)}{dt} = C_C \frac{dv_O(t)}{dt} \tag{17.185}$$

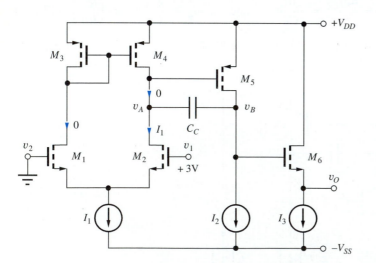

Figure 17.76 Operational amplifier with input stage overload.

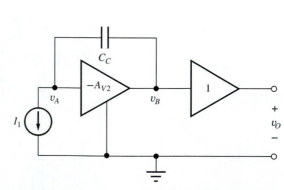

Figure 17.77 Simplified model for three-stage op amp.

The slew rate is the maximum rate of change of the output signal, and

$$\text{SR} = \left.\frac{dv_O(t)}{dt}\right|_{\text{max}} = \frac{I_1}{C_C} \tag{17.186}$$

The slew rate is determined by the total input stage bias current and the value of the compensation capacitor C_C. (It is seldom pointed out that this derivation tacitly assumes that the output of amplifier A_{V2} is capable of sourcing or sinking the current I_1. This requirement will be met as long as the amplifier is designed with $I_2 \geq I_1$.)

> **EXERCISE:** Show that the slew rate is symmetrical in the CMOS amplifier in Fig. 17.76; that is, what is the current in capacitor C_C if $v_1 = 0$ V and $v_2 = +3$ V?
>
> **ANSWER:** I_1

Relationships Between Slew Rate and Gain-Bandwidth Product

Equation (17.186) can be related directly to the unity gain bandwidth of the amplifier using Eq. (17.179):

$$\text{SR} = \frac{I_1}{C_C} = \frac{I_1}{\left(\dfrac{G_m}{\omega_T}\right)} = \frac{\omega_T}{\left(\dfrac{G_m}{I_1}\right)} \tag{17.187}$$

For the simple CMOS amplifier in Fig. 17.69, the input stage transconductance is equal to that of transistors M_1 and M_2,

$$\left(\frac{G_m}{I_1}\right) = \frac{1}{I_1}\sqrt{2K_{n2}\frac{I_1}{2}} = \sqrt{\frac{2K_{n2}}{I_1}}$$

and $\hspace{12cm}$ (17.188)

$$\text{SR} = \omega_T\sqrt{\frac{I_1}{K_{n2}}}$$

For a given desired value of ω_T, the slew rate increases with the square root of the bias current in the input stage.

For the bipolar amplifier in Fig. 17.75,

$$\left(\frac{G_m}{I_1}\right) = \left(\frac{40\dfrac{I_1}{2}}{I_1}\right) = 20 \quad \text{and} \quad \text{SR} = \frac{\omega_T}{20} \tag{17.189}$$

In this case, the slew rate is related to the choice of unity gain frequency by a fixed factor.

> **EXERCISE:** What is the slew rate of the CMOS amplifier in Fig. 17.69 if $K_{n2} = 1$ mA/V^2, $K_{p5} = 1$ mA/V^2, $C_C = 20$ pF, $\lambda = 0.02$ V^{-1}, $I_1 = 100$ μA, and $I_2 = 500$ μA?
>
> **ANSWER:** 5.00 V/μS

> **EXERCISE:** What is the slew rate of the bipolar amplifier in Fig. 17.75 if $C_C = 20$ pF, $I_1 = 100$ μA, and $I_2 = 500$ μA?
>
> **ANSWER:** 5.00 V/μS

17.11 TUNED AMPLIFIERS

In radio-frequency (RF) applications, amplifiers with narrow bandwidths are needed in order to be able to select one signal from the large number that may be present (from an antenna, for example). The frequencies of interest are typically well above the unity gain frequency of operational amplifiers so that RC active filters cannot be used. These amplifiers often have high Q; that is, f_H and f_L are very close together relative to the midband or center frequency of the amplifier. For example, a bandwidth of 20 kHz may be desired at a frequency of 1 MHz for an AM broadcast receiver application ($Q = 50$), or a bandwidth of 200 kHz could be needed at 100 MHz for an FM broadcast receiver ($Q = 500$). These applications often use resonant *RLC* circuits to form frequency selective **tuned amplifiers.**

Figure 17.78 is an example of a simple narrow-band tuned amplifier. A JFET has been chosen for this example to simplify the biasing, but any type of transistor could be used. The *RLC* network in the drain of the amplifier represents the frequency-selective portion of the circuit, and the parallel combination of resistors R_D, R_3, and the output resistance r_o of the transistor set the Q and bandwidth of the circuit. Although resistor R_D is not needed for biasing, it is often included to control the Q of the circuit.

The operating point of the transistor can be found from analysis of the dc equivalent circuit in Fig. 17.78(b). Bias current is supplied through the inductor, which represents a direct short-circuit connection between the drain and V_{DD} at dc, and all capacitors C_1, C_2, C_S, and C have been replaced by open circuits. The actual Q-point can easily be found from Fig. 17.78(b) using the methods presented in previous chapters, so this discussion focuses only on the ac behavior of the tuned amplifier using the ac equivalent circuit in Fig. 17.79.

Writing a single nodal equation at the output node v_o of the circuit in Fig. 17.79(b) and observing that $v = v_s$ yields

$$(sC_{GD} - g_m)\mathbf{V_s}(s) = \mathbf{V_o}(s)\left[g_o + G_D + G_3 + s(C + C_{GD}) + \frac{1}{sL}\right] \quad (17.190)$$

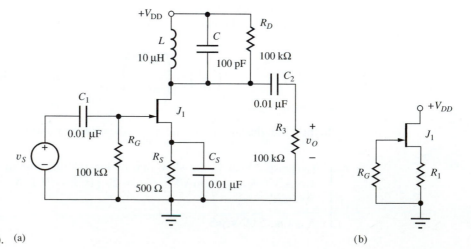

Figure 17.78 (a) Tuned amplifier using a JFET. (b) dc Equivalent circuit for the tuned amplifier in Fig. 17.78(a).   (a)   (b)

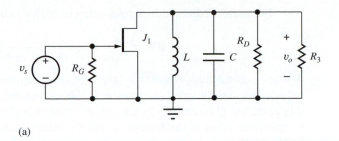

(a)

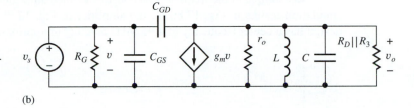

(b)

Figure 17.79 (a) High-frequency ac equivalent circuit and (b) small-signal model for the tuned amplifier in Fig. 17.78.

Making the substitution $G_P = g_o + G_D + G_3$, and then solving for the voltage transfer function:

$$A_V(s) = \frac{\mathbf{V_o}(s)}{\mathbf{V_s}(s)} = \frac{(sC_{GD} - g_m)}{G_P + s(C + C_{GD}) + \dfrac{1}{sL}}$$

$$= \frac{\mathbf{V_o}(s)}{\mathbf{V_s}(s)} = (sC_{GD} - g_m)R_P \frac{\dfrac{s}{R_P(C + C_{GD})}}{s^2 + \dfrac{s}{R_P(C + C_{GD})} + \dfrac{1}{L(C + C_{GD})}} \qquad (17.191)$$

If we neglect the right-half-plane zero, then Eq. (17.191) can be rewritten as

$$A_V(s) = \frac{\mathbf{V_o}(s)}{\mathbf{V_s}(s)} \approx A_{\text{mid}} \frac{s\dfrac{\omega_o}{Q}}{s^2 + s\dfrac{\omega_o}{Q} + \omega_o^2} \qquad (17.192)$$

in which

$$\omega_o = \frac{1}{\sqrt{L(C + C_{GD})}}$$

is the **center frequency** of the amplifier, and the Q is given by

$$Q = \omega_o R_P(C + C_{GD}) = \frac{R_P}{\omega_o L}$$

The center or midband frequency of the amplifier is equal to the resonant frequency ω_o of the LC network. At the center frequency, $s = j\omega_o$, and Eq. (17.192) reduces to

$$A_V(j\omega_o) = A_{\text{mid}} \frac{j\omega_o \dfrac{\omega_o}{Q}}{(j\omega_o)^2 + j\omega_o \dfrac{\omega_o}{Q} + \omega_o^2} = A_{\text{mid}} \frac{j\omega_o \dfrac{\omega_o}{Q}}{-\omega_o^2 + j\omega_o \dfrac{\omega_o}{Q} + \omega_o^2} = A_{\text{mid}}$$

$$A_{\text{mid}} = -g_m R_P = -g_m(r_o \| R_D \| R_3) \qquad (17.193)$$

For narrow bandwidth circuits—that is, high-Q circuits—the bandwidth is equal to

$$\text{BW} = \frac{\omega_o}{Q} = \frac{1}{R_P(C + C_{GD})} = \frac{\omega_o^2 L}{R_P} \tag{17.194}$$

A narrow bandwidth requires a large value of equivalent parallel resistance R_P, large capacitance, and/or small inductance. In this circuit, the maximum value of $R_P = r_o$. For this case, the Q is limited by the output resistance of the transistor and thus the choice of operating point of the transistor, and the midband gain A_{mid} equals the amplification factor μ_f.

An example of the frequency response of a tuned amplifier is presented in the SPICE simulation results in Fig. 17.80 for the amplifier in Fig. 17.79. This particular amplifier design has a center frequency of 4.91 MHz and a Q of approximately 50.

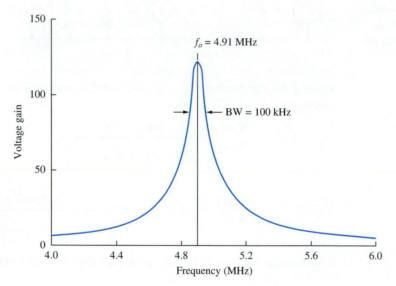

Figure 17.80 Simulated frequency response for the tuned amplifier in Fig. 17.78 with $C_{GS} = 50$ pF, $C_{GD} = 20$ pF, $V_{DD} = 15$ V, $I_{DSS} = 20$ mA, $V_P = -2$ V, and $\lambda = 0.02$ V^{-1}.

EXERCISE: What is the impedance of the 0.01-μF coupling and bypass capacitors in Fig. 17.78 at a frequency of 5 MHz?

ANSWERS: $-j3.18\ \Omega$ (note that $X_C \ll R_G$ and $X_C \ll R_3$)

EXERCISE: Find the center frequency, bandwidth, Q, and midband gain for the amplifier in Fig. 17.78 using the parameters in Fig. 17.80, assuming $I_D = 3.20$ mA. (Remember that C_{GD} is Q-point dependent. Use $\phi_j = 0.9$ V.)

ANSWERS: 4.92 MHz, 105 kHz, 46.9, -116

EXERCISE: What is the new value of the center frequency if V_{DD} is reduced to 10 V?

ANSWER: 4.89 MHz

Use of a Tapped Inductor—The Auto Transformer

The impedance of the gate-drain capacitance and output resistance of the transistor, C_{GD}, and r_o, can often be small enough in magnitude to degrade the characteristics of the tuned amplifier. The problem can be solved by connecting the transistor to a tap on the inductor instead of across the full inductor, as indicated in Fig. 17.81. In this case, the inductor

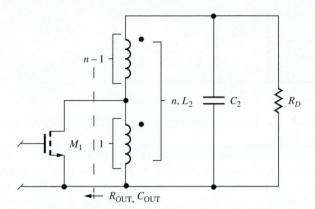

Figure 17.81 Use of a tapped inductor as an impedance transformer.

functions as an auto transformer and changes the effective impedance reflected into the resonant circuit.

The n-turn auto transformer can be modeled by its total magnetizing inductance L_2 in parallel with an ideal transformer having a turns ratio of $(n-1):1$. The ideal transformer has its primary and secondary windings interconnected, as in Fig. 17.82(b). Impedances are transformed by a factor of n^2 by the ideal transformer configuration:

$$\mathbf{V_o}(s) = \mathbf{V_2}(s) + \mathbf{V_1}(s) = (n-1)\mathbf{V_1}(s) + \mathbf{V_1}(s) = n\mathbf{V_1}(s)$$
$$\mathbf{I_s}(s) = \mathbf{I_1}(s) + \mathbf{I_2}(s) = (n-1)\mathbf{I_2}(s) + \mathbf{I_2}(s) = n\mathbf{I_2}(s)$$
(17.195)

and

$$\frac{\mathbf{V_o}(s)}{\mathbf{I_2}(s)} = \frac{n\mathbf{V_1}(s)}{\dfrac{\mathbf{I_s}(s)}{n}} = n^2\frac{\mathbf{V_1}(s)}{\mathbf{I_s}(s)} \qquad Z_s(s) = n^2 Z_p(s)$$
(17.196)

Thus, the impedance $Z_s(s)$ reflected into the secondary of the transformer is n^2 times larger than the impedance $Z_p(s)$ connected to the primary.

Using the result in Eq. (17.196), the resonant circuit in Fig. 17.81 can be transformed into the circuit representation in Fig. 17.83. L_2 represents the total inductance of the transformer. The equivalent output capacitance of the transistor is reduced by the factor of n^2 and the output resistance is increased by this same factor. Thus, a much higher Q can be

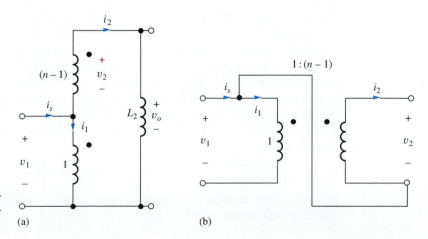

Figure 17.82 (a) Tapped inductor and (b) its representation by an ideal transformer.

(a)   (b)

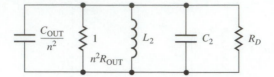

obtained, and the center frequency is not shifted (detuned) significantly by changes in the value of C_{GD}.

A similar problem often occurs if the tuned circuit is placed at the input of the amplifier rather than the output, as in Fig. 17.84. For the case of the bipolar transistor in particular, the equivalent input impedance of Q_1 represented by R_{IN} and C_{IN} can be quite low due to r_π and the large input capacitance resulting from the Miller effect. The tapped inductor increases the impedance to that in Fig. 17.85 in which L_1 now represents the total inductance of the transformer.

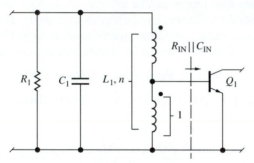

Figure 17.84 Use of an auto transformer at the input of transistor Q_1.

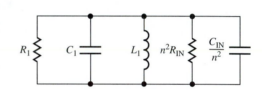

Figure 17.85 Transformed circuit model for the tuned circuit in Fig. 17.84.

Multiple Tuned Circuits—Synchronous and Stagger Tuning

Multiple RLC circuits are often needed to tailor the frequency response of tuned amplifiers, as in Fig. 17.86, which has tuned circuits at both the amplifier input and output. The high-frequency ac equivalent circuit for the double-tuned amplifier appears in Fig. 17.86(b). The source resistor is bypassed by capacitor C_S, and C_C is a coupling capacitor. The **radio frequency choke (RFC)** is used for biasing and is designed to represent a very high impedance (an open circuit) at the operating frequency of the amplifier.

Two tuned circuits can be used to achieve higher Q than that of a single LC circuit if both are tuned to the same center frequency **(synchronous tuning),** or a broader band amplifier can be realized if the circuits are tuned to slightly different center frequencies **(stagger tuning),** as shown in Fig. 17.87. For the case of synchronous tuning, the overall bandwidth can be calculated using the bandwidth shrinkage factor that was developed in Chapter 12:

$$\text{BW}_n = \text{BW}_1 \sqrt{2^{\frac{1}{n}} - 1} \qquad (17.197)$$

in which n is the number of synchronous tuned circuits and BW_1 is the bandwidth for the case of a single tuned circuit.

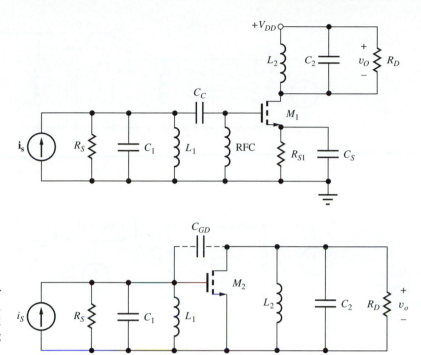

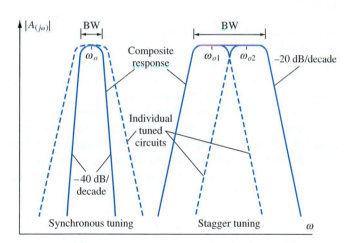

Figure 17.86 (a) Amplifier employing two tuned circuits. (b) High-frequency ac model for the amplifier employing two tuned circuits.

Figure 17.87 Examples of tuned amplifiers employing synchronous and stagger tuning of two tuned circuits.

However, two significant problems can occur in the amplifier in Fig. 17.86, particularly for the case of synchronous tuning. First, alignment of the two tuned circuits is difficult because of interaction between the two tuned circuits due to the Miller multiplication of C_{GD}. Second, the amplifier can easily become an oscillator due to the coupling of signal energy from the output of the amplifier back to the input through C_{GD}. (A discussion of oscillators is in the next chapter.)

A technique called **neutralization** can be used to solve this feedback problem but is beyond the scope of this discussion. However, two alternative approaches are shown in Fig. 17.88, in which the feedback path is eliminated. In Fig. 17.88(a), a cascode stage is used. Common-base transistor Q_2 effectively eliminates Miller multiplication and provides excellent isolation between the two tuned circuits. In Fig. 17.88(b), the C-C/C-B cascade is used to minimize the coupling between the output and input.

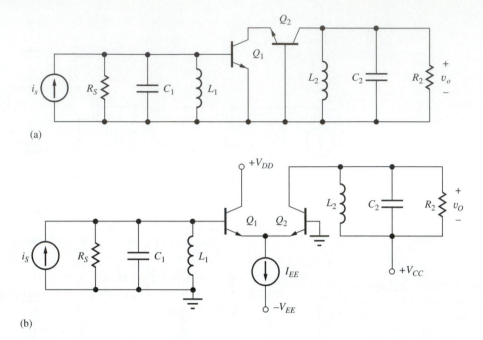

(a)

(b)

Figure 17.88 (a) Double-tuned cascode and (b) C-C/C-B cascade circuits that provide inherent isolation between input and output.

SUMMARY

Amplifier frequency response is normally determined by splitting the circuit into two models, one valid at low frequencies, where coupling and bypass capacitors are most important, and a second valid at high frequencies, in which the internal device capacitances control the frequency-dependent behavior of the circuit. Direct analysis of these circuits in the frequency domain, although usually possible for single-transistor amplifiers, becomes impractical for multistage amplifiers. In most cases, however, we are primarily interested in the midband gain and the upper- and lower-cutoff frequencies of the amplifier, and estimates of f_H and f_L can be obtained using the open-circuit and short-circuit time-constant methods. More accurate results can be obtained using SPICE circuit simulation.

Frequency behavior of the bipolar transistor is modeled by adding the base-emitter and base-collector capacitors C_π and C_μ and the base resistance r_x to the hybrid-pi model. The value of C_π is proportional to collector current I_C, whereas C_μ is weakly dependent on collector-base voltage. The $r_x C_\mu$ product is an important figure of merit for the frequency characteristics of the bipolar transistor. The frequency dependence of the FET is modeled by adding gate-source and gate-drain capacitances, C_{GS} and C_{GD}, to the pi-model of the FET. The values of C_{GS} and C_{GD} are independent of operating point when the FET is operating in its saturation region.

Both the BJT and FET have finite current gain at high frequencies, and the unity gain-bandwidth product ω_T for both devices is determined by the device capacitances and the transconductance of the transistor. In the bipolar transistor, the β-cutoff frequency ω_β represents the frequency at which the current gain is 3 dB below its low-frequency value.

If all the poles and zeros of the transfer function can be found from the low- and high-frequency equivalent circuits, then f_H and f_L can be accurately estimated using Eqs. (17.16) and (17.23). In many cases, a dominant pole exists in the low- and/or high-frequency responses, and this pole controls f_H or f_L. Unfortunately, the complexity of most amplifiers precludes finding the exact locations of all the poles and zeros except through numerical means.

For design purposes, however, one needs to understand the relationship between the device and circuit parameters and f_H and f_L. The short-circuit time-constant (SCTC) and open-circuit time-constant (OCTC) approaches provide the needed information and are used to find detailed expressions for f_H and f_L for the three classes of single-stage amplifiers, the inverting, noninverting, and follower stages. It was found that the inverting amplifiers provide high gain but the most limited bandwidth. Noninverting amplifiers can provide improved bandwidth for a given voltage gain, but it is important to remember that these stages have a much lower input resistance. The follower configurations provide unity gain over an extremely wide bandwidth. The three basic classes of amplifiers show the direct tradeoff that occurs between voltage gain and bandwidth. The OCTC and SCTC methods can also be used to determine the upper- and lower-cutoff frequencies of multistage amplifiers, and the frequency response of the differential, cascode, and C-C/C-B cascade amplifiers and the current mirror were all discussed, as well as an example of a three-stage amplifier.

The input impedance of an amplifier is decreased as a result of Miller multiplication, and the expression for the dominant pole of an inverting amplifier can be cast in terms of the Miller effect. Miller multiplication is a useful method for setting the unity gain frequency of internally compensated operational amplifiers. This technique is often called Miller compensation. In these op amps, slew rate is directly proportional to the unity-gain frequency.

Tuned amplifiers employing *RLC* circuits can be used to achieve narrow-band amplifiers at radio frequencies. Designs can use either single- or multiple-tuned circuits. If the circuits in a multiple-tuned amplifier are all designed to have the same center frequency, the circuit is referred to as synchronously tuned. If the tuned circuits are adjusted to different center frequencies, the circuit is referred to as stagger-tuned. Care must be taken to ensure that tuned amplifiers do not become oscillators, and the use of the cascode and C-C/C-B cascade configurations offer improved isolation between multiple-tuned circuits.

Key Terms

Beta-cutoff frequency	Midband gain	Radio frequency choke (RFC)
Cascode amplifier	Miller compensation	Short-circuit time-constant
Center frequency	Miller effect	(SCTC) method
Compensation capacitor	Miller integrator	Slew rate
Dominant high-frequency pole	Miller multiplication	Stagger tuning
Dominant low-frequency pole	Neutralization	Synchronous tuning
Dominant pole	Open-circuit time-constant (OCTC)	Tuned amplifiers
Frequency compensation	method	Unity-gain-bandwidth product
Lower-cutoff frequency	Pole frequencies	Upper-cutoff frequency

Reference

P. E. Gray and C. L. Searle, *Electronic Principles,* Wiley, New York: 1969.

PSPICE Simulation Data Figure 17.4 C-S Amplifier Frequency Response

```
VDD 7 0 DC 12
VS 1 0 AC 1
```

```
RS 1 2 1K
C1 2 3 0.1UF
R1 3 0 430K
R2 7 3 560K
RD 7 4 4.3K
R4 5 0 1.3K
C3 5 0 10UF
C2 4 6 0.1UF
R3 6 0 100K
M1 4 3 5 5 MOS1
.MODEL MOS1 NMOS KP=500U VTO = 1 LAMBDA=0.0133
.OP
.AC DEC 20 0.01HZ 10KHZ
.PRINT AC VDB(6) VP(6)
.PROBE V(6)
.END
```

Figure 17.6 C-E Amplifier Frequency Response

```
VCC 7 0 DC 12
VS 1 0 AC 1
Q1 4 3 5 N1
RS 1 2 1K
C1 2 3 2UF
R1 3 0 10K
R2 7 3 30K
RC 7 4 4.3K
RE 5 0 1.3K
C3 5 0 10UF
C2 4 6 0.1UF
R3 6 0 100K
.MODEL N1 NPN BF=100 IS=1FA VAF = 75
.OP
.AC DEC 20 1HZ 10KHZ
.PRINT AC VDB(6) VP(6)
.PROBE V(6)
.END
```

Figure 17.65 Three-Stage Amplifier Frequency Response

```
VCC 12 0 DC 15
VS 1 0 AC 1
RS 1 2 10K
C1 2 3 0.01UF
RG 3 0 1MEG
*
J1 5 3 4 JN1
*The JFET Model is being used for M1 to simplify the input data description
RD1 12 5 620
RS1 4 0 200
C2 4 0 47UF
```

C3 5 6 1UF
Q2 8 6 7 BJT1
R1 12 6 78K
R2 6 0 22K
RC2 12 8 4.7K
RE2 7 0 1.5K
C4 7 0 22UF
C5 8 9 1UF
Q3 12 9 10 BJT2
R3 12 9 91K
R4 9 0 120K
RE3 10 0 3.3K
C6 10 11 22UF
RL 11 0 250
.MODEL JN1 NJF BETA=.005 VTO=-2 LAMBDA=0.02 CGS=7PF CGD=4PF
.MODEL BJT1 NPN BF=150 IS=1FA VAF = 80 RB=250 TF=0.65NS CJC=2PF
.MODEL BJT2 NPN BF=80 IS=1FA VAF = 60 RB=250 TF=0.65NS CJC=2PF
.OP
.AC DEC 50 1HZ 10MEG
.PRINT AC VDB(11) VP(11)
.PROBE V(11)
.END

Figures 17.78 to 17.80 JFET-Tuned Amplifier Frequency Response

VCC 5 0 DC 15
VS 1 0 AC 1
C1 1 2 0.01UF
RG 2 0 100K
RS 3 0 500
CS 3 0 0.01UF
J1 4 2 3 JN1
RD 5 4 100K
L 5 4 10UH
C 5 4 100PF
C2 4 6 0.01UF
RL 6 0 100K
.MODEL JN1 NJF BETA=.005 VTO=-2 LAMBDA=0.02 CGS=50PF CGD=20PF
.OP
.AC DEC 1000 4MEG 6MEG
.PRINT AC VDB(6) VP(6)
.PROBE V(6)
.END

Problems

17.1 Amplifier Frequency Response

17.1. Find A_{mid} and $F_L(s)$ for the following transfer function. Is there a dominant pole? If so, what is the dominant-pole approximation of $A_V(s)$? What is the cutoff frequency f_L of the dominant-pole approxi-mation? What is the exact cutoff frequency using the complete transfer function?

$$A_V(s) = \frac{25s^2}{(s + 1)(s + 20)}$$

17.2. Find A_{mid} and $F_L(s)$ for the following transfer function. Is there a dominant pole? If so, what is the dominant-pole approximation of $A_V(s)$? What is the cutoff frequency f_L of the dominant-pole approximation? What is the exact cutoff frequency using the complete transfer function?

$$A_V(s) = \frac{250s^2}{(s + 100)(s + 500)}$$

17.3. Find A_{mid} and $F_L(s)$ for the following transfer function. Is there a dominant pole? Use Eq. (17.16) to estimate f_L. Use the computer to find the exact cutoff frequency f_L.

$$A_V(s) = -\frac{150s(s + 15)}{(s + 12)(s + 20)}$$

17.4. Find A_{mid} and $F_H(s)$ for the following transfer function. Is there a dominant pole? If so, what is the dominant-pole approximation of $A_V(s)$? What is the cutoff frequency f_H of the dominant-pole approximation? What is the exact cutoff frequency using the complete transfer function?

$$A_V(s) = \frac{2 \times 10^{11}}{(s + 10^4)(s + 10^5)}$$

17.5. Find A_{mid} and $F_H(s)$ for the following transfer function. Is there a dominant pole? If so, what is the dominant-pole approximation of $A_V(s)$? What is the cutoff frequency f_H of the dominant-pole approximation? What is the exact cutoff frequency using the complete transfer function?

$$A_V(s) = \frac{(s + 2 \times 10^9)}{(s + 10^7)\left(1 + \dfrac{s}{10^9}\right)}$$

17.6. Find A_{mid} and $F_H(s)$ for the following transfer function. Is there a dominant pole? Use Eq. (17.16) to estimate f_H. Use the computer to find the exact cutoff frequency f_H.

$$A_V(s) = \frac{4 \times 10^9(s + 5 \times 10^5)}{(s + 1.3 \times 10^5)(s + 2 \times 10^6)}$$

17.7. Find A_{mid}, $F_L(s)$, and $F_H(s)$ for the following transfer function. Is there a dominant pole at low frequencies? At high frequencies? Use Eqs. (17.16) and (17.23) to estimate f_L and f_H. Use the computer to find the exact cutoff frequencies and compare to the estimates.

$$A_V(s) = -\frac{10^8 s^2}{(s + 1)(s + 2)(s + 500)(s + 1000)}$$

*17.8. Find A_{mid}, $F_L(s)$ and $F_H(s)$ for the following transfer function. Is there a dominant pole at low frequencies? At high frequencies? Use Eqs. (17.16) and (17.23) to estimate f_L and f_H. Use the computer

to find the exact cutoff frequencies and compare to the estimates.

$$A_V(s) = \frac{10^{10}s^2(s + 1)(s + 200)}{(s + 3)(s + 5)(s + 7)(s + 100)^2(s + 300)}$$

17.2 Direct Determination of the Low-Frequency Poles and Zeros

17.9. (a) Draw the low-frequency and midband equivalent circuits for the common-source amplifier in Fig. P17.9 if $R_S = 1$ kΩ, $R_1 = 4.3$ MΩ, $R_2 = 5.6$ MΩ, $R_4 = 13$ kΩ, $R_D = 43$ kΩ, and $R_3 = 1$ MΩ. (b) What are the lower-cutoff frequency and midband gain of the amplifier if the Q-point = (0.2 mA, 5 V) and $V_{GS} - V_{TN} = 1$ V?

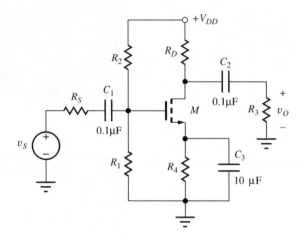

Figure P17.9

17.10. (a) Draw the low-frequency and midband equivalent circuits for the common-source amplifier in Fig. P17.9 if $R_S = 5$ kΩ, $R_1 = 430$ kΩ, $R_2 = 560$ kΩ, $R_4 = 13$ kΩ, $R_D = 43$ kΩ, and $R_3 = 220$ kΩ. (b) What are the lower-cutoff frequency and midband gain of the amplifier if the Q-point = (0.2mA, 5V) and $V_{GS} - V_{TN} = 1$ V?

17.11. (a) Draw the low-frequency ac and midband equivalent circuits for the common-base amplifier in Fig. P17.11 if $R_S = 200$ Ω, $R_E = 4.3$ kΩ, $R_C = 2.2$ kΩ, $R_3 = 51$ kΩ, and $\beta_o = 100$. (b) Write

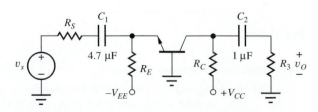

Figure P17.11

an expression for the transfer function of the amplifier and identify the location of the two low-frequency poles and two low-frequency zeros. Assume $r_o = \infty$. (c) What are the lower-cutoff frequency and midband gain of the amplifier if the Q-point = (1 mA, 5 V)? (d) What are the lower-cutoff frequency and midband gain of the amplifier if $R_E = 430$ kΩ, $R_C = 220$ kΩ, $R_3 = 510$ kΩ, and the Q-point is (10 μA, 5 V)?

17.12. (a) Draw the low-frequency equivalent circuit for the common-gate amplifier in Fig. P17.12. (b) Write an expression for the transfer function of the amplifier and identify the location of the two low-frequency poles and two low-frequency zeros. Assume $r_o = \infty$. (c) What are the lower-cutoff frequency and midband gain of the amplifier if $g_m = 5$ mS?

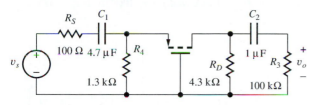

Figure P17.12

17.3 Estimation of ω_L Using the Short-Circuit Time-Constant Method

17.13. (a) Draw the low-frequency and midband equivalent circuits for the common-emitter amplifier in Fig. P17.13 if $R_S = 1$ kΩ, $R_1 = 100$ kΩ, $R_2 = 300$ kΩ, $R_E = 13$ kΩ, $R_C = 43$ kΩ, and $R_3 = 43$ kΩ. (b) What are the lower-cutoff frequency and midband gain of the amplifier assuming a Q-point of (0.164 mA, 2.79 V) and $\beta_o = 100$?

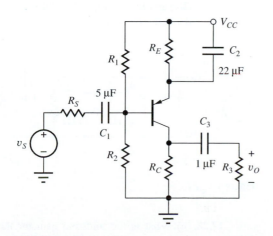

Figure P17.13

17.14. (a) Draw the low-frequency and midband equivalent circuits for the common-gate amplifier in Fig. P17.14. (b) What are the lower-cutoff frequency and midband gain of the amplifier if the Q-point = (0.1 mA, 8.6 V), $V_{GS} - V_{TN} = 1$ V, $C_1 = 4.7$ μF, $C_2 = 0.1$ μF, and $C_3 = 0.1$ μF?

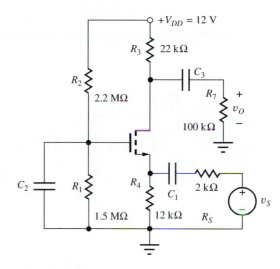

Figure P17.14

17.15. (a) Draw the low-frequency and midband equivalent circuits for the source follower in Fig. P17.15. (b) What are the lower-cutoff frequency and midband gain of the amplifier if the transistor is biased at 0.75 V above threshold with a Q-point = (0.1 mA, 8.8 V), $C_1 = 4.7$ μF, and $C_3 = 0.1$ μF?

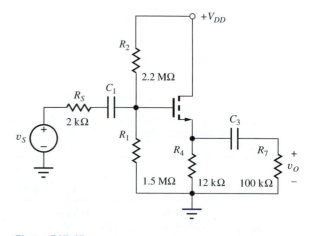

Figure P17.15

17.16. (a) Draw the low-frequency and midband equivalent circuits for the emitter follower in Fig. P17.16. (b) What are the lower-cutoff frequency and midband gain of the amplifier if the Q-point is (0.25 mA, 12 V), $\beta_o = 100$, $C_1 = 4.7\ \mu F$, and $C_3 = 10\ \mu F$?

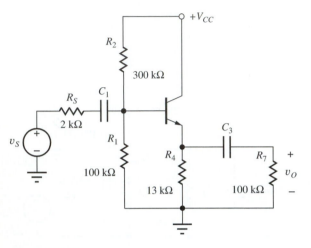

Figure P17.16

17.17. Redesign the value of C_3 in the C-S stage in Prob. 17.9 to set $f_L = 500$ Hz.

17.18. Redesign the value of C_1 in the C-B stage in Prob. 17.11 to set $f_L = 100$ Hz.

17.19. Redesign the value of C_2 in the C-E stage in Prob. 17.13 to set $f_L = 20$ Hz.

17.20. Redesign the value of C_1 in the C-G stage in Prob. 17.14 to set $f_L = 1$ Hz.

17.21. Redesign the value of C_3 in the C-D stage in Prob. 17.15 to set $f_L = 10$ Hz.

17.22. Redesign the value of C_3 in the C-C stage in Prob. 17.16 to set $f_L = 5$ Hz.

17.4 Transistor Models at High Frequencies

17.23. Fill in the missing parameter values for the BJT in the following table if $r_x = 250\ \Omega$.

I_C	f_T	C_π	C_μ	$\dfrac{1}{2\pi r_x C_\mu}$
10 μA	50 MHz		0.50 pF	
100 μA	300 MHz	0.75 pF		
500 μA	1 GHz		0.25 pF	
10 mA		10 pF		1.59 GHz
1 μA		1 pF	1 pF	
	5 GHz	1 pF	0.5 pF	

17.24. Fill in the missing parameter values for the MOS-FET in the following table if $K_n = 1\ mA/V^2$.

I_D	f_T	C_{GS}	C_{GD}
10 μA		1.5 pF	0.5 pF
250 μA		1.5 pF	0.5 pF
	250 MHz	1.5 pF	0.5 pf

17.25. A transistor with $f_T = 500$ MHz and $\mathbf{C}_{\mu o} = 2$ pF is biased at a Q-point of (2 mA, 5 V). What is the forward-transit time τ_F if $\phi_{jc} = 0.9$ V?

17.5 Base Resistance in the Hybrid-Pi Model

17.26. (a) What is the midband gain for the common-emitter amplifier in Fig. P17.26 if $r_x = 250\ \Omega$, $I_C = 1$ mA, and $\beta_o = 100$? (b) If $r_x = 0$?

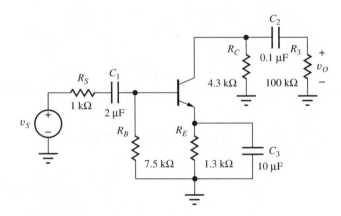

Figure P17.26

17.27. (a) What is the midband gain for the common-base amplifier in Fig. P17.27 if $r_x = 250\ \Omega$, $I_C = 0.1$ mA, and $\beta_o = 100$? (b) If $r_x = 0$?

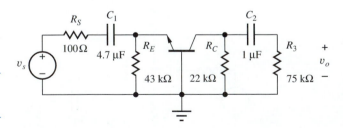

Figure P17.27

17.28. (a) What is the midband gain for the common-collector amplifier in Fig. P17.28 if $r_x = 250\ \Omega$, $I_C = 1$ mA, and $\beta_o = 100$? (b) If $r_x = 0$?

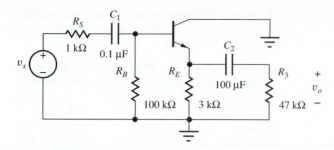

Figure P17.28

17.6 High-Frequency Limitations of Single-Stage Amplifiers

Factorization

17.29. Use dominant root factorization techniques to estimate the roots of the following quadratic equations and compare the results to the exact roots: (a) $s^2 + 5100s + 500,000$; (b) $2s^2 + 700s + 30,000$.

17.30. (a) Use dominant root factorization techniques to estimate the roots of the following equation. (b) Compare the results to the exact roots.

$$s^3 + 1110s^2 + 111,000s + 1,000,000$$

**17.31. Use Newton's method to help find the roots of the following polynomial. (*Hint:* Find the roots one at a time. Once a root is found, factor it out to reduce the order of the polynomial. Use approximate factorization to find starting points for iteration.)

$$s^6 + 138s^5 + 4263s^4 + 4760s^3$$
$$+ 235,550s^2 + 94,000s + 300,000$$

For Probs. 17.32 to 17.36, use $f_T = 500$ MHz, $r_x = 300\ \Omega$, $C_\mu = 0.75$ pF, $C_{GS} = C_{GD} = 2.5$ pF.

17.32. What are the midband gain and upper-cutoff frequency for the common-source amplifier in Prob. 17.9?

17.33. Simulate the frequency response of the amplifier in Prob. 17.9 and determine A_{mid}, f_L, and f_H.

17.34. What are the midband gain and upper-cutoff frequency for the common-emitter amplifier in Prob. 17.26 if $I_C = 1$ mA and $\beta_o = 100$?

17.35. What are the midband gain and upper-cutoff frequency for the common-emitter amplifier in Prob. 17.13?

17.36. Simulate the frequency response of the amplifier in Prob. 17.13 and determine A_{mid}, f_L, and f_H.

17.7 Miller Multiplication

**17.37. (a) Find the transfer function of the Miller integrator in Fig. 17.39 if $A(s) = 10A_o/(s + 10)$. The

transfer function is really that of a low-pass amplifier. What is the cutoff frequency if $A_o = 10^5$? (b) For $A_o = 10^6$? (c) Show that the transfer function approaches that of the ideal integrator if $A_o \to \infty$.

*17.38. (a) What is the input capacitance of the circuit in Fig. P17.38 if Z is a 100-pF capacitor and the amplifier is an op amp with a gain of 100,000? (**b) What is the input impedance of the circuit in Fig. P17.38 at $f = 1$ kHz if element Z is a 100-kΩ resistor and $A(s) = 10^6/(s + 10)$? (c) At 50 kHz? (d) At 1 MHz?

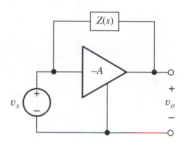

Figure P17.38

17.39. Use the C_T approximation to calculate the impedance presented to v_s by the circuit in Fig. P17.39 at $f = 1$ kHz if $r_x = 250\ \Omega$, $r_\pi = 2.5$ kΩ, $g_m = 0.04$ S, $R_L = 2.5$ kΩ, $C_\pi = 15$ pF, and $C_\mu = 1$ pF. (b) At 50 kHz. (c) At 1 MHz. (d) Compare your results to SPICE.

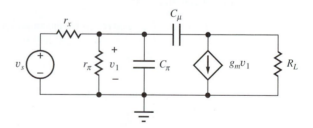

Figure P17.39

17.8 Estimation of ω_H Using the Open-Circuit Time-Constant Method

17.40. (a) Redesign the common-emitter amplifier in Fig. 17.31 to have an upper-cutoff frequency of 5 MHz by changing the value of the collector resistor R_C. What is the new value of the midband voltage gain? What is the gain-bandwidth product?

17.41. What are the values of (a) A_{mid}, f_L, and f_H for the common-emitter amplifier in Fig. P17.41 if $C_1 = 1$ μF, $C_2 = 0.1$ μF, $C_3 = 2.2$ μF, $R_3 = $

$100 \text{ k}\Omega$, $\beta_o = 100$, $f_T = 300$ MHz, $r_x = 300 \,\Omega$, and $C_\mu = 0.5$ pF? (b) What is the gain-bandwidth product?

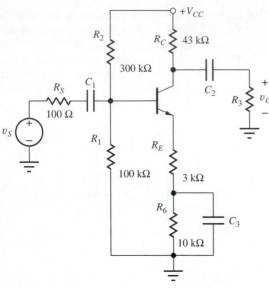

Figure P17.41

17.42. (a) Redesign the common-emitter amplifier in Fig. P17.41 to have an upper-cutoff frequency of 7.5 MHz by selecting a new value for R_E. Maintain the sum $R_E + R_6 = 13$ kΩ. What is the new value of the midband voltage gain? What is the gain-bandwidth product?

17.43. Find (a) A_{mid}, (b) f_L, and (c) f_H for the amplifier in Fig. P17.43 if $\beta_o = 100$, $f_T = 200$ MHz, $C_\mu = 1$ pF, and $r_x = 300 \,\Omega$.

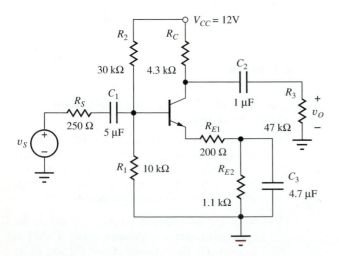

Figure P17.43

 17.44. Redesign the values of R_{E1} and R_{E2} in the amplifier in Prob. 17.43 to achieve $f_H = 10$ MHz. Do not change the Q-point.

*17.45. The network in Fig. P17.45 has two poles. (a) Estimate the lower-pole frequency using the short-circuit time-constant technique if $C_1 = 1 \,\mu$F, $C_2 = 10 \,\mu$F, $R_1 = 10$ kΩ, $R_2 = 1$ kΩ, and $R_3 = 1$ kΩ. (b) Estimate the upper-pole frequency using the open-circuit time-constant technique. (c) Why do the positions of the poles seem to be backward? (d) Find the system determinant and compare its exact roots to those in (a) and (b).

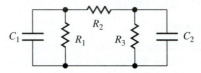

Figure P17.45

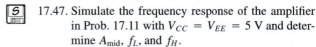

For Probs. 17.46 to 17.53, use $f_T = 500$ MHz, $r_x = 300 \,\Omega$, $C_\mu = 0.60$ pF for the BJT, and $C_{GS} = 3$ pF and $C_{GD} = 0.60$ pF for the FET.

17.46. What are the midband gain and upper-cutoff frequency for the common-base amplifier in Prob. 17.11(c)?

17.47. Simulate the frequency response of the amplifier in Prob. 17.11 with $V_{CC} = V_{EE} = 5$ V and determine A_{mid}, f_L, and f_H.

17.48. What are the midband gain and cutoff frequency for the common-gate amplifier in Prob. 17.14?

17.49. Simulate the frequency response of the amplifier in Prob. 17.14 and determine A_{mid}, f_L, and f_H.

17.50. (a) What are the midband gain and upper-cutoff frequency for the source follower in Prob. 17.15? (b) Simulate the frequency response of the amplifier in Prob. 17.15 with $V_{DD} = 10$ V and determine A_{mid}, f_L, and f_H.

17.51. (a) What are the midband gain and upper-cutoff frequency for the emitter follower in Prob. 17.16? (b) Simulate the frequency response of the amplifier in Prob. 17.16 with $V_{CC} = 15$ V and determine A_{mid}, f_L, and f_H.

*17.52. Derive an expression for the total capacitance looking into the gate of the FET in Fig. 17.56(b). Use it to interpret Eq. (17.132).

**17.53. Derive an expression for the total input capacitance of the BJT in Fig. 17.52(c). Use it to interpret Eq. (17.130).

17.9 Frequency Response of Multistage Amplifiers

17.54. What is the minimum bandwidth of the NMOS current mirror in Fig. P17.54 if $I_S = 100\ \mu$A, $K'_n = 25\ \mu$A/V^2, $\lambda = 0.02$ V^{-1}, $C_{GS1} = 3$ pF, $C_{GD1} = 0.5$ pF, and $(W/L)_1 = 5/1 = (W/L)_2$?

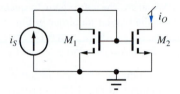

Figure P17.54

17.55. What is the minimum bandwidth of the MOS current mirror in Fig. P17.54 if $I_S = 200\ \mu$A, $K'_n = 25\ \mu$A/V^2, $\lambda = 0.02$ V^{-1}, $C_{GS1} = 3$ pF, $C_{GD1} = 1$ pF, $(W/L)_1 = 5/1$, and $(W/L)_2 = 25/1$?

17.56. What is the minimum bandwidth of the *pnp* current mirror in Fig. P17.56 if $I_S = 100\ \mu$A, $\beta_o = 50$, $V_A = 60$ V, $f_T = 50$ MHz, $C_\mu = 2$ pF, and $A_{E2} = A_{E1}$?

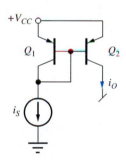

Figure P17.56

17.57. What is the minimum bandwidth of the *npn* current mirror in Fig. P17.57 if $I_S = 100\ \mu$A, $\beta_o = 100$, $V_A = 60$ V, $f_T = 600$ MHz, $C_\mu = 0.5$ pF, and $A_{E2} = 10\ A_{E1}$?

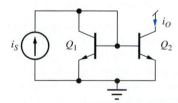

Figure P17.57

*17.58. What is the minimum bandwidth of the bipolar current mirror in Fig. P17.57 if $I_S = 250\ \mu$A, $\beta_o =$

100, $V_A = 50$ V, $f_T = 500$ MHz, $C_\mu = 0.3$ pF, $r_x = 175\ \Omega$, and $A_{E2} = 4A_{E1}$?

**17.59. Use the OCTC approach to find the minimum bandwidth of the Wilson current mirror in Fig. P17.59 if $I_{REF} = 250\ \mu$A, $K_n = 250\ \mu$A/V^2, $V_{TN} = 0.75$ V, $\lambda = 0.02$ V^{-1}, $C_{GS} = 3$ pF, and $C_{GD} = 1$ pF.

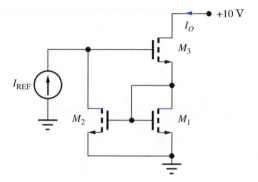

Figure P17.59

Gain-Bandwidth Product

17.60. A bipolar transistor must be selected for use in a common-emitter amplifier with a gain of 40 dB and a bandwidth of 5 MHz. What should be the minimum specification for the transistor's f_T? What should be the minimum $r_x C_\mu$ product? (Use a factor of 2 safety margin for each estimate.)

17.61. A bipolar transistor must be selected for use in a common-base amplifier with a gain of 40 dB and a bandwidth of 20 MHz. What should be the minimum specification for the transistor's f_T? What should be the minimum $r_x C_\mu$ product? (Use a factor of 2 safety margin for each estimate.)

17.62. A FET with $C_{GS} = 10$ pF and $C_{GD} = 3$ pF will be used in a common-gate amplifier with a source resistance of 100 Ω, $A_{mid} = 20$, and a bandwidth of 25 MHz. Estimate the Q-point current needed to achieve these specifications if $K_n = 25$ mA/V^2 and $V_{DD} = 15$ V.

17.63. A BJT will be used in a differential amplifier with load resistors of 100 kΩ. What are the maximum values of r_x and C_μ that can be tolerated if the gain and bandwidth are to be 100 and 1 MHz, respectively?

*17.64. A FET with $C_{GS} = 15$ pF and $C_{GD} = 5$ pF will be used in a common-source amplifier with a source resistance of 100 Ω and a bandwidth of 25 MHz. Estimate the minimum Q-point current needed to achieve this bandwidth if $K_n = 25$ mA/V^2 and $V_{GS} - V_{TN} \geq 0.25$ V.

17.65. What is the upper bound on the bandwidth of the circuit in Fig. P17.11 if $R_C = 12$ kΩ, $R_3 = 47$ kΩ, and $C_\mu = 2$ pF?

**17.66. (a) Use the OCTC approach to estimate the cut-off frequency of the Darlington stage in Fig. P17.66(a). Assume $I_{C1} = 0.1$ mA, $I_{C2} = 1$ mA, $\beta_o = 100$, $f_T = 300$ MHz, $C_\mu = 0.5$ pF, $V_A = 50$ V, $r_x = 300$ Ω, and $R_L = \infty$. (b) Use the OCTC approach to estimate the cutoff frequency of the C-C/C-E cascade in Fig. P17.66(b). (c) Which configuration offers better bandwidth? (d) Which configuration is used in the second stage in the μA-741 amplifier in Chapter 16? Why do you think it was used?

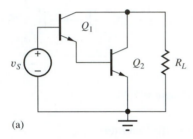

(a)

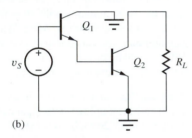

(b)

Figure P17.66

17.67. Draw a Bode plot for the common-mode rejection ratio for the differential amplifier in Fig. 17.57 if $I_C = 100$ μA, $R_{EE} = 10$ MΩ, $C_{EE} = 1$ pF, $\beta_o = 100$, $V_A = 50$ V, $f_T = 200$ MHz, $C_\mu = 0.3$ pF, $r_x = 175$ Ω, and $R_L = 100$kΩ

17.68. Use SPICE to plot the graph for Prob. 17.67.

17.10 Single-Pole Operational Amplifier Compensation

17.69. (a) What are the unity-gain frequency and positive and negative slew rates for the CMOS amplifier in Fig. 17.69 if $I_1 = 250$ μA, $I_2 = 500$ μA, $K_{n1} = 1$ mA/V^2, and $C_C = 7.5$ pF? (b) If $I_1 = 500$ μA, $I_2 = 250$ μA, and $C_C = 10$ pF?

17.70. Simulate the frequency response of the CMOS amplifier in Fig. 17.74 for $R_Z = 0$ and for $R_Z = 1$ kΩ. Compare the values of the unity-

gain frequency and phase shift of the amplifier at the unity gain frequency. Use $I_1 = 250$ μA, $I_2 = 500$ μA, $I_3 = 2$mA, $(W/L)_1 = 20/1$, $(W/L)_3 = 40/1$, $(W/L)_5 = 160/1$, $(W/L)_6 = 60/1$, and $C_C = 7.5$ pF. $V_{DD} = V_{SS} = 10$ V. Use CMOS models from Chapter 9.

17.71. (a) What are the unity-gain frequency and slew rate of the bipolar amplifier in Fig. 17.75 if $I_1 = 50$ μA, $I_2 = 500$ μA, and $C_C = 12$ pF? (b) If $I_1 = 200$ μA, $I_2 = 250$ μA, and $C_C = 12$ pF?

17.72. What are the positive and negative slew rates of the amplifier in Fig. P17.72 just after a 2-V step function is applied to input v_2 if $I_1 = 40$ μA, $I_2 = 400$ μA, $I_3 = 500$ μA, and $C_C = 5$ pF? Assume v_1 is grounded. (b) Check your answers with SPICE.

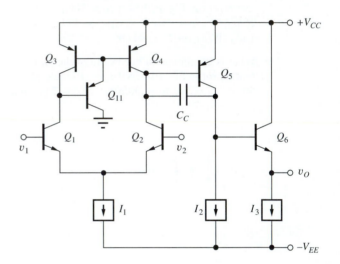

Figure P17.72

*17.73. (a) Use SPICE to calculate the frequency response of the amplifier in Fig. P17.72 for $I_1 = 100$ μA, $I_2 = 500$ μA, $I_3 = 500$ μA, and $C_C = 15$ pF. (b) Repeat for $I_1 = 100$ μA, $I_2 = 50$ μA, and $C_C = 15$ pF. Compare the unity-gain frequency to that predicted by Eq. (17.183). Discuss the reasons for any discrepancy. Use $V_{CC} = V_{EE} = 15$ V.

**17.74. Perform an analysis that shows that the compensation network with C_C and R_Z also improves the response of the CMOS amplifier in Fig. 17.74 for the case in which C_{GD} is included in the analysis. (*Hint:* Use dominant root factorization of the numerator polynomial.)

17.11 Tuned Amplifiers

17.75. What are the center frequency, Q, and midband gain for the amplifier in Fig. P17.75 if the FET has $C_{GS} = 50$ pF, $C_{GD} = 5$ pF, $\lambda = 0.0167$ V^{-1},

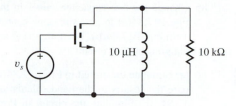

Figure P17.75

and it is biased at 2 V above threshold with $I_D = 10$ mA and $V_{DS} = 10$ V.

17.76. (a) What is the value of C required for $f_o = 10.7$ MHz in the circuit in Fig. P17.76 if $I_C = 10$ mA, $V_{CE} = 10$ V, $\beta_o = 100$, $C_\mu = 2$ pF, $f_T = 500$ MHz, and $V_A = 75$ V? (b) What is the Q of the amplifier? (c) Where should a tap be placed on the inductor to achieve a Q of 100? (d) What is the new value of C required to achieve $f_o = 10.7$ MHz?

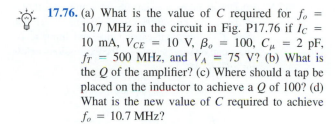

Figure P17.76

17.77. Simulate the characteristics and find the center frequency and bandwidth for the double-tuned amplifier in Fig. P17.77 if $K_n = 20$ mA/V^2, $V_{TN} = -1$ V, $\lambda = 0.02$ V^{-1}, $C_{GS} = 25$ pF, and (a) $C_{GD} = 0$ pF and (b) $C_{GD} = 1$ pF.

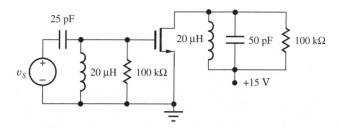

Figure P17.77

17.78. (a) Draw the dc and high-frequency ac equivalent circuits for the circuit in Fig. P17.78. (b) What is the resonant frequency of the circuit for $V_C = 0$ V if the diode is modeled by $C_{jo} = 20$ pF and $\phi_j = 0.9$ V? (c) For $V_C = 10$ V?

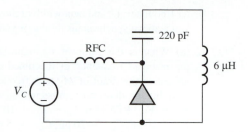

Figure P17.78

*17.79. (a) What are the center frequency, Q, and midband gain for the tuned amplifier in Fig. P17.79 if $L_1 = 5$ μH, $C_1 = 10$ pF, $C_2 = 10$ pF, $I_C = 1$ mA, $C_\pi = 5$ pF, $C_\mu = 1$ pF, $R_L = 5$ kΩ, $r_\pi = 2.5$ kΩ, and $r_x = 0$ Ω? (b) What would be the answers if the base terminal of the transistor were connected to the top of the inductor?

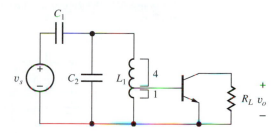

Figure P17.79

17.80. (a) What is the value of C_2 required to achieve synchronous tuning of the circuit in Fig. P17.80 if $L_1 = L_2 = 10$ μH, $C_1 = C_3 = 20$ pF, $C_{GS} = 20$ pF, $C_{GD} = 5$ pF, $V_{TN1} = -1$ V, $K_{n1} = 10$ mA/V^2, $V_{TN2} = -4$ V, $K_{n2} = 10$ mA/V^2, and $R_G = R_D = 100$ kΩ? (b) What are the Q, midband gain, and bandwidth of your design?

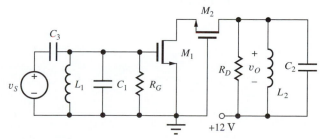

Figure P17.80

17.81. Simulate the frequency response of the circuit design in Prob. 17.80 and find the midband gain, cen-

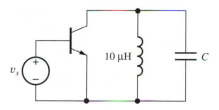

ter frequency, Q, and bandwidth of the circuit. Did you achieve synchronous tuning of your design?

 **17.82. (a) What is the value of C_2 required to adjust the resonant frequency of the tuned circuit connected to the drain of M_2 to a frequency 2 percent higher than that connected at the gate of M_1 in Fig. P17.80 if $L_1 = L_2 = 10$ μH, $C_1 = C_3 = 20$ pF, $C_{GS} = 20$ pF, $C_{GD} = 5$ pF, $V_{TN1} = -1$ V, $K_{n1} = 10$ mA/V^2, $V_{TN2} = -4$ V, $K_{n2} = 10$ mA/V^2, and $R_G = R_D = 100$ kΩ? (b) What are the Q and bandwidth of your design?

*17.83. Simulate the frequency response of the circuit design in Prob. 17.82 and find the midband gain, center frequency, Q and bandwidth, and the Q of the circuit. Was the desired stagger tuning achieved?

17.84. (a) What are the midband gain, center frequency, bandwidth, and Q for the circuit in Fig. P17.84(a) if $I_D = 20$ mA, $\lambda = 0.02$ V^{-1}, $C_{GD} = 5$ pF, and $K_n = 5$ mA/V^2? (b) Repeat for the circuit in Fig. P17.84(b).

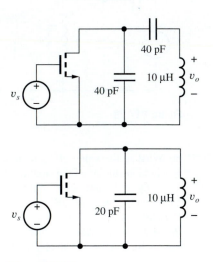

Figure P17.84

 17.85 Change the two capacitor values in the circuit in Fig. P17.84(a) to give the same center frequency as in Fig. P17.84(b). What are the Q and midband gain for the new circuit?

 17.86 (a) Simulate the circuit in Prob. 17.84(a) and compare the results to the hand calculations in Prob. 17.84. (b) Simulate the circuit in Prob. 17.84(b) and compare the results to the hand calculations in Prob. 17.84. (c) Simulate the circuit in Prob. 17.85 and compare the results to the hand calculations in Prob. 17.85

*17.87 (a) Derive an expression for the input admittance of the common-emitter circuit in Fig. 17.21 and show that the input capacitance and input resistance can be represented by the expressions below for $\omega C_\mu R_L \ll 1$.

$$C_{in} = C_\pi + C_\mu(1 + g_m R_L)$$

$$R_{in} = r_\pi \left\| \frac{R_L}{(1 + g_m R_L)(\omega C_\mu R_L)^2} \right.$$

(b) A MOSFET has $C_{GS} = 6$ pF, $C_{GD} = 2$ pF, $g_m = 5$ mS, and $R_L = 10$ kΩ. What are the values of C_{in} and R_{in} at a frequency of 5 MHz?

Feedback, Stability, and Oscillators

Examples of feedback systems abound in daily life. The thermostat that senses the temperature of a room and turns the air-conditioning system on and off is one example. Another is the remote control that we use to select a channel on the television or set the volume at an acceptable level. The heating and cooling system uses a simple temperature transducer to compare the temperature with a fixed set point. However, we are part of the TV remote control feedback system; we operate the control until our senses tell us that the audio and optical information is what we want.

The theory of negative feedback in electronic systems was first developed by Harold Black of the Bell Telephone System. In 1928, he invented the feedback amplifier to stabilize the gain of early telephone repeaters. Today, some form of feedback is used in virtually every electronic system. This chapter formally develops the concept of feedback, which is an invaluable tool in the design of electronic systems. Valuable insight into the operation of many common electronic circuits can be gained by recasting the circuits as feedback amplifiers.

We already encountered **negative** (or **degenerative**) **feedback** in several forms. The four-resistor bias network uses negative feedback to achieve an operating point that is independent of variations in device characteristics. We also found that a source or emitter resistor can be used in an inverting amplifier to control the gain and bandwidth of the stage. Many of the advantages of negative feedback were actually uncovered during the discussion of operational-amplifier circuit design. Generally, feedback can be used to achieve a tradeoff between gain and many of the other properties of amplifiers:

1. *Gain stability*: Feedback reduces the sensitivity of gain to variations in the values of transistor parameters and circuit elements.

2. *Input and output impedances*: Feedback can increase or decrease the input and output resistances of an amplifier.

3. *Bandwidth*: The bandwidth of an amplifier can be extended using feedback.

4. *Nonlinear distortion*: Feedback reduces the effects of nonlinear distortion. (For example, feedback can be used to minimize the effects of the dead zone in a class-B amplifier stage.)

Feedback may also be **positive** (or **regenerative**), and we explore the use of positive feedback in sinusoidal **oscillator circuits** in this chapter. We encountered the use of a combination of negative and positive feedback in the discussion of *RC* active filters and multivibrator circuits in Chapter 12. Sinusoidal oscillators use positive feedback to generate signals at specific desired frequencies; they use negative feedback to stabilize the amplitude of the oscillations.

Positive feedback in amplifiers is usually undesirable. Excess phase shift in a feedback amplifier may cause the feedback to become regenerative and cause the feedback amplifier to break into oscillation. Remember that positive feedback was identified in Chapter 17 as a potential source of oscillation problems in tuned amplifiers.

18.1 CLASSIC FEEDBACK SYSTEM

Figure 18.1 is the block diagram for a classic feedback system. This diagram may represent a simple feedback amplifier or a complex feedback control system. It consists of an amplifier with transfer function $A(s)$, referred to as the **open-loop amplifier,** a **feedback network** with transfer function $\beta(s)$, and a summing block indicated by Σ. The variables in this diagram are represented as voltages but could equally well be currents or even other physical quantities such as temperature, velocity, distance, and so on.

In Fig. 18.1, the input to the open-loop amplifier A is provided by the subtractor, which develops the difference between the input signal v_s and the feedback signal v_f. In

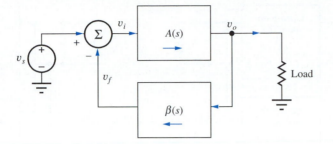

Figure 18.1 Classic block diagram for a feedback system

the frequency domain,

$$\mathbf{V_i}(s) = \mathbf{V_s}(s) - \mathbf{V_f}(s) \tag{18.1}$$

The output signal is equal to the product of the open-loop amplifier gain and the input signal to the amplifier:

$$\mathbf{V_o}(s) = A(s)\mathbf{V_i}(s) \tag{18.2}$$

The signal fed back to the input is given by

$$\mathbf{V_f}(s) = \beta(s)\mathbf{V_o}(s) \tag{18.3}$$

Combining Eqs. (18.1) to (18.3) and solving for the overall voltage gain of the system yields the classic expression for the **closed-loop gain** of a feedback amplifier:

$$A_V(s) = \frac{\mathbf{V_o}(s)}{\mathbf{V_s}(s)} = \frac{A(s)}{1 + A(s)\beta(s)} = \frac{A(s)}{1 + T(s)} \tag{18.4}$$

Equation (18.4) was encountered in Chapter 12, where $A(s)$ was identified as the **open-loop gain** and the product $T(s) = A(s)\beta(s)$ was defined as the **loop gain.** For the block diagram in Fig. 18.1, negative feedback requires $T(s) > 0$, whereas $T(s) < 0$ corresponds to the positive feedback condition.

A number of assumptions are implicit in this derivation. It is assumed that the blocks can be interconnected, as shown in Fig. 18.1, without affecting each other. That is, connecting the feedback network and the load to the output of the amplifier does not change the characteristics of the amplifier, nor does the interconnection of the subtractor, feedback network and input of the open-loop amplifier modify the characteristics of either the amplifier or feedback network. In addition, it is tacitly assumed that signals flow only in the forward direction through the amplifier, and only in the reverse direction through the feedback network, as indicated by the arrows in Fig. 18.1.

Implementation of this block diagram with operational amplifiers having large input resistances, low output resistances, and essentially zero reverse-voltage gain is one method of satisfying these unstated assumptions. However, most general amplifiers and feedback networks do not necessarily satisfy these assumptions. The theory developed in the next several sections explores the analysis and design of more general feedback systems that do not satisfy the implicit restrictions just outlined.

18.2 FEEDBACK AMPLIFIER DESIGN USING TWO-PORT NETWORK THEORY

If we consider both the amplifier and feedback networks to be represented as a two-port, then four basic feedback amplifier topologies can be defined: voltage, transresistance, current, and transconductance amplifiers. Figure 18.2 shows these four amplifiers in block

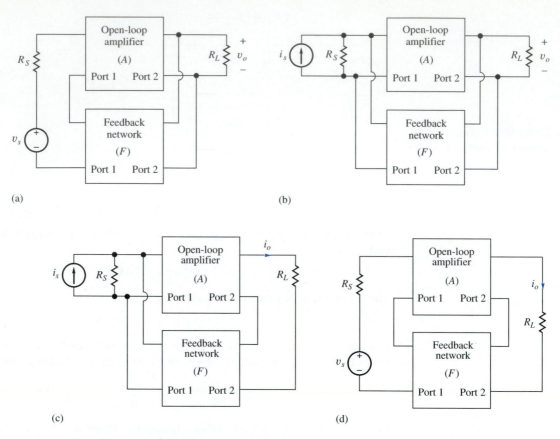

Figure 18.2 (a) Series-shunt feedback amplifier (*h*-parameters). Voltage amplifier topology: $A_V = \mathbf{v_o}/\mathbf{v_s}$. (b) Shunt-shunt feedback amplifier (*y*-parameters). Transresistance amplifier topology: $A_{TR} = \mathbf{v_o}/\mathbf{i_s}$. (c) Shunt-series feedback amplifier (*g*-parameters). Current amplifier topology: $A_I = \mathbf{i_o}/\mathbf{i_s}$. (d) Series-series feedback amplifier (*z*-parameters). Transconductance amplifier topology: $A_{TC} = \mathbf{i_o}/\mathbf{v_s}$.

diagram form; each is characterized by a specific combination of the input and output port connections. Port voltages are summed by connecting the ports in series, and port currents are summed by connecting the ports in parallel, usually termed a **shunt connection.**

In the voltage amplifier topology in Fig. 18.2(a), the input port of the feedback network is connected in series with the input port of the amplifier, and the output ports of the amplifier and feedback network form a parallel or shunt connection. Thus this topology is referred to as a **series-shunt feedback** amplifier. The first adjective refers to the input port configuration and the second refers to the output.

In the transresistance topology in Fig. 18.2(b), shunt connections are used at both the input and output ports; thus this circuit is referred to as a **shunt-shunt feedback** amplifier. The current amplifier topology in Fig. 18.2(c) connects the input ports in parallel and the output ports in series and so is usually referred to as a **shunt-series feedback** amplifier. Finally, for the transconductance amplifier topology in Fig. 18.2(d), the ports of the amplifier and feedback network are connected in series at both the input and output, so this topology is referred to as the **series-series feedback** amplifier.

We analyze the behavior of these amplifiers using two-port descriptions for the amplifiers and feedback networks. Based on the various port connections, analysis of each type uses a different set of two-port parameters.

18.3 VOLTAGE AMPLIFIERS—SERIES-SHUNT FEEDBACK

Because of our study of op-amp circuits, we are, in general, most familiar with **voltage amplifiers,** and we start our analysis with this configuration (see Fig. 18.3). As will become apparent during the analysis, the *h*-parameters are the appropriate two-port parameters for analyzing this configuration.

Analysis begins by describing the amplifier and feedback network by their individual *h*-parameter two-port descriptions:

$$\mathbf{v_1^A} = h_{11}^A \mathbf{i_1} + h_{12}^A \mathbf{v_2}$$
$$\mathbf{i_2^A} = h_{21}^A \mathbf{i_1} + h_{22}^A \mathbf{v_2} \tag{18.5}$$

and

$$\mathbf{v_1^F} = h_{11}^F \mathbf{i_1} + h_{12}^F \mathbf{v_2}$$
$$\mathbf{i_2^F} = h_{21}^F \mathbf{i_1} + h_{22}^F \mathbf{v_2} \tag{18.6}$$

in which the superscripts indicate the amplifier (*A*) and feedback network (*F*), respectively. Next, we proceed to find the two-port parameters of the overall feedback amplifier based on these individual *h*-parameter descriptions. Because of the series connection at the input, the overall input voltage v_1 of the feedback amplifier is just the sum of the input voltages of the individual two-ports:

$$\mathbf{v_1} = \mathbf{v_1^A} + \mathbf{v_1^F} \tag{18.7}$$

and, because of the shunt connection at the output, the overall current i_2 into the output port is the sum of the currents at the output of the individual two-ports:

$$\mathbf{i_2} = \mathbf{i_2^A} + \mathbf{i_2^F} \tag{18.8}$$

Substituting Eqs. (18.5) and (18.6) into Eqs. (18.7) and (18.8) yields a two-port description for the overall feedback amplifier:

$$\mathbf{v_1} = (h_{11}^A + h_{11}^F)\mathbf{i_1} + (h_{12}^A + h_{12}^F)\mathbf{v_2}$$
$$\mathbf{i_2} = (h_{21}^A + h_{21}^F)\mathbf{i_1} + (h_{22}^A + h_{22}^F)\mathbf{v_2} \tag{18.9}$$

Here we see the reasoning behind the choice of the *h*-parameters, which allows the two sets of network parameters to be conveniently added together. Because the corresponding parameters of both networks always appear together in Eq. (18.9), a more compact notation is achieved by defining

$$h_{ij}^T = h_{ij}^A + h_{ij}^F \tag{18.10}$$

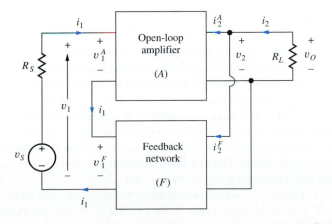

Figure 18.3 Series-shunt feedback amplifier.

so that the two-port equations become

$$\mathbf{v_1} = h_{11}^T \mathbf{i_1} + h_{12}^T \mathbf{v_2}$$
$$\mathbf{i_2} = h_{21}^T \mathbf{i_1} + h_{22}^T \mathbf{v_2}$$

$$(18.11)$$

Normally, the forward current gain of the amplifier far exceeds that of the feedback network, $h_{21}^A \gg h_{21}^F$, and the reverse voltage gain of the feedback network is much greater than that of the amplifier, $h_{12}^F \gg h_{12}^A$. Using these approximations to simplify Eq. (18.11) yields

$$\mathbf{v_1} = h_{11}^T \mathbf{i_1} + h_{12}^F \mathbf{v_2}$$
$$\mathbf{i_2} = h_{21}^A \mathbf{i_1} + h_{22}^T \mathbf{v_2}$$

$$(18.12)$$

An expression for the closed-loop gain of the feedback amplifier, including the effects of R_S and R_L, can now be found using Eq. (18.12). At the input port in Fig. 18.3, $\mathbf{v_1}$ and $\mathbf{i_1}$ are related by

$$\mathbf{v_1} = \mathbf{v_s} - \mathbf{i_1} R_S$$

$$(18.13)$$

and $\mathbf{v_2}$ and $\mathbf{i_2}$ at the output port are related by

$$\mathbf{i_2} = -\frac{\mathbf{v_2}}{R_L} = -G_L \mathbf{v_2}$$

$$(18.14)$$

Substituting Eqs. (18.13) and (18.14) into Eq. (18.12) yields

$$\mathbf{v_s} = (R_s + h_{11}^T)\mathbf{i_1} + h_{12}^F \mathbf{v_2}$$
$$0 = h_{21}^A \mathbf{i_1} + (h_{22}^T + G_L)\mathbf{v_2}$$

$$(18.15)$$

The source and load resistors, R_S and R_L, are absorbed into the expressions in Eq. (18.15) to develop a consistent set of equations for overall feedback amplifier gain, input resistance, and output resistance calculations.

The closed-loop voltage gain is found from Eq. (18.15) by solving for $\mathbf{v_2}$ in terms of $\mathbf{v_s}$:

$$A_V = \frac{\mathbf{v_2}}{\mathbf{v_s}} = \frac{h_{21}^A}{h_{21}^A h_{12}^F - (R_S + h_{11}^T)(h_{22}^T + G_L)}$$

$$(18.16)$$

By dividing numerator and denominator by the second denominator term, Eq. (18.16) can be rearranged into the standard form for a feedback system:

$$A_V = \frac{\dfrac{-h_{21}^A}{(R_S + h_{11}^T)(h_{22}^T + G_L)}}{1 + \dfrac{-h_{21}^A}{(R_S + h_{11}^T)(h_{22}^T + G_L)}h_{12}^F} = \frac{A}{1 + A\beta}$$

$$(18.17)$$

in which $$A = -\frac{h_{21}^A}{(R_S + h_{11}^T)(h_{22}^T + G_L)} \qquad \text{and} \qquad \beta = h_{12}^F$$

$$(18.18)$$

Figure 18.4(a) and (b) provide an interpretation of Eqs. (18.17) and (18.18) and a general methodology for analyzing feedback amplifiers. Figure 18.4(a) shows the feedback amplifier with an explicit representation of the two-port parameters of the feedback network with $h_{21}^F = 0$. Equations (18.17) and (18.18) indicate that the gain of the amplifier A should be calculated including the effects of h_{11}^F, h_{22}^F, R_S, and R_L. A schematic representation of these equations is given by redrawing the circuit of Fig. 18.4(a) as in Fig. 18.4(b). Although the position of feedback elements h_{11}^F and h_{22}^F in the drawing has changed, the actual circuit remains the same. The amplifier circuit, the A-circuit, now includes h_{11}^F, h_{22}^F, R_S, and R_L, and the feedback network contains only h_{12}^F.

Figure 18.5 reinforces the analysis technique. The three required h-parameters of the feedback network are found based on their individual definitions. Then the voltage gain of

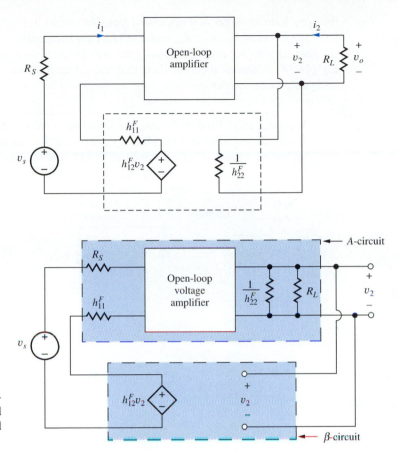

Figure 18.4 Schematic interpretation of the amplifier and feedback circuits described by Eqs. (18.17) and (18.18).

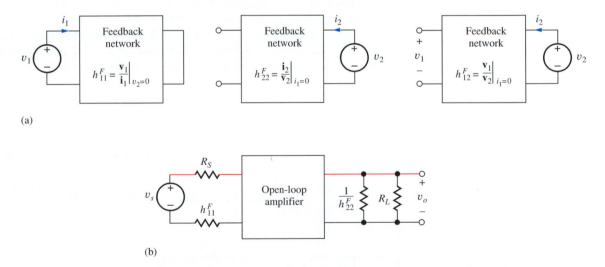

Figure 18.5 Subcircuits used for analysis of the series-shunt feedback amplifier: (a) circuits for determining the *h*-parameters of the feedback network, and (b) the A-circuit for finding the amplifier gain.

the open-loop amplifier A is calculated from the circuit in Fig. 18.5(b), which includes the loading effects of h_{11}^F, h_{22}^F, R_S, and R_L. The gain is calculated directly from the A-circuit; we generally *do not* evaluate A using the mathematical two-port parameter description in Eq. (18.18) (although it can be done that way). Our first example helps make the overall analysis process clearer.

EXAMPLE 18.1: Find A, β, and the closed-loop voltage gain A_V for the series-shunt feedback amplifier in Fig. 18.6 if the op amp has an open-loop gain of 80 dB, a differential-mode input resistance of 25 kΩ, and an output resistance of 1 kΩ.

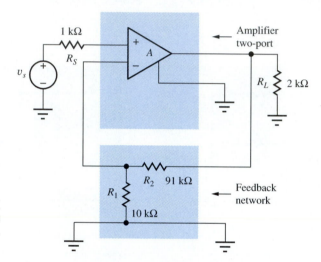

Figure 18.6 Series-shunt feedback amplifier example with the two two-ports identified.

SOLUTION: The first step in the analysis is to draw the amplifier as a pair of interconnected two-ports, as in Fig. 18.6, to ensure that the theory can actually be applied to the amplifier configuration. The importance of this step must not be overlooked.

The two-port representation in Fig. 18.6 also helps in the explicit identification of the feedback network components. The values of h_{11}^F, h_{12}^F, and h_{22}^F, corresponding to the feedback network, are found from the three circuits in Fig. 18.7:

$$h_{11}^F = \left.\frac{\mathbf{v_1}}{\mathbf{i_1}}\right|_{\mathbf{v_2}=0} = R_1\|R_2 = 10\text{ k}\Omega\|91\text{ k}\Omega = 9.01\text{ k}\Omega$$

$$h_{22}^F = \left.\frac{\mathbf{i_2}}{\mathbf{v_2}}\right|_{\mathbf{i_1}=0} = \frac{1}{R_1 + R_2} = \frac{1}{10\text{ k}\Omega + 91\text{ k}\Omega} = \frac{1}{101\text{ k}\Omega}$$

$$h_{12}^F = \left.\frac{\mathbf{v_1}}{\mathbf{v_2}}\right|_{\mathbf{i_1}=0} = \frac{R_1}{R_1 + R_2} = \frac{10\text{ k}\Omega}{10\text{ k}\Omega + 91\text{ k}\Omega} = 0.0990$$

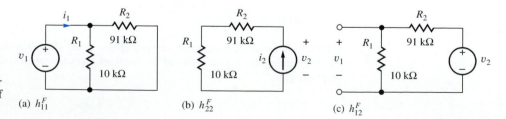

Figure 18.7 Circuits for determining the h-parameters of the feedback network.

(a) h_{11}^F (b) h_{22}^F (c) h_{12}^F

The forward gain of the amplifier can now be found using the A-circuit in Fig. 18.8. R_S and h_{11}^F have been added in series with the amplifier input, and R_L and h_{22}^F are placed in parallel with the amplifier output. The voltage gain of the A-circuit is

$$A = \frac{\mathbf{v_o}}{\mathbf{v_s}} = \frac{25\,k\Omega}{1\,k\Omega + 25\,k\Omega + 9.01\,k\Omega}(10^4)\frac{1.96\,k\Omega}{1.96\,k\Omega + 1.00\,k\Omega} = 4730$$

and the feedback factor is $\beta = h_{12}^F = 0.0990$. Using these results, the closed loop is

$$A_V = \frac{A}{1 + A\beta} = \frac{4730}{1 + 4730\,(0.0990)} = 10.1$$

In this case, the loop gain is much larger than 1, $A\beta = (4730)(0.0990) = 468$, and

$$A_V = \frac{A}{1 + A\beta} \approx \frac{1}{\beta} = 10.1$$

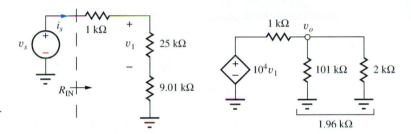

Figure 18.8 Augmented amplifier circuit (the A-circuit).

Input Resistance

The input resistance of the closed-loop series-shunt feedback amplifier can be calculated from the two-port description for the overall amplifier in Fig. 18.4(b), repeated from Eq. (18.15):

$$\mathbf{v_s} = (R_S + h_{11}^T)\mathbf{i_1} + h_{12}^F\mathbf{v_2} \tag{18.19}$$
$$0 = h_{21}^A\mathbf{i_1} + (h_{22}^T + G_L)\mathbf{v_2}$$

This time, solving the second equation for v_2 in terms of i_1 and substituting the result back into the first gives

$$\mathbf{v_s} = (R_S + h_{11}^T)\mathbf{i_1} + h_{12}^F\frac{-h_{21}^A}{(h_{22}^T + G_L)}\mathbf{i_1} \tag{18.20}$$

which can be rearranged as

$$R_{IN} = \frac{\mathbf{v_s}}{\mathbf{i_1}} = (R_S + h_{11}^T)\left[1 + \frac{-h_{21}^A}{(R_S + h_{11}^T)(h_{22}^T + G_L)}h_{12}^F\right] = (R_S + h_{11}^T)[1 + A\beta] \tag{18.21}$$

or

$$R_{IN} = R_{IN}^A(1 + A\beta) \tag{18.22}$$

From Eq. (18.22), we see that series feedback at a port increases the input resistance at that port by the factor $(1 + A\beta)$. Note that this equation has exactly the same form as that obtained in Chapter 12.

EXAMPLE 18.2: Calculate the input resistance for the series-shunt feedback amplifier in Fig. 18.6.

SOLUTION: From Fig. 18.8 and Example 18.1:

$$R_{IN}^A = 1\,\text{k}\Omega + 25\,\text{k}\Omega + 9.01\,\text{k}\Omega = 35.0\,\text{k}\Omega \qquad \text{and} \qquad (1 + A\beta) = 469$$

which yields

$$R_{IN} = R_{IN}^A(1 + A\beta) = 35.0\,\text{k}\Omega(469) = 16.4\,\text{M}\Omega \qquad \blacklozenge$$

Output Resistance

The output resistance of the closed-loop amplifier can be calculated in a manner similar to the input resistance calculation, based on the circuit in Fig. 18.9. The signal source v_s is set to zero, a test source v_x is applied to the output, and i_x must be determined. For Fig. 18.9,

$$\mathbf{v_1} = -\mathbf{i_1}R_S \qquad \mathbf{v_2} = \mathbf{v_x} \qquad \mathbf{i_2} = \mathbf{i_x} - G_L\mathbf{v_2} \tag{18.23}$$

Substituting these constraints into Eq. (18.12) yields

$$0 = (R_S + h_{11}^T)\mathbf{i_1} + h_{12}^F\mathbf{v_x}$$
$$\mathbf{i_x} = h_{21}^A\mathbf{i_1} + (h_{22}^T + G_L)\mathbf{v_x} \tag{18.24}$$

and solving for $\mathbf{i_x}$ in terms of $\mathbf{v_x}$ yields

$$\mathbf{i_x} = h_{21}^A \frac{-h_{12}^F}{(R_S + h_{11}^T)}\mathbf{v_x} + (h_{22}^T + G_L)\mathbf{v_x} \tag{18.25}$$

Rearranging Eq. (18.25) yields an expression for the output resistance of the overall amplifier, which again is in the same form as that derived in Chapter 12.

$$R_{\text{OUT}} = \frac{\mathbf{v_x}}{\mathbf{i_x}} = \frac{1}{(h_{22}^T + G_L)\left[1 + \dfrac{-h_{21}^A}{(R_S + h_{11}^T)(h_{22}^T + G_L)}h_{12}^F\right]} = \frac{\left(\dfrac{1}{h_{22}^T + G_L}\right)}{1 + A\beta} \tag{18.26}$$

$$R_{\text{OUT}} = \frac{R_{\text{OUT}}^A}{1 + A\beta} \tag{18.27}$$

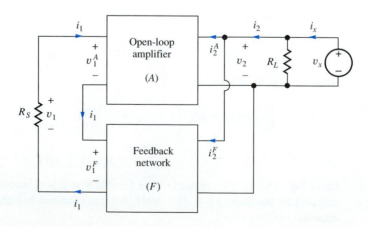

Figure 18.9 Output resistance of the series-shunt feedback network.

The output resistance of the closed-loop amplifier is equal to the output resistance of the A-circuit, including the effects of R_S and R_L, reduced by the amount of feedback $(1 + A\beta)$. Shunt feedback reduces the impedance level at a port.

EXAMPLE 18.3: Calculate the output resistance for the series-shunt feedback amplifier in Fig. 18.6.

SOLUTION: From the A-circuit in Fig. 18.8,

$$R_{\text{OUT}}^A = 2\text{ k}\Omega\|101\text{ k}\Omega\|1\text{ k}\Omega = 662\Omega$$

and

$$R_{\text{OUT}} = \frac{R_{\text{OUT}}^A}{1 + A\beta} = \frac{662}{469} = 1.41\Omega$$

◆

EXERCISE: What would the closed-loop gain, input resistance, and output resistance of the series-shunt feedback amplifier example have been if the loading effects of h_{11}^F, h_{22}^F, R_S, and R_L on the feedback network had all been ignored?

ANSWERS: 10.1, 24.8 MΩ, 1.01Ω

DISCUSSION: Note that the closed-loop gain is essentially unchanged because of the high value of loop gain, but the values of R_{IN} and R_{OUT} differ by substantial percentages. Feedback stabilizes the value of the voltage gain but not those of the input and output resistances.

18.4 TRANSRESISTANCE AMPLIFIERS —SHUNT-SHUNT FEEDBACK

The **transresistance amplifier** is another important class of amplifier, widely used in optical communications systems to convert optical signals from a fiber into an electrical signal. For example, i_S and R_S are one model for a photodiode detector at the output of an optical fiber. The transresistance amplifier is formed using the shunt-shunt feedback configuration in Fig. 18.10. Because the input port voltages are the same and the output port voltages are the same for the amplifier and feedback two-ports, the y-parameters are appropriate for analyzing this configuration.

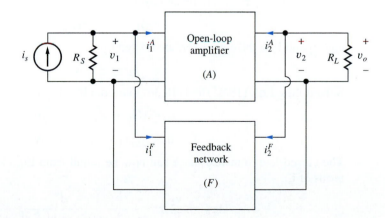

Figure 18.10 Shunt-shunt feedback amplifier.

The analysis mirrors that in Sec. 18.3. In this case, the amplifier and feedback network are represented by their individual y-parameters:

$$\mathbf{i}_1^A = y_{11}^A \mathbf{v}_1 + y_{12}^A \mathbf{v}_2$$
$$\mathbf{i}_2^A = y_{21}^A \mathbf{v}_1 + y_{22}^A \mathbf{v}_2 \tag{18.28}$$

and

$$\mathbf{i}_1^F = y_{11}^F \mathbf{v}_1 + y_{12}^F \mathbf{v}_2$$
$$\mathbf{i}_2^F = y_{21}^F \mathbf{v}_1 + y_{22}^F \mathbf{v}_2 \tag{18.29}$$

in which the superscripts again indicate the amplifier (A) and feedback network (F), respectively.

Based on the connections at the input and output ports, the overall input current $\mathbf{i}_1$ and output current $\mathbf{i}_2$ can be written as

$$\mathbf{i}_1 = \mathbf{i}_1^A + \mathbf{i}_1^F \qquad \text{and} \qquad \mathbf{i}_2 = \mathbf{i}_2^A + \mathbf{i}_2^F \tag{18.30}$$

Substituting Eqs. (18.28) and (18.29) into Eq. (18.30) yields the two-port description for the overall shunt-shunt feedback amplifier:

$$\mathbf{i}_1 = (y_{11}^A + y_{11}^F)\mathbf{v}_1 + (y_{12}^A + y_{12}^F)\mathbf{v}_2$$
$$\mathbf{i}_2 = (y_{21}^A + y_{21}^F)\mathbf{v}_1 + (y_{22}^A + y_{22}^F)\mathbf{v}_2 \tag{18.31}$$

Because the corresponding parameters of both networks again appear together in Eq. (18.31), a more compact notation is achieved by defining

$$y_{ij}^T = y_{ij}^A + y_{ij}^F \tag{18.32}$$

and

$$\mathbf{i}_1 = y_{11}^T \mathbf{v}_1 + y_{12}^T \mathbf{v}_2$$
$$\mathbf{i}_2 = y_{21}^T \mathbf{v}_1 + y_{22}^T \mathbf{v}_2 \tag{18.33}$$

Once again assuming that $y_{21}^A \gg y_{21}^F$ and $y_{12}^F \gg y_{12}^A$, Eq. (18.33) is represented in simplified form as

$$\mathbf{i}_1 = y_{11}^T \mathbf{v}_1 + y_{12}^F \mathbf{v}_2$$
$$\mathbf{i}_2 = y_{21}^A \mathbf{v}_1 + y_{22}^T \mathbf{v}_2 \tag{18.34}$$

The expression for the closed-loop gain of the shunt-shunt feedback amplifier including the effects of R_S and R_L can now be found with the aid of Eq. (18.34). At the input port in Fig. 18.10, $\mathbf{v}_1$ and $\mathbf{i}_1$ are related by

$$\mathbf{i}_1 = \mathbf{i}_s - \mathbf{v}_1 G_S \tag{18.35}$$

and $\mathbf{v}_2$ and $\mathbf{i}_2$ at the output port are related by

$$\mathbf{i}_2 = -G_L \mathbf{v}_2 \tag{18.36}$$

Substituting Eqs. (18.35) and (18.36) into Eq. (18.34) yields

$$\mathbf{i}_s = (G_S + y_{11}^T)\mathbf{v}_1 + y_{12}^T \mathbf{v}_2$$
$$0 = y_{21}^T \mathbf{v}_1 + (y_{22}^T + G_L)\mathbf{v}_2 \tag{18.37}$$

The closed-loop transresistance can now be found from Eq. (18.37) by solving for $\mathbf{v}_2$ in terms of $\mathbf{i}_s$:

$$A_{TR} = \frac{\mathbf{v}_2}{\mathbf{i}_s} = \frac{y_{21}^F}{y_{21}^F y_{12}^A - (G_S + y_{11}^T)(y_{22}^T + G_L)} \tag{18.38}$$

Rearranging Eq. (18.38) into the standard form for a feedback amplifier gives

$$A_{TR} = \frac{\mathbf{v_2}}{\mathbf{i_s}} = \frac{\dfrac{-y_{21}^A}{(G_S + y_{11}^T)(y_{22}^T + G_L)}}{1 + \dfrac{-y_{21}^A}{(G_S + y_{11}^T)(y_{22}^T + G_L)} y_{12}^F} = \frac{A}{1 + A\beta} \qquad (18.39)$$

in which $\qquad A = \dfrac{\mathbf{v_o}}{\mathbf{i_s}} = -\dfrac{y_{21}^A}{(G_S + y_{11}^T)(y_{22}^T + G_L)} \qquad$ and $\qquad \beta = y_{12}^F \qquad (18.40)$

Figure 18.11 provides the interpretation of Eqs. (18.39) and (18.40) for the case of shunt-shunt feedback. Figure 18.11(a) shows the feedback amplifier with an explicit representation of the two-port parameters of the feedback network with $y_{21}^F = 0$. Equations (18.39) and (18.40) indicate that the gain of the amplifier A should be calculated including the effects of y_{11}^F, y_{22}^F, R_S, and R_L, and a schematic representation of these equations is given by redrawing the amplifier, as in the circuit in Fig. 18.11(b). The position of feedback circuit elements y_{11}^F and y_{22}^F has been changed, but the overall circuit is once again the same. The amplifier A-circuit now includes y_{11}^F, y_{22}^F, R_S, and R_L, whereas the feedback network consists only of y_{12}^F.

Figure 18.12 reinforces the analysis technique. The three required y-parameters of the feedback network are found based on their individual definitions. Then the transresistance of the open-loop amplifier A is calculated from the circuit in Fig. 18.12(d), which includes the loading effects of y_{11}^F, y_{22}^F, R_S, and R_L. The gain is calculated directly from

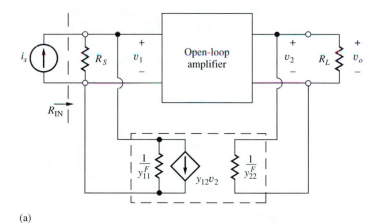

(a)

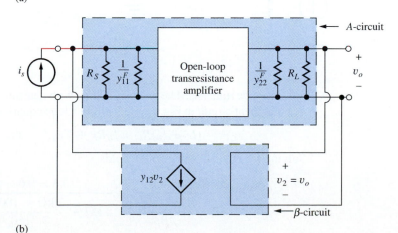

(b)

Figure 18.11 Schematic interpretation of the amplifier and feedback circuits described by Eqs. (18.39) and (18.40).

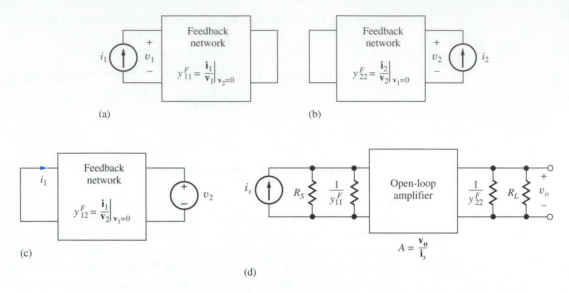

Figure 18.12 (a–c) Feedback circuits and (d) A-circuit for the shunt-shunt feedback amplifier.

the A-circuit; remember, we normally *do not* evaluate A using the mathematical two-port parameter description given in Eq. (18.40).

EXAMPLE 18.4:   Analysis of the shunt-shunt feedback amplifier in Fig. 18.13 provides an example of applying the two-port theory to a practical single-transistor amplifier. Let us find A, β, and the closed-loop transresistance A_{TR} for the shunt-shunt feedback amplifier in Fig. 18.13 assuming $\beta_F = 150$ and $V_A = 50$ V.

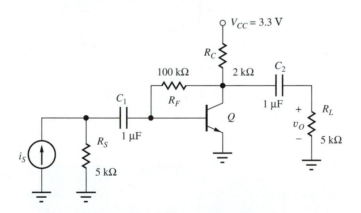

Figure 18.13 Shunt-shunt feedback amplifier.

SOLUTION: *dc Analysis.* The analysis begins with determination of the Q-point for the dc equivalent circuit in Fig. 18.14. Writing a loop equation following the dashed line,

$$V_{CC} = (I_C + I_B)R_C + I_B R_F + V_{BE} \qquad \text{and} \qquad I_C = \beta_F I_B$$

Solving for the collector current yields

$$I_C = \frac{V_{CC} - V_{BE}}{R_C + \dfrac{R_C + R_F}{\beta_F}} = \frac{3.3 - 0.6}{2\text{ k}\Omega + \dfrac{2\text{ k}\Omega + 100\text{ k}\Omega}{150}} = 1.01\text{ mA}$$

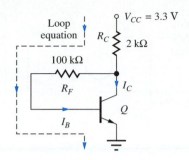

Figure 18.14 dc Equivalent circuit.

The collector-emitter voltage is

$$V_{CE} = V_{CC} - (I_C + I_B)R_C = 3.3 \text{ V} - (1.02 \text{ mA})2 \text{ k}\Omega = 1.27 \text{ V}$$

For this collector current, the small-signal parameters are

$$g_m = 40I_C = 40.3 \text{ mS} \qquad r_\pi = \frac{\beta_o}{g_m} = 3.72 \text{ k}\Omega \qquad r_o = \frac{V_A + V_{CE}}{I_C} = 50.8 \text{ k}\Omega$$

ac Analysis: The first step in the ac analysis is to make sure that the amplifier is indeed a shunt-shunt configuration. The midband ac equivalent circuit of the feedback amplifier is redrawn in Fig. 18.15, clearly identifying the two interconnected two-ports that compose the open-loop amplifier and feedback network.

The parameters y_{11}^F, y_{22}^F, and y_{12}^F are next found by applying the y-parameter definitions to the feedback network, as in the circuits of Fig. 18.16.

$$A: \quad y_{11}^F = \left.\frac{\mathbf{i_1}}{\mathbf{v_1}}\right|_{\mathbf{v_2}=0} = \frac{1}{R_F} = 10^{-5} \text{ S}$$

$$B: \quad y_{22}^F = \left.\frac{\mathbf{i_2}}{\mathbf{v_2}}\right|_{\mathbf{i_1}=0} = \frac{1}{R_F} = 10^{-5} \text{ S}$$

$$C: \quad y_{12}^F = \left.\frac{\mathbf{i_1}}{\mathbf{v_2}}\right|_{\mathbf{v_1}=0} = -\frac{1}{R_F} = -10^{-5} \text{ S}$$

The A-circuit is constructed in Fig. 18.17 by placing R_S and $[y_{11}^F]^{-1} = R_F$ in parallel with the amplifier input and R_L and $[y_{22}^F]^{-1} = R_F$ in parallel with the amplifier output. The transresistance of the augmented open-loop amplifier is then found from the figure. Applying current division at the input,

$$\mathbf{i_b} = \mathbf{i_s}\frac{4.76 \text{ k}\Omega}{4.76 \text{ k}\Omega + r_\pi} \qquad \text{and} \qquad \mathbf{v_o} = -\beta_o\mathbf{i_b}(1.41 \text{ k}\Omega)$$

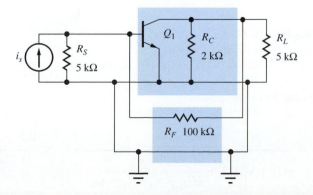

Figure 18.15 Amplifier decomposed into two-ports.

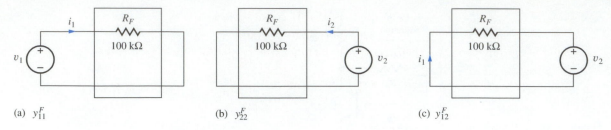

Figure 18.16 Circuits for finding the y-parameters of the feedback network.

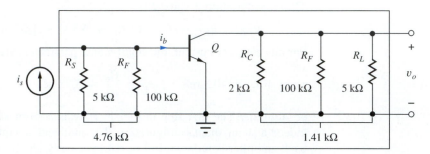

Figure 18.17 The augmented open-loop amplifier circuit (the A-circuit).

Solving for A yields

$$A = \frac{\mathbf{v_o}}{\mathbf{i_s}} = -\frac{4.76 \text{ k}\Omega}{4.76 \text{ k}\Omega + 3.72 \text{ k}\Omega}(150)1.41 \text{ k}\Omega = 119 \text{ k}\Omega$$

The feedback factor is $\beta = y_{12}^F = 10^{-5}$ S. Using these results, the closed-loop trans-resistance is

$$A_{TR} = \frac{A}{1 + A\beta} = \frac{119 \text{ k}\Omega}{1 + 119 \text{ k}\Omega(0.01 \text{ mS})} = 54.4 \text{ k}\Omega$$

Note that the loop gain is low in this case, $A\beta = 1.19$, and the transresistance of the amplifier differs significantly from the ideal value of $100 \text{ k}\Omega (A_{TR} = 1/\beta = R_F)$. ◆

Input Resistance

The input resistance R_{IN} of the closed-loop shunt-shunt feedback amplifier can be calculated for the overall amplifier in Fig. 18.11 using the two-port description in Eq. (18.37). The input resistance is

$$R_{\text{IN}} = \frac{\mathbf{v_1}}{\mathbf{i_s}} \tag{18.41}$$

Solving Eq. (18.37) for $\mathbf{i_s}$ in terms of $\mathbf{v_1}$ gives

$$\mathbf{i_s} = (G_S + y_{11}^T)\mathbf{v_1} + y_{12}^F \frac{-y_{21}^A}{(y_{22}^T + G_L)}\mathbf{v_1} \tag{18.42}$$

which can be rearranged as

$$R_{\text{IN}} = \frac{1}{(G_S + y_{11}^T)\left[1 + \dfrac{-y_{21}^A}{(G_S + y_{11}^T)(y_{22}^T + G_L)}y_{12}^F\right]} = \frac{\left(\dfrac{1}{G_S + y_{11}^T}\right)}{1 + A\beta} = \frac{R_{\text{IN}}^A}{1 + A\beta} \tag{18.43}$$

Again, we see that shunt feedback reduces the resistance at the port by the factor $(1 + A\beta)$. As the loop gain approaches infinity—for an ideal op amp, for example—the input resistance of the closed-loop transconductance amplifier approaches zero.

> **EXERCISE:** Calculate the R_{IN}^A and R_{IN} for the shunt-shunt feedback amplifier in Fig. 18.13. Use the numeric results from the example.
>
> **ANSWER:** 2.09 kΩ, 954 Ω

Output Resistance

The output resistance of the closed-loop amplifier can be calculated in a manner similar to the input resistance calculation, but using the circuit in Fig. 18.18. We start with Eq. (18.34) and apply a test source i_x to the output of the amplifier:

$$\mathbf{i_1} = y_{11}^T \mathbf{v_1} + y_{12}^F \mathbf{v_2}$$
$$\mathbf{i_2} = y_{21}^A \mathbf{v_1} + y_{22}^T \mathbf{v_2}$$

$$(18.44)$$

The voltage and current at the input port are related by

$$\mathbf{i_1} = -\mathbf{v_1} G_S \tag{18.45}$$

and at the output port,

$$\mathbf{i_2} = \mathbf{i_x} - G_L \mathbf{v_2} \tag{18.46}$$

Substituting Eqs. (18.46) and (18.45) into Eq. (18.44) gives

$$0 = (G_S + y_{11}^T)\mathbf{v_1} + y_{12}^F \mathbf{v_x}$$
$$\mathbf{i_x} = y_{21}^A \mathbf{v_1} + (y_{22}^T + G_L)\mathbf{v_x}$$

$$(18.47)$$

and solving for $\mathbf{i_x}$ in terms of $\mathbf{v_x}$ yields

$$\mathbf{i_x} = y_{21}^A \frac{-y_{12}^F}{(G_S + y_{11}^T)}\mathbf{v_x} + (y_{22}^T + G_L)\mathbf{v_x} \tag{18.48}$$

Rearranging Eq. (18.48) yields an expression for the output resistance of the overall amplifier:

$$R_{\text{OUT}} = \frac{\mathbf{v_x}}{\mathbf{i_x}} = \frac{1}{(y_{22}^T + G_L)\left[1 + \dfrac{-y_{21}^A}{(G_S + y_{11}^T)(y_{22}^T + G_L)}y_{12}^F\right]} = \frac{\dfrac{1}{(y_{22}^T + G_L)}}{1 + A\beta} = \frac{R_{\text{OUT}}^A}{1 + A\beta}$$

$$(18.49)$$

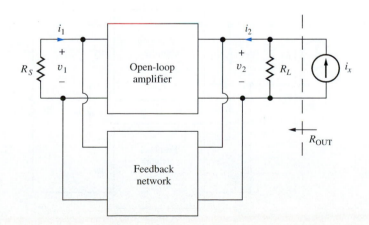

Figure 18.18 Output resistance of the shunt-shunt feedback amplifier.

The output resistance of the closed-loop amplifier is equal to the output resistance of the A-circuit decreased by the amount of feedback $(1 + A\beta)$. In the ideal case, the output resistance of the transresistance amplifier approaches zero as the loop gain approaches infinity.

EXERCISE: Calculate the R_{OUT}^A and R_{OUT} for the shunt-shunt feedback amplifier in Fig. 18.13.

ANSWERS: 1.37 kΩ, 626 Ω

18.5 CURRENT AMPLIFIERS—SHUNT-SERIES FEEDBACK

Current amplifiers are another useful category of amplifiers; we encountered the most common application of open-loop current amplifiers in the form of current mirrors. Analysis of the feedback current amplifier in Fig. 18.19 mirrors those presented in Secs. 18.3 and 18.4 and will only be summarized in this section. Based on the connections at the input and output ports, the overall input current $\mathbf{i_1}$ and output voltage $\mathbf{v_2}$ can be written as

$$\mathbf{i_1} = \mathbf{i_1^A} + \mathbf{i_1^F} \quad \text{and} \quad \mathbf{v_2} = \mathbf{v_2^A} + \mathbf{v_2^F} \tag{18.50}$$

For this case, the amplifier and feedback network are represented by their individual g-parameters. Assuming $g_{21}^A \gg g_{21}^F$ and $g_{12}^F \gg g_{12}^A$ yields

$$\mathbf{i_1} = g_{11}^T \mathbf{v_1} + g_{12}^F \mathbf{i_2}$$
$$\mathbf{v_2} = g_{21}^A \mathbf{v_1} + g_{22}^T \mathbf{i_2} \tag{18.51}$$

where

$$g_{ij}^T = g_{ij}^A + g_{ij}^F \tag{18.52}$$

Substituting $\mathbf{i_1} = \mathbf{i_s} - \mathbf{v_1} G_S$ and $\mathbf{v_2} = -\mathbf{i_2} R_L$ into Eq. (18.51) yields

$$\mathbf{i_s} = (G_S + g_{11}^T)\mathbf{v_1} + g_{12}^F \mathbf{i_2}$$
$$0 = g_{21}^A \mathbf{v_1} + (g_{22}^T + R_L)\mathbf{i_2} \tag{18.53}$$

The closed-loop current gain is found directly from Eq. (18.53):

$$A_I = \frac{\mathbf{i_2}}{\mathbf{i_s}} = \frac{g_{21}^A}{g_{21}^A g_{12}^F - (G_S + g_{11}^T)(g_{22}^T + R_L)} \tag{18.54}$$

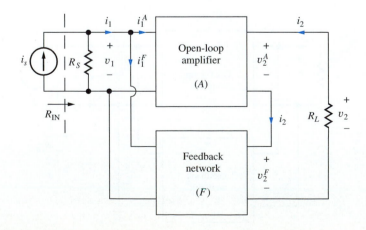

Figure 18.19 Shunt-series feedback amplifier.

Rearranging Eq. (18.54) into the standard form for a feedback amplifier gives

$$A_1 = \frac{\dfrac{-g_{21}^A}{(G_S + g_{11}^T)(g_{22}^T + R_L)}}{1 + \dfrac{-g_{21}^A}{(G_S + g_{11}^T)(g_{22}^T + R_L)}g_{12}^F} = \frac{A}{1 + A\beta} \qquad (18.55)$$

in which $\qquad A = -\dfrac{g_{21}^A}{(G_S + g_{11}^T)(g_{22}^T + R_L)} \qquad$ and $\qquad \beta = g_{12}^F \qquad (18.56)$

Figure 18.20 presents the interpretation of Eqs. (18.55) and (18.56). The forward current gain of the amplifier should be calculated using the A-circuit in Fig. 18.20(b), in which the original amplifier is augmented by absorbing g_{11}^F and g_{22}^F of the feedback network as well as R_S and R_L, and the feedback factor is simply $\beta = g_{12}^F$. Based on the g-parameter definitions, the A-circuit and three g-parameters of the feedback network are found using the circuits in Fig. 18.21.

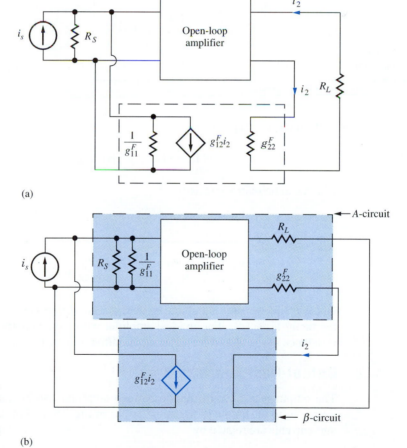

Figure 18.20 Schematic interpretation of the amplifier and feedback circuits described by Eqs. (18.55) and (18.56).

(a)

(b)

Input Resistance

The input resistance of the closed-loop shunt-series feedback amplifier can be calculated from the two-port description in Eq. (18.53) for the overall amplifier in Fig. 18.19. Solving

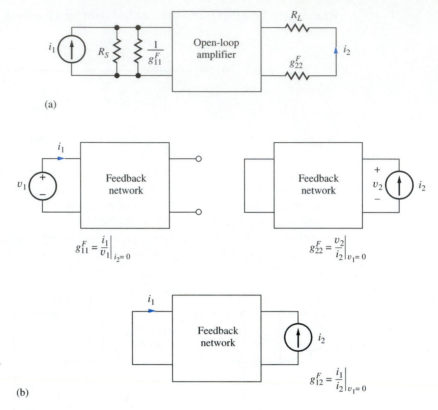

(a)

Figure 18.21 (a) *A*-circuit and (b) feedback circuits for the shunt-series feedback amplifier.

(b)

for $\mathbf{i_s}$ in terms of $\mathbf{v_1}$:

$$\mathbf{i_s} = (G_S + g_{11}^T)\mathbf{v_1} + g_{12}^F \frac{-g_{21}^A}{(g_{22}^T + R_L)}\mathbf{v_1} \tag{18.57}$$

which can be rearranged as

$$R_{\text{IN}} = \frac{\mathbf{v_1}}{\mathbf{i_s}} = \frac{1}{(G_S + g_{11}^T)\left[1 + \dfrac{-g_{21}^A}{(G_S + g_{11}^T)(g_{22}^T + R_L)}g_{12}^F\right]} = \frac{\left(\dfrac{1}{G_S + g_{11}^T}\right)}{1 + A\beta} = \frac{R_{\text{IN}}^A}{1 + A\beta} \tag{18.58}$$

Once again, we see that shunt feedback at a port reduces the resistance at the port by the factor $(1 + A\beta)$. For an ideal amplifier with loop gain approaching infinity, the input resistance of the closed-loop current amplifier approaches zero.

Output Resistance

The output resistance of the closed-loop amplifier can be calculated by applying a test source v_x to the output of the amplifier, as in Fig. 18.22. For this circuit, the port voltages and currents are related by

$$\mathbf{i_1} = -\mathbf{v_1}G_S \qquad \text{and} \qquad \mathbf{v_2} = \mathbf{v_x} - \mathbf{i_2}R_L \tag{18.59}$$

Substituting Eq. (18.59) into (18.51) gives

$$0 = (G_S + g_{11}^T)\mathbf{v_1} + g_{12}^F\mathbf{i_2}$$

$$\mathbf{v_x} = g_{21}^A\mathbf{v_1} + (g_{22}^T + R_L)\mathbf{i_2} \tag{18.60}$$

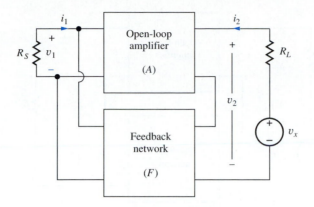

Figure 18.22 Output resistance of the shunt-series feedback amplifier.

and solving for $\mathbf{v_x}$ in terms of $\mathbf{i_2}$ yields

$$\mathbf{v_x} = g_{21}^A \frac{-g_{12}^F}{(G_S + g_{11}^T)}\mathbf{i_2} + (g_{22}^T + R_L)\mathbf{i_2} \tag{18.61}$$

Rearranging Eq. (18.61) yields an expression for the output resistance of the overall amplifier:

$$R_{\text{OUT}} = \frac{\mathbf{v_x}}{\mathbf{i_2}} = (g_{22}^T + R_L)\left[1 + \frac{-g_{21}^A}{(G_S + g_{11}^T)(g_{22}^T + R_L)}g_{12}^F\right] = (g_{22}^T + R_L)(1 + A\beta)$$

or $R_{\text{OUT}} = R_{\text{OUT}}^A(1 + A\beta)$

$$\tag{18.62}$$

The output resistance of the closed-loop amplifier is equal to the output resistance of the A-circuit increased by the feedback factor $(1 + A\beta)$. As the loop gain approaches infinity in an ideal amplifier, the output resistance of the current amplifier also approaches infinity.

Common errors occur in applying the two-port theory to transistor amplifiers, particularly in circuits that use series feedback at the output port. We delay presentation of examples until Sec. 18.7, following completion of the development of the mathematical description of the series-series feedback amplifier in Sec. 18.6.

18.6 TRANSCONDUCTANCE AMPLIFIERS —SERIES-SERIES FEEDBACK

The final configuration considered is the **transconductance amplifier,** which produces an output current proportional to the input voltage. Thus, it should have very high input resistance as well as very high output resistance. To achieve these characteristics, series feedback is utilized at both the input and output ports, as in Fig. 18.23. For this case, the input port currents are equal and the output port currents are equal for the amplifier and feedback two-ports; z-parameters are appropriate for analyzing this configuration.

For the circuit in Fig. 18.23, the overall input voltage $\mathbf{v_1}$ and output voltage $\mathbf{v_2}$ can be written as

$$\mathbf{v_1} = \mathbf{v_1^A} + \mathbf{v_1^F} \qquad \text{and} \qquad \mathbf{v_2} = \mathbf{v_2^A} + \mathbf{v_2^F} \tag{18.63}$$

and the z-parameter description of the overall circuit is

$$\mathbf{v_1} = z_{11}^T\mathbf{i_1} + z_{12}^T\mathbf{i_2}$$
$$\mathbf{v_2} = z_{21}^T\mathbf{i_1} + z_{22}^T\mathbf{i_2} \tag{18.64}$$

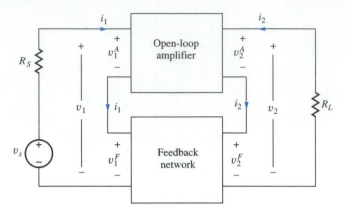

Figure 18.23 Series-series feedback amplifier (transconductance amplifier).

where
$$z_{ij}^T = z_{ij}^A + z_{ij}^F \tag{18.65}$$

Using $\mathbf{v_1} = \mathbf{v_s} - \mathbf{i_1}R_S$ and $\mathbf{v_2} = -\mathbf{i_2}R_L$, and assuming $z_{21}^A \gg z_{21}^F$ and $z_{12}^F \gg z_{12}^A$, yields the standard simplified form:

$$\mathbf{v_S} = (R_S + z_{11}^T)\mathbf{i_1} + z_{12}^T\mathbf{i_2} \tag{18.66}$$

$$0 = z_{21}^T\mathbf{i_1} + (z_{22}^T + R_L)\mathbf{i_2}$$

The closed-loop gain of the transconductance amplifier can be found from Eq. (18.66):

$$A_{TC} = \frac{\mathbf{i_2}}{\mathbf{v_s}} = \frac{\dfrac{-z_{21}^A}{(R_S + z_{11}^T)(z_{22}^T + R_L)}}{1 + \dfrac{-z_{21}^A}{(R_S + z_{11}^T)(z_{22}^T + R_L)}z_{12}^F} = \frac{A}{1 + A\beta} \tag{18.67}$$

in which
$$A = -\frac{z_{21}^A}{(R_S + z_{11}^T)(z_{22}^T + R_L)} \qquad \text{and} \qquad \beta = z_{12}^F \tag{18.68}$$

Figure 18.24 is the schematic interpretation of Eqs. (18.67) and (18.68). The forward transconductance of the amplifier should be calculated using the A-circuit in which the original amplifier is augmented by absorbing z_{11}^F and z_{22}^F of the feedback network as well as R_S and R_L, and the feedback factor is given by $\beta = z_{12}^F$.

Input and Output Resistances

The input and output resistances of the closed-loop series-series feedback amplifier can be calculated from the two-port description for the overall amplifier in a manner similar to that used to derive results in the previous three sections:

$$R_{\text{IN}} = \frac{\mathbf{v_s}}{\mathbf{i_1}} = (R_S + z_{11}^T)\left[1 + \frac{-z_{21}^A}{(R_S + z_{11}^T)(z_{22}^T + R_L)}z_{12}^F\right] \tag{18.69}$$

$$R_{\text{IN}} = (R_S + z_{11}^T)(1 + A\beta) = R_{\text{IN}}^A(1 + A\beta) \tag{18.70}$$

and

$$R_{\text{OUT}} = \frac{\mathbf{v_x}}{\mathbf{i_2}} = (z_{22}^T + R_L)\left[1 + \frac{-z_{21}^A}{(R_S + z_{11}^T)(z_{22}^T + R_L)}z_{12}^F\right] \tag{18.71}$$

$$R_{\text{OUT}} = (z_{22}^T + R_L)(1 + A\beta) = R_{\text{OUT}}^A(1 + a\beta) \tag{18.72}$$

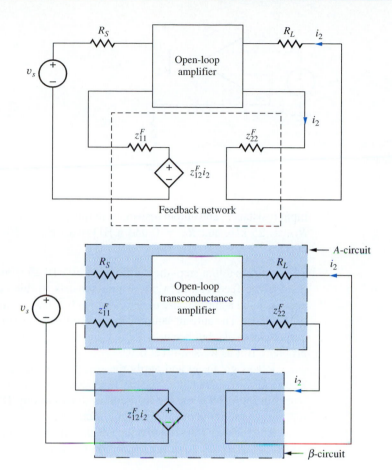

Figure 18.24 Schematic interpretation of the amplifier and feedback circuits described by Eqs. (18.67) and (18.68).

As we should expect by now, series feedback increases the impedance levels at both ports by the factor $(1 + A\beta)$. For very large loop gain, the input and output resistances of the closed-loop transconductance amplifier both approach infinity.

18.7 COMMON ERRORS IN APPLYING FEEDBACK THEORY

Great care must be exercised in applying the two-port theory to ensure that the amplifier and feedback networks can actually be represented as two-ports. This is particularly true for the case of amplifiers that appear to use series feedback at the output port. Many popular textbooks incorrectly apply the feedback theory to these amplifiers because a simple relationship seems to relate the output current to the feedback current. The best way to illustrate the problem is through an example that produces erroneous results.

EXAMPLE 18.5:   We use the basic implementation of the transconductance amplifier in Fig. 18.25 as an example of the series-series feedback configuration. Direct analysis of the circuit using ideal op-amp theory indicates that the circuit develops an output current equal to $i_O = v_{REF}/R$ with an infinite input resistance and an output resistance approaching $\beta_o r_o$ of the BJT. Let us use feedback theory to find the output current,

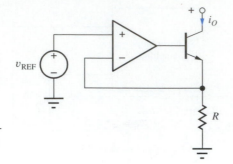

Figure 18.25 "Simple" series-series feedback amplifier ($V_{\mathrm{REF}} = 5$ V, $R = 5$ kΩ).

input resistance, and output resistance of this circuit for an op amp with $A_o = 10{,}000$, $R_{ID} = 25$ kΩ, and $R_O = 0$ and a BJT with $\beta_o = 100$, $r_\pi = 2.5$ kΩ, and $r_o = 50$ kΩ.

SOLUTION: As a first step, the amplifier in Fig. 18.25 is redrawn in Fig. 18.26 to emphasize the feedback network, which consists in this case of just resistor R. This appears to be a simple case of series-series feedback. A minor problem seems to exist, however. The current sampled by the feedback network is i_e rather than the actual output current i_o, but because $\alpha_o \approx 1$ and $i_e \approx i_o$, this does not appear to be a major problem. But as we shall see, *it is!*

Let us go ahead and apply the series-series feedback theory to the amplifier. The required z-parameters for the feedback network are found from the three networks in Fig. 18.27, and the A-circuit is shown in Fig. 18.28, including the two-port representation of the operational amplifier.

The forward transconductance of the amplifier can now be found using the A-circuit in Fig. 18.28. Assuming $R = 5$ kΩ, $V_{\mathrm{REF}} = 5$ V, $I_C = 1$ mA, and $\beta_o = 100$,

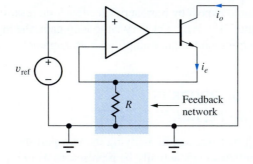

Figure 18.26 Feedback representation of circuit in Fig. 18.25.

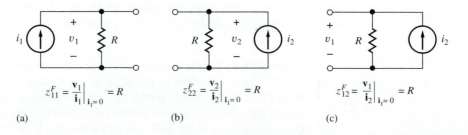

Figure 18.27 z-Parameter calculations for the feedback network.

(a) $\quad z_{11}^F = \left.\dfrac{\mathbf{v_1}}{\mathbf{i_1}}\right|_{\mathbf{i_1} = 0} = R$

(b) $\quad z_{22}^F = \left.\dfrac{\mathbf{v_2}}{\mathbf{i_2}}\right|_{\mathbf{i_1} = 0} = R$

(c) $\quad z_{12}^F = \left.\dfrac{\mathbf{v_1}}{\mathbf{i_2}}\right|_{\mathbf{i_1} = 0} = R$

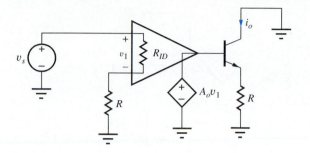

Figure 18.28 *A-circuit, including the model for the op amp.*

$$\mathbf{i_o} = \mathbf{v_s}\frac{R_{ID}}{R_{ID} + R}A_o\frac{\beta_o}{r_\pi + (\beta_o + 1)R}$$

$$A = \frac{\mathbf{i_o}}{\mathbf{v_s}} = \frac{25\text{ k}\Omega}{25\text{ k}\Omega + 5\text{ k}\Omega}10^4\frac{100}{2.5\text{ k}\Omega + (101)5\text{ k}\Omega} = 1.64\text{ S}$$

$$R_{IN}^A = R_{ID} + R = 25\text{ k}\Omega + 5\text{ k}\Omega = 30\text{ k}\Omega \tag{18.73}$$

$$R_{OUT}^A = r_o\left[1 + \frac{g_m R}{1 + \dfrac{R}{r_\pi}}\right] = 50\text{ k}\Omega\left[1 + \frac{0.04(5\text{ k}\Omega)}{1 + \dfrac{5\text{ k}\Omega}{2.5\text{ k}\Omega}}\right] = 3.38\text{ M}\Omega$$

Using these results, the closed-loop feedback amplifier predictions are

$$A_{TR} = \frac{\mathbf{i_o}}{\mathbf{v_s}} = \frac{A}{1 + A\beta} = \frac{1.64}{1 + 1.64(5000)} = \frac{1.64}{8200} = 0.200\text{ mS}$$

$$R_{IN} = R_{IN}^A(1 + A\beta) = 30\text{ k}\Omega(8200) = 246\text{ M}\Omega \tag{18.74}$$

$$R_{OUT} = R_{OUT}^A(1 + A\beta) = 3.38\text{ M}\Omega(8200) = 27.7\text{ G}\Omega$$

Now, suppose we routinely check our hand calculations with SPICE. Here we compare the SPICE results with the hand calculations in Table 18.1. The transconductance and input resistance are correct, but the output resistance is off by a factor of 5000.

Figure 18.29 illustrates the cause of this problem. We (deliberately) violated our rule of being sure to draw the circuit in two-port form before proceeding with the analysis, blindly assuming that the amplifier could be represented as a two-port network. The problem occurs because the output of the op amp is referenced to ground, and the base current of the BJT escapes from the output port (and feedback loop). This base current loss limits the output resistance of the overall circuit to approximately

Table 18.1		
Series-Series Feedback Amplifier		
	Two-Port Theory	**SPICE**
A_{TC}	0.200 mS	0.198 mS
R_{IN}	246 MΩ	249 MΩ
R_{OUT}	27.7 GΩ	6.43 MΩ—*Oops!*

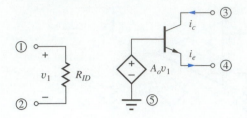

Figure 18.29 Five distinct terminals of the amplifier.

$$R_{\text{OUT}} \le \beta_o r_o = (100)50 \text{ k}\Omega = 5.00 \text{ M}\Omega^{[1]} \tag{18.75}$$

Terminals 3 and 4 do not represent valid terminals of a two-port network because the current entering terminal 3 is not equal to that exiting terminal 4. The amplifier is actually a three-port. It has five distinct terminals, not four, and cannot be reduced to a two-port.

If the output of the op-amp could somehow be referenced to the emitter of the transistor, as in the hypothetical A-circuit shown in Fig. 18.30, then the forward amplifier could be represented as a two-port. Figure 18.31 gives the new A-circuit for this hypothetical case; the new values for the A-circuit are

$$\mathbf{i_o} = \beta_o \mathbf{i_b} = \mathbf{v_s} \frac{R_{ID}}{R_{ID} + R} \frac{A_o}{r_\pi} \beta_o$$

$$A = \frac{\mathbf{i_o}}{\mathbf{v_s}} = \frac{25 \text{ k}\Omega}{25 \text{ k}\Omega + 5 \text{ k}\Omega} \frac{10^4}{2.5 \text{ k}\Omega} 100 = 333 \text{ S} \tag{18.76}$$

$$R_{\text{IN}}^A = R_{ID} + R = 30 \text{ k}\Omega$$

$$R_{\text{OUT}}^A = r_o + R = 55 \text{ k}\Omega$$

The closed-loop feedback amplifier parameters become

$$A_{TC} = \frac{\mathbf{i_o}}{\mathbf{v_s}} = \frac{A}{1 + A\beta} = \frac{333}{1 + 333(5000)} = \frac{333}{1.67 \times 10^6} = 0.2 \text{ mS}$$

$$R_{\text{IN}} = R_{\text{IN}}^A(1 + A\beta) = 30 \text{ k}\Omega(1.67 \times 10^6) = 50.1 \text{ G}\Omega \tag{18.77}$$

$$R_{\text{OUT}} = R_{\text{OUT}}^A(1 + A\beta) = 55 \text{ k}\Omega(1.67 \times 10^6) = 91.9 \text{ G}\Omega$$

[1] The actual values used by SPICE are $\beta_o r_o = 112(56.7 \text{ k}\Omega) = 6.35 \text{ M}\Omega$.

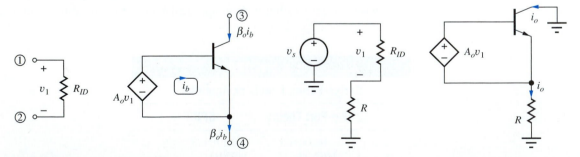

Figure 18.30 A different amplifier circuit that can be represented as a two-port.

Figure 18.31 The A-circuit using the amplifier in Fig. 18.30.

SPICE simulation of this circuit yields $A_{TC} = 0.2$ mS, $R_{IN} = 42.3$ GΩ, and $R_{OUT} = 87.3$ GΩ. We see that the theory and SPICE simulation are now in reasonable agreement.

From the results in Table 18.1, the question of why A_{TC} and R_{IN} are approximately correct naturally arises, and this is addressed in Fig. 18.32. As far as R_{IN} and A_{TC} are concerned, the amplifier can be properly represented as the series-shunt feedback amplifier in Fig. 18.32, because the collector of Q_1 can be connected directly to ground for these calculations, and a valid two-port representation exists. Thus, the A_{TC} and R_{IN} calculations are not in error. Because $i_o = \alpha_o i_e$, and $\alpha_o \approx 1$, the transconductance from input to i_e and from input to i_o have essentially the same value.

One final comment before we leave this example. If transistor Q_1 were replaced by a MOSFET, then the improperly applied feedback analysis would *appear* to work correctly. Consider the new A-circuit in Fig. 18.33. Because the current in the gate terminal is zero at dc, no current escapes through the ground terminal, and the calculations appear to be correct (although they are still actually imprecise). Although the improper two-port analysis seems to give correct answers at dc, the analysis is still incorrect at higher frequencies for which the gate current is no longer zero due to currents through C_{GS} and C_{GD}. Significant errors can also occur if the MOSFET is modeled as a four-terminal device with the substrate connected to ac ground.

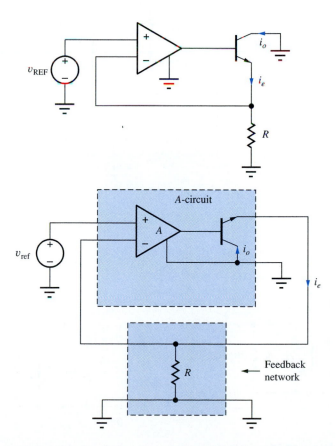

Figure 18.32 Circuit of Fig. 18.25 represented as a series-shunt feedback amplifier.

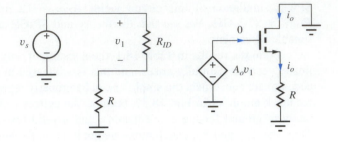

Figure 18.33 Transconductance amplifier with the BJT replaced by a MOSFET.

EXAMPLE 18.6: A popular form of transconductance amplifier is the shunt-series feedback pair in Fig. 18.34. In trying to apply our basic rule, however, we find that the amplifier cannot be drawn as a pair of two-ports in a shunt-series configuration, as indicated in Fig. 18.35. In defining the ports, we see that the currents entering the ports are not equal to those leaving the ports. The problem is even clearer in the small-signal model in Fig. 18.35(b). Transistors are inherently three-terminal devices, and the input and output ports of the device are not fully isolated from each other.

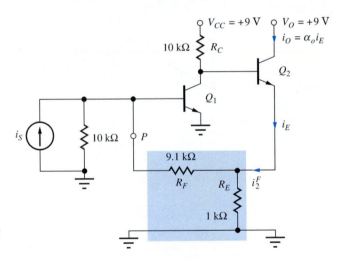

Figure 18.34 Shunt-series feedback pair using bipolar transistors.

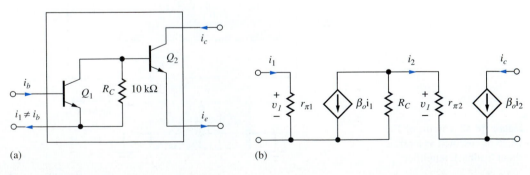

(a)

(b)

Figure 18.35 (a) Failed attempt to represent the amplifier as a two-port. (b) Small-signal model showing common terminal between input and output.

However, the shunt-series feedback pair can be properly represented as the shunt-shunt transresistance configuration in Fig. 18.36. Thus we can use the y-parameter theory to find the transresistance and input resistance, but we cannot properly calculate the output resistance of the transconductance configuration using the two-port theory when the output is defined at the collector. Therefore, let us analyze the circuit using the shunt-shunt feedback theory and compare the results to SPICE.

We assume that we have found the Q-points and use the small-signal parameters given in Table 18.2. The A-circuit for the amplifier is given in Fig. 18.37, in which $[y_{11}^F]^{-1}$ and $[y_{22}^F]^{-1}$ are placed in parallel with the input and output of the amplifier. We find the transresistance of the amplifier by finding Thévenin equivalent of the first stage, as indicated in Figs. 18.37 and 18.38. Cutting the circuit at the dashed line in Fig. 18.37 and finding the open-circuit voltage at v_1:

$$\mathbf{v_1} = -\beta_{o1}\mathbf{i_b}(r_{o1}\|R_C) \quad \text{and} \quad \mathbf{i_b} = \mathbf{i_s}\frac{R_B}{R_B + r_{\pi 1}} \tag{18.78}$$

Combining these equations and evaluating:

$$\mathbf{v_1} = -\mathbf{i_s}\frac{R_B}{R_B + r_{\pi 1}}\beta_{o1}(r_{o1}\|R_C) = -\mathbf{i_s}\frac{4.76\ \text{k}\Omega}{4.76\ \text{k}\Omega + 3.79\ \text{k}\Omega}100(8.88\ \text{k}\Omega) \tag{18.79}$$

$$\mathbf{v_1} = -4.94 \times 10^5\mathbf{i_s}$$

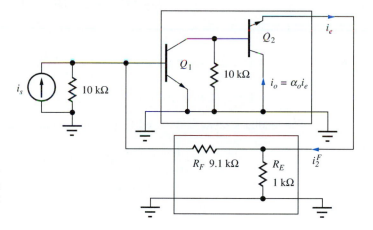

Figure 18.36 Successful representation of the circuit in Fig. 18.34 as a shunt-shunt feedback amplifier.

T a b l e 18.2		
Transistor Parameters		
$\beta_o = 100$ $V_A = 100\ \text{V}$	r_π	r_o
Q_1 (0.66 mA, 2.3 V)	3.79 kΩ	79.2 kΩ
Q_2 (1.6 mA, 7.5 V)	1.56 kΩ	35.9 kΩ

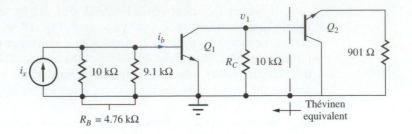

Figure 18.37 *A*-circuit for the shunt-series feedback pair.

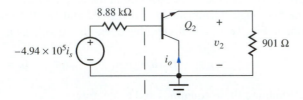

Figure 18.38 Simplified *A*-circuit using Thévenin equivalent circuit.

The Thévenin equivalent resistance is $R_{\text{th}} = 10\,\text{k}\Omega \| r_{o1} = 8.88\,\text{k}\Omega$. The output voltage v_2 in Fig. 18.38 is expressed as

$$\mathbf{v_2} = \mathbf{v_1} \frac{(\beta_{o2} + 1)(0.901\,\text{k}\Omega)}{8.88\,\text{k}\Omega + r_{\pi 2} + (\beta_{o2} + 1)(0.901\,\text{k}\Omega)} \tag{18.80}$$

and the overall transresistance of the *A*-circuit is

$$A = \frac{\mathbf{v_2}}{\mathbf{i_s}} = -4.94 \times 10^5 \frac{(101)(0.901\,\text{k}\Omega)}{8.88\,\text{k}\Omega + 1.56\,\text{k}\Omega + (101)(0.901\,\text{k}\Omega)} \tag{18.81}$$

$$A = -4.43 \times 10^5 \; \Omega$$

The feedback factor and closed-loop transresistance are

$$\beta = y_{12}^F = -\frac{1}{9100}\,\text{S} \quad \text{and} \quad (1 + A\beta) = 1 + \frac{4.43 \times 10^5}{9100} = 49.7$$

$$A_{TR} = \frac{A}{1 + A\beta} = \frac{-4.43 \times 10^5 \; \Omega}{49.7} = -8910\;\Omega \tag{18.82}$$

and the closed-loop input and output resistance are

$$R_{\text{IN}} = \frac{R_{\text{IN}}^A}{1 + A\beta} = \frac{R_B \| r_{\pi 1}}{1 + A\beta} = \frac{4.76\,\text{k}\Omega \| 3.79\,\text{k}\Omega}{49.7} = 42.5\;\Omega$$

$$R_{\text{OUT}} = \frac{R_{\text{OUT}}^A}{1 + A\beta} = \frac{901\,\Omega \left\| \dfrac{r_{\pi 2} + 8.88\,\text{k}\Omega}{\beta_{o2} + 1} \right.}{1 + A\beta} \tag{18.83}$$

$$= \frac{901\,\Omega \left\| \dfrac{1.56\,\text{k}\Omega + 8.88\,\text{k}\Omega}{101} \right.}{49.7} = 1.86\;\Omega$$

In the original circuit, the desired output was actually the collector current of Q_2. The desired closed-loop current gain A_I can be found using the preceding results with a relationship between v_2 and i_o derived from the A-circuit:

$$A_1 = \frac{i_o}{i_s} = \frac{\alpha_o i_e}{i_s} = \frac{\alpha_o \dfrac{v_2}{901}}{i_s} = \frac{\alpha_o}{901}\frac{v_2}{i_s} = \frac{\alpha_o}{901}A_{TR} \tag{18.84}$$

$$A_I = \frac{0.99}{901}(-8910) = -9.79$$

Table 18.3 compares the results of these calculations with those of SPICE and includes similar calculations based on analysis of the amplifier as a shunt-series configuration using g-parameters. We see that the g-parameter description would erroneously overestimate the output resistance of the amplifier. In addition, there is a small but perceptible discrepancy in the calculated value of the current gain A_I.

Table 18.3

Shunt-Series Feedback Pair Results

	Shunt-shunt Theory (y-parameters)	SPICE	Shunt-series Theory (g-parameters)	SPICE
A_{TR}	-8910	-8910	—	—
R_{IN}	$42.5\ \Omega$	$43.9\ \Omega$	$41.5\ \Omega$	$43.9\ \Omega$
R_{OUT}	$1.86\ \Omega$	$1.70\ \Omega$	$18.0\ \text{M}\Omega$	$3.39\ \text{M}\Omega$
A_I	9.79	—	9.90	9.81

In summary, the key to analyzing feedback amplifiers using two-port theory is to be certain before beginning the analysis that the overall network can be properly represented as a pair of two-ports. When the theory is applied properly, the results will be correct. ◆

18.8   USING FEEDBACK TO CONTROL FREQUENCY RESPONSE

In Secs. 18.3 to 18.6, we found that feedback can be used to stabilize the gain and improve the input and output resistances of an amplifier, and in Chapter 12, we found, in the discussion of operational amplifiers, that feedback can be used to trade reduced gain for increased bandwidth in low-pass amplifiers. A similar effect was noted in Sec. 17.8 in the discussion of the gain-bandwidth limitations of the inverting amplifiers. In this section, we extend the analysis to more general feedback amplifiers.

The closed-loop gain for all the feedback amplifiers in this chapter can be written as

$$A_V = \frac{A}{1+A\beta} \quad \text{or} \quad A_V(s) = \frac{A(s)}{1+A(s)\beta(s)} \tag{18.85}$$

Up to now, we have worked with the midband value of A and assumed it to be a constant. However, we can explore the frequency response of the general closed-loop feedback amplifier by substituting a frequency-dependent voltage gain expression for A into Eq. (18.85).

Suppose that amplifier A is an amplifier with cutoff frequencies of ω_H and ω_L and midband gain A_o as described by

$$A(s) = \frac{A_o \omega_H s}{(s + \omega_L)(s + \omega_H)} \tag{18.86}$$

Substituting Eq. (18.86) into Eq. (18.85) and simplifying the expression yields

$$A_V(s) = \frac{\dfrac{A_o \omega_H s}{(s + \omega_L)(s + \omega_H)}}{1 + \dfrac{A_o \omega_H s}{(s + \omega_L)(s + \omega_H)}\beta} = \frac{A_o \omega_H s}{s^2 + [\omega_L + \omega_H(1 + A_o\beta)]s + \omega_L \omega_H} \tag{18.87}$$

Assuming that $\omega_H(1 + A_o\beta) \gg \omega_L$, then dominant-root factorization (see Sec. 17.6) yields the following estimates of the upper- and lower-cutoff frequencies and bandwidth of the closed-loop feedback amplifier:

$$\omega_L^F \approx \frac{\omega_L \omega_H}{\omega_L + \omega_H(1 + A_o\beta)} \approx \frac{\omega_L}{1 + A_o\beta}$$

$$\omega_H^F \approx \omega_L + \omega_H(1 + A_o\beta) \approx \omega_H(1 + A_o\beta) \tag{18.88}$$

$$\mathrm{BW}_F = \omega_H^F - \omega_L^F \approx \omega_H(1 + A_o\beta)$$

The upper- and lower-cutoff frequencies and bandwidth of the feedback amplifier are all improved by the factor $(1 + A_o\beta)$. Using the approximations in Eq. (18.88), we find that the transfer function in Eq. (18.87) can be rewritten approximately as

$$A_V(s) \approx \frac{\dfrac{A_o}{(1 + A_o\beta)}\omega_H(1 + A_o\beta)s}{\left(s + \dfrac{\omega_L}{(1 + A_o\beta)}\right)[s + \omega_H(1 + A_o\beta)]} \tag{18.89}$$

As expected, the midband gain is stabilized at

$$A_{\mathrm{mid}} = \frac{A_o}{1 + A_o\beta} \approx \frac{1}{\beta} \tag{18.90}$$

It should once again be recognized that the gain-bandwidth product of the closed-loop amplifier remains constant:

$$\mathrm{GBW} = A_{\mathrm{mid}} \times \mathrm{BW}_F \approx \frac{A_o}{1 + A_o\beta}\omega_H(1 + A_o\beta) = A_o\omega_H \tag{18.91}$$

These results are displayed graphically in Fig. 18.39 for an amplifier with $1/\beta = 20$ dB. The open-loop amplifier has $A_o = 40$ dB, $\omega_L = 100$ rad/s, and $\omega_H = 10,000$ rad/s, whereas the closed-loop amplifier has $A_V = 19.2$ dB, $\omega_L = 9.1$ rad/s, and $\omega_H = 110,000$ rad/s.

> **EXERCISE:** An op amp has a dc gain of 100 dB and a unity-gain frequency of 10 MHz. What is the upper-cutoff frequency of the op amp itself? If the op amp is used to build a noninverting amplifier with a closed-loop gain of 60 dB, what is the bandwidth of the feedback amplifier? Write an expression for the transfer function of the op amp. Write an expression for the transfer function of the noninverting amplifier.
>
> **ANSWERS:** 100 Hz; 10 kHz; $A(s) = 2\pi \times 10^7/(s + 200\pi)$; $A(s) = 2\pi \times 10^7/(s + 2\pi \times 10^4)$

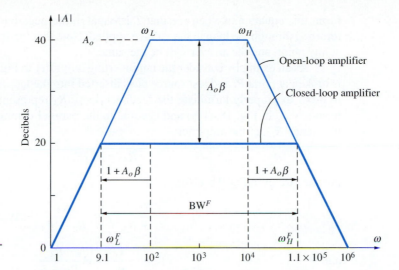

Figure 18.39 Graphical interpretation of feedback amplifier frequency response.

18.9 FINDING THE LOOP GAIN

In the previous sections, as well as in Chapter 12, we discovered the important role loop
gain in feedback amplifiers plays. In Sec. 18.10, we will find that the stability of feedback
amplifiers can be determined by analyzing the loop gain. Thus it is important to know how
to determine the loop gain directly from the circuit, not only theoretically but computation-
ally, using SPICE and actual circuit measurements.

Direct Calculation of the Loop Gain

Figure 18.40 illustrates a direct method of calculating the loop gain. The original input
source v_s in Fig. 18.1 is first set to zero. Then, the feedback loop is opened at some arbitrary
point, and a test source v_x is inserted into the loop. It is important to note that the output of
the feedback network must be properly terminated. In Fig. 18.40, the loop has been broken
at the output of the feedback network $\beta(s)$. In this case, the termination R_{IS} is equivalent
to the input resistance of the summing circuit that would be connected to the feedback
network when the loop is closed.

   The loop gain T can now be calculated from Fig. 18.40 by finding the return voltage $\mathbf{v_r}$:

$$\mathbf{v_r} = \beta \mathbf{v_o} = \beta A(0 - \mathbf{v_x}) = -A\beta \mathbf{v_x} \qquad \text{and} \qquad T = A\beta = -\frac{\mathbf{v_r}}{\mathbf{v_x}} \qquad (18.92)$$

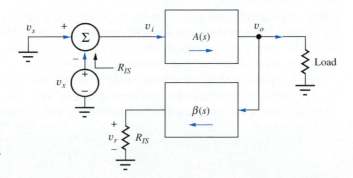

Figure 18.40 Direct calculation of the loop gain.

From this equation, we can see that T is equal to the negative of the ratio of the voltage returned through the loop to the voltage applied. Note that the feedback loop can be broken at any point, and the answer will be the same.

As an example, consider the noninverting amplifier in Fig. 18.41. The feedback loop is broken at point P, and test source v_x is inserted into the loop. Resistor R_3 must be added in order to properly terminate the feedback loop. R_3 represents the resistance presented to source v_x in Fig. 18.41(b) and is equal to the parallel combination of R_1 and the input resistance R_{ID} of the amplifier:

$$R_3 = R_1 \| R_{ID} \tag{18.93}$$

For the circuit in Fig. 18.41(b),

$$\mathbf{v_r} = \frac{R_3}{R_2 + R_3}\mathbf{v_o} = \frac{R_3}{R_2 + R_3}(-A\mathbf{v_x}) \tag{18.94}$$

and

$$T = -\frac{\mathbf{v_r}}{\mathbf{v_x}} = A\frac{R_3}{R_2 + R_3} \tag{18.95}$$

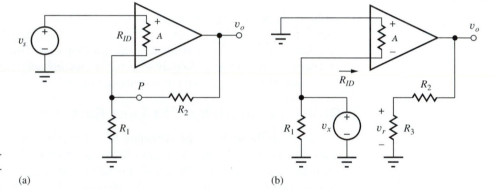

Figure 18.41 (a) Noninverting amplifier with (b) feedback loop broken at point P.

(a)   (b)

Finding the Loop Gain Using Successive Voltage and Current Injection

In many practical cases, particularly when the loop gain is large, the feedback loop cannot be opened to measure the loop gain because a closed loop is required to maintain a correct dc operating point. Another problem is electrical noise, which may cause an open-loop amplifier to saturate. A similar problem occurs in SPICE simulation of high-gain circuits such as operational amplifiers, in which the circuit amplifies the numerical noise present in the calculations, and the analysis is unable to converge to a stable operating point. Fortunately, the method of **successive voltage and current injection** [1] can be used to measure the loop gain without opening the feedback loop, even in unstable systems.

Again consider the basic feedback amplifier in Fig. 18.41. To use the voltage and current injection method, an arbitrary point P within the feedback loop is selected, and a voltage source v_x is inserted into the loop, as in Fig. 18.42(a). The two voltages v_2 and v_1 on either side of the inserted source are measured, and T_V is calculated:

$$T_V = -\frac{\mathbf{v_2}}{\mathbf{v_1}} \tag{18.96}$$

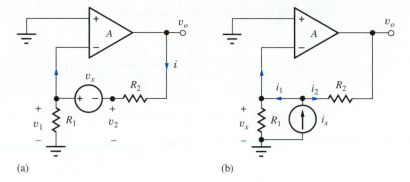

Figure 18.42 (a) Voltage injection at point P and (b) current injection at point P. $R_{ID} = \infty$.

(a)   (b)

Next, the voltage source is removed, a current i_x is injected into the same point P, and the ratio T_I of currents i_2 and i_1 is determined.

$$T_I = \frac{i_2}{i_1} \qquad (18.97)$$

These two sets of measurements yield two equations in two unknowns: the loop gain T and the resistance ratio R_2/R_1.

For the voltage injection case in Fig. 18.42(a),

$$\mathbf{v_1} = \mathbf{i}R_1 = \frac{\mathbf{v_o} + \mathbf{v_x}}{R_1 + R_2} R_1 \qquad \text{and} \qquad \mathbf{v_o} = -\mathbf{A}\mathbf{v_1} \qquad (18.98)$$

Combining these two expressions yields

$$\mathbf{v_o} = -\frac{A\beta}{1 + A\beta}\mathbf{v_x} \qquad \text{where } \beta = \frac{R_1}{R_1 + R_2} \qquad (18.99)$$

After some algebra, voltages v_1 and v_2 are found to be given by

$$\mathbf{v_1} = \beta(\mathbf{v_o} + \mathbf{v_x}) = \frac{\beta}{1 + A\beta}\mathbf{v_x} \qquad \text{and} \qquad \mathbf{v_2} = \mathbf{v_1} - \mathbf{v_x} = \frac{\beta - (1 + A\beta)}{1 + A\beta}\mathbf{v_x} \qquad (18.100)$$

and T_V is equal to

$$T_V = \frac{1 + A\beta - \beta}{\beta} \qquad (18.101)$$

We recognize the $A\beta$ product as the loop gain T, and using $1/\beta = 1 + R_2/R_1$, T_V can be rewritten as

$$T_V = T\left(1 + \frac{R_2}{R_1}\right) + \frac{R_2}{R_1} \qquad (18.102)$$

The current injection circuit in Fig. 18.42(b) provides the second equation in two unknowns. Injection of current i_x causes a voltage v_x to develop across the current generator; currents i_1 and i_2 can each be expressed in terms of this voltage:

$$\mathbf{i_1} = \frac{\mathbf{v_x}}{R_1} \qquad \text{and} \qquad \mathbf{i_2} = \frac{\mathbf{v_x} - \mathbf{v_o}}{R_2} = \mathbf{v_x}\frac{1 + A}{R_2} \qquad (18.103)$$

Taking the ratio of these two expressions yields T_I

$$T_I = \frac{\mathbf{i_2}}{\mathbf{i_1}} = \frac{\dfrac{1+A}{R_2}}{\dfrac{1}{R_1}} = (1+A)\frac{R_1}{R_2} = \frac{R_1}{R_2} + A\frac{R_1}{R_2} \qquad (18.104)$$

Multiplying the last term by β and again using $1/\beta = 1 + R_2/R_1$ yields

$$T_I = \frac{R_1}{R_2} + A\beta\frac{R_1}{R_2}\frac{1}{\beta} = \frac{R_1}{R_2} + T\left(1 + \frac{R_1}{R_2}\right) \qquad (18.105)$$

Simultaneous solution of Eqs. (18.105) and (18.102) gives the desired result:

$$T = \frac{T_V T_I - 1}{2 + T_V + T_I} \qquad \text{and} \qquad \frac{R_2}{R_1} = \frac{1 + T_V}{1 + T_I} \qquad (18.106)$$

Using this technique, we can find both the loop gain T and the resistance (or impedance) ratio at point P.

Although the resistance ratio was determined by R_2 and R_1 in the circuit in Fig. 18.42, R_2 and R_1 in the general case actually represent the two equivalent resistances that would be calculated looking to the right and left of the point P, where the loop is broken. This fact is illustrated more clearly by the SPICE analysis in Example 18.7.

EXAMPLE 18.7: Let us find the loop gain T and the resistance ratio for the shunt-series feedback pair of Fig. 18.34, using the method of successive voltage and current injection at point P. In the dc-coupled case, we can insert zero valued sources into the circuit and use the .TF function to find the sensitivity of voltages v_1 and v_2 to changes in v_x and the sensitivity of i_1 and i_2 to changes in i_x. Alternatively, v_x and i_x can be made 1-V and 1-A ac sources, and two ac analyses can be performed. This method has the advantage of finding the loop gain and impedance ratio as a function of frequency.

For this example, we use the .TF function in SPICE, and the amplifier circuit is redrawn in Fig. 18.43 with sources V_{x1}, V_{x2}, and I_x added to the circuit. V_{x2}

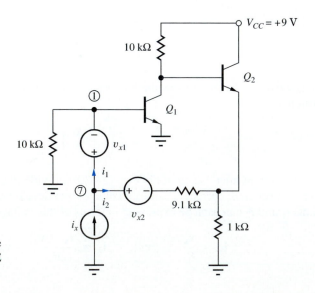

Figure 18.43 Shunt-series feedback pair with zero value sources added for SPICE analysis.

is added so that current i_2 can be determined by SPICE. The results of the four SPICE transfer function analyses (using the .TF function) are

$$\frac{V(7)}{VX1} = 0.995 \qquad \frac{V(1)}{VX1} = -4.78 \times 10^{-3}$$

$$\frac{I(VX2)}{IX} = 0.985 \qquad \frac{I(VX1)}{IX} = 0.0152$$

and the loop gain and resistance ratio calculated using these four values are

$$T_V = -\frac{0.995}{-4.78 \times 10^{-3}} = 208$$

$$T_I = \frac{0.985}{.0152} = 64.8$$

$$T = \frac{T_V T_I - 1}{2 + T_V + T_I} = \frac{208(64.8) - 1}{2 + 208 + 64.8} = 49.0$$

$$\frac{R_2}{R_1} = \frac{1 + T_V}{1 + T_I} = \frac{1 + 208}{1 + 64.8} = 3.18$$

The value of T computed by hand in Eq. (18.82) was 48.7 and compares very well to the result based on SPICE.

The two resistances R_1 and R_2 associated with the open feedback loop are identified in Fig. 18.44. Calculating these resistances and their ratio by hand gives

$$R_1 = 10 \text{ k}\Omega \| r_{\pi 1} = 10 \text{ k}\Omega \| 3.79 \text{ k}\Omega = 2.75 \text{ k}\Omega$$

$$R_2 \approx 9.1 \text{ k}\Omega + 1 \text{ k}\Omega \left\| \frac{10 \text{ k}\Omega + r_{\pi 2}}{\beta_{o2} + 1} \right. = 9.1 \text{ k}\Omega + 1 \text{ k}\Omega \| 116 \text{ }\Omega = 9200 \text{ }\Omega$$

$$\frac{R_2}{R_1} = 3.35$$

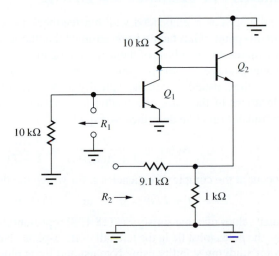

Figure 18.44 Definition of resistances R_1 and R_2.

The small difference in the resistance ratio is caused by the slightly different values of r_π and β_o calculated by SPICE and by neglecting r_{o1}. If the exact values from the simulation are used, then the calculated resistance ratio is precisely 3.18. ◆

Simplifications

Although analysis of the successive voltage and current injection method was performed using ideal sources, Middlebrook's analysis [1] shows that the technique is valid even if source resistances are included with both v_x and i_x. In addition, if point P is chosen at a position in the circuit where R_2 is zero or R_1 is infinite, then the equations can be simplified and T can be found from only one measurement. For example, if a point is found where R_1 is infinite, then Eq. (18.102) reduces to $T = T_V$. In an ideal op-amp circuit, such a point exists at the input of the op amp, as in Fig. 18.45(a).

Alternatively, if a point can be found where $R_2 = 0$, then Eq. (18.102) also reduces to $T = T_V$. In an ideal op-amp circuit, such a point exists at the output of the op amp, as in Fig. 18.45(b). A similar set of simplifications can be used for the current injection case. If $R_1 = 0$ or R_2 is infinite, then $T = T_I$.

In practice, the conditions $R_2 \gg R_1$ or $R_1 \gg R_2$ are sufficient to permit the use of the simplified expressions [2]. In the general case, where these conditions are not met, or we are not sure of the exact impedance levels, then the general method can always be applied.

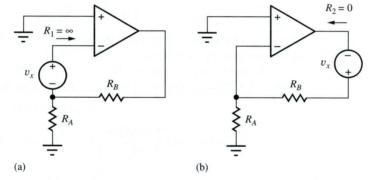

Figure 18.45 (a) Voltage injection at a point P_1, where $R_1 = \infty$ and (b) voltage injection at a point P_2, where $R_2 = 0$. (An ideal op amp is assumed.)

18.10 STABILITY OF FEEDBACK AMPLIFIERS

Whenever an amplifier is embedded within a feedback network, a question of **stability** arises. Up to this point, it has tacitly been assumed that the feedback is negative. However, as frequency increases, the phase of the loop gain changes, and it is possible for the feedback to become positive at some frequency. If the gain is also greater than or equal to 1 at this frequency, then instability occurs, typically in the form of oscillation.

The locations of the poles of a feedback amplifier can be found by analysis of the closed-loop transfer function described by Eq. (18.107):

$$A_V(s) = \frac{A(s)}{1 + A(s)\beta(s)} = \frac{A(s)}{1 + T(s)} \tag{18.107}$$

The poles occur at the complex frequencies s, for which the denominator becomes zero:

$$1 + T(s) = 0 \quad \text{or} \quad T(s) = -1 \tag{18.108}$$

The particular values of s that satisfy Eq. (18.108) represent the poles of $A_V(s)$. For amplifier stability, the poles must lie in the left half of the s-plane. Now we discuss two graphical approaches for studying stability using Nyquist and Bode plots.

The Nyquist Plot

The **Nyquist plot** is a useful graphical method for qualitatively studying the locations of the poles of a feedback amplifier. The graph represents a mapping of the right half of the

s-plane (RHP) onto the $T(s)$-plane, as in Fig. 18.46. Every value of s in the s-plane has a corresponding value of $T(s)$. The critical issue is whether any value of s in the RHP corresponds to $T(s) = -1$. However, checking every possible value of s would take a rather long time. Nyquist realized that to simplify the process, we need only plot $T(s)$ for values of s on the $j\omega$ axis:

$$T(j\omega) = A(j\omega)\beta(j\omega) = |T(j\omega)| \angle T(j\omega) \tag{18.109}$$

which represents the boundary between the RHP and LHP. $T(j\omega)$ is normally graphed using the polar coordinate form of Eq. (18.109). If the **−1 point** is enclosed by this boundary, then there must be some value of s for which $T(s) = -1$, a pole exists in the RHP, and the amplifier is not stable.[2] However, if -1 lies outside the interior of the Nyquist plot, then the poles of the closed-loop amplifier are all in the left-half plane and the amplifier is stable.

Today, we are fortunate to have computer tools such as MATLAB, which can quickly construct the Nyquist plot for us. These tools eliminate the tedious work involved in creating the graphs, so that we can concentrate on interpretation of the information. Let us consider examples of basic first-, second-, and third-order systems.

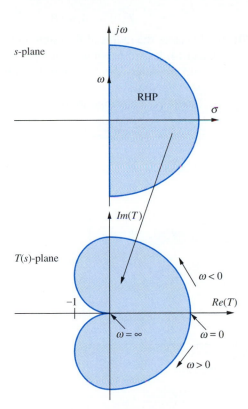

Figure 18.46 Nyquist plot as a mapping between the s-plane and the $T(s)$-plane.

First-Order System

In most of the feedback amplifiers we considered, β was a constant and $A(s)$ was the frequency-dependent part of the loop gain $T(s)$. However, the important thing is the overall behavior of $T(s)$. The simplest case of $T(s)$ is that of a basic low-pass amplifier with a

---

[2] If we mentally "walk" around the s-plane, keeping the shaded region on our right, then the corresponding region in the $T(s)$-plane will also be on our right as we "walk" in the $T(s)$-plane.

loop-gain described by

$$T(s) = \frac{A_o \omega_o}{s + \omega_o}\beta = \frac{T_o}{s + \omega_o} \tag{18.110}$$

For example, Eq. (18.110) might correspond to a single-pole operational amplifier with resistive feedback. The Nyquist plot for

$$T(j\omega) = \frac{T_o}{j\omega + 1} \tag{18.111}$$

is given in Fig. 18.47. At dc, $T(0) = T_o$, whereas for $\omega \gg 1$,

$$T(j\omega) \approx -j\frac{T_o}{\omega} \tag{18.112}$$

As frequency increases, the magnitude monotonically approaches zero, and the phase asymptotically approaches $-90°$.

From Eq. (18.110), we see that changing the feedback factor β scales the value of $T_o = T(0)$,

$$T(0) = A_o\omega_o\beta \tag{18.113}$$

but changing $T(0)$ simply scales the radius of the circle in Fig. 18.47, as indicated by the curves for $T_o = 5$, 10, and 14. It is impossible for the graph in Fig. 18.47 to ever enclose the $T = -1$ point, and the amplifier is stable regardless of the value of T_o. This is one reason why general-purpose op amps are often internally compensated to have a single-pole low-pass response. Single-pole op amps are stable for any fixed value of β.

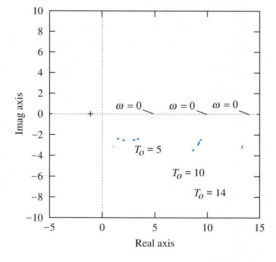

Nyquist plot for first-order $T(s)$ for $T_o = 5$, 10, and 14. (Nyquist plots are easily made using MAT-LAB. This figure is generated by three simple MATLAB statements: nyquist(14,[1 1]), nyquist(10,[1 1]), and ny-quist(5,[1 1]).)

A second-order loop-gain function can be described by

$$T(s) = \frac{A_o}{\left(1 + \dfrac{s}{\omega_1}\right)\left(1 + \dfrac{s}{\omega_2}\right)}\beta = \frac{T_o}{\left(1 + \dfrac{s}{\omega_1}\right)\left(1 + \dfrac{s}{\omega_2}\right)} \tag{18.114}$$

An example appears in Fig. 18.48 for

$$T(s) = \frac{14}{(s + 1)^2} \qquad T(j\omega) = \frac{14}{(j\omega + 1)^2} \tag{18.115}$$

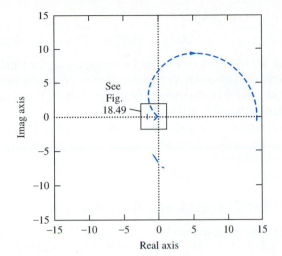

Nyquist plot for second-order $T(s)$. (Generated using MATLAB command: nyquist(14, [1 2 1]).)

In this case, T_o is 14, but at high frequencies

$$T(j\omega) \approx (-j)^2 \frac{14}{\omega^2} = -\frac{14}{\omega^2} \qquad (18.116)$$

As frequency increases, the magnitude decreases monotonically from 14 toward 0, and the phase asymptotically approaches $-180°$. Again, it is theoretically impossible for this transfer function to encircle the -1 point. However, the second-order system can come arbitrarily close to this point, as indicated in Fig. 18.49, which is a blowup of the Nyquist plot in the region near the -1 point. The larger the value of T_o, the closer the curve will come to the -1 point. The curve in Fig. 18.49 is plotted for a T_o value of only 14, whereas an actual op-amp circuit could easily have a T_o value of 1000 or more.

Although technically stable, the second-order system can have essentially zero **phase margin,** as defined in Fig. 18.50. Phase margin Φ_M represents the maximum increase in phase shift (phase lag) that can be tolerated before the system becomes unstable. Φ_M is

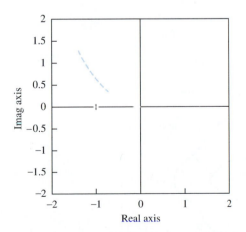

Blowup of Fig. 18.48 near the -1 point. The second-order system does not enclose the -1 point but may come arbitrarily close to doing so.

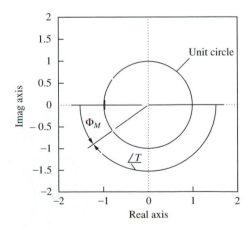

Definition of phase margin Φ_M.

defined as

$$\Phi_M = \angle T(j\omega_1) - (-180°) = 180° + \angle T(j\omega_1) \qquad \text{where } |T(j\omega_1)| = 1 \quad (18.117)$$

To find Φ_M, we first must determine the frequency ω_1 for which the magnitude of the loop gain is unity, corresponding to the intersection of the Nyquist plot with the unit circuit in Fig. 18.48, and then determine the phase shift of T at this frequency. The difference between this angle and $-180°$ is Φ_M.

Small phase margin leads to excessive peaking in the closed-loop frequency response and undesirable ringing in the step response. In addition, any rotation of the Nyquist plot due to additional phase shift (from poles that may have been neglected in the model, for example) can lead to instability.

Third-Order Systems and Gain Margin

Third-order systems described by

$$T(s) = \frac{A_o}{\left(1 + \dfrac{s}{\omega_1}\right)\left(1 + \dfrac{s}{\omega_2}\right)\left(1 + \dfrac{s}{\omega_3}\right)} \beta = \frac{T_o}{\left(1 + \dfrac{s}{\omega_1}\right)\left(1 + \dfrac{s}{\omega_2}\right)\left(1 + \dfrac{s}{\omega_3}\right)} \quad (18.118)$$

can easily have stability problems. Consider the example in Fig. 18.51, for

$$T(s) = \frac{14}{s^3 + s^2 + 3s + 2} \quad (18.119)$$

For this case, $T(0) = 7$, and at high frequencies

$$T(j\omega) \approx (-j)^3 \frac{14}{\omega^3} = +j\frac{14}{\omega^3} \quad (18.120)$$

At high frequencies, the polar plot asymptotically approaches zero along the positive imaginary axis, and the plot can enclose the critical -1 point under many circumstances. The particular case in Fig. 18.51 represents an unstable closed-loop system.

Gain margin is another important concept and is defined as the reciprocal of the magnitude of $T(j\omega)$ evaluated at the frequency for which the phase shift is 180°:

$$\text{GM} = \frac{1}{|T(j\omega_{180})|} \qquad \text{where } \angle T(j\omega_{180}) = -180° \quad (18.121)$$

Gain margin is often expressed in dB as $\text{GM}_{\text{dB}} = 20\log(\text{GM})$.

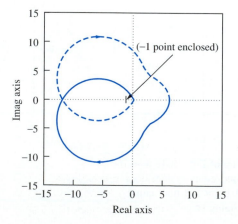

Figure 18.51 Nyquist plot for third-order $T(s)$. (Using MATLAB: nyquist(14, [1 1 3 2]).)

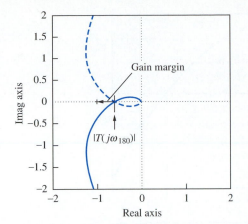

Figure 18.52 Nyquist plot showing gain margin of a third-order system. (Using MATLAB: nyquist(5, [1 3 3 1]).)

Equation (18.121) is interpreted graphically in Fig. 18.52. If the magnitude of $T(s)$ is increased by a factor equal to or exceeding the gain margin, then the closed-loop system becomes unstable, because the Nyquist plot then encloses the -1 point.

EXERCISE: Find the gain margin for the system in Fig. 18.46 described by

$$T(s) = \frac{5}{s^3 + 3s^2 + 3s + 1} = \frac{5}{(s+1)^3}$$

ANSWER: 4.08 dB

18.11 DETERMINING STABILITY FROM THE BODE PLOT

Phase and gain margin can also be determined directly from a **Bode plot** of the loop gain, as indicated in Fig. 18.53. This figure represents $A\beta$ for a third-order transfer function:

$$A\beta = \frac{2 \times 10^{19}}{(s + 10^5)(s + 10^6)(s + 10^7)} = \frac{2 \times 10^{19}}{s^3 + 11.1 \times 10^6 s^2 + 11.1 \times 10^{12} s + 10^{18}}$$

Phase margin is found by first identifying the frequency at which $|A\beta| = 1$ or 0 dB. For the case in Fig. 18.53, this frequency is approximately 1.2×10^6 rad/s. At this frequency, the phase shift is $-145°$, and the phase margin is $\Phi_M = 180° - 145° = 35°$. The amplifier can tolerate an additional phase shift of approximately $35°$ before it becomes unstable.

Gain margin is found by identifying the frequency at which the phase shift of the amplifier is exactly $180°$. In Fig. 18.53, this frequency is approximately 3.2×10^6 rad/s. The loop gain at this frequency is -17 dB, and the gain margin is therefore $+17$ dB. The gain must increase by 17 dB before the amplifier becomes unstable.

Using a tool like MATLAB, we can easily construct the Bode plot for the gain of the amplifier and use it to determine the range of closed-loop gains for which the amplifier will be stable. Stability can be determined by properly interpreting the Bode magnitude plot. We use the following mathematical approach:

$$20 \log|A\beta| = 20 \log|A| - 20 \log\left|\frac{1}{\beta}\right| \tag{18.122}$$

Rather than plotting the loop gain $A\beta$ itself, the magnitude of the open-loop gain A and the reciprocal of the feedback factor β are plotted separately. (Remember, $A_V \approx 1/\beta$.) The frequency at which these two curves intersect is the point at which $|A\beta| = 1$, and

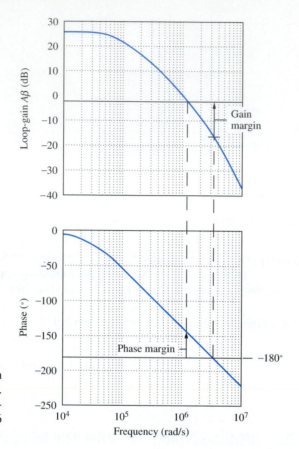

Figure 18.53 Phase and gain margin on the Bode plot. (Graph plotted using MATLAB: bode(2E19,[1 11.1E6 11.1E12 1E18]).)

the phase margin of the closed-loop amplifier can easily be determined from the phase plot.

Let us use the Bode plot in Fig. 18.54 as an example. In this case,

$$A(s) = \frac{2 \times 10^{23}}{(s + 10^5)(s + 3 \times 10^6)(s + 10^8)} \tag{18.123}$$

The asymptotes from Eq. (18.123) have also been included on the graph. For simplicity in this example, we assume that the feedback is independent of frequency (for example, a resistive voltage divider) so that $1/\beta$ is a straight line.

Three closed-loop gains are indicated. For the largest closed-loop gain, $(1/\beta) = 80$ dB, the phase margin is approximately 85°, and stability is not a problem. The second case corresponds to a closed-loop gain of 50 dB and has a phase margin of only 15°. Although stable, the amplifier operating at a closed-loop gain of 50 dB exhibits significant overshoot and "ringing" in its step response. Finally, if an attempt is made to use the amplifier as a unity gain voltage follower, the amplifier will be unstable (negative phase margin). We see that the phase margin is zero for a closed-loop gain of approximately 35 dB.

Relative stability can be inferred directly from the magnitude plot. If the graphs of A and $1/\beta$ intersect at a "rate of closure" of 20 dB/decade, then the amplifier will be stable. However, if the two curves intersect in a region of 40 dB/decade, then the closed-loop amplifier will have poor phase margin (in the best case) or be unstable (in the worst case). Finally, if the rate of closure is 60 dB or greater, the closed-loop system will be unstable. The closure rate criterion is equally applicable to frequency-dependent feedback as well.

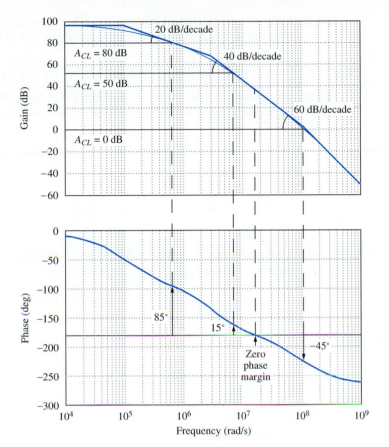

18.12 OSCILLATORS

Oscillators are an important class of feedback circuits that are used for signal generation. We saw one form of oscillator, the nonlinear multivibrator, in Chapter 12. However, that circuit is limited to relatively low frequency operation by the characteristics of the operational amplifier. In Secs. 18.13 to 18.15, we consider **sinusoidal oscillators,** which are based on linear amplifiers suitable for signal generation at frequencies up to at least 0.5 to 1 GHz.

The Barkhausen Criteria for Oscillation

The oscillator can be described by a positive (or regenerative) feedback system using the block diagram in Fig. 18.55. A frequency-selective feedback network is used, and the oscillator is designed to produce an output even though the input is zero.

For a sinusoidal oscillator, we want the poles of the closed-loop amplifier to be located at a frequency ω_o, precisely on the $j\omega$ axis. These circuits use positive feedback through

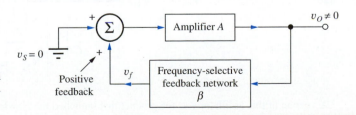

Figure 18.55 Block diagram for a positive feedback system.

the frequency-selective feedback network to ensure sustained oscillation at the frequency ω_o. Consider the feedback system in Fig. 18.55, which is described by

$$A_v(s) = \frac{A(s)}{1 - A(s)\beta(s)} = \frac{A(s)}{1 - T(s)} \tag{18.124}$$

The use of positive feedback results in the minus sign in the denominator. For sinusoidal oscillations, the denominator of Eq. (18.124) must be zero for a particular frequency ω_o on the $j\omega$ axis:

$$1 - T(j\omega_o) = 0 \qquad \text{or} \qquad T(j\omega_o) = +1 \tag{18.125}$$

The **Barkhausen criteria for oscillation** are a statement of the two conditions necessary to satisfy Eq. (18.125):

$$\begin{aligned} &1. \ \angle T(j\omega_o) = 0° \qquad \text{or even multiples of } 360°\text{---}2n\pi \text{ rad} \\ &2. \ |T(j\omega_o)| = 1 \end{aligned} \tag{18.126}$$

These two criteria state that the phase shift around the feedback loop must be zero degrees, and the magnitude of the loop gain must be unity. Unity loop gain corresponds to a truly sinusoidal oscillator. A loop gain greater than 1 causes a distorted oscillation to occur.

In the next sections we look at several RC oscillators that are useful at frequencies below a few megahertz. Following that discussion, LC and crystal oscillators, both suitable for use at much higher frequencies, are presented.

18.13 OSCILLATORS EMPLOYING FREQUENCY-SELECTIVE RC NETWORKS

RC networks can be used to provide the required frequency-selective feedback at frequencies below a few megahertz. This section introduces two RC **oscillator** circuits: the Wien-bridge oscillator and the phase-shift oscillator. Another example, the quadrature oscillator, is in Prob. 18.61.

The Wien-Bridge Oscillator

The **Wien-bridge oscillator**[3] in Fig. 18.56 uses two RC networks to form the frequency-selective feedback network. The loop gain $T(s)$ for the Wien-bridge circuit can be found by breaking the loop at point P, as redrawn in Fig. 18.57. The operational amplifier is operating as a noninverting amplifier with a gain $G = \mathbf{V_1}(s)/\mathbf{V_s}(s) = 1 + R_2/R_1$. The loop gain can be found using voltage division between $Z_1(s)$ and $Z_2(s)$:

$$\mathbf{V_o}(s) = \mathbf{V_1}(s)\frac{Z_2(s)}{Z_1(s) + Z_2(s)} \tag{18.127}$$

and
$$\mathbf{V_o}(s) = \mathbf{V_1}(s)\frac{\left[\dfrac{R\left(\dfrac{1}{sC}\right)}{R + \dfrac{1}{sC}}\right]}{\left[R + \dfrac{1}{sC}\right] + \left[\dfrac{R\left(\dfrac{1}{sC}\right)}{R + \dfrac{1}{sC}}\right]} \tag{18.128}$$

[3] A version of this oscillator was the product that launched the Hewlett-Packard Company.

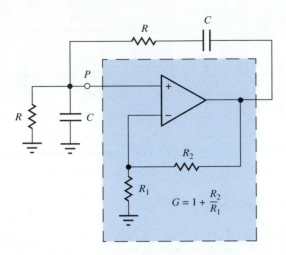

Figure 18.56 Wien-bridge oscillator circuit.

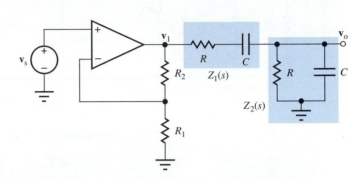

Figure 18.57 Circuit for finding the loop gain of the Wien-bridge oscillator.

Simplifying Eq. (18.128) yields the transfer function for the loop gain:

$$\mathbf{V_o}(s) = G\mathbf{V_s}(s)\frac{sRC}{s^2R^2C^2 + 3sRC + 1}$$

$$T(s) = \frac{\mathbf{V_o}(s)}{\mathbf{V_s}(s)} = \frac{sRCG}{s^2R^2C^2 + 3sRC + 1} \tag{18.129}$$

For $s = j\omega$,

$$T(j\omega) = \frac{j\omega RCG}{(1 - \omega^2 R^2 C^2) + 3jwRC} \tag{18.130}$$

Applying the first Barkhausen criterion, we see that the phase shift will be zero if $(1 - \omega_o^2 R^2 C^2) = 0$. At the frequency $\omega_o = 1/RC$,

$$T(j\omega_o) = +\frac{G}{3} \qquad \angle T(j\omega_o) = 0° \qquad |T(j\omega_o)| = \frac{G}{3} \tag{18.131}$$

At $\omega = \omega_o$, the phase shift is zero degrees. If the gain of the amplifier is set to $G = 3$, then $|T(j\omega_o)| = 1$, and sinusoidal oscillations will be achieved.

The Wien-bridge oscillator is useful up to frequencies of a few megahertz, limited primarily by the characteristics of the amplifier. In signal generator applications, capacitor values are often switched by decade values to achieve a wide range of oscillation frequencies. The resistors can be replaced with potentiometers to provide continuous frequency adjustment within a given range.

The Phase-Shift Oscillator

A second type of *RC* oscillator is the **phase-shift oscillator** depicted in Fig. 18.58. A three-section *RC* network is used to achieve a phase shift of 180°, which, added to the 180° phase shift of the inverting amplifier, results in a total phase shift of 360°.

The phase-shift oscillator has many practical implementations. One possible implementation combines a portion of the phase-shift function with an op-amp gain block, as in Fig. 18.59. The loop gain can be found by breaking the feedback loop at x–x' and calculating $\mathbf{V_o}(s)$ in terms of $\mathbf{V'_o}(s)$.

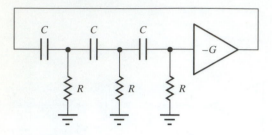

Figure 18.58 Basic concept for the phase-shift oscillator.

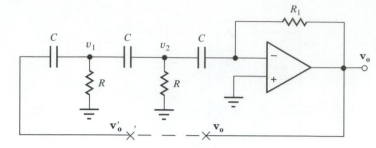

Figure 18.59 One possible realization of the phase-shift oscillator.

Writing the nodal equations for voltages $\mathbf{V_1}$ and $\mathbf{V_2}$,

$$\begin{bmatrix} sC\mathbf{V'_o}(s) \\ 0 \end{bmatrix} = \begin{bmatrix} (2sC + G) & -sC \\ -sC & (2sC + G) \end{bmatrix} \begin{bmatrix} \mathbf{V_1}(s) \\ \mathbf{V_2}(s) \end{bmatrix} \qquad (18.132)$$

and using standard op-amp theory:

$$\frac{\mathbf{V_o}(s)}{\mathbf{V_2}(s)} = -sCR_1 \qquad (18.133)$$

Combining Eqs. (18.132) and (18.133) and solving for $\mathbf{V_o}(s)$ in terms of $\mathbf{V'_o}(s)$ yields

$$T(s) = \frac{\mathbf{V_o}(s)}{\mathbf{V'_o}(s)} - \frac{s^3 C^3 R^2 R_1}{3s^2 R^2 C^2 + 4sRC + 1} \qquad (18.134)$$

and

$$T(j\omega) = -\frac{(j\omega)^3 C^3 R^2 R_1}{(1 - 3\omega^2 R^2 C^2) + j4\omega RC} = \frac{j\omega^3 C^3 R^2 R_1}{(1 - 3\omega^2 R^2 C^2) + j4\omega RC} \qquad (18.135)$$

We can see from Eq. (18.135) that the phase shift of $T(j\omega)$ will be zero if the real term in the denominator is zero:

$$1 - 3\omega_o^2 R^2 C^2 = 0 \qquad \text{or} \qquad \omega_o = \frac{1}{\sqrt{3}RC} \qquad (18.136)$$

and

$$T(j\omega_o) = +\frac{\omega_o^2 C^2 R R_1}{4} = +\frac{1}{12}\frac{R_1}{R} \qquad (18.137)$$

For $R_1 = 12R$, the second Barkhausen criterion is met.

Amplitude Stabilization in *RC* Oscillators

As power supply voltages, component values, and/or temperature change with time, the loop gain of an oscillator also changes. If the loop gain becomes too small, then the desired oscillation decays; if the loop gain is too large, waveform distortion occurs. Therefore, some form of **amplitude stabilization,** or gain control, is often used in oscillators to automatically control the loop gain and place the poles exactly on the $j\omega$ axis. Circuits will be designed so that, when power is first applied, the loop gain will be larger than the minimum needed for oscillation. As the amplitude of the oscillation grows, the gain control circuit reduces the gain to the minimum needed to sustain oscillation.

Two possible forms of amplitude stabilization are shown in Figs. 18.60 to 18.63. In the original Hewlett-Packard Wien-bridge oscillator, resistor R_1 was replaced by a

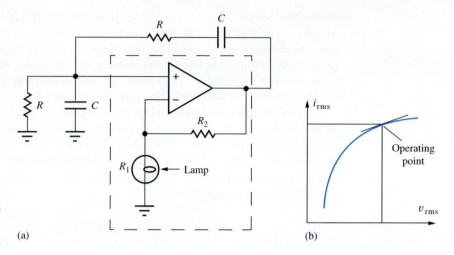

Figure 18.60 (a) Wien-bridge with amplitude stabilization. (b) Bulb *i-v* characteristic.

(a)

(b)

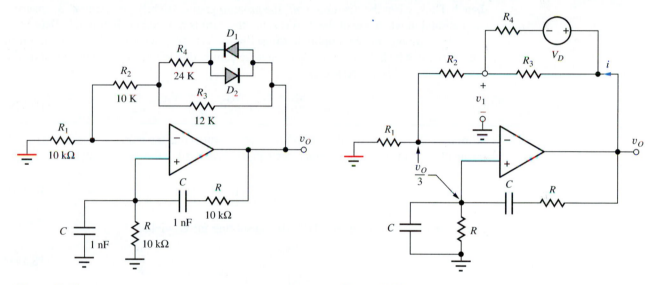

Figure 18.61 Diode amplitude stabilization of a Wien-bridge oscillator.

Figure 18.62 Equivalent circuit with diode D_1 on.

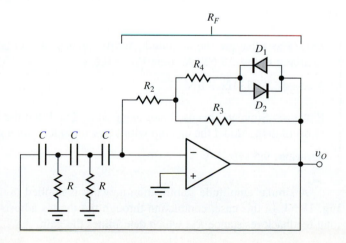

Figure 18.63 Diode amplitude stabilization of a phase-shift oscillator.

nonlinear element, the light bulb in Fig. 18.60. The small-signal resistance of the lamp is strongly dependent on the temperature of the filament of the bulb. If the amplitude is too high, the current is too large and the resistance of the lamp increases, thereby reducing the gain. If the amplitude is low, the lamp cools, the resistance decreases, and the loop gain increases. The thermal time constant of the bulb effectively averages the signal current, and the amplitude is stabilized using this clever technique.

In the Wien-bridge circuit in Fig. 18.61, diodes D_1 and D_2 and resistors R_1 to R_4 form an amplitude control network. For a positive output signal at node v_O, diode D_1 turns on as the voltage across R_3 exceeds the diode turn-on voltage. When the diode is on, resistor R_4 is switched in parallel with R_3, reducing the effective value of the loop gain. Diode D_2 functions in a similar manner on the negative peak of the signal. The values of the resistors should be chosen so that

$$\frac{R_2 + R_3}{R_1} > 2 \quad \text{and} \quad \frac{R_2 + R_3 \| R_4}{R_1} < 2 \tag{18.138}$$

The first ratio should be set to be slightly greater than 2, and the second to slightly less than 2. Thus, when the diodes are off, the op-amp gain is slightly greater than 3, ensuring oscillation, but when one of the diodes is on, the gain is reduced to slightly less than 3.

An estimate for the amplitude of oscillation can be determined from the circuit in Fig. 18.62, in which diode D_1 is assumed to be conducting with an on-voltage equal to V_D. The current i can be expressed as

$$\mathbf{i} = \frac{\mathbf{v_O} - \mathbf{v_1}}{R_3} + \frac{\mathbf{v_O} - \mathbf{v_1} - V_D}{R_4} \tag{18.139}$$

From Eq. (18.131) and ideal op-amp behavior, we know that the voltages at both the inverting and noninverting input terminals are equal to one-third of the output voltage. Therefore,

$$\mathbf{v_1} = \frac{\mathbf{v_O}}{3}\left(1 + \frac{R_2}{R_1}\right) \tag{18.140}$$

Combining Eqs. (18.139) and (18.140) and solving for $\mathbf{v_O}$ yields

$$\mathbf{v_O} = \frac{3V_D}{\left(2 - \dfrac{R_2}{R_1}\right)\left(1 + \dfrac{R_4}{R_3}\right) - \dfrac{R_4}{R_1}} \quad \text{where } \frac{R_2}{R_1} < 2 \tag{18.141}$$

Because the gain control circuit is actually a nonlinear circuit, Eq. (18.141) is only an estimate of the actual output amplitude; nevertheless, it does provide a good basis for circuit design.

> **EXERCISE:** What are the amplitude and frequency of oscillation for the Wien-bridge oscillator in Fig. 18.62? Assume $V_D = 0.6$ V.
>
> **ANSWERS:** 9.95 kHz, 3.0 V

> **EXERCISE:** Simulate this oscillator using SPICE and find the frequency and amplitude of oscillation. Model the op amp with a macromodel with a gain of 100,000.
>
> **ANSWERS:** 9.5 kHz, 3 V

A similar amplitude stabilization network is applied to the phase-shift oscillator in Fig. 18.63. In this case, conduction through the diodes adjusts the effective value of the total feedback resistance R_F, which determines the gain.

18.14 *LC* OSCILLATORS

Individual transistors are used in oscillators designed for high-frequency operation, and the frequency-selective feedback network is formed from a high-Q LC network or a quartz crystal resonant element. Two classic forms of *LC* **oscillator** are introduced here: The Colpitts oscillator uses capacitive voltage division to adjust the amount of feedback, and the Hartley oscillator employs an inductive voltage divider. Crystal oscillators are discussed in Sec. 18.15.

The Colpitts Oscillator

Figure 18.64 shows the basic **Colpitts oscillator.** A resonant circuit is formed by inductor L and the series combination of C_1 and C_2; C_1, C_2, or L can be made variable elements in order to adjust the frequency of oscillation. The dc equivalent circuit is shown in Fig. 18.64(b). The gate of the FET is maintained at dc ground through inductor L, and the Q-point can be determined using standard techniques. In the small-signal model in Fig. 18.64(c), the gate-source capacitance C_{GS} appears in parallel with C_2 and the gate-drain capacitance C_{GD} appears in parallel with the inductor.

This circuit is used to illustrate another approach to finding the conditions for oscillation. The algebra in the analysis can be simplified by defining $G = 1/(R_S \| r_o)$ and $C_3 = C_2 + C_{GS}$. Writing nodal equations for $\mathbf{V_g}(s)$ and $\mathbf{V_s}(s)$ yields

$$\begin{bmatrix} 0 \\ 0 \end{bmatrix} = \left[\begin{matrix} \left(s(C_3 + C_{GD}) + \dfrac{1}{sL} \right) & -sC_3 \\ -(sC_3 + g_m) & (s(C_1 + C_3) + g_m + G) \end{matrix} \right] \begin{bmatrix} \mathbf{V_g}(s) \\ \mathbf{V_s}(s) \end{bmatrix} \quad (18.142)$$

The determinant of this system of equations is

$$\Delta = s^2[C_1C_3 + C_{GD}(C_1 + C_3)] + s[(C_3 + C_{GD})G + GC_3] + \frac{(g_m + G)}{sL} + \frac{(C_1 + C_3)}{L} \quad (18.143)$$

Because the oscillator circuit has no external excitation, we must require $\Delta = 0$ for a nonzero output voltage to exist. For $s = j\omega$, the determinant becomes

$$\Delta = \left(\frac{(C_1 + C_3)}{L} - \omega^2[C_1C_3 + C_{GD}(C_1 + C_3)] \right)$$

$$+ j\left(\omega[(g_m + G)C_{GD} + GC_3] - \frac{(g_m + G)}{\omega L} \right) = 0 \quad (18.144)$$

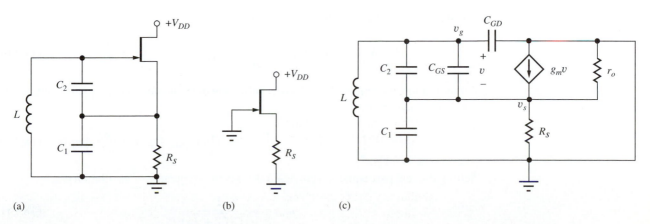

Figure 18.64 (a) Colpitts oscillator and (b) its dc and (c) small-signal models.

after collecting the real and imaginary parts. Setting the real part equal to zero defines the frequency of oscillation ω_o,

$$\omega_o = \frac{1}{\sqrt{L\left(C_{GD} + \dfrac{C_1 C_3}{C_1 + C_3}\right)}} = \frac{1}{\sqrt{LC_{TC}}} \qquad \text{where } C_{TC} = C_{GD} + \frac{C_1 C_3}{C_1 + C_3} \tag{18.145}$$

and setting the imaginary part equal to zero yields a constraint on the gain of the FET circuit:

$$\omega^2 L\left[C_{GD} + \frac{G}{(g_m + G)}C_3\right] = 1 \tag{18.146}$$

At $\omega = \omega_o$, the gain requirement expressed by Eq. (18.146) can be simplified to yield

$$g_m R = \frac{C_3}{C_1} \qquad \left(g_m R \geq \frac{C_3}{C_1}\right) \tag{18.147}$$

From Eq. (18.145), we see that the frequency of oscillation is determined by the resonant frequency of the inductor L and the total capacitance C_{TC} in parallel with the inductor. The feedback is set by the capacitance ratio and must be large enough to satisfy the condition in Eq. (18.147). A gain that satisfies the equality places the oscillator poles exactly on the $j\omega$ axis. However, normally, more gain is used to ensure oscillation, and some form of amplitude stabilization is used.

The Hartley Oscillator

Feedback in the **Hartley oscillator** circuit in Fig. 18.65 is set by the ratio of the two inductors L_1 and L_2. The dc circuit in this case, Fig. 18.65(b), is particularly simple with the Q-point equal to (I_{DSS}, V_{DD}).

The conditions for oscillation can be found in a manner similar to that used for the Colpitts oscillator. For simplicity, the gate-source and gate-drain capacitances have been neglected, and no mutual coupling appears between the inductors. Writing the nodal equations for the small-signal model in Fig. 18.65(c):

$$\begin{bmatrix} 0 \\ 0 \end{bmatrix} = \begin{bmatrix} sC + \dfrac{1}{sL_2} & -\dfrac{1}{sL_2} \\[2ex] -\left(\dfrac{1}{sL_2} + g_m\right) & \dfrac{1}{sL_1} + \dfrac{1}{sL_2} + g_m + g_o \end{bmatrix} \begin{bmatrix} \mathbf{V_g}(s) \\ \mathbf{V_s}(s) \end{bmatrix} \tag{18.148}$$

The determinant of this system of equations is

$$\Delta = sC(g_m + g_o) + \frac{g_o}{sL_2} + \frac{1}{s^2 L_1 L_2} + C\left(\frac{1}{L_1} + \frac{1}{L_2}\right) \tag{18.149}$$

For oscillation, we require $\Delta = 0$. After collecting the real and imaginary parts for $s = j\omega$, the determinant becomes

$$\Delta = \left[C\left(\frac{1}{L_1} + \frac{1}{L_2}\right) - \frac{1}{\omega^2 L_1 L_2}\right] + j\left(\omega C(g_m + g_o) - \frac{g_o}{\omega L_2}\right) = 0 \tag{18.150}$$

Setting the real part equal to zero again defines the frequency of oscillation ω_o,

$$\omega_o = \frac{1}{\sqrt{C(L_1 + L_2)}} \tag{18.151}$$

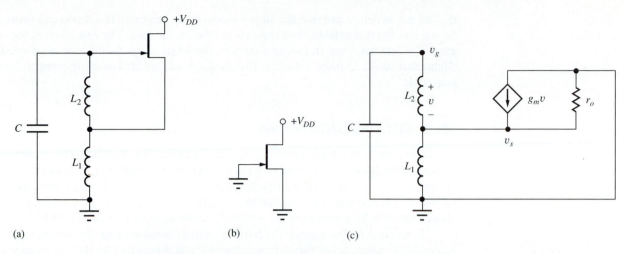

(a)   (b)   (c)

Figure 18.65 (a) Hartley oscillator using a JFET. (b) dc Equivalent circuit. (c) Small-signal model (C_{GS} and C_{GD} have been neglected for simplicity).

and setting the imaginary part equal to zero yields a constraint on the amplification factor of the FET:

$$1 + g_m r_o = \frac{1}{\omega_2 C L_2} \tag{18.152}$$

At $\omega = \omega_o$, the gain requirement expressed by Eq. (18.152) becomes

$$\mu_f = \frac{L_1}{L_2} \quad \left(\mu_f \geq \frac{L_1}{L_2} \right) \tag{18.153}$$

The frequency of oscillation is set by the resonant frequency of the capacitor and the total inductance, $L_1 + L_2$. The feedback is set by the ratio of the two inductors and must satisfy the condition in Eq. (18.153). For poles on the $j\omega$ axis, the amplification factor must be large enough to satisfy the equality. Generally, more gain is used to ensure oscillation, and some form of amplitude stabilization is used.

Amplitude Stabilization in *LC* Oscillators

The inherently nonlinear characteristics of the transistors are often used to limit amplitude. For example, the JFET gate diode can be used to form a peak detector that limits amplitude. In bipolar circuits, rectification by the base-emitter diode often performs the same function. In the MOS version of the Colpitts oscillator in Fig. 18.66, a diode and

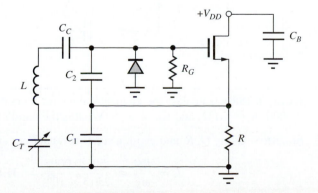

Figure 18.66 Tunable MOS-FET version of the Colpitts oscillator with a diode rectifier for amplitude limiting.

resistor are added to provide the amplitude-limiting function. The diode and resistor R_G form a rectifier that establishes a negative dc bias on the gate. The capacitors in the circuit act as the rectifier filter. In practical circuits, the onset of oscillation is accompanied by a slight shift in the Q-point values as the oscillator adjusts its operating point to limit the amplitude.

18.15 CRYSTAL OSCILLATORS

Oscillators with very high frequency accuracy and stability can be formed using quartz crystals as the frequency-determining element (**crystal oscillators**). The crystal is a piezo-electric device that vibrates in response to electrical stimulus. Although the frequency of vibration of the crystal is determined by its mechanical properties, the crystal can be modeled electrically by a very high Q ($> 10{,}000$) resonant circuit, as in Fig. 18.67.

L, C_S, and R characterize the intrinsic series resonance path through the crystal element itself, whereas the parallel capacitance C_P is dominated by the capacitance of the package containing the quartz element. The equivalent impedance of this network exhibits a series resonant frequency ω_S at which C_S resonates with L, and a parallel resonant frequency ω_P that is determined by L resonating with the series combination of C_S and C_P.

The impedance of the crystal versus frequency can easily be calculated using the circuit model in Fig. 18.67:

$$Z_C = \frac{Z_P Z_S}{Z_P + Z_S} = \frac{\dfrac{1}{sC_P}\left(sL + R + \dfrac{1}{sC_S}\right)}{\dfrac{1}{sC_P} + \left(sL + R + \dfrac{1}{sC_S}\right)} = \frac{1}{sC_P}\left(\frac{s^2 + s\dfrac{R}{L} + \dfrac{1}{LC_S}}{s^2 + s\dfrac{R}{L} + \dfrac{1}{LC_T}}\right) \quad (18.154)$$

where $C_T = \dfrac{C_S C_P}{C_S + C_P}$

Figure 18.68 is an example of the variation of crystal impedance with frequency. Below ω_S and above ω_P, the crystal appears capacitive; between ω_S and ω_P, it exhibits an inductive reactance. As can be observed in the figure, the region between ω_S and ω_P is quite narrow. If the crystal is used to replace the inductor in the Colpitts oscillator, a well-defined frequency of oscillation will exist. In most crystal oscillators, the crystal operates between the two resonant points and represents an inductive reactance, replacing the inductor in the circuit.

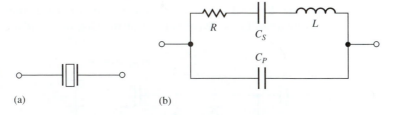

Figure 18.67 Symbol and electrical equivalent circuit for a quartz crystal.

(a)   (b)

EXAMPLE 18.8: Calculate the element values for a crystal with $f_S = 5$ MHz, $Q = 20{,}000$, $R = 50\ \Omega$, and $C_P = 5$ pF. What is the parallel resonant frequency?

SOLUTION: Using Q, R, and f_S for a series resonant circuit,

$$L = \frac{RQ}{\omega_S} = \frac{50(20{,}000)}{2\pi(5 \times 10^6)} = 31.8\text{ mH}$$

$$C_S = \frac{1}{\omega_S^2 L} = \frac{1}{(10^7\pi)^2(0.0318)} = 31.8 \text{ fF}$$

Typical values of C_P fall in the range of 5 to 20 pF. For $C_P = 5$ pF, the parallel resonant frequency will be

$$f_P = \frac{1}{2\pi\sqrt{L\dfrac{C_S C_P}{C_S + C_P}}} = \frac{1}{2\pi\sqrt{(31.8 \text{ mH})(31.6 \text{ fF})}} = 5.02 \text{ MHz}$$

whereas

$$f_S = 5.00 \text{ MHz}$$

The two resonant frequencies differ by only 0.4%. Note that the high Q of the crystal results in a relatively large effective value for L and a small value for C_S. ◆

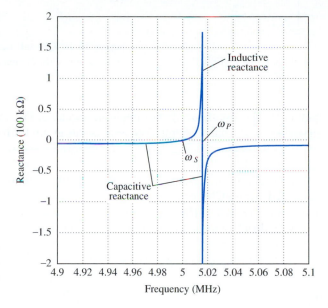

Figure 18.68 Reactance versus frequency for crystal parameters calculated in the example.

Several examples of crystal oscillators are given in Figs. 18.69 to 18.72. Many variations are possible, but most of these oscillators are topological transformations of the

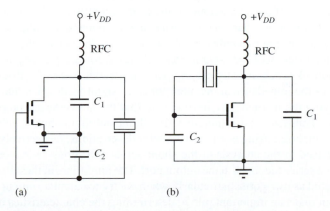

(a)   (b)

Figure 18.69 Two forms of the same Colpitts crystal oscillator.

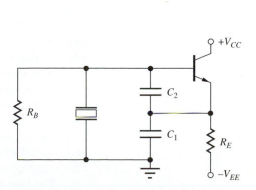

Figure 18.70 Crystal oscillator using a bipolar transistor.

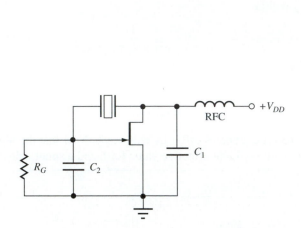

Figure 18.71 Crystal oscillator using a JFET.

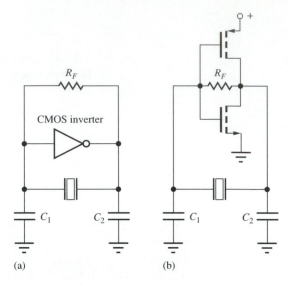

(a)   (b)

Figure 18.72 Crystal oscillator using a CMOS inverter as the gain element.

Colpitts or Hartley oscillators. For example, the circuit in Fig. 18.69(a) represents a Colpitts oscillator with the source terminal chosen as the ground reference. The same circuit is drawn in a different form in Fig. 18.69(b). Figures 18.70 and 18.71 show Colpitts oscillators using bipolar and JFET devices.

The final crystal oscillator, shown in Fig. 18.72, represents a circuit that is often implemented using a CMOS logic inverter. The circuit forms yet another Colpitts oscillator, similar to Fig. 18.69(b). The inverter is initially biased into the middle of its operating region by feedback resistor R_F to ensure that the Q-point of the gate is in a region of high gain.

SUMMARY

The characteristics of general feedback amplifiers can be expressed in terms of the two-port model parameters for the individual open-loop amplifier and feedback network. Analysis of each of the four different interconnections of the amplifier and feedback network uses a particular set of two-port parameters: series-shunt feedback uses the h-parameters; shunt-shunt feedback uses the y-parameters; shunt-series feedback uses the g-parameters; and series-series feedback uses the z-parameters. Series feedback places ports in series, whereas shunt feedback is achieved by placing ports in parallel. Series feedback at an amplifier port increases the impedance at that port, whereas shunt feedback reduces it.

Before applying the methods, we must ensure that the networks are properly represented as two-ports. Transistor realizations of series-shunt and shunt-shunt feedback amplifiers can readily be analyzed using h- and y-parameter descriptions, respectively. However, care must be exercised in the analysis of the shunt-series and series-series feedback circuits, which involve series feedback at the output port. The amplifiers in these circuits often cannot be represented as two-ports, particularly when we try to calculate output resistance.

The loop gain plays an important role in determining the characteristics of feedback amplifiers. For theoretical calculations, the loop gain may be found by breaking the feedback loop at some arbitrary point and directly calculating the voltage returned around the loop. However, the loop must be properly terminated before the loop-gain calculation is attempted. When using SPICE or making experimental measurements, it is often impossible to break the feedback loop. The method of successive voltage and current injection is a powerful method for determining the loop gain without the need for opening the feedback loop.

Whenever feedback is applied to an amplifier, stability becomes a concern. In most cases, a negative or degenerative feedback condition is desired. Stability can be determined by studying the characteristics of the loop gain $T(s) = A(s)\beta(s)$ of the feedback amplifier as a function of frequency, and stability criteria can be evaluated from either Nyquist diagrams or Bode plots. In the Nyquist case, stability requires that the plot of $T(j\omega)$ not enclose the $T = -1$ point. On the Bode plot, the asymptotes of the magnitudes of $A(j\omega)$ and $1/\beta(j\omega)$ must not intersect with a rate of closure exceeding 20 dB/decade. Phase margin and gain margin, which can be found from either the Nyquist or Bode plot, are important measures of stability.

In circuits called oscillators, feedback is actually designed to be positive or regenerative so that an output signal can be produced by the circuit without an input being present. The Barkhausen criteria for oscillation state that the phase shift around the feedback loop must be an even multiple of 360° at some frequency, and the loop gain at that frequency must be equal to 1.

Oscillators use some form of frequency-selective feedback to determine the frequency of oscillation; RC and LC networks and quartz crystals can all be used to set the frequency. The Wien-bridge and phase-shift oscillators are examples of oscillators employing RC networks to set the frequency of oscillation. Most LC oscillators are versions of either the Colpitts or Hartley oscillators. In the Colpitts oscillator, the feedback factor is set by the ratio of two capacitors; in the Hartley case, a pair of inductors determines the feedback. Crystal oscillators use a quartz crystal to replace the inductor in LC oscillators. A crystal can be modeled electrically as a very high-Q resonant circuit, and when used in an oscillator, the crystal accurately controls the frequency of oscillation.

For true sinusoidal oscillation, the poles of the oscillator must be located precisely on the $j\omega$ axis in the s-plane. Otherwise, distortion occurs. To achieve sinusoidal oscillation, some form of amplitude stabilization is normally required. Such stabilization may result simply from the inherent nonlinear characteristics of the transistors used in the circuit, or from explicitly added gain control circuitry.

Key Terms

Amplitude stabilization	Hartley oscillator	Regenerative feedback
Barkhausen criteria for oscillation	LC oscillators	Series-series feedback
Bode plot	Loop gain	Series-shunt feedback
Closed-loop bandwidth	-1 Point	Shunt connection
Closed-loop gain	Negative feedback	Shunt-series feedback
Closed-loop input resistance	Nyquist plot	Shunt-shunt feedback
Closed-loop output resistance	Open-loop amplifier	Sinusoidal oscillator
Colpitts oscillator	Open-loop gain	Stability
Crystal oscillator	Oscillator circuits	Successive voltage and current
Current amplifier	Oscillators	injection technique
Degenerative feedback	Phase margin	Transconductance amplifier
Feedback amplifier stability	Phase-shift oscillator	Transresistance amplifier
Feedback network	Positive feedback	Voltage amplifier
Gain margin (GM)	RC oscillators	Wien-bridge oscillator

References

1. R. D. Middlebrook, "Measurement of loop gain in feedback systems," *International Journal of Electronics,* vol. 38, no. 4, pp. 485–512, April 1975. Middlebrook credits a 1965 Hewlett-Packard Application Note as the original source of this technique.
2. R. C. Jaeger, S. W. Director, and A. J. Brodersen, "Computer-aided characterization of differential amplifiers," *IEEE JSSC,* vol. SC-12, pp. 83–86, February 1977.

PSPICE Simulation Data *Figure 18.25 Series-Series Feedback Amplifier
*An output resistance $RO = 100\Omega$ has been added to the op-amp model

```
VCC 5 0 10
VREF 1 0 DC 5
RID 1 2 25K
R 2 0 5K
E1 4 0 1 2 10K
RO 4 3 100
Q1 5 3 2 N1
.MODEL N1 NPN BF = 93 VA = 50
.OP
.TF I(VCC) VREF
.END
```

*Figure 18.31 Improved Series-Series Feedback Amplifier
*An output resistance $RO = 100\ \Omega$ has been added to the op-amp model

```
VCC 5 0 12
VREF 1 0 DC 5
RID 1 2 25K
R 2 0 5K
E1 4 2 1 2 10K
RO 4 3 100
Q1 5 3 2 N1
.MODEL N1 NPN BF = 93 VA = 50
.OP
.TF I(VCC) VREF
.END
```

*Figure 18.34 Shunt-Series Feedback Pair

```
*
VCC 3 0 DC 9
VO 4 0 DC 9
IS 0 1 DC 0
RB 1 0 10K
RF 1 5 9.1K
RE 5 0 1K
RC 3 2 10K
Q1 2 1 0 N1
Q2 4 2 5 N1
.MODEL N1 NPN BF = 100 VA = 50
```

```
.OP
*.TF V(5) IS
.TF I(VO) IS
.END
```

*Figure 18.43 DC Loop Gain of the Shunt-Series Feedback Pair

```
*
VCC 3 0 DC 9
VO 4 0 DC 9
VX1 7 1 DC 0
VX2 7 6 DC 0
IX 0 7 DC 0
IS 0 1 DC 0
RB 1 0 10K
RF 6 5 9.1K
RE 5 0 1K
RC 3 2 10K
Q1 2 1 0 N1
Q2 4 2 5 N1
.MODEL N1 NPN BF = 100 VA = 50
.OP
.TF V(1) VX1
*.TF V(7) VX1
*.TF I(VX1) IX
*.TF I(VX2) IX
.END
```

Problems

18.1 Classic Feedback System

18.1. (a) Calculate the sensitivity of the closed-loop gain A_V with respect to changes in open-loop gain A, $S_A^{A_V}$, using Eq. (18.4) and the definition of sensitivity originally presented in Chapter 12:

$$S_A^{A_V} = \frac{A}{A_V} \frac{\partial A_V}{\partial A}$$

(b) Use this formula to estimate the percentage change in closed-loop gain if the open-loop gain A changes by 10 percent for an amplifier with $A = 100$ dB and $\beta = 0.01$.

18.2. An amplifier's closed-loop voltage gain A_V is described by Eq. (18.4). What is the minimum value of open-loop gain needed if the gain error is to be less than 0.01 percent for a voltage follower ($A_{CL} \approx 1$ with $\beta = 1$)?

 18.3. Use SPICE to simulate and compare the transfer characteristics of the two class-B output stages in Fig. P18.3 if the op amp is described by $A_o =$

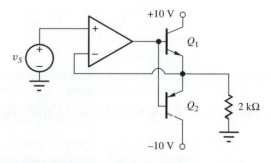

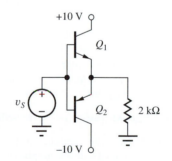

Figure P18.3

1000, $R_{ID} = 100$ kΩ, and $R_O = 100$ Ω. Assume $V_S = 0$.

18.4. An amplifier's closed-loop voltage gain is described by Eq. (18.4). What is the minimum value of open-loop gain needed if the gain error is to be less than 0.2 percent for an ideal gain of 200?

18.2 Feedback Amplifier Design Using Two-Port Network Theory

 18.5. Identify the type of negative feedback that should be used to achieve the following design goals: (a) high input resistance and high output resistance, (b) low input resistance and high output resistance, (c) low input resistance and low output resistance, (d) high input resistance and low output resistance.

18.6. Identify the type of feedback being used in the four circuits in Fig. P18.6.

 18.7. An amplifier has an open-loop voltage gain of 86 dB, $R_{ID} = 40$ kΩ, and $R_O = 1000$ Ω. The amplifier is used in a feedback configuration with a resistive feedback network. (a) What is the largest value of input resistance that can be achieved in the feedback amplifier? (b) What is the smallest value of input resistance that can be achieved? (c) What is the largest value of output resistance that can be achieved? (d) What is the smallest value of output resistance that can be achieved?

18.8. An amplifier has an open-loop voltage gain of 86 dB, $R_{ID} = 40$ kΩ, and $R_O = 1000$ Ω. The amplifier is used in a feedback configuration with a resistive feedback network. (a) What is the largest current gain that can be achieved with this feedback amplifier? (b) What is the largest transconductance that can be achieved with this feedback amplifier?

18.3 Voltage Amplifiers—Series-Shunt Feedback

*18.9. Draw the amplifier in Fig. P18.6(a) as a *series-shunt* feedback amplifier. (a) Find h_{11}^T, h_{22}^T, h_{21}^A, and h_{12}^F. (b) Calculate $A = -h_{21}^A/(R_S + h_{11}^T)(h_{22}^T + G_L)$ and β using these values. (c) Find the closed-loop gain. (d) Compare the values of h_{12}^F to h_{12}^A and the value of h_{21}^A to h_{21}^F. $R_L = 5.6$ kΩ, $R_1 = 4.3$ kΩ, $R_2 = 39$ kΩ, and $R_s = 1$ kΩ.

18.10. Use the two-port approach to find the voltage gain, input resistance, and output resistance of the feedback amplifier in Fig. P18.6(a). Assume $R_S = 1$ kΩ, $R_L = 5$ kΩ, $R_1 = 5$ kΩ, and $R_2 = 45$ kΩ.

18.11. Draw the amplifier in Fig. P18.11 as a series-shunt feedback amplifier, and use two-port

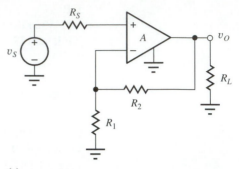

(a)

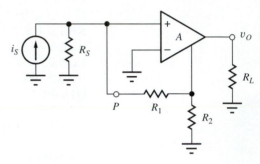

(b)

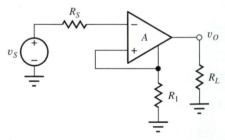

(c)

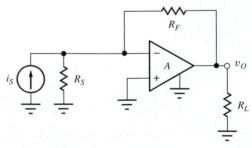

(d)

Figure P18.6 For each amplifier A: $A_o = 5000$, $R_{ID} = 15$ kΩ, $R_O = 1$ kΩ.

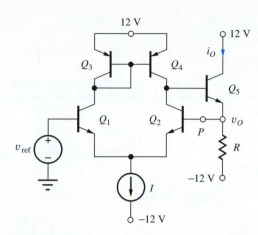

Figure P18.11

theory to find the voltage gain $A_V = v_o/v_{\text{ref}}$, input resistance, and output resistance. Use the results of these calculations to find the transconductance $A_{TC} = i_o/v_{\text{ref}}$. Assume $\beta_o = 100$, $V_A = 50$ V, $I = 200$ μA, $V_{\text{REF}} = 0$ V, and $R = 10$ kΩ.

18.12. Use the two-port approach to find the voltage gain, input resistance, and output resistance of the feedback amplifier in Fig. P18.12 if $R_1 = 1$ kΩ, $R_2 = 7.5$ kΩ, $\beta_o = 100$, $V_A = 50$ V, $I = 200$ μA, $V_{CC} = 10$ V, $A = 50$ dB, $R_{ID} = 40$ kΩ, and $R_O = 1$ kΩ.

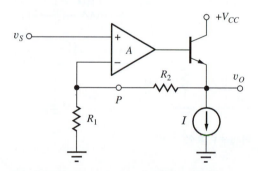

Figure P18.12

18.13. (a) Calculate the sensitivity of the closed-loop input resistance of the series-shunt feedback amplifier with respect to changes in open-loop gain A:

$$S_A^{R_{\text{IN}}} = \frac{A}{R_{\text{IN}}} \frac{\partial R_{\text{IN}}}{\partial A}$$

(b) Use this formula to estimate the percentage change in closed-loop input resistance if the open-loop gain A changes by 10 percent for an amplifier with $A = 100$ dB and $\beta = 0.01$.

18.14. (a) Calculate the sensitivity of the closed-loop output resistance of the series-shunt feedback amplifier with respect to changes in open-loop gain A:

$$S_A^{R_{\text{OUT}}} = \frac{A}{R_{\text{OUT}}} \frac{\partial R_{\text{OUT}}}{\partial A}$$

(b) Use this formula to estimate the percentage change in closed-loop output resistance if the open-loop gain A changes by 10 percent for an amplifier with $A = 100$ dB and $\beta = 0.01$.

18.4 Transresistance Amplifiers —Shunt-Shunt Feedback

18.15. Use the two-port approach to find the transresistance, input resistance, and output resistance of the feedback amplifier in Fig. P18.6(d). Assume $R_S = 100$ kΩ, $R_L = 5$ kΩ, and $R_F = 33$ kΩ.

18.16. The circuit in Fig. P18.16 is a shunt-shunt feedback amplifier. Use the two-port method to find the input resistance, output resistance, and transresistance of the amplifier if $R_S = 1$ kΩ, $R_E = 1$ kΩ, $\beta_o = 100$, $V_A = 50$ V, $R_L = 4.7$ kΩ, and $R_F = 36$ kΩ. What is the voltage gain of this amplifier? (*Note:* Represent v_s and R_s by a Norton equivalent circuit.)

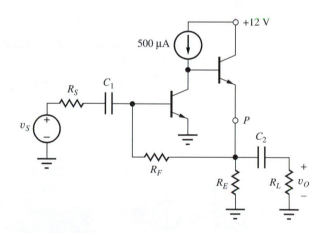

Figure P18.16

18.17. Use SPICE to find the input resistance, output resistance, and transresistance of the amplifier in Fig. P18.16 and compare the results to those in Prob. 18.16. $C_1 = 82$ μF and $C_2 = 47$ μF.

*18.18. Use two-port theory to derive an expression for the input impedance of the shunt-shunt feedback amplifier in Fig. P18.18.

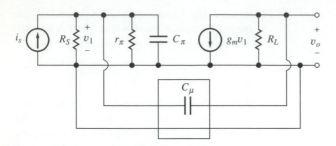

Figure P18.18

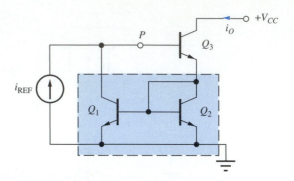

Figure P18.20

*18.19. Draw the Wilson current source in Fig. P18.19 as a shunt-shunt feedback amplifier and find the current gain i_o/i_{ref} and input resistance of the source. Use the two-port model for the current mirror. For simplicity, assume all transistors have the same W/L ratio. Assume $g_m = 2$ mS and $r_o = 36$ kΩ.

18.21. Use SPICE to simulate the Wilson BJT source with $i_{REF} = 100$ μA, $V_{CC} = 6$ V, and $V_A = 50$ V for current gains of 10^2, 10^4, and 10^6 and show that R_{OUT} goes from a limit of $\beta_o r_o/2$ to $\mu_f r_o$.

18.5 Current Amplifiers—Shunt-Series Feedback

18.22. Use two-port analysis to find the midband transresistance, input resistance, and output resistance of the amplifier in Fig. P18.22 if $g_m = 2$ mS and $r_o = 40$ kΩ.

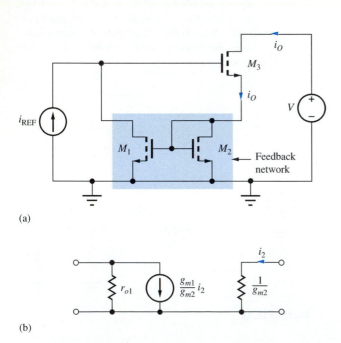

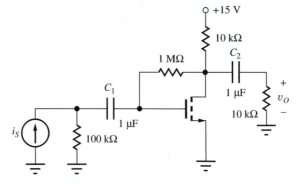

Figure P18.22

18.23. Use the two-port approach to find the current gain, input resistance, and output resistance of the feedback amplifier in Fig. P18.6(b). Assume $R_S = 100$ kΩ, $R_L = 5$ kΩ, $R_1 = 10$ kΩ, and $R_2 = 1$ kΩ.

18.24. Analyze the amplifier in Prob. 18.16 as a shunt-series feedback amplifier.

18.6 Transconductance Amplifiers—Series-Series Feedback

18.25. (a) Draw the emitter follower as a *series-series* feedback amplifier. (b) Draw the A-circuit and β-network. (c) Use these circuits to find ex-

Figure P18.19

*18.20. Draw the Wilson current source in Fig. P18.20 as a shunt-shunt feedback amplifier and find the current gain i_o/i_{ref} and input resistance of the source. Use the two-port model, Fig. P18.19(b), for the current mirror. For simplicity, assume all transistors have the same emitter area with $\beta_o = 100$, $V_A = 50$, $g_m = 50$ mS, and $V_{CC} \ll V_A$.

pressions for the voltage gain and input resistance of the amplifier.

18.26. Use the two-port approach to find the voltage gain, input resistance, and output resistance of the feedback amplifier in Fig. P18.6(c). Assume $R_S = 2\ \text{k}\Omega$, $R_L = 5\ \text{k}\Omega$, and $R_1 = 5\ \text{k}\Omega$.

*18.27. In Chapter 15, the gain of the bipolar inverting amplifier was expressed as

$$A_V = -\frac{\beta_o R_L}{R_S + r_\pi + (\beta_o + 1)R_E}$$

(a) Show that this expression can be written as

$$A_V = \left(\frac{A}{1 + A\beta}\right)R_L$$

What are the expressions for A and β? (b) Show that the amplifier can be represented as a series-series connection of two-ports.

18.7 Common Errors in Applying Feedback Theory

18.28. Draw the Wilson current source in Fig. P18.20 as a shunt-series feedback amplifier and find the current gain, input resistance, and *incorrect value* of the output resistance of the source. Use the two-port model for the current mirror.

18.29. Draw the small-signal model for the "series-series feedback triple" in Fig. P18.29 and show that it cannot be drawn as a series-series feedback amplifier for two-port analysis.

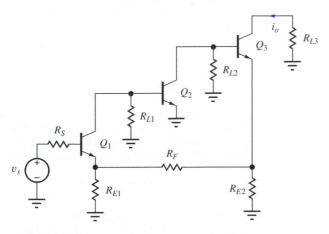

Figure P18.29

18.8 Using Feedback to Control Frequency Response

18.30. (a) Find f_H and f_L for the A-circuit for the shunt-shunt feedback circuit in Fig. P18.22 if $g_m =$

2 mS, $r_o = 25\ \text{k}\Omega$, $C_{GD} = 3$ pF, and $C_{GS} = 10$ pF. (b) What are the closed-loop values of f_H and f_L?

18.31. (a) Calculate the sensitivity of the closed-loop bandwidth of a low-pass amplifier with respect to changes in open-loop gain A_o:

$$S_{A_o}^{\omega_H^F} = \frac{A}{\omega_H^F}\frac{\partial \omega_H^F}{\partial A_o}$$

(b) Use this formula to estimate the percentage change in closed-loop bandwidth if the open-loop gain A_o changes by 10 percent for an amplifier with $A = 100$ dB and $\beta = 0.01$.

18.32. The voltage gain of an amplifier is described by

$$A(s) = \frac{2 \times 10^{14}\pi^2}{(s + 2\pi \times 10^3)(s + 2\pi \times 10^5)}$$

(a) What are the open-loop gain and upper- and lower-cutoff frequencies of this amplifier? (b) If this amplifier is used in a feedback amplifier with a closed-loop gain of 100, what are the upper- and lower-cutoff frequencies of the closed-loop amplifier?

18.33. (a) Find f_H, and f_L for the A-circuit for the BJT shunt-shunt feedback example in Fig. 18.13 if $f_T = 500$ MHz, $r_x = 0$, and $C_\mu = 0.75$ pF. (b) What are the closed-loop values of f_H and f_L?

18.34. Find f_H for the A-circuit for the series-shunt feedback amplifier in Example 18.1 and Fig. 18.6 if the amplifier has $f_T = 10$ MHz. What is the closed-loop value of f_H? (*Hint:* Include the frequency dependence in the controlled voltage source.)

18.9 Finding the Loop Gain
Direct Calculation

18.35. Break the feedback loop of the amplifier in Fig. P18.11 at point P and calculate the loop gain. Assume $\beta_o = 100$, $V_A = 50$ V, $I = 200\ \mu\text{A}$, $V_{\text{REF}} = 0$ V, and $R = 10\ \text{k}\Omega$.

*18.36. Break the feedback loop of the amplifier in Fig. P18.12 at point P and calculate the loop gain. Assume $R_1 = 1\ \text{k}\Omega$, $R_2 = 7.5\ \text{k}\Omega$, $\beta_o = 100$, $V_A = 50$ V, $I = 200\ \mu\text{A}$, $V_{CC} = 10$ V, $A_o = 50$ dB, $R_{ID} = 40\ \text{k}\Omega$, and $R_O = 1\ \text{k}\Omega$.

18.37. Break the feedback loop of the amplifier in Fig. P18.16 at point P and calculate the loop gain. Assume $R_S = 1\ \text{k}\Omega$, $R_E = 1\ \text{k}\Omega$, $\beta_o = 100$, $V_A = 50$ V, $R_L = 4.7\ \text{k}\Omega$, and $R_F = 36\ \text{k}\Omega$.

18.38. Break the feedback loop of the Wilson current source in Fig. P18.20 at point P and calculate the loop gain (current gain). Use the two-port model, Fig. P18.19(b), for the current mirror. Assume all transistors have the same emitter area with $\beta_o = 100$, $V_A = 50$, and $g_m = 50$ mS.

*18.39. Break the feedback loop at point P in the active low-pass filter in Fig. P18.39 and write an expression for the loop gain of the circuit.

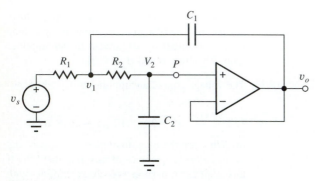

Figure P18.39

18.40. Break the feedback loop at point P in the active high-pass filter in Fig. P18.40 and write an expression for the loop gain of the circuit.

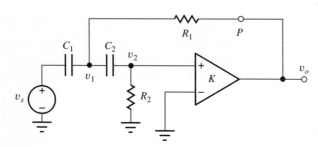

Figure P18.40

Voltage and Current Injection

 18.41. Use the successive voltage and current injection technique at point P with SPICE to calculate the loop gain of the amplifier in Fig. P18.11. Assume $\beta_o = 100$, $V_A = 50$ V, $I = 200$ μA, $V_{\text{REF}} = 0$ V, and $R = 10$ kΩ.

 18.42. Use the successive voltage and current injection technique at point P with SPICE to calculate the loop gain of the amplifier in Fig. P18.12. Assume $R_1 = 1$ kΩ, $R_2 = 7.5$ kΩ, $\beta_o = 100$, $V_A = 50$ V, $I = 200$ μA, $V_{CC} = 10$ V, $A_o = 50$ dB, $R_{ID} = 40$ kΩ, and $R_O = 1$ kΩ.

 18.43. Use the successive voltage and current injection technique at point P with SPICE to calculate the loop gain of the amplifier in Fig. P18.12. Assume $R_1 = 40$ kΩ, $R_2 = 300$ kΩ, $\beta_o = 100$, $V_A = 50$ V, $I = 200$ μA, $V_{CC} = 10$ V, $A_{vo} = 50$ dB, $R_{ID} = 40$ kΩ, and $R_O = 1$ kΩ.

18.44. Use the successive voltage and current injection technique at point P with SPICE to calculate the loop gain of the amplifier in Fig. P18.6(b). Assume $R_S = 1$ kΩ, $R_2 = 1$ kΩ, $R_L = 4.7$ kΩ, and $R_1 = 36$ kΩ.

18.45. Use the successive voltage and current injection technique at point P with SPICE to calculate the loop gain of the Wilson current source in Fig. P18.20. Assume all transistors have the same emitter area with $\beta_o = 100$, $V_A = 50$ V, $i_{\text{REF}} = 100$ μA, and $V_{CC} = 6$ V.

18.46. Use voltage injection at point P in Fig. P18.40 with SPICE to find the loop gain versus frequency for frequencies from 1 Hz to 1 MHz. Assume $C_1 = C_2 = 0.005$ μF, $R_1 = R_2 = 2$ kΩ, and the amplifier can be modeled by the transfer function

$$K(s) = \frac{10^7}{(s + 5 \times 10^6)}$$

18.10 to 18.11 Stability of Feedback Amplifiers/ Determining Stability from the Bode Plot

18.47. The voltage gain of an amplifier is described by

$$A(s) = \frac{4 \times 10^{19} \pi^3}{(s + 2\pi \times 10^4)(s + 2\pi \times 10^5)^2}$$

(a) If resistive feedback is used, find the frequency at which the loop gain will have a phase shift of 180°. (b) At what value of closed-loop gain will the amplifier break into oscillation? (c) Is the amplifier stable for larger or smaller values of closed-loop gain?

*18.48. What is the maximum load capacitance C_L that can be connected to the output of the voltage follower in Fig. P18.48 if the phase margin of the

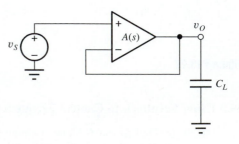

Figure P18.48

amplifier is to be 60°? Assume that the amplifier voltage gain is described by the following transfer function, and that it has an output resistance of $R_o = 500 \ \Omega$:

$$A(s) = \frac{10^7}{(s + 50)}$$

18.49. The voltage gain of an amplifier is described by

$$A(s) = \frac{2 \times 10^{14} \pi^2}{(s + 2\pi \times 10^3)(s + 2\pi \times 10^5)}$$

(a) Will this amplifier be stable for a closed-loop gain of 5? (b) If so, what is the phase margin?

18.50. (a) Use MATLAB to make a Bode plot for the amplifier in Prob. 18.49 for a closed-loop gain of 5. Is the amplifier stable? What is the phase margin? (b) Repeat for the unity-gain case.

18.51. Find the loop gain for an integrator that uses a single-pole op amp with $A_o = 100$ dB and $f_T = 1$ MHz. Assume the integrator feedback elements are $R = 100 \ \text{k}\Omega$ and $C = 0.01 \ \mu\text{F}$. What is the phase margin of the integrator?

*18.52. Find the closed-loop transfer function of an integrator that uses a two-pole op amp with $A_o = 100$ dB, $f_{p1} = 1$ kHz, and $f_{p2} = 100$ kHz. Assume the integrator feedback elements are $R = 100 \ \text{k}\Omega$ and $C = 0.01 \ \mu\text{F}$. What is the phase margin of the integrator?

*18.53. (a) Write an expression for the loop gain $T(s)$ of the amplifier in Fig. P18.53 if $R_1 = 1 \ \text{k}\Omega$, $R_2 = 20 \ \text{k}\Omega$, $C_C = 0$, and the op-amp transfer function is

$$A(s) = \frac{2 \times 10^{11} \pi^2}{(s + 2\pi \times 10^2)(s + 2\pi \times 10^4)}$$

(b) Use MATLAB to make a Bode plot of $T(s)$. What is the phase margin of this circuit? (c)

Can compensation capacitor C_C be added to achieve a phase margin of 45°? If so, what is the value of C_C?

18.54. (a) Use MATLAB to make a Bode plot for the amplifier in Prob. 18.47. Find the frequency for which the phase shift is 180°. (b) At what value of closed-loop gain will the amplifier break into oscillation?

18.55. Use MATLAB to make a Bode plot for the amplifier in Prob. 18.53 for a closed-loop gain of 100. Is the amplifier stable? What is the phase margin?

18.56. Use MATLAB to make a Bode plot for the loop gain of the active low-pass filter in Fig. P18.39 if the op amp can be modeled as a single-pole amplifier with $A_o = 100$ dB and $f_T = 1$ MHz. Assume $C_1 = 0.05 \ \mu\text{F}$, $C_2 = 0.01 \ \mu\text{F}$, and $R_1 = R_2 = 2 \ \text{k}\Omega$. What is the phase margin of this circuit? What is the gain margin?

18.57. Use MATLAB to make a Bode plot for the loop gain of the active high-pass filter in Fig. P18.40 if the amplifier is modeled by $K(s)$ in Prob. 18.46. Assume $C_1 = C_2 = 0.005 \ \mu\text{F}$, $R_1 = R_2 = 2 \ \text{k}\Omega$. What is the phase margin of this circuit? What is the gain margin?

18.58. Use MATLAB to make a Bode plot for the integrator in Prob. 18.51. What is the phase margin of the integrator?

*18.59. Use MATLAB to make a Bode plot for the integrator in Prob. 18.52. What is the phase margin of the integrator?

18.60. The noninverting amplifier in Fig. P18.60 has $R_1 = 47 \ \text{k}\Omega$, $R_2 = 390 \ \text{k}\Omega$, and $C_S = 45$ pF. What is the phase margin of the amplifier if amplifier voltage gain is described by the following transfer function:

$$A(s) = \frac{10^7}{(s + 50)}$$

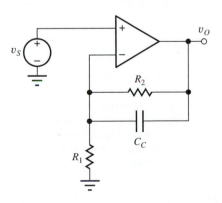

Figure P18.53

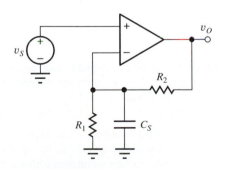

Figure P18.60

18.13 Oscillators Employing Frequency-Selective *RC* Networks

18.61. The circuit in Fig. P18.61 is called a quadrature oscillator. Derive an expression for its frequency of oscillation. What is the value of R_F required for sinusoidal oscillation?

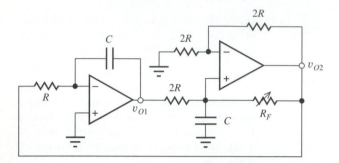

Figure P18.61

18.62. Derive an expression for the frequency of oscillation of the three-stage phase-shift oscillator in Fig. P18.62. What is the ratio R_2/R_1 required for oscillation?

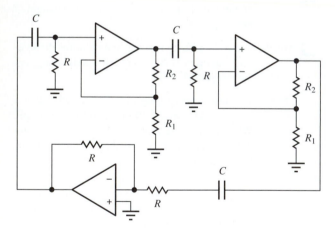

Figure P18.62

18.63. Calculate the frequency and amplitude of oscillation of the Wien-bridge oscillator in Fig. 18.61 if $R = 5$ kΩ, $C = 500$ pF, $R_1 = 10$ kΩ, $R_2 = 15$ kΩ, $R_3 = 6.2$ kΩ, and $R_4 = 10$ kΩ.

 18.64. Use SPICE transient simulation to find the frequency and amplitude of the oscillator in Prob. 18.63. Start the simulation with a 1-V initial condition on the grounded capacitor C.

18.65. Calculate the frequency and amplitude of oscillation of the phase-shift oscillator in Fig. 18.63 if $R = 5$ kΩ, $C = 1000$ pF, $R_2 = 47$ kΩ, $R_3 = 15$ kΩ, and $R_4 = 68$ kΩ.

 18.66. Use SPICE transient simulation to find the frequency and amplitude of the oscillator in Prob. 18.65. Start the simulation with a 1-V initial condition on the capacitor connected to the inverting input of the amplifier.

18.14 *LC* Oscillators

Colpitts Oscillators

**18.67. The ac equivalent circuit for a Colpitts oscillator is given in Fig. P18.67. (a) What is the frequency of oscillation if $g_m = 10$ mS, $\beta_o = 100$, $R_E = 1$ kΩ, $L = 5$ μH, $C_1 = 20$ pF, $C_2 = 100$ pF, $C_4 = 0.01$ μF, and $C_3 = $ infinity? Assume that the capacitances of the transistor can be neglected (see Prob. 18.68). (b) A variable capacitor C_3 is added to the circuit and has a range of 5–50 pF. What range of frequencies of oscillation can be achieved? (c) What is the minimum transconductance needed to ensure oscillation in part (a)? What is the minimum collector current required in the transistor?

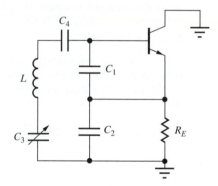

Figure P18.67

18.68. The ac equivalent circuit for a Colpitts oscillator is given in Fig. P18.67. (a) What is the frequency of oscillation if $L = 20$ μH, $C_1 = 20$ pF, $C_2 = 100$ pF, $C_3 = $ infinity, $C_4 = 0.01$ μF, $f_T = 500$ MHz, $r_\pi = \infty$, $V_A = 50$ V, $r_x = 0$, $R_E = 1$ kΩ, $C_\mu = 3$ pF, and the transistor is operating at a Q-point of (5 mA, 5 V)? (b) What is the frequency of oscillation if the Q-point current is doubled?

18.69. Design a Colpitts oscillator for operation at a frequency of 20 MHz using the circuit in Fig. 18.64(a). Assume $L = 3 \,\mu H$, $I_{DSS} = 10$ mA, and $V_P = -4$ V. Ignore the device capacitances.

18.70. What is the frequency of oscillation of the MOS-FET Colpitts oscillator in Fig. P18.70 if $L = 10 \,\mu H$, $C_1 = 50$ pF, $C_2 = 50$ pF, $C_3 = 0$ pF, $C_{GS} = 10$ pF, and $C_{GD} = 4$ pF? What is the minimum amplification factor of the transistor?

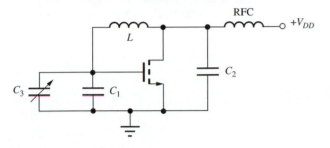

Figure P18.70

18.71. Capacitor C_3 is added to the Colpitts oscillator in Prob. 18.70 to allow tuning the oscillator. (a) Assume C_3 can vary from 5 to 50 pF and calculate the frequencies of oscillation for the two adjustment extremes. (b) What is the minimum value of amplification factor needed to ensure oscillation throughout the full tuning range?

18.72. A variable-capacitance diode is added to the Colpitts oscillator in Fig. P18.72 to form a voltage tunable oscillator. (a) The parameters of the diode are $C_{jo} = 20$ pF and $\phi_j = 0.8$ V (see Eq. 3.21). Calculate the frequencies of oscillation for $V_{TUNE} = 2$ V and 20 V if $L = 10 \,\mu H$, $C_1 = 75$ pF, and $C_2 = 75$ pF. Assume the RFC has infinite impedance and C_C has zero impedance. (b) What is the minimum value of voltage gain needed to ensure oscillation throughout the full tuning range?

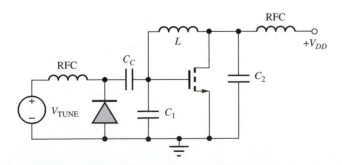

Figure P18.72

18.73. (a) Perform a SPICE transient simulation of the Colpitts oscillator in Fig. 18.64 and compare its frequency of oscillation to hand calculations if $V_{DD} = 10$ V, $I_{DSS} = 10$ mA, $V_P = -4$ V, $R = 820 \,\Omega$, $C_2 = 220$ pF, $C_1 = 470$ pF, and $L = 10 \,\mu H$. (b) Repeat if $C_2 = 470$ pF and $C_1 = 220$ pF.

18.74. Perform a SPICE transient simulation of the Colpitts oscillator in Fig. P18.70 if $L = 10 \,\mu H$, $C_1 = 50$ pF, $C_2 = 50$ pF, $C_3 = 0$ pF, $RFC = 20$ mH, $V_{DD} = 12$ V, $K_n = 10$ mA/V^2, $V_{TN} = 1$ V, $C_{GS} = 10$ pF, and $C_{GD} = 4$ pF. What are the amplitude and frequency of oscillation?

Hartley Oscillators

18.75. What is the frequency of oscillation of the Hartley oscillator in Fig. P18.75 if the diode is replaced by a short circuit and $L_1 = 10 \,\mu H$, $L_2 = 10 \,\mu H$, and $C = 20$ pF?

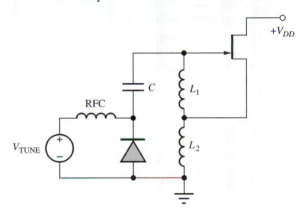

Figure P18.75

18.76. A variable-capacitance diode is added to the Hartley oscillator in Prob. P18.75 to form a voltage-tunable oscillator, and the value of C is changed to 220 pF. (a) If the parameters of the diode are $C_{jo} = 20$ pF and $\phi_j = 0.8$ V (see Eq. 3.21), calculate the frequencies of oscillation for $V_{TUNE} = 2$ V and 20 V. Assume the RFC has infinite impedance. (b) What is the minimum value of amplification factor of the FET needed to ensure oscillation throughout the full tuning range?

18.15 Crystal Oscillators

18.77. A crystal has a series resonant frequency of 10 MHz, series resistance of 40Ω, Q of 25,000, and parallel capacitance of 10 pF. (a) What are the values of L and C_S for this crystal? (b) What is the parallel resonant frequency of the crystal? (c) The crystal is placed in an oscillator circuit in parallel with a total capacitance of 22 pF. What will be the frequency of oscillation?

18.78. The crystal in the oscillator in Fig. P18.78 has $L = 15$ mH, $C_S = 20$ fF, and $R = 50\Omega$. (a) What is the frequency of oscillation if $R_E = 1$ kΩ, $R_B = 100$ kΩ, $V_{CC} = V_{EE} = 5$ V, $C_1 = 100$ pF, $C_2 = 470$ pF, and $C_3 = \infty$. Assume the transistor has $\beta_f = 100$, $V_A = 50$ V, and infinite f_T. (b) Repeat if $C_\mu = 5$ pF and $f_T = 250$ MHz.

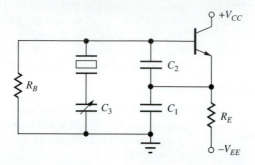

Figure P18.78

18.79. A variable capacitor C_3 is placed in series with the crystal in the oscillator in Prob. 18.78(a) to provide a calibration adjustment. Assume C_3 can vary from 1 pF to 35 pF and calculate the frequencies of oscillation for the two adjustment extremes.

18.80. Simulate the crystal oscillator in Fig. P18.78 and find the frequency of oscillation if $R_E = 1$kΩ, $R_B = 100$ kΩ, $V_{CC} = V_{EE} = 5$ V, $C_1 = 100$ pF, $C_2 = 470$ pF, and $C_3 = \infty$. The crystal has $L = 15$ mH, $C_S = 20$ fF, $R = 50$ Ω, and $C_P = 20$ pF. Assume the transistor has $\beta_F = 100$, $V_A = 50$ V, $C_\mu = 5$ pF, and $\tau_F = 1$ ns.

Integrated Circuit Fabrication

Monolithic integrated circuit fabrication is illustrated by the device cross sections in Figs. A.1 and A.2.[1] The n-channel MOS transistor in Fig. A.1 is constructed in a p-type substrate. Source and drain regions are formed by selectively converting shallow regions at the surface into heavily-doped n-type (n^+) material. Silicon dioxide regions on the surface form the gate insulator of the MOS device and serve to isolate one transistor from another. A thin film of polysilicon becomes the gate of the transistor, and aluminum metallization makes contact to the source and drain. Interconnections between devices can be made using the source/drain regions, the polysilicon layer, and the metallization layer.

The bipolar transistor in Fig. A.2 has alternating n- and p-type regions selectively fabricated in a p-type substrate. The heavily doped n^+ buried layer is used to reduce the resistance of the collector region. Silicon dioxide is again used as an electrical insulator, and aluminum is used to make electrical connections to the collector, base, emitter, and substrate terminals of the transistor.

When the MOS or bipolar process is finished, the complete silicon wafer typically contains hundreds of virtually identical copies of the integrated circuit design. All the dice on the wafer are tested, and any bad die is marked with ink. The wafer is then sawed apart. Good dice are mounted in various packages for final testing and subsequent sale or use.

Integrated Circuit Processes

These complicated IC structures are fabricated through repeated application of a number of basic processing steps: oxidation, photolithography, etching, ion implantation, diffusion, evaporation, sputtering, chemical vapor deposition (CVD), and epitaxial growth. Silicon dioxide (S_iO_2) layers are formed by heating silicon wafers to a high temperature (1000 to 1200°C) in the presence of pure oxygen or water vapor. This process is called *oxidation*. Thin layers of metal films are deposited through *evaporation* by heating the metal to its melting point in a vacuum. Both conducting metal films and insulators may be deposited through a process called *sputtering,* which uses physical ion bombardment to effect transfer of atoms from a source target to the wafer surface.

---

[1] Adapted from *Introduction to Microelectronic Fabrication* by Richard C. Jaeger. Copyright ©1988 by Addison-Wesley Publishing Co. Reprinted by permission.

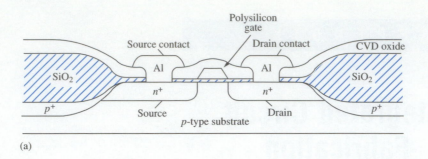

Figure A.1 The structure of an *n*-channel metal-oxide-semiconductor (NMOS) field-effect transistor structure with recessed oxide isolation. (a) A vertical cross section through the NMOS FET. (b) A composite top view of the masks used to fabricate the transistor.

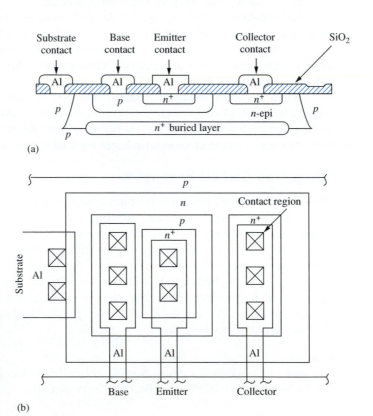

Figure A.2 The structure of a junction-isolated bipolar transistor. (a) A vertical cross section through the BJT. (b) A composite top view of the masks used to fabricate the transistor.

Thin films of polysilicon, silicon dioxide, and silicon nitride can all be formed through *chemical vapor deposition* (CVD), in which the material is precipitated from a gaseous mixture directly onto the surface of the silicon wafer. Shallow *n*- and *p*-type layers are formed by *ion implantation,* where the wafer is bombarded by high-energy (50 keV to 1 MeV) acceptor or donor impurity atoms generated by a high-voltage particle accelerator. Greater depth of the impurity layers may be achieved by *diffusion* of the impurities at high temperature, typically 1000 to 1200°C, in either an inert or oxidizing environment. Bipolar processes, as well as some CMOS processes, employ the *epitaxial growth* technique to form thin high-quality layers of crystalline silicon on top of the wafer. The epitaxial layer replicates the crystal structure of the original silicon substrate.

In order to build devices and circuits, *n*- and *p*-type regions must be formed selectively in the silicon surface. Silicon dioxide, silicon nitride, polysilicon, photoresist, and other materials can all be used to block out areas of the wafer surface to prevent penetration of impurity atoms during implantation and/or diffusion. *Masks* containing window patterns to be opened in the protective layers are produced using a combination of computer-aided design systems and photographic reduction techniques. The patterns are transferred from the mask to the wafer surface through the use of high-resolution optical photographic techniques, a process called *photolithography.* The windows defined by the masks are cut through the protective layers by wet-chemical etching using acids or by dry-plasma etching.

The fabrication steps just outlined can be combined in many different ways to form integrated circuits. Bipolar processing was used in the fabrication of the first successful ICs in the early 1960s. Processes were subsequently developed in the late 1960s and early 1970s for PMOS and then NMOS technologies; CMOS technologies came into widespread use by the mid-1980s. BICMOS processes, including NMOS and PMOS devices as well as bipolar-junction transistors, began to appear in 1990.

A Simple NMOS Process

A process flow for a basic recessed-oxide NMOS process is defined in the flowchart in Fig. A.3, and the process cross sections appear in Fig. A.4, p. 1055. To begin the process, a clean silicon wafer is oxidized to produce a thin layer of silicon dioxide that protects the silicon surface. A layer of silicon nitride is then deposited by chemical vapor deposition. The first mask defines the active transistor areas, and the nitride/oxide sandwich is etched away everywhere except where transistors are to be formed.

Next, a boron implantation, used to enhance device isolation, is performed and followed by an oxidation step. The unetched nitride serves to block both implantation and oxidation. The nitride and oxide layers are removed, and a thin layer of silicon dioxide is regrown; this subsequently becomes the gate insulator for the MOS transistors. Following gate-oxide growth, a boron implantation may be used to adjust the MOSFET threshold voltage.

Polysilicon is now deposited over the entire wafer using CVD processing. Mask 2 defines the polysilicon gate region of the transistors, and the polysilicon layer is etched away everywhere except over the gate regions of the NMOS transistors and any areas to be used for polysilicon interconnections. Next, donor impurities are ion-implanted into the polysilicon and through the thin oxide to form the source and drain regions. The implanted impurities may be driven in deeper during a subsequent high-temperature annealing and diffusion step.

An additional layer of oxide is deposited on the surface, and contact openings are defined by the third mask step. Metal is deposited over the entire wafer surface by evaporation or sputtering, and the fourth mask step is used to define the electrical interconnection and

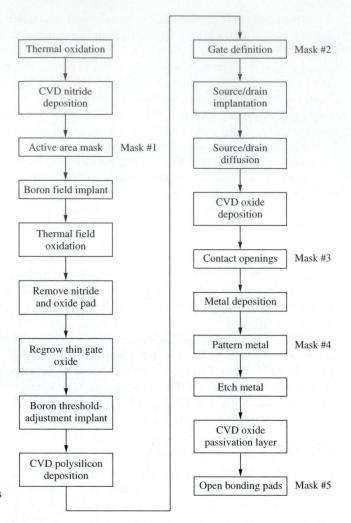

Figure A.3 NMOS process flowchart.

pad patterns that will be etched in the metal. A passivation layer of phosphosilicate glass or polyimide (not shown in Fig. A.4) is deposited on the wafer surface, and the fifth and final mask is used to open windows over the pads so that bonding wires can be attached to the periphery of the IC die.

This simple process requires five mask steps. Note that these mask steps all use subtractive processes. The entire surface of the wafer is first coated with a desired material, and then most of the material is removed by wet-chemical or dry-plasma etching.

Complementary MOS (CMOS) Process Flow

Figure A.5 (p. 1056) shows the mask sequence for a basic complementary MOS or CMOS process. The process steps are similar to those of the NMOS process, except the first mask step defines the "*p*-well" or "*p*-tub," which serves as the substrate for the *n*-channel devices, and a second new mask step is required to define the source/drain regions for the *p*-channel transistors. Additional masks may be used separately to adjust the threshold voltage of each type of MOS transistor; these are very common in state-of-the-art CMOS processes. The complete CMOS process typically requires at least nine mask levels.

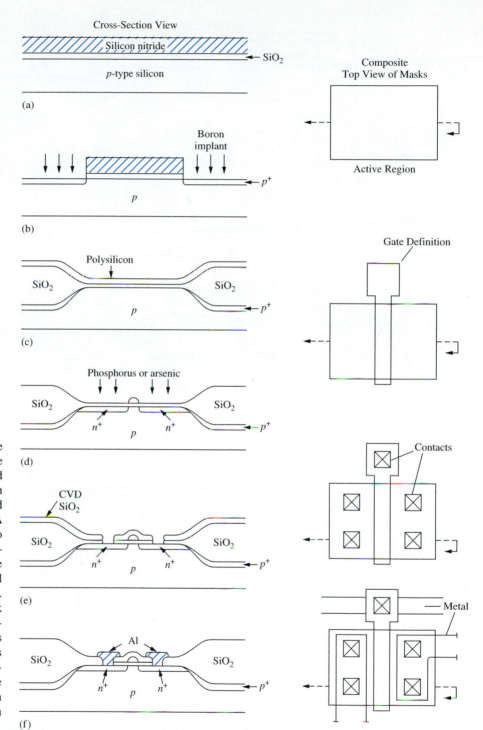

Figure A.4 Process sequence for a semirecessed oxide NMOS process. (a) Oxidized silicon wafer covered with silicon nitride. (b) Etched wafer after first mask step. A boron implantation is used to adjust the field-oxide threshold voltage. (c) Structure following nitride removal and polysilicon deposition. (d) Wafer after second mask step and etching of polysilicon. (e) The third mask step is used to open contact windows following silicon dioxide deposition. (f) Final structure following metal deposition and patterning with fourth photolithography step.

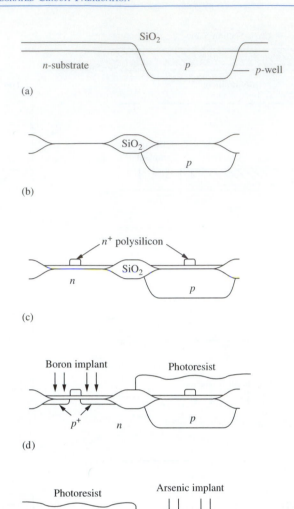

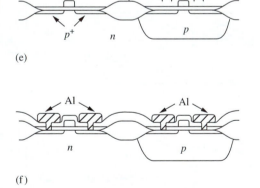

Figure A.5   Cross-sectional views at the major steps in a basic CMOS process: (a) Following formation of the p-well; (b) after selective oxidation; (c) after gate oxidation and polysilicon gate definition; (d) p-type source/drain implantation; (e) n-type source/drain implantation; and (f) final structure following metal deposition and patterning.

Alternate process designs use an n-well instead of a p-well. The n-well process permits realization of high-performance NMOS transistors. Advanced twin-well processes have also been developed. In this case, both p- and n-wells are formed in a lightly-doped substrate, and the n- and p-channel devices can then each be optimized for best performance. Twin-well processes for VLSI often start with a lightly doped epitaxial layer grown on a heavily doped substrate to help suppress CMOS latchup (see Sec. 8.10).

Bipolar Transistor Fabrication

Basic bipolar fabrication is somewhat more complex than single-channel MOS processing, as indicated in Figs. A.6 and A.7. A p-type silicon wafer is oxidized, and the first mask is used to define a diffused region called the buried layer or subcollector. This buried layer is used to reduce series resistance in the collector of the bipolar transistor. Following the buried-layer diffusion, epitaxial growth is used to add an n-type silicon layer to the top of the original wafer. An oxide layer is then grown on the surface, and mask 2 is used to define windows for a deep p-diffusion that isolates one bipolar transistor from another. Another oxidation step follows the isolation diffusion.

Mask 3 creates windows in the oxide for a p-type base diffusion. The wafer is usually oxidized during the base diffusion, and mask 4 defines the emitter diffusion and places an n^+ region under the collector contact to ensure formation of a good ohmic contact to the subsequent aluminum metallization. Masks 5, 6, and 7 are used to open contact windows, pattern the metallization layer, and open windows in the passivation layer, just as described for the NMOS process. Thus, the basic bipolar process requires seven mask levels compared with five for the NMOS process and nine or more for the CMOS process.

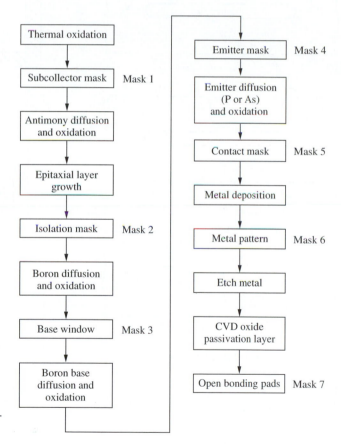

Figure A.6 Bipolar technology process flow.

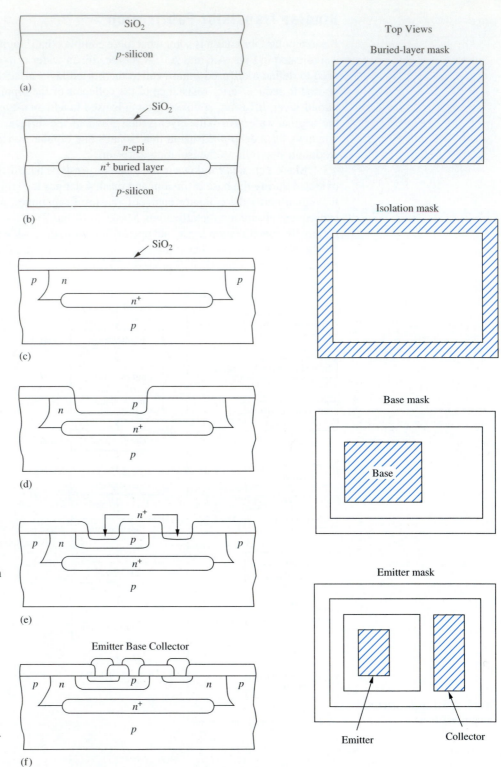

Figure A.7 Cross-sectional views at the major steps in a junction-isolated bipolar process: (a) Oxidized silicon wafer; (b) after buried-layer diffusion using first mask, and subsequent epitaxial layer growth and oxidation; (c) following the deep isolation diffusion using the second mask; (d) after base diffusion using the third mask; (e) the fourth mask defines the emitter and collector contact regions; (f) final structure following contact and metal mask steps.

Solid-State Device Models and SPICE Simulation Parameters

B.1 *pn* JUNCTION DIODES

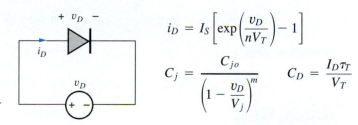

$$i_D = I_S \left[\exp\left(\frac{v_D}{nV_T}\right) - 1 \right]$$

$$C_j = \frac{C_{jo}}{\left(1 - \dfrac{v_D}{V_j}\right)^m} \qquad C_D = \frac{I_D \tau_T}{V_T}$$

Figure B.1 Diode with applied voltage v_D.

	Table B.1		
	Diode Parameters for Circuit Simulation		
Parameter	**Name**	**Default**	**Typical Value**
Saturation current	IS	1×10^{-14} A	3×10^{-17} A
Emission coefficient (ideality factor—n)	N	1	1
Transit time (τ_T)	TT	0	0.15 nS
Series resistance	RS	0	10 Ω
Junction capacitance	CJO	0	1.0 pF
Junction potential (V_j)	VJ	1 V	0.8 V
Grading coefficient (m)	M	0.5	0.5

B.2 MOS FIELD-EFFECT TRANSISTORS (MOSFETs)

A summary of the mathematical models for both the NMOS and PMOS transistors follows. The terminal voltages and currents are defined in Fig. B.2.

1059

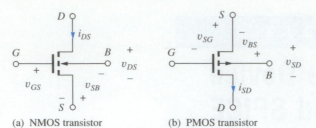

Figure B.2 NMOS and PMOS transistor circuit symbols.

(a) NMOS transistor   (b) PMOS transistor

NMOS Transistor Model Summary

$$K_n = K_n' \frac{W}{L} = \mu_n C_{ox}'' \frac{W}{L}$$

$$i_G = 0 \text{ and } i_B = 0 \quad \text{for all regions}$$

Cutoff Region

$$i_{DS} = 0 \quad \text{for } v_{GS} \leq V_{TN}$$

Linear Region

$$i_{DS} = K_n \left(v_{GS} - V_{TN} - \frac{v_{DS}}{2} \right) v_{DS} \quad \text{for } v_{GS} - V_{TN} \geq v_{DS} \geq 0$$

Saturation Region

$$i_{DS} = \frac{K_n}{2} (v_{GS} - V_{TN})^2 (1 + \lambda v_{DS}) \quad \text{for } v_{DS} \geq (v_{GS} - V_{TN}) \geq 0$$

Threshold Voltage

$$V_{TN} = V_{TO} + \gamma \left(\sqrt{v_{SB} + 2\phi_F} - \sqrt{2\phi_F} \right)$$

PMOS Transistor Model Summary

$$K_p = K_p' \frac{W}{L} = \mu_p C_{ox}'' \frac{W}{L}$$

$$i_G = 0 \text{ and } i_B = 0 \quad \text{for all regions}$$

Cutoff Region

$$i_{SD} = 0 \quad \text{for } v_{SG} \leq -V_{TP}$$

Linear Region

$$i_{SD} = K_p \left(v_{SG} + V_{TP} - \frac{v_{SD}}{2} \right) v_{SD} \quad \text{for } v_{SG} + V_{TP} \geq v_{SD} \geq 0$$

Saturation Region

$$i_{SD} = \frac{K_p}{2} (v_{SG} + V_{TP})^2 (1 + \lambda v_{SD}) \quad \text{for } v_{SD} \geq (v_{SG} + V_{TP}) \geq 0$$

Threshold Voltage

$$V_{TP} = V_{TO} - \gamma \left(\sqrt{v_{BS} + 2\phi_F} - \sqrt{2\phi_F} \right)$$

Table B.2

Types of MOSFET Transistors

NMOS Device		PMOS Device
Enhancement-Mode	$V_{TN} > 0$	$V_{TP} < 0$
Depletion-Mode	$V_{TN} \leq 0$	$V_{TP} \geq 0$

MOS Transistor Parameters for Circuit Simulation

For simulation purposes, use the LEVEL=1 models in SPICE with the following SPICE parameters in your NMOS and PMOS devices:

Table B.3

MOS Device Parameters for SPICE Simulation
(MOSIS 2-μm p-well process)

Parameter	Symbol	NMOS Transistor	PMOS Transistor
Threshold voltage	VTO	0.91 V	−0.77 V
Transconductance	KP	50 μA/V²	20 μA/V²
Body effect	GAMMA	$0.99 \sqrt{V}$	$0.53 \sqrt{V}$
Surface potential	PHI	0.7 V	0.7 V
Channel-length modulation	LAMBDA	0.02 V⁻¹	0.05 V⁻¹
Mobility	UO	615 cm²	235 cm²/s
Ohmic drain resistance	RD	0	0
Ohmic source resistance	RS	0	0
Junction saturation current	IS	0	0
Built-in potential	PB	0	0
Gate-drain capacitance per unit width	CGDO	330 pF/m	315 pF/m
Gate-source capacitance per unit width	CGSO	330 pF/m	315 pF/m
Gate-bulk capacitance per unit width	CGBO	395 pF/m	415 pF/m
Junction bottom capacitance per unit area	CJ	3.9×10^{-4} F/m²	2×10^{-4} F/m²
Grading coefficient	MJ	0.45	0.47
Sidewall capacitance	CJSW	510 pF/m	180 pF/m
Sidewall grading coefficient	MJSW	0.36	0.09
Source-drain sheet resistance	RSH	22 Ω/square	70 Ω/square
Oxide thickness	TOX	4.15×10^{-6} cm	4.15×10^{-6} cm
Junction depth	XJ	0.23 μm	0.23 μm

T a b l e B.3 *(Continued)*			
MOS Device Parameters for SPICE Simulation **(MOSIS 2-μm *p*-well process)**			
Parameter	**Symbol**	**NMOS Transistor**	**PMOS Transistor**
Lateral diffusion	LD	0.26 μm	0.25 μm
Substrate doping	NSUB	$2.1 \times 10^{16}/\text{cm}^3$	$5.9 \times 10^{16}/\text{cm}^3$
Critical field	UCRIT	9.6×10^5 V/cm	6×10^5 V/cm
Critical field exponent	UEXP	0.18	0.28
Saturation velocity	VMAX	7.6×10^7 cm/s	6.5×10^7 cm/s
Fast surface state density	NFS	$9 \times 10^{11}/\text{cm}^2$	$3 \times 10^{11}/\text{cm}^2$
Surface state density	NSS	$1 \times 10^{10}/\text{cm}^2$	$1 \times 10^{10}/\text{cm}^2$

B.3 JUNCTION FIELD-EFFECT TRANSISTORS (JFETs)

Circuit Symbols and JFET Model Summary

Figure B.3 presents the circuit symbols and terminal voltages and currents for *n*-channel and *p*-channel JFETs.

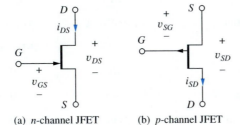

(a) *n*-channel JFET   (b) *p*-channel JFET

Figure B.3 *n*-channel and *p*-channel JFET circuit symbols.

n-Channel JFET

$$i_G \approx 0 \qquad \text{for } v_{GS} \leq 0; \ V_P < 0$$

Cutoff Region

$$i_{DS} = 0 \qquad \text{for } v_{GS} \leq V_P$$

Linear Region

$$i_{DS} = \frac{2I_{DSS}}{V_P^2}\left(v_{GS} - V_P - \frac{v_{DS}}{2}\right)v_{DS} \qquad \text{for } v_{GS} - V_P \geq v_{DS} \geq 0$$

Saturation Region

$$i_{DS} = I_{DSS}\left(1 - \frac{v_{GS}}{V_P}\right)^2 (1 + \lambda v_{DS}) \qquad \text{for } v_{DS} \geq v_{GS} - V_P \geq 0$$

p-Channel JFET

$$i_G \approx 0 \qquad \text{for } v_{SG} \le 0; \ V_P > 0$$

Cutoff Region

$$i_{SD} = 0 \qquad \text{for } v_{SG} \le -V_P$$

Linear Region

$$i_{SD} = \frac{2I_{DSS}}{V_P^2}\left(v_{SG} + V_P - \frac{v_{SD}}{2}\right)v_{SD} \qquad \text{for } v_{SG} + V_P \ge v_{SD} \ge 0$$

Saturation Region

$$i_{SD} = I_{DSS}\left(1 + \frac{v_{SG}}{V_P}\right)^2 (1 + \lambda v_{SD}) \qquad \text{for } v_{SD} \ge v_{SG} + V_P \ge 0$$

Table B.4

JFET Device Parameters for SPICE Simulation (NJF/PJF)

Parameter	Symbol	NJF Default	NJF Example
Pinchoff voltage (V_P)	VTO	-2 V	-2 V ($+2$ V for PJF)
Transconductance parameter	BETA $= \left(\dfrac{2I_{DSS}}{V_P^2}\right)$	100 μA/V^2	250 μA/V^2
Channel-length modulation	LAMBDA	0 V^{-1}	0.02 V^{-1}
Ohmic drain resistance	RD	0	100 Ω
Ohmic source resistance	RS	0	100 Ω
Zero-bias gate-source capacitance	CGS	0	10 pF
Zero-bias gate-drain capacitance	CGD	0	5 pF
Gate built-in potential	PB	1 V	0.75 V
Gate saturation current	IS	10^{-14} A	10^{-14} A

B.4 BIPOLAR-JUNCTION TRANSISTORS (BJTs)

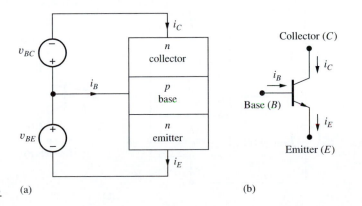

Figure B.4 *npn* Transistor. (a)   (b)

Transport Model Equations

$$i_E = I_S \left[\exp\left(\frac{v_{BE}}{V_T}\right) - \exp\left(\frac{v_{BC}}{V_T}\right) \right] + \frac{I_S}{\beta_F} \left[\exp\left(\frac{v_{BE}}{v_T}\right) - 1 \right]$$

$$i_C = I_S \left[\exp\left(\frac{v_{BE}}{V_T}\right) - \exp\left(\frac{v_{BC}}{V_T}\right) \right] - \frac{I_S}{\beta_R} \left[\exp\left(\frac{v_{BC}}{V_T}\right) - 1 \right]$$

$$i_B = \frac{I_S}{\beta_F} \left[\exp\left(\frac{v_{BE}}{V_T}\right) - 1 \right] + \frac{I_S}{\beta_R} \left[\exp\left(\frac{v_{BC}}{V_T}\right) - 1 \right]$$

$$\beta_F = \frac{\alpha_F}{1 - \alpha_F} \quad \text{and} \quad \beta_R = \frac{\alpha_R}{1 - \alpha_R}$$

Table B.5

Regions of Operation of the Bipolar Transistor

Base-Emitter Junction	Base-Collector Junction	
	Forward Bias	**Reverse Bias**
Forward bias	**Saturation region** (closed switch)	**Forward active region** (good amplifier)
Reverse bias	**Reverse active region** (poor amplifier)	**Cutoff region** (open switch)

Forward-Active Region, Including Early Effect

$$i_C = I_S \left[\exp\left(\frac{v_{BE}}{V_T}\right) \right] \left[1 + \frac{v_{CE}}{V_A} \right]$$

$$\beta_F = \beta_{FO} \left[1 + \frac{v_{CE}}{V_A} \right]$$

$$i_B = \frac{I_S}{\beta_{FO}} \left[\exp\left(\frac{v_{BE}}{V_T}\right) \right]$$

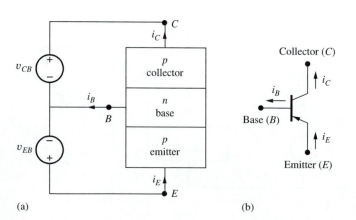

Figure B.5 *pnp* Transistor.   (a)   (b)

Transport Model Equations

$$i_E = I_S\left[\exp\left(\frac{v_{EB}}{V_T}\right) - \exp\left(\frac{v_{CB}}{V_T}\right)\right] + \frac{I_S}{\beta_F}\left[\exp\left(\frac{v_{EB}}{V_T}\right) - 1\right]$$

$$i_C = I_S\left[\exp\left(\frac{v_{EB}}{V_T}\right) - \exp\left(\frac{v_{CB}}{V_T}\right)\right] - \frac{I_S}{\beta_R}\left[\exp\left(\frac{v_{CB}}{V_T}\right) - 1\right]$$

$$i_B = \frac{I_S}{\beta_F}\left[\exp\left(\frac{v_{EB}}{V_T}\right) - 1\right] + \frac{I_S}{\beta_R}\left[\exp\left(\frac{v_{CB}}{V_T}\right) - 1\right]$$

$$\beta_F = \frac{\alpha_F}{1 - \alpha_F} \quad \text{and} \quad \beta_R = \frac{\alpha_R}{1 - \alpha_R}$$

pnp Forward-Active Region, Including Early Effect

$$i_C = I_S\left[\exp\left(\frac{v_{EB}}{V_T}\right)\right]\left[1 + \frac{v_{EC}}{V_A}\right]$$

$$\beta_F = \beta_{FO}\left[1 + \frac{v_{EC}}{V_A}\right]$$

$$i_B = \frac{I_S}{\beta_{FO}}\left[\exp\left(\frac{v_{EB}}{V_T}\right)\right]$$

Table B.6

Bipolar Device Parameters for Circuit Simulation (*npn/pnp*)

Parameter	Name	Default	Typical *npn* Values
Saturation current	IS	10^{-16} A	3×10^{-17} A
Forward current gain	BF	100	100
Forward emission coefficient	NF	1	1.03
Forward early voltage	VAF	∞	75 V
Reverse current gain	BR	1	0.5
Base resistance	RB	0	100 Ω
Collector resistance	RC	0	10 Ω
Emitter resistance	RE	0	1 Ω
Forward transit time	TF	0	0.15 nS
Reverse transit time	TR	0	15 nS
Base-emitter junction capacitance	CJE	0	0.5 pF
Base-emitter junction potential	PHIE	0.75 V	0.8 V

T a b l e B.6 (*Continued*)

Bipolar Device Parameters for Circuit Simulation (*npn/pnp*)

Parameter	Name	Default	Typical *npn* Values
Base-emitter grading coefficient	ME	0.5	0.5
Base-collector junction capacitance	CJC	0	1 pF
Base-collector junction potential	PHIC	0.75 V	0.7 V
Base-collector grading coefficient	MC	0.33	0.33
Collector substrate junction capacitance	CJS	0	3 pF

Standard Discrete Component Values

Standard resistor values: All values available with a 5 percent tolerance. Bold values are available with 10 percent tolerance.

Ohms							
1.0	**5.6**	**33**	**180**	**1000**	**5600**	**33000**	**180000**
1.1	6.2	36	200	1100	6200	36000	200000
1.2	**6.8**	**39**	**220**	**1200**	**6800**	**39000**	**220000**
1.3	7.5	43	240	1300	7500	43000	240000
1.5	**8.2**	**47**	**270**	**1500**	**8200**	**47000**	**270000**
1.6	9.1	51	300	1600	9100	51000	300000
1.8	**10**	**56**	**330**	**1800**	**10000**	**56000**	**330000**
2.0	11	62	360	2000	11000	62000	360000
2.2	**12**	**68**	**390**	**2200**	**12000**	**68000**	**390000**
2.4	13	75	430	2400	13000	75000	430000
2.7	**15**	**82**	**470**	**2700**	**15000**	**82000**	**470000**
3.0	16	91	510	3000	16000	91000	510000
3.3	**18**	**100**	**560**	**3300**	**18000**	**100000**	**560000**
3.6	20	110	620	3600	20000	110000	620000
3.9	**22**	**120**	**680**	**3900**	**22000**	**120000**	**680000**
4.3	24	130	750	4300	24000	130000	750000
4.7	**27**	**150**	**820**	**4700**	**27000**	**150000**	**820000**
5.1	30	160	910	5100	30000	160000	910000

Megohms						
1.0	1.6	**2.7**	4.3	**6.8**	11.0	**18.0**
1.1	**1.8**	3.0	**4.7**	7.5	**12.0**	20.0
1.2	2.0	**3.3**	5.1	**8.2**	13.0	**22.0**
1.3	**2.2**	3.6	**5.6**	9.1	**15.0**	
1.5	2.4	**3.9**	6.2	**10.0**	16.0	

Precision (1%) Resistors

10.0	19.1	36.5	69.8	133	255	487	931	1.78K	3.40K	6.49K	12.4K	23.7K	45.3K	84.5K	158K	294K	549K
10.2	19.6	37.4	71.5	137	261	499	953	1.82K	3.48K	6.65K	12.7K	24.3K	46.4K	86.6K	162K	301K	562K
10.5	20.0	38.3	73.2	140	267	511	976	1.87K	3.57K	6.81K	13.0K	24.9K	47.5K	88.7K	165K	309K	576K
10.7	20.5	39.2	75.0	143	274	523	1.00K	1.91K	3.65K	6.98K	13.3K	25.5K	48.7K	90.9K	169K	316K	590K
11.0	21.0	40.2	76.8	147	280	536	1.02K	1.96K	3.74K	7.15K	13.7K	26.1K	49.9K	93.1K	174K	324K	604K
11.3	21.5	41.2	78.7	150	287	549	1.05K	2.00K	3.83K	7.32K	14.0K	26.7K	51.1K	95.3K	178K	332K	619K
11.5	22.1	42.2	80.6	154	294	562	1.07K	2.05K	3.92K	7.50K	14.3K	27.4K	52.3K	97.6K	182K	340K	634K
11.8	22.6	43.2	82.5	158	301	576	1.10K	2.10K	4.02K	7.68K	14.7K	28.0K	53.6K	100K	187K	348K	649K
12.1	23.2	44.2	84.5	162	309	590	1.13K	2.15K	4.12K	7.87K	15.0K	28.7K	54.9K	102K	191K	357K	665K
12.4	23.7	45.3	86.6	165	316	604	1.15K	2.21K	4.22K	8.06K	15.4K	29.4K	56.2K	105K	196K	365K	681K
12.7	24.3	46.4	88.7	169	324	619	1.18K	2.26K	4.32K	8.25K	15.8K	30.1K	57.6K	107K	200K	374K	698K
13.0	24.9	47.5	90.9	174	332	634	1.21K	2.32K	4.42K	8.45K	16.2K	30.9K	59.0K	110K	205K	383K	715K
13.3	25.5	48.7	93.1	178	340	649	1.24K	2.37K	4.53K	8.66K	16.5K	31.6K	60.4K	113K	210K	392K	732K
13.7	26.1	49.9	95.3	182	348	665	1.27K	2.43K	4.64K	8.87K	16.9K	32.4K	61.9K	115K	215K	402K	750K
14.0	26.7	51.1	97.6	187	357	681	1.30K	2.49K	4.75K	9.09K	17.4K	33.2K	63.4K	118K	221K	412K	768K
14.3	27.4	52.3	100	191	365	698	1.33K	2.55K	4.87K	9.31K	17.8K	34.0K	64.9K	121K	226K	422K	787K
14.7	28.0	53.6	102	196	374	715	1.37K	2.61K	4.99K	9.53K	18.2K	34.8K	66.5K	124K	232K	432K	806K
15.0	28.8	54.9	105	200	383	732	1.40K	2.67K	5.11K	9.76K	18.7K	35.7K	68.1K	127K	237K	442K	825K
15.4	29.4	56.2	107	205	392	750	1.43K	2.74K	5.23K	10.0K	19.1K	36.5K	69.8K	130K	243K	453K	845K
15.8	30.1	57.6	110	210	402	768	1.47K	2.80K	5.36K	10.2K	19.6K	37.4K	71.5K	133K	249K	464K	866K
16.2	30.9	59.0	113	215	412	787	1.50K	2.87K	5.49K	10.5K	20.0K	38.3K	73.2K	137K	255K	475K	887K
16.5	31.6	60.4	115	221	422	806	1.54K	2.94K	5.62K	10.7K	20.5K	39.2K	75.0K	140K	261K	487K	909K
16.9	32.4	61.9	118	226	432	825	1.58K	3.01K	5.76K	11.0K	21.0K	40.2K	76.8K	143K	267K	499K	931K
17.4	33.2	63.4	121	232	443	845	1.62K	3.09K	5.90K	11.3K	21.5K	41.2K	78.7K	147K	274K	511K	953K
17.8	34.0	64.9	124	237	453	866	1.65K	3.16K	6.04K	11.5K	22.1K	42.2K	80.6K	150K	280K	523K	976K
18.2	34.8	66.5	127	243	464	887	1.69K	3.24K	6.19K	11.8K	22.6K	43.2K	82.5K	154K	287K	536K	1.00M
18.7	35.7	68.1	130	249	475	909	1.74K	3.32K	6.34K	12.1K	23.2K	44.2K					

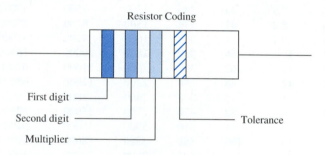

Resistor Coding

First digit —
Second digit —
Multiplier —
— Tolerance

Resistor Color Code

Color	Digit	Multiplier	Tolerance, %
Silver	· · ·	0.01	10
Gold	· · ·	0.1	5
Black	0	1	
Brown	1	10	
Red	2	10^2	
Orange	3	10^3	
Yellow	4	10^4	
Green	5	10^5	
Blue	6	10^6	
Violet	7	10^7	
Gray	8	10^8	
White	9	10^9	

Standard Capacitor Values (Larger values are also available)

pF	pF	pF	pF	μF	μF	μF	μF	μF	μF	μF
1	10	100	1000	0.01	0.1	1	10	100	1000	10000
	12	120	1200	0.012	0.12	1.2	12	120	1200	12000
1.5	15	150	1500	0.015	0.15	1.5	15	150	1500	15000
	18	180	1800	0.018	0.18	1.8	18	180	1800	
	20	200	2000	0.020	0.20				2000	20000
2.2	22	220	2200	0.022	0.22	2.2	22	220	2200	22000
	27	270	2700	0.027	0.27	2.7	27	270	2700	
3.3	33	330	3300	0.033	0.33	3.3	33	330	3300	33000
	39	390	3900	0.039	0.39	3.9	39	390	3900	
4.7	47	470	4700	0.047	0.47	4.7	47	470	4700	47000
5.0	50	500	5000	0.050	0.50					50000
5.6	56	560	5600	0.056	0.56	5.6	56	560	5600	
6.8	68	680	6800	0.068	0.68	6.8	68	680	6800	68000
8.2	82	820	8200	0.082	0.82	8.2	82	820	8200	

Standard Inductor Values

μH	μH	μH	μH	mH	mH	mH
0.10	1.0	10	100	1.0	10	100
	1.1	11	110			
	1.2	12	120	1.2	12	120
0.15	1.5	15	150	1.5	15	
0.18	1.8	18	180	1.8	18	
	2.0	20	200			
0.22	2.2	22	220	2.2	22	
	2.4	24	240			
0.27	2.7	27	270	2.7	27	
0.33	3.3	33	330	3.3	33	
0.39	3.9	39	390	3.9	39	
	4.3	43	430			
0.47	4.7	47	470	4.7	47	
0.56	5.6	56	560	5.6	56	
	6.2	62	620			
0.68	6.8	68	680	6.8	68	
	7.5	75	750			
0.82	8.2	82	820	8.2	82	
	9.1	91	910			

Data Sheets

D.1 DIODES

IN4001–IN4007 Lead Mounted Silicon Rectifiers*

GENERAL-PURPOSE RECTIFIERS

. . . subminiature size, axial lead mounted rectifiers for general-purpose low-power applications.

**LEAD MOUNTED
SILICON RECTIFIERS**

**50-1000 VOLTS
DIFFUSED JUNCTION**

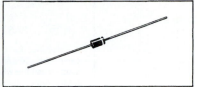

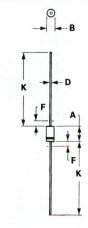

*MAXIMUM RATINGS

Rating	Symbol	1N4001	1N4002	1N4003	1N4004	1N4005	1N4006	1N4007	Unit
Peak Repetitive Reverse Voltage Working Peak Reverse Voltage DC Blocking Voltage	V_{RRM} V_{RWM} V_R	50	100	200	400	600	800	1000	Volts
Non-Repetitive Peak Reverse Voltage (halfwave, single phase, 60 Hz)	V_{RSM}	60	120	240	480	720	1000	1200	Volts
RMS Reverse Voltage	$V_{R(RMS)}$	35	70	140	280	420	560	700	Volts
Average Rectified Forward Current (single phase, resistive load, 60 Hz, see Figure 8, $T_A = 75^O$C)	I_O	← 1.0 →							Amp
Non-Repetitive Peak Surge Current (surge applied at rated load conditions, see Figure 2)	I_{FSM}	← 30 (for 1 cycle) →							Amp
Operating and Storage Junction Temperature Range	T_J, T_{stg}	← 65 to +175 →							^{O}C

*ELECTRICAL CHARACTERISTICS

Characteristic and Conditions	Symbol	Typ	Max	Unit
Maximum Instantaneous Forward Voltage Drop ($i_F = 1.0$ Amp, $T_J = 25^O$C) Figure 1	v_F	0.93	1.1	Volts
Maximum Full-Cycle Average Forward Voltage Drop ($I_O = 1.0$ Amp, $T_L = 75^O$C, 1 inch leads)	$V_{F(AV)}$	–	0.8	Volts
Maximum Reverse Current (rated dc voltage) $T_J = 25^O$C $T_J = 100^O$C	I_R	0.05 1.0	10 50	μA
Maximum Full-Cycle Average Reverse Current ($I_O = 1.0$ Amp, $T_L = 75^O$C, 1 inch leads	$I_{R(AV)}$	–	30	μA

*Indicates JEDEC Registered Data.

NOTES:
1. ALL RULES AND NOTES ASSOCIATED WITH JEDEC DO-41 OUTLINE SHALL APPLY.
2. POLARITY DENOTED BY CATHODE BAND.
3. LEAD DIAMETER NOT CONTROLLED WITHIN "F" DIMENSION.

MECHANICAL CHARACTERISTICS

CASE: Transfer Molded Plastic

MAXIMUM LEAD TEMPERATURE FOR SOLDERING PURPOSES: 350°C, 3/8" from case for 10 seconds at 5 lbs. tension

FINISH: All external surfaces are corrosion-resistant, leads are readily solderable

POLARITY: Cathode indicated by color band

WEIGHT: 0.40 Grams (approximately)

DIM	MILLIMETERS		INCHES	
	MIN	MAX	MIN	MAX
A	4.07	5.20	0.160	0.205
B	2.04	2.71	0.080	0.107
D	0.71	0.86	0.028	0.034
F	—	1.27	—	0.050
K	27.94	—	1.100	—

**CASE 59-03
DO-41
PLASTIC**

*Copyright of Motorola, used by permission.

IN3909–IN3913 Fast Recovery Power Rectifiers*

MOTOROLA SEMICONDUCTOR TECHNICAL DATA

1N3909 thru 1N3913
MR1396

Designers Data Sheet

STUD MOUNTED
FAST RECOVERY POWER RECTIFIERS

. . . designed for special applications such as dc power supplies, inverters, converters, ultrasonic systems, choppers, low RF interference, sonar power supplies and free wheeling diodes. A complete line of fast recovery rectifiers having typical recovery time of 150 nanoseconds providing high efficiency at frequencies to 250 kHz.

Designer's Data for "Worst Case" Conditions

The Designers Data sheets permit the design of most circuits entirely from the information presented. Limit curves — representing boundaries on device characteristics -- are given to facilitate "worst case" design.

FAST RECOVERY POWER RECTIFIERS
50-600 VOLTS
30 AMPERES

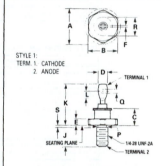

STYLE 1:
TERM. 1. CATHODE
2. ANODE

*MAXIMUM RATINGS

Rating	Symbol	1N3909	1N3910	1N3911	1N3912	1N3913	MR1396	Unit
Peak Repetitive Reverse Voltage Working Peak Reverse Voltage DC Blocking Voltage	V_{RRM} V_{RWM} V_R	50	100	200	300	400	600	Volts
Non-Repetitive Peak Reverse Voltage	V_{RSM}	75	150	250	350	450	650	Volts
RMS Reverse Voltage	$V_{R(RMS)}$	35	70	140	210	280	420	Volts
Average Rectified Forward Current (Single phase, resistive load, $T_C = 100°C$)	I_O				30			Amps
Non-Repetitive Peak Surge Current (surge applied at rated load conditions)	I_{FSM}				300			Amp
Operating Junction Temperature Range	T_J				– 65 to +150			°C
Storage Temperature Range	T_{stg}				– 65 to +175			°C

THERMAL CHARACTERISTICS

Characteristic	Symbol	Max	Unit
Thermal Resistance, Junction to Case	$R_{\theta JC}$	1.2	°C/W

*ELECTRICAL CHARACTERISTICS

Characteristic	Symbol	Min	Typ	Max	Unit
Instantaneous Forward Voltage (I_F = 93 Amp, $T_J = 150°C$)	v_F	–	1.2	1.5	Volts
Forward Voltage (I_F = 30 Amp, $T_C = 25°C$)	V_F	–	1.1	1.4	Volts
Reverse Current (rated dc voltage) $T_C = 25°C$ $T_C = 100°C$	I_R	– –	10 0.5	25 1.0	µA mA

*REVERSE RECOVERY CHARACTERISTICS

Characteristic	Symbol	Min	Typ	Max	Unit
Reverse Recovery Time (I_F = 1.0 Amp to V_R = 30 Vdc, Figure 16) (I_{FM} = 36 Amp, di/dt = 25 A/µs, Figure 17)	t_{rr}	– –	150 200	200 400	ns
Reverse Recovery Current (I_F = 1.0 Amp to V_R = 30 Vdc, Figure 16)	$I_{RM(REC)}$	–	1.5	2.0	Amp

*Indicates JEDEC Registered Data for 1N3909 Series.

DIM	MILLIMETERS MIN	MILLIMETERS MAX	INCHES MIN	INCHES MAX
A	—	20.07	—	0.790
B	16.94	17.45	0.669	0.687
C	—	11.43	—	0.450
D	—	9.53	—	0.375
E	2.92	5.08	0.115	0.200
F	—	2.03	—	0.080
J	10.72	11.51	0.422	0.453
K	19.05	25.40	0.750	1.00
L	3.96		0.156	—
P	5.59	6.32	0.220	0.249
Q	3.56	4.45	0.140	0.175
R	—	16.94	—	0.667
S	—	2.26	—	0.089

CASE 42A-01
DO-203AB
METAL

MECHANICAL CHARACTERISTICS

CASE: Welded, hermetically sealed

FINISH: All external surfaces corrosion resistant and readily solderable

POLARITY: Cathode to Case

WEIGHT: 17 Grams (Approximately)

MOUNTING TORQUE: 25 in-lbs max.

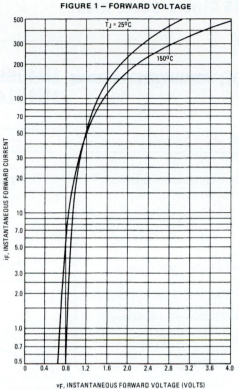

FIGURE 1 – FORWARD VOLTAGE

i_F, INSTANTANEOUS FORWARD CURRENT

$T_J = 25°C$

150°C

v_F, INSTANTANEOUS FORWARD VOLTAGE (VOLTS)

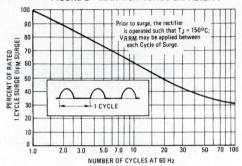

FIGURE 2 – MAXIMUM SURGE CAPABILITY

PERCENT OF RATED 1 CYCLE SURGE (I_{FM} SURGE)

Prior to surge, the rectifier is operated such that $T_J = 150°C$; V_{RRM} may be applied between each Cycle of Surge.

1 CYCLE

NUMBER OF CYCLES AT 60 Hz

NOTE 1

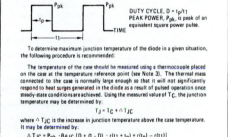

P_{pk} P_{pk}
TIME

DUTY CYCLE, $D = t_p/t_1$
PEAK POWER, P_{pk}, is peak of an equivalent square power pulse.

To determine maximum junction temperature of the diode in a given situation, the following procedure is recommended:

The temperature of the case should be measured using a thermocouple placed on the case at the temperature reference point (see Note 3). The thermal mass connected to the case is normally large enough so that it will not significantly respond to heat surges generated in the diode as a result of pulsed operation once steady-state conditions are achieved. Using the measured value of T_C, the junction temperature may be determined by:

$$T_J = T_C + \triangle T_{JC}$$

where $\triangle T_{JC}$ is the increase in junction temperature above the case temperature. It may be determined by:

$$\triangle T_{JC} = P_{pk} \cdot R_{\theta JC} [D + (1 - D) \cdot r(t_1 + t_p) + r(t_p) - r(t_1)]$$

where
$r(t)$ = normalized value of transient thermal resistance at time, t, from Figure 3, i.e.:
$r(t_1 + t_p)$ = normalized value of transient thermal resistance at time $t_1 + t_p$.

FIGURE 3 – THERMAL RESPONSE

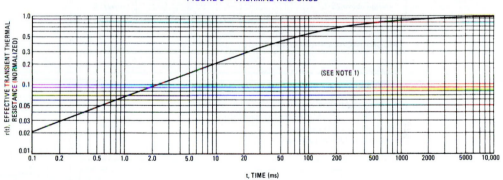

$r(t)$, EFFECTIVE TRANSIENT THERMAL RESISTANCE (NORMALIZED)

(SEE NOTE 1)

t, TIME (ms)

*Courtesy of Motorola, used by permission.

IN4099–IN4135 Silicon Zener Diodes*

MOTOROLA
SEMICONDUCTOR
TECHNICAL DATA

1N4099 thru 1N4135
1N4614 thru 1N4627

LOW-LEVEL SILICON PASSIVATED ZENER DIODES

. . . designed for 250 mW applications requiring low leakage, low impedance, and low noise.

- Voltage Range from 1.8 to 100 Volts
- First Zener Diode Series to Specify Noise — 50% Lower than Conventional Diffused Zeners
- Zener Impedance and Zener Voltage Specified for Low-Level Operation at I_{ZT} = 250 μA
- Low Leakage Current — I_R from 0.01 to 10 μA over Voltage Range

SILICON ZENER DIODES
(±5.0% TOLERANCE)

250 MILLIWATTS
1.8–100 VOLTS

SILICON OXIDE
PASSIVATED JUNCTION

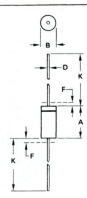

MAXIMUM RATINGS

Rating	Symbol	Value	Unit
DC Power Dissipation @ T_A = 25°C	P_D	250	mW
Derate above 25°C		1.43	mW/°C
Junction and Storage Temperature Range	T_J, T_{stg}	–65 to +200	°C

MECHANICAL CHARACTERISTICS

CASE: Hermetically sealed, all-glass.

DIMENSIONS: See outline drawing.

FINISH: All external surfaces are corrosion resistant and leads are readily solderable and weldable.

POLARITY: Cathode indicated by polarity band.

WEIGHT: 0.2 gram (approx.)

MOUNTING POSITION: Any

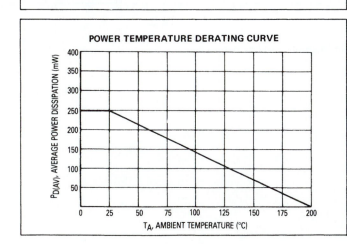

POWER TEMPERATURE DERATING CURVE

NOTES:
1. PACKAGE CONTOUR OPTIONAL WITHIN A AND B. HEAT SLUGS, IF ANY, SHALL BE INCLUDED WITHIN THIS CYLINDER, BUT NOT SUBJECT TO THE MINIMUM LIMIT OF B.
2. LEAD DIAMETER NOT CONTROLLED IN ZONE F TO ALLOW FOR FLASH, LEAD FINISH BUILDUP AND MINOR IRREGULARITIES OTHER THAN HEAT SLUGS.
3. POLARITY DENOTED BY CATHODE BAND.
4. DIMENSIONING AND TOLERANCING PER ANSI Y14.5, 1973.

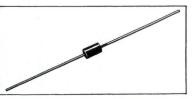

DIM	MILLIMETERS		INCHES	
	MIN	MAX	MIN	MAX
A	3.05	5.08	0.120	0.200
B	1.52	2.29	0.060	0.090
D	0.46	0.56	0.018	0.022
F	–	1.27	–	0.050
K	25.40	38.10	1.000	1.500

All JEDEC dimensions and notes apply.

CASE 299-02
DO-204AH
GLASS

ELECTRICAL CHARACTERISTICS

(At 25°C Ambient temperature unless otherwise specified) I_{ZT} = 250 μA and V_F = 1.0 V max @ I_F = 200 mA on all Types

Type Number (Note 1)	Nominal Zener Voltage V_Z (Note 1) (Volts)	Max Zener Impedance Z_{ZT} (Note 2) (Ohms)	Max Reverse Current I_R (Note 4) (μA)	@	Test Voltage V_R (Volts)	Max Noise Density At I_{ZT} = 250 μA N_D (Fig 1) (micro-volts per Square Root Cycle)	Max Zener Current I_{ZM} (Note 3) (mA)
1N4614	1.8	1200	7.5		1.0	1.0	120
1N4615	2.0	1250	5.0		1.0	1.0	110
1N4616	2.2	1300	4.0		1.0	1.0	100
1N4617	2.4	1400	2.0		1.0	1.0	95
1N4618	2.7	1500	1.0		1.0	1.0	90
1N4619	3.0	1600	0.8		1.0	1.0	85
1N4620	3.3	1650	7.5		1.5	1.0	80
1N4621	3.6	1700	7.5		2.0	1.0	75
1N4622	3.9	1650	5.0		2.0	1.0	70
1N4623	4.3	1600	4.0		2.0	1.0	65
1N4624	4.7	1550	10		3.0	1.0	60
1N4625	5.1	1500	10		3.0	2.0	55
1N4626	5.6	1400	10		4.0	4.0	50
1N4627	6.2	1200	10		5.0	5.0	45
1N4099	6.8	200	10		5.2	40	35
1N4100	7.5	200	10		5.7	40	31.8
1N4101	8.2	200	1.0		6.3	40	29.0
1N4102	8.7	200	1.0		6.7	40	27.4
1N4103	9.1	200	1.0		7.0	40	26.2
1N4104	10	200	1.0		7.6	40	24.8
1N4105	11	200	0.05		8.5	40	21.6
1N4106	12	200	0.05		9.2	40	20.4
1N4107	13	200	0.05		9.9	40	19.0
1N4108	14	200	0.05		10.7	40	17.5
1N4109	15	100	0.05		11.4	40	16.3
1N4110	16	100	0.05		12.2	40	15.4
1N4111	17	100	0.05		13.0	40	14.5
1N4112	18	100	0.05		13.7	40	13.2
1N4113	19	150	0.05		14.5	40	12.5
1N4114	20	150	0.01		15.2	40	11.9
1N4115	22	150	0.01		16.8	40	10.8
1N4116	24	150	0.01		18.3	40	9.9
1N4117	25	150	0.01		19.0	40	9.5
1N4118	27	150	0.01		20.5	40	8.8
1N4119	28	200	0.01		21.3	40	8.5
1N4120	30	200	0.01		22.8	40	7.9
1N4121	33	200	0.01		25.1	40	7.2
1N4122	36	200	0.01		27.4	40	6.6
1N4123	39	200	0.01		29.7	40	6.1
1N4124	43	250	0.01		32.7	40	5.5
1N4125	47	250	0.01		35.8	40	5.1
1N4126	51	300	0.01		38.8	40	4.6
1N4127	56	300	0.01		42.6	40	4.2
1N4128	60	400	0.01		45.6	40	4.0
1N4129	62	500	0.01		47.1	40	3.8
1N4130	68	700	0.01		51.7	40	3.5
1N4131	75	700	0.01		57.0	40	3.1
1N4132	82	800	0.01		62.4	40	2.9
1N4133	87	1000	0.01		66.2	40	2.7
1N4134	91	1200	0.01		69.2	40	2.6
1N4135	100	1500	0.01		76.0	40	2.3

NOTE 1: TOLERANCE AND VOLTAGE DESIGNATION

The type numbers shown have a standard tolerance of ±5.0% on the nominal zener voltage. C for ±2.0%, D for ±1%.

NOTE 2: ZENER IMPEDANCE (Z_{ZT}) DERIVATION

The zener impedance is derived from the 60 cycle ac voltage, which results when an ac current having an rms value equal to 10% of the dc zener current (I_{ZT}) is superimposed on I_{ZT}.

NOTE 3: MAXIMUM ZENER CURRENT RATINGS (I_{ZM})

Maximum zener current ratings are based on maximum zener voltage of the individual units.

NOTE 4: REVERSE LEAKAGE CURRENT I_R

Reverse leakage currents are guaranteed and are measured at V_R as shown on the table.

*Courtesy of Motorola, used by permission.

IN5441–IN5456 Voltage-Variable Capacitance Diodes*

MOTOROLA
SEMICONDUCTOR
TECHNICAL DATA

1N5441A,B
thru
1N5456A,B

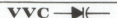

VVC ⟶ ▷|◁

**VOLTAGE-VARIABLE
CAPACITANCE DIODES**

6.8 – 100 pF
30 VOLTS

SILICON EPICAP DIODES

. . . epitaxial passivated abrupt junction tuning diodes designed for electronic tuning, FM, AFC and harmonic-generation applications in AM through UHF ranges, providing solid-state reliability to replace mechanical tuning methods.

- Excellent Q Factor at High Frequencies
- Guaranteed Capacitance Change — 2.0 to 30 V
- Guaranteed Temperature Coefficient
- Capacitance Tolerance — 10% and 5.0%
- Complete Typical Design Curves

DO-204AA GLASS

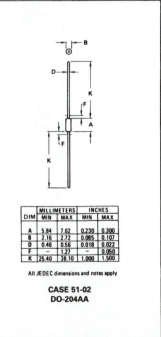

*MAXIMUM RATINGS

Rating	Symbol	Value	Unit
Reverse Voltage	V_R	30	Volts
Device Dissipation @ T_A = 25°C Derate above 25°C	P_D	400 2.67	mW mW/°C
Operating Junction Temperature Range	T_J	+175	°C
Storage Temperature Range	T_{stg}	–65 to +200	°C

*Indicates JEDEC Registered Data.

DIM	MILLIMETERS		INCHES	
	MIN	MAX	MIN	MAX
A	5.84	7.62	0.230	0.300
B	2.16	2.72	0.085	0.107
D	0.46	0.56	0.018	0.022
F	–	1.27	–	0.050
K	25.40	38.10	1.000	1.500

All JEDEC dimensions and notes apply

**CASE 51-02
DO-204AA**

*ELECTRICAL CHARACTERISTICS (T_A = 25°C unless otherwise noted)

Characteristic — All Types	Test Conditions	Symbol	Min	Typ	Max	Unit
Reverse Breakdown Voltage	I_R = 10 μAdc	$V_{(BR)R}$	30	—	—	Vdc
Reverse Voltage Leakage Current	V_R = 25 Vdc, T_A = 25°C V_R = 25 Vdc, T_A = 150°C	I_R	— —	— —	0.02 20	μAdc
Series Inductance	f = 250 MHz, lead length ≈ 1/16"	L_S	—	4.0	—	nH
Case Capacitance	f = 1.0 MHz, lead length ≈ 1/16"	C_C	—	0.17	—	pF
Diode Capacitance Temperature Coefficient (Note 6)	V_R = 4.0 Vdc, f = 1.0 MHz	TC_c	—	300	—	ppm/°C

Device	C_T, Diode Capacitance (1) V_R = 4.0 Vdc, f = 1.0 MHz pF			TR, Tuning Ratio C_2/C_{30} f = 1.0 MHz		Q, Figure of Merit V_R = 4.0 Vdc f = 50 MHz
	Min (Nom − 10%)	Nom	Max (Nom + 10%)	Min	Max	Min
1N5441A	6.1	6.8	7.5	2.5	3.2	450
1N5443A	9.0	10.0	11.0	2.6	3.2	400
1N5444A	10.8	12.0	13.2	2.6	3.2	400
1N5445A	13.5	15.0	16.5	2.6	3.2	400
1N5446A	16.2	18.0	19.8	2.6	3.2	350
1N5448A	19.8	22.0	24.2	2.6	3.2	350
1N5449A	24.3	27.0	29.7	2.6	3.2	350
1N5450A	29.7	33.0	36.3	2.6	3.2	350
1N5451A	35.1	39.0	42.9	2.6	3.2	300
1N5452A	42.3	47.0	51.7	2.6	3.2	250
1N5453A	50.4	56.0	61.6	2.6	3.3	200
1N5455A	73.8	82.0	90.2	2.7	3.3	175
1N5456A	90.0	100.0	110.0	2.7	3.3	175

(1) To order devices with C_T Nom ±5.0% add Suffix B.
*Indicates JEDEC Registered Data.

PARAMETER TEST METHODS

1. **L_S, Series Inductance**
   L_S is measured on a shorted package at 250 MHz using an impedance bridge (Boonton Radio Model 250A RX Meter or equivalent).

2. **C_C, Case Capacitance**
   C_C is measured on an open package at 1.0 MHz using a capacitance bridge (Boonton Electronics Model 75A or equivalent).

3. **C_T, Diode Capacitance**
   (C_T = C_C + C_J). C_T is measured at 1.0 MHz using a capacitance bridge (Boonton Electronics Model 75A or equivalent).

4. **TR, Tuning Ratio**
   TR is the ratio of C_T measured at 2.0 Vdc divided by C_T measured at 30 Vdc.

5. **Q, Figure of Merit**
   Q is calculated by taking the G and C readings of an admittance bridge at the specified frequency and substituting in the following equations:

   $$Q = \frac{2\pi f C}{G}$$

   (Boonton Electronics Model 33AS8 or equivalent).

6. **TC_c, Diode Capacitance Temperature Coefficient**
   TC_c is guaranteed by comparing C_T at V_R = 4.0 Vdc, f = 1.0 MHz, T_A = −65°C with C_T at V_R = 4.0 Vdc, f = 1.0 MHz, T_A = +85°C in the following equation, which defines TC_c:

   $$TC_c = \left| \frac{C_T(+85°C) - C_T(-65°C)}{85 + 65} \right| \frac{10^6}{C_T(25°C)}$$

   Accuracy limited by C_T measurement to ±0.1 pF.

FIGURE 1 – NORMALIZED DIODE CAPACITANCE versus JUNCTION TEMPERATURE

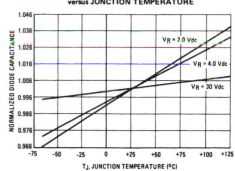

MOTOROLA RF DEVICE DATA

*Courtesy of Motorola, used by permission.

D.2 BIPOLAR TRANSISTORS
2N3903/2N3904 General-Purpose *npn* Transistors*

2N3903
2N3904

CASE 29-02, STYLE 1
TO-92 (TO-226AA)

GENERAL PURPOSE TRANSISTOR

NPN SILICON

MAXIMUM RATINGS

Rating	Symbol	Value	Unit
Collector-Emitter Voltage	V_{CEO}	40	Vdc
Collector-Base Voltge	V_{CBO}	60	Vdc
Emitter-Base Voltage	V_{EBO}	6.0	Vdc
Collector Current — Continuous	I_C	200	mAdc
Total Device Dissipation @ T_A = 25°C Derate above 25°C	P_D	625 2.8	mW mW/°C
*Total Device Dissipation @ T_C = 25°C Derate above 25°C	P_D	1.5 12	Watts mW/°C
Operating and Storage Junction Temperature Range	T_J, T_{stg}	−55 to +150	°C

*THERMAL CHARACTERISTICS

Characteristic	Symbol	Max	Unit
Thermal Resistance, Junction to Case	$R_{\theta JC}$	83.3	°C/W
Thermal Resistance, Junction to Ambient	$R_{\theta JA}$	200	°C/W

*Indicates Data in addition to JEDEC Requirements.

ELECTRICAL CHARACTERISTICS (T_A = 25°C unless otherwise noted.)

Characteristic		Symbol	Min	Max	Unit
OFF CHARACTERISTICS					
Collector-Emitter Breakdown Voltage(1) (I_C = 1.0 mAdc, I_B = 0)		$V_{(BR)CEO}$	40	—	Vdc
Collector-Base Breakdown Voltage (I_C = 10 μAdc, I_E = 0)		$V_{(BR)CBO}$	60	—	Vdc
Emitter-Base Breakdown Voltage (I_E = 10 μAdc, I_C = 0)		$V_{(BR)EBO}$	6.0	—	Vdc
Base Cutoff Current (V_{CE} = 30 Vdc, V_{EB} = 3.0 Vdc)		I_{BL}	—	50	nAdc
Collector Cutoff Current (V_{CE} = 30 Vdc, V_{EB} = 3.0 Vdc)		I_{CEX}	—	50	nAdc
ON CHARACTERISTICS					
DC Current Gain(1)		h_{FE}			—
(I_C = 0.1 mAdc, V_{CE} = 1.0 Vdc)	2N3903 2N3904		20 40	— —	
(I_C = 1.0 mAdc, V_{CE} = 1.0 Vdc)	2N3903 2N3904		35 70	— —	
(I_C = 10 mAdc, V_{CE} = 1.0 Vdc)	2N3903 2N3904		50 100	150 300	
(I_C = 50 mAdc, V_{CE} = 1.0 Vdc)	2N3903 2N3904		30 60	— —	
(I_C = 100 mAdc, V_{CE} = 1.0 Vdc)	2N3903 2N3904		15 30	— —	
Collector-Emitter Saturation Voltage(1) (I_C = 10 mAdc, I_B = 1.0 mAdc) (I_C = 50 mAdc, I_B = 5.0 mAdc)		$V_{CE(sat)}$	— —	0.2 0.3	Vdc
Base-Emitter Saturation Voltage(1) (I_C = 10 mAdc, I_B = 1.0 mAdc) (I_C = 50 mAdc, I_B = 5.0 mAdc)		$V_{BE(sat)}$	0.65 —	0.85 0.95	Vdc
SMALL-SIGNAL CHARACTERISTICS					
Current-Gain — Bandwidth Product (I_C = 10 mAdc, V_{CE} = 20 Vdc, f = 100 MHz)	2N3903 2N3904	f_T	250 300	— —	MHz

2N3903, 2N3904

ELECTRICAL CHARACTERISTICS (continued) (T_A = 25°C unless otherwise noted.)

Characteristic		Symbol	Min	Max	Unit
Output Capacitance (V_{CB} = 5.0 Vdc, I_E = 0, f = 1.0 MHz)		C_{obo}	—	4.0	pF
Input Capacitance (V_{BE} = 0.5 Vdc, I_C = 0, f = 1.0 MHz)		C_{ibo}	—	8.0	pF
Input Impedance (I_C = 1.0 mAdc, V_{CE} = 10 Vdc, f = 1.0 kHz)	2N3903 2N3904	h_{ie}	1.0 1.0	8.0 10	k ohms
Voltage Feedback Ratio (I_C = 1.0 mAdc, V_{CE} = 10 Vdc, f = 1.0 kHz)	2N3903 2N3904	h_{re}	0.1 0.5	5.0 8.0	X 10^{-4}
Small-Signal Current Gain (I_C = 1.0 mAdc, V_{CE} = 10 Vdc, f = 1.0 kHz)	2N3903 2N3904	h_{fe}	50 100	200 400	—
Output Admittance (I_C = 1.0 mAdc, V_{CE} = 10 Vdc, f = 1.0 kHz)		h_{oe}	1.0	40	μmhos
Noise Figure (I_C = 100 μAdc, V_{CE} = 5.0 Vdc, R_S = 1.0 k ohms, f = 10 Hz to 15.7 kHz)	2N3903 2N3904	NF	— —	6.0 5.0	dB

SWITCHING CHARACTERISTICS

			Symbol	Min	Max	Unit
Delay Time	(V_{CC} = 3.0 Vdc, V_{BE} = 0.5 Vdc,		t_d	—	35	ns
Rise Time	I_C = 10 mAdc, I_{B1} = 1.0 mAdc)		t_r	—	35	ns
Storage Time	(V_{CC} = 3.0 Vdc, I_C = 10 mAdc,	2N3903	t_s	—	175	ns
	I_{B1} = I_{B2} = 1.0 mAdc)	2N3904		—	200	
Fall Time			t_f	—	50	ns

(1) Pulse Test: Pulse Width ≤ 300 μs, Duty Cycle ≤ 2.0%.

*Courtesy of Motorola, used by permission.

2N3905/2N3906 General-Purpose *pnp* Transistors*

MAXIMUM RATINGS

Rating	Symbol	Value	Unit
Collector-Emitter Voltage	V_{CEO}	40	Vdc
Collector-Base Voltage	V_{CBO}	40	Vdc
Emitter-Base Voltage	V_{EBO}	5.0	Vdc
Collector Current — Continuous	I_C	200	mAdc
Total Device Dissipation @ T_A = 25°C Derate above 25°C	P_D	625 5.0	mW mW/°C
Total Power Dissipation @ T_A = 60°C	P_D	250	mW
Total Device Dissipation @ T_C = 25°C Derate above 25°C	P_D	1.5 12	Watts mW/°C
Operating and Storage Junction Temperature Range	T_J, T_{stg}	−55 to +150	°C

*THERMAL CHARACTERISTICS

Characteristic	Symbol	Max	Unit
Thermal Resistance, Junction to Case	$R_{\theta JC}$	83.3	°C/W
Thermal Resistance, Junction to Ambient	$R_{\theta JA}$	200	°C/W

2N3905
2N3906

CASE 29-02, STYLE 1
TO-92 (TO-226AA)

GENERAL PURPOSE TRANSISTOR

PNP SILICON

ELECTRICAL CHARACTERISTICS (T_A = 25°C unless otherwise noted.)

Characteristic		Symbol	Min	Max	Unit
OFF CHARACTERISTICS					
Collector-Emitter Breakdown Voltage(1) (I_C = 1.0 mAdc, I_B = 0)		$V_{(BR)CEO}$	40	—	Vdc
Collector-Base Breakdown Voltage (I_C = 10 μAdc, I_E = 0)		$V_{(BR)CBO}$	40	—	Vdc
Emitter-Base Breakdown Voltage (I_E = 10 μAdc, I_C = 0)		$V_{(BR)EBO}$	5.0	—	Vdc
Base Cutoff Current (V_{CE} = 30 Vdc, V_{BE} = 3.0 Vdc)		I_{BL}	—	50	nAdc
Collector Cutoff Current (V_{CE} = 30 Vdc, V_{BE} = 3.0 Vdc)		I_{CEX}	—	50	nAdc
ON CHARACTERISTICS(1)					
DC Current Gain		h_{FE}			—
(I_C = 0.1 mAdc, V_{CE} = 1.0 Vdc)	2N3905 2N3906		30 60	— —	
(I_C = 1.0 mAdc, V_{CE} = 1.0 Vdc)	2N3905 2N3906		40 80	— —	
(I_C = 10 mAdc, V_{CE} = 1.0 Vdc)	2N3905 2N3906		50 100	150 300	
(I_C = 50 mAdc, V_{CE} = 1.0 Vdc)	2N3905 2N3906		30 60	— —	
(I_C = 100 mAdc, V_{CE} = 1.0 Vdc)	2N3905 2N3906		15 30	— —	
Collector-Emitter Saturation Voltage (I_C = 10 mAdc, I_B = 1.0 mAdc) (I_C = 50 mAdc, I_B = 5.0 mAdc)		$V_{CE(sat)}$	— —	0.25 0.4	Vdc
Base-Emitter Saturation Voltage (I_C = 10 mAdc, I_B = 1.0 mAdc) (I_C = 50 mAdc, I_B = 5.0 mAdc)		$V_{BE(sat)}$	0.65 —	0.85 0.95	Vdc
SMALL-SIGNAL CHARACTERISTICS					
Current-Gain — Bandwidth Product (I_C = 10 mAdc, V_{CE} = 20 Vdc, f = 100 MHz)	2N3905 2N3906	f_T	200 250	— —	MHz
Output Capacitance (V_{CB} = 5.0 Vdc, I_E = 0, f = 100 kHz)		C_{obo}	—	4.5	pF

2N3905, 2N3906

ELECTRICAL CHARACTERISTICS (continued) (T_A = 25°C unless otherwise noted.)

Characteristic		Symbol	Min	Max	Unit
Input Capacitance (V_{BE} = 0.5 Vdc, I_C = 0, f = 100 kHz)		C_{ibo}	—	10.0	pF
Input Impedance (I_C = 1.0 mAdc, V_{CE} = 10 Vdc, f = 1.0 kHz)	2N3905 2N3906	h_{ie}	0.5 2.0	8.0 12	k ohms
Voltage Feedback Ratio (I_C = 1.0 mAdc, V_{CE} = 10 Vdc, f = 1.0 kHz)	2N3905 2N3906	h_{re}	0.1 0.1	5.0 10	X 10^{-4}
Small-Signal Current Gain (I_C = 1.0 mAdc, V_{CE} = 10 Vdc, f = 1.0 kHz)	2N3905 2N3906	h_{fe}	50 100	200 400	—
Output Admittance (I_C = 1.0 mAdc, V_{CE} = 10 Vdc, f = 1.0 kHz)	2N3905 2N3906	h_{oe}	1.0 3.0	40 60	μmhos
Noise Figure (I_C = 100 μAdc, V_{CE} = 5.0 Vdc, R_S = 1.0 k ohm, f = 10 Hz to 15.7 kHz)	2N3905 2N3906	NF	— —	5.0 4.0	dB

SWITCHING CHARACTERISTICS

			Symbol	Min	Max	Unit
Delay Time	(V_{CC} = 3.0 Vdc, V_{BE} = 0.5 Vdc		t_d	—	35	ns
Rise Time	I_C = 10 mAdc, I_{B1} = 1.0 mAdc)		t_r	—	35	ns
Storage Time		2N3905 2N3906	t_s	— —	200 225	ns
Fall Time	(V_{CC} = 3.0 Vdc, I_C = 10 mAdc, I_{B1} = I_{B2} = 1.0 mAdc)	2N3905 2N3906	t_f	— —	60 75	ns

(1) Pulse Width ≤ 300 μs, Duty Cycle ≤ 2.0%.

*Courtesy of Motorola, used by permission.

2N3055 *npn* Power Transistors*

MOTOROLA
■ SEMICONDUCTOR ■■■■■■■■■■■■■
TECHNICAL DATA

NPN
2N3055
PNP
MJ2955

COMPLEMENTARY SILICON POWER TRANSISTORS

. . . designed for general-purpose switching and amplifier applications.

- DC Current Gain — h_{FE} = 20-70 @ I_C = 4 Adc

- Collector-Emitter Saturation Voltage —
  $V_{CE(sat)}$ = 1.1 Vdc (Max) @ I_C = 4 Adc

- Excellent Safe Operating Area

15 AMPERE
POWER TRANSISTORS
COMPLEMENTARY SILICON

60 VOLTS
115 WATTS

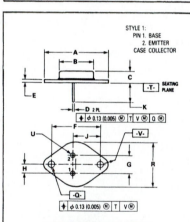

MAXIMUM RATINGS

Rating	Symbol	Value	Unit
Collector-Emitter Voltage	V_{CEO}	60	Vdc
Collector-Emitter Voltage	V_{CER}	70	Vdc
Collector-Base Voltage	V_{CB}	100	Vdc
Emitter-Base Voltage	V_{EB}	7	Vdc
Collector Current — Continuous	I_C	15	Adc
Base Current	I_B	7	Adc
Total Power Dissipation @ T_C = 25°C Derate above 25°C	P_D	115 0.657	Watts W/°C
Operating and Storage Junction Temperature Range	T_J, T_{stg}	−65 to +200	°C

THERMAL CHARACTERISTICS

Characteristic	Symbol	Max	Unit
Thermal Resistance, Junction to Case	$R_{\theta JC}$	1.52	°C/W

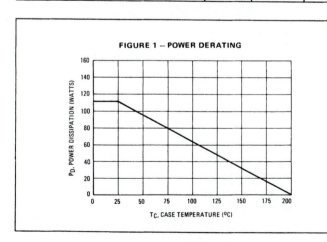

FIGURE 1 — POWER DERATING

STYLE 1:
PIN 1. BASE
2. EMITTER
CASE COLLECTOR

DIM	MILLIMETERS		INCHES	
	MIN	MAX	MIN	MAX
A	—	39.37	—	1.550
B	—	21.08	—	0.830
C	6.35	8.25	0.250	0.325
D	0.97	1.09	0.038	0.043
E	1.40	1.77	0.055	0.070
F	30.15 BSC		1.187 BSC	
G	10.92 BSC		0.430 BSC	
H	5.46 BSC		0.215 BSC	
J	16.89 BSC		0.665 BSC	
K	11.18	12.19	0.440	0.480
Q	3.84	4.19	0.151	0.165
R	—	26.67	—	1.050
U	4.83	5.33	0.190	0.210
V	3.84	4.19	0.151	0.165

NOTES:
1. DIMENSIONING AND TOLERANCING PER ANSI
   Y14.5M, 1982.
2. CONTROLLING DIMENSION: INCH.
3. ALL RULES AND NOTES ASSOCIATED WITH
   REFERENCED TO-204AA OUTLINE SHALL APPLY.

CASE 1-06
TO-204AA
(TO-3)

ELECTRICAL CHARACTERISTICS (T_C = 25°C unless otherwise noted)

Characteristic	Symbol	Min	Max	Unit
*OFF CHARACTERISTICS				
Collector-Emitter Sustaining Voltage (1) (I_C = 200 mAdc, I_B = 0)	$V_{CEO(sus)}$	60	—	Vdc
Collector-Emitter Sustaining Voltage (1) (I_C = 200 mAdc, R_{BE} = 100 Ohms)	$V_{CER(sus)}$	70	—	Vdc
Collector Cutoff Current (V_{CE} = 30 Vdc, I_B = 0)	I_{CEO}	—	0.7	mAdc
Collector Cutoff Current (V_{CE} = 100 Vdc, $V_{BE(off)}$ = 1.5 Vdc) (V_{CE} = 100 Vdc, $V_{BE(off)}$ = 1.5 Vdc, T_C = 150°C)	I_{CEX}	— —	1.0 5.0	mAdc
Emitter Cutoff Current (V_{BE} = 7.0 Vdc, I_C = 0)	I_{EBO}	—	5.0	mAdc
*ON CHARACTERISTICS (1)				
DC Current Gain (I_C = 4.0 Adc, V_{CE} = 4.0 Vdc) (I_C = 10 Adc, V_{CE} = 4.0 Vdc)	h_{FE}	20 5.0	70 —	—
Collector-Emitter Saturation Voltage (I_C = 4.0 Adc, I_B = 400 mAdc) (I_C = 10 Adc, I_B = 3.3 Adc)	$V_{CE(sat)}$	—	1.1 3.0	Vdc
Base-Emitter On Voltage (I_C = 4.0 Adc, V_{CE} = 4.0 Vdc)	$V_{BE(on)}$	—	1.5	Vdc
SECOND BREAKDOWN				
Second Breakdown Collector Current with Base Forward Biased (V_{CE} = 40 Vdc, t = 1.0 s; Nonrepetitive)	$I_{s/b}$	2.87	—	Adc
DYNAMIC CHARACTERISTICS				
Current Gain — Bandwidth Product (I_C = 0.5 Adc, V_{CE} = 10 Vdc, f = 1.0 MHz)	f_T	2.5	—	MHz
*Small-Signal Current Gain (I_C = 1.0 Adc, V_{CE} = 4.0 Vdc, f = 1.0 kHz)	h_{fe}	15	120	—
*Small-Signal Current Gain Cutoff Frequency (V_{CE} = 4.0 Vdc, I_C = 1.0 Adc, f = 1.0 kHz)	f_{hfe}	10	—	kHz

* Indicates Within JEDEC Registration. (2N3055)

(1) Pulse Test: Pulse Width ≤ 300 μs, Duty Cycle ≤ 2.0%.

FIGURE 2 —   ACTIVE REGION SAFE OPERATING AREA

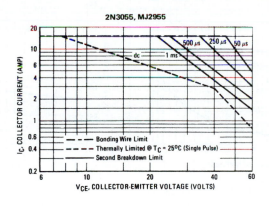

2N3055, MJ2955

There are two limitations on the power handling ability of a transistor: average junction temperature and second breakdown. Safe operating area curves indicate I_C-V_{CE} limits of the transistor that must be observed for reliable operation; i.e., the transistor must not be subjected to greater dissipation than the curves indicate.

The data of Figure 2 is based on T_C = 25°C; $T_{J(pk)}$ is variable depending on power level. Second breakdown pulse limits are valid for duty cycles to 10% but must be derated for temperature according to Figure 1.

NPN
2N3055

PNP
MJ2955

FIGURE 3 – DC CURRENT GAIN

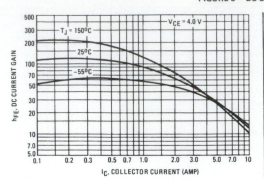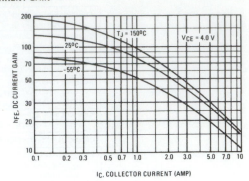

FIGURE 4 – COLLECTOR SATURATION REGION

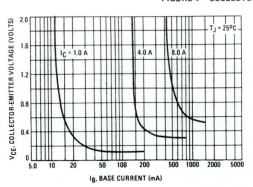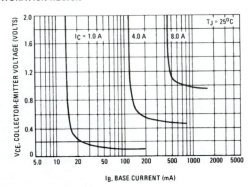

FIGURE 5 – "ON" VOLTAGES

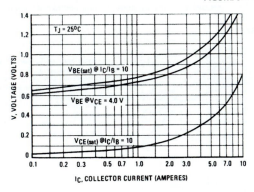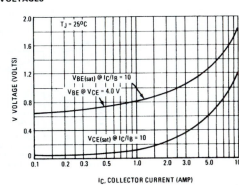

*Courtesy of Motorola, used by permission.

Specialized Two-Port Parameter Definitions for Bipolar Transistors

Common Emitter

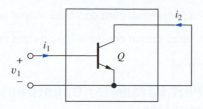

h_{ie} = short-circuit common-emitter input impedance

h_{fe} = short-circuit common-emitter forward current gain

$$h_{ie} = h_{11} = \left.\frac{\mathbf{v_1}}{\mathbf{i_1}}\right|_{v_2=0} = r_x + r_\pi \qquad h_{fe} = h_{21} = \left.\frac{\mathbf{i_2}}{\mathbf{i_1}}\right|_{v_2=0} = \beta_o$$

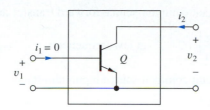

h_{oe} = open-circuit common-emitter output impedance

h_{re} = open-circuit common-emitter reverse voltage gain

$$h_{oe} = h_{22} = \left.\frac{\mathbf{i_2}}{\mathbf{v_2}}\right|_{i_1=0} = \frac{1}{r_o} \qquad h_{re} = h_{12} = \left.\frac{\mathbf{v_1}}{\mathbf{v_2}}\right|_{i_1=0}$$

Common-Base

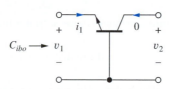

z_{ib} = open-circuit common-base input impedance

C_{ibo} = open-circuit common-base input capacitance

$$C_{ibo} = C_\pi$$

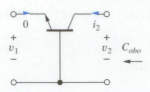

z_{ob} = open-circuit common-base output impedance

C_{obo} = open-circuit common-base output capacitance

$C_{obo} = C_\mu$

Specialized Two-Port Parameter Definitions for Field-Effect Transistors

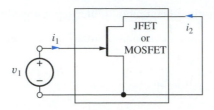

y_{fs} = short-circuit common-source forward transfer admittance

$$y_{fs} = y_{21} = \left. \frac{\mathbf{i_2}}{\mathbf{v_1}} \right|_{v_2 = 0} \qquad \text{at low frequencies, } y_{fs} = g_m$$

y_{is} = short-circuit common-source input admittance

$$y_{is} = y_{11} = \left. \frac{\mathbf{i_1}}{\mathbf{v_1}} \right|_{v_2 = 0} \qquad y_{iss} = g_{iss} + sC_{iss}$$

C_{iss} = short-circuit common-source input capacitance ($C_{iss} = C_{GS} + C_{GD}$)

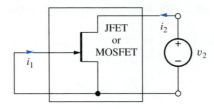

y_{os} = short-circuit common-source output admittance

$$y_{os} = y_{22} = \left. \frac{\mathbf{i_2}}{\mathbf{v_2}} \right|_{v_1 = 0} \qquad \text{at low frequencies, } y_{os} = g_o$$

y_{rs} = short-circuit common-source reverse transfer admittance

$$y_{rs} = y_{12} = \left. \frac{\mathbf{i_1}}{\mathbf{v_2}} \right|_{v_1 = 0}$$

$$-y_{rss} = g_{rss} + sC_{rss} \qquad (C_{rss} = C_{GD})$$

C_{rss} = short-circuit common-source reverse transfer capacitance

D.3 JFETs

2N5457–2N5459 General-Purpose
n-Channel JFET*

2N5457
2N5458
2N5459

CASE 29-05, STYLE 5
TO-92 (TO-226AA)

JFET
GENERAL PURPOSE

N-CHANNEL — DEPLETION

Refer to 2N4220 for graphs.

MAXIMUM RATINGS

Rating	Symbol	Value	Unit
Drain-Source Voltage	V_{DS}	25	Vdc
Drain-Gate Voltage	V_{DG}	25	Vdc
Reverse Gate-Source Voltage	V_{GSR}	−25	Vdc
Gate Current	I_G	10	mAdc
Total Device Dissipation @ $T_A = 25°C$ Derate above 25°C	P_D	310 2.82	mW mW/°C
Junction Temperature Range	T_J	125	°C
Storage Channel Temperature Range	T_{stg}	−65 to +150	°C

ELECTRICAL CHARACTERISTICS ($T_A = 25°C$ unless otherwise noted.)

Characteristic		Symbol	Min	Typ	Max	Unit
OFF CHARACTERISTICS						
Gate-Source Breakdown Voltage ($I_G = -10\ \mu Adc$, $V_{DS} = 0$)		$V_{(BR)GSS}$	−25	—	—	Vdc
Gate Reverse Current ($V_{GS} = -15$ Vdc, $V_{DS} = 0$) ($V_{GS} = -15$ Vdc, $V_{DS} = 0$, $T_A = 100°C$)		I_{GSS}	— —	— —	−1.0 −200	nAdc
Gate Source Cutoff Voltage ($V_{DS} = 15$ Vdc, $I_D = 10$ nAdc)	2N5457 2N5458 2N5459	$V_{GS(off)}$	−0.5 −1.0 −2.0	— — —	−6.0 −7.0 −8.0	Vdc
Gate Source Voltage ($V_{DS} = 15$ Vdc, $I_D = 100\ \mu Adc$) ($V_{DS} = 15$ Vdc, $I_D = 200\ \mu Adc$) ($V_{DS} = 15$ Vdc, $I_D = 400\ \mu Adc$)	2N5457 2N5458 2N5459	V_{GS}	— — —	−2.5 −3.5 −4.5	— — —	Vdc
ON CHARACTERISTICS						
Zero-Gate-Voltage Drain Current* ($V_{DS} = 15$ Vdc, $V_{GS} = 0$)	2N5457 2N5458 2N5459	I_{DSS}	1.0 2.0 4.0	3.0 6.0 9.0	5.0 9.0 16	mAdc
SMALL-SIGNAL CHARACTERISTICS						
Forward Transfer Admittance Common Source* ($V_{DS} = 15$ Vdc, $V_{GS} = 0$, $f = 1.0$ kHz)	2N5457 2N5458 2N5459	$\|Y_{fs}\|$	1000 1500 2000	— — —	5000 5500 6000	μmhos
Output Admittance Common Source* ($V_{DS} = 15$ Vdc, $V_{GS} = 0$, $f = 1.0$ kHz)		$\|Y_{os}\|$	—	10	50	μmhos
Input Capacitance ($V_{DS} = 15$ Vdc, $V_{GS} = 0$, $f = 1.0$ MHz)		C_{iss}	—	4.5	7.0	pF
Reverse Transfer Capacitance ($V_{DS} = 15$ Vdc, $V_{GS} = 0$, $f = 1.0$ MHz)		C_{rss}	—	1.5	3.0	pF

*Pulse Test: Pulse Width ≤ 630 ms; Duty Cycle ≤ 10%.

*Courtesy of Motorola, used by permission.

2N5265–2N5270 General-Purpose p-Channel JFET*

**2N5265
thru
2N5270**

**CASE 20-05, STYLE 5
TO-72 (TO-206AF)**

**JFET
GENERAL PURPOSE**

P-CHANNEL — DEPLETION

MAXIMUM RATINGS

Rating	Symbol	Value	Unit
Drain-Source Voltage	V_{DS}	60	Vdc
Drain-Gate Voltage	V_{DG}	60	Vdc
Reverse Gate-Source Voltage	V_{GSR}	60	Vdc
Drain Current	I_D	20	mAdc
Forward Gate Current	I_{GF}	10	mAdc
Total Device Dissipation @ T_A = 25°C Derate above 25°C	P_D	300 2.0	mW mW/°C
Junction Temperature Range	T_J	− 65 to + 175	°C
Storage Temperature Range	T_{stg}	− 65 to + 200	°C

ELECTRICAL CHARACTERISTICS (T_A = 25°C unless otherwise noted.)

Characteristic		Symbol	Min	Max	Unit
OFF CHARACTERISTICS					
Gate-Source Breakdown Voltage (I_G = 10 μAdc, V_{DS} = 0)		$V_{(BR)GSS}$	60	—	Vdc
Gate Reverse Current (V_{GS} = 30 Vdc, V_{DS} = 0) (V_{GS} = 30 Vdc, V_{DS} = 0, T_A = 150°C)		I_{GSS}	 — —	 2.0 2.0	 nAdc μAdc
Gate Source Cutoff Voltage (V_{DS} = 15 Vdc, I_D = 1.0 μAdc)	2N5265, 2N5266 2N5267, 2N5268 2N5269, 2N5270	$V_{GS(off)}$	 — — —	 3.0 6.0 8.0	Vdc
Gate Source Voltage (V_{DS} = 15 Vdc, I_D = 0.05 mAdc) (V_{DS} = 15 Vdc, I_D = 0.08 mAdc) (V_{DS} = 15 Vdc, I_D = 0.15 mAdc) (V_{DS} = 15 Vdc, I_D = 0.25 mAdc) (V_{DS} = 15 Vdc, I_D = 0.4 mAdc) (V_{DS} = 15 Vdc, I_D = 0.7 mAdc)	 2N5265 2N5266 2N5267 2N5268 2N5269 2N5270	V_{GS}	 0.3 0.4 1.0 1.0 2.0 2.0	 1.5 2.0 4.0 4.0 6.0 6.0	Vdc
ON CHARACTERISTICS					
Zero-Gate-Voltage Drain Current (V_{DS} = 15 Vdc, V_{GS} = 0)	 2N5265 2N5266 2N5267 2N5268 2N5269 2N5270	I_{DSS}	 0.5 0.8 1.5 2.5 4.0 7.0	 1.0 1.6 3.0 5.0 8.0 14	mAdc
SMALL-SIGNAL CHARACTERISTICS					
Forward Transfer Admittance (V_{DS} = 15 Vdc, V_{GS} = 0, f = 1.0 kHz)	 2N5265 2N5266 2N5267 2N5268 2N5269 2N5270	$\|y_{fs}\|$	 900 1000 1500 2000 2200 2500	 2700 3000 3500 4000 4500 5000	μmhos
Output Admittance Common Source (V_{DS} = 15 Vdc, V_{GS} = 0, f = 1.0 kHz)		$\|y_{os}\|$	—	75	μmhos

*Courtesy of Motorola, used by permission.

D.4 MOSFETs

2N7000 *n*-Channel MOSFET*

2N7000

CASE 29-04, STYLE 7
TO-92 (TO-226AA)

3 Drain

1
2
3

2 Gate

1 Source

TMOS FET
TRANSISTOR

N-CHANNEL — ENHANCEMENT

MAXIMUM RATINGS

Rating	Symbol	Value	Unit
Drain-Source Voltage	V_{DSS}	60	Vdc
Drain-Gate Voltage ($R_{GS} = 1\ M\Omega$)	V_{DGR}	60	Vdc
Gate-Source Voltage	V_{GS}	±40	Vdc
Drain Current Continuous Pulsed	 I_D I_{DM}	 200 500	mAdc
Total Power Dissipation @ T_C = 25°C Derate above 25°C	P_D	400 3.2	mW mW/°C
Operating and Storage Temperature Range	T_J, T_{stg}	−55 to +150	°C

THERMAL CHARACTERISTICS

Thermal Resistance Junction to Ambient	$R_{\theta JA}$	312.5	°C/W
Maximum Lead Temperature for Soldering Purposes, 1/16″ from case for 10 seconds	T_L	300	°C

ELECTRICAL CHARACTERISTICS (T_C = 25°C unless otherwise noted.)

Characteristic	Symbol	Min	Max	Unit
OFF CHARACTERISTICS				
Drain-Source Breakdown Voltage (V_{GS} = 0, I_D = 10 μA)	$V_{(BR)DSS}$	60	—	Vdc
Zero Gate Voltage Drain Current (V_{DS} = 48 V, V_{GS} = 0) (V_{DS} = 48 V, V_{GS} = 0, T_J = 125°C)	I_{DSS}	 — —	 1.0 1.0	 μAdc mA
Gate-Body Leakage Current, Forward (V_{GSF} = 15 Vdc, V_{DS} = 0)	I_{GSSF}	—	−10	nAdc
ON CHARACTERISTICS*				
Gate Threshold Voltage (V_{DS} = V_{GS}, I_D = 1.0 mA)	$V_{GS(th)}$	0.8	3.0	Vdc
Static Drain-Source On-Resistance (V_{GS} = 10 Vdc, I_D = 0.5 Adc) (V_{GS} = 10 Vdc, I_D = 0.5 V, T_C = 125°C)	$r_{DS(on)}$	 — —	 5.0 9.0	Ohm
Drain-Source On-Voltage (V_{GS} = 10 V, I_D = 0.5 Adc) (V_{GS} = 4.5 V, I_D = 75 mA)	$V_{DS(on)}$	 — —	 2.5 0.4	Vdc
On-State Drain Current (V_{GS} = 4.5 V, V_{DS} = 10 V)	$I_{d(on)}$	75	—	mA
Forward Transconductance (V_{DS} = 10 V, I_D = 200 mA)	g_{fs}	100	—	μmhos
DYNAMIC CHARACTERISTICS				
Input Capacitance	(V_{DS} = 25 V, V_{GS} = 0 f = 1.0 MHz)	C_{iss}	—	60	pF
Output Capacitance		C_{oss}	—	25	
Reverse Transfer Capacitance		C_{rss}	—	5.0	
SWITCHING CHARACTERISTICS*				
Turn-On Delay Time	(V_{DD} = 15 V, I_D = 600 mA R_{gen} = 25 ohms, R_L = 25 ohms)	t_{on}	—	10	ns
Turn-Off Delay Time		t_{off}	—	10	

(1) Pulse Test: Pulse Width ≤ 300 μs, Duty Cycle ≤ 2.0%.

*Courtesy of Motorola, used by permission.

MTM8P08, MTM8P10 *p*-Channel Power MOSFET*

MTM8P08, MTM8P10 MTP8P08, MTP8P10

(Formerly MTM/MTP 814, 815)

Designer's Data Sheet

P-CHANNEL ENHANCEMENT MODE SILICON GATE TMOS POWER FIELD EFFECT TRANSISTOR

These TMOS Power FETs are designed for low voltage, high speed power switching applications such as switching regulators, converters, solenoid and relay drivers.

- Silicon Gate for Fast Switching Speeds — Switching Times Specified at 100°C
- Designer's Data — I_{DSS}, $V_{DS(on)}$, $V_{GS(th)}$ and SOA Specified at Elevated Temperature
- Rugged — SOA is Power Dissipation Limited
- Source-to-Drain Diode Characterized for Use With Inductive Loads

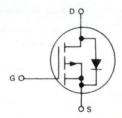

8.0 AMPERE

P-CHANNEL TMOS POWER FET

$r_{DS(on)} = 0.4$ OHMS
80 and 100 VOLTS

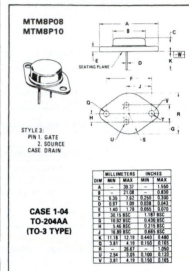

MAXIMUM RATINGS

Rating	Symbol	MTM8P08 MTP8P08	MTM8P10 MTP8P10	Unit
Drain-Source Voltage	V_{DSS}	80	100	Vdc
Drain-Gate Voltage ($R_{GS} = 1.0$ MΩ)	V_{DGR}	80	100	Vdc
Gate-Source Voltage e	V_{GS}	±20		Vdc
Drain Current Continuous Pulsed	I_D I_{DM}	8.0 25		Adc
Gate Current — Pulsed	I_{GM}	1.5		Adc
Total Power Dissipation @ $T_C = 25°C$ Derate above 25°C	P_D	75 0.6		Watts W/°C
Operating and Storage Temperature Range	T_J, T_{stg}	–65 to 150		°C

THERMAL CHARACTERISTICS

Thermal Resistance Junction to Case	$R_{\theta JC}$	1.67	°C/W
Maximum Lead Temp. for Soldering Purposes, 1/8" from case for 5 seconds	T_L	275	°C

Designer's Data for "Worst Case" Conditions

The Designer's Data Sheet permits the design of most circuits entirely from the information presented. Limit data — representing device characteristics boundaries — are given to facilitate "worst case" design.

MTM8P08
MTM8P10

STYLE 3:
PIN 1. GATE
2. SOURCE
CASE DRAIN

DIM	MILLIMETERS MIN	MAX	INCHES MIN	MAX
A	–	39.37	–	1.550
B	–	21.08	–	0.830
C	6.35	7.62	0.250	0.300
D	0.97	1.09	0.038	0.043
E	1.40	1.78	0.055	0.070
F	30.15 BSC		1.187 BSC	
G	10.92 BSC		0.430 BSC	
H	5.46 BSC		0.215 BSC	
J	16.89 BSC		0.665 BSC	
K	11.18	12.19	0.440	0.480
Q	3.81	4.19	0.150	0.165
R	–	26.67	–	1.050
U	2.54	3.05	0.100	0.120
V	3.81	4.19	0.150	0.165

CASE 1-04 TO-204AA (TO-3 TYPE)

MTP8P08
MTP8P10

STYLE 5:
PIN 1. GATE
2. DRAIN
3. SOURCE
4. DRAIN

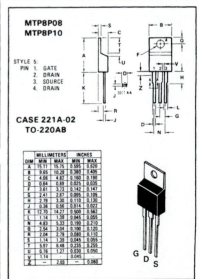

DIM	MILLIMETERS MIN	MAX	INCHES MIN	MAX
A	15.11	15.75	0.595	0.620
B	9.65	10.29	0.380	0.405
C	4.06	4.82	0.160	0.190
D	0.64	0.89	0.025	0.035
F	3.61	3.73	0.142	0.147
G	2.41	2.67	0.095	0.105
H	2.79	3.30	0.110	0.130
J	0.36	0.56	0.014	0.022
K	12.70	14.27	0.500	0.562
L	1.14	1.39	0.045	0.055
N	4.83	5.33	0.190	0.210
Q	2.54	3.04	0.100	0.120
R	2.04	2.79	0.080	0.110
S	1.14	1.39	0.045	0.055
T	5.97	6.48	0.235	0.255
U	0.76	1.27	0.030	0.050
V	1.14	?	0.045	–
Z	–	2.03	–	0.080

CASE 221A-02 TO-220AB

MOTOROLA TMOS POWER MOSFET DATA

MTM/MTP8P08, 10

ELECTRICAL CHARACTERISTICS (T_C = 25°C unless otherwise noted)

Characteristic		Symbol	Min	Max	Unit
OFF CHARACTERISTICS					
Drain-Source Breakdown Voltage (V_{GS} = 0, I_D = 5.0 mA) MTM8P08/MTP8P08 MTM8P10/MTP8P10		$V_{(BR)DSS}$	80 100	— —	Vdc
Zero Gate Voltage Drain Current (V_{DS} = 0.85 Rated V_{DSS}, V_{GS} = 0) T_J = 100°C		I_{DSS}	— —	0.25 2.5	mAdc
Gate-Body Leakage Current (V_{GS} = 20 Vdc, V_{DS} = 0)		I_{GSS}	—	500	nAdc
ON CHARACTERISTICS*					
Gate Threshold Voltage (I_D = 1.0 mA, V_{DS} = V_{GS}) T_J = 100°C		$V_{GS(th)}$	2.0 1.5	4.5 4.0	Vdc
Drain-Source On-Voltage (V_{GS} = 10 V) (I_D = 4.0 Adc) (I_D = 8.0 Adc) (I_D = 4.0 Adc, T_J = 100°C)		$V_{DS(on)}$	— — —	1.6 4.8 3.0	Vdc
Static Drain-Source On-Resistance (V_{GS} = 10 Vdc, I_D = 4.0 Adc)		$r_{DS(on)}$	—	0.4	Ohms
Forward Transconductance (V_{DS} = 15 V, I_D = 4.0 A)		g_{fs}	2.0	—	mhos
SAFE OPERATING AREAS					
Forward Biased Safe Operating Area		FBSOA	See Figure 13		
Switching Safe Operating Area		SSOA	See Figure 14		
DYNAMIC CHARACTERISTICS					
Input Capacitance	(V_{DS} = 25 V, V_{GS} = 0, f = 1.0 MHz)	C_{iss}	—	1200	pF
Output Capacitance		C_{oss}	—	600	pF
Reverse Transfer Capacitance		C_{rss}	—	180	pF
SWITCHING CHARACTERISTICS* (T_J = 100°C)					
Turn-On Delay Time	(V_{DS} = 25 V, I_D = 4.0 A, R_{gen} = 50 ohms)	$t_{d(on)}$	—	80	ns
Rise Time		t_r	—	150	ns
Turn-Off Delay Time		$t_{d(off)}$	—	200	ns
Fall Time		t_f	—	150	ns

SOURCE DRAIN DIODE CHARACTERISTICS*

Characteristic		Symbol	Typ	Unit
Forward On-Voltage	I_S = 8.0 A	V_{SD}	1.3	Vdc
Forward Turn-On Time	V_{GS} = 0	t_{on}	250	ns
Reverse Recovery Time		t_{rr}	325	ns

*Pulse Test: Pulse Width ≤ 300 μs, Duty Cycle ≤ 2%.

RESISTIVE SWITCHING

FIGURE 1 — SWITCHING TEST CIRCUIT

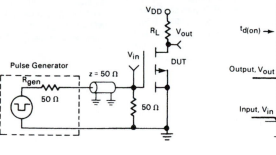

FIGURE 2 — SWITCHING WAVEFORMS

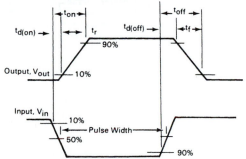

*Courtesy of Motorola, used by permission.

D.5 OPERATIONAL AMPLIFIERS

AD-741 Low-Cost General-Purpose Bipolar Op Amp*

ANALOG DEVICES

Low Cost, High Accuracy IC Op Amps

AD741 Series

FEATURES
Precision Input Characteristics
  Low V_{OS}: 0.5 mV max (L)
  Low V_{OS} Drift: 5 μV/°C max (L)
  Low I_b: 50 nA max (L)
  Low I_{OS}: 5 nA max (L)
  High CMRR: 90 dB min (K, L)
High Output Capability
  A_{OL} = 25,000 min, 1 kΩ Load (J, S)
    T_{min} to T_{max}
  V_O = ±10 V min, 1 kΩ Load (J, S)
Chips and MIL-STD-883B Parts Available

FUNCTIONAL BLOCK DIAGRAMS

TO-99 (H) Package

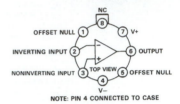

NOTE: PIN 4 CONNECTED TO CASE

Mini-DIP (N) Package

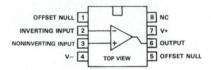

GENERAL DESCRIPTION

The Analog Devices AD741 Series are high performance monolithic operational amplifiers. All the devices feature full short circuit protection and internal compensation.

The Analog Devices AD741J, AD741K, AD741L, and AD741S are specially tested and selected versions of the standard AD741 operational amplifier. Improved processing and additional electrical testing guarantee the user precision performance at a very-low cost. The AD741J, K and L substantially increase overall accuracy over the standard AD741C by providing maximum limits on offset voltage drift and significantly reducing the errors due to offset voltage, bias current, offset current, voltage gain, power supply rejection, and common-mode rejection. For example, the AD741L features maximum offset voltage drift of 5 μV/°C, offset voltage of 0.5 mV max, offset current of 5 nA max, bias current of 50 nA max, and a CMRR of 90 dB min. The AD741S offers guaranteed performance over the extended temperature range of −55°C to +125°C, with max offset voltage drift of 15 μV/°C, max offset voltage of 4 mV, max offset current of 25 nA, and a minimum CMRR of 80 dB.

HIGH OUTPUT CAPABILITY

Both the AD741J and AD741S offer the user the additional advantages of high guaranteed output current and gain at low values of load impedance. The AD741J guarantees a minimum gain of 25,000 swinging ±10 V into a 1 kΩ load from 0 to +70°C. The AD741S guarantees a minimum gain of 25,000 swinging ±10 V into a 1 kΩ load from −55°C to +125°C.

All devices feature full short circuit protection, high gain, high common-mode range, and internal compensation. The AD741J, K and L are specified for operation from 0 to +70°C, and are available in both the TO-99 and mini-DIP packages. The AD741S is specified for operation from −55°C to +125°C, and is available in the TO-99 package.

AD741 Series—SPECIFICATIONS (typical @ +25°C and ±15 V dc, unless otherwise specified)

Model	AD741C Min	Typ	Max	AD741 Min	Typ	Max	AD741J Min	Typ	Max	Units
OPEN-LOOP GAIN										
R_L = 1 kΩ, V_O = ±10 V							50,000	200,000		V/V
R_L = 2 kΩ, V_O = ±10 V	20,000	200,000		50,000	200,000					V/V
T_A = min to max R_L = 2 kΩ	15,000			25,000			25,000			V/V
OUTPUT CHARACTERISTICS										
Voltage @ R_L = 1 kΩ, T_A = min to max							±10	±13		V
Voltage @ R_L = 2 kΩ, T_A = min to max	±10	±13		±10	±13					V
Short Circuit Current		25			25			25		mA
FREQUENCY RESPONSE										
Unity Gain, Small Signal		1			1			1		MHz
Full Power Response		10			10			10		kHz
Slew Rate		0.5			0.5			0.5		V/μs
Transient Response (Unity Gain)										
Rise Time C_L ≤ 10 V p–p		0.3			0.3			0.3		μs
Overshoot		5.0			5.0			5.0		%
INPUT OFFSET VOLTAGE										
Initial, R_S ≤ 10 kΩ, Adjust to Zero		1.0	6.0		1.0	5.0		1.0	3.0	mV
T_A = min to max		1.0	7.5		1.0	6.0			4.0	mV
Average vs. Temperature (Untrimmed)									20	μV/°C
vs. Supply, T_A = min to max								30	100	μV/V
INPUT OFFSET CURRENT										
Initial		20	200		20	200		5	50	nA
T_A = min to max		40	300		85	500			100	nA
Average vs. Temperature								0.1		nA/°C
INPUT BIAS CURRENT										
Initial		80	500		80	500		40	200	nA
T_A = min to max		120	800		300	1,500			400	nA
Average vs. Temperature								0.6		nA/°C
INPUT IMPEDANCE DIFFERENTIAL	0.3	2.0		0.3	2.0			1.0		MΩ
INPUT VOLTAGE RANGE[1]										
Differential, max Safe									±30	V
Common-Mode, max Safe	±12	±13		±12	±13			±15		V
Common-Mode Rejection,										
R_S = ≤ 10 kΩ, T_A = min to max,										
V_{IN} = ±12 V	70	90		70	90		80	90		dB
POWER SUPPLY										
Rated Performance		±15			±15			±15		V
Operating							±5		±18	V
Power Supply Rejection Ratio		30	150		30	150				μV/V
Quiescent Current		1.7	2.8		1.7	2.8		2.2	3.3	mA
Power Consumption		50	85		50	85		50	85	mW
T_A = min					60	100				mW
T_A = max					45	75				mW
TEMPERATURE RANGE										
Operating Rated Performance	0		+70	−55		+125	0		+70	°C
Storage	−65		+150	−65		+150	−65		+150	°C

NOTES
[1]For supply voltages less than ±15 V, the absolute maximum input voltage is equal to the supply voltage.
Specifications subject to change without notice.
All min and max specifications are guaranteed. Specifications shown in **boldface** are tested on all production units at final electrical test. Results from those tests are used to calculate outgoing quality levels.

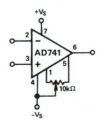

Standard Nulling Offset Circuit

METALIZATION PHOTOGRAPH
All versions of the AD741 are available in chip form.
Contact factory for latest dimensions.
Dimensions shown in inches and (mm).

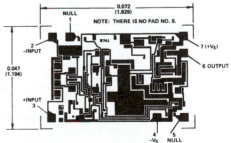

PAD NUMBERS CORRESPOND TO PIN NUMBERS FOR THE TO-99 8 PIN METAL PACKAGE.

AD741 Series—Typical Performance Curves

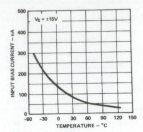

Figure 1. Input Bias Current vs. Temperature

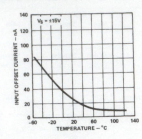

Figure 2. Input Offset Current vs. Temperature

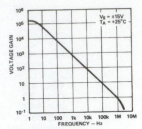

Figure 3. Open-Loop Gain vs. Frequency

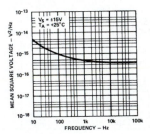

Figure 4. Open-Loop Phase Response vs. Frequency

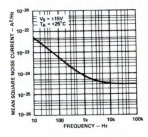

Figure 5. Common-Mode Rejection vs. Frequency

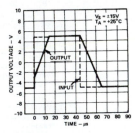

Figure 6. Broad Band Noise vs. Source Resistance

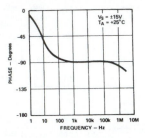

Figure 7. Input Noise Voltage vs. Frequency

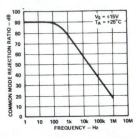

Figure 8. Input Noise Current vs. Frequency

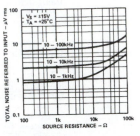

Figure 9. Voltage Follower Large Signal Pulse Response

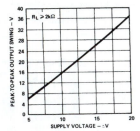

Figure 10. Output Voltage Swing vs. Supply Voltage

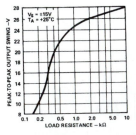

Figure 11. Output Voltage Swing vs. Load Resistance

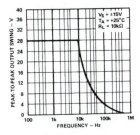

Figure 12. Output Voltage Swing vs. Frequency

*With permission of Analog Devices.

LF-155/LF156/LF157 General-Purpose JFET Input-Op Amp (see Chapter 12)

OP-77 Precision Op Amp*

ANALOG DEVICES

Next Generation OP-07, Ultra-Low Offset Voltage Operational Amplifier

OP-77

FEATURES
- Outstanding Gain Linearity
- Ultra High Gain .... 5000V/mV Min
- Low V_{OS} Over Temperature .... 60µV Max
- Excellent TCV_{OS} · .... 0.3µV/°C Max
- High PSRR .... 3µV/V Max
- Low Power Consumption .... 60mW Max
- Fits OP-07, 725, 108A/308A, 741 Sockets
- Available in Die Form

ORDERING INFORMATION †

	PACKAGE			OPERATING TEMPERATURE RANGE
TO-99	CERDIP 8-PIN	PLASTIC 8-PIN	LCC 20-PIN	
OP77AJ*	OP77AZ*	–	–	MIL
OP77EJ	OP77EZ	–	–	IND
–	–	OP77EP	–	COM
OP77BJ*	OP77BZ*	–	OP77BRC/883	MIL
OP77FJ	OP77FZ	–	–	IND
–	–	OP77FP	–	COM
–	–	OP77GP	–	COM
–	–	OP77GS††	–	COM
–	–	OP77HP	–	XIND
–	–	OP77HS††	–	XIND

*   For devices processed in total compliance to MIL-SDT-883, add /883 after part number. Consult factory for 883 data sheet.

†   Burn-in is available on commercial and industrial temperature range parts in CerDIP, plastic DIP, and TO-can packages.

†† For availability and burn-in information on SO and PLCC packages, contact your local sales office.

GENERAL DESCRIPTION

The OP-77 significantly advances the state-of-the-art in precision op amps. The OP-77's outstanding gain of 10,000,000 or more is maintained over the full ±10V output range. This exceptional gain-linearity eliminates incorrectable system nonlinearities common in previous monolithic op amps, and provides superior performance in high closed-loop-gain applications. Low initial V_{OS} drift and rapid stabilization time, combined with only 50mW power consumption, are significant improvements over previous designs. These characteristics, plus the exceptional TCV_{OS} of 0.3µV/°C maximum and the low V_{OS} of 25µV maximum, eliminates the need for V_{OS} adjustment and increases system accuracy over temperature.

PSRR of 3µV/V (110dB) and CMRR of 1.0µV/V maximum virtually eliminiate errors caused by power supply drifts and common-mode signals. This combination of outstanding characteristics makes the OP-77 ideally suited for high-resolution instrumentation and other tight error budget systems.

Continued

PIN CONNECTIONS

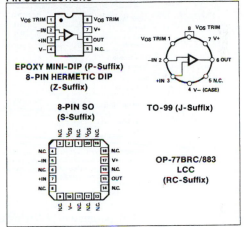

SIMPLIFIED SCHEMATIC

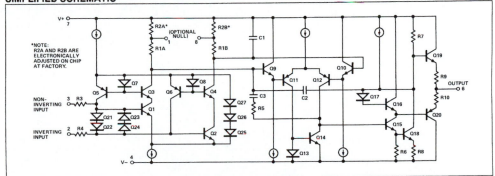

OP-77

ELECTRICAL CHARACTERISTICS at $V_S = \pm 15V$, $T_A = 25°C$, unless otherwise noted.

PARAMETER	SYMBOL	CONDITIONS	OP-77E MIN	OP-77E TYP	OP-77E MAX	OP-77F MIN	OP-77F TYP	OP-77F MAX	OP-77G/H MIN	OP-77G/H TYP	OP-77G/H MAX	UNITS
Input Offset Voltage	V_{OS}		—	10	25	—	20	60	—	50	100	μV
Long-Term V_{OS} Stability	V_{OS}/Time	(Note 1)	—	0.3	—	—	0.4	—	—	0.4	—	μV/Mo
Input Offset Current	I_{OS}		—	0.3	1.5	—	0.3	2.8	—	0.3	2.8	nA
Input Bias Current	I_B		−0.2	1.2	2.0	−0.2	1.2	2.8	−0.2	1.2	2.8	nA
Input Noise Voltage	e_{np-p}	0.1Hz to 10Hz (Note 2)	—	0.35	0.6	—	0.38	0.65	—	0.38	0.65	μV_{p-p}
Input Noise Voltage Density	e_n	$f_O = 10Hz$	—	10.3	18.0	—	10.5	20.0	—	10.5	20.0	$nV/\sqrt{Hz}$
		$f_O = 100Hz$ (Note 2)	—	10.0	13.0	—	10.2	13.5	—	10.2	13.5	
		$f_O = 1000Hz$	—	9.6	11.0	—	9.8	11.5	—	9.8	11.5	
Input Noise Current	i_{np-p}	0.1Hz to 10Hz (Note 2)	—	14	30	—	15	35	—	15	35	pA_{p-p}
Input Noise Current Density	i_n	$f_O = 10Hz$	—	0.32	0.80	—	0.35	0.90	—	0.35	0.90	$pA/\sqrt{Hz}$
		$f_O = 100Hz$ (Note 2)	—	0.14	0.23	—	0.15	0.27	—	0.15	0.27	
		$f_O = 1000Hz$	—	0.12	0.17	—	0.13	0.18	—	0.13	0.18	
Input Resistance — Differential-Mode	R_{IN}	(Note 3)	26	45	—	18.5	45	—	18.5	45	—	$M\Omega$
Input Resistance — Common-Mode	R_{INCM}		—	200	—	—	200	—	—	200	—	$G\Omega$
Input Voltage Range	IVR		± 13	± 14	—	± 13	± 14	—	± 13	± 14	—	V
Common-Mode Rejection Ratio	CMRR	$V_{CM} = \pm 13V$	—	0.1	1.0	—	0.1	1.6	—	0.1	1.6	$\mu V/V$
Power Supply Rejection Ratio	PSRR	$V_S = \pm 3V$ to $\pm 18V$	—	0.7	3.0	—	0.7	3.0	—	0.7	3.0	$\mu V/V$
Large-Signal Voltage Gain	A_{VO}	$R_L \geq 2k\Omega$, $V_O = \pm 10V$	5000	12000	—	2000	6000	—	2000	6000	—	V/mV
Output Voltage Swing	V_O	$R_L \geq 10k\Omega$	± 13.5	± 14.0	—	± 13.5	± 14.0	—	± 13.5	± 14.0	—	V
		$R_L \geq 2k\Omega$	± 12.5	± 13.0	—	± 12.5	± 13.0	—	± 12.5	± 13.0	—	
		$R_L \geq 1k\Omega$	± 12.0	± 12.5	—	± 12.0	± 12.5	—	± 12.0	± 12.5	—	
Slew Rate	SR	$R_L \geq 2k\Omega$ (Note 2)	0.1	0.3	—	0.1	0.3	—	0.1	0.3	—	$V/\mu s$
Closed-Loop Bandwidth	BW	$A_{VCL} = +1$ (Note 2)	0.4	0.6	—	0.4	0.6	—	0.4	0.6	—	MHz
Open-Loop Output Resistance	R_O		—	60	—	—	60	—	—	60	—	Ω
Power Consumption	P_d	$V_S = \pm 15V$, No Load	—	50	60	—	50	60	—	50	60	mW
		$V_S = \pm 3V$, No Load	—	3.5	4.5	—	3.5	4.5	—	3.5	4.5	
Offset Adjustment Range		$R_P = 20k\Omega$	—	± 3	—	—	± 3	—	—	± 3	—	mV

NOTES:
1. Long-Term Input Offset Voltage Stability refers to the averaged trend line of V_{OS} vs. Time over extended periods after the first 30 days of operation. Excluding the initial hour of operation, changes in V_{OS} during the first 30 operating days are typically 2.5μV.
2. Sample tested.
3. Guaranteed by design.

*With permission of Analog Devices.

Physical Constants and Conversion Factors

Physical Constants

Symbol	Quantity	Value
N_{AV}	Avogadro constant	6.022×10^{26}/kg·mole
c	Speed of light in a vacuum	2.998×10^{10} cm/s
ε_o	Permittivity of free space	8.854×10^{-14} F/cm
ε_S	Relative permittivity of silicon	11.7
ε_{OX}	Relative permittivity of silicon dioxide	3.9
E_G	Bandgap of silicon	1.12 eV
h	Planck's constant	6.625×10^{-34} J·s
		4.135×10^{-15} eV·s
k	Boltzmann's constant	1.381×10^{-23} J/K
		8.617×10^{-5} eV/K
$\dfrac{kT}{q}$	Thermal voltage at 300K	0.0259 V
m_o	Electron rest mass	9.1095×10^{-31} kg
M_p	Proton rest mass	1.6726×10^{-27} kg
n_i	Silicon intrinsic carrier density at room temperature	10^{10}/cm^3
q	Electronic charge	1.602×10^{-19} C

Conversion Factors

1 angstrom = 10^{-8} cm	$\mu = 10^{-6}$
1 μm = 10^{-4} cm	n = 10^{-9}
1 mil = 25.4 μm	p = 10^{-12}
1 eV = 1.602×10^{-19} J	f = 10^{-15}
	k = 10^{3}
	M = 10^{6}

Answers to Selected Problems

Chapter 1

1.3. 1.26 years, 4.18 years

1.5. 2.01 years, 6.67 years

1.7. 113 MW, 511 kA

1.9. 2.44 mV, 5.71 V

1.11. 19.53 mV/bit, 10001110_2

1.13. 0.002 A, 0.002 cos (1000t) A

1.15. $[5 + 2\sin(2500t) + 4\sin(1000t)]$ V

1.17. 14.7 V, 3.30 V, 76.7 μA, 300 μA

1.19. 150 μA, 100 μA, 8.20 V

1.21. 40 Ω, 0.025 v_s

1.23. 56 kΩ, $1.07 \times 10^{-3}v_s$

1.25. 1.00 MΩ, $-2.00 \times 10^8 i_s$

1.28. $5\underline{/-45°}$, $100\underline{/-12°}$

1.31. Bandpass amplifier

1.33. $25.0\sin(2000\pi t) + 15.0\cos(8000\pi t)$ V

1.35. 0 V

1.37. 3.29, 0.995, −6.16; 3.295, 0.9952, −6.155

Chapter 2

2.2. 305.2 K

2.4. -5×10^4 cm/s

2.5. For Ge: 35.9/cm³, 2.27×10^{13}/cm³, 8.04×10^{15}/cm³

2.7. 2.13×10^6 cm/s, 7.80×10^5 cm/s, 3.41×10^4 A/cm², 1.25×10^{-10} A/cm²

2.9. 316.6 K

2.12. 100 V/cm

2.15. 3.00×10^{16}/cm³, 3.33×10^5/cm³

2.19. 1.11 μm

2.21. 10^2/cm³, 10^{18}/cm³, 350cm²/V · s, 150 cm²/V · s, 0.042 Ω · cm, p-type

2.23. 10^{16}/cm³, 10^4/cm³, 710 cm²/V · s, 260 cm²/V · s, 2.40 Ω · cm, p-type

2.27. 2.5×10^{15}/cm³

2.29. Yes—add equal amounts of donor and acceptor impurities. Then $n = n_i = p$, but the mobilities are reduced. See Prob. 2.26.

2.31. 1.4×10^{17}/cm³

2.33. 6.64 mV, 12.9 mV, 25.9 mV

2.35. $12.0 \times 10^3 \exp(-5000x)$ A/cm²; 1.20 mA

2.37. −553 A/cm², −603 A/cm², +20 A/cm², −7 A/cm², +46.7 A/cm²

Chapter 3

3.1. 10^{18}/cm³, 10^2/cm³, 10^{15}/cm³, 10^5/cm³, 0.748 V, 0.984 μm

3.3. 0.806 V, 1.02 μm, 1.02 μm, 1.02×10^{-4} μm, 15.8 kV/cm

3.5. 1.80 V, 3.06 μm

3.7. 160 A/cm^2

3.9. 5×10^{20}/cm^4

3.14. 1.39, 3.17 pA

3.15. 0.748 V; 0.691 V; 0 A; -0.909×10^{-17} A; -1.00×10^{-17} A

3.17. 1.35 V; 1.38 V

3.19. 0.518 V; 0.633 V

3.21. 0.757 V; 0.721 V

3.23. -1.96 mV/K

3.25. 374 V

3.27. 4 V, 0 Ω

3.29. 9.80 nF/cm^2; 37.6 pF

3.30. 400 fF, 10 fC; 100 pF, 2.5 pC

3.32. 13.9 MHz; 21.9 MHz

3.35. SPICE: (441 μA, 0.693 V); Load line: (450 μA, 0.500 V)

3.41. Load line: (51 μA, 0.49 V); Mathematical model: (49.93 μA, 0.5007 V); Ideal diode model: (100 μA, 0 V); CVD model: (40.0 μA, 0.600 V)

3.44. (a) (0.500 mA, 0 V); (0.465 mA, 0.700 V)

3.45. (a) (-6.67 V, 0 A), (0 V, 1.67 mA); (-6.15 V, 0 A), (0.75 V, 1.62 mA)

3.50. (I_Z, V_Z) = (343 μA, 4.00 V)

3.53. 12.6 mW

3.57. 0.975 ($V_P - V_{on}$)

3.60. -7.91 V; 1.05 F; 17.8 V; 3530 A; 841 A ($\Delta T = 0.628$ ms)

3.65. 3.33 F; 12 V; 4.24 V; 1540 A; 7530 A

3.69. 7.91 V; 0.527 F; 17.8 V; 420 A; 1770 A

3.73. 417 μF; 2000 V; 1410 V; 44.4 A; 314 A

3.77. $\delta = 2/3$; $C = 74.1\ \mu$F $\to 82\ \mu$F; $L = 1.48$ mH $\to$ 1.5 mH

3.79. $V_O = \dfrac{V_S}{1 - \delta} - V_{on}$; 6.75 V; 37.5 mV; 44.4 mA

3.80. $\eta = \dfrac{100\%}{1 + (1 - \delta)\dfrac{V_{on}}{V_S}}$; 96.4%;

$\eta = \dfrac{100\%}{1 + (1 - \delta)\dfrac{V_{onD}}{V_S} + \delta\dfrac{V_{onS}}{V_S}}$

3.83. $\delta = 0.300$; $C = 2.08\ \mu$F $\to$ 2.2 μF; $L = 7.00$ mH $\to$ 6.8 mH

3.85. $V_O = V_S\delta - V_{on}(1 - \delta)$; 4.63 V; 116 mV; 46.3 mA; slightly reduced output voltage, <50 percent of ripple voltage and current

3.98. Slopes: 0, +0.5, 0.667; breakpoints: -2 V, 0 V

3.101. Slopes: +0.25, +0.5, +0.25, 0; breakpoints: 0 V, 2 V, 4 V

3.103. 5 mA, 4.4 mA, 3.6 mA, 5.6 ns

3.106. (0.969 A, 0.777 V); 0.753 W; 1 A, 0.864 V

3.107. 1.11 μm, 0.875 μm; far infrared, near infrared

Chapter 4

4.1. 34.5 μA/V^2; 86.3 μA/V^2; 173 μA/V^2

4.3. 208 μA; -218 μA

4.5. 94.1 Ω

4.7. 94.1 Ω; 235 Ω; 250/1

4.12. 125 μA/V^2; 1.5 V; enhancement mode; 5/1

4.14. 57.5 μA, linear region; 195 μA, saturation region; 0 A, cutoff

4.15. saturation; cutoff; saturation; linear; linear; saturation

4.19. 1.72 mA; 1.56 mA

4.21. 2.26 mA; 2.48 mA

4.23. 6.00 mA; 6.00 mA (our linear region model does not contain λ)

4.25. 97.9 μA; 98.1 μA

4.27. 31.5 μA; 28.8 μA

4.29. 4.85 V

4.31. 13.8 μA/V^2; 34.5 μA/V^2; 69.0 μA/V^2

4.33. 5.00 μA; 9100 μA; 0.550 μA; 4.10 μA

4.36. $V_{TN} > 0$; depletion mode; no

4.37. Cutoff; 0 A

4.39. (1.12 mA, 1.75 V); linear region

4.43. 134 μA; 116 μA

4.51. (a) (1.03 μA, 1.7 V)

4.52. (70.2 μA, 9.47 V)

4.55. (a) (144 μA, 4.20 V) (b) (193 μA, 0.56 V)

4.57. 4.04 V, 2.71 mA, 10.8 mA

4.59. 4.52 mA; 10.8 mA

4.61. 3.61 mA; 6.77 mA; 2.61 mA

4.63. (59.8 μA, 6.03 V), 138 kΩ

4.69. (227 μA, 3.18 V)

4.71. (102 μA, 3.98 V)

4.73. (9/10) = 1.11/1

4.75. (36.3 μA, 12.9 mV); (31.7 μA, 1.54 V); (28.2 μA, 2.69 V)

4.77. 1.73×10^{-7} F/cm^2; 4.32 fF

4.81. (500 μA, 5.00 V); (79.9 μA, 0.250 V); (159 μA, 3.70 V)

4.83. 2.50 kΩ; 10.0 kΩ

4.84. 0.5 mA, 0, 1.17 V; 1.38 mA, 0.62 mA, −0.7 V

4.86 (76.4 μA, 9.21 V), (76.4 μA, 5.03 V); 5.18 V

4.87. (a) (69.5 μA, 3.52 V)

4.89. (a) (69.5 μA, 5.05 V)

Chapter 5

5.3. 0.0167, 0.667, 3.00, 0.909, 49.0, 0.9950, 0.9990, 5000

5.4. 2 fA; 1.01 fA, −0.115 V

5.6. 2.02 fA

5.7. 1.07 mA; −1.07 mA

5.13. saturation, forward-active region, reverse-active region, cutoff

5.15. 2.31 mA; 388 μA; 0

5.19. 12 fF; 1.2 pF; 120 pF

5.21. 0.282 μm

5.23. $I_C = 16.3$ pA, $I_E = 17.1$ pA, $I_B = 0.857$ pA, forward-active region; although I_C, I_E, I_B are all very small, the Transport model still yields $I_C \cong \beta_F I_B$

5.25. 50, 1.73 fA

5.27. 6.25 MHz

5.29. 0.500, 17.3 aA

5.31. −23.7 μA, +31.6 μA, −55.3 μA

5.33. v_{ECSAT} is identical to Eq. (5.46)

5.37. 0.812 V, 0.723 V

5.39. 71.7, 43.1 V

5.41. 100 μA, 4.52 μA, 95.5 μA, 0.589 V, 0.593 V; 2.19 mA, 0.100 mA, 2.09 mA, 0.666 V, 0.666 V

5.43. (80.9 μA, 3.80 V); (404 μA, 3.80 V)

5.47. (42.2 μA, 4.39 V)

5.53. 101 μA, 98.4 μA

5.59. (7.8 mA, 4.1 V)

5.61. (5.0 mA, 1.3 V)

5.63. 56 kΩ (or 62 kΩ), 1.5 MΩ; 12.4 μA, 0.799 V

5.65. 60.7 μA, 86.0 μA, 4.00 V, 5.95 V

5.69. 4.4 percent; 70 percent

5.71. 4.74 mA, 9.71 mA, 1.28 V, 3.73 V

5.73. 5.24 V

5.75. 3.21 Ω

Chapter 6

6.1. 10 μW/gate, 2 μA

6.3. 5 V, 0 V, 0 W, 0.25 mW; 3.3 V, 0 V, 0 V, 0.11 mW

6.5. ⌐, $V_{OL} = 0$ V, $V_{OH} = 3.3$ V, $V_{REF} = 1.1$ V; $Z = A$

6.7. 3 V, 0 V, 2 V, 1 V, −3

6.9. 2 V, 2 V, 3 V, 2 V

6.11. 3.3 V, 0 V, 1.8 V, 1.5 V, 1.5 V, 1.5 V

6.13. −0.78 V, −1.36 V

6.15. 1 ns

6.17. 5 μW, 1.52 μA, 5 fJ

6.19. 2.20 RC; 2.20 RC

6.21. −0.78 V, −1.36 V, 0.5 ns, 0.5 ns, 8 ns, 9 ns, 4 ns, 4 ns

6.24. $Z = 0\ 0\ 0\ 1\ 0\ 0\ 1\ 1$

6.26. $Z = 0\ 1\ 0\ 1\ 0\ 1\ 0\ 1$

6.29. 2; 1

6.31. $Z = AB$; $Z = A + B$

6.33. 16.2

6.35. $Y = \overline{ABC}$

6.37. $V_{REF} = 2.8$ V

6.39. 0.583 pF

Chapter 7

7.1. 20 μW/gate, 4 μA/gate

7.3. 86.3 μS/V, 34.5 μS/V

7.5. 0.984 V, 3.13 V

7.7. 40.3 kΩ; 4.90/1; 1.47 V, 0.653 V

7.9. 1000 Ω; 2500 Ω; a resistive channel exists connecting the source and drain; 20/1

7.11. 1.83 V

7.13. 0.774 V, 0.610 V

7.15. 3.74/1, 1/1.41

7.17. 0.190 V

7.19. ratioed logic so $V_{OH} = 3.39$ V, $V_{OL} = 0.25$ V; $P = 0.18$ mW

7.21. 6.80 V

7.23. 1.89

7.25. 4.90/1, 1/1.41, 0.777 V, 1.36 V

7.29. 3.53/1, 1/3.39

7.31. +5 V, 0.163 V

7.33. $Y = \overline{(A + B)(C + D)(E + F)}$, 6.18/1, 1/2.15

7.40. $Y = \overline{(C + E)[A(B + D) + G] + F}$;   1/1.08, 4.12/1, 6.18/1, 12.4/1

7.43. 3.15/1, 6.06/1, 6.24/1, 6.42/1

7.47. 1.86/1, 8.24/1, 12.4/1, 24.7/1

7.49. $I'_{DS} = 2I_{DS}$, $P'_D = 2P_D$

7.54. 60.2 ns, a potentially stable state exists with no oscillation

7.55. 105 ns, 6.23 ns, 17.9 ns

7.57. 192 ns, 4.44 ns, 11.8 ns

7.63. 2.63/1, 25.3/1, 13.6 ns, 2.07 ns

7.69. −4.00 V, −0.300 V

7.71. 1.28/1, 7.09/1

7.73. 1.61 V, 4.68 V

7.75. $Y = \overline{A + B}$

Chapter 8

8.1. 108 μA/V²; 43.2 μA/V²

8.3. 250 pA; 450 pA; 450 pA

8.5. 2.5 V; 2.16 V

8.7. 2.1628 V, 2.16 V

8.9. 27.0/1, 1/1.17

8.11. 2.57 V, 1.70 V

8.13. 1.69 V, 1.17 V

8.15. 4.29/1, 10.7/1

8.17. 0.75 ns, 0.90 ns, 0.40 ns, 0.35 ns, $\langle C \rangle = 121$ fF

8.19. 2 μW/gate, 16.0 fF, 36.7 fF

8.21. 4 W; 1.74 W

8.23. 22.6 μA; 2.25 μA

8.25. 5/1, 8/1; 15/1, 24/1

8.30. 8.05 ns, 16.1 ns, 16.1 ns

8.31. (a) 5 transistors

8.33. $Y = \overline{(A + B)(C + D)E} = \overline{ACE + ADE + BDE + BCE}$, 15/1, 18/1, 30/1

8.35. 4/1, 15/1

8.37. 4/1, 6/1, 10/1

8.39. 20/1, 24/1, 40/1

8.41. 10.9 ns, 2.58 ns

8.43. 19.3 ns, 48.3 ns

8.51. 500 Ω, 1250 Ω

8.53. ≈160/1

Chapter 9

9.1. 268,435,456; 1,073,741,824

9.3. 3.73 pA

9.9. "1" level is discharged by junction leakage current

9.11. −19.8 mV; 2.48 V

9.15. 1.60 V, +5.00 V; −1.83 V

9.19. 110 μA

9.21. 361 μA, 1.85 W

9.23. 0.266 V

9.24. 0.95 V

9.31. 11,304; 11,304

9.35. $V_{DD} \rightarrow \frac{2}{3}V_{DD} \rightarrow \frac{1}{2}V_{DD}$; $R \geq \dfrac{2V_{IH}}{V_{DD} - V_{IH}} = \dfrac{2V_{IH}}{NM_H}$

9.37. $W_3 = 00101011_2$

9.42. $O_5 = \overline{A + C}$

9.46. 1.16/1

Chapter 10

10.1. 1.38 V, 1.12

10.3. −1.75 V, 0 V

10.5. −1.0 V, −1.4 V, −1.2 V, 132 mV, 10.4 mW

10.7. −0.700 V, −1.70 V, −1.20 V, 1.00 V

10.9. −0.700 V, −1.50 V, −1.10 V, 2.67 kΩ; 0.314 V, −0.100 V, +0.300 V

10.10. 53.3 μA

10.13. 4.20 kΩ, 1.17 kΩ, 200 Ω, 185 Ω

10.15. 0.324 V

10.19. 0.340 V

10.21. 50.0 μA, −2.30 V

10.25. +0.600 V, −0.560 V, 314 Ω

10.29. 500 Ω, 60.0 mA

10.31. $Y = A + \overline{B}$

10.35. −0.892 V; −1.14 V

10.39. −1.00 V; −0.974 V; −0.948 V; −0.922 V

10.43. 23.2 μA

10.45. −0.850 V; 3.59 pJ

10.47. 0 V, −0.600 V, 5.67 mW; $Y = A + B + C$, $Y = \overline{A + B + C}$, 5 vs. 6

10.53. 2.23 kΩ, 4.84 kΩ, 60.1 kΩ

10.55. 2.98 pA, 74.5 fA

10.57. 160; 0.976; 5; 0.773 V

10.59. 0.691 V, 0.710 V

10.60. 40.2 mV, 0.617 mV

10.61. 3 V, 0.15 V, 0.66 V, 0.80 V, 33

10.63. 0.682 V, 2.47 mA

10.69. 5 V, 0.15 V, 0; −1.06 mA, 31; −1.06 mA vs. −1.01 mA, 0 mA vs. 0.2 mA

10.77. 8

10.79. 234 mA, 34.9 mA

10.83. (I_B, I_C): (a) (135 μA, −169 μA); (515 μA, 0); (169 μA, 506 μA); (0, 0) (b) all 0 except $I_{B1} = I_{E1} = 203$ μA

10.89. 1.85 V, 0.15 V; 62.5 μA, −650 μA; 13

10.91. $Y = \overline{ABC}$; 1.9 V; 0.15 V; 0, −408 μA

10.93. 1.5 V, 0.25 V; 0, −1.00 mA; 16

10.95. 963 μA, 963 μA, 0

10.100. (I_B, I_C): (532 μA, 0); (0, 0); (0, 0); (3.75 μA, 150 μA)

10.103. $Y = A + B + C$; 0 V, −1.0 V; 0, −0.90 V

10.104. $Y = A + B + C$; 0 V, −0.80 V; −0.40 V

Chapter 11

11.3. Using MATLAB:

```
t=linspace(0,.004);
vs=sin(1000*pi*t)+0.333*sin(3000*pi*t)+0.200*sin(5000*pi*t);
vo=2*sin(1000*pi*t+pi/6)+sin(3000*pi*t+pi/6)+sin(5000*pi*t+pi/6);
plot(t,vs,t,vo)
```

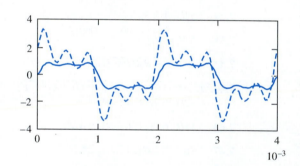

500 Hz: $1\underline{/0°}$, 1500 Hz: $0.333\underline{/0°}$, 2500 Hz: $0.200\underline{/0°}$; $2\underline{/30°}$, $1\underline{/30°}$, $1\underline{/30°}$; $2\underline{/30°}$, $3\underline{/30°}$, $5\underline{/30°}$; yes

11.7. −10 (20 dB), 0.1 V

11.9. $8 - \sin(1000\,t)$; there are only two components; dc: 8 V, 159 Hz: −4 V

11.11. $y_{11} - \dfrac{y_{12}y_{21}}{y_{22}} \rightarrow y_{11}$; $\dfrac{y_{12}}{y_{22}} \rightarrow 0$; $-\dfrac{y_{21}}{y_{22}}$; $\dfrac{1}{y_{22}}$

11.13. $\left(g_{11} - \dfrac{g_{12}g_{21}}{g_{22}}\right)^{-1} \rightarrow \dfrac{1}{g_{11}}$; $\left(g_{21} - \dfrac{g_{22}g_{11}}{g_{12}}\right)^{-1} \rightarrow$ 0; $\left(g_{12} - \dfrac{g_{11}g_{22}}{g_{21}}\right)^{-1} \rightarrow -\dfrac{g_{21}}{g_{11}g_{22}}$; $\left(g_{22} - \dfrac{g_{21}g_{12}}{g_{11}}\right)^{-1} \rightarrow \dfrac{1}{g_{22}}$;

11.17. 10 kΩ, 1, −101, 4.17 μS

11.19. 24.3 MΩ, 240 kΩ, 24.2 MΩ, 240 kΩ

11.21. 102 kΩ, 0.0164, 98.3, 16.4 μS

11.23. 3.50 kΩ, 1.00 kΩ, −6.00 MΩ, 61.0 kΩ

11.24. 1 mS, −1, 2001, 20 kΩ

11.26. 0.101 S, 50.0 μS, −0.100 S, 50.0 μS

11.29. 45.3 mV; 1.00 W

11.31. −8180

11.33. 0, ∞, 125 mW, ∞

11.37. 60 dB, 10 kHz, 10 Hz, 9.99 kHz, band-pass amplifier

11.39. 80 dB, ∞, 50 Hz, ∞, high-pass amplifier

11.49. 0.477 sin (10πt + 63.4°) V, 0.999 sin (1000πt − 1.72°) V, 0.477 sin (10^5πt − 78.7°) V

11.51. 0.06 sin (2πt + 88.9°) V, 2.12 sin (100πt + 45.0°) V, 3.00 sin (10^4πt + 0.57°) V

11.55. $\dfrac{10^8\pi}{s + 10^7\pi}$; $-\dfrac{10^8\pi}{s + 10^7\pi}$

11.59. 10 sin (1000πt + 10°) + 3.33 sin (3000πt + 30°) + 3.00 sin (5000πt + 50°) V;
Using MATLAB:

```
t = linspace(0,.004);
vs = sin(1000*pi*t)+0.333*sin(3000*pi*t)+0.200*sin(5000*pi*t);
vo = 10*sin(1000*pi*t+pi/18)+3.33*sin(3000*pi*t+3*pi/18)+
2.00*sin(5000*pi*t+5*pi/18);
plot(t, 10*vs, t, vo)
```

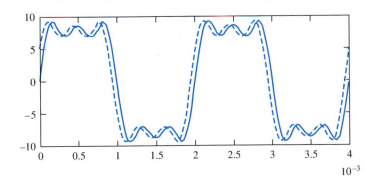

Chapter 12

12.1. 79.9 dB, 120 dB, 89.9 dB; 5.05 mV

12.3. ≥4.95 MΩ

12.5. 0.100 mV, 140 dB

12.7. −46.8, 4.7 kΩ, 0, 33.4 dB

12.9. 83.9, ∞, 0, 83.9 dB

12.11. (0.510 sin 3770t − 1.02 sin 10000t) V, 0

12.13. −10, 110 kΩ, 10 kΩ

12.15. −5.00, 20.0 kΩ; +6.00, 27.0 kΩ, 0, 33.0 kΩ (not a useful circuit)

12.17. 0.484 A; 0.730 V; 0.730 V; ≥ 7.03 W (choose 10 W), 7.27 W

12.19. $\dfrac{v_1 - v_2}{R}$; ∞; R(1 + A)

12.21. 3.99 V, 3.99 V, 1.99 V, 1.99 V, 3.99 V, 199 μA; −5 MΩ

12.23. 3.6 kΩ, 49.6 kΩ

12.25. −1.20 V; −1.80 V; 0 to −3.00 V in 0.20-V steps

12.27. One solution: 1.07 percent, 1 percent, 2 percent, 4 percent, 8 percent, 16 percent

12.29. −0.300 V, −0.600 V, −1.20 V, −2.40 V

12.30. A and B taken together, B and C taken together

12.35. 785 MΩ, 3.75 mΩ

12.37. Noninverting to achieve R_{IN} with an acceptable value for resistor R_2: R_{OUT} can be met; R_{IN} is not achievable

12.39. −16.2 v_S, 85.9 mΩ

12.41. 0.25 percent

12.43. 60 dB

12.45. 0.500 sin 5000πt, 10 sin 120πt; −10, −0.037; 48.6 dB; −5.00 sin 5000πt − 0.370 sin 120πt

12.47. −26.0 mV, 0, −26.0 mV, yes, 90.9 kΩ

12.49. $A_V = 10{,}000 [u(v_{ID} + 0.0005) - u(v_{ID} - 0.0015)]$

12.51. 10.1 kΩ, 1.00 MΩ

12.53. −0.460 V; −0.546 V; −18.7 percent

12.55. 10.0 V, 0 V; 15.0 V, 0.125 V

12.57. One possibility: 1 kΩ, 20 kΩ

12.63. $\left(1 + \dfrac{R_2}{R_1}\right)\dfrac{sC(R_1 \| R_2) + 1}{sCR_2 + 1}$

12.65. 3 stages: 1 kΩ, 20 kΩ, 200 pF

12.70. $A_V(s) = -\dfrac{3.653 \times 10^{13}}{s^2 + 3.142 \times 10^7 s + 1.916 \times 10^{12}}$;

bode(−3.65e13,[1 3.142e7 1.916e12])

12.73. 20 kΩ, 200 kΩ, 796 pF

12.74. −20, 143 kHz; 78.1 dB, 72.9 kHz

12.77. Two stages

12.81. 6.91, 145 kHz, [6.35, 7.53], [133 kHz, 157 kHz]

12.83. 1.89 V/μs

12.85. 10 V/μs

12.86. 250 kΩ, 1 kΩ, 2.55 μF, 8×10^4, 50 Ω; add two 10^9-Ω resistors

12.91. 200,000, 10^{12} Ω, 1 kΩ, unspecified, 12.7 μF

12.93. 0.010 μF, 0.005 μF, 1.13 kΩ, 20.0 kHz; 0.005 μF, 0.0025 μF

12.97. $\dfrac{K}{s^2 R_1 R_2 C_1 C_2 + s[R_1 C_1 (1 - K) + C_2 (R_1 + R_2)] + 1}$;

$\dfrac{K}{3 - K}$

12.99. −1, −1

12.103. 1 kΩ, 100 kΩ, 0.0159 μF

12.105. 1 rad/s, 0.0640 rad/s, 15.6; $\left(\dfrac{20}{s^2 + 0.1s + 1}\right)^2$

12.107. 5.48 kHz, 1.34 kHz, 4.05, 63.1 dB

12.113. (0, $T/2$): 0 V, ($T/2$, $3T/2$): 1 V, ($3T/2$, $5T/2$): 4 V, ($5T/2$, $7T/2$): 8 V, ($7T/2$, $9T/2$): 12 V, ($9T/2$, $5T$): 15 V

12.116. 12.6 kHz, 1.58, 7.96 kHz

12.118. $-V_1 V_2/(10^4 I_S)$

12.121. 2.40 Hz

12.126. 2.38 V, 2.62 V, 0.240 V

12.128. 0.487 V, −0.487 V, 0.974 V

12.131. 0 Hz

Chapter 13

13.1. $0.700 + 0.005 \sin 2000\pi t$ V; $-1.03 \sin 2000\pi t$ V; $5.00 - 1.03 \sin 2000\pi t$ V; 2.82 mA

13.3. Bypass, coupling, coupling; 0 V

13.6. Coupling, bypass, coupling; 0 V

13.9. (1.78 mA, 6.08 V)

13.13. (98.4 μA, 4.96 V)

13.17. (82.2 μA, 6.04 V)

13.23. (338 μA, 5.40 V)

13.27. (1.00 mA, 7.50 V)

13.37. Thévenin equivalent source resistance, gate-bias voltage divider, gate-bias voltage divider, source-bias resistor—sets source current, drain-bias resistor—sets drain-source voltage, load resistor

13.40. 11.3 μA, 50 mV

13.43. (188 μA, $V_{CE} \geq 0.7$ V), 7.52 mS, 532 kΩ

13.47. 90, 120; 95, 75

13.51. −120

13.53. Yes, using $I_C R_C = (V_{CC} + V_{CE})/2$

13.55. 2.5 mA; 30.7 V

13.57. −314, −314

13.59. −95

13.60. (−95.0, −94.1)

13.64. 3

13.67. 1.25 A

13.71. Virtually any desired Q-point

13.72. (156 μA, 9 V)

13.78. 400 = 133,000 $i_P + v_{PK}$; (1.4 mA, 215 V); 1.6 mS, 55.6 kΩ, 89, −62.7

13.80. FET

13.81. 111 μA, 1400

13.84. Yes, it is possible although the required value of $V_{GS} - V_{TN}$ (6.70 V) is getting rather large

13.85. 0.5 V, (125 μA, 7.5 V)

13.87. 2.5 V, 25 V

13.89. 3

13.91. −10.9

13.94. −7.27

13.99. 833 μA

13.101. 33.3 kΩ, 94.4 kΩ

13.103. 647 Ω, 3.62 kΩ

13.106. 1 MΩ, 0, −7.45 MΩ, 3.53 kΩ

13.108. 6.8 MΩ, 45.8 kΩ

13.115. $-15.0\, v_S$, 45.8 kΩ

13.119. -60.7, 630 Ω, 960 Ω; gain reduced by 25 percent due to lower input resistance

13.123. 50 mA/V^2, 842 kΩ

13.129. 1.38 μW, 0.581 mW, 0.960 mW, 0.887 mW, 2.43 mW

13.136. $V_{CC}/15$

13.137. 3.38 V, 13.6 V

13.139. 356 μA, 2.02 V

13.141. 32.9 μA, 2.30 V

13.143. 500 μA, 1.76 V

Chapter 14

14.1. (a) C-C, (d) not useful, (k) C-B, (o) C-D

14.5. -5.00, ∞, 20.0 kΩ, ∞; -10.0, ∞, 10.0 kΩ, ∞

14.7. (a) -6.91 (e) -120

14.8. 6.58 kΩ, 66.7 kΩ

14.12. -120, -60.9, 2.83 kΩ, 8.20 kΩ, 6.76 mV

14.13. -14.7, -11.6, 368 kΩ, 75 kΩ, 183 mV

14.15. -3.07, 84.9, 1.00 MΩ, 39.0 kΩ, 1.49 V

14.19. 0.909, ∞, 100 Ω, ∞

14.21. 0.978, 1.31, 31.6 kΩ, 29.6 Ω, 0.867 V

14.23. 0.956, 9.56, 1.00 MΩ, 555 Ω, 6.28 V

14.25. $(0.005 + 0.2V_{R4})$ V

14.28. 48.8, 2.00 kΩ, ∞, 1; 14.3, 2.00 kΩ, ∞, 1

14.29. 48.8, 1.98 kΩ, 4.92 MΩ, 1; 23.7, 1.98 kΩ, 10.1 MΩ, 1

14.31. 5.51, 0.178, 2.73 kΩ, 24.0 kΩ, 0.398 V

14.33. 36.5, 0.274, 252 Ω, 39.0 kΩ, 14.9 mV

14.37. 44.5 Ω

14.39. 632 Ω

14.41. $(\beta_o + 1)r_o = 153$ MΩ

14.43. $A_V = 398$ with $R_{\mathrm{IN}} = 1$ MΩ: A C-E amplifier operating at low current should be able to achieve both high A_V and high R_{IN}. It would be difficult to achieve $A_V = 52$ dB with an FET stage.

14.45. A follower has a gain of approximately 0 dB. The input resistance of a C-C amplifier is approximately $(\beta_o + 1)R_L \approx 101(10 \text{ k}\Omega) = 1$ MΩ.

Therefore a C-D stage would be preferred to achieve the gain of approximately 1 with $R_{\mathrm{IN}} = 25$ MΩ.

14.47. A noninverting amplifier is needed. Either the C-B or C-S amplifier should be able to achieve $A_V = +10$ with $R_{\mathrm{IN}} = 2$ kΩ with proper choice of the Q-point.

14.49. 1.66 Ω

14.53. $\mu_f \mathbf{v}_s$, $r_o(1 + g_m R_5)$

14.55. v_s, $(R_{\mathrm{th}} + r_\pi)/(\beta_o + 1)$

14.56. (b) $-(g_m/\alpha_o)$, $-g_\pi$, $y_{21} = (\beta_o + 1)y_{12}$
(d) $-(g_m + g_o)$, $y_{21} = \mu_f y_{12}$

14.57. $(1/g_m)(1 + R_L/r_o)$ for $\mu_f \gg 1$

14.58. -0.984, 0.993, 0.703 V

14.61. SPICE: (9.81 μA, 5.74 V), 0.983, 11.0 MΩ, 2.58 kΩ

14.63. SPICE: (106 μA, 7.14 V), -14.2, 369 kΩ, 65.8 kΩ

14.64. SPICE: (268 μA, 8.60 V), 4.26, 1.27 kΩ, 18.8 kΩ

14.68. SPICE: (5.59 mA, 5.93 V), -3.27, 10.0 MΩ, 1.53 kΩ

14.70. SPICE: (3.84 mA, 10.0 V), 0.953, 1.00 MΩ, 504 Ω

14.72. 33.3 mA

14.75. $A_V^{\mathrm{max}} = 54.8$, $A_V^{\mathrm{min}} = 44.8$, beyond Monte Carlo results by approximately 2 percent of nominal gain.

14.79. Voltage is not sufficient—transistor will be saturated.

14.83. 95.2, 1000 Ω, ∞, 1; A_V is 2$\times$ larger, R_{IN} is 2$\times$ smaller

Chapter 15

15.1. 4.12, 1 MΩ, 64.3 Ω

15.2. 4.44

15.5. 2.19

15.7. 711, 8.29 kΩ, 401 Ω

15.9. 466, 73.8 kΩ, 20 kΩ

15.13. (a) (5.00 mA, 10.3 V), (1.88 mA, 3.21 V), (2.47 mA, 6.86 V) (b) (5.00 mA, 9.45 V), (2.38 mA, 0.108 V), (3.15 mA, 4.60 V) Q_2 is saturated! The circuit will no longer function properly as an amplifier.

15.14. (325 μA, 7.14 V), (184 μA, 7.85 V), 86.1 dB

15.17. (50.0 μA, 1.58 V), (215 μA, 13.2 V), −63.2, 1 MΩ, 1.91 kΩ

15.19. (a) (223 μA, 2.87 V), (1.96 mA, 5.00 V), −218, 7.61 kΩ, 241 Ω (b) −1.49, 75.6 kΩ

15.21. (a) (4.44 μA, 1.40 V), (23.3 μA, 2.30 V) (b) (4.08 μA, 1.42 V), (23.6 μA, 2.28 V)

15.25. $I_{C2} = \beta_F I_{C1}$, $g'_m = g_m$, $r'_\pi = \beta_o r_\pi$, $r'_o = \dfrac{r_o}{2}$, $\beta'_o = \beta_o(\beta_o + 1)$, $\mu'_f = \dfrac{\mu_f}{2}$

15.27. $I_{C2} = \beta_F I_{C1}$, $g'_m = g_m$, $r'_\pi = \beta_o r_\pi$, $r'_o = r_o$, $\beta'_o = \beta_o^2$, $\mu'_f = \mu_f$

15.29. (8.52 μA, 1.42 V), (8.40 μA, 0.940 V), −48.1, cascode amplifier

15.30. (a) (20.7 μA, 5.87 V) (b) −273, 243 kΩ, 660 kΩ (c) −0.604, 47.1 dB, 27.3 MΩ

15.34. (a) (8.43 μA, 1.36 V) (b) −33.7, −1.02 kΩ, ∞ for differential output, 24.4 dB for single-ended output, 594 kΩ, 200 kΩ, 4.90 MΩ, 50 kΩ

15.35. $R_{EE} = 1.1$ MΩ, $R_C = 1.0$ MΩ

15.37. (198 μA, 4.98 V); differential output: −309, 0, ∞; single-ended output: −155, −0.0965, 64.1 dB; 25.2 kΩ, 20.2 MΩ, 78.0 kΩ, 19.5 kΩ

15.41. $V_O = 1.09$ V, $v_o = 0$; $V_O = 1.09$ V, $v_o = 219$ mV; 5.00 mV

15.43. (47.4 μA, 6.23 V); Differential output: −380, 0, ∞; single-ended output: −190, −0.661, 49.2 dB; 158 kΩ, 22.7 MΩ

15.47. −16.1 V, −13.1 V, −3.00 V

15.48. −283, 4.94×10^{-3}, 95.2 dB

15.52. (24.2 μA, 5.36 V); $A_{dd} = -45.9$, $A_{cc} = -0.738$, differential CMRR = ∞, single-ended CMRR = 29.7 dB, ∞, ∞

15.55. (91.3 μA, 12.9 V); $A_{dd} = -16.7$, $A_{cc} = -0.486$, differential CMRR = ∞, single-ended CMRR = 24.7 dB, ∞, ∞

15.60. (150 μA, 7.61 V); $A_{dd} = -26.0$, $A_{cc} = -0.233$, differential CMRR = ∞, single-ended CMRR = 34.9 dB, ∞, ∞

15.63. (142 μA, 7.27 V); $A_{dd} = -21.7$, $A_{cc} = -0.785$, differential CMRR = ∞, single-ended CMRR = 22.9 dB, ∞, ∞

15.65. (20.0 μA, 6.67 V); $A_{dd} = -26.8$, $A_{cc} = -0.119$, differential CMRR = ∞, single-ended CMRR = 41.0 dB, ∞, ∞

15.66. −3.08 V, −1.22 V, 62.1 mV

15.69. (99.0 μA, 10.8 V); $A_{dd} = -30.1$, $A_{cc} = -0.165$, 554 kΩ

15.73. (24.8 μA, 12.0 V), (500 μA, 12.0 V), 893, 202 kΩ, 20.6 kΩ, 147 MΩ, v_2

15.75. (a) (98.8 μA, 14.3 V), (300 μA, 14.3 V) (b) 551, 40.5 kΩ, (c) 49.0 kΩ (d) 34.6 MΩ, (e) v_2

15.79. (98.8 μA, 14.3 V), (300 μA, 14.3 V), 27,800, 40.5 kΩ

15.82. (a) (250 μA, 15.6 V), (500 μA, 15.0 V) (b) 4300, ∞, 165 kΩ (c) v_2 (d) v_1

15.85. (250 μA, 4.92 V), (6.10 μA, 4.30 V), (494 μA, 5.00 V), 17,000, ∞, 196 kΩ

15.89. (250 μA, 10.9 V), (2.00 mA, 9.84 V), (5.00 mA, 12.0 V), 866, ∞, 127 Ω

15.91. (300 μA, 5.10 V), (500 μA, 2.89 V), (2.00 mA, 5.00 V), 1220, ∞, 341 Ω

15.93. (99.0 μA, 4.96 V), (500 μA, 3.41 V), (2.00 mA, 5.00 V), 11,400, 50.5 kΩ, 224 Ω

15.95. (4.95 μA, 2.36 V), (24.5 μA, 3.07 V), (245 μA, 3.00 V), 182, 1.01 MΩ, 1.63 kΩ, v_B, v_A, 900, $r_{\pi 3}$ and $r_{\pi 4}$ are low, R_{IN5} is low.

15.98. (99.0 μA, 1.40 V), (990 μA, 12.0 V), 189, 50.6 kΩ, 1.06 kΩ

15.101. (24.8 μA, 17.3 V), (24.8 μA, 17.3 V), (9.62 μA, 15.9 V), (490 μA, 16.6 V), (49.0 μA, 17.3 V), (4.95 mA, 18.0 V), 88.5 dB, 202 kΩ, 18.1 Ω

15.103. 36.8 μA

15.105. 196 μA

15.109. 22.8 μA

15.111. 5 mA, 0 mA, 10 mA, 12.5 percent

15.112. 100 percent

15.115. 70 mA, 19.6 V

15.117. 6.98 mA, 0 mA

15.119. 25.0 mΩ

15.121. 22.8 μA, 43.9 MΩ

15.123. Two of many: 75 kΩ, 62 kΩ, 150 Ω; 68 kΩ, 12 kΩ, 1 kΩ

15.125. 96.7 μA, 16.3 MΩ

15.126. 20.2 μA, 101 MΩ

15.129. 16.9 μA, 168 MΩ, 5.11 μA, 555 MΩ, 16.9 μA, 168 MΩ

15.131. 44.1 μA, 22.1 MΩ, 10.0 μA, 210 MΩ

15.133. 100 μA, 657 GΩ

15.136. (9.34 μA, 9.03 V), (4.62 μA, 7.62 V), 96.5 dB

15.138. $\beta_{o1}\mu_{f1}/2$

15.139. 3.16 V

Chapter 16

16.1. 4.06 kΩ ≤ R ≤ 4.37 kΩ

16.3. 19.8 percent, 13.3 percent

16.5. 7.69 percent, 0.813 μA, 0.855 μA

16.7. 274 μA, 383 kΩ, 574 μA, 192 kΩ

16.11. (a) 994 μA, 68.9 kΩ, 1.52 mA, 41.5 kΩ

16.14. 125 μA, 690 μA, 1.31 mA, 600 kΩ, 100 kΩ, 66.4 kΩ

16.16. 10

16.19. 12.3 μA, 31.3 MΩ, 29.3 μA, 15.2 MΩ

16.23. 172 kΩ, 9.78 kΩ, 0.445

16.27. $-V_{EE}$ + 1.16 V for V_{CB3} ≥ 0

16.30. $-V_{EE}$ + 1.91 V = −8.09 V

16.31. 3.80/1

16.33. 17.5 μA, 1.16 GΩ; 20.3 kV; 2.11 V

16.35. 16.9 μA, 163 MΩ, 2750 V; $2V_{BE}$ = 1.4 V

16.39. 318 μA, 295 μA, 66.5 μA

16.41. 187 μA

16.43. 46.5 μA, 140 μA

16.45. 26.4 μA

16.49. 16.9 μA, 16.9 μA

16.51. 30.7 μA, 15.3 μA

16.53. 79.1, 6.28 × 10⁻⁵, 122 dB

16.55. 1200, 0, ∞

16.57. (100 μA, 8.70 V), (100 μA, 7.45 V), (100 μA, 2.50 V), (100 μA, 1.25 V), 323, 152

16.58. (125 μA, 1.54 V), (125 μA, 2.79 V), (125 μA, 2.50 V), (125 μA, 1.25 V); 19,600

16.61. 171 μA

16.63. 100 μA

16.64. (125 μA, 8.63 V), (125 μA, 1.31 V), (125 μA, 10.0 V), (125 μA, 8.71 V), (125 μA, 1.29 V), (125 μA, 6.00 V), (125 μA, 2.75 V); 43.4; 14,900

16.66. 10,800

16.71. 6400; 80,000

16.72. 7500; 7500

16.75. 7.78, 574 Ω, 1.65 × 10⁶, 60.0 kΩ

16.77. ±1.4 V, ± 2.4 V

16.79. 271 kΩ, 255 Ω

16.81. V_{EE} ≥ 2.8 V, V_{CC} ≥ 1.4 V; 3.8 V, 1.7 V

16.82. 0.406 mS, 2.83 MΩ

16.86. (100 μA, 15.7 V), (50 μA, 12.9 V), (50 μA, 0.700 V), (50 μA, 1.40 V), (50 μA, 29.3 V), (100 μA, 0.700 V), (100 μA, 13.6 V), 1 mS, 752 kΩ

16.89. −1.125 V; −1.668 V; $n \times (-0.1875)$ V

16.92. 000: 0, 001: 0.1220, 010: 0.2564, 100: 0.5000; 0.0716 LSB, 0.0434 LSB; 0.376 LSB, 0.188 LSB

16.95. 1.43 percent, 2.5 percent, 5 percent, 10 percent

16.97. −0.3125 V, −0.6250 V, −1.250 V, −2.500 V

16.99. 1.0742 kΩ, 0.188 LSB, 0.094 LSB; 1.2929 kΩ, 0.224 LSB, 0.417 LSB

16.105. −2.500 V, −1.875 V, −1.250 V, −0.625 V, 0 V, +0.625 V, 1.250 V, +1.875 V

16.107. (3.415468 V, 3.415781 V)

16.111. 0001011111, 95 μs

16.113. 167 ns

16.115. RC ≥ 0.0448 s; v_O (200 ms) = 22.32 V

Chapter 17

17.1. 25, $\dfrac{s^2}{(s + 1)(s + 20)}$, yes, $\dfrac{25s}{(s + 20)}$, 3.18 Hz, 3.19 Hz

17.4. 200, $\dfrac{1}{\left(1 + \dfrac{s}{10^4}\right)\left(1 + \dfrac{s}{10^5}\right)}$, yes, 1.59 kHz, 1.58 kHz

17.7. 200, $\dfrac{s^2}{(s + 1)(s + 2)}$, $\dfrac{1}{\left(1 + \dfrac{s}{500}\right)\left(1 + \dfrac{s}{1000}\right)}$, 0.356 Hz, 71.2 Hz; 0.380 Hz, 66.7 Hz

17.10. (b) −14.1 (23.0 dB), 11.8 Hz

17.11. 19.3 dB, 151 Hz; 35.0 dB, 12.6 Hz

17.14. 7.24 dB, 19.2 Hz

17.16. 0.964, 0.627 Hz

17.17. 0.152 μF

17.20. Cannot reach 1 Hz; f_L = 13.1 Hz for $C_1 = \infty$, limited by C_3

17.22. 0.351 μF

17.25. 308 ps

17.26. −100; −107

17.28. 0.977; 0.978

17.29. −5100, −98.0, −5000, −100; −350, −42.9, −300, −50

17.34. −98.7, 1.42 MHz

17.35. −129, 1.10 MHz

17.37. $1/10^5 RC$; $1/10^6 RC$; $1/sRC$

17.39. $(2750 - j4.99)\ \Omega$, $(2730 - j226)\ \Omega$, $(836 - j1040)\ \Omega$

17.41. −9.44, 43.9 Hz, 9.02 MHz; 85.1 MHz

17.45. −1300; −92.3; −100, −1200

17.46. 9.13, 40.9 MHz

17.48. 2.30, 10.9 MHz

17.51. 0.964, 114 MHz

17.52. $C_{GD} + C_{GS}/(1 + g_m R_L)$ for $\omega \ll \omega_T$

17.55. 99.3 kHz

17.57. 48.2 kHz

17.61. 4 GHz, 39.8 ps

17.64. 781 μA

17.65. 8.33 MHz

17.69. 7.96 MHz, 25V/μs

17.72. 8 V/μs

17.75. 22.5 MHz, 6.06, −85.7

17.76. 20.1 pF, 12.6, n = 2.81, 21.9 pF

17.78. 15.2 MHz; 27.5 MHz

17.79. 13.4 MHz, 7.98, 112$\underline{/-90°}$; 4.74 MHz, 5.21, 46.1$\underline{/-90°}$

17.84. 10.9 MHz, 30.9, −75.0; 10.1 MHz, 15.8, −35.4

Chapter 18

18.1. $1/(1 + A\beta)$; 9.99×10^{-3} percent

18.4. 100 dB

18.7. 800 MΩ; 2.00 Ω; 20.0 MΩ; 50 mΩ

18.9. 18.8 kΩ, 1.02 mS, -75.0×10^3, 3140, 0.0993, 10.0; 0.0993 ≫ 0; 75,000 ≫ 0.0993

18.11. 0.999, 43.9 MΩ, 2.49 Ω, 98.9 μS

18.13. $A\beta/(1 + A\beta)$; 99.9 percent

18.15. −33.0 kΩ; 8.11 kΩ; 0.705 Ω

18.16. 82.2 Ω; 46.2 Ω; −32.4 kΩ; −32.4

18.17. 36.8 Ω; 18.6 Ω; −34.4 kΩ

18.19. 0.973, 973 Ω

18.22. −446 kΩ, 50.4 kΩ, 2.45 kΩ

18.23. −11.0, 15.2 Ω, 2.72 MΩ

18.24. 22.0 Ω; 12.5 Ω; −35.0

18.28. $\beta_o/(\beta_o + 1)$, $2/g_m$, $(\beta_o + 1)r_o$

18.30. 46.1 kHz, 9.31 Hz, 81.0 kHz, 5.29 Hz

18.32. 114 dB, 0 Hz, 1000 Hz, 0 Hz, 101 kHz

18.35. 58.9 dB

18.38. 91.8

18.39. $(s/R_2 C_2)/[s^2 + s(1/R_2 C_2 + 1/(R_1 \| R_2)C_1) + 1/R_1 R_2 C_1 C_2]$

18.45. T_V = 987, T_I = 110, T = 98.8

18.47. 110 kHz; $A \le 2050$; larger

18.49. yes, but almost no phase margin; 1.83°

18.51. 90.0°

18.53. 12°; yes

18.56. phase margin is undefined; $|T(j\omega)| < 1$ for all ω; gain margin = 3 dB

18.60. 38.4°

18.61. $\omega = 1/RC$, $R_F = 2R$

18.63. 63.7 kHz, 6.85 V

18.65. 18.4 kHz, 10.7 V

18.70. 9.00 MHz, 1.20

18.76. 11.1 MHz, 18.1 MHz, 1.00

18.77. 15.915 mH, 15.916 fF; 10.008 MHz, 10.003 MHz

18.78. 9.190 MHz; 9.190 MHz

Index